KU-530-483

SECOND EDITION

CORPORATE FINANCIAL MANAGEMENT

DOUGLAS R. EMERY

BANK OF AMERICA SCHOLAR AND PROFESSOR OF FINANCE
UNIVERSITY OF MIAMI

JOHN D. FINNERTY

PRINCIPAL, ANALYSIS GROUP | ECONOMICS
AND
PROFESSOR OF FINANCE, FORDHAM UNIVERSITY

JOHN D. STOWE

PROFESSOR OF FINANCE
UNIVERSITY OF MISSOURI–COLUMBIA

PEARSON
Prentice Hall

PRENTICE HALL, UPPER SADDLE RIVER, NJ 07458

To our families with love and appreciation
Cindy, Ryan, Lacey, and Logan   Louise and Will
Adette, Doug, David, Jason, and Laura

Library of Congress Cataloging-in-Publication Data
Emery, Douglas R.
Corporate financial management / Douglas R. Emery, John D. Finnerty, John D. Stowe
p. cm.
Includes bibliographical references and index.
ISBN 0-13-083226-X
1. Corporations--Finance. I. Finnerty, John D. II. Stowe, John D. III. Title.

HG4026.E468 2004
658.15--dc21   2002193122

Executive Editor: Mickey Cox
Editor-in-Chief: P. J. Boardman
Managing Editor: Gladys Soto
Assistant Editor: Erika Rusnak
Editorial Assistant: Francesca Calogero
Project Manager, Media: Victoria Anderson
Executive Marketing Manager: Kathleen McLellan
Marketing Assistant: Christopher Bath
Managing Editor (Production): Cynthia Regan
Production Editor: Michael Reynolds
Production Assistant: Joe DeProspero
Permissions Supervisor: Suzanne Grappi
Associate Director, Manufacturing: Vinnie Scelta
Buyer: Diane Peirano
Design Manager: Maria Lange
Art Director: Kevin Kall
Interior Design: Donna Wicks/Dorothy Bungert
Cover Design: Kevin Kall
Manager, Print Production: Christy Mahon
Print Production Liaison: Suzanne Duda
Composition: Carlisle Publishers Services
Full-Service Project Management: Carlisle Publishers Services
Printer/Binder: Von Hoffman
Cover Printer: Phoenix

Credits and acknowledgments borrowed from other sources and reproduced, with permission, in this textbook appear on appropriate page within text.

Pearson Education LTD.
Pearson Education Australia PTY, Limited
Pearson Education Singapore, Pte. Ltd
Pearson Education North Asia Ltd
Pearson Education, Canada, Ltd
Pearson Educación de Mexico, S.A. de C.V.
Pearson Education–Japan
Pearson Education Malaysia, Pte. Ltd

PEARSON
Prentice Hall

10 9 8 7 6 5 4 3 2 1
ISBN 0-13-083226-X

BRIEF CONTENTS

CONTENTS

PREFACE

The field of finance has evolved over the past 50 years from basic descriptions of observed practice. Today, it is a sound body of concepts and theory that helps us understand finance. The world of finance continues to evolve at a dizzying pace. Changes in the economic environment and in the practice of finance occur daily. Consider stock price movements over the last several years and scandals at Enron, ImClone, Tyco, and WorldCom. How can you prepare for such a rapidly changing field? This text offers a set of fundamental tenets designed to help you develop intuition about decision making that will hold true through future evolutions in the financial world. Our *principles* of finance provide an integrated view of the theory of finance so that financial decision making can be treated as an application of this basic understanding.

Corporate Financial Management shows how to apply this 'ready intuition' to the world of financial management. For example, the first principle, the Principle of Self-Interested Behavior, is the most basic. Without this principle, we cannot explain financial behavior. Regrettably, some people misapply this principle. In your career, you are likely to face illegal "opportunities" to make literally millions of dollars by, for example, insider trading. Our Principle of Self-Interested Behavior explicitly excludes such behavior: individuals should obey the rules and regulations to ensure legal—and ethically sound—behavior. There is nothing wrong with pursuing self-interested behavior—provided you play by the rules. Recent scandals demonstrate the importance of corporate governance, and highlight the relevance of our chapter on agency theory, which is based on the Principle of Self-Interested Behavior.

The applications in this text come from the real business world—many pulled from today's headlines—and are designed to illustrate how financial principles are useful and immediately applicable. We tell you about executive stock options at McDonalds, financing decisions by firms such as PepsiCo, American Airlines, and CBS, and investment decisions made by firms such as Boeing and Disney.

Whether it is a corporate treasurer deciding what type of security to issue, an investment banker determining the structure of a new security, a bond trader deciding which bonds to buy, or a stock portfolio manager deciding which stocks to sell, it is their grasp of financial theory and their ability to apply it in *any* situation that distinguishes the successful people.

INTENDED AUDIENCE

Corporate Financial Management was written for use in corporate finance and financial management courses in MBA and undergraduate programs. There is an abundance of material, so the book can be used in the introductory course, and/or as a text for advanced classes as well as being a reference for other work in the business school curriculum.

We assume throughout the book a familiarity with the standard prerequisites in business/management programs: college-level algebra, financial accounting, microeconomics, and statistics. Although we assume students have this background, we provide reminders of basic definitions and concepts that were covered in prerequisite courses. Also, although an understanding of mathematics is necessary, we facilitate the learning process by providing simple examples and analogies. By providing both verbal/logical and mathematical descriptions, we hope to enlist each student's "learning strength," as well as have the descriptions reinforce one another.

Finally, this book has been written with the intent that it will become a useful future reference tool for students as they move through their business careers. The explanations, information, applications, minicases, and problem sets provide a valuable reference source for material not covered in class; and the chapter summaries provide an easily accessed summary of the important dimensions and concepts connected with particular topics.

IMPORTANT CHANGES AND IMPROVEMENTS IN THE SECOND EDITION

This edition reflects feedback from users and changes within the corporate world and the issues students encounter today.

- **REAL OPTIONS**. We use the term option in its broadest sense: any right without an obligation attached to it. This definition allows us to apply the important insights of option theory to a wide variety of topics and provides a natural introduction into real options. For example, we use option concepts in agency theory, capital budgeting, and capital structure, among many others. Options analysis is one of the most valuable technologies available in finance.
- **AGENCY THEORY**. We include a separate chapter on agency theory and principal-agent problems. Throughout the book, we explicitly show how the important insights from this material can be used to solve many practical problems throughout the rest of the book.
- **CORPORATE GOVERNANCE**. Corporate governance issues are examined in the context of agency theory. For example, we describe some of the manager-stockholder conflicts that contributed to the downfall of Enron.
- **CAPITAL BUDGETING**. In response to users and reviews, capital budgeting is covered earlier in this edition.
- **MINICASES.** A Minicase has been added to the end of almost every chapter as a direct application of the material in that chapter.
- **BULLETED SUMMARIES.** The chapter summaries are given in bulleted, rather than narrative, format to facilitate student review.
- **PROBLEM SETS**. Problems are organized into three different levels of difficulty, from basic to advanced, to help faculty and students determine appropriate material to review more efficiently. Level A problems are basic. They review the chapter material and can be answered by direct reference to the text material. Level B problems also relate fairly closely to the material in the chapter but are somewhat more complex. Level C problems are advanced extensions of material presented in the chapter. The level C problems are designed to challenge the students with complex situations, puzzles, or the examination of more subtle implications of the material in the chapter. Occasionally, problems are drawn from material in earlier chapters to reinforce the retention of important concepts. Selected solutions are included at the end of the text.
- **QUESTIONS**. These are in addition to the problem sets. The questions are intended to be answered verbally, without calculations. The questions are divided by level of difficulty into two groups. The first group of questions should be answerable by direct reference to the chapter. Questions in the second group may require a little more thought because they are more complex, more subtle, or, occasionally, sneaky.
- **CURRENCY**. All of the examples, tables, and figures have been updated to include the current laws, regulations, and data.

- **FOCUS ON PRINCIPLES**. These boxes set the stage in the beginning of each chapter by highlighting how particular finance principles apply to the chapter material. They highlight such things as looking for capital budgeting projects that offer a valuable new idea or use a firm's comparative advantage, and seeing the value of real options in a capital budgeting project. The *Focus on Principles* boxes also help students develop and apply financial intuition.

OTHER FEATURES

- **KEY TERMS.** Important words and phrases are bolded the first time they appear and included in the glossary.
- **PRINCIPLES OF FINANCE**. In Chapter 2, we describe the 12 principles of finance that provide the foundation for learning finance.
- **EXAMPLES**. Numerous examples are included in each chapter. They illustrate the concepts as well as the computational details needed to apply the concepts. Good numerical examples are a fundamental learning device for many business students.
- **NUMBERED EQUATIONS.** Important equations are numbered when they appear in the text.
- **EQUATION SUMMARIES**. Following each chapter is an equation summary that reprints all of the numbered equations in the chapter. Students can use these to study, and many professors expressed the importance of these summaries for their classroom instruction. We have provided the equation summaries on the website for this second edition.
- **INTERNATIONALIZATION**. It is imperative that today's companies incorporate into their decision making the specific constraints and additional market imperfections introduced by operating in an international economy. The principles of finance do not stop at the border. Therefore, the concepts and principles developed in this book are readily applicable to international transactions. With this in mind, we treat the international aspects of finance throughout the book as both a point of view and a particular market environment in which to operate.
- **A PRACTITIONER'S PERSPECTIVE**. John Finnerty has worked almost 30 years in the world of finance and, thus, brings a unique perspective to this book. Based on this first-hand experience, John brings the real world of business into the classroom.

THIS BOOK'S OVERRIDING GOAL

We wrote *Corporate Financial Management* with an overriding goal of modernizing the teaching of finance. In particular, we believe the revolution in financial research involving asymmetric information, options, and agency theory should be brought into the classroom. Since the first edition was written, the Nobel prize in economics has offered substantial validation for our view: two of the latest six prizes have been awarded for work in the area of asymmetric information, and one has been awarded for work in options. This book can enrich the teaching of finance by weaving these important research advances into the very fabric of the traditional financial management course.

Certainly these research advances are very important—but they are *also* fascinating. They are immediately applicable and relevant to the real world, as we have witnessed with scandals at Enron, ImClone, Tyco, and WorldCom. This edition offers the excitement of this profoundly important material directly to the student. These concepts, integrated throughout, can and should be understood within the context of finance.

The other business/management disciplines have enthusiastically embraced the idea of a corporation as a set of stakeholders. Beyond accounting, areas such as organizational behavior, strategic management, business law, marketing, and production are currently working to incorporate the implications of agency theory, options, and asymmetric information into their views of the organizational world. This makes the principal-agent framework a natural way for integrating the business/management areas. Therefore, this book offers the chance for the core finance class to play a central role in the curriculum.

This book lends itself very comfortably to the new environment in which many of us find ourselves. This new environment sometimes forces us to rethink, and change, how we teach finance. With change comes opportunity. We believe this new environment provides an excellent opportunity for the finance discipline to provide a leadership role.

SUPPLEMENTARY MATERIALS

- **INSTRUCTOR'S RESOURCE CD-ROM**. The instructor's resource CD-ROM contains the following resources for instructors: solutions to questions and problem sets; minicases and solutions to minicases; PowerPoint presentations; test bank; TestGen-EQ; Excel solutions; complete set of tables and figures from the text; equation summaries. Other instructor resources include teaching notes and alternative class syllabi with suggested problem assignments for alternative course lengths and coverage.
- **POWERPOINT NOTES**. The PowerPoint notes on the instructor's resource CD-ROM provide a complete set of color slide presentations for lecturing on the material and a second set of reduced notes for teaching the core MBA class.
- **TEST BANK**. The test bank provides a wide variety of problems like those at the back of the chapters as well as multiple-choice and essay questions, designed to test student comprehension. The test bank is available in both Word form and as a computerized test bank.
- **TESTGEN-EQ**. The test bank is designed for use with the TestGen-EQ test generating software. This computerized package allows instructors to custom design, save, and generate classroom tests. The test program permits instructors to edit, add, or delete questions from the test banks; edit existing graphics and create new graphics; analyze test results; and organize a database of tests and student results. This new software allows for greater flexibility and ease of use. It provides many options for organizing and displaying tests, along with a search-and-sort feature.
- **FINCOACH**, version 2.0, written by Puneet Handa, is an easy-to-install and user-friendly Windows product that covers topics including: single cash flows, infinite cash flows, bond valuation, stock valuation, porfolio diversification, CAPM, cost of capital, project and firm valuation, and financial statement analysis. This algorithmic software program provides a large number of problems with randomly generated inputs so that an almost infinite number of problems are available to the student.

Companion Website (http://www.prenhall.com/emery)

- **Online Study Guide.** This content-rich, interactive website is a great starting point for teaching and learning resources, including: an interactive study guide featuring multiple-choice, short answer/problem solving, and essay questions.
- **Links to Web Exercises.** These web exercises are keyed to each chapter and direct the student to an updated, economics-related website to gather data on and analyze a specific financial problem.
- **Syllabus Manager** allows instructors to enhance their lectures with all the resources available with this text. Instructors can post their own syllabus and link to any of the material on the site. A faculty lounge area includes teaching resources and faculty chat rooms.

- **Interactive Financial Calculators.** With this edition, we have included access to web-based financial calculators that bring the material alive in a way that today's student can easily relate to. Many of these calculators include interactive slider controls, allowing you to instantly see the impact of a change in one of the variables.
- **Downloadable Supplements** allow instructors to access the book's solutions to questions and problem sets; minicases and solutions to minicases; PowerPoint presentations; and test bank. Please contact your Prentice Hall sales representative for password information.

Online Course Offerings

To accommodate various teaching styles, we offer a complete range of technology-support materials.

WEBCT Developed by educators, WebCt provides faculty with easy-to-use Internet tools to create online courses. Prentice Hall provides the content and enhanced features to help instructors create a complete online course. Online courses are free when shrinkwrapped with the text and contain the online study guide and all test questions from the test item files. Please visit our website at http://www.prenhall.com/webct for more information or contact your local Prentice Hall sales representative.

BLACKBOARD Easy to use, Blackboard's simple templates and tools make it easy to create, manage, and use online course materials. Prentice Hall provides the content and instructors can create online courses using the Blackboard tools, which include design, communications, testing, and course-management tools. Please visit our website location at http://www.prenhall.com/blackboard for more information.

COURSECOMPASS This customizable, interactive online course-management tool, powered by Blackboard, provides the most intuitive teaching and learning environment available. Instructors can communicate with students, distribute course material, and access student progress online. For further information, please visit our website located at http://www.prenhall.com/coursecompass or contact your Prentice Hall sales representative.

ACKNOWLEDGEMENTS

As with any book, this book is not simply the work of its authors. Many people have contributed to our work over the years. We deeply appreciate the invaluable comments and suggestions we have received from the following people:

Sankar Acharya, University of Illinois—Chicago; Kofi Amoateng, North Carolina Central University; James S. Ang, Florida State University; Robert J. Angell, North Carolina A&T State University; Mary M. Bange, University of South Carolina; Shyam B. Bhandari, Bradley University; Robert Boldin, Indiana University of Pennsylvania; Elizabeth B. Booth, Michigan State University; Victor Marek Borun, Fordham University; Ronald C. Braswell, Florida State University; Greggory A. Brauer, European School of Management—Paris; Ivan E. Brick, Rutgers University; Timothy R. Burch, University of Miami; Theodore F. Byrley, Buffalo State University; Julie Cagle, Xavier University; Cynthia J. Campbell, Iowa State University; Douglas Carman, Southwest Texas State University; Richard P. Castanias, University of California—Davis; Mary C. Chaffin, University of Texas—Dallas; Susan Chaplinsky, University of Virginia; Gil Charney, Webster University; Sris Chatterjee, Fordham University; K.C. Chen, California State University—Fresno; Su-Jane Chen, Metropolitan State College of Denver; Elizabeth S. Cooperman, University of Colorado—Denver; James J. Cordeiro, SUNY—Brockport; Cynthia L. Cordes, University of Miami; Claire Crutchley, Auburn University; Larry Y. Dann, University of Oregon; Anand S. Desai, Kansas State University; Diane K. Denis, Purdue University; Upinder S. Dhillon, SUNY—Binghamton; Louis H. Ederington, University of Oklahoma; Eldon L. Erickson, SUNY—Buffalo; John R. Ezzell, Pennsylvania State University; Richard J. Fendler, Georgia State University; M. Andrew Fields, University of Delaware; Michael E. Fuerst, University of Miami; Mona J. Gardner, Illinois Wesleyan University; Adam K. Gehr, Jr., DePaul University; Chinmoy Ghosh, University of Connecticut; Atul Gupta, Bentley College; Puneet Handa, University of Iowa; Delvin D. Hawley, University of Mississippi; James D. Harriss, Campbell University; Kathleen L. Henebry, University of Nebraska at Omaha; J. Lawrence Hexter, Kent State University; Shalom J. Hochman, Mercantile Discount Bank Ltd.; Keith M. Howe, DePaul University; Jim Hsieh, Ohio State University; Rob Hull, Washburn University; Mai E. Iskandar, Suffolk University; Robert R. Johnson, Association for Investment Management and Research; Steve A. Johnson, University of Texas—El Paso; Daniel P. Klein, Bowling Green State University; Ronald J. Kudla, The University of Akron; Lynn Phllips Kugele, Christian Brothers University; Bruce R. Kuhlman, University of Toledo; Raman Kumar, Virginia Polytechnic Institute and State University; Francis E. (Frank) Laatsch, Bowling Green State University; William F. Landsea, University of Miami; Dennis Lasser, SUNY—Binghamton; Edward C. Lawrence, University of Missouri—St. Louis; Dean Leistikow, Fordham University; Richard D. MacMinn, Illinois State University; Judy E. Maese, New Mexico State University; J. Robert Malko, Utah State University; Gershon N. Mandelker, University of Pittsburgh; Terry Maness, Baylor University; Surendra K. Mansinghka, Hong Kong University of Science and Technology; David C. Mauer, Southern Methodist University; Ronald W. Melicher, University of Colorado; Roni Michaely, Cornell University; Edward M. Miller, University of New Orleans; Dina Naples, SUNY—Binghamton; William Nelson, Indiana University Northwest; Dennis T. Officer, University of Kentucky; Roger R. Palmer, University of St. Thomas; Yun W. Park, California State University—Fullerton; Robert M. Pavlik, Southwest Texas State University; Ralph A. Pope, California State University—Sacramento; Annette B. Poulson, University of Georgia; Gabriel Ramirez, Virginia Commonwealth University; Raghavendra Rau, Purdue University; Bill Reese, Tulane University; Jong-Chul Rhim, University of Southern Indiana; Kimberly Rodgers, Penn State University; Martin Ruckes, University of Wisconsin—Madison; Anthony Saunders, New York University; Barry Schachter, Office of the Comptroller; Lemma W. Senbet, University of Maryland; Dennis P. Sheehan, Pennsylvania State University; D. Katherine Spiess, University of Notre Dame; Suresh C. Srivastava, University of Alaska—Anchorage; Swapan K. Sen, Christopher Newport University; Jan R. Squires, Association for Investment Management and Research; Tie Su, University of Miami; Robert J. Sweeney, Wright State University; John Thatcher, University of Wisconsin—Whitewater; Ray E. Whitmire, Texas A&M University; Daniel T. Winkler, University of North Carolina—Greensboro; Joseph Vu, DePaul University; Robert P. Yuyuenyongwatana, Cameron University; Emilio Zarruk, Florida Atlantic University.

We also thank Mark Lerch of Thomson Financial for providing data for several tables, and Stephen B. Land, Esq., of Linklaters and Robert E. McGrath of PricewaterhouseCoopers, both of whom reviewed portions of the manuscript dealing with tax issues. As we remind you repeatedly in the book, taxes play an important role in financial decision making, and the tax law changes frequently. It is therefore important to check on the current tax provisions that may affect a financial decision when you undertake a financial analysis.

We are grateful to too many other people for their help and encouragement to mention them all individually. We thank our friends and colleagues at our respective institutions for their support and encouragement, especially Dean Paul K. Sugrue, Dean Sharon P. Smith, and Dean Bruce J. Walker. We appreciate the helpful discussions we have had with our many colleagues and friends over the years, many of whom are listed above. Some of those individuals are not associated with a university. They include, among others, Lawrence A. Darby, III, Karen K. Dixon, Philip C. Parr, and F. Katherine Warne.

We thank John Finnerty's partners at Analysis Group|Economics, especially Martha Samuelson, Bruce Stangle, and Atanu Saha, who provide a stimulating environment within which to apply the principles of finance and a laboratory for testing new analytical techniques based on these principles.

We thank all of the people at Prentice Hall who helped with the project, especially Mickey Cox, executive editor for this edition, Gladys Soto, our managing editor, Erika Rusnak, our assistant editor who handled the supplements package, Torie Anderson, media project manager, and Francesca Calogero, editorial assistant.

Lifelong appreciation goes to our parents; to Doug Emery's undergraduate professor, mentor, and friend, William Graziano of Baker University; and to John Finnerty's great uncle, O. K. Taylor, who started his career at what is now Exxon Mobil Corporation as an office boy and retired many years later as deputy treasurer. After years of trying, they finally got it across to us: "When in doubt, always go back to first principles."

The first edition was perhaps the most error-free first edition of a corporate finance textbook. Nevertheless, readers have provided assistance in detecting and reporting the little errors that plague published work. Our goal is to offer the best corporate financial management textbook available, and we want to ensure that all future editions are error free. Therefore, we are offering a reward of $10 per arithmetic error to the first individual reporting it. Any arithmetic error resulting in follow-on errors will be counted double. All errors of any sort should be reported on the form provide on our website www.prenhall.com/emery.

In this book, we say a great deal about the 12 principles of finance that are explained in Chapter 2. In writing this book, we regularly encountered a 13th principle—the unlucky one that is the bane of all authors. We call it the Underestimation Principle. Its circularity highlights its inevitability: Writing a book always takes longer than you think—even when you take into account the Underestimation Principle! So, we sincerely thank our spouses and families for their tremendous forbearance during the long and arduous process that culminated in this book.

Douglas R. Emery	John D. Finnerty	John D. Stowe
Miami, Florida	New York, New York	Columbia, Missouri

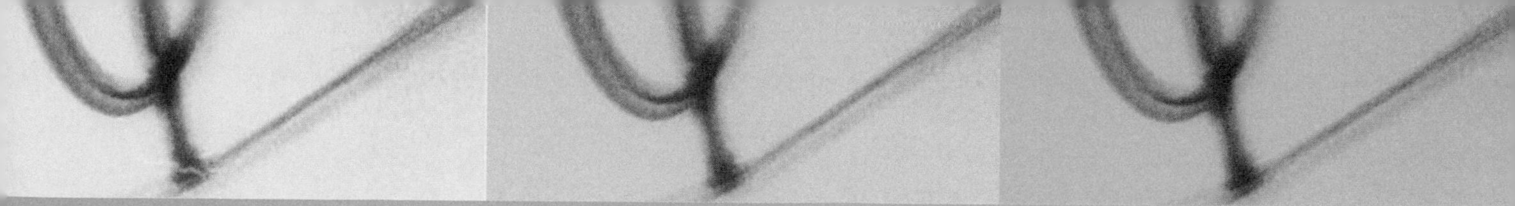

PART I

FOUNDATIONS

1

Introduction and Overview

Most of us have some interest in money. Money, and therefore finance, is an integral part of life. Understanding finance can empower you. It can help you to use money more efficiently and, yes, it can even help you make *more* money.

Perhaps you have a great idea for a new product or service. It might even be as "big" as the compact disc and how it replaced vinyl records for playing music. If you want to make money on your great new idea, how will you go about it? If you don't already have a lot of money, you will need financing—and critical business know-how. Among other things, you will need to understand finance. But even if you are not destined to become a business tycoon like Bill Gates, founder of Microsoft Corporation, you can benefit from finance.

Finance is not as specialized or complex as you might think. In fact, it is a daily concern of people and organizations, such as businesses and governments. The study of finance can benefit anyone. It can help with your career and your personal financial transactions, such as taking out a loan. It can also help when you are trying to understand world economic events or thinking about investing some money. Learning the ins and outs of finance will widen your perspective on important aspects of your present and future life.

1.1 WHAT IS FINANCE?

Finance is primarily concerned with determining value. The question "What is something worth?" is asked again and again. Finance is also concerned with how to make the best decisions. For example, should you make an investment? The decision rule in finance says you should buy an asset if it is worth more than it costs. Though seemingly obvious, this principle can easily be overlooked in a complex situation, as in the heat of a corporate takeover battle, such as when Viacom took over Paramount.

There are three main areas of finance: corporate financial management, investments, and financial markets and intermediaries. These areas often involve the same financial transactions, but each area deals with them from a different viewpoint.

This book focuses on corporate financial management. However, you can apply the principles and theories of finance to any area, including your personal financial transactions. For example, we will show you how to calculate which is more valuable when you buy a car, special financing such as a 0.9% APR loan or a special price such as $1,500 cash back.

Corporate Financial Management

Corporate financial management focuses on how a corporation can create and maintain value. The amounts of money at stake can be huge. For example, Microsoft invested more than $1 billion developing and marketing Windows XP. More generally, *financial management* decisions are based on the fundamental concepts described in this book.

EXAMPLE eBay's Decision to Go Public

You have probably heard of eBay, the largest and most popular Internet auction market for person-to-person trading in golf clubs, collectibles, memorabilia, antiques, and lots more. It harnessed the power of the Internet to develop a global market for the exchange of goods between individuals.

eBay was founded by Pierre Omidyar, who put up $14,262. In return, he got 14.7 million shares of eBay common stock. Initially he owned 100% of the firm's stock, but eBay sold stock to finance development, which reduced Omidyar's ownership to 42%. As eBay's growth strategy began working, it again needed capital.

eBay had been successful in using the Internet, and investors were very interested in buying Internet stocks. As a result, eBay was considering *going public.* That is, it was considering selling shares of its common stock to the general public for the first time. Even though eBay was a very new firm, it was already profitable. Profitable Internet firms were rare, and eBay sensed an opportunity to make as big a splash in the stock market as it had in the auction market.

eBay went to *underwriters* for advice. Underwriters specialize in selling new shares of stock. The underwriters saw the potential in the new idea. They estimated that eBay could sell 3.5 million shares for between $14 and $16 per share. That would provide about $45 to $55 million in additional financing. eBay's owners decided to go for it.

The underwriters soon discovered the extent of Wall Street's fascination with firms that could exploit the power of the Internet and make money at it. Anticipated demand for the shares was building. As the issue date approached, the underwriters raised the target price range to $16 to $18 per share. At $17, eBay would be worth $675 million. Not bad for a firm whose gross sales in the first half of that year were only $14.9 million! But it didn't stop there.

Demand for eBay's shares continued to build. When eBay went public, it sold the 3.5 million shares at $18 per share. But when the stock started public trading, it was at $53.50 per share, nearly three times the price the underwriters had paid for it. At that price, eBay was worth more than $2 billion! The stock closed at $47.375. Its first day's volume was more than 9 million shares—almost three times the number of shares available for trading! You might think of this as a sharks' feeding frenzy.

Based on the first day's closing stock price, Omidyar's stake was worth over $720 million, more than 50,000 times his initial investment just 28 months earlier. Omidyar's new idea, a web-based auction market for person-to-person trading, proved valuable indeed!

Corporate financial management decisions fall into three major categories. The first two reflect the two sides of a *balance sheet.* **Investment decisions** are primarily concerned with the asset (left) side. They address questions such as: Should we buy new computers or a warehouse? Should we invest more in inventory, receivables, or marketable securities? These questions are critical because a business is what it owns, whether it is a trucking firm, a movie theater, or a clothing store.

Financing decisions are primarily concerned with the liabilities and stockholders' equity (right) side. They determine how the firm will obtain the money to make its investments. For example, eBay obtained additional money for investing by selling new shares of its common stock. Other financing questions are: Should debt be short- or long-term? Should we borrow in foreign currency, such as the Japanese Yen?

Managerial decisions are the third major type of corporate financial management decisions. Such decisions include the firm's numerous day-to-day operating and financing decisions. How large should the firm be, and how fast should it grow? Should the firm grant credit to a customer? Should the firm change its advertising program? How should the firm compensate its managers and other employees?

Investments

The area of **investments** studies financial transactions from the viewpoint of investors outside the firm. Investors provide funds when they *invest* in (buy) financial securities, such as stocks and bonds. Formally, **financial securities** are contracts that provide for the exchange of money at various times. The positions of the issuing firm and investor are mirror images. You can see this clearly with a bond: It is an asset for the investor, but a liability for the firm. We can therefore view our eBay example from the "other side" of the transaction: Should you have bought some of the eBay stock being offered?

Capital Markets and Financial Intermediaries

The area of capital markets and intermediaries explores the firm's financing decision from yet another viewpoint, that of a third party. This area is that of a go-between who facilitates transactions between investors and corporations.

Capital markets are markets where financial securities, such as stocks and bonds, are bought and sold. Some market participants, such as brokers and dealers, facilitate the purchases and sales of securities by other parties. They charge fees or commissions for their services. For example, they helped bring eBay's stock offering to market. In contrast, **financial intermediaries** purchase financial securities such as stocks and bonds of other firms, but hold them as investments instead of reselling them. Financial intermediaries finance these investments by issuing claims against themselves (for example, shares of stock in themselves).

The Science of Finance

Finance is a science. Like other sciences, it has fundamental concepts, principles, and theories. In Chapter 2, we describe the Principles of Finance, which we will apply throughout the book. A downward-sloping demand curve is an example of an economic principle you already know: If you lower a product's price, you will sell more of it.

An important tool of science is called modeling. Modeling is a method of describing reality. There are different types of models. Many of our finance models are mathematical models, like a downward-sloping demand curve. The primary benefit of using a mathematical model is its precision in specifying relationships. To the extent we can control the inputs, we can use a model to predict outcomes.

There are many ways to establish relationships within a model. One method is empirical estimation. For example, often a firm will estimate future sales of a new product using sales observed during test marketing. Other relationships are contractually specified, such as repaying borrowed money according to a loan agreement. Finally, many relationships come from logical, conceptual, or theoretical ideas, as in the case of expecting a downward-sloping demand curve.

But models have limitations. A famous marketing example cites a case of an *upward-*sloping demand curve. A firm sold more after raising its price. The product was the beach sandal, flip-flops.[1] Very few people would buy them at first. Apparently, they thought the sandals could not be worth much if they did not cost very much. When marketers figured out the problem, they raised the price. Sales then increased as people tried the new product. Of course, after flip-flops caught on, competition drove the price back down. Today, flip-flops have a downward-sloping demand curve, as we would expect.[2]

Does this temporary upward-sloping demand curve invalidate the principle of a downward-sloping demand curve? Of course not. The problem was caused by **asymmetric information:** some people knew things others did not know. In this case, some people had the impression that a low price identified a poorly made product. But something can be cheap because it is inexpensive to make—rather than because it is poorly made. Once this impression was corrected, flip-flops became extraordinarily popular—and cheap.

Despite its problems, an imperfect model can provide useful insights, and can be the best starting point for solving new and challenging problems.

The Art of Finance

In some situations, precise models cannot be created, and people may refer to using intuition, experience, or a "gut feel" to make decisions. Such intuition is the "art" of finance. It is important to understand that, despite the seeming imprecision, often decision makers are actually using intuition from the Principles of Finance. They are using scientific valuation concepts, but not exact quantities. In such cases, the "trick" is to use the intuition and experience to enhance the science.

Finance and Accounting

Finance frequently uses accounting information. Consequently, people often ask: How is finance different from accounting?

The fundamental difference between finance and accounting is the viewpoint. Accounting generally has a historical outlook. Its major purpose is to account for past activities. In marked contrast, finance's emphasis on determining value and making decisions focuses solidly on the future. Starting from an accounting view brings us to the current position; finance concentrates on the implications for the future. Finance asks questions like, "What do we do now?" and "Where do we go from here?"

Review

1. What is finance, and what are its major concerns?
2. What are the three main areas of finance?
3. Describe the three types of questions corporate financial management addresses.
4. How are finance and accounting fundamentally different?

---

[1]A friend of ours, Phil Parr, calls them "go-aheads." He says, "Did you ever try going backwards in them?"
[2]You might say the demand curve for flip-flops flip-flopped.

1.2 OWNERSHIP, CONTROL, AND RISK

Businesses are often very large and complex organizations. However, by tracing the development of a firm from one person's idea into a major corporation, we gain insights into that complexity. Consider the following fictionalized account of Henry Ford's automobile manufacturing firm. Note how each decision in the firm's evolution can affect the firm's value and future decisions. Each step adds additional interested parties, called stakeholders. A **stakeholder** is an entity that has a legitimate claim of any sort on the firm.

Start-up

Henry started with the idea of making an affordable car. Using his own money, he bought raw materials, built a car, sold it, and earned a profit. He reinvested the money from the sale, bought more raw materials, and made more cars. Figure 1.1 shows Henry's first *balance sheet.* Note that the **balance sheet identity,**

$$\text{Total Assets} = \text{Liabilities} + \text{Stockholders' Equity}$$

must always hold. Note also that the financing decision is represented by the right-hand side of the balance sheet.

Henry provided the entire financing himself. (Hence, liabilities and stockholders' equity is made up solely of Henry's equity, HE.) Henry is also the manager of the firm. At this point, Henry is the only person within the firm.

Henry's primary motivation was to earn money. But what happens if the firm is unsuccessful? That is, what happens if Henry cannot sell his cars for a profit? Eventually, Henry would run out of money. Under some circumstances, Henry could lose the money he invested, but no one else would lose anything.

At this initial point, we want to note three things: First, Henry has exclusive *ownership* of the firm and its assets. Second, Henry has complete *control* of the firm and its assets (within legal limits). Third, Henry is bearing all the *risk* associated with the firm's investment.

Debt

Building one car at a time was OK, but it occurred to Henry that if he could buy more raw materials with each order, he could save money on shipping charges. Henry (and therefore the firm) did not have enough money to make such large orders, so Henry went to a bank and borrowed some money. He promised to repay the money out of revenues from future car sales. Figure 1.2 shows the revised balance sheet for Henry's firm.

Note that the firm's financing—its *capital structure*—is now made up of two parts. (We use TA' to represent the liabilities plus stockholders' equity to emphasize that the accounting identity

FIGURE 1.1
Start-up balance sheet for Henry Ford's fictionalized firm.

Cash	C		
Raw materials	R		
Tools	T		
Garage	G	Henry's equity	HE
Total Assets	TA	Liabilities + Stockholders' Equity	TA

FIGURE 1.2
Revised balance sheet for Henry's firm, right after the bank loan.

Cash	C′		
Raw materials	R′		
Tools	T′	Bank loan	B′
Garage	G′	Henry's equity	HE′
Total Assets	TA′	Liabilities + Stockholders' Equity	TA′

must always hold.) The two parts of the firm's new financing are debt and equity. **Equity** represents ownership, whereas **debt** is a legal obligation to repay borrowed money. As the only **shareholder** (or **stockholder** or **equityholder**[3]), Henry still has exclusive ownership of the firm and its assets. Henry also retains direct control over the firm and its assets because he manages the firm. However, Henry is now constrained by bank loan obligations. His firm is required to pay interest on the loan and repay the money it borrowed. The bank has become a stakeholder in Henry's firm.

As with Henry, the bank's primary motivation for making this loan was to earn money. Because of this, Henry agreed to pay interest in addition to repaying the loan. But now what happens if the firm is unsuccessful? That is, what if Henry cannot sell his cars for a profit? Under some circumstances, the firm might not have enough cash to fully repay the bank. Because of this possibility, the bank is bearing some risk. But how much risk?

On the downside, if the loan is not fully paid, the bank may still get something, whereas Henry will have lost all of the money he invested. On the upside, if the firm does well, the bank will receive only the loan repayment plus promised interest, whereas Henry will get all of the "excess net revenue"—everything above the amount promised to the bank. Therefore, Henry does worse than the bank on the downside and better than the bank on the upside. So Henry is bearing more of the risk than the bank. Of course, the bank must trust Henry to act responsibly and not run off without repaying.

You can see that this situation is more complex than in the start-up, where Henry provided all the financing. Determining the values of the claims on the firm is more difficult. The firm's decisions are more complex because they affect more stakeholders. To review the current situation: First, Henry retains exclusive ownership of the firm. Second, Henry still controls the firm's assets, but he is constrained by bank-loan obligations. Third, the bank now bears some of the risk. Fourth, Henry bears all the *residual* (remaining) risk, which is the majority of the firm's risk.

Employees

After a while, Henry has so many orders that it would take him longer than the rest of his life to build those cars—and more orders are coming. To fill them, Henry hires employees. Although the balance sheet does not change, Henry's firm now has obligations to its employees. For example, its employees would be upset if the firm delayed wage payments. And the employees have obligations to the firm. For example, an employee should not use an expense account for personal benefit. Although neither the balance sheet nor the ownership of the firm has changed, Henry's control over the firm's assets has been further constrained.

Multiple Equityholders

Demand for Henry's cars continues to grow. Now, even though Henry has employees to build the cars on backorder, he is again short of money to buy raw materials. The bank refuses to loan more money because of the risk. The bank tells Henry to get other equity financing, and Henry does. Just like eBay, he sells shares in his firm to new equityholders. He also creates a board of directors. Figure 1.3 illustrates the firm's new balance sheet.

Where do Henry and his firm stand now? First, the firm is no longer exclusively Henry's. The firm has other equityholders who are part owners. Second, although Henry is still the manager and still has control over the firm's assets, he is now even more constrained. In addition to the bank loan and employee obligations, Henry now has an obligation to act in the best interests of the other equityholders. Third, the bank continues to bear some of the risk of the firm. Fourth, Henry and the new equityholders now share the firm's residual risk in direct proportion to the number of shares each person owns.

As with Henry and the bank, the new equityholders' motivation is to make money. And, the more money the firm makes, the more money each equityholder makes (in proportion to the

[3]We follow financial industry practice and use the terms *shareholder, stockholder,* and *equityholder* interchangeably.

FIGURE 1.3
Revised balance sheet for Henry's firm, right after going public.

Cash	C″		
Raw materials	R″	Bank loan	B″
Tools	T″	New stockholders' equity	O″
Garage	G″	Henry's equity	HE″
Total Assets	TA″	Liabilities + Stockholders' Equity	TA″

number of shares each person owns). Because all the equityholders have the same motivation, it might appear that all their interests are identical. Not so. Henry is the only equityholder who has *direct* control over the firm's assets. Therefore, the other equityholders have to trust Henry to act in their best interests and not, for example, pay himself a huge inappropriate salary.

Separating Ownership from Control

Henry's firm operates successfully, but now he has decided to retire and live off investment returns. So Henry hires special employees, *managers,* to run the firm.

As with other employees, hiring managers does not change the balance sheet. Nevertheless, this change is *very important:* The managers now control the firm. Henry must trust the managers to run the firm for his benefit, just as the other equityholders trusted him.

At the start, the right side of the balance sheet was very simple, just Henry's equity. Now, it has become complex, involving explicit as well as implicit contracts among its many stakeholders. Each change added potential conflicts of interest.

For example, an equityholder who owns only a few shares may be willing to place the firm at great risk to have a chance at earning a high return because he has other assets and can "afford" to take the risk. Contrast this equityholder with the firm's manager. If the firm goes bankrupt, the managers can lose their jobs. Because of this, the managers may limit the firm's risk—even by passing up investments that have great potential returns.

Review

1. What are some of the conflicts of interest between Henry and the bank?
2. Describe some of the conflicts of interest between Henry and the other shareholders.
3. What are some of the conflicts of interest between the managers and the other shareholders of Henry's firm?

1.3 THREE DIFFERENT VIEWS OF A FIRM

The evolution of Henry's firm highlights three different models of the firm, the *investment-vehicle, accounting,* and *set-of-contracts models.* Each model provides powerful insights into particular problems.

The Investment-Vehicle Model

The investment-vehicle model shown in Figure 1.4 is the most basic view of the firm. Investors provide funds (financing) in exchange for financial securities. The firm then invests those funds and pays investors the returns.

We have identified the two basic types of financial securities: equity and debt. Equity is the firm's ownership. It is typically represented by shares of **common stock.** A person who owns all the shares of common stock owns the firm. With multiple shareholders, ownership is proportional. For example, if a shareholder owns 350 of a firm's total 1,000 shares, that person owns 35% of the firm.

Debt is a legal obligation to make contractually agreed upon future payments, identified as interest and repayment of the principal (original debt amount). Debtholders have loaned the firm

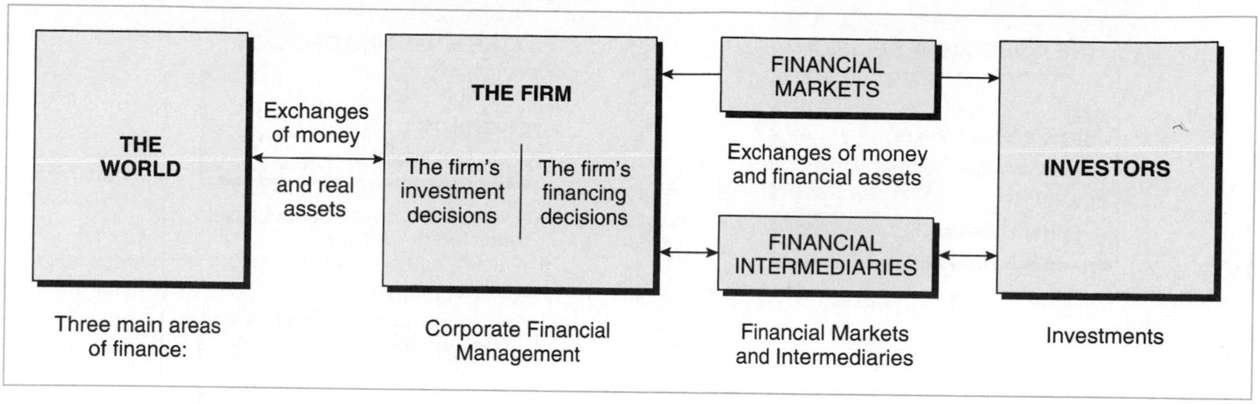

FIGURE 1.4
The investment-vehicle model of the firm, and the three main areas of finance.

money. They have no claim of ownership as long as the firm meets its payment obligations. The firm controls the use of the funds.

In the investment-vehicle model, the firm's managers are neutral intermediaries who act only in the best interest of the shareholders. Sometimes, especially in the case of small firms, the owner is the manager. In such cases, there is obviously no conflict between the owner and the manager because they are the same person.

The investment-vehicle model of the firm is embodied in an often-stated goal that managers should *maximize shareholder wealth.* In a "perfect" world (one without owner-manager conflicts) maximizing shareholder wealth is the theoretically correct managerial goal. Because of this, the investment-vehicle model is the best starting point for analyzing financial decisions.

The Accounting Model

In a sense, the U.S. accounting model is a way to operationalize and approximate the investment-vehicle model. It is embodied in the balance sheet view of the firm, an abbreviated version of which is shown in Figure 1.5. The firm's investment decisions concern the asset side, and the firm's financing decisions concern the liabilities and stockholders' equity side. Many day-to-day operating and financial policies (managerial decisions) can be seen on the balance sheet, the *income statement,* and the *statement of cash flows.*

One advantage of the accounting model is that it is highly integrated, showing how the firm's pieces fit together. Another advantage is that accounting is widely familiar, which makes it a good way to communicate.

There are disadvantages to the accounting model, however. A major one is accounting's primarily historical viewpoint. A lot of the information you use to make decisions is simply not in the accounting system. Although the accounting perspective is important and often helpful, it is frequently inadequate by itself for many corporate decisions.

The Set-of-Contracts Model

The set-of-contracts model is a refinement of the investment-vehicle model. It starts with the investment-vehicle model, but recognizes imperfections that can arise in the contracts (relationships) among the firm's many stakeholders. Figure 1.6 shows many of the firm's major stakeholders.

Contracts in the set-of-contracts model are both *explicit* and *implicit.* In an explicit contract, the firm makes specific promises. Explicit contracts include such things as bonds, outstanding guarantees on previously sold products, severance agreements for terminated employees, and pension obligations. There are implicit contracts to be honest and disclose relevant information. Employees have implicit contracts to give their best effort. Managers have implicit contracts with

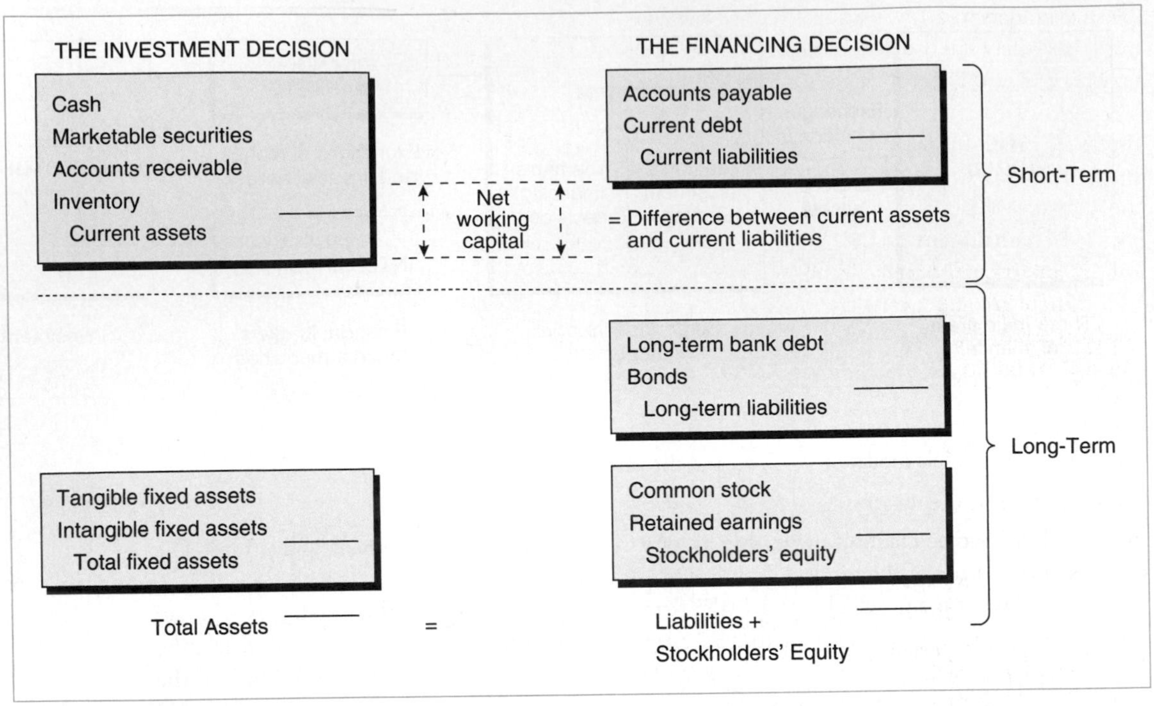

FIGURE 1.5
The accounting model of the firm.

FIGURE 1.6
The set-of-contracts model of the firm.

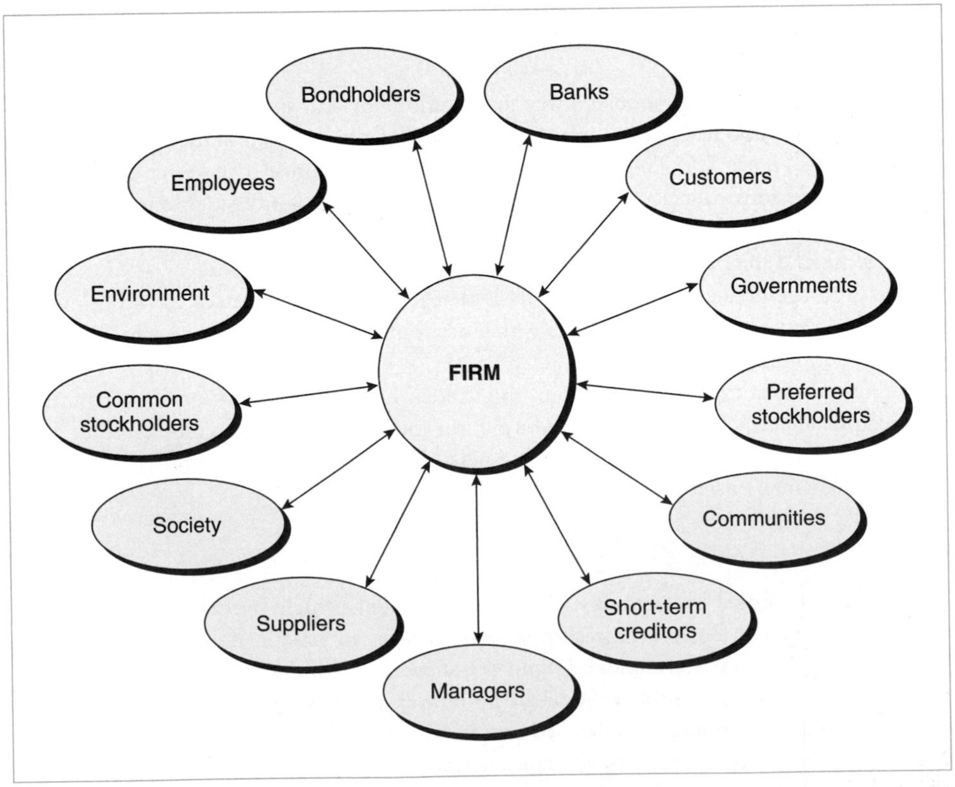

the shareholders to act in the shareholders' best interests. Regulatory and legal requirements, such as workplace safety standards and product liability, include both explicit and implicit contracts. At times, a court of law may have to determine the specific obligations of both explicit and implicit contracts.

Many contracts depend on the occurrence of particular future outcomes, such as an employee bonus if profits reach a certain level. The bonus is *contingent* on reaching this profit amount. There are many such contingent contracts. Participation in a retirement plan may be contingent on having worked for the firm for a minimum number of years. This type of contract is called a **contingent claim.** The contract's outcome is contingent on the value of some other asset or a particular occurrence.

There are many contingent claims in business. A loan can be a contingent claim. If a firm does not repay, the lender can seize the collateral. However, that claim is contingent on the firm's contractual failure. Without such a failure, the lender cannot take the collateral.

Review

1. What is the major difference between debt and equity?
2. How is the accounting model a subset of the investment-vehicle model?
3. How does the set-of-contracts model of the firm build on the investment-vehicle model of the firm?
4. Which two types of contracts are important according to the set-of-contracts model?
5. What is a contingent claim? Give an example.

1.4 THE ROLE OF THE CORPORATION

We focus on the corporation because it is the predominant form of business organization in the United States. Corporations issue a variety of financial securities, many of which are publicly traded. This section discusses the advantages of the corporate form over the primary alternative forms.

The Corporate Form

There are four basic forms of business organization: sole proprietorship, partnership, corporation, and limited liability company. In a **sole proprietorship,** a single individual owns all the firm's assets directly and is directly responsible for all its liabilities. The sole proprietor has *unlimited liability.* That is, the sole proprietor's entire personal wealth is at risk. But a sole proprietorship is not a taxable entity. Instead, the proprietorship's income is added to the owner's other income to determine income taxes due. Most small businesses are set up as proprietorships because they are easy to organize.

A **partnership** is similar to a sole proprietorship except that there are two or more owners. In a *general partnership* all partners have unlimited liability, including unlimited liability for actions taken entirely by other general partners. The partners share in profits and losses, often in proportion to their respective capital contributions to the partnership. As with a proprietorship, the income from the business is taxed directly to the general partners; a partnership does not pay income taxes. Oil and gas ventures and real estate ventures are often organized as partnerships because of tax laws.

The partnership form has another disadvantage besides unlimited liability. If a general partner leaves the partnership or dies, the partnership must be dissolved. This is very inconvenient if there are many partners. Many states permit *limited partnerships,* in which there are one or more limited partners in addition to the general partners. The general partners run the partnership with unlimited liability. The limited partners contribute capital and share in partnership profits or losses. But a limited partner's liability is limited to the invested capital. In addition, limited partners are typically allowed to withdraw by selling their partnership interest, which avoids the need to dissolve the partnership when someone dies or wishes to withdraw.

A **corporation** is legally a "person" that is separate and distinct from its owners, the shareholders. Among other things, it is allowed to own assets, incur liabilities, and sell securities. Corporate officers are agents who are authorized to act for the corporation.

The **limited liability company** form has recently emerged as a viable alternative to the corporate and partnership forms. It offers limited liability, like a corporation, but is normally taxed like a partnership. Its main disadvantage is that it is taxed like a corporation if its shares are allowed to trade in the open market. Table 1.1 compares the corporate form of organization to three other forms of organization.

The corporate form of organization has four major advantages over the other three forms:

- **Limited liability**. Shareholders' liability for corporate obligations is limited to the loss of the shares. If a corporation goes bankrupt, as Enron did in 2001 and WorldCom and Conseco did in 2002, or loses a large product-liability suit, as many asbestos producers have, the most its shareholders can lose is their invested capital. In a sole proprietorship or a general partnership, the owners can lose considerably more—in the extreme case, virtually everything they own.
- **Permanency.** A corporation's legal existence is not affected when some of its shareholders die or sell their shares. It is more permanent than a proprietorship or a partnership.
- **Transferability of ownership.** Selling shares in a corporation is normally easier than selling a proprietorship, a general-partnership interest, or shares of a limited liability company.
- **Better access to external sources of capital.** Because of its permanency and its ability to borrow money or to sell additional shares, a corporation has greater financing flexibility.

The corporate form does have a significant drawback, however. A corporation must pay taxes on its income. Operating income paid to shareholders through cash dividends is taxed twice, first to the corporation and then to the shareholder.

Of course, there are many other forms of organization. These include master limited partnerships, mutual organizations, religious organizations, fraternal organizations, not-for-profit corporations, and many kinds of governmental organizations. Although we focus mostly on profit-making corporations, the principles of finance apply equally well to other forms of organizations.

Ownership Rights

A corporation's shareholders, its owners, have the following rights:

- **Dividend rights.** Shareholders get an identical per-share amount of any dividends.[4] However, the decision to pay dividends is made by the firm's board of directors and is subject to legal and other restrictions.
- **Voting rights.** Shareholders have the right to vote on certain matters, such as the annual election of directors. In most cases, each share of common stock entitles its holder to one vote. A corporation's *articles of incorporation* typically specify either of two voting procedures: majority voting or cumulative voting. Under *majority voting,* shareholders vote for each director separately, casting one vote per share for each director they support. The candidates receiving the largest numbers of votes are elected to the board. Alternatively, under *cumulative voting,* the directors are voted on jointly, and a shareholder can cast all his votes in favor of a single candidate. Cumulative voting makes it easier for a minority-shareholder group to elect a particular representative to the board.
- **Liquidation rights.** Shareholders have the right to a proportional share of the firm's residual value in the event of liquidation. The residual value is what remains after all the corporation's other obligations have been settled.
- **Preemptive rights.** In some corporations, shareholders have the right to subscribe proportionally to any new issue of the corporation's shares. Such offerings are called *rights offerings.*

---

[4]Some corporations have more than one class of common stock. The classes may have different dividend rights. But within each class, the stockholders share equally on a per-share basis in any dividends.

TABLE 1.1
Comparison of alternative forms of organization.

	SOLE PROPRIETORSHIP	CORPORATION	PARTNERSHIP	LIMITED LIABILITY COMPANY
Management:	The sole proprietor owns and operates the business.	The corporation owns and operates the business. Employees of the corporation manage the business. The shareholders are represented by the corporation's board of directors.	The partnership owns and operates the business. One of the general partners is usually designated the manager of partnership operations. The partnership agreement specifies who exercises operating and management authority.	The company owns and operates the business. Employees of the company manage the business.
Liability for Financial Obligations:				
-Nature of liability	The sole proprietor bears full liability.	The shareholders have no direct liability for the corporation's financial obligations.	The general partners are jointly and severally liable for all obligations of the partnership as well as for certain liabilities incurred by any general partner. Limited partners have no liability for partnership obligations except obligations they specifically undertake.	The shareholders have no direct liability for the company's financial obligations.
-Dollar amount of exposure	Liability is unlimited.	Liability is limited to equity invested.	Liability is unlimited for general partners. Liability is limited to equity invested for limited partners.	Liability is limited to equity invested.
Income Tax Treatment:				
-Taxable entity	Sole proprietor.	Corporation.	Partners.	Shareholders in the company, which is treated as a partnership for federal income tax purposes provided it is privately held.[a]
-Deductibility, depreciation, and interest expense	All tax consequences of business flow through directly to the sole proprietor. The sole proprietorship is not a taxable entity.	The tax benefits of ownership are claimed by the corporation.	The tax benefits of ownership usually flow through to partners in the same proportion as ownership percentages.	Tax benefits of ownership usually flow through to shareholders in the same proportion as ownership percentages.
-Limitation on tax deductions	No limitations.	Deductions may not be taken directly by the shareholders.	Deductions are usually limited to the tax basis of each partner's investment.	Deductions are usually limited to the tax basis of each shareholder's investment.
-Income taxation	Income is taxed at the sole proprietor level only.	Income is taxed at the corporate level. Dividends are taxable to the shareholders as ordinary income	Income is taxed at the partner level only.	Income is taxed at the shareholder level only.

[a]A limited liability company is taxed as a corporation if its shares are traded in the public securities market.

When a firm has two or more classes of common stock with differences in dividend, voting, liquidation, or preemptive rights, the different classes of stock will usually trade at different prices. The prices reflect the differential rights.

The Goal of a Business

Many people say a firm's goal is profit. More carefully stated, according to the investment-vehicle model, a firm's goal is to *maximize shareholder wealth.* Shareholder wealth maximization is a more specific form of profit maximization.

WHY NOT PROFIT MAXIMIZATION? There are at least three important reasons why profit maximization is not an operational goal. First, profit maximization is vague. *Profit* has many different definitions. Do we mean accounting profits (based on book values) or economic profits (based on market values, and beyond a fair return)? Are we measuring private profits or social profits, which include any impacts on all parts of society? Are we maximizing short-run profits or long-run profits?

Second, profit maximization ignores differences in when we get the money. These differences are important because of the *time value of money.* Profit maximization does not clearly distinguish between getting money today and getting it in the future. When costs and benefits extend over time, such as a few years, profit measures fail to properly adjust for differences in value.

Third, profit maximization ignores risk differences between alternative courses of action. When given a choice between two alternatives that have the same return but different risk, most people will take the less risky one. This makes the less risky alternative more valuable. Profit maximization ignores such differences in value.

SHAREHOLDER WEALTH MAXIMIZATION **Shareholder wealth maximization** focuses the profit motive squarely on the owners. By maximizing shareholder wealth, we are directly addressing the problems of profit maximization. First, shareholder wealth is unambiguous. It is based on the future cash flows that are expected to come to the shareholders, rather than an ambiguous notion of profit. (A cash flow is a transfer of money from one party to another.) Second, shareholder wealth depends explicitly on the timing of future cash flows. Finally, our process for measuring shareholder wealth accounts for risk differences.

Review

1. Discuss the major advantages and disadvantages of the corporation as compared to sole proprietorships, partnerships, and limited liability companies.
2. Explain how limited partnerships differ from general partnerships.
3. What are the four types of rights corporate stockholders have?
4. State the goal of the firm. How is this different from the goal of profit maximization?

1.5 THE EVOLUTION OF FINANCE

Finance has evolved by addressing important business, economic, and social problems. For example, finance has long been concerned with the role of the firm in allocating society's resources. Recently, some have begun to question whether the modern corporate form, as we know it, will be eclipsed by a more efficient organizational form. Another form may be better able to function in a global environment and better serve the needs of all its stakeholders.

Historical Development

During the Great Depression in the 1930s, finance was very legalistic and descriptive, dealing with the bankruptcies and reorganizations that were rampant at that time. Following World War II, it remained descriptive, but focused on business investment decisions to assist in the postwar economic boom. In the late 1950s, finance took a radical turn. It moved beyond simply describing current practice. It became a science, and endeavored to explain the causes and consequences of financial transactions. During the 1960s and 1970s, there were important advances in the pricing of risky assets and in valuing contingent claims. Since then, the field has investigated asymmetric information and the problems of agency theory. The focus has been on efficient contracts that achieve the various participants' objectives.

The scientific quest for understanding has paid off. Several people have been awarded Nobel Prizes for their contributions to finance. Nobel Prize winners to date whose work has contributed to understanding finance are shown below in the box.

Contemporary Trends

Three important trends in finance are globalization, computerization, and corporate reorganization. These trends are rapidly changing the business world.

GLOBALIZATION Lower trade barriers, cheaper and more reliable transportation, and instantaneous electronic communication have transformed business into a global marketplace. Large securities firms, such as Salomon Smith Barney, trade U.S. Treasury securities "around the clock." They transfer the "trading book" from New York to Tokyo to London and back to New York in order to maintain continuous markets. Don't think of globalization solely as the importing and exporting of such things as cars and wheat. Globalization is much more.

Almost every product and service has some international content. Financial services are now an important part of the global marketplace. Even corporations themselves are more international. Ownership transcends national boundaries, as do the capital markets. Your working environment is likely to be multinational and diverse in many ways.

COMPUTERIZATION AND TELECOMMUNICATIONS Powerful, low-cost computing has become a fact of life. Securities trade in electronic markets. Most analysts have more computing capacity on their desks than was available in the highest-capacity computer in existence not many

Nobel Prize Winners Whose Work Has Contributed Significantly to Finance

James Tobin, 1981—Liquidity and behavior under risk

Franco Modigliani, 1985—Capital structure and dividend policy

Harry M. Markowitz, 1990—Portfolio theory

Merton H. Miller, 1990—Capital structure and dividend policy

William F. Sharpe, 1990—Capital asset pricing

John Nash, 1994—Game theory

James A. Mirrlees, 1996—Asymmetric information

William S. Vickrey, 1996—Asymmetric information

Robert C. Merton, 1997—Option pricing

Myron S. Scholes, 1997—Option pricing

George A. Ackerloff, 2001—Adverse selection

A. Michael Spence, 2001—Asymmetric information

Joseph E. Stiglitz, 2001—Asymmetric information

Daniel Kahneman, 2002—Behavioral finance

Vernon L. Smith, 2002—Behavioral finance

Other winners whose related work has also been particularly important to finance include Kenneth Arrow, 1972; Milton Friedman, 1976; Herbert Simon, 1978; George Stigler, 1982; Gerald Debreu, 1983; and Ronald Coase, 1992.

years ago! In addition, there has been a simultaneous development of telecommunications media that share databases, information, images, and conferencing almost anywhere in the world. It is hard to imagine how many people in the world knew within minutes about the attack on the World Trade Center—including those on the doomed fourth hijacked plane that crashed in Pennsylvania.

Individual firms have thrived and disappeared because of their ability, or inability, to use technology effectively. Likewise, individual managers have thrived—or lost their jobs—because of their willingness and ability, or lack of, to use computing and telecommunications technology. If you become a financial analyst, you will have access to vastly more information at the push of a button than could have been obtained by any means not long ago.

CORPORATE REORGANIZATION AND RESTRUCTURING We have seen a procession of corporate reorganizations, bankruptcies, mergers, acquisitions, and spinoffs. Just think of Enron, WorldCom, Conseco, and the "dot-com" craze. Hundreds of firms saw their shares soar in value only to plunge into bankruptcy and disappear just a few years later. Within large and small firms, the managerial and professional staffs have, at times, been in turmoil. During a recent period, the Fortune 500 corporations (the 500 largest industrial corporations in the U.S.) laid off over 5 million employees. People can no longer expect their jobs to be secure, and they are not as likely to spend an entire career with one firm.

In the past, professionals had one or possibly two distinct careers during their working lives, and only a couple of different employers. Today's generation of managers may have very different career paths. You may go through three, four, or even more, distinct careers, and you may work in shorter stretches for more employers before you retire.

Today, a corporation may be less willing to hire, train, and work to retain employees who are not well trained and highly motivated. We sincerely believe that sound training in finance is critical to your career. Such training provides valuable skills and insights that will enhance your understanding of the nature of business, the marketplace, and your place in it.

Review

1. How have the trends in globalization, computerization and telecommunications, and corporate reorganization affected the business world?
2. Is a recent graduate more or less likely than in the past to spend an entire career with a single firm?
3. How can sound training in corporate financial management affect your career?

1.6 A FEW WORDS OF ADVICE

There are some things we encourage you to keep in mind as you study. These are things we have found to be helpful to our students.

Financial Principles

This book was written with an overriding belief that if you understand the "first principles," every problem and issue can be solved using these principles. Essentially, we believe that if you understand general concepts, you can always apply that understanding to a specific situation. And once you understand the principles and the structure of the financial world, using those principles can be interesting and even fun.

Financial Jargon

When you first encounter a subject, you must learn new terms. Finance is no exception. It has its own language, or jargon. And when you learn a new language, it is better to add vocabulary in sequence, rather than trying to learn all of it at once. A rich language has many terms for essentially the same thing, but each term has subtle differences that make it the "best" term to use in a particular situation. This richness provides more precise communication and is welcome in technical situations. However, it can be overwhelming at first.

Toward this end, we will help you avoid getting bogged down in terminology. For now, we'll keep it simple, concentrating on helping you understand the basic concepts rather than forcing you to memorize new terms. Although the new terminology is essential, we will endeavor to familiarize you with the terminology of finance in a way that promotes your understanding of the basics. In the longer term, however, it is very important that you learn the language of finance. Unless you do, it can be very difficult to comprehend fully the more subtle concepts.

Business Calculators

We recommend you purchase a good business calculator. You may have a calculator that will add, subtract, multiply, and divide or a "scientific" calculator with complex math functions. These calculators are good for balancing your checkbook or for courses in statistics, engineering, chemistry, and the like. However, this is a finance course, and we have written this book with a business calculator in mind.

Business calculators are necessary equipment in the business world. For convenience, we will simply say "calculator" when we mean a business calculator. Such a calculator will also serve you well in other classes, in your professional life, and in your personal financial transactions, such as your investments and loans.

Finance Isn't Just for Finance Majors

Regardless of your major, we believe this will be an important and worthwhile course for you. The principles can be immediately used in your personal financial transactions, such as borrowing money or using a credit card. This course will also provide important preparation for additional study. Even if you are majoring in another subject, this course will provide you with the ability to apply financial principles in that field. If you are undecided about a major, this course could help you decide on a major. We are admittedly biased, but we encourage you to consider finance.

We appreciate the opportunity to teach you about finance. We believe finance can enhance your professional and personal lives in many ways. We hope your finance studies pay you generous dividends.

SUMMARY

The purpose of Chapter 1 is to introduce you to the field of finance and the objective of corporate financial management. Some of the key concepts covered in the chapter are:

- Finance is the field concerned with acquiring, investing, and managing capital.
- The fundamental questions that finance addresses are: (1) What assets should the firm acquire? (2) How should the firm be financed? (3) What operating and financial decisions are consistent with the goal of the firm to maximize shareholder wealth?
- The three basic areas of finance are corporate finance, investments, and capital markets and financial intermediaries.
- Three basic models of the firm are: (1) the investment-vehicle model, which views the firm from the viewpoint of stockholders, (2) the accounting model, which represents the firm as a set of financial statements, and (3) the set-of-contracts model, which views the firm as a set of contracts among its various stakeholders.
- The corporate form of organization benefits from limited liability, permanency, transferability of ownership, and better access to capital markets. A big disadvantage can be double taxation of income.

- The rights of stockholders include dividend rights, voting rights, liquidation rights, and (sometimes) preemptive rights.
- Profit maximization suffers from vagueness, not accounting for the time value of money, and not accounting for risk.
- Shareholder wealth maximization is the goal of the firm in the investment-vehicle view of the firm. Shareholder wealth maximization means maximizing the value of the firm to its owners.
- The field of finance has evolved in response to the major societal and economic needs of the times.
- Current significant trends in finance involve globalization, computerization and telecommunications, and restructuring of the business environment and the workplace.

QUESTIONS

1. What is finance? What is corporate financial management? What are the three major questions that financial managers deal with?
2. What are the two basic types of financial securities that firms issue? What are the differences between them?
3. What are three problems associated with using profit maximization as the goal of the firm? What is shareholder wealth maximization? How does shareholder wealth maximization deal with these three problems?
4. What are the advantages of the corporate form of organization over the sole proprietorship and partnership forms? What is the primary disadvantage of the corporate form?
5. Distinguish between investing decisions and financing decisions within the area of corporate financial management. Give one example of each.
6. Give examples of a firm's stakeholders in the set-of-contracts view of the firm. Distinguish between an explicit contract and an implicit contract and give an example of each.
7. What is a contingent claim? Give an example of a contingent claim.
8. Explain the four rights of common stockholders. Which of the four rights is often not offered to common stockholders by modern corporations?

CHALLENGING QUESTIONS

9. Classify each of the following jobs into one of the three areas of finance (1) corporate finance, (2) investments, or (3) capital markets and financial intermediaries.
   a. A credit analyst for a manufacturing firm who decides which customers receive credit.
   b. A financial planner who advises individuals on how to invest to achieve their long-term financial needs.
   c. An individual who is looking at several stocks as potential additions to an investment portfolio.
   d. A manager who is evaluating long-term equipment purchases for an employer.
   e. A stockbroker who helps clients buy and sell securities.
   f. A bank loan officer who attempts to identify good customers to whom the bank should lend money.
   g. A manager who is deciding how an expansion of a business should be financed.
10. Consider the fictionalized account of Henry's car firm.
    a. Describe some of the conflicts of interest between Henry and the bank.
    b. Describe some of the conflicts of interest between Henry and the other shareholders.
    c. Describe some of the conflicts of interest between the managers and the other shareholders of Henry's firm.

2

The Financial Environment: Concepts and Principles

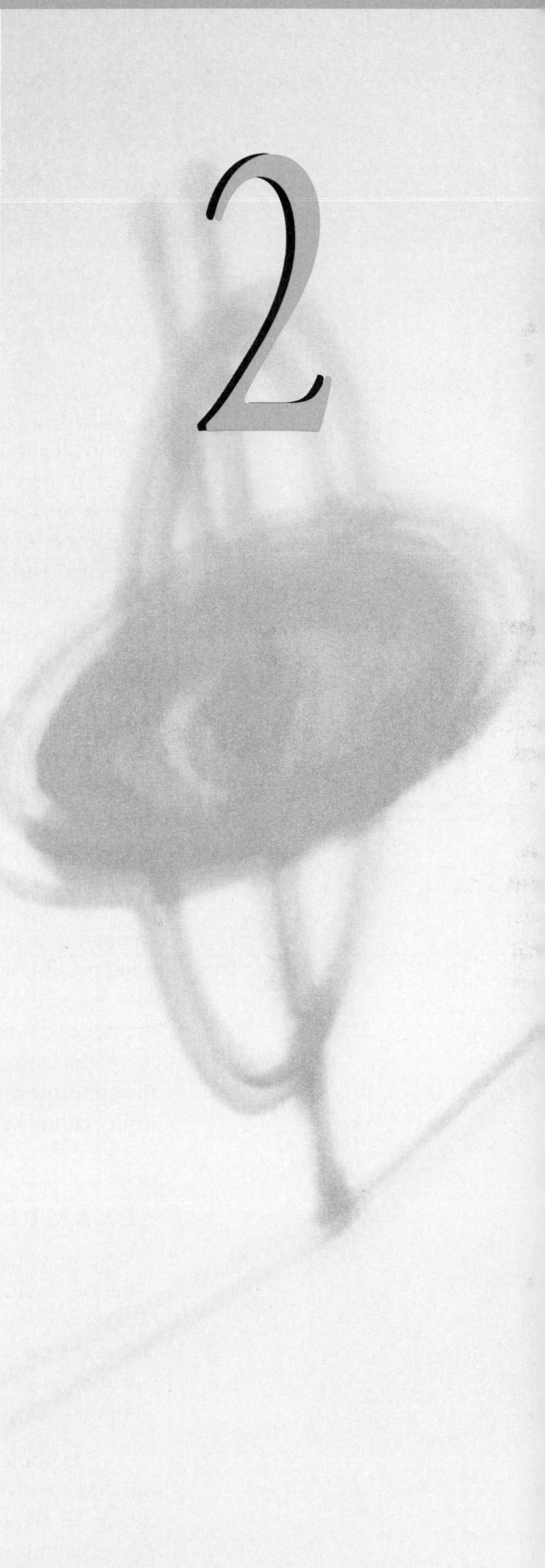

Every field of endeavor has fundamental laws, principles, or tenets that help guide you in understanding that field. Finance is no exception. There are important, basic principles that can help you understand mundane practices in finance as well as new and complex situations.

If you wanted to sell your car, would you want to get the highest possible price? Sure. Do you think a person who wanted to buy it would want to pay the lowest possible price? Undoubtedly. Suppose you wanted to invest some money. Would you like to triple your money in the next year? That would be nice. But do you want to risk losing all your money? Not really. Do you think you might have to take some risk to get a superior return? Probably. If someone guaranteed to double your money in six months with absolutely no risk, would you doubt them? We hope so. If we owed you $100, would you rather have it today or in three years? Today, of course.

The answers to these questions are obvious in such straightforward situations. They come from intuition you have developed, based on an understanding of the world. In more complex situations, answers are not always so easy. So you need principles to help you.

In this chapter we describe the principles of finance. They are the foundations on which financial management is built. We will help you understand their application to the practice of finance.

We also take a quick look at the capital markets. Recall that a financial security, which we will call simply a *security*, is issued by a firm to finance itself. A security, such as a stock or bond, is essentially a claim on future cash flows, such as dividend and interest payments. Capital market transactions (buying and selling securities) are important, both as a part of financial management and as a place to observe and apply the principles of finance.

2.1 PRINCIPLES OF FINANCE: THE COMPETITIVE ECONOMIC ENVIRONMENT

The principles of finance, described in this section and the two that follow, are based on logical deduction and on empirical observation. Even if every principle is not absolutely correct in every case, most practitioners accept the principles as a valid way to describe their world.

Our first group of principles deals with competition in an economic environment.

The Principle of Self-Interested Behavior: People Act in Their Own Financial Self-Interest

To make good business decisions, you need to understand human behavior. Although there may be individual exceptions, we assume that people act in an economically rational way. That is, people act in their own financial self-interest.

It may be hard to swallow the Principle of Self-Interested Behavior at first. One reason is that most of us realize money is not everything. The Principle of Self-Interested Behavior does not deny this truth; nor does it deny the importance of "human" considerations. It is not saying money is *the most important thing* in life.

This principle says that when all else is equal, all parties to a financial transaction will choose the course of action most financially advantageous to themselves. It explains actual behavior very well. This is because most business interactions are "arm's-length" transactions. In such impersonal transactions, getting the most good out of available resources is the primary consideration.

You might think that giving money to a charity, having children, and being honest on your tax return are violations of the Principle of Self-Interested Behavior. They are not. These decisions involve more than money. But even if certain actions do violate the Principle of Self-Interested Behavior, the principle is still useful for our purposes. This is because it is a very good approximation of human behavior.

There is an important corollary to the Principle of Self-Interested Behavior. Frequently, competing desirable actions can be taken. When someone takes an action, that action eliminates other possible actions. Informally, people often refer to an unused opportunity as an opportunity cost. More precisely, an **opportunity cost** is the difference between the value of one action and the value of the best alternative.

An opportunity cost provides an indication of the relative importance of a decision. When the opportunity cost is small, the cost of an incorrect choice is small. Similarly, when the opportunity cost is large, the cost of not making the best choice is large.

EXAMPLE The Opportunity Cost of Selling a Used Car

Suppose you sell a car for $3,200 without much forethought. You find out the next day that the car could have been sold for $3,300. You have incurred an opportunity cost of at least $100. You might not consider that very significant. But suppose you discovered the next day that the car could have been sold for $4,500. You probably would consider the opportunity cost of $1,300 on an asset worth $4,500 significant.

Do not let the simplicity of our used-car example lull you into thinking such costs are obvious and easy to calculate. In some cases, opportunity costs are very subtle and difficult even to define, let alone calculate. However, the importance of opportunity costs cannot be overstated.

An important application of the Principle of Self-Interested Behavior is called **agency theory.** Agency theory analyzes conflicts of interest and behavior in a principal-agent relationship. Broadly speaking, a **principal-agent relationship** is a relationship in which one entity, an **agent,** makes decisions that affect another entity, a **principal.**

The set-of-contracts model we discussed in Chapter 1 views contracts as principal-agent relationships. Examples include those between the firm (as the principal) and its employees (agents), such as its managers, salespeople, and others. There are also principal-agent relationships involving pension fund managers, lawyers, and real estate, travel, and insurance agents. Important principal-agent relationships include those involving the firm's stockholders, managers, and bondholders.

EXAMPLE Death of Occidental Petroleum's Founder

Armand Hammer was the long-time chairman of Occidental Petroleum Corporation. Hammer's name had come to be synonymous with Occidental. He had built it into a major corporation. What do you think happened to Occidental's stock price when Armand Hammer's death was announced? It jumped up 9%. Trading volume exceeded 8 million shares, many times the stock's average trading volume, making it the most active stock on the New York Stock Exchange that day. Why?

Many oil industry analysts felt that Hammer had begun to operate the firm as his personal fiefdom. They accused him of using the firm's resources to support his own pet projects (such as an art museum to house his collection), even when investing in them was not in the best interests of stockholders. Stockholders believed his successor, Ray Irani, would make better business decisions. And indeed, most would agree that the firm fared much better under Irani.

The problem of **moral hazard** is a critical consideration in principal-agent relationships. Like our flip-flop example in Chapter 1, this problem is caused by *asymmetric information.* Moral hazard refers to situations wherein the agent can take unseen actions for personal benefit even though such actions are costly to the principal. By carefully analyzing individual behavior, agency theory helps us develop more effective provisions for contracts between a principal and an agent. A typical goal of such contract provisions is to reduce conflicts of interest, thereby reducing moral hazard problems.

The Principle of Two-Sided Transactions: Each Financial Transaction Has at Least Two Sides

The Principle of Two-Sided Transactions may seem very straightforward, yet it is sometimes forgotten when things become complex. Understanding financial transactions requires that we not become self-centered. Don't forget, while we are following self-interested behavior, others are also acting in *their own* financial self-interest. That includes those with whom we are transacting business. Consider the sale of an asset—or should we say the purchase? And that is just the point. For every sale, there is a purchase. For each buyer, there is a seller.

EXAMPLE So Who Was Buying?

Media reports of stock market transactions sometimes refer to "profit takers *selling off* their holdings" and causing a decline in the price of a particular common stock. The implication is that there was more selling than buying. You may even read in the newspaper that changes in market prices are the result of an "imbalance" between the amount of buying and the amount of selling that is taking place. This, of course, is not true.

When stocks are traded, there is a buyer and a seller for each share that changes hands. If you will recall the Principle of Self-Interested Behavior, you know the buyers did not deliberately buy a stock that was going to decline in value. They thought the stock would maintain or increase its value. It just happened that the buyers turned out to be wrong! Quite simply, it is these differences in expectations that lead to many of the securities trades in the first place.

We can describe this sort of situation as one where more people believe the stock is overvalued than believe the stock is undervalued. This difference in beliefs may lead to more *sell orders* than *buy orders.* However, in spite of the disequilibrium in orders (those *willing* to buy or sell), there is *exactly* one share purchased for each share sold. In such situations, people buy or sell until the market price reaches what they think is the correct value.

Most financial transactions are zero-sum games. A **zero-sum game** is a situation in which one player can gain *only* at the expense of another player. In these situations, my gain is your loss, and vice versa. This is exactly the case with most buyer-seller relations. A higher price costs the buyer and benefits the seller, and vice versa. Nevertheless, some transactions may not appear to be zero-sum games. Consider the case of municipal bonds (*munis;* pronounced "mu-nees").

EXAMPLE Tax-Free Municipal Bonds

Municipal bonds are issued by state and local governments. The interest payments on such bonds are exempt from federal taxes. This allows state and local governments to issue munis at a lower interest rate than they would have to pay if the interest were taxable. Purchasers of munis will get a higher after-tax return than they would if they had bought otherwise similar but fully taxable bonds. It appears, then, that this is not a zero-sum game. Both sides are better off. However, this is not so clear when you consider some other parties to the transaction. How about other taxpayers? Reducing one group of taxpayers' tax payments may cause others to bear a larger portion of the cost of running the government.

Many transactions that are not zero-sum games result from provisions in the tax code. We will not debate whether these provisions are good or bad. However, consistent with the Principle of Self-Interested Behavior, people actively seek out and exploit tax-created exceptions to the usual zero-sum-game condition.

Sometimes, people overlook the Principle of Two-Sided Transactions. Egotistical people can suffer from *hubris,* an arrogance due to excessive pride and an insolence toward others. They believe, mistakenly, that they are superior to those with whom they are doing business. Such hubris has led to many unfortunate decisions. For example, firms have often paid what seems to be an excessive amount to buy another firm. Such firms are implicitly saying that the marketplace is stupid. Unfortunately, often an accurate assessment is possible only after the fact. Empirical evidence shows successes and failures. However, on average, a firm's value does not increase by acquiring another firm.

EXAMPLE Hewlett-Packard's Offer to Take Over Compaq Computer

The management of Hewlett-Packard Company met with executives of Compaq Computer Corporation to discretely discuss a possible business combination. Within a few months, the firms announced their plan to merge to the world. What do you think happened to their stock prices when the plan was announced? HP's fell 19% and Compaq's fell 10%, for a combined $10.6 billion loss the next day. Investors apparently thought the merger would be bad for both firms. They registered that opinion "loudly" with the drop in price they were willing to pay for stock. Despite this reaction, the merger was ultimately accomplished—but only after HP's management fought and won a highly publicized battle of epic proportions to carry out their decision.

There are at least two sides to every transaction, and the parties on the other side can be just as bright, hardworking, and creative as you are. Underestimating your competitors can lead to disaster.

The Signaling Principle: Actions Convey Information

The Signaling Principle is another extension of the Principle of Self-Interested Behavior. It addresses the problem of *asymmetric information.* Assuming self-interested behavior, we can guess at the information or opinions behind the decisions we observe. For example, a decision to sell an asset might imply that the asset is in poor condition. Likewise, a firm's decision to enter a new line of business may reveal something about the firm's position and its belief in the venture's potential. Similarly, when a firm announces a dividend, stock split, or a new securities issue, people often interpret these actions as signals about the firm's future earnings. In fact, when actions are at odds with announcements, the actions are usually louder than words.

EXAMPLE Actions Versus Words

In the months before Enron collapsed, its executives actively discouraged other employees from selling their shares of Enron. Those other employees did not find out until later that, at the same time, some of those same executives were actively selling their own shares. Understandably, the other employees were outraged. If they had known of the actions, they could have "listened" to the actions instead of the words!

In another situation a few years earlier, K-mart's stock was trading around $16 per share, and said to be worth at least $20 by some retail-industry analysts. Meanwhile, corporate insiders sold 250,000 shares in one month, and 200,000 shares the next month, most of it at about $17. Some K-mart executives exercised stock options that were not scheduled to expire for another six years, and provided them only a small gain. One investment manager asked, "If the company is worth $20 or $30 per share, why are insiders selling the stock?" And once again, actions offered better information than words. Within a couple of years, K-mart filed for bankruptcy.

Of course, decisions can be misinterpreted. For example, recall the temporarily upward-sloping demand curve for flip-flops, discussed in Chapter 1. Many consumers incorrectly thought the incredibly low price signaled that the product was worthless.

The flip-flop example illustrates what is known as adverse selection. The problem of **adverse selection** occurs when offering something to the market seems to indicate something negative about the item being offered. Adverse selection discourages people from offering to sell good-quality products. This problem is common in used-equipment markets because the equipment offered for sale can be broken or even worthless as opposed to no longer needed.

The Behavioral Principle: When All Else Fails, Look at What Others Are Doing for Guidance

The Behavioral Principle is a direct application of the Signaling Principle. The Signaling Principle says that actions convey information. The Behavioral Principle says, in essence, "Let's try to use such information."

To help you understand the Behavioral Principle, we want you to imagine that you have already earned your degree and have been working for a medium-size corporation for about a year and a half in three different positions. Recently, your hard work and the long hours you have been putting in have been noticed by your boss, Mr. Womack, the financial vice president. In recognition of your accomplishments, Mr. Womack has invited you and your spouse to his home for dinner, along with several other members of the department and their spouses.

You and your spouse are just congratulating each other for having successfully navigated the very formal cocktail hour when you arrive at the dining room. It is larger than your whole apartment. As you seat yourselves in your assigned seats, you and your spouse simultaneously nudge each other, motioning toward the silverware. There is more silverware at your place setting alone than you have in your entire kitchen. You have no clue about which piece should be used for which food. What do you do?

There is only one reasonable way to proceed. Discreetly look down the table as each course is served and use the same piece of silverware that Mr. Womack is using. But suppose this is not possible—you cannot see Mr. Womack very well from where you sit. What should you do? You can simply "check out" the people immediately around you. Most of us will go with the majority if there is not someone we especially trust.

Now change the scenario from dinner to finance. Suppose you are a financial manager. You are facing a major decision that seems to have no single, clearly correct course of action. For example, suppose the board of directors has asked you to assess how the firm is currently being financed and perhaps recommend changes. As it turns out, there is no prescribed single optimal capital structure for a firm; managers must make an informed judgment. What should you do?

One reasonable approach is to look for guidance in what other firms similar to your firm are currently doing and have done in the recent past. You can imitate the firms that you feel are most likely to be the best guides, or you can imitate the majority. In particular, the policy choices made by other firms in the same industry can provide useful guidance. This form of behavior is sometimes referred to as the "industry effect." This is what we mean by the Behavioral Principle of Finance: When all else fails, look at what others are doing for guidance.

In practice, the Behavioral Principle is typically applied in two types of situations. In some cases, such as the choice of a capital structure, theory does not provide a clear solution to the problem. In other cases, theory provides a clear solution, but the cost of gathering the necessary information outweighs the potential benefit. Valuing certain assets is an example of the latter case. The value of some assets, such as stock or a piece of real estate, can often be estimated at relatively low cost from the observed recent purchase prices of similar assets. In cases such as these, managers use the Behavioral Principle to arrive at an inexpensive approximation of the correct answer.

We have just cited two appropriate applications of the Behavioral Principle: (1) the case where there is a limit to our understanding and (2) the case where its use is more cost-effective than the most accurate method. Both cases require thought and judgment. An application that is *not* appropriate is "blind imitation." Some people attempt to minimize personal cost and risk (cover their backside) by copying someone else. We want to leave you with an important warning to avoid this misapplication.

The Behavioral Principle can be tricky to apply. You have to decide when there is no single, clearly correct, best course of action. Further, having decided this, you must decide whether there is a "best" other or group of others to look to for guidance. Finally, you must determine from their actions what your best course of action would be. The Behavioral Principle is, admittedly, a second-best principle. It leads to approximate solutions in the best of situations and, in the worst, to imitating the errors of others. Despite its potential shortcomings, it can be very useful at times.

This principle also has an important corollary. Its application can lead to the **free-rider problem.** In such situations, a "leader" expends resources to determine a best course of action, and a "follower" receives the benefit of the expenditure by simply imitating. So the leader is subsidizing the follower. For example, McDonald's does extensive research and analysis concerning the placement of its restaurants. Other fast-food chains have at times chosen their new restaurant locations by simply building near a McDonald's restaurant. Patent and copyright laws are designed to protect innovators, at least to some extent, from the free-rider problem and to reward the introduction of valuable new ideas that improve society.

Review

1. Explain in your own words the Principle of Self-Interested Behavior.
2. What is a principal-agent relationship? Give some examples.
3. Why is it important to remember the Principle of Two-Sided Transactions?
4. Give an example of the Signaling Principle, where actions convey information.
5. What are two good reasons for using the Behavioral Principle?
6. Define the following concepts: *opportunity cost, zero-sum game, adverse selection,* and *free rider.*

2.2 PRINCIPLES OF FINANCE: VALUE

Our second group of principles deals with ways of creating value and economic efficiency.

The Principle of Valuable Ideas: Extraordinary Returns Are Achievable with New Ideas

The Principle of Valuable Ideas says you might find a way to get rich! New products or services can create value, so if you have a new idea, you might then transform it into *extraordinary positive value* for yourself.

Thomas Edison became a very wealthy man from having invented a large number of unique products, such as the light bulb, the phonograph, the motion picture, and many others. The ability to hold a patent granting the exclusive rights to produce a unique product further enhances the product's value. Even without patent protection, some firms have been successful at building brand loyalty. They convince consumers that they are the only firms that can produce particular types of products, and this conviction generates more repeat purchases and purchases of related products.

New ideas may also take the form of improved business practices or marketing. For example, a man named Ray Kroc bought a small chain of hamburger stands. By applying his ideas about how to operate the business, he made himself and a large number of other people very wealthy. You might have heard of Ray's little chain—it is called McDonald's. The list of such products and services is almost endless, and the potential for new products and services *is* endless.

The Principle of Comparative Advantage: Expertise Can Create Value

The Principle of Comparative Advantage may be familiar. In a broad sense, it is the very idea underlying our economic system. If everyone does what they do best, we will have the most qualified people doing each type of work. This creates economic efficiency: We pay others to do what they can do better than we can, and they pay us to do what we can do better than they can.

The Principle of Comparative Advantage is the basis for foreign trade. Each country produces the goods and services that it can make most efficiently. Then, when countries trade, each can be better off.

EXAMPLE Michael Jordan Plays Better Basketball

Michael Jordan is arguably the best basketball player ever, but for personal reasons, he left basketball and tried out for a baseball team. He then played only one season of minor league baseball before "throwing in the towel." He left baseball to others who play better than he does, and he went back to playing basketball, which he does better than anyone else.

The Options Principle: Options Are Valuable

An **option** is a right, without an obligation, to do something. In other words, the owner (the buyer of the option) can require the writer (the seller of the option) to make the transaction specified in the option contract (for example, sell a parcel of land). However, the writer cannot require the owner to do anything. Often, in finance, an explicit option contract refers to the right to buy or sell an asset for a prespecified price.

The right to buy is a **call option,** and the right to sell is a **put option.** Call options are frequently used by real estate developers. A call option allows the developer to gain the consent of all necessary parties *before* investing a large amount of money—money that could be lost if any of the parties later refused to sell their land.

Insurance is a kind of put option. Suppose you have insurance on your car, and the car is destroyed by a cement truck while it is parked. The insurance settlement can be viewed as selling the destroyed car to the insurance firm. Now you may or may not decide to buy another car, but that is your choice.

The Options Principle also has a corollary: An option cannot have a negative value to the owner. This is because the owner can always decide to do nothing. Of course, the option can be worthless. However, even the smallest chance of a positive payoff at *any* time in the future gives the option some positive value, however tiny that value might be.

The word *options* makes some people think of explicit financial contracts such as call options and put options. However, we use the term in its broadest sense: a right with no obligation attached. With such a broad definition, you can see that options are widespread. In fact, they exist in many situations without being noticed. The importance of options extends well beyond their easily identified existence because many assets contain "hidden" options.

One important hidden option is created by what is called limited liability. **Limited liability** is a legal concept within bankruptcy that limits an investor's possible loss to what has already been invested. For example, suppose a corporation fails to repay a debt. The debtholder cannot sue the stockholders for the money. So the most the stockholders can lose is the money they have already invested.

Limited liability creates the option to default, the *option* not to fully repay a debt. Of course, this is not an option you think of right away as being valuable. Nevertheless, it is a valuable option.

EXAMPLE Conseco Uses Its Option to Default

When Conseco, Inc. was unable to meet its financial obligations, it filed for protection from its creditors and reorganization under what is called *Chapter 11 of the U.S. Bankruptcy Code.* The result was that some of Conseco's creditors did not—and never will—get all the money they are owed. Of course, such situations are complex, and they have many other negative consequences and related problems. However, the fact of the matter is that Conseco, once one of the largest corporations in the U.S., failed to make legally required payments, it *defaulted,* and yet it continued to operate.

Hidden options dramatically complicate the process of measuring value. In some cases, such options actually provide an alternative way to value an asset, as we will see when we consider valuing shares of common stock. We discuss options in greater detail at several points in this text. For now, we hope you can see that an asset plus an option is more valuable than the asset alone.

The Principle of Incremental Benefits: Financial Decisions Are Based on Incremental Benefits

The Principle of Incremental Benefits states that the value derived from choosing a particular alternative is determined by the net extra—that is, incremental—benefit the decision provides compared to its alternative. The term *incremental* is very important. The incremental costs and benefits are those that would occur *with* a particular course of action but would not occur *without* taking that course of action.

For example, if General Motors spends nothing this year on advertising its products, some people will nevertheless buy GM products. Thus, the value to GM of advertising its products is based on the difference between whatever future sales they would make *with* the advertising expenditure and whatever future sales they would make *without* the advertising expenditure. And GM's decision, whether and how much to advertise, is based on the profit from the incremental sales that result from the advertising when compared to the cost of the advertising. In other words, the advertising decision is based on the *net* (incremental) change in profit.

The incremental benefits are cash flows in many situations. The incremental cash flow is the cash flow that would occur as a result of the decision minus the cash flow that would occur without the decision.

As with other principles, the Principle of Incremental Benefits can get lost when things become complex. But this principle is easily overlooked even in some relatively simple situations. There is one situation in which it may be difficult to accept and apply this principle. It involves the concept of a sunk cost. A **sunk cost** is a cost that has already been incurred; subsequent decisions cannot change it.

EXAMPLE Creating the Lockheed Tri-Star

When Lockheed Corporation developed its L-1011 tri-star jet, critical decisions were made about whether to continue the project. When the wide-body jet was first proposed, there was enthusiasm in the corporation about its potential. But after considerable work on the project, it became clear that the tri-star project would not be nearly as valuable as expected. Some decision makers at Lockheed proposed abandoning the tri-star. Others argued against such a strategy, because so much had already been spent on its development. The decision to continue with the project proved to be a disaster for Lockheed. Bankruptcy was only narrowly avoided, and the tri-star project was eventually scrapped.[1]

If Lockheed decision makers had applied the Principle of Incremental Benefits, they might have saved a lot of money. At some point, the potential benefits from finishing the project were insufficient to justify the remaining development costs. Concentrating on previous expenditures can obscure the fact that, in such cases, the firm should proceed with a project only if the necessary *remaining* costs are less than the projected final benefits from the project. Whatever expenditures have already been incurred—sunk costs—are not relevant to the decision to continue the project because they cannot be changed.

In spite of the Principle of Incremental Benefits, some individuals seem to have an emotional attachment to sunk costs. These people continue to own an asset even though they know they could sell the asset and reinvest their money more profitably elsewhere. Clearly, these individuals are not applying the Principle of Incremental Benefits. They are continuing to incur an opportunity cost. Unfortunately, identifying such situations can be very difficult. Still, remember that an asset is not like a family member. Most of us are emotional about people, but we recommend that you not be emotional about your investments.

[1]It was said by someone other than us: "Sunk costs nearly sunk Lockheed."

Review

1. Explain in your own words the Principle of Comparative Advantage.
2. What is the main difference between a call option and a put option?
3. Give an example of a successful business that illustrates the Principle of Valuable Ideas.
4. Which principle does the following situation violate? A firm has invested $50 million in a new computer chip. Its chief scientist wants to abandon the effort, but the vice president for research and development tells securities analysts that the firm "can't afford to abandon the project now."
5. Define the following terms: *incremental costs and benefits, sunk costs, option, call option,* and *put option.*

2.3 PRINCIPLES OF FINANCE: FINANCIAL TRANSACTIONS

Our last group of principles emerges from observing financial transactions.

The Principle of Risk-Return Trade-Off: There Is a Trade-Off Between Risk and Return

The Principle of Risk-Return Trade-Off says that if you want to have a chance at some really great outcomes, you have to take a chance on having a really bad outcome. In a financial transaction, we assume that *when all else is equal, people prefer higher return and lower risk.* To appreciate the justification for this assumption, simply ask yourself this question: If you are faced with two identical (including their riskiness) alternatives, except that alternative A provides a higher return than B, which alternative will you choose? We predict you will choose A.

Similarly, if you are offered two identical (including their return) alternatives, except that A is riskier than B, which alternative will you choose? If you are like most people, you will choose B. This behavior is called **risk aversion:** avoiding risk when all else is equal. In other words, investors are not indifferent to risk but require compensation for bearing it.

People generally behave as though they are averse to risk. Almost any decision or choice you make involves risk. For example, decisions to make an investment, take a job, or lend money involve varying degrees of risk. Personal decisions also involve risk, and your personal choices will generally reflect your attitude toward risk.

If people prefer higher return and lower risk and they act in their own financial self-interest, competition then creates the Principle of Risk-Return Trade-Off. Competition forces people to make a trade-off between the return and the risk of their investment. You just cannot get high returns and low risk simultaneously because that is what *everyone* wants. Therefore, to get a higher expected return, you will have to take more risk.

A corollary to the Principle of Risk-Return Trade-Off is that most people are willing to take less return in exchange for less risk. When an asset is bought or sold, its return can be adjusted by altering its sale price. A lower (higher) purchase price increases (decreases) the return. Capital markets, such as the stock market, offer such opportunities, and each participant makes his risk-return trade-off.

The Principle of Diversification: Diversification Is Beneficial

The Principle of Diversification is really quite straightforward, and requires little explanation. Prudent investors will not invest their entire wealth in a single firm. That would expose their entire wealth to the risk that the firm might fail. But if the investment is divided among many firms, the entire investment will not be lost unless all of those firms fail. This is much less likely than one of them failing. Spreading investments around, instead of concentrating them, is called

diversification. We will explain in Chapter 9 how investors can lower their risk by investing in a group of securities, called a **portfolio,** rather than by investing exclusively in one security.

EXAMPLE Examples of Diversification

Mutual funds, commercial banks, and other financial intermediaries all have very diversified portfolios. No single investment makes up a very large part of their overall portfolios. Individual investors are advised to diversify their portfolios broadly. Operating businesses diversify themselves in many ways. They operate in different business segments. They try to diversify their customer base; that is, they try not to depend too heavily on only a few customers. They diversify their sources of supply. Your college curriculum is diversified, because you cannot concentrate too heavily in one area of study to the exclusion of others. Even a healthy diet should be diversified.

Why is diversification so widespread? Quite simply, because it reduces risk.

The Principle of Capital Market Efficiency: The Capital Markets Reflect All Information Quickly

Buying and selling securities is referred to as **trading.** Probably the best-known capital markets are in New York, London, and Tokyo. The New York Stock Exchange (NYSE) and NASDAQ (National Association of Securities Dealers Automated Quotation) stock markets are the most widely known in the United States. Together with other stock exchanges around the world and smaller ones around the country, they are collectively referred to as the *stock market.* There are many other capital markets as well.

The Principle of Capital Market Efficiency says the capital markets are *informationally efficient.* More formally, *market prices of financial assets that are traded regularly in the capital markets reflect all publicly available information and adjust fully and quickly to "new" information.*

EXAMPLE Capital Markets React to New Information

Suppose an oil company announced the discovery of a massive new oil field. What stock market trading prices would change? Clearly, the share price of the discovering firm would rise. But what about other oil company stocks? Because of the increase in the supply of oil, the price of oil would decline, bringing down the value of the oil reserves owned by other firms. Therefore, we would expect that the share prices of the other oil companies would tend to fall (unless they were participating in the new discovery). Other share prices might change as well.

For example, cheaper oil should lead to cheaper plastic and increased business for a plastics manufacturer. That would suggest higher share prices for plastics manufacturers. However, the share prices of banks that have loaned Mexico a lot of money might decrease. The lower price of oil would reduce Mexico's oil revenue and increase the likelihood that those banks would not be fully repaid.

Alert traders who recognize these effects would act upon the information. Among other things, they might (1) buy the shares of the oil company that made the discovery, (2) sell the shares of oil companies not involved in the discovery, (3) buy the shares of firms such as plastics manufacturers that would benefit from the lower price of oil, and (4) sell the shares of lenders to Mexico that would be hurt by a lower price of oil.

This active trading is the mechanism by which new information becomes reflected in share prices. As you may have gathered by now, an event like a major oil discovery would provide opportunities to make a great deal of money quickly in many different capital markets. This opportunity to profit from new information provides the incentive to act (recall the Principle of Self-Interested Behavior) that causes share prices to respond to new information.

Capital market efficiency depends on how quickly new information is reflected in share prices. The capital markets in the U.S., Europe, and Japan are well organized. It is generally much easier, cheaper, and faster to buy and sell financial assets in these markets than to buy and sell real assets. For example, the cost of making a stock transaction (buying or selling) is very low, especially when compared to transaction costs in the real-asset markets (such as machines, real estate, and raw materials).

In addition to offering convenience, low cost, and high speed, the world capital markets are unimaginably large, with total transactions in the tens of billions of dollars each day. There are numerous participants, and competition is intense. When new information arrives, there are plenty of people paying close attention because there is a lot of money at stake. The lower the transaction costs and the easier it is to trade, the easier it is to act on new information, and the more quickly share prices adjust to reflect the new information.

In an efficient market that had no impediments to trading, the price of each asset would be the same everywhere in the market, except for temporary differences during periods of disequilibrium. In such a market environment, if price differentials existed, traders would take immediate actions to benefit from those differences through arbitrage. **Arbitrage** is the act of buying and selling an asset simultaneously, where the sale price is greater than the purchase price, so that the difference provides a riskless profit. As long as selling prices exceed buying prices, traders can earn a riskless arbitrage profit. And they can continue to do so until the price differential no longer exists.

Arbitrage enforces the economic principle called the *law of one price.* This law states that equivalent securities must trade at the same price. The law of one price may not hold strictly when there are transaction costs or other impediments to trading, but it is a good approximation of reality.

It is easy to accept the Principle of Capital Market Efficiency. Yet it is probably the hardest to "internalize" of all of the Principles of Finance. We all know there are people who win the lottery and people who occasionally amass vast fortunes trading in the stock market. How can we become a winner? How can we start with a small sum and amass a great fortune trading in stocks? (The answer to both questions is the same: only with luck or illegal activity!) If there were a reliable way to amass such a fortune, of course, everyone would do it, and then, instead of one great fortune, there would be a multitude of smaller "fortunes." Yet hope springs eternal!

EXAMPLE Hot Tips and Easy Money

The logic of the Principle of Capital Market Efficiency is impeccable, and a lot of empirical research supports it. Nevertheless, investors gobble up hot tips and continue to search for "bargains" in the stock market. Just about every major brokerage house regularly publishes a list of "undervalued stocks." If a stock appears on such a list, investors will evaluate the security and bid up the stock's price if they agree with the brokerage analysts' conclusion. In an efficient market, a stock does not remain undervalued for very long. So how can brokerage houses regularly identify and publish extensive lists of them? What special powers do their analysts possess that enable them to identify such undervalued firms?

If you are skeptical of the value of such lists, you are not alone. Empirical research has not shown them to provide extra value. People who seem to have the gift of "second sight" are more likely to trade for their own account (take the profits for themselves) than to publish a list so that other people can help themselves to the money. Why? You guessed it—the Principle of Self-Interested Behavior.

Competition, size, and the similarity of assets combine to make the capital markets informationally efficient for actively traded securities. Sometimes, we assume that the capital markets are *perfect* (100% efficient—no losses due to friction) in order to build a decision model. However, the dot-com bubble reminds us that the capital markets are not 100% efficient, even for actively traded stocks. And there are many stocks that seldom trade and whose prices may not accurately reflect their value. But a perfect market is still the best approximation we have of the capital markets. The assumption of perfect capital markets is like the assumption of risk aversion. Though not 100% correct, it is useful in many situations.

RECONCILING CAPITAL MARKET EFFICIENCY WITH VALUABLE NEW IDEAS You may find it difficult to reconcile the Principle of Valuable Ideas with the Principle of Capital Market Efficiency. Together, they state that the capital markets are efficient, but that even in the capital markets, with all the competition that exists, a *new* market, product, or service can be created that provides an extraordinary return.

Here is the critical difference between the two principles. The Principle of Valuable Ideas applies to the return associated with being part of the creation of the opportunity. The Principle of Capital Market Efficiency involves the return associated with simply purchasing part of an opportunity that has become known to everyone. The founders of Microsoft earned a tremendous rate of return on their investment as a result of their innovations. But what happened as other people became aware of the unique advantages that Microsoft's software offered? Those advantages became fully reflected in Microsoft's share price. Thus, once the stock became actively traded, a purchaser of Microsoft common stock could expect, because of capital market efficiency, to earn only a rate of return commensurate with the risk of the investment. Of course, because of the very nature of risk, the outcome could be quite different from what was expected.

The Time-Value-of-Money Principle: Money Has a Time Value

If you own some money, you can "rent" it to someone else. The borrower must pay you interest for the use of your money (or you will not make the loan). Simply stated, the time value of money is how much it costs to "rent" money.

You can think of the time value of money as the opportunity to earn interest on a bank savings account. Keeping money as cash creates an opportunity cost, not earning interest on the money. For this reason, we think of the interest rate as a measure of the opportunity cost. In fact, because of capital market efficiency, we use capital market alternatives as benchmarks against which to measure other investment opportunities: Do not make the investment unless it is at least as good as comparable capital market investments.

Suppose you deposit \$1,000 today in a bank savings account that is paying 7% per year. One year from today, the account will have \$1,070. We can call the starting amount PV (for present value) and next year's account balance FV (for future value). Let r be the interest rate. The interest earned over a time period is the interest rate times the amount deposited initially, $r(\text{PV})$. Then FV is the sum of the starting amount, PV, plus the interest, or

$$\text{FV} = \text{PV} + r(\text{PV}) = \text{PV}(1 + r) \tag{2.1}$$

For PV = \$1,000 and $r = 0.07$, in one year FV is \$1,070 (= 1,000(1.07)). In words, Equation (2.1) says the future value equals the present value times 1 plus the interest rate.

Equation (2.1) is based on *per-year* interest. But suppose you save the money for two years? At the end of the first year, the account contains \$1,070. By reapplying Equation (2.1) at the end of two years, you will have

$$\text{FV} = \$1{,}070(1.07) = \$1{,}144.90$$

Note that the account will earn \$70 interest the first year and an additional \$74.90 interest the second year. This is because the interest paid at the end of the first year itself earns interest the second year, amounting to \$4.90 (7% of \$70). Paying interest on interest already earned is called paying **compound interest.** The process of compounding interest can be handled by extending Equation (2.1). Let n be the number of time periods the money remains in the account. Thus

$$\text{FV} = \text{PV}(1 + r)^n \tag{2.2}$$

Now let us reverse the logic of Equation (2.2). This time, we rewrite the equation so that we can solve for PV (instead of FV).

$$\text{PV} = \frac{\text{FV}}{(1+r)^n} \tag{2.3}$$

In words, Equation (2.3) says a dollar today is worth more than a dollar in the future. This is because today's dollar can be invested to earn interest until tomorrow. The future amount is *discounted* to calculate the present value by dividing it by the quantity $(1 + r)^n$. This adjustment reflects the cost to rent money at an interest rate of r per period for n periods.

To compute a present value, you must estimate the amounts to be received in the future. The future amounts are referred to as *expected future cash flows.* Next, you must estimate the appropriate "rental" rate for each of the expected future cash flows from now until you expect to receive them. This rental rate has many different names, but the generic term for it is the **discount rate.**

EXAMPLE Present and Future Values

What is the future value of $1,000 invested today if it earns 10% interest for one year? for two years?

Using equation (2.2) where $FV = PV(1 + r)^n$:

$$FV = 1{,}000(1 + 0.10)^1 = 1{,}000(1.10) = 1{,}100$$

$$FV = 1{,}000(1 + 0.10)^2 = 1{,}000(1.21) = 1{,}210$$

What is the present value of $1,000 discounted at 10% if it is received in one year? in two years?

Using Equation (2.3):

$$PV = \frac{FV}{(1+r)^n} = \frac{1{,}000}{(1+0.10)^1} = \$909.09$$

$$PV = \frac{FV}{(1+r)^n} = \frac{1{,}000}{(1+0.10)^2} = \$826.45$$

Equation (2.3) is often referred to as the basic **discounted cash flow (DCF) framework** for valuation. It is simple in the form given, but it can become complex as we combine multiple expected future cash flows and allow the discount rate to change over time. Equation (2.3) can be used to value any asset, provided we can estimate the expected future cash flows and determine an appropriate discount rate for each cash flow. The discount rate must accurately reflect each cash flow's riskiness. Selecting the appropriate discount rate and estimating expected future cash flows is often difficult, even for an expert.

The Time-Value-of-Money Principle is probably the most useful concept you can learn in this class. The importance of this principle (and for that matter, of all the principles) rests on its ability to keep our thinking clear and logical. Chapter 4 is devoted to the time value of money, and applications of the principle appear throughout the book. You will encounter the time value of money repeatedly for the rest of your life.

Review

1. What does it mean to say an investor is risk averse?
2. Why do investors diversify their investment portfolios? (Answer in three words or less.)
3. Explain the Principle of Capital Market Efficiency in your own words.
4. Why is a dollar today worth more than a dollar to be received a year from today?
5. Compute the present value of $100 due in one year if the discount rate is 10%.
6. Define the following terms: *risk aversion, portfolio, diversification, arbitrage, compound interest,* and *discount rate.*

2.4 CAPITAL MARKETS

The capital markets are important and are watched very carefully by financial managers for several reasons. One reason is simply that firms make direct transactions in financial markets, such as issuing their own securities, redeeming or repurchasing their own securities, and investing in other firms' securities. A second reason is that many of the concepts and principles that apply to financial markets are concepts and principles that managers also apply to the management of the firm's real assets. Finally, capital markets provide information and signals that help managers make decisions.

Money Market Securities

Money market securities are short-term claims with an original maturity that is generally one year or less. The largest markets for money market securities are for Treasury bills, commercial paper, certificates of deposit, and bankers' acceptances. Money market securities tend to be high-grade securities with little risk of default. Because of the short maturities involved, the amount of interest earned simply does not allow much margin for default or for expensive credit investigations. Similarly, the securities rarely offer **collateral,** assets that can be claimed if the borrower defaults. The risk and amount of interest income are too small to justify the added expense involved with collateral.

TREASURY BILLS A Treasury bill (T-bill) is a short-term security issued by the U.S. government. The government regularly issues T-bills with original maturities of 13 weeks, 26 weeks, and 52 weeks. Most T-bills are sold in $10,000 denominations. T-bills do not have explicitly stated interest. Instead, they are sold on what is called a **discount basis.** For example, suppose a 52-week T-bill that will pay $10,000 at maturity is sold for $9,400. The $600 discount is the implicit interest the investor would earn.

COMMERCIAL PAPER Commercial paper is a promissory note sold by very large, creditworthy corporations. The minimum size is typically $100,000. Maturities range from 1 day to 270 days. Longer maturities require registration with the Securities and Exchange Commission, which is a fairly expensive process, so corporations simply do not issue maturities longer than 270 days. Corporations that issue commercial paper typically have a standby line of credit from a major bank. That way, if the firm finds itself short of the cash it needs to redeem the commercial paper, it can quickly and easily borrow the necessary funds to fulfill its obligation.

CERTIFICATES OF DEPOSIT Certificates of deposit (CDs) are promises to pay, written by a commercial bank, with maturities typically ranging between six months and five years. CDs are sold at face value and pay a fixed interest rate. The principal and the last period's interest are paid to the lender at maturity. Negotiable CDs have denominations of $100,000 or more and can be traded in the capital markets.

BANKERS' ACCEPTANCES Bankers' acceptances are short-term loans made to importers and exporters. They help facilitate international trade. The acceptance occurs when the bank "accepts" a customer's promise to pay. The bankers' acceptance is a guarantee that promises to pay the face amount of the security to whomever presents it for payment. The bank customer uses the bankers' acceptance to finance a transaction by giving the security to a supplier in exchange for goods or services. The supplier can either hold the acceptance until maturity and collect from the bank or sell it at a discount. Bankers' acceptances usually have short maturities (180 days or less). The security is a two-party obligation, a direct customer liability, and a contingent liability for the bank. Therefore, the risk of default is very low.

Bonds and Stocks

Bonds and stocks are long-term securities issued by corporations or governments.

LONG-TERM DEBT Bonds are long-term debt securities. Recall that debt is a legal obligation for borrowed money. A debt security is a promise to pay interest and to repay the borrowed money, the *principal,* on prespecified terms. Failure to make the promised payments is default. It can lead to bankruptcy. *Bonds* have maturities of ten or more years. *Notes* have maturities between one and ten years. Bonds and notes are often referred to as fixed-income securities, because they promise to pay specific (fixed) amounts to their owners.

STOCKS A share of stock is equity in a corporation. Recall that equity represents ownership. *Common stock* is the residual interest in the firm. It is residual because it is a claim on the earnings and assets of the firm *after* all of the firm's other, more senior obligations have been met. The common shareholders have the dividend rights, voting rights, liquidation rights, and preemptive rights we described in Chapter 1. Common stock does not have a maturity.

Preferred stock also represents an equity claim. There are some important differences between common stock and preferred stock. Preferred stockholders are promised a specific periodic dividend, whereas common stockholders receive whatever dividends are decided on (perhaps none) by the board of directors of the corporation each quarter. Preferred stockholders have a higher priority with respect to the payment of dividends and the distribution of liquidation proceeds. This means that preferred stockholders must be paid their dividends before common stockholders can be paid any dividends, and must receive their stated liquidation preference before the common stockholders get anything. However, if the firm is unable to pay its preferred dividends, it cannot be forced into bankruptcy. Preferred stockholders normally do not have a right to vote on general corporate matters.

Derivative Securities

A **derivative** is a security that derives its value from the value of another asset or an index value. Options, forward contracts, futures, and swaps are among the most common derivatives.

OPTIONS Call options and put options, which we described with the Options Principle, are very visible examples of derivatives. For example, suppose you own a call option on a share of stock giving you the right to buy the stock at a fixed price of $20 any time during the next three months. The value of your call option depends on the value of the underlying stock. The current stock price is $15. If the stock goes up to $35 per share, you can exercise your call option, and the payoff on the call will be $15 (the $35 value of the stock minus the $20 you pay to exercise your call option). By contrast, if the stock stays at $15, you will not exercise your right to buy the stock at $20 because the option would be worthless.

There are many securities with option-like features in addition to puts and calls. A warrant is a long-term call option issued by a corporation giving its holder the right to buy stock at a fixed price directly from the corporation. A convertible security gives holders the right to exchange the security for common shares. Employee stock options give employees the right to buy their employer's stock at stated exercise prices.

FUTURES AND FORWARDS A **futures contract** is a standardized **forward contract** that is traded in a futures market. A forward contract is an agreement to buy or sell something for a particular price at a future point in time. Note that a forward contract is not an option—the owner has the obligation to make the transaction. Futures are traded on commodities such as corn, oil, and gold. Futures are also traded on financial assets such as bonds, stocks, and foreign currencies. It may seem odd at first to contract to buy something in the future. Why not simply buy it now or wait and buy it when you need it?

The answer lies in the need to plan. Suppose you do not have a way to store what you are going to need. Or suppose what you are going to need has not been produced yet, as in the case of next fall's crop of corn. Market prices change according to supply and demand, so prices may be different in the future from what we expect. By making the contract now, we can lock in our future needs at an agreed-upon price.

For example, a food company such as Kraft Foods can plan for its needs for corn meal, and farmers can sell their corn before it is harvested. This enables both parties to benefit from the Principle of Comparative Advantage. By arranging the sale-purchase ahead of time, each side of the transaction can concentrate its efforts on what it does best. It need not worry constantly about what it will pay or earn for corn.

Forward contracts are also traded in private transactions. Though useful and common, such nonstandard contracts do not have the liquidity that the futures market provides.

SWAPS A swap is an agreement to exchange payments. For example, a typical interest-rate swap is the exchange of fixed-rate interest payments for floating-rate interest payments. An issuer of fixed-rate debt can enter into an interest-rate swap to transform the debt into floating-rate debt if that better suits its needs. A swap is usually cheaper than paying off the old debt and issuing new debt.

A **spot market** is a market in which assets are bought/sold for immediate delivery. Some of the same assets traded in spot markets are also traded in the futures markets.

Primary and Secondary Market Transactions

A **primary market** transaction is a firm's sale of newly created securities to get additional financing. The issuing firm receives the proceeds from the sale of the securities. The **secondary market** is where previously issued securities are bought and sold. Secondary market transactions account for the vast majority of trading in the capital markets. This is because a primary transaction takes place only once, when the securities are issued.

Brokers, Dealers, and Investment Bankers

Brokers, dealers, and investment bankers facilitate securities trading. Brokers and dealers are middlemen who assist investors in trading securities in the secondary market. A broker *helps* investors sell or buy securities, charging a sales commission. A broker does not take ownership of the shares, but a dealer does. Dealers buy securities for, and sell them from, their own accounts. Suppose you buy 100 shares of Sears stock through a broker. The broker arranges the purchase from someone else, typically through a stock exchange. If, instead, you buy the shares from a dealer, you are buying the shares from that person.

Although some firms get additional financing by selling securities directly to investors, many others raise capital with the assistance of investment bankers, who specialize in marketing new securities. The people who buy the securities can be individuals or financial institutions, such as pension funds, mutual funds, and insurance companies. In some cases, the investment banker acts as a broker, without taking ownership of the securities. In other cases, the investment banker acts as an **underwriter,** who guarantees a minimum price, thereby acting, in effect, as a dealer. The first time a firm issues shares to the public is called an **initial public offering (IPO).** If the firm later issues additional shares to the public, it is called a **seasoned offering.**

Financial Intermediaries

Financial intermediaries are *institutions* that assist in the financing of firms. Financial intermediaries include commercial banks and pension funds. They invest in securities but are themselves financed by issuing their own financial claims to others.

Commercial banks invest primarily in business and personal loans and in marketable securities. They finance their assets by selling various kinds of deposits, such as checking accounts, money market accounts, savings accounts, and certificates of deposit. Pension funds invest primarily in stocks, bonds, and mortgages. They finance their portfolios with the cash contributions made on behalf of pension beneficiaries and keep the funds invested until it is time to pay them

TABLE 2.1
Examples of financial intermediaries.

TYPE OF FINANCIAL INTERMEDIARY	PRIMARY KINDS OF INVESTMENTS	TYPES OF OBLIGATIONS
Commercial banks	Business and personal loans and securities	Deposit liabilities and bonds
Pension funds	Stocks, bonds, mortgages	Obligations to pension beneficiaries
Savings and loans	Mortgages	Certificates of deposit
Mutual savings banks	Mortgages	Certificates of deposit
Credit unions	Personal loans, car loans	Share deposits
Mutual funds	Stocks, bonds, or money market securities	Mutual fund shares
Insurance companies	Bonds, mortgages, stocks	Policy obligations

out as benefits. With financial intermediaries, savers invest in securities indirectly because the intermediary uses their savings to buy securities. Table 2.1 lists examples of the assets and obligations of various financial intermediaries.

Review

1. What are the primary kinds of money market securities?
2. How is preferred stock different from common stock?
3. What is a derivative? What are options, forwards, and swaps? What is a spot market, a forward market, and a futures market?
4. Distinguish between primary and secondary market transactions.
5. What are investment bankers, brokers, dealers, and financial intermediaries?

2.5 THE TERM STRUCTURE OF INTEREST RATES

One way to describe the market for debt securities is to graph the relationship between interest rate and maturity for a particular class of debt securities, such as U.S. Treasury securities. This shows how the interest rate depends on maturity. This relationship is called a *yield curve.* One form of yield curve has a special name. The yield curve for zero-coupon U.S. Treasury securities is called the *term structure of interest rates.* (Zero coupon means there are no payments until maturity, so that such securities always trade on a discount basis.) Informally, the phrase **term structure** is sometimes used to refer to the general relationship between debt maturity and interest rates. We will use this phrase as well.

Available maturities vary widely. At one extreme, investors borrow for less than a day. For example, banks borrow overnight in the federal funds market. At the other extreme, governments and firms regularly issue bonds with maturities of up to 30 years, and sometimes even as long as 100 years. A virtual continuum of maturities exists between these extremes.

More often than not, interest rates increase with maturity. Figure 2.1 shows an example of the common upward-sloping term structure of interest rates. There also are much less frequent periods when the reverse is true; the term structure is downward sloping. Figure 2.2 illustrates this unusual structure. Note that in both cases the curve flattens out as maturity increases, because differences in interest rates typically become smaller with longer maturity.

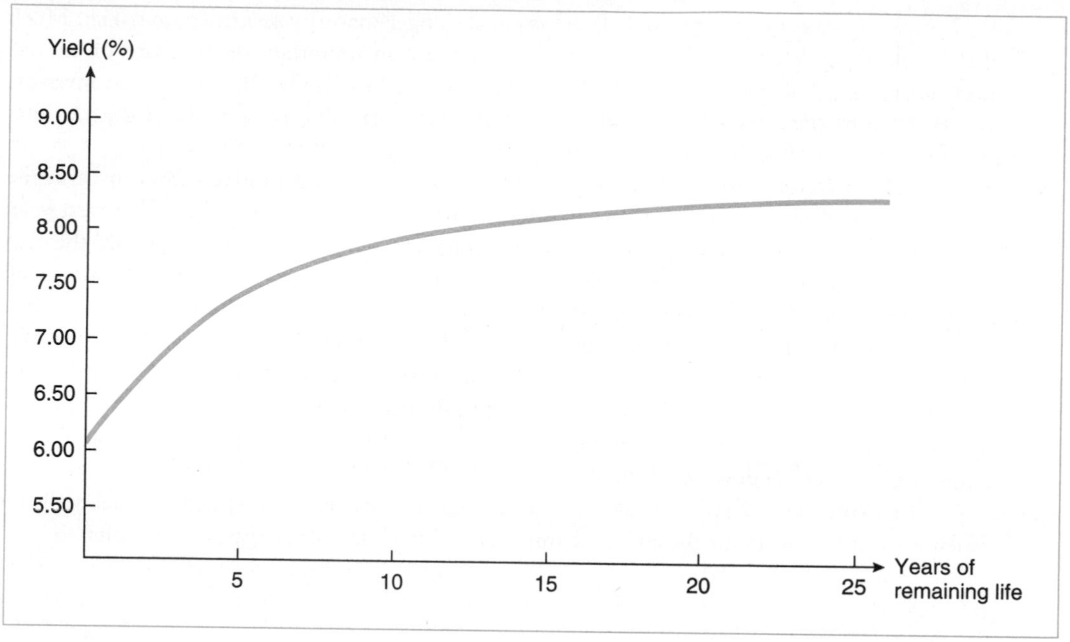

FIGURE 2.1
An example of the common upward-sloping term structure of interest rates.

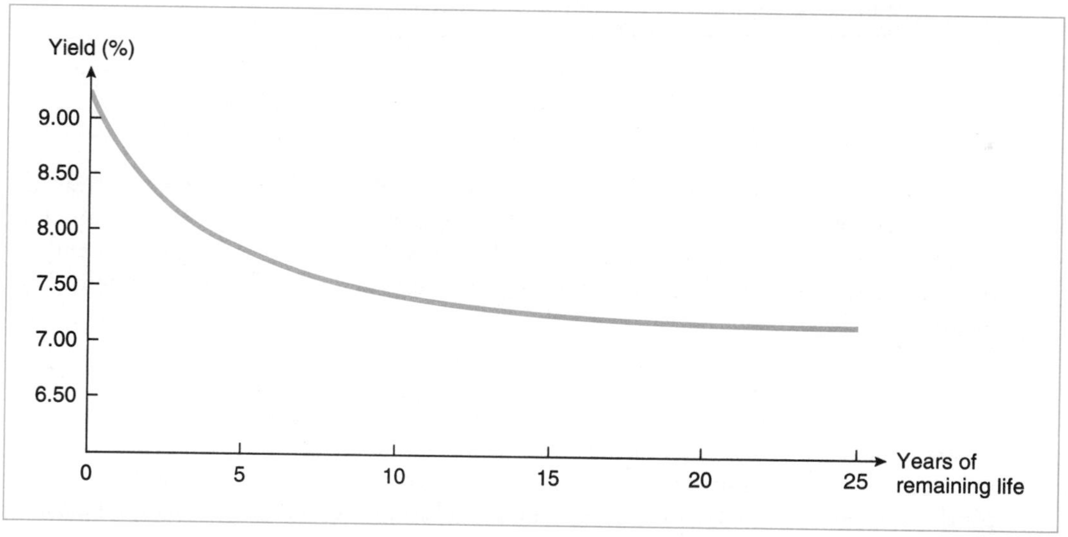

FIGURE 2.2
An example of the uncommon downward-sloping term structure of interest rates.

Interest rates are affected by the risk of default and the taxability of the returns. Investors require higher rates to offset tax liabilities and the possibility of default. For this reason, the securities used to compile a yield curve must all have the same default risk and tax status, such as the zero-coupon U.S. Treasury securities used to create the term structure of interest rates. In addition to tax considerations, several other factors affect the term structure of interest rates.

At the most basic level, a particular maturity may be desirable for specific needs, such as retirement or a down payment on a house. So investors may seek to invest in maturities that match their needs. Beyond specific needs, shorter maturities provide more liquidity and greater financial flexibility, a form of option that the Options Principle tells us is valuable.

As we explain in Chapter 5, if all else is equal, longer-maturity securities are riskier. Much of this risk depends on inflation expectations, which are an important determinant of interest rates. Therefore, if all else is equal, the Principle of Risk-Return Trade-Off implies that investors will require a higher interest rate (return) to bear the extra risk. This is the basis for the idea that the term structure *should* usually be upward sloping.

Finally, investors also take into consideration what they expect interest rates to be in the future. That is, if investors believe that long-term interest rates are going to be higher next year, they will want to wait to make a long-term investment. Of course, investors do not hold the cash in a cookie jar while they wait. They put the money in short-term investments, such as money market securities. This kind of "waiting" increases the supply of short-term funds and at the same time decreases the supply of long-term funds. The shift in these supplies lowers the short-term rate and increases the long-term rate, which increases the upward slope of the curve. The reverse happens when investors believe interest rates are going to decrease. This can bring about a downward-sloping term structure. Unusual expectations can even lead to oddly shaped curves that are not consistently upward or downward sloping.

The Principle of Capital Market Efficiency tells us that the term structure reflects all the available information about the collective impact of all these factors at any point in time.

Review

1. What is a yield curve?
2. What class of securities is used to compile the term structure of interest rates?
3. Why is the term structure usually upward sloping?

2.6 BUSINESS ETHICS

Ethics consists of standards of conduct or moral judgment. Business ethics is a topic of great concern because of the complexity of business relationships. Recall the set-of-contracts model of the firm. The firm is at the center of relationships with many stakeholders, such as customers, employees, managers, shareholders, creditors, suppliers, the community, and governmental units. High standards of ethical conduct require that each stakeholder deal, and be dealt with, in an honest and fair manner.

There are different levels of ethical behavior. At the most basic level, ethical behavior requires that you comply fully with all of the rules and regulations that apply to your behavior. Failure to do so can result in substantial penalties that include time in jail and fines assessed by regulatory agencies and by the courts. The financial consequences often go far beyond these penalties. Many individuals have lost their careers, and businesses have gone bankrupt, because of unethical behavior. The gains from unethical behavior sometimes have been small compared to the ultimate losses due to the loss of trust and reputation.

Behaving ethically means much more than simply following rules and regulations—it requires making personal judgments about right and wrong. Some people believe business is inherently corrupt, immoral, and unethical. Unfortunately, actions by firms such as WorldCom, Enron, and Arthur Andersen have lent support for this view. However, many others assert that high ethical standards are essential to the profitability and survival of the firm and that ethics in business may be higher than in other segments of society. Why do so many feel that ethical behavior is essential to profitability? There are some clear answers.

1. Ethical behavior avoids fines and legal expenses.
2. It builds customer loyalty and sales.
3. It helps attract and keep high-quality employees and managers.

4. It builds public confidence and adds to the economic development of the communities in which the firm operates.
5. A good reputation enhances relations with the firm's investors.

Ethical behavior can be a necessity for firms to operate profitably and to survive.

Many firms have formal codes of conduct that are a prominent part of their corporate cultures. Managers are often very careful to explore the ethical dimensions of their decisions. Furthermore, if you join a profession—such as appraisal, financial analysis, personnel management, or real estate brokerage—there are professional societies with codes of ethics you must know and follow. In addition, professionals in many fields, such as the accounting profession and the securities industry, are regulated by government agencies and are thus subject to special licensing procedures and rules of conduct. Failure to behave ethically can cost you your license to practice your profession—or worse.

Code of Ethics for Chartered Financial Analysts

The Association for Investment Management and Research requires that Chartered Financial Analysts adhere to a detailed set of Standards of Professional Conduct that cover the relationships of CFAs with the public, clients, customers, employers, employees, and fellow analysts. The topics covered in the Standards of Professional Conduct are:

I. Fundamental Responsibilities
II. Relationships with and Responsibilities to the Profession
  A. Use of Professional Designation
  B. Professional Misconduct
  C. Prohibition against Plagiarism
III. Relationships with and Responsibilities to the Employer
  A. Obligation to Inform Employer of Code and Standards
  B. Duty to Employer
  C. Disclosure of Conflicts to Employer
  D. Disclosure of Additional Compensation Arrangements
  E. Responsibilities of Supervisors
IV. Relationships with and Responsibilities to Clients and Prospects
  A. Investment Process
    A1. Reasonable Basis and Representations
    A2. Research Reports
    A3. Independence and Objectivity
  B. Interactions with Clients and Prospects
    B1. Fiduciary Duties
    B2. Portfolio Investment Recommendations and Actions
    B3. Fair Dealing
    B4. Priority of Transactions
    B5. Preservation of Confidentiality
    B6. Prohibition against Misrepresentation
    B7. Disclosure of Conflicts to Clients and Prospects
    B8. Disclosure of Referral Fees
V. Relationships with and Responsibilities to the Investing Public
  A. Prohibition against Use of Material Nonpublic Information
  B. Performance Presentation

Source: *Standards of Practice Handbook,* Charlottesville, VA: Association for Investment Management and Research.

Review

1. Why should a financial manager be concerned with business ethics?
2. Why is ethical behavior essential to profitability?

SUMMARY

Financial markets, financial principles, and business ethics are all a foundation for the financial decisions that managers routinely make.

- The principles of finance describe typical behavior in financial transactions and provide guidance for decision making:
  - Financial self-interest guides rational decision making.
  - Many financial decisions must consider the time value of money.
  - All transactions are two sided, with each party considering their self-interest.
  - Incremental costs and benefits are the basis for choices among alternatives.
  - Investors are risk averse.
  - The marketplace rewards risk because rational investors require a reward to bear it.
  - Diversification can reduce risk.
  - Options are valuable because they contain rights, but not obligations.
  - Market prices in an efficient market reflect all available information.
  - Actions can be valuable signals.
  - Look to what others are doing for guidance.
  - Extraordinary returns are possible with new ideas.
- Money markets are short-term markets where Treasury bills, commercial paper, certificates of deposit, and bankers' acceptances are traded.
- Capital markets are long-term markets where stocks and bonds trade.
- Derivative markets trade derivative instruments such as options, futures, forwards, and swaps.
- Corporations raise capital by issuing securities in primary transactions, and previously issued securities trade in secondary transactions.
- Investment bankers, brokers, and dealers primarily facilitate the trading of securities. Financial intermediaries buy and hold the securities of others while issuing claims against themselves.
- The term structure of interest rates represents the relationship between interest rates and maturity. The main factors that affect the term structure include expected future changes in interest rates, taxes, and default risk.
- Business ethics, standards of conduct, and moral judgment are central to the operations and profitability of many businesses.

EQUATION SUMMARY

$$FV = PV + r(PV) = PV(1 + r) \tag{2.1}$$

$$FV = PV(1 + r)^n \tag{2.2}$$

$$PV = \frac{FV}{(1 + r)^n} \tag{2.3}$$

QUESTIONS

1. Define these terms: *opportunity cost, principal-agent relationship, moral hazard, zero-sum game, sunk cost, hubris, adverse selection.*
2. Cite an example in which the problem of moral hazard can arise in a principal-agent relationship.
3. Define the terms *option, call option,* and *put option.*
4. What is a portfolio? Why is diversification beneficial?
5. Distinguish between each of the following pairs:
   a. Spot market and futures market
   b. Call option and put option
   c. Option contract and futures contract
   d. Broker and dealer
   e. Investment banker and financial intermediary
   f. Primary market and secondary market
   g. Initial public offering and seasoned equity offering
   h. Forward contract and futures contract
   i. Stock and bond.
6. Define the term *limited liability.* How does limited liability create an option for a borrower?
7. Describe in your own words what is meant by the term *efficient capital market.* What is arbitrage?
8. Explain in your own words the idea of compound interest.
9. What are the factors that cause the term structure to be upward sloping or downward sloping?
10. What is ethics? If you follow all applicable rules and regulations, are you an ethical person?
11. Why do many business managers feel that ethical behavior is essential to the profitability and survival of their firm?
12. Describe in your own words why financial decisions are based on incremental benefits? How does a sunk cost affect the incremental benefit from a decision?
13. What is the major distinction between debt and equity? Why is it so important?

CHALLENGING QUESTIONS

14. Cite an example that involves information signaling.
15. Describe a situation in which the problem of adverse selection can arise.
16. Explain why the Principle of Two-Sided Transactions is important to financial decision making.
17. *USA Today* once reported that executives of Teradyne had told Wall Street analysts that "business was jumping," but the next day the firm's chairman sold 24,800 shares of his stock in the firm for $32 each, or $793,600. The chairman's secretary said the shares belonged to his daughter. Interpret these events in light of the Signaling Principle.
18. Explain how the Behavioral Principle is derived directly from the Signaling Principle.
19. Cite two appropriate applications and one inappropriate application of the Behavioral Principle.

20. Explain how the Signaling Principle is derived directly from the Principle of Self-Interested Behavior.
21. Describe a situation where you might want to guard against the free-rider problem.
22. Suppose buy orders are placed for twice as many shares of a stock as the number of shares offered for sale in a one-hour period. What would be the relationship (higher, lower, or the same) between the reported trading price just before and just after that one-hour period, assuming no other events occurred?
23. When IBM introduced a new line of personal computers, the *Wall Street Journal* reported that this event would trigger "a new phase of competition in the computer industry." How would you expect the prices of other personal computer manufacturers' common stocks to react to this announcement?
24. How are the Principles of Self-Interested Behavior and Two-Sided Transactions related to the Principle of Capital Market Efficiency?
25. Cite an example in which it is not possible to measure exactly the opportunity cost of an alternative. Is it possible to measure exactly the opportunity cost of an alternative in most situations?
26. Suppose you are a manager in a manufacturing business. How are the capital markets relevant to the effective performance of your job?
27. In our discussion of the Principle of Capital Market Efficiency, we introduced the concept of arbitrage. We also said we would later on assume that the capital markets are perfect. How can the concept of arbitrage be used as the basis for a definition of a perfect capital market?
28. When McDermott International Inc. announced a few years ago that its chairman and CEO would soon retire and that it had hired an investment banker to review its strategic alternatives, its share price rose 9.5%. Securities analysts had been critical of the chairman, and the firm's performance had lagged behind that of its competitors. What signals did the announcement convey?
29. Several years ago, IBM had a chief financial officer whose quarterly earnings announcements and analysis could "move the market" for technology stocks. His quarterly conferences became so popular, IBM moved them from its headquarters to a hotel ballroom. How does signaling theory help us understand why these quarterly announcements affected other technology stocks?

PROBLEMS

LEVEL A (BASIC)

A1. (Present and future values)
   a. What is the future value of $1,000 invested today if it earns 25% interest for 1 year? for 2 years?
   b. What is the present value of $1,000 discounted at 25% if it is received in 1 year? in 2 years?

A2. (Present and future values)
   a. What is the future value of $2,000 invested today if it earns 20% interest for 1 year? for 2 years?
   b. What is the present value of $2,000 discounted at 20% if it is received in 1 year? in 2 years?

A3. (Future value) An investor deposits $1,000 into a bank account that pays interest at the rate of 10% per year (payable at the end of each year). She leaves the money and all accrued interest in the account for 5 years.
   a. How much money does she have after 1 year?
   b. How much money does she have at the end of year 5?
   c. If the bank instead paid only 6% interest, how much less money does she have after 1 year and after year 5?

A4. (Future value) An investor deposits $5,000 into a bank account that pays interest at the rate of 4% per year (payable at the end of each year). She leaves the money and all accrued interest in the account for 5 years.

a. How much money does she have after 1 year?

b. How much money does she have at the end of year 5?

c. If the bank instead paid 8% interest, how much additional money does she have after 1 year and after year 5?

A5. (Present value) What is the present value of $10,000 to be received 7 years from today when the annual discount rate is 12%?

A6. (Present and future values) Assume you are starting with an investment of $20,000.

a. What is the future value of the investment after 1 year if it earns 12% per year? What is the present value of this future value discounted at 12%?

b. What is the future value of the investment after 1 year if it earns 15% per year? What is the present value of this future value discounted at 15%?

c. What is the future value of the investment after 1 year if it earns 15% per year? What is the present value of this future value discounted at 20%?

LEVEL B

B1. (Present value) What is the present value of $15,000 to be received 11 years from today when the annual discount rate is 10%?

B2. (Future value) What is the future value in 7 years of $10,000 invested today when the annual interest rate is 12%?

B3. (Future value) What is the future value in 3 years of $30,000 invested today when the annual interest rate is 10%?

B4. (Present and future values) Assume that you are starting with an investment of $10,000.

a. What is the future value of the investment after 1 year if it earns 10% per year? What is the present value of this future value discounted at 10%?

b. What is the future value of the investment after 1 year if it earns 20% per year? What is the present value of this future value discounted at 10%?

c. What is the future value of the investment after 1 year if it earns 10% per year? What is the present value of this future value discounted at 20%?

B5. (Present value) What is the present value of $5,000 to be received in two equal installments ($2,500 each), 4 years and 5 years from today, when the annual discount rate is 10%?

B6. (Options) Assume you pay $1,000 for a call option that gives you the right to buy a piece of property for $20,000 any time within the next year.

a. Assume the property appreciates and you can sell it for $30,000 at the end of the year. If you use the option, what is your gain (the difference between the property value and the price using the option)? Will you use your call option? What is your profit in dollars after you subtract the cost of the option? What is your realized return?

b. Assume the property can be sold for $15,000 at the end of the year. If you use the option, what is your gain? Will you use your call option?

B7. (Options) Assume you pay $1,500 for a call option that gives you the right to buy a piece of property for $100,000 any time within the next year.

a. Assume the property appreciates and you can sell it for $150,000 at the end of the year. If you use the option, what is your gain (the difference between the property value and the price using the option)? Will you use your call option? What is your profit in dollars after you subtract the cost of the option? What is your realized return?

b. Assume the property can be sold for $85,000 at the end of the year. If you use the option, what is your gain? Will you use your call option?

B8. (Opportunity cost) You own a small duplex near campus. You bought it several years ago for $120,000. You can sell the duplex today for $160,000, or you can add on to the duplex and sell it for $220,000. The addition would cost $80,000. Should you sell the duplex "as is," or should you invest in the addition and then sell? At what selling price would you change your mind?

B9. (Opportunity cost) You own a small apartment complex near campus. You bought it several years ago for $1,000,000. You can sell the complex today for $1,600,000, or you can add on to the complex and sell it for $2,000,000. The addition would cost $500,000. Should you sell the complex "as is," or should you invest in the addition and then sell? At what selling price would you change your mind?

LEVEL C (ADVANCED)

C1. (Options) Assume you buy a call option for $2.00 that gives you the right to buy a share of stock for its current price of $20.00 at any time during the next year. You can buy a put option for $1.00 to sell the same stock for $20.00 at any time during the next year. The stock does not pay a dividend.

a. At the end of the year, the stock is selling for $24. What is the realized return on the stock, the call option, and the put option?

b. At the end of the year, the stock is selling for $17. What is the realized return on the stock, the call option, and the put option?

C2. (Options) Assume you buy a call option for $3.00 that gives you the right to buy a share of stock for its current price of $35.00 at any time during the next year. You can buy a put option for $2.00 to sell the same stock for $35.00 at any time during the next year. The stock does not pay a dividend.

a. At the end of the year, the stock is selling for $40. What is the realized return on the stock, the call option, and the put option?

b. At the end of the year, the stock is selling for $30. What is the realized return on the stock, the call option, and the put option?

3

Accounting, Cash Flows, and Taxes

No matter how large and complex it is, a firm's accounting system serves two basic purposes:

- reporting the firm's financial activities to its various stakeholders, and
- providing information to assist the firm's decision makers.

This chapter reviews material from basic accounting classes. We outline the basics of the accounting statements, without going into the details of how they are prepared. We describe important differences between accounting and economic information. Our focus in financial management is on how to use and interpret this information, rather than on operating an accounting system and creating financial reports.

Accounting statements are important, as actions by firms such as WorldCom, Enron, and Arthur Andersen, among others, have often demonstrated. Accounting statements are used to communicate with stakeholders outside the firm, such as stockholders, bondholders, and other creditors. They are used within the firm to help plan and organize its activities. Accounting statements are used to monitor employees in connection with such things as performance or even theft. And they are used by the Internal Revenue Service to determine the firm's taxes.

Finally, we review the federal income tax system. Because taxes affect value, they affect many of a firm's financial management decisions. At the most basic level, taxes are a significant cost of doing business. Throughout the book, we point out situations where taxes can affect decisions.

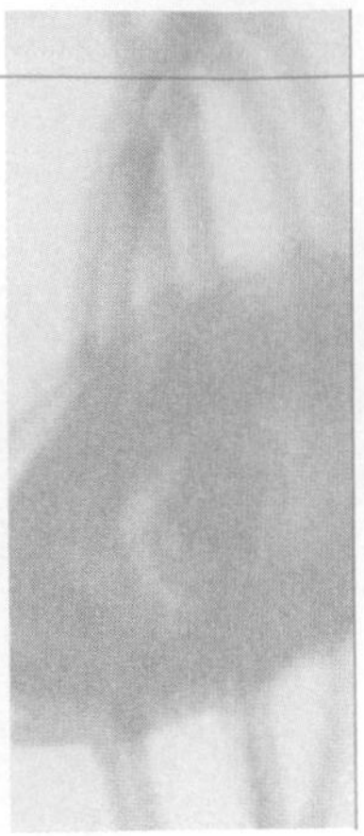

FOCUS ON PRINCIPLES

- *Two-Sided Transactions:* Recognize that the accounting system always records two sides to every transaction, a debit and a credit, and there are real people or real firms on each side of the transaction.
- *Incremental Benefits:* Use financial statements and the accounting system to help identify and estimate the incremental expected cash flows for making financial decisions.
- *Risk-Return Trade-Off:* Keep in mind that managerial decisions are based on future risks and returns. Accounting tends to measure historical or past returns. Consequently, many decisions require information and perspectives that are unavailable from the accounting system.
- *Behavioral Principle:* Use the wealth of financial information available from thousands of other firms to apply this principle.
- *Signaling:* Recognize that financial information provides many observable signals about customers, competitors, and suppliers.

3.1 THE LAYOUT OF ACCOUNTING STATEMENTS

Accounting statements in the United States are prepared according to **generally accepted accounting principles (GAAP).** GAAP includes the conventions, rules, and procedures that define how firms should maintain records and prepare financial reports.[1] In the United States, these rules and procedures are based on guidelines issued by the *Financial Accounting Standards Board (FASB).* FASB is the U.S. accounting profession's rule-making organization.

Internationally, the set of generally accepted accounting principles varies from one country to another. In some cases U.S. GAAP is different from another country's GAAP. British GAAP, for example, differ substantially from U.S. GAAP. As a result, a firm's financial statements can look quite different depending on which country's GAAP is used to prepare them. In any case, you cannot compare the information contained in the financial statements of two firms when the statements were prepared under different systems of GAAP until you first adjust for the differences.

Even under U.S. GAAP, it is possible for accounting numbers to distort economic reality. One of the tasks facing a good manager is to use accounting information effectively. Managers must know what accounting information can—and cannot—be used for. This is a balancing act. They have to combine their knowledge of accounting with other sources of information to make sound business decisions.

Financial Statements

A firm's published **annual report** includes, at a minimum, an income statement, a balance sheet, a statement of cash flows, and accompanying notes.[2] We review these statements, using a basic set of statements for OutBack SportWear, Inc. as an example.[3] They are the "raw material" for a variety

[1]According to the American Institute of Certified Public Accountants (AICPA), the "phrase 'generally accepted accounting principles' is a technical accounting term that encompasses the conventions, rules, and procedures necessary to define accepted accounting practice at a particular time. It includes not only broad guidelines of general application, but also detailed practices and procedures. . . . Those conventions, rules, and procedures provide a standard by which to measure financial presentations."

[2]A firm's annual report includes income statements and statements of cash flows for the latest three years and balance sheets for the latest two years. It also includes a separate statement of stockholders' equity. This shows how the firm's total stockholders' equity changed from one balance sheet to the next during the past three years.

[3]Publicly traded firms also publish quarterly reports and make public announcements of important information. And they file, with the Securities and Exchange Commission (SEC), disclosures that investors use. Such disclosures include 10-K annual reports (the information in the annual report plus more disclosures), 10-Q reports (the information in quarterly reports plus more), 8-K statements (describing significant events of interest to investors as the events occur), and registration statements (large documents containing financial and business information that must be filed before new securities can be publicly issued).

of techniques and procedures that managers and analysts use in financial statement analysis. But first, let us introduce some basic terms we will need.

The **maturity** of an asset is the end of its life. When a financial asset is issued (created), the length of its life is called its **original maturity.** The amount of time remaining until maturity is called the **remaining maturity.** Often, "maturity" is used to mean remaining maturity.

The **liquidity** of an asset expresses how quickly and easily it can be sold without loss of value. Cash is the most liquid asset.

Market value is the price for which something could be bought or sold in a "reasonable" length of time. A reasonable length of time is defined in terms of the asset's liquidity. It might be several months or even a year for buildings and land, but only a few days for publicly traded stocks and bonds. **Book value (net book value)** is a net amount shown in the accounting statements.

Balance Sheet

The **balance sheet** reports the financial position of a firm at a particular point in time. The balance sheet shows the firm's **assets,** which are the productive resources used in its operations. The balance sheet also shows the firm's **liabilities and stockholders' equity,** which are the total claims of creditors and owners against the assets.

A typical balance sheet, that of OutBack SportWear, is shown in Table 3.1. Note that the *balance sheet identity* is satisfied:

$$\text{Assets} = \text{Liabilities} + \text{Stockholders' equity} \tag{3.1}$$

Assets and liabilities are both broken down into short-term and long-term parts. In accounting statements, **current (short-term)** refers to a period of up to one year. **Long-term** refers to more than one year. Current assets are expected to become cash within one year. Current liabilities mature or are expected to be paid off with cash within one year. A long-term asset and a long-term liability have remaining maturities of more than one year. Current assets and liabilities are usually arranged in approximate order of remaining maturity, from shortest to longest. This arrangement reflects the fact that, generally, the book values of the short-remaining-maturity assets and liabilities tend to be closer to their current market values than those that have long maturities. For example, the book value of receivables may be fairly close to the market value. In contrast, the current market value of net fixed assets can be very different from the book value.

TABLE 3.1
OutBack SportWear, Inc. annual balance sheet ($ millions) December 31.

	LATEST YEAR	PREVIOUS YEAR		LATEST YEAR	PREVIOUS YEAR
ASSETS			LIABILITIES & STOCKHOLDERS' EQUITY		
Cash and equivalents	$ 9.5	$ 12.0	Accounts payable	$ 18.8	$ 14.7
Accounts receivable	233.2	203.3	Notes payable	66.2	33.2
Inventories	133.9	118.8	Accrued expenses	77.7	62.0
Total current assets	$376.6	$334.1	Total current liabilities	$162.7	$109.9
Net plant and equipment	203.8	167.0	Long-term bonds	74.4	70.2
Total assets	$580.4	$501.1	Other long-term liabilities	19.6	17.7
			Total liabilities	$256.7	$197.8
			Preferred stock	10.0	10.0
			Common stock	45.4	45.4
			Retained earnings	268.3	247.9
			Total common equity	$323.7	$303.3
			Liabilities and stockholders' equity	$580.4	$501.1

The liabilities and stockholders' equity (right-hand) side of the balance sheet shows the firm's choice of its **capital structure:** the proportions of debt versus equity financing and the mixture of debt maturities, short-term versus long-term.

The difference between current assets and current liabilities is the firm's net working capital, often simply called **working capital:**

$$\text{Working capital} = \text{Current assets} - \text{Current liabilities} \tag{3.2}$$

Working capital provides a measure of the business's liquidity, or its ability to meet its short-term obligations as they come due.

Income Statement

The **income statement** reports the revenues, expenses, and profit (or loss) for a firm over a specific interval of time, typically a year or a quarter of a year. Net income, sometimes referred to as profit, is the difference between total revenue and total cost during the period. Table 3.2 shows the income statement for OutBack SportWear. In this income statement, the gross profit is the net sales minus the cost of goods sold. The cost of goods sold is the direct cost for the materials, labor, and other expenses directly associated with the production of the goods or services sold by the firm.

To compute the operating profit, subtract from gross profit (1) the indirect costs associated with selling, general, and administrative expenses and (2) depreciation and amortization (which are noncash items). **Earnings before interest and taxes (EBIT)** equals operating profit plus nonoperating profit (such as investment income). Subtracting interest expense from EBIT gives pretax income

TABLE 3.2
OutBack SportWear, Inc. annual income statement
($ millions, except per-share data) years ended December 31.

	LATEST YEAR	PREVIOUS YEAR
Sales	$546.9	$485.8
Cost of goods sold	286.3	247.3
Gross profit	$260.6	$238.5
Selling, general & administrative exp.	186.2	180.5
Depreciation & amortization	22.7	20.1
Earnings before interest and taxes (EBIT)	$ 51.7	$ 37.9
Interest expense	7.7	8.0
Earnings before tax	$ 44.0	$ 29.9
Total income tax	18.1	11.9
Net income	$ 25.9	$ 18.0
Preferred dividends	1.0	1.0
Net income available for common	$ 24.9	$ 17.0
Dividends on common stock	4.5	3.6
Addition to retained earnings	$ 20.4	$ 13.4
Per-share data:		
Earnings per-share	$ 2.77	$ 1.89
Dividends per-share	$ 0.50	$ 0.40
Shares outstanding (millions)	9.000	9.000

of $44.0 million in the latest year. Finally, subtracting income taxes yields net income: $25.9 million, up from $18.0 million in the previous year.

If the firm has preferred stock outstanding, preferred dividends paid are subtracted from net income to get net income available for common stock. After subtracting whatever common stock dividends the firm paid, the remaining earnings are the current period's addition to retained earnings on the balance sheet.

Dividends per-share and earnings per-share (EPS) are given in the bottom part of the income statement. The firm's common stockholders have a residual claim to the firm's assets after all debts and preferred stock dividends have been paid. The stockholders' welfare, then, depends on the current and future profitability and dividends of the firm. The per-share figures indicate how large the net income is relative to the number of common shares.[4] With nine million shares outstanding, OutBack shows $2.77 in EPS in the latest year.

Corporations occasionally declare an extraordinary gain or loss in addition to income or loss from their normal operations. OutBack SportWear did not report any extraordinary income. If a corporation had an extraordinary gain or loss, the income statement would show net income before and after (that is, without and with) the extraordinary gain or loss. In addition, EPS would be reported before and after the extraordinary income. For valuation purposes, EPS before extraordinary items (without taking them into account) is a more meaningful measure of the firm's sustainable profit.

Finally, dividends per-share divided by EPS gives the firm's **payout ratio.** The payout ratio is the proportion of earnings that the firm paid out to common shareholders as cash dividends. OutBack's latest payout ratio is about 18% (= 0.50/2.77).

Statement of Cash Flows

The **statement of cash flows** indicates how the cash position of the firm has changed during the period covered by the income statement. Thus, it complements the income statement and the balance sheet. Changes in a firm's cash position can be the result of any of the firm's many transactions.

The statement of cash flows breaks down the sources and uses of cash into three components. These are cash flows from (1) operating, (2) investing, and (3) financing activities. The flows of funds between a firm and its investors, creditors, workers, customers, and other stakeholders serve as a fundamental starting point for the analysis of the firm, its capital investment projects, corporate acquisitions, and many other decisions.

Table 3.3 shows the statement of cash flows for OutBack SportWear. The sources and amounts of cash flows from operating activities, investing activities, and financing activities are itemized.[5]

Let us look more closely at the cash flow from operating activities. The net income is taken from OutBack's income statement (Table 3.2). To arrive at net income, various items are

---

[4]The earnings-per-share calculation can be fairly complicated. Basic earnings per-share is net income divided by the weighted average number of common shares outstanding during the period. Other definitions, such as diluted earnings per-share, take into account what are called the *dilutive effects* of option-like instruments (warrants, convertibles, executive stock options). The rules for computing earnings per-share are given in Accounting Principles Board, "Earnings per-share," APB Opinion No. 15 (New York: AICPA, 1969). Most analysts regard diluted earnings per-share as more informative than basic earnings per-share.

[5]The format of the statement of cash flows shown in Table 3.3 is a presentation called the *indirect* method. Another method, called the *direct method,* sums the cash inflows and outflows associated with operating the firm. The first part of the statement of cash flows (cash flows from operating activities) looks different depending on whether the direct or the indirect method is used; the other two parts are the same. Although their formats differ, the methods give the same numerical result. We use the indirect method here because it is used most widely in published financial statements.

TABLE 3.3
OutBack SportWear, Inc. statement of cash flows ($ millions) year ended December 31.

Cash Flows from Operating Activities	
Net income	$ 25.9
Depreciation and amortization	22.7
Accounts receivable decrease (increase)	(29.9)
Inventories decrease (increase)	(15.1)
Accounts payable increase (decrease)	4.1
Accrued expenses increase (decrease)	15.7
Net cash provided by (used in) operating activities	23.4
Cash Flows from Investing Activities	
Purchase of plant and equipment	(59.5)
Net cash provided by (used in) investing activities	(59.5)
Cash Flows from Financing Activities	
Notes payable increase (decrease)	33.0
Issuance of long-term debt, net	4.2
Increase in other long-term liabilities	1.9
Cash dividends (preferred and common)	(5.5)
Net cash provided by (used in) financing activities	33.6
Net increase (decrease) in cash and equivalents	(2.5)
Cash and equivalents, beginning of year	12.0
Cash and equivalents, end of year	$ 9.5

deducted from sales, including some that are noncash expenses. Depreciation is usually the largest of these items. Because these items are not cash flows, they must be added back to net income to determine cash flow. Dividends are *not* subtracted from operating activities. Instead, they are a discretionary part of financing activities. The other items represent changes in several working capital accounts, which are part of operating activities. Decreases (increases) in asset (liability) accounts are positive cash flows (*inflows*). The opposites are negative cash flows (*outflows*). One short-term liability, notes payable, is considered a financing activity and is not included in operating activities.

Investing activities cash flows include those connected with buying or selling long-term assets, acquiring other firms, and selling subsidiaries. OutBack used $59.5 million to purchase plant and equipment, which is an outflow (negative cash flow).

Financing activities cash flows include those connected with selling or repurchasing common and preferred stock, issuing or retiring long-term debt, issuing and repaying short-term notes, and paying dividends on common and preferred stock. For example, OutBack borrowed $33.0 million in notes payable, which was an inflow.

Net increase (decrease) in cash and equivalents is the sum of the cash flows from the three sections: $23.4 - 59.5 + 33.6 = \$(2.5)$ million. This change is then added to the beginning cash balance of $12.0 million, leaving the ending cash balance of $9.5 million.

In many financial decisions, such as long-term investments, we separate the investing, financing, and operating cash flows. It is important to understand that such separations in the statement of cash flows are somewhat arbitrary, particularly in the case of the first part of the statement, which shows the cash flows from operating activities. For example, dividends are included with financing cash flows, whereas interest expense is treated as an operating cash flow.

TABLE 3.4
Subjects typically covered as notes to financial statements in annual reports.

- Summary of significant accounting policies
- More detailed breakdowns of other income, interest and other financial charges, and provision for income taxes
- A description of the earnings-per-share calculation
- Details concerning any extraordinary items, such as gain (or loss) on sales of assets or subsidiaries, and foreign exchange gains or losses
- Breakdown of inventories, investments (including nonconsolidated subsidiaries), property, plant, and equipment, and other assets
- Costs and amounts of short-term borrowings
- Schedules of long-term debt, preferred stock, and capitalized and operating lease obligations
- Schedule of capital stock issued or reserved for issuance and statement of changes in shareholders' equity (which is often included as a separate financial statement)
- Details concerning significant acquisitions or disposals of assets
- Details concerning the use of derivatives
- Information concerning employee pension and stock option plans
- Commitments and contingent liabilities
- Events subsequent to the balance sheet date, but prior to the release of the financial statements to the public, that might significantly affect their interpretation
- Quarterly operating results
- Business segment information (by line of business and by geographical region)
- A five-year summary comparison of financial performance and financial position

Notes to the Financial Statements

The **notes to the financial statements** are an integral part of the statements. The notes disclose the significant accounting policies used to prepare the financial statements. They also provide additional detail concerning several of the items in the accounting statements. Table 3.4 lists subjects usually included in such notes.

Published annual reports also include **management's discussion** of recent operating results. Management's discussion is included along with the financial statements. Usually there is also a letter to the stockholders, which appears at the front of the annual report. This letter and the management's discussion can help you interpret the accounting statements. They can also provide insights into management's philosophy and strategy that simply do not appear in the numerical sections of the annual report.

The notes to the financial statements and management's discussion contain a wealth of useful information. You cannot fully appreciate the information contained in a firm's accounting statements unless you read the notes to the financial statements and the management's discussion.[6]

As you may have learned in your accounting class, the Enron and Arthur Andersen debacle engendered extensive debate over the rules of financial disclosure by public firms. The SEC wants a separate section of the annual report to disclose in plain English all the factors that can affect the firm's future performance and all the accounting policies and assumptions that affect how its performance is reported. The FASB is also working on projects to bring reported financial information more in line with what investors and creditors need. This will include better information about intangible assets and more forward-looking information.

---

[6]This is why accounting and securities regulations require firms to furnish this information!

Review

1. A firm issues $10 million of new bonds and repurchases $10 million of its common stock. What happens to Total Assets, Net Working Capital, and to Common Stockholders' Equity?
2. A firm issues $10 million of new bonds. It then pays off $2 million of accounts payable, purchases $6 million of capital equipment, and purchases $2 million of additional inventory. What happens to Total Assets, Net Working Capital, and to Common Stockholders' Equity?
3. Sales increase by $100. The cost of goods sold goes up by $60, and depreciation and interest expenses are unchanged. The tax rate is 40% and the firm does not change its dividend. What happens to Net Income and the Addition to Retained Earnings as a result of the increased sales?
4. Indicate whether each of the following transactions is classified as a cash flow in the firm's operating activities, investing activities, or financing activities and whether it increases or decreases the firm's cash balance.
   1. Increases inventory
   2. Decreases accounts receivable
   3. Increases accounts payable
   4. Sells some of its long-term plant and equipment
   5. Reduces the balance on its long-term mortgage
   6. Issues some additional common stock

3.2 MARKET VALUES VERSUS BOOK VALUES

Accounting statements are invaluable aids to analysts and managers. But the statements do not provide certain critical information, and as a result they have inherent limitations. Accounting statements are historical. They do not provide any information about cash flows that might be expected in the future. They also do not provide critically important information about the *current* market values of assets and liabilities. Thus, accounting statements not only fail to look ahead, they do not even report the current situation. Such missing information limits the usefulness of accounting information.

There are several reasons why accounting statements are historical, but we will not contribute here to the debate over how accounting statements might be better prepared. We will simply review the information accounting statements provide, based on today's practice, and note important implications of the procedures.

Market Versus Book Value of Assets

The current market value of an asset can be *very* different from its book value. Four factors affect the likelihood of a difference between market and book values: the time since the asset was acquired, inflation, the asset's liquidity, and whether the asset is tangible or intangible.

TIME SINCE ACQUISITION As a rule, the more time that has passed since an asset was acquired, the greater the chance that the asset's current market value will be more or less than its book value. When an asset is acquired, it is recorded in the accounting statements at its cost. And that cost is a market value, at least in some sense. Therefore, the initial book value is quite likely to be similar to the market value of the asset *at the time it is acquired.* Over time, however, the market value can diverge significantly from the book value. This is because changes in the book value (depreciation each period) are specified by GAAP rather than by economic considerations.

EXAMPLE Differences in Car Usage

Two firms buy identical cars. In one case, a sales representative is going to drive the car about 10,000 miles per month. In the other, a manager is going to drive the car about 1,000 miles per month. GAAP specifies identical depreciation rules for these cars. The rule is based on the type of asset (an automobile), not on how it will be used. Thus, after any significant time, say a year, the book values of the cars will be identical, but the more heavily used car will have a much lower market value. The more time that passes, the larger the difference is likely to be.

EXAMPLE The Sampson Company Waterfront Warehouse

The Sampson Company purchased a warehouse 15 years ago. Since then, the area surrounding the building has changed dramatically from an industrial area of factories and shipping warehouses into an exclusive high-rise condominium area overlooking the waterfront. Sampson's building and land currently have a combined book value of $231,000 (after accounting for depreciation on the building; depreciation cannot be claimed on land). Today the building could be sold for $15 million. Such a difference fundamentally changes the value of the firm. It also has profound implications for the best use of the firm's assets at this point in time. Sampson should consider moving its operations elsewhere and selling the current location. Of course, in other cases the market value may be well *below* the book value, which could have very different policy implications!

INFLATION Inflation during the time since the asset was acquired is a second important factor that can cause a significant difference between market value and book value. When prices change because of inflation, the market values of existing assets also change to reflect the difference in purchasing power. Such changes can be dramatic. For example, from 1964 until 2003, inflation caused the purchasing power of a dollar to change by about a factor of 8. This means that what could be purchased for $1.00 in 1964 cost about $8.00 in 2003.

EXAMPLE SunTrust's Shares of Coca-Cola Stock

Many years ago, when the Coca-Cola Company first issued shares of its common stock to the public, some of the shares went to a predecessor of SunTrust Banks in Atlanta. At the time, the value of the stock was recorded at its current market value of $100,000. Until relatively recently, the stock was shown on SunTrust's balance sheet as an asset with a book value of $100,000. However, the stock had since gone up in value. Seventy-five years later, those shares were worth about $1.5 billion, an increase of about 15,000 times over their original value. We know that the stock value increased well in excess of inflation over the intervening years. However, inflation during the same time period was substantial, perhaps changing purchasing power by a factor of 50 or more. Therefore, even if the value of the shares had increased only in step with inflation, the shares would be worth in excess of $5 million. In that case, then, only the remaining 300-times increase (= 15,000/50) is due to the success of the Coca-Cola Company!

LIQUIDITY An asset's liquidity is a third factor that affects the likelihood that the asset's current market value will differ from its book value. Less liquid assets have higher transaction costs when they are sold, so there is greater uncertainty about the *net* proceeds from a sale. As a consequence, if all else is equal, the current market values of less liquid assets can differ more from their book values than those of more liquid assets.

For example, compare a two-year-old pickup truck to a unique patented process for producing plastic bags. The pickup truck is a more liquid asset, because it could be easily sold in a used-truck market with low transaction costs. Contrast this with the plastic-bag-production process. Such a production process may be worth much more than its book value if it is the leading production technology. Or it may be essentially worthless if another technology has made it obsolete. But in either case, it could be very costly and time consuming to find the buyer who will pay the most for the process because there is not an established market for used plastic-bag-production processes.

TANGIBLE VERSUS INTANGIBLE ASSETS Whether an asset is tangible or intangible affects the likelihood of there being a significant difference between market and book values. The market values of intangible assets are much more variable than those of tangible assets. As with our example of the plastic-bag-production process, intangible assets can be extremely valuable or essentially worthless. Intangible assets also tend to be extremely illiquid. Even long-term assets such as plant and equipment are more likely to have established markets (real estate and used equipment) than are intangible assets such as patents or the design for a new product. Intangible assets tend to be unique. There are no active markets for selling them. Therefore, the current market value of an intangible asset is especially likely to differ from its book value.

EXAMPLE Developing a New Product at Murray Corporation

Murray Corporation has spent $14 million developing a new product. Now, it can more accurately estimate that the product will provide only about $5 million in profit to offset the development cost. At this point, Murray would like to sell the rights to its product to another firm and let that firm manufacture and market the new product. Would you pay $14 million for something that is worth only $5 million? Despite the $14 million historical cost on Murray's balance sheet, a potential buyer will assess the value of the new product on the basis of its *future* potential.[7]

We noted earlier that placement on the balance sheet reflects the general remaining maturity of the assets. We should now point out that balance sheet placement also reflects the general likelihood that there will be a difference between the asset's book value and its market value. As you move down the list of assets, they are less liquid and have generally been held longer. Intangible assets are shown last.

Consider two types of assets that represent opposite extremes in liquidity: cash and a manufacturing plant. Cash is extremely liquid (actually, it is the very *definition* of liquidity), whereas it would probably require considerable effort to find a buyer for the plant.[8] However, despite the fact that the market values of other current assets are generally less likely to differ from their book values, care is always in order when valuing a firm. Accounts receivable can include bad debts. Inventory can be obsolete or can be shown at very low values because of a "last-in–first-out" policy of accounting for inventory. Thus, even the book values of current assets other than cash and equivalents can be poor approximations of market value. Therefore, it is wise to look especially carefully at assets other than cash and equivalents when trying to value them.

---

[7]This problem is a major reason why GAAP calls for expensing (depreciating) research and development costs over a relatively short time period. Of course, the other side to this is that when a firm does make a great and valuable discovery, its book value grossly *under*states its market value.

[8]Of course, if the firm really wanted to sell the plant quickly, it could probably find a buyer almost instantly for a low enough price, say $1.00. (But even this price might be too high if the plant sat on top of a chemical waste dump that would cost the new owner $100 million to clean up.)

Market Versus Book Value of Liabilities

As with assets, the current market value of a liability can differ from its book value. Generally, however, the potential divergence is smaller, and the relationship between the market and book values is less complex.

REMAINING MATURITY The time until a liability must be paid off—its remaining maturity—is the main factor that affects the difference between the market and book values of a healthy firm's liabilities. Liabilities have explicit contractual amounts that must be paid at specific points in time. Failure to meet these contractual obligations creates the possibility of bankruptcy. Therefore, when a liability becomes due, the market value of the liability is essentially equal to its book value. In contrast, the market value of liabilities that do not have to be repaid for a long time reflects current economic conditions, as well as expectations about the future.

Consider a loan for $10 million that is due to be paid off in four months. Because the remaining maturity is short, the cost of interest is relatively insignificant compared to the amount borrowed. Now consider a long-term loan for $10 million at 6% interest per year that does not have to be repaid for another 25 years, except for yearly interest. If the borrowing rate today is 10%, the market value of this liability is smaller than its book value because its remaining maturity of 25 years provides the firm with 25 more years over which to enjoy the low 6% interest cost on the existing loan.

FINANCIAL DISTRESS In our discussion of the impact of remaining maturity, we referred to a *healthy* firm's liabilities. A second factor that affects the difference between the market and book values of liabilities is the firm's financial health. The market values of a financially distressed firm's liabilities are likely to be below their book values because of the uncertainty about the firm's long-term viability, and the likelihood that liabilities holders will not get fully repaid. Thus financial distress can intensify the effect of remaining maturity on the market value of a firm's liabilities.

Total Value

The total value of a firm is simply the sum of the market values of all its assets. Because the market values of the individual assets can be very different from their book values, the balance sheet amount *Total Assets* should *never* be taken as a reliable estimate of the current value of the firm.

Equity Value

The current book value of the firm's equity is probably the least informative item on a balance sheet. Every factor that affects the difference between the market and book values of each individual item on the balance sheet affects the difference between the market and book values of the firm's equity. This is because the difference between the market and book values of equity is the sum of the differences between the market and book values of all the other items on the balance sheet.

Look back at Equation (3.1), the balance sheet identity. We can rewrite that equation as

$$\text{Stockholders' equity} = \text{Assets} - \text{Liabilities}$$

This form makes it is easy to see the residual nature of the equity value. We have just said that the Assets amount is not the market value of the firm's assets and that the Liabilities amount is not the market value of the firm's liabilities. Therefore, it should be clear that the difference between the two is not miraculously going to become an accurate measure of market value, either!

If instead of being book (historical) values, the Assets and Liabilities amounts were current market values, this equation would provide the true residual value of the stockholders' equity. In a GAAP balance sheet, however, the value of Stockholders' Equity is simply the result of applying the required rules to the historical cost of the assets and liabilities—in essence, an amount that forces the balance sheet identity to hold. In a sense, the book value of stockholders' equity is a "plug" figure that enforces the balance sheet identity.

As we will explain in detail later, stock prices observed in public market trading are a much more accurate basis for estimating the current market value of a firm.

Review

1. Why might the market value of an asset differ from its book value?
2. Why is the difference between market value and book value likely to be greater for intangible assets than tangible assets?
3. How does the maturity of a liability affect the difference between its book and market value?
4. Your friend believes that the book value of Microsoft Corporation's stockholders' equity is a good measure of what Microsoft's equity is really worth. Do you agree? Explain.
5. The book value of the firm's assets is $100 and the market value of the assets is $200. The book value of the firm's liabilities is $40 and the market value is $44. What is the book value of stockholder's equity and the market value of equity?

3.3 ACCOUNTING NET INCOME VERSUS CASH FLOW

The income statement contains noncash expenses and accruals. Because of this, net income is not an accurate measure of cash inflow. In fact, this is part of the reason for requiring a Statement of Cash Flows.

Noncash Items

Certain items in the income statement are called noncash items, wherein the cash flow for the expense occurs outside of the reporting period. Depreciation is the most significant of these items. The use of certain assets, such as plant and equipment, spans multiple income statement periods. GAAP requires that the total expense be spread over multiple income periods, such as five, ten, or even 30 years.

The only thing at issue here is *timing*. The claim of expense for accounting purposes is separated in time from when the cash flow actually occurs. The cash flow for the item occurs at the time of purchase. The expense charged against income occurs in stages over several income statement periods. Therefore, noncash items make the firm's net income figure very different from its cash inflow. Deferred and accrued taxes are two other examples of noncash items.

Accruals

The revenues and expenses on the income statement include items for which no cash has yet been received. For example, a sale of merchandise that has been agreed to and perhaps even been delivered, but that the customer has not yet paid for, can be included. Also, a sale for which some cash has already been received may not be included, because it has not met certain GAAP requirements. Despite this, the revenues shown over a long time are a good estimate of the actual revenue that will *ultimately* be collected. However, within a limited time period of, say, one or two years, the revenue shown on the income statement can be significantly different from the cash revenue that actually came into the firm.

Estimating Cash Flow

Cash flow is often estimated by adding back noncash items to the net income, as in the first two lines of the operating activities part of the statement of cash flows (Table 3.3). This is because the distortion from accruals is typically relatively small.

Accounting Income Versus Economic Income

A firm's economic income is its total realized profit on an investment. It is made up of the cash inflow plus the change in the market value of the assets and liabilities. As we have just discussed, net income is not cash flow, and book changes in the firm's assets and liabilities do not reflect changes in market values. Thus Net Income is not economic income. As with the balance sheet, however, some items on the income statement are more or less likely than others to be good estimates of economic reality.

OPERATING INCOME Operating income can be a good estimate of economic operating income, provided that (1) the firm has made no changes in its accounting procedures, such as switching inventory accounting from a "last-in–first-out" (LIFO) to a "first-in–first-out" (FIFO) basis, and (2) the accounting period is sufficiently long. Changes in accounting procedures can increase or decrease the amounts reported in that period. With respect to the length of the accounting period, several years is preferable. Good or poor performance may not be revealed in income statements of one or two years. However, over time, significant changes in performance are likely to be revealed in any extended series of income statements.

EXTRAORDINARY INCOME Interpreting the economic meaning of extraordinary income requires an understanding of its nature and origin. For example, consider an extraordinary item that is the sale of some land that was worth much more than its current book value. This windfall could have come from good decision making—or dumb luck. If it was good decision making, it may mean a brighter future. Luck may not continue.

In general, extraordinary items occur only once. They do not reflect the firm's *sustainable net income.* We therefore recommend that you use *net income before extraordinary items* when doing calculations that involve net income.

Review

1. What are the main differences between net income and cash flows?
2. Why might the economic income of the firm differ significantly from its net income?
3. Why should you use net income *before extraordinary items* when doing calculations that involve net income?
4. How would it be possible for a firm to report positive accounting income, and yet have negative economic income?

3.4 CORPORATE AND PERSONAL INCOME TAXES

Taxes make the federal government, and any state and local government that levies income taxes, a partner with every firm. With so much money at stake, taxes can have a significant impact on financial decisions. Both corporate and personal taxes are relevant to corporate financial management. We focus here on income taxes for illustrative purposes and because they are currently the most significant form of taxes.

Corporate Income Taxes

As shown in Table 3.5, the federal tax rate generally increases with the level of income. The tax rate applied to the last dollar of income is called the **marginal tax rate.** The **average tax rate** is the total taxes paid divided by taxable income. A **progressive tax system** has an average tax rate that increases for some increases in the level of income but never decreases with such increases. The marginal tax rate is never less than the average tax rate in a progressive tax system.

TABLE 3.5
Corporate income tax rates.

CORPORATE TAXABLE INCOME ($)	PAY THIS AMOUNT ON THE BASE OF THE RANGE ($)	PLUS THIS RATE TIMES THE EXCESS OVER THE BASE (%)
0–50,000	0	15
50,000–75,000	7,500	25
75,000–100,000	13,750	34
100,000–335,000	22,250	39
335,000–10,000,000	113,900	34
10,000,000–15,000,000	3,400,000	35
15,000,000–18,333,333	5,150,000	38
over 18,333,333	6,416,667	35

EXAMPLE Corporate Income Taxes for Sidewell, Inc.

Suppose Sidewell, Inc. has taxable corporate income of $200,000. What will be the corporation's federal corporate income tax liability on this amount?

From the tax rates in Table 3.5, the tax liability will be

$$\text{Tax} = 22{,}250 + 0.39(200{,}000 - 100{,}000) = 22{,}250 + 39{,}000 = \$61{,}250$$

The marginal tax rate is 39%, but the average tax rate on this level of income is 30.625% (= 61,250/200,000).

As income is taxed at the higher marginal tax rate in a progressive tax system, the average tax rate continues to increase. Figure 3.1 shows the marginal and average corporate tax rates based on Table 3.5.

There are two more important complications. First, tax structures are often modified. Thus, the average and marginal tax rates that apply to a corporation can and do change from time to time, sometimes dramatically. Second, state and local governments often impose additional income (and other) taxes on corporations, so the total tax is the sum of the federal, state, and local tax levies. The result is that no single tax rate will endure through time, and no single tax rate will apply across all geographical locations.

Throughout this book, we will simply specify an income tax rate, such as 40%. We intend whatever rate we specify to reflect all taxes from all levels. The single rate is a simplified approximation of taxes. We use different tax rates to emphasize that actual tax rates vary over time and from one location to another.

CORPORATE CAPITAL GAINS A long-term capital gain or loss, referred to simply as a **capital gain,** occurs *for tax purposes* when an asset that has been owned for a sufficiently long time (currently, more than one year) is sold for more or less than its tax basis (that is, its net book value for tax purposes). Although an actual gain or loss occurs every time the market value of the asset changes, the gain or loss is not recognized *for tax purposes* until the asset is sold. This means that the tax on the gain is postponed—indefinitely—until the asset is sold. Of course, this also means no tax-reducing losses can be claimed until the asset is sold. This is an important complicating feature of the tax system. It creates what is called a **tax-timing option.** We will describe and discuss tax-timing options in more detail later.

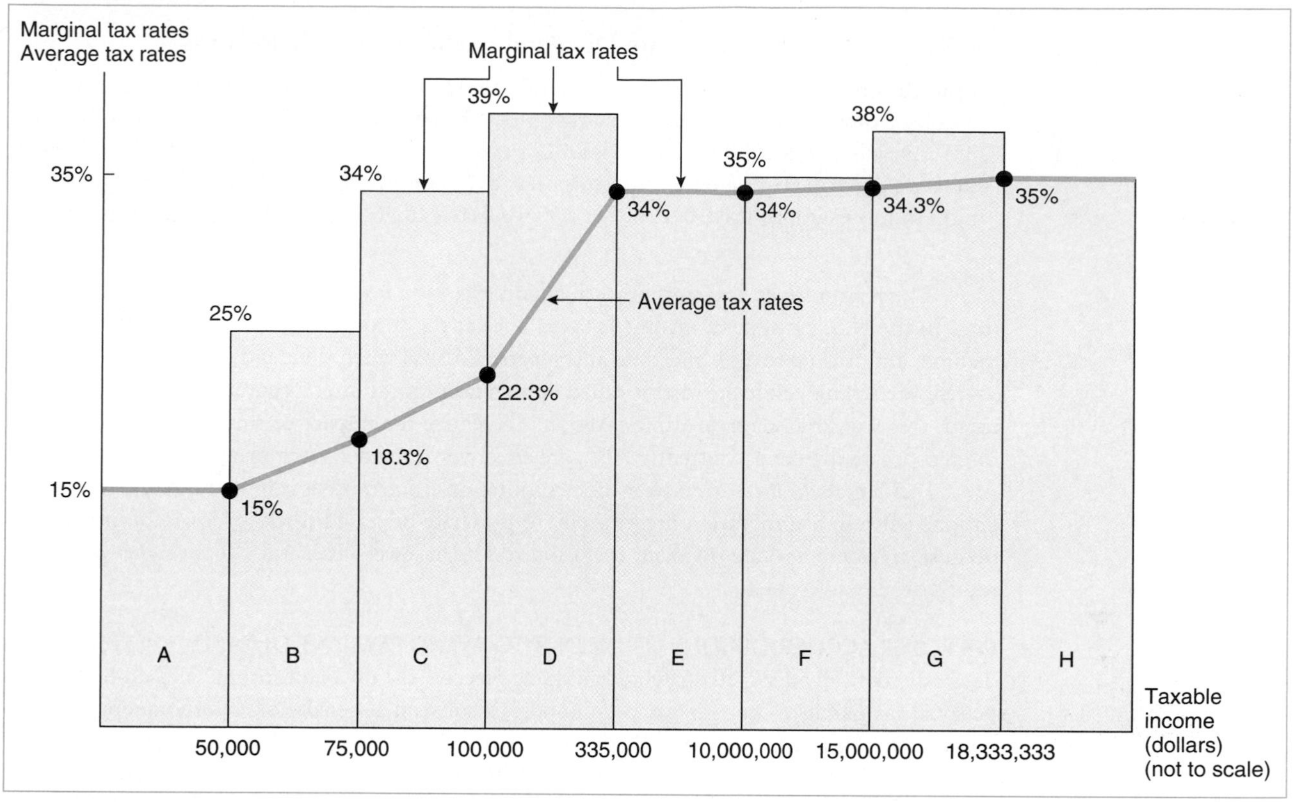

FIGURE 3.1
Marginal and average corporate income tax rates.

Corporate capital gains are currently taxed at the same rates as regular income. Before 1987, corporate capital gains were taxed at a lower rate. A lower tax rate on capital gains provides extra incentive to invest in capital assets. Short-term capital gains (losses) that result from holding assets for less than the required year are taxed as regular income.

TAX TREATMENT OF INTEREST EXPENSE AND DIVIDENDS PAID Interest paid on debt obligations is a tax-deductible expense. Dividends paid to common and preferred stockholders are not. If a firm is to pay $100 of interest, the firm needs $100 of earnings before interest and taxes (EBIT). However, if a firm is to pay $100 of dividends, it will need more than $100 of EBIT, because taxes will be deducted from EBIT. For example, suppose the tax rate is 40%. Taxes of $40 will be paid out of the $100 of EBIT. This will leave only $60 to pay the planned $100 of dividends. To find the amount of EBIT necessary to cover the dividends, simply divide the dividend amount by 1 minus the marginal tax rate. In our example,

$$\text{EBIT needed} = 100/(1 - 0.40) = 100/0.6 = \$166.67$$

If EBIT is $166.67, taxes due on this will be $66.67 (= [0.40]166.67). This will leave $100 (= 166.67 − 66.67) after taxes to pay the dividend.

This unequal, or **asymmetric,** treatment of interest expense and dividend payments effectively lowers the tax bills of corporations that use more debt financing. Conversely, it increases the tax bills of corporations that use more equity financing.

INTERCORPORATE DIVIDEND EXCLUSION At least 70% of dividends *received* by a corporation from another corporation are not taxed.[9] The remaining dividends received are taxed at ordinary rates.

[9]The proportion not taxed ranges from 70% to 100%, depending on the percentage of ownership.

EXAMPLE Intercorporate Dividend Exclusion at Epic Records

Epic Records receives $10,000 of dividend income from Columbia Music. It can deduct $7,000 from its taxable income, leaving $3,000 to be taxed.[10] If Epic's marginal tax rate is 35%, it will owe $1,050 (= [0.35]3,000) in taxes on the $10,000 of dividends. This means that the *effective* tax rate on an intercorporate dividend payment is 30% of the marginal tax rate. In this example, it is 10.5% (= 1,050/10,000 = 0.30 × 35%) for Epic Records.

The reason for an intercorporate dividend exclusion involves the concept of multiple taxation. In the U.S. tax system, income is taxed once at the corporate level when the firm earns the income, and it is taxed a second time at the personal level when dividends are paid to individual shareholders. This results in what is called double taxation. If intercorporate dividends were fully taxed, this would amount to triple taxation. To reduce the impact of this, a substantial part of intercorporate dividends, currently 70%, are effectively excluded from taxation.

Incidentally, *interest received* by one corporation from another is fully taxable. There are situations wherein a corporation might prefer to purchase preferred stock (over a debt instrument) because an intercorporate dividend exclusion results in lower taxes and a higher *after-tax* rate of return on the investment.

IMPROPER ACCUMULATIONS OF INCOME TO AVOID PAYMENT OF TAXES If a corporation does not pay a dividend, its shareholders do not receive the dividend income and do not incur a personal tax liability. The U.S. tax code imposes a substantial penalty on a corporation if it accumulates earnings simply to avoid shareholder personal income taxes. A corporation is allowed to accumulate $250,000 of retained earnings without being subject to this tax. Accumulations above $250,000 are subject to the penalty tax if they are considered unnecessary for the reasonable needs of the business. However, if these funds are reinvested in the firm to buy more assets, to pay off debt obligations, or to provide a reasonable amount of liquidity, the improper-accumulations tax is not imposed. Although this penalty tax is very rarely imposed, the threat of the penalty is real. It encourages corporations either to use the funds in the firm or to distribute them as dividends.

TAX LOSS CARRY-BACKS AND CARRY-FORWARDS If a corporation shows a loss (has negative net income), this loss can be "carried back" as much as two years or "carried forward" for as much as 20 years to offset taxable income in those years. For example, suppose a corporation has negative net income this year but had positive net income and paid taxes within the prior two years. This year's loss can be used to offset previous profits (carried back), and the government will refund some previously paid taxes. If the corporation's current loss exceeds its previous income, the firm can use the loss to offset future profits (carry the loss forward) and reduce its future taxes.

S CORPORATIONS The so-called Subchapter S regulation permits small businesses that meet certain requirements to choose to be taxed as partnerships or proprietorships instead of as corporations. This allows the corporation to receive some of the benefits of the corporate form of organization and yet avoid the double taxation of income. Subchapter S corporate income is reported as personal income by its owners. The individual owners then pay personal income taxes on the part of the income that is allocated to each of them.

Personal Income Taxes

Personal income taxes are the federal government's largest source of income. In a recent year, they made up 36% of its total income. Here we will look at some of the features of the personal income tax system that have implications for financial management.

[10]The effect of the intercorporate dividend exclusion is to exclude the amount from income. It is as though the deducted amount is simply not counted as part of Epic's income.

PERSONAL INCOME TAX RATES Like corporate income tax rates, personal income tax rates increase with income, going from zero to a maximum of 39.1%. The marginal tax rates for the two most common filing status categories ("single" and "married, filing jointly") are shown in Table 3.6. There are other schedules for people classified as "married, filing separately" or as "head of household." Personal tax rates are further complicated by the elimination of certain exemptions and deductions for higher incomes. The elimination of an exemption or deduction raises the effective tax rate. In addition, individuals pay social security and medicare taxes and income taxes to state and local governments, so the effective tax rates for individuals can be much higher than the rates in Table 3.6.

EXEMPTIONS AND DEDUCTIONS Taxable income is equal to gross income minus allowable exemptions and deductions. For each dependent there is an exemption, which was $2,900 in 2001 and increases each year with inflation. In addition, you can choose either to itemize your deductions or to take a standard deduction that is based on your filing status. Itemized deductions include such things as home mortgage interest, gifts to charity, state and local income taxes paid, real estate taxes paid, and some medical and job-related expenses. As mentioned above, some exemptions and deductions are eliminated for incomes above certain levels.

DIVIDEND AND INTEREST INCOME Dividend income received from common stock and preferred stock is fully taxable. Income from interest paid by corporations, financial institutions, and individuals is also fully taxable. However, recall from our discussion of the Principle of Two-Sided Transactions that interest on munis (municipal bonds), certain state and local government bonds, is not taxable by the federal government. Consequently, munis can be attractive investments. The after-income-tax yield on the muni equals its before-income-tax yield, whereas the after-income-tax yield on the taxable bond is

$$\text{After-income-tax yield} = \text{Before-income-tax yield}(1 - \text{Marginal income tax rate}) \quad (3.3)$$

Note, however, that the relative attractiveness of a muni depends on one's marginal income tax rate. With a zero income tax rate, a taxable bond's after-income-tax yield is the same as its before-income-tax yield.

TABLE 3.6
Personal income tax rates.

PERSONAL TAXABLE INCOME ($)	PAY THIS AMOUNT ON THE BASE OF THE RANGE ($)	PLUS THIS RATE TIMES THE EXCESS OVER THE BASE (%)
Single Taxpayer		
0–27,050	0	15
27,050–65,550	4,057.50	27.5
65,550–136,750	14,645.00	30.5
136,750–297,350	36,361.00	35.5
over 297,350	93,374.00	39.1
Married Taxpayers Filing Jointly		
0–45,200	0	15
45,200–109,250	6,780.00	27.5
109,250–166,500	24,393.75	30.5
166,500–297,350	41,855.00	35.5
over 297,350	88,306.75	39.1

EXAMPLE Yields on Munis Versus Taxable Securities

Suppose Phil and Marcia can invest in a taxable bond yielding 8.0% or a muni yielding 6.5%. Phil's marginal income tax rate is 15%, whereas Marcia's is 30%. Which bond should each one invest in?

The after-income-tax muni yield is 6.5% for both of them. If Marcia invests in the taxable bond, she will have an after-income-tax yield of 5.6%:

$$\text{After-income-tax yield} = 8.0(1 - 0.30) = 8.0(0.70) = 5.6\%$$

Therefore, the muni is more attractive for Marcia.

However, if Phil invests in the taxable bond, he will have an after-income-tax yield of 6.80%:

$$\text{After-income-tax yield} = 8.0(1 - 0.15) = 8.0(0.85) = 6.80\%$$

So Phil is better off investing in the taxable bond, despite the taxation on its interest.

PERSONAL CAPITAL GAINS TAXES Like corporate income, the personal income tax system has special provisions for long-term capital gains that result from owning assets for more than one year. And they also lead to tax-timing options.

EXAMPLE A Capital Gain Tax-Timing Option on Goodyear Stock

Suppose you bought 100 shares of Goodyear for $3,000 a little more than a year ago and the shares are worth $4,500 today. If you sell the shares for $4,500, you will be taxed on a $1,500 capital gain. But for as long as you continue to own the shares, you will not have to pay a capital gains tax. Now suppose instead that your shares have gone down in value to $2,200. If you sell the shares for $2,200, you will be able to claim a capital loss of $800, which could reduce your taxes this year.

As with corporate income, short-term capital gains (losses) are taxed as regular income. However, personal (long-term) capital gains may be taxed at a lower rate because the maximum capital gains rate is currently 20%.[11] Thus, if your marginal ordinary rate is above 20%, your capital gains are taxed at the lower rate of 20%. The lower capital gains tax rate provides extra incentive to make long-term investments.

Review

1. What is a progressive tax system? How do the marginal and average tax rates usually compare in such a system?
2. Explain an important difference in corporate income taxes between interest expense and dividends paid.
3. How does the intercorporate dividend exclusion work?
4. Explain how capital gains are taxed differently from ordinary income.
5. What is a tax-timing option?

[11]A lower tax rate of 18% applies to gains on capital assets held more than 5 years.

SUMMARY

The purpose of Chapter 3 is to review the major financial statements, emphasize the difference between accounting and economic concepts of value and income, and detail the major corporate and personal tax features that affect a firm's financial policy.

- The primary financial statements are the balance sheet, income statement, and statement of cash flows. The footnotes and management's discussion are also important parts of the firm's annual report.
- The balance sheet shows the assets, liabilities, and stockholders' equity of the firm. The balance sheet shows the firm's financial position at a specific point in time.
- The income statement reports the firm's revenues, costs, and net income for a period of time, such as during one year or one quarter.
- The statement of cash flows shows the cash flows that result in a period's change in cash balances. The cash flows are broken into three parts, cash flows from operating activities, investing activities, and financing activities.
- Market values are based on expected future cash flows. Book values are based on historical costs. The market values and book values of assets, liabilities, and stockholders' equity can be substantially different.
- Economic income (cash flow plus capital gain) differs from accounting income.
- Corporate and personal income taxes are levied by the federal government as well as by most states and many local governments.
- Marginal and average tax rates for both corporations and individuals are fairly high and taxes are a major expense of doing business.
- Currently, corporate capital gains tax rates are the same as ordinary income rates. When they exist, lower capital gains rates are an incentive to invest in capital assets. Personal capital gains tax rates are lower than ordinary income tax rates.
- For corporations, interest paid is a tax-deductible expense, but dividends paid are not tax deductible. This encourages the use of debt financing.
- Double taxation is the system of taxing income twice, once at the corporate level and a second time when dividends are paid to stockholders. At least seventy percent of intercorporate dividends are excluded from taxable income to avoid triple taxation.
- S Corporations are certain small businesses that can avoid double taxation (if they qualify) by allocating their income to their owners who pay personal taxes on the corporation's income.
- Personal tax rates and corporate tax rates are progressive, where low-income individuals and corporations have lower marginal and average tax rates.
- Interest income on municipal bonds is not taxable by the federal government.

EQUATION SUMMARY

$$\text{Assets} = \text{Liabilities} + \text{Stockholders' equity} \tag{3.1}$$

$$\text{Working capital} = \text{Current assets} - \text{Current liabilities} \tag{3.2}$$

$$\text{After-income-tax yield} = \text{Before-income-tax yield}(1 - \text{Marginal income tax rate}) \tag{3.3}$$

QUESTIONS

1. Explain the purpose of each of the following financial statements: income statement, balance sheet, and statement of cash flows.
2. What is the balance sheet identity?
3. Assume that interest rates have increased substantially. Would this tend to increase or decrease the market value of a firm's liabilities (relative to the book value of liabilities)?
4. Assume that inflation rates have been fairly high. Would this tend to increase or decrease the market value of a firm's assets (relative to their book values)?
5. Describe the difference between economic income and accounting net income.
6. Explain why the notes to a firm's financial statements are an integral part of the financial statements.
7. What primarily distinguishes:
   a. Current assets from the other classes of assets on the balance sheet?
   b. Current liabilities from the other classes of liabilities on the balance sheet?
8. Define the term *cash flow.* Explain the difference between cash flow and earnings.
9. Define the term *working capital.* How is working capital calculated? What does working capital measure?

CHALLENGING QUESTIONS

10. In a corporation's annual report, what do you think would be the order of presentation of the following items: balance sheet, income statement, statement of cash flows, management's discussion, notes to the financial statements?
11. What important feature of the corporate tax system tends to favor the use of debt financing over equity financing?
12. Why do you think each of the following features is part of the tax code applied to corporations?
    a. Progressive tax rates (low rates for low levels of corporate income).
    b. Intercorporate dividend exclusion.
    c. A tax on improper accumulations of income to avoid payment of personal taxes on dividends.
13. "For high-income individuals, capital gains are taxed at a lower rate than ordinary income. Additionally, the payment of a capital gains tax can be deferred by postponing the sale of an asset that has gone up in value." Do you agree with this opinion?
14. "Because interest on municipal bonds is not taxable, individuals should always buy municipal bonds instead of taxable corporate bonds." Is this advice sound? Do munis always have a higher after-tax yield? When do munis have a higher after-tax yield?
15. Cite and briefly discuss four factors that affect the likelihood that the market and book values of an asset will differ.
16. Cite and briefly discuss two factors that affect the likelihood that the market and book values of a liability will differ.

PROBLEMS

LEVEL A (BASIC)

A1. (Balance sheet and income statement) Johnson's Scuba Co. has a weird accountant who reported the balance sheet and income statement items in alphabetical order. Please put these items in the correct format for a balance sheet and income statement for Johnson's Scuba Co. for the year ending January 31. All of the data are in thousands of dollars.

Accounts payable	500
Accounts receivable	700
Addition to retained earnings	400
Cash and equivalents	300
Common stock	500
Cost of goods sold	2,000
Depreciation	200
Dividends on common shares	100
Earnings before interest and taxes	800
Earnings before taxes	750
Gross profit	2,000
Interest expense	50
Inventories	500
Long-term debt	1,000
Net income	500
Net plant and equipment	3,000
Notes payable	250
Other current liabilities	400
Retained earnings	1,850
Sales	4,000
Selling, general, and administrative expenses	1,000
Taxes	250
Total assets	4,500
Total current assets	1,500
Total liabilities and equity	4,500
Total current liabilities	1,150
Total liabilities	2,150

A2. (Balance sheet and income statement) Rimbey Sporting Goods has a weird accountant who reported the balance sheet and income statement items in alphabetical order. Please put these items in the correct format for a balance sheet and income statement for Rimbey Sporting Goods for the year ending January 31. All of the data are in thousands of dollars.

Accounts payable	500
Accounts receivable	600
Addition to retained earnings	250
Cash and equivalents	200
Common stock	100
Cost of goods sold	3,700
Depreciation	300
Dividends on common shares	150
Earnings before interest and taxes	800
Earnings before taxes	700
Gross profit	2,300
Interest expense	100
Inventories	700
Long-term debt	1,100
Net income	400
Net plant and equipment	2,500
Notes payable	300
Other current liabilities	500
Retained earnings	1,500
Sales	6,000
Selling, general, and administrative expenses	1,200

Taxes	300
Total assets	4,000
Total current assets	1,500
Total liabilities and equity	4,000
Total current liabilities	1,300
Total liabilities	2,400

A3. (Statement of cash flows) Johnson's accountant also presented all of the items in the statement of cash flows in alphabetical order. Please put these items in the correct format for a statement of cash flows for Johnson's Scuba Co. for the year ending January 31. All data are in thousands of dollars.

Accounts payable increase	100
Accounts receivable increase	(50)
Cash dividends (common stock)	(200)
Cash and equivalents at beginning of year	300
Cash and equivalents at end of year	150
Depreciation and amortization	200
Increase in other long-term liabilities	0
Inventories increase	(200)
Issuance of long-term debt, net	100
Net cash provided by (used in) financing activities	0
Net cash provided by (used in) investing activities	(700)
Net cash provided by (used in) operating activities	550
Net income	500
Net increase in cash and equivalents	(150)
Notes payable increase	100
Purchase of plant and equipment	(700)

A4. (Statement of cash flows) Rimbey's accountant also presented all of the items in the statement of cash flows in alphabetical order. Please put these items in the correct format for a statement of cash flows for Rimbey Sporting Goods for the year ending January 31. All data are in thousands of dollars.

Accounts payable increase	50
Accounts receivable increase	(100)
Cash dividends (common stock)	(150)
Cash and equivalents at beginning of year	100
Cash and equivalents at end of year	200
Depreciation and amortization	300
Increase in other long-term liabilities	0
Inventories increase	(150)
Issuance of long-term debt, net	200
Net cash provided by (used in) financing activities	100
Net cash provided by (used in) investing activities	(500)
Net cash provided by (used in) operating activities	500
Net income	400
Net increase in cash and equivalents	100
Notes payable increase	50
Purchase of plant and equipment	(500)

A5. (Financial statements) For the year ended December 31, Dutch Retail, Inc. recorded the items listed below. Prepare an income statement for the year ended December 31, for Dutch Retail, Inc. Please use an appropriate format, such as the one in Table 3.2.

Cost of goods sold	$ 200
Interest expense	100
Preferred dividends paid	50
Common dividends paid	100
Selling expenses	65
Administrative expenses	100

Depreciation expense	150
Sales revenues	900
Taxes = 40% of taxable income	

A6. (Financial statements) For the year ended December 31, Dominion Resources, Inc. recorded the items listed below. Prepare an income statement for the year ended December 31 for Dominion Resources, Inc. Please use an appropriate format, such as the one in Table 3.2.

Cost of goods sold	$485
Interest expense	20
Preferred dividends paid	5
Common dividends paid	10
Selling expenses	30
Administrative expenses	125
Depreciation expense	100
Sales revenues	700
Taxes = 40% of taxable income	

A7. (Financial statements) Construct a balance sheet for Falken Computers, Inc. from the following data. Use a format similar to the balance sheet in Table 3.1. What is stockholders' equity?

Cash	$500
Inventory	100
Accounts receivable	300
Fixed assets	700
Accounts payable	300
Accrued expenses	100
Long-term debt	500

A8. (Financial statements) Construct a balance sheet for Solomon Mines from the following data. Use a format similar to the balance sheet in Table 3.1. What is stockholders' equity?

Cash	$100
Inventory	200
Accounts receivable	200
Fixed assets	400
Accounts payable	100
Accrued expenses	50
Long-term debt	300

A9. (Financial statements) For the year, Pennsylvania Construction has a cash flow from operating activities of $1,000,000, a cash flow from investing activities of −$600,000, and a cash flow from financing activities of −$200,000. If Pennsylvania Construction has a beginning cash balance for the year of $500,000, what is the company's ending cash balance?

A10. (Financial statements) For the year, Utah Ski Tours has a cash flow from operating activities of $700,000, a cash flow from investing activities of −$450,000, and a cash flow from financing activities of −$100,000. If Utah Ski Tours has a beginning cash balance for the year of $300,000, what is the firm's ending cash balance?

A11. (Financial statements) Ivan Brick Company earned net income after taxes of $850,000 during the latest year. Retained earnings on its balance sheet equaled $1,740,000 on December 31, last year and $2,040,000 on December 31, the latest year. What cash dividends did Ivan Brick Company pay during the latest year?

A12. (Corporate taxes) The Boston Publishing Company has taxable income of $250,000.

a. What is its federal corporate tax liability?

b. What are its average and marginal tax rates?

c. If Boston had an additional $10,000 from interest income, what additional taxes would be owed?

d. If Boston had an additional $10,000 of dividend income (from other corporations), what additional taxes would be owed?

A13. (Corporate taxes) The Sherman Electronics Company has taxable income of $300,000.

a. What is its federal corporate tax liability?

b. What are its average and marginal tax rates?

c. If Sherman had an additional $20,000 from interest income, what additional taxes would be owed?

d. If Sherman had an additional $25,000 of dividend income (from other corporations), what additional taxes would be owed?

A14. (Corporate taxes) Newbould Industries, Inc. has earnings before interest and taxes of $1,500,000. Newbould has interest expense of $300,000, and paid cash dividends of $200,000 to its common stockholders. Newbould received no dividends from other corporations. Its income tax rate is 35%.

a. What is Newbould's income tax liability?

b. What is Newbould's after-tax income?

A15. (Corporate taxes) Oleson, Inc. has earnings before interest and taxes of $500,000. Oleson has interest expense of $200,000, and paid cash dividends of $200,000 to its common stockholders. Oleson received no dividends from other corporations. Its income tax rate is 35%.

a. What is Oleson's income tax liability?

b. What is Oleson's after-tax income?

A16. (Corporate taxes) The Welch Trading Corporation is in the 35% marginal tax bracket. What would be its after-tax yield from investing in each of the following securities?

a. A Treasury bond paying 8.0% interest.

b. A municipal bond paying 5.2% interest.

c. Preferred stock paying a 5.81% dividend yield. Don't forget the 70% intercorporate dividend exclusion.

A17. (Corporate taxes) Alaskan Industries is in the 40% marginal tax bracket. What would be its after-tax yield from investing in each of the following securities?

a. A Treasury bond paying 7.5% interest.

b. A municipal bond paying 5.6% interest.

c. Preferred stock paying a 6% dividend yield. Note the 70% intercorporate dividend exclusion.

A18. (Personal taxes) Two of your friends are trying to decide between buying taxable bonds yielding 8.0% and municipal bonds yielding 6.0%. Gary is in the 20% marginal tax bracket, which includes the combined effect of federal and state personal income taxes. Anna is in the 40% marginal tax bracket.

a. What are the after-tax yields of the two kinds of bonds for Gary?

b. What are the after-tax yields of the two kinds of bonds for Anna?

c. What marginal tax rate would cause both bonds to have the same after-tax yield?

A19. (Personal taxes) Two of your friends are trying to decide between buying taxable bonds yielding 7.5% and municipal bonds yielding 5.0%. John is in the 25% marginal tax bracket, which includes the combined effect of federal and state personal income taxes. Kate is in the 38% marginal tax bracket.

a. What are the after-tax yields of the two kinds of bonds for John?

b. What are the after-tax yields of the two kinds of bonds for Kate?

c. What marginal tax rate would cause both bonds to have the same after-tax yield?

LEVEL B

B1. (Financial statements) Consider the following financial information for Spartan Video.

Balance Sheet, December 31
(Figures in millions of dollars)

ASSETS	LATEST YEAR	PREVIOUS YEAR	LIABILITIES AND STOCKHOLDERS' EQUITY	LATEST YEAR	PREVIOUS YEAR
Current assets	$200	$150	Current liabilities	$100	$ 80
Net fixed assets	500	400	Long-term debt	300	300

Partial Income Statement, latest year ending December 31

(Figures in millions of dollars)

Sales	$1,000
Cost of goods sold	300
Selling and administrative expenses	100
Depreciation	60
Interest expense	40

a. What is stockholders' equity in the previous and latest years?

b. Assume a tax rate of 40%. What are income taxes paid and net income after taxes for the latest year?

c. The firm did not issue or repurchase any stock during the latest year. What dividend was paid?

d. Given the change in net fixed assets and depreciation expense, what is the amount of fixed assets purchased during the latest year?

e. What is net working capital in the previous and latest years?

f. What is cash provided (used) by operations during the latest year (the increase in working capital is a use of cash)? What is cash provided (used) by investing activities? What is cash provided (used) by financing activities?

B2. (Financial statements) Consider the following financial information for Sunny Fruit Co.

Balance Sheet, December 31
(Figures in millions of dollars)

ASSETS	LATEST YEAR	PREVIOUS YEAR	LIABILITIES AND STOCKHOLDERS' EQUITY	LATEST YEAR	PREVIOUS YEAR
Current assets	$400	$200	Current liabilities	$150	$195
Net fixed assets	600	400	Long-term debt	500	100

Partial Income Statement, latest year ending December 31

(Figures in millions of dollars)

Sales	$900
Cost of goods sold	200
Selling and administrative expenses	200
Depreciation	100
Interest expense	50

a. What is stockholders' equity in the previous and latest years?

b. Assume a tax rate of 40%. What are income taxes paid and net income after taxes for the latest year?

c. The company did not issue or repurchase any stock during the latest year. What dividend was paid?

d. Given the change in net fixed assets and depreciation expense, what is the amount of fixed assets purchased during the latest year?

e. What is net working capital in the previous and latest years?

f. What is cash provided (used) by operations during the latest year (the increase in working capital is a use of cash)? What is cash provided (used) by investing activities? What is cash provided (used) by financing activities?

B3. (Book and market values) Bill's Lanes, a Louisiana corporation that owns several bowling alleys, has the following balance sheet:

Bill's Lanes Corporation
Balance Sheet, December 31
(Figures in thousands of dollars)

ASSETS		**LIABILITIES AND STOCKHOLDERS' EQUITY**	
Current assets	$1,200	Current liabilities	$ 800
Net fixed assets	3,000	Long-term debt	1,000
Total	$4,200	Stockholders' equity	2,400
		Total	$4,200

Assume that the market value of the current assets is equal to the book value and that the market value of the net fixed assets is three times the book value. The market value of current liabilities is equal to the book value and the market value of long-term debt is 90% of its book value.

a. What is the market value of Bill's Lanes' assets?

b. What is the market value of Bill's Lanes' liabilities?

c. If the market value of equity is equal to the market value of assets minus the market value of liabilities, what is the market value of the equity in Bill's Lanes?

B4. (Book and market values) Newport Mining, a Tennessee corporation that owns several mining operations, has the following balance sheet:

Newport Mining
Balance Sheet, December 31
(Figures in thousands of dollars)

ASSETS		**LIABILITIES AND STOCKHOLDERS' EQUITY**	
Current assets	$2,000	Current liabilities	$ 500
Net fixed assets	5,000	Long-term debt	2,000
Total	$7,000	Stockholders' equity	4,500
		Total	$7,000

Assume the market value of the current assets is equal to the book value and that the market value of the net fixed assets is three times the book value. The market value of current liabilities is equal to the book value and the market value of long-term debt is 90% of its book value.

a. What is the market value of Newport's assets?

b. What is the market value of Newport's liabilities?

c. If the market value of equity is equal to the market value of assets minus the market value of liabilities, what is the market value of the equity in Newport Mining?

B5. (Book and market values) Consider the following information about the Peachtree Construction Company. All data are in millions of dollars.

	BOOK VALUE	MARKET VALUE
Assets, December 31, previous year	800	1,400
Assets, December 31, latest year	900	1,650
Liabilities, December 31, previous year	400	425
Liabilities, December 31, latest year	425	475

a. What is the book value of stockholders' equity at the end of the previous and latest years?

b. What is the market value of stockholders' equity at the end of the previous and latest years?

c. For the latest year ending December 31, net income was $150 million. If Peachtree paid its stockholders cash dividends of $75 million, what is the total economic income of the stockholders during this year?

B6. (Book and market values) Consider the following information about the Dilbert Printing Company. All data are in millions of dollars.

	BOOK VALUE	MARKET VALUE
Assets, December 31, previous year	1,000	2,000
Assets, December 31, latest year	1,200	1,400
Liabilities, December 31, previous year	600	900
Liabilities, December 31, latest year	650	1,050

a. What is the book value of stockholders' equity at the end of the previous and latest years?

b. What is the market value of stockholders' equity at the end of the previous and latest years?

c. For the latest year ending December 31, net income was $175 million. If Dilbert paid its stockholders cash dividends of $50 million, what is the total economic income of the stockholders during this year?

B7. (Corporate income taxes) Santiago's Chile Company has sales of $15,000,000, cost of goods sold of $6,000,000, selling and administrative costs of $2,500,000, and depreciation expenses of $500,000. Santiago's also paid $200,000 of interest expense and received $150,000 of dividends from other corporations. Santiago's Chile had a realized long-term capital gain of $400,000 and paid dividends of $250,000 to shareholders. Use the corporate income tax rates given in Table 3.5.

a. What is the federal income tax liability for Santiago's Chile Company?

b. What are the marginal and average tax rates for Santiago's?

B8. (Corporate income taxes) Phil's Trucking Co. has sales of $12,000,000, cost of goods sold of $3,000,000, selling and administrative costs of $2,000,000, and depreciation expenses of $600,000. Phil's also paid $100,000 of interest expense and received $150,000 of dividends from other corporations. Phil's had a realized long-term capital gain of $250,000 and paid dividends of $400,000 to shareholders. Use the corporate income tax rates given in Table 3.5.

a. What is the federal income tax liability for Phil's Trucking Co.?

b. What are the marginal and average tax rates for Phil's?

B9. (Personal income taxes) Assume that you are a single taxpayer and have one personal exemption for $2,500 and itemized deductions of $7,500. Calculate your federal income tax liability for the three cases given below. What is your marginal income tax rate and your average income tax rate for each case? Use the personal tax rate schedule in Table 3.6.

a. Your taxable income is $25,000.

b. Your taxable income is $75,000.

c. Your taxable income is $125,000. In addition, you lose your personal exemption (for $2,500) and all but $3,000 of your itemized deductions.

B10. (Personal income taxes) Assume you are a single taxpayer and have one personal exemption for $2,500 and itemized deductions of $8,500. Calculate your federal income tax liability for the three cases given below. What is your marginal income tax rate and your average income tax rate for each case? Use the personal tax rate schedule in Table 3.6.

a. Your taxable income is $30,000.

b. Your taxable income is $100,000.

c. Your taxable income is $175,000.

LEVEL C (ADVANCED)

C1. (Accounting versus economic income) During the latest year, McGowan Construction earned net income of $250,000. The firm neither bought nor sold any capital assets, and the book value of its assets declined by the year's depreciation charge, which was $200,000. The firm's operating cash flow for the year was $450,000, and the market value of its assets increased by $300,000. What was McGowan Construction's economic income for the year? Why is this figure different from its accounting net income?

C2. (Accounting versus economic income) During the latest year, McDonald Construction earned net income of $500,000. The company neither bought nor sold any capital assets, and the book value of its assets declined by the year's depreciation charge, which was $150,000. The company's operating cash flow for the year was $800,000, and the market value of its assets increased by $400,000. What was McDonald Construction's economic income for the year? Why is this figure different from its accounting net income?

C3. (Personal taxes and return on investment) Ed Lawrence invests $100,000, buying 2,000 shares of Yolo Freight for $50 per-share. After one year, he receives a cash dividend of $1.50 per-share and sells the stock for $62.00 per-share.

a. Assume no taxes. What is the ending value of Ed's investment (including the value of the stock and the cash dividend)? What is the rate of return on his investment?

b. Assume that Ed pays taxes of 39.6% on dividends and 28% on capital gains. After taxes, what is the ending value of his portfolio? What is the after-tax rate of return on his investment?

C4. (Personal taxes and return on investment) Brandon invests $300,000, buying 10,000 shares of WABC for $30 per-share. After one year, he receives a cash dividend of $2 per-share and sells the stock for $42.00 per-share.

a. Assume no taxes. What is the ending value of Brandon's investment (including the value of the stock and the cash dividend)? What is the realized return on his investment?

b. Assume Brandon pays taxes of 39.6% on dividends and 28% on capital gains. After taxes, what is the ending value of his portfolio? What is the realized after-tax return on his investment?

APPENDIX
ANALYZING FINANCIAL STATEMENTS

Despite the built-in limitations of accounting information, published accounting statements can reveal a great deal about a firm. Financial analysts and managers find it helpful to calculate financial ratios when interpreting a firm's accounting statements. A **financial ratio** is simply one quantity divided by another. Financial statement analysis can be useful in at least two ways. First, it can help structure your thinking about business decisions. Second, it can provide some information that is helpful in making those decisions.

The number of financial ratios that could be created is virtually limitless, but certain basic ratios are used frequently. These ratios fall into six classes: *liquidity ratios, asset activity ratios, leverage ratios, coverage ratios, profitability ratios, and market value ratios.* The calculation and interpretation of these six classes of ratios are discussed here. Our sample calculations are made on an actual balance sheet and income statement of Anheuser-Busch, which are shown in Tables 3A.1 and 3A.2.

TABLE 3A.1

Anheuser-Busch Companies, Inc. annual balance sheet (millions of dollars, rounded), December 31.

	LATEST YEAR	PREVIOUS YEAR	2 YEARS AGO
ASSETS			
Cash and equivalents	$ 127.4	$ 215.0	$ 97.3
Accounts receivable	751.1	649.8	654.8
Inventories	626.7	660.7	635.6
Other current assets	290.0	290.3	240.0
Total current assets	$ 1,795.2	$ 1,815.8	$ 1,627.7
Gross fixed assets	11,727.1	11,385.1	10,589.6
Accumulated depreciation	(4,230.0)	(3,861.4)	(3,393.1)
Net fixed assets	7,497.1	7,523.7	7,196.5
Other assets	1,588.0	1,198.4	1,162.3
Total assets	$10,880.3	$10,537.9	$ 9,986.5
LIABILITIES & STOCKHOLDERS' EQUITY			
Accounts payable	$ 812.5	$ 737.4	$ 709.8
Taxes payable	91.0	38.8	45.2
Accrued expenses	609.7	426.7	392.7
Other current liabilities	302.4	256.9	255.1
Total current liabilities	$ 1,815.6	$ 1,459.8	$ 1,402.8
Long-term debt	3,031.7	2,642.5	2,644.9
Deferred taxes	1,170.4	1,276.9	1,500.7
Other liabilities	607.1	538.3	0.0
Total liabilities	$ 6,624.8	$ 5,917.5	$ 5,548.4
Preferred stock	$ 0.0	$ 0.0	$ 0.0
Common stock	342.5	341.3	338.5
Capital surplus	402.2	328.5	193.3
Retained earnings	5,990.4	5,793.5	5,230.5
Less: Treasury stock	(2,479.6)	(1,842.9)	(1,324.2)
Total common equity	$ 4,255.5	$ 4,620.4	$ 4,438.1
Total liabilities & stockholders' equity	$10,880.3	$10,537.9	$ 9,986.5

TABLE 3A.2
Anheuser-Busch Companies, Inc. annual income statement (millions of dollars, rounded, except per-share amounts), December 31.

	LATEST YEAR	PREVIOUS YEAR	2 YEARS AGO
Sales	$ 11,505	$ 11,394	$ 10,996
Cost of goods sold	6,811	6,742	6,614
Gross profit	4,694	4,652	4,382
Selling, general, & administrative expenses	2,309	2,309	2,126
Depreciation, depletion, & amortization	608	567	534
Operating profit	1,777	1,776	1,722
Interest expense	(208)	(200)	(239)
Capitalized interest	37	48	47
Nonoperating profit (loss)	(556)	(9)	(9)
Earnings before tax	1,050	1,615	1,521
Total income tax	456	621	581
Net income	594	994	940
Preferred dividends	0	0	0
Available for common	$ 594	$ 994	$ 940
Earnings per share	$2.17	$3.48	$3.26
Dividends per share	$1.36	$1.20	$1.06
Shares outstanding (000)	273,963	285,690	288,282

Liquidity Ratios

Liquidity ratios measure a firm's liquidity. The purpose is to assess the firm's ability to meet its financial obligations on time. Four widely used liquidity ratios are the current ratio, the quick ratio, the working capital ratio, and the cash ratio. The most commonly used measure of overall liquidity is the **current ratio.**

$$\text{Current ratio} = \frac{\text{Current assets}}{\text{Current liabilities}} = \frac{1{,}816}{1{,}460} = 1.24x$$

The current ratio measures the number of times the firm's current assets "cover" its current liabilities. Presumably, the higher the current ratio, the greater the firm's ability to meet its short-term obligations as they come due. A widely held but rough rule of thumb is that a current ratio of 2.0 is an appropriate target for most firms.

Inventories are considered current assets, so they are included in the current ratio calculation. Inventories, however, are less liquid than marketable securities and accounts receivable. This is because it is normally more difficult to turn inventory into cash on short notice. Thus, analysts often exclude inventories from the numerator in the current ratio and calculate the **quick ratio** (also called the **acid test ratio**).

$$\text{Quick (Acid Test) ratio} = \frac{\text{Current assets} - \text{Inventories}}{\text{Current liabilities}} = \frac{1{,}816 - 661}{1{,}460} = 0.79x$$

Another widely held but rough rule of thumb says a quick ratio of 1.0 or more is healthy.

Equation (3.2) defines working capital as the difference between current assets and current liabilities. The **working capital ratio** is working capital expressed as a proportion of sales.

$$\text{Working capital ratio} = \frac{\text{Current assets} - \text{Current liabilities}}{\text{Sales}} = \frac{1{,}816 - 1{,}460}{11{,}394} = 3.1\%$$

Working capital is often considered a measure of liquidity by itself. This ratio shows the amount of liquidity relative to sales.

The **cash ratio** is calculated by dividing cash and equivalents by total assets.

$$\text{Cash ratio} = \frac{\text{Cash and equivalents}}{\text{Total assets}} = \frac{215}{10{,}538} = 2.0\%$$

Cash and equivalents (such as marketable securities) are the most liquid assets. The cash ratio shows the proportion of assets held in the most liquid possible form.

Ratios for other firms in the same industry and time period are often compared to judge a firm's relative strengths and weaknesses. For example, we can compare Anheuser-Busch's ratios to average ratios for the other large firms in the alcoholic beverages industry.[12]

	ANHEUSER-BUSCH	OTHER ALCOHOLIC BEVERAGE FIRMS
Current ratio	1.24x	2.12x
Quick ratio	0.79x	0.93x
Working capital ratio	3.1%	24.0%
Cash ratio	2.0%	3.0%

Anheuser-Busch has lower liquidity ratios than the other alcoholic beverage firms. Nevertheless, Anheuser-Busch is a healthy firm; nobody expects it to have trouble meeting its obligations as they come due. Its health allows it to carry much greater current liabilities, and it simply does not need as much liquidity as the rules of thumb prescribe, a current ratio of 2.0 and a quick ratio of 1.0. Note that the other alcoholic beverage firms have current and quick ratios that are very close to 2.0 and 1.0, respectively.

Asset Activity Ratios

Asset activity ratios are designed to measure how effectively a firm manages its assets. There are several ratios focusing on the management of specific assets as well as total assets.

The **receivables turnover ratio** is

$$\text{Receivables turnover} = \frac{\text{Annual credit sales}}{\text{Accounts receivable}} = \frac{11{,}394}{650} = 17.53x$$

It measures the number of times the accounts receivable balance "turns over" during the year. Note that annual credit sales, which give rise to receivables, are used in the numerator. If a figure for annual credit sales is not available, the firm's net sales figure is used instead. Making that substitution is like assuming that all sales were credit sales.

[12]Brown-Forman Corporation, Canandaigua Wine Co., Adolph Coors Company, The Molson Companies Ltd., and Seagram Co. are the other firms followed by *The Value Line Investment Survey.* The enormous difference between the working capital ratios for Anheuser-Busch and the other alcoholic beverage firms may look odd. You will find in a moment that Anheuser-Busch also has relatively high receivables and inventory turnover ratios.

TABLE 3A.3
Accounts receivable aging schedule.

AGE (DAYS)	ACCOUNTS RECEIVABLE	PERCENTAGE OF TOTAL
0–30	$1,500	50.0%
30–60	900	30.0
60–90	450	15.0
over 90	150	5.0
Total	$3,000	100.0%

A closely related figure is the **days' sales outstanding** (DSO). It is the number of days in a year divided by the receivables turnover ratio.[13]

$$\text{Days' sales outstanding} = \frac{365}{\text{Receivables turnover}} = \frac{\text{Accounts receivable}}{\text{Annual credit sales}/365} = \frac{365}{17.53} = 20.8 \text{ days}$$

The days' sales outstanding shows approximately how long it takes, on average, to collect a receivable. The days' sales outstanding is also called the **average collection period.**

A more detailed picture of the firm's accounts receivable can be obtained by preparing an **aging schedule.** An aging schedule shows the amounts of receivables that have been outstanding for different periods, such as 0 to 30 days, 30 to 60 days, 60 to 90 days, and more than 90 days. An example of an accounts receivable aging schedule is given in Table 3A.3. An external analyst typically lacks the detailed information in an aging schedule unless the firm has chosen to provide it. Of course, managers within the firm want this information to help monitor their accounts receivable.

A measure of the effectiveness of inventory management is the **inventory turnover ratio,** which is calculated as follows:

$$\text{Inventory turnover} = \frac{\text{Cost of goods sold}}{\text{Inventory}} = \frac{6,742}{661} = 10.20x$$

Inventory turnover is a good estimate of how many times per year the inventory is physically turning over. In the past, some analysts calculated the inventory turnover by dividing net sales by inventory. However, this calculation overstates the turnover rate of physical inventory.[14]

Another way to measure inventory turnover is the **days' sales in inventory ratio.** This is the time for "one turnover." For example, if inventory turnover were 12.0*x*, one turnover would be 1/12 of a year, which in days is 30.42 (= 365/12). For Anheuser-Busch, it is

$$\text{Days' sales in inventory} = \frac{365}{\text{Inventory turnover}} = \frac{365}{10.20} = 35.8 \text{ days}$$

The days' sales in inventory ratio estimates the average time, in days, that inventory stays with the firm before it is sold.

---

[13]Before calculators and computers were widely used, analysts often used a 360-day year for simplicity. Although much of the financial press has continued this practice so far, it is becoming less popular. We always use a 365-day year.

[14]An example illustrates the problem: 60 units of the firm's product were sold last year; sales were $600; cost of goods sold on these units was $360; and inventory was $120 with 20 units in it. Dividing *sales* by inventory, 600/120 = 5.0*x*. Dividing *cost of goods sold* by inventory, 360/120 = 3.0*x*. From knowing the number of units, we can see that the physical turnover rate is in fact 60/20 = 3.0*x*. The turnover rate of 5.0*x* is larger than the physical turnover rate, because sales are on a different basis; sales include profit. Cost of goods sold does not include profit. Cost of goods sold is on the same cost basis as inventory.

Finally, two other ratios show how productively the firm is using its assets. These are the **fixed asset turnover ratio** and the **total asset turnover ratio.**

$$\text{Fixed asset turnover} = \frac{\text{Sales}}{\text{Net fixed assets}} = \frac{11,394}{7,524} = 1.51x$$

$$\text{Total asset turnover} = \frac{\text{Sales}}{\text{Total assets}} = \frac{11,394}{10,538} = 1.08x$$

These ratios show the sales generated per book-value dollar of fixed assets and total assets, respectively.

We can again compare Anheuser-Busch's ratios to those of the other alcoholic beverage firms.

	ANHEUSER-BUSCH	OTHER ALCOHOLIC BEVERAGE FIRMS
Receivables turnover	17.53x	8.11x
Days' sales outstanding	20.8 days	50.9 days
Inventory turnover	10.20x	2.89x
Days' sales in inventory	35.8 days	189.2 days
Fixed asset turnover	1.51x	3.84x
Total asset turnover	1.08x	1.01x

Anheuser-Busch turns over its receivables and inventory more rapidly than the other firms.[15] Anheuser-Busch's fixed assets turn over more slowly. This implies that Anheuser-Busch requires a larger investment in fixed assets (relative to sales) than these other firms.

Leverage Ratios

Financial leverage is the extent to which a firm is financed with debt. The amount of debt a firm uses has both positive and negative effects. The more debt, the more likely it is that the firm will have trouble meeting its obligations. Thus the more debt, the higher the probability of financial distress and even bankruptcy. Furthermore, the chance of financial distress, and even the existence of debt obligations, can create conflicts of interest among the stakeholders.

Despite this, debt is a major source of financing. It provides a significant tax advantage because interest is tax deductible, as we noted in this chapter. Debt also has lower transaction costs and is generally easier to arrange. Finally, debt affects how the firm's stakeholders bear the risk of the firm. One particular effect is that debt makes the stock riskier because of the increased chance of financial distress. These factors are discussed at length later in the book. At this point, suffice it to say that leverage is very important. **Leverage ratios** measure the amount of (financial) leverage.

Three common leverage ratios are the debt ratio, the debt/equity ratio, and the equity multiplier. The **debt ratio** is the proportion of debt financing.

$$\text{Debt ratio} = \frac{\text{Total debt}}{\text{Total assets}} = \frac{5,918}{10,538} = 0.56x$$

The **debt/equity ratio** is a simple rearrangement of the debt ratio and expresses the same information on a different scale. Whereas the debt ratio can be as small as zero but, assuming positive equity, is always less than 1.0, the debt/equity ratio ranges from zero to infinity. The debt/equity ratio is

$$\text{Debt/equity ratio} = \frac{\text{Total debt}}{\text{Stockholders' equity}} = \frac{5,918}{4,620} = 1.28x$$

[15]We suggest you draw your own conclusions concerning the reasons for this rapid turnover in inventory.

The **equity multiplier** is yet another representation of the same information. It shows how much total assets the firm has for each dollar of equity.

$$\text{Equity multiplier} = \frac{\text{Total assets}}{\text{Stockholders' equity}} = \frac{10,538}{4,620} = 2.28x$$

All three of these leverage ratios are widely used. As we have said, they are simply different representations of the same information. If you know any one of them, you can derive the other two. For example, suppose a firm has a debt ratio of 0.40x and so is 40% debt financed. From this we know that the firm is 60% equity financed. Therefore, the firm's debt/equity ratio is 40/60 = 0.67x. Because total assets equal 100% of the financing (the balance sheet equation, A = L + OE), the equity multiplier is 100/60 = 1.67. Generalizing, we have

$$\text{Debt/equity ratio} = \frac{\text{Debt ratio}}{1.0 - \text{Debt ratio}}$$

$$\text{Equity multiplier} = \text{Debt/equity ratio} + 1.0 = \frac{1}{1 - \text{Debt ratio}}$$

Because it does not make any difference which of the three measures is used, we use the debt ratio throughout this book for simplicity and consistency.

Here again we compare Anheuser-Busch to the other alcoholic beverage firms.

	ANHEUSER-BUSCH	OTHER ALCOHOLIC BEVERAGE FIRMS
Debt ratio	0.56x	0.24x
Debt/equity ratio	1.28x	0.51x
Equity multiplier	2.28x	1.51x

The debt ratio shows that Anheuser-Busch is 56% debt financed. The debt/equity ratio shows that the firm has $1.28 in debt for each $1.00 of equity. The equity multiplier shows that the firm has about $2.28 in total assets for each $1.00 of equity. The comparison shows that Anheuser-Busch has more leverage than the other firms.

Coverage Ratios

Coverage ratios show the number of times a firm can "cover" or meet a particular financial obligation. The **interest coverage ratio,** which is also called the **times-interest-earned ratio,** measures the coverage of the firm's interest expense. It is earnings before interest and income taxes (EBIT) divided by the firm's interest expense. For Anheuser-Busch, EBIT equals operating profit (1,776) plus nonoperating profit (−9):

$$\text{EBIT} = 1{,}776 - 9 = 1{,}767$$

The interest coverage ratio is

$$\text{Times-interest-earned ratio} = \text{Interest coverage ratio} = \frac{\text{EBIT}}{\text{Interest expense}} = \frac{1,767}{200} = 8.84x$$

Many firms lease or rent assets that require contractual payments. Long-term leases are reported on the balance sheet, and the periodic lease payments are included in the firm's interest expense. Rental agreements are different. They are not on the balance sheet. Renting an asset is an alternative to owning it. (Rental payments are therefore an alternative to the interest payments the firm would make if it borrowed the money to buy the same assets.) Rental expense is reported in the notes to the financial statements. For these firms, the **fixed-charge coverage ratio** is useful, where fixed charges consist of interest expense plus rental payments:[16]

$$\text{Fixed charge coverage ratio} = \frac{\text{EBIT} + \text{Rental payments}}{\text{Interest expense} + \text{Rental payments}} = \frac{1,767 + 5}{200 + 5} = 8.64x$$

The **cash flow coverage ratio** is the firm's operating cash flows divided by its payment obligations for interest, principal, preferred stock dividends, and rent.[17]

$$\text{Cash flow coverage ratio} = \frac{\text{EBIT} + \text{Rental payments} + \text{Depreciation}}{\text{Rental payments} + \text{Interest expense} + \dfrac{\text{Preferred stock dividends}}{1-T} + \dfrac{\text{Debt repayment}}{1-T}}$$

$$\text{Cash flow coverage ratio} = \frac{1,767 + 5 + 567}{5 + 200 + \dfrac{0}{1 - 0.4} + \dfrac{344}{1 - 0.4}} = 3.01x$$

Note that two of the financial obligations in the denominator of the cash flow coverage ratio are divided by $(1 - T)$, where T is the marginal income tax rate. Rental payments and interest charges are tax-deductible expenses. Only one dollar of before-tax cash flow is required to meet one dollar of these obligations. In contrast, preferred stock dividends and principal repayments must be made out of after-tax cash flows. They are divided by $(1 - T)$ to get the equivalent before-tax operating cash flow necessary to meet them. This is similar to the difference in tax treatment between interest expense and dividends that we noted in the chapter.

We can compare Anheuser-Busch's coverage ratios with those of the other alcoholic beverage firms.

	ANHEUSER-BUSCH	OTHER ALCOHOLIC BEVERAGE FIRMS
Interest coverage ratio	8.84x	6.28x
Fixed charge coverage ratio	8.64x	6.17x
Cash flow coverage ratio	3.01x	8.26x

Anheuser-Busch has comparatively better coverage of its interest and fixed-charge obligations. Its cash flow coverage ratio is lower because it had greater long-term debt repayment obligations.

Profitability Ratios

Profitability ratios focus on the profit-generating performance of the firm. These ratios measure how effectively the firm is able to generate profits. They reflect the operating performance, its riskiness, and the effect of leverage. We will look at two kinds of profitability ratios. These are *profit margins,* which measure performance in relation to sales, and *rate of return ratios,* which measure performance relative to some measure of the size of the investment.

Gross profit is the difference between sales and the cost of goods sold. Gross profit is critical to the firm because it represents the amount of money remaining to pay operating costs,

[16]Rental expense in the previous year is \$5 million.

[17]Debt repayment in the previous year is \$344 million.

financing costs, and taxes and to provide for profit. The **gross profit margin** is the amount of each sales dollar left after paying the cost of goods sold.

$$\text{Gross profit margin} = \frac{\text{Gross profit}}{\text{Sales}} = \frac{\text{Sales} - \text{Cost of goods sold}}{\text{Sales}} = \frac{4,652}{11,394} = 40.8\%$$

The **net profit margin** measures the profit that is available from each dollar of sales after *all* expenses have been paid, including cost of goods sold; selling, general, and administrative expenses; depreciation; interest; and taxes.

$$\text{Net profit margin} = \frac{\text{Net income before extraordinary items}}{\text{Sales}} = \frac{994}{11,394} = 8.7\%$$

Here is how Anheuser-Busch stacks up against the other alcoholic beverage firms:

	ANHEUSER-BUSCH	OTHER ALCOHOLIC BEVERAGE FIRMS
Gross profit margin	40.8%	40.5%
Net profit margin	8.7%	7.2%

Anheuser-Busch has done well. Its gross profit margin is about the same, but its net profit margin is higher.

Unlike profit margins, *rate of return ratios* express profitability in relation to various measures of investment in the firm. Their potential usefulness is inherently limited, however, because they are based on book values. Three ratios are commonly used: return on assets, earning power, and return on equity.

Return on assets (ROA) corresponds to the net profit margin, except that net income is expressed as a proportion of total assets.

$$\text{ROA} = \text{Return on assets} = \frac{\text{Net income}}{\text{Total assets}} = \frac{994}{10,538} = 9.4\%$$

Earning power is EBIT divided by total assets.

$$\text{Earning power} = \frac{\text{EBIT}}{\text{Total assets}} = \frac{1,767}{10,538} = 16.8\%$$

The difference between ROA and earning power is due to debt financing. Net income is EBIT minus interest and taxes, so ROA will always be less than earning power. Earning power represents the "raw" operating results, whereas ROA represents the combined results of operating and financing.

Return on equity (ROE) is the rate of return on the common stockholders' equity:

$$\begin{aligned}\text{ROE} &= \text{Return on common stockholders' equity} \\ &= \frac{\text{Earnings available for common stock before extraordinary items}}{\text{Common stockholders' equity}} = \frac{994}{4,620} = 21.5\%\end{aligned}$$

where common stockholders' equity includes common stock (at par value), capital surplus, and retained earnings. ROE shows the residual profits of the firm as a proportion of the book value of common stockholders' equity. The amount of leverage affects both the numerator and the denominator of ROE. Typically, ROE is greater than ROA for healthy firms. In bad years, however, ROE can fall below ROA. This is because financial leverage increases the risk of the stock, as we noted earlier.

Comparing Anheuser-Busch to the other alcoholic beverage firms, we have

	ANHEUSER-BUSCH	OTHER ALCOHOLIC BEVERAGE FIRMS
Return on assets (ROA)	9.4%	5.8%
Earning power	16.8%	10.6%
Return on equity (ROE)	21.5%	11.4%

Anheuser-Busch has higher profitability than the other firms. Note once again, however, that these ratios collectively reflect not only the operating performance and its riskiness but also the effect of the firm's leverage.

Market Value Ratios

Analysts use several **market value ratios** that relate the market value of the firm's common stock to earnings per share (EPS), dividends per share (DPS), and book value per share, which is total common equity divided by the number of common shares outstanding. Book value per share is \$16.17 (= 4,620/285.69). At the time the statements were prepared, the market price of Anheuser-Busch common stock was \$58.50 per share.

The **price/earnings ratio (P/E)** is the market price per share of common stock divided by the earnings per share (EPS).

$$\text{P/E} = \text{Price/earnings ratio} = \frac{\text{Market price per share}}{\text{Earnings per share}} = \frac{58.50}{3.48} = 16.8x$$

When earnings are negative, EPS is of course negative, which makes the P/E negative as well. Also, when EPS gets close to zero, the P/E becomes extremely large because of dividing by the EPS. The P/E is not generally reported when EPS is negative or very small, because it is not considered to be economically meaningful under those conditions.

Another form of the same information is **earnings yield,** which is the reciprocal of the P/E.

$$\text{Earnings yield} = \frac{\text{Earnings per share}}{\text{Market price per share}} = \frac{3.48}{58.50} = 5.95\%$$

Unlike the P/E, earnings yield does not "break down" when EPS is very small or negative. EPS is the numerator, avoiding the division-by-zero problem. A negative EPS is a loss per share, in which case earnings yield is a negative rate of return, a rate of losing value.

The **dividend yield** is the ratio of the dividends per share to the market price per share.

$$\text{Dividend yield} = \frac{\text{Dividend per share}}{\text{Market price per share}} = \frac{1.20}{58.50} = 2.05\%$$

Many firms do not pay a cash dividend. Such firms simply have a dividend yield of zero. The decision to pay cash dividends is essentially a choice between paying out earnings to the owners or reinvesting the money in the firm. We will have more to say about dividends later on.

Finally, the **market-to-book ratio** is the market price per share divided by the book value per share.

$$\text{Market-to-book ratio} = \frac{\text{Market price per share}}{\text{Book value per share}} = \frac{58.50}{16.17} = 3.62x$$

The market-to-book ratio is a very rough index of a firm's historical performance. The higher the ratio, the greater is market value relative to book value. A high ratio says the firm has created more in market value than the GAAP rules have recorded in book value. The implied message is that the firm has done well. Of course, as we noted earlier, there are many possible explanations for a difference between market and book values. Although the implied message of a high market-to-book ratio is likely to be correct in most cases, additional information is generally needed to reach a confident conclusion.

Comparing Anheuser-Busch with other alcoholic beverage firms, we have:

	ANHEUSER-BUSCH	OTHER ALCOHOLIC BEVERAGE FIRMS
Price/earnings ratio	16.8*x*	15.4*x*
Earnings yield	5.95%	6.40%
Dividend yield	2.05%	2.00%
Market-to-book ratio	3.62*x*	1.93*x*

Past increases in the market value of Anheuser-Busch's common stock have significantly exceeded increases in the book value per-share. This makes Anheuser-Busch's P/E and market-to-book ratios higher than those of the other firms. Its earnings yield and dividend yield are about the same.

Common-Statement Analysis

Another technique used in financial statement analysis is called common-statement analysis. Common-statement analysis makes some comparisons more meaningful because it puts the things being compared on a common basis. There are two widely used methods of common-statement analysis. **Common-size analysis** shows items as percentages rather than as amounts of money. Balance sheet items are expressed as percentages of total assets, and income statement items are expressed as percentages of sales. Common-size analysis makes possible a more meaningful comparison of firms that are of significantly different sizes and enables us to track a single firm through time.

Common-base-year analysis shows each item as a percentage of its amount in an initial year, such as five years ago. Common-base-year analysis makes it easy to see which items are growing relatively faster or slower, because items that are more (less) than 100% have increased (declined).

SUMMARY

Despite the inherent limitations of accounting information, financial statement analysis can provide additional insights into the firm. Numerous widely used financial ratios are given in Table 3A.4.

- Financial statement analysis can be useful in two fundamental ways. First, it can help structure your thinking about business decisions. Second, it can provide some information that is helpful in making those decisions.
- Financial ratio analysis focuses on specific relationships in the financial statements.
- Liquidity ratios show the firm's ability to meet its maturing short-term obligations. These ratios include the current ratio, the quick ratio, the working capital ratio, and the cash ratio.
- Asset turnover ratios show how effectively the firm is using its assets. These ratios include the receivables turnover, days' sales outstanding, inventory turnover, days' sales in inventory, fixed asset turnover, and total asset turnover ratios.
- Leverage ratios show the relative contribution of creditors and owners to the firm's financing. These include ratios such as the debt ratio, debt-to-equity ratio, and the equity multiplier.
- Coverage ratios show the amount of funds available to "cover" a particular financial obligation compared to the size of that obligation. These include interest coverage, fixed charge coverage, and cash flow coverage ratios.
- Profitability ratios include profit margins and rate of return ratios. The profit margin ratios are the gross profit margin and the net profit margin. The rate of return ratios include the return on assets, earning power ratio, and return on equity.

- Market-value ratios are based on the market price of the company's common stock. These ratios include the price/earnings ratio, the earnings yield, the dividend yield, and the market-to-book ratio.
- Common-size financial statements show percentage breakdowns of the income statement and balance sheet that allow easier comparisons across companies.
- Common-base-year financial statements show each item as a percentage of its amount in an initial year.

TABLE 3A.4
Summary of financial ratios.

LIQUIDITY RATIOS

$$\text{Current ratio} = \frac{\text{Current assets}}{\text{Current liabilities}}$$

$$\text{Quick ratio} = \frac{\text{Current assets} - \text{Inventories}}{\text{Current liabilities}}$$

$$\text{Working capital ratio} = \frac{\text{Current assets} - \text{Current liabilities}}{\text{Sales}}$$

$$\text{Cash ratio} = \frac{\text{Cash and equivalents}}{\text{Total assets}}$$

ASSET ACTIVITY RATIOS

$$\text{Receivables turnover} = \frac{\text{Annual credit sales}}{\text{Accounts receivable}}$$

$$\text{Days' sales outstanding} = \frac{365}{\text{Receivables turnover}}$$

$$\text{Inventory turnover} = \frac{\text{Cost of goods sold}}{\text{Inventory}}$$

$$\text{Days' sales in inventory} = \frac{365}{\text{Inventory turnover}}$$

$$\text{Fixed asset turnover} = \frac{\text{Sales}}{\text{Net fixed assets}}$$

$$\text{Total asset turnover} = \frac{\text{Sales}}{\text{Total assets}}$$

LEVERAGE RATIOS

$$\text{Debt ratio} = \frac{\text{Total debt}}{\text{Total assets}}$$

$$\text{Debt/equity ratio} = \frac{\text{Total debt}}{\text{Stockholders' equity}} = \frac{\text{Debt ratio}}{1.0 - \text{Debt ratio}}$$

$$\text{Equity multiplier} = \frac{\text{Total assets}}{\text{Stockholders' equity}} = \text{Debt/equity ratio} + 1.0$$

(continued)

COVERAGE RATIOS

$$\text{Interest coverage ratio} = \frac{\text{EBIT}}{\text{Interest expense}}$$

$$\begin{matrix}\text{Fixed charge} \\ \text{coverage ratio}\end{matrix} = \frac{\text{EBIT} + \text{Rental payments}}{\text{Interest expense} + \text{Rental payments}}$$

$$\begin{matrix}\text{Cash flow} \\ \text{coverage ratio}\end{matrix} = \frac{\text{EBIT} + \text{Rental payments} + \text{Depreciation}}{\begin{matrix}\text{Rental} \\ \text{payments}\end{matrix} + \begin{matrix}\text{Interest} \\ \text{expense}\end{matrix} + \frac{\begin{matrix}\text{Preferred stock} \\ \text{dividends}\end{matrix}}{1 - T} + \frac{\begin{matrix}\text{Debt} \\ \text{repayment}\end{matrix}}{1 - T}}$$

PROFITABILITY RATIOS

$$\text{Gross profit margin} = \frac{\text{Gross profit}}{\text{Sales}} = \frac{\text{Sales} - \text{Cost of goods sold}}{\text{Sales}}$$

$$\text{Net profit margin} = \frac{\text{Net income before extraordinary items}}{\text{Sales}}$$

$$\text{Return on assets} = \frac{\text{Net income}}{\text{Total assets}}$$

$$\text{Earning power} = \frac{\text{EBIT}}{\text{Total assets}}$$

$$\text{Return on equity} = \frac{\begin{matrix}\text{Earnings available for common stock} \\ \text{before extraordinary items}\end{matrix}}{\text{Common stockholders' equity}}$$

MARKET VALUE RATIOS

$$\text{P/E} = \text{Price/earnings ratio} = \frac{\text{Market price per share}}{\text{Earnings per share}}$$

$$\text{Earnings yield} = \frac{\text{Earnings per share}}{\text{Market price per share}}$$

$$\text{Dividend yield} = \frac{\text{Dividend per share}}{\text{Market price per share}}$$

$$\text{Market-to-book ratio} = \frac{\text{Market price per share}}{\text{Book value per share}}$$

APPENDIX REVIEW

Compute each of the ratios in Table 3A.4 for OutBack SportWear, using the information given in Tables 3.1, 3.2, and 3.3, and assuming the common stock has a current market value of $47.25. To calculate the book value per-share, subtract the preferred stock from total stockholders' equity to get common stockholders' equity.

PART II

VALUE AND CAPITAL BUDGETING

Capital budgeting is the process of choosing the firm's long-term capital investments. This includes investments in such things as land, plant, and equipment. Capital budgeting is fundamental because a firm is essentially defined by its assets and the products and services those assets produce. For example, Ford makes cars, regardless of how the firm is financed. A firm's choices of which products to produce and which services to offer, then, are capital budgeting decisions—and those choices are intertwined with all the other decisions facing the firm.

A firm has an almost limitless number of possible investments, but past and current choices constrain its future choices. The strategic nature of these choices can be seen in the time horizons of capital assets, which may span years or even decades. In some cases, such as forest product management, capital assets may not produce returns for generations.

Regardless of their time horizons, capital budgeting projects are judged by the value they create. When you buy a stock or bond that is worth more than it costs—one with a positive NPV—your wealth will increase by the amount of the difference. When a firm undertakes a capital budgeting project with a positive NPV, the value of the firm's stock will increase by that amount. And, of course, a negative-NPV project will decrease its stock value.

So you can see why we say capital budgeting decisions are the most important decisions facing a firm. Capital budgeting has a direct link to shareholder wealth. The more successful a firm's capital budgeting decisions, the higher the value of the firm's stock.

THE TIME VALUE OF MONEY

4

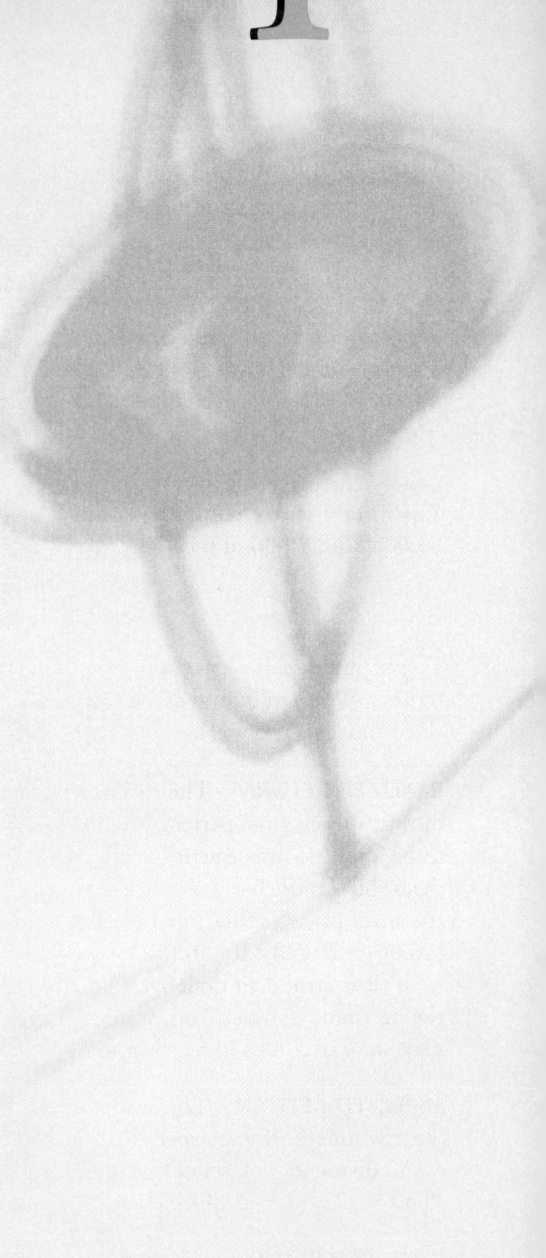

Have you ever paid for something with monthly payments? Suppose you wanted to buy a $30,000 car and were told the payments would be $656.10 per month for 48 months. How would you know whether you were being offered a great deal, a fair deal, or a bad deal?

Now suppose you have $30,000 to invest for a long time, and someone tells you about an investment that will double your money without any risk: Invest your $30,000 now, and you will get back $60,000 in 15 years. How does this compare with other no-risk investments?

This chapter will teach you how to answer such questions; it is devoted entirely to the Time-Value-of-Money Principle. You will learn how to determine the present value of future cash flows and, more generally, how to value at one point in time cash flows that actually occur at other points in time. We develop the logic underlying these calculations and show you procedures for solving problems using a financial calculator. We urge you, however, not to use these calculator procedures like cookbook recipes. Understanding the logic will prepare you to apply the Time-Value-of-Money Principle in the business world to new types of problems, ones that don't fit neatly into classroom examples.

Like you, firms also have to choose among investments and borrowing alternatives. In fact, their success *depends* on those choices. Financial decisions are measured by their net present value (NPV). NPV is the present value of the expected future cash flows minus the cost. The NPV is the value created or lost by a decision. Therefore, to be successful, firms must find positive-NPV opportunities and avoid negative-NPV choices.

FOCUS ON PRINCIPLES

- *Time Value of Money:* Note that the value of a cash flow depends on when it will occur.
- *Two-Sided Transactions:* Be specific about the timing of cash flows to be fair to both sides of a transaction.
- *Risk-Return Trade-Off:* Recognize that a higher-risk investment has a higher required return. Therefore, the time value of money is especially important to the profitability of long-term investments.
- *Capital Market Efficiency:* Use efficient capital markets to estimate an investment's expected and required returns.

4.1 RATES OF RETURN AND NET PRESENT VALUE

Most investors want to know about an investment's rate of return. An investment's *return* for a period equals its income during the period (its cash flows plus its increase or decrease in value) divided by its starting value. Thus,

$$\text{Return} = \text{Rate of return} = \frac{\text{Cash flow} + (\text{Ending value} - \text{Beginning value})}{\text{Beginning value}} \tag{4.1}$$

For example, suppose you bought a share of stock for \$20, it paid you a \$0.50 dividend during the next year, and was worth \$24.50 at the end of one year. Your rate of return for the year would be

$$\text{Return} = \frac{0.50 + (24.50 - 20.00)}{20.00} = \frac{5.00}{20.00} = 25\%$$

Your total income consists of \$0.50 of dividends and \$4.50 in increased value, for a total of \$5.00. With \$5.00 of income and an original investment of \$20.00, your rate of return is 25%.

Realized, Expected, and Required Returns

The example we just gave is of a realized (or actual) return. There are, however, other concepts of returns. We describe and discuss here three different rates of returns. Distinguishing among these three concepts is critical.

REALIZED RETURN The **realized return** is the rate of return actually earned on an investment during a given time period. The realized return depends on what the future cash flows turn out to be after the investment is made. In the preceding return example, with the same \$0.50 dividend, but an unchanged stock price, the realized return would be 2.5% (= 0.50/20.00). Or, if the stock price had declined to \$16.00, the realized return would be *minus* 17.5% (= [0.50 + (16.00 − 20.00)]/20.00).

It is critical to understand that a realized return is an outcome, the result of having made the decision to invest. You cannot go back and change the realized rate of return. You can only make new decisions in reaction to it.

EXPECTED RETURN The **expected return** is the rate of return you expect to earn if you make the investment. If you expected to make 15% in our example investment, including an expected \$0.50 dividend, you would be expecting the value of the stock next year to be \$22.50 (15% = [0.50 + (22.50 − 20.00)]/20.00).

REQUIRED RETURN The **required return** is the rate of return that exactly reflects the riskiness of the expected future cash flows. This is the return the market would require of an investment of identical risk. The market evaluates all of the available information about an investment and prices it in comparison with all other investments. This pricing process establishes an investment's required return, the fair return for an investment.

EXAMPLE Stock Investment Rates of Return

An investment of \$20 in K-Tron common stock is expected to pay no dividend and have a value of \$24 in one year. An investment of \$70 in GM is expected to generate a \$2.50 dividend next year and the price of the stock is expected to be \$78. What are the expected returns for these investments? If the required return is 10%, which stocks should be profitable investments? One year from now, K-Tron has paid no dividend and is selling for \$19. GM has paid a \$3.00 dividend and is selling for \$81. What are the realized returns for the two stocks?

Using Equation (4.1):

$$\text{Expected return for K-Tron} = [0 + (24 - 20)]/20 = 4/20 = 20\%$$

$$\text{Expected return for GM} = [2.50 + (78 - 70)]/70 = 10.5/70 = 15\%$$

Both stocks are good investments because in each case the expected return exceeds the required return.

Finally, again using Equation (4.1):

$$\text{Realized return for K-Tron} = [0 + (19 - 20)]/20 = -1/20 = -5\%$$

$$\text{Realized return for GM} = [3.00 + (81 - 70)]/70 = 14.00/70 = 20\%$$

Net Present Value

Using the required return to calculate the present value of an asset's expected future cash flows—Equation (2.3)—is one way to value the asset. Another way is to find out what it would cost to *buy* such an asset. The difference between an asset's value (the present value of its expected future cash flows) and its cost is the asset's **net present value (NPV).**

$$\text{NPV} = \text{Present value of expected future cash flows} - \text{Cost} \tag{4.2}$$

A positive NPV increases wealth because the asset is worth more than it costs. A negative NPV decreases wealth because the asset costs more than it is worth.

The net-present-value concept is important because it provides a framework for decision making. NPV appears in connection with virtually every topic in this book, and most financial decisions can be viewed in terms of net present value. NPV measures the value created or lost by a financial decision. However, NPV is measured from the benchmark of a "normal" market return. Therefore, a zero-NPV decision earns the required return and is "fair." A decision that earns less than the required return is undesirable and has a negative NPV. Positive-NPV decisions earn more than the appropriate return. Firms that pursue the goal of maximizing shareholder wealth seek to make positive-NPV decisions.

Another way to state the Principle of Capital Market Efficiency is to say that financial securities are priced fairly. A **fair price** is a price that does not favor either the buyer's or seller's side of the transaction. A fair price makes the NPV from investing equal zero. Sometimes, people ask, "If the NPV is zero, why would anyone purchase a financial security?" The answer is to earn a profit. Remember, a zero NPV implies that the investor will earn the required return for the investment risk, *not* a zero return.

The Principle of Risk-Return Trade-Off implies that investors who take more risk will earn a larger profit, on average. The decision to invest in (purchase) a financial security with NPV = 0 often involves risk. But in exchange for that risk, you get a higher expected return.

EXPECTED VERSUS REQUIRED RETURNS Confusion between the expected and required returns arises because, if capital markets were *perfect,* an investment's expected return would *always* equal its required return and the investment's NPV would be zero. In fact, financial analysis often starts off assuming a perfect capital market environment, where everyone can expect to earn the required return for the risk they bear. Although this is a good starting place for analysis, and the capital markets are efficient, we must add that they are not, in fact, perfect.

EXPECTED VERSUS REALIZED RETURNS Confusion between the expected and realized returns is created by risk. Because of risk, the outcome rarely equals the expected amount. In fact, one way to think about risk is to consider how different the outcome can be from the expected amount. The risk is high when the difference can be great. The risk is low when there cannot be much difference.

AN ILLUSTRATION Let us review and summarize the relationships among these concepts by using an investment you might make. First, on the basis of alternative market investments of the same risk, you determine a minimum return you would have to earn to be willing to invest. (Otherwise, you would simply invest your money in one of these alternatives.) This is the *required* return. Next, you estimate the return if you were to make the investment. This is the *expected* return. Then you decide whether to make the investment. If the expected return is more than the required return, the investment is worth more than its cost, and the NPV is positive. A positive NPV creates value, whereas a negative NPV loses value. Let us say the NPV is positive, and you make the investment.

Later, the investment pays off. The payoff is the *realized* return. If the realized return is bad (low, negative, or perhaps even −100%—you get nothing back), you are not happy, but that is the fundamental nature of risk! After the return is realized, you cannot turn back the clock and decide not to make the investment after all. Of course, if the realized return is good (equal to or greater than the expected return), you are glad you made the investment. Therefore, the realized return is disconnected—by risk—from the required and expected returns, despite its vital importance and our desire for it to be large.

Review

1. Distinguish among the concepts of *realized, expected,* and *required returns.*
2. Assume you buy a share of General Motors stock for $48.00. During the next year, you receive $2.25 in cash dividends and sell the stock for $55.00 per share at the end of the year. What is your realized return?
3. If the required return is 12% and projects A, B, and C have expected returns of 15%, 9%, and 13%, respectively, in which, if any, projects should you invest?
4. If the expected return is above the required return, does this mean that the realized return also will be above the required return?
5. Why would anyone ever make a *zero*-NPV investment?

4.2 VALUING SINGLE CASH FLOWS

In this section, we explain how time affects the value of a cash flow. That is, given a cash flow at one point in time, we show how to determine its value at some other point in time. For example, suppose you expect to receive $10,000 six years from today. We show how to calculate what that expected $10,000 is worth now.

Assumptions, Notation, and Some Advice

We need several additional definitions and underlying assumptions. Please read through the complete list of notation and assumptions now, even though we will not explain some of the terms until later.

Cash Flows Occur at the End of the Time Period Unless otherwise stated, cash flows occur at the end of the time period.

Cash Outflows Are Negative Values From the decision maker's viewpoint, positive cash flows are inflows and negative cash flows are outflows. The decision maker can be a firm or an individual. In other words, the algebraic sign indicates whether the amount is an inflow (+) or an outflow (−) to the decision maker.

The Decision Point Is $t = 0$ Unless otherwise stated, "now" is the instant before $t = 0$. That is, $t = 0$ cash flows (in or out) are just about to occur. In other words, you can still make a decision that affects them, such as choosing to make an investment.

Compounding Frequency Is the Same as Payment Frequency

Unless otherwise stated, financial transactions assume the compounding frequency is identical to the payment frequency. For example, if payments are monthly, compounding is also monthly.

Notation

APR	The annual percentage rate (nominal annual rate). The APR equals r times m.
APY	The annual percentage yield (effective annual rate). The APY is the amount you would actually earn if you invested for exactly one year and if the investment paid interest at r per period for m periods.
CF_t	The net cash flow at time t. For example, CF_3 is the net cash flow at the end of time period 3.
FV	A future value amount.
$FVAF_{r,n}$	The future-value-annuity factor for an n-period annuity at r per period.
FVA_n	The future value of an n-period annuity (at $t = n$).
$FVF_{r,n}$	The future-value factor for n periods at r per period.
FV_n	A future value at time n. For example, FV_5 is a future value at the end of time period 5.
I	The discount rate per period for a calculator. For example, $i = 2$ is 2% per time period.
m	The number of compounding periods per year.
n	A number of time periods. For example, n might be 36 months.
N	The number of periods for a calculator.
NPV	The net present value.
PMT	The net cash flow each period for an annuity in a calculator.
PV	A present-value amount.
$PVAF_{r,n}$	The present-value-annuity factor for an n-period annuity at r per period.
PVA_n	The present value of an n-period annuity.
$PVF_{r,n}$	The present-value factor for n periods at r per period.
r	The discount rate per period. For example, $r = 0.02$ is 2% per time period.
t	A time period. For example, $t = 3$ is time period 3.

Advice

1. Always use a time line. Valuation problems are easier to understand and the error rate is lower with the visual aid of a time line.
2. When making calculations, be careful to match the rate of return with the size of time periods. For example, use a monthly rate of return when periods are in months.
3. Make the calculations in the chapter yourself. Doing so is critical to help develop your abilities.
4. Follow the conceptual development carefully to build your understanding of the concepts.

Future Values

A future value (FV) is a value at the end of a given time period. If you invest $1,000 today, Table 4.1 shows the amount of money you will have at the end of each of the next six years if you earn 10% interest per year. After one year:

$$FV_1 = \$1{,}000 + \$100 = \$1{,}100$$

In the second year, you will earn $110 more—10% interest on your accumulated investment (= [0.10]1,100), for a total of

$$FV_2 = \$1{,}100 + \$110 = \$1{,}210$$

The extra $10 of interest earned in the second year is called compound interest. **Compound interest** is a method of interest computation wherein interest is earned on both the original investment *and* on the reinvested interest. As you can see in Table 4.1, the interest earned each year grows because of compound interest.

Table 4.1 also shows how fast your $1,000 investment grows if invested funds earn simple interest instead of compound interest. **Simple interest** is a method of interest computation wherein interest is earned on *only* the original investment. Note that in year 1 with simple interest, the interest earned is $100, the same as with compound interest. However, after that, the story changes. In year 2 with simple interest, the interest earned is again $100. No interest is earned on the first year's $100 interest. All other years also earn only $100, 10% of the original investment.

TABLE 4.1
Future value of an investment of $1,000.

	COMPOUND INTEREST, $r = 10\%$			SIMPLE INTEREST, $r = 10\%$		
YEAR	BEGINNING BALANCE	INTEREST EARNED	ENDING BALANCE	BEGINNING BALANCE	INTEREST EARNED	ENDING BALANCE
1	$1,000	$100	$1,100	$1,000	$100	$1,100
2	1,100	110	1,210	1,100	100	1,200
3	1,210	121	1,331	1,200	100	1,300
4	1,331	133.10	1,464.10	1,300	100	1,400
5	1,464.10	146.41	1,610.51	1,400	100	1,500
6	1,610.51	161.05	1,771.56	1,500	100	1,600

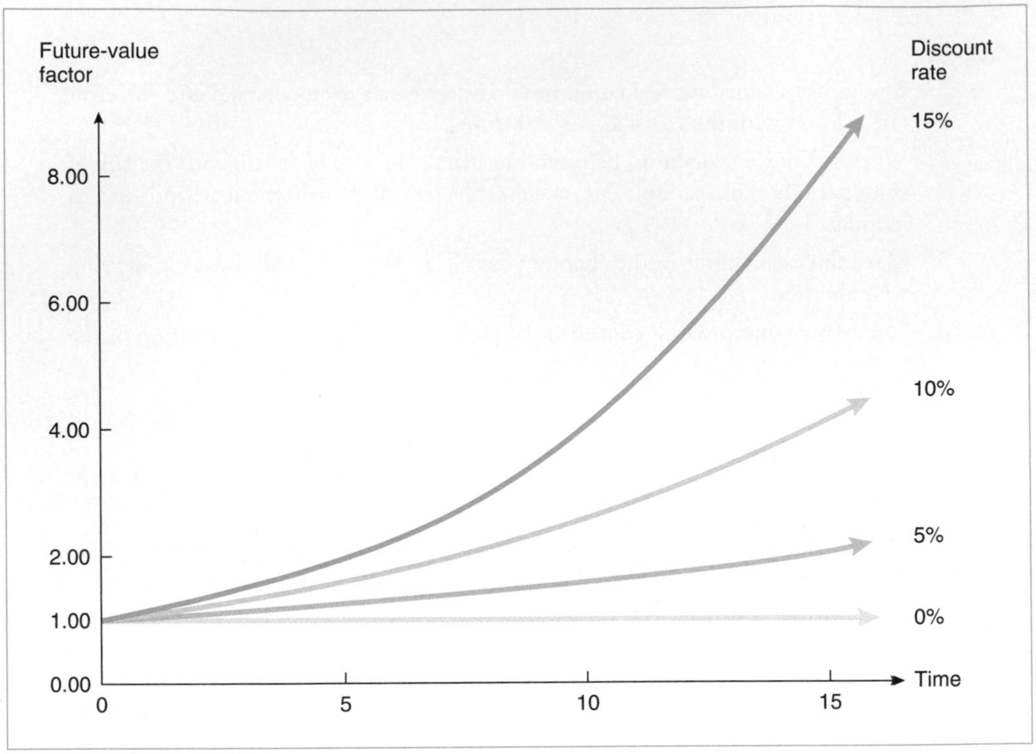

FIGURE 4.1
The future-value factor, $FVF_{r,n}$, as a function of time and various discount rates.

Would you rather earn compound interest or simple interest? Obviously, if the interest rates are the same, you will have more money with compound interest than with simple interest. Because of today's technology, the use of simple interest has largely disappeared.

One way to find a future value is to calculate interest each year, adding it to the previous year's balance, and accumulating the result for the desired number of years. In Table 4.1, we stopped at six years. Suppose you were investing for twenty years. Calculating the value would be tedious and error prone. Consequently, we use shortcut methods whenever we can. One shortcut method of finding future values is to use the **future-value formula:**

The Future-Value Formula

$$FV_n = PV(1 + r)^n = PV(FVF_{r,n}) \tag{4.3}$$

The amount $(1 + r)^n$ is called the future-value factor. The **future-value factor,** $FVF_{r,n}$, is the value \$1.00 will grow to if it is invested at r per period for n periods. Figure 4.1 is a graph of $FVF_{r,n}$ as a function of n and r. As you can see, future value is directly related to both time and the discount rate. The larger the discount rate, the larger the future value. For positive discount rates, the more time, the larger the future value.

EXAMPLE Calculating a Future Value

Let us redo one of the calculations in Table 4.1. What is the future value of \$1,000 invested at 10% per year for six years?

Use the future-value formula with these values:

$$FV_n = PV(FVF_{r,n}) = PV(1 + r)^n = 1{,}000(1.10)^6 = 1{,}000(1.771561) = \$1{,}771.56$$

To do this on a calculator, you can first raise 1.10 (= 1 + the discount rate) to the power six, using the y^x key where y = 1.10 and x = 6. Then multiply the answer by 1,000 to get 1771.56.

Financial Calculators

There are five basic input variables to a financial (sometimes called business) calculator:

PV	Present value
FV	Future value
N	The number of time periods
I	The discount rate per period. This corresponds to the r in the text's equations. (Note that the calculator key will show I/YR.)
PMT	The cash flow (payment) for an annuity

The basic calculator formula encompasses each of the four basic time-value-of-money formulas we explain in this chapter. For this reason, in many cases, you need to put in a zero for some variables—especially if we have not explained the variable yet. Even though you may not fully appreciate the basic calculator formula right away, we state it now so you can refer back to it. Then, you can see how each of the basic time-value-of-money formulas is part of it, as we explain that formula.

The Basic Calculator Formula

$$PV + PMT\left[\frac{(1+I)^N - 1}{I(1+I)^N}\right] + FV\left[\frac{1}{(1+I)^N}\right] = 0$$

The calculator solves this equation for each time-value-of-money calculation. It computes the variable you want on the basis of the values you put in for all the other variables. Amounts can be positive or negative. However, to use your calculator, you must understand how it handles positive and negative amounts.

Confusion about positives and negatives can occur because the basic calculator formula sums to zero. As a result, the three terms cannot all be positive. You can think of this in terms of the decision maker's cash flows we described earlier: You are paying out (−) one amount to get in (+) another. For example, if you borrow $10,000 (PV), the money is an inflow, which is a positive. But when you pay back $248.85 per month for 48 months, the payments are outflows, which are negatives. If you enter PV as a positive value, the calculator calculates FV (or PMT) as a negative value. Appendix A at the end of the book shows the key strokes for standard calculations on a calculator of this type, the BAII PLUS.

Another common problem that can arise is when a calculator retains one or more values from previous calculations. If you do not put in a value for a variable, your calculator may use a value from a previous calculation and give you an incorrect answer. You can avoid this problem in two ways. One way is to push the "clear-all" button to zero all the variables. (Be sure to use the "clear-all" rather than the "clear-the-latest-entry" button. The calculator's "how-to" book will describe both procedures.) Another way to avoid the problem is to enter a zero for any variables not otherwise used. We will use this approach for our calculator computations.

CALCULATOR SOLUTION

Data Input	Function Key
6	N
10	I
1,000	PV
0	PMT
−1,771.56	**FV**

An easier way to make our future-value calculation is to use a financial calculator: Put in PV = 1,000, N = 6, I = 10%, and PMT = 0, then compute FV = −1,771.56. Note that the discount rate is entered as a percent, 10, *not* as a decimal number, 0.10. Throughout the rest of the book, we will show such calculations in a standardized format. The amount the calculator solves for is in bold type. The other amounts are inputs.

Let us practice on another example.

CALCULATOR SOLUTION

Data Input	Function Key
15	N
6	I
1,000	PV
0	PMT
−2,396.56	**FV**

EXAMPLE Grandma's Savings Bond

Suppose your grandma just gave you a $1,000 savings bond. If the bond earns 6% interest, what will the bond be worth in 15 years?

Using the future-value formula, the bond will be worth:

$$FV_n = PV(FVF_{r,n}) = PV(1 + r)^n$$
$$FV_{15} = 1{,}000(1.06)^{15} = 1{,}000(2.39656) = \$2{,}396.56$$

What would your bond be worth if it earned 10% instead of 6%? Do this one on your calculator. The answer is $4,177.25.

CALCULATOR SOLUTION

Data Input	Function Key
15	N
10	I
1,000	PV
0	PMT
−4,177.25	**FV**

Present Values

Now, let us find the *present* value of an expected *future* cash flow. A present value (PV) is an amount invested today at r per period that would provide a given future value at time n. We can compute a PV using the **present-value formula:**

The Present-Value Formula

$$PV = FV_n\left[\frac{1}{(1 + r)^n}\right] = FV_n(PVF_{r,n}) \tag{4.4}$$

The present-value formula is simply a rearrangement of the future-value formula where we solve for PV instead of FV. In the present-value formula, the amount $[1/(1 + r)^n]$ is called the present-value factor. The **present-value factor,** $PVF_{r,n}$, is the amount that, if invested today at r per period, will grow to exactly $1.00 n years from today.

Figure 4.2 is a graph of $PVF_{r,n}$ as a function of time and various discount rates. It shows that present value is inversely related to both time and the discount rate. That is, the larger the discount rate, the smaller the present value. For positive discount rates, the more time until the cash flow, the smaller is the present value. Like two kids on a seesaw, when one goes up the other goes down.

EXAMPLE Present Value of a Future Cash Flow

CALCULATOR SOLUTION

Data Input	Function Key
2	N
8	I
0	PMT
2,000	FV
−1,714.68	**PV**

What is the present value of $2,000 to be received two years from today if the required return is 8% per year?

Using the present-value formula,

$$PV = FV_n(PVF_{r,n}) = FV_n\left[\frac{1}{(1 + r)^n}\right] = 2{,}000\left[\frac{1}{(1.08)^2}\right] = 2{,}000(0.857339) = \$1{,}714.68$$

$PVF_{8\%,2}$ is 0.857339, and the present value of the future $2,000 is $1,714.68.

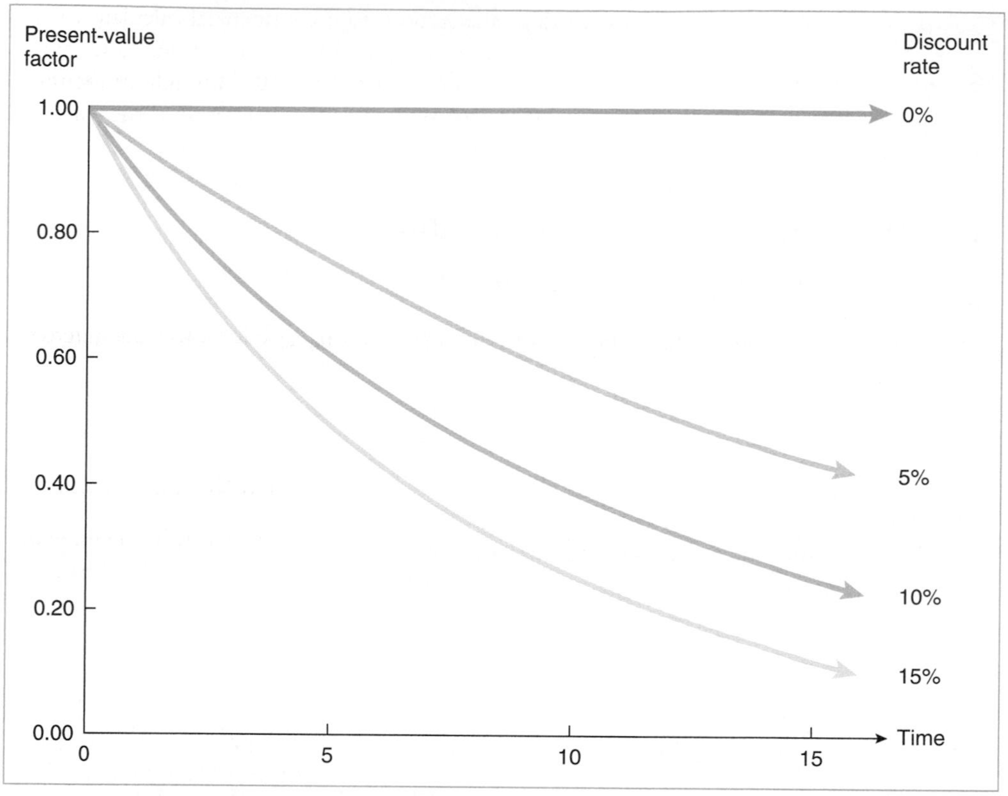

FIGURE 4.2
The present-value factor, $PVF_{r,n}$, as a function of time and various discount rates.

Solving for a Return

If you look back at the basic calculator formula, you can see how the present-value formula is part of it. You can also see that if you know any four of the five input variables, the formula can be solved for the fifth.

For example, to find a PV, we put in FV (the expected future cash flow), N (the time the cash flow will occur), I (the required return), and PMT = 0. However, suppose you already know PV, but you do not know the discount rate. You can rearrange the present value formula (4.4) and solve for the expected return. Solving for r, with PMT = 0, we get

$$r = \left[\frac{FV}{PV}\right]^{1/n} - 1$$

EXAMPLE The Expected Return for a Bank One Certificate of Deposit

Suppose Bank One offers a certificate of deposit that pays $10,000 in three years in exchange for $7,938.32 today. What interest rate is Bank One offering? In other words, what is the expected return from investing in this certificate of deposit?

Using our rearranged formula, with $n = 3$, FV = 10,000, and PV = 7,938.32, we find that the expected return is

$$r = \left[\frac{10{,}000}{7{,}938.32}\right]^{0.3333} - 1 = 1.08 - 1 = 8.00\%$$

CALCULATOR SOLUTION

Data Input	Function Key
3	N
7,938.32	PV
0	PMT
−10,000	FV
8.00	I

Solving for the Number of Time Periods

We could also rearrange the basic calculator formula to solve for n using natural logarithms. However, it is much easier to let the calculator do the work.

CALCULATOR SOLUTION

Data Input	Function Key
6	I
1	PV
0	PMT
−2	FV
11.9	N

EXAMPLE How Long to Double Your Salary?

Are you earning a salary currently? If you are, and your salary grew at 6% per year, how many years would it take to double?

Even though we do not know how much you make, so long as it is more than zero, we can tell you it will take 11.9 years to double if it is growing at 6% per year. Try it.

Review

1. What is the future-value formula? What is the present-value formula?
2. Is the present-value factor the reciprocal of the future-value factor?
3. What is the future value of $100 invested for one year at 0%? What is the present value of $100 received in one year discounted back at 100%?
4. Choose the correct word in each set of parentheses: The future-value factor is (positively/negatively) related to the discount rate, and the present-value factor is (positively/negatively) related to the discount rate. The future-value factor is (positively/negatively) related to the number of time periods, and the present-value factor is (positively/negatively) related to the number of time periods.
5. Explain why present value and the discount rate are inversely related.

4.3 VALUING ANNUITIES

Annuity payments are a very common financial arrangement. An **annuity** is a series of equal, periodic cash flows. The cash flows occur regularly, such as every month or every year.

Annuities occur in many different financial transactions. Monthly payments on a car loan, a student loan, or a mortgage are annuities. Monthly rent is an annuity. A paycheck, with a fixed salary, is an annuity. Lease, interest, and dividend payments are annuities. Any series of equal, periodic cash flows is an annuity.

The majority of annuities have end-of-period payments. For example, car loans usually require end-of-month payments. For a 48-month loan, the first payment is made at the end of the first month and the 48th (and last) is made at the end of month 48. This kind of annuity, where payments occur at the end of each period, is called an **ordinary annuity.** An annuity where the first payment is more than one period in the future is called a **deferred annuity.**

Other annuities, such as a rental, require beginning-of-period payments. For a 12-month apartment lease, the first rent payment is due at the beginning of the first month, and the 12th (and last) is due at the beginning of the 12th month. This kind of annuity, where payments occur at the beginning of each period, is called an **annuity due.**

We know the timing of payments affects value. Therefore, it is critical to know whether you are dealing with an ordinary annuity or an annuity due. We will start by analyzing the future and present values of an ordinary annuity. Later, we will show you how to handle an annuity due.

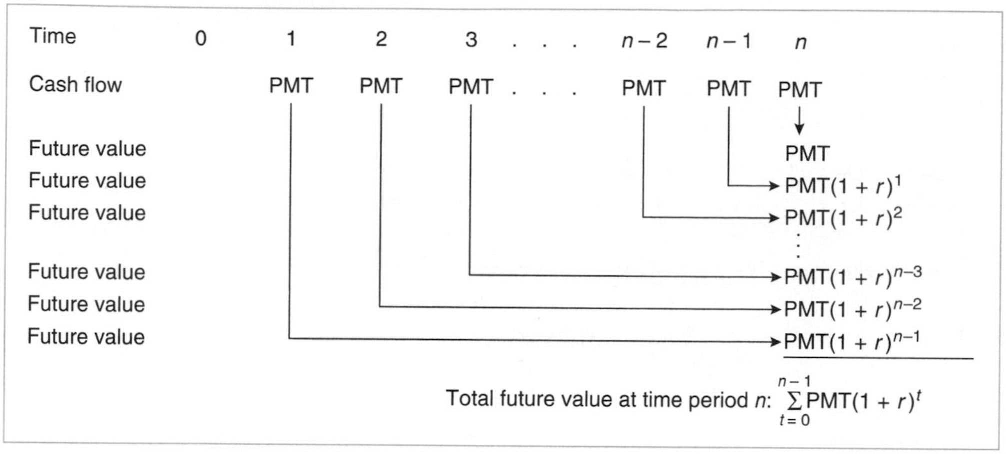

FIGURE 4.3
The future value of an n-period annuity.

The Future Value of an Annuity

We started our discussion of the time value of money in Chapter 2 with an example of depositing money in a savings account. Now consider a savings plan for depositing the same amount every period for n periods. How much will you have at the end of the n periods?

Let the periodic cash flow, PMT, be the amount deposited at the end of each time period (that is, $CF_1 = CF_2 = \cdots = CF_n = PMT$). Figure 4.3 illustrates the future value of an n-period annuity.

The future value of an annuity is the total value that will have accumulated at the end of the annuity if the annuity payments are all invested at r per period. The future value of an annuity can be computed using the future value formula to value each payment and then adding up the individual values to get the total. If we start with the last payment at time $t = n$ and proceed backwards to the first payment at time $t = 1$, the future value of the annuity at time n, FVA_n, is

$$FVA_n = PMT(1 + r)^0 + PMT(1 + r)^1 + \cdots + PMT(1 + r)^{n-1}$$

Figure 4.3 illustrates this calculation. Note that the first payment (at $t = 1$) earns interest for $(n - 1)$ periods, *not n* periods. Each subsequent payment earns interest for one less period than the previous one. Note that the last payment occurs exactly at the end of the annuity, so it does not earn any interest—$(1 + r)^0 = 1$.

The equation for FVA_n has a PMT in every term on the right-hand side. If the PMT is factored out, the equation can be rewritten as

$$FVA_n = PMT[(1 + r)^0 + (1 + r)^1 + \cdots + (1 + r)^{n-1}] = PMT\sum_{t=0}^{n-1}(1 + r)^t$$

where Σ is a summation. This equation can be simplified to

$$FVA_n = PMT\sum_{t=0}^{n-1}(1 + r)^t = PMT\left[\frac{(1 + r)^n - 1}{r}\right] = PMT(FVAF_{r,n}) \qquad (4.5)$$

The quantity in large brackets in Equation (4.5) is called the future-value-annuity factor. The **future-value-annuity factor,** $FVAF_{r,n}$, is the total future value of \$1.00 per period for n periods invested at r per period. The particular values for PMT, n, and r along with Equation (4.5) are all that are needed to determine the future value of the annuity.

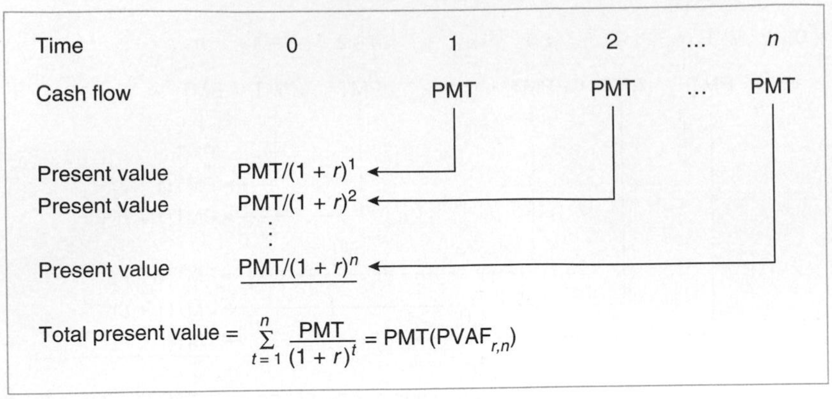

FIGURE 4.4
The present value of an *n*-period annuity.

CALCULATOR SOLUTION

Data Input	Function Key
30	N
5	I
0	PV
2,000	PMT
−132,877.70	**FV**

CALCULATOR SOLUTION

Data Input	Function Key
30	N
6	I
0	PV
2,000	PMT
−158,116.37	**FV**

EXAMPLE Saving for Retirement at Citibank

Suppose you save \$2,000 per year at the end of each year for 30 years at Citibank, and the money earns 5% interest per year. How much will you have at the end of the 30 years?

The cash flows are like those in Figure 4.3 with $n = 30$. Therefore, using Equation (4.5)

$$FVA_{30} = PMT(FVAF_{5\%,30}) = 2{,}000\left[\frac{(1.05)^{30} - 1}{0.05}\right] = 2{,}000(66.43885) = \$132{,}877.70$$

$FVAF_{5\%,30}$ is 66.43885, and the future value of the annuity is \$132,877.70.

What would be the future value if the interest rate was 6% instead of 5%? Compute the answer of \$158,116.37 on your calculator.

The Present Value of an Annuity

The present value of an annuity is the amount that, if invested today at *r* per period, could exactly provide equal payments every period for *n* periods. The present value of an annuity, PVA_n, is simply the sum of the present values of the *n* individual payments:

$$PVA_n = PMT\frac{1}{(1+r)^1} + PMT\frac{1}{(1+r)^2} + \cdots + PMT\frac{1}{(1+r)^n}$$

The present value of an *n*-period annuity is illustrated in Figure 4.4. Because the cash flows or payments are all identical, we can rewrite this as

$$PVA_n = PMT\left[\frac{1}{(1+r)^1} + \frac{1}{(1+r)^2} + \cdots + \frac{1}{(1+r)^n}\right] = PMT\sum_{t=1}^{n}\frac{1}{(1+r)^t}$$

This equation for PVA_n can be simplified to

$$PVA_n = PMT\sum_{t=1}^{n}\frac{1}{(1+r)^t} = PMT\left[\frac{(1+r)^n - 1}{r(1+r)^n}\right] = PMT(PVAF_{r,n}) \qquad (4.6)$$

The quantity in large brackets in Equation (4.6) is called the present-value-annuity factor.[1] The **present-value-annuity factor,** $PVAF_{r,n}$, is the total present value of an annuity of \$1.00 per period for *n* periods discounted at *r* per period. The particular values for PMT, *n*, and *r* are all that are needed to determine the present value of the annuity.

---

[1]The present value of an annuity can also be expressed as the PV of FVA_n. To see this, show that $PVAF_{r,n}$ = $FVAF_{r,n}$ times $PVF_{r,n}$.

EXAMPLE Computing the Present Value of a Car Loan from GMAC

Suppose General Motors Acceptance Corporation (GMAC) expects to receive future car-loan payments of $200 per month for the next 36 months from one of its customers. The first payment is due one month from today. The interest rate on the loan is 1% per month. How much money is being borrowed? In other words, what is the present value of the loan?

Using Equation (4.6) with PMT = $200, $n = 36$, and $r = 1\%$:

$$PVA_{36} = PMT(PVAF_{1\%,36}) = 200\left[\frac{(1.01)^{36} - 1}{0.01(1.01)^{36}}\right] = 200(30.1075) = \$6,021.50$$

$PVAF_{1\%,36}$ is 30.1075, and the present value is $6,021.50.

CALCULATOR SOLUTION

Data Input	Function Key
30	N
1	I
200	PMT
0	FV
−6,021.50	**PV**

Calculating Annuity Payments

We have shown how to compute the present and future values of an annuity, given a set of payments and a discount rate. When you borrow money, the amount is the present value, and the annuity is the loan payments. We can solve for the payments by rearranging Equation (4.6):

$$PMT = PVA_n\left[\frac{r(1 + r)^n}{(1 + r)^n - 1}\right] = \frac{PVA_n}{PVAF_{r,n}} \tag{4.7}$$

EXAMPLE Computing Annual Loan Payments

Consider a $10,000 loan requiring equal payments at the end of each of the next five years. If the interest rate is 9% per year, what are the payments?

Using Equation (4.7), we get:

$$PMT = PVA_5\left[\frac{(0.09)(1.09)^5}{(1.09)^5 - 1}\right] = \$2,570.92$$

$PVAF_{9\%,5}$ is 3.88965, and the payments are $2,570.92.

CALCULATOR SOLUTION

Data Input	Function Key
5	N
9	I
10,000	PV
0	FV
−2,570.92	**PMT**

Now suppose you are getting ahead of the game and saving money regularly rather than paying off a loan. The accumulated amount is a future value. We can solve for the amount that must be saved regularly to accumulate a given future value, this time by rearranging Equation (4.5):

$$PMT = FVA_n\left[\frac{r}{(1 + r)^n - 1}\right] = \frac{FVA_n}{FVAF_{r,n}} \tag{4.8}$$

EXAMPLE Saving at the IBM Credit Union for a Down Payment on a House

Dina Naples is saving money at the IBM Credit Union for a down payment on a house. How much does she have to save at the end of every month to accumulate a total of $12,000 at the end of five years if the money is invested at 0.5% per month?

CALCULATOR SOLUTION

Data Input	Function Key
60	N
0.5	I
0	PV
12,000	FV
−171.99	PMT

Using Equation (4.8), we get:

$$\text{PMT} = \text{FVA}_{60}\left[\frac{(0.005)}{(1.005)^{60} - 1}\right] = \$171.99$$

$\text{FVAF}_{0.5\%,60}$ is 69.77, and the payments are $171.99.

Review

1. What is an annuity?
2. What is the future value of an annuity? What is the present value of an annuity?
3. Explain why the future value of an annuity, FVA_n, discounted back over n periods at r per period must equal the present value of the annuity, PVA_n.

Amortizing a Loan

A **loan amortization schedule** shows how a loan is paid off over time. That is, it shows the relationships among a loan's payments, principal, and interest rate.

To create an amortization schedule, start with the amount borrowed. Add the first period's interest, and then subtract the first period's payment. The result is the remaining balance, which is the starting amount for the second period. Repeat this procedure each period until the remainder becomes zero at the end of the last period.

EXAMPLE Amortizing a Loan

CALCULATOR SOLUTION

Data Input	Function Key
3	N
8.5	I
1,000	PV
0	FV
−391.54	PMT

Suppose a $1,000 loan with an interest rate of 8.5% requires equal payments at the end of each of the next three years. The annual loan payments will be $391.54.

What is this loan's amortization schedule?

This loan's amortization schedule is given in Table 4.2. Each period's interest increases the remaining balance by the interest rate times the previous period's remaining balance. The loan payment then reduces the remaining balance. Because the loan payment exceeds the first year's interest charge, the remaining balance is sequentially reduced to zero after n periods. Note how the interest amount declines and the principal reduction increases over the loan's life.

TABLE 4.2
A loan amortization schedule.

YEAR	1	2	3
a. Principal at start of period	$1,000.00	$693.46	360.86
b. Interest for the period (8.5% of starting principal)	85.00	58.94	30.68
c. Balance (a + b)	1,085.00	752.40	391.54
d. Payment	−391.54	−391.54	−391.54
e. Principal at end of this period and start of next period (c − d)	693.46	360.86	0.00
f. Principal reduction (d − b)	306.54	332.60	360.86

Calculating the Discount Rate and Number of Annuity Payments

In addition to solving for the payments, future value, or present value of an annuity, we can solve for the discount rate or the number of annuity payments. However, unlike the payments, we cannot always rearrange our equation to solve for these variables. Instead, the equation must be solved using trial and error. A financial calculator is especially convenient for calculating these variables because it performs the tedious trial-and-error calculations automatically.

EXAMPLE Computing the Interest Rate on a Mortgage from Chase Home Mortgage

Chase Home Mortgage offers a $100,000 home mortgage loan. Payments will be $678.79 per month for 30 years (360 payments). What interest rate is Chase charging?

Using Equation (4.6):

$$100{,}000 = 678.79(\text{PVAF}_{r,360}) - 678.98\left[\frac{(1+r)^{360} - 1}{r(1+r)^{360}}\right]$$

An r of 0.6% solves this equation, so Chase is charging 0.6% per month.

CALCULATOR SOLUTION

Data Input	Function Key
360	N
100,000	PV
−678.79	PMT
0	FV
0.6	**I**

CALCULATOR SOLUTION

Data Input	Function Key
48	N
0.75	I
15,000	PV
0	FV
−373.28	**PMT**

EXAMPLE Computing the Remaining Life of a Car Loan

Let us say you borrowed $15,000 to buy a car. The loan was originally a 48-month loan charging 0.75% per month on the unpaid balance. Your monthly payment is $373.28.

Now you do not remember how many payments are remaining, but your statement says that your remaining balance is now $9,092.81. How many more monthly payments are left?

Again, using Equation (4.6):

$$9{,}092.81 = 373.28(\text{PVAF}_{0.75\%,n}) = 373.28\left[\frac{(1+0.0075)^n - 1}{0.0075(1+0.0075)^n}\right]$$

An n of 27 solves this equation, so you have to make 27 more monthly payments.

CALCULATOR SOLUTION

Data Input	Function Key
0.75	I
9,092.81	PV
373.28	PMT
0	FV
27	**N**

Valuing Deferred Annuities

Sometimes, annuities start at a time other than right away (where the first payment is at $t = 1$). The present value of such an annuity can be computed by first calculating the annuity's future value, and then calculating the present value of that lump sum future value.

EXAMPLE Computing the Present Value of an Annuity Starting in the Future

What is the present value of $5,000 per year to be received at the end of each of the years 4 through 7 if the required return is 12% per year?

This deferred annuity, one not starting until sometime in the future, is equivalent to its future value at the end of its life, year 7, which is $23,896.64.

The present value of the annuity is then the present value of this lump sum, $10,809.63.

Figure 4.5 shows the equivalence of the three amounts: annuity cash flows, lump sum value at year 7, and present value.

CALCULATOR SOLUTION

Data Input	Function Key
4	N
12	I
0	PV
5,000	PMT
−23,896.64	**FV**

CALCULATOR SOLUTION

Data Input	Function Key
7	N
12	I
0	PMT
−23,896.64	FV
10,809.63	**PV**

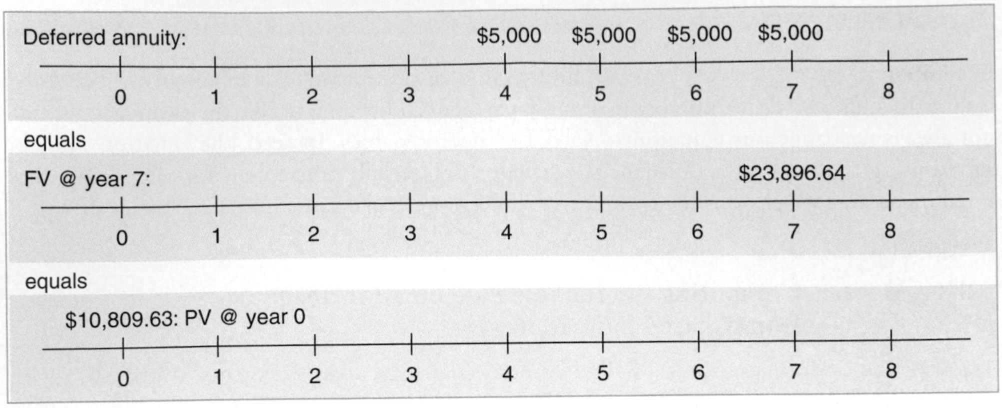

FIGURE 4.5
Valuing a deferred annuity.

Perpetuities

An annuity that goes on forever is called a **perpetuity.** Although perpetuities actually exist in some situations, the most important reason for studying them is that they can be used as a simple and fairly accurate approximation of a long-term annuity.

Figure 4.2 showed that the present-value factor becomes smaller as n becomes larger. Therefore, later payments in a long annuity add little to the present value of the annuity. For example, at a required return of 10% per year, the present value of getting \$100 in 30 years is only \$5.73. It is a mere 85 cents if payment is going to take 50 years.

To examine the present value of a perpetuity, we can start with the present value of an annuity and see what happens when the life of the annuity, n, becomes very large. Let us start by rewriting Equation (4.6), the present value of an annuity formula:

$$PVA_n = PMT\left[\frac{(1+r)^n - 1}{r(1+r)^n}\right] = PMT\left[\frac{(1+r)^n}{r(1+r)^n}\right] - PMT\left[\frac{1}{r(1+r)^n}\right]$$

$$PVA_n = \left[\frac{PMT}{r}\right] - \left[\frac{PMT}{r(1+r)^n}\right]$$

Written this way, you can see what happens when n becomes large. The first term on the right-hand side of the last line is not affected by n. But the second term gets smaller because $(1 + r)^n$ gets larger when n increases. As n gets really big, the second term goes to zero. Therefore, the present value of a perpetuity is

$$PVA_{perpetuity} = \frac{PMT}{r} \tag{4.9}$$

EXAMPLE Present Value of a Perpetuity

What is the present value of \$1,000 per year, forever, if the required return is 8% per year? Using Equation (4.9):

$$PVA_{perpetuity} = \frac{PMT}{r} = \frac{1{,}000}{0.08} = \$12{,}500.00$$

Now let us say the \$1,000 per year only lasted for 50 years. What would be the present value, and how well does the present value of the perpetuity approximate this present value?

The actual present value for the 50-year annuity is

$$PVA_{50} = PMT(PVAF_{8\%,50}) = 1{,}000\left[\frac{(1.08)^{50} - 1}{(0.08)(1.08)^{50}}\right] = 1{,}000(12.23348) = \$12{,}233.48$$

In this case, the perpetuity is worth only about 2% more than a 50-year annuity. This is because the present value of the very distant (the fifty-first and subsequent) payments is very small.

CALCULATOR SOLUTION

Data Input	Function Key
50	N
8	I
1,000	PMT
0	FV
−12,233.48	**PV**

Valuing an Annuity Due

The payments for an annuity due occur at the beginning of each period instead of at the end. Because each payment occurs one period earlier, an annuity due has a higher present value than a comparable ordinary annuity. Likewise, an annuity due has a higher future value than a comparable ordinary annuity because each payment has an additional period to compound. In fact, a simple way to value an annuity due is to multiply the value of a comparable ordinary annuity by $(1 + r)$.

EXAMPLE Computing the Future Value and Present Value of an Annuity Due

What are the future and present values of an annuity due of $100 per year for seven years, if the required return is 10% per year?

If this were an ordinary annuity, the future and present values would be:

$$FVA_n = PMT(FVAF_{10\%,7}) = 100\left[\frac{(1.10)^7 - 1}{0.10}\right] = \$948.72$$

$$PVA_n = PMT(PVAF_{10\%,7}) = 100\left[\frac{(1.10)^7 - 1}{0.10(1.10)^7}\right] = \$486.84$$

CALCULATOR SOLUTION

Data Input	Function Key
7	N
10	I
0	PV
100	PMT
−948.72	**FV**

CALCULATOR SOLUTION

Data Input	Function Key
7	N
10	I
100	PMT
0	FV
−486.84	**PV**

Then, for the annuity due:

$$\text{Future value of annuity due} = FVA_n(1 + r) = 948.72(1.10) = \$1{,}043.59$$
$$\text{Present value of annuity due} = PVA_n(1 + r) = 486.84(1.10) = \$535.53$$

You can also use a financial calculator to compute the FV and PV of an annuity due directly. To do so, put your calculator into the BEGIN mode, and make the FV and PV calculations in the usual way.

Review

1. Describe the layout of a loan amortization schedule.
2. Why is the value of a perpetuity a good estimate of the value of an otherwise comparable long-term annuity?
3. Indicate whether each of the following is typically an ordinary annuity or an annuity due:
   a. Monthly installment on a car loan;
   b. Monthly rent payment on an apartment;
   c. Monthly paycheck for someone on a fixed monthly salary;
   d. The monthly payment on your cable television hookup.

4.4 MULTIPLE EXPECTED FUTURE CASH FLOWS

Unlike an annuity, in some cases, future cash flows vary in size. In this section, we demonstrate a few common-sense methods for computing the value of a set of unequal future cash flows. We describe three such methods using the following example.

EXAMPLE Computing the Present Value of a Set of Unequal Future Cash Flows

You have an opportunity to invest $10,000. If you make the investment, you expect to get $2,000 next year, $8,000 the year after, and $5,000 in the third year. If the required return is 10%, what is the net present value (NPV) of your investment?

The NPV is the sum of the present values of all the cash flows:

$$\text{NPV} = \frac{-10{,}000}{(1.1)^0} + \frac{2{,}000}{(1.1)^1} + \frac{8{,}000}{(1.1)^2} + \frac{5{,}000}{(1.1)^3}$$

$$\text{NPV} = -10{,}000 + 1{,}818.182 + 6{,}611.570 + 3{,}756.574 = \$2{,}186.326$$

This calculation is illustrated in Figure 4.6.

A second method for calculating the total present value of our set of unequal future cash flows is called the "rollback" method: Start with the most distant cash flow ($5,000 at time 3) and discount it back one period (at 10%). Its value at $t = 2$ is $4,545.45 (= 5,000/1.10). Add this amount to the time 2 cash flow of $8,000 to get $12,545.45. Discount this amount back one period. Its value at $t = 1$ is $11,404.96 (= 12,545.45/1.10). Add the time 1 cash flow to this amount to get $13,404.96. Discount this amount back one period. Its value is $12,186.33 (= 13,404.96/1.10). Finally, this amount minus the $10,000 time 0 cash flow equals the total present value of $2,186.33. Figure 4.7 illustrates the rollback method of calculating a present value.

Finally, many financial calculators provide a third method for valuing this unequal set of future cash flows. Because calculators are not identical, you will have to use your own calcu-

FIGURE 4.6
Computing the present value of a set of unequal future cash flows.

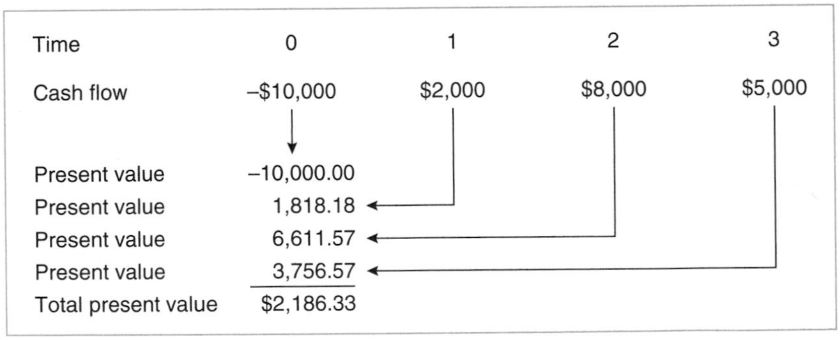

FIGURE 4.7
The rollback method for calculating a present value.

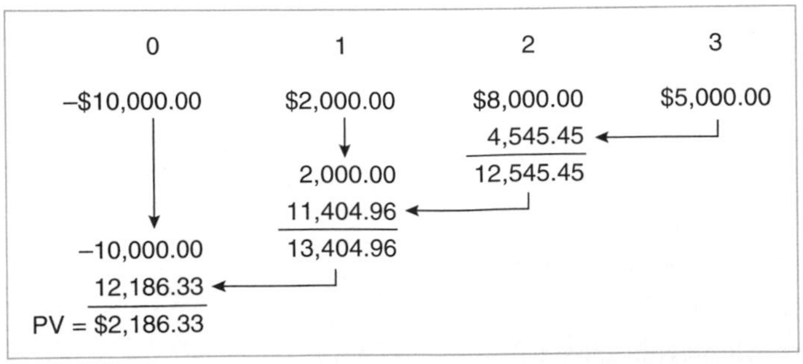

lator's manual to learn how to use this method. There is an important advantage to using this calculator feature: If you already know the present value, but do not know the discount rate, the calculator can automatically compute the expected return for the set of unequal cash flows. This can eliminate the hassle of very tedious trial-and-error calculations.

Valuing Cash Flows at Other Points Along the Time Line

Thus far, we have calculated a present value ($t = 0$) or a future value at $t = n$. But suppose we want to know the total value of a set of cash flows at some other point in time. Calculating such a value directly may require extra care, but it uses the same formulas. And if you already know the present or future value, calculating such values is quite straightforward. Our next example illustrates this process, by building on our last example.

EXAMPLE Computing Total Value at Other Points in Time

Let us reconsider the value of our set of unequal cash flows. What is their total value at $t = 2$? Cash flows before $t = 2$ must be compounded forward. Cash flows on or after $t = 2$ must be discounted back. The sum of these compounded and discounted cash flows plus the $t = 2$ cash flow equals FV_2, the total value at $t = 2$:

$$FV_2 = -10{,}000(1.10)^2 + 2{,}000(1.10)^1 + 8{,}000(1.10)^0 + 5{,}000\frac{1}{(1.10)^1}$$

$$= -12{,}100 + 2{,}200 + 8{,}000 + 4{,}545.45 = \$2{,}645.45$$

This calculation is illustrated in Figure 4.8.

In this case, there is a shortcut for computing FV_2. In our previous example, we computed the present of this set of cash flows. This value can be used directly to find FV_2. Simply compound the total present value forward two periods, just as though it is a single cash flow at $t = 0$:

$$FV_n = PV(FVF_{r,n}) = PV(1 + r)^n$$

$$FV_2 = 2{,}186.326(1.10)^2 = \$2{,}645.45$$

CALCULATOR SOLUTION

Data Input	Function Key
2	N
10	I
2,186.326	PV
0	PMT
−2,645.45	**FV**

In a parallel way, FV_2 can also be used directly to find FV_3. Simply compound 2,645.45 forward one period, just as though it is a single cash flow at $t = 2$:

$$FV_3 = FV_2(FVF_{10\%,1}) = 2{,}645.45(1.10)^1 = \$2{,}910.00$$

CALCULATOR SOLUTION

Data Input	Function Key
1	N
10	I
2,645.45	PV
0	PMT
2,910.00	**FV**

This example illustrates a very important point we want to emphasize. Once you have the total value of a set of cash flows at *any* point in time, you can easily compute the total value at any *other* point in time. Simply *treat the value you know as though it is a single cash flow* and compound or discount it for the difference in time to compute the value you are looking for.

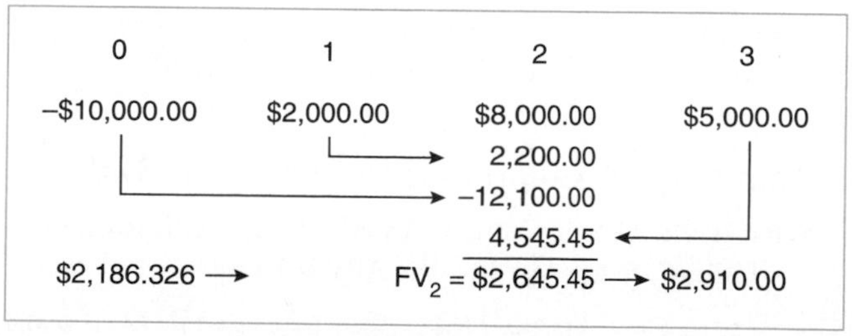

FIGURE 4.8
Computing the future value at time period 2 of an unequal set of future cash flows.

Review

1. How can you compute the present value of an unequal set of future cash flows?
2. Assume you have an unequal set of cash flows extending from $t = 1$ through $t = 10$. How can you find the value of this stream at $t = 4$?

4.5 COMPOUNDING FREQUENCY

Thus far, we have been careful to use a discount rate that is consistent with the frequency of the cash flows—for example, 1% per *month* with *monthly* payments or 10% per *year* with *annual* payments. In practice, interest rates are typically stated in one of two ways, as an annual percentage rate (APR) or as an annual percentage yield (APY), even though interest may be calculated and paid more often than annually.

Annual Percentage Rate (APR)

The **annual percentage rate (APR)** is the periodic rate times the number of periods in a year. The APR is a nominal rate, a rate "in name only." The true (effective) annual rate may be different from the APR because of the compounding frequency.

The **compounding frequency** is how often interest is compounded. For example, the compounding frequency might be monthly (12 times per year), quarterly (4 times), or annually (once). The periodic rate is an effective rate, but recall that two periods of interest is more than double one. The second period's interest includes interest on the first period's interest.

With m compounding periods per year and a periodic rate of r, the APR is:

$$\text{APR} = (m)(r) \tag{4.10}$$

EXAMPLE Computing an APR at Bank of America

Bank of America offers a loan, charging 1% per month. What is the APR?

Using Equation (4.10), the APR is 12%:

$$\text{APR} = 12(0.01) = 0.12 = 12.00\%$$

Note: The compounding frequency is the same as the payment frequency, unless it is otherwise specified.

Annual Percentage Yield (APY)

The **annual percentage yield (APY)** is the effective (true) annual rate of return. It is the rate you *actually* earn or pay in one year, taking into account the effect of compounding. The APY is computed by compounding the periodic rate for the compounding frequency:

$$\text{APY} = \left[1 + \frac{\text{APR}}{m}\right]^m - 1 \tag{4.11}$$

If interest is compounded once per year, $m = 1$, the APY equals the APR. When compounding is more often, the APY, the true rate, exceeds the APR.

EXAMPLE Computing the APY from Bank of America's APR

What is the APY on Bank of America's 12% APR loan, with monthly compounding?

Using Equation (4.11), the APY is 12.68%:

$$\text{APY} = (1 + r)^m - 1 = (1.01)^{12} - 1 = 0.1268 = 12.68\%$$

CALCULATING THE APY USING A CALCULATOR We can also compute the APY using the future value. If you start with 100% of your money and compound it at r for m periods (one year), the increase is the true rate of return.

After one year, you would have 112.68% of the 100% you started with, so you would earn an APY of 12.68%.

CALCULATOR SOLUTION

Data Input	Function Key
12	N
1	I
100	PV
0	PMT
−112.68	**FV**

EXAMPLE Computing the APY for a Credit Card

A credit card charges 1.50% per month on unpaid balances. The periodic rate $r = 1.5\%$ and $m = 12$. The APR $= 0.015(12) = 0.18 = 18.00\%$. What is the APY? That is, what is the true, or effective, annual return?

The credit card is charging 19.562% per year.

CALCULATOR SOLUTION

Data Input	Function Key
12	N
1.5	I
100	PV
0	PMT
−119.562	**FV**

The Effect of Compounding Frequency on Future Value

How does compounding frequency affect future value? To answer this question, let us compare yearly, semiannually, quarterly, monthly, weekly, daily, and continuous compounding for saving $10,000 for a year at a 12% APR.

The future value of $10,000 in one year is shown in Table 4.3 for all of these compounding frequencies. The APY equals the 12% APR for yearly compounding. But the table shows how the future value and APY increase as the compounding frequency increases.

Another way to understand an APY is to say that it is the total interest earned in a year (annual interest) divided by the principal. That is

$$\text{APY} = \frac{\text{Annual interest}}{\text{Principal}}$$

For example, the annual interest for monthly compounding is $1,268.25, which, divided by $10,000, gives the same 12.68% we got using Equation (4.11).

Continuous Compounding

If more frequent compounding increases the future value, what if we compound daily, hourly, or even every minute? These are all examples of *discrete compounding,* where interest is compounded a finite number of times per year. If interest is compounded an infinite number of times per year, we have *continuous compounding.*

THE APR AND APY WITH CONTINUOUS COMPOUNDING When m, the compounding frequency, becomes large enough, compounding becomes essentially continuous. Without giving the proof, it turns out that with continuous compounding:

$$\text{APY} = e^{\text{APR}} - 1 \qquad (4.12)$$

where e is approximately 2.718.[2] The function e^x is called an exponential function. It is usually found on a calculator with either an "e^x" or "exp" on the key.

[2]This number occurs frequently in the mathematical and natural sciences. It is the base for what are called *natural logarithms,* usually denoted *ln; ln* is the inverse function of *e*. That is, $ln(e^x) = x$.

TABLE 4.3
Future values and APYs for various compounding frequencies.

COMPOUNDING FREQUENCY	m	PV	FV_{YEAR}	ANNUAL INTEREST	APY
Yearly	1	$10,000	$11,200.00	$1,200.00	12.0000%
Semiannually	2	10,000	11,236.00	1,236.00	12.3600
Quarterly	4	10,000	11,255.09	1,255.09	12.5509
Monthly	12	10,000	11,268.25	1,268.25	12.6825
Weekly	52	10,000	11,273.41	1,273.41	12.7341
Daily	365	10,000	11,274.75	1,274.75	12.7475
Continuous	∞	10,000	11,274.97	1,274.97	12.7497

The APR is 12%.
m = number of times interest is compounded per year
When $t = 1$, $FV = PV(1 + APR/m)^m = 10{,}000(1 + 0.12/m)^m$
Interest = FV − PV
$APY = (1 + APR/m)^m - 1$
For continuous compounding, $FV = PV\, e^{APR} = 10{,}000e^{0.12}$
For continuous compounding, $APY = e^{APR} - 1 = e^{0.12} - 1$

CALCULATOR SOLUTION

Data Input	Function Key
100,000	N
12/100,000	I
100	PV
0	PMT
−112.74968	**FV**

EXAMPLE Computing an APY with Continuous Compounding

What is the APY for a 12% APR continuously compounded?

Using Equation (4.12), we have

$$APY = e^{APR} - 1 = e^{0.12} - 1 = 0.1274969 = 12.74969\%$$

An alternative to the above calculation is to approximate APY using a very large value for m. For example, $m = 100{,}000$ (compounding about 274 times per day) yields APY = 12.74968%.

Figure 4.9 shows how compounding frequency affects future value by graphing future value as a function of annual, semiannual, and continuous compounding for 20% APR. Note how the "stair steps" are smaller and more frequent for semiannual compounding and how they become a smooth curve with continuous compounding. Note also that the amount increases faster with more frequent compounding.

Review

1. What is the APR (annual percentage rate)? Does it reflect the frequency of compounding?
2. What is the APY (annual percentage yield)? How does it take into account the effect of compounding?
3. Explain in your own words the meaning of continuous compounding.
4. Suppose a bank offers you a 10% APR certificate of deposit. You can specify annual, semiannual, quarterly, monthly, or daily compounding. Which would you choose?
5. Suppose you are going to borrow from a bank at 10% APR. You can specify annual, semiannual, quarterly, monthly, or daily compounding. Which would you choose?

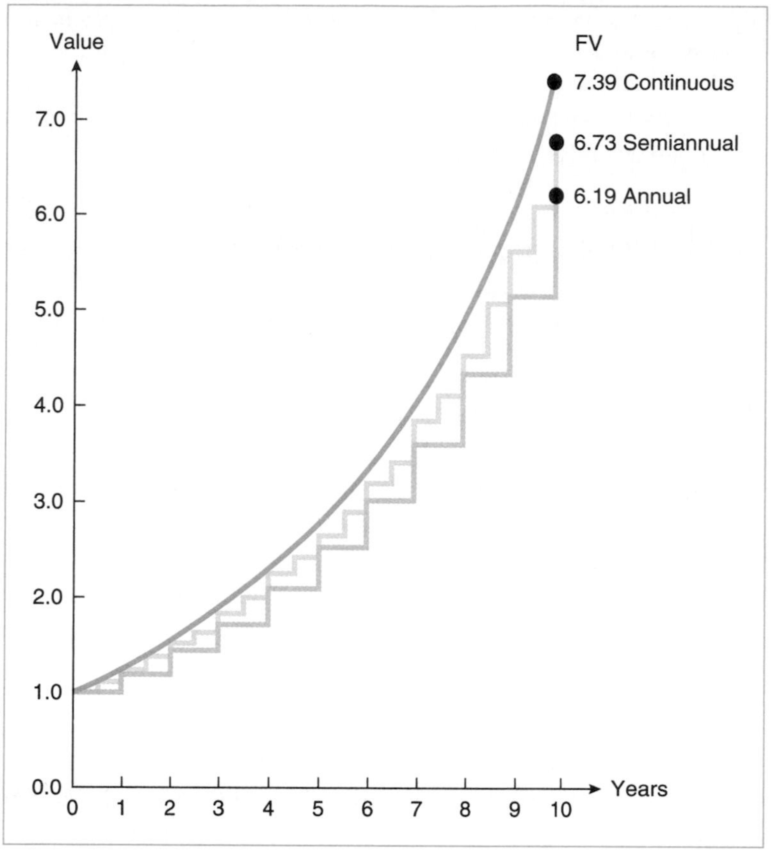

FIGURE 4.9
Future value as a function of annual, semiannual, and continuous compounding for 20% APR.

4.6 PARTIAL TIME PERIODS

Using the time-value-of-money formulas with partial time periods requires care and an understanding of the assumptions underlying the formulas. A time line can be essential to solving problems involving partial time periods.

Single Cash Flows

Computing present and/or future values of single cash flows between partial time periods is straightforward because a fractional exponent can be used directly in modern calculators.

EXAMPLE Computing the Present Value of a Single Future Cash Flow

What is the present value of $1,000 to be received 46 months from today if the required return is 12% APY?

Using the present value formula with $n = 3.8333$ (= 46/12):

$$PV = 1{,}000\left[\frac{1}{(1.12)^{3.8333}}\right] = \$647.64$$

CALCULATOR SOLUTION

Data Input	Function Key
3.8333	N
12	I
1,000	PMT
0	FV
−647.64	**PV**

Annuities with Partial Time Periods

Unfortunately, calculator treatment of annuities with partial time periods is not consistent. Some "round down," and treat the partial time period and payment as though it is not there. Others "round up," and treat the partial time period and payment as though it is a full period and payment.

CALCULATOR SOLUTION

Data Input	Function Key
3	N
10	I
0	PV
1,000	PMT
−3,310.00	**FV**

Still others account for the partial time period but assume no payment. Our advice is to either (1) carefully study how your calculator works and use it successfully, or (2) "take matters into your own hands" and account for annuities with partial time periods in other ways. Here are two examples of how to compute a future value using a two-step process, without relying on whatever assumptions are programmed into your calculator.

EXAMPLE Computing the Future Value of an Annuity after It Has Ended

CALCULATOR SOLUTION

Data Input	Function Key
0.75	N
10	I
3,310	PV
0	PMT
−3,555.27	**FV**

What is the value 3.75 years from now of a three-year annuity, with the first $1,000 payment being made one year from today, if the expected return is 10% APY?

The value in three years is: $1{,}000(\text{FVAF}_{10\%,3}) = \$3{,}310.00$.

The future value in 3.75 years can then be computed by simply treating the $3,310 as though it is a single cash flow at $t = 3$ and compounding that amount for 0.75 time periods to get: $3{,}310(\text{FVAF}_{10\%,0.75}) = 3{,}310[1.1]^{0.75} = \$3{,}555.27$.

Figure 4.10 illustrates the solution to this example using a time line.

EXAMPLE Computing the Present Value of an Annuity with Early Cash Flows

CALCULATOR SOLUTION

Data Input	Function Key
4	N
8	I
5,000	PMT
0	FV
−16,560.63	**PV**

What is the present value of a four-year annuity, with the first $5,000 payment being made nine months from today, if the required return is 8% APY?

Three months ago, this annuity would be a "normal" four-year annuity. So its value as of three months ago (at $t = -0.25$) is $5{,}000(\text{PVAF}_{8\%,4}) = \$16{,}560.63$.

The present value can then be computed by simply treating $16,560.63 as a single cash flow, and compounding it forward to the present for 0.25 time periods, to get $16{,}560.63(\text{FVF}_{8\%,0.25}) = 16{,}560.63[1.08]^{0.25} = \$16{,}882.35$.

Figure 4.11 illustrates the solution using a time line.

CALCULATOR SOLUTION

Data Input	Function Key
0.25	N
8	I
16,560.63	PV
0	PMT
−16,882.35	**FV**

Review

1. How can you compute the present or future value of a single cash flow when there is a partial time period involved?
2. Why must you be especially careful when using a calculator to compute the present or future value of an annuity when there is a partial time period involved?

FIGURE 4.10
Solution using a time line.

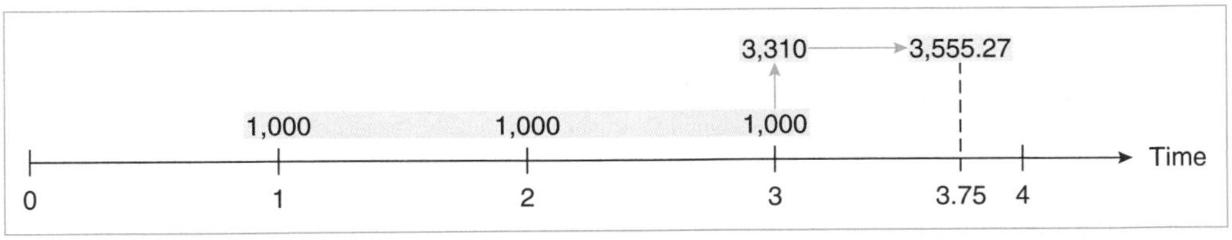

FIGURE 4.11
Solution using a time line.

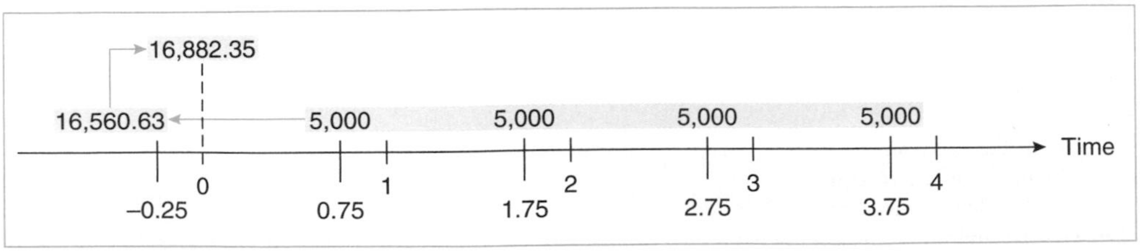

4.7 EVALUATING "SPECIAL-FINANCING" OFFERS

"Special-financing" offers are often used as part of a sales promotion for consumer goods, such as cars, furniture, and even condominiums. In short, special financing has become part of the package in many types of consumer purchases. But how can you tell whether the financing is really special in anything but name only? In this section, we provide an example and some guidelines for dealing with special financing.

Often the interest rate creates the most confusion with special financing. This is because the special rate offered, such as 0.9% APR, is not the opportunity cost for borrowing money. You cannot really borrow money at that rate. The special financing is simply a promotional gimmick. In essence, the firm is lowering the effective price to encourage sales. It is just that the lower price is expressed in the form of special financing. The key question, then, is how much does the interest savings lower the price?

To evaluate a special financing deal, you need the interest rate at which you can borrow money for *any* comparable use. That is, you need the market interest rate for such loans. The market interest rate provides a way to measure the opportunity cost of the special financing. You use the market rate to compute the "real" price for the product. The real price is the present value of the payments you would have to make using the special-financing offer. If the present value is smaller than the cash price, the special financing is a better deal; the real price with special financing is lower than the cash price.

CALCULATOR SOLUTION

Data Input	Function Key
36	N
0.075	I
20,000	PV
0	FV
−563.30	**PMT**

EXAMPLE Cash Back or 0.9% APR from Chevy

Chevy is offering a choice of either "special financing" or "cash back" to buy a car you have already decided to buy. The stated price is $20,000. Either you can have $2,000 cash back, for a cash price of $18,000, or you can borrow the "$20,000" at 0.9% APR, 0.075% per month (= 0.9/12). Monthly payments would be $563.30 for the next 36 months.

Or, you could borrow $18,000 from Citibank (or any of several other banks) at 7.2% APR and pay cash for the car. Should you take the special-financing offer or take the cash-back offer and borrow from a bank?

The best choice has the lowest present-value cost. The difference between the two costs is the NPV of the choice. On the basis of 7.2% APR (0.60% per month), the present value of the special-financing loan payments is $18,189.38.

CALCULATOR SOLUTION

Data Input	Function Key
36	N
0.60	I
−563.30	PMT
0	FV
18,189.38	**PV**

This is more than the $18,000 cash-back-offer price, so taking the cash-back offer and borrowing from the bank is the better deal. The NPV is $189.38.

There is another way to see the difference between the two alternatives: Compute what the payments would be on the Citibank loan if Citibank required the same 36 monthly payments.[3] The payments for such a Citibank loan would be $557.44.

CALCULATOR SOLUTION

Data Input	Function Key
36	N
0.60	I
18,000	PV
0	FV
−557.435	**PMT**

So the bank loan would be $5.865 per month cheaper (= 563.30 − 557.435). Note that the monthly savings have a present value of $189.38, which is the NPV for the bank loan.

CALCULATOR SOLUTION

Data Input	Function Key
36	N
0.60	I
5,865	PMT
0	FV
−189.38	PV

In the preceding example, you had already decided to purchase that particular car. But what if you are still shopping? In the next example, we will show how to evaluate competing product offers.

[3]To make a "fair" comparison possible, the repayment process for the bank loan *must* be identical to that for the special-financing offer: 36 equal monthly payments. If the length of the period is different (say weekly), if the maturity of the loan is different (say 48 months), or if the payments are not identical each period, a comparison of payments can lead to the wrong choice.

CALCULATOR SOLUTION

Data Input	Function Key
48	N
0.0	I
22,000	PV
0	FV
−458.33	**PMT**

CALCULATOR SOLUTION

Data Input	Function Key
48	N
0.60	I
−458.33	PMT
0	FV
19,065.99	**PV**

EXAMPLE Computing the Value of a Special-Financing Offer from Chrysler

Suppose that just before you "sign on the dotted line" for the Chevy, you hear about another offer from Chrysler. It is a nicer model that you actually like better—except for its higher price of $22,000. Now Chrysler is offering 0% APR for 48 months on this "$22,000" model. Therefore, you could buy the nicer model for $458.33 per month for the next 48 months.

However, because the loan on the more expensive model is over a different period, the lower monthly payment is not necessarily the best deal.[4]

Is Chrysler's price on the better model less than the $18,000 cash price on Chevy's more basic model? It is a lower monthly payment at a "lower" interest rate, but it is for 12 more months. What is the real price for the Chrysler? There is no cash-back offer on this nicer model to give a guideline for the price discount.

Again, the real price with the special financing is the present value of the loan payments at the opportunity cost (market) interest rate. On the basis of the bank's 7.2% APR interest rate, the real price is $19,065.99.

Therefore, Chrysler's 0% APR special-financing offer on the nicer model costs $1,065.99 more (= 19,065.99 − 18,000) than the best deal (cash back) on Chevy's model.

Review

1. Why is "special financing" just like a reduction in the real price of the car?
2. Why is it so important to calculate the value of special-financing offers correctly when deciding which brand to buy?

SUMMARY

This chapter explored the Time-Value-of-Money Principle and established the following concepts:

- The expected rate of return is what you expect to earn, the required rate of return is the return the marketplace demands for securities with similar characteristics, and the realized rate of return is what you actually get.
- NPV (net present value) is the present value minus the cost. NPV measures the value created by a financial decision. A positive (negative) NPV creates (destroys) value.
- The present value and future value formulas can be used to compute the value of cash flows at times other than when they will be paid or received. These formulas can be used to find the PV (present value), FV (future value), PMT (annuity cash flow), n (number of periods), or r (the periodic rate of return).
- An annuity is a set of equal periodic payments for a given number of periods. Annuities are common in financial contracts. Annuity formulas allow complex problems to be solved in a routine manner.
- Time-value-of-money formulas can also be used to find a loan's payments or true interest cost—its APY.
- A loan's APY—its true annual cost—can differ from its APR, which is a nominal rate.
- Present value and the discount rate are inversely related: Present value goes down when r goes up, and vice versa—like two kids on a seesaw.

[4]We also want to caution that you must *never* multiply the payment amount times the number of payments. Remember, even identical cash flows, if they occur at different times, do not have the same value—because of the time value of money.

EQUATION SUMMARY

The Basic Calculator Formula

$$PV + PMT\left[\frac{(1+I)^N - 1}{I(1+I)^N}\right] + FV\left[\frac{1}{(1+I)^N}\right] = 0$$

$$\text{Return} = \text{Rate of return} = \frac{\text{Cash flow} + (\text{Ending value} - \text{Beginning value})}{\text{Beginning value}} \tag{4.1}$$

$$\text{NPV} = \text{Net present value} = \text{Present value of expected future cash flows} - \text{Cost} \tag{4.2}$$

The Future-Value Formula

$$FV_n = PV(1+r)^n = PV(FVF_{r,n}) \tag{4.3}$$

The Present-Value Formula

$$PV = FV_n\left[\frac{1}{(1+r)^n}\right] = FV_n(PVF_{r,n}) \tag{4.4}$$

$$FVA_n = PMT\left[\frac{(1+r)^n - 1}{r}\right] = PMT(FVAF_{r,n}) \tag{4.5}$$

$$PVA_n = PMT\left[\frac{(1+r)^n - 1}{r(1+r)^n}\right] = PMT(PVAF_{r,n}) \tag{4.6}$$

$$PMT = PVA_n\left[\frac{r(1+r)^n}{(1+r)^n - 1}\right] = \frac{PVA_n}{PVAF_{r,n}} \tag{4.7}$$

$$PMT = FVA_n\left[\frac{r}{(1+r)^n - 1}\right] = \frac{FVA_n}{FVAF_{r,n}} \tag{4.8}$$

$$PVA_{perpetuity} = \frac{PMT}{r} \tag{4.9}$$

$$APR = (m)(r) \tag{4.10}$$

$$APY = \left[1 + \frac{APR}{m}\right]^m - 1 \tag{4.11}$$

$$APY = e^{APR} - 1 \tag{4.12}$$

QUESTIONS

1. Assume that the rate of return r is equal to zero.
   a. What is the future value of \$1.00 in five years?
   b. What is the present value of \$1.00 received five years in the future?
   c. What is the future value of an ordinary annuity of \$1.00 per year for five years?
   d. What is the present value of an ordinary annuity of \$1.00 per year for five years?

2. Why is the present value of a future cash flow inversely related to the discount rate?
3. What is an ordinary annuity? What is an annuity due? Why is the present value of an annuity due greater than the present value of an ordinary annuity?
4. Give a formula for each of the following:
   a. Future value formula
   b. Present value formula
   c. Future value of an annuity formula
   d. Present value of an annuity formula
5. Indicate which of the following pairs is larger. Answer without computing the results.
   a. The FV of $100 invested at 10% compounded annually for three years OR the FV of $100 invested at 10% compounded monthly for three years.
   b. The PV of $100 received in three years discounted back at 10% compounded annually OR the PV of $100 received in three years discounted back at 10% compounded monthly.
   c. The FV of an ordinary annuity OR the FV of an annuity due.
   d. The PV of an ordinary annuity OR the PV of an annuity due.
6. Dewey Noe computed the value of a 10-year annuity of $100 per year. The value was $700. Now he cannot remember whether it was a *present* value or a *future* value. Which is it? Why?
7. Why should a business undertake an investment that has a positive net present value?

CHALLENGING QUESTIONS

8. Explain the format or layout of a loan amortization table.
9. Assume that you extend the life of an annuity by one year. For example, assume that you increase the life from 10 years to 11 years. How much does this increase the present value of the annuity?

PROBLEMS

LEVEL A (BASIC)

A1. ***(PV and FV of single payments)*** Fill in the missing information below:

	PV	FV	*r*	*n*	
a.		—	20	10%	10
b.		10	—	10%	10
c.		10	20	—	10
d.		10	20	10%	—

A2. ***(PV and FV of single payments)*** Fill in the missing information below:

	PV	FV	*r*	*n*	
a.		—	20	10%	15
b.		10	—	10%	15
c.		10	20	—	15
d.		15	20	10%	—

A3. ***(PV and FV of single payments)*** Fill in the missing information:

	PV	FV	*r*	*n*	
a.		—	22,000	5.6%	3.0
b.		1,000	—	12.1%	5.5
c.		400	400	—	4.0
d.		25,000	50,000	7.75%	—

A4. ***(PV and FV of single payments)*** Fill in the missing information:

	PV	FV	r	n
a.	—	45,000	5.6%	3.0
b.	250	—	12.1%	5.5
c.	500	500	—	4.0
d.	25,000	78,000	7.75%	—

A5. (Calculating FVs) If you invest $1,000 in a savings account paying 12% APY, what will be your account balance at the end of the following periods?

a. one year
b. five years
c. 1.75 years

A6. (Calculating PVs) What is the present value of $20,000 discounted back at 6 percent if the money is received at the end of the following periods?

a. one year
b. five years
c. 1.75 years

A7. (Calculating the PV) A scam artist collected $20 million from gullible investors for an oil-well-drilling scheme. The scam artist promised that he would pay off the investors in full within eight years if the oil wells, for some reason, were not drilled. He purchased zero-coupon bonds that paid off the $20 million in a single payment at the end of eight years. He then mailed the bonds to his investors, pocketing the difference between the price of the bonds and the $20 million, and skipped the country. The rate of return on the bonds was 9%.

a. What is the present value of $20 in 8 years discounted at 9%?
b. How much did the scam artist pocket?

A8. (Expected, required, and realized returns) If you buy shares of Rivas Resorts, it will cost you $45 per share and you expect to receive $1.00 in dividends and sell the stock for $56 in one year. If you invest in Carreras Holdings, the investment would be $125 per share with an expected dividend of $5.00 and stock price of $132 in one year.

a. What are the expected returns for Rivas and Carreras?
b. If the required rate of return is 15%, which stocks should be profitable investments?
c. One year from now, Rivas has paid a $1.00 dividend and is selling for $52. Carreras has paid a $5.00 dividend and is selling for $155. What were the realized returns for the two stocks?

A9. (Expected, required, and realized returns) If you buy shares of MacroComputer Inc., it will cost you $55 per share and you expect to receive $2.00 in dividends and sell the stock for $60 in one year. If you invest in Minnesota Instruments, the investment would be $100 per share with an expected dividend of $4.00 and stock price of $115 in one year.

a. What are the expected returns for MacroComputer and Minnesota?
b. If the required return is 20%, which stocks should be profitable investments?
c. One year from now, MacroComputer has paid a $2.00 dividend and is selling for $60. Minnesota has paid a $4.00 dividend and is selling for $125. What were the realized returns for the two stocks?

A10. (Rate of return) Adrian Trennepohl bought shares of a small firm's stock three years ago for $12.00 per share. What would be Adrian's annual rate of return if she sells the stock today for each of the following prices?

a. $72.00
b. $13.50
c. $15.00
d. $6.00

A11. (Rate of return) Mary M. Contrary bought shares of a small firm's stock three years ago for $12.00 per share. What would be Mary's annual realized return if she sells the stock today for each of the following prices?

a. $36.00

b. $17.50

c. $13.75

d. $8.00

A12. (Rate of return) After graduation, Florence moved across the country to Greenville and bought a small house for $108,000. Clarence moved to Columbia and bought a house for $145,000. Four years later, they both sold their houses. Florence netted $135,000 when she sold her house and Clarence netted $115,000 on his.

a. What annual rate of return did Florence realize on her house?

b. What annual rate of return did Clarence realize on his house?

A13. (Rate of return) After graduation, Adrian moved across the country to Brownville and bought a small house for $208,000. Bill moved to Columbus and bought a house for $195,000. Four years later, they both sold their houses. Adrian netted $256,000 when she sold her house and Bill netted $168,000 on his.

a. What annual rate of return did Adrian realize on her house?

b. What annual rate of return did Bill realize on his house?

A14. (PV of lump sum) George Jetson invests $100 for one year at 10%. He expects to have $110 in one year.

a. What is the present value of this future amount discounted at 10%?

b. What is the present value discounted at 8%?

c. What is the present value discounted at 12%?

A15. (PV of lump sum) George Jingle invests $500 for one year at 10%. He expects to have $550 in one year.

a. What is the present value of this future amount discounted at 10%?

b. What is the present value discounted at 8%?

c. What is the present value discounted at 12%?

A16. (Calculating the PV and FV of an annuity) Assume an ordinary annuity of $500 at the end of each of the next three years.

a. What is the future value at the end of year 3 if cash flows can be invested at 10%?

b. What is the present value discounted at 10%?

A17. (PV of an annuity) What is the present value of $500 per year for eight years if the required return is 8.5% per year?

A18. (PV of an annuity) What is the present value of $100 per year for 10 years if the required return is 6.5% per year?

A19. (FV of an annuity) What is the future value at the end of year 6 of a six-year annuity of $1,000 per year if the expected return is 10%?

A20. (FV of an annuity) What is the future value at the end of year 8 of an eight-year annuity of $1,000 per year if the expected return is 10%?

A21. (FV of an annuity) What is the future value, at the end of year 5, of $1,200 per year for each of the next five years if the expected return is 7% per year?

A22. (FV of an annuity) What is the future value, at the end of year 7, of $1,500 per year for each of the next seven years if the expected return is 9% per year?

A23. (FV of an annuity) What is the future value 10 years from now of an annuity of $350 per year for each of the next 10 years if the expected return is 10% per year?

A24. (FV of an annuity) What is the future value 25 years from now of an annuity of $600 per year for each of the next 25 years if the expected return is 10% per year?

A25. (PV of an annuity) What is the present value of a six-year annuity of $1,000 per year, if the required return is 10% per year?

A26. (PV of an annuity) What is the present value of a five-year annuity of $1,000 per year, if the required return is 15% per year?

A27. (Remaining life of an annuity) You borrowed $25,000 to buy a car. The loan was originally a 48-month loan charging 0.65% per month on the unpaid balance. Your monthly payment is $607.98. Now you do not remember how many payments are remaining, but your statement says that your remaining balance is now $16,022.03. How many more monthly payments are left?

A28. (Remaining life of an annuity) You borrowed $225,000 to buy a house. The loan was originally a 30-year loan charging 0.60% per month on the unpaid balance. Your monthly payment is $1,527.27. Now you do not remember how many payments are remaining, but your statement says that your remaining balance is now $215,407.67. How many more monthly payments are left?

A29. (Finding loan payments) What are the monthly payments on a three-year $5,000 loan if the interest rate is 1% per month?

A30. (Finding loan payments) What are the monthly payments on a 15-year $35,000 loan if the interest rate is 1% per month?

A31. (Loan payments and amortization schedule) What are the annual payments for a four-year $4,000 loan if the interest rate is 9% per year? Make up a loan amortization schedule for this loan.

A32. (Loan payments and amortization schedule) Create a loan amortization schedule for borrowing $9,500 at an interest rate of 15% per year, to be paid off in four equal annual payments.

A33. (Loan payments and amortization schedule) Create a loan amortization schedule for borrowing $7,500 at an interest rate of 20% per year, to be paid off in four equal annual payments.

A34. (Ordinary annuity and annuity due) Assume an annuity payment of $125, an annuity life of 10 years, and a discount rate of 10%.

a. If the annuity is an ordinary annuity, what is the future value of the annuity?
b. If the annuity is an ordinary annuity, what is its present value?
c. If the annuity is an annuity due, what is its future value?
d. If the annuity is an annuity due, what is its present value?

A35. (Ordinary annuity and annuity due) Assume an annuity payment of $300, an annuity life of 10 years, and a required return of 8%.

a. If the annuity is an ordinary annuity, what is the future value of the annuity?
b. If the annuity is an ordinary annuity, what is its present value?
c. If the annuity is an annuity due, what is its future value?
d. If the annuity is an annuity due, what is its present value?

A36. (PV of a perpetuity) What is the present value of a perpetuity of $800 per year if the required return is 11% per year?

A37. (PV of a perpetuity) What is the present value of a perpetuity of $2,500 per year if the required return is 15% per year?

A38. (Loan payment) What are the monthly payments on a $15,000 four-year loan if the required return is 9% APR?

A39. (Loan payment) What are the monthly payments on a $30,000 five-year loan if the required return is 9% APR?

A40. (PV of loan) What is the present value of $100 per week for five years if the required return is 10% APR?

A41. (PV of loan) What is the present value of $300 per week for three years if the required return is 8.5 APR?

A42. (FV of an annuity) What is the future value after 10 years of $200 per month if the expected return is 6% APR?

A43. (FV of an annuity) What is the future value after 15 years of $250 per month if the expected return is 5% APR?

A44. (Finding mortgage payment) What are the monthly payments on a $150,000 25-year mortgage if the required return is 7.5% APR?

A45. (Finding mortgage payment) What are the monthly payments on a $98,000 30-year mortgage if the required return is 9.5% APR?

A46. (Value of cash flows at various points in time) You expect to receive the following future cash flows at the end of the years indicated: $500 in year 2, $1,200 in year 4, $800 in year 5, and $1,500 in year 6. If the discount rate is 7% per year,

a. What is the present value of all four expected future cash flows?
b. What is the value of the four flows at year 5?
c. What is the value of the four flows at year 10?

A47. (Value of cash flows at various points in time) You expect to receive the following future cash flows at the end of the years indicated: $1,500 in year 2, $1,300 in year 4, $600 in year 5, and $1,700 in year 6. If the discount rate is 9% per year,

a. What is the present value of all four expected future cash flows?
b. What is the value of the four flows at year 5?
c. What is the value of the four flows at year 10?

A48. (Value of cash flows at various points in time) The following future cash flows will be received at the end of the years indicated: $1,000 in year 1, $1,400 in year 2, $900 in year 4, and $600 in year 5. If the discount rate is 8% per year;

a. What is the present value of all four expected future cash flows?
b. What is the value of the four flows at year 5?
c. What is the value of the four flows at year 3?

A49. (Value of cash flows at various points in time) The following future cash flows will be received at the end of the years indicated: $2,000 in year 1, $1,200 in year 2, $400 in year 4, and $600 in year 5. If the discount rate is 7% per year,

a. What is the present value of all four expected future cash flows?
b. What is the value of the four flows at year 5?
c. What is the value of the four flows at year 3?

A50. (PV of single payment) What is the present value of $10,000 to be received 7.8 years from today, if the required return is 8.2% APY?

A51. (PV of single payment) What is the present value of $10,000 to be received 9.2 years from today, if the required return is 6.8% APY?

A52. (PV of a perpetuity) What is the present value of $10,000 per year received at the end of each year in perpetuity with a required return of 7.4% APR?

A53. (PV of a perpetuity) What is the present value of $200,000 per year received at the end of each year in perpetuity with a required return of 4% APR?

LEVEL B

B1. (Finding the APY) You expect to receive $16,000 three years from today. If the present value of this amount is $12,701.13, what is the APY?

B2. (PV of an annuity) What is the present value of a stream of $1,500 payments received at the end of each of years 3 through 9 if the required return is 10% per year?

B23. (Finding the APR and APY for a mortgage) Suppose a bank offers a $125,000 20-year mortgage if you will pay back $1,000 per month.

a. What monthly interest rate is the bank charging?

b. What APR interest rate is the bank charging on this mortgage?

c. What APY interest rate is the bank charging on this loan?

B24. (PV of single payment with continuous compounding) What is the present value of $3,400 to be received three years from today if the required return is 11% APR compounded continuously?

B25. (PV of single payment with continuous compounding) What is the present value of $6,900 to be received three years from today if the required return is 10% APR compounded continuously?

B26. (PV of a single payment) What is the present value of $4,500 to be received 31 months from today if the required return is 10% APY?

B27. (PV of a single payment) What is the present value of $900 to be received 31 months from today if the required return is 10% APY?

B28. (PV of discrete payments with continuous compounding) What is the future value of $20,000 received as a lump sum at the end of each year for five years if the expected return is 10% per year compounded continuously?

B29. (PV of discrete payments with continuous compounding) What is the future value of $9,000 received as a lump sum at the end of each year for five years if the expected return is 10% per year compounded continuously?

B30. (PV of an annuity) What is the present value of a five-year annuity, with the first $3,000 payment being made three months from today, if the required return is 7% APY?

B31. (PV of an annuity) What is the present value of a five-year annuity, with the first $5,000 payment being made three months from today, if the required return is 7% APY?

B32. (FV of an annuity) What is the value 4.35 years from now of a four-year annuity, with the first $1,200 payment being made one year from today, if the expected return is APY = 10%?

B33. (FV of an annuity) What is the value seven years from now of a four-year annuity, with the first $1,600 payment being made one year from today, if the expected return is APY = 10%?

B34. (PV of an annuity) What is the present value of a six-year annuity, with the first $2,500 payment being made seven months from today, if the required return is APY = 12%?

B35. (PV of an annuity) What is the present value of a six-year annuity, with the first $3,000 payment being made four months from today, if the required return is APY = 12%?

B36. (PV of an annuity) What is the present value of a stream of $1,900 payments received at the end of each of years 3 through 9 if the required return is 10% per year?

B37. (Finding the APY) You expect to receive $2,000 three years from today. If the present value of this amount is $1,423.56, what is the APY?

B38. (Finding the time period) You expect to receive $1,000 sometime in the future. If the present value of this amount is $592.03 and the discount rate is 10% APY, when is the cash flow expected to occur?

B39. (Finding the time period) You expect to receive $5,000 sometime in the future. If the present value of this amount is $2,332.54 and the discount rate is 10% APY, when is the cash flow expected to occur?

B40. (Time to double your money) How long does it take a present value amount to double if the expected return is

a. 4%?

b. 9%?

c. 15%?

B41. (Times to double your money) How long does it take a present value amount to double if the expected return is

a. 10%?

b. 12%?

c. 16%?

B42. (Finding the APY) If an annuity of $5,000 per year for eight years has a present value of $27,469.57, what is the expected APY?

B43. (Finding the APY) If an annuity of $8,000 per year for eight years has a present value of $33,657.30, what is the expected APY?

B44. (PV of a delayed annuity) What is the present value of a 15-year annuity with payments of $1,800 per year, where the first payment is expected to occur four years from today and the required return is 7.3% APY?

B45. (PV of a delayed annuity) What is the present value of a 13-year annuity with payments of $2,700 per year, where the first payment is expected to occur four years from today and the required return is 8.5% APY?

B46. (Finding the PV of an annuity with missing payments) Suppose you expect to receive $1,000 per year for each of the next 15 years, except that you will not receive any payments in years 3 and 5. What is the present value of this stream if the required return is 12% APR?

B47. (Finding the PV of an annuity with missing payments) Suppose you expect to receive $1,000 per year for each of the next 13 years, except that you will not receive any payments in years 3 and 5. What is the present value of this stream if the required return is 11% APR?

B48. (Mortgage loan interest rates) Bob's Bank has offered you a $40,000 mortgage on a house. Payments are to be $374.90 per month for 30 years.

a. What monthly interest rate is Bob charging?

b. What is the APR on this loan?

c. What is the APY on this loan?

B49. (Mortgage loan interest rates) Peter's Bank has offered you a $200,000 mortgage on a house. Payments are to be $2,057.23 per month for 30 years.

a. What monthly interest rate is Peter charging?

b. What is the APR on this loan?

c. What is the APY on this loan?

B50. (Special-financing offer) Chrysler is offering "42-month 2.2% APR" financing or "$2,000 cash back" on a car you have decided to buy. The stated price for the car is $23,000.

a. What are the monthly payments required for Chrysler's special-financing deal?

b. If you can borrow the cash to buy the car from several different banks at 8.3% APR, would you be better off taking the cash-back offer?

B51. (Special-financing offer) Honda is offering "42-month 2.5% APR" financing or "$2,000 cash back" on a car you have decided to buy. The stated price for the car is $23,000.

a. What are the monthly payments required for Honda's special-financing deal?

b. If you can borrow the cash to buy the car from several different banks at 8.3% APR, would you be better off taking the cash-back offer?

B52. (Special-financing offer) You have negotiated a price of $20,000 to buy a car. Ford will either give you $1,500 cash back, or a 48-month loan of the "$20,000" at 3.9% APR. Alternatively, you can borrow $18,500 from Citibank (or any of several other banks) at 8% APR and pay cash for the car.

a. What are the monthly payments required for Ford's special-financing deal?

b. If you can borrow the cash to buy the car from several different banks at 8.0% APR, would you be better off taking the cash-back offer?

B53. (Special-financing offer) Performance Auto is offering you a choice of either special financing or a price discount on their new sports car, the QT-123. The stated price for the car is $31,000, but you can pay $25,500 cash and "drive it home today." Alternatively, you can borrow the $31,000 from Performance Auto and make monthly payments for three years with a 1% APR. Suppose the best financing currently available is to borrow money from Bob's Bank for three years at 12% APR with monthly installment payments, and you have decided to buy a QT-123 from Performance Auto. Should you take the special financing or borrow the money from Bob's Bank and pay the cash price?

B54. (Special-financing offer) Performance Auto is offering you a choice of either special financing or a price discount on their new van, the Van-Go. The stated price for the van is $23,000, but you can pay $19,500 cash and "drive it home today." Alternatively, you can borrow the $23,000 from Performance Auto and make monthly payments for four years with a 0.9% APR. Suppose the best financing currently available is to borrow money from Barb's Bank for four years at 7.2% APR with monthly installment payments, and you have decided to buy a Van-Go from Performance Auto. Should you take the special financing or borrow the money from Barb's Bank and pay the cash price?

B55. (Monthly loan installment) What are the monthly payments on a three-year $10,000 loan (36 equal payments) if the interest rate is a 10% APY?

B56. (Monthly loan installment) What are the monthly payments on a three-year $20,000 loan (36 equal payments) if the interest rate is a 8% APY?

B57. (FV and PV of an annuity) Suppose you would like to be paid $20,000 per year during your retirement, which starts in 20 years. Assume the $20,000 is an annual perpetuity and that the expected return is 4% APY. How much should you save per year for the next 20 years so that you can achieve your retirement goal?

B58. (FV and PV of an annuity) Suppose you would like to be paid $40,000 per year during your retirement, which starts in 20 years. Assume the $40,000 is an annual perpetuity and that the expected return is 5% APY. How much should you save per year for the next 20 years so that you can achieve your retirement goal?

B59. (Special-financing offer) Let us say Toyota is offering "36-month 1.9% APR" financing or "$1,400 cash back" on a car you have decided to buy. The stated price for the car is $18,000. You can borrow the cash to buy the car from several different banks at 8.1% APR. Which alternative has the lower "real" price, the special-financing deal or the cash-back offer?

B60. (Special-financing offer) Let's say Toyota is offering "36-month 3% APR" financing or "$1,400 cash back" on a car you have decided to buy. The stated price for the car is $18,000. You can borrow the cash to buy the car from several different banks at 8% APR. Which alternative has the lower "real" price, the special-financing deal or the cash-back offer?

B61. (Excel: amortization table) You borrow $20,000 for a 36-month car loan.

a. If the APR is 9.00%, what is your monthly loan payment?

b. Prepare a loan amortization schedule that shows, for each month, your loan payment, interest expense, loan amortization, and remaining loan balance.

c. What is the APY on your loan?

B62. (Excel: amortization table) Bill Welch is buying out his partner in an avocado orchard. Bill is borrowing $200,000 and will pay 10% interest on the outstanding balance. Bill has agreed to pay $25,000 per year for the first five years, $30,000 for the next four, and then will pay off the remaining balance at the end of the 10th year.

a. Prepare a loan amortization schedule that shows, for the next 10 years, Bill's loan payment, interest expense, loan amortization, and remaining loan balance.

b. What is the final (10th) loan payment?

LEVEL C (ADVANCED)

C1. (Loan payments) Harry's Home Finance is offering to loan you $10,000 for a home improvement. The loan is to be repaid in monthly installments over nine years. If the interest rate on this loan is 15% APR, compounded continuously, what would your monthly payments be if you accepted Harry's offer?

C2. (Loan payments) Barry's Home Finance is offering to loan you $19,000 for a home improvement. The loan is to be repaid in monthly installments over nine years. If the interest rate on this loan is 12% APR, compounded continuously, what would your monthly payments be if you accepted Barry's offer?

C3. (PV of an annuity) Billy Bob won a lottery that will pay him $10,000 per year for 10 years. He got the first payment nine months ago, so the second payment will occur three months from today. Billy Bob has decided to sell the rest of the payments. He is offering them to you for $61,825.00. If the appropriate required return on this stream of expected future cash flows is 10% APY,

a. What is the present value of this set of cash flows?

b. What is the net present value of buying this set of expected future cash flows from Billy Bob for $61,825.00?

C4. (PV of an annuity) Jason won a lottery that will pay him $100,000 per year for 10 years. He got the first payment nine months ago, so the second payment will occur three months from today. Jason has decided to sell the rest of the payments. He is offering them to you for $602,000.00. If the appropriate required return on this stream of expected future cash flows is 10.8% APY,

a. What is the present value of this set of cash flows?

b. What is the net present value of buying this set of expected future cash flows from Jason for $602,000.00?

C5. (PV of an annuity) What is the present value of $5,000 per year received at the end of each year for 20 years if the required return is 8% APR, compounded continuously?

C6. (PV of an annuity) What is the present value of $2,000 per year received at the end of each year for 15 years if the required return is 6% APR, compounded continuously?

C7. (Annuity payments) Suppose your parents have decided that after you graduate at the end of this year, they will start saving money to help pay for your younger brother to attend college. They plan to save money for five years before he starts college and to continue to save during his college years. They plan to give your brother $8,000 per year at the start of each of his four college years. Your parents will thus make monthly savings payments for eight years, five prior to and three during your brother's college education. (The sixtieth monthly savings payment happens simultaneously with the first $8,000 college payment.) The monthly interest rate earned on their savings is 0.45%. How much must the monthly savings be under these conditions?

C8. (FV and PV of an annuity) Suppose your parents have decided that after you graduate at the end of this year, they will start saving money to help pay for your younger sister to attend college. They plan to save money for five years before she starts college. The instant after they make the last payment, they will withdraw the first payment for her. The payments to her will be $8,000 per year at the start of each of her four college years. They will save an equal amount at the end of every month for five years. The monthly interest rate they will earn on their savings is 0.45%. How much must they save each month in order to be able to make the four payments with no money left over?

C9. (Annuity payments) Suppose your parents have decided that after you graduate at the end of this year, they will start saving money to help pay for your younger brother to attend college. They plan to save money for five years before he starts college and to continue to save during his college years. They plan to give your brother $10,000 per year at the start of each of his four college years. Your parents will thus make monthly payments for eight years, five prior to and three during your brother's college education. The monthly interest rate earned on their savings is 0.45%. How much must the monthly savings be under these conditions?

C10. (PV of a perpetuity) What is the present value of $1,000 every two years forever, with the first payment two years from today, if the required return is 12% APY?

C11. (PV of a perpetuity) What is the present value of $5,500 every two years forever, with the first payment two years from today, if the required return is 8% APY?

C12. (PV of an accelerated perpetuity) What is the present value of $500 every four years forever, with the first payment two years from today, if the required return is 12% APY?

C13. (PV of a deferred perpetuity) What is the present value of $6,500 every four years forever, with the first payment six years from today, if the required return is 11% APY?

C14. (Finding an APY) A firm advertising early-retirement programs promises to repay you forever, whatever amount you pay them per year for 12 years. What interest rate are they promising?

C15. (Finding an APY) A firm advertising early-retirement programs promises to repay you forever, whatever amount you pay them per year for 20 years. What interest rate are they promising?

C16. (Finding an annuity payment) Suppose you would like to be paid $30,000 per year during your retirement, which starts in 25 years. Assume the $30,000 is an annual perpetuity and that the expected return is 6% APY. What should you save *per month* for the next 25 years so that you can achieve your retirement goal?

C17. (Finding an annuity payment) Suppose you would like to be paid $50,000 per year during your retirement, which starts in 20 years. Assume the $50,000 is an annual perpetuity and that the expected return is 5.5% APY. What should you save *per month* for the next 20 years so that you can achieve your retirement goal?

C18. (Finding loan payments) What are the monthly payments on a $50,000 25-year loan if the interest rate is 13% APR with continuous compounding?

C19. (Finding loan payments) What are the monthly payments on a $5,000 10-year loan if the interest rate is 14% APR with continuous compounding?

C20. (Excel: PV of income stream) Cynthia Fisher is purchasing an asset that will pay her $1,000 in one year, $1,500 in two years, $2,000 in three years, and $2,500 in four years.

a. If the required rate of return is 10%, what is the present value of this income stream?

b. If Cynthia purchases this asset for $3,500, what rate of return will she earn on her investment?

C21. (Excel: PV of income stream) Eduardo Garcia has a starting salary of $45,000. He expects the salary to grow at 10% annually for the following nine years. Then for years 11 through 30, the salary will grow at 8% annually. Finally, for years 31 through 35, the salary will decline by 5% annually. Assume that the payments are received at the end of the year and that the required rate of return is 6%. What is the PV of Eduardo's projected income stream?

C22. (Excel: FV of variable cash flows) Gary French wants to have $1.0 million in ten years. Currently, he has an investment portfolio of $200,000. He will also invest an additional $25,000 at the end of each of the next ten years. If he has the following annual returns, how much will his investment portfolio be worth at the end of ten years?

Year 1	12%	Year 6	8%
Year 2	−6%	Year 7	4%
Year 3	3%	Year 8	1%
Year 4	9%	Year 9	14%
Year 5	−17%	Year 10	11%

MINICASE THE $125 BILLION SWISS SURPRISE

Imagine getting a bill for $125 billion you did not know you owed. That actually happened to the residents, called "burghers," of the town of Ticino, Switzerland. The New York Supreme Court in Brooklyn ordered Ticino to pay a group of American investors. The investors had sued in the Brooklyn court over a loss they claimed in connection with the failure 27 years earlier of Inter Change Bank, a tiny bank in Ticino. The burghers had known about the suit, but thought the matter was trivial, and were naturally stunned by the bill. Their lead lawyer quipped that "if the judgment was upheld by the higher courts, all of Ticino's citizens would have to spend the rest of their lives flipping real burgers (the kind you eat) at McDonald's and Burger King to pay off the debt."

The root of Ticino's problem was a deposit made 28 years earlier, one year before the bank failed. The estate of one Sterling Granville Higgins deposited $600 million of options on Venezuelan oil and mineral deposits. The bank agreed to pay an interest rate of 1% per week. (No wonder the bank failed the next year!) The Brooklyn court ruled that Ticino had to pay 1% interest per week compounded weekly for the seven years between the date of deposit and the date Ticino had the bank liquidated and interest at the rate of 8.54% APY for the subsequent 21 years.

QUESTIONS

1. The $125 billion reported in the press was rounded, but the original amount was precisely $600 million. Assuming the time periods are exactly seven years at 1% per week and exactly 21 years at 8.54% APY, how much was the bill to the nearest dollar?
2. What is the APY over the entire 28 years as the $600 million grows to the exact amount you calculated in question 1?
3. Suppose Ticino could pay $5 billion per year. How long would it take to pay off the debt, assuming interest continued to be charged at 8.54% APY? How long would it take at $12 billion per year?

Postscript: To the burghers' relief, the judgment was thrown out on appeal. This no doubt restored the confidence of the good burghers of Ticino in the American system of justice!

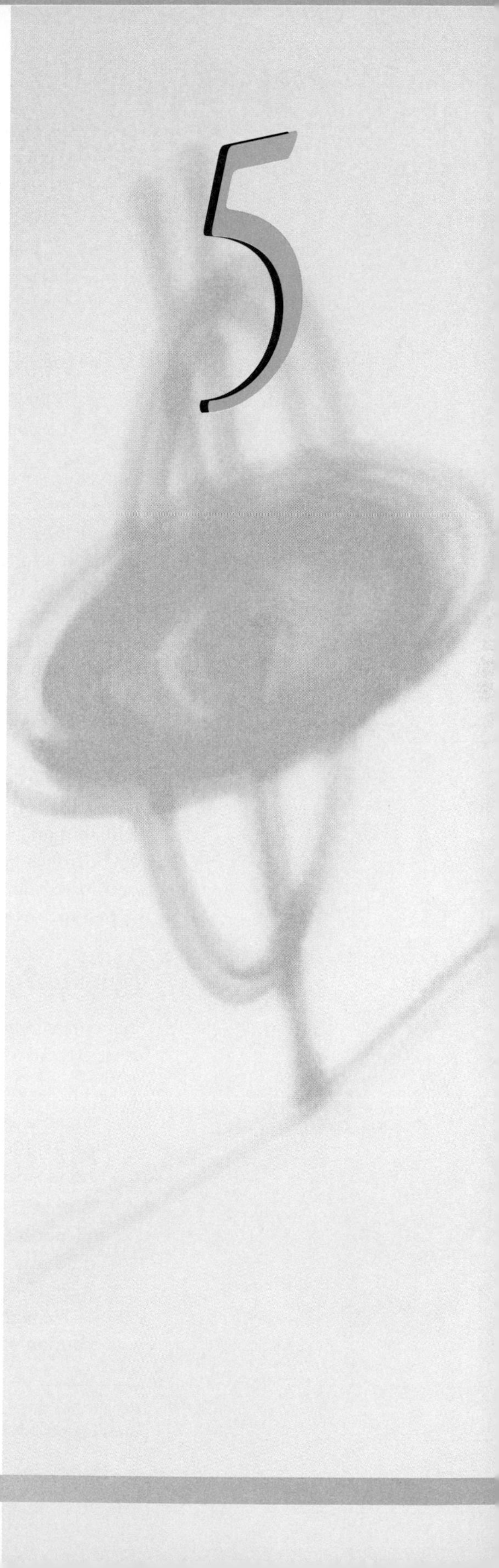

5 VALUING BONDS AND STOCKS

Bonds and stocks are the most common and basic types of financial securities. Financial securities provide much of the financing (liabilities and stockholders' equity) for firms. When a firm decides to expand and lacks the necessary cash, it can obtain the money it needs by selling new securities.

In this chapter, we cover the basics of how bonds and stocks are valued. Recall that stocks and bonds have a fundamental difference. A bond is debt, a type of loan. Stock is equity, a form of ownership. In later chapters, we will examine many important details about the numerous alternatives firms have for financing and explore theories about how firms should be financed.

We know from previous chapters that the value of something can be expressed as the present value of its expected future cash flows. This is especially convenient for financial securities because they are nothing but a claim on future cash flows. We can make immediate use of the time-value-of-money tools from the previous chapter to value bonds and stocks.

For a bond, the periodic expected future cash flows are the contractually promised interest and principal payments. For a stock, the periodic expected future cash flows are cash dividends. Both have one additional expected future cash flow, the cash received if the bond is paid off or sold or if the stock is sold. The steps in the basic valuation procedure for any asset are as follows:

1. Estimate the expected future cash flows.
2. Determine the required return, which depends on the riskiness of the expected future cash flows.
3. Compute the present value, which is what the asset is worth.

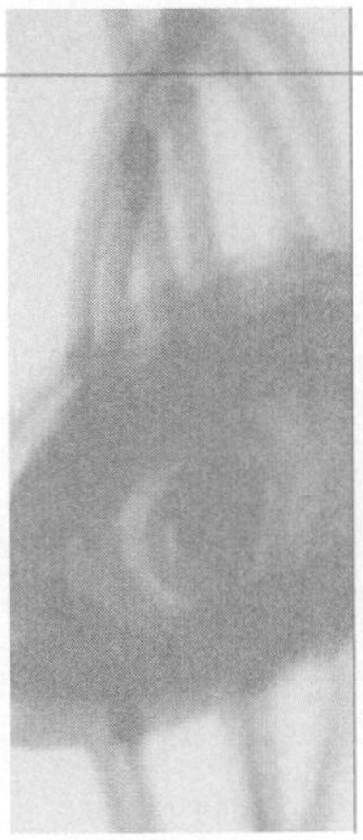

FOCUS ON PRINCIPLES

- *Incremental Benefits:* Note that the incremental benefits from owning a financial security are its expected future cash flows.
- *Time Value of Money:* Determine the value of a financial security by computing the present value of its expected future cash flows.
- *Risk-Return Trade-Off:* Recognize that a financial security's value and required return reflect its risk.
- *Two-Sided Transactions:* Use the fair price of a financial security to compute its expected return, because the fair price does not favor either side of the transaction.
- *Efficient Capital Markets:* Estimate the required return for a financial security with its expected return.
- *Options:* Recognize a call provision's value to the issuing firm.

5.1 BONDS

A **bond** is a long-term obligation for borrowed money. It is a promise to pay interest and repay the borrowed money on terms specified in a contract called a **bond indenture.** The indenture is the legal contract between the issuing corporation and the bondholders.

In addition to U.S. corporations, many other entities sell bonds to borrow money. The U.S. Government, federal agencies, state governments, municipalities, non-U.S. firms, foreign governments, and international agencies account for most other bond issues. We will use U.S. corporate bonds for illustrative purposes. These same bond valuation techniques apply to virtually any bond.

We start with an example. A bond contract for a six-year $100 million loan specifies an interest rate of 7% per year payable semiannually (7% APR[1]). It also requires principal repayment in equal installments three, four, five, and six years from the date the bond was issued. The borrower would then be obligated to pay the lender 3.5% (one-half of 7%) of the unpaid bond loan balance every six months. Table 5.1 specifies the bond's future cash flows promised by the borrower.

Typical Bond Features

There are many different types of bonds. They can be described by their pattern of promised future payments. A typical bond indenture includes the following provisions:

1. The **par value,** which is also called the **face value,** specifies the amount of money that must be repaid at the end of the bond's life. Most U.S. corporate bonds have a par value of $1,000. A bond issue of $100,000,000 would involve the sale of 100,000 such bonds, each with a par value of $1,000.
2. A promise to make **coupon payments** periodically over the life of the bond. Coupon payments are the finance term for what people call interest payments in everyday language. The large majority of U.S. corporate bonds make semiannual coupon payments. Coupon payments are determined by the **coupon rate.** In the preceding example, the coupon rate is 7% and, assuming a $1,000 par value and semiannual interest payments, calls for coupon payments of $35 (one-half the coupon rate times the par value) every six months.

[1]Recall that the APR, annual percentage rate, is the rate per compounding period times the number of compounding periods in a year.

TABLE 5.1
Schedule of semiannual bond payments.

PERIOD	INITIAL LOAN BALANCE	INTEREST PAYMENT	PRINCIPAL REPAYMENT	ENDING LOAN BALANCE	TOTAL DEBT SERVICE PAYMENT
0.5	$100,000,000	$3,500,000	—	$100,000,000	$3,500,000
1.0	100,000,000	3,500,000	—	100,000,000	3,500,000
1.5	100,000,000	3,500,000	—	100,000,000	3,500,000
2.0	100,000,000	3,500,000	—	100,000,000	3,500,000
2.5	100,000,000	3,500,000	—	100,000,000	3,500,000
3.0	100,000,000	3,500,000	$25,000,000	75,000,000	28,500,000
3.5	75,000,000	2,625,000	—	75,000,000	2,625,000
4.0	75,000,000	2,625,000	25,000,000	50,000,000	27,625,000
4.5	50,000,000	1,750,000	—	50,000,000	1,750,000
5.0	50,000,000	1,750,000	25,000,000	25,000,000	26,750,000
5.5	25,000,000	875,000	—	25,000,000	875,000
6.0	25,000,000	875,000	25,000,000	—	25,875,000

3. A promise to repay the **principal** of the bond issue in one or more installments over the life of the bond issue. The principal is the total amount of money being borrowed. Typically, it is simply the total of the par values of all the bonds that make up the bond issue.
4. The **maturity** of a bond is the end of its life, which occurs at the **maturity date.** When a bond is issued (created), the length of its life is its **original maturity.** The amount of time remaining until maturity is called the **remaining maturity.** Virtually any original maturity is possible, but most U.S. corporate bonds issued in recent years have had original maturities between 5 and 30 years.
5. A **call provision** gives the issuer (the firm) the right (option) to pay off the bonds prior to their maturity. When you first think about it, it may seem odd to need the right to pay back the money you owe. After all, if you do not need the borrowed money anymore, just return it. But, like other options, this one is valuable. Let us step to the other side of the transaction to see how.

If you buy a bond that pays 8% interest and then market interest rates go down, you would be pretty happy to continue to earn 8%. That would be more than you could get in other comparable market investments. But the firm would want to repay you and reborrow the money from others at the new lower interest rate. If interest rates instead went up, the opinions on repayment would be reversed. Because of this difference in view from the two sides of the transaction, the contract must carefully specify the rights of each side. Call provisions typically have a "grace period" of several years after issuance during which the firm cannot repay the bonds. A bond's call price usually starts at a premium above the bond's par value (typically one year's interest) and then declines over time, reaching par value at or near maturity.

A bond issue that requires the repayment of the entire principal amount at maturity is said to have a **bullet maturity.** When a bond issue is repaid in multiple installments, the method of repayment is called a **sinking fund.** Typically, bond issues that have a sinking fund require annual payments that begin after some specified "grace period." Sinking fund payments are a fixed obligation from the firm's viewpoint, but not from the bondholder's. The bonds to be repaid in a given year are chosen by lottery. So any particular bondholder does not know their bond will be repaid until just

FIGURE 5.1
Hypothetical bond quotes with a Coca-Cola Enterprises bond highlighted.

Bonds	Cur Yld	Vol	Close	Net Chg.
CaterpInc 9 3/8 11	9.1	30	103.50	−1.50
Chrylslr 9.95s17	8.7	37	114.13	...
Citicp 6.50s13	6.6	8	98.25	+0.13
ClevEl 6.75s15	6.9	10	98.38	−0.63
Coca-Cola Ent. 6.95s26	7.1	49	98	+0.50
CrayRs 6.13s22	cv	31	85.25	−0.75

before it happens.[2] Sometimes firms repurchase the bonds in the capital markets from owners wanting to sell them, rather than by lottery selection. This is especially likely when a bond is selling for less than its par value.[3]

The final repayment of principal is typically larger than the others. When it is, it is called the **balloon payment** (or balloon, for short).

Obtaining Bond Information

Suppose you wanted to find out information about a publicly traded bond. One source is a current *Wall Street Journal.* It has bond quotes similar to those shown in Figure 5.1.

From the highlighted Coca-Cola Enterprises bond quote, you know the

1. *Coupon rate.* Coca-Cola Ent. pays a coupon rate of 6.95% (indicated by the 6.95% after the name) on these bonds, or $34.75 (one-half of 6.95% of $1,000) every six months.
2. *Maturity year.* Assuming the bonds do not have a sinking fund, Coca-Cola Ent. will pay owners $1,000 per bond at the bond's maturity in 2026 (indicated by the 26 following the 6.95%).
3. *Current yield.* The bond's current yield is 7.1%. This is a measure of return based on the current price.
4. *Trading volume.* Yesterday, 49 of these bonds were traded.
5. *Closing price.* Yesterday's **closing price** for this bond was 98. The closing price is simply the price of a financial security in the last trade before the market closed. Bond prices are quoted as a percentage of the par value. The Coca-Cola Ent. bond was selling for 98% of its face value. The quote indicates a dollar price of $980.00 (98.00% of $1,000).
6. *Net change in price.* The closing price is $5 higher than the previous day's closing price (1/2% of $1,000).

A variety of additional symbols and notations can provide further information in the quote. For example, the Cray Bond has cv for its current yield. This means the bond is a convertible bond. It can be exchanged at the bondholder's option for a given number of shares of Cray common stock.

A **stock and bond guide,** such as those published by *Standard & Poor's* or *Moody's,* provides more information about this and other bonds. For example, you can determine the exact date a bond pays interest, its maturity date, and its sinking fund provisions (that is, how the principal is to be repaid). Figure 5.2 illustrates information from a bond guide. Check the highlighted bond.

From this quote, you know that

1. Coca-Cola Ent. pays interest on March 15 and November 15 of each year.
2. Coca-Cola Ent.'s 6.95s 2026 bonds mature on November 15, 2026.

---

[2]This is frequently the opposite of the typical lottery: In this case, you win by *not* being picked!

[3]A sinking fund effectively changes the maturity of the total bond issue. This is because some of the bonds are repaid before the stated maturity date. A calculation that takes this difference into account is called *duration.* Duration provides a measure of the "effective" length of a bond issue's life.

FIGURE 5.2

A page from a Standard & Poor's Stock and Bond Guide with a Coca-Cola Enterprises bond highlighted. Standard & Poor's *Stock and Bond Guide*, 2002 Edition, p. 302.

Standard & Poor's

Title-Industry Code & Co. Finances (In Italics) / Individual Issue Statistics: Exchange ↓	Ind / Interest Dates	S&P Rating	Fixed Charge Coverage 1998 / Date of Last Rating Change	Fixed Charge Coverage 1999 / Prior Rating	Fixed Charge Coverage 2000 / Eligible ↓	Year End / Bond Form	Million $ Cash & Equiv. / Redemption Provisions: Regular Price	Million $ Curr. Assets / Regular (Begins) Thru	Curr. Liab. / Sinking Fund Price	Balance Sheet Date / Sinking Fund (Begins) Thru	Refund/Other Restriction Price	L. Term Debt (Mil $) / Refund/Other Restriction (Begins) Thru	Capitalization (Mil $) / Outst'g (Mil $)	Underwriting Firm	Total Debt % Capital / Underwriting Year	Price Range 2001 High	Price Range 2001 Low	Mo. End Price Sale(s) or Bid	Curr. Yield	Yield to Mat.
***Coca-Cola Bott Consol** (Cont.)*																				
Deb 6⅜s 2009	Mn	**BBB**			X	BE	[1]Z100	....	....	....	....	....	250	S4	'99	103.72	90.96	98.86	6.45	6.55
Deb 7.20s 2009	jJ	**BBB**			X	BE	NC	....	....	....	....	....	100	C4	'97	108.13	95.36	103.50	6.96	6.65
Coca-Cola Co	***11e***		***19.55***	***12.88***	***9.25***	***Dc***	***2567***	***7665***	***8768***	***9-30-01***		***1399***	***16364***		***32.3***					
Deb 7⅜s 2093	jJ29	**A+**	12/99	AA−	X	R	NC	....	....	....	....	....	116	M2	'93	113.32	91.43	104.66	7.05	7.05
Nts 6⅝s 2002	aO	**A+**	12/99	AA−	X	R	NC	....	....	....	....	....	150	G1	'92	103.77	101.24	103.11	6.42	4.74
Nts 6s 2003	jJ15	**A+**	12/99	AA−	X	R	NC	....	....	....	....	....	150	M2	'93	105.32	100.06	104.47	5.74	4.12
Nts[2] 5s 2011	Ms15	**A+**			X	BE	[1]Z100	....	....	....	....	....	500	S4	2001	103.92	94.93	98.88	5.82	5.90
Coca-Cola Enterprises	***11f***		***1.24***	***1.18***	....	***Dc***	***180.0***	***2875***	***3477***	***9-28-01***		***11193***	***15470***		***78.7***					
Deb 8½s 2012	Fa	**A**	12/99	A+	X	BE	NC	....	....	....	....	....	250	S1	'92	122.90	114.08	117.74	7.22	6.25
Deb 7⅛s 2017	fA	**A**	12/99	A+	X	BE	NC	....	....	....	....	....	300		'97	109.90	99.23	106.62	6.68	6.47
Deb 8½s 2022	Fa	**A**	12/99	A+	X	BE	NC	....	....	....	....	....	750	S1	'92	123.79	112.20	120.12	7.08	6.70
Deb 8s 2022	mS15	**A**	12/99	A+	X	BE	NC	....	....	....	....	....	250	S1	'92	118.47	106.92	114.80	6.97	6.69
Deb 6¾s 2023	mS15	**A**	12/99	A+	X	BE	NC	....	....	....	....	....	250	S1	'93	104.66	93.41	100.89	6.69	6.67
Deb[3] 7s 2026	aO	**A**	12/99	A+	X	BE	NC	....	....	....	....	....	300	L3	'96	109.99	102.95	107.60	6.51	6.39
Deb 6.95s 2026	mN15	**A**	12/99	A+	X	BE	NC	....	....	....	....	....	250	U1	'96	107.84	95.38	103.81	6.69	6.64
Deb 6¾s 2028	mS15	**A**	12/99	A+	X	BE	[1]Z100	....	....	....	....	....	400	C6	'98	105.52	92.90	101.34	6.66	6.64
Deb 6.70s 2036	aO15	**A**	12/99	A+	X	BE	NC	....	....	....	....	....	300	S1	'96	105.92	101.47	105.40	6.36	6.32
Deb 6¾s 2038	Jj15	**A**	12/99	A+	X	BE	NC	....	....	....	....	....	250	L3	'98	104.64	91.05	99.07	6.81	6.82
Deb[4] 7s 2098	Mn15	**A**	12/99	A+	X	BE	NC	....	....	....	....	....	250	L3	'98	103.89	89.18	96.03	7.29	7.29
Nts 7⅞s 2002	Fa	**A**	12/99	A+	X	BE	NC	....	....	....	....	....	500	S1	'92	102.52	100.46	100.46	7.84	7.41
Nts 6⅝s 2004	fA	**A**	12/99	A+	X	BE	NC	....	....	....	....	....	200	L3	'97	107.81	102.32	106.60	6.21	4.60
Nts[5] 8s 2005	Jj4	**A**	12/99	A+	X	BE	NC	....	....	....	....	....	250	M2	'92	110.43	106.39	109.94	7.28	5.22
Nts 5¾s 2008	mN	**A**	12/99	A+	X	BE	NC	....	....	....	....	....	600	L3	'98	103.95	95.84	100.36	5.73	5.69
Nts 7⅛s 2009	mS30	**A**	12/99	A+	X	BE	NC	....	....	....	....	....	300		'99	111.17	103.44	107.10	6.65	6.06
Cogentrix Energy	***72b***		***2.00***	***1.90***	....	***Dc***	***118.0***	***209.0***	***176.0***	***6-30-00***		***1650***	***1961***		***88.7***					
Sr Nts[6] 8.10s 2004	Ms15	**BB+**	8/98	BBB−	Y	R	[7]Z100	....	100	....	....	....	100	S1	'94	104.80	101.55	104.24	7.77	6.60
Sr Nts[6] 8¾s 2008	aO15	**BB+**			Y	BE	[8]Z100	....	....	....	....	....	220	Exch.	'99	107.98	96.95	98.84	8.85	8.95
[9]Coinmach Corp.	***63***		***0.84***	***0.67***	....	***Mr***	***23.20***			***3-31-00***		***692.0***	***724.0***		***95.6***					
Sr Nts[6]'D' 11¾s 2005	mN15	**B**	9/99	B+	Y	BE	102.9375	11-14-02	....	....	....	....	297	Exch.	'98	103.50	101.00	102.50	11.46	11.06
Cole Nat'l Group	***591***		***2.51***	***1.17***	....	***Ja***	***21.60***	***218.0***	***143.0***	***11-3-01***		***284.0***	***333.0***		***87.1***					
Sr Sub Nts[6] 9⅞s 2006	jD31	**B**	8/99	B+	Y	BE	102.4688	12-30-03	....	....	....	....	150	W6	'96	100.00	75.00	97.50	10.13	10.45
Sr Sub Nts[6] 8⅝s 2007	fA15	**B**	8/99	B+	Y	BE	104.3125	(8-15-02)	....	....	....	....	125	Exch.	'98	95.50	70.00	92.50	9.32	10.21
Colgate-Palmolive Co	***33***		***6.81***	***7.29***	....	***Dc***	***292.0***	***2405***	***2156***	***9-30-01***		***3083***	***4355***		***81.4***					
M-T Nts 'B' 7.54s 2002	[10]jd	**AA−**	5/01	A+	X	BE	NC	....	....	....	....	....	10.0	C4	'94	103.10	101.98	101.98	7.39	6.03
M-T Nts 'B' 7.60s 2004	[11]jd	**AA−**	5/01	A+	X	BE	NC	....	....	....	....	....	22.0	G1	'94	110.26	105.15	108.18	7.02	4.95
M-T Nts 'B' 7.64s 2004	[11]jd	**AA−**	5/01	A+	X	BE	NC	....	....	....	....	....	20.0	M2	'94	110.36	105.27	108.27	7.06	4.96
M-T Nts 'C' 6.58s 2002	mN5	**AA−**	5/01	A+	X	BE	NC	....	....	....	....	....	150	C1	'99	104.04	101.51	103.29	6.37	4.69
M-T Nts 'C' 5.58s 2008	[12]jd	**AA−**	5/01	A+	X	BE	NC	....	....	....	....	....	50.0	G1	'98	104.76	94.74	100.55	5.55	5.49
M-T Nts 'C' 6.45s 2028	[13]jd	**AA−**	5/01	A+	X	BE	NC	....	....	....	....	....	102	M2	'98	100.42	88.42	93.58	6.89	6.98
M-T Nts 'D' 7.84s 2007	Mn15	**AA−**	5/01	AA−	X	BE	NC	....	....	....	....	....	175	M2	2000	115.84	108.42	112.07	7.00	5.56
Collins & Aikman Products	***8***		***1.06***	***1.35***	....	***Dc***	***58.20***	***429.0***	***413.0***	***9-30-01***		***779.0***	***765.0***		***119.7***					
Sr[14] Sub[15] Nts[6] 11½s 2006	Ao15	**B**			Y	BE	105.75	4-14-02	....	....	....	....	400		'96	102.25	75.00	97.50	11.79	12.14
Colonial Realty LP	***57***		***2.32***	***2.49***	....	***Dc***	***10.10***			***6-30-00***		***1069***	***1831***		***58.4***					
Sr Nts 8.05s 2006	jJ15	**BBB−**			X	BE	[16]Z100	....	....	....	....	....	65.0	L3	'96	108.18	100.83	105.58	7.62	6.82

Uniform Footnote Explanations-See Page 260. Other: [1] Red at greater of 100 or amt based on formula. [2] Co may red in whole, at 100, for tax law chge. [3] (HRO)On 10-01-06 at 100. [4] Co may red in whole for tax event. [5] (HRO)On ea Jan 4 at 100. [6] (HRO)On Chge of Ctrl at 101. [7] Plus premium. [8] Plus Make-Whole Amt. [9] Subsid & data of Coinmach Laundry. [10] Due 5-23-02. [11] Due 5-24-04. [12] Due 11-06-08. [13] Due 6-16-28. [14] Gtd by Collins & Aikman Corp. [15] Co may red at 100 On Chge of Ctrl. [16] Plus make whole Amt.

Source: Reprinted by permission of Standard & Poors

3. Coca-Cola Ent. has $250 million worth of these bonds outstanding.
4. This bond issue does not include a sinking-fund provision.

CURRENT YIELD The **current yield** equals the annual coupon payment divided by the closing dollar price. It is a measure of the rate of income from the coupon payments. However, it ignores the gain or loss that will result from the difference between the purchase price and the principal repayment. The yield to maturity, which is discussed in the next section, is a better measure of the return because it measures the *total* return from owning a bond, including changes in market value. Given that current computer and information technology could easily provide the yield to maturity, there is little need for the bond quote to include the current yield. It appears that the current yield is still in the bond quote simply because of tradition. Traditions are often hard to break!

Review

1. Define the following terms: *bond indenture, par* or *face value, coupon, principal, maturity, call provision,* and *sinking fund.*
2. What is the par value of most U.S. corporate bonds?
3. How often do U.S. corporate bonds usually pay interest?
4. A corporate bond is quoted at a price of 95 in a newspaper. What is its dollar price?

5.2 BOND VALUATION

The value of a bond, its fair price, is the present value of its promised future coupon and principal repayments. This present value is determined by the bond's required return. Recall again that the required return is the minimum rate of return you must expect to be willing to make the investment (buy the bond).

When a bond is issued, its terms are set by the issuing firm to achieve a particular fair price for the bond. Most often, firms set the terms so that, when the bond is issued, the fair price will be very close to the bond's par value. However, after the bonds have been issued, their fair price will reflect current market conditions for that contract.

In other words, bond values change over time. This is because the contract terms, especially the schedule of payments, are usually fixed. But the required return always reflects *current* market conditions. As a result, whenever the interest rate (required return) changes, the bond price (the present value of its future payments) changes.

CALCULATOR SOLUTION

Data Input	Function Key
4	N
3.5	I
30	PMT
1,000	FV
−981.63	PV

Valuing a Bond

Consider a two-year bond with a 6% coupon rate. The bond pays $30 every six months for the next two years plus a $1,000 principal repayment at maturity, the time of the last coupon payment. Currently, the bond's required return equals 3.5% per six-month period. So the fair price of the bond, B_0, is:

$$B_0 = \frac{30}{(1.035)} + \frac{30}{(1.035)^2} + \frac{30}{(1.035)^3} + \frac{30}{(1.035)^4} + \frac{1{,}000}{(1.035)^4} = \$981.63$$

Figure 5.3 illustrates this present value computation.

Note that in this case we are not putting in zero for one of the calculator inputs. This case further illustrates the power of a financial calculator and demonstrates the logic of the Basic

	Now	6 months	1 year	18 months	2 years
Time	0	1	2	3	4
Cash flow		30.00	30.00	30.00	1,030.00
Present value	28.99 ←	30.00			
Present value	28.00 ←		30.00		
Present value	27.06 ←			30.00	
Present value	897.58 ←				1,030.00
Total present value:	$981.63				
Required return:	7% APR				

FIGURE 5.3
The present value of a bond's expected future cash flows.

Calculator Formula, given in Chapter 4. The calculator computes the sum of these two present values in one calculation.

Note also that for all bonds of this type, it is always the case that *when the required return equals the coupon rate, the fair price equals the par value.*

Another way to make this same computation is to view the expected future cash flows as two parts: (1) a four-period annuity of \$30 every six months and (2) a single \$1,000 payment two years from today. The bond's value is the present value of the two parts:

$$B_0 = \text{PV(coupon payments)} + \text{PV(par value)} = 30\text{PVAF}_{3.5\%,4} + 1{,}000\text{PVF}_{3.5\%,4}$$

$$B_0 = 30\left[\frac{(1.035)^4 - 1}{(0.035)(1.035)^4}\right] + \frac{1{,}000}{(1.035)^4} = 110.19 + 871.44 = \$981.63$$

A BOND VALUATION FORMULA FOR A BOND WITH SEMIANNUAL COUPON PAYMENTS
To generalize our valuation method to value any bond of this type:

$$B_0 = \text{PV(coupon payments)} + \text{PV(par value)}$$

$$B_0 = \left[\frac{\text{CPN}}{2}\right]\text{PVAF}_{(r/2)\%,2N} + 1{,}000\,\text{PVF}_{(r/2)\%,2N}$$

$$B_0 = \left[\frac{\text{CPN}}{2}\right]\left[\frac{(1 + r/2)^{2N} - 1}{(r/2)(1 + r/2)^{2N}}\right] + \frac{1{,}000}{(1 + r/2)^{2N}} \tag{5.1}$$

where

CPN = the coupon rate times the par value
N = the number of remaining years until maturity
r = the bond's current required return

In practice, bond returns are normally quoted as an APR with semiannual compounding. For example, in Equation (5.1), if the bond's required return is quoted as 10%, that means 5% per six-month period. That is why we use $r/2$ in the formula. Of course, when compounding is more frequent than once a year, the APY (the true, or effective, return) exceeds the APR. A 10% APR with semiannual compounding provides an APY of 10.25% ($= [1.05]^2 - 1 = 0.1025 = 10.25\%$).

CALCULATOR SOLUTION

Data Input	Function Key
2	N
5.0	I
100	PV
0	PMT
−110.25	FV

EXAMPLE Computing the Fair Price of a Ford Credit Bond

A Ford Credit bond has a coupon rate of 8.5% and a remaining maturity of exactly 12 years. If the required return on this bond is 10% APR, what is the bond's current fair price?

The semiannual coupon payments in this case will be $42.50 (= one-half of 8.5% of $1,000 = 85/2), and the semiannual required return is 5%. Using Equation (5.1), the fair price of the bond—the present value of its expected future cash flows—is

$$B_0 = 42.50\text{PVAF}_{5\%,24} + 1000\text{PVF}_{5\%,24} = (42.50)\left[\frac{(1.05)^{24} - 1}{(0.05)(1.05)^{24}}\right] + \frac{1{,}000}{(1.05)^{24}}$$

$$B_0 = 586.44 + 310.07 = \$896.51$$

CALCULATOR SOLUTION

Data Input	Function Key
24	N
5	I
42.50	PMT
1,000	FV
–896.51	PV

Buying this bond for less than $896.51 would be a positive-NPV investment because it is worth more than it cost. Paying more than $896.51 would be a negative-NPV investment. At its fair price of exactly $896.51, buying the bond would be a zero-NPV investment.

Estimating a Bond's Expected Return: The Yield to Maturity

The expected return is the rate of return you expect to earn if you make the investment (buy the bond). A bond's expected return can be estimated by its yield to maturity. The **yield to maturity (YTM)** is the return that will be earned if all the payments are made exactly as promised. Therefore, the YTM is the APR that makes the bond's market price equal the present value of its promised future cash flows.[4]

This relationship is again given by Equation (5.1). But instead of putting in the required return and solving for B_0, we put in the current market price and solve for r, which is the YTM.

EXAMPLE Computing the YTM of a Coca-Cola Bond

What is the YTM of a Coca-Cola bond that is currently selling for $782.50, has a 6% coupon rate, and matures in exactly six years?

The inputs are B_0 = 782.50, CPN/2 = 30.00 (one-half of 6.0% of $1,000), and $2N$ = 12. Putting these into Equation (5.1), we have:

$$782.50 = 30.00\left[\frac{(1 + r/2)^{12} - 1}{(r/2)(1 + r/2)^{12}}\right] + \frac{1{,}000}{(1 + r/2)^{12}}$$

The $r/2$ that solves this equation is 5.528%. r is the YTM.

CALCULATOR SOLUTION

Data Input	Function Key
12	N
–782.50	PV
30.00	PMT
1,000	FV
5.528	I

So the YTM for this bond is two times $r/2$ or 11.056%. Practitioners would say the bond's YTM is about 11.1%.

This example is another case where a financial calculator really pays off. After you key in the inputs, the calculator will automatically perform the trial-and-error process needed to solve for the expected return.[5]

---

[4]The YTM is only an estimate of the expected return because it ignores risk. We discuss bond risk in the next section.

[5]The trial-and-error process without a financial calculator is as follows: Pick a discount rate and calculate the present value. If the present value is above the price, choose a higher discount rate and try again. If the present value is below the price, choose a lower discount rate and try again. Continue trying discount rates until one provides a price that is "close enough" to the target price.

ZERO-COUPON BONDS A **zero-coupon bond** (also called a **pure-discount bond**) is a bond that makes no payments until its maturity. Its par value, which is paid at maturity, is the combined repayment of principal and all the interest over the bond's life. Despite the seeming difference, Equation (5.1) can be used to value a zero-coupon bond, or to determine its YTM.

EXAMPLE Computing the YTM of a J.C. Penney Zero-Coupon Bond

J.C. Penney has a zero-coupon bond that will pay $1,000 at maturity in exactly 20 years. The bond is selling for $178.43. What is its YTM?

Using Equation (5.1) with semiannual compounding[6] and CPN/2 = 0

$$\frac{1{,}000}{(1 + r/2)^{40}} = \$178.43$$

The $r/2$ that solves this is 4.40, so the YTM is 8.8% (= 2[4.4]).

CALCULATOR SOLUTION

Data Input	Function Key
40	N
−178.43	PV
0.00	PMT
1,000	FV
4.403	I

Review

1. A recent bond quote provides a good estimate of a bond's value. How else can you estimate the value of a bond?
2. What is the fair price of a Texaco bond that has an 8% coupon rate, a required return of 10%, and matures in exactly 4 years?
3. What is a yield to maturity (YTM)? How do you compute it?

5.3 BOND RISKINESS

The YTM is the bond's *promised* return, which is its expected return—if the payments are certain. But what if the bond issuer may not make all the payments exactly as promised?

If the firm fails to make a payment, or even if it is just late making a payment, the investor's realized return will be less than the promised return. But the firm is not going to pay more than the contract requires, so the realized return will never be more than the promised return. Therefore, when there is any chance the payments will not be made exactly as promised—any payment risk—the expected return is less than the YTM.

Nevertheless, the YTM is a good estimate of the expected return on high-grade bonds because the payment risk is low. The YTM is not always a good estimate of the expected return on so-called "junk" bonds, named for precisely their higher level of payment risk.

Interest-Rate Risk

Bonds rarely sell for exactly face (par) value, even if that was their original selling price. Whenever a bond's required return changes, the bond's fair price also changes. A bond selling below its par value is called a **discount bond.** A bond selling above its par value is called a **premium bond.**

In Chapter 2, we described the *term structure of interest rates*. The term structure shows how interest rates depend on maturity. We described several factors that affect the term structure. A

[6]We chose semiannual compounding for comparability with other bonds. You could use annual compounding, in which case the calculation would provide the bond's APY.

very important factor is the risk of interest rate changes. As we said, changes in required returns most often result from changes in the expected rate of inflation.

With contractually fixed cash flows (interest and principal payments), a drop in the required return raises the present value, and vice versa. Because of this, owning a bond is risky. This risk, that market prices will fluctuate, exists even if the firm is healthy and makes all of the required payments. This risk is called **interest-rate risk.** Because of interest-rate risk, even bonds that are guaranteed against default have some risk.

A bond can be riskless (or as close as possible to being riskless) *only* in the sense that the future cash flows will occur as promised. If you sell the bond before its maturity, it is likely to be for a price that differs from your purchase price. In fact, a decline in market value can easily exceed the income received from the interest payments while you own the bond!

How much interest-rate risk is there? It depends primarily on the bond's remaining maturity. When all else is equal, interest-rate risk is greater with a longer remaining maturity.

Remaining Maturity and Interest-Rate Risk

The present value of a payment due in the distant future changes more with a change in the required return than does a payment due in the near future. To see this, compare a one-year bond and a ten-year bond, both with an 8% coupon rate. Table 5.2 compares the values of these bonds at the required returns of 4% through 15%.

At 4% per year, the one-year bond is worth \$1,038.83 and the ten-year bond is worth \$1,327.03. At 15% per year, the one-year bond is worth \$937.16 and the ten-year bond is worth

TABLE 5.2
A comparison of bond value sensitivity to changes in the required return.

REQUIRED RETURN	FAIR PRICE FOR AN 8% COUPON BOND WITH A ONE-YEAR REMAINING MATURITY	FAIR PRICE FOR AN 8% COUPON BOND WITH A TEN-YEAR REMAINING MATURITY
4%	\$1,038.83	\$1,327.03
5%	1,028.92	1,233.84
6%	1,019.14	1,148.77
7%	1,009.51	1,071.06
8%	1,000.00	1,000.00
9%	990.64	934.96
10%	981.41	875.38
11%	972.31	820.74
12%	963.33	770.60
13%	954.48	724.54
14%	945.76	682.18
15%	937.16	643.19
Interest rate *increases* from 4% to 15%:		
Decrease in value:	\$101.67	\$683.84
Percentage decrease:	9.8%	51.5%
Interest rate *increases* from 8% to 12%:		
Decrease in value:	\$36.67	\$229.40
Percentage decrease:	3.7%	22.9%
Interest rate *decreases* from 8% to 4%:		
Increase in value:	\$38.83	\$327.03
Percentage increase:	3.9%	32.7%

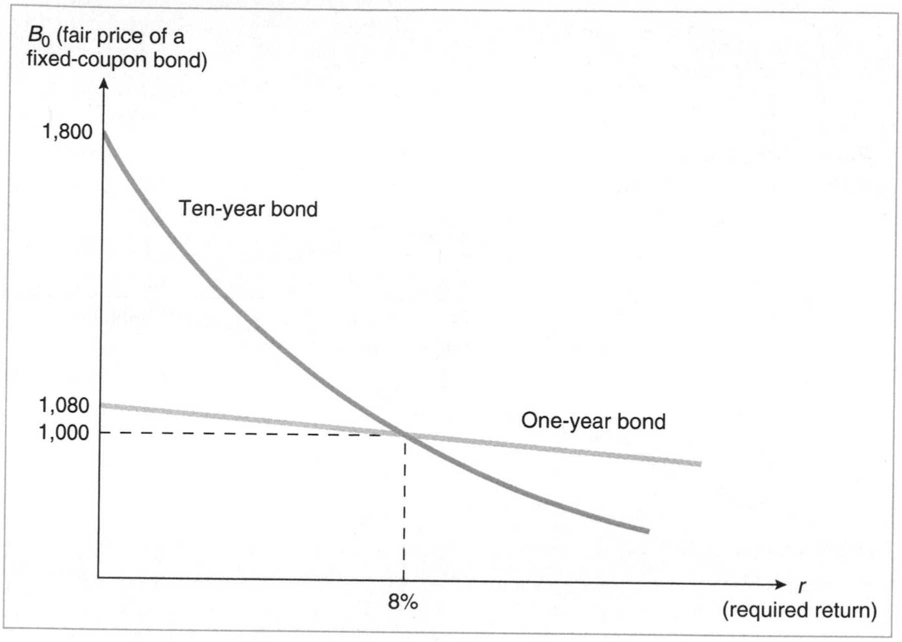

FIGURE 5.4
A comparison of bond value sensitivity to changes in the required return.

\$643.19. Therefore, an increase in the required return on these bonds from 4% to 15% causes less than a 10% drop in the value of the one-year bond. In contrast, that same rate change causes more than a 50% drop in the value of the ten-year bond.

Figure 5.4 graphs the values of these same bonds as a function of required return. The slope of the curve for the value of the ten-year bond is much steeper. As a result, any change in the required return will cause a larger change in its value than in the value of the one-year bond.

Bond Values, Maturity, and Default

Although a bond's value may vary over time, it is constrained by its *terminal value.* In most cases, a bond's terminal value is simply its par value to be paid at maturity. As a result, the bond's price will tend to converge to its par value as the bond matures. Therefore, although a bond's value may fluctuate (due to changes in interest rates), the typical path of a bond's value is somewhat constrained because it ends at its par value. This concept is illustrated in Figure 5.5 by hypothetical price paths for both a discount bond (selling below par) and a premium bond (selling above par).

The price paths shown in Figure 5.5 ignore two alternative outcomes: *default* and *early repayment.* We consider the possibility of default now, and discuss the issue of early repayment in the next section.

Suppose there is a significant chance that the firm won't be able to pay off its bonds at maturity. If you were going to purchase one of these bonds, how would you take this potential problem into account? You would offer a lower price. Because others will have the same reaction, the bond will be worth less than it would be if full repayment were not in doubt. If the firm did pay off the bonds on time, you would earn a higher return (having paid less for the bond). But this possibility is your reward for taking the higher risk that you may not get the full promised payments on time. This is another illustration of the Principle of Risk-Return Trade-Off.

If repayment continues to be in doubt as the bond approaches maturity, the bond's price will converge to a lower value. The bond's price at maturity will be the discounted value of the payment the bondholders expect to receive eventually (when the firm makes a settlement after defaulting).

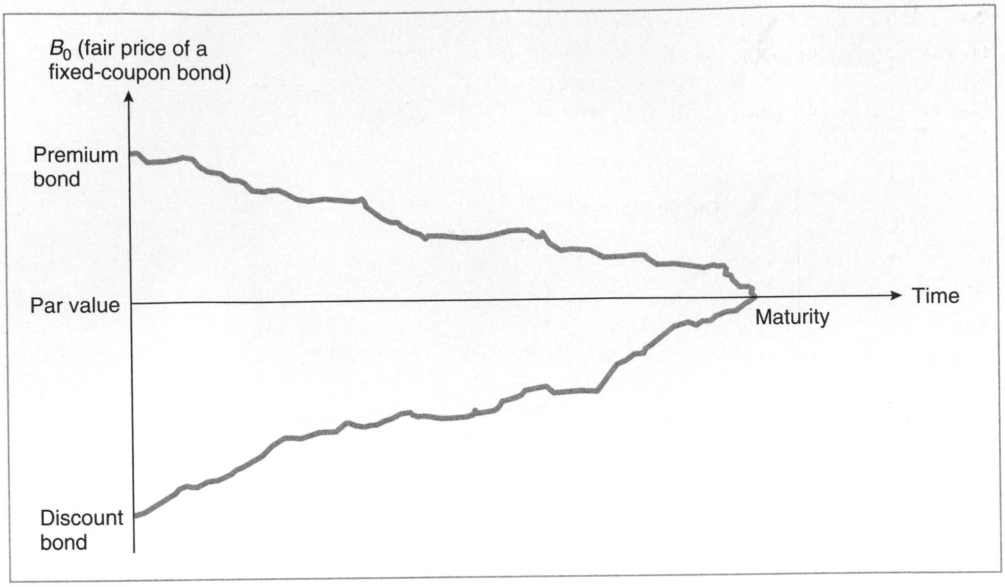

FIGURE 5.5
Hypothetical price paths for a discount bond and a premium bond.

Bond Values and Call Provisions

The call provision (the firm's option to pay off the bonds early) can also change the bond's terminal value and its maturity. This is because the firm can repay the bonds early by paying the call price to the bondholders. If you know this, you would not pay much more than the call price for the bond, because the firm could call the bonds right after you buy one.

For example, suppose you could buy a bond for $1,230, but it could be called for $1,080 anytime after you buy it. If you pay $1,230 for the bond today, tomorrow you could be forced to sell it back to the firm for only $1,080, producing a one-day loss of $150, or −12.2%. So it is clear you do not want to pay much more than the call price for a bond.

But what if the bond can't be called now but could be called five years from today? In such cases, practitioners compute the **yield to call (YTC)** on bonds selling above their call price. The YTC is a bond's promised return, assuming the firm will pay off the bonds (pay the bondholders the call price) on a specified call date.

EXAMPLE Computing the YTC of an IBM Bond

Suppose IBM has a bond that can't be called today but can be called in three years at a call price of $1,090. The bond has a remaining maturity of 18 years and a coupon rate of 12%. It currently sells for $1,175.97. What is the bond's YTC? In other words, what return will be earned from buying this bond today for $1,175.97, if the firm makes all promised payments and redeems the bonds in three years by paying $1,090?

Once again we apply Equation (5.1), but with the call price in place of the par value. The inputs are $B_0 = 1{,}175.97$, CPN/2 is 60.00 (one-half of 12% of $1,000), future value is 1,090, and $2N = 6$ (3 years until the call):

CALCULATOR SOLUTION

Data Input	Function Key
6	N
−1,175.97	PV
60.00	PMT
1,090	FV
4.00	I

$$\$1{,}175.97 = 60.00\left[\frac{(1+r/2)^6 - 1)}{(r/2)(1+r/2)^6}\right] + \frac{1{,}090}{(1+r/2)^6}$$

The $r/2$ that solves the equation is 4.0%. Therefore, this bond's YTC is 8.0%.

If IBM does not call the bond three years from now, but continues to make all the required payments throughout the life of the bond, the realized return will be the YTM, which is higher than the YTC. Of course, that is a "big if" you might not want to count on!

You can verify that the bond's YTM is currently 9.89%.

CALCULATOR SOLUTION

Data Input	Function Key
36	N
−1,175.97	PV
60.00	PMT
1,000	FV
4.94	I

The key point in the IBM bond example is that if the firm calls the bond at its earliest chance, you will earn only an 8% yield, not the 9.89% YTM. This is an important risk to take into account. This risk of calling is why the YTC is, and the YTM is not, the appropriate measure of return when a bond is selling above its call price.

Of course, we cannot know for certain now if the bonds will be called. As with every option, the outcome is contingent on the decision of the optionholder—in this case, the firm. And that decision in turn depends on other contingencies—in this case, future market interest rates.

Other Bond Risks

There are several other risks that bondholders are taking, including inflation risk, currency risk, and marketability risk.

INFLATION RISK Bond payments are stated in nominal dollars. That is, they ignore inflation—and the decreasing purchasing power it causes. Current inflationary expectations are built into the required return. If inflation turns out to be less than expected, the future cash flows will have more purchasing power than had been expected, which would be a gain. On the other hand, if inflation turns out to be more than expected, the future cash flows will have less purchasing power, a loss. Fixed income securities can have considerable inflation risk.

CURRENCY RISK Many people invest in foreign securities. Payments from foreign securities are usually made in a foreign currency. If the value of that currency changes, relative to the value of a dollar, the dollar-denominated value of your investment will change. For example, suppose you buy a Japanese bond that makes payments in Yen. If the Yen appreciates (depreciates) relative to the dollar, the bond's payments will be worth more (less) when you convert them into dollars.

MARKETABILITY RISK The volume of trading in corporate bonds is lower than the volume in common stocks. Bonds are less liquid and have larger trading costs. This reduces the bond's return. If a bond's liquidity changes significantly, the bond's required return will change to reflect the change in trading costs. The possibility of significant changes in liquidity creates marketability risk, which affects bond values.

Review

1. Define interest-rate risk, default risk, call risk, inflation risk, currency risk, and marketability risk.
2. Suppose you buy a bond that has some default risk. If the bond does not default, is the realized return above or below the expected return?
3. What is a YTC, yield to call? How is it different from a YTM?

5.4 STOCK VALUATION

Stocks are of two basic types, common stock and preferred stock. *Common stock* represents the residual ownership interest in a firm. Collectively, the common stockholders are the owners of the firm. They elect the firm's directors. In the event the firm is liquidated, they share proportionately in what is left after the bondholders and other higher-legal-priority claimants are legally satisfied (for example, the government gets any taxes owed).

The common stockholders may receive cash dividends, which the firm pays out of its cash, presumably from profits it earns. But dividends are not a contractual obligation of the firm. As a result, the common stockholders bear more risk than the bondholders. There is greater uncertainty about the payments they will receive. In fact, common stock has no explicitly promised future payments. Of course, we expect the firm to pay cash dividends to its common stockholders, at least at some point in the future.

Preferred Stock

Preferred stock has a claim higher in priority than the firm's common stock but lower in priority than the firm's debt. There is a stated cash dividend rate, which is like the stated interest rate on debt. But if the firm fails to pay the dividends, the preferred stockholders cannot force the firm into bankruptcy. Compared to common stockholders, preferred stockholders typically have only very limited rights to vote on corporate matters.

Preferred stock is therefore a hybrid; it falls between bonds and common stock in the legal-priority hierarchy of financial securities. The risk of preferred stock also falls between that of the firm's common stock and that of its bonds. Of course, a firm that wants to keep a good financial reputation will make every effort to pay its preferred stock obligations.

Preferred stock payment obligations are typically viewed like debt obligations, and they look like debt payment obligations. As a result, the bond valuation model can also be used to value preferred stock—under the assumption that the firm will meet its preferred stock payment obligations. However, an adjustment is required. Preferred stock pays dividends quarterly, whereas bonds pay interest semiannually.

EXAMPLE Valuing New York Edison Preferred Stock

New York Edison has preferred stock outstanding that pays a \$2.00 per quarter dividend. New York Edison must repay the \$100 par value 20 years from today. The market price of the stock is \$97.50. What is the stock's YTM?

The formula is like Equation (5.1), but with quarterly payments and compounding:

$$\text{Preferred stock value} = (\text{Coupon payment})\text{PVAF}_{(r/4)\%,4N} + (\text{Par value})\text{PVF}_{(r/4)\%,4N}$$

$$\$97.50 = 2.00\left[\frac{(1+r/4)^{4N}-1}{(r/4)(1+r/4)^{4N}}\right] + \frac{100}{(1+r/4)^{4N}}$$

The YTM on this preferred stock equals 4 times the quarterly rate, or 8.256%.

CALCULATOR SOLUTION

Data Input	Function Key
80	N
−97.50	PV
2.00	PMT
100	FV
2.064	I

Some preferred stocks never mature. Such a perpetual preferred stock therefore has no final principal payment and is expected to pay dividends every period into the future. In such situations, the valuation formula collapses to the simpler perpetuity formula (Equation 4.9), and stock value equals dividend/required return.

EXAMPLE Valuing United Airlines Perpetual Preferred Stock

United Airlines has perpetual preferred stock outstanding that pays a \$0.40 quarterly dividend. It has a required return of 12% APR (3% per quarter). What is the stock worth?

Using Equation (4.9), with PMT = 0.40 and $r = 0.03$, the stock's value is

$$\text{Stock value} = \text{PVA}_{\text{perpetuity}} = \frac{\text{dividend}}{r} = \frac{0.40}{0.03} = \$13.33$$

Valuing Common Stock

There are two important differences between the factors for valuing common stock and those for valuing bonds. First, because corporations have potentially infinite life, common stocks have infinite lives: Unlike most bonds, corporations never have to redeem common stock. When an investor sells a stock, its value depends on future expected cash flows, which theoretically continue forever.

Second, as previously mentioned, the future cash flows are not explicitly promised. The future cash flows must be estimated on the basis of expectations about the firm's future earnings and dividend policy.

From a financial viewpoint, common stock value depends *entirely* on the cash flows the firm will distribute to its owners and the required return on such cash flows. This is a strong statement, but it is the fundamental way in which stocks are valued.

The Fair Price of a Share of Common Stock

When you own a stock, you know that its future sale price can largely determine your profit or loss. During your investment horizon, you expect to receive cash dividends plus the sale price at the end of the horizon.

Let the value of a share of common stock today be P_0. The expected future cash dividends are $D_1, D_2, \ldots, D_n$, for time periods $1, 2, \ldots, n$. The cash dividend just paid by the firm is D_0. P_0 is the present value of the expected future cash dividends plus the present value of P_n, the expected future cash sale price of the share of stock at time n, or

$$P_0 = \frac{D_1}{(1+r)^1} + \frac{D_2}{(1+r)^2} + \cdots + \frac{D_n}{(1+r)^n} + \frac{P_n}{(1+r)^n} \tag{5.2}$$

where r is the stock's required return.[7]

If Equation (5.2) looks suspiciously like the bond valuation model, that's because it involves the same valuation concept: The price of a financial security equals the present value of its expected future cash flows. For a share of common stock, these are its periodic dividends plus a terminal amount. Valuing a share of common stock is more difficult than valuing a bond because its expected future cash flows are so uncertain.

A stock's value has two components. Its dividends are often called the income component. Cash dividends are similar to other income sources. The second component is the change in value, which is often called the capital gain component. Capital gain represents the growth (or loss) in stock value from the time of purchase until the time of sale.

[7]For now, we are ignoring tax considerations and treating cash dividends as though payments occur annually rather than quarterly as they typically do, and thus compounding yearly. These simplifications might significantly affect valuation in practice, but they are useful simplifications that allow us to concentrate on the important concepts.

For an investor who has a one-year horizon, $n = 1$, the value of the stock is:

$$P_0 = \frac{D_1}{(1+r)^1} + \frac{P_1}{(1+r)^1}$$

For an investor with a two-year horizon, $n = 2$, the value of the stock is:

$$P_0 = \frac{D_1}{(1+r)^1} + \frac{D_2}{(1+r)^2} + \frac{P_2}{(1+r)^2}$$

and so forth.

EXAMPLE Investing in Pepperidge Farm Common Stock

Steve Wyatt is considering an investment in Pepperidge Farm common stock. He expects Pepperidge Farm to pay a \$1.48 dividend in one year and \$1.80 in two years. He believes Pepperidge Farm will sell for \$26.00 in two years. What is the stock worth if its required return is 12%?

The present value of Steve's investment is:

$$P_0 = \frac{1.48}{(1.12)^1} + \frac{1.80}{(1.12)^2} + \frac{26.00}{(1.12)^2} = 1.32 + 1.43 + 20.73 = \$23.48$$

So the stock is worth \$23.48 to Steve.

You might wonder how Steve estimated that the stock would sell for \$26 in two years. That is, what determines the stock price at time n? The answer is that the value at time n is once again the present value (as of time n) of the expected future (after time n) dividends and eventual selling price.

Therefore, P_0 depends *directly* on the dividends the investor receives for n periods and *indirectly* on dividends after time n. That is, the dividends after time n determine the stock price at n. This concept holds regardless of how many times the stock might be sold in the future. For example, Joe can buy the stock now. Joe can sell it to Mary in the future. Mary can later sell it to Gordo. Gordo can sell it to you. You can sell it to someone else, and so forth. At any point in time, the stock's value depends on the dividends and future sale price the investor expects to receive. But the expected future sale price in turn depends on subsequent dividends and another selling price. Conceptually, then, the expected future sale price drops out.

As a result, a stock's fair price can be expressed as the present value of *all* its expected future dividends, that is, of an *infinite* stream of expected future cash dividend payments, or

$$P_0 = \frac{D_1}{(1+r)^1} + \frac{D_2}{(1+r)^2} + \cdots = \sum_{t=1}^{\infty} \frac{D_t}{(1+r)^t} \tag{5.3}$$

Equation (5.3) is a very general expression for the value of a share of stock. It does not assume any specific pattern of future cash dividends. And it makes no specific assumption about when the share of stock will be sold; the share might be sold any number of future times—or never.

What Determines Future Dividends?

If the value of a share of common stock is based on expected future cash dividends, a logical next question is: What determines future dividends? There are two factors that determine cash dividends: (1) the firm's earnings and (2) its dividend policy. A firm's future profitability ultimately determines how much income the firm has available to distribute as dividends.

The decision to distribute cash dividends to stockholders is made by the board of directors. The board must choose between either reinvesting or paying out the earnings as dividends. A firm's **dividend policy** guides its payment of cash dividends.

A simple but convenient way to describe a dividend policy is to compute the payout ratio. The **payout ratio** expresses the firm's cash dividend as a proportion of its earnings:

$$\text{Payout ratio} = \frac{\text{Dividends}}{\text{Earnings}}$$

Although a payout ratio is an oversimplification of a firm's dividend policy, we can use this measure to analyze stock valuation. Chapter 17 examines dividend policy in more depth.

Review

1. Why is preferred stock often called a hybrid security?
2. Why is the bond valuation model useful for valuing preferred stock?
3. What are the two components of a stock's value?
4. How can a share of common stock be valued without regard to a future sale price?
5. Why might a payout ratio be a kind of indicator of a firm's emphasis on growth?

5.5 APPLYING THE DIVIDEND VALUATION MODEL

Investors look at a firm (and its stock) as a source of growing wealth. Therefore, they are interested in the underlying rate of growth of a firm and the implications of that growth rate for the stock's value. We are going to assume cash dividends will change at some average rate g from one period to the next, forever into the future. This characterization of cash dividends is very useful. It is general enough to apply to many situations (for example, the rate of change can be positive or negative). It is also a good *approximation* of actual patterns of dividends.

Although an infinite horizon may seem to be unbelievable (after all, corporations do not really live forever, or at least none has yet), it is a good approximation. This is because most of a stock's value is determined by the value of its nearest dividends. As with any cash flow, the further in the future a dividend will occur, the smaller is its present value. As Figure 5.6 shows, very distant future dividends contribute little to the present value of the stock. For example, the present value at 10% of a $2 dividend, expected 60 years from now, is less than a penny.

CALCULATOR SOLUTION

Data Input	Function Key
60	N
10	I
0	PMT
2.00	FV
−0.007	PV

The Constant Growth Model

Assume cash dividend payments change at the rate of g from one period to the next forever into the future. For example, suppose the latest year's dividends totaled $1.00 and dividends are growing 5% per year. Future dividends would then total $1.05 next year, $1.1025 the year after, $1.158 in the third year, and so on. Then the dividend payment for period t, D_t, can be expressed as the previous dividend, D_{t-1}, times (1 plus g). Thus, D_t can be expressed as a function of any dividend between now and time t, or

$$D_t = D_0(1 + g)^t$$

If each future dividend in Equation (5.3) is represented in this way, P_0, the current price, can be rewritten as the sum of the growing dividends, discounted by the required return, r:

$$P_0 = \frac{D_0(1 + g)}{(1 + r)} + \frac{D_0(1 + g)^2}{(1 + r)^2} + \frac{D_0(1 + g)^3}{(1 + r)^3} + \cdots = D_0\sum_{t=1}^{\infty}\frac{(1 + g)^t}{(1 + r)^t}$$

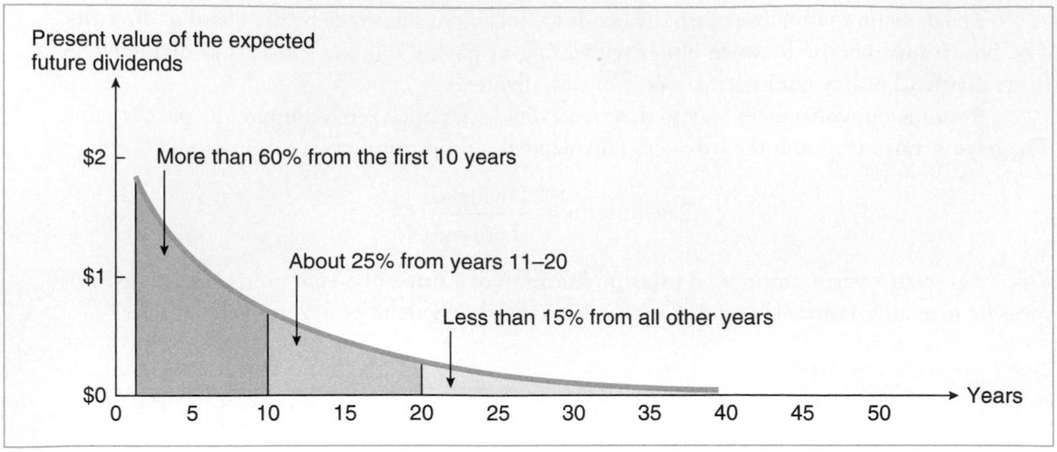

FIGURE 5.6
Relative contribution to stock price of near and distant future dividends at a 10% required return.

This is an infinite geometric series, like the perpetuity we described in Chapter 4 (Equation 4.9). This one simplifies to

$$P_0 = \frac{D_1}{(r - g)}$$

In this situation, D_1 is a *growing* perpetuity. It grows at the rate of g forever. A positive growth rate ($g > 0$) makes the denominator less than r. This in turn makes the present value, P_0, larger than it would be if the perpetual cash flow were not growing. The positive growth increases the value of the stock. Logically, the higher the growth rate, the greater the stock's value.

We can use this same notion to determine a stock's fair price at any point in time. That price, P_t, can be expressed in two different ways. The first is in terms of the next period's dividend (D_{t+1}), the growth rate (g), and the required return (r), whenever dividends from D_{t+1} on are expected to grow by g every period forever into the future. So whenever g is expected to be constant from time $t + 1$ on, P_t can be written as

$$P_t = \frac{D_{t+1}}{(r - g)} \tag{5.4}$$

The second way to express P_t is in terms of the previous period's price, P_{t-1}. By substituting $(1 + g)D_t$ for D_{t+1} and P_{t-1} for $D_t/(r - g)$ into the above equation, we get:

$$P_t = (1 + g)P_{t-1}$$

Therefore, just like dividends, P_t also grows by g each period.

EXAMPLE Valuing a Constant Growth Stock: Procter & Gamble

Suppose Procter & Gamble (P&G) is expected to pay a dividend of $3.00 next year on its common stock, the required return is 12%, and dividend payments are expected to grow at 4% per year forever. What is the fair price for a share of P&G common stock?

Using Equation (5.4) with $t = 0$, $D_1 = \$3.00$, $r = 0.12$, and $g = 0.04$, we have

$$P_0 = \frac{3.00}{(0.12 - 0.04)} = \$37.50$$

What if P&G had no growth prospects whatsoever? Then what would a share be worth?

Using Equation (5.4) again, this time with $t = 0$, $D_1 = \$3.00$, $r = 0.12$, and $g = 0$, we have

$$P_0 = \frac{3.00}{(0.12 - 0)} = \$25.00$$

So in this example, the 4% growth increases stock value by 50%, from \$25.00 to \$37.50.

AN IMPORTANT COMMENT ON THE RELATIONSHIP BETWEEN g AND R One of the first questions about Equation (5.4) is what happens if g equals r, or if g is greater than r. The question arises because if we blindly apply Equation (5.4), it would imply that the stock's value is infinite if g equals r and that it is negative if g is greater than r. Neither situation makes economic sense. A faster-growing firm is riskier and will have a higher required return, so the larger g is, the larger r will be.

Quite simply, g can never be greater than or equal to r. Although we won't prove this, consider the following argument: g is the rate at which cash dividends are expected to grow *every period, forever.* r is the stock's required rate of return, essentially its earnings. In the long run, dividends are paid from earnings. For dividends to grow at g, earnings must grow just as fast. Of course, it is easy to imagine very high earnings growth. However, any such situation involves a *limited* time period. Earnings cannot grow faster than the economy forever, otherwise the firm's total revenue would equal the economy's total output. In the limit, the firm would become the entire economy. After that, it could not grow faster than itself!

One other comment concerning g might be helpful. Even though g acts like a discount rate in that it compounds amounts, it is a *growth* rate. Be careful to distinguish between the two; it is easy to mix up the rates when you are working problems.

Estimating a Stock's Required Return Using the Constant Growth Model

For a publicly traded stock, the most recent price paid is the best available estimate of its value. This price can be used in the constant growth model, Equation (5.4), to estimate the required return for a stock. A stock's required return is often called its **capitalization rate.**

Rearranging Equation (5.4) provides a model for computing a stock's expected return. Based on the Principle of Capital Market Efficiency, a stock's expected return is in turn a good estimate of its required return, or capitalization rate:

$$r = \frac{D_1}{P_0} + g \tag{5.5}$$

Earlier, we referred to the two components of a stock's value: income and capital gains. You see these in Equation (5.5). The income component is also called the **dividend yield,** which is the dividend divided by the price. The capital gains component, or **capital gains yield,** is g. The total return is simply the sum of the two.

EXAMPLE Estimating International Paper's Capitalization Rate

Suppose you look in today's *Wall Street Journal* and see that International Paper's stock price is \$51.00 and its last year's dividend was \$1.52. If International Paper's dividend growth rate is expected to be 5.25% per year forever, what is the capitalization rate on its common stock?

First, note that next year's dividend, D_1, is expected to be \$1.60 (= 1.52[1.0525]). Then, with a price of 51 for P_0, and $g = 0.0525$ in Equation (5.5), the expected return is

$$r = \frac{D_1}{P_0} + g = \frac{1.60}{51.00} + 0.0525 = 0.0315 + 0.0525 = 0.084$$

So the implied capitalization rate, our estimate of International Paper's required return, is 8.4%. This rate consists of a 3.15% dividend yield plus a 5.25% capital gains yield.

Valuing a Supernormal Growth Stock

Consider a firm that is currently experiencing high dividend growth, which is expected to continue for some finite time. After this period of "supernormal" growth, dividend growth will be at a "normal" rate forever into the future. We can compute the value of this firm's stock by using Equation (5.2) and breaking the dividend stream into two parts: a normal growth part, which goes on forever into the future, and a supernormal growth part, which is finite. The normal growth part makes up the sale price, P_n, which can be computed using Equation (5.4). The supernormal growth part is D_1 through D_{n-1}. Applying Equation (5.2), then, P_0 equals the present value of the two parts.

EXAMPLE Valuing a Supernormal Growth Stock: Meridian Research

Sales at Meridian Research are growing 80% per year. This high sales growth rate is expected to translate into a 25% growth rate in cash dividends for each of the next four years. After that, the dividend growth rate is expected to be 5% per year forever. The latest annual dividend, paid yesterday, is \$0.75. The stock's required return is 22%. What is a share of Meridian common stock worth?

First, compute the expected future cash dividends, which are

Time	0	1	2	3	4	5	. . .
Dividend	0.75	0.938	1.172	1.465	1.831	1.923	. . .
Growth	25%	25%	25%	25%	5%	5%	. . .

Second, compute the stock's fair price at a future point in time, using Equation (5.4). To be able to use Equation (5.4), you must pick a point after the dividend growth rate has become constant forever. Using dividend 4, which is the first dividend that will grow at the constant rate of $g = 5\%$, the hypothetical sale value of the stock, P_3, is

$$P_3 = \frac{D_4}{r - g} + \frac{1.831}{0.22 - 0.05} = \$10.771$$

Finally, compute the present value of the expected future sale price and add that to the present value of all the expected cash dividends between now and then. Using Equation (5.2), with $n = 3$, we have

$$P_0 = \frac{0.938}{(1.22)} + \frac{1.172}{(1.22)^2} + \frac{1.465}{(1.22)^3} = \frac{10.771}{(1.22)^3}$$

$$= 0.768 + 0.787 + 0.807 + 4.394 = \$8.294$$

Note that if we choose a hypothetical sale point that is after period 3, we will get the same present value for the stock. Try it using period 4.

Valuing an Erratic Growth Stock

Now consider a firm that is expected to have erratic dividend growth for some finite time, followed by a normal rate forever into the future. We can again break the dividend stream into two parts and use Equation (5.2). In fact, we can generalize our procedure further.

Suppose expected dividend growth varies for n periods but is constant at g forever after that. At time n, the dividend D_n, can be used to calculate a price at time $n - 1$, using Equation (5.4):

$$P_{n-1} = \frac{D_n}{r - g}$$

We can now use this expression in Equation (5.2), which gives

$$P_0 = \frac{D_1}{(1 + r)} + \frac{D_2}{(1 + r)^2} + \cdots + \frac{D_{n-1}}{(1 + r)^{n-1}} + \frac{D_n}{(1 + r)^{n-1}(r - g)} \tag{5.6}$$

Equation (5.6) is a general formula for valuing common stocks with *any* variable dividend growth rates over a finite time period that is followed by a constant growth rate forever. It simply combines Equation (5.4) and (5.2) into a single formula.

EXAMPLE Valuing an Erratic Growth Stock: Novell

Novell is currently in a building stage. It is not expected to change its annual cash dividend while new projects are being developed over the next three years. Its dividend was $1 last year and is to be $1 for each of the next three years. After the projects have been developed, earnings are expected to grow at a high rate for two years as the sales resulting from the new projects are realized. The higher earnings are expected to result in a 40% increase in dividends for two years. After these two extraordinary increases in dividends, the dividend growth rate is expected to be 3% per year forever. If Novell's common stock required return is 12%, what is a share worth today?

As with our Meridian Research example, first compute the expected future dividends.

Time	0	1	2	3	4	5	. . .
Dividend	1.00	1.00	1.00	1.00	1.40	1.96	. . .
Growth	0%	0%	0%	40%	40%	3%	. . .

Second, note that D_5 is where the growth rate in the dividends is expected to become constant forever. This is the earliest point that satisfies the constant growth assumption. Using Equation (5.6) with $D_5 = \$1.96$, $g = 3\%$, and $r = 12\%$, we have

$$P_0 = \frac{1.00}{(1.12)} + \frac{1.00}{(1.12)^2} + \frac{1.00}{(1.12)^3} + \frac{1.40}{(1.12)^4} + \frac{1.96}{(1.12)^4(0.12 - 0.03)} = \$17.13$$

Review

1. With constant dividend growth, as in Equation (5.4), what is the relationship between one dividend and the next, such as between D_t and D_{t+1}? What is the relationship between one price and the previous price?
2. Why is it that g can never equal or exceed r when dividend growth is constant forever?
3. What is a stock's capitalization rate?
4. Explain in your own words how Equation (5.6) combines Equations (5.4) and (5.2).

5.6 OBTAINING COMMON STOCK INFORMATION

Suppose you wanted to get information about a particular common stock, say PepsiCo, makers of Pepsi-Cola. You could look in a newspaper, such as the *Wall Street Journal* or *The New York Times,* and find New York Stock Exchange quotes like those in Figure 5.7.

From the PepsiCo quote, you know PepsiCo's

1. *Year-to-date % change.* The percentage change in PepsiCo's stock price for the calendar year to date is 4.5%.
2. *Latest 52 weeks' price range.* The highest and lowest prices paid in the prior 52 weeks for a share of PepsiCo common stock were $53.50 and $43.08, respectively.
3. *Stock symbol.* PepsiCo's stock symbol on the NYSE is PEP.
4. *Dividend rate.* PepsiCo's annual dividend rate (based on the latest quarter's dividend) is $0.60. The f indicates that the annual rate increased on the latest declaration.
5. *Dividend yield.* PepsiCo's dividend yield is 1.2%, which is the dividend rate divided by the closing price (= 0.60/50.90).
6. *Price-earnings ratio.* PepsiCo's P/E is 34; it is the closing price divided by the latest 12 months' earnings per share.
7. *Trading volume.* 4,222,400 shares (= [42,224]100) changed ownership yesterday.
8. *Closing price.* The last price paid yesterday for PepsiCo common stock was $50.90.
9. *Change in closing price.* Yesterday's closing price was $0.67 higher than the previous day's closing price.

A variety of additional symbols and notation can provide further information in the quote. For example, the s indicates that the firm had a stock split or stock dividend, or cash or cash equivalent distribution, amounting to 10% or more during the past 52 weeks. The high and low prices have been adjusted to reflect this. Other notations indicate such things as a new 52-week high or low price, or that dividends and earnings are given in Canadian dollars.

You can find out more about these and other items by looking in a **stock and bond guide,** such as *Standard & Poor's.* Additional information published in a guide includes the number of shares outstanding and the stated dividend rate for preferred stock. Figure 5.8 illustrates a page from a stock and bond guide.

From this page, we know that

1. PepsiCo has 1,749,594,000 shares of common stock outstanding and no publicly traded preferred stock.
2. PepsiCo has paid $0.57 per share in dividends this year so far.
3. PepsiCo has $2.559 billion in long-term debt.
4. PepsiCo had $2.630 billion in cash and equivalents on September 8 of the year.

FIGURE 5.7
Hypothetical stock quote with PepsiCo highlighted.

YTD % CHG	52-WEEK HI	52-WEEK LO	STOCK (SYM)	DIV	YLD %	PE	VOL 100s	CLOSE	NET CHG
−13.2	29.50	18.64	Penny JC **JCP**	.50	2.1	56	24351	23.35	−1.15
49.9	21.75	9	PennzQuak **PZL**	.10	.5	dd	6258	21.66	...
−8.2	19.39	8	Pepboys **PBY**	.27	1.7	20	6179	15.75	−0.51
37.9	34.80	19.48	PepsiBttlng **PBG** s	.04	.1	28	17109	32.40	−0.93
4.5	53.50	43.08	PepsiCo **PEP**	.60f	1.2	34	42224	50.90	0.67
−59.9	38.27	11.78	PerkinElmer **PKI** s	.28	2.0	...	3913	14.03	−0.05
13.7	28.80	21.16	PetroCnda g **PCZ**	.40g	...	...	204	27.86	−0.15
−12.7	45	34	Pfizer **PFE**	.52	1.5	27	128060	34.79	−0.70
20.2	56.69	43	PhlpMor **MO**	2.32	4.2	13	39763	55.10	−0.01

FIGURE 5.8

A page from a Standard & Poor's Stock and Bond Guide with PepsiCo highlighted. Standard & Poor's *Stock and Bond Guide,* 2002 Edition, pp. 148–149.

¶ S&P 500 # MidCap 400 ✤ SmallCap 600 • Options Index	Ticker	Name of Issue (Call Price of Ptd. Stocks)	Market	Com. Rank. & Ptd. Rating	Inst. Hold Cos	Inst. Hold Shs. (000)	Principal Business	Price Range 1971-99 High	1971-99 Low	2000 High	2000 Low	2001 High	2001 Low	Dec. Sales in 100s	December, 2001 Last Sale or Bid High	Low	Last	% Div Yield	P-E Ratio	EPS 5 Yr Growth	% Annualized Total Return 12 Mo	36 Mo	60 Mo
¶1 •[1]	PAYX	✓Paychex Inc	NNM	A+	927	213689	Computer payroll acctg svcs	29.91	0.13	61.25	24.16	51.00	28.27	604992	39.47	34.17	34.85	1.3	48	31	−27.6	16.0	29.0
#2 •[2]	PSS	✓Payless ShoeSource	NY,P	NR	284	18936	Footwear retailer U.S.	77.00	20.00	71.68	38.75	78.22	51.50	26689	56.70	52.70	56.15	...	12	11	−20.6	5.8	8.4
3 •[3]	PCCC	✓PC Connection	NNM	NR	76	4797	Direct mkt computers/pds	26.66	4.00	70.25	8.62	20.56	6.00	13546	17.79	14.00	14.83	...	34	...	42.9	8.1	...
4	MALL	PC Mall	NNM	C	19	1160	Direct mkt computer products	63.00	3.00	15.50	0.50	4.20	0.62	7451	4.20	2.85	4.06	...	9	57	261	−49.5	−11.1
✤5 •[4]	PCTI	✓PC-Tel Inc	NNM	NR	124	14179	Dvlp data communic solutions	54.00	17.00	98.00	8.43	12.50	6.37	29546	10.50	8.57	9.71	...	d	...	−9.7	...	...
6	PDSG	✓PDS Gaming	NSC	B−	5	175	Finance gaming eqp.furniture	10.50	1.00	2.75	1.00	5.29	1.21	8393	3.38	2.45	3.20	...	8	2	163	0.8	12.8
7 •[5]	BTU	✓Peabody Energy	NY	NR	164	13418	Coal exploration/mining	...	...	...	...	38.05	22.20	39536	28.70	24.55	28.19	1.4	..	...	...	...	...
8	PAE	✓Peace Arch Entertainment'B'	AS,To	NR	1	5.5	Dvlp mkt TV programming	5.18	2.75	7.25	1.25	3.62	0.50	1742	0.73	0.50	0.61	...	d	...	−68.5	...	...
9	PGC	Peapack-Gladstone Fin'l	AS	NR	11	537	Commercial bank, N.J.	...	...	41.81	31.81	42.27	32.27	116	37.25	36.50	36.50B	1.6	15	...	1.2	...	...
10	PSO	✓Pearson pc ADR[51]	NY	NR	29	9552	Fin'l, media publishing/TV	...	...	30.56	22.37	26.25	9.28	17155	13.02	10.95	12.28	2.5	34	...	−46.7	...	...
11	PY	✓Pechiney ADS[52]	NY,Ch,Ph,P	NR	20	4676	Aluminum production/products	36.43	14.12	41.25	16.37	30.00	16.05	1651	26.05	24.00	25.18	1.5	13	NM	12.2	18.0	6.7
12	PIII	✓PECO II	NNM	NR	72	7427	Mfr communic pwr sys/eq	...	...	47.50	12.00	25.75	2.96	7450	6.44	5.25	5.96	...	..	...	−77.0	...	...
✤13 •[6]	PDX	✓Pediatrix Medical Group	NY,Ch	NR	224	16307	Physician mgmt svs-NICU	65.56	6.00	25.68	6.43	43.17	18.98	70169	38.78	31.45	33.92	...	28	−2	41.0	−17.3	−1.7
14	PMFG	Peerless Mfg	NNM	B	16	591	Mfr Industrial filters	12.50	0.71	12.18	5.75	23.50	6.25	2856	18.73	15.02	18.05	...	12	34	133	51.9	27.7
15 •[7]	PRLS	Peerless Systems	NNM	NR	26	4719	Digital document pd softwr	24.37	2.81	8.25	0.43	2.27	0.50	25230	1.50	0.91	1.25	...	d	Neg	29.0	−47.2	−40.7
16 •[8]	PGTV	✓Pegasus Communications'A'	NNM	NR	236	34418	Broadcast/satellite/cable T.V.	51.37	4.06	77.50	18.25	32.75	4.69	84563	11.17	9.20	10.41	...	5	NM	−59.6	−6.0	8.7
17	PEGA	Pegasystems Inc	NNM	NR	32	4527	Customer svc mgmt softwr	40.00	3.43	26.06	1.81	6.43	1.93	3501	4.60	3.75	4.35	...	87	−49	88.1	1.5	−32.1
18	PFI	Pelican Financial	AS	NR	3	58	Finance & banking services	6.81	3.29	4.77	1.36	6.75	1.93	516	5.70	5.00	5.64	...	7	...	267	...	...
19	PAGI	✓Pemco Aviation Group	NNM	B−	14	690	Aircraft maintenance/systems	24.50	1.12	18.93	7.87	18.00	8.12	1485	18.00	12.75	15.85	...	7	NM	26.8	63.5	23.6
20 •[3]	PMTR	✓Pemstar Inc	NNM	NR	150	25336	Electronics mfr svcs	...	...	25.87	5.50	18.55	6.25	63619	15.97	10.95	12.00	...	33	...	36.2	...	...
21	PNG	✓Penn-America Group	NY	NR	34	3335	Insur. commercial prop/liab'y	23.00	4.33	9.75	6.62	10.60	6.93	606	10.55	9.80	10.55	2.0	21	Neg	42.1	7.9	1.7
22	PNN.A	✓Penn Engr & Mfg'A'	NY,Ch	A−	26	1713	Captive fasteners: DC motors	13.62	0.53	17.15	10.00	19.95	14.31	163	17.00	16.35	16.51B	1.9	15	9	7.9	20.9	11.9
23	PNN	✓Com(non-vtg)	NY	B+	101	10604		14.25	7.50	19.62	10.81	22.00	14.00	1673	17.75	15.40	16.75	1.9	15	9	−3.6	16.4	12.3
24	PTA	Penn Treaty American	NY	B	41	6138	Accident & health Insurance	35.50	3.00	21.56	12.25	19.75	2.10	28729	6.43	3.50	6.35	...	7	1	−63.7	−38.2	−24.6
25	PVA	✓Penn Virginia	NY,Ph	B	156	5668	Nat'l resources: O&G: Inv'mnt	34.50	4.37	33.37	15.56	45.40	26.25	9156	34.80	29.52	34.10	2.6	4	41	5.5	27.5	11.9
26	PVR	Penn Virginia Resource Ptnrs L.P.	NY	NR	..	...	Manage coal prop, U.S.	...	...	...	...	25.80	21.00	12140	25.80	23.20	25.80	7.8	..	...	...	...	...
¶27 •[6]	JCP	✓Penney (J.C.)	Ny,B,C,Ch,Ph,P	B−	599	211497	Dept stores, disc: mail order	78.75	4.90	22.50	8.62	29.50	10.50	443570	27.40	22.38	26.90	1.9	82	Neg	153	−12.8	−7.2
28	KTP	Penney(J.C.) 7.625% CortTs Tr Debs	NY	...[55]	..	...	Corporate-Backed Trust Sec	25.12	16.50	19.87	10.50	22.39	10.81	1081	21.00	20.29	20.84	9.2	..	...	116	...	...
29	PEI	Pennsylvania RE Inv Tr SBI	NY,Ph	NR	97	2897	Real estate Investment trust	30.37	2.00	19.75	14.62	25.05	18.25	8195	23.35	22.15	23.20	8.8	18	5	33.0	17.3	8.7
#30 •[9]	PZL	✓Pennzoil-Quaker State	NY	NR	256	52061	Motor oil/refin pd/auto svcs	18.00	8.50	13.25	8.37	16.00	9.00	57168	15.14	12.50	14.45	0.7	d	...	15.6	4.7	...
31	PTAC	Pentacon Inc	BB	NR	11	738	Dist hardware/fasteners	14.68	2.06	5.68	0.56	1.49	0.15	3518	0.33	0.20	0.21	...	d	...	−73.6	−63.2	...
#32 •[10]	PNR	✓Pentair, Inc	NY,Ch,Ph	A	322	32996	Mfr Indl eqp/specialty prod	49.43	0.09	44.62	20.62	39.60	21.87	36049	39.60	33.70	36.51	2.0	21	−7	54.2	−1.0	4.3
✤33	PME	✓Penton Media	NY	NR	207	27453	Publishing/information svcs	29.62	12.50	36.37	21.25	27.18	3.25	50936	7.13	5.20	6.26	...	d	...	−76.6	−32.0	...
34	PEOP	✓PeoplePC Inc	NNM	NR	18	6173	Internet access services	...	...	10.37	0.68	2.37	0.06	258120	0.38	0.20	0.22	...	d	...	−70.0	...	...
¶35 •[11]	PGL	✓Peoples Energy	NY,B,C,Ch,P,Ph	B+	415	18579	Gas utility in Chicago	62.87	7.00	46.93	26.18	44.62	34.35	29441	38.68	35.40	37.93	5.4	14	−2	−10.7	4.0	8.0
36	PHC	✓Peoples Holding	AS	A−	30	323	Commercial banking, Mississippi	46.00	10.04	28.62	17.00	37.75	16.37	537	37.75	32.50	37.00	2.7	17	5	114	8.3	11.0
¶37 •[12]	PSFT	✓PeopleSoft Inc	NNM,Ch	B+	895	211216	Mfr human resource mgmt softwr	57.43	1.06	50.00	12.00	53.87	15.78	1282129	42.73	34.05	40.20	...	72	−4	8.1	...	...
✤38 •[3]	PBY	✓Pep Boys-Manny,Mo,Jack	NY,B,Ch,P,Ph	B+	216	28321	Retail chain: auto parts, etc.	38.25	0.20	9.37	3.31	18.49	3.75	90312	18.49	15.90	17.15	1.6	25	Neg	392	6.6	−8.8
¶39 •[5]	PBG	✓Pepsi Bottling Group	NY,Ph	NR	585	175186	Mfr,dstr Pepsi-Cola beverages	12.62	7.75	21.25	8.12	25.00	15.81	168600	24.10	22.02	23.50	0.2	25	...	18.3	...	...
40	GEM	✓Pepsi-Gemex [61]S.A.	NY,Ch,Ph,P	NR	35	9084	Soft drink bottler, Mexico	31.12	4.50	6.62	3.75	7.49	3.81	14492	6.80	4.52	6.68	...	...	...	52.7	−5.1	−4.0
#41 •[13]	PAS	✓PepsiAmericas Inc	NY,B,Ch,P,Ph	B−	268	69984	Prod/distr Pepsi	41.25	2.59	16.43	10.37	17.00	12.25	60015	14.26	12.40	13.80	0.3	23	−10	−15.5	...	...
¶42 •[12]	PEP	✓PepsiCo Inc	NY,B,C,Ch,P,Ph	A	2179	1148028	Soft drink: snack foods	44.81	0.54	49.93	29.68	50.46	40.25	814458	49.80	46.45	48.69	1.2	29	13	−0.5	7.4	...
43 •[14]	PSTI	✓Per-Se Technologies	NNM,Ch	C	118	17021	Hospital/Dr. acc rec mgmt svcs	159.76	6.00	13.87	2.12	10.77	3.21	29688	10.77	8.35	10.75	...	d	85	209	3.0	−20.4
44	PRCP	✓Perceptron Inc	NNM	C	28	2884	Design,mfr measurement sys	39.25	3.00	7.50	1.25	2.37	0.87	4117	1.48	1.10	1.32	...	d	Neg	−12.0	−41.6	−47.9
45	PDA	✓Perdigao S.A. ADS[65]	NY	NR	3	41	Produce pork & poultry prd	...	...	15.00	12.37	16.50	7.85	1353	13.15	12.00	12.60B	3.2	..	...	−9.8	...	...

Uniform Footnote Explanations-See Page 1. Other: [1]CBOE,P,Ph:Cycle 3. [2]CBOE:Cycle 3. [3]CBOE:Cycle 1. [4]ASE,P:Cycle 3. [5]ASE,CBOE,P,Ph:Cycle 3. [6]ASE,CBOE,P:Cycle 2. [7]CBOE:Cycle 2. [8]ASE,CBOE,Ph:Cycle 3. [9]ASE,CBOE:Cycle 1. [10]Ph:Cycle 2. [11]P:Cycle 3. [12]ASE,CBOE,P,Ph:Cycle 1. [13]CBOE,P:Cycle 1. [14]ASE:Cycle 3. [51]Ea ADR rep 1 ord shr,25p. [52]Ea ADS rep 0.5 Ord'A'shr,EC15.24. [53]Reported in Euros. [54]To be determined. [55]Rate'A'by S&P. [56]12 Mo Dec'97: Fiscal Aug'97 earn $1.18. [57]Fiscal Sep'97 & prior. [58]Fiscal Sep'98 earn $0.54. [59]10 Mo Dec'99. [60]Stk dstr of Momentum Business Applications, '99. [61]Global Dep shrs, rep 6ord Ptd Ctf rep1B, 1L&1Dshr. [62]Pfd in $M. [63]Fiscal Dec'98 & prior. [64]12 Mo Jun'99. [65]Ea ADS rep 2 Pfd Shrs, no par. [66]Approx. [67]Shrs in millions, incl 145902M pfd shrs.

(continued)

FIGURE 5.8
(continued)

Common and Convertible Preferred Stocks — PAY-PER 149

Index	Splits ◆ Cash Divs. Ea. Yr. Since	Dividends: Latest Payment Period $	Date	Ex. Div.	Total $ So Far 2001	Ind. Rate	Paid 2000	Financial Position Mil-$: Cash& Equiv.	Curr. Assets	Curr. Liab.	Balance Sheet Date	Capitalization: Lg Trm Debt Mil-$	Shs. 000 Pfd.	Com.	Earnings $ Per Shr. Years End	1997	1998	1999	2000	2001	Last 12 Mos.	Interim Earnings Period	$ per Shr. 2000	2001	Index
1◆	1988	Q0.11	11-15-01	10-30	0.38	0.44	0.27	660	2647	1920	11-30-01	....	...	374740	My	v0.21	v0.27	v0.37	v0.51	v0.68	0.73	6 Mo Nov	v0.32	v0.37	1
2	....	None Since Public			...	Nil	....	52.7	522	264	11-03-01	260	...	22225	Ja	v3.31	v3.78	v4.35	v□5.16	E4.75	4.19	9 Mo Oct	v∆4.54	v3.57	2
3◆	....	None Since Public			...	Nil	....	53.3	210	92.9	9-30-01	6.67	...	24456	Dc	pv0.51	vp0.65	v0.94	v1.23	....	0.44	9 Mo Sep	v1.02	v0.23	3
4◆	....	None Since Public			...	Nil	....	6.44	84.1	67.7	9-30-01	0.73	...	10440	Dc	v0.41	vd1.75	vd1.05	v□d0.83	....	0.45	9 Mo Sep	v□d1.06	v0.22	4
5	....	None Since Public			...	Nil	....	129	139	32.9	9-30-01	....	...	19475	Dc	...	v0.04	v□0.48	v0.30	....	d2.81	9 Mo Sep	v0.38	vd2.73	5
6	....	None Since Public			...	Nil	....	Total Assets $111M			9-30-01	88.1	...	3746	Dc	v0.28	v0.09	vd0.20	v0.20	....	0.40	9 Mo Sep	v0.16	v0.36	6
7	2001	Q0.10	11-28-01	11-2	0.20	0.40	....	44.2	557	673	9-30-01	1010	...	51945	Mr	...	...	...	pv0.12	....	....	6 Mo Sep	n/a	v□0.29	7
8	....	None Since Public			...	Nil	....	Total Assets $76.7M			j5-31-01	26.6	...	± 3888	Au	...	±v0.63	v±0.58	v±0.21	vPd3.71	jd3.71				8
9◆	2000	Q0.15	2-1-02	12-28	0.532	0.60	0.482	Total Deposits $597M			9-30-01	....	...	3327	Dc	...	...	v2.27	v2.26	....	2.44	9 Mo Sep	v1.74	v1.92	9
10	1995	0.124	11-5-01	8-8	0.311	0.31	0.32¼	528	2573	1484	j12-31-00	2715	...	798000	Dc	...	...	0.78	v0.36	....	0.36				10
11	1996	0.378	5-23-01	4-30	0.378	0.38	0.327	461	3815	2725	[53]12-31-00	734	1091	78000	Dc	v1.91	v2.22	v1.58	v1.83	....	2.01	9 Mo Sep	v1.09	v1.27	11
12	....	None Since Public			...	Nil	....	46.1	98.9	14.2	9-30-01	10.5	...	21799	Dc	...	...	v0.42	v0.68	....	0.05	9 Mo Sep	v0.49	vd0.14	12
13	....	....			...	Nil	....	3.54	78.0	59.8	9-30-01	14.7	...	24452	Dc	v1.33	v1.82	v1.58	v0.68	....	1.21	9 Mo Sep	v0.43	v0.96	13
14◆	1954	Div Omitted 1-30-01			...	Nil	0.25	0.53	42.3	28.4	9-30-01	....	...	2977	Je	v0.19	v0.84	v0.64	v0.32	v1.02	1.45	3 Mo Sep	vd0.18	v0.25	14
15	....	None Since Public			...	Nil	....	16.2	19.8	6.94	10-31-01	....	...	15373	Ja	v0.42	v0.39	v0.22	vd1.19	....	d1.05	9 Mo Oct	vd0.71	vd0.57	15
16◆	....	None Since Public			...	Nil	....	89.0	184	278	9-30-01	1142	163	± 56933	Dc	v□d1.51	vd3.32	±vd5.17	v∆3.86	....	1.98	9 Mo Sep	v□d2.51	v□d4.39	16
17	....	None Since Public			...	Nil	....	26.2	73.4	20.4	9-30-01	....	...	32694	Dc	v0.04	vd0.46	vd0.08	vd0.71	....	0.05	9 Mo Sep	vd0.53	v0.23	17
18◆	2001	0.05	12-28-01	12-10	0.05	[54]....	....	Total Deposits $94.1M			9-30-01	151	...	4393	Dc	...	v1.16	v□1.01	v0.05	....	0.78	9 Mo Sep	v0.05	v□0.78	18
19◆	....	None Paid			...	Nil	....	1.99	44.7	41.8	9-30-01	4.38	...	4036	Dc	vd2.30	v2.53	v1.52	v2.23	....	2.21	9 Mo Sep	v1.85	v1.83	19
20	....	None Since Public			...	Nil	....	12.6	291	115	9-30-01	70.9	...	36477	Mr	...	...	pv0.08	v0.25	....	0.36	6 Mo Sep	v0.05	v0.16	20
21◆	1995	Q0.053	12-12-01	11-26	0.21	0.21	0.21	Total Assets $242M			9-30-01	1.61	...	7651	Dc	v1.17	v0.90	v0.24	vd0.50	....	0.50	9 Mo Sep	vd0.54	v0.46	21
22◆	1967	Q0.08	1-15-02	12-12	0.24	0.32	0.26	9.90	104	33.8	9-30-01	....	...	±17315	Dc	±v0.84	±v0.96	v±0.99	v±1.57	....	1.14	9 Mo Sep	v±1.11	v±0.68	22
23◆	1996	Q0.08	1-15-02	12-12	0.24	0.32	0.26	....	...	...			...	13965	Dc	±v0.84	v±0.96	±v0.99	v±1.57	....	1.14	9 Mo Sep	v±1.11	v±0.68	23
24	....	None Paid			...	Nil	....	Total Assets $968M			9-30-01	79.2	...	p19368	Dc	v0.98	v2.64	v2.40	v2.61	....	0.98	9 Mo Sep	v1.96	v0.33	24
25◆	1984	Q0.22½	12-6-01	11-13	0.90	0.90	0.90	....	18.1	20.3	9-30-01	135	...	8922	Dc	v1.88	v1.13	v1.71	v4.69	....	8.97	9 Mo Sep	v2.25	v6.53	25
26	....	Plan qtly div			...	2.00	....	25.0	26.2	0.55	p6-30-01	24.3	...	±★15300	Dc	...	...	...	±vp1.29	....	....	6 Mo Jun	n/a	v±p0.84	26
27	1922	Q0.12½	2-1-02	1-8	0.50	0.50	0.98¾	1791	9061	4999	10-27-01	5193	600	263812	Ja	v2.10	v2.19	v1.16	vd2.81	E0.33	d2.31	9 Mo Oct	vd0.57	vd0.07	27
28	1999	S0.953	9-4-01	8-29	1.906	1.91	1.906	Co option to redm at $25				....	...	★4000	Ja	...	...	...	....	....	....	Due 3-1-2097			28
29	1962	Q0.51	12-17-01	11-28	2.04	2.04	1.92	Total Assets $595M			9-30-01	351	...	15865	Dc	□v[56]1.31	v□1.76	v1.56	v2.41	....	1.26	9 Mo Sep	v2.07	v0.92	29
30	1999	Q0.02½	12-15-01	11-28	0.425	0.10	0.75	0.58	654	484	9-30-01	1035	...	79515	Dc	vNil	vd0.96	vd4.12	vd1.10	....	d1.25	9 Mo Sep	v0.20	v0.05	30
31	....	None Since Public			...	Nil	....	0.11	170	101	9-30-01	99.1	...	16959	Dc	p[57]0.41	v[58]0.56	v0.05	vd0.05	....	d0.31	9 Mo Sep	v0.02	vd0.24	31
32	1976	Q0.18	11-9-01	10-24	0.70	0.72	0.66	32.8	1045	531	9-29-01	781	...	49058	Dc	v2.11	v2.46	v2.33	v□1.17	E1.75↓	1.50	9 Mo Sep	v□1.17	v1.50	32
33	1998	Div Omitted 7-31-01			0.09	Nil	0.12	28.4	146	132	9-30-01	353	...	31935	Dc	pv0.66	v0.50	v□0.59	v2.49	....	d0.95	9 Mo Sep	v2.30	vd1.14	33
34	....	None Since Public			...	Nil	....	18.0	27.1	46.9	9-30-01	....	...	114002	Dc	...	...	vp[59]d1.15	v□d4.09	....	d0.52	9 Mo Sep	vd4.16	vd0.59	34
35	1937	Q0.51	1-15-02	12-19	2.03	2.04	1.99	51.6	830	744	6-30-01	744	...	35399	Sp	v2.81	v2.25	v2.61	v2.44	vP2.74	2.74				35
36◆	1987	Q0.25	1-2-02	12-18	0.93	1.00	0.87	Total Deposits $1087.6M			9-30-01	24.4	...	5723	Dc	v1.82	v1.94	v2.38	v1.83	....	2.19	9 Mo Sep	v1.45	v1.81	36
37◆	....	h[60]....	1-15-99	1-19	...	Nil	....	1421	1963	819	9-30-01	....	...	302875	Dc	v0.44	v0.55	vd0.67	v0.48	E0.56	0.55	9 Mo Sep	v0.35	v0.42	37
38	1950	Q0.068	1-28-02	1-10	0.27	0.27	0.27	23.0	671	598	11-03-01	522	...	51401	Ja	v0.80	v0.08	v0.58	∆vd1.00	E0.70	0.70	9 Mo Oct	v□d1.07	v□0.63	38
39◆	1999	Q0.01	1-2-02	12-11	0.04	0.04	0.04	191	1730	1145	6-16-01	3282	...	285296	Dc	...	pvd0.39	v0.46	v0.77	E0.94	1.05	9 Mo Sep	v0.76	v1.04	39
40	....	0.145	7-2-98	6-18	...	Nil	....	22.5	233	204	12-31-00	328	...	1501167	Dc	v0.78	v0.30	v1.15	v0.71	....	....	6 Mo Jun	n/a	v0.53	40
41◆	1950	A0.04	4-3-01	3-7	0.04	0.04	0.05	86.6	540	646	9-30-01	1091	...	155879	Dc	v0.04	v□0.60	vd0.07	v0.51	E0.60	0.46	9 Mo Sep	v0.57	v0.52	41
42◆	1952	Q0.145	1-2-02	12-5	0.57	0.58	0.55	2630	7457	5204	9-08-01	2559	...	1749594	Dc	v1.36	v1.31	v1.37	v1.48	E1.66	1.55	9 Mo Sep	v1.03	v1.10	42
43◆	....	None Since Public			...	Nil	....	26.7	84.9	64.4	9-30-01	175	...	29926	Dc	∆vd3.84	v□d21.51	vd1.20	vd0.36	....	d0.58	9 Mo Sep	v□d0.06	vd0.28	43
44	....	None Since Public			...	Nil	....	6.42	46.9	23.8	9-30-01	1.04	...	8185	Je	v1.28	v[63]d0.41	v[64]d0.56	v0.23	vd0.76	d0.62	3 Mo Sep	v□d0.30	vd0.16	44
45	2000	[66]0.335	3-11-02	12-12	0.39	0.40	0.06	190	414	397	12-31-99	291	...	[67]223262	Dc	...	...	...	....	....	....	No EPS Reported			45

◆ **Stock Splits & Divs By Line Reference Index** [1]3-for-2,'97,'98,'99,'00. [3]3-for-2,'00. [4]No adj for stk dstr,'99. [9]10%,'01. [14]2-for-1,'01. [16]2-for-1,'00. [18]10%,'01. [19]1-for-4 REVERSE,'98. [21]3-for-2,'97. [22]2-for-1,'01. [23]2-for-1,'01. [25]2-for-1,'97. [36]3-for-2,'98. [37]2-for-1,'97. [39]2-for-1,'01. [41]No adj for stk dstr,'98. [42]No adj for stk dstr,'97. [43]t-for-3 REVERSE,'99.

Source: Reprinted by permission of Standard & Poors

Review

1. Define the following terms: *exchange symbol, dividend yield, trading volume, closing price.*
2. Assume you have a copy of the *Wall Street Journal* and *Standard and Poor's Stock and Bond Guide.* Which one would you look in to find each of the following pieces of information? 1. Yesterday's closing stock price; 2. The number of outstanding shares; 3. Yesterday's trading volume in a stock; 4. A corporation's total long-term debt; 5. The stock's exchange symbol.
3. A share of stock is quoted at 24.25 in the newspaper. What is its dollar price?

5.7 THE PRICE-EARNINGS RATIO

Like participants in conversations about football and the weather, many investors will join into a discussion concerning the investment potential of a stock and feel good about their contribution, regardless of any knowledge they might have about the stock. In this type of conversation, a statistic that is often mentioned as a measure of a stock's investment potential is the **price/earnings (P/E) ratio,** commonly referred to as the **P/E ratio,** or simply **P/E.** Recall that stock quotations in the financial press list a stock's P/E. It is the market price per share divided by the firm's annual earnings per share.

Often investors will refer to a stock as selling at a "high" or "low" P/E to indicate that the stock has good or bad investment potential. But what does that mean? As with many things, it is unclear what a high or low P/E really indicates without obtaining additional information. Let us work through the relationships to find out why conventional wisdom holds that a high P/E is good and a low P/E is bad in a stable market environment. Then we will show you how the reasoning connected with this conventional wisdom is muddled by illustrating some situations that can reverse that conventional wisdom.

Dividend Growth

Earlier, we used Equation (5.5) to estimate International Paper's capitalization rate. In that example, we asserted that g was 5.25%. But where does that growth come from? Money not paid out in dividends is retained and invested in other assets. This money—retained earnings—is the source of the firm's growth in earnings, which provides for the growth in the firm's dividends. Recall that the firm's payout ratio (POR) is the proportion of earnings it pays out in dividends. Therefore, (1 − POR) is the amount the firm retains and reinvests. Let i represent the expected return on the money retained. Growth is then the product of the two:

$$g = (1 - \text{POR})i \tag{5.7}$$

The Logic of the P/E Ratio

With POR constant, the next dividend (D_1) is simply that proportion of the next period's expected earnings per share, (EPS_1), or $D_1 = \text{POR}(EPS_1)$. Substituting this and Equation (5.7) into Equation (5.5), we can express the firm's expected return as

$$r = \frac{D_1}{P_0} + g = \frac{(\text{POR})(EPS_1)}{P_0} + (1 - \text{POR})i$$

Rearranging this equation, we have

$$r = (\text{POR})\left(\frac{\text{EPS}_1}{P_0}\right) + (1 - \text{POR})i \tag{5.8}$$

$$r = \text{dividend yield} + \text{capital gains yield}$$

Note how POR determines the split between the dividend and capital gains yields. The dividend yield is based on the firm's earnings from its current operations. The capital gains yield is the growth from reinvested earnings. Of course, there is a tradeoff. More of one requires less of the other. Each dollar of earnings can be either paid out or retained and reinvested, but not both.

Look at Equation (5.8). If we hold r and POR constant, then the smaller [EPS_1/P_0] is, the larger i must be. Because [EPS_1/P_0] is the inverse of the P/E, a small [EPS_1/P_0] corresponds to a high P/E. Therefore, the conventional wisdom is that, with all else equal, the higher the P/E, the higher the expected return on future investments. So conventional wisdom holds that a "high" P/E corresponds to good future investment opportunities.

An Important Warning About the Conventional Wisdom

Although the conventional wisdom is that a high P/E is good and a low P/E is bad, we must hasten to add that this does not always hold. The valuation formulas rely on expectations (averages). But the price and earnings are historical. They are not expectations—they have already been realized. Moreover, actual values almost never equal the average.

A firm's earnings vary from year to year, and yet the firm's value may be much less variable. In such cases, a firm can have a high P/E during a bad year when earnings are low and a low P/E during a good year. Yet in both cases, the firm may not have changed fundamentally. Therefore, a high P/E can be the result of low earnings rather than a high expected return on future investments.

In addition, recall that earnings do not reflect the actual timing of income. For example, a firm might be recognizing (in the accounting sense) a bad debt that has existed for several years. Or a firm might now sell a piece of land that had become very valuable a long time ago. Selling the land would appear to create a large profit. Of course, you don't have to sell something for it to be worth more or less than what you paid for it. And for a firm, the profits from such a sale may be unrelated to its future earnings.

We explained in Chapter 3 that accounting net income is different from economic income. Economic income is what determines stock value. In recent years, many public firms have begun to report their own measures of net income, such as 'core' income and 'pro forma' income. These measures lack standard definitions. As a result of having multiple versions of 'net income,' comparisons based on P/E ratios can be very misleading.

Therefore, maintain a healthy skepticism about P/Es. You need a lot more information than just a P/E to estimate the value of a share of stock. After all, if all you needed was a P/E, you probably would not need this course! Still, when discussing football, the weather, or stock values, it is nice to have an opinion.

Measuring the Expected NPV of Growth Opportunities

Another way to think about the difference between the required and expected returns, and measure how that difference affects stock value, is to compute the expected NPV of the firm's growth opportunities. The NPV of growth opportunities for a firm is just what the name implies. As you should expect, it is positive if the expected return exceeds the required return and negative if the expected return is less than the required return.

If the expected return, i, equals the required return, r, Equation (5.8) becomes:

$$r = (\text{POR})\left(\frac{\text{EPS}_1}{P_0}\right) + (1 - \text{POR})r$$

Solving this for P_0, we get:

$$P_0 = \frac{\text{EPS}_1}{r} \tag{5.9}$$

If we view the firm's earnings as a perpetuity, Equation (5.9) is the present value of the equity-owned portion of the firm's current operations.

But suppose i does not equal r? In such cases, P_0 is higher or lower than the present value of the firm's current operations by however much the firm is expected to gain or lose on its future investments. P_0 can be expressed as the value of the firm's current operations plus NPVGO, the expected NPV of the firm's future growth opportunities:

$$P_0 = \frac{\text{EPS}_1}{r} + \text{NPVGO} \tag{5.10}$$

EXAMPLE Estimating NPVGO: McHandy

A financial analyst has just told you that she has analyzed the fast-hardware industry and estimated that the capitalization rate for the industry is currently 15%. You are thinking of buying stock in McHandy, a firm that is invested solely in this industry. McHandy expects to earn \$4.20 per share next year (which you feel represents a good estimate of the firm's long-run prospects). McHandy's stock is selling for \$30.50. What is McHandy's NPVGO?

From Equation (5.9), McHandy's stock is worth \$28.00 (= 4.20/0.15) on the basis of its current operations alone. From Equation (5.10), NPVGO is positive and equals \$2.50 (= 30.50 − 28.00). Therefore, McHandy is expected to make good future investments, ones that are expected to earn more than their required returns and thus have a positive NPV.

Review

1. How is the price-earnings ratio computed? What does it signify?
2. Explain why a high P/E ratio does not always imply good future investment opportunities.
3. When is the NPV of future investments positive? When is it negative?
4. How does the expected NPV of the firm's future investments (NPVGO) affect the value of its shares (P_0)?

SUMMARY

This chapter describes the typical features of bonds and stocks and presents valuation models for both securities. Fundamental points in the chapter include:

- Information about bonds and stocks is readily available from a variety of sources.
- A security's fair price is the present value of its expected future cash flows.

- Conversely, we can compute a security's expected return from its market price. The expected return is called the yield to maturity, YTM, for a bond and the capitalization rate for a stock.
- A bond's expected future cash flows are its future coupon payments and terminal value.
- Interest-rate risk is the sensitivity of a bond's value to interest-rate changes. Interest-rate risk depends primarily on a bond's remaining maturity.
- Bonds are also subject to inflation risk, currency risk, and marketability risk.
- If an investor's bond is likely to be called, its yield to call, YTC, may be more relevant than its YTM.
- A stock's expected future cash flows are more uncertain and are more difficult to estimate than those of a bond. A stock's expected future cash flows are its cash dividends and selling price.
- A stock's value can be expressed as the present value of all its expected future cash dividends.
- A high P/E ratio is generally thought to be a positive indicator of expected future investment potential, but you need a lot more information than just a P/E ratio to estimate the value of a share of stock.

EQUATION SUMMARY

$$B_0 = \text{PV(coupon payments)} + \text{PV(par value)}$$

$$B_0 = \left[\frac{\text{CPN}}{2}\right]\text{PVAF}_{(r/2)\%,2N} + 1{,}000\,\text{PVF}_{(r/2)\%,2N}$$

$$B_0 = \left[\frac{\text{CPN}}{2}\right]\left[\frac{(1+r/2)^{2N}-1}{(r/2)(1+r/2)^{2N}}\right] + \frac{1{,}000}{(1+r/2)^{2N}} \tag{5.1}$$

$$P_0 = \frac{D_1}{(1+r)^1} + \frac{D_2}{(1+r)^2} + \cdots + \frac{D_n}{(1+r)^n} + \frac{P_n}{(1+r)^n} \tag{5.2}$$

$$P_0 = \frac{D_1}{(1+r)} + \frac{D_2}{(1+r)^2} + \cdots = \sum_{t=1}^{\infty} \frac{D_t}{(1+r)^t} \tag{5.3}$$

$$P_t = \frac{D_{t+1}}{(r-g)} \tag{5.4}$$

$$r = \frac{D_1}{P_0} + g \tag{5.5}$$

$$P_0 = \frac{D_1}{(1+r)} + \frac{D_2}{(1+r)^2} + \cdots + \frac{D_{n-1}}{(1+r)^{n-1}} + \frac{D_n}{(1+r)^{n-1}(r-g)} \tag{5.6}$$

$$g = (1 - \text{POR})i \tag{5.7}$$

$$r = (\text{POR})\left(\frac{\text{EPS}_1}{P_0}\right) + (1 - \text{POR})i \tag{5.8}$$

$$P_0 = \frac{\text{EPS}_1}{r} \tag{5.9}$$

$$P_0 = \frac{\text{EPS}_1}{r} + \text{NPVGO} \tag{5.10}$$

QUESTIONS

1. What is a required return?
2. Define the term *expected return.*
3. What are coupon payments, and what is a coupon rate?
4. What is the maturity of a bond?
5. What does the term *payout ratio* mean?
6. What is the basic approach that is used to value any asset, including bonds and common stocks?
7. What information is needed to calculate the yield to maturity for a bond? Once you have this information, how do you calculate the yield to maturity?
8. Assume that a long-term bond is selling for a discount. If you calculate the current yield and yield to maturity, which will have the highest value? Which will have the lowest value?
9. What is a yield to call? When is a yield to call a more reasonable estimate of your expected return than the yield to maturity?
10. What are the assumptions behind the dividend growth model? What is the value of a share of stock using the dividend growth model? What is the required return for a stock using the dividend growth model?

CHALLENGING QUESTIONS

11. What is interest-rate risk? How is interest-rate risk related to the maturity of a bond and to the coupon rate for a bond?
12. Assume that the Federal Reserve unexpectedly raises interest rates. As a result, bond prices and stock prices both fall. What explanation can you give for this?
13. Cite and explain three reasons why a P/E ratio may not be a reliable indicator of a stock's expected future performance.
14. Cite and discuss two important factors that limit the usefulness of the stock valuation model.
15. Explain in your own words why the growth rate in the dividend growth model, g, cannot be larger than the required return, r.

PROBLEMS

LEVEL A (Basic)

A1. (Bond valuation) A $1,000 face value bond has a remaining maturity of 10 years and a required return of 9%. The bond's coupon rate is 7.4%. What is the fair value of this bond?

A2. (Bond valuation) Find the missing information for each of the following bonds. The coupons are paid in semiannual installments, so the number of payments is equal to twice the bond's life in years. The YTM is compounded semiannually.

BOND	N (YEARS)	YIELD TO MATURITY	PRESENT VALUE	COUPON RATE	FACE VALUE
1	10	7.8%	—	7.8%	$1,000
2	5	10.5%	—	9.5%	$1,000
3	25	8.2%	—	5.5%	$1,000
4	15	—	$1,050.00	7.4%	$1,000
5	—	9.0%	$977.20	8.5%	$1,000
6	8	7.0%	$1,120.94	—	$1,000

A3. (Bond valuation) Find the missing information for each of the following bonds. The coupons are paid in semiannual installments, so the number of payments is equal to twice the bond's life in years. The YTM is compounded semiannually.

BOND	N (YEARS)	YIELD TO MATURITY	PRESENT VALUE	COUPON RATE	FACE VALUE
1	8	10.2%	—	8.0%	$1,000
2	7	8.0%	—	9.0%	$1,000
3	15	9.5%	—	7.5%	$1,000
4	20	—	$1,075.00	8.5%	$1,000
5	—	7.0%	$963.80	6.49%	$1,000
6	13	7.8%	$1,140.60	—	$1,000

A4. (Bond valuation) General Electric made a coupon payment yesterday on its "6.75s13" bonds that mature on October 9, 2013. If the required return on these bonds is 8% APR and today is April 10, 2005, what should be the market price of these bonds?

A5. (Bond valuation) RCA made a coupon payment yesterday on its "6.25s16" bonds that mature on November 9, 2016. If the required return on these bonds is 9.2% nominal annual and today is May 10, 2005, what should be the market price of these bonds?

A6. (Bond valuation) Dow made a coupon payment yesterday on its "7.75s17" bonds that mature on April 18, 2017. If the required return on these bonds is 8.4% nominal annual and today is April 19, 2005, what should be the market price of these bonds?

A7. (Bond valuation) IBM made a coupon payment yesterday on its "7.00s20" bonds that mature on August 9, 2020. If the required return on these bonds is 8% APR and today is August 10, 2005, what should be the market price of these bonds?

A8. (Yield to maturity) New Jersey Lighting has a 7% coupon bond maturing in 17 years. The current market price of the bond is $975. What is the bond's yield to maturity?

A9. (Yield to maturity) Marstel Industries has a 9.2% bond maturing in 15 years. What is the yield to maturity if the current market price of the bond is: a. $1,120? b. $1,000? c. $785?

A10. (Yield to maturity) Long Island Lighting has a 8.9% coupon bond maturing in 20 years. The current market price of the bond is $915. What is the bond's yield to maturity?

A11. (Yield to maturity) Kraft's 5.75% coupon bond that matures in five years is selling for 98. a. What is the yield to maturity? b. What is the current yield?

A12. (One-period dividend discount model) Mead is expected to pay a $1.40 dividend in the next year and to sell for $68.00 in one year. Discounted at a required return of 12%, what is the value of one share of Mead today?

A13. (One-period dividend discount model) Hoover is expected to pay a $1.25 dividend in the next year and to sell for $55.00 in one year. Discounted at a required return of 8%, what is the value of one share of Hoover today?

A14. (Two-period dividend discount model) New England Electric has projected dividends of $2.72 in one year and $3.10 in two years. If the stock is projected to sell for $48.00 in two years, what is the value of the stock today if the required return is 10%?

A15. (Two-period dividend discount model) Pacific Utility has projected dividends of $2.00 in one year and $2.55 in two years. If the stock is projected to sell for $36.00 in two years, what is the value of the stock today if the required return is 10%?

A16. (Dividend discount model) Assume that IBM is expected to pay a total cash dividend of $5.60 next year and that dividends are expected to grow at a rate of 6% per year forever. Assuming annual dividend payments, what is the current market value of a share of IBM stock if the required return on IBM common stock is 10%?

A17. (Dividend discount model) Assume Microsoft is expected to pay a total cash dividend of $4.50 next year and that dividends are expected to grow at a rate of 7% per year forever. Assuming annual dividend payments, what is the current market value of a share of Microsoft stock if the required return on Microsoft common stock is 12%?

A18. (Expected return) Northern States Power has a projected dividend of $3.60 next year. The current stock price is $50.50 per share. If the dividend is projected to grow at 3.5% annually, what is the expected return on Northern States stock?

A19. (Expected return) East Atlantic has a projected dividend of $1.85 next year. The current stock price is $42.25 per share. If the dividend is projected to grow at 4.7% annually, what is the expected return on East Atlantic stock?

A20. (Required return for a preferred stock) James River $3.38 preferred is selling for $45.25. The preferred dividend is nongrowing. What is the required return on James River preferred stock?

A21. (Required return for a preferred stock) Sony $4.50 preferred is selling for $65.50. The preferred dividend is nongrowing. What is the required return on Sony preferred stock?

A22. (Stock valuation) Suppose Toyota has nonmaturing (perpetual) preferred stock outstanding that pays a $1.00 quarterly dividend and has a required return of 12% APR (3% per quarter). What is the stock worth?

A23. (Stock valuation) If Footlocker has perpetual preferred stock outstanding that pays a $0.60 quarterly dividend and has a required return of 13.2% APR (3.3% per quarter), what is the stock worth?

A24. (Stock valuation) Let's say the Mill Due Corporation is expected to pay a dividend of $5.00 per year on its common stock forever into the future. It has no growth prospects whatsoever. If the required return on Mill Due's common stock is 14%, what is the share worth?

A25. (Growth rate) Suppose Toshiba has a payout ratio of 55% and an expected return on its future investments of 15%. What is Toshiba's expected growth rate?

A26. (Valuing a perpetual bond) Suppose a bond pays $90 per year forever. If the bond's required return is 10.3%, what is the bond selling for in the capital markets?

A27. (Valuing a perpetual bond) Suppose a bond pays $100 per year forever. If the bond's required return is 9%, what is the bond selling for in the capital markets?

LEVEL B

B1. (Yield to maturity) DuPont's "8.45s20" bonds closed yesterday at 103. If these bonds mature on October 9, 2020, and today is April 10, 2005, what is the yield to maturity of these bonds? What is their APY?

B2. (Yield to maturity) GMAC's "8.75s16" bonds closed yesterday at 95.25. If these bonds mature on April 18, 2016, and today is April 19, 2005, what is the yield to maturity of these bonds? What is their APY?

B3. (Yield to maturity) Mitsubishi's "6.25s10" bonds closed yesterday at 105.8. If these bonds mature on November 9, 2010, and today is May 10, 2005, what is the yield to maturity of these bonds? What is their APY?

B4. (Yield to maturity) Toyota's "7.5s28" bonds closed yesterday at 88.25. If these bonds mature on August 9, 2028, and today is August 10, 2005, what is the yield to maturity of these bonds? What is their APY?

B5. (Remaining maturity) IBM's "9.375s" bonds closed yesterday at 95.13. If a coupon payment was made yesterday, April 9, 2005, and the yield to maturity on these bonds is 10%, when do these bonds mature?

B6. (Remaining maturity) ATT's "7.125% coupon" bonds closed yesterday at 92.75. If a coupon payment was made yesterday, May 9, 2005, and the yield to maturity on these bonds is 8%, when do these bonds mature?

B7. (Remaining maturity) Intel's "6.875s" bonds closed yesterday at 92.13. If a coupon payment was made yesterday, April 18, 2005, and the yield to maturity on these bonds is 12%, when do these bonds mature?

B8. (Remaining maturity) MCI's "6.5s" bonds closed yesterday at $948.90. If a coupon payment was made yesterday, August 9, 2005, and the yield to maturity on these bonds is 7.4, when do these bonds mature?

B9. (Yield to call) Bowen Mills has a 10.5% coupon bond that has a remaining maturity of 14 years. The bond is callable in four years at a price of $1,080. Its current market price is $1,090.

a. If the required return for this bond is 8.0% (assuming that it is not callable), what would be the value of the bond?

b. What is the yield to maturity (based on its current market price)?

c. What is the yield to call?

B10. (Yield to call) Xerox has a 8.5% coupon bond that has a remaining maturity of 16 years. The bond is callable in three years at a price of $1,100. Its current market price is $1,250.

a. If the required return for this bond is 10.0% (assuming it's not callable), what would be the value of the bond?

b. What is the yield to maturity (based on current market price)?

c. What is the yield to call?

B11. (Yield to maturity) Suppose Coca-Cola has a zero-coupon bond that will pay $1,000 at maturity on May 9, 2010. Today is May 9, 2005, and the bond is selling for $790.09. What is the YTM?

B12. (Yield to maturity) Assume J.C. Penney has a zero-coupon bond that will pay $1,000 at maturity on April 18, 2030. Today is April 18, 2005, and the bond is selling for $98.24. What is its YTM?

B13. (Yield to call) Suppose Samsung has a bond that cannot be called today but can be called in four years at a call price of $1,080. The bond has a remaining maturity of 16 years, has a coupon rate of 14%, and is currently selling for $1,107.67. What is the bond's YTC?

B14. (Yield to call) Assume MCI has a bond that cannot be called today. It can, however, be called in two years at a call price of $1,050. The bond has a remaining maturity of eight years, has a coupon rate of 14%, and is currently selling for $1,112.05. What is the bond's YTC?

B15. (Required return) What required return is implied by the constant growth model for a stock that is selling for $25.00 per share, is expected to pay a single cash dividend next year of $1.80, and whose growth in dividend payments is expected to be 2% per year forever?

B16. (Required return) What required return is implied by the constant growth model for a stock that is selling for $47.00 per share, is expected to pay a single cash dividend next year of $0.75, and whose growth in dividend payments is expected to be 1.5% per year forever?

B17. (Expected dividend growth rate) Suppose that GM is expected to pay $4.00 in cash dividends next year at the rate of $1.00 per quarter and that the required return on GM stock is 14%. If GM is currently selling for $37.50 per share, what is the expected growth rate in dividends for GM based on the constant growth model?

B18. (Expected dividend growth rate) Suppose that Ford is expected to pay $6.00 in cash dividends next year at the rate of $1.50 per quarter and that the required return on Ford stock is 12%. If Ford is currently selling for $65.00 per share, what is the expected growth rate in dividends for Ford based on the constant growth model?

B19. (Expected dividend growth rate) Let's say Daimler-Benz, the builder of Mercedes cars and trucks, is expected to pay $4.00 (or the equivalent in euros) in cash dividends next year at the rate of $1.00 per quarter. The required return on Daimler-Benz stock is 14%. The stock is currently selling for the equivalent of $37.50 per share on the Frankfurt Stock Exchange. What is the expected growth rate in dividends for Daimler-Benz on the basis of the constant growth model?

B20. (Interest-rate risk) A quick look in the NYSE bond-quote section will tell you that GMAC has many different issues of bonds outstanding. Suppose that four of them have identical coupon rates of 7.25% but mature on four different dates. One matures in 2 years, one in 5 years, one in 10 years, and the last in 20 years. Assume that they all made coupon payments yesterday.

a. If the yield curve was flat and all four bonds had the same yield to maturity of 9%, what is the fair price of each bond today?

b. Suppose that during the first hour of operation of the capital markets today, the term structure shifts and the yield to maturity of all these bonds changes to 10%. What is the fair price of each bond now?

c. Suppose that in the second hour of trading, the yield to maturity of all these bonds changes once more to 8%. Now what is the fair price of each bond?

d. Based on the price changes in response to the changes in yield to maturity, how is interest-rate risk a function of the bond's maturity? That is, is interest-rate risk the same for all four bonds, or does it depend on the bond's maturity?

B21. (Interest-rate risk) Philadelphia Electric has many bonds trading on the New York Stock Exchange. Suppose PhilEl's bonds have identical coupon rates of 9.125% but that one issue matures in 1 year, one in 7 years, and the third in 15 years. Assume that a coupon payment was made yesterday.

a. If the yield to maturity for all three bonds is 8%, what is the fair price of each bond?

b. Suppose that the yield to maturity for all of these bonds changed instantaneously to 7%. What is the fair price of each bond now?

c. Suppose that the yield to maturity for all of these bonds changed instantaneously again, this time to 9%. Now what is the fair price of each bond?

d. Based on the fair prices at the various yields to maturity, is interest-rate risk the same, higher, or lower for longer- versus shorter-maturity bonds?

B22. (Interest-rate risk) A quick look in the NYSE bond-quote section will tell you that IBM has many different issues of bonds outstanding. Suppose that four of them have identical coupon rates of 6% but mature on four different dates. One matures in 4 years, one in 7 years, one in 15 years, and the last in 30 years. Assume they all made coupon payments yesterday.

a. If the yield curve was flat and all four bonds had the same yield to maturity of 8%, what is the fair price of each bond today?

b. Suppose that during the first hour of operation of the capital markets today, the term structure shifts and the yield to maturity of all these bonds changes to 11%. What is the fair price of each bond now?

c. Suppose that in the second hour of trading, the yield to maturity of all these bonds changes once more to 7%. Now what is the fair price of each bond?

d. Based on the price changes in response to the changes in yield to maturity, how is interest-rate risk a function of the bond's maturity? That is, is interest-rate risk the same for all four bonds, or does it depend on the bond's maturity?

B23. (Interest-rate risk) NYSEG has many bonds trading on the New York Stock Exchange. Suppose NYSEG's bonds have identical coupon rates of 7% but that one issue matures in 1 year, one in 8 years, and the third in 20 years. Assume a coupon payment was made yesterday.

a. If the yield to maturity for all three bonds is 6%, what is the fair price of each bond?

b. Suppose that the yield to maturity for all of these bonds changed instantaneously to 8%. What is the fair price of each bond now?

c. Suppose that the yield to maturity for all of these bonds changed instantaneously again, this time to 12%. Now what is the fair price of each bond?

d. Based on the fair prices at the various yields to maturity, is interest-rate risk the same, higher, or lower, for longer- versus shorter-maturity bonds?

B24. (Default risk) You buy a very risky bond that promises an 8.8% coupon and return of the $1,000 principal in ten years. You pay only $500 for the bond.

a. You receive the coupon payments for two years and the bond defaults. After liquidating the firm, the bondholders receive a distribution of $150 per bond at the end of 2.5 years. What is the realized return on your investment?

b. The firm does far better than expected and bondholders receive all of the promised interest and principal payments. What is the realized return on your investment?

B25. (Default risk) You buy a very risky bond that promises a 9.5% coupon and return of the $1,000 principal in 10 years. You pay only $500 for the bond.

a. You receive the coupon payments for three years and the bond defaults. After liquidating the firm, the bondholders receive a distribution of $150 per bond at the end of 3.5 years. What is the realized return on your investment?

b. The firm does far better than expected and bondholders receive all of the promised interest and principal payments. What is the realized return on your investment?

B26. (Constant growth model)

a. The current dividend for Birmingham Electric is $2.40 and is growing at 5% annually. If the required return is 13%, what is the value of one share of stock?

b. Montgomery Audio is expected to pay a $1.30 dividend next year. The dividend is expected to grow at 6% annually. If the current stock price is $21.25, what is Montgomery's required return?

B27. (Constant growth model) Medtrans is a profitable firm that is not paying a dividend on its common stock. James Weber, an analyst for A. G. Edwards, believes that Medtrans will begin paying a $1.00 per share dividend in two years and that the dividend will increase 6% annually thereafter. Bret Kimes, one of James' colleagues at the same firm, is less optimistic. Bret thinks that Medtrans will begin paying a dividend in four years, that the dividend will be $1.00, and that it will grow at 4% annually. James and Bret agree that the required return for Medtrans is 13%.

a. What value would James estimate for this firm?

b. What value would Bret assign to the Medtrans stock?

B28. (Dividend valuation) Wichita Realty Trust is expected to pay a modest dividend of $1.00 per share for two years and then $2.00 per share for years three through five. Then in year six, Wichita Realty Trust is planning to pay a $40.00 per share liquidating dividend and to go out of business. What is the value of a share of this firm if the required return is 10%?

B29. (Dividend valuation) TransAmerican is a profitable firm that is not paying a dividend on its common stock. Phil Parr believes that TransAmerican will begin paying a $2.00 per share dividend in two years and that the dividend will increase 8% annually thereafter. Rich Andrews is less optimistic. Rich thinks that TransAmerican will begin paying a dividend in four years, that the dividend will be $2.00, and that it will grow at 5% annually. Phil and Rich agree that the required return for TransAmerican is 15%.

a. What value would Phil estimate for this firm?

b. What value would Rich assign to the TransAmerican stock?

B30. (Dividend valuation) San Francisco Bank is expected to pay a dividend of $1.50 per share for two years and then $2.00 per share for years three through five. Then in year six, San Francisco Bank is planning to pay a $37.00 per share liquidating dividend and to go out of business. What is the value of a share of this firm if the required return is 13%?

B31. (Supernormal growth model) Crockett Paintball Company has a current dividend of $1.00. The dividend is expected to grow at 40% annually for three years, and then to grow thereafter at 5% per year. If the required return is 14%, what is the value per share?

B32. (Supernormal growth model) Gebhardt Corp. has recently undertaken a major expansion project that is expected to provide growth in earnings per share of 400% within the coming year and 75% growth in each of the subsequent three years. After that time, normal growth of 3% per year forever is expected. The cash dividend was 10 cents per share this last year and is expected to be that amount for each of the next five years. In the sixth year, it is expected that the payout ratio will be 80% of the earnings per share, and the payout ratio is expected to remain at that level forever. If the required return on Gebhardt common stock is 32% per year and the latest earnings per share was 25 cents, at what price should Gebhardt Corp. common stock be selling in the market?

B33. (Supernormal growth model) Microsoft Corp. has recently undertaken a major expansion project that is expected to provide growth in earnings per share of 300% within the coming year and 50% growth in each of the subsequent three years. After that time, normal growth of 7% per year forever is expected. The cash dividend was $3.00 per share this last year and is expected to be that amount for each of the next five years. In the sixth year, it is expected that the payout ratio will be 70% of the earnings per share, and the payout ratio is expected to remain at that level forever. If the required return on Microsoft common stock is 20% per year and the latest earnings per share was $5.00, at what price should Microsoft Corp. common stock be selling in the market?

B34. (Excel: Supernormal growth model) Key Marketing Corporation common stock is selling for $23.37 per share with an expected cash dividend next year of $1. Short-term prospects are excellent for Key Marketing: A 20% annual growth rate in dividend payments is expected for the three years following next year's dividend. After that, a normal growth rate of 6% per year forever is expected. What required return is implied by the current $23.37 price?

B35. (Excel: Required return with supernormal growth) Losh Key Corporation common stock is selling for $25.00 per share with an expected cash dividend next year of $1. Short-term prospects are excellent for Losh Key: A 25% annual growth rate in dividend payments is expected for the three years following next year's dividend. After that, a normal growth rate of 4% per year forever is expected. What required return does the current price of Losh Key's stock imply?

B36. (Excel: Constant growth model) RONAC Corporation will pay a $1.00 cash dividend in one year. The dividend is expected to grow forever at 7% annually, and the required rate of return is 12%.

a. What is the value of one share of RONAC?

b. What is the cumulative present value of the first five dividends? The first 10, 20, 30, 40, and 50? What are the percentages of the value of one share represented by these cumulative present values?

c. There is a formula for the value of a growing perpetuity that has a finite life of n years. The present value of the first n dividends, using this formula, is

$$PV = \frac{D_1}{r-g}\left[1 - \frac{(1+g)^n}{(1+r)^n}\right]$$

Use this formula to verify that the PV of the first 50 dividends agrees with what you found in part b.

B37. (Excel: Bond valuation) Norman Electric bonds have a \$1,000 face value, mature in 20 years, and have an 8% coupon (paid semiannually).

a. What is the value of the bond if the required rate of return is 9.5% (APR)?

b. If the bond can be purchased for \$850, what is the yield to maturity?

B38. (Excel: Supernormal growth model) The current ($t = 0$) dividend is \$2.20. The dividend will grow at 20% annually for three years, 12% annually for the following three years, and then grow at 6% forever after that. If the required return is 11%, what is the value of one share?

LEVEL C (Advanced)

C1. (Bond valuation between coupon payments) Gehr's Gears, Inc. has bonds outstanding that mature in 14 years and 3 months from today. The bonds have an annual coupon rate of 15% and pay interest every six months. The bonds are currently selling for \$1,100.

a. Assuming a coupon payment was made yesterday and there are 29 more coupon payments remaining to be paid in the life of the bond, what is the YTM on this bond? What is the APY for this bond under these assumptions?

b. Assuming a coupon payment was made yesterday and there are 28 more coupon payments remaining to be paid in the life of the bond, what is the YTM on this bond? What is the APY for this bond under these assumptions?

c. Assuming a coupon payment was made, as it actually was, three months ago and there are 29 more coupon payments remaining to be paid in the life of the bond, what is the YTM on this bond? What is the APY for this bond under these assumptions?

C2. (Bond valuation between coupon payments) Kay Patteris owns a bond that matures in six years and four months from today. The bond has an annual coupon rate of 6% and pays interest every six months. Currently, the bond is selling for \$825.

a. Assuming a coupon payment was made yesterday and there are 13 more coupon payments remaining to be paid in the life of the bond, what is the YTM on this bond? What is the APY for this bond under these assumptions?

b. Assuming a coupon payment was made yesterday and there are 12 more coupon payments remaining to be paid in the life of the bond, what is the YTM on this bond? What is the APY for this bond under these assumptions?

c. Assuming a coupon payment was made, as it actually was, two months ago and there are 13 more coupon payments remaining to be paid in the life of the bond, what is the YTM on this bond? What is the APY for this bond under these assumptions?

C3. (Supernormal growth model) Managers of The Biden-Time Co., makers of Mickey Moose watches, are currently considering suspending the firm's cash dividends for the next three years to invest the money in a project they call Court Jesters. Biden-Time's *current* operations are expected to earn \$.85 per share next year and with a constant payout ratio of 75% are expected to grow at 5% per year forever. Under the *proposed* Court Jesters plan, earnings are expected to grow at 17% per year for the investment years. After the investment, the firm expects to have a payout ratio of 70% and a growth rate in earnings of 6.5% forever. If the required return on Biden-Time's stock is 20% per year, what is the NPV per share of the Court Jesters plan?

C4. (Dividend discount model) The copy service Quick Quality in Quantity (Q3) has a payout ratio of 80%, a required return of 10%, and is expected to pay a dividend next year of \$2.00. If Q3 is selling for \$25 per share, what is its expected return? What is the expected market value of a share of Q3 four years from now?

C5. (Dividend discount model) Philip Quick, owner of a chain of self-service gas stations, has several investments. One of them is 2,000 shares of Getty Oil. Getty is expected to pay a dividend next year of \$2.38 and has expected growth of 6% per year forever. If Getty is selling for \$19.45 per share, what is Phil's expected return on Getty Oil? Another of Phil's investments is 1,200 shares of ConEdison, which has an expected growth rate in dividends of 4% per year forever, sells for \$41.88, and is expected to pay a dividend of \$3.35 per share next year. What is Phil's expected return on ConEdison? Now the real question: How can Phil's expected returns be different for these two investments? Why doesn't Phil sell the one with the lower expected return and buy more of the one with the higher return?

C6. (Bond yield) In 1998, the U.S. Treasury discovered that it had been paying Social Security and other trust funds hundreds of millions of dollars a year in extra interest because of a mistake a computer programmer had made in 1980. The Treasury pays interest on special nonmarketable bonds issued to the trust funds based on the average market yield of outstanding Treasury debt with more than four years to maturity as calculated by a computer program. Market practice is to assume that callable Treasury bonds that are trading at a premium to face value will be called for face value as soon as they become callable. However, the Treasury's computer program assumed that premium bonds would not be called before maturity.

a. Calculate the YTM (yield to maturity) for a 10% Treasury bond with a price of 130 that matures in 15 years, assuming annual payments and compounding.

b. Calculate the YTC (yield to call) on the same bond, assuming it is callable at par in 10 years.

c. Explain why the Treasury's mistake was so costly.

C7. (Excel: Rate of return for supernormal growth stock) PM Enterprises has paid a \$2.00 dividend in the year just ended. The dividend will grow at 20% annually for the next four years and then grow at 5% thereafter. The stock price is \$30.

a. Estimate the rate of return you will earn if you purchase PM Enterprises at its current stock price. Use trial and error with the supernormal growth model equation to find the answer.

b. Forecast dividends for the next 100 years. Find the discount rate that makes the present value of the dividend stream equal the stock price.

C8. (Excel: Bond prices) Cincinnati Engines has a six-year bond outstanding. It has a 6% coupon (paid semiannually) and \$1,000 face value. Assume that the yield to maturity (APR) follows one of the three paths below. What will be the value of the bond at the beginning of each of the next six years, assuming these price paths?

PATH	TIME TO MATURITY					
	6	5	4	3	2	1
1	10%	10%	10%	10%	10%	10%
2	10%	9%	8%	7%	6%	5%
3	10%	11%	12%	13%	14%	15%

MINICASE BOND YIELDS FOR JOHNSON & JOHNSON

Johnson & Johnson is a well known, large, and financially sophisticated global corporation. When it borrows money, it works to get the best deal. Sometimes it sells domestic bonds, and other times it sells Eurodollar bonds. The main difference between these two types of bonds is that domestic bonds pay interest semiannually, whereas Eurobonds pay annually. Because of this, if you want to determine the lowest-cost alternative, you must compare the bonds' APYs. Below is information about five Johnson & Johnson debt issues.

There is another complication in calculating bond yields. Throughout the chapter, we valued bonds at the beginning of an interest period. In reality, of course, bonds can trade throughout a period. In practice, a bond's price is quoted without accrued interest. However, the *invoice price* the buyer pays the seller is the quoted price plus pro rata accrued interest. For example, suppose a 7% semiannual bond trades at a quoted price of 95 on day 108 of a 182-day interest period. The pro rata accrued interest will be \$20.77 (108/182 of the \$35 semiannual interest payment), and therefore the invoice price is \$970.77.

Let f represent the fraction of an interest period since the last interest payment. The present value of the bond's coupon payments can be calculated by adjusting the bond valuation formula, Equation (5.1), for the fractional period. The adjustment is the same as the one illustrated in Figure 4.11 in Chapter 4. The bond value given in Equation (5.1) is compounded forward by f, the fraction of the interest period. Setting this adjusted present value equal to the invoice price, we have:

$$B_0 + f(\text{PMT}) = \left((\text{PMT}) \left[\frac{(1+r)^n - 1}{(r)(1+r)^n} \right] + \frac{1{,}000}{(1+r)^n} \right) (1+r)^f$$

where B_0 is the quoted bond price, PMT is the bond interest payment per period, n is the number of remaining periods, and r is the yield per period.

If you know r, you can rearrange this equation and solve for B_0 using trial and error with a calculator. However, solving for r using a calculator is very tedious. Therefore, we recommend you use a spreadsheet to solve for r.

ISSUE	MARKET	FREQUENCY	MATURITY	PRICE (% OF PAR)
7.375s20	Eurobond	Annual	11/09/20	101.9785
7.375s19	Domestic	Semiannual	06/29/19	103.2288
8.25s28	Eurobond	Annual	04/30/28	110.1563
6.73s17	Domestic	Semiannual	09/15/17	98.1535
6.85s32	Domestic	Semiannual	01/01/32	97.0501

QUESTIONS

1. Calculate the APY for each of Johnson & Johnson's bonds and identify which one has the lowest APY, assuming today is January 15, 2006.
2. The 8.25s28 can be called in 2018 at par. Calculate the YTC (yield to call), assuming today is January 15, 2006. Does this change your answer to question 1?

6

BUSINESS INVESTMENT RULES

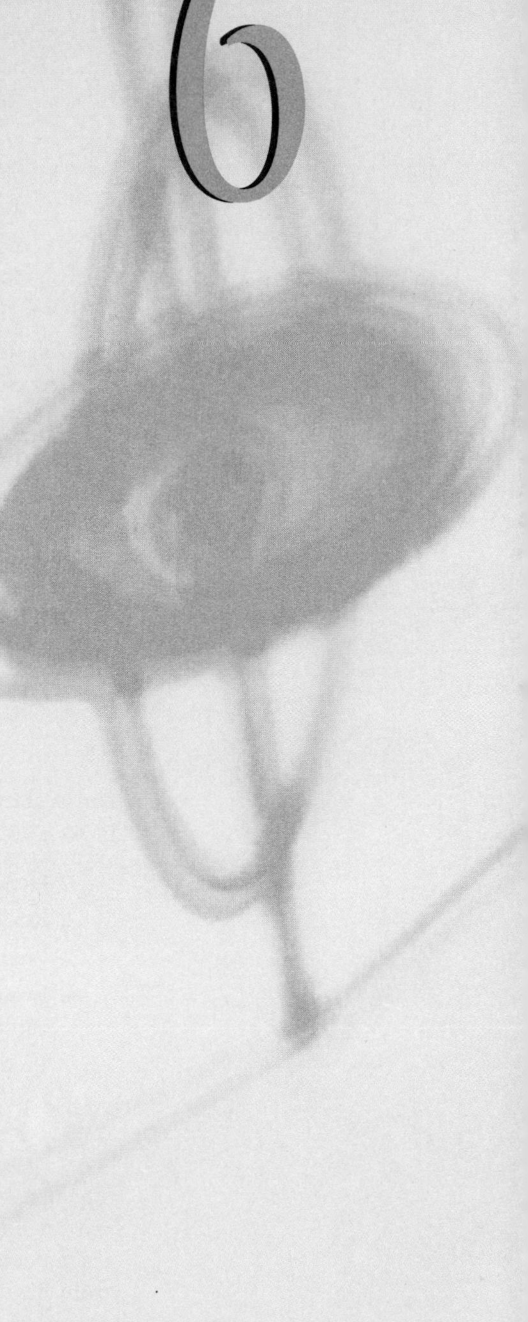

When making capital budgeting decisions, a firm evaluates the expected future cash flows in relation to the required initial investment. The objective is to find investment projects that will add value to the firm. These are projects that are worth more to the firm than they cost—projects that have a positive NPV.

The pivotal role of capital budgeting, and the risks associated with capital investments, are dramatically demonstrated by comparing the initial cash outflow, which can be huge, to that of the relatively much smaller expected periodic future cash inflows. The risk is especially obvious if you consider the tremendous uncertainty associated with the timing and size of the future cash flows. A firm might invest $200 million now, *hoping* to net $30 million per year *after* several years of development!

A firm's evaluation of a long-term investment project is like an individual's investment decision. The steps are the same:

1. Estimate the expected future cash flows from the project, like estimating the coupon payments for a bond or the dividend stream for a stock, and a maturity value or terminal sale price.
2. Assess the risk and determine a required return for discounting the expected future cash flows.
3. Compute the present value of the expected future cash flows.
4. Determine the cost of the project and compare it to what the project is worth. If the project is worth more than it costs—if it has a positive NPV—it will create value.

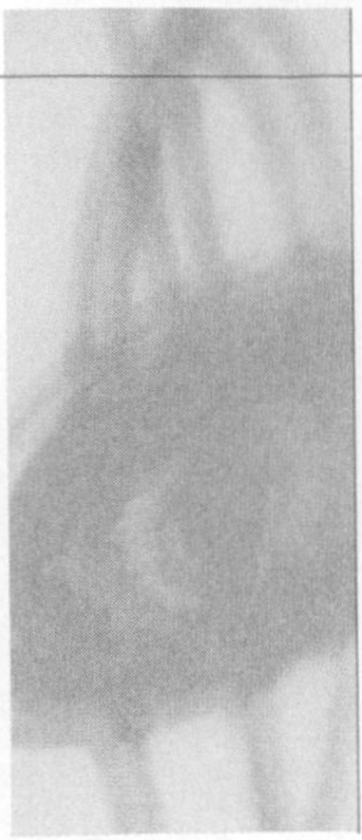

FOCUS ON PRINCIPLES

- *Valuable Ideas:* Look for new ideas to use as a basis for capital budgeting projects that will create value.
- *Comparative Advantage:* Look for capital budgeting projects that will use the firm's comparative advantage to create value.
- *Incremental Benefits:* Identify and estimate the expected future cash flows for a capital budgeting project on an incremental basis.
- *Risk-Return Trade-Off:* Incorporate the risk of a capital budgeting project into its *cost of capital*—the project's required return.
- *Time Value of Money:* Measure the current value a capital budgeting project will create, its NPV.
- *Options:* Recognize the value of options, such as the options to expand, postpone, or abandon a capital budgeting project.
- *Two-Sided Transactions:* Consider why the other party to a transaction is willing to participate.
- *Signaling:* Consider the products and actions of competitors.

In this chapter we will present the process of capital budgeting as it is practiced in most corporations. We will show you ways to measure the attractiveness of projects. As you will see, some badly flawed methods remain in practice and can lead to bad decisions. We will also show how sound methods of evaluating business investments can be applied to both proposed projects and to current operations. When combined with reasonable estimates of future outcomes, these methods support good decisions.

Throughout this first chapter on capital budgeting, we will ignore taxes and certain other complications to focus on basic investment criteria and the process of capital budgeting.

6.1 THE CAPITAL BUDGETING PROCESS

Let us start by looking at how **capital budgeting** works in practice. The overall process can be broken down into five steps as a project moves from idea to reality:

1. Generating ideas for capital budgeting projects
2. Reviewing existing projects and facilities
3. Preparing proposals
4. Evaluating proposed projects and creating the **capital budget,** the firm's set of planned capital expenditures
5. Preparing appropriation requests

Idea Generation

The first—and most important—part of the capital budgeting process is generating new ideas. Its critical importance is obvious from the Principle of Valuable Ideas. Unfortunately, we cannot teach people how to come up with valuable new ideas. If we could, we would already be wealthy from having followed the procedure ourselves! However, although we don't have a process that ensures the creation of new ideas, it is important to stress their value. Such an emphasis makes it more likely that those ideas that do occur to us and to others will be given serious consideration.

Where do new ideas come from? Ideas for capital budgeting projects come from all levels within an organization. Figure 6.1 shows the typical flow of capital investment ideas within a firm. Often plant managers are responsible for identifying potential projects that will enable their plants to operate on a different scale or on a more efficient basis. For instance, a plant manager

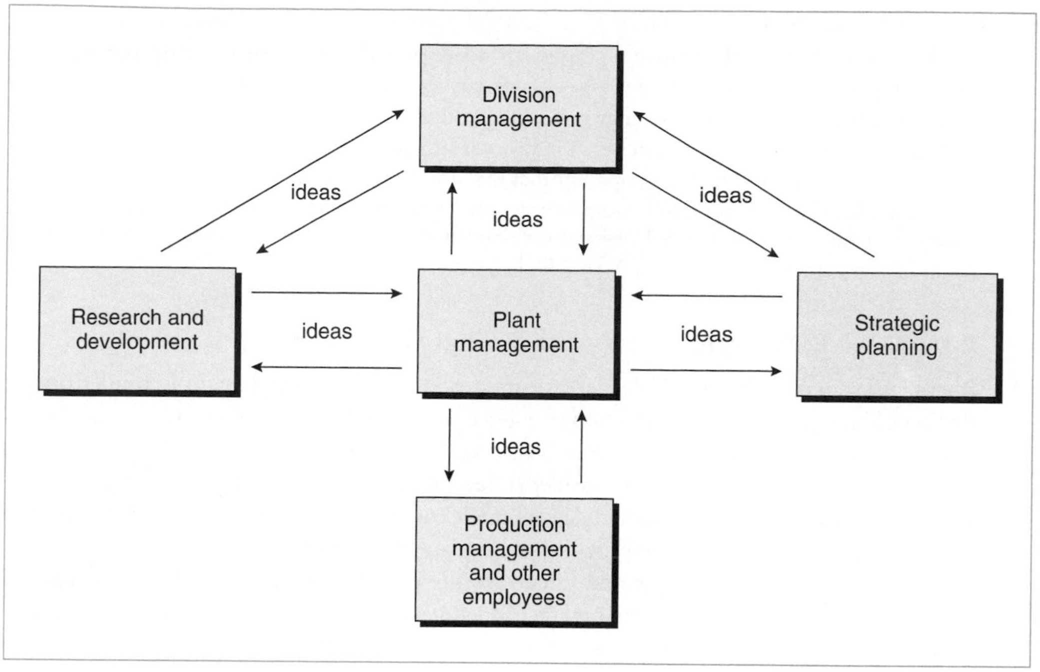

FIGURE 6.1
The typical flow of capital budgeting ideas within a firm.

might suggest adding 10,000 square feet of production space to a plant or replacing a piece of equipment with a newer, more efficient machine. After screening out the less advantageous or less attractive ideas, the manager would send the ones that appear to be attractive to the divisional level, along with supporting documentation.

Division management not only reviews such proposals, but also adds ideas of its own. For example, division management may propose the introduction of a new product line or combining two plants and eliminating the less efficient one. Such ideas are less likely to come from the plant managers!

This bottom-up process results in ideas percolating upward through the organization. At each level, ideas submitted by lower-level managers are screened; some are forwarded to the next level. In addition, the managers at successively higher levels, who are in a position to take a broader view of the firm's business, add ideas that may not be visible to lower-level managers.

At the same time, there is also a top-down process at work in most firms. Strategic planners will generate ideas regarding new businesses the firm should enter, other firms it might acquire, and ways to modify its existing businesses to achieve greater profitability. Strategic planning is a critical element in the capital budgeting process. The processes complement one another; the top-down process generates ideas of a broader, more strategic nature, whereas the bottom-up process generates ideas of a more project-specific nature.

In addition, some firms have a research-and-development group, either within a production division or as a separate department. A research-and-development group often provides new ideas for products that can be sent on to a marketing research department. Table 6.1 lists the typical stages for the development and approval of a capital investment proposal.

Each stage in Table 6.1 involves a capital budgeting decision at one or more levels of the firm. Therefore, at each stage, the firm re-estimates the NPV of going ahead. With this kind of sequential appropriation of funds, an automatic progress review is enforced, which enables early cancellation of unsuccessful projects. So each stage includes options, for example, to abandon, postpone, change, or continue.

TABLE 6.1
Development and approval stages for a proposed capital budgeting project.

1. Approve funds for research that may result in a product *idea.*
2. Approve funds for market research that may result in a product *proposal.*
3. Approve funds for product development that may result in a usable *product.*
4. Approve funds for plant and/or equipment for the *production* and sale of the new product.

EXAMPLE Strategic Decisions at Boeing: Will It Fly?

Boeing Corporation is a world leader in commercial aircraft. In the heat of competition, Boeing often faces a critical capital budgeting decision: whether to develop a new generation of passenger aircraft. Developing new aircraft is very expensive.

For example, recently, Boeing considered developing a new generation of its highly successful 747 jumbo jet. The estimated development cost was $7 billion. Its major competitor, Airbus Industrie, was also considering developing larger, longer-range aircraft.

Boeing announced that it would undertake the project only if it would benefit shareholders. After sizing up the potential market, Boeing scrapped plans for the new 747 because of rising development costs and weak demand for the plane.

Classifying Capital Budgeting Projects

Analysis costs money. Therefore, certain types of projects receive only cursory checks before approval, whereas others are subjected to extensive analysis. Generally, less costly and more routine projects are subjected to less extensive evaluation. As a result, firms typically categorize projects and analyze them at the level judged appropriate to their category. Investments in each category may have a lot in common and can be analyzed similarly. A useful set of investment classifications is:

Maintenance projects
Cost-saving/revenue-enhancing projects
Capacity expansions in current businesses
New products and new businesses
Projects required by government regulation or firm policy

MAINTENANCE EXPENDITURES At a most basic level, a firm must make certain investments to continue to be a healthy, profitable business. Replacing worn-out or damaged equipment is necessary to continue in business. Therefore, the major questions concerning such investments are: "Should we continue in this business?" and if so, "Should we continue to use the same production process?" Because the answers to these questions are so frequently "yes," an elaborate decision-making process is not a good use of resources. Typically, such decisions are approved with only routine review.

COST SAVINGS/REVENUE ENHANCEMENT These projects include improvements in production technology to realize cost savings and marketing campaigns to achieve revenue enhancement. The central issue is increasing the difference between revenue and cost; the result must be sufficient to justify the investment. Cost-reducing investments involve not only the requirement that the purchase and installation of the equipment must be profitable, but also that current action is better than waiting until a later time—there may be a valuable option to postpone.

CAPACITY EXPANSION IN CURRENT BUSINESSES Deciding to expand the current business is inherently more difficult than approving maintenance or cost-savings proposals. Firms have to consider the economics of expanding or adding new facilities and must also prepare demand forecasts. The Principle of Two-Sided Transactions reminds us to consider competitors' likely strategies. Marketing consultants may help, but the cash flow projections for this type of project have naturally greater uncertainty than do maintenance or replacement projects.

NEW PRODUCTS AND NEW BUSINESSES These projects, which include research-and-development activities, are among the most difficult to evaluate. Their newness and long lead times make it very difficult to forecast product demand accurately. In many cases, the project may be of special interest because it would give the firm an option to break into a new market. For example, a firm that possesses a proprietary technology might spend additional research-and-development funds trying to develop new products based on this technology. If successful, these new products could pave the way for future profitable investment opportunities. Access to such follow-up opportunities creates options for the firm, which you know are valuable.

MEETING REGULATORY AND POLICY REQUIREMENTS Government regulations and/or firm policies concerning such things as pollution control and health or safety factors are viewed as costs. Often, the critical issue in such projects is meeting the standards in the most efficient manner—at the minimum present-value cost—rather than realizing the value added by the project. Engineering analyses of alternative technologies often provide critical information in such cases. Of course, the firm must also consider the possibility that the option to abandon the business is worth more than making the required investments and continuing.

Capital Budgeting Proposals

Small expenditures may be handled informally but, in general, the originator presents a proposal in writing. Sometimes proposals are not formally written in smaller, privately owned firms, which tend to have relatively informal organizational structures. Most firms use standard forms, and these are typically supplemented by written memoranda for larger, more complex projects. Also, there may be consulting or other studies prepared by outside experts; for example, economic forecasts from economic consultants.

For a healthy firm, a maintenance project might require only limited supporting information. In contrast, a new product would require extensive information gathering and analysis. At the same time, within a category, managers at each level typically have upper limits on their authority regarding both expenditures on individual assets and the total expenditure for a budgeting period. In this way, larger projects require the approval of higher authority.

For example, at the lowest level, a department head may have the authority to approve \$25,000 in total equipment purchases for the year but must obtain specific approval from higher authority for any single piece of equipment costing more than \$5,000. A plant manager might have authorization limits of \$250,000 per year and \$50,000 per piece of equipment, and so forth.

A system of authorization such as this requires more extensive review and a greater number of inputs to improve important ideas. Multiple reviews make sense because a firm wishes to avoid making a negative-NPV investment. The hierarchical review structure reflects the obvious fact that misjudging a larger project is potentially more costly than misjudging a smaller one, hence, the need for a greater number of reviews before deciding to proceed.

Capital Budgeting and the Required Return

Recall that the required return is the minimum rate of return that you need to earn to be willing to make an investment. It is the rate of return that exactly reflects the riskiness of the expected future cash flows. In capital budgeting, the required return has several different names. The most widely used term is the **cost of capital.** Other names are the *hurdle rate* and the *appropriate discount rate,* or simply the *discount rate.* Although these terms may be used interchangeably, it is important to remember that the cost of capital reflects the riskiness of the capital budgeting project's cash flows, not the interest rate on its bonds or the riskiness of the firm's *existing* assets.

Review

1. What are the five steps in the capital budgeting process? Which is most important?
2. Why are capital budgeting projects frequently classified into groups such as maintenance projects, cost savings/revenue enhancement projects, capacity expansion projects, new product/new business projects, and projects mandated by regulation or firm policy?
3. What other names are used to refer to the cost of capital, a capital budgeting project's required return?

6.2 NET PRESENT VALUE (NPV)

Recall that an asset's net present value (NPV) is the difference between what it is worth (the present value of its expected future cash flows—its market value) and what it costs. A capital budgeting project is a collection of assets.

Can something really be worth more than it costs? Yes, it happens. But being the skeptical and insightful person you are, you know that we are not going to give you a list of such opportunities; we would rather keep it for ourselves. In fact, the major difficulty of finding a project's NPV rests on the need to see situations differently from other people in the market. That means taking some risk based on special knowledge or valuable ideas. At best, we can estimate a project's NPV in advance. We will not know its true market value, or what it is *really* worth, until the project is completed and the returns are collected.

EXAMPLE Discovering a Positive-NPV Opportunity

Suppose you have noticed a run-down office building in downtown Asbury Park that you think has possibilities. You decide to buy it for $420,000 and invest $300,000 more in renovations over the next six months. After this, you offer the building for sale and sell it to the highest bidder for $910,000. Because the building turned out to be worth more than you paid for it, that is, its market value of $910,000 exceeded its cost of $720,000 (= $420,000 + 300,000), your management will have created about $190,000 (= $910,000 − 720,000) in value.

Although it is delightful to contemplate the money you made in our example, think about how you could have known enough to undertake this capital budgeting project in the first place. To estimate the market value after renovation, you might have looked at other buildings in good repair to see what they were worth and then adjusted for differences between these buildings and the run-down one you were thinking of buying. You would also estimate the cost of the needed renovations and add that to the cost of buying the building, to determine the total cost. Finally, you would compare your market value estimate to your total cost estimate.

If the estimates tell you the project creates value, and your estimates are correct, then you get the value that is created. You can see right away how important accurate estimates are!

Let us generalize from our building renovation example. You could find the building's market value by offering it for sale—the highest offer you get is its market value. However, that is possible only after doing the renovations. Although you might be able to offer the building for sale before doing the renovations by describing your plans, at best this would be awkward, time consuming, and expensive. Furthermore, keep in mind the Principle of Two-Sided Transactions: Once you pointed out the potential value of renovating the building to other people, some of them might decide to bid on the building now for more than the $420,000 you hoped to pay for it.

As an alternative, the example mentioned a method of estimating market value without offering it for sale: Find the market value of a similar asset and adjust for whatever differences there are between the two.

Yet another way to determine value is to use **discounted-cash-flow (DCF) analysis** and compute the present value of all the cash flows connected with ownership. This is like discounting the interest payments on a bond or dividends on a stock.

The NPV of a capital budgeting project is the present value of *all* of the cash flows connected with the project, all its costs and revenues, now and in the future:

$$\text{NPV} = \text{CF}_0 + \frac{\text{CF}_1}{(1+r)} + \frac{\text{CF}_2}{(1+r)^2} + \cdots + \frac{\text{CF}_n}{(1+r)^n}$$

$$= \sum_{t=0}^{n} \frac{\text{CF}_t}{(1+r)^t} \qquad (6.1)$$

DECISION RULE for net present value: Undertake a capital budgeting project if the NPV is positive.

EXAMPLE Computing an NPV

Suppose that instead of expecting to sell the building after you renovate it, you expect to lease it out for 20 years and then sell the building for $250,000. You expect the lease to pay you $110,000 per year. Finally, the cost of capital in this case is 12%. What is the NPV of this renovation project?

Using Equation (6.1), the NPV is $127,555.49:

$$\text{NPV} = -[420,000 + 300,000] + 110,000 \sum_{t=1}^{20} \frac{1}{(1.12)^t} + 250,000 \frac{1}{(1.12)^{20}}$$

$$= -720,000 + 821,639.80 + 25,916.69 = \$127,555.49$$

The NPV is the present value of the future cash flows, which is $847,555.49 minus the initial cost of $720,000.

CALCULATOR SOLUTION

Data Input	Function Key
20	N
12	I
110,000	PMT
250,000	FV
847,555.49	**PV**

It is important to note that the uncertainty connected with the assumptions about revenues, costs, and selling price are included in the cost of capital (required return). That is to say, computing the NPV does *not* reduce the risk. If the assumptions work out, however, you will be richer for undertaking the project.

Adding Value per Share

If the firm undertook the building renovation project, how much value does it add to a share of its stock? Typically, each share has a $1/n$ claim on the firm's value, where n is the number of outstanding shares. This claim extends to the project's NPV. In concept then, if the firm had 100,000 shares of common stock outstanding, and our estimates are correct, the project would add $1.28 per share (= 127,555.49/100,000). If the project were completely unanticipated by the market, and the market agreed with the NPV estimate, the price of the stock would jump by $1.28 per share. In practice, a share of stock does not typically change precisely by its fractional claim on the NPV of a new project. This is because prices are made on expectations, and rarely is it the case where the project is a complete surprise and the market makes the identical estimate of NPV.

Review

1. What is the NPV of a capital budgeting project?
2. State the decision rule for net present value.
3. What is discounted-cash-flow analysis?

6.3 INTERNAL RATE OF RETURN (IRR)

Another method of evaluating a capital budgeting project is called the internal-rate-of-return method. The **internal rate of return (IRR)** is the project's expected return. If the cost of capital (required return) equals the IRR (expected return), the NPV equals zero. So, one way of viewing the IRR is to say that it is the discount rate that makes the total present value of all of a project's cash flows sum to zero. Of course, because of risk, the project's realized return will almost surely be different from its IRR. Recall from Chapter 5 how to compute a bond's yield to maturity (YTM). We use the same sort of procedure to compute an IRR:

$$CF_0 + \frac{CF_1}{(1 + IRR)} + \frac{CF_2}{(1 + IRR)^2} + \cdots + \frac{CF_n}{(1 + IRR)^n} = 0$$

$$\sum_{t=0}^{n} \frac{CF_t}{(1 + IRR)^t} = 0 \qquad (6.2)$$

DECISION RULE for internal rate of return: Undertake the capital budgeting project if the IRR exceeds *r*, the project's cost of capital.

In its simplest form, the IRR rule is intuitively appealing. In essence, it asks whether the capital budgeting project's expected return exceeds its required return. In other words, will it create value?

At first glance, this seems to be saying the same thing the NPV rule says. As we will see, this is generally true—but not always. The intuitive appeal of the IRR rule, however, probably accounts for its widespread use (in fact, many practitioners even prefer it).

Like other expected returns, the IRR must be calculated by trial and error. Although many calculators and spreadsheets can solve for the IRR, they also are using trial and error. Let us work through a detailed trial-and-error calculation to help you understand the problem.

EXAMPLE Computing an IRR for Reebok

Suppose Reebok can invest in a capital budgeting project that has a 12% cost of capital. The project's expected future net cash flows are shown in Figure 6.2. What is the IRR of Reebok's capital budgeting project?

When in doubt, start by trying 10%. At a discount rate of 10%, the NPV of this project would be

$$NPV_{10\%} = -800 + \frac{300}{(1.10)^1} + \frac{300}{(1.10)^2} + \frac{300}{(1.10)^3} + \frac{150}{(1.10)^4} = +\ 48.51$$

FIGURE 6.2
Expected future net cash flows for Reebok's capital budgeting project.

Year	0	1	2	3	4
Cash flows	−800	300	300	300	150

Because $NPV_{10\%}$ is positive, we need a larger rate. Let us try 14%.

$$NPV_{14\%} = -800 + \frac{300}{(1.14)^1} + \frac{300}{(1.14)^2} + \frac{300}{(1.14)^3} + \frac{150}{(1.14)^4} = -14.70$$

Because 14% would make the NPV negative, it is too high. Let us try 13%:

$$NPV_{13\%} = -800 + \frac{300}{(1.13)^1} + \frac{300}{(1.13)^2} + \frac{300}{(1.13)^3} + \frac{150}{(1.13)^4} = +0.34$$

This is pretty close, but you could keep going with this process and be more accurate. In this particular case, you could notice that the cash flows are very even and can be represented as an annuity of +300 per year for four years plus a terminal cash flow of −150. Then, using a calculator, calculate IRR = 13.0225%. With a cost of capital of 12%, then, the IRR decision rule would tell us to undertake this project, which is the same advice the NPV decision rule offers.

CALCULATOR SOLUTION

Data Input	Function Key
4	N
−800	PV
300	PMT
−150	FV
13.0225	I

If you consider a project where the cash flows are more complex and uneven, you can see the value of a spreadsheet. In practice, spreadsheets are used for all but the simplest projects.

Review

1. What is a capital budgeting project's IRR?
2. State the decision rule for internal rate of return. What does it mean in practical terms?
3. Does the IRR rule usually lead to the same investment decisions as the NPV rule?

6.4 USING THE NPV AND IRR CRITERIA

In many applications, the NPV and IRR are both valuable guides to making capital budgeting decisions. Frequently, both the NPV and IRR agree and can be trusted to provide a valid assessment. There are some instances, however, where the NPV and IRR disagree on the relative merits of projects, and there are other instances where the IRR is very difficult to interpret. In this section, we discuss when both methods can be trusted. We also show cases where they disagree. When in doubt, as we show, use the NPV rule.

When the IRR and NPV Methods Agree: Independent, Conventional Projects

In the example just given, the IRR and NPV methods agree. This will happen whenever the projects are both independent and conventional. An **independent project** is one that can be chosen independently of other projects. That is, undertaking it neither requires nor precludes any other investment. A project that requires other investments is simply part of a larger capital budgeting project, which must be evaluated together with all of its parts. When undertaking one project prevents investing in another project, and vice versa, the projects are said to be **mutually exclusive projects.**

A **conventional project** is a project with an initial cash outflow that is followed by one or more expected future cash inflows. That is, after making the investment, the total cash flow in each future year is expected to be positive. Purchasing a stock or bond is a simple example of a conventional capital budgeting project: You buy the security (a negative cash flow), and the terminal sale price and any dividends or interest payments while you own it will not be negative (you have limited liability).

NPV Profile

Another way to look at this problem is to graph NPV as a function of the discount rate. This graph is called an **NPV profile,** which is a very useful tool.

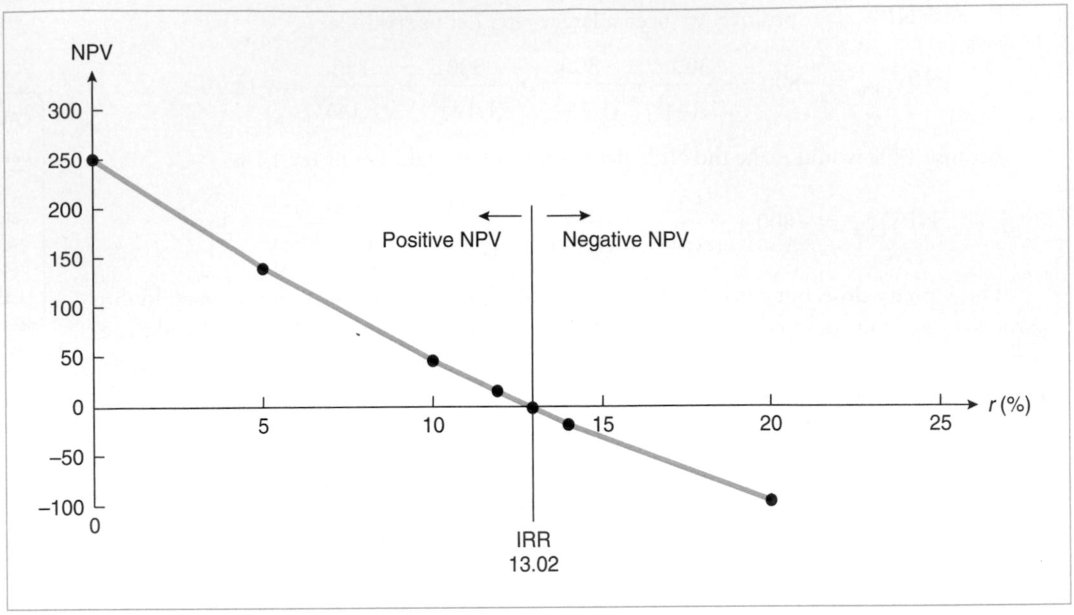

FIGURE 6.3
An NPV profile.

The NPV profile includes both NPV and IRR, as well as the project's value at various costs of capital. Therefore, if you are unsure about the project's cost of capital, you can use the NPV profile to identify costs of capital at which the project would not create value.

An NPV profile for our IRR computation example is presented in Figure 6.3. To construct this NPV profile, we use the calculations in the example and a couple more. One of the additional calculations assumes a cost of capital of 0%, in which case the NPV would be +250. This calculation is straightforward because it is simply the undiscounted sum of all the cash flows. We also calculated what the NPV would be at discount rates of 5% and 20%, to fill in the graph.

The NPV profile in Figure 6.3 shows the general relationship between IRR and NPV for independent, conventional projects. If the IRR exceeds the cost of capital, the NPV is positive. If the IRR is less than the cost of capital, the NPV is negative.

When IRR and NPV Can Differ: Mutually Exclusive Capital Budgeting Projects

Thus far, we have looked only at the question of whether or not to undertake an independent project. But often we must choose from a set of mutually exclusive projects. If we undertake one, we cannot undertake any of the others.

For example, a firm that plans to build a new assembly plant might have three possible locations and four possible plant configurations. But the firm needs only *one* plant. Therefore, it must choose one configuration in one location, and the alternatives are effectively mutually exclusive. In such cases, we can get conflicting recommendations from the IRR and NPV methods.

Conflicting recommendations can occur because there is a difference in (1) the *size* of the projects, or (2) the *cash flow timing*. An example of the latter occurs when cash flows from one project come in mostly early and cash flows from the other project come in later. We will look at each of these types of differences in turn.

SIZE DIFFERENCES When one project is larger than another, the smaller project can have a larger IRR but a smaller NPV. For example, suppose project A has an IRR of 30% and an NPV of $100, and project B has an IRR of 20% and an NPV of $200. The choice between these two

Year	0	1	2	3	4	5	6	IRR	NPV
Project S	−250	100	100	75	75	50	25	22.08%	76.29
Project L	−250	50	50	75	100	100	125	20.01%	94.08

FIGURE 6.4
Alternative short- and long-term capital budgeting projects for Guess.

projects—and therefore the resolution of such conflicts—is fairly straightforward: You need only decide whether you would rather have more wealth or a larger IRR. Like you, we will take the wealth, thank you. Therefore, the NPV decision rule is the better rule to follow when mutually exclusive projects differ in size.

CASH FLOW TIMING DIFFERENCES The problem of cash flow timing can arise because of the **reinvestment rate assumption.** The question is: "What will the cash inflows from the investment earn when they are subsequently reinvested in other projects?" The IRR method assumes the future cash inflows will earn the project's IRR. The NPV method assumes they will earn the cost of capital.

The following example illustrates the conflict in the reinvestment rate assumption that results from a difference in cash flow timing. As you will see, the NPV profiles diverge at a **crossover point,** a cost of capital at which the two projects have equal NPV.

EXAMPLE Comparing IRR with NPV at Guess, Inc.

Suppose Guess, Inc. can invest in only one of two projects, S (for short term) and L (for long term). The cost of capital is 10%, and the projects have the expected future cash flows shown in Figure 6.4. Which is the better project?

Project S has an IRR of 22.08%, and project L has an IRR of 20.01%. But project S has an NPV of \$76.29, and project L has an NPV of \$94.08. Thus, the IRR method tells us to choose S, but the NPV method says choose L.

Take a look at Figure 6.5. It compares NPV and IRR. You can see there that project S will have a higher NPV than project L whenever the cost of capital is higher than 15.40%, the crossover point.[1] Both projects would have an NPV of \$37.86 if the cost of capital were 15.40%. You can also see that project L has a steeper NPV profile than project S. This is because the present values of cash flows farther in the future are more sensitive to the discount rate. We saw this in the case of bonds, where the market value of a long-term bond changes more than that of a short-term bond in response to a given interest rate change.

Which method makes the better assumption about what the reinvested cash flows will earn? If the cost of capital is computed correctly, it is the project's required return. In equilibrium, the required return equals the expected return and, over time, competitive forces drive investment returns to equilibrium.

Although new ideas can be very valuable, after awhile most people will be using them, and they will no longer command a positive NPV. So the NPV from future projects based on the

[1]You can compute the crossover point by finding the rate that makes the present value of the cash flow differences equal zero. Thus, for this example, the yearly differences are:

Year	0	1	2	3	4	5	6
Cash flow difference	0	50	50	0	−25	−50	−100

You can verify that 15.3985% will make the present value of this cash flow stream equal zero.

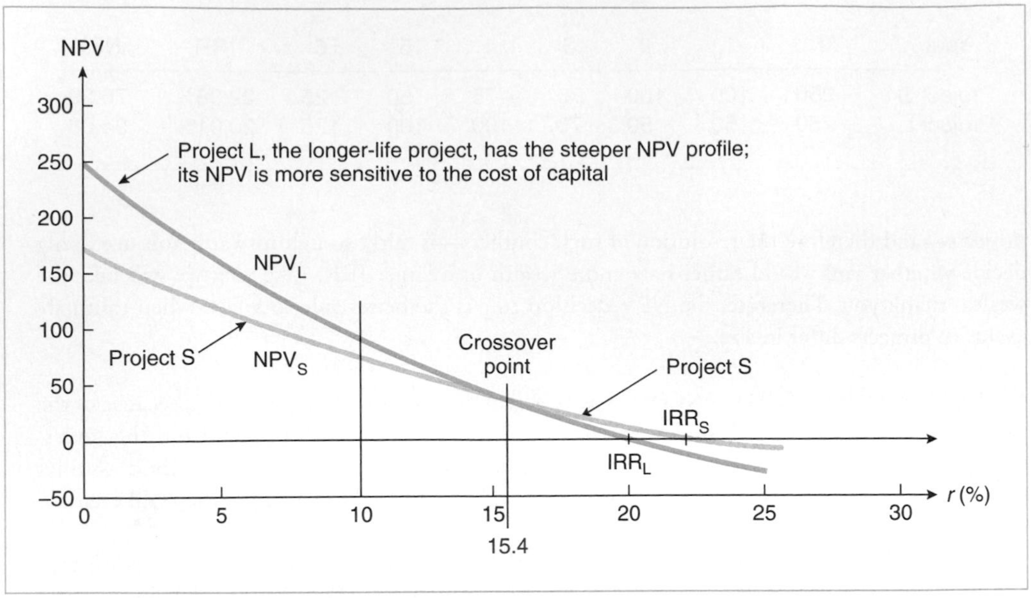

FIGURE 6.5
A comparison of NPV and IRR.

same sort of idea will tend toward zero. In the long run, then, reinvested cash flows can earn the cost of capital, but not the extra, positive, NPV. So the NPV method's assumption that the reinvestment rate will equal the cost of capital is the better assumption. And, again, the NPV decision rule is superior to the IRR decision rule.

Another Case Where IRR and NPV Can Differ: Nonconventional Projects

We defined a conventional capital budgeting project earlier in the chapter. A **nonconventional project** has a cash flow pattern that is different in some way from conventional projects. Nonconventional projects can create a conflict between the NPV and IRR decision rules.

In some cases, a nonconventional project is simply the reverse conventional project, one in which the initial cash flow is positive and the subsequent flows are all negative. A lifetime annuity, which insurance firms sell to retired persons, is an example. From the insurance firm's viewpoint, it receives a lump-sum amount at the start of the investment. It then makes monthly payments to the annuity's owner for the rest of that person's life.

Analyzing such cases using IRR is straightforward: Simply reverse the IRR decision rule. That is, for a reverse conventional project, undertake the project if the IRR is *less than* the cost of capital. Of course, if you forget to reverse the IRR rule in such cases, you will make exactly the wrong decision.

Unfortunately, complications can arise. When some future cash flows are expected to be positive and others negative, there can be multiple IRRs. Such cases can occur, for example, when an environmental cleanup is necessary at the end of the project. The firm makes an initial investment, receives positive cash flows while the project is operating, and then must make a cash outlay to clean up when the project is terminated. Another example is a project that requires one or more major renovations during its life. Let's take a look at the kinds of conflicts that can arise in these more complex situations.

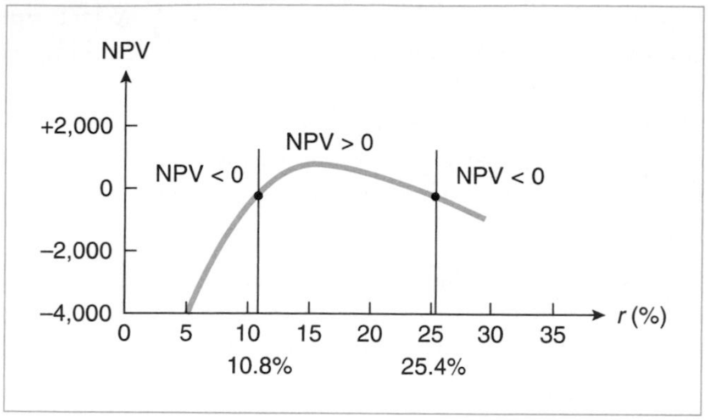

FIGURE 6.6
A capital budgeting project with multiple IRRs.

EXAMPLE Multiple IRRs for Triborg, Inc.

Triborg, Inc. can invest in a project that has an initial cost of −$24,000, with expected future cash flows of $58,000 after three years and −$51,000 after 10 years. So the net expected cash flows are negative, positive, and negative. Is this a problem? It can be.

The best way to see the problem we are illustrating here is to look at the NPV profile for this project, which is shown in Figure 6.6. You can see the problem right away. With possible discount rates from 0 to 30%, the NPV goes from negative to positive, and back to negative again. The project has two IRRs, 10.8% and 25.4%. That is, there are two points where the NPV would be zero if those points were the cost of capital.[2]

In this case, the IRR decision rule breaks down completely. If we applied the IRR decision rule blindly to this choice, we could make a serious mistake.

For example, if the cost of capital were 10% and both IRRs exceed this, we would undertake the project because both IRRs exceed this. However, at a 10% cost of capital, the project has a negative NPV. Reversing the rule as we did with reverse conventional projects does not help either. If the cost of capital exceeded 26%, the rule would again lead to an incorrect decision. Finally, even in the range where the NPV is positive, it is not very large, and the project would not create much wealth, anyway.

Unfortunately, calculators and currently available PC software generally are not fully equipped to handle the problem of multiple IRRs. They often report only the IRR their trial-and-error process happens to find first. However, they can be used to create an NPV profile. And, in any case, that provides a much more complete view of the project's potential value.

IRR, on Balance

At this point, you may ask, "Why use the IRR rule, when you may have to make several NPV calculations in the course of computing the IRR?" Our answer is that you should not use the IRR rule. Use NPV, instead.

In practice, however, the IRR rule is more widely used than the NPV rule. Many people prefer the intuitive feel of the IRR rule: After all, if the expected return is big enough, it will surely exceed the required return, and the project is a good investment. Such straightforward simplicity is

[2]The number of IRRs is never more than the number of sign reversals in the stream of cash flows. So conventional projects and reverse conventional projects have only one IRR because they have only one sign reversal—a negative followed by all positives, or a positive followed by all negatives. In this example, there can be at most two IRRs because there are two reversals, the flows go from negative to positive, and back to negative.

appealing. For example, in cases where the cost of capital is especially uncertain, as in the case of an entirely new product, using the IRR rule gets around having to compute the cost of capital carefully.

Also, if the IRR for a conventional project is large enough, say 88%, it is probably not worth the trouble to estimate the cost of capital accurately. Because the cost of capital would virtually never be that high, we can simply undertake the project without wasting additional resources on analysis. Those resources can be spent instead on making the project successful!

Review

1. What is the difference between mutually exclusive projects and independent projects?
2. Distinguish between a conventional project and a nonconventional project.
3. When do the NPV and IRR methods agree? Under what circumstances can they differ?
4. When the NPV and IRR methods disagree, which is usually more reliable?
5. Describe an NPV profile in your own words. Why is it so useful?

6.5 OTHER WIDELY USED CAPITAL BUDGETING CRITERIA

Several capital budgeting criteria besides the NPV and IRR are widely used. These include the *modified internal rate of return, profitability index, payback, discounted payback,* and *urgency.* We will describe them here as background in case you encounter them. Because some of these are not economically sound, it is critical to know their strengths and weaknesses.

Profitability Index

Another time-value-of-money-adjusted method that can be used to evaluate capital budgeting projects is the **profitability index (PI),** or **benefit-cost ratio** as it is sometimes called. The PI for a project equals the present value of the future cash flows divided by the initial investment. One way to view the PI is that it is 1 plus the NPV divided by the initial investment:

$$\text{Profitability Index} = \text{PI} = \frac{\text{PV(future cash flows)}}{\text{Initial investment}} = 1 + \frac{\text{NPV}}{\text{Initial investment}} \tag{6.3}$$

If a project had an NPV of \$240, and required an initial cash flow of −\$1,000, the project's PI would be 1.24 (= 1 + 240/1,000).

DECISION RULE for the profitability index: Undertake the capital budgeting project if the PI is greater than 1.0.

You probably wonder why we bother introducing this method, because it is obvious the NPV decision rule will give you the identical recommendation.[3] The idea underlying the PI is to measure the capital budgeting project's "bang for the buck." By scaling (dividing) the present value of the future cash flows by the initial outlay, you can see how much return is obtained *per dollar* invested. For example, with a PI of 1.24, you get \$1.24 of present value back for each \$1 invested, or an NPV of \$0.24 for each \$1 invested.

[3]In fact, some people define the PI as simply the NPV divided by the initial investment. Such a definition changes the scale to center on zero, rather than 1.0. There is no substantive difference because such a definition simply changes the cutoff for the PI rule to zero from 1.0.

Although the PI works fine for independent projects, the scale problem of mutually exclusive projects we saw with IRR also occurs with PI. For example, suppose project A has a PI of 1.6 and an NPV of $100. Project B has a PI of 1.3 and an NPV of $200. The choice between these two projects is again straightforward: Would you rather have more wealth or a larger PI? (Again, like you, we will take the wealth.) Therefore, the NPV decision rule is the better rule to follow when mutually exclusive projects differ in size.

PROFITABILITY INDEX, ON BALANCE Although PI offers a perspective on "bang for the buck," it is best used in conjunction with NPV, rather than in place of NPV. PI gets some use in practice, but less than IRR. Its most beneficial use is in situations where the firm is restricting the amount of investment it makes, rather than investing in all worthwhile projects. Such a situation is called *capital rationing,* which we discuss in Chapter 8.

Modified Internal Rate of Return (MIRR)

We noted earlier that many practitioners prefer IRR because of its intuitive appeal. Modified internal rate of return (MIRR) was developed to have the same intuitive feel, but provide a better measure of relative profitability than IRR. This method calculates the present value of all the cash outflows and the future value of all the cash inflows using the cost of capital. The MIRR is the rate of return that equates the two over the project life of N, so that

$$\text{PV(cash outflows)} = \frac{\text{FV(cash inflows)}}{(1 + \text{MIRR})^N} \tag{6.4}$$

MIRR is used by some firms, such as FedEx, because it is a better measure than IRR, but has the same intuitive appeal. The decision rule for MIRR is the same as it is for IRR.

> **DECISION RULE** for modified internal rate of return: Undertake the capital budgeting project if the MIRR exceeds r, the project's cost of capital.

Let us use an example to illustrate the MIRR method.

EXAMPLE Computing the MIRR for Reebok's Project

The cash flows for this project for times 0 through 4 are, respectively, −800, 300, 300, 300, 150, and the cost of capital is 12%. The present value of the cash outflows is simply the 800 at time 0. The future value of 300 per year for four years at 12% is 1,433.80.

So the future value of all the cash flows is 1,283.80 (= 1,433.80 − 150). The MIRR, which equates the present and future values, is 12.5516%.

CALCULATOR SOLUTION

Data Input	Function Key
4	N
12	I
0	PV
300	PMT
1,433.80	**FV**

CALCULATOR SOLUTION

Data Input	Function Key
4	N
−800	PV
0	PMT
1,283.80	FV
12.5516	**I**

MIRR, ON BALANCE MIRR is a better measure than IRR, but offers the same intuitive appeal. Still, like IRR and PI, although MIRR offers a good measure of "bang for the buck," it is best used in conjunction with NPV.

Payback

An appealing investment concept is that of "getting your money back." Of course, risk may intervene, but investors often want an estimate of the time it will take to recover the initial cash outflow. When this amount of time is calculated without regard to the time value of money, it is called a project's payback. **Payback** is computed by simply summing all the expected cash flows (without discounting them) in sequential order until the sum equals the initial outflow.

> **DECISION RULE** for payback: Undertake the capital budgeting project if the payback is less than a preset number of years.

EXAMPLE Computing a Payback

Let us turn again to the building renovation example we used earlier in the chapter to illustrate the NPV method. We expected to purchase the building for $420,000 and spend $300,000 on renovations. After renovation, we expected to be able to lease the building out for $110,000 per year. Ignoring taxes, this would give the cash flows in Figure 6.7. What is this project's payback?

The payback is 6.55 years (= 720,000/110,000), because $110,000 per year for 6.55 years equals $720,000, the initial investment.

The idea underlying the payback method is simple: The shorter the payback the better. But, there are serious deficiencies in the payback method. You are probably already saying, "But, but, but—it ignores the time value of money!" This is true. And it also ignores risk differences. In fact, the cutoff is entirely arbitrary, and all cash flows beyond the cutoff are ignored. Let us compare the payback method with the NPV method.

EXAMPLE Payback and NPV at Neiman Marcus

Let us say Neiman Marcus requires a two-year payback. The cost of capital is 15% for two projects it is considering, S (for short-term) and L (for long-term). These projects have the expected future cash flows given in Figure 6.8. What does the payback rule advise in this case?

Project S has a two-year payback, and project L has a three-year payback. Therefore, the payback rule would tell us to invest in project S, but not in project L. But is this good advice? Frankly, no. First, consider the projects' NPVs:

$$NPV_S = -1,000 + \frac{500}{(1.15)^1} + \frac{500}{(1.15)^2} + \frac{150}{(1.15)^3} + \frac{100}{(1.15)^4} = -31.34$$

$$NPV_L = -1,000 + \frac{300}{(1.15)^1} + \frac{300}{(1.15)^2} + \frac{400}{(1.15)^3} + \frac{500}{(1.15)^4} + \frac{500}{(1.15)^5} = +285$$

Is this a problem? Of course it is. Project S will actually decrease shareholder wealth, despite its shorter payback; and the opposite holds for L. We would urge the firm to undertake L and "pass" on S. In practice, most firms require that projects meet multiple tests. In this case, a firm that used both NPV and a two-year payback rule might discard both projects.

FIGURE 6.7
Payback for the building renovation project.

Year	0	1	2	3	4	5	6	7	8
Cash flows	−720	110	110	110	110	110	110	110	110
Cumulative	−720	−610	−500	−390	−280	−170	−60	+50	
Payback:								↑6.55 years	

FIGURE 6.8
Short- and long-term investment alternatives for Neiman Marcus.

Year	0	1	2	3	4	5
Project S	−1,000	500	500	150	100	0
Project L	−1,000	300	300	400	500	500

As we have seen, payback ignores the time value of money. In effect, it assumes the cost of capital is 0%. This underestimates the time required to recover the real (present) value of the initial investment. It can even recommend projects that actually decrease wealth. In addition, managers who use payback set an arbitrary cutoff for project profitability. If the payback exceeds the maximum time, the project is rejected—period. Furthermore, it is impossible to estimate the project's value using payback alone, because all cash flows beyond the payback cutoff are ignored. Obviously, this method has major deficiencies: It can rule out attractive long-term opportunities.

PRACTICAL VALUE OF PAYBACK Despite the drawbacks of the payback method, the gut reaction of wanting to "at least get your money back" is a powerful feeling to overcome. Moreover, payback provides a control on liquidity, offers a different type of risk control, is easy to compute, and is simple to understand.

Payback controls liquidity because it rejects excessively long-term projects. This may be important for a smaller, less liquid firm because it favors investments that will return cash sooner. That cash can be reinvested in other profitable projects.

Cash flows further in the future are arguably more risky. As a risk control device, payback addresses this harshly by simply ignoring those beyond the payback period.

Finally, we would add two other practical considerations: First, most investments with a short payback, and additional benefits beyond that, will also have a positive NPV. Second, for relatively small investments, the cost of extensive analysis can exceed the potential loss from a mistake. This can make the simplicity of payback attractive.

PAYBACK, ON BALANCE Probably because of the practical considerations just noted, the payback rule is still widely used in practice despite its serious deficiencies. However, very few firms use payback by itself. Most firms also require investments to be acceptable on the basis of other rules, such as NPV. Because of its weaknesses, payback should be viewed, at best, as a supplement to the discounted-cash-flow techniques.

Discounted Payback

If a firm wants to use the payback method, a better measure is a variation of payback called **discounted payback.** The discounted payback is the amount of time it takes for the project's *discounted* cash flows to equal the project's initial cost. The idea underlying the discounted payback period is to incorporate the time value of money into the basic notion of getting your money back.

> **DECISION RULE** for discounted payback: Undertake the capital budgeting project if the discounted payback is less than a preset cutoff.

EXAMPLE Discounted Payback at Neiman Marcus

Let us look again at Neiman Marcus's two alternative projects and apply a discounted payback cutoff of four years. What are the discounted paybacks for these investments? What investment decisions would the discounted payback rule imply?

Discounted payback computations for the projects are shown in Figure 6.9. Project S has an infinite discounted payback, whereas project L has a 3.87-year discounted payback. The prorated portion of the fourth year is determined by the amount of the year-4 benefit needed to sum to the initial cost. In this case, it is 0.87 (= [286 − 37]/286). Therefore, the discounted payback rule would tell us to invest in project L, but not in project S.

Is this good advice? We know from the past calculations that NPV_S is negative and NPV_L is positive, so this advice matches that of the NPV rule. In fact, you can probably see that for

FIGURE 6.9
Discounted payback for Neiman Marcus's alternative short- and long-term capital budgeting projects.

Project S

Year	**0**	**1**	**2**	**3**	**4**	**5**
Cash flows	−1,000	500	500	150	100	0
PV	−1,000	435	378	99	57	0
Cumulative	−1,000	−565	−187	−88	−31	−31
Discounted payback: infinite because the initial investment is not returned						

Project L

Year	**0**	**1**	**2**	**3**	**4**	**5**
Cash flows	−1,000	300	300	400	500	500
PV	−1,000	261	227	263	286	248
Cumulative	−1,000	−739	−512	−249	+37	+285
Discounted payback:					↑3.87 years	

conventional projects, which are the most common type, a project that meets a discounted payback cutoff will always have a positive NPV. This is because the present value of the future cash flows during the discounted payback period alone cover the initial cost.

The project's NPV, then, is the present value of the remaining cash flows—those ignored by the discounted payback period computation. You can see this by noting that the cumulative sum for all the project cash flows equals the NPV of the project, \$285. Figure 6.10 illustrates the cumulative present values of the cash flows for project L.

Discounted payback is superior to the payback method because it includes the effects of the time value of money. However, it too is arbitrary and suffers from the weakness of ignoring all cash flows beyond the cutoff. This can be a significant problem when there are negative expected future cash flows. The rule can break down in such cases.

For example, let us say project L had a year-6 cash flow of −\$700, such as might be connected with the cost of cleaning up an environmental hazard after the project was done. If that were the case, the project would have an NPV of −\$18, but the discounted payback rule would still favor undertaking the project because the discounted payback period would still be 3.87 years, less than the four-year cutoff. So the discounted payback rule can break down with nonconventional projects.

DISCOUNTED PAYBACK, ON BALANCE Although it is better than payback, the discounted payback method is still not an adequate indicator by itself. It too should be viewed as, at best, a supplement to the NPV method. Discounted payback is neither as conceptually correct as NPV nor as simple as payback. If you can understand the notion of discounted payback, you can understand and use net present value. So why bother with discounted payback? This is probably why discounted payback is not very widely used in practice.

Urgency

The final method we look at can be described by inverting Ben Franklin's advice and asking, "Why do today what you can put off until tomorrow?" The corollary to this perverse statement as applied to capital budgeting is "Do not replace it until we *absolutely* have to." No need for replacement studies. Wait until the machine breaks down, then air-freight in a new one. At that point, the specter of costly downtime will be sufficient to convince management to skip the analysis and simply order the replacement equipment.

Such a policy has obvious disadvantages, yet stories of plants that have critical equipment held together by "chewing gum and baling wire" loom large in industrial folklore. Capital budgeting projects and key pieces of equipment should be reviewed at regular intervals. A firm should

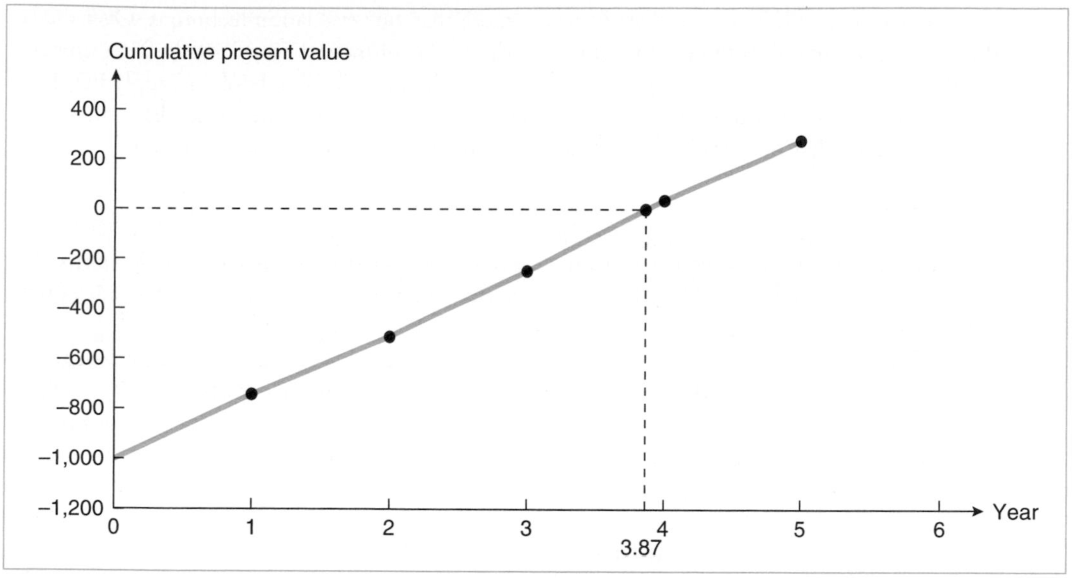

FIGURE 6.10
Neiman Marcus's long-term investment, cumulative present values of the cash flows for project L.

develop a program of preventive maintenance and should estimate a probable replacement date each time it acquires a significant piece of equipment. This will help to ensure that the assets are used with maximum efficiency and that equipment is replaced when it is most advantageous to do so—rather than when the baling wire finally snaps and the equipment stops working!

URGENCY, ON BALANCE Urgency is a frequently used but extremely poor basis for making important decisions. Firms should instead plan ahead. Drawing on Ben Franklin again, with accuracy this time, "An ounce of prevention is worth a pound of cure."

Review

1. What is the profitability index? How is it calculated? What is its decision rule?
2. Explain how the profitability index rule breaks down when there is a size difference between mutually exclusive projects.
3. What is the payback rule? Why is it inferior to NPV? Does it have any practical value? Does the discounted payback method avoid the shortcomings of the simple payback method?

6.6 BUSINESS INVESTMENT IN PRACTICE

In this section, we will look at some other practical aspects of capital budgeting and provide some perspective on how it is actually done.

Methods of Evaluation

Just about all firms use the evaluation methods we have discussed, in one form or another. *The single most useful tool is the NPV profile.* This is because it provides the most complete view of the project. It incorporates both NPV and IRR, and also sheds light on the problem of an uncertain required return.

Understandably, however, most firms use more than one evaluation technique. Over the last thirty years, the use of techniques based on the time value of money, especially the NPV method, has increased substantially. We hope that means that when you finish school and apply the things you have learned here, you will be able to convince your employer to use the better discounted-cash-flow techniques that are available for capital budgeting if they are not already being used.

Appropriations

A decision to include an investment in the capital budget seldom means automatic approval of the required expenditures. Most firms require that plant managers or division heads submit detailed appropriation requests before funds can be released for a project.

Firms often create manuals that specify how appropriation requests must be prepared. This helps maintain managerial control over investments and their associated costs.

Conducting a review of budgeted capital expenditures just prior to releasing funds provides one last check before making the expenditure. This can be valuable in cases where new information has come to light that might make one or more changes advantageous.

Review and Performance Measurement

As we have said, capital budgeting has a critical role in the firm's strategic plan. Therefore, firms must systematically review the status of all projects. Such a process is sometimes called a **postaudit.** Managers should examine projects not yet completely underway to determine whether or not development should continue.

They also must assess the performance of the firm's existing assets. Consideration should be given to whether projects should, for example, be expanded, contracted, liquidated, sold off, reconfigured, or simply continued. The basic capital budgeting techniques discussed in this chapter can be applied to the review and performance-measurement process.

The major goal of the postaudit is improvement. Improvements can come primarily in two areas: (1) forecasting and (2) operations. When people know that records of estimates, either forecasts or operational goals, will be maintained and later compared to the actual outcomes, they tend to be more careful making their estimates. The fact that they are being monitored and will be evaluated and held accountable for their work tends to motivate people to seek better methods and work to eliminate both conscious and unconscious biases. This kind of process is sometimes referred to as *continuous improvement,* and it is part of the concept of *total quality management (TQM).*

Although very difficult in some situations, postaudits are extremely important because of their potential impact on value. In Chapter 8, we will discuss postaudits further.

Review

1. What is the single most useful capital budgeting evaluation tool?
2. Why are appropriation requests useful in the capital budgeting process?
3. What is a postaudit? Why are postaudits useful in the capital budgeting process?

SUMMARY

The capital budgeting process and the investment criteria used to make capital budgeting decisions are critical because firms are effectively defined by the products and services they provide using their capital assets.

- **Idea generation** is the first and most important part of the capital budgeting process. Sources of potential valuable ideas include production employees, managers at all levels, sales and marketing staff, research and development groups, and the strategic planning process.

- The **net present value** (NPV) method discounts all cash flows at the project's required return—its *cost of capital.* The NPV measures the value the project will create, which is the difference between what the project is worth and what it will cost to undertake. The NPV method recommends that all independent projects with a positive NPV be undertaken. The NPV method is widely used in practice.
- The **internal rate of return** (IRR) is the project's expected return. It is the return that would make the NPV zero if it were the project's cost of capital. The IRR method recommends that every conventional capital budgeting project with an IRR greater than its cost of capital be undertaken. Caution is needed because the IRR decision rule can break down when projects are mutually exclusive or nonconventional. IRR is widely used in practice, probably because of its "intuitive feel."
- The **profitability index** (PI) method calculates one plus the project's NPV divided by its initial cost. The idea is to measure the project's "bang for the buck." The PI rule can break down when projects are mutually exclusive.
- The **payback** method finds the length of time it takes to recover the initial investment, without regard to the time value of money. It recommends acceptance of projects that "return the investment" quickly. The payback method has several serious deficiencies that can cause bad recommendations, but it may have some practical value. In particular, it can provide a liquidity screen, which might be desirable in some situations. Although widely used in conjunction with other methods, payback is rarely used alone.
- The **discounted payback** method is like payback but incorporates the effect of the time value of money. The discounted payback is the time it takes the project to earn a present value equal to its initial cost. Although this method is superior to the payback method, it is still inferior to NPV because it ignores the value of cash flows after the payback point. Discounted payback is not widely used in practice, probably because it is neither as conceptually correct as NPV nor as simple as payback.
- **Urgency** is a dangerous but widely used method of allocating resources. Its use is shortsighted. Many potential crises can be avoided through good planning.
- In practice, most firms use multiple evaluation methods for investments of any significance. However, the **NPV profile** is the single most useful tool. It provides the project's NPV, IRR, and sensitivity to the discount rate at a glance.
- The **postaudit** is a critical and ongoing part of capital budgeting. It provides a significant opportunity to create value through *continuous improvement* in forecasting outcomes and in choosing and operating projects.

EQUATION SUMMARY

$$\begin{aligned} NPV &= CF_0 + \frac{CF_1}{(1+r)} + \frac{CF_2}{(1+r)^2} + \cdots + \frac{CF_n}{(1+r)^n} \\ &= \sum_{t=0}^{n} \frac{CF_t}{(1+r)^t} \end{aligned} \tag{6.1}$$

$$\begin{aligned} CF_0 + \frac{CF_1}{(1+IRR)} + \frac{CF_2}{(1+IRR)^2} + \cdots + \frac{CF_n}{(1+IRR)^n} &= 0 \\ \sum_{t=0}^{n} \frac{CF_t}{(1+IRR)^t} &= 0 \end{aligned} \tag{6.2}$$

$$\text{Profitability Index} = \text{PI} = \frac{\text{PV(future cash flows)}}{\text{Initial investment}} = 1 + \frac{\text{NPV}}{\text{Initial investment}} \tag{6.3}$$

$$\text{PV(cash outflows)} = \frac{\text{FV(cash inflows)}}{(1 + \text{MIRR})^N} \tag{6.4}$$

QUESTIONS

1. Briefly describe the five steps in the capital budgeting process.
2. Why is the Principle of Valuable Ideas of critical importance to the capital budgeting process?
3. Define the term *independent project.*
4. Define the terms *conventional project* and *nonconventional project.*
5. Define the term *mutually exclusive projects.*
6. Define the term *profitability index* and describe the concept.
7. Define the term *payback* and describe the concept.
8. What is an internal rate of return (IRR)?
9. Briefly explain why capital budgeting projects are frequently classified into groups such as maintenance projects, cost savings/revenue enhancement projects, capacity expansion projects, new product/new business projects, and projects mandated by regulation or firm policy.
10. Why can the NPV and IRR methods disagree on the rankings for mutually exclusive projects?
11. What are the strengths and weaknesses of the payback and the discounted payback?
12. Which of the capital budgeting criteria are the most sound? Which are the least sound?
13. Suppose you were restricted to using only one method of analysis to evaluate a capital budgeting project. Briefly explain why the NPV profile is the best method to use.
14. Why do firms perform postaudits, reviewing and measuring the performance of their previous capital investments?

PROBLEMS

LEVEL A (BASIC)

A1. (NPV and IRR) An investment of $100 at time 0 generates a cash flow of $150 at time 1. If the cost of capital is 10%, what is the NPV? What is the IRR?

A2. (NPV and IRR) An investment of $500 at time 0 generates a cash flow of $1,000 at time 1. If the cost of capital is 12%, what is the NPV? What is the IRR?

A3. (Mutually exclusive projects) Consider the cash flows given below for the mutually exclusive projects, S and L.

a. If the cost of capital is 10%, what is the NPV of each investment?
b. What is the IRR of each investment?
c. Which investment should you accept?

YEAR	0	1	2
Project S	−100	160	0
Project L	−100	0	200

A4. (Mutually exclusive projects) Consider the cash flows given below for the mutually exclusive projects, S and L.

a. If the cost of capital is 8%, what is the NPV of each investment?

b. What is the IRR of each investment?

c. Which investment should you accept?

YEAR	0	1	2
Project S	−200	300	0
Project L	−200	0	300

A5. (NPV and PI) Vu Trading Company is evaluating a project that has the estimated cash flows given below. The cost of capital is 14%.

a. What is the project's NPV?

b. What is the profitability index?

YEAR	0	1	2	3	4
Cash flow	−100,000	30,000	30,000	60,000	60,000

A6. (NPV and PI) HH&R Holdings Corp. is evaluating a project that has the estimated cash flows given below. The cost of capital is 11%.

a. What is the project's NPV?

b. What is the profitability index?

YEAR	0	1	2	3	4
Cash flow	−50,000	20,000	20,000	50,000	50,000

A7. (Investment criteria) An investment of $100 returns exactly $100 in one year. The cost of capital is 10%.

a. What is the payback, NPV, and IRR for this investment?

b. Is this a profitable investment?

A8. (Investment criteria) Compute the NPV, IRR, and payback period for the following investment. The cost of capital is 10%.

YEAR	0	1	2	3
Cash flow	−200	100	100	150

A9. (Investment criteria) An investment of $50 returns exactly $50 in one year. The cost of capital is 9%.

a. What is the payback, NPV, and IRR for this investment?

b. Is this a profitable investment?

A10. (Payback and discounted payback) Find the payback and the discounted payback for a project with the cash flows given below. The cost of capital is 12%.

YEAR	0	1	2	3	4
Cash flow	−10	3	3	4	6

A11. (Payback and discounted payback) Find the payback and the discounted payback for a project with the cash flows given below. The cost of capital is 12%.

YEAR	**0**	**1**	**2**	**3**	**4**
Cash flow	−15	5	5	5	10

A12. (NPV and IRR) A project is expected to generate cash flows of $50,000 annually for five years plus an additional $100,000 in year 6. The cost of capital is 10%.

a. What is the most that you can invest in this project at time 0 and still have a positive NPV?

b. What is the most that you can invest in this project at time 0 if you want to have a 15% IRR?

A13. (NPV and IRR) A project is expected to generate cash flows of $14,000 annually for five years plus an additional $27,000 in year 6. The cost of capital is 10%.

a. What is the most that you can invest in this project at time 0 and still have a positive NPV?

b. What is the most that you can invest in this project at time 0 if you want to have a 15% IRR?

A14. (Investment criteria) Compute the NPV, IRR, and payback period for a project with the cash flows given below. The cost of capital is 10%.

YEAR	**0**	**1**	**2**	**3**
Cash flow	−250,000	100,000	200,000	100,000

A15. (Investment criteria) Compute the NPV, IRR, and payback period for a project with the cash flows given below. The cost of capital is 10%.

YEAR	**0**	**1**	**2**	**3**
Cash flow	−80,000	40,000	30,000	50,000

A16. (Investment criteria) An investment of $100,000 generates cash flows of $30,000 annually for the next three years. Find the NPV using a 10% cost of capital, the internal rate of return, and the payback period.

A17. (Investment criteria) An investment of $93,000 generates cash flows of $25,000 annually for the next three years. Find the NPV using an 11% cost of capital, the internal rate of return, and the payback period.

A18. (Investment criteria) Consider an investment that has the following cash flows:

YEAR	**0**	**1**	**2**	**3**	**4**
Cash flow	−1,000	300	400	500	500

The cost of capital is 10%. Compute the:

a. Payback

b. Discounted payback

c. Net present value

d. Profitability index

e. Internal rate of return

A19. (NPV) An investment of $10 will generate an annual cash flow of $1 forever. If the cost of capital is 8%, what is the NPV of this investment?

A20. (NPV) An investment of $25 will generate an annual cash flow of $2 forever. If the cost of capital is 7%, what is the NPV of this investment?

A21. (Payback and NPV) Three projects have the cash flows given below. The cost of capital is 10%.

a. Calculate the paybacks for all three projects. Rank the projects from best to worst based on their paybacks.

b. Calculate the NPVs for all three projects. Rank the projects from best to worst based on their NPVs.

c. Why are these two sets of rankings different?

YEAR	0	1	2	3	4	5
Project 1	−10	4	3	2	1	5
Project 2	−10	1	2	3	4	5
Project 3	−10	4	3	2	1	10

A22. (Payback and NPV) Three projects have the cash flows given below. The cost of capital is 10%.

a. Calculate the payback for each of the three projects. Rank the projects from best to worst based on their payback.

b. Calculate the NPVs for all three projects. Rank the projects from best to worst based on their NPVs.

c. Why are these two sets of rankings different?

YEAR	0	1	2	3	4	5
Project 1	−20	5	5	5	5	5
Project 2	−20	8	3	4	5	0
Project 3	−20	5	6	5	4	14

LEVEL B

B1. (Reverse conventional project) You have an opportunity to undertake a project that has a positive cash flow of $100 at time 0 and a negative cash flow of $100 at time 1. The cost of capital is 10%.

a. What is the IRR?

b. What is the NPV?

c. Should you accept this project?

B2. (Reverse conventional project) You have an opportunity to undertake a project that has a positive cash flow of $500 at time 0 and a negative cash flow of $500 at time 1. The cost of capital is 14%.

a. What is the IRR?

b. What is the NPV?

c. Should you accept this project?

B3. (Reverse conventional project) You can undertake a project with the following cash flows:

CF_0	CF_1	CF_2
+5,000	+5,000	−12,500

The cost of capital is 10%. The internal rate of return is 15.8%. Should you accept this project? Why or why not?

B4. (Reverse conventional project) You can undertake a project with the following cash flows:

CF_0	CF_1	CF_2
+1,000	+1,000	−2,500

The cost of capital is 10%. The internal rate of return is 15.83%. Should you accept this project? Why or why not?

B5. (NPV) Truman State University is evaluating an investment in new air handling systems for some of its major buildings. The expected outlays and the expected savings, in millions of dollars, are given below:

TIME	0	1	2	3	4 THROUGH 10
Outlays	2.0	3.0	4.0	0	0
Savings	0	0.5	1.0	1.5	2.0

What is the net present value of this investment if the required return is 8%?

B6. (NPV) Charleston Treatment Plant is evaluating an investment in new water handling systems for the Charleston area. The expected outlays and the expected savings, in millions of dollars, are given below:

TIME	0	1	2	3	4 THROUGH 10
Outlays	5.0	4.0	3.0	0	0
Savings	0	1.0	2.0	3.0	4.0

What is the net present value of this investment if the required return is 6%?

B7. (NPV and shareholder wealth) Stockholders are surprised to learn that the firm has invested $43 million in a project that has an expected payoff of $8 million per year for six years. The project's cost of capital is 12%.

a. What is the project's NPV?

b. There are 3 million outstanding shares. What should be the direct impact of this investment on the per share value of the common stock?

B8. (NPV and shareholder wealth) Stockholders are surprised to learn that the company has invested $27 million in a project that has an expected payoff of $5 million per year for seven years. The project's cost of capital is 12%.

a. What is the project's NPV?

b. There are 4 million outstanding shares. What should be the direct impact of this investment on the per share value of the common stock?

B9. (Investment criteria) Pierre Bouvier is evaluating four projects. The cash flows for the four projects are given below.

a. Pierre thinks you can rank these projects from best to worst by simply inspecting the cash flows (and not calculating anything). Try to do so.

b. Pierre next found the NPV of each project, discounting future cash flows at 10%. What is the NPV for each project?

c. Do your rankings in parts a and b agree?

TIME	0	1	2	3	4
Project K	−100	40	40	40	40
Project L	−100	40	80	0	40
Project M	−90	40	80	0	30
Project N	−90	40	80	0	40

B10. (Investment criteria) Wallace is evaluating four projects. The cash flows for the four projects are given below.

a. Wallace thinks you can rank these projects from best to worst by simply inspecting the cash flows (and not calculating anything). Try to do so.

b. Wallace next found the NPV of each project, discounting future cash flows at 10%. What is the NPV for each project?

c. Do your rankings in parts a and b agree?

TIME	0	1	2	3	4
Project K	−400	100	100	100	100
Project L	−400	100	500	0	100
Project M	−200	100	500	0	300
Project N	−200	100	500	0	100

B11. (Investment criteria) Consider the cash flows for the two capital budgeting projects given below. The cost of capital is 10%.

a. Calculate the NPV for both projects.

b. Calculate the IRR for both.

c. Calculate the PI for both.

d. Calculate the MIRR for both.

e. Calculate the payback for both.

f. Which is the better project? Why?

YEAR	0	1	2	3	4
Project A	−10,000	4,000	4,000	4,000	4,000
Project B	−5,000	2,000	2,000	2,000	2,000

B12. (Investment criteria) Consider the cash flows for the two capital budgeting projects given below. The cost of capital is 10%.

a. Calculate the NPV for both projects.

b. Calculate the IRR for both.

c. Calculate the PI for both.

d. Calculate the MIRR for both.

e. Calculate the payback for both.

f. Which is the better project? Why?

YEAR	0	1	2	3	4
Project A	−25,000	10,000	10,000	10,000	10,000
Project B	−12,500	5,000	5,000	5,000	5,000

B13. (NPV profile) Consider the projects shown below.

a. Which is the better project?

b. Is this an example of size differences or cash flow timing differences?

c. What is the crossover point, the discount rate that would have the same NPV for both projects? (Hint: Find the differential cash flows between the two projects. Then find the IRR for the differential cash flows.)

	CASH FLOWS ($)				
PROJECT	CF_0	CF_1	CF_2	NPV @ 10%	IRR
R1	−100	70	70	$21.49	25.7%
R2	−150	100	100	$23.55	21.5%

B14. (NPV profile) Consider the projects shown below.

a. Which is the better project?

b. Is this an example of size differences or cash flow timing differences?

c. What is the crossover point, the discount rate that would have the same NPV for both projects? (Hint: Find the differential cash flows between the two projects. Then find the IRR for the differential cash flows.)

	CASH FLOWS ($)				
PROJECT	CF_0	CF_1	CF_2	NPV @ 10%	IRR
R1	−300	200	200	$47.11	21.53%
R2	−3,000	1,800	1,800	$123.97	13.07%

B15. (Investment criteria) Consider a project that has the cash flows shown below. The required return on the investment is 10%. Compute the:

a. Payback

b. Discounted payback

c. NPV

d. Profitability index

e. IRR

f. MIRR

YEAR	0	1	2	3	4
Cash flow	−175,000	30,000	80,000	65,000	95,000

B16. (Investment criteria) Consider a project that has the cash flows shown below. The required return on the investment is 10%. Compute the:

a. Payback

b. Discounted payback

c. NPV

d. Profitability index

e. IRR

f. MIRR

YEAR	0	1	2	3	4
Cash flow	−70,000	40,000	30,000	30,000	30,000

B17. (NPV) Bill Scott estimates that a project will involve an outlay of $125,000 and will return $40,000 per year for six years. The required return is 12%.

a. What is the NPV using Bill's estimates?

b. David Scott is less optimistic about the project. David thinks the outlay will be 10% higher, the annual cash flows will be 5% lower, and that the project will have a five-year life. David does agree with Bill's required return. What is the NPV using David's estimates?

B18. (NPV) James Hall estimates that a project will involve an outlay of $500,000 and will return $150,000 per year for six years. The required return is 11%.

a. What is the NPV using James' estimates?

b. Brandon Hall is less optimistic about the project. Brandon thinks the outlay will be 10% higher, the annual cash flows will be 5% lower, and that the project will have a five-year life. Brandon does agree with James' required return. What is the NPV using Brandon's estimates?

B19. (Investment criteria) Suppose Reebok has a possible capital budgeting project with a cost of capital of 10%, and the expected cash flows shown below.

a. Calculate the project's NPV. Should Reebok accept the project?

b. Calculate the project's IRR. Should Reebok accept the project according to the IRR rule?

c. Calculate the project's payback. What does payback tell you about the project's acceptability?

YEAR	**0**	**1**	**2**	**3**	**4**	**5**
Cash flow	−100	25	50	50	25	10

B20. (Investment criteria) Suppose Coca-Cola has a possible capital budgeting project with a cost of capital of 10%, and the expected cash flows shown below.

a. Calculate the project's NPV. Should Coca-Cola accept the project?

b. Calculate the project's IRR. Should Coca-Cola accept the project according to the IRR rule?

c. Calculate the project's payback. What does payback tell you about the project's acceptability?

YEAR	**0**	**1**	**2**	**3**	**4**	**5**
Cash flow	−333	78	68	54	120	145

B21. (Investment criteria) Texaco has a capital budgeting project with a cost of capital of 12%, and the following expected cash flow pattern:

a. Calculate NPV. Should the firm accept the project?

b. Calculate IRR. Should the firm accept the project?

c. Calculate payback period.

d. How would your answers to parts a or b change if you were told that the project is one of two mutually exclusive projects the firm has under consideration?

YEAR	**0**	**1**	**2**	**3**
Cash flow	50	100	−20	−50

B22. (Investment criteria) National Fuel has a capital budgeting project with a cost of capital of 12%, and the following expected cash flow pattern:

a. Calculate NPV. Should the company accept the project?

b. Calculate IRR. Should the company accept the project?

YEAR	0	1	2	3
Cash flow	150	250	−100	−300

B23. (Mutually exclusive projects) Sperry is considering two mutually exclusive capital budgeting projects with a cost of capital of 14%, and the expected cash flows shown below. Which, if either, project should Sperry undertake? Justify your answer.

YEAR	0	1	2	3	4	5
Project A	−100	30	40	50	40	30
Project B	−150	45	60	75	60	60

B24. (Mutually exclusive projects) P&G is considering two mutually exclusive capital budgeting projects with a cost of capital of 14%, and the expected cash flows shown below. Which, if either, project should P&G undertake? Justify your answer.

YEAR	0	1	2	3	4	5
Project A	−1,000	250	250	250	250	250
Project B	−500	300	300	300	300	300

B25. (Excel: NPV profile) Helix Inc. is considering two mutually exclusive one-time projects. Both require an initial investment of $80,000. Project A will last for six years and has expected net future cash flows of $40,222 per year. Project B will last for five years and has expected net future cash flows of $44,967 per year. The cost of capital for this project is 12%.

a. Calculate the NPV for each project.

b. Calculate the IRR for each project.

c. Graph the NPV of the projects as a function of the discount rate, including solving for the crossover point by trial and error.

d. Which project should Helix take?

B26. (Excel: NPV profile) Watson Inc. is considering two mutually exclusive one-time projects. Both require an initial investment of $50,000. Project A will last for six years and has expected net future cash flows of $25,000 per year. Project B will last for five years and has expected net future cash flows of $20,000 per year. The cost of capital for this project is 10%.

a. Calculate the NPV for each project.

b. Calculate the IRR for each project.

c. Which project should Watson, Inc. take?

B27. (Excel: Choosing among mutually exclusive projects) The cash flows for two mutually exclusive investments are:

YEAR	0	1	2	3	4
Project A	−500	200	200	200	200
Project B	−500	0	0	0	1,000

a. Compute the total present value of each project's cash flows discounted at 0%, 5%, 10%, 15%, 20%, and 25%.

b. What is the NPV of each project assuming a 10% cost of capital?

c. What is the IRR for each project?

d. What is the crossover rate (the discount rate that gives the same NPV for both projects)?

e. What is the NPV discounted at the crossover rate?

f. Which project should be chosen?

B28. (Excel: Choosing among mutually exclusive projects) Suppose Kodak is considering two mutually exclusive capital budgeting projects with the following expected cash flow patterns:

TIME	0	1	2	3	4	5	6
Project A	−350	140	140	100	100	65	30
Project B	−350	65	65	100	140	140	175

a. Compute the IRR for each project.

b. Compute the NPV for each project, assuming the cost of capital is 10%.

c. Compute the NPV for each project, assuming costs of capital of 14%, 18%, and 22%. Create NPV profiles comparing the projects.

d. If the cost of capital is precisely 12%, which project should Kodak undertake?

B29. (Excel: Finding NPV and IRR) Use the worksheet functions in your spreadsheet to find the NPV, IRR, and PI of the following project. The cost of capital is 10%. Are you getting the correct values in your spreadsheet?

Time	0	1
Cash flow	−100	+120

B30. (Excel: Finding NPV and IRR) Kennesaw Instrument Company is looking at six projects with the following cash flows (investment outlays are negative cash flows):

TIME	0	1	2	3	4	5	6	7	8
Project A	−10	2	3	4	5	4	3	2	1
Project B	−8	−3	5	5	5	2	0	0	0
Project C	−45	25	20	15	5	0	0	0	0
Project D	−1	2	2	2	0	0	0	0	0
Project E	−30	6	6	6	6	6	0	0	0
Project F	−10	−20	5	5	8	8	8	8	8

The cost of capital for all of the projects is 10%.

a. Calculate the NPV for the six projects.

b. Calculate the IRR for the six projects.

c. Calculate the MIRR for the six projects.

B31. (Excel: Mutually exclusive projects) Gloria Brick is preparing an economic analysis of two mutually exclusive projects shown below:

PROJECT	CF_0	CF_1	CF_2	CF_3
1	−200	300	0	0
2	−200	0	0	400

The cost of capital is 10%.

a. What is the NPV and IRR for each project?

b. Calculate the NPV for each project assuming required rates of return of 0%, 5%, 10%, etc. up to 50%.

c. Graph the NPV profile for each project.

LEVEL C (ADVANCED)

C1. (Investment criteria) Nassau Manufacturing Company is considering two capital budgeting projects with a cost of capital of 15%, and the expected cash flows shown below.

a. Calculate the NPV and IRR for each project.

Which project(s) should Nassau accept, assuming they are:

b. Independent?

c. Dependent (both or neither are required)?

d. Mutually exclusive?

YEAR	0	1	2	3	4	5
Project A	−100	25	30	40	30	25
Project B	−50	10	15	25	15	15

C2. (Investment criteria) Westbury Manufacturing is considering two capital budgeting projects with a cost of capital of 8%, and the expected cash flows shown below.

a. Calculate the NPV and IRR for each project.

Which project(s) should Westbury accept, assuming they are:

b. Independent?

c. Dependent (both or neither are required)?

d. Mutually exclusive?

YEAR	0	1	2	3	4	5
Project A	−200	80	65	85	100	115
Project B	−150	30	55	75	95	105

C3. (Discounted payback) A staff analyst has just brought you an incomplete capital budgeting analysis that shows you only that the discounted payback of this conventional project is 5.24 years. A moment later, before you can fully collect your thoughts and ask the analyst any questions, the marketing vice president calls you and asks if the project analysis shows a positive NPV. You answer yes. Explain how you know this.

C4. (Excel: Multiple rates of return) Consider the oil pump cash flows below:

TIME	0	1	2
Cash flow	−1,600	10,000	−10,000

a. Calculate the NPV for the oil pump using discount rates between 0% and 500%, in 25% increments.

b. What are the two internal rates of return?

c. Where is the highest NPV?

d. Graph the NPV profile.

MINICASE GETTING OFF THE GROUND AT BOEING

When the Boeing Corporation announced its intention to build a new plane, the project was an enormous undertaking. Research and development had already begun two and a half years earlier, and Boeing had already spent $873 million. Aggregate development cost, disregarding the time value of money, was expected to be between $4 billion and $5 billion. Production facilities and personnel training would require an additional investment of $2.0 billion, and they would need $1.7 billion in working capital when deliveries began in six years. The table below shows projected future cash flows for the project at the time of Boeing's announcement. Boeing's cost of capital was 18%.

CASH FLOW PROJECTIONS FOR THE BOEING PROJECT (DOLLAR AMOUNTS IN MILLIONS)

Year	After-tax Profit[a]	Depreciation	Capital Expenditures[b]	Year	After-tax Profit[a]	Depreciation	Capital Expenditures[b]
1	(597.30)	40.00	400.00	18	1,691.19	129.20	178.41
2	(947.76)	96.00	600.00	19	1,208.64	96.99	627.70
3	(895.22)	116.40	300.00	20	1,954.39	76.84	144.27
4	(636.74)	124.76	200.00	21	2,366.03	65.81	100.51
5	(159.34)	112.28	182.91	22	2,051.46	61.68	(463.32)
6	958.62	101.06	1,741.42	23	1,920.65	57.96	(234.57)
7	1,718.14	90.95	2.12	24	2,244.05	54.61	193.92
8	1,503.46	82.72	(327.88)	25	2,313.63	52.83	80.68
9	1,665.46	77.75	67.16	26	2,384.08	52.83	83.10
10	1,670.49	75.63	(75.21)	27	2,456.65	52.83	85.59
11	1,553.76	75.00	(88.04)	28	2,531.39	52.83	88.16
12	1,698.99	75.00	56.73	29	2,611.89	47.52	90.80
13	1,981.75	99.46	491.21	30	2,699.26	35.28	93.53
14	1,709.71	121.48	32.22	31	2,785.50	28.36	96.33
15	950.83	116.83	450.88	32	2,869.63	28.36	99.22
16	1,771.61	112.65	399.53	33	2,956.28	28.36	102.20
17	1,958.48	100.20	(114.91)	34	3,053.65	16.05	105.26

[a]Includes expenditure for research and development.
[b]Includes changes in working capital. Negative values are caused by reductions in working capital.

QUESTIONS

1. Calculate the NPV, IRR, and payback for the project.
2. On the basis of your analysis, do you think Boeing should have continued with this project? Explain your reasoning.

7

CAPITAL BUDGETING CASH FLOWS

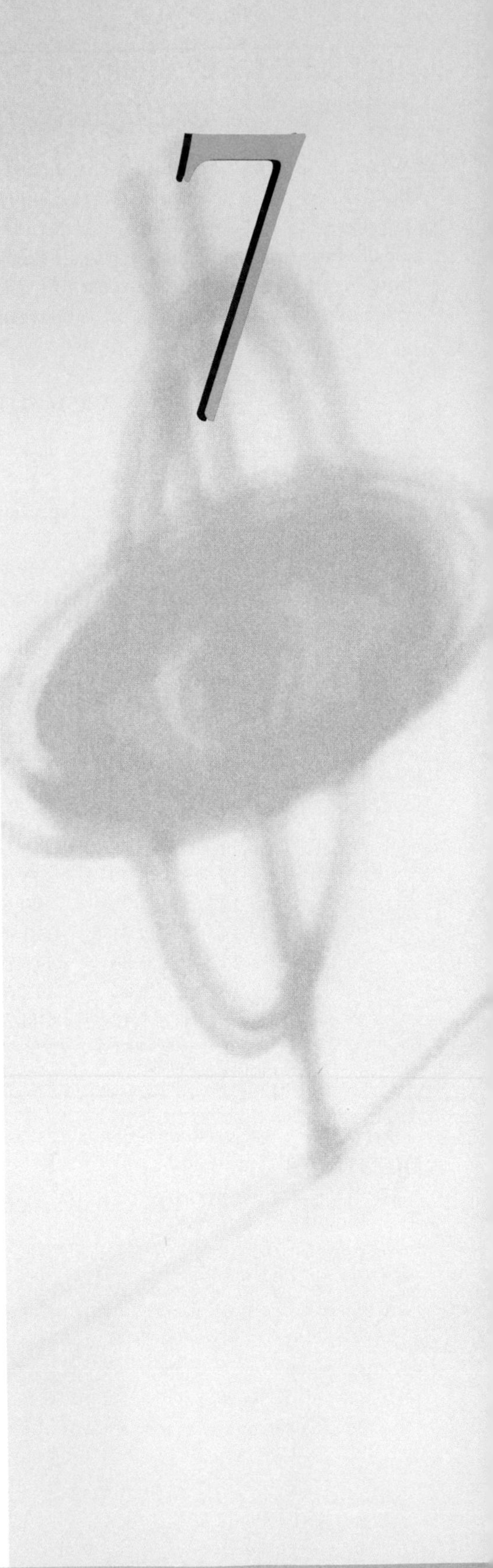

This chapter continues our investigation of capital budgeting. In the previous chapter we described the capital budgeting process and examined several investment criteria. Most investment criteria, such as NPV and IRR, depend on a project's expected future cash flows.

In this chapter we will show you how to estimate a capital budgeting project's expected future cash flows—its incremental after-tax cash flows. Such estimates critically affect the accuracy of the various capital budgeting investment criteria. As you read the chapter, there are five very important things to remember about cash flow estimation. The phrase *incremental after-tax cash flows* actually includes three of them.

First, cash flow is what is relevant. Second, these cash flows are measured on an after-tax basis. Third, the Principle of Incremental Benefits reminds us that it is the incremental cash flow that is relevant. Fourth, the Time-Value-of-Money Principle reminds us that the value of a cash flow depends on its timing. Fifth, incremental financing costs are implicitly included in the project's cost of capital—its required return—not in the cash flows.

We will also look at inflation and optimal replacement cycles. These things can complicate capital budgeting. However, as we will see, the key to proper treatment of these considerations in a capital budgeting analysis is carefully applying the Time-Value-of-Money Principle.

FOCUS ON PRINCIPLES

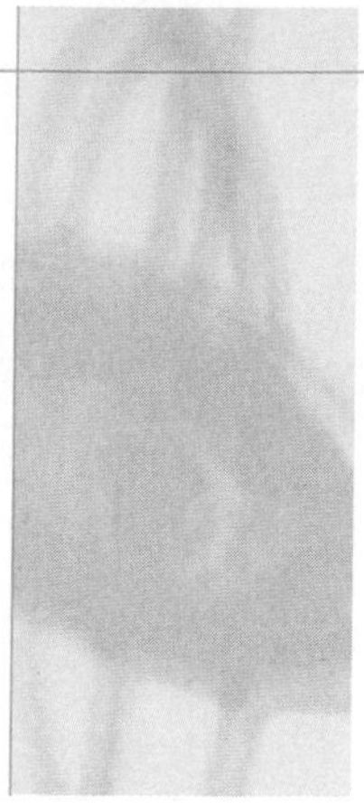

- *Incremental Benefits:* Identify and estimate the incremental expected *after-tax* future cash flows for a capital budgeting project. Special care is necessary to deal with projects that will erode or enhance the firm's current operations.
- *Time Value of Money:* Measure the value the capital budgeting project will create—its NPV.
- *Risk-Return Trade-Off:* Incorporate the risk of a capital budgeting project into its cost of capital, its required return.
- *Valuable Ideas:* Look for new ideas to use as a basis for capital budgeting projects that will create value.
- *Comparative Advantage:* Look for capital budgeting projects that use the firm's comparative advantage to add value.
- *Options:* Recognize the value of options, such as the options to expand, postpone, or abandon a capital budgeting project.
- *Two-Sided Transactions:* Consider why the other party to a transaction is willing to participate.
- *Signaling:* Consider the actions and products of competitors.

7.1 AN OVERVIEW OF ESTIMATING CASH FLOWS

As a prelude to the more detailed analysis of estimating cash flows given in this chapter, we would first like to cover some of the basic concepts used in estimating these cash flows and then give a simple numerical example. After this quick preview, we will go into more detail.

Basic Concepts Behind Capital Budgeting Cash Flows

There are five basic concepts to keep in mind when calculating a project's cash flows.

First, costs and benefits are measured in terms of cash flow—not income. This distinction is critical because, among other things, income calculations reflect noncash items and ignore the time value of money. Also, including indirect (noncash) benefits and costs leads to ambiguity and subjective (nonfinancial) choices that might hide any principal-agent problems between the managers and shareholders.[1]

Second, cash flow timing is critical because money is worth more the sooner you get it. But timing affects value even beyond simple time-value-of-money considerations. Firms often depend on expected cash inflows to meet their financial obligations. Insufficient cash inflow can cause failure to meet these obligations, which in turn can lead to penalty fees and even bankruptcy.

The third important concept is embodied in the Principle of Incremental Benefits: Cash flows must be measured on an incremental, or marginal, basis. They are the difference between the firm's cash flows with and without the project. For example, consider a sequential set of capital budgeting decisions concerning the research and development of a new product. Initial funds are spent for research; subsequent funds may or may not be approved for product development, test marketing, and production. At each stage, previous expenditures are sunk costs. Therefore, at each stage of the decision-making process, only *future* expenditures and revenues are relevant to the decision whether to proceed with product development.

---

[1] Nonquantified items can be a valid and very important part of a capital budgeting project. However, such items should be introduced into the analysis only *after* the direct cash flows have been identified and incorporated. This is so that the nonquantified items are not double counted, yet still get proper consideration. This also minimizes potential principal-agent conflicts by explicitly identifying these items.

Fourth, the Principle of Incremental Benefits further requires that expected future cash flows are measured on an after-tax basis. A firm is concerned with after-tax cash flows for the same reason that you, as an individual, are interested in take-home pay: Ultimately, that is what you can spend. Shareholders are interested in the *net* gain in wealth, and taxes take away from the wealth gain.

Finally, we want to alert you to a subtle aspect of the standard capital budgeting analysis: Financing costs are not explicitly identified. However, please do not think they have been left out. The incremental financing costs are implicitly included in the project's cost of capital—its required return. In other words, when we compute a project's NPV or IRR, the discount rate includes in it the opportunity cost for obtaining financing for the project.

An Example Comparing Project Cash Flows and Income

Let us look at a simplified example first, to give you the "big picture" before delving into the details.

A firm has the following capital budgeting project:

1. The initial outlay is $5,000.
2. The investment is depreciated straight-line to a salvage value of $1,000 in four years, so depreciation is $1,000 per year (= [5,000 − 1,000]/4).
3. At the end of the four years, the investment will be sold for exactly its net book value of $1,000.
4. Each year for four years, the investment will generate incremental sales of $4,000 and cash operating expenses of $1,500.
5. The firm pays income taxes at the rate of 40% of taxable income.
6. The project's cost of capital is 10%.

What are the project's cash flows? What are the project's NPV and IRR?

In this case, we can identify three different types of cash flows: an initial outlay (the "cost" of the investment), annual after-tax operating cash flows, and a salvage value. The initial outlay (at time 0) is $5,000 and the salvage (at time 4) is $1,000. That leaves the operating cash flows.

As part of the firm's operations, we can think of the project's contribution to the firm's income statement as though it were its own "mini" income statement, shown in Table 7.1. The project's net income is its revenue minus all its expenses (cash operating expenses, depreciation, and income taxes). Project net income is $900.

Now let us examine the income statement for those transactions that are cash flows. You can see that sales are a cash *inflow* of $4,000, cash operating expenses an *outflow* of $1,500, and taxes an *outflow* of $600. So the net cash flow is +$1,900.

TABLE 7.1
"Mini" income statement for the project.

	INCOME STATEMENT	CASH FLOWS
Sales	$4,000	+$4,000
Cash operating costs	1,500	−1,500
Depreciation	1,000	
Taxable income	$1,500	
Taxes at 40%	600	−600
Net income	$ 900	
		+$1,900 = Net cash flow

Note that we did not include any financing or interest expenses in the project's hypothetical mini income statement. This income statement shows operating revenues and costs only. Notice also that the $1,900 net cash flow is equal to net income + depreciation (= 900 + 1,000). Depreciation is a noncash charge, so we add it back to net income to get the cash flow.

Over the project's four-year life, the cash flows for our investment are as follows:

TIME	0	1	2	3	4
(1) Investment	−5,000				
(2) Annual operating cash flows		+1,900	+1,900	+1,900	+1,900
(3) Salvage					+1,000
Totals	−5,000	+1,900	+1,900	+1,900	+2,900

For these cash flows, the NPV (using the 10% cost of capital) is the present value of the future cash flows ($6,705.76) minus the initial cost of $5,000, or $1,705.76. The IRR is 23.91%. Because the NPV is positive, this is a profitable investment.

CALCULATOR SOLUTION

Data Input	Function Key
4	N
10	I
1,900	PMT
1,000	FV
6,705.76	**PV**

CALCULATOR SOLUTION

Data Input	Function Key
4	N
−5,000	PV
1,900	PMT
1,000	FV
23.91	**I**

Review

1. What are the five basic concepts to keep in mind when calculating a project's cash flows?
2. Why do we explicitly not include financing costs when estimating a project's cash flows?
3. What three types of project cash flows are identified in the example?

7.2 CALCULATING A PROJECT'S INCREMENTAL CASH FLOWS

In addition to the three types of cash flows identified in the example, a fourth type is nonoperating cash flows during the project's life. Therefore, a capital budgeting project's cash flows fall into four basic categories:

1. Net initial investment outlay
2. Expected future net operating cash flows
3. Nonoperating cash flows to support the project, such as those for an overhaul
4. Net salvage value, which is the after-tax total amount of cash received and/or spent when the project ends.

In this section, we look at each type of cash flow.

Net Initial Outlay

The net initial outlay can be broken down into cash expenditures for the new capital assets, changes in net working capital, cash flow from the sale of old equipment, and the tax impact of the sale of old equipment:

(1) Cash paid for new capital assets	$-I$	
(2) Increase in net working capital	$-\Delta W$	
(3) Cash received on sale of old equipment	S	
(4) Tax paid (saved) on sale of old equipment	$-T(S-B)$	
Net cash flow for initial investment =	$-I-\Delta W+S-T(S-B)$	(7.1)

Negative (positive) signs indicate cash outflows (inflows). The first item includes the purchase price, freight or shipping costs, and setup costs. An increase in net working capital is also part of the project's initial outlay. Additional production and sales usually require additional inventory and accounts receivable, which must be financed. Of course, if a project would reduce the firm's net working capital, those funds would be freed up to be invested elsewhere.

The third item in the initial outlay is the net cash flow from the sale of old equipment, and the fourth item is any tax effect on that sale. A tax effect occurs whenever an asset is sold for a net sale price other than the asset's net book value.[2] The taxes due are the tax rate times the excess of the sale price over the net book value, which is $T(S - B)$.

For example, suppose an asset was purchased five years ago for $2,000 and there has been $300 of depreciation expense claimed for tax purposes for each of the five years. The net book value of that asset is currently $500 (= 2,000 − 5[300]). If the asset is sold today for more than $500, then "too much" depreciation was claimed. In such a case, the government will "recapture" the excess depreciation by taxing the amount above the net book value. In the same way, if the asset is sold today for less than $500, "too little" depreciation was claimed, and the firm now claims the amount below the net book value as an expense.[3]

A potential fifth item, an investment tax credit, is not currently in effect. We describe the investment tax credit later.

The Investment in Net Working Capital

The investment in net working capital can be easily overlooked. In order to operate a new project, additional investments in short-term assets such as cash, receivables, and inventory may be required. Some spontaneous short-term financing, such as from accounts payable, may also occur with the new project. The increase in net working capital is the additional short-term assets required minus the additional short-term liabilities generated.

Recall that net working capital is current assets minus current liabilities. But exactly what is working capital? To get a better understanding, consider the following simple (even silly) example about an entrepreneurial child named Terry.

It is a hot summer afternoon, and after watching people walk uncomfortably through the neighborhood because of the heat, Terry decides there is money to be made selling lemonade. Terry makes some lemonade and a sign, *Lemonade: 50 cents.*[4] After Terry has made several trips to the curb in front of the house—taking the sign, a table, a chair, some cups, and the lemonade—a customer walks by and asks Terry for a glass of lemonade. Terry pours the glass and says, "That will be 50 cents, please." The customer hands over a $1 bill, to which Terry responds, "Would you like to buy two glasses?" The customer is not that thirsty and asks for change. Terry puts the customer on hold, runs into the house, and borrows $3 worth of change from Mom. After returning and making change for the customer, Terry settles into selling lemonade all afternoon.

That evening at the dinner table, Dad asks about everyone's day. Terry proudly reports making $11 selling lemonade. This prompts Mom to ask about the $3 in change. Terry hands $3 to Mom and revises the profit estimate down to $8. Mom, however, points out that money has a time value and that Terry had the use of her money all afternoon. Terry agrees and pays Mom the loan-shark rate of 5 cents interest on the $3 loan.

---

[2]This is the net book value for tax purposes, often called the asset's *tax basis.*

[3]The gain is taxed at ordinary income tax rates until all prior depreciation deductions have been fully "recaptured." If, for example, as a result of inflation, the asset is sold for more than was initially paid for it, all prior depreciation deductions are recaptured, and the excess above the original purchase price is taxed as a capital gain.

[4]Terry considered charging $50 per glass. That way, selling only one glass would make a successful day. Then Terry remembered about price elasticity and downward-sloping demand curves: There would be no demand with such a high price.

Terry's working capital was the $3 in change. It was put in at the start, and at the end when operations were shut down, it was there in the bottom of the cash register. The only cost of having the working capital was the time value of money. However, Terry could not operate the lemonade stand without the working capital. And although the time value of money is trivial for $3 for an afternoon, it *can* be a substantial cost, as in the case of a 10-year project that requires $5 million in working capital.

When we analyze a capital budgeting project, the cost of the investment in working capital due to the time value of money is accounted for by the incremental cash flows. Increases in working capital are outflows. Decreases in, and releases of, working capital are inflows. The difference in the present values of these cash flows is the time-value-of-money cost of using the working capital during the project's life.

Tax Considerations

Two important tax considerations for a capital budgeting project are whether the assets will be expensed or capitalized and the tax consequences of selling old assets. Other tax regulations may also be relevant to the investment cash flows.

EXPENSING OR CAPITALIZING THE NEW INVESTMENT When a firm buys a capital asset, the cost is not usually recognized immediately. **Capitalizing** an asset involves recording the outlay as an asset and allocating (depreciating) the cost over future time periods. Capitalizing leads to depreciation expense. It allocates the cost of the asset to two or more time periods.

In contrast, cash expenditures that are **expensed** are immediately recognized for tax purposes. Expensed items do not have any *subsequent* tax consequences. Generally, the earlier an expense is recognized, the earlier the tax savings will occur. The importance of this is seen in the next example.

EXAMPLE Capitalizing Versus Expensing at Boeing

The Boeing Corporation is going to purchase an asset that costs $1 million. Boeing's marginal tax rate is 40%. How does the pattern of expenses recognized for tax purposes differ between (1) capitalizing the asset on a straight-line basis over four years and (2) expensing the $1 million right now? What are the tax savings generated by these expenses? What is the present value of the tax savings discounted at 8%?

The answers to these questions are shown in Table 7.2. If the investment is capitalized and depreciated, the total expense of $1,000,000 is allocated over the next four years, or $250,000 per year. The tax savings are equal to 40% of the depreciation charge, which is $100,000 per year. The present value of the tax savings equals $331,213. If Boeing can expense this item, the full cost is deducted immediately, resulting in tax savings with a present value of $400,000. Expensing the item increases the present value of the tax savings by $68,787, from $331,213 to $400,000. Clearly, Boeing would be better off expensing rather than capitalizing the asset.

The present value of taxes saved is greater the sooner the expense is allowed as a tax-deductible expense. To the extent a firm can expense instead of capitalize an outlay, it will effectively reduce its taxes.

For example, assume that you are investing $100,000, and that you are able to expense $20,000 and are capitalizing the balance of $80,000. This additional expense reduces your current outlay by the tax rate times the $20,000. With a 40% tax rate, your outlay is reduced by $8,000, making your outlay $92,000 instead of $100,000. Of course, expensing part of the investment results in a smaller capitalized investment and smaller depreciation charges in the future.

TABLE 7.2
Capitalizing versus expensing an investment at Boeing.

Capitalizing and depreciating a $1,000,000 investment:

TIME	0	1	2	3	4	TOTAL
Expense	0	250,000	250,000	250,000	250,000	1,000,000
Tax savings	0	100,000	100,000	100,000	100,000	400,000
PV of tax savings	0	92,593	85,734	79,383	73,503	331,213

Expensing a $1,000,000 investment:

TIME	0	1	2	3	4	TOTAL
Expense	1,000,000	0	0	0	0	1,000,000
Tax savings	400,000	0	0	0	0	400,000
PV of tax savings	400,000	0	0	0	0	400,000

As the Boeing example demonstrates, firms will not generally choose to capitalize rather than expense an asset. However, the tax code *requires* that certain assets be capitalized.[5]

TAX ON SALE OF EXISTING ASSETS If a project involves selling or disposing of existing assets, often there are tax consequences. The tax effect equals the tax rate times the difference between the selling price and the net book value, $T(S - B)$. The tax effect can be a tax liability or a tax credit, depending on whether the selling price is more or less than the net book value. For example, suppose that the net book value B is $200 and the tax rate is 40%. The tax effect for various selling prices between 0 and $400 is shown:

Selling price: (S)	Difference: ($S - B$)	Tax liability:[6] $T(S - B)$	Net cash flow: $S - T(S - B)$
$400	$200	$80	$320
300	100	40	260
200	0	0	200
100	−100	−40	140
0	−200	−80	80

OTHER TAXES There are other taxes that can also affect business investments. One of these that is not currently in effect is the **investment tax credit,** which is a credit against taxes due based on new capital investment. For example, with a 10% investment tax credit, businesses receive a tax credit equal to 10% of new capital outlays. This tax credit is applied to a firm's tax bill, reducing it by the amount of the credit. The effect of such a credit is to reduce the cost of purchasing the assets. For example, a 10% investment tax credit would reduce the cost by 10%. The stated government purpose of having an investment tax credit is to stimulate business investment.

Other taxes that can affect a firm include sales taxes, property taxes, payroll taxes, and many others. These are typically included as a cost of doing business. Businesses also receive subsidies from the federal and state and local governments that can reduce the cost of doing business.

---

[5]We are assuming the firm has sufficient income to use the tax credit or that loss carrybacks and carryforwards work properly. Exceptions to this generalization rarely occur, but when they do, it is often a unique situation that requires careful analysis.

[6]A negative tax liability is a tax credit.

Review

1. What is the net cash flow for the initial investment and how is it calculated?
2. What is the difference between capitalizing an expenditure and expensing it for tax purposes? Which is more advantageous to the firm?
3. How can taxes affect the initial investment?
4. What is the net investment in working capital?

Net Operating Cash Flow

After the initial investment, a project generates future cash inflows and outflows. Let ΔR be the change in periodic revenue and ΔE be the change in periodic cash operating expense connected with undertaking the project in each period. The **net operating cash flow, CFAT (cash flow after tax),** can then be expressed as $\Delta R - \Delta E$ minus the tax liability on this amount:

$$\text{Net operating cash flow} = \text{CFAT} = \Delta R - \Delta E - \text{tax liability}$$

The tax liability depends on the change in depreciation as well as ΔR and ΔE. Let ΔD be the depreciation change, then the tax liability will be $T(\Delta R - \Delta E - \Delta D)$, and the net operating cash flow will be

$$\text{CFAT} = \Delta R - \Delta E - T(\Delta R - \Delta E - \Delta D)$$

This equation is typically rearranged into two other forms. The first is:

$$\text{CFAT} = (\Delta R - \Delta E)(1 - T) + T\Delta D \tag{7.2}$$

In this form, CFAT is after-tax cash revenues and cash expenses plus the "tax shield" from the depreciation expense. Equation (7.2) can be viewed as the *operating cash flows after tax plus the depreciation tax shield.*

The other form in which CFAT is commonly expressed is:

$$\text{CFAT} = (\Delta R - \Delta E - \Delta D)(1 - T) + \Delta D \tag{7.3}$$

In this form, CFAT can be thought of as *net income plus depreciation.* This is because $(\Delta R - \Delta E - \Delta D)(1 - T)$ would be the net income from the project if the firm were all-equity financed (and therefore had no interest expense). Depreciation is added back to net income because it is a non-cash charge. The following example shows that the two methods of finding CFAT produce the same results.

EXAMPLE Equivalence of Two Methods of Computing CFAT

In order to illustrate the equivalence of the two methods of computing CFAT, let us assume that $\Delta R = \$4{,}000$, $\Delta E = \$1{,}500$, $\Delta D = \$1{,}000$, and $T = 40\%$. You may recognize these values from the numerical example earlier in this chapter.

The first method, Equation (7.2), finds the cash flow as *operating cash flows after tax plus the depreciation tax shield:*

$$\text{CFAT} = (\Delta R - \Delta E)(1 - T) + T\Delta D$$
$$\text{CFAT} = (4{,}000 - 1{,}500)(1 - 0.40) + 0.40(1{,}000)$$
$$\text{CFAT} = 2{,}500(0.60) + 0.40(1{,}000) = 1{,}500 + 400 = \$1{,}900$$

Operating cash flows before tax are \$2,500, and after paying the 40% tax, operating cash flows after tax are \$1,500. The depreciation is \$1,000, which, at the 40% tax rate, provides a \$400 tax shield. The cash flow is \$1,500 plus \$400, or \$1,900.

The second method, Equation (7.3), finds the cash flow as *net income plus depreciation:*

$$\text{CFAT} = (\Delta R - \Delta E - \Delta D)(1 - T) + \Delta D$$
$$\text{CFAT} = (4{,}000 - 1{,}500 - 1{,}000)(1 - 0.40) + 1{,}000$$
$$\text{CFAT} = 1{,}500(0.60) + 1{,}000 = 900 + 1{,}000 = \$1{,}900$$

Income before taxes is $1,500. Income after taxes is $900. Adding the net income and the depreciation gives the net cash flow of $1,900. Thus, CFAT calculated as operating cash flows after tax plus the depreciation tax shield is identical to CFAT calculated as net income plus depreciation.

Nonoperating Cash Flows

Nonoperating cash flows, cash flows that are not associated with operations, can occur at various points during the life of a capital project. For example, equipment such as boats, trucks, or airplanes can require engine overhauls every few years. The rest of the boat, truck, or airplane may also need major repair, but on a less frequent basis. Expensed nonoperating cash flows are multiplied by $(1 - T)$ to adjust for taxes. Nonoperating cash flows that are required to be capitalized have a cash outflow when they occur and depreciation expenses that follow.

Future changes in net working capital are another common nonoperating cash flow. A future increase in net working capital is a cash outflow and a future decrease in net working capital is a cash inflow. These future nonoperating cash flows, just like future operating cash flows, are discounted back to find a project's NPV.

Net Salvage Value

The **net salvage value** is the after-tax net cash flow from terminating the project. It can be broken into four parts: sale of assets, taxes owed or saved on the sale, cleanup and removal expenses, and release of net working capital.

The tax liability on the sale of assets is computed exactly as described earlier in our discussion of the net initial outlay. The tax liability is $T(S - B)$. Cleanup and removal expenses are generally expensed immediately. Therefore, they are multiplied by $(1 - T)$ to adjust for taxes. The release of net working capital is unaffected by taxes. Tax law treats it as an internal transfer of funds. Therefore, the release of net working capital is simply an added cash flow. With cleanup and removal expenses represented as REX, net salvage value can be broken into four parts:

(1) Cash received on sale of old equipment	S
(2) Tax paid (saved) on sale of old equipment	$-T(S - B)$
(3) After-tax cleanup and removal expenses	$-(1 - T)\text{REX}$
(4) Release of investment in working capital	ΔW

$$\text{Net salvage value} = S - T(S - B) - (1 - T)\,\text{REX} + \Delta W \quad (7.4)$$

The term **salvage value** typically refers to the before-tax difference between the sale price (S) and the clean up and removal expense (REX). That is, salvage value $= S -$ REX. You can see that this is an incomplete view of the cash flows at the end of a project's life. It ignores the taxes due (or saved) when the sale price differs from the net book value, it ignores the tax deductibility of the cleanup and removal expenses, and it ignores the working capital that is released when the investment is no longer in service.

Review

1. There are two equivalent equations for calculating the net operating cash flow after tax (CFAT). Give the equation for *operating cash flows after tax plus the depreciation tax shield.* Give the equation for *net income plus depreciation.*
2. If the tax rate increases, will CFAT increase or decrease? Why?
3. What are the two types of nonoperating cash flows?
4. What is net salvage value? Give the equation for net salvage value and explain each of its four parts. Under what circumstances would taxes not affect the net salvage value?

7.3 AN EXAMPLE OF INCREMENTAL CASH FLOW ANALYSIS

Rocky Mountain Chemical Corporation (RMC) is thinking of replacing the packaging machines in its Texas plant. Each packaging machine currently in use has a net book value of \$1 million and will continue to be depreciated on a straight-line basis to a net book value of zero over the next five years. The plant engineer estimates that the old machines could be used for as many as 10 more years. The purchase price for the new machines is \$5 million apiece, which would be depreciated over a 10-year period on a straight-line basis to a net book value of \$500,000 each. Each new machine is expected to produce a pretax operating savings of \$1.5 million per year over the machine it would replace.

RMC estimates that it could sell the old packaging machines for \$250,000 each. Installation of each new machine would be expected to cost \$600,000 in addition to the purchase price. Of this amount \$500,000 would be capitalized in the same way as the purchase price, and the remaining \$100,000 will be expensed immediately. Because the new machines are so much faster than the ones they would replace, the firm's average raw materials inventory account would need to be increased by \$30,000 for each new machine. Simultaneously, because of trade credit, accounts payable would increase by \$10,000. Finally, management believes that even though the new machines would have a net book value of \$500,000 at the end of 10 years, it would be possible to sell them for only \$300,000, with removal and cleanup cost of \$40,000.

If RMC has a marginal tax rate of 40%, what would be the after-tax incremental expected future cash flows associated with each new machine?

The Net Cash Flow for the Initial Investment

The net cash flow for the initial investment includes the \$5 million purchase price, the \$500,000 capitalized installation cost, and the \$100,000 expensed installation cost, which sums to \$5.6 million. Of this amount, \$5.5 million will be depreciated over the life of the investment. The \$100,000 expensed installation cost creates an immediate tax saving of \$40,000 (the tax rate times the expense, 0.40(100,000)). Thus, the initial cash investment for the new equipment is \$5.56 million (5,600,000 − 40,000). The increases in inventory and accounts payable cause a required increase in net working capital of $\Delta W = \$20{,}000$. The sale of the machine currently in use would have two effects on future cash flows. First, we receive a cash inflow of the sale price of \$250,000, along with the taxes due or saved on the sale. In this case, we have a tax *loss* on the sale of \$750,000 ($S - B = 250{,}000 - 1{,}000{,}000$). With a marginal tax rate of 40%, this creates a tax saving of \$300,000 (= 0.40(750,000)). This tax saving is a positive cash flow of this amount. The second tax effect occurs in the depreciation expenses that would *not* be claimed for the old machine in each of the next five years. This effect would be accounted for in the expected future annual cash flows. We can compute the net initial outlay using Equation (7.1):

$$\text{Net cash flow for initial outlay} = -I - \Delta W + S - T(S - B)$$
$$= -5{,}560{,}000 - 20{,}000 + 250{,}000 - .40(250{,}000 - 1{,}000{,}000)$$
$$= -5{,}560{,}000 - 20{,}000 + 250{,}000 + 300{,}000 = -\$5{,}030{,}000$$

So the net cash outlay on the investment is $5.03 million.

Note that the original purchase price of the old machine does not enter into this calculation. The original cost is a *sunk cost.* It was incurred in the past and therefore cannot be affected by the decision to replace the old machine. Similarly, care must be taken to correctly treat sunk costs that have been incurred more recently. Dollars that have already been spent—for example, on feasibility studies, prior research and development, and site preparation—are irrelevant for purposes of capital budgeting analysis. They are also sunk costs. Whether or not the firm proceeds with the project, the timing and amounts of prior capital expenditures cannot change because these expenditures have already been made.

The Annual Operating Cash Flows (CFAT)

The net operating cash flows resulting from purchasing the new machine can be calculated using either Equation (7.2) or (7.3). The change in revenue, ΔR, is zero. The change in expenses, ΔE, is −$1.5 million. Depreciation would increase $500,000 per year (= [5,500,000 − 500,000]/10) for the next 10 years because of the new machine. It would decrease $200,000 per year (1,000,000/5) for the next five years because of the sale of the old machine. Therefore, ΔD is $300,000 (= 500,000 − 200,000) for years 1 through 5 and then ΔD is $500,000 for years 6 through 10.

Now let us use Equation (7.2), the *operating cash flows after tax plus the depreciation tax shield.* For years 1 through 5,

$$\text{CFAT} = (\Delta R - \Delta E)(1 - T) + T\Delta D$$
$$\text{CFAT(1 through 5)} = (0 - (-1{,}500{,}000))(1 - 0.4) + (0.4)(300{,}000) = \$1{,}020{,}000$$

For years 6 through 10, $\Delta D = \$500{,}000$, and

$$\text{CFAT(6 through 10)} = (0 - (-1{,}500{,}000))(1 - 0.4) + (0.4)(500{,}000) = \$1{,}100{,}000$$

If you prefer, you can also use Equation (7.3), the *net income plus depreciation* method. For years 1 through 5:

$$\text{CFAT} = (\Delta R - \Delta E - \Delta D)(1 - T) + \Delta D$$
$$\text{CFAT(1 through 5)} = (0 - (-1{,}500{,}000) - 300{,}000)(1 - 0.4) + (300{,}000) = \$1{,}020{,}000$$

For years 6 through 10:

$$\text{CFAT(6 through 10)} = (0 - (-\ 1{,}500{,}000) - 500{,}000))(1 - 0.4) + (500{,}000) = \$1{,}100{,}000$$

No nonoperating cash flows are expected over the life of this project, so no nonoperating cash flows need be included in the project's cash flow stream.

Salvage Value

Even though these machines will be depreciated to a book value of $500,000 over 10 years, they are expected to have a market value of $300,000 at the end of the project's life. A removal and cleanup expenditure of $40,000 is expected, which is tax deductible. In addition, the $20,000 investment in net working capital is recovered. From Equation (7.4), the net salvage value is

$$\text{Net salvage value} = S - T(S - B) - (1 - T)\text{REX} + \Delta W$$
$$= 300{,}000 - 0.4(300{,}000 - 500{,}000) - 0.6(40{,}000) + 20{,}000$$
$$= 300{,}000 - (-80{,}000) - 24{,}000 + 20{,}000 = \$376{,}000$$

Over the next ten years, the incremental cash flows for this project are then (in $ millions):

YEAR	0	1	2	3	4	5	6	7	8	9	10
	−5.03	1.02	1.02	1.02	1.02	1.02	1.1	1.1	1.1	1.1	1.476

The final step, calculating the net present value from the expected cash flows, is shown in the following example.

EXAMPLE Computing the NPV of Rocky Mountain's Packaging Machine

Let us continue our earlier example of RMC's packaging-machine replacement. If the project's required return is 12%, what is the NPV?

Computing the NPV of the project's annual incremental cash flows, we have

$$\text{NPV} = \sum_{t=0}^{n} \frac{\text{CF}_t}{(1+r)^t} = -5.03 + \sum_{t=1}^{5} \frac{1.02}{(1.12)^t} + \sum_{t=6}^{9} \frac{1.10}{(1.12)^t} + \frac{1.476}{(1.12)^{10}} = \$1{,}017{,}925$$

So the project should be accepted because the NPV is positive.

A More Convenient Computation Procedure

Our computation of the NPV for the packaging machine is partitioned by years. That is, the after-tax cash flow for each year is computed, and then the NPV is the sum of the present values of the after-tax cash flows.

An alternative to this procedure is to compute the after-tax cash flow (ATCF) for each item (for example, the initial cost, the change in working capital, and so on), in which case the NPV is the sum of the present values of the ATCFs for the items. Most people make fewer mistakes grouping by item because we think in terms of items rather than annual cash flows.

Naturally, the total discounted cash flows will be the same, regardless of whether we group them by year or by item. In the previous example we totaled the cash flows in each year, discounted their values, and summed them. The column totals in Table 7.3 show these cash flows by year before discounting. The row totals in Table 7.3 show them undiscounted by item. Table 7.4 then shows the NPV calculation for the example, using item cash flow groupings. In Table 7.4, BTCF refers to the item's before-tax cash flow, and the formula for each item's BTCF and ATCF are shown below the amount.

Erosion and Enhancement

RMC's decision to replace its packaging machines involves many aspects of the firm's operations. And yet all the incremental cash flows were identified, and the decision could be made separately

TABLE 7.3
Alternative groupings of the cash flows for RMC's packaging-machine replacement, by years and by items (in $ thousands).

ITEM	TIME 0	1	2	3	4	5	6	7	8	9	10	TOTAL BY ITEM	
Capitalized installation and equipment cost	−5,500											−5,500	$t = 0$
Expensed installation cost	−60											−60	$t = 0$
Change in net working capital	−20											−20	$t = 0$
Sale of old equipment	550											550	$t = 0$
Investment tax credit	0											0	$t = 0$
Lost depreciation from sale of old equipment		−80	−80	−80	−80	−80						−80/yr	$t = 1–5$
Depreciation		200	200	200	200	200	200	200	200	200	200	200/yr	$t = 1–10$
Change in revenues minus expenses		900	900	900	900	900	900	900	900	900	900	900/yr	$t = 1–10$
Sale of equipment											380	380	$t = 10$
Removal expense											−24	−24	$t = 10$
Return of net working capital											20	20	$t = 10$
Total by year	−5,030	1,020	1,020	1,020	1,020	1,020	1,100	1,100	1,100	1,100	1,476		

TABLE 7.4
Alternative NPV calculation for RMC's packaging-machine replacement, with the cash flows grouped by item (in $ thousands).

TIME	ITEM	BTCF[a]	ATCF	PV AT 12%
0	Capitalized installation and equipment cost	−5,500 $-I_0$	−5,500 $-I_0$	−5,500.000
0	Expensed installation cost	−100 $-E_0$	−60 $-(1-T)E_0$	−60.000
0	Change in net working capital	−20 $-\Delta W$	−20 $-\Delta W$	−20.000
0	Sale of old equipment	250 S_0	550 $S_0(1-T)+TB_0$	550.000
0	Investment tax credit	0	0 I_c	0.000
1–5	Lost depreciation from sale of old equipment	0	−80/yr $-TD_{old}$	−288.382
1–10	Depreciation	0	200/yr TD_{new}	6,215.245 (Depreciation and Change in revenues minus expenses)
1–10	Change in revenues minus expenses	1,500/yr $\Delta R-\Delta E$	900/yr $(1-T)(\Delta R-\Delta E)$	
10	Sale of equipment	300 S	380 $S(1-T)+TB$	121.062 (Sale of equipment, Removal expense and Return of net working capital)
10	Removal expense	−40 −REX	−24 $-(1-T)$REX	
10	Return of net working capital	20 ΔW	20 ΔW	
				NPV = $1,017.925

[a]Note that noncash items have zero before-tax cash flow.

from other decisions. Some capital budgeting decisions cannot be made so independently. For example, a new product can interact with the firm's existing products and services.

Suppose a firm has discovered how to make a product that would be better than one of its existing products. For example, suppose Proctor & Gamble created a new soap. Such a new product can cause what is called **erosion** of one or more existing products. Sales of the new product will erode (reduce) sales of the existing products.

EXAMPLE New Computer Game Systems at Nintendo

When Nintendo discovers a computer graphics innovation that will require a new type of machine, the firm faces the problems of erosion and enhancement. Sales of existing products and the value of existing production facilities, for Nintendo and its competitors, will probably be eroded by a superior system. At the same time, a new system might provide Nintendo with an enhancement of some existing and potential future products. The firm could develop the new system to facilitate such enhancement.

Perhaps less obvious is the decline in the market value of the production facilities for existing products caused by the innovation. Because of reduced or eliminated sales opportunities, the value of plant and equipment used by *other firms,* as well as that of the firm introducing the innovation, declines. Therefore, as perverse as it might seem, a firm may be best served by delaying introduction of an innovation until it can be incorporated into the firm's natural replacement of equipment. Of course, a firm might also introduce the innovation sooner than it might have otherwise, as a defensive move against competitors.

Just as one interaction among products may cause a decrease in value, another interaction may cause an increase in value. Such an increase is called **enhancement.** For example, an innovation that causes a reduction in the cost of making or installing a home swimming pool may cause an increase in the sales of swimming pool maintenance equipment.

It is vital to include dependencies that cause significant erosion or enhancement in order to correctly measure a project's NPV. Without their inclusion, you will not have measured the NPV, even though you think you have! The next chapter examines several project interdependencies.

Review

1. In an equipment-replacement decision, explain how the incremental cash flows are measured for the initial outlay, annual net operating cash flows, and net salvage value.
2. Describe two alternative ways of grouping a project's incremental after-tax cash flows. Why are they equivalent?
3. Explain the concepts of erosion and enhancement.
4. Why is it so important to include any significant effects of erosion and enhancement?

7.4 INFLATION

Expectations about inflation affect required returns. So a project's required return—its cost of capital—depends on inflation expectations. And, of course, expectations about inflation also affect the project's expected future cash flows. Therefore, it seems obvious that inflation expectations can affect a project's value. However, surprisingly, the changes may actually cancel each other out.

It is very important to keep in mind the relationship among the required return, expected cash flows, and present value. Present value depends on both the required return *and* the expected cash flows. When any one of these three things changes, at least one of the others must also change.

For example, if the required return increases, present value will decrease if the expected cash flows do not also change. This is the case for bonds. With fixed coupon payments, the market value of a bond changes whenever market interest rates change. As a result, even U.S. government bonds are not truly riskless because of inflation uncertainty.[7] Similarly, an increase in the expected cash flows will increase present value *if* the required return (and therefore risk) has not changed.

A possibility easily forgotten is that changes in both the expected cash flows and the required return can offset each other exactly, and *present value can be constant—despite the changes.*

Capital Budgeting and Inflation

Inflation effects can be complex because asset value is a function of both the required return and the expected future cash flows. And, as we noted, inflation affects the project's expected future cash flows as well as its required return. Yet, as we also noted, the changes can cancel each other out, leaving the project's NPV unchanged.

When an estimate includes inflation, it is in *nominal* terms. When an estimate excludes inflation, it is in *real* terms.[8] To analyze a capital budgeting decision, discount nominal expected future cash flows at the nominal required return. Discount real expected future cash flows at the real required return.

Let us look first at the effect of inflation on the required return. Let the required return in real terms be r_r, the required return in nominal terms be r_n, and the inflation rate be i. The nominal rate can be obtained by simply compounding the real rate and the inflation rate, or

$$(1 + r_n) = (1 + r_r)(1 + i)$$

Multiplying the right-hand side and rearranging, the nominal rate can be expressed as a function of the real and inflation rates:

$$r_n = r_r + i + ir_r \tag{7.5}$$

This relationship may surprise you. You may have seen the nominal rate expressed simply as the sum of the real and inflation rates, without including the cross-term, ir_r. Because the cross-term is relatively small compared to the other terms, the sum is a good approximation and is often used in practice. However, Equation (7.5) is the correct expression.

A major inflation effect is that while revenues and expenses inflate, depreciation tax credits do not inflate. This is because depreciation expense is based on the historical cost of the equipment. Thus, depreciation tax credits must be discounted at the nominal cost of capital. Expected revenue and expense cash flows are often expressed in real terms and must be discounted at the real cost of capital. You can see this problem in the following example.

EXAMPLE Monogramming at Christian Dior

Christian Dior is thinking of buying a monogramming machine. The machine has a four-year useful life and would require an initial outlay of $100,000. The machine would be depreciated to a zero book value over four years on a straight-line basis, so depreciation would

[7]It is very important to note that the relevant measure is the *expected* future inflation rate. This can be quite different from the realized inflation rate, even though expected future inflation rates are often highly correlated with recent realized inflation rates.

[8]The term *nominal* means that the value is a value "in name only." Future cash flows that are expressed in nominal dollar terms may not have the same purchasing power as today's dollars, which is why "constant purchasing power dollars" is another phrase for "real."

TABLE 7.5
NPV calculation for Christian Dior's monogramming machine.

TIME	ITEM	BTCF	ATCF	PV
0	Initial cost	−100,000	−100,000	−100,000
1–4	$\Delta R - \Delta E$	50,000/yr	30,000/yr	95,096 @ 10%
1–4	Depreciation	0	10,000/yr	26,487 @ 18.8%
				NPV = \$21,583

be \$25,000 per year. The machine would generate an incremental increase in operating income of \$50,000 per year in real terms before taxes, and the relevant tax rate is 40%. Inflation is expected to be 8% per year, and the project's required return in real terms would be $r_r = 10\%$. What is the NPV of purchasing this machine?

The real operating cash flow ($\Delta R - \Delta E$) before taxes is \$50,000, which is \$30,000 after taxes (= (1 − 0.4)50,000). These real cash flows are discounted at the real cost of capital of 10%.

To compute the present values of *nominal* after-tax cash flows, we need the *nominal* cost of capital. The nominal discount rate is found with Equation (7.5):

$$r_n = r_r + i + ir_r = 0.10 + 0.08 + (0.08)(0.10) = 18.8\%$$

The nominal depreciation tax credit is $T\Delta D = 0.4(25{,}000) = \$10{,}000$ per year and is discounted at the nominal cost of capital, 18.8%. Table 7.5 shows that the project's NPV is \$21,583.

If inflation affects various component cash flows differently—for example, if revenues are expected to increase 6% per year, but expenses are expected to increase 9%—those differences must be incorporated into the analysis. Although this adds complexity, such complexity does not change the way we incorporate the effects of inflation. Nominal cash flows are discounted at the nominal cost of capital, and real cash flows are discounted at the real cost of capital.

Review

1. Why is the nominal cost of capital not simply the sum of the real cost of capital and the expected inflation rate?
2. True or false? Nominal cash flows can be discounted at the real cost of capital.

7.5 A LITTLE MORE ABOUT TAXES

Early in the previous century, Congress instituted a procedure for collecting taxes, now familiar to most Americans, called the income tax. Since that time, the income tax has become the primary source of tax revenue for the federal government. Income tax provisions and rates have changed frequently. Table 7.6 shows the statutory federal tax rates on corporate income over the years since the income tax was initiated in 1909.

Another way tax laws have changed over the years is in the provisions for capitalizing equipment expense—depreciation—and for claiming investment tax credit. In the past three decades there have been no less than five major—and numerous minor—changes in depreciation rules. MACRS (pronounced "makers"), which stands for *Modified* ACRS (accelerated cost recovery system, pronounced "acres") is the latest provision. ACRS was originally introduced to replace the

TABLE 7.6
Statutory corporate income tax rates from 1909 through 2001.

YEAR	RATE BRACKETS OR EXEMPTIONS	RATE[a] (PERCENT)
1909–1913	$5,000 exemption	1
1913–1915	No exemption after March 1, 1913	1
1916	None	2
1917	None	6
1918	$2,000 exemption	12
1919–1921	$2,000 exemption	10
1922–1924	$2,000 exemption	12.5
1925	$2,000 exemption	13
1926–1927	$2,000 exemption	13.5
1928	$3,000 exemption	12
1929	$3,000 exemption	11
1930–1931	$3,000 exemption	12
1932–1935	None	13.75
1936–1937	Graduated normal tax	
	First $2,000	8
	Over $40,000	15
	Graduated surtax on undistributed profits ranging from —	7–27
1938–1939	First $25,000	12.5–16
	Over $25,000	19[b]
1940	First $25,000	14.85–18.7
	$25,000 to $31,964.30	38.3
	$31,964.30 to $38,565.89	36.9
	Over $38,565.89	24
1941	First $25,000	21–25
	$25,000 to $38,461.54	44
	Over $38,461.54	31
1942–1945	First $25,000	25–29
	$25,000 to $50,000	53
	Over $50,000	40
1946–1949	First $25,000	21–25
	$25,000 to $50,000	53
	Over $50,000	38
1950	First $25,000	23
	Over $25,000	42
1951	First $25,000	28.75
	Over $25,000	50.75
1952–1963	First $25,000	30
	Over $25,000	52
1964	First $25,000	22
	Over $25,000	50
1965–1967	First $25,000	22
	Over $25,000	48
1968–1969	First $25,000	24.2[c]
	Over $25,000	52.8[c]
1970	First $25,000	22.55[c]
	Over $25,000	49.2[c]

(continued)

TABLE 7.6 *(Continued)*

YEAR	RATE BRACKETS OR EXEMPTIONS	RATE[a] (PERCENT)
1971–1974	First $25,000	22
	Over $25,000	48
1975–1978	First $25,000	20
	Next $25,000	22
	Over $50,000	48
1979–1981	First $25,000	17
	$25,000 to $50,000	20
	$50,000 to $75,000	30
	$75,000 to $100,000	40
	Over $100,000	46
1982	First $25,000	16
	$25,000 to $50,000	19
	$50,000 to $75,000	30
	$75,000 to $100,000	40
	Over $100,000	46
1983–1986	First $25,000	15
	$25,000 to $50,000	18
	$50,000 to $75,000	30
	$75,000 to $100,000	40
	Over $100,000	46
1987–1990[d]	First $50,000	15
	$50,000 to $75,000	25
	Over $75,000[e]	34
1991–1992	First $50,000	15
	$50,000 to $75,000	25
	$75,000 to $100,000	34
	$100,000 to $335,000	39
	Over $335,000	34
1993–2001	First $50,000	15
	$50,000 to $75,000	25
	$75,000 to $100,000	34
	$100,000 to $335,000	39
	$335,000 to $10,000,000	34
	$10,000,000 to $15,000,000	35
	$15,000,000 to $18,333,333	38
	Over $18,333,333	35

[a]In addition to the rates shown, certain types of "excess profits" levies were in effect in 1917–1921, 1933–1945, and 1950–1953.
[b]Less adjustments: 14.025% of dividends received and 2.5% of dividends paid.
[c]Includes surcharge of 10% in 1968 and 1969 and 2.5% in 1970.
[d]Rates shown effective for tax years beginning on or after July 1, 1987. Income in taxable years that include July 1, 1987 (other than as the first date of such year) is subject to a blended rate.
[e]An additional 5% tax is imposed on a corporation's taxable income in excess of $100,000. Maximum additional tax is $11,750; this provision phases out the benefit of graduated rates for corporations with taxable income between $100,000 and $335,000; corporations with income above $335,000, in effect, pay a flat tax at a 34% rate.
Source: Treasury Department, Office of Tax Analysis.

asset depreciation range (ADR) method. ADR had been an attempt to specify carefully (once and for all!) the rules for using the three allowable depreciation methods, which were, at that time, *double declining balance, sum of the years' digits,* and *straight line.* The designation of these three depreciation methods as the allowable methods for federal income tax purposes had occurred many years earlier, but the rules governing their use had changed often.

Looking at this past history of change, we see little reason to assume that any procedure is permanent.

Because tax law changes occur often, it is critical to *use the **current** tax laws to determine after-tax cash flows* for a capital budgeting decision (or for that matter, for any financial decision). However, because of the frequency of changes, there is not much point in memorizing all of the tax provisions. When you make a financial decision, determine exactly what the treatment for each item will be under current tax law by consulting current tax guides (federal, state, or private) or tax experts within or outside your organization.

Even though federal corporate income taxes are the largest part of a business's total tax bill, there are other tax provisions. Most states have an income tax. Consequently, the marginal tax rate usually is not the federal income tax rate, but is a higher rate that reflects the combined effect of federal, state, and local taxes. A business may also face other taxes that are not directly related to its income. These include federal and state excise taxes, payroll taxes, property taxes, and state and local sales taxes. The effect of these taxes is included by reducing revenues or increasing cash expenses (ΔR and ΔE) by the amount of the tax.

Because of the complexity of the tax laws, we do not attempt to specify taxes perfectly. In our presentations, we follow the convention of using a single marginal tax rate that people often think of as the federal income tax rate. To remind us that normally the rate is larger than the federal rate, we generally use a tax rate in our examples that is different from the most common corporate tax rate (before surtax) of 35%.

Depreciation

In many of the examples and problems in this book, we use straight-line depreciation, even though firms actually use the MACRS system, an accelerated depreciation method, for tax purposes or capital budgeting analysis. (Most firms *do* use straight-line depreciation for financial reporting purposes.) Straight-line depreciation is not used for tax purposes because of the time value of money. As long as a firm has enough income that it can fully use all of its tax credits and deductions, the sooner it claims the depreciation, the sooner it can put the money from the tax shield to work earning more money. Over the life of an investment, the total amount of depreciation tax deductions will be the same, regardless of the depreciation schedule that is used. However, the *present values* of the alternative tax credit patterns can differ substantially.

Under current tax laws, an investment is assigned to a property class, and each class of property has a separate depreciation schedule. Property is put into a class based on a rough estimate of its useful life. Some of the asset classes are shown in Table 7.7. Each MACRS property class has a separate depreciation schedule, which is shown in Table 7.8. MACRS is an accelerated depreciation method, which results in higher depreciation charges in the early years of a project's life. This reduces taxable income, taxes, and net income during the early years. But it also results in a higher after-tax cash flow because of the lower taxes.

Which depreciation method is best? The answer comes from determining which provides the largest present value of the tax credits (the depreciation deduction times the marginal tax rate). The answer is not necessarily the same from year to year, because the allowable methods and procedures change with disturbing regularity. Therefore, there is little point in memorizing the fact that a particular method is optimal now, because it probably will not be by the time you get around to using it.

There is considerable value, however, in describing a general method for identifying the optimal depreciation schedule from whatever schedules are allowable at the time you have to choose one. Despite all the changes, the way to determine the best method has not changed since the income tax laws first began requiring firms to capitalize equipment costs. *A firm should use the depreciation method that provides the largest present value of depreciation tax credits.*

TABLE 7.7
MACRS asset classes.

MACRS ASSET CLASSES	TYPES OF PROPERTY
3-year	Tractor units, racehorses over two years old, rent-to-own consumer durables
5-year	Cars, light and heavy trucks, computer and office equipment
7-year	Office furniture and fixtures, railroad property, and any property that does not have a designated class life
10-year	Fruit trees, water transportation (boats)
15-year	Depreciable land improvements, wastewater plants, pipelines
20-year	Farm buildings, municipal sewers
27.5-year	Residential property
39-year	Nonresidential real property

TABLE 7.8
Depreciation rates under MACRS (modified accelerated cost recovery system).

	RECOVERY PERIOD CLASS					
YEARS	3-YEAR	5-YEAR	7-YEAR	10-YEAR	15-YEAR	20-YEAR
1	33.33%	20.00%	14.29%	10.00%	5.00%	3.75%
2	44.45	32.00	24.49	18.00	9.50	7.22
3	14.81	19.20	17.49	14.40	8.55	6.68
4	7.41	11.52	12.49	11.52	7.70	6.18
5		11.52	8.93	9.22	6.93	5.71
6		5.76	8.93	7.37	6.23	5.28
7			8.93	6.55	5.90	4.89
8			4.45	6.55	5.90	4.52
9				6.55	5.90	4.46
10				6.55	5.90	4.46
11				3.29	5.90	4.46
12					5.90	4.46
13					5.90	4.46
14					5.90	4.46
15					5.90	4.46
16					2.99	4.46
17						4.46
18						4.46
19						4.46
20						4.46
21						2.25

Notes:
1. Depreciation is lower in year 1 because assets are assumed to be in service for only six months. Note that this assumption means that depreciation is over n + 1 years so, for example, a 5-year asset is depreciated over 6 years.
2. Rates for four asset classes (3-year, 5-year, 7-year, and 10-year) are 200% declining balance with a half-year convention and a switch to straight-line when optimal. Only half the formula amount is claimed the first year.
3. Rates for 10-year and 15-year property are 150% declining balance with a half-year convention and a switch to straight-line when optimal.
4. Residential real property is depreciated straight-line over 27.5 years. Nonresidential real property is depreciated straight-line over 39 years.

TABLE 7.9
GE depreciation.

	MACRS DEPRECIATION				STRAIGHT-LINE DEPRECIATION		
YEAR	MACRS PERCENTAGE	DEPRECIATION	TAX SHIELD	PV @ 10%	DEPRECIATION	TAX SHIELD	PV @ 10%
1	20.00	$20,000	$8,000	$ 7,273	$20,000	$8,000	$7,273
2	32.00	32,000	12,800	10,579	20,000	8,000	6,611
3	19.20	19,200	7,680	5,770	20,000	8,000	6,011
4	11.52	11,520	4,608	3,147	20,000	8,000	5,464
5	11.52	11,520	4,608	2,861	20,000	8,000	4,967
6	5.76	5,760	2,304	1,301			
Totals	100.00%	$100,000	$40,000	$30,931	$100,000	$40,000	$30,326

EXAMPLE Alternative Depreciation Methods at General Electric

General Electric invests in a capital asset that costs $100,000. GE must depreciate this asset as five-year property using the MACRS schedule. Assume GE's marginal tax rate is 40% and the asset's required return is 10%. What are the asset's annual depreciation charges, its annual tax shields, and the present value of the tax shields?

They are shown in Table 7.9. As you can see, the total depreciation charge using the MACRS schedule is $100,000 and the tax credits, undiscounted, total $40,000. The present value of the tax credits is $30,931. But what if GE used straight line depreciation instead?

Table 7.9 also shows the comparable calculations using straight-line depreciation. Although the *total* depreciation and undiscounted tax credits are the same, the present value of the tax credits, $30,326, is less. MACRS provides greater depreciation in the project's early years, which increases the present value.

Based on the general superiority of expensing over capitalizing (which we illustrated earlier in the Boeing example), we could have predicted the superiority of the MACRS method in the GE example. The comparison in the General Electric example was between straight-line and an "accelerated" method. Although not as quick as expensing, an accelerated method allows depreciation to be claimed more quickly than straight line. As long as a firm can use the tax credits, accelerated depreciation provides the more advantageous treatment.

Review

1. When is the effective income tax rate higher than the federal rate?
2. Explain how to calculate MACRS depreciation.

7.6 EVALUATING REPLACEMENT CYCLES

RMC's packaging-machine replacement involved replacing specialized equipment that is subject to periodic technological design improvements. In such cases, the replacement decision is basically a one-time decision. Later, when the chosen machine becomes worn out or technologically obsolete, its replacement is essentially a new project. Such a project is, in effect, a decision whether to continue producing a product or even to remain in that line of business.

But many replacement decisions are instead routine decisions, involving machinery and equipment that does not change very much over time. The asset is replaced or overhauled because of worn-out parts rather than technological improvement. Essentially, the new asset is identical to the one it replaces. In such cases, there is a routine pattern, or **replacement cycle.** The asset is purchased, maintained, and replaced on a regular basis. An example would be a delivery vehicle for Federal Express.

When alternatives in a routine replacement decision do not have identical life cycles, the asset with the largest single-cycle NPV is not necessarily the best choice. Instead, the choice must be made on a comparable basis. For example, if a firm is choosing between two assets, one with a 5-year life and the other with a 10-year life, two sequential 5-year assets would be needed to do the job of one 10-year asset.

One way to choose among alternatives in a replacement cycle decision, then, is to find a common horizon where some number of sequential replacements of one asset equals that for the alternative.[9] This approach can be cumbersome, however.

For example, comparing a six-year type A asset with a seven-year type B asset would involve a horizon of 42 years—seven sequential purchases of A types versus six of B types. If there was a C-type alternative with an eight-year life, the process would become even more tedious. A more convenient method of choosing among alternatives in such situations is on the basis of equivalent annual cost.

Equivalent Annual Cost

Equivalent annual cost (EAC) is the *equivalent* cost per year of owning an asset over its entire life. The method is a simple two-step application of time-value-of-money mathematics. The first step is to compute the present value of all costs associated with owning the asset over its entire life. These costs include the purchase price, maintenance costs, and operating costs over the period of expected ownership. Let the net initial outlay be C_0 and the yearly CFAT costs be $C_1, C_2, \ldots, C_n$, where n is the length of the asset's life. The cost of capital is r. The total present value of costs over the life of the asset, TC, is

$$\text{TC} = C_0 + \sum_{t=1}^{n} \frac{C_t}{(1+r)^t}$$

The second step is to determine the cash flow that, if paid each year, would have the same present value, TC. In other words, what annuity payment has a present value of TC? This cash flow is the equivalent annual cost (EAC) and is calculated like the payments of an ordinary annuity, Equation (4.7). In EAC notation, it is:

$$\text{EAC} = \text{TC}\left[\frac{r(1+r)^n}{(1+r)^n - 1}\right] \tag{7.6}$$

EXAMPLE Replacing Production Machines at Hoover

Hoover Inc. is considering replacing a set of its production machines. Hoover can buy two alternative machines, A or B. Hoover should choose the machine with the lower equivalent annual cost, so we must calculate each machine's EAC.

Machine A costs $49,000 to purchase and install, has a five-year life, and will be depreciated over five years on a straight-line basis to a book value of $4,000, so depreciation will be $9,000 per year for five years (= [49,000 − 4,000]/5). At the end of the five years, Hoover expects to be able to sell machine A for $10,000. For the expected production level, it will cost $25,000 per year to operate machine A. The relevant tax rate is 40%, and the project's cost of capital is 12%.

---

[9] This is called the "common horizon" approach.

TABLE 7.10
Present value of the total cost for Hoover's machine A.

TIME	ITEM	CFBT	CFAT	PV AT 12%
0	I_0	−49,000	−49,000	−49,000
1–5	$-\Delta E$	−25,000/yr	−15,000/yr	−54,072
1–5	Depreciation	0/yr	3,600/yr	12,977
5	Salvage	10,000	7,600	4,312
		(B = 4,000)	$(1 - T)S + TB$	
				TC = −$85,783

TABLE 7.11
Present value of the total cost for Hoover's machine B.

TIME	ITEM	CFBT	CFAT	PV AT 12%
0	I_0	−72,000	−72,000	−72,000
1–10	$-\Delta E$	−24,000/yr	−14,400/yr	−81,363
1–8	Depreciation	0/yr	3,600/yr	17,883
6	Overhaul	−18,000	−10,800	−5,472
				TC = −$140,952

CALCULATOR SOLUTION

Data Input	Function Key
5	N
12	I
85,783	PV
0	FV
−23,797	PMT

CALCULATOR SOLUTION

Data Input	Function Key
10	N
12	I
140,952	PV
0	FV
−24,946	PMT

The present value of all of machine A's costs is −$85,783, as given in Table 7.10. The EAC can then be calculated using Equation (7.6):

$$\text{EAC} = \text{TC}\left[\frac{r(1+r)^n}{(1+r)^n - 1}\right] = -85{,}783\left[\frac{.12(1.12)^5}{(1.12)^5 - 1}\right] = -\$23{,}797$$

Machine B has a 10-year life but costs $72,000 to purchase and install. It will be depreciated over eight years on a straight-line basis to a book value of zero, so depreciation will be $9,000 per year for the first eight years (= 72,000/8) and zero for the last two years of use. Machine B is expected to require an overhaul at the end of year 6 that will cost $18,000 and will be expensed, rather than capitalized. At the end of the 10 years, Hoover expects to be able to sell machine B for a scrap value that will equal the cost of removal and cleanup. Machine B is slightly less expensive to run than machine A, costing $24,000 per year to operate.

The present value of all the costs for machine B is − $140,952, as given in Table 7.11 (a one-stop convenience table). The EAC can then be calculated using Equation (7.6) as –$24,946.

Based on the EACs then, Hoover should buy machine A with its smaller EAC. Note that we disregarded the revenues, because both alternatives have the same revenues and risk.

Figure 7.1 compares the costs over 10 years of using the two machines. The comparison shows both the EACs and the present values of total cost outlays over a common 10-year horizon. Figure 7.1 illustrates how comparing EACs is equivalent to comparing costs over a common horizon, which happens in all cases. However, as we noted earlier, the EAC method is more convenient, especially with more than two alternatives.

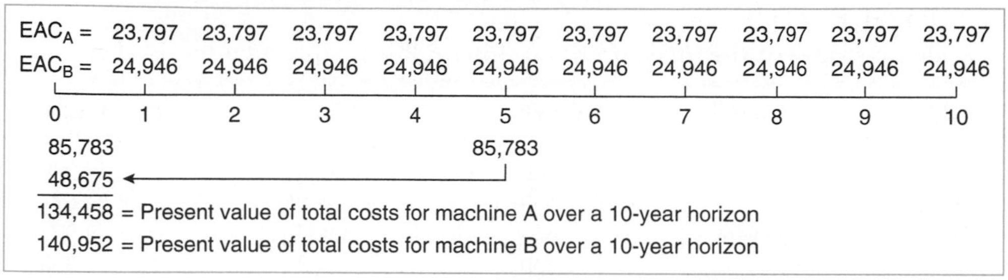

FIGURE 7.1
Comparison of the equivalent annual cost and common horizon methods.

Replacement Frequency

The preferred shorter replacement cycle in the Hoover example has an additional option associated with it. Because of the shorter life cycle, there is less chance that a mechanically sound machine will be made useless by a technological advance. In essence, the firm has the option to change production technologies more often when it purchases the machine with the shorter life cycle. Therefore, if the two machines had identical EACs (including removal costs), the machine with the shorter life cycle would be preferred. Although we do not have an option pricing model to conveniently estimate the value of more frequent replacement, it is nevertheless a valuable option. Other capital budgeting options are discussed in the next chapter.

The Hoover example compared two alternative machines. It is also useful to consider alternative replacement cycles for a given machine. The optimal replacement cycle is the one that minimizes the EAC. Salvage values and maintenance costs vary with the type and usage of a machine. (Salvage value is also a function of the potential future uses of the equipment.) One life cycle is not necessarily optimal for *all* situations. Let us investigate replacement cycle frequency by extending the Hoover example to consider various life cycles for machine A. Note that the depreciation schedule does not change, despite the change in usage.

EXAMPLE Replacement Cycle Frequency at Hoover

Let us say that instead of replacing it after five years, machine A could be replaced early at the end of four years. Or it could be used an extra year and replaced after six years. With less use, the machine would have an expected $16,000 resale value at the end of four years. With more use, the machine would require maintenance costing $1,000 at the end of year 5 and is expected to have a zero salvage value at the end of year 6. Which replacement cycle is best?

The total cost over one four-year life cycle is −$74,220, as given in Table 7.12. From Equation (7.6), the EAC for a four-year cycle is −$24,436.

CALCULATOR SOLUTION

Data Input	Function Key
4	N
12	I
74,220	PV
0	FV
−24,436	PMT

TABLE 7.12
Present value of the total cost of machine A if it is replaced after four years.

TIME	ITEM	CFBT	CFAT	PV AT 12%
0	I_0	−49,000	−49,000	−49,000
1–4	$-\Delta E$	−25,000/yr	−15,000/yr	−45,560
1–4	Depreciation	0/yr	3,600/yr	10,934
4	Salvage	16,000	14,800	9,406
		$(B = 13{,}000)$	$(1 - T)S + TB$	
				TC = −$74,220

TABLE 7.13
Present value of the total cost of machine A if it is replaced after six years.

TIME	ITEM	CFBT	CFAT	PV AT 12%
0	I_0	−49,000	−49,000	−49,000
1–6	$-\Delta E$	−25,000/yr	−15,000/yr	−61,671
1–5	Depreciation	0/yr	3,600/yr	12,977
5	Maintenance	−1,000	−600	−340
6	Salvage	0	1,600	811
		(B = 4,000)	$(1 - T)S + TB$	
				TC = −$97,223

CALCULATOR SOLUTION

Data Input	Function Key
6	N
12	I
97,223	PV
0	FV
−23,647	**PMT**

The total cost over one six-year life cycle is −$97,223, as given in Table 7.13. Earlier we found that the EAC for the five-year cycle is −$23,797. From Equation (7.6), the EAC for a six-year cycle is −$23,647.

So the six-year replacement cycle is best.

As we pointed out earlier, the choice of machine A (over B), with its shorter replacement cycle, provides more flexibility with respect to technological innovations. Similarly, flexibility in a machine's replacement cycle is also valuable because even if one cycle is projected at one point in time, the firm has the option to change when replacement will occur, depending upon conditions that develop.

In the replacement-cycle-frequency example, the alternative EACs are very similar. Therefore, the firm can purchase machine A, run it for four years, and reevaluate the replacement decision then. The reevaluation would include technological considerations, the condition of the machine, replacement cost, salvage values, maintenance experience over the four years, and more accurate maintenance cost projections for its continued use, among other things.

Equivalent Annual Annuities

The EAC calculation annualizes the total cost of a project over its life. The same type of calculation can be used to annualize *any* amount, such as a project's NPV, its total revenue, and so on. In such cases, the amount is called an *equivalent annual benefit.* The general term for an annualized amount is **equivalent annual annuity (EAA).** The EAA is a useful measure whenever the project horizon is indefinitely long, such that the assumption of an infinite, or permanent, stream is a good characterization of the situation.

CALCULATOR SOLUTION

Data Input	Function Key
5	N
11	I
2,800	PV
0	FV
−757.60	**PMT**

EXAMPLE Computing an Equivalent Annual Annuity (EAA)

Suppose one five-year cycle of a machine has an NPV of $2,800. Assuming a required return of 11%, what is the project's EAA?

Using Equation (7.6) with EAA in place of EAC and NPV in place of TC, the EAA for this project's NPV would be $757.60. With an infinite horizon of sequential replacement, the NPV from the sequence would be the present value of a perpetuity of EAA inflows, or $6,887.27 (= 757.60/0.11).

Other Replacement Scenarios

One-time replacement decisions should be made using the one-time NPV decision criterion: Choose the asset with the largest NPV. In this section on replacement cycles, we assume an asset will be replaced periodically, with an infinitely long horizon. The choice of replacement cycle for the *routine* like-for-like replacement of assets is made on the basis of equivalent annual cost: *Choose the asset with the lowest EAC or the highest EAA.*

When future significant technological advances are likely, the replacement cycle decision becomes more complex. Among other things, the decision must include the option, connected with a shorter replacement cycle, to make technological change sooner. In practice, technological advances can be difficult to predict. Nevertheless, their possible occurrence can materially affect a firm's choice of asset.

Review

1. How do periodic replacement decisions differ from one-time replacement decisions? What is the best way to handle assets with replacement cycles in capital budgeting analysis?
2. What is the equivalent annual cost of owning an asset? How is it related to an ordinary annuity?
3. How is the EAC (equivalent annual cost) approach used to decide which of two machines to purchase?
4. What is an equivalent annual annuity (EAA)? How can it be used in capital budgeting analysis?

SUMMARY

This chapter describes the critical problem of estimating a capital budgeting project's incremental cash flows. We want to leave you with one final observation. ***The accuracy of the estimates used in capital budgeting is critically important.*** Bad estimates will not lead to good decisions, regardless of the evaluation methods you choose or how well you apply them. Having said that, however, we must sadly note that no one ever has completely accurate estimates of investment outcomes.

- A project's net initial outlay includes cash expenditures, changes in net working capital, after-tax cash flows from selling old equipment, and any investment tax credits. The net cash flow for initial investment $= -I - \Delta W + S - T(S - B)$.
- A project's periodic net operating cash flow, its CFAT, can be described as *operating cash flows after tax plus the depreciation tax shield:* CFAT $= (\Delta R - \Delta E)(1 - T) + T\Delta D$.
- Net operating cash flow can also be described as incremental *net income plus depreciation:* CFAT $= (\Delta R - \Delta E - \Delta D)(1 - T) + \Delta D$.
- A project's nonoperating cash flows, nonregular cash flows during its life, must be included.
- A project's net salvage value includes the after-tax cash flow from the sale of assets, all cleanup and removal expenses, and any release of net working capital. Net salvage value $= S - T(S - B) - (1 - T)REX + \Delta W$.
- Be sure to include the effects of all economic dependencies that cause erosion or enhancement in the value of existing or potential projects.

- Be sure to use the *current* tax laws to determine after-tax cash flows.
- For tax and capital budgeting purposes, a firm should use the depreciation method that provides the largest present value of depreciation tax credits.
- The Modified Accelerated Cost Recovery System, MACRS, is required under current tax laws. Corporations usually use straight-line depreciation for financial reporting. In the text, we use straight-line tax depreciation to simplify the calculations.
- Include the effect of inflation by representing all cash flows and discount rates for a decision on a consistent basis—in either real *or* nominal terms.
- The nominal discount rate depends on the real rate and the expected inflation rate: $r_n = r_r + i + ir_r$.
- Because present value is a function of both cash flow and required return, in many cases inflation does not have a significant effect on the capital budgeting decision, although it can increase the complexity of calculations.
- When an investment is part of a replacement cycle, the correct method for evaluating alternative investments is the Equivalent Annual Cost (EAC) or the Equivalent Annual Annuity (EAA).

EQUATION SUMMARY

$$\text{Net cash flow for initial investment} = -I - \Delta W + S - T(S - B) \tag{7.1}$$

$$\text{CFAT} = (\Delta R - \Delta E)(1 - T) + T\Delta D \tag{7.2}$$

$$\text{CFAT} = (\Delta R - \Delta E - \Delta D)(1 - T) + \Delta D \tag{7.3}$$

$$\text{Net salvage value} = S - T(S - B) - (1 - T)\,\text{REX} + \Delta W \tag{7.4}$$

$$r_n = r_r + i + ir_r \tag{7.5}$$

$$\text{EAC} = \text{TC}\left[\frac{r(1+r)^n}{(1+r)^n - 1}\right] \tag{7.6}$$

QUESTIONS

1. Choose one of each of the bracketed terms that correctly states a concept used in assembling project cash flows.

   The costs and benefits should be measured in terms of [cash flow/net income].

   Cash flows are measured on an [incremental/total] basis.

   Future cash flows are measured on a [before-tax/after-tax] basis.

   Financing costs are [ignored/included].
2. Explain the basic cash flows that are included in the net cash flow for the initial investment.
3. Why is it important to recognize and exclude sunk costs from a capital budgeting analysis?
4. Describe the calculation of the net operating cash flow as operating cash flows after tax plus the depreciation tax shield. Describe the calculation of the net operating cash flow as net income plus depreciation.
5. What are two types of nonoperating cash flows that can occur during a project's life?
6. Explain the calculation of a project's net salvage value.
7. How are financing charges normally accounted for in a capital budgeting analysis?
8. Why is a change in net working capital an important and necessary part of the incremental cost of a capital budgeting project?

9. What is the relationship between the nominal rate of return, the real rate of return, and the rate of inflation?
10. Why are *current* tax laws very important to the proper evaluation of a capital investment project?
11. Explain the concept of an equivalent annual cost in your own words.
12. Suppose that you invested $10,000 in an asset that is depreciated as five-year property under the modified accelerated cost recovery system. Explain how you would calculate the investment's depreciation charges.
13. Define the terms *erosion* and *enhancement* as they relate to the firm's capital investment decisions.

CHALLENGING QUESTIONS

14. Phyllis believes that the firm should use straight-line depreciation for a capital project because it results in higher net income during the early years of the project's life. Joanna believes that the firm should use the modified accelerated cost recovery system depreciation because it reduces the tax liability during the early years of the project's life. Assuming you have a choice between depreciation methods, whose advice should you follow? Why?
15. From one point of view, inflation does not create a problem in the evaluation of a capital budgeting project. From another point of view, inflation creates tremendous problems in the evaluation of a capital budgeting project. What are these two points of view?

PROBLEMS

LEVEL A (BASIC)

A1. (Net income and net cash flows) Julie Stansfield has a bicycle rental shop with annual revenues of $200,000. Cash operating expenses for rent, labor, and utilities are $70,000. Depreciation is $40,000. Julie's tax rate is 40%.

a. What should be Julie's net income?

b. What is her net cash flow?

A2. (Net income and net cash flows) Annual revenues are $100, cash operating expenses are $40, depreciation is $10, and the tax rate is 40%.

a. What is net income?

b. What is the net cash flow?

A3. (MACRS depreciation) Modigliani Jet Ski Company has purchased several firm cars for a total of $150,000. They are classed as five-year property.

a. What is the annual depreciation charge for these assets?

b. If Modigliani's marginal tax rate is 40%, what is the annual depreciation tax shield?

c. Discounted at 8%, what is the present value of the depreciation tax shields?

A4. (MACRS depreciation) Modigliani Jet Ski Company also purchased some special tools for a total of $150,000. The tools are classed as three-year property.

a. What is the annual depreciation charge for these assets?

b. If Modigliani's marginal tax rate is 40%, what is the annual depreciation tax shield?

c. Discounted at 8%, what is the present value of the depreciation tax shields?

A5. (Capitalizing versus expensing) Suppose the Caltron Corporation is going to purchase an asset that costs $0.5 million. Caltron's marginal tax rate is 35%. How does the pattern of expenses recognized for tax purposes differ between (1) capitalizing the asset and depreciating it on a straight-line basis over five years and (2) expensing the $0.5 million right now?

A6. (Net investment outlay) You purchase a new machine for $100. You pay an additional $30 for freight and setup costs. The old machine that is being replaced has a book value of $10 and can be sold for $20. An investment of $40 in working capital is also required. The marginal tax rate is 30%. What is the net investment outlay?

A7. (Net investment outlay) The cost of a new machine is $70,000 plus an additional $8,000 for freight and setup costs. The old machine that is being replaced has a book value of $15,000 and can be sold for $7,000. An investment of $15,000 in working capital is also required. The marginal tax rate is 30%. What is the net investment outlay?

A8. (Cash flows after tax) Assume that revenues increase by $400,000, cash operating expenses increase by $180,000, and depreciation increases by $45,000. The tax rate is 34%.

a. Calculate the cash flow after tax using the formula where CFAT is operating cash flows after tax plus the depreciation tax shield.

b. Calculate the cash flow after tax using the formula where CFAT is net income plus depreciation.

c. Should the answers to a. and b. be the same?

A9. (Cash flows after tax) Revenues increase by $16,000, cash operating expenses increase by $6,000, and depreciation increases by $2,000. The tax rate is 45%.

a. Calculate the cash flow after tax using the formula where CFAT is operating cash flows after tax plus the depreciation tax shield.

b. Calculate the cash flow after tax using the formula where CFAT is net income plus depreciation.

c. Should the answers to a. and b. be the same?

A10. (Salvage value) Suppose Intel Corporation is contemplating a capital budgeting project with capital assets that will be depreciated to a book value of $100,000 but that Intel expects to have a salvage value of $180,000. Intel's marginal tax rate is 40%. Cleanup and removal expenses are expected to be $11,000, and there will be a $20,000 return of working capital. What is the net salvage value?

A11. (Salvage value) Zydeco Shrimping is selling off one of its boats. The boat has been depreciated to a $100,000 book value and can be sold for $150,000. Net working capital of $20,000 can be liquidated. Zydeco will have before-tax cleanup and removal expenses of $5,000. If Zydeco is in the 40% tax bracket, what is the net salvage value?

A12. (Salvage value) At the end of its economic life, Booth Broadcasting will decommission one of its southwestern radio stations. The equipment and building have been depreciated to zero and the land has a $400,000 book value. Working capital of $200,000 can be liquidated. Booth has before-tax cleanup and removal expenses of $100,000. Booth is selling the property to an Australian investor for $1,500,000. If Booth Broadcasting is in the 45% tax bracket, what is the net salvage value?

A13. (Investment in working capital) Nelson Store's expansion plans are expected to increase its inventories by $30 million. Nelson will also increase its accounts receivable by $15 million and its accounts payable by $8 million. What investment in net working capital is required?

A14. (Nominal and real discount rates) The real required rate of return is 8% and the inflation rate is 5%.

a. What is the nominal required rate of return if you add the two rates and ignore the cross-term?

b. What is the nominal required rate of return including the cross-term?

A15. (Nominal and real discount rates) The nominal and real discount rates are 18% and 8%.

a. What is the expected inflation rate (ignoring the cross-term)?

b. What is the expected inflation rate (including the effect of the cross-term)?

A16. (EAC) The total present value of all costs associated with an asset over a seven-year life is $73,285. If the asset has a cost of capital of 11%, what is the EAC of using this asset?

A17. (EAC) A machine that costs \$10,000 new can be replaced after being used from four to seven years. Annual maintenance costs are identical for all possible replacement cycles. The machine has a cost of capital of 12%. The alternative net salvage values at the end of four to seven years of use are, respectively, \$3,800, \$2,800, \$1,000, −\$1,000. Ignoring taxes and inflation, what is the optimal replacement cycle?

A18. (Basic capital budgeting) The investment is \$3,000,000, which is depreciated straight line for 10 years down to a zero salvage value. For its 10-year life, the investment will generate annual sales of \$600,000 and annual cash operating expenses of \$100,000. Although the investment is depreciated to a zero book value, you expect to sell it for \$500,000 in 10 years. The marginal income tax rate is 30% and the cost of capital is 10%.

a. What are the net operating cash flows after tax?

b. What is the net present value of the investment?

A19. (Basic capital budgeting) An investment of \$30,000 will be depreciated straight line for 10 years down to a zero salvage value. For its 10-year life, the investment will generate annual sales of \$12,000 and annual cash operating expenses of \$2,000. Although the investment is depreciated to a zero book value, it should sell for \$3,000 in ten years. The marginal income tax rate is 40% and the cost of capital is 10%.

a. What are the net operating cash flows after tax?

b. What is the net present value of the investment?

LEVEL B

B1. (Capitalizing versus expensing) Bey Travel Agency is a small firm owned by David Bey that has just purchased \$20,000 worth of computer upgrades. Under current tax laws, Bey has a choice of expensing or depreciating a small investment such as this. Bey's marginal tax rate is 40%.

a. What is the present value of the depreciation tax shield if the computers are depreciated straight line over the next five years? The cost of capital is 10%.

b. What is the present value of the tax saving if the computers are expensed immediately?

c. Would you recommend that Bey expense or capitalize this investment?

B2. (Incremental cash flows and NPV) The Canton Sundae Corporation is considering the replacement of an existing machine. The new machine, called an X-tender, would provide better sundaes, but it costs \$120,000. The X-tender requires \$20,000 in setup costs that are expensed immediately and \$20,000 in additional working capital. The X-tender's useful life is 10 years, after which it can be sold for a salvage value of \$40,000. Canton uses straight-line depreciation, and the machine will be depreciated to a book value of zero on a six-year basis. Canton has a tax rate of 45% and a 16% cost of capital on projects like this one. The X-tender is expected to increase revenues minus expenses by \$35,000 per year. What is the NPV of buying the X-tender?

B3. (Replacement frequency) In the section on replacement frequency in this chapter, the example considered Hoover's inventory equipment. Suppose that machine A could be used for a seventh year if \$18,000 is spent for maintenance at the end of year 6. This is in addition to \$1,000 necessary at the end of year 5 to use the machine a sixth year. The net salvage value will be zero. What is the EAC for a seven-year replacement cycle?

B4. (Incremental cash flows and NPV) Johnson & Johnson currently has a machine that has five years of useful life remaining. Its current net book value is \$50,000, and it is being straight-line depreciated to its expected zero salvage value in five years. It generates \$60,000 per year in sales revenue, requiring \$30,000 in operating expenses, excluding depreciation. If the firm sells the machine now, it could get \$30,000 for it. The firm is considering buying a new machine to replace this one. The new machine will have a useful life of five years and a salvage value of \$5,000. It costs \$65,000. It is expected to generate \$70,000 in sales revenue and require \$25,000 in operating expenses annually, excluding depreciation. The project's cost of capital is 10%, the firm will use straight-line depreciation to $5,000 over five years, and the relevant tax rate is 40%. Compute the NPV from replacing the old machine.

B5. (Cash flows and NPV for a new project) Syracuse Roadbuilding Company is considering the purchase of a new tandem box dump truck. The truck costs $95,000, and an additional $5,000 is needed to paint it with the firm logo and install radio equipment. Assume the truck falls into the MACRS three-year class. The truck will generate no additional revenues, but it will reduce cash operating expenses by $35,000 per year. The truck will be sold for $40,000 after its five-year life. An inventory investment of $4,000 is required during the life of the investment. Syracuse Roadbuilding is in the 45% income tax bracket.

a. What is the net investment?

b. What is the after-tax net operating cash flow for each of the five years?

c. What is the after-tax salvage value?

d. Assuming a 10% cost of capital, what is the net present value of this investment?

B6. (Cash flows and NPV for a replacement decision) Andrew Thompson Interests (ATI) is using a mechanical switching system that it bought five years ago for $400,000. This mechanical system is being depreciated straight line to an estimated salvage value of zero over a 10-year life. Thus, the annual depreciation charge is $40,000 and current book value is $200,000. At the end of its life, the actual salvage value is expected to be $25,000. If ATI sold this equipment today, it would fetch $100,000.

ATI is evaluating a new digital switching system that will cost $500,000. The digital system is depreciated straight line to a zero salvage value over a five year life. At the end of the five years, ATI expects to sell the system for $150,000. The new digital system should have a favorable impact on operating cash flows, increasing revenues by $100,000 annually and decreasing cash operating expenses by $50,000 annually. The new equipment has no effect on the investment in working capital.

ATI is in the 40% tax bracket and has a 12% cost of capital. Consider each of the following questions assuming that ATI sells the old mechanical switching system and replaces it with the new digital system.

a. What is the net investment?

b. What is the after-tax net operating cash flow for each of the five years?

c. What is the after-tax salvage value?

d. What is the net present value of this investment?

B7. (Incremental cash flows and NPV) Procter & Gamble is considering buying a new machine that costs $100,000. The machine requires $8,000 in setup costs that are expensed immediately and $12,000 in additional working capital. The machine's useful life is 10 years, after which it can be sold for a salvage value of $30,000. The machine requires a maintenance overhaul costing $14,000 at the end of year 7. The overhaul is fully expensed when it is done. P&G uses straight-line depreciation, and the machine will be depreciated to a book value of zero on a six-year basis. P&G has a tax rate of 40% and the project's cost of capital is 13%. The machine is expected to increase revenues minus expenses by $55,000 per year. What is the NPV of buying the machine?

B8. (Incremental cash flows and NPV) The Miller Corporation is considering a new product. An outlay of $6 million is required for equipment to produce the new product, and additional net working capital of $500,000 is required to support production and marketing. The equipment will be depreciated on a straight-line basis to a zero book value over eight years. Although the depreciable life is eight years, the project is expected to have a productive life of only six years, and it will have a salvage value of zero at that time (removal cost = scrap value). Revenues minus expenses for the first two years of the project will be $5 million per year but, because of competition, revenues minus expenses in years 3 through 6 will be only $3 million. The cost of capital for this project is 16%, and the relevant tax rate is 35%. Compute the NPV of Miller's new product.

B9. (Incremental cash flows and NPV) The Simon Corporation is considering a new product. An outlay of $2 million is required for equipment to produce the new product, and additional net working capital of $100,000 is required to support production and marketing. The equipment will be depreciated on a straight-line basis to a zero book value over eight years. Although the depreciable life is eight years, the project is expected to have a productive life of only six years, and it will have a salvage value of zero at that time (removal cost = scrap value). Revenues minus expenses for the first two years of the project will be $0.5 million per year but, because of competition, revenues minus expenses in years 3 through 6 will be only $0.4 million. The cost of capital for this project is 11%, and the relevant tax rate is 35%. Compute the NPV of Simon's new product.

B10. (Inflation) Suppose Starter, makers of athletic wear, is considering purchasing a new knitting machine that will cost $250,000. It will have an eight-year useful life. It can be depreciated to a $10,000 book value on a straight-line basis. Incremental operating income will be $100,000 per year before taxes, in real terms. Starter's marginal tax rate is 40%. Inflation is expected to average 5% per year, and the project's cost of capital in real terms is 8%. The salvage value will be $10,000.

a. Calculate the NPV in real terms.

b. Calculate the NPV in nominal terms.

B11. (Inflation) Dominick's is considering buying a new machine that will cost $350,000, and will have an eight-year useful life. It can be depreciated to a $110,000 book value on a straight-line basis. Incremental operating income will be $100,000 per year before taxes in real terms. Dominick's marginal tax rate is 40%. Inflation is expected to average 5% per year, and the project's cost of capital in real terms is 8%. The salvage value will be $110,000.

a. Calculate the NPV in real terms.

b. Calculate the NPV in nominal terms.

B12. (Replacement cycle) Barry Marks is looking for the optimal replacement cycle for his firm's towmotors. New towmotors cost $70,000 apiece. Their resale value, like that of new cars, drops rapidly at first and then declines more slowly. However, annual operating costs increase with age. Barry has carefully assessed these factors and boiled down the cash flows from various replacement cycles to the following:

YEAR	**1**	**2**	**3**	**4**
Operating costs each year after purchase	20	30	40	50
Salvage value if held for this time period	45	30	25	20

The data are in $1,000s. The operating costs are after taxes and after the effect of the depreciation tax shield. The salvage value is also after taxes. The cost of capital is 10%. What is the equivalent annual cost (EAC) for replacing the towmotors after every one, two, three, or four years?

B13. (Capitalizing versus expensing) Suppose Hydrex can either expense or capitalize an asset it has just purchased for $9,000. If it capitalizes the asset, it will depreciate the asset to a book value of zero on a straight-line basis over three years. Hydrex has a marginal tax rate of 38%, and the cost of capital for this asset is 12%. What is the present-value difference to Hydrex between expensing and capitalizing the asset? Assume Hydrex will have sufficient income over the next three years to use all possible tax credits.

B14. (Inflation) A project's initial investment is $40,000, and it has a five-year life. At the end of the fifth year, the equipment is expected to be sold for $12,000, at which time its net book value will be $5,000. The CFATs (including inflation, depreciation, and net salvage value) for the next five years are expected to be $20,000, $25,000, $10,000, $10,000, and $10,000. In real terms, the project's cost of capital is 10%, and the riskless return is 7%. The tax rate is 46%, and the inflation rate is 3%. What is the project's NPV?

B15. (Incremental cash flows and NPV) A new product called AW-SUM is being considered by Egg Streams, Unlimited. An outlay of $16 million is required for equipment to produce the new product, and additional net working capital in the amount of $3.2 million is also required. The project is expected to have an eight-year life and the equipment will be depreciated on a straight-line basis to a zero book value over eight years. Although the equipment will be depreciated to a zero book value, it is expected to have a salvage value of $2 million. Revenues minus expenses for the project are expected to be $5 million per year. The project's cost of capital is 16%, and the relevant tax rate is 35%. Compute the NPV of the AW-SUM project.

B16. (Taxes and NPV) Depreciation provides a sort of shield against taxes. If there were no taxes, there would be no depreciation tax shields.

a. Does this mean that the NPV of the AW-SUM project in problem B15 would be less if there were no taxes?

b. Compute the NPV of the AW-SUM project in problem B15, assuming a tax rate of 0% and a cost of capital of 16%.

B17. (Taxes) The investment is $1,000,000, which is depreciated straight line to a zero salvage value over a 10-year life. The asset will be worthless in 10 years. The project will generate, annually, revenues of $800,000, cash operating expenses of $500,000, and depreciation of $100,000. The tax rate is 30%, and the cost of capital is 10%.

a. What is the annual cash flow and NPV?

b. What would be the annual cash flow and NPV if the tax rate were 0%?

c. What tax rate would result in a zero NPV?

B18. (Investment in net working capital) You are reviewing the project analysis submitted by one of your staff analysts. You find the analysis to be correct except that the analyst ignored the effects of changes in net working capital. You expect an increase in net working capital of $400,000 at time 0, another increase of $400,000 in one year, a decrease of $200,000 in five years, and a liquidation of remaining working capital at the end of 10 years. If the analyst had calculated an NPV of $360,000, what should be the project's NPV including the effect of changes in net working capital? The cost of capital is 10%.

B19. (Analysis of cash flows) Corpus Christi Partners has evaluated a major expansion that had a positive NPV of $4,500,000. Joe Whitman believes that if the Partners invest an additional $500,000 in net working capital, the annual revenues would be increased by $140,000 per year and the annual cash operating expenses would be increased by $40,000 per year. These changes would persist over the 10-year life of the project. The investment in net working capital would not affect depreciation schedules and would be reversed at the end of 10 years. Corpus Christi Partners is in the 30% tax bracket and has a 10% cost of capital.

a. Assuming that Joe's estimates are correct, what is the outlay, annual net operating cash flow, and after-tax salvage value?

b. What is the net present value of the additional investment in net working capital?

c. What is the total NPV of the project including the additional investment in working capital?

B20. (EAC) Y.B. Blue Corporation is considering two alternative machines. Machine A will cost $50,000, have expenses (excluding depreciation) of $34,000 per year, and have a useful life of six years. Machine B will cost $70,000, have a useful life of five years, and will have expenses (excluding depreciation) of $26,000 per year. Y.B. uses straight-line depreciation and pays taxes at the rate of 35%. The project's cost of capital is 13%. Net salvage value is zero for each machine at the end of its useful life. Assuming the project for which the machine will be used is profitable, which machine should be purchased?

B21. (EAC) Billy Bob's Big Eat'n Place has decided to purchase a new cornhusker. Billy Bob will buy one of two machines. Each machine costs $1,500. Machine A has a four-year life, a salvage value of $1,000, and expenses of $475 per year. Machine B has a five-year life, a salvage value of $500, and expenses of $460 per year. Whichever machine is used, revenues for this project are $1,200 per year, and machines will be replaced at the end of their lives. Using straight-line depreciation to the salvage value, a tax rate of 35%, and a cost of capital of 20%, which machine should Billy Bob buy, and why?

B22. (Excel: NPV and product pricing) You are bidding on a contract to supply 10,000 Lat Blasters per year for five years. The cash expenses are $200 per Lat Blaster, or $2,000,000 per year. This contract would require an investment of $5,000,000, which would be depreciated straight line over the five-year life of the project. The salvage value will be zero. Your marginal tax rate is 40% and cost of capital is 10%. Your annual revenue is the price per Lat Blaster times 10,000 units per year. What minimum annual revenue and what price per Lat Blaster is required to produce a zero net present value?

B23. (Excel: Solving for an unknown salvage value) Wendy Guo is investing $800,000 in a property that will generate fairly low profits for two years, at which time she plans to sell the project. The profitability of her investment hinges on the selling price. For the two years while she owns the project, annual revenues of $80,000, cash expenses of $30,000, and depreciation of $30,000 are expected. Wendy's tax rate is 40% and her cost of capital is 12%. What minimum selling price for the property is needed for Wendy to make a profit (have a zero NPV)? Do not forget the taxes that Wendy must pay if she sells the property for more than book value.

B24. (Excel: Capital budgeting cash flows) Racine Machine is in the 40% tax bracket and has an 11% cost of capital. Racine is considering a capital project that involves a $100,000 investment outlay and a 10-year life. Operating revenues will be increased by $55,000 annually, and cash operating costs will be increased by $25,000 annually. Salvage value is zero.

a. Assume straight-line depreciation over a six-year life. Calculate the annual net operating cash flows after tax. Calculate the investment's NPV and IRR.

b. Assume depreciation is based on the rates for five-year property under MACRS. Calculate the annual net operating cash flows after tax. Calculate the investment's NPV and IRR.

c. Assume depreciation is based on the rates for three-year property under MACRS. Calculate the annual net operating cash flows after tax. Calculate the investment's NPV and IRR.

d. Which depreciation schedule results in the highest NPV and IRR?

B25. (Excel: Capital budgeting cash flows) You have an assignment to calculate the NPV and IRR for a capital budgeting project. The information you have assembled is: 1. The outlay for capital equipment is $1,000,000. It will be depreciated as five-year property under MACRS. After 10 years, it will be salvaged for $200,000 (before taxes). 2. The investment in working capital is $250,000, which will be recovered in 10 years. 3. Sales revenues will be $500,000 in year 1. Sales will grow 10% annually for years 2–5. Sales will grow at 0% for years 6–10. 4. There are two components to cash operating expenses. Fixed expenses will be $100,000 in year 1, and these will grow at 2% annually for the entire life of the project. Variable cash operating expenses of 10% of the current year's sales are also incurred. 5. The income tax rate is 34%. 6. The cost of capital is 11%.

a. What is the net operating cash flow for years 1–10? What are the total cash flows, inclusive of investing cash flows and operating cash flows, for years 0–10?

b. What is the NPV and IRR?

LEVEL C (ADVANCED)

C1. (Replacement cycles) Suppose Federal Express is considering which of two delivery trucks to purchase. The German model will cost $75,000, will have expenses (excluding depreciation) of $250,000 per year, and will have a useful life of three years. The Japanese model will cost

$100,000, will have expenses (excluding depreciation) of $240,000 per year, and will have a useful life of four years. Suppose Federal Express uses straight-line depreciation and pays taxes at a 40% rate. The cost of capital for the project is 12%. The salvage values are $15,000 for the German model and $12,000 for the Japanese model. Which model of delivery truck should Federal Express purchase?

C2. (Replacement cycles) Suppose Federal Express in problem C1 could refit either model of delivery truck at the end of its estimated useful life. An expenditure of $5,000 would extend either truck's useful life by one year. Operating expenses would be $10,000 higher in the extra year for either truck. Alternatively, spending $10,000 would extend either truck's original estimated useful life by two years. Operating expenses would be $20,000 per year higher in the extra years under this alternative. The depreciation schedules would remain as given in C1. Estimated salvage values for the one- and two-year extensions are, respectively, $12,000 and $10,000 for the German truck, and $10,000 and $8,000 for the Japanese truck.

a. What is the optimal replacement cycle for each truck?

b. Which one should Federal Express purchase?

C3. (Incremental cash flows and NPV) Ivan's Onion-Brick Restaurant has been very successful for 10 years. However, the growth potential in Ivan's area has declined, and therefore Ivan is contemplating investment in a new business line: consulting. Ivan can enter this new field by purchasing and renovating a small building in downtown Newark at a cost of $100,000, all of which will be depreciated on a straight-line basis to a zero book value over 10 years. Although it will be depreciated to a zero book value, the entire project is expected to be sold off for a salvage value of $65,000 at the end of eight years. It is estimated that the revenues from the project will be $100,000 per year during the next two years and $150,000 in years 3 through 8. Variable costs (including all labor and material) will be 65% of revenues. At the expected revenue levels, Ivan expects to average about $30,000 in receivables, and accounts payable are expected to average $5,000. Ivan has determined that the project's cost of capital is 17.31%, and the tax rate is 35%. What is the NPV of this project?

C4. (Excel: Inflation) Letter-Fly, Unlimited, a conglomerate corporation with investments in overnight mail service and skeet-shooting franchises, is contemplating a five-year investment project that requires an initial investment of $200,000 for equipment (depreciated over five years on a straight-line basis to a zero salvage value). The project also requires $25,000 in additional net working capital and is expected to have a salvage value of zero. The revenues from the project are expected to be $100,000 in the first year and are expected to have an inflation rate of 3.5% per year over the life of the project. Expenses are expected to be $25,000 in the first year and are expected to have an inflation rate of 6% per year. The general level of inflation for the economy is expected to be 5% per year. If the required return on this project in real terms is 8% and taxes are paid at the rate of 32%, should Letter-Fly undertake the investment project?

C5. (Excel: Equivalent annual cost) The Kelly Cab Company wishes to replace its cabs regularly, after two, three, four, or five years. The Kelly Cab accountant has put together several cost estimates for our use: 1. The investment in a cab is $25,000. 2. The after-tax costs of operating a cab are $12,000 the first year, $13,000 the second, $15,000 the third, $18,000 the fourth, and $24,000 the fifth. 3. Some fixed costs (like driver salaries, licenses, and insurance) can be ignored for this analysis. 4. If a cab is sold for salvage, the after-tax salvage value is $10,000 in two years. If sold after three, four, or five years, respectively, the after-tax salvage value is $8,000, $5,000, and $3,000. 5. The opportunity cost of funds is 10%.

a. Calculate the total present value and the equivalent annual cost of operating a cab two years, three years, four years, or five years.

b. How frequently should Kelly Cab replace its cabs?

MINICASE THE POWER TO COOL OFF IN FLORIDA

The Indiantown Cogeneration Project involved the construction and operation of a coal-fired plant in Martin County, Florida, that produces electricity and steam. The capital cost (including interest during construction) was approximately $770 million. Since completion, it has an electric generating capacity of 330 megawatts (net) and a steam capacity of 175,000 pounds per hour. The project sells the electric power to Florida Power & Light Company (FPL) under a 30-year contract and the steam to Caulkins Indiantown Citrus Company under a 15-year contract. FPL's electricity payments have two parts: one for electric capacity and the other for the electric energy that it receives.

The project's financing consisted of $630 million of 30-year 9% APR interest rate debt and $140 million of equity. The debt requires equal annual sinking fund payments of $31.5 million beginning in year 11. Depreciation is straight line to zero over 20 years. The tax rate is 40%. Other information about the project is:

OUTPUT/INPUT		
Electricity	2,500,000	megawatt-hours per year
Steam	525,000,000	pounds per year
Coal consumption	1,000,000	tons per year
PRICES IN YEAR 1, AND ANNUAL ESCALATION RATES (IN PARENTHESES)		
Electric capacity payment	$375,000.00	per megawatt (1% per year)
Electric energy payment	24.00	per megawatt-hour (4% per year)
Steam price	0.20	per thousand pounds (7% per year)
Coal price	29.00	per ton (4.5% per year)
FIRST YEAR OPERATING COSTS AND ANNUAL ESCALATION RATES		
Fuel delivery and waste disposal	$20	per ton of coal (4.5% per year)
Operations and maintenance	$15	million (3% per year)
Other operating expenses	$15	million (3% per year)

QUESTIONS

1. Estimate the project's CFATs for each of the 30 years.
2. Using a 7.15% cost of capital, and assuming a zero salvage value, calculate the project's NPV and IRR.
3. The debt was issued a year before the project was completed. Calculate the interest coverage ratio and cash flow coverage ratio for each of years 10 (the first year of the sinking fund, year 11 of the debt) through 20.
4. Will the project be able to meet its annual debt service obligations?

8

Capital Budgeting in Practice

The capital budgeting principles and techniques we have learned so far provide an excellent framework. However, we do not want you to think that capital budgeting decisions are mechanical and straightforward. Practical realities introduce complexities that can make capital budgeting decision making intellectually challenging.

For example, the principle that options are valuable is straightforward, but applying it in valuing a capital budgeting project can be challenging. Similarly, opportunity costs play a very important role in determining the value of a project, but first we have to identify them. This chapter suggests places to look for options and opportunity costs caused by interaction among existing operations and new projects.

Another kind of interaction among projects comes from *capital rationing*. Capital rationing places limits on what a firm spends, such as placing a cap on the amount available to spend on projects this year. On the one hand, such limits can seem bad, because they might eliminate positive-NPV projects. On the other hand, there are good reasons for such limits; *"soft" capital rationing* can be a practical tool for planning and coordinating a firm's capital budget. Controlling managerial responsibility and incentives are two other useful tools for managing a firm's capital budgeting decisions.

The chapter ends with a discussion of additional practical considerations in the capital budgeting process. We examine several factors that can be subtle and difficult to deal with in practice. Finally, we provide an overview with practical reminders of the importance of the Principles of Finance.

FOCUS ON PRINCIPLES

- *Options:* Recognize the value of options, such as the options to expand, postpone, or abandon a capital budgeting project.
- *Two-Sided Transactions:* Consider why the other party to a transaction is willing to participate.
- *Signaling:* Consider the actions and products of competitors.
- *Valuable Ideas:* Look for new ideas to use as a basis for capital budgeting projects that will create value.
- *Comparative Advantage:* Look for capital budgeting projects that use the firm's comparative advantage to add value.
- *Incremental Benefits:* Identify and estimate a project's incremental expected future cash flows.
- *Risk-Return Trade-Off:* Consider the risk of the capital budgeting project when determining the project's cost of capital, its required return.
- *Time Value of Money:* Measure the value the capital budgeting project will create—its NPV.

8.1 A PROPOSAL FOR CAPACITY EXPANSION: THE PRICE-SETTING OPTION

Remember Rocky Mountain Chemical Corporation's packaging-machine proposal, which we analyzed in the previous chapter? Well, let us assume that besides the new packaging-machine proposal, RMC has several other projects under consideration. If undertaken, these projects will be financed with funds from a new bond issue RMC made earlier this month.

One project is an expansion of RMC's production capacity for a consumer product produced at its Colorado plant, a specialty facial soap called Smooooth. This year's sales are running substantially ahead of last year's and are currently just about at the plant capacity of 10 million bars per year. Next year's sales might top 11 million bars if RMC has the production capacity to produce that much soap. Furthermore, management estimates that if RMC spent an additional $500,000 per year on advertising in each of the next three years, sales would rise to 12 million bars next year, 13 million the year after, and 14.5 million per year following that for the foreseeable future.

The proposal under consideration is to increase RMC's production capacity for Smooooth soap by 65%. Before-tax initial outlays for the project are expected to total $1.85 million. Of this amount, $50,000 would be an increase in working capital. Capitalized space and equipment costs would be $1.45 million. Of $350,000 in installation costs, $250,000 would have to be capitalized and $100,000 could be expensed immediately. This last amount could be expensed immediately because it would stem from the temporary reassignment of current employees.[1]

The capitalized expenses would be depreciated to a zero book value on a straight-line basis over eight years. However, the additional facility is expected to be able to produce for 10 years if a substantial overhaul of the equipment is done at the end of the sixth year. The overhaul would be expected to cost $200,000 and would be expensed (rather than capitalized) when it is done. Depreciation, therefore, would be $212,500 per year (= [1.45 + 0.25]/8) for the first eight years and zero for the last two years of the project. The salvage value of the new equipment (scrap value minus the cost of removal and cleanup) would be zero at the end of the 10 years.

[1]Although these employees will be paid anyway, their wages become an opportunity cost if the project is undertaken. This is because the firm will lose the work normally done by these employees while they help with the installation process. This phenomenon can also occur with respect to managerial time.

The wholesale price for Smooooth is \$0.612 per bar, and the variable cost of production is \$0.387 per bar. So RMC earns a contribution margin of \$0.225 per bar on Smooooth. The additional 4.5 million bars sold in years 3 through 10 would therefore generate an increase of \$1,012,500 (= [0.225]4.5 million) in revenue minus expenses each year. The increase for years 1 and 2 would be \$450,000 and \$675,000, respectively. RMC's marginal tax rate is 40%, and the project's required return is 16%. What's the project's NPV?

Table 8.1 shows the NPV calculation for the proposed expansion. Note once again that financing charges do not appear explicitly anywhere in the analysis, even though we know the incremental funds for the project will come from RMC's recent bond issue. The financing opportunity costs are part of the project's required return. The NPV is \$342,266. By trial and error, the IRR is found to be about 19.7%, which exceeds the 16% required return. Finally, because the NPV is positive, the profitability index is also positive and equals 1.189 (= 1 + 342,266/[1,700,000 + 60,000 + 50,000]).

At this point, it would be easy to say, "Let's do it!" However, although the project looks good so far, we have left an important option out of the analysis.

The Price-Setting Option

What we did not consider in our NPV calculation is the option to raise the Smooooth's wholesale price. That option creates a significant opportunity cost.

What if we raised the price less than 2 cents, from \$0.612 to \$0.629 per bar? If this price increase decreased next year's demand to 10.2 million bars, the current plant's entire capacity of 10 million bars could be sold at the higher price. And this would be possible without *any* additional cash outflows!

TABLE 8.1
NPV calculation for smooooth production capacity expansion.

TIME	ITEM	BTCF	ATCF	PV
0	Capitalized installation and equipment cost	−1,700,000 $-I_0$	−1,700,000 $-I_0$	−1,700,000
0	Expensed installation cost	−100,000 $-E_0$	−60,000 $-(1-T)E_0$	−60,000
0	Change in net working capital	−50,000 $-\Delta W$	− 50,000 $-\Delta W$	−50,000
1–3	Additional advertising expense	−500,000/yr $-\Delta E$	−300,000/yr $-(1-T)\Delta E$	−673,767
1–8	Depreciation	0 0	85,000/yr TD	369,205
1	Change in revenues minus expenses	450,000/yr $\Delta R - \Delta E$	270,000/yr $(1-T)(\Delta R - \Delta E)$	232,759
2	Change in revenues minus expenses	675,000/yr $\Delta R - \Delta E$	405,000/yr $(1-T)(\Delta R - \Delta E)$	300,981
3–10	Change in revenues minus expenses	1,012,000/yr $\Delta R - \Delta E$	607,500/yr $(1-T)(\Delta R - \Delta E)$	1,961,007
6	Overhaul expense	−200,000 $-\Delta E$	−120,000 $-(1-T)\Delta E$	−49,253
10	Return of net working capital	50,000 ΔW	50,000 ΔW	11,334
				NPV = \$342,266

Based on the sales projections, demand at a wholesale price of \$0.629 is expected to exceed 10 million bars per year for the next 10 years. With an increase of \$0.017 over the current price, RMC would have additional before-tax revenues of \$170,000 (= 0.017[10 million]) per year. This translates into an increase in after-tax revenues of \$102,000 (= 170,000[1 − 0.4]) per year.

As an alternative to the expansion plan, then, RMC could increase its wholesale price and obtain an increase of \$102,000 in its annual net CFAT—*with no other changes whatsoever in its after-tax cash flows.* You can verify that the present value of \$102,000 per year for 10 years at 16% is \$492,989, which exceeds the \$342,266 from the expansion plan. Therefore, although the expansion plan is better than the status quo, the alternative of increasing the price is even better than expansion.

Based on marketing research, RMC estimates that the demand curve for Smooooth soap (the quantity sold at a given price) is 2.538 million/price^3. RMC can optimize its price setting based on its *current* production capacity. Set the demand equal to the maximum production (10 million bars) and solve for the price, which is \$0.633. This is the highest possible price that will produce the desired 10 million in demand.

Of course, estimating a demand curve is not easy. Many dimensions must be taken into account, such as consumers substituting other products and the likelihood that a competing product will become available. But in spite of the cost and difficulty of obtaining it, an estimate of the demand curve for a product may be very valuable. In any case, the analysis for a proposed expansion should always include consideration of the price-setting option, and the opportunity costs associated with it.

Another thing to consider is the cost of capital. The required return for RMC's proposed wholesale price change would probably be less than it is for the capacity expansion proposal because it is a less risky alternative. The firm will have to commit more fixed costs for plant and equipment if it undertakes the expansion. If demand were to decline in the future, the price could be reduced under either alternative to stimulate demand. However, the firm's fixed costs would be higher under the expansion alternative. A lower cost of capital would of course raise the NPV of the price-increase alternative. The cost of capital is examined in Chapter 11.

Flexibility in product pricing is another illustration of the importance of hidden options and demonstrates once again the value of options. Price flexibility is a very valuable tool. Automobile manufacturers have exercised this option, popularizing cash rebates and "special financing" as forms of price reduction to stimulate demand. Similarly, firms should consider price *increases* among their alternative actions. Of course, in some cases, keeping a constant price can have benefit as well.

Review

1. Define the price-setting option, and explain why it can be so valuable.
2. Explain why expanding production facilities would involve greater business risk than raising the price of the product.
3. Why might the cost of capital for a proposed price change be less than the cost of capital for a proposed capacity expansion?

8.2 CAPITAL BUDGETING OPTIONS

Numerous options can be connected with any investment a firm might make. In the expansion example just given, we saw the value of the price-setting option. When we analyzed the replacement decision, we noted the options a firm has in connection with equipment replacement. If an option is ignored, the firm may be incurring an opportunity cost. We must consider the value of all options connected with a capital budgeting project in order to correctly measure the project's NPV.

What are capital budgeting options worth? An option is the right to do something without any obligation to do it. When the option is costless, it simply adds to the project's value. Not all options are costless. Therefore, a project's NPV can be expressed as its "basic" NPV from discounted cash flows (DCF-NPV) *plus* the value of all options associated with the project *minus* any costs connected with getting or maintaining those options:

$$\text{NPV} = \text{DCF-NPV} + \text{Value of options} - \text{Cost of options} \tag{8.1}$$

Unfortunately, we do not have an option pricing model for all options and cannot always accurately estimate the "value of options." However, it is important to understand that the lack of a convenient option pricing model does not diminish the importance of an option.

Managerial options have been shown to have substantial value. For example, consider mineral mining operations. A mining firm has the option to suspend mining operations during times when the price of the mineral is too low to make extraction profitable. The firm can then restart operations whenever mineral prices rise and extraction becomes profitable again. This option substantially increases the value of the mine.

Options are valuable, but there are certain problems associated with combining option values. When a capital budgeting option is exercised, other options are often precluded. In effect, when one option is exercised, other options are eliminated, and simultaneously many costs become sunk costs. Thus, the decision to exercise an option must include the value of all alternative actions in the analysis. Otherwise, a firm may incur an opportunity cost by choosing an alternative that was not the best.

We will now discuss three other capital budgeting options: (1) future investment opportunities, (2) the abandonment option, and (3) the postponement option.

Future Investment Opportunities

Future investment opportunities are options to identify additional, more valuable investment possibilities in the future that result from a current investment. For example, manufacturing and distributing a product now puts a distribution and marketing network in place. This creates an option to sell additional products, should they be developed from valuable new ideas or a comparative advantage.

Money is spent on research and development in the hope of being first to discover a new idea. Being first secures the option of developing the idea into a product, production technique, or service.

Chapter 5 presented a dividend growth method for valuing stock. We found that an important factor in determining a stock's value is the growth created by reinvesting the firm's earnings. In fact, managers often say that the largest part of a project's value comes from its future investment opportunities. Unfortunately, we must emphasize that accurately measuring such future investment opportunities can be a difficult, if not impossible, task.

EXAMPLE Future Investment Option for Kosky Financial Advising

Tom Kosky is considering the expansion of his financial advising business by opening an office in Naples. Tom has carefully considered the revenues and costs this office might generate and found that it is somewhat unprofitable; the DCF-NPV is −\$50,000. However, by investing today, Tom thinks he might have a future option to expand into providing retirement services. It would cost Tom an additional \$100,000 in personnel, licensing, and facilities costs to have this option for future growth. Does the growth option make the current investment have a positive NPV?

If this future opportunity occurs, Tom estimates the present value of this option to be \$500,000. There is a 60% chance of this occurring and a 40% chance that this investment will not be worthwhile. So the expected value of the future investment option is \$300,000 (= 0.6[500,000]).

Using Equation (8.1), then, the NPV is actually $150,000:

$$\begin{aligned}\text{NPV} &= \text{DCF-NPV} + \text{Value of option} - \text{Cost of option} \\ &= -50{,}000 + 300{,}000 - 100{,}000 = \$150{,}000\end{aligned}$$

So the future investment option makes the new office an attractive investment.

The Abandonment Option

Another option to consider in capital budgeting is the possibility of stopping a project earlier than originally planned. This is the **abandonment option.** The abandonment value of a project is simply the NPV from terminating the project by selling or scrapping its assets. The decision rule on abandonment is simple. Abandon only if the abandonment value is greater than the present value of the future cash flows without abandonment.

A project's or asset's abandonment value depends on a number of things, but it is higher when there is an active used-equipment market. Generic and widely used brands of tangible assets, such as cars and trucks, are more likely to have such markets.

Intangible assets—such as special production processes, patents, and copyrights—are less likely to have organized markets. Therefore, intangible assets usually have higher transaction costs to find buyers and are more difficult to sell than generic, tangible assets. Of course, there are rarely any cleanup or removal costs associated with disposing of an intangible asset. Consequently, highly specialized tangible assets subject to technological obsolescence tend to have even higher transaction costs than intangible assets.[2]

We considered the importance of deciding whether to *continue to develop* an investment project in Chapter 6's discussion of the capital budgeting process. This is simply the abandonment option during the development stage of a project. In addition to its importance during development, the abandonment option should be considered periodically after a project is actually under way. It is possible that abandonment of part, or even all, of its operations could have a positive NPV (bearing in mind that sunk costs should be ignored).

EXAMPLE To Sell or Not to Sell Joe's Diner

Joe's Diner has been operating for about as long as anyone can remember. Pete has run it for the last 18 years since he took it over from his father, Jack. Last month, Pete was approached by a developer about selling the place. Diane, the developer, would not say exactly what she had in mind, except that Pete could move the diner if he wanted to. She was interested only in the land. At the end of their conversation, Diane offered Pete $1,000,000 for the land.

Pete was confident that this was a fair price—indeed, the most he could hope to get for the place at this time. Pete thought about moving the diner, but he found out that it was not feasible to move the physical structure. Also, there was no place he could move into that was close enough to keep the clientele and good name of Joe's Diner. If he sold, he would have no choice but to abandon the business.

---

[2]Mainframe computers in the 1970s are an example of such highly specialized equipment subject to technological obsolescence. Many universities were offered mainframe computers as "gifts" if the university would pay the cost of removal and reinstallation. Several universities made the mistake of accepting such "gifts," only to discover that they could have gotten greater computing capability for less money by purchasing a new machine! Corporations were sorry when universities began refusing such "gifts," because not only did the corporation then have to pay the removal cost, but in many cases it also lost a significant tax benefit from having made a "gift" to a nonprofit organization.

TABLE 8.2
NPV calculation for abandoning Joe's Diner.

TIME	ITEM	BTCF	ATCF	PV @ 12%
0	Land sale	1,000,000	840,000	840,000
0	Equipment sale	90,000	75,000	75,000
1–12	EAC-building (saved)	72,000/yr	54,000/yr	334,496
1–12	$\Delta R - \Delta E$ (forgone)	−300,000/yr	−225,000/yr	−1,393,734
1–12	Wages	100,000/yr	80,000/yr	495,550
12	Land sale (forgone)	−1,000,000	−840,000	−215,607
				NPV = $135,705

Pete gathered the following information to analyze his decision whether to sell the diner: The sale price of $1,000,000 would provide an after-tax amount of $840,000. The equipment could be sold at auction for about $90,000, on which he would have to pay $15,000 in taxes. The building needed renovation about every 10 years. The before-tax equivalent annual cost (EAC) of this periodic maintenance was $72,000, and the after-tax EAC, including the effect of depreciation, was $54,000. The annual revenues minus expenses from running the diner were $300,000 per year, on which Pete paid taxes at the rate of 25%. Pete determined that his required return is 12%. The one thing Pete almost forgot to include in the analysis was the opportunity cost for his time.

A friend recently offered Pete $100,000 per year, including retirement and other benefits, to come and work for him. Pete figured that it would not be exactly a 40-hour work week, but it would average less than his 55-hour work week in the diner. With the change in income sources, Pete's tax specialist estimated that the $100,000 per year would be taxed at an average rate of 20%. Finally, Pete had been planning for quite a while to sell the diner and retire 12 years from now. He estimated that the land would sell for the same price then as now, after adjusting for the effect of inflation.

From this information, and help from a friend who had taken a finance class, Pete created the NPV calculation for abandoning his investment in the diner (Table 8.2). Note that the positive and negative signs are reversed from what they would normally be, because Pete is selling, rather than undertaking, the project.

So the "basic" NPV—the DCF-NPV—of abandonment was positive, $135,705. But in spite of this, Pete turned Diane down. He decided he enjoyed what he was doing more than he would enjoy increasing his wealth by $135,705.

We want to emphasize that this was *not* necessarily an irrational choice on Pete's part. For him, the nonmonetary values he received from owning the diner exceeded $135,705. Pete said he was just relieved that his opportunity cost of staying in the diner was not larger, because at some amount, he would have had to sell the diner, because the nonmonetary values would not have been large enough to overcome the opportunity cost.

Postscript: Two years later, Diane came back and offered Pete $2,000,000 for the diner. He took it!

It is important to understand in the preceding example that Pete needed to have an accurate estimate of the monetary opportunity cost of continuing to own the diner in order to make a rational decision about whether the nonmonetary values exceeded that cost. The nonmonetary values are not irrelevant, but it is simply more accurate to include them after all other costs that are more easily quantified have been included.

The Postponement Option

We illustrated the price-setting option earlier in the chapter. Another logical option to consider is the **postponement option,** which is the option to postpone, rather than cancel, an expansion alternative. A price increase now, followed by an expansion in production capacity, additional advertising, and perhaps even a price *decrease* later, might be superior to a simple price increase now. Because of interactions among the various alternatives, the analysis can become very complex.

There are many postponement decisions in your personal life. Should you study for an exam now or postpone your studying? Should you try to enter an MBA program now or delay for a period of time. In business, the timing of investments is critical. A profitable investment is sometimes more profitable if it is delayed. Timing decisions are not easy, as the following example reminds us. The example is about a college basketball player considering entering the pro draft before his college eligibility has been completed.

EXAMPLE Entering the NBA Draft Early

After three years of college ball, Arnell Johnson owns most of his college's offensive records. Arnell is considering declaring himself eligible for the NBA draft and skipping his senior year. If he goes pro now, agents tell him that his likely contract and the rest of his basketball earnings will have a present value of around $10 million. What should Arnell do?

Arnell needs to compare the benefits of going pro now versus the benefits of postponing for a year. If he waits, he might actually get a smaller contract next year. He loses a year's earnings, and he might be injured. On the other hand, a year of weight lifting and additional basketball experience might result in a substantially better contract.

Many professional prospects weigh the costs and benefits and find that acting now is preferred to postponement. Others choose to postpone.

A Warning About Capital Budgeting Options

In Chapter 6, we discussed different decision rules used in making capital budgeting decisions. Often, people in practice talk about the "gut feel," or special expertise, that allows them to say a project should be undertaken even though it does not appear to have a positive NPV. Options are frequently at the heart of the matter. It is difficult to quantify their value, so the "gut feel" approach is often simply to "guesstimate" that the project is profitable and then to go ahead with it. Although the "gut feel" approach is not entirely wrong, it should be applied very sparingly. Otherwise, the value of one or more vague options can be used to justify undertaking *any* project, no matter how unprofitable it might appear or actually be.

It is best to quantify the additional value for the options that would be necessary to justify the project. Then you can see if that additional value is at all reasonable.

EXAMPLE Follow-on Markets at Hess, Inc.

Suppose Hess, Inc. has a project with a DCF-NPV of −$1 million, before adding the value of a significant option to the NPV calculation. Therefore, if that option is worth more than $1 million, the project would actually have a positive NPV and should be undertaken.

The option that exists for Hess consists of a 25% chance of gaining entry into a new market five years from now. The project's required return is 20%. What must be the future value of the follow-on market entry, in order to make the current project's NPV positive?

For the present value of the option to exceed \$1 million, the expected future value (five years from now) must be greater than about \$2.5 million (= $[1.2]^5 1{,}000{,}000 = 2{,}488{,}320$). With a 25% chance of achieving market entry, the future project within the option must then be expected to produce almost \$10 million (= 0.25[10] + 0.75[0] = 2.5 million) in additional NPV (five years from now) for the current project to have a positive total NPV. This might be possible—but that is a lot of NPV!

Review

1. Why is it important to consider all options connected with a proposed capital budgeting project?
2. What is the relationship between the "basic" NPV of a project, its DCF-NPV, and the value and cost of project related options?
3. List three capital budgeting options. Describe each one.
4. What is the major pitfall that can result from hidden options?

8.3 CAPITAL RATIONING

As the name implies, **capital rationing** limits (rations) the firm's capital expenditures. A firm can impose such limits in a number of different ways, but two are widely used.

One method is to use a cost of capital that exceeds the project's required return by, for example, 3%. Although this is a form of rationing, the use of a "higher" rate can be subtle, because in many cases it is not explicitly acknowledged. Often, management argues on the basis of "conservatism," and a "few points" are added, or the number is "rounded up" when a required return is established. Obviously, the effect of increasing the discount rate is to reduce the calculated NPVs of conventional projects. Many projects that had positive NPVs will have negative NPVs at the higher rate, and thereby be rationed out of the firm's planned capital expenditures.

Note that for reverse-conventional projects (starting with an inflow followed by future outflows), the "conservatism" is backwards. The higher cost of capital could make a negative NPV incorrectly seem to be positive.

EXAMPLE Rationing Capital with Artificially High Discount Rates

Chula Vista Entertainment has five capital budgeting projects that have positive NPVs using a cost of capital that equals the required return. Management wants to raise the cost of capital by three percentage points and invest only in those projects that still have a positive NPV at the higher cost of capital. The projects and their NPVs are shown in Table 8.3.

TABLE 8.3
Chula Vista's capital budgeting projects.

PROJECT	INITIAL OUTLAY	NPV AT COST OF CAPITAL	NPV AT COST OF CAPITAL + 3%
1	\$1,000,000	\$440,000	\$310,000
2	500,000	105,000	50,000
3	750,000	122,000	−40,000
4	1,250,000	210,000	110,000
5	700,000	66,000	−90,000

Without rationing capital by using a higher cost of capital, all five projects have a positive NPV and the total outlay for the five projects is $4,200,000. When the cost of capital is raised 3%, projects 3 and 5 have negative NPVs and would be rejected. Rejecting these projects reduces the total capital outlay by $1,450,000, to $2,750,000.

A second method of capital rationing is to set a maximum on parts of, or the total, capital budget. For example, a firm decides that it will invest a maximum of $1.2 million in new projects this year. This second method is more visible because rationing is explicitly acknowledged. And because of this acknowledgment, although it may not actually be, it seems to be the more widely used of the two methods.

EXAMPLE Capital Rationing with a Budget Constraint

Bayless Enterprises has the six projects listed in Table 8.4. The six projects require a total outlay of $1,550,000 if they are all accepted. Bayless has chosen to invest only $1,000,000 and would like the set of projects from this list that would have the highest total NPV without exceeding this budget.

One way to find the optimal set of projects is to enumerate all possible sets of projects and take the one with the highest total NPV. This can be tedious. As a guide, you can use the PI (Profitability Index) to try to find the best projects. Recall that the PI is the project's total present value divided by the initial outlay, or one plus the NPV divided by the initial outlay. The PIs are also shown in Table 8.4, along with how their PIs rank, from best (1) to worst (6).

In lucky cases, the projects with the highest ranking PIs make up the best set. In this case, however, the optimal set of projects is not so easy. Projects A, B, C, and E have a total outlay of $900,000 and total NPV of $271,000. Projects C, D, and E have a total outlay of $1,000,000 and total NPV of $291,000. Projects A, D, and E have a total outlay of $950,000 and NPV of $246,000. So the optimal set of projects is C, D, and E.

More complex situations, including multiple period constraints, can be solved using a form of linear programming called zero-one integer programming. A variety of user-friendly software is available for this purpose.

Pitfalls of Capital Rationing

One obvious consequence of using a higher discount rate is that a conventional project's NPV will be understated. Some financial managers are not bothered by this fact, because they like the idea that value is being "conservatively" measured. Likewise, limiting the total amount of money spent on new capital budgeting projects can also be viewed as being "conservative." This conservatism, however, can create opportunity costs if the firm passes up positive-NPV projects.

TABLE 8.4
Bayless Enterprises's six capital budgeting projects.

PROJECT	OUTLAY	NPV	PV	PI	PI RANK
A	$250,000	$ 75,000	$325,000	1.30	2
B	150,000	30,000	180,000	1.20	5
C	300,000	120,000	420,000	1.40	1
D	500,000	125,000	625,000	1.25	3
E	200,000	46,000	246,000	1.23	4
F	150,000	15,000	165,000	1.10	6

Unfortunately, management may be eager to incur this opportunity cost because of an agency cost. In Chapter 13, we describe the nondiversifiability of human capital. This is the difficulty people have in diversifying their unique capabilities and expertise (human capital). This difficulty causes a divergence of incentives between shareholders and managers over the choice of capital budgeting projects.

Shareholders hold diversified investment portfolios, and are concerned only about nondiversifiable risk. But because managers' human capital is not well diversified, they can be "wiped out" if the firm goes bankrupt. Therefore, managers are concerned about the firm's total risk (diversifiable plus nondiversifiable).

As a result, managers may want to choose projects "conservatively" so that only projects with a greater margin of safety will be chosen. In this way, managers reduce the likelihood of bankruptcy, the firm's total risk, and the likelihood they will lose their jobs. When managers choose projects "conservatively" to reduce their personal risk, such choices create opportunity costs, which add to the firm's agency costs.

Capital Rationing and Capital Market Efficiency

Capital rationing has been widely criticized because of capital market efficiency, which should make rationing unnecessary. In a perfect capital market, a firm could *always* obtain funds needed to undertake a positive-NPV project, because the project would be better than other capital market opportunities. Therefore, given that existing capital markets are very efficient, academics argue that firms should simply obtain whatever additional funds are needed to undertake all positive-NPV projects.

In practice, however, firms regularly ration their capital expenditures. And, as it turns out, there can be some practical benefits from capital rationing.

Benefits of Capital Rationing

In Chapter 14, we identify three persistent capital market imperfections: tax asymmetries, information asymmetries, and transaction costs. We show here how two of these imperfections, information asymmetries and transaction costs, can make capital rationing beneficial for a firm.

To obtain funds from the capital market, a firm must convince investors that they can expect to earn at least their required return. However, recall the problem of *adverse selection* from our discussion of the Signaling Principle, where offering something for sale appears to be a negative signal. Adverse selection leads investors to ask, "If this investment is so good, why is the firm willing to let me in on it? Why doesn't the firm want to keep all of the positive NPV for itself?"

Of course, only the managers know the answer, so there is *asymmetric information* between investors and the firm. Recall that asymmetric information is a situation where information is known to some participants but not others. Investors will raise their required return to protect themselves from the risk of being "taken." The higher required return lowers the amount of funds obtained from selling new securities to the outside investors. As a result, the firm must have "special circumstances" to make the sale of new securities attractive.

Two such special circumstances include a "really great" new investment opportunity and a "really bad" set of current operations. The benefits from really great new investment opportunities are obvious, but let us examine the second case. Additional funds can help a troubled firm in the following way.

When people learn that a firm's current operations are worth less than was previously believed, the firm's market value declines, and investors incur a loss. By bringing in new investors prior to such a decline in value, the new investors help the existing investors by sharing in the value loss, so the existing investors' loss is smaller than it would have been.

Without going on to explain this idea fully, this brief discussion should help you to appreciate the importance of problems of asymmetric information. Capital rationing can be beneficial because it is a way a firm can manage the problems and costs of asymmetric information connected with getting additional financing for new projects.

The direct transaction costs of obtaining additional financing, such as the issuance costs of new bonds, provide another way in which capital rationing can benefit a firm. As with asymmetric information considerations in the capital markets, we look at the impact of transaction costs in depth in later chapters. We provide some insight into the problem here because it relates to the use of capital rationing.

Simply stated, the cost of obtaining additional financing is a declining function of the amount of new financing. That is, the cost, as a percentage of the amount of new financing, is lower when more funds are obtained. For example, the total flotation costs for $200 million worth of bonds might be only 1% of the value of the new bonds. In contrast, $10 million worth of bonds might have total flotation costs of 6% or more of the value of the bonds.

Let us say a firm has a project with a "basic" NPV that is positive but insufficient funds to undertake it. If the transaction costs of obtaining the needed funds exceed the project's NPV, the project's true NPV would be negative, and the project is undesirable after all. A capital rationing process can help avoid such situations.[3]

Another market imperfection that can make capital rationing beneficial takes place in the labor, as opposed to the capital, markets. When a firm invests, it must have a manager for the project. Existing managers may be able to manage additional small projects; however, a large new project can swamp an existing manager and hurt current operations.

In addition, a new project might require managerial expertise beyond what the firm's existing employees can provide.[4] Although a firm may be confident of the high quality of certain current employees, it cannot be so confident of being able to hire similar employees off the street. Everyone is not equally qualified, but the firm knows more about its current employees. There is an information asymmetry between the firm and potential new employees needed to allow the firm to undertake the project. This creates an added transaction cost and decreases the project's NPV. Capital rationing can provide a way to include these otherwise ignored costs and measure the project's NPV more accurately.

CAPITAL RATIONING, ON BALANCE Agency costs create pitfalls for the use of capital rationing. But other market imperfections can make capital rationing beneficial. We suspect both factors contribute to the fact that almost all firms engage in some sort of capital rationing process.

We will build on this later in the chapter and show how capital rationing can also be beneficial in planning and managing capital expenditures.

Review

1. What is capital rationing?
2. What are two methods firms use to impose capital rationing? Which method is more widely used?
3. Explain how the profitability index can serve as a useful tool for identifying the best projects under capital rationing.
4. What are some of the pitfalls of capital rationing?
5. Explain why capital rationing would be unnecessary in a perfect capital market environment.
6. Are there any practical benefits to capital rationing? Explain.

[3]It might be argued that, in such cases, the firm would not really be capital rationing. It would simply be measuring the project's NPV more accurately by including all the costs, including those of obtaining the needed financing. As a practical matter, however, the process used would look like capital rationing.

[4]Of course, new employees may be assigned to current operations to allow existing employees to manage the new operations. Whatever the distribution of assignments, however, the firm must hire additional qualified managers.

8.4 MANAGING THE FIRM'S CAPITAL BUDGET

Earlier, we discussed the abandonment option. We noted that replacement decisions often provide natural opportunities for considering abandonment. However, the abandonment option probably should be considered with respect to a firm's ongoing operations more frequently and systematically than simply whenever a replacement decision is being considered.

We also said earlier that capital rationing can create opportunity costs if it causes the firm to pass up positive-NPV projects. This can be even more significant if forgone projects are more valuable than the firm's current operations. This opportunity cost can be controlled by the effective use of the abandonment option. The firm can abandon less profitable current operations and use the freed-up funds to increase its (rationed) capital budget and undertake more new positive-NPV projects.

As you can see, there is an important interaction between capital rationing and abandonment. In fact, there are many interactions between capital rationing and the various options of price flexibility and replacing, postponing, accelerating, or abandoning projects. These interactions lead to the idea of a planning horizon, whereby capital rationing can be used as a tool for managing interactions between a firm's investment and financing decisions. For example, capital rationing this year can ensure the availability of funds for a project planned to be undertaken next year.

Of course, plans can change for any number of reasons. For example, a competitor can make a project unattractive by changing a price or introducing a new product. Although planning cannot guarantee a great outcome, it can improve the expected value of the outcome. Therefore, planning is critical to good financial management.

Capital Rationing as a Planning Tool

Capital rationing can be of two types. **"Hard" capital rationing** refers to how the maximum total expenditure is viewed, implying that under no circumstances can that maximum be exceeded. Alternatively, management may consider exceeding its self-imposed capital expenditure limit, a condition called **"soft" capital rationing:** The firm sets a spending limit, but depending upon project desirability and the firm's condition at the time decisions are actually made, the firm may over- or underspend relative to that limit.

A firm can get a good picture of the trade-offs among alternative projects using *sensitivity analysis,* which entails varying the maximum expenditure limit. For example, a firm may find that a small increase in the total expenditure would allow it to undertake the next most desirable project, which may be a worthwhile trade-off. Computer software is particularly useful for soft capital rationing and sensitivity analysis. Once the problem has been formulated, the computer can be conveniently used to obtain alternative solutions simply by changing the constraint values.

Managerial Authority and Responsibility

Good decision making requires cooperation. This holds for capital budgeting as well. Interpersonal relationships can play a key role. Feuds between people and/or divisions hurt the firm. People within the same functional area, such as marketing research, obviously must be able to work together successfully. In addition, cooperation among the various decision-making *levels* plays a critical role.

Good capital budgeting decisions also require members of different functional areas to work together successfully. For example, marketing research and finance must exchange information to estimate project cash flows. Procedures that provide authority by area and amount, with a hierarchy of amounts, are designed to minimize problems among individuals, levels, and areas. Unfortunately, although such procedures generally provide a net gain by reducing or eliminating certain kinds of problems, they may create others.

Chapter 6 described a typical budgetary authority system where a manager could approve capital expenditures—but only within certain limits. However, a manager can break up expenditures that exceed the limit into smaller ones that do not require additional approval, spread them out over time, or both. In this way, a manager can undertake a project without having to obtain prior approval from a higher decision-making level.

It may sound extreme, yet cases have been cited where a division of a corporation actually built and equipped a whole new plant using plant expense orders. In one such case, corporate headquarters discovered the new plant only after its managers submitted an expenditure request for a chimney. They had to. They could not figure out how to break a key component of the chimney expense into smaller amounts!

The problem illustrated by this example is that the division thought the firm needed the new plant but felt that corporate headquarters would turn down the project. In essence, the division thought it knew better than headquarters. The division managers probably felt that corporate-level managers lacked the hands-on viewpoint. Of course, they might have been right, but they might just as easily have been wrong. The responsibility for that decision was not theirs. The viewpoint from the division level does not encompass the breadth of the higher level of decision-making authority.

This example illustrates a tremendous breakdown of the system of authority and responsibility. The division's responsibility was to communicate its viewpoint to higher levels. Headquarters had the responsibility of trying to understand that viewpoint, weighing it along with other information, and deciding on the best course of action.

At the other extreme, having top management review all decisions could lead to the absurd case where the CEO has to approve a salesperson's purchase of a new pencil. In essence, budgetary authority is designed to reduce transaction costs. Lowering the level of decision-making authority within a firm may reduce the net cost of making decisions, including the opportunity cost of delay when time is critical.

The problems just cited point out the need to balance decision-making authority against transaction costs. In spite of these and other problems that can arise, recall from Chapter 6 that multiple layers of decision-making authority provide a monitoring function that can reduce agency costs. The multiple layers and divisions of authority make collusion among employees more difficult, and it is less likely that employees will take self-interested actions at the expense of the shareholders. Therefore, the multiple layers may provide a form of agency cost reduction that also enters into the choice of decision-making authority for each level of the firm.

In practice, the procedures outlined in Chapters 6 and 7, along with intelligent, honest, and hard-working employees, provide methods of coping with the complexities encountered in practice and generally produce sensible capital budgeting decisions.

Managerial Incentives and Performance Evaluation

Capital rationing can provide additional opportunities for managers to take self-interested actions, thus increasing the firm's agency costs. This points out once again the value of managerial incentives that reduce agency costs.

A typical example of poor incentives is the case where managers are evaluated on the basis of the firm's or the division's return on the book value of assets. This rate is often called a return on investment (ROI). In practice, ROI has several different definitions. Thus, the definition for ROI does not have a consistent relationship with NPV. Therefore, it does not measure managerial success in choosing projects that create value.

When managers are evaluated and rewarded for a measure of performance, self-interested behavior leads them to actions that will improve the performance measure and increase their reward. Consequently, it is important to choose performance measures that are consistent with the firm's goals. Otherwise, you might get exactly what you asked for—even though it was not at all what you wanted!

Postaudits

A **postaudit** is a set of procedures for evaluating a capital budgeting decision after the fact. Postaudits are valuable. However, some words of caution are in order because postaudits can pose practical challenges and must be done carefully. Sometimes the opportunity costs of forgone alternatives and options are simply impossible to measure. Also, as the cliché "hindsight is better than foresight" points out, using hindsight to evaluate foresight is not reasonable. Outcomes can occur that were not even thought possible, let alone predicted. In some cases, as in the following example, identifying and measuring the incremental cash flows that actually resulted from a decision can be impossible.

EXAMPLE Kroger's New Optical Scanners

Kroger installed a new generation of optical scanners in its grocery checkout counters. The new scanners were installed for a variety of reasons. It was argued that they would improve the store's inventory management by reducing the chance of over- and understocking, reducing the time to take inventory, and reducing the cost of ordering. In addition, the scanners were expected to improve customer service by reducing the time for customers to check out. If Kroger is now interested in determining whether installing the scanners was a good decision, what can be determined from a postaudit?

The current costs of ordering and taking inventory can be compared to such costs before the scanners were installed to measure any savings. Also, it might be possible to establish a cost savings for any reduction in overstocking. However, estimating the incremental revenues associated with a reduction in the number of stockouts would be very difficult at best—how many sales would have been lost?

Suppose total sales have not increased. We cannot establish what the sales level would have been if the new scanners had not been installed. After all, competitors may also have put in new scanners, so the store might have experienced a substantial drop in sales had the scanners *not* been installed. Alternatively, an observed increase in sales could have been caused by many things, such as improved economy-wide conditions. Similarly, connecting the new scanners directly to an improvement in the customer service level is not possible.

In this case, it is just not possible to measure exactly the incremental cash inflows that were generated by installing the new scanners. At this point, only the financial condition of the entire store can be meaningfully established.

In spite of the problems of evaluating a decision after the fact, postaudits made up of sensible evaluation procedures can be useful and are often undertaken in practice. One valuable and typical procedure is to evaluate some or all of the expected future cash flow estimates. This process is often aimed more at improving the analyst's ability to forecast expected future cash flows on current and future projects than simply evaluating the analyst's performance. Some analysts have relatively consistent biases in their estimates (either optimistically above or pessimistically below the expected value). It might be possible to correct such a bias over time through the review and evaluation of the analyst's work.

A second form of postaudit is to determine the value of abandonment, versus continued operation, of an entire project. Often, as in the optical-scanner example, determining the value of the entire operation is the only reasonable method of evaluating a project. Of course, although this may determine the project's current value, it does not indicate whether a particular decision was good or bad. The current value provides a measure of the outcome from the entire set of past decisions, but that outcome could be more the result of good or bad luck than good or bad decision making.

The Capital Budgeting Framework

The capital budgeting/NPV framework is a useful decision-making tool. It is based on sound principles and techniques. However, practical realities can significantly complicate its use. In practice, there can be a great deal of "squish" in the decision-making process. But it is important to have a rationally based system for making decisions as a guide. Otherwise, managers could justify self-interested choices with enough "subjective add-ons." Recall our warning about this problem in our discussion of the value that options add to a project's DCF-NPV.

Do not be swayed by the following kind of argument: Because estimating and planning are complex, difficult, and uncertain, in the final analysis, decisions are subjective. Therefore, forget all the complex analysis—"Just take your best shot." Although the first statement is true, the conclusion does not follow. A decision is certainly easier to make if it is simply the result of a coin flip or a "gut-feel best guess," but it can lead to disaster.

If a decision is worth considering and can benefit from additional information, gather the most cost-efficient information set and make the decision based on that information. Sometimes the most cost-efficient information is what you already have. In such cases, choose the optimal alternative based on that information. But often, gathering extra information is a cost-effective method of making a better decision, even if the information is not perfect.

Remember, if capital budgeting decisions were trivial, there would not be much reason to study the process. Framing the analysis and decision properly improves understanding and subjective judgments and puts them in proper context. Of course, using the NPV framework will not save you from the effects of inaccurate forecasts of incremental cash flows, or from the effects of using the wrong cost of capital.

Review

1. What is hard capital rationing? How is soft capital rationing different?
2. Are different analytical techniques required to apply the two types of capital rationing?
3. Why is soft capital rationing a useful managerial tool for planning?
4. What is the purpose of having multiple layers of decision-making authority within a firm?
5. What is a postaudit? How is it useful in capital budgeting?

8.5 OTHER FACTORS THAT ARE DIFFICULT TO QUANTIFY

We have already mentioned several factors that are difficult to quantify in a capital budgeting analysis, such as options, incorporating the effects of erosion and enhancement, predicting the likelihood of technological advances, and hiring qualified managers.

Overlooking such factors that create opportunity costs can lead to bad decision making. However, we have emphasized the importance of care in performing incremental analysis to reflect such factors (when they are important) while avoiding double counting and/or overestimating the impact of these factors, particularly with respect to options.

Here is a list of some other factors that can also increase or decrease project value. For the most part, these factors have a much smaller impact on project value than those already mentioned.

1. *Working relationships with suppliers*—either good or bad. The importance of interpersonal relationships within a firm extends to relationships with individuals and departments in other firms. An individual working for a supplier can cause a costly delay (provide special help) because of a personal vendetta (great relationship).

2. *Particular expertise* concerning a project, or the lack of it, among current employees. In our discussion of capital rationing, we pointed out the problems of information asymmetry in the labor markets and noted the difficulty of identifying high-quality employees. When transaction costs must be incurred to identify and hire additional employees, those costs decrease the project's NPV. Similarly, when existing employees have expertise that can be used for a project, transaction costs associated with undertaking the project, such as training, will be lower, which in turn increases the project's NPV.
3. *Experience* with the quality of machines and/or service from particular manufacturers. As with relationships with suppliers, good or bad service or parts availability from a manufacturer can decrease or increase the firm's expenses. Likewise, when a machine is known to have a better or worse "cost/quality" relationship, it will increase or decrease the project's NPV. Also, improved knowledge of the expenses connected with using a machine may increase the accuracy of the forecast cash flows. Such improved knowledge is more likely when dealing with machines that use existing technology than machines using innovative technology.

The same warning we gave about options applies to these and similar factors: As long as a person does not provide specific values that can be carefully examined, a proponent of a project can always find a long enough list of vague add-ons with which to "shout down" an opponent of the project. Do not be fooled. *A long list is not a substitute for a large NPV!*

Review

1. Name three factors that can have an important effect on the NPV of a capital budgeting project but are difficult to quantify.
2. Explain why it is important to describe thoroughly the benefits that you expect to result from a factor that cannot be readily quantified. What problem do vague add-ons present?

8.6 SOME PRACTICAL ADVICE

Decision making in a complex world is difficult because no single approach *always* works best. As with earning extraordinary returns in the stock market, if it were that easy, everyone would already be doing it. At one extreme, the decision maker should gather all the relevant information to make the optimal choice. But, of course, there is more information that could be gathered in just about every situation, and so, with that strategy, the decision maker would never make a decision.

At the other extreme, gathering information costs money and takes time. Therefore, in order to minimize cost, one could conclude that the decision maker should never gather more information.

Either approach may in fact be best in a particular situation, but both are too extreme to be applied to every situation. Extreme solutions involving "always" or "never"—such as always wait (or never wait), always purchase more information (or never purchase more information)—are too simplistic to be consistently successful in complex situations. Our advice is to be wary of simplistic decision-making procedures that are like cure-all medicines, claimed to be appropriate for all situations.

Despite the need to be wary, the capital budgeting/NPV framework for decision making described in Chapters 6 and 7 is *always* correct! The problem is that following the framework is sometimes extremely difficult because of a variety of complicating factors, such as opportunity costs, options, erosion, and enhancement. The tools we have described provide methods of coping in an environment where it is not only impossible to predict future outcomes, but often impossible even to describe the possible outcomes. In other words, in some cases, we cannot even imagine some of the outcomes.

When your investment depends on unknown future events, you simply do the best you can. We can talk about the possibility of a technological advance, but often we cannot say anything more about it than to make some general statements about rendering an existing product obsolete. Also, some possible outcomes are so unlikely that they have no significant effect on the analysis, yet if one occurs, its effect will be catastrophic. This was the case when the New York World Trade Center was destroyed on 9-11-01. Although the possibility of a terrorist attack was known, the outcome of complete destruction might have been one in a million.

As we have said, we know of no way to teach a person how to generate new ideas. Our ability to teach a person to assimilate information is also limited.

Applying the Principles of Finance

Despite all the difficulties, several Principles of Finance are especially important to remember with respect to capital budgeting decisions.

VALUABLE NEW IDEAS Bad financing decisions can destroy a firm. On the other hand, although good financing decisions can contribute to a firm's profitability, the possibility of extraordinary success rests primarily on investment decisions. Because of capital market efficiency, great financial management rarely makes a firm extraordinarily profitable. The Principle of Valuable Ideas is alive and well. ***Pursuing valuable ideas is the best way to achieve extraordinary returns.***

Valuable new ideas are not necessarily limited to new products. A valuable new idea can be related to many dimensions of the business. For example, internet transactions are replacing many store transactions.

At the same time, a firm must adjust for erosion or enhancement. Introducing new ideas in the form of products, services, management, and/or technology can erode (reduce) the value of current ideas or even render current ideas worthless. For example, HDTV is replacing conventional TV, the same way color TV replaced black and white.

COMPARATIVE ADVANTAGE Beyond new ideas, a firm should look for ways to make good use of its comparative advantages or current expertise. Promising places to look for opportunities include the use of patents and marketing or distribution networks.

MARKET EFFICIENCY In Chapter 5, we showed how bond and stock values can be easily found by looking at their latest trading price. And yet we have noted that the physical asset markets are not as efficient as the capital markets. In spite of lower efficiency, there is useful information contained in a physical asset's market-traded price.

If you are not going to trust a market price, you should have a very good reason. This is true in the physical asset markets as well as the capital markets. Beware of an analysis that places a value on an asset that is very different from prices observed in a competitive market. Even if the market is less efficient than the capital markets, you need to have one or more good reasons why it should be different, such as a new idea or comparative advantage.

When there is a competitive market for an asset, ***you should think long and hard before you conclude that a market price is "wrong."*** Ask yourself what value you are bringing to the asset. That is, how will your use of the asset be different, so that the asset is worth more to you than it is to other people? And if an asset will be used more profitably by others because, for example, they hold a patent, it is probably not good to compete with them for the use of that asset.

TWO-SIDED TRANSACTIONS Why is the other party to the transaction willing to sell the asset to you or purchase it from you? Remember, those on the other side of the transaction are acting in their self-interest. Establishing reasons for the willingness to transact can help you understand the project you are analyzing.

SIGNALING Watch the competition. Try to understand their actions. Often, but not always, their actions contain information. The question is: What information do the actions contain? The actions could simply be application of the Behavioral Principle, which can lead to a "herd" mentality. If you are the first to recognize such behavior, you can profit from it by doing something different.

Finally, ***plan ahead.*** Undertaking a major project is not as simple as discounting cash flows. It requires management. The capital budgeting/NPV framework is useful for making decisions. It is always correct. The difficulty is in correctly estimating future values. But just because it is difficult or the process becomes complex, do not blow it off and flip a coin. Use the information you have in the best way you can to decide whether to go ahead, quit, or seek additional information.

Review

1. Which capital budgeting decision criterion is always correct?
2. What is the most promising way to achieve extraordinary returns?
3. True or false? You should *always* think long and hard before concluding that the market price of an asset is wrong.

SUMMARY

When businesses are actually making capital budgeting decisions, factors such as project interactions and investment options can greatly complicate the process. However, the decision-making process based on maximizing NPV provides a *framework* for making the best possible capital budgeting decisions.

- Options and the opportunity costs they create play a very important role in capital budgeting decisions. The following capital budgeting options were identified: Expansion option, Price-setting option, Abandonment option, Postponement option, Replacement option, and Future investment opportunities.
- When options exist, the NPV of a project is its DCF-NPV plus the expected value of the options minus the cost of the options.
- "Soft" capital rationing is a useful framework for the planning process and can be conveniently accomplished using specialized software packages.
- Pursuing valuable new ideas and using the firm's comparative advantages are the best ways to achieve extraordinary returns.
- Factors such as employee expertise, working relationships with other firms, and past experience with machines and/or services can play valuable, but lesser, roles in capital budgeting decisions.
- Watch how other people and firms act for useful information—the competition and those on the other side of your transactions.
- Have good reasons why you should be able to get a positive NPV from a project, especially if there is no innovative idea or comparative advantage involved.
- The framework presented in this chapter for making capital budgeting decisions helps structure the decision and can enhance one's understanding of complex situations, even though its application is not as simple as hastily calculating an NPV.

EQUATION SUMMARY

$$\text{NPV} = \text{DCF-NPV} + \text{Value of options} - \text{Cost of options} \tag{8.1}$$

QUESTIONS

1. Cite and briefly discuss six areas to look for options that might be connected with a firm's capital budgeting opportunities.
2. Define *capital rationing.*
3. Contrast the concepts of "soft" and "hard" capital rationing.
4. How can capital rationing be used as a tool for managerial planning?
5. Why might it be important to review and assess (postaudit) a firm's decisions? What are some of the pitfalls associated with such a task?
6. Briefly explain how the pricing of a product can interact with a firm's decision to expand production capacity.
7. Why might the consideration of abandonment value be more important for a firm engaging in capital rationing than for firms that simply take on all positive-NPV projects?
8. Cite and briefly discuss six factors that can be especially difficult to quantify for inclusion in a capital budgeting NPV calculation.
9. Respond to the following comment: First you tell us the value of a project is its NPV. Now you say that the project's value is its NPV plus the value of its options minus the cost of those options. Which is right?
10. Cite and briefly discuss potential pitfalls encountered in estimating the value of future investment options, in the context of our warning about capital budgeting options.
11. Explain why no single approach will always work in a complex and competitive business world.

CHALLENGING QUESTIONS

12. Based on the Principle of Two-Sided Transactions, what would you tell a firm that has "discovered" a large positive-NPV project that requires the firm to purchase the assets (which are necessary to undertake the project) from another corporation?
13. Cite an example of a situation in which "hard" capital rationing would be appropriate for at least a limited time.
14. Suppose you are a manager considering a capital budgeting project. You have examined the proposed project and, according to every relevant piece of information you can find, you feel the project should be undertaken. After submitting your analysis, the division head informs you that the project has not been approved for funding. Briefly discuss the possible causes of the difference between your opinion of the project and that of upper management.
15. We have said that abandonment should always be considered with respect to a firm's current operations. Suppose a firm has the opportunity to sell one of its subsidiaries that is doing poorly. As a general rule, why would it *not* be likely that a firm can "limit its losses" by selling off such subsidiaries?
16. Cite and discuss four broad factors that can cause the NPV of a capital budgeting project to be incorrectly measured.
17. Capital rationing would not be a shareholder wealth-maximizing strategy in a perfect capital market. How might the capital market imperfections, such as information asymmetries and transaction costs, render capital rationing a rational tool?
18. Discuss the importance of erosion and enhancement to a firm such as IBM when it considers introducing a new product.
19. How might the agency costs associated with the separation of ownership and control contribute to a tendency for firms to expand rather than raise the prices of their products?

PROBLEMS

LEVEL A (BASIC)

A1. (Future investment option) You are evaluating an investment in a very nice Indian restaurant in Wichita Falls. The NPV of the investment is −\$1.5 million. For an additional outlay of \$0.2 million, you will have the option to add additional restaurants in the region. If circumstances are favorable (probability = 0.5), the expansion option has an NPV of \$6 million. If circumstances are unfavorable (probability = 0.5), the expansion option has an NPV of 0. What is the total NPV of the investment, including the cost and expected value of the expansion option?

A2. (Future investment option) You are evaluating an investment in a carpet cleaning business in Plattsburgh, NY. The NPV of the investment is −\$2 million. For an additional outlay of \$0.1 million, you will have the option to add additional carpet cleaning businesses in the region. If circumstances are favorable (probability = 0.5), the expansion option has an NPV of \$5 million. If circumstances are unfavorable (probability = 0.5), the expansion option has an NPV of 0. What is the total NPV of the investment, including the cost and expected value of the expansion option?

A3. (Capital rationing) Consider the following capital projects:

PROJECT	OUTLAY	NPV	PV	PROFITABILITY INDEX	RANK (1 = HIGHEST PI)
A	\$150	\$ 60	\$210	1.40	1
B	300	105	405	1.35	2
C	200	60	260	1.30	3

a. With no limit on capital outlays, which projects should be accepted? What is the total outlay and the total NPV?

b. Assume the capital budget is limited to \$450. Which projects should be accepted? What is the total outlay and the total NPV?

c. Assume the capital budget is limited to \$400. Which projects should be accepted? What is the total outlay and the total NPV?

A4. (Postponement option) A real estate developer can build a golf course now or wait one year. The cash flows for investing now or postponing one year are:

TIME	0	1	2	3	4	5	6
Invest now	−50	10	20	20	20	20	20
Invest in one year		−55	24	24	24	24	24

If the cost of capital is 10%, should the developer invest now or postpone and invest in one year?

A5. (Postponement option) Suppose IBM can introduce a new technology now or wait one year. The cash flows for investing now or postponing one year are:

TIME	0	1	2	3	4	5	6
Invest now	−200	50	100	100	100	100	100
Invest in one year		−400	150	150	150	150	150

If the cost of capital is 10%, should IBM invest now or postpone and invest in one year?

A6. (Abandonment) Five years ago, your firm installed a quick-lube store on Connolly Avenue. Southwest Cellular would like your store to convert to one of its own outlets. They have made you an offer that nets you \$600,000 after taxes. Your required return is 12%.

a. You expect \$75,000 cash flow after tax for the next ten years. Should you abandon?

b. Assume your annual cash flow is \$120,000. What is the minimum offer you would accept?

A7. (Abandonment) Seven years ago, your firm started a car wash on 3rd Street. Exxon Mobil would like to convert the car wash to a gas station. They have made you an offer that nets you $800,000 after taxes. Your required return is 12%.

a. You expect a $125,000 cash flow after tax for the next ten years. Should you abandon?

b. Assume your annual cash flow is $175,000. What is the minimum offer you would accept?

A8. (Capital rationing) Consider the projects shown below (amounts in $1,000).

a. Compute the profitability index for each project.

b. If you were rationed to $115,000 for the initial investment, which projects should you choose?

c. If you were rationed to $95,000 for the initial investment, which projects should you choose?

PROJECT	A	B	C	D	E	F	G
Initial cost	10	20	20	15	30	40	20
NPV	1.1	3.6	0.8	1.6	4.0	3.0	1.4

A9. (Capital rationing) Consider the projects shown below (amounts in $1,000).

a. Compute the profitability index for each project.

b. If you were rationed to $145,000 for the initial investment, which projects should you choose?

c. If you were rationed to $100,000 for the initial investment, which projects should you choose?

PROJECT	A	B	C	D	E	F	G
Initial cost	15	20	25	30	35	40	45
NPV	2.5	3	1.5	3.2	2.8	2.1	3.1

A10. (Salvage value) Suppose GAF Corporation is contemplating a capital budgeting project with capital assets that will be depreciated to a book value of $10,000 but are expected to have a salvage value of $18,000. GAF's marginal tax rate is 34%. Cleanup and removal expenses are expected to be $1,000, and there will be a $2,000 return of working capital. What is the net salvage value?

A11. (Basic capital budgeting) The investment is $1,000,000, which is depreciated straight line for 10 years down to a zero salvage value. For its 10-year life, the investment will generate annual sales of $800,000 and annual cash operating expenses of $250,000. Although the investment is depreciated to a zero book value, you expect to sell it for $200,000 in 10 years. The marginal income tax rate is 30% and the cost of capital is 10%.

a. What after-tax net cash flows are expected?

b. What is the net present value of the investment?

A12. (Basic capital budgeting) An investment of $60,000 will be depreciated straight line for 10 years down to a zero salvage value. For its 10-year life, the investment will generate annual sales of $30,000 and annual cash operating expenses of $12,000. Although the investment is depreciated to a zero book value, it should sell for $10,000 in 10 years. The marginal income tax rate is 40% and the cost of capital is 10%.

a. What after-tax net cash flows are expected?

b. What is the net present value of the investment?

LEVEL B

B1. (Mutually exclusive projects) The current level of production for Adam's Gears, Inc. (the original gear) is limited by its production facilities, so Adam is considering an expansion of the firm's production capacity. Because the product has become essentially generic, raising the price is not an option for Adam. There are two types of processes that can be installed for the expansion.

One process is considerably more automated than the other, and therefore the operating leverage of the expansion project would be higher if the more automated process were chosen. The total production capacity is the same for the two processes, as is the expected value of the additional gear sales ($1.3 million per year). Process A costs $1.56 million to install and has variable costs of $740,000 per year, whereas process B costs $390,000 to install and has variable costs of $935,000 per year. Both investments would be depreciated on a straight-line basis to a zero book value over 8 years, but both have a 10-year useful life and expected salvage values of zero at the end of 10 years. Required returns are 15% for process A and 12% for process B. If Adam's Gears has a marginal tax rate of 30%, which, if either, project should Adam undertake?

B2. (Future investment option) Virginia Matteson is considering a major investment in new technology for her executive recruiting business. Virginia has carefully considered the revenues and costs that this investment will generate and finds that it is unprofitable. Her discounted cash flow analysis reveals an expected NPV of −$100,000. However, Virginia believes that this new technology could enable her to expand her business into a new area, that of renting professional staff such as accountants, lawyers, and computer specialists to her clients. The additional cost of preparing for the temporary professional business would have a present value of $100,000. Virginia believes that this new business, if future conditions justified it, would be worth a present value of $1,000,000. The probability of the temporary professional business becoming a reality, she estimates, is about 40%. What is the NPV of the investment in new technology if you include the cost and expected value of the future investment option?

B3. (Future investment option) John Williams is considering an investment in a new computer network for his financial consulting business. John has carefully considered the revenues and costs that this investment will generate and finds that it is unprofitable. His discounted cash flow analysis reveals an expected NPV of −$600,000. However, John believes that this new technology could enable him to expand his business into a new area, that of accounting consulting. The additional cost of preparing for the accounting business would have a present value of $200,000. John believes that this new business, if future conditions justified it, would be worth a present value of $1,600,000. The probability of the accounting business becoming a reality, he estimates, is about 50%. What is the NPV of the investment in the new computer network if you include the cost and expected value of the future investment option?

B4. (Abandonment) You can invest $1.0 million in a new business. There is a 50% probability that the business will be worth $1.6 million and a 50% probability that it will be worth $0.6 million.

a. What is your expected NPV?

b. After you invest in the business, you can abandon it for $0.9 million. If you use the abandonment option rationally, what is your expected NPV?

B5. (Abandonment) You can invest $2.0 million in a new business. There is a 50% probability that the business will be worth $3.2 million and a 50% probability that it will be worth $1.2 million.

a. What is your expected NPV?

b. After you invest in the business, you can abandon it for $1.5 million. If you use the abandonment option rationally, what is your expected NPV?

B6. (Abandonment) Your dance/karate studio generates a cash flow after taxes of $220,000 per year. A national chain wants to purchase your studio for $1.5 million. You believe the fair value of your business is the capitalized cash flow for 10 years, discounted at 14%. Should you keep the business or sell out?

B7. (Abandonment) Your office furniture business generates a cash flow after taxes of $150,000 per year. A national chain wants to purchase your business for $1.0 million. You believe the fair value of your business is the capitalized cash flow for 10 years, discounted at 12%. Should you keep the business or sell out?

B8. (Incremental cash flows and NPV) The Howe Fix-It Corp. is considering buying a new machine called a TX2 that costs $60,000. The TX2 requires $10,000 in setup costs that are expensed immediately and $10,000 in additional working capital. The TX2's useful life is 10 years, after which it can be sold for a salvage value of $20,000. The TX2 requires a maintenance overhaul costing $30,000 at the end of year 7. The overhaul is fully expensed when it is done. Howe uses straight-line depreciation, and the machine will be depreciated to a book value of zero on a six-year basis. Howe has a tax rate of 40% and the project's cost of capital is 15%. The TX2 is expected to increase revenues minus expenses by $17,500 per year. What is the NPV of buying the TX2?

B9. (NPV and abandonment) The owners of Egg Sauce, Ltd. are tired of their business. In fact, they are so *exhausted* that they are considering abandoning the business. The building and land could be sold for $700,000 and would provide an after-tax amount of $640,000. The equipment could be sold at auction for about $55,000 and, at that price, they could claim a tax credit of $5,000. The building needs renovation about every 10 years. The before-tax EAC of this periodic maintenance is $40,000, and the after-tax EAC, including the effect of depreciation, is $30,000. The annual revenues minus expenses (including all employee costs) from running Egg Sauce are $200,000 per year, and the firm pays taxes at the rate of 35% on this amount. The investment's cost of capital is 15%. What is the NPV from abandoning Egg Sauce?

B10. (NPV and abandonment) The owners of Reynold Simulation are considering abandoning the business. The building and land could be sold for $900,000 and would provide an after-tax amount of $540,000. The equipment could be sold for about $80,000 and, at that price, they could claim a tax credit of $7,000. The building needs renovation about every 10 years. The before-tax EAC of this periodic maintenance is $35,000, and the after-tax EAC, including the effect of depreciation, is $25,000. The annual revenues minus expenses (including all employee costs) from running Reynold Simulation are $200,000 per year, and the firm pays taxes at the rate of 40% on this amount. The investment's cost of capital is 15%. What is the NPV from abandoning the business?

B11. (Future investment option) Suppose Upjohn's research team would like to spend $50 million on final development and testing of a new kidney drug. The DCF-NPV is −$10 million. Production cannot begin until testing has been completed, which will take several years, and success is not assured. There is a 40% chance that the research might also give Upjohn the option to produce a related drug that could stimulate hair growth and eliminate baldness.

a. Suppose the hair growth stimulant could be marketable within three years and yield CFATs of $5 million per year forever. If the cost of capital for the research project is 15%, should Upjohn proceed with it?

b. What is the minimum option value necessary to justify the research project?

c. What is the minimum level of perpetual annual CFATs needed to justify the research project?

B12. (Future investment option) Suppose Cyrix's development department would like to spend $35 million on final development and testing of a microprocessor. The DCF-NPV is −$12 million. Production cannot begin until testing has been completed, which will take several years, and success is not assured. There is a 50% chance that the research might also give Cyrix the option to produce a coprocessor that could significantly speed up old processors.

a. Suppose the coprocessor could be marketable within two years and yield CFATs of $4 million per year forever. If the cost of capital for the research project is 10%, should Cyrix proceed with it?

b. What is the minimum option value necessary to justify development?

c. What is the minimum level of perpetual annual CFATs needed to justify development?

B13. (Replacement cycles) Suppose Daimler Chrysler is considering which of two emission testing devices to buy. Machine A costs $100,000, has a five-year useful life, and has operating expenses of $40,000 per year. Machine B costs $36,000, has a six-year useful life, and has operating expenses of $62,000 per year. Both machines will have zero salvage value, revenues of $85,000 per year, straight-line depreciation to a zero book value, and both will be replaced at the end of their lives. Daimler Chrysler's tax rate is 35%.

a. Assume a 12% cost of capital for each machine. Which one should Daimler Chrysler buy?

b. Suppose instead that machine A requires a higher cost of capital, 15%, because it's a riskier process. Machine B's cost of capital is still 12%. Which machine should Daimler Chrysler buy?

B14. (Replacement cycles) Suppose Dell is considering which of two computer diagnostics machines to buy. Machine A costs $60,000, has a five-year useful life, and has operating expenses of $15,000 per year. Machine B costs $30,000, has a six-year useful life, and has operating expenses of $25,000 per year. Both machines will have zero salvage value, revenues of $75,000 per year, straight-line depreciation to a zero book value, and both will be replaced at the end of their lives. Dell's tax rate is 35%.

a. Assume a 12% cost of capital for each machine. Which one should Dell buy?

b. Suppose instead that machine A requires a higher cost of capital, 15%, because it's a riskier process. Machine B's cost of capital is still 12%. Which machine should Dell buy?

B15. (Excel: Incremental cash flows and NPV) A Wendy's franchisee is considering replacing his kitchen equipment. The equipment currently has a net book value of $60,000, and will continue to be depreciated on a straight-line basis to a net book value of zero over the next three years. The franchisee estimates that the current equipment could be used for up to an additional six years. The purchase price for the new equipment is $300,000, and it would be depreciated over a six-year period on a straight-line basis to a net book value of $50,000. The new equipment would produce pretax operating savings of $80,000 per year as compared to the replaced equipment. The old equipment can be sold for $25,000. Installation would cost $30,000 in addition to the purchase price, all of which would be expensed immediately. The franchisee believes the equipment would have a net salvage value of $40,000 at the end of six years.

a. If the franchisee has a marginal tax rate of 30%, what would be the after-tax incremental expected future cash flows associated with the new equipment by year and by item?

b. Approximately what is the IRR for the project?

c. If the cost of capital for the project is 12%, what is the NPV?

d. Compute the NPV assuming costs of capital of 0%, 4%, 8%, 12%, and 16%. Prepare an NPV profile for the project.

LEVEL C (ADVANCED)

C1. (Price-Setting) RMC's Smooooth soap has a marginal cost of $0.387 per bar. Given the demand function we used in the chapter (Demand = 2.538 million/price^3), express total revenue as a function of quantity demanded. Show that marginal revenue equals marginal cost when the quantity demanded is 12,974,330. Demonstrate that the optimal price is $0.5805 per bar.

C2. (Abandonment) An investment of $200 will generate one of two outcomes: $144 in one year and $172.80 in two years OR $120 in one year and $120 in two years. Each outcome has a 50% probability. The cost of capital is 20%.

a. What is the expected NPV?

b. Assume you have the option to abandon in one year for $120. If you abandon, you keep the year 1 cash flow and give up the year 2 cash flow. Is abandonment rational for either outcome? What is the NPV of the investment assuming rational abandonment?

C3. (Abandonment) An investment of $500 will generate one of two outcomes: $400 in one year and $500 in two years OR $300 in one year and $300 in two years. Each outcome has a 50% probability. The cost of capital is 15%.

a. What is the expected NPV?

b. Assume you have the option to abandon in one year for $300. If you abandon, you keep the year 1 cash flow and give up the year 2 cash flow. Is abandonment rational for either outcome? What is the NPV of the investment assuming rational abandonment?

MINICASE BUILDING THE EUROTUNNEL

The Eurotunnel Project took 10 years to complete. It involved the construction of a twin-bore rail tunnel with associated infrastructure, rolling stock ("railroad cars"), and terminals. It joined the United Kingdom's rail system with those of France and the rest of continental Europe. It provides comfortable, fast, frequent, and reliable rail service that is competitive with air travel between London and Paris.

The project was technically straightforward from an engineering standpoint. It was initially expected to cost £4.8 billion (£ stands for British pounds). The cost estimate was later increased to £6.0 billion. This construction cost was spread more or less evenly over eight years. The sponsors raised £1.0 billion of equity and £5.0 billion of debt. Most of the debt was floating rate (the rate is reset regularly to current market rates).

In return for building the project, the sponsors received authority to operate it for 48 years. They would receive all the revenues and pay all the costs. At the end, the governments of Great Britain and France would become the owners without any further compensation to the project sponsors.

The table below provides project projections. For years not listed, assume each item increases by equal annual amounts between the years given. The tax rate is 40%. Using an 8% cost of capital, and assuming the £6 billion construction cost is spread evenly over the eight years of construction, calculate the project's NPV and IRR.

CASH FLOW PROJECTIONS FOR THE EUROTUNNEL PROJECT (MILLIONS OF BRITISH POUNDS)

YEAR	1	2	3	4	5	6	7	8	9	10	20	30	40	48
Revenue:														
Shuttle	£384	£423	£463	£505	£551	£599	£652	£709	£770	£836	£1,763	£3,527	£6,682	£10,650
Rail	314	341	368	396	430	459	493	530	569	612	1,191	2,105	3,641	5,526
Ancillary	64	71	77	85	91	100	109	117	127	138	282	552	1,033	1,648
Total Revenue	762	835	908	986	1,072	1,158	1,254	1,356	1,466	1,586	3,236	6,184	11,356	17,824
Operating Costs:														
Fixed expenses	88	92	99	107	117	126	137	148	161	174	314	562	1,006	1,604
Variable expenses	57	63	69	76	89	90	98	107	116	130	317	645	1,240	2,000
Total Operating Costs	145	155	168	183	206	216	235	255	277	304	631	1,207	2,246	3,604
Depreciation	158	159	160	162	167	169	171	173	176	184	234	271	328	383
Interest, net	351	322	307	291	277	265	234	212	190	171	39	173	370	616
Profit before taxes	108	199	273	350	422	508	614	716	823	927	2,410	4,879	9,152	14,453
Income taxes	18	38	53	69	88	198	240	279	321	361	934	1,893	3,547	5,573
Profit after taxes	£90	£161	£220	£281	£334	£310	£374	£437	£502	£566	£1,476	£2,986	£5,605	£8,880

APPENDIX
ADDITIONAL METHODS OF PROJECT ANALYSIS

Thus far, we have not explicitly defined risk. It has been accounted for by the project's cost of capital, its required return. When the cash flows are discounted at the risk-adjusted cost of capital, the effect of risk is thereby included in the calculation of the project's NPV.

Here, we look at some other methods that are sometimes used to incorporate risk into capital budgeting decisions. In particular, we examine NPV break-even analysis, sensitivity analysis, scenario analysis, and Monte Carlo simulation.

Before proceeding, we need to alert you to a major problem with using these methods: They can make it difficult or even impossible to separate two kinds of risk, diversifiable and nondiversifiable. Therefore, the distinction between them can be overlooked in the analysis. As we explain in Chapter 10, diversifiable risk is not relevant to shareholders. However, it can be very relevant to managers personally because of the difficulty of diversifying the managers' human capital, which we describe in Chapter 13.

The use of the methods discussed in this appendix, then, presents a particular problem because managers have an incentive to use them improperly. By focusing on total risk (and deliberately including diversifiable risk), managers may be able to use risk as a basis for rejecting projects that may be good for the shareholders—but bad for the managers. This aspect of capital budgeting analysis is another case where divergent interests can cause a conflict between shareholders and managers.

Despite this problem, the methods presented here can be useful when it is not possible to determine a market-based estimate of a project's cost of capital. Generally, using these techniques takes more expertise than is provided here. However, it is important to know of their existence and their potential benefits and problems. Additional expertise can be obtained from further study or from support staff who are well versed in such quantitative methods. You may have encountered (or will encounter) some or all of these methods in other course work.

Break-Even Analysis

The **break-even point** is where the total contribution margin exactly equals the total fixed cost of producing a product or service. The contribution margin is the difference between revenue and variable cost. For example, if revenue is $15 per unit for a product, and the variable cost of producing a unit of the product is $10, the contribution margin is $5 per unit. With a total fixed cost of $500,000, the break-even point is 100,000 units (= 500,000/5).

Break-even is the point at which the accounting income is zero. But accounting income ignores the project's other costs, so break-even is *not* the point at which the NPV equals zero. In spite of this, break-even is an important point of analysis, so it is important to understand the break-even concept.

It is easy for people to believe that as long as sales stay above the break-even point, the firm is "making money." But this is not true. Consider the break-even example just given. Suppose the firm could sell the entire project and everything connected with it for an after-tax net salvage value of $1.2 million. Then selling the project would be a positive-NPV decision if sales would fall exactly at the break-even point forever into the future. With sales forever at the break-even point, the firm's net cash flow from the project each year would equal the tax credit from the depreciation. The firm could sell the project and create value by investing the money elsewhere.

The financial indifference point is the sales level at which the NPV from selling or abandoning the project is zero. We need more information to determine that point.

TABLE 8.6
NPV calculation for the production amount that will yield a zero NPV.

TIME	ITEM	BTCF	ATCF	PV AT 12%
0	Salvage	1,200,000	1,200,000	1,200,000
1–6	$\Delta R - \Delta E$	?	?	?
1–4	Depreciation (lost)	0	−60,000/yr	−182,241
				NPV = 0

EXAMPLE Determining the Financial Indifference Point (Zero-NPV Sales Level)

Suppose our project has six more years of useful life, after which it will have a net salvage value of zero. Also assume that depreciation would be $150,000 per year for the next four years and zero for the last two years, that the relevant tax rate is 40%, and that the project's required return is 12%. To determine the zero-NPV sales level, first set the NPV from selling equal to zero. Next, work backwards to the present value of the after-tax cash flows it would require, and the particular value of $\Delta R - \Delta E$ before taxes. Finally, use the necessary $\Delta R - \Delta E$ before taxes and the contribution margin per unit to solve for the zero-NPV sales level.

The NPV calculation with these unknowns is shown in Table 8.6. To have a zero NPV, $\Delta R - \Delta E$ after taxes must produce a present value of $1,017,759 (= 1,200,000 − 182,241). Solving for the corresponding annuity payment implies $247,545 per year. Therefore, $\Delta R - \Delta E$ before taxes equals $412,575 per year (= 247,545/[1 − 0.4]). $\Delta R - \Delta E$ before taxes is the total contribution margin minus the fixed cost. So with Q as the number of units sold, c as the contribution margin per unit, and F as the fixed cost per year, $\Delta R - \Delta E$ before taxes is

$$\Delta R - \Delta E \text{ before taxes} = cQ - F \tag{8.2}$$

Solving for Q, we have

$$Q = \frac{\Delta R - \Delta E \text{ before taxes} + F}{c} = \frac{412{,}575 + 500{,}000}{5} = 182{,}515$$

Therefore, the financial indifference point, the sales level at which the firm is actually indifferent to having the project, is 182,515 units per year for the next six years. This is almost twice the 100,000 units at which accounting income is zero. Although the precise relationship between the financial indifference point and the break-even point is situation specific, the sales level for the financial indifference point is always much larger.

Determining a project's indifference point—the unit sales level per period at which the project's NPV is zero—provides a feel for the project by putting the NPV in terms of the minimum number of units that must be sold per year to have a positive-NPV investment. This applies to prospective, as well as ongoing, projects. And you can get still more of a feel for a project by determining how sensitive the project's NPV is to variations in sales.

TABLE 8.7
NPV calculation for keeping the project, at the expected sales level.

TIME	ITEM	BTCF	ATCF	PV AT 12%
0	Salvage (foregone)	−1,200,000	−1,200,000	−1,200,000
1–6	$\Delta R - \Delta E$	500,000/yr	300,000/yr	1,233,422
1–4	Depreciation	0	60,000/yr	182,241
				NPV = $215,663

Sensitivity Analysis

Sensitivity analysis varies key parameters in a process to determine the sensitivity of outcomes to the variation and addresses the question: "What if things do not go as predicted?"

NPV sensitivity to sales is determined by the relationship between profit and sales, which is largely determined by the contribution margin. A large contribution margin makes a steep slope, in which case profits are very sensitive to changes in sales. A small contribution margin makes a flatter slope, and profits are less sensitive to changes in sales.

EXAMPLE Sensitivity Analysis

A common way to examine profit sensitivity is to estimate optimistic, expected, and pessimistic sales levels. Extending our break-even example, suppose optimistic, expected, and pessimistic sales levels are 250,000, 200,000, and 150,000, respectively. At the expected sales level, yearly BTCF for $\Delta R - \Delta E$ is given by Equation (8.2):

$$\Delta R - \Delta E \text{ before taxes} = cQ - F = 5(200{,}000) - 500{,}000 = \$500{,}000$$

The NPV at the expected sales level is shown in Table 8.7. Similar calculations for $Q =$ 250,000 and $Q =$ 150,000 show that the NPV ranges from −$401,048 to $832,374.

If the optimistic and pessimistic sales estimates had been 75,000 and 400,000 instead of 150,000 and 250,000, respectively, the variation in the NPV would have been from −$1,326,115 to +$3,195,930. Such comparisons can provide further insight into a project.

Obviously, you can perform sensitivity analysis with respect to any parameter in the NPV computation. However, as we said earlier, great care is necessary to identify the nondiversifiable risk in the analysis. And this is especially difficult when combining optimistic and pessimistic estimates for multiple parts.

Scenario Analysis

Sensitivity analysis measures the sensitivity of NPV by varying one variable at a time. In contrast, **scenario analysis** constructs scenarios where *several* variables change in each scenario. A project is evaluated by looking at its NPVs in all of the constructed scenarios.

Although it is possible to create a large number of alternative scenarios, it is very common to use only three or four. The scenarios are constructed to span the good and bad outcomes that the project might encounter.

TABLE 8.8
Kingdom Catheter's three possible investment scenarios.

SCENARIO	WORST CASE	MOST LIKELY	BEST CASE
Unit sales	10,000	14,000	18,000
Unit price	\$150	\$170	\$190
Sales revenue	\$1,500,000	\$2,380,000	\$3,420,000
Variable cost per unit	\$105	\$100	\$95
Variable cash expenses	\$1,050,000	\$1,400,000	\$1,710,000
Fixed cash expenses	\$70,000	\$80,000	\$90,000
ATCF	\$326,000	\$690,000	\$1,190,000
NPV	−\$158,027	\$1,898,654	\$4,723,765

EXAMPLE Scenario Analysis at Kingdom Catheter

Kingdom Catheter Company is considering an investment in a new product where future cash flows are hard to predict. The team leader has constructed three possible scenarios for future sales, which are shown in Table 8.8. Annual sales and costs are projected to be constant over the 10-year life. The project requires a \$2,000,000 investment, which is depreciated straight line to zero over 10 years (depreciation is \$200,000 per year). Salvage value will be zero. The required rate of return is 12% and the marginal tax rate is 30%. What is the NPV for each scenario?

CALCULATOR SOLUTION	
Data Input	**Function Key**
10	N
12	I
326,000	PMT
0	FV
−1,841,973	**PV**

For the worst-case scenario, the annual CFAT is:

$$\text{CFAT} = (\Delta R - \Delta E - \Delta D)(1 - T) + \Delta D$$

$$\text{CFAT} = (1{,}500{,}000 - 1{,}050{,}000 - 70{,}000 - 200{,}000)(1 - 0.3) + 200{,}000$$
$$= \$326{,}000$$

The present value of a 10-year annuity of \$326,000 at 12% is \$1,841,973, and the NPV is −\$158,027 (= 1,841,973 − 2,000,000).

CALCULATOR SOLUTION	
Data Input	**Function Key**
10	N
12	I
690,000	PMT
0	FV
−3,898,654	**PV**

For the most likely scenario, the annual CFAT is:

$$\text{CFAT} = (2{,}380{,}000 - 1{,}400{,}000 - 80{,}000 - 200{,}000)(1 - 0.3) + 200{,}000$$
$$= \$690{,}000$$

The present value of this cash flow stream is \$3,898,654, and the NPV is \$1,898,654 (= 3,898,654 − 2,000,000).

CALCULATOR SOLUTION	
Data Input	**Function Key**
10	N
12	I
1,190,000	PMT
0	FV
−6,723,765	**PV**

Finally, for the best-case scenario, the annual ATCF is \$1,190,000. The present value of this cash flow stream is \$6,723,765, and the NPV is \$4,723,765 (= 6,723,765 − 2,000,000).

So this project has a somewhat negative NPV for the worst-case scenario. But it has very large positive NPVs in the most likely and best-case scenarios.

Monte Carlo Simulation

Airline pilots get some of their training on flight simulators. A flight simulator is a physical model that simulates or imitates (as realistically as possible) what it is like to fly an airplane in a variety of circumstances. Physically, the pilot sits in the model, which is an exact replica of the cockpit of the plane being simulated. Video equipment provides a visual scene that appears for the pilot through the cockpit windows. The model is mounted on a complex construction of hydraulic equipment that creates motion like that of flying. Although expensive, flight simulators help train pilots in a variety of situations. Inexpensive computer programs are also available that can make a computer seem like a flight simulator, minus the physical movement.

Monte Carlo simulation, or more simply, **simulation,** is a technique that uses a mathematical model to represent a financial decision or other phenomenon. Simulation imitates a risky situation many times to build a distribution of the possible outcomes. As with a flight simulator, the intention is to make good decisions without having to risk life and limb actually flying the thing in the air (or in this case, making the financial decision).

A simulation model is similar to sensitivity analysis, in that it can be used to attempt to answer "what-if" questions. The model relies on random sampling from probability distributions of outcomes. Using a computer, a simulation model can assess the likelihood of particular outcomes by trying out a large number of possible outcomes.

Often, in statistics courses, a coin is flipped a number of times to illustrate that the number of resulting heads actually does turn out to be very close to the 50% that is theoretically estimated using probability theory. This is a simple simulation experiment. Flipping two coins and observing that both are heads about 25% of the time is a slightly more complex simulation experiment. With two coins, of course, the probability of two heads can be calculated by multiplying the probabilities of the individual outcomes together—0.5 for the occurrence of heads on the first coin times 0.5 for heads on the second coin equals 0.25 for the combined event. Although we can use probability theory to determine the probabilities of combined outcomes in simple cases like these coin examples, it is not hard to imagine situations too complex to mathematically derive the probabilities of all possible outcomes. By making assumptions about the joint probability distributions of the random variables, outcome probabilities can be determined for complex situations using a simulation model.

The major drawback to simulation is that it may be simply impossible to identify the nondiversifiable risk in the analysis. In such cases, simulation cannot provide a clear picture of the true riskiness of a project.

SUMMARY

- Be sure to distinguish between the break-even point and the zero-NPV sales level, the financial indifference point.
- Sensitivity analysis can provide insight into a project's profitability by examining "what-if" questions, such as how does the NPV respond to specific changes in a variable?
- Scenario analysis provides an overview of a project's profitability under different possible scenarios.
- Be careful when using break-even analysis, sensitivity analysis, scenario analysis, and Monte Carlo simulation because these techniques do not separate diversifiable from nondiversifiable risk.

APPENDIX QUESTIONS

1. What is a break-even point? How is it different from the zero-NPV sales level?
2. What is sensitivity analysis?
3. What is scenario analysis?
4. What is Monte Carlo simulation? How is simulation similar to scenario analysis?

APPENDIX PROBLEM SET

B1. (Excel: Sensitivity analysis) The project has expected sales of 1,000 units, price of $500 per unit, cash operating expenses of $200 per unit, straight-line depreciation to zero over a 10-year life, a cost of capital of 10%, investment of $100,000, and tax rate of 40%.

a. What is the project's NPV?

b. Calculate the effect on NPV of each of the following changes: Sales are 1,100 units; cost of capital is 11%; initial outlay is $110,000; tax rate is 45%. In each case, assume other values are as expected.

B2. (Excel: Sensitivity analysis) Expected sales are 100,000 units, the price is $60 per unit, cash operating expenses are $25 per unit, straight-line depreciation to zero over a 10-year life will be used, the required rate of return is 10%, the investment is $9,000,000, and the tax rate is 40%.

a. What is the NPV?

b. Calculate the effect on NPV of each of the following changes: Unit sales are 10% higher than expected; the price is 10% higher than expected; the unit costs are 10% higher than expected; the required rate of return is 11%; the initial outlay is $10,000,000; the tax rate is 45%. In each case, assume other values are as expected.

B3. (Excel: Scenario analysis) An analyst at Centenary Cement Company is evaluating a new plant. The plant will cost $2 million and be depreciated straight line to zero over the plant's 10-year life. The analyst developed the three scenarios given below, based on the outlook for highway and commercial construction. Calculate the NPV and IRR for each scenario.

	WORST-CASE SCENARIO	MOST LIKELY SCENARIO	BEST-CASE SCENARIO
Unit sales volume	500	600	700
Unit price	$2,000	$2,200	$2,500
Variable cash expenses per unit	$1,000	$1,000	$900
Fixed cash expenses	$400,000	$500,000	$600,000
Tax rate	40%	40%	40%
Cost of capital	12%	12%	12%

B4. (Excel: Break-even) Patty's Stores is evaluating a $4,000,000 outlay for a new store. The investment will be depreciated straight line over 10 years to a zero salvage value. Annual cash operating expenses will be $200,000 plus 60% of sales. Patty's marginal tax rate is 40%, and the required rate of return is 10%.

a. What annual sales volume is required for accounting break-even (zero profits)?

b. What annual sales volume is required for a zero NPV?

B5. (Excel: Break-even) Pledge Macrobiotics is a new firm investing $800,000 in itself. The investment will be depreciated straight line to zero over the expected 10-year life of the business. Fixed cash operating expenses will be $170,000 annually. Variable cash expenses should be equal to 75% of sales. Pledge is in the 40% tax bracket and has a 14% required rate of return.

a. What is the accounting break-even sales volume?

b. What is the NPV break-even sales volume?

B6. (Excel: Break-even) Florida Avocado Products is investing $4,000,000 in a new project. The investment will be depreciated straight line to zero over the expected 10-year life. Fixed cash operating expenses will be $500,000 annually. Variable cash expenses should be equal to 40% of sales. Florida Avocado is in the 40% tax bracket and has a 12% cost of capital.

a. What is the accounting break-even sales volume?

b. What is the NPV break-even sales volume?

C1. (Excel: Sensitivity analysis) Extension of the Eurotunnel *Minicase:*

1. Recalculate the NPV assuming construction costs are 10% and 25% higher than projected (6.6 and 7.5 billion spread evenly over the eight years).
2. Recalculate the NPV assuming annual revenues are 10% and 25% lower than projected.
3. Recalculate the NPV assuming annual operating costs are 10% and 25% higher than projected.
4. Finally, recalculate the NPV assuming the worst case of each of questions 2, 3, and 4. That is, assume construction costs and annual operating costs are 25% higher than projected, and annual revenues are 25% lower than projected.

PART III

RISK AND RETURN

In Part III, we explore more fully the Principle of Risk-Return Trade-Off. Chapter 9 starts with a brief look at the realized returns and risk connected with stock ownership. We show how investing in portfolios of stocks alters the risk of owning a single stock and describe the risk-return trade-off for portfolios. Finally, we develop a prescription for investing in stocks: Invest some of your money in the market portfolio of stocks and the rest of your money in a riskless asset.

Chapter 10 builds on Chapter 9 and develops the capital-asset-pricing model (CAPM). It shows how, in equilibrium, capital markets determine the trade-off between the expected return and risk of an individual stock when it is part of the market portfolio.

The shareholders' required return is the firm's cost of equity capital. This is a key component of the required return for a capital budgeting project that is called the *cost of capital.* Chapter 11 shows how to determine a cost of capital.

Chapter 12 is a broad overview of the Options Principle. Options are sometimes called contingent claims, because they are valuable only under specific (contingent) circumstances. Options occur naturally in the course of business dealings; however, they are not always easy to spot. So we point out several "hidden options" that can affect value and decision making.

Part III finishes with an exploration of agency theory in Chapter 13. There are important potential conflicts of interest among the firm's many stakeholders. We illustrate how these conflicts give rise to *agency costs* that affect the firm's value, and we explain how proper financial contracting can minimize these costs.

9

RISK AND RETURN: STOCKS

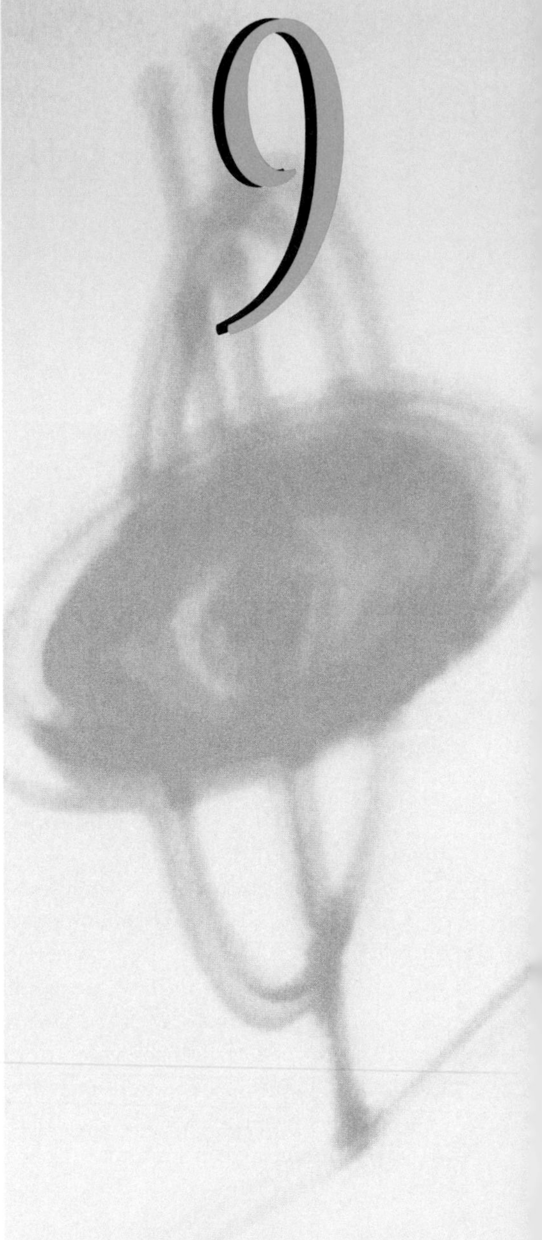

Everyone knows about risk. Some people will not skydive because they think it is too risky. Others will not even fly in an airplane because of risk. Most of us would say there is more risk in jumping out of a flying airplane (even with a parachute) than simply being up in the plane, but *how much* more risk? We do not know how to measure this risk difference. We cannot even measure the amount of risk connected with getting in the plane in the first place. But you do not need to measure the risk precisely to decide whether you will fly in an airplane—and, once you are flying, whether you will jump out.

Now think about investing. It too can be risky. But, as in skydiving, you could invest without measuring the risk precisely. Most of us, however, would want to know about the risk and would consider an investment in terms of its opportunity costs. That is, we would ask, "Compared to what?" To do that, we must measure the risk.

In this chapter and the next, we tackle the problem of measuring risk. We start with realized stock returns. Calculating realized returns precisely is important so that we can communicate with one another. Realized stock returns provide a valuable perspective on investing, and a starting point for our analysis.

Surprisingly, the variability of individual security returns is not the best way to measure risk. Investors typically hold groups of assets called *diversified portfolios.* An investor is therefore concerned with each security's incremental contribution to the risk of the entire portfolio.

If the returns from a particular security are highly variable, is it a high-risk security? Suppose the security's returns tend to be high when the returns on the rest of the portfolio are low. Adding that security to the portfolio could actually reduce the risk of the portfolio because of the Principle of Diversification. We would say such a security has high *specific risk* when the security is considered in isolation but that it has low *market risk* when placed in the portfolio. We will show you how a security's risk within a portfolio depends on the correlation between that security's returns and the returns on the rest of the portfolio.

FOCUS ON PRINCIPLES

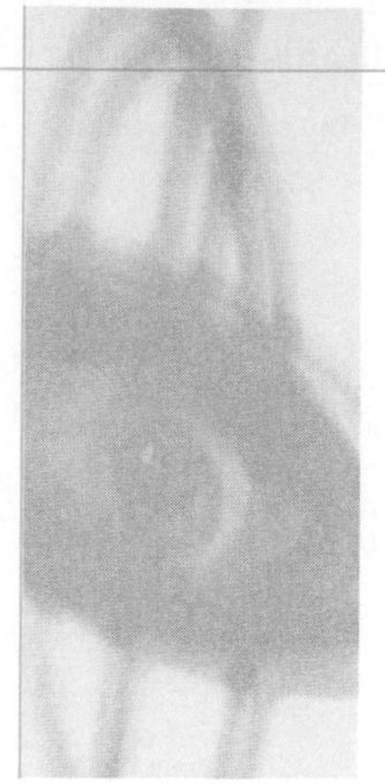

- *Diversification:* Invest in a group of assets, a *portfolio,* to reduce the total risk of your entire investment.
- *Risk-Return Trade-Off:* Invest in the amounts of the risky *market portfolio* and the *riskless asset* that provide the investment risk level you choose.
- *Efficient Capital Markets:* Estimate a security's risk and required return from its past realized returns.
- *Incremental Benefits:* Measure the incremental benefits from owning a security, which are its expected future cash flows.
- *Time Value of Money:* Determine the value of a security by computing the present value of its expected future cash flows.
- *Two-Sided Transactions:* Use a security's fair price to compute its expected return, because the fair price does not favor either side of the transaction.
- *Self-Interested Behavior:* Recognize that prices will be set by the highest bidder, because owners will sell to the highest bidder.
- *Valuable Ideas:* Look for innovative management or information services that might provide a positive NPV by creating value for capital market participants.

9.1 HISTORICAL SECURITY RETURNS IN THE UNITED STATES

We are going to start by looking at past returns to investing in U.S. bonds and stocks. But first, we need to talk about how to measure those returns. Suppose someone earned 10% on one security and 20% on another. Which was the better investment? The answer seems obvious. But what if the 10% was earned over the last six months and the 20% was over the last six years? Clearly, the amount of time the money was invested affects our opinion of the investment. This amount of time is called the **holding period.**

A realized return—the rate of return actually earned on an investment—has little meaning without knowing the holding period. To standardize comparisons of realized returns, investors often calculate an annual equivalent return, a realized APY. In Chapter 4, we showed how to compute an APY using Equation (4.11). But when cash flows and time periods are irregular, things are more complex.

Suppose someone tells you a particular investment produced a return r_1 the first year, r_2 the second year, . . . , and r_N in year N when it was sold. The N-year realized return, r, is simply the result of compounding the N annual returns:

$$r = (1 + r_1)(1 + r_2) \ldots (1 + r_N) - 1$$

But what is the realized APY for the holding period in this case?

Normally, we think of compounding from the smaller period to the larger. So for an N-year holding period, we can compound the APY for N years to compute the holding period realized return:

$$1 + r = (1 + \text{realized APY})^N \qquad (9.1)$$

EXAMPLE Calculating a Realized APY for the Hasbin Corporation

Suppose a friend told you he bought $12,000 worth of Hasbin Corporation common stock 45 months (3.75 years) ago. Hasbin has paid no dividends since he bought the stock. Your friend's stock is currently worth $13,680. What is his realized holding period APY?

CALCULATOR SOLUTION

Data Input	Function Key
3.75	N
−100	PV
0	PMT
114.00	FV
3.56	**I**

First, the realized return for the 3.75-year holding period is 14% (= [13,680/12,000] − 1). Using Equation (9.1), we have a realized APY of 3.56%:

$$1.14 = (1 + 0.0356)^{3.75}$$

Our next example is more realistic, but also more complex.

CALCULATOR SOLUTION

Data Input	Function Key
46/365	N
30	I
0	PMT
0.45	FV
0.435	**PV**

CALCULATOR SOLUTION

Data Input	Function Key
137/365	N
30	I
0	PMT
0.45	FV
0.408	**PV**

CALCULATOR SOLUTION

Data Input	Function Key
187/365	N
30	I
0	PMT
37.25	FV
32.565	**PV**

EXAMPLE Calculating a Purchase Price from a Realized APY

A friend tells you she sold some stock on August 20 for $37.25 per share. The stock paid her $0.45 per share in cash dividends on April 1 and July 1. She does not remember what she paid for the stock, but her investment advisor said she bought the stock on February 14 and earned a 30% realized APY for the holding period. How much did she pay for the stock?

The sale price and cash dividends are cash inflows received after buying the stock. The dividends came 46 and 137 days, and the sale price 187 days, after the stock purchase. We can calculate the price paid by discounting the cash inflows back to February 14 at the realized APY. Their combined present values must equal the cash outflow for buying the stock, $33.408:

$$\frac{0.45}{(1+0.30)^{(46/365)}} + \frac{0.45}{(1+0.30)^{(137/365)}} + \frac{37.25}{(1+0.30)^{(187/365)}} = \$33.408$$

$$0.435 + 0.408 + 32.565 = \$33.408$$

The problem becomes even more complex if we have to calculate such an investment's realized APY for the holding period. Trial and error is generally necessary. Such calculations are done using spreadsheets or other available software.

The Long View

CALCULATOR SOLUTION

Data Input	Function Key
75	N
1.00	PV
0	PMT
2,586.45	FV
11.05	**I**

Figure 9.1 compares the cumulative returns, 1926 to 2000, from investing $1 in each of six classes of securities: large-firm common stocks, small-firm common stocks, long-term corporate bonds, long-term U.S. government bonds, intermediate-term U.S. government bonds, and U.S. Treasury bills. The vertical (y) axis shows the realized returns for all holding periods starting from the end of 1925.

For example, if one dollar had been invested in large-firm common stocks at year-end 1925, with all dividends reinvested in additional shares of common stock, the investment would have grown to $2,586.45 by year-end 2000. This is a 75-year holding period with a realized return of 258,545% (= [2,586.45 − 1.00]/1.00) and a realized APY of 11.05%.

Small-firm common stocks produced the greatest cumulative return, and Treasury bills produced the smallest. But the small-firm stock returns also have the most variability.

Table 9.1 shows the average annual total percentage returns. It also shows the standard deviations of these returns. Standard deviation is a measure of variability. We explain the standard deviation and how it serves as a measure of risk shortly.

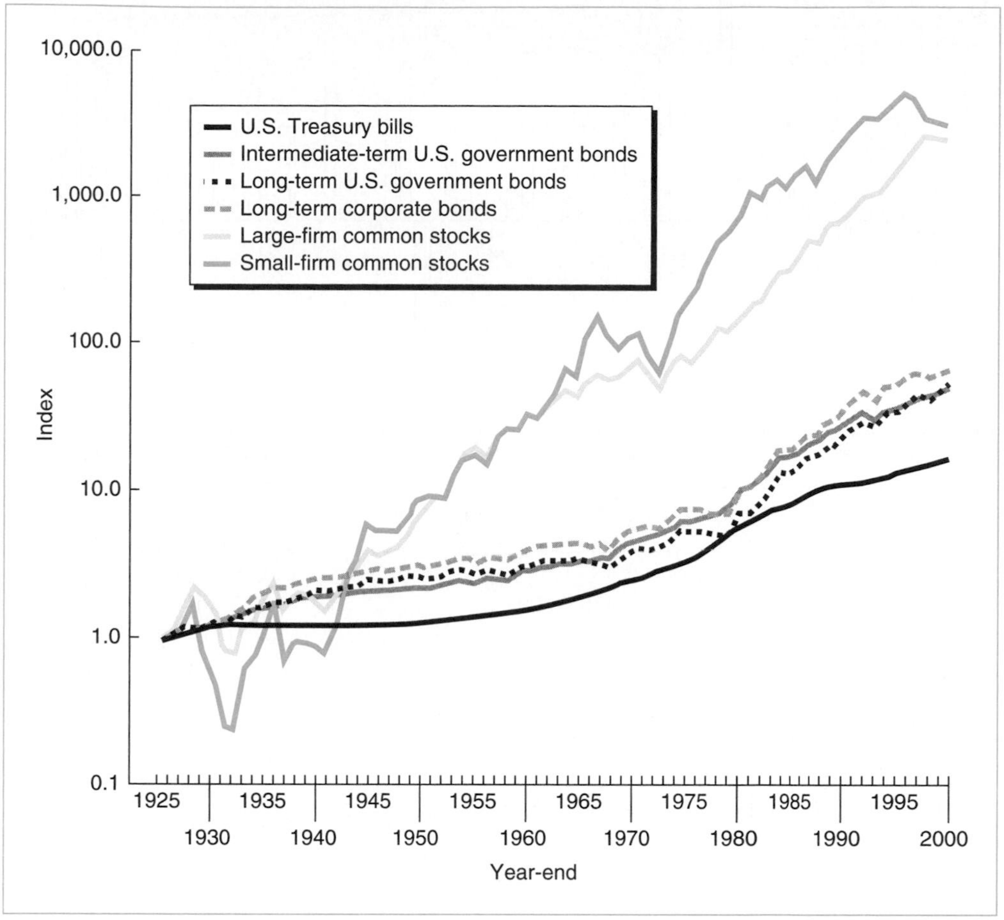

FIGURE 9.1
Cumulative returns from investing in different classes of securities, 1926–2000.

TABLE 9.1
Average annual realized returns for different classes of securities, 1926–2000.

CLASS OF SECURITY	GEOMETRIC MEAN	ARITHMETIC MEAN	STANDARD DEVIATION
Large-firm common stocks	11.0%	13.0%	20.2%
Small-firm common stocks	12.4	17.3	33.4
Long-term corporate bonds	5.7	6.0	8.7
Long-term U.S. government bonds	5.3	5.7	9.4
Intermediate-term U.S. government bonds	5.3	5.5	5.8
U.S. Treasury bills	3.8	3.9	3.2

Source: *Stocks, Bonds, Bills, and Inflation 2001 Yearbook* (Chicago, Ill.: Ibbotson Associates, 2001), p. 14.

Common Stock Realized APYs

Figure 9.2 shows average yearly realized APYs for common stocks in each year from 1926 to 2000. The highest (53.99%) occurred in 1933 and the lowest (−43.34%) in 1931. Figure 9.3 shows the frequency of these APYs. You can see that realized returns from investing in large-firm common stocks are spread out over a wide range.

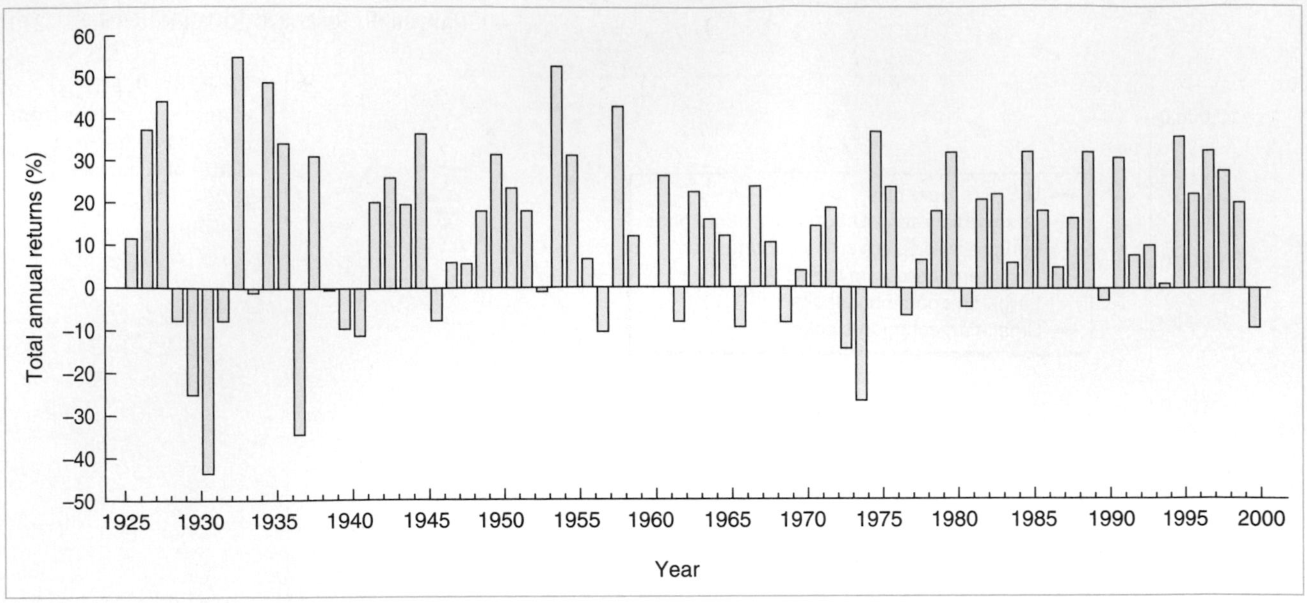

FIGURE 9.2
Yearly realized APYs from investing in large-firm common stocks, 1926–2000.

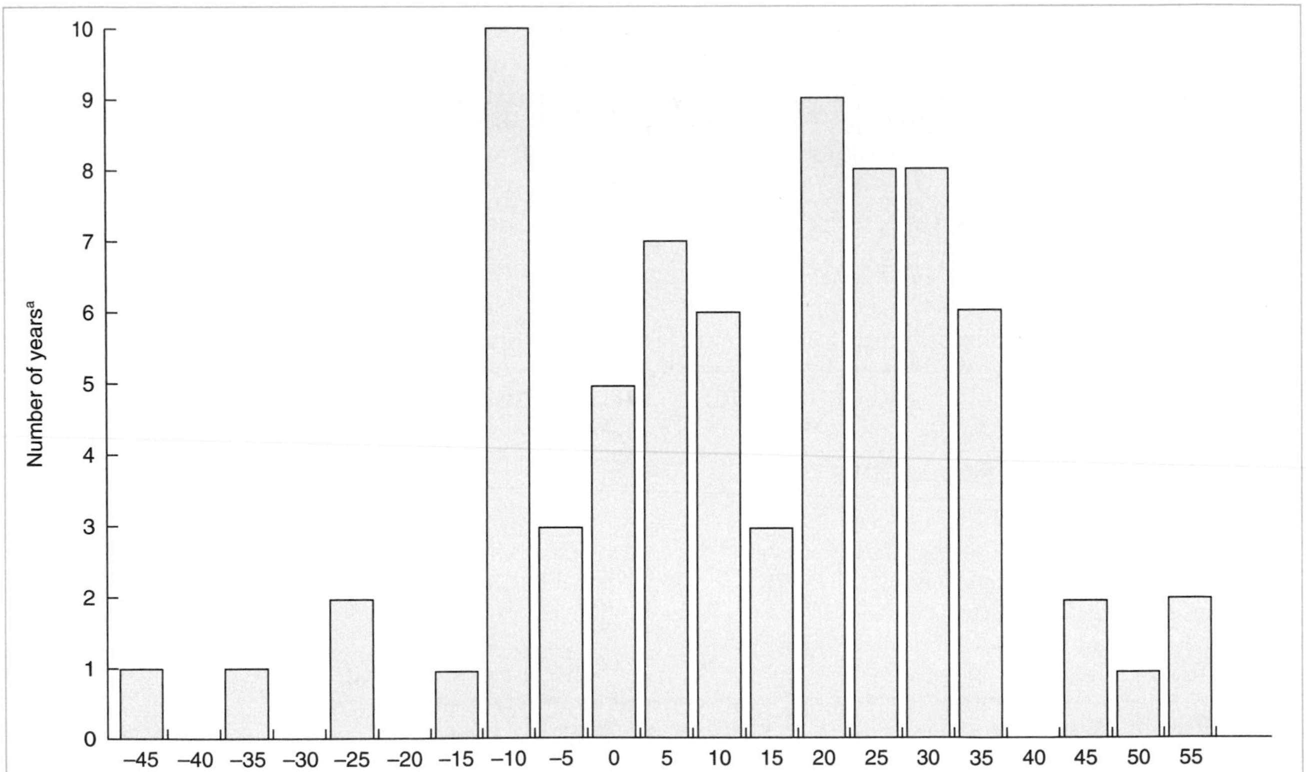

[a]Each interval is centered over the number that appears beneath it. For example, the height of the bar over the number 10 (meaning 10% return) indicates that 6 of the realized APYs were between 7.5% and 12.5%. The numbers beneath the horizontal axis are the midpoints of the indicated ranges.

FIGURE 9.3
The frequency of the APYs shown in Figure 9.2.

Review

1. What are the realized return and realized APY from an investment that cost $10,000 and returned $13,000 27 months later?
2. In how many years did the average realized APY for large-firm common stocks exceed 40 percent? In how many was it below 30 percent?
3. For large-firm common stocks, what was the longest period without a negative annual return? What was the longest period of consecutive losing years?

9.2 PROBABILITY AND STATISTICS

Intuitively, the risk of an asset is the likelihood its realized return will vary substantially from its expected return. That is, an important dimension of risk is the probability (chance) a really bad outcome will occur. In this section we show how some basic concepts from probability and statistics are applied to risk and return.

Random Variables

A *random variable* is not perfectly predictable. For example, the amount of Ford Motor Company's earnings for next year is a random variable. We might have in mind some possible outcomes for this random variable, but we cannot know the value for sure until the year ends and Ford reports its earnings.

Probabilities

Because the value of a random variable is uncertain, we need a way to measure the relative likelihood of each possible outcome. We do this by assigning a *probability* to each possible outcome. Probabilities must satisfy two conditions: (1) A probability cannot be negative and (2) the probabilities of all possible outcomes must sum to 1.0.

The first condition says we are interested only in possible (positive probability) outcomes. The second ensures that the specified set includes all possible values.

EXAMPLE Ford's EPS for Next Year

Jones Securities Service gathers earnings forecasts and analyzes them for its subscribers. Ten analysts forecast Ford's earnings. Three predict earnings per share (EPS) next year of $5.75, two forecast $5.90, one predicts $6.25, and four forecast $6.30. What are the probabilities associated with these forecasts?

There are four different predictions: $5.75, $5.90, $6.25, and $6.30. For simplicity, assume these are the only possible outcomes and the analysts are equally likely to be correct. Then the probability of an outcome is its frequency divided by the total number of predictions. So Ford's EPS for next year will be $5.75 with probability 0.3(= 3/10), $5.90 with probability 0.2(= 2/10), $6.25 with probability 0.1(= 1/10), and $6.30 with probability 0.4(= 4/10).

The Mean

Thus far, we have talked about expected cash flows without really defining the term *expected.* An expected amount is the mean of the random variable. The **mean** of a random variable is its long-run average. It is the average value we would get if we repeated the random experiment a very large number of times.[1] The mean is usually shown by writing a lower case letter with a bar over it. For example $\bar{x}$ is the mean of X.

Suppose a random variable X can take on N possible values x_n, where $n = 1, 2, \ldots, N$. If the probability associated with x_n is p_n, then

$$\bar{x} = \sum_{n=1}^{N} p_n x_n \tag{9.2}$$

In words, Equation (9.2) says to multiply each possible outcome x_n by its probability of occurrence p_n, and then to sum the products. The mean is the weighted average of the possible outcomes, where the weights are the probabilities.

EXAMPLE Calculating the Mean of Ford's EPS

Let us continue our previous example. The mean of Ford's EPS for next year is

$$\bar{x} = (0.3)(5.75) + (0.2)(5.90) + 0.1(6.25) + 0.4(6.30) = \$6.05$$

Figure 9.4 shows how the mean locates the "weighted center" of the probability distribution. The mean is like a fulcrum that balances the probability weighted value on either side of it.

We have said the mean is the average outcome when an experiment is repeated many times (actually, an infinite number of times). However, suppose we can have only one outcome, such as Ford's actual realized EPS next year. The mean does not provide a complete picture of what might happen when there can be many outcomes. Any single outcome might vary tremendously from its mean. In spite of this and other limitations, the mean is very useful as a *summary statistical measure.*

FIGURE 9.4
Mean value of Ford's earnings per share.

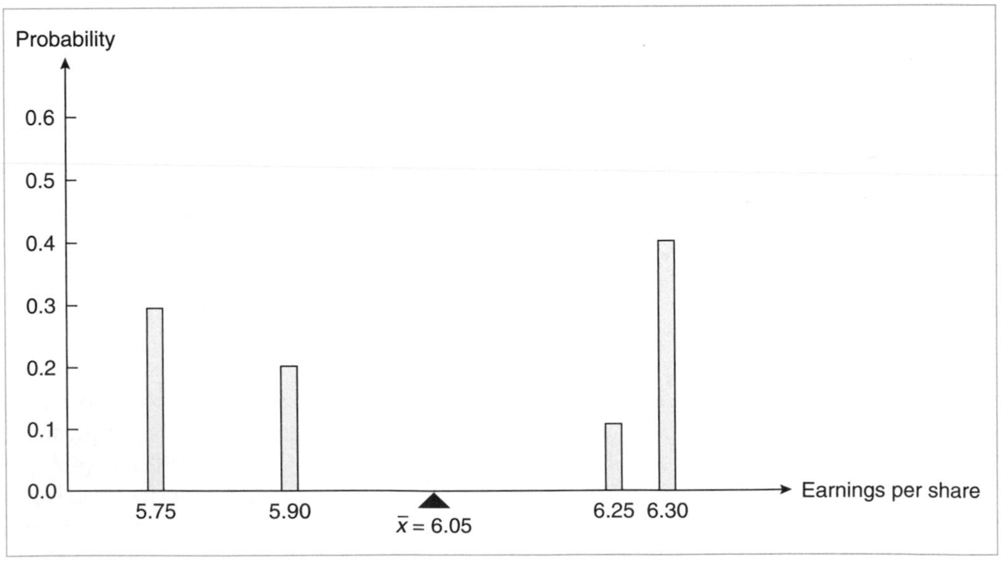

[1]In your statistics class, you might have flipped coins or rolled dice. What is the mean value for rolling a pair of dice? It is 7.0. If you roll a pair of dice many, many times, the average of all the rolls will get closer and closer to 7.0 as you continue rolling.

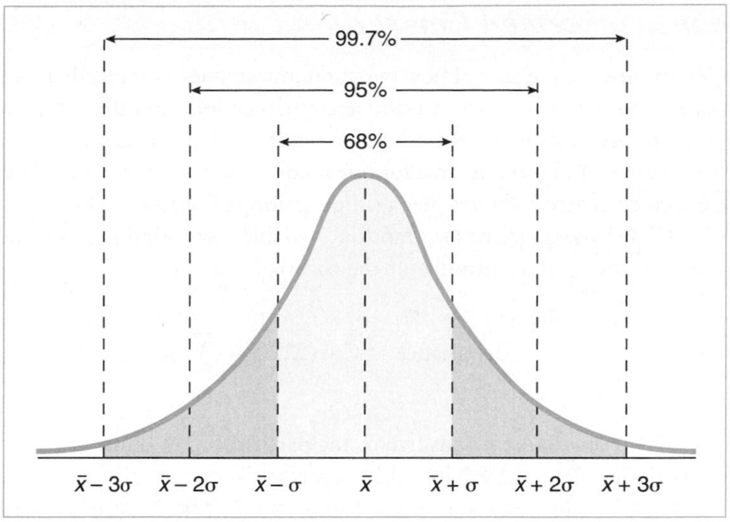

FIGURE 9.5
Dispersion of possible outcomes for a normal random variable (normal pdf).

Variance and Standard Deviation

The **variance** is a measure of the dispersion of all possible outcomes around the mean. Variance is typically shown using a Greek letter, σ^2 (sigma squared), sometimes with an identifying subscript. The formula for variance is

$$\sigma_x^2 = \sum_{n=1}^{N} p_n(x_n - \bar{x})^2 \tag{9.3}$$

The **standard deviation** is the square root of the variance, sometimes with an identifying subscript. For example, σ_x is the standard deviation of X.

Figure 9.5 shows the bell-shaped probability density function (pdf) for what is known as the *normal random variable.* The normal pdf is frequently encountered in finance. In such situations, we know that there is a 68% probability that any single outcome will fall within one standard deviation (plus or minus) of the mean, a 95% probability that it will fall within two standard deviations of the mean, and a 99.7% probability that it will fall within three standard deviations of the mean.

Suppose we know the variance (or standard deviation), but nothing else. Like a mean, variance provides limited insight without other information. For example, suppose we told you the variance of X is 100. That does not mean much by itself. Suppose the variance of television prices for all current models is 100, or the variance of prices for all fast food hamburgers is 100. In the first case, the variance would be small. In the second case, it would be large.

Because of this problem, the mean and variance are used *together.* Look at Figure 9.5. Knowing $\bar{x}$ and σ_x would enable you to draw the normal pdf *exactly.*

EXAMPLE Computing the Variance and Standard Deviation of Ford's EPS

Continuing our Ford example, the variance of possible earnings per share next year is

$$\sigma^2 = (0.3)(5.75 - 6.05)^2 + (0.2)(5.90 - 6.05)^2 + (0.1)(6.25 - 6.05)^2 + (0.4)(6.30 - 6.05)^2$$
$$= 0.0605$$

The standard deviation is

$$\sigma = \sqrt{0.0605} = 0.2460$$

Covariance and Correlation Coefficient

Covariance is a measure of how two random variables vary together, or "covary." Covariance can be positive, negative, or zero. A positive covariance indicates that when one random variable has an outcome above its mean, the other also tends to be above its mean. A negative covariance indicates the reverse—a higher outcome for one tends to be associated with a lower outcome for the other. A covariance of zero indicates that a simple pairing of outcomes does not reveal any regular pattern.

The covariance of two random variables, say X and Y, is usually shown as Cov(X, Y), or sometimes σ_{XY}. The formula for the covariance is

$$\text{Covariance} = \text{Cov}(X,Y) = \sum_{n=1}^{N} p_n(x_n - \bar{x})(y_n - \bar{y}) \tag{9.4}$$

The covariance is sensitive to the particular unit of measurement. The **correlation coefficient** removes this sensitivity. Although covariance can take on any value, the correlation coefficient can be only between minus 1 and plus 1. The correlation coefficient is usually shown as Corr (X, Y). The formula for the correlation coefficient is

$$\text{Corr}(X,Y) = \frac{\text{Cov}(X,Y)}{\sigma_X \sigma_Y} \tag{9.5}$$

Dividing by the standard deviations cancels out the units of measurement, leaving Corr(X, Y) unit free.

Review

1. Explain the meaning of the terms *mean* and *standard deviation.*
2. What does a positive correlation coefficient between two random variables signify? What does a negative correlation coefficient between them signify?

9.3 EXPECTED RETURN AND SPECIFIC RISK

Earlier, we showed how to compute a realized APY. However, in selecting investments, we are concerned with the *future* returns, which are uncertain. Therefore, in making an investment, we are interested in the expected return.

Measuring the Expected Future Return

One measure of the expected return is the mean of future possible returns. Remember, however, the drawback to using the mean. It represents the average outcome when the experiment is repeated many times. But suppose you can get only *one* of those outcomes?

Recall that risk disconnects the expected and realized returns. If you own an asset for the next year, it will provide you with *one* realized return, which may turn out to be positive, zero, or negative. More important, it can turn out to be very different from its mean. And once next year's outcome is realized, the experiment is not repeated. (The second year might be considered a repeat. However, conditions may have changed so much that the possible outcomes are quite different from those of the first year.) After the fact, when you have the outcome, it does not really matter what the mean was.

Despite this drawback, investment decisions must be made before the outcome is known. You may remember the *law of large numbers* from your statistics class. Applied to finance, it says that if you have a large enough group of investments, the good and bad outcomes tend to cancel each other out. In that way, the average of the outcomes will approximate the mean of the group more and more closely as the number of investments increases.[2] In this sense, the mean is a good measure of the expected return when you have a large number of investments.

A DEFINITION OF EXPECTED RETURN We can finally give you a precise definition of expected return: An asset's **expected return** is the mean of its future possible returns.

EXAMPLE Calculating IBM's Expected Return

During work one day, suppose a friend recommends investing in IBM common stock. She has researched it for her finance class. She thinks it has a 0.35 probability of producing a 15% return, a 0.25 probability of a 25% return, and a 0.10 probability of a 40% return. However, she says a bad outcome of −10% is also possible, with probability 0.30. What is the expected return?

Using Equation (9.2), we get

$$\text{Expected return} = (0.30)(-10) + (0.35)(15) + (0.25)(25) + (0.10)(40) = 12.5\%$$

Measuring Specific Risk

The other aspect of the risk-return trade-off is risk. First, we will consider the risk of an investment by itself, its *specific risk*. Later, we will consider the risk of an asset that belongs to a group, called a *portfolio*, of assets.

People usually come up with two notions when they think about why an investment is risky: (1) uncertainty about the future return and (2) the possibility of a large negative return—that is, a bad outcome. For example, losing an entire investment—say your life savings of $280,000—because the firm went bankrupt would be a bad outcome!

Standard deviation reflects variability both above and below the mean return. When an asset has a return distribution that is approximately symmetrical around the mean (like the normal pdf in Figure 9.5), the larger the standard deviation, the riskier the investment.

Despite potential shortcomings, the standard deviation of the return (just "standard deviation," for short) is a pretty good measure of risk. First, return distributions tend to be approximately symmetrical. Second, evidence indicates that, as a practical matter, other conceptually superior measures do not perform any better.

A DEFINITION OF RISK An investment's **specific risk** is its standard deviation.

Review

1. Explain the drawbacks to using the historical mean return when evaluating next year's expected return from investing in AT&T common stock.
2. Explain why the mean is a good measure of expected return when you have a large number of different investments.
3. According to your broker, a share of Microsoft common stock might produce three possible returns next year: 15%, 25% or 50%. The respective probabilities, again according to your broker, are: 0.20, 0.45, and 0.35. What is the expected return?
4. What are the two dimensions of risk? Explain the practical meaning of each.

[2]Literally, the law of large numbers states that the average of the outcomes approaches the mean in the limit (that is, as the number of trials increases without limit).

9.4 INVESTMENT PORTFOLIOS

An investment made up of a group of assets is called a **portfolio.** Combining securities into portfolios reduces risk. This follows from the Principle of Diversification. Stocks with "good" returns tend to cancel out those with "bad" returns. Rational investors hold a portfolio of stocks rather than "put all their eggs in one basket."

EFFICIENT PORTFOLIOS An **efficient portfolio** is one that provides the highest expected return for a given amount of risk and the lowest risk for a given expected return. According to the Principle of Risk-Return Trade-Off, investors want high return and low risk. Therefore, investors will want to invest only in efficient portfolios.

Risk and Return in Two-Asset Portfolios

Now let us see how the risks and expected returns of individual assets combine to create a portfolio's risk and expected return.

Let the return to asset 1 be R_1 with expected return r_1 and specific risk σ_1. The return to asset 2 is R_2 with expected return r_2 and specific risk σ_2. Suppose a proportion w_1 of portfolio value is invested in asset 1, and the remainder $(1 - w_1)$ is invested in asset 2. The *portfolio's expected return,* r_p, is

$$r_p = w_1 r_1 + (1 - w_1) r_2 \tag{9.6}$$

Equation (9.6) says the portfolio's expected return is simply the weighted average of the individual assets' expected returns. The weights are the proportions of money invested in each asset. Therefore, r_p is a linear function of r_1 and r_2.

The portfolio's risk is related to the individual assets' risks in a more complex way. The portfolio's standard deviation, σ_p, is

$$\sigma_p = \{w_1^2\sigma_1^2 + (1 - w_1)^2\sigma_2^2 + 2w_1(1 - w_1)\text{Corr}(R_1,R_2)\sigma_1\sigma_2\}^{1/2} \tag{9.7}$$

where $\text{Corr}(R_1,R_2)$ stands for the correlation coefficient between the returns on the two assets. As you can see, σ_p is not a simple weighted average of σ_1 and σ_2.

EXAMPLE Calculating a Portfolio's Risk and Expected Return

Table 9.2 provides the possible returns and their probability for two assets, "mature stock" and "growth stock," in each of four scenarios. Equation (9.2) is used to calculate the expected returns, which are 5.4% for the mature stock and 9.4% for the growth stock. Equation (9.3) is used to calculate the variance, the square root of which is the standard deviation, σ. The standard deviations are 3.7% for the mature stock and 6.1% for the growth stock.

Suppose equal amounts are invested in the two stocks. What will be the portfolio's expected return and risk? Because the stocks are equally weighted, $w_1 = 0.5$. Therefore, using Equation (9.6), we find that the portfolio's expected return is

$$r_p = 0.5(5.4) + 0.5(9.4) = 7.4\%$$

Next, we calculate the covariance and correlation coefficient using Equations (9.4) and (9.5).

$$\text{Cov}(R_1,R_2) = 0.1(-8.4)(-7.4) + 0.3(-2.4)(-5.4) + 0.4(1.6)(0.6) + 0.2(4.6)(10.6) = 20.24$$

$$\text{Corr}(R_1, R_2) = \frac{20.24}{(3.7)(6.1)} = 0.90$$

TABLE 9.2
Return estimates for two stocks.

STATE OF THE ECONOMY	PROBABILITY OF OCCURRENCE	MATURE STOCK		GROWTH STOCK
Recession	0.10	−3.0%		2.0%
Stable	0.30	3.0		4.0
Moderate growth	0.40	7.0		10.0
Boom	0.20	10.0		20.0
	1.00			
Expected return, $\bar{r}$		5.4%		9.4%
Standard deviation, σ		3.7%		6.1%
Correlation coefficient, Corr			0.90	

Finally, using Equation (9.7), the portfolio's standard deviation is

$$\sigma_p = \{(0.5)^2(3.7)^2 + (0.5)^2(6.1)^2 + 2(0.5)(0.5)(0.90)(3.7)(6.1)\}^{1/2} = 4.8\%$$

Portfolio-Asset Risk-Return Interactions

Our portfolio example looked at an equally weighted two-asset portfolio. But what about other, unequal combinations? Figure 9.6 graphs the expected return and risk for each asset. Expected return is measured along the vertical (*y*) axis, and risk (standard deviation) along the horizontal (*x*) axis. Suppose all the money is invested in either asset 1 or asset 2. Then the risk-return combinations are at A_1 and at A_2, respectively. But we are more interested in "true" portfolios involving both assets. These are cases where money is invested in each asset.

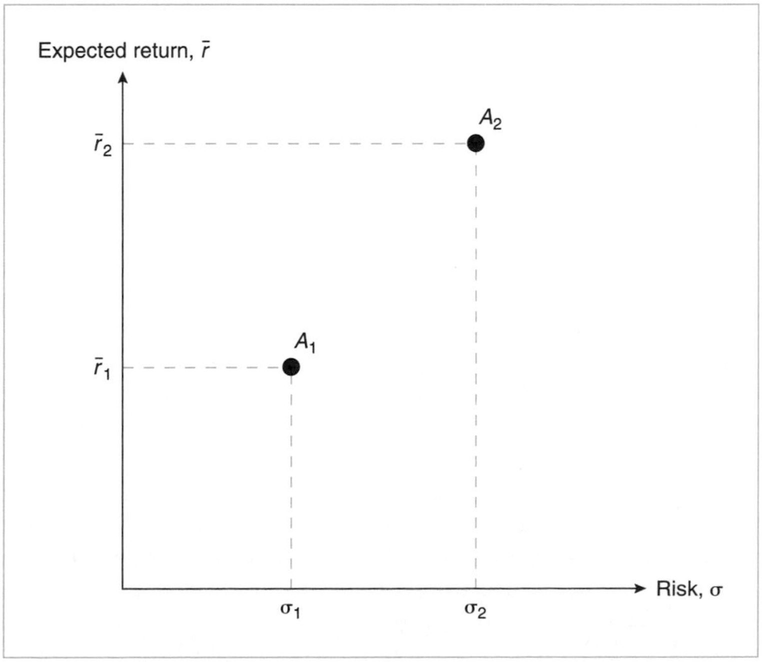

FIGURE 9.6
Expected return and risk of asset 1 and asset 2.

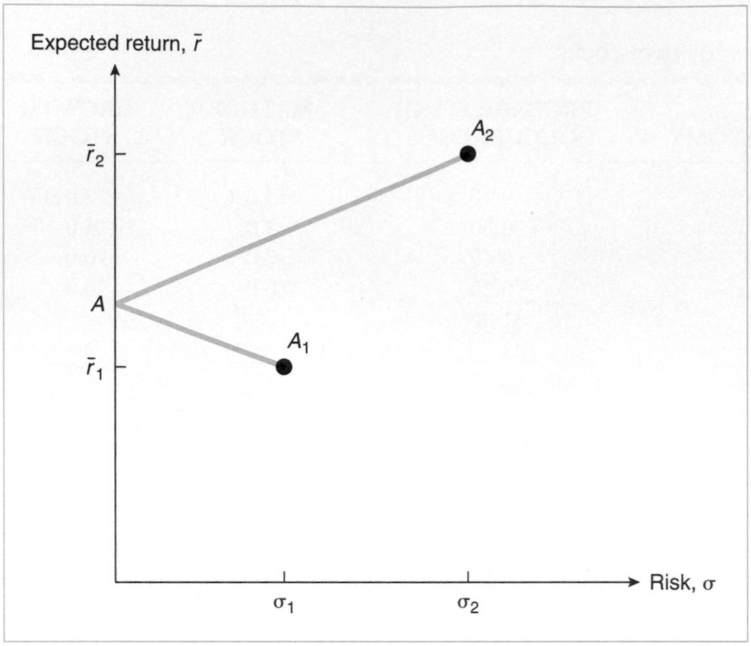

FIGURE 9.7
Perfect negative correlation ($Corr(R_1,R_2) = -1.0$).

Equation (9.6) shows r_p in terms of the assets' expected returns. Equation (9.7) shows σ_p in terms of σ_1 and σ_2. Let us explore the combined effect of Equations (9.6) and (9.7) by substituting a value for the correlation coefficient, $Corr(R_1,R_2)$, and looking at all possible values for w_1 between 0 and 1.

PERFECT NEGATIVE CORRELATION Figure 9.7 graphs the portfolio risk-return combinations given by Equations (9.6) and (9.7) for $0 \leq w_1 \leq 1.0$ when $Corr(R_1,R_2) = -1.0$. Note in Figure 9.7 that it is possible to combine investments in the two risky assets so that the portfolio risk is zero. This result is a direct consequence of the perfect negative correlation. When asset 1's realized return is high, asset 2's realized return is low, and vice versa. When asset 1 has a "medium return," so does asset 2. Therefore, when the two assets are combined in the proportions represented by portfolio *A* in Figure 9.7, high and low returns always cancel each other out *exactly.* The portfolio earns the same return every period and has a zero standard deviation.

The idea that you might be able to invest in two assets, both of which are risky, and yet have your total investment be riskless is not at all intuitive. Harry Markowitz pointed out this phenomenon in 1952 and started a revolution in the way people think about investing.

Figure 9.7 illustrates the special case in which the minimum value of portfolio risk is $\sigma_p = 0$. When Corr $= -1.0$, we can determine analytically the exact proportions to invest in the two risky assets, w_1 and $(1 - w_1)$, so that the portfolio is riskless. For any specific case, these proportions can be derived by setting Equation (9.7) equal to zero and solving for w_1.

Are there two securities to invest in that are perfectly negatively correlated? Probably not. However, this provides a very powerful starting point, which we are going to build on. Let us next consider the other extreme possibility.

PERFECT POSITIVE CORRELATION Unlike our first case, it is both realistic and easy to find two assets that have perfect positive correlation between their returns. A simple example is two identical securities, such as two shares of Procter & Gamble common stock. When $Corr(R_1,R_2) = +1.0$, Equation (9.7) reduces to

$$\sigma_p = w_1\sigma_1 + (1 - w_1)\sigma_2$$

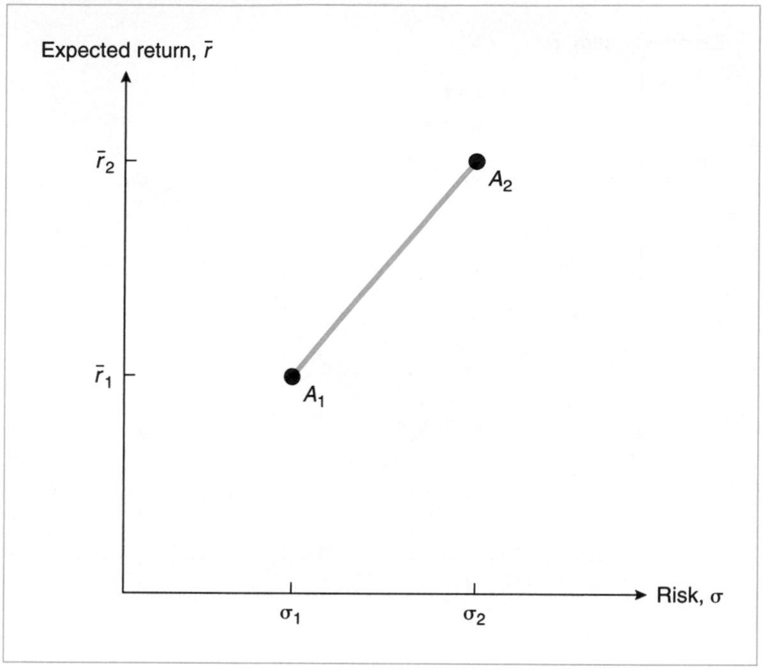

FIGURE 9.8
Perfect positive correlation ($\text{Corr}(R_1,R_2) = +1.0$).

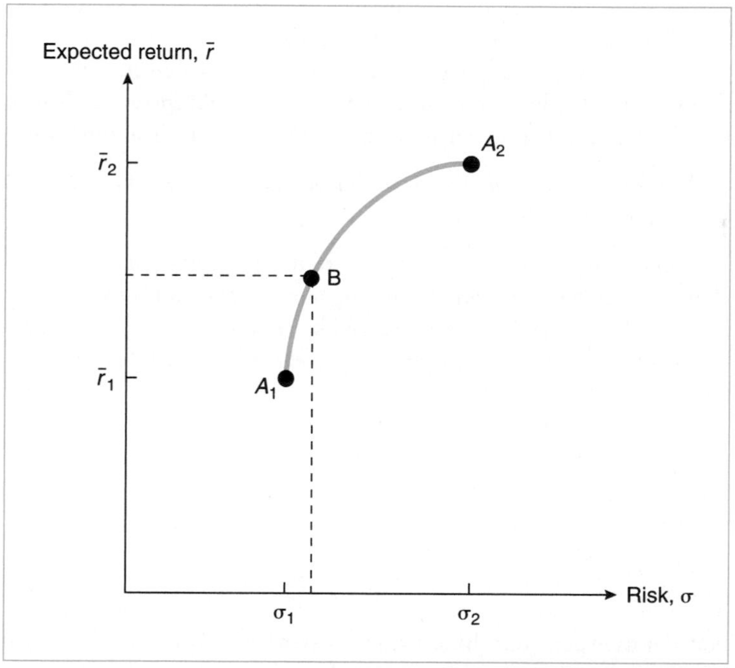

FIGURE 9.9
Positive correlation ($\text{Corr}(R_1,R_2) = 0.4$).

Figure 9.8 shows the possible expected returns and risks to portfolio combinations for values of w_1 between 0.0 and 1.0, when $\text{Corr}(R_1,R_2) = +1.0$, which is a straight line between A_1 and A_2.

POSITIVE CORRELATION Figure 9.9 shows the curve linking all possible combinations of portfolio risk and return for assets 1 and 2 when $\text{Corr}(R_1,R_2) = 0.4$. It is not a straight line. Compare portfolios with $w_1 = 1.0$ (all the money invested in asset 1) and $w_1 = 0.5$ shown by portfolio B. A portfolio with $w_1 = 0.5$ has an expected return exactly halfway between the expected returns of assets 1 and 2. However, its standard deviation is only about one-fifth of the way from asset 1 to asset 2.

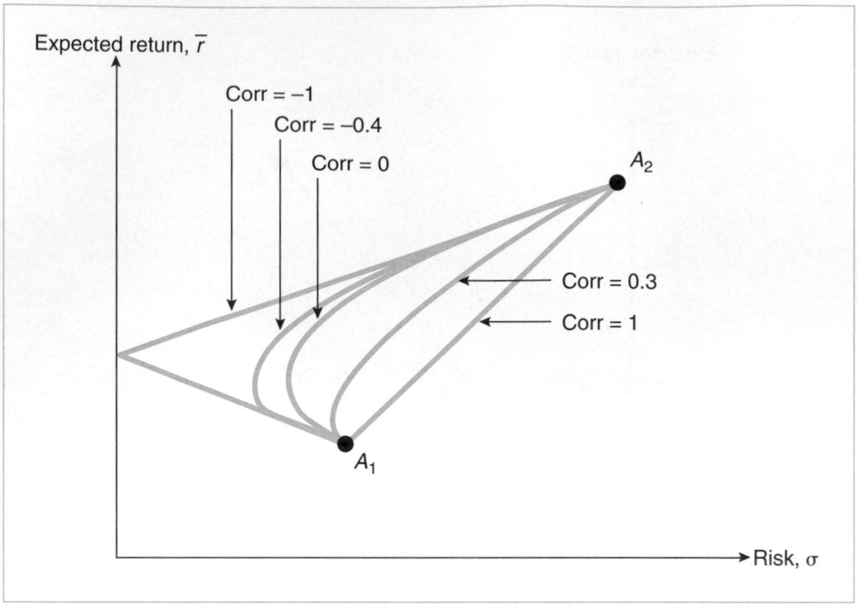

FIGURE 9.10
How the set of all possible combinations for two-asset portfolios depends on Corr.

In this case, the trade-off between how much expected return you get and how much risk you take on is more favorable where w_1 is greater than 0.5 than it is where w_1 is less than 0.5. In mathematical terms, the slope is greater when w_1 is close to 1.0 and smaller when it is near zero.

Some people might be so risk averse they would not invest anything in asset 2. Others might have such little risk aversion that they would invest all their money in asset 2. But most people will find it attractive to diversify. This leads us to an interesting generalization:

When asset returns are not perfectly positively correlated, diversification can reduce the portfolio's risk for a given level of return.

In other words, when asset returns are not perfectly positively correlated, diversification can change the risk-return trade-off among our set of possible investments as we move along the curve in Figure 9.9. Note that risk is reduced by combining stocks into portfolios: $\text{Corr}(R_1,R_2) < 1$, risk is reduced, but it *cannot* be completely eliminated (except for the unlikely case where $\text{Corr}(R_1,R_2) = -1$).

Figure 9.10 provides a graphic picture of how the set of all possible combinations for two-asset portfolios depends on Corr. The higher Corr is, the straighter the curve. It is important to understand that each case has only one value for Corr. The set of all possible risk-return combinations for each correlation is represented by one line.

An Expanded Framework: Portfolios with More Than Two Assets

Now let us expand our thinking from two assets. Consider all of the stocks that are traded on the NYSE and NASDAQ stock markets. That gives us more than 10,000 stocks. In addition to these individual assets, we can form an infinite number of portfolios containing different proportions of these stocks.

It is impossible to list all the possible asset combinations. Nevertheless, we can show you what it generally looks like, based on past realized stock returns. Figure 9.11 illustrates the returns of all possible portfolios of stocks. (It reminds us of an umbrella without a handle.)

The really important thing here is what we can say about how investors should invest their money when they face this set of alternatives. Should they invest in portfolio *G*, which lies in the middle of the umbrella in Figure 9.11? No, because *G* is not an *efficient portfolio,* one that pro-

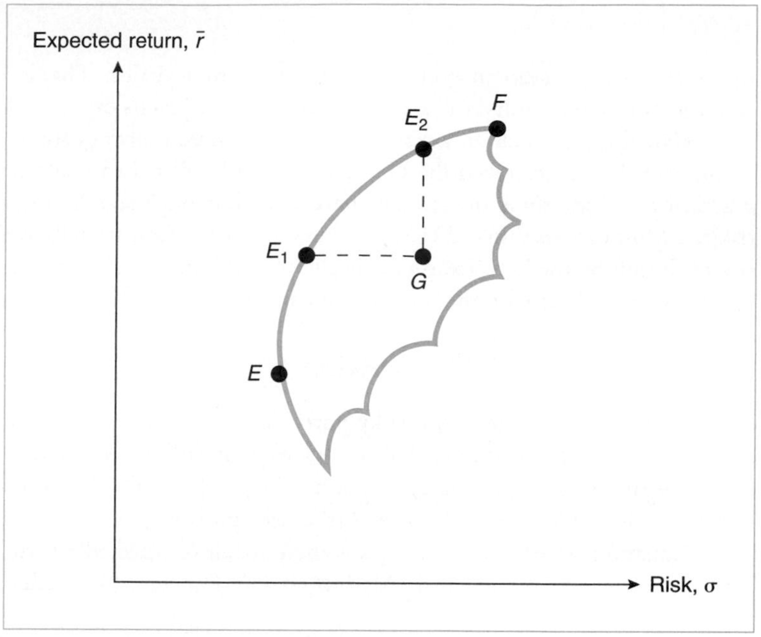

FIGURE 9.11
The expected returns to all possible combinations of risky assets.

vides the highest return for a given level of risk. They can instead invest in portfolio E_2. It has the same risk, but a higher expected return. Or, they can invest in the efficient portfolio E_1, which has the same expected return, but the lowest possible risk for that expected return.

As we noted, investors will want to invest only in efficient portfolios, those with the highest possible expected return for a given risk level. The set of efficient portfolios—those on the curve between E and F—is called the **efficient frontier.** This leads to an important recommendation:

You should not invest in a portfolio that lies below the efficient frontier—regardless of how much or how little risk you are willing to take.

Review

1. Define the term *portfolio.* Can a portfolio contain just one asset?
2. If the returns from two assets are perfectly negatively correlated, how can it be possible to find a combination of investments in these two assets that has zero portfolio risk?
3. When the returns from two assets are less than perfectly positively correlated, how can diversification be beneficial?
4. What is an efficient portfolio? What is the efficient frontier?
5. Explain why a rational investor would never knowingly invest money in a portfolio that is below the efficient frontier.

9.5 A PRESCRIPTION FOR INVESTING

Another element of investing is a *riskless asset.* Surprisingly, the "riskless" asset's return critically affects how everyone should invest their money in *risky* assets. The existence of a riskless asset also allows us to establish the market-determined trade-off between risk and expected return. This risk-return trade-off provides the key to pricing individual risky assets.

A Riskless Asset

By *riskless asset,* we mean an asset with a zero standard deviation. That is, one with no uncertainty about its future return. Its realized return will always equal its expected return.

Can there be such an asset? Literally, no. There is always some chance, no matter how small, that the debtor (even the U.S. government) will fail to make timely payment.[3] But for practical purposes, some investments have a small enough standard deviation to be considered riskless. Most experts think of U.S. government 90-day Treasury bills as riskless investments. The risk of default by the U.S. Treasury is negligible. Although such investments are not *literally* riskless, we will go along with the majority and assume them to be essentially riskless.

Investing in the Riskless Asset

Combining one investment in a risky portfolio of assets with a second investment in a riskless asset is the two-asset portfolio problem we looked at earlier. Let us build on what we learned. Let asset 1 be the riskless asset and asset 2 be a risky portfolio. The (total) portfolio is a combination of asset 1 (the riskless asset) and asset 2 (the risky portfolio).

Equations (9.6) and (9.7) express the portfolio's expected return and standard deviation. But we can simplify things a little. With $\sigma_1 = 0.0$, Equation (9.7) reduces to

$$\sigma_p = \{(1 - w_1)^2\sigma_2^{\,2}\}^{1/2} = (1 - w_1)\sigma_2$$

This equation shows that the (total) portfolio's risk (that of the combined investments in the riskless asset and the risky portfolio), σ_p, is a simple linear function of σ_2. Therefore, the set of all possible combinations of asset 1 and asset 2 forms a straight line between the riskless asset and the chosen risky portfolio (asset 2). Figure 9.12 shows this relationship for an arbitrarily chosen risky portfolio, *G,* from among our "umbrella set" of all possible portfolios.

Note that some of the line from the riskless return, r_f, to *G*'s return dominates part of the efficient frontier.[4] The problem is further complicated because the amount it dominates depends on the choice of *G.* This brings up a logical question: Is there a "best" risky portfolio? Yes. Now let us see why, and what that portfolio is.

Choosing the Best Risky Portfolio

Figure 9.12 suggests the following decision rule: Choose the risky portfolio that dominates the largest portion of the efficient frontier. If we follow this rule, the *best* risky portfolio is the one that produces a line of combinations tangent to the efficient frontier. This best risky portfolio is identified as *M* in Figure 9.13.

Lending and Borrowing

Investing in the riskless asset is really simply lending money. The opposite, borrowing, is like having a *negative* investment in the riskless asset (asset 1). That is, borrowing money to invest makes the proportion invested in the riskless asset, w_1, negative. In effect, what we owe you is negative to us—but positive to you. (The Principle of Two-Sided Transactions strikes again!) So borrowed money is simply a negative investment.

One problem with using negative values for w_1 to represent a borrowed amount is that the implied borrowing rate of interest is the same as the lending rate of interest. At first, this may

---

[3]You never know—the eastern U.S. might be destroyed by a huge meteorite during the next period. Or, as nearly happened a few years ago, the federal government might default because the U.S. Congress refuses to raise the debt ceiling and the U.S. Treasury runs out of cash.

[4]The *f* in r_f is to indicate that the return is *free* of risk.

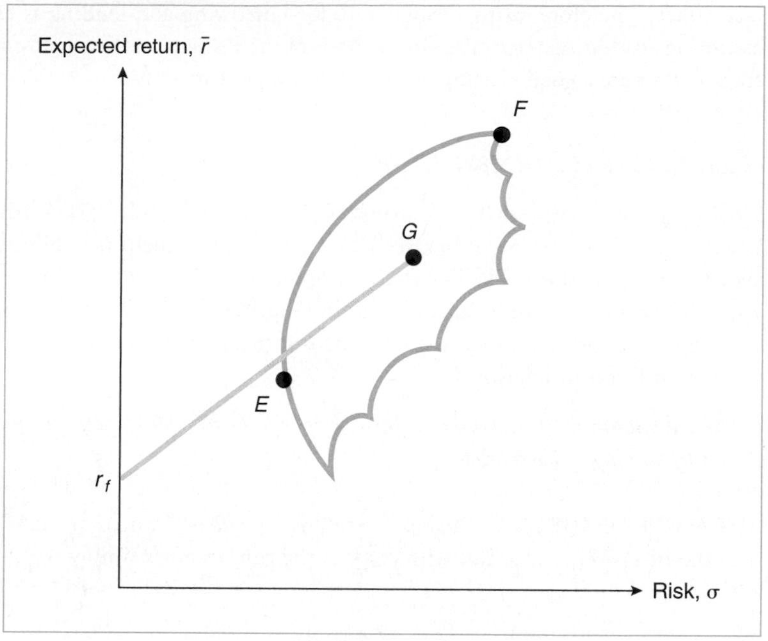

FIGURE 9.12
Combinations of a risky portfolio and the riskless asset.

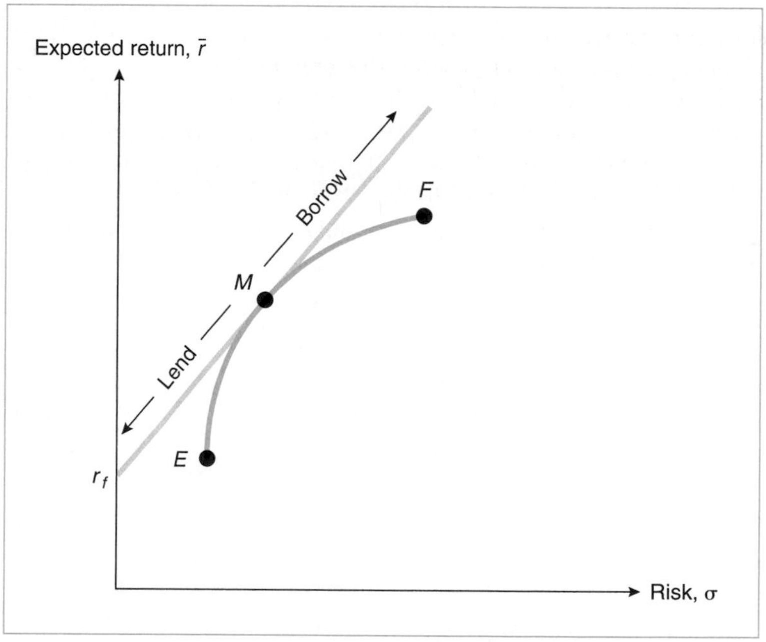

FIGURE 9.13
Combinations of the risky portfolio *M* and the riskless asset, making up the capital market line (CML).

seem very troublesome. We know that banks we go to charge a higher rate for borrowing than they pay for lending (the rate paid on deposits).

Different borrowing and lending rates are certainly a fact of life for most of us. However, consider large corporations. Many invest and borrow in the commercial paper market. One day a firm is a lender, but the next day that same firm may be a borrower. The commercial paper rate is generally quoted as a single rate.

The main difference between the bank's borrowing and lending rates in practice is the charge for transacting in small amounts. In other words, the bank is simply charging (a transaction cost) for separating large amounts into small ones or putting small amounts together to make large ones. Therefore, using a single rate for borrowing and lending is essentially equivalent to assuming costless transactions. On the basis of the Principle of Capital Market Efficiency, costless transactions are a good starting point for forming estimations.

The Capital Market Line

Letting w_1 be negative does not change Equations (9.6) and (9.7). With the possibility of borrowing (negative investment in asset 1), the line of investment possibilities simply continues past M with the same slope. The line that links possible investment combinations when you can borrow at the riskless return is called the **capital market line (CML).** The CML touches the efficient frontier at M and dominates the efficient frontier everywhere else. The CML provides another important recommendation:

> *You should invest your money in the risky portfolio M, and set your portfolio's return and risk levels by lending or borrowing.*

THE SLOPE OF THE CML A slope is the "rise" over the "run." For the CML, the rise is $r_M - r_f$, and the run is $\sigma_M - \sigma_f$. But with $\sigma_f = 0$, the run becomes simply σ_M. Therefore,

$$\text{CML slope} = \frac{r_M - r_f}{\sigma_M} \tag{9.8}$$

The slope of the CML is the amount of expected return per unit of risk. The numerator of the slope, $r_M - r_f$, is called the **market risk premium.**

EXAMPLE Calculating the Slope of the CML

Let us say that $r_M = 15\%$, $r_f = 7\%$, and $\sigma_M = 16\%$. What is the slope of the CML?

Using Equation (9.8), it is

$$\text{CML slope} = \frac{r_M - r_f}{\sigma_M} = \frac{15 - 7}{16} = 0.50$$

When you really think about it, Figure 9.13 suggests a startling approach to picking investments. It is extremely unlikely that anyone would arrive at such an approach intuitively. However, a careful modeling of the world of stock investments has produced surprising conclusions about how everyone should invest. Everyone should invest in M. But what is M?

The Market Portfolio

Because everyone invests in the same set of risky assets, everyone will own a portion of every asset in this special portfolio M (for "market"). Any asset in the market that is not in M cannot have an owner. This is because everyone owns a part of the same set of assets. But every asset in the market must have an owner. Therefore, every asset must be included in M. Because M includes every risky asset in the market, it is called the **market portfolio.**

In this view, all investors diversify their ownership of risky assets by owning some of everything. But what proportion of their money should they invest in each asset? This question is more easily analyzed by examining a simplified example of a market, rather than the stock market with its more than 10,000 stocks.

EXAMPLE The Market Portfolio's Composition

Consider a market with three risky assets: 1, 2, and 3. They are worth \$100, \$200, and \$300, respectively, for a total market value of \$600. Suppose there are two investors, A and B. Investor A owns \$450 worth of the market portfolio, *M,* and B owns \$150 worth. They invest the rest of their money in the riskless asset. Because investor A owns 75% of *M,* A will own 75% of each asset. Similarly, B owns 25% of *M* and 25% of each asset. The investors own identical mixes of risky assets. But what proportion of each investor's risky assets is invested in asset 1?

The answer is one-sixth, because asset 1 is one-sixth (= 100/600) of the total market value. If an investor C decides to invest in this market, she should invest one-sixth of her money in asset 1, one-third (= 200/600) in asset 2, and one-half (= 300/600) in asset 3. In this way, C would be investing in the market portfolio.

If we translate our three-asset example into a large market of risky assets such as the stock market, the principle for determining the market portfolio is the same. However, identifying the value of each asset can be tricky. An asset's value is not the market value *per share.* Instead, it is the total market value of all the firm's stock.

That is, the asset value to use in determining the proper investment proportions is the market value per share multiplied by the number of shares the corporation has outstanding. For example, if IBM is selling for \$80 per share and there are 1.5 billion shares of IBM, the stock market value of IBM is \$120 billion.

We determine the proportion of money to invest in each stock in the following manner. First, sum the stock market values of all the corporations in the market. Then divide the corporation's stock market value by the sum of all the values. The resulting fraction is the proportion of the market portfolio to invest in the stock. Continuing our hypothetical example of IBM, suppose the sum of the values for all stocks is \$8.5 trillion. Then *M* would contain 1.41% (= 120 billion/8.5 trillion) invested in IBM stock.

If finding the proportions to invest in each stock sounds tedious, that is because it would be! Fortunately, when such information is valuable to one set of people, other people apply the Principle of Valuable Ideas. They recognize the potential to make a positive NPV by producing the information for a profit, or by creating investment funds that approximate the market portfolio.

Currently, information about the market portfolio's make up can be purchased from a variety of information services. Also, many so-called stock index funds have been created. The fund's portfolio of common stocks matches the composition of an index, such as the Standard & Poor's 500 Index, which is a diversified set of common stocks that is generally accepted as a good estimate for the (common stock) market. For example, the oldest and largest of the S&P 500 mutual funds, the Vanguard Index Trust-500 Portfolio, had approximately \$73.2 billion under management at December 31, 2001. The 181 S&P 500 mutual funds tracked by Lipper Inc. had \$243.3 billion under management at December 31, 2001.

Review

1. What is a riskless asset?
2. In what sense is a 90-day Treasury bill a riskless asset? In what sense is a 30-year Treasury bond *not* a riskless asset?
3. Explain how the existence of a riskless asset alters an investor's set of investment opportunities.
4. What is the CML?
5. Which assets are in the market portfolio, *M*?

SUMMARY

An asset's expected return and risk are based on its future possible returns.

- The analysis of risk and return uses several basic statistical concepts, including the mean, variance, standard deviation, covariance, and correlation coefficient.
- An investment's expected return is its mean or weighted value of its possible future returns. The weights are the probabilities of each possible future return.
- Risk has two dimensions: (1) the degree of uncertainty about future outcomes and (2) the possibility of a negative outcome. The standard deviation of a distribution of future returns that is approximately symmetrical around the mean captures both dimensions. Thus, in most cases, we can use an asset's standard deviation of return to measure its specific risk.
- Combining stocks into portfolios reduces risk because of the Principle of Diversification. The returns from stocks that perform better than expected tend to offset the returns from stocks that perform worse than expected.
- A portfolio's expected return is the weighted average of its individual security expected returns. The proportions of portfolio value invested in each security are the weights.
- The portfolio's standard deviation of return depends on (1) the proportions invested in each security, (2) the standard deviations of the individual securities in the portfolio, and (3) the correlation coefficients between the returns of the securities that compose the portfolio. It is *not* simply a weighted average of the standard deviations of the individual securities.
- The amount of risk reduction in a two-asset portfolio depends on the correlation between the two assets' returns. In a portfolio consisting of two assets whose returns are perfectly negatively correlated, it is possible to find a set of investment proportions for which the portfolio is riskless. If the two assets are perfectly positively correlated, the risk-return trade-off is a straight line with no risk reduction from diversification. With correlations between -1 and $+1$, the risk-return trade-off is usually a curved, nonlinear function.
- An efficient portfolio is one that provides the greatest possible expected return for a given risk level and the smallest risk level for a given expected return. The set of efficient portfolios makes up the efficient frontier.
- By combining the efficient frontier with the possibility of lending or borrowing at the riskless return, the best investment strategy is to invest part of the money in the market portfolio and the rest in the riskless asset.
- The capital market line (CML), which goes through the riskless return and is tangent to the efficient frontier at *M*, traces out the available risk-return possibilities. Investors should invest in the risky portfolio *M* and set their return and risk levels by lending or borrowing to achieve their most desired position on the CML. As a result, investors' choices of which risky portfolio to invest in are not based on their attitude toward risk. Everyone should invest in *M*.

EQUATION SUMMARY

$$1 + r = (1 + \text{realized APY})^N \tag{9.1}$$

$$\bar{x} = \sum_{n=1}^{N} p_n x_n \tag{9.2}$$

$$\sigma_x^2 = \sum_{n=1}^{N} p_n (x_n - \bar{x})^2 \tag{9.3}$$

$$\text{Covariance} = \text{Cov}(X,Y) = \sum_{n=1}^{N} p_n(x_n - \bar{x})(y_n - \bar{y}) \tag{9.4}$$

$$\text{Corr}(X,Y) = \frac{\text{Cov}(X,Y)}{\sigma_X \sigma_Y} \tag{9.5}$$

$$r_p = w_1 r_1 + (1 - w_1) r_2 \tag{9.6}$$

$$\sigma_p = \{w_1^2\sigma_1^2 + (1 - w_1)^2\sigma_2^2 + 2w_1(1 - w_1)\text{Corr}(R_1,R_2)\sigma_1\sigma_2\}^{1/2} \tag{9.7}$$

$$\text{CML slope} = \frac{r_M - r_f}{\sigma_M} \tag{9.8}$$

QUESTIONS

1. What is meant by the term *expected return?*
2. Define the term *mean.*
3. What are the two dimensions of risk?
4. How is *risk* defined in this chapter?
5. Define the term *efficient frontier.* Why is it desirable to invest in a portfolio that lies on the efficient frontier?
6. Define the term *capital market line (CML).*

CHALLENGING QUESTIONS

7. a. Suppose you own $1 million worth of 30-year Treasury bonds. Is this asset riskless?
   b. Let us say you own $1 million worth of 90-day Treasury bills. You "roll over" this investment every 90 days by reinvesting the proceeds in another issue of 90-day Treasury bills. Is this investment riskless?
   c. Can you think of an asset that is truly riskless?
8. Explain the fallacy in the following statement: "I bought the stock for $30 per share. It is now selling for $20 per share. But I have not lost anything because I have not sold it yet."
9. Explain how it is possible to invest in two risky assets that are perfectly negatively correlated (i.e., $\text{Corr}(R_1,R_2) = -1.0$) and earn a riskless return.
10. Figure 9.11 shows what the group of all possible portfolio combinations for stocks in the stock market looks like. Is it possible that any two of these portfolios have a correlation coefficient between them that is equal to *minus* 1.0? If it is possible, give an example. If it is not possible, explain why.

PROBLEMS

LEVEL A (BASIC)

A1. (Realized return) Tie Su bought $5,000 worth of stock 22 months ago. The firm has paid no dividends since he bought the stock. The stock is currently worth $5,680. What is Tie's realized APY?

A2. (Realized return) Andy Fields bought $15,000 worth of stock 37 months ago. The firm has paid no dividends since he bought the stock. The stock is currently worth $20,400. What is Andy's realized APY?

A3. (Expected return and standard deviation) An investment has four possible returns, each with its own probability given below.

a. What is the expected return?

b. What are the variance and the standard deviation of returns?

Return	−7.5%	0%	10%	20%
Probability	0.20	0.25	0.35	0.20

A4. (Expected return and standard deviation) An investment has four possible returns, each with its own probability given below.

a. What is the expected return?

b. What are the variance and the standard deviation of returns?

Return	−12%	−2%	8%	30%
Probability	0.20	0.25	0.35	0.20

A5. (Portfolio return and standard deviation) Two stocks have the expected returns and standard deviations shown below. The correlation between the returns of the two stocks is 0.50.

a. What is the expected portfolio return?

b. What is the portfolio standard deviation?

STOCK	EXPECTED RETURN	STANDARD DEVIATION	PORTFOLIO WEIGHTS
1	12%	10%	0.40
2	16%	20%	0.60

A6. (Portfolio return and standard deviation) Two stocks have the expected returns and standard deviations shown below. The correlation between the returns of the two stocks is 0.45.

a. What is the expected portfolio return?

b. What is the portfolio standard deviation?

STOCK	EXPECTED RETURN	STANDARD DEVIATION	PORTFOLIO WEIGHTS
1	15%	15%	0.70
2	21%	25%	0.30

A7. (Calculating portfolio weights) Consider a market with four risky assets, 1, 2, 3, and 4, worth $1,000, $2,500, $1,500, and $5,000, respectively. If an investor wants to replicate the market portfolio, what proportion of the investor's portfolio should be invested in each risky asset?

A8. (Calculating portfolio weights) Consider a market with four risky assets, 1, 2, 3, and 4, worth $3,000, $2,000, $1,000, and $1,500, respectively. If an investor wants to replicate the market portfolio, what proportion of the investor's portfolio should be invested in each risky asset?

A9. (Expected portfolio return) Musumeci Capital Management has invested its portfolio as shown below. What is Musumeci's expected portfolio return?

ASSET	PORTFOLIO WEIGHT	EXPECTED RETURN
Money market securities	10%	4%
Corporate bonds	20	8
Equities	70	12

A10. (Expected portfolio return) National Investment Corp. has invested its portfolio as shown below. What is National's expected portfolio return?

ASSET	PORTFOLIO WEIGHT	EXPECTED RETURN
Money market securities	25%	8%
Corporate bonds	30	12
Equities	45	9

LEVEL B

B1. (Realized return) Tim Burch sold some stock on September 11 for $52.50 per share. The stock paid him $1.05 per share in cash dividends on April 1 and July 1. He does not remember what he paid for the stock, but his investment advisor said he bought the stock on February 22 and had a 20% realized APY. What did Tim pay for the stock?

B2. (Realized return) Janet Todd sold some stock on December 7 for $22.75 per share. The stock paid her $0.35 per share in cash dividends on October 1. She does not remember what she paid for the stock, but her investment advisor said she bought the stock on September 11 and had a 50% realized APY. What did Janet pay for the stock?

B3. (Expected return and standard deviation) What is the expected return and standard deviation of the return for the next year on a stock that is selling for $30 now and has probabilities of 0.2, 0.6, and 0.2 of selling one year from now at $24, $33, and $39, respectively? Assume that no dividends will be paid on the stock during the next year and ignore taxes.

B4. (Expected return and standard deviation) What is the expected return and standard deviation of the return for the next year on a stock that is selling for $100 now and has probabilities of 0.3, 0.5, and 0.2 of selling one year from now at $92, $101, and $120, respectively? Assume no dividends will be paid on the stock during the next year and ignore taxes.

B5. (Expected return and risk) General Eclectic Corporation is considering three possible capital investment projects. The projected returns depend on the future state of the economy as given below.

a. Calculate each project's expected return, variance, and standard deviation.

b. Rank the projects on the basis of (1) expected return and (2) risk. Which project would you choose?

State of the Economy	Probability of Occurrence	PROJECTED RETURN 1	2	3
Recession	0.20	10%	8%	12%
Stable	0.60	15	13	10
Boom	0.20	21	25	8

B6. (Expected return and risk) Procter & Gamble is considering three possible capital investment projects. The projected returns depend on the future state of the economy as given below.

a. Calculate each project's expected return, variance, and standard deviation.

b. Rank the projects on the basis of (1) expected return and (2) risk. Which project would you choose?

State of the Economy	Probability of Occurrence	PROJECTED RETURN 1	2	3
Recession	0.1	9%	3%	15%
Stable	0.7	13	10	11
Boom	0.2	17	22	5

B7. (Realized return) Cynthia Campbell bought some stock on June 17 for $72.25 per share. The stock paid her $1.52 per share in cash dividends on July 1, October 1, and January 1. Cynthia sold the stock on February 14 and earned a 25% realized APY. For what price did Cynthia sell the stock?

B8. (Realized return) John Howe bought some stock on March 10 for $32.50 per share. The stock paid him $1.15 per share in cash dividends on April 1 and July 1. John sold the stock on September 22 and earned a 15% realized APY. For what price did John sell the stock?

B9. (Excel: Calculating means, standard deviations, covariance, and correlation) Given the probability distributions of returns for stock X and stock Y, compute:

a. the expected return for each stock, $\bar{x}$ and $\bar{y}$

b. the variance of the return for each stock

c. the covariance between the returns for stock X and stock Y

d. the correlation coefficient between the returns for stock X and stock Y.

Probability	RETURNS Stock X	Stock Y
0.1	−10%	4%
0.3	0	8
0.3	6	0
0.2	10	−5
0.1	20	15

B10. (Excel: Calculating means, standard deviations, covariance, and correlation) Given the probability distributions of returns for stock X and stock Y, compute:

a. the expected return for each stock, $\bar{x}$ and $\bar{y}$ here

b. the variance of the return for each stock

c. the covariance between the returns for stock X and stock Y

d. the correlation coefficient between the returns for stock X and stock Y.

Probability	RETURNS Stock X	Stock Y
0.2	5%	12%
0.2	10	10
0.4	12	8
0.15	14	0
0.05	18	2

B11. (Excel: Portfolio returns and standard deviations) ARC has an expected return of 9% and standard deviation of 10%, and HMT has an expected return of 12% and a standard deviation of 20%. The portfolio return and risk, of course, depend on the portfolio weights and the correlation between ARC and HMT returns. Calculate the portfolio returns and standard deviations for the weights and correlations shown in the table below:

WEIGHTS		PORTFOLIO	PORTFOLIO STANDARD DEVIATION FOR CORRELATIONS BELOW				
ARC	**HMT**	**RETURN**	**1.0**	**0.5**	**0.0**	**−0.5**	**−1.0**
1.0	0.0						
0.9	0.1						
0.8	0.2						
0.7	0.3						
0.6	0.4						
0.5	0.5						
0.4	0.6						
0.3	0.7						
0.2	0.8						
0.1	0.9						
0.0	1.0						

LEVEL C (ADVANCED)

C1. (Capital market line) Plot the 10 investment portfolio risks and returns given below.

a. Identify the efficient portfolios and plot the efficient frontier.

b. Suppose the riskless return is 10%. Which is the best portfolio?

c. Suppose you are prepared to experience a standard deviation of 10%. What is your best investment strategy? What is your expected return?

d. Suppose you are prepared to experience a standard deviation of 30%. What is your best investment strategy? What is your expected return?

PORTFOLIO	1	2	3	4	5	6	7	8	9	10
Expected return	10.0	12.0	7.5	8.3	6.1	13.2	14.1	7.9	9.2	13.1
Risk	15.5	18.7	14.3	17.2	22.3	23.0	25.2	17.1	16.7	23.4

C2. (Calculating expected returns, standard deviations, covariance, and correlation) The following table provides one full year of actual monthly returns for Microsoft Corp. (symbol MSFT) common stock and the S&P 500 Index. Compute:

a. the average monthly return for the market and for MSFT over these 12 months

b. the variance of the monthly return for each over these 12 months

c. the covariance between the returns for the market and MSFT over these 12 months

d. the correlation coefficient between the returns for the market and MSFT for these 12 months.

MONTH	MARKET (S&P 500)	MSFT	MONTH	MARKET (S&P 500)	MSFT
JAN	3.25%	5.58%	JUL	3.15%	−0.24%
FEB	−3.00	−3.08	AUG	3.76	12.86
MAR	−4.58	2.73	SEP	−2.69	−3.44
APR	1.16	9.14	OCT	2.08	12.25
MAY	1.24	16.22	NOV	−3.95	−0.20
JUN	−2.68	−3.95	DEC	1.23	−2.78

C3. (Portfolio returns and risk) There are four securities and five possible economic scenarios. The probability of occurrence and security returns are given below.

a. Calculate the expected return and standard deviation of returns for each security.
b. Calculate the correlation coefficient for each pair of securities.
c. Assuming the four securities are weighted equally, calculate the expected return to the portfolio and the standard deviation of the return to the portfolio.
d. Assuming 20% of the portfolio is invested in each of U.S. T-bills and government bonds and 30% is invested in each of corporate bonds and common stock, calculate the expected return to the portfolio and the standard deviation of the return to the portfolio.

STATE OF THE ECONOMY	PROBABILITY OF OCCURRENCE	U.S. T-BILLS	GOVERNMENT BONDS	CORPORATE BONDS	COMMON STOCK
High growth	0.10	6.0%	8.0%	10.0%	25.0%
Moderate growth	0.25	6.0	7.5	9.0	15.5
Slow growth	0.35	6.0	7.0	8.5	11.5
Stagnation	0.15	6.0	6.0	6.0	−1.0
Recession	0.15	6.0	4.0	−2.0	−11.5
	1.00				

C4. (Excel: Realized return) Wayne Ferson bought some stock on June 21 for $43.75 per share. The stock paid him $1.22 per share in cash dividends on July 1, October 1, and January 1. Wayne sold the stock on February 21 for $51.00 per share. What was Wayne's realized holding period APY?

C5. (Excel: Realized return) Nancy Jacobs bought some stock on March 5 for $13.00 per share. The stock paid her $0.32 per share in cash dividends on April 1, July 1, and October 1. Nancy sold the stock on December 25 for $31.25 per share. What was Nancy's realized holding period APY?

10

Risk and Return: Asset Pricing Models

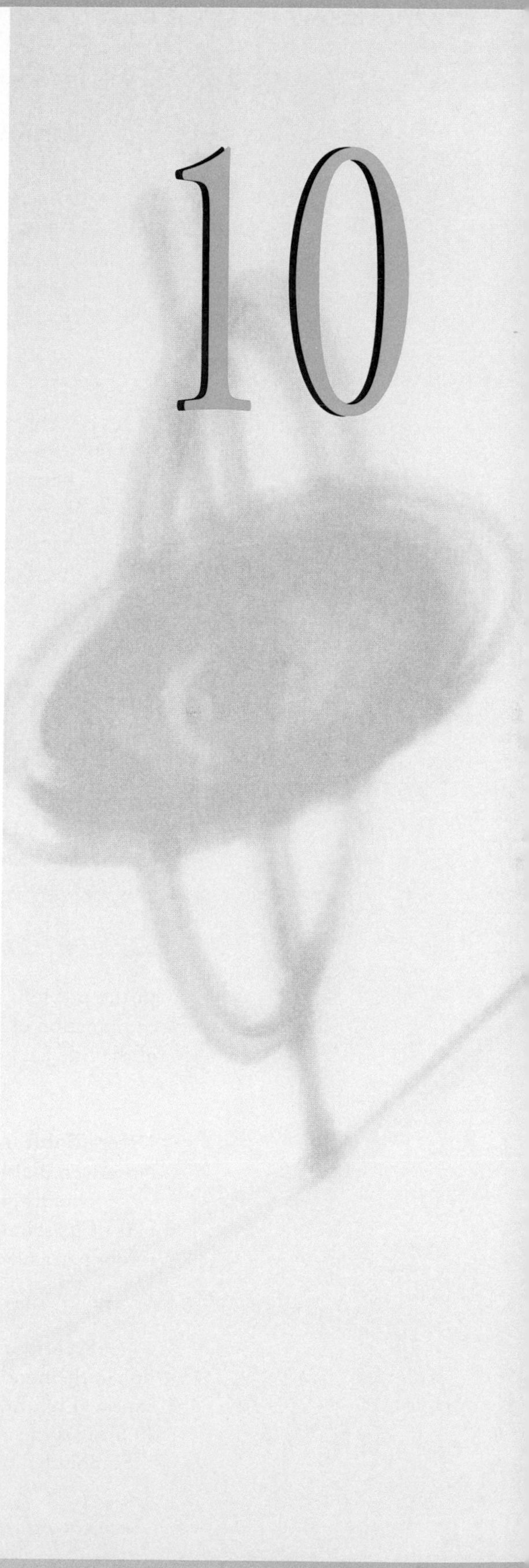

The Principle of Risk-Return Trade-Off says the greater the risk, the higher the required return. But how much higher for a particular amount of risk? Because a required return is an opportunity cost, sometimes we can use comparable investments to estimate a required return. But suppose there is no comparable investment. This was the case when COMSAT launched the first communications satellite. It could not look at comparable investments, because there were none! So what determines a required return?

This chapter builds on the previous chapter and develops an intuitively appealing model, called the *capital-asset-pricing model* (CAPM), for estimating required returns. In the CAPM, the required return is the riskless return *plus* a premium for the asset's risk:

$$\begin{matrix}\text{Required}\\ \text{return}\end{matrix} = \text{Riskless return} + \text{Beta}\left[\begin{matrix}\text{Market portfolio's}\\ \text{expected return}\end{matrix} - \text{Riskless return}\right]$$

The risk premium is a function of two variables. Beta (pronounced "bay-tah") measures the asset's incremental contribution to the risk of a diversified portfolio. Beta measures the asset's *market risk.* Beta reflects the correlation between an asset's returns and those of the market portfolio. The market portfolio's expected return minus the riskless return can be thought of as the price per risk unit. That is, it is the (additional) required return the market will pay you for bearing one unit of market risk.

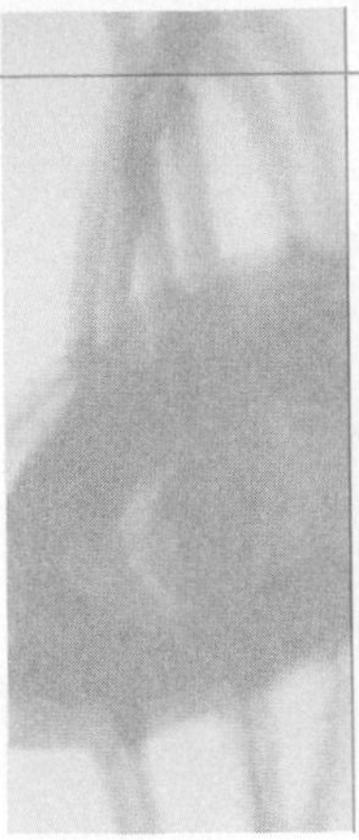

FOCUS ON PRINCIPLES

- *Diversification:* Invest in a group of assets, a *portfolio,* to reduce the total risk of your entire investment.
- *Risk-Return Trade-Off:* Invest in the amounts of the risky *market portfolio* and the *riskless asset* that provide the investment risk level you choose.
- *Efficient Capital Markets:* Estimate a security's risk and required return from its past realized returns.
- *Incremental Benefits:* Measure the incremental benefits from owning a security, which are its expected future cash flows.
- *Time Value of Money:* Determine the value of a security by computing the present value of its expected future cash flows.
- *Two-Sided Transactions:* Use a security's fair price to compute its expected return, because the fair price does not favor either side of the transaction.
- *Self-Interested Behavior:* Recognize that prices will be set by the highest bidder, because owners will sell to the highest bidder.
- *Valuable Ideas:* Look for innovative management or information services that might provide a positive NPV by creating value for capital market participants.

10.1 THE CAPITAL-ASSET-PRICING MODEL (CAPM)

The investment prescription developed in the previous chapter is to own a portfolio on the CML by investing in some mix of the market portfolio and the riskless asset. We arrived at this prescription without really saying much about the risk and return of the individual stocks. Now, we can do that by building on what we have learned. We can, in a sense, reverse our thought process; we can invert the CML. That is, we can ask, "What must a particular security's risk and expected return be, given the CML?"

Diversifiable and Nondiversifiable Risk

In the previous chapter, we showed that a portfolio's standard deviation is not a simple linear combination of its assets' standard deviations. The Principle of Diversification asserts itself. Some of the risk can be diversified away. So a security's specific risk is the sum of two parts:

$$\text{Specific risk} = \text{Diversifiable risk} + \text{Nondiversifiable risk} \tag{10.1}$$

Diversifiable risk (or *unsystematic risk*) is risk that can be eliminated by diversification. **Nondiversifiable risk** (or *systematic risk*) is risk that cannot be eliminated by diversification.

Nondiversifiable risk is really *market risk.* Therefore, a security's nondiversifiable risk is the part of its standard deviation that correlates with the market portfolio. So the nondiversifiable risk of particular security j is its correlation with the market times its standard deviation

$$\text{Nondiversifiable risk of security } j = [\text{Corr}(j,M)]\sigma_j$$

Security j's nondiversifiable risk is the amount of risk it contributes to the market portfolio. So the nondiversifiable risk sets its expected return. But how much does the market "pay" in expected return for taking on risk? The price for market risk is the slope of the CML, Equation (9.8). It is the amount of expected return per unit of risk. Therefore, security j's risk premium, the amount above the riskless return, is its nondiversifiable risk times the slope of the CML:

$$\text{Security } j\text{'s risk premium} = (\text{Nondiversifiable risk})(\text{CML slope}) = [\text{Corr}(j, M)]\sigma_j \left[\frac{r_M - r_f}{\sigma_M}\right]$$

This relationship is typically rearranged and expressed in terms of a variable, β_j, the Greek letter beta subscripted to identify the asset *j*:

$$\text{Security } j\text{'s risk premium} = [\text{Corr}(j, M)]\sigma_j\left[\frac{r_M - r_f}{\sigma_M}\right]$$

$$= \left[\frac{[\text{Corr}(j, M)]\sigma_j}{\sigma_M}\right](r_M - r_f) = \beta_j(r_M - r_f)$$

A stock's **beta** is a measure of its market—that is, nondiversifiable—risk. Beta can be expressed either in terms of Corr(*j*,*M*) or in terms of Cov(*j*,*M*):

$$\beta_j = \frac{\text{Corr}(j, M)\sigma_j}{\sigma_M} = \frac{\text{Corr}(j, M)\sigma_j\sigma_M}{\sigma_M\sigma_M} = \frac{\text{Cov}(j, M)}{\sigma_M^2} \qquad (10.2)$$

The Security Market Line

Security *j*'s total expected return, r_j, is the sum of the riskless return and its risk premium:

$$r_j = r_f + \beta_j(r_M - r_f) \qquad (10.3)$$

When the capital market is in equilibrium, Equation (10.3) is called the **security market line (SML).** Based on the Principle of Capital Market Efficiency, when in an equilibrium, the required return equals the expected return. Therefore, the SML also identifies the required return for security *j* that is implied by the CML. Let us compute an expected/required return.

EXAMPLE Computing an Expected Return

Suppose $r_f = 7\%$, Cov(*j*,*M*) = 250, $\sigma_M^2 = 225$, and $r_M = 15\%$. What is security *j*'s required return?

First, using Equation (10.2), β_j is 1.11:

$$\beta_j = \frac{\text{Cov}(j, M)}{\sigma_M^2} = \frac{250}{225} = 1.11$$

Second, using Equation (10.3), security *j*'s required return equals 15.88%:

$$r_j = r_f + \beta_j(r_M - r_f) = 7\% + 1.11(15\% - 7\%) = 15.88\%$$

The SML, Equation (10.3), expresses the security's return as thc sum of the riskless return and a risk premium. The risk premium is the product of two factors. The first is β_j (beta). The second is the market risk premium $(r_M - r_f)$, which is the slope of the SML.[1] The slope of the SML is the amount of return per unit of *nondiversifiable* (market) risk, just as the CML slope is the amount of return per unit of specific (total) risk. The greater the degree of collective risk aversion, the higher the market risk premium, and the steeper the slope of the SML.

[1]It is especially important to understand that beta is *not* the slope of the SML. Beta is the variable plotted along the horizontal axis in Figure 10.1.

FIGURE 10.1
The security market line on December 29, 2000.

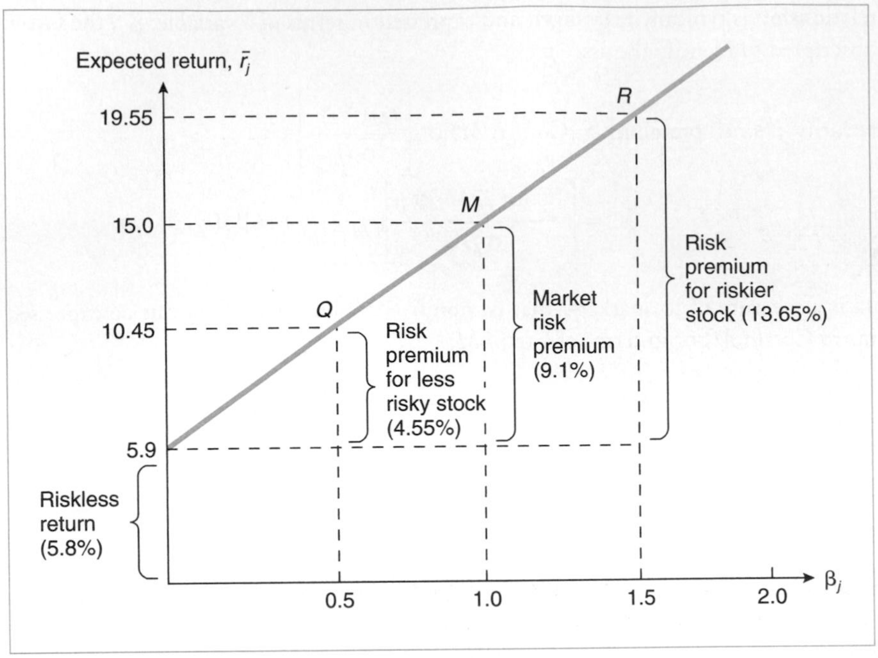

Figure 10.1 shows the SML as a function of β_j on December 29, 2000. The riskless return—the yield on three-month Treasury bills is used as the estimate—was 5.9%. The riskless return has a beta of zero, where the SML crosses the expected return (*y*) axis. The expected return on the market portfolio (which has a beta of 1.0) was 9.1%, which means that the market risk premium (slope) was 9.1% (= 15.0% − 5.9%). The return on the market portfolio is:

$$r_M = 5.9\% + (1.0)9.1\% = 15.0\%$$

EXAMPLE The Stock Market Risk-Return Trade-Off

What risk-return trade-off is reflected in Figure 10.1?

Riskier (higher beta) stocks have higher required returns. Consider point R, where $\beta_R = 1.50$. Using Equation (10.3), we find that

$$r_R = 5.9 + 1.5(9.1) = 19.55\%$$

Next consider point Q. Less risky (lower beta) stocks have lower required returns. Point Q has a beta of 0.50, and a required return of

$$r_Q = 5.9 + 0.5(9.1) = 10.45\%$$

In more general terms, a stock is a *capital asset.* The SML (in conjunction with the Principle of Capital Market Efficiency) prices stocks by specifying a required (equal to the expected) return. Can we generalize and use it to specify a required return to *any* capital asset? Yes, if the model is appropriate to the situation.

When we use the more general concept that *j* is a capital asset, rather than specifically a stock, Equation (10.3) becomes one form of what is called the **capital-asset-pricing model (CAPM).** Just as the name implies, it is a model for pricing capital assets. In it, an asset's required return is simply the sum of the riskless return and an asset-specific risk premium.

The CAPM is so simple, you might wonder why we go to such great lengths to explain it. The answer is that it shows that the appropriate risk adjustment is not immediately obvious. The risk adjustment in the CAPM is based on how an asset's return *covaries* with the return on the market portfolio. It shows how an individual asset contributes to the risk of an investor's total portfolio.

Review

1. What is the difference between diversifiable and nondiversifiable risk?
2. Does beta measure specific risk or market risk?
3. What is the SML?
4. What is the slope of the SML, and how is it a kind of "price" for risk?
5. What is the difference between the CML and the SML?

10.2 ESTIMATING AND USING THE CAPM

Suppose we knew every asset return distribution in the market and the covariance of each asset's return with the market portfolio's return. Then we could specify a required return for every asset using Equation (10.3). In practice, we do not have this information.

In applying the CAPM to real-world situations, we are taking it out of the perfect capital market environment in which it was derived. Nevertheless, the CAPM is still useful in estimating required returns. We can measure how stock returns vary with respect to the market portfolio's return by applying a statistical method called *linear regression.* We can express stock j's realized return, R_j, as a linear function of the realized market risk premium $(R_M - r_f)$, so that

$$R_j = r_f + \tilde{\beta}_j(R_M - r_f) \tag{10.4}$$

We use the tilde (~) to indicate that $\tilde{\beta}_j$ is a random variable.

To estimate β_j from historical data, collect a sample of simultaneous observations of R_j, R_M, and r_f. Then use Equation (10.4) to estimate the linear regression slope coefficient, β_j.

Linear regression is why the coefficient β_j came to be called the common stock's *beta.* Beta is a *linear measure* of how much an individual asset contributes to the market portfolio's standard deviation (specific risk). So an asset's beta is a simple, well-behaved measure of the asset's market risk.

EXAMPLE Computing a Beta

Table 10.1 provides a recent year of monthly returns for General Electric common stock (symbol GE) and the market (with the Standard & Poor's 500 Index as the market portfolio estimate). GE's beta is calculated by using linear regression to estimate Equation (10.4):

$$R_{GE,t} - r_{f,t} = \beta(R_{M,t} - r_{f,t}) + \varepsilon_t$$

where $R_{GE,t}$ is the realized return (including dividends) on GE during month t, $r_{f,t}$ is the realized return on Treasury bills during month t, $R_{M,t}$ is the realized return on the S&P 500 Index during month t, β is the regression coefficient, and ε_t is the error term. In this example, the y intercept is constrained to equal zero.

We applied ordinary least squares regression analysis (using the data regression function in a spreadsheet package). The estimated β coefficient for GE, based on this year of data, is 1.47.

TABLE 10.1
A recent year of monthly returns for General Electric common stock, the S&P 500 index, and treasury bills.

MONTH	GE	MARKET (S&P 500)	RISKLESS SECURITY	MONTH	GE	MARKET (S&P 500)	RISKLESS SECURITY
JAN	−13.41%	−5.36%	0.41%	JUL	−2.50%	−1.66%	0.48%
FEB	−1.22	2.05	0.43	AUG	13.42	5.72	0.50
MAR	17.56	8.82	0.47	SEP	−1.16	−5.65	0.51
APR	1.05	3.18	0.46	OCT	−5.19	−0.50	0.56
MAY	0.39	2.24	0.50	NOV	−9.58	−8.70	0.51
JUN	0.72	2.34	0.40	DEC	−2.95	0.40	0.50

Sources: *Bloomberg L.P.* and *Stocks, Bonds, Bills, and Inflation 2001 Yearbook* (Chicago, III.: Ibbotson Associates), p. 225.

FIGURE 10.2
A stock's characteristic line.

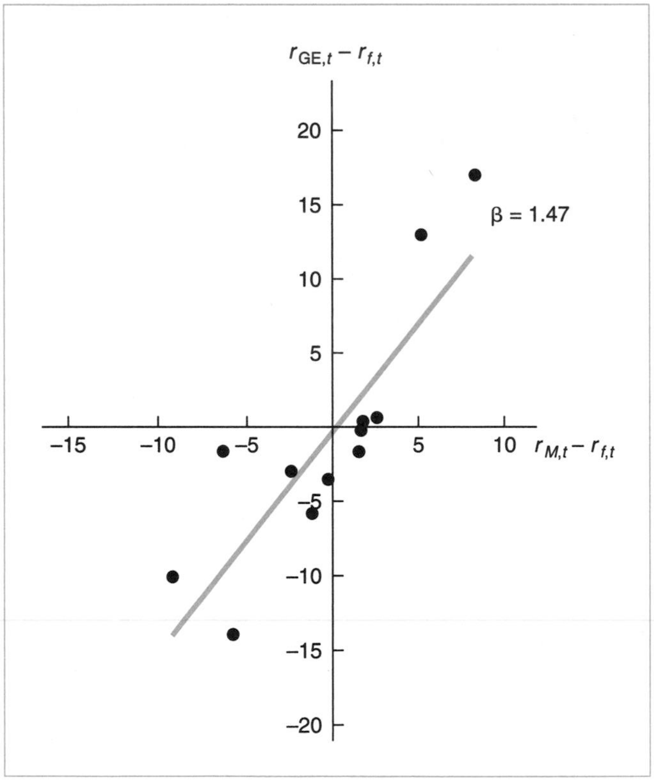

Figure 10.2 plots the regression equation. This plot is called the stock's **characteristic line.** A security's beta is thus the slope of the stock's characteristic line.

Most experts use a larger number of observations, although we used 12 monthly observations to simplify the example.

Table 10.2 shows the beta coefficients for a cross-section of 40 firms, many of which are familiar to you. (Having lunch at McDonald's anytime this week? Had a Coke lately?)

Beta indicates how sensitive a security's returns are to changes in the returns on the market portfolio. If a security's beta is 1.0, its returns tend to track the market portfolio. If the market portfolio increases or decreases by 10%, the stock also tends to move up or down by 10%.

TABLE 10.2
Beta coefficients for selected firms.

COMMON STOCK	BETA	COMMON STOCK	BETA
eBay Inc.	2.20	International Business Machines	1.05
Morgan Stanley Dean Witter	2.14	Walt Disney Company	1.05
Yahoo! Inc.	2.00	Ford Motor Company	1.01
Amazon.com	1.95	AT&T Corporation	1.00
Merrill Lynch & Co.	1.76	Dow Chemical	1.00
American Express	1.50	Neiman Marcus Group Inc. "A"	0.98
J.P. Morgan Chase & Co.	1.50	Berkshire Hathaway "A"	0.95
Cisco Systems	1.50	Merck & Co.	0.95
Home Depot	1.50	British Petroleum plc	0.90
Pearson Group plc	1.40	3M Company	0.90
General Electric	1.30	Coca-Cola	0.85
Intel Corporation	1.30	McDonald's Corporation	0.85
Nippon Telephone & Telegraph	1.21	Exxon Mobil	0.80
Hewlett-Packard	1.20	Nike, Inc. "B"	0.77
Microsoft Corporation	1.20	Procter & Gamble	0.65
DaimlerChrysler	1.15	Philip Morris Companies	0.65
Wal-Mart Stores	1.15	New York Times Co.	0.63
Boeing	1.10	Pfizer Inc.	0.58
General Motors	1.10	American Greetings Corp. "A"	0.41
Roche Holding AG	1.08	Idaho Corporation	0.36

Sources: *Bloomberg L.P.* and *Valueline Investment Survey.*

If a stock has a beta less than 1.0, it will tend to rise or fall less than the market. For example, suppose a stock has a beta of 0.5. If the market portfolio increases or decreases by 10%, the stock will tend to move up or down only 5%.

A stock with a beta greater than 1.0 will rise or fall more than the market. For example, a stock with a beta of 1.5 will tend to rise or fall by 15% when the market portfolio increases or decreases 10%. Values of beta for most common stocks fall within the range from 0.75 to 1.50.

Take note that beta can be negative. Accordingly, an asset with a negative beta can have a required return that is *less* than the riskless return. At first glance, this seems counterintuitive: How can any asset have an expected return that is less than the riskless return?

Remember, these are assets held in a fully diversified portfolio, the market portfolio. Therefore, the measure of risk for the individual asset depends on how the standard deviation of the portfolio return changes when that asset is added to the portfolio. When a negative-beta asset is added to the market portfolio, it actually lowers the market portfolio's standard deviation. So although the notion of negative risk is counterintuitive, it makes sense in this context.

Arbitrage and the SML

As the name *security market line* suggests, the [beta/expected return] combinations of all securities in the market portfolio must lie along the SML. Consider a security l whose [beta/expected return] combination lies below the SML, as represented by the point l in Figure 10.3. Would anyone want to invest in asset l? No.

There is an asset whose [beta/expected return] combination, located at l' on the SML, is superior. Asset l' has the same β as asset l. Thus, both contribute identically to portfolio risk. However, asset l' has a higher expected return. In a perfect capital market, an asset such as l

FIGURE 10.3
The SML and arbitrage.

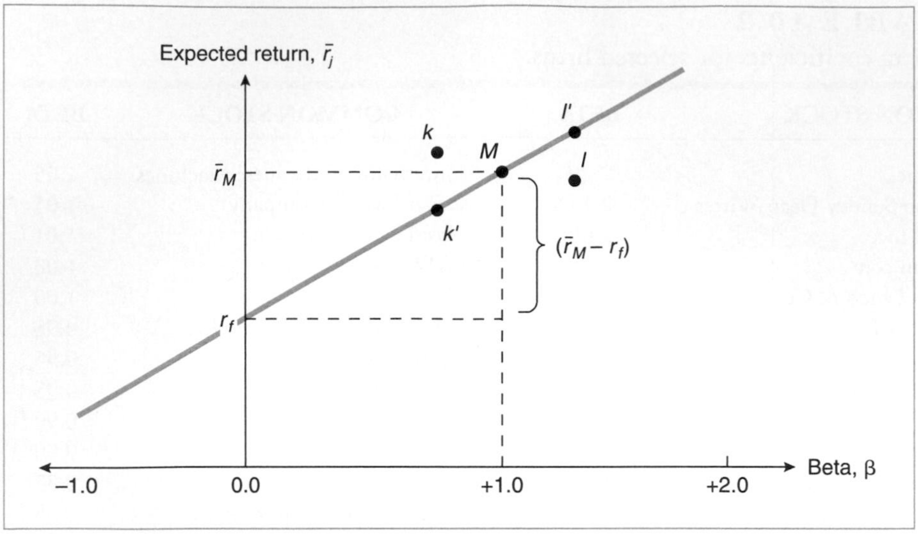

would give rise to an *arbitrage opportunity.* Investors could earn an *arbitrage profit,* without changing their portfolio's risk, by selling l short and buying asset l'.

Selling short is borrowing a security and selling it with the expectation of buying it back later at a lower price (to make a profit). Brokerage firms arrange the borrowing from the pool of securities investors have invested with them. Selling short is "owing" the stock, whereas buying long is owning the stock. The expected profit from the short sale is based on how large a position the investor takes and the size of the difference, $r_{l'} - r_l$.

How long would such an arbitrage opportunity continue to exist? Until the price of asset l has been driven down to such an extent that the [beta/expected return] combination for asset l shifts up to the SML. That is, until the [beta/expected return] combinations for assets l and l' are equal.

Can a security whose [beta/expected return] combination lies above the SML, such as security k depicted in Figure 10.3, exist for long? Again, not in a perfect capital market. Investors would purchase asset k and sell asset k' short, thereby earning an arbitrage profit without changing their portfolio's risk. The expected profit is based on the spread $r_k - r_{k'}$. Arbitrage activity would continue until the market value of the asset k had been driven up to such an extent that the [beta/expected return] combination for asset k shifts down to the SML.

In a perfect capital market environment, one with no impediments to arbitrage activity (no restrictions on short selling, for example), the [beta/expected return] combinations for all securities *and* for all portfolios of securities must lie along the SML.

Approximating the Market Portfolio

We previously cited the law of large numbers as a justification for using the mean of the distribution to represent a portfolio's expected return. The concept of large numbers, and more specifically random samples, can also be used here. The law of large numbers can help determine an accurate approximation of the market portfolio.

When we want to estimate the unknown mean of a probability distribution, we compute the sample mean for a reasonably large random sample. And the definition of "large" does not necessarily depend on the size of the underlying population. A large sample in statistics may contain only 25 to 30 independent observations.

Therefore, we can predict that the realized return to a portfolio of approximately equal investments in 25 to 30 *randomly* chosen stocks will be consistently close to the market portfolio's realized return. And, in fact, this result has been shown empirically countless times. The accuracy

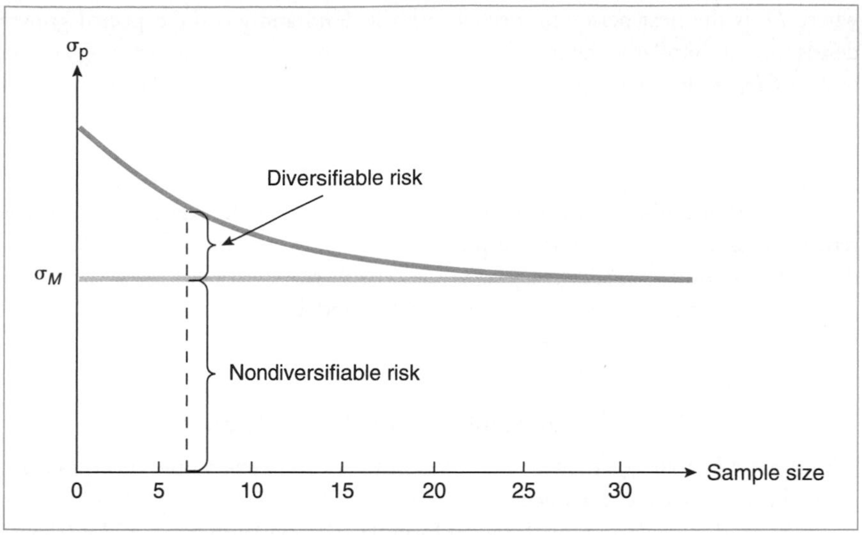

FIGURE 10.4
Portfolio standard deviation as a function of portfolio size.

of this approximation depends on the size of the random sample. Figure 10.4 graphs portfolio standard deviation as a function of the number of randomly selected securities in the portfolio. As the number of securities increases, the portfolio standard deviation approaches the market standard deviation, which is the nondiversifiable risk level. If the number of securities is not large, the extra risk borne by the portfolio is its diversifiable risk.

Prices Are Set by Diversified Investors

Figure 10.4 is another way of showing how diversification reduces portfolio risk. Recall that every asset has both diversifiable and nondiversifiable risk. Adding securities reduces diversifiable risk. Look back at Equation (10.4). The market compensates investors only for taking on nondiversifiable risk. It will not pay them for taking on diversifiable risk. Why is this?

Nondiversified investors will be taking more risk than diversified investors. For nondiversified investors, the added (diversifiable) risk lowers the value of, and the price they should pay for, the security. Diversified investors will be taking less risk and can afford to pay more for the security. People wanting to sell the security will follow the Principle of Self-Interested Behavior and sell to the highest bidders—diversified investors. Therefore, the market price will reflect the security's higher value to diversified investors.

This point can be seen in another way. With a large number of assets, such as in the U.S. stock market, it is both easy and relatively inexpensive to diversify. So U.S. investors are not able to require compensation for diversifiable risk when they can easily (and virtually costlessly) eliminate it. In other words, investors can choose whether to take on diversifiable risk. Consequently, they cannot require payment for taking it on.

What Happens If You Do Not Diversify?

The constant growth model (Chapter 5) offers a method of converting a stock's required return, r, into its market value. Let us use the constant growth model to value a security for two prospective buyers. One investor will add this to a diversified portfolio. The other will invest only in this security. The security's value to the diversified investor, P, can be expressed as

$$P = \frac{D_1}{r - g}$$

where D_1 is the next period's expected cash dividend and g is the expected growth rate of dividends forever. Similarly, the security's value to the nondiversified investor, P_n, can be expressed in terms of D_1, g, and the required rate of return to the nondiversified investor, r_n, as

$$P_n = \frac{D_1}{r_n - g}$$

The relationship between P_n and P is determined by the relationship between the required returns, r_n and r. Equation (10.3) expresses r in terms of nondiversifiable risk. However, r_n reflects the security's nondiversifiable risk *plus* its diversifiable risk. Therefore, its risk premium will be larger, and r_n will be larger than r_j. Consequently, with g and D_1 identical in both cases, P_n is less than P.

EXAMPLE Stock Value and Investor Diversification

Suppose $r = 10\%$, $r_n = 14\%$, $D_1 = \$2$, and $g = 5\%$. How would diversified and nondiversified investors value this stock?

From the dividend growth model formula, $P = \$40$ and $P_n = \$22.22$. The value of the security to the diversified investor is greater than it is to the nondiversified investor.

But what about the value to the seller of the stock? Following the Principle of Self-Interested Behavior, sellers will sell to the highest bidder. In a bidding competition between diversified and nondiversified purchasers, diversified investors can "afford to" bid a higher price. Therefore, observed stock prices reflect the higher value that diversified investors are willing to pay for the shares. Nondiversified investors who are going to purchase shares must pay the higher (diversified) price.

A nondiversified investor, then, faces three alternatives: (1) do not invest in the stock, (2) receive a lower return (by paying a higher price) than is appropriate for the risk, or (3) diversify. We need to emphasize that under the second alternative, nondiversified investors *must* pay the higher prices appropriate for a diversified investor. Otherwise, they will be outbid. And this holds even if there are a sizable number of nondiversified investors.

This is a striking example of the robustness of the conclusions of the CAPM. It is assumed that all investors invest in the market portfolio. However, even if that assumption is violated, competition ensures that *prices will be set as though all investors did invest in the market portfolio.*

A WORD OF WARNING The CAPM appears to work reasonably well in most situations. However, there are two situations we must warn you about. The CAPM tends to *understate* the required return for common stocks of firms that are *small* or are *highly leveraged* (a firm with a comparatively large proportion of debt financing). Using the CAPM in such situations requires adjustments for these effects. The bibliography, available at our web site, contains sources for learning more about these issues and how to make such adjustments.

Review

1. Is all the information we need for using the CAPM readily available?
2. Do returns on a stock with a beta greater than 1.0 tend to vary more or less than the market return?
3. If you cannot duplicate the market portfolio exactly, how can you approximate it?
4. Why is it that prices are set by diversified investors?

10.3 MULTIFACTOR MODELS

An important assumption underlying the CAPM is that the mean and standard deviation contain all relevant information about an asset's future return. But suppose there is more to an asset's expected return? Essentially, the CAPM says an asset's expected return depends on a single factor: the market portfolio's expected return. But what if other factors affect required returns?

Consider the return on the common stock of a firm, GIOC (for Great Investment Opportunity Corporation). The return on GIOC stock can be expressed as the sum of two components, the riskless return r_f, plus an uncertain, or risky component, which we will call R (for risky). Letting r_G represent the return on GIOC stock, we have

$$r_G = r_f + R$$

The uncertain component R is affected by a variety of factors. Some factors affect all firms, whereas others are specific to GIOC (and perhaps a handful of similar firms). To be perfectly general, suppose that there are K independent factors that contribute to nondiversifiable risk. In that case, the stock return would be expressed by a *multifactor model:*

$$r_G = r_f + R(F_1, F_2, \ldots, F_K) + \varepsilon \qquad (10.5)$$

where F_k denotes factor k ($k = 1, 2, \ldots, K$), $R(F_1 \ldots)$ is some function of the factors, and ε denotes the incremental return due to nondiversifiable risk.

Review

1. How does a multifactor model differ from the CAPM?

10.4 ARBITRAGE PRICING THEORY

Equation (10.5) is a more general model of a required return than the CAPM. But exactly what do the F_k's consist of? And what does the function $R(F_1 \ldots)$ look like? There is considerable debate about these questions. For example, are multiple factors being approximated by the market portfolio's expected return in the CAPM, thereby masking the *true* determinants of a required return? At this point, no single opinion has emerged.

There is, however, one model that has received considerable attention because it relaxes the assumption of a single determinant. This alternative model is called the **arbitrage pricing theory (APT).** As the name implies, the APT relies on the concept of arbitrage. It is a model based on a market that is in equilibrium and free of arbitrage opportunities.

A Multifactor Linear Model

Like the CAPM, the APT is built on the Principle of Capital Market Efficiency. The APT simply represents an alternative approach to securities valuation within the same framework. The APT relates asset returns within a multivariate framework in which the return relationships are linear.

Although the APT takes the Principle of Capital Market Efficiency as its starting point, it does not attempt to specify any particular set of determinants on the basis of conceptual arguments. Instead, the APT asserts that an asset's expected return depends on a linear combination of some set of factors. The factors must be identified empirically.

Thus far, in empirical tests of the APT, a variety of different factors have emerged as possible determinants of actual common stock returns. A statistical method called *factor analysis* has been used to attempt to identify relevant factors.[2]

The APT model looks strikingly like an "extended" CAPM. However, it is derived in a very different way. We will not derive the APT model here, but we will show you its operational form:

$$r_j = r_f + \beta_{j1}(r_{f1} - r_f) + \beta_{j2}(r_{f2} - r_f) + \cdots + \beta_{jK}(r_{jK} - r_f) \tag{10.6}$$

where K is the number of factors that affect an asset's return; $r_{f1}, r_{f2}, \ldots, r_{fK}$ are the expected returns to factors 1, 2, . . . , K, respectively; and $\beta_{j1}, \beta_{j2}, \ldots, \beta_{jK}$, are the asset's sensitivities to factors 1, 2, . . . , K, respectively. APT formulations typically include the market risk premium, the sole factor in the CAPM, as an explanatory variable.

The APT, then, is a multifactor model of the general form of Equation (10.5). The F_k's are identified empirically, by assuming $R(F_1 \ldots)$ is a simple linear function.

Applications

To illustrate the APT, let us assume there are five relevant factors: confidence risk, time horizon risk, inflation risk, business-cycle risk, and market-timing risk. The expected returns to the five factors are, respectively, 2.70%, −0.70%, −4.30%, 1.50%, and 3.60%. Note that the respective impact of each factor is incremental to the impact of the other factors. The size of this impact depends on the asset's factor sensitivity and the expected return to the factor. The factor sensitivities and the returns to each factor are identified empirically.

EXAMPLE Applying the APT

Suppose the riskless return is 4% and the factor sensitivities and factor returns for Merck are given here:

RISK FACTOR	MERCK'S FACTOR SENSITIVITY	EXPECTED FACTOR RETURNS
Confidence risk	0.18	2.70%
Time horizon risk	0.66	−0.70%
Inflation risk	−0.20	−4.30%
Business-cycle risk	1.20	1.50%
Market-timing risk	0.75	3.60%

Using Equation (10.6), the required return for Merck should be:

$$\begin{aligned} r_{\text{MERCK}} &= 4.0\% + 0.18(2.70\%) + 0.66(-0.70\%) - 0.20(-4.30\%) + 1.20(1.50\%) \\ &\quad + 0.75(3.60\%) \\ r_{\text{MERCK}} &= 9.04\% \end{aligned}$$

Merck's required return is slightly over 9%.

[2]One of the difficulties that arises with this research is that, in some cases, the quantified factors have not appeared to be associated with identifiable real-world factors. That is, some quantified factors cannot be identified as something familiar, such as a measure of inflation or unemployment.

APT Versus the CAPM

As a practical matter, the APT is simply an alternative model that describes actual stock returns about as well as the CAPM. The CAPM endures probably because it is relatively simple and it was the first one put forth. Alternatives have not provided significantly better descriptions of realized returns. Neither have they provided such an increase in understanding that one of them is unequivocally superior in a conceptual sense. Perhaps the market risk premium adequately incorporates the effect of the plausible alternative factors. Perhaps additional factors are yet to be identified. Or, maybe the return relationships are significantly nonlinear. Hopefully, future research will eventually answer these important questions.

Review

1. Describe the meaning and significance of the arbitrage pricing theory (APT).
2. How does the APT differ from the CAPM? In what sense is it an "extended CAPM"?
3. How is the APT applied in practice?

10.5 INTERNATIONAL CONSIDERATIONS

There are many multinational firms making investments in more than one country. Should the required return on such foreign investments be greater than the required return on an otherwise identical domestic investment? Many believe a risk premium should be added when evaluating foreign investments, because of higher economic and political risks. This could be a mistake because an international investment's required return may actually be *less* than that for an otherwise identical domestic investment.

International Diversification

Just as firms invest internationally, investors purchase both domestic and foreign securities. We know that the relevant risk for pricing an asset is its nondiversifiable risk.

Suppose there is a single world capital market. In such a market, most of the economic and political risk is specific to the investment and can be eliminated by diversification. Consequently, investors face the same nondiversifiable risk on a foreign investment as on an otherwise identical domestic project. Therefore, the required return for the two projects would be the same. We could still use the CAPM, but *M* would be a **world market portfolio.** It would include all the capital assets in the world. Beta would be based on the world market portfolio return.

Now let us consider the opposite of a single world market. Suppose the various national capital markets are essentially separated and investors mostly purchase domestic stocks in their own countries. Suppose you get a chance to make either a domestic or foreign investment. The investments are otherwise identical. Because the Principle of Diversification does not depend on national boundaries, you may be better off making the international investment.

International investment has two benefits: (1) the "basic" required return may be lower than that from an otherwise identical domestic investment, and (2) there are potential risk-reducing benefits from international diversification. With separated capital markets, investors may not be able to get this specific diversification in other ways. In such a case, therefore, the foreign investment may be more valuable than the otherwise identical domestic investment.

International Opportunities

In reality, the world capital markets are not fully integrated. Certain countries have restrictions. And, in practice, U.S. investors have not invested very much internationally. We do not know why. Possible factors include problems obtaining foreign financial information,[3] foreign tax considerations, costs of converting currencies, higher transaction costs, expropriation risk, as well as legal and other forms of political risk. But things seem to be changing.

In recent years, U.S. financial institutions have increased their foreign investing. In addition, many foreign firms have listed their shares on the NYSE. Mutual funds have been created that invest in firms located in a specific region (for example, there are several Latin American funds) or in a particular country (there are dozens of country funds, including funds investing in Argentina, India, Korea, Mexico, and Spain). These changes have made it easier and less expensive for Americans to make foreign investments.

Unfortunately, the "bottom line" is that we do not have an exact formula for a foreign investment's required return. However, we can say that it is *not* the required return for an otherwise identical domestic investment plus a "tacked-on" risk premium.

Review

1. Describe what is meant by the term *world market portfolio.*
2. Should a foreign investment have an extra risk premium added to its required return compared to a domestic investment?

SUMMARY

The risk-return trade-off is fundamental to many business and personal decisions.

- For diversified investors, the proper measure of a stock's risk is its nondiversifiable risk, not its specific risk. Nondiversifiable risk is also called market risk or systematic risk. A stock's required return is based on its nondiversifiable risk.
- The capital-asset-pricing model (CAPM) expresses the required return as the riskless return plus a risk premium. The risk premium is a function of two variables, the investment's beta and the market price of risk. Beta is a measure of market risk. Beta is the covariance between the security's return and the market return divided by the variance of the market portfolio's future return. The market price of risk is the difference between the expected market return and the riskless return.
- The CAPM expresses an asset's required return as the riskless return plus a risk premium

$$r_j = r_f + \beta_j(r_M - r_f)$$

where r_j is the expected return on security j, r_f is the riskless return, β_j is the security's beta, and r_M is the expected return on the market portfolio.
- The CAPM prices only nondiversifiable risk. U.S. investors can easily eliminate diversifiable risk at low cost. Therefore, stock prices reflect the stock's value to diversified investors.
- Beta can be estimated using linear regression. Many analytical services provide beta estimates for actively traded common stocks.
- The market portfolio includes all assets. In practice, a stock market index, such as the S&P 500, is used as a proxy for the market portfolio.
- The CAPM appears to work reasonably well in most situations. However, there is evidence that it tends to *understate* the required return for the common shares of firms that

[3]Foreign countries generally impose less exacting disclosure requirements than exist in the United States.

are *small* or are *highly leveraged* (a firm with a comparatively large proportion of debt financing). Using the CAPM in such situations requires adjustments for these effects.

- International investing may provide benefits from diversification. A foreign investment's required return is not found by "tacking on" an additional risk premium to the required return for an otherwise identical domestic investment.

EQUATION SUMMARY

$$\text{Specific risk} = \text{Diversifiable risk} + \text{Nondiversifiable risk} \tag{10.1}$$

$$\beta_j = \frac{\text{Corr}(j,M)\sigma_j}{\sigma_M} = \frac{\text{Corr}(j,M)\sigma_j\sigma_M}{\sigma_M\sigma_M} = \frac{\text{Cov}(j,M)}{\sigma_M^2} \tag{10.2}$$

$$r_j = r_f + \beta_j(r_M - r_f) \tag{10.3}$$

$$R_j = r_f + \tilde{\beta}_j(R_M - r_f) \tag{10.4}$$

$$r_G = r_f + R(F_1, F_2, \ldots, F_K) + \varepsilon \tag{10.5}$$

$$r_j = r_f + \beta_{j1}(r_{f1} - r_f) + \beta_{j2}(r_{f2} - r_f) + \cdots + \beta_{jK}(r_{jK} - r_f) \tag{10.6}$$

QUESTIONS

1. Define *beta* and briefly describe what it measures.
2. What does the term *market price of risk* mean?
3. Common stock A has an expected return of 10%, a standard deviation of future returns of 25%, and a beta of 1.25. Common stock B has an expected return of 12%, a standard deviation of future returns of 15%, and a beta of 1.50. Which stock is riskier? Explain.
4. a. Define the term *capital market line, CML.*
   b. Define the term *security market line, SML.*
   c. What is the difference between the CML and the SML?
5. Describe the CAPM.
6. What is a *characteristic line*?
7. What is the difference between diversifiable risk and nondiversifiable risk?
8. Why is it that the market will pay an investor for taking on nondiversifiable risk, but will not pay an investor for taking on diversifiable risk?
9. What is a *world market portfolio?*

CHALLENGING QUESTIONS

10. Respond to the following statement: First you say σ measures the risk of investing. Then you say β measures the risk of investing. Which is right?
11. Explain why a foreign investment project might have a lower required return than an otherwise identical domestic project.

12. According to the CAPM, an asset with a beta of zero has a required return equal to the riskless return, r_f. Does this mean that the asset is riskless? Can an asset with a positive standard deviation of return, σ, have a beta of zero?
13. Suppose r_f is 5% and r_M is 10%. According to the SML and the CAPM, an asset with a beta of -2.0 has a required return of ***negative*** 5% (= 5 − 2[10 − 5]). Can this be possible? Does this mean that the asset has negative risk? Why would anyone ever invest in an asset that has an expected and required return that is negative? Explain.

PROBLEMS

LEVEL A (BASIC)

A1. (Calculating beta) What is the beta of a stock whose covariance with the market portfolio return is 0.0045 if the variance of the return on the market portfolio is 0.002?

A2. (Calculating beta) What is the beta of a stock whose covariance with the market portfolio return is 0.0068 if the variance of the return on the market portfolio is 0.008?

A3. (Calculating beta) Malhotra Computers has a standard deviation of monthly returns of 9% and has a 0.70 correlation with market returns. The standard deviation of market monthly returns is 6%. What is Malhotra's beta?

A4. (Calculating beta) Colorado Delivery Services, Inc. has a standard deviation of monthly returns of 11% and has a 0.85 correlation with market returns. The standard deviation of market monthly returns is 7%. What is Colorado Delivery Services' beta?

A5. (Required return) According to the CAPM, what would be the required return on an asset that has a beta of 1.35 when the expected return on the market portfolio is 12% and the riskless return is 7%?

A6. (Required return) According to the CAPM, what would be the required return on an asset that has a beta of 1.25 when the expected return on the market portfolio is 12% and the riskless return is 5%?

A7. (Market price of risk) The market portfolio has an expected return of 12.4% and a standard deviation of 20%. The riskless return is 4.4%.
   a. What is the market price of risk $(r_M - r_f)$?
   b. What is the slope of the capital market line (which is the price of market risk divided by the standard deviation of the market return)?

A8. (Market price of risk) The market portfolio has an expected return of 14% and a standard deviation of 15%. The riskless return is 5%.
   a. What is the market price of risk $(r_M - r_f)$?
   b. What is the slope of the capital market line (which is the price of market risk divided by the standard deviation of the market return)?

LEVEL B

B1. (Beta) What is the beta of an asset whose correlation coefficient with the market portfolio's returns is 0.62 and variance is 0.1 if the variance of the market portfolio's return is 0.0025?

B2. (Beta) What is the beta of an asset whose correlation coefficient with the market portfolio's returns is 0.80 and variance is 0.12 if the variance of the market portfolio's return is 0.04?

B3. (CAPM) The required return on an asset with a beta of 1.4 is 17% and the riskless rate of return is 7%. What is the expected return on the market portfolio?

B4. (CAPM) The required return on an asset with a beta of 0.95 is 7.9% and the riskless rate of return is 6%. What is the expected return on the market portfolio?

B5. (CAPM) Suppose the expected return and variance of the market portfolio are 0.11 and 0.0016, respectively. If the riskless return is 0.06, what will be the required return on a stock whose return variance is 0.12 and correlation with the market portfolio's returns is 0.46?

B6. (CAPM) Suppose the expected return and variance of the market portfolio are 0.15 and 0.002, respectively. If the riskless return is 0.055, what will be the required return on a stock whose return variance is 0.12 and correlation with the market portfolio's returns is 0.6?

B7. (CAPM) What is the beta of a stock when its expected return is 15%, its standard deviation of return is 25%, its correlation coefficient with the market is 0.2, and the return to the market portfolio is 14% with a standard deviation of 4%? Assuming the market for this stock is in equilibrium, what is the riskless return that is implied by the information given?

B8. (CAPM) What is the beta of a stock when its expected return is 30%, its standard deviation of return is 32%, its correlation coefficient with the market is 0.4, and the return to the market portfolio is 22% with a standard deviation of 8%? Assuming the market for this stock is in equilibrium, what is the riskless return that is implied by the information given?

B9. (CAPM) Stock A has a beta of 2.0 and a required return of 15%. The market return is 10%. What will be the required return on stock B, which has a beta of 1.4?

B10. (CAPM) Stock A has a beta of 1.4 and a required return of 18.5%. The market return is 15%. What will be the required return on stock B, which has a beta of 1.9?

B11. (CAPM) Not-So-Swift Meat Processors is considering building a new meat processing facility in Omaha, Nebraska. Not-So-Swift has 75 million common shares outstanding. The share price is $25. Assume $r_f = 6.5\%$, $\beta = 0.95$, and $r_M - r_f = 8.4\%$. Estimate Not-So-Swift's required return on its equity investment in the new facility.

B12. (CAPM) Owego Storage and Housing, Inc. is considering building a new warehouse in Endicott, New York. Owego Storage has 2 million common shares outstanding. The share price is $11. Assume $r_f = 4.5\%$, $\beta = 0.75$, and $r_M - r_f = 11.5\%$. Estimate Owego Storage's required return on its equity investment in the new warehouse.

B13. (CAPM) The riskless return is 6% and the expected market return is 14%. The market standard deviation is 20% and the standard deviation for Uplift stock is 36%. The correlation between market and Uplift returns is 0.80.

a. What is the beta for shares of Uplift stock?

b. Using the CAPM, what is the required return on Uplift?

B14. (Excel: Plotting GE's characteristic line) Obtain 50 observations of recent return data for General Electric, the S&P 500, and Treasury bills from a reputable source, for example, Value Line Investment Survey, Bloomberg L.P., *Stocks, Bonds, Bills, and Inflation Yearbook*, CRSP, or your professor. Plot the regression equation and estimate General Electric's required return.

LEVEL C (ADVANCED)

C1. (Beta and required return) The riskless return is currently 6%, and Chicago Gear has estimated the contingent returns given here.

a. Calculate the expected returns on the stock market and on Chicago Gear stock.

b. What is Chicago Gear's beta?

c. What is Chicago Gear's required return according to the CAPM?

		REALIZED RETURN	
State of the Market	**Probability that State Occurs**	**Stock Market**	**Chicago Gear**
Stagnant	0.20	(10%)	(15%)
Slow growth	0.35	10	15
Average growth	0.30	15	25
Rapid growth	0.15	25	35

C2. (Arbitrage pricing theory) Suppose the riskless return is 4.5% and the factor sensitivities and factor returns for BioTherm and the S&P 500 Index are given below. Using the APT, what should be the required returns for BioTherm shares and for the S&P 500 Stock Index?

RISK FACTOR	BIOTHERM FACTOR SENSITIVITY	S&P 500 FACTOR SENSITIVITY	EXPECTED FACTOR RETURNS
Confidence risk	0.15	0.30	2.70%
Time horizon risk	0.70	0.56	−0.70%
Inflation risk	−0.40	−0.35	−4.30%
Business-cycle risk	1.45	1.75	1.50%
Market-timing risk	1.20	1.00	3.60%

C3. (Excel: Beta and required return) Will Eatem, a portfolio manager for the Conservative Retirement Equity Fund (CREF), is considering investing in the common stock of Big Caesar's Pizza (stock symbol PIES). His analysts have compiled the return data given here.

a. Calculate the beta coefficient for PIES.

b. The riskless return is 6% and the market risk premium is 8.4%. Plot the SML.

c. You have recently met with the management of PIES. You are favorably impressed, and you estimate that the stock will earn a return of 19% over the next 12 months. Should you invest in PIES?

YEAR	1	2	3	4	5	6	7	8	9	10
S&P 500	−10.2	5.8	12.2	−7.3	−1.5	10.5	8.3	15.7	−2.1	8.6
PIES	−5.3	13.2	6.1	2.1	−8.8	15.7	3.9	12.6	−7.3	10.2

C4. (Excel: Calculating beta from historical returns) Many analysts subtract the riskless return from the market and security returns and use these excess returns to calculate betas. Use this convention for this problem. The following table provides the monthly returns for Exxon Mobil common stock (symbol XOM) and the market as approximated by the S&P 500 Index for a recent year. Compute the following.

a. The average monthly return for the market and for XOM over these 12 months.

b. The variance of the monthly return for each over these 12 months.

c. The covariance between the returns for the market and XOM over these 12 months.

d. The correlation coefficient between the returns for the market and XOM for these 12 months.

e. The beta for XOM using linear regression for these 12 months.

MONTH	MARKET (S&P 500)	XOM	RISKLESS SECURITY	MONTH	MARLET (S&P 500)	XOM	RISKLESS SECURITY
JAN	3.25%	5.35%	0.25%	JUL	3.15%	4.85%	0.28%
FEB	−3.00	−1.36	0.21	AUG	3.76	1.21	0.37
MAR	−4.58	−4.15	0.27	SEP	−2.69	−4.52	0.37
APR	1.16	0.00	0.27	OCT	2.08	9.35	0.38
MAY	1.24	−1.64	0.32	NOV	−3.95	−2.78	0.37
JUN	−2.68	−8.24	0.31	DEC	1.23	−0.61	0.44

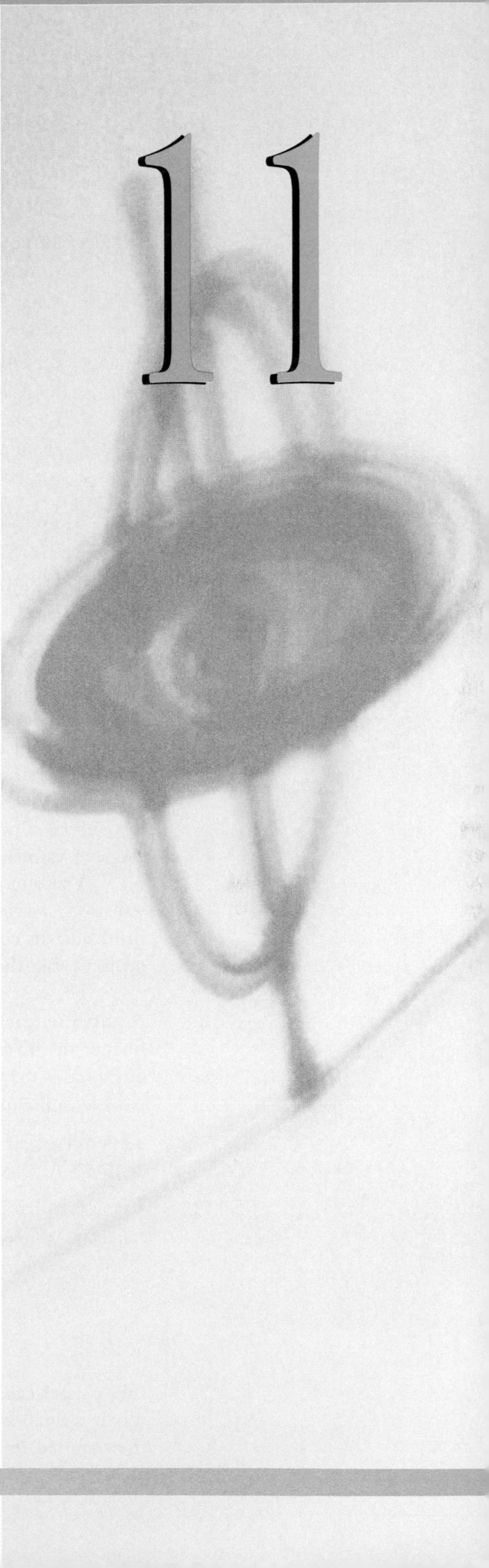

11

Risk, Return, and Capital Budgeting

In Chapter 1, we described the investment-vehicle model. In that model, the firm's managers are intermediaries who act only in the best interest of the shareholders. In such a world, the firm is simply a conduit for shareholders to invest in the firm's assets. Figure 1.4 in Chapter 1 shows this "investment-pass-through" effect.

In a perfect capital market environment, the cost of capital—a capital budgeting project's required return—would be the investors' required return for investing in the firm's assets. The required return is perfectly "passed through" from investors to the firm's choice of assets—its capital budgeting decisions. In other words, the cost of capital would be the investors' required return for the project. Because of this, and the Principle of Capital Market Efficiency, we start our analysis of the cost of capital assuming a perfect capital market environment. Subsequently, in Part IV, we examine how capital market imperfections affect the cost of capital.

Another way to view the cost of capital is to say it is an opportunity cost. If a firm undertakes a project, it creates an opportunity cost: It gives up the chance to make other investments—including investments in publicly traded financial securities. So the cost of capital is the required return on comparable publicly traded securities.[1] In this chapter, we use the idea of comparable publicly traded securities to determine the cost of capital. We will use what we learned about required returns in Chapters 9 and 10 to estimate a capital budgeting project's required return.

[1] Such comparability is admittedly difficult to define in some cases. However, recall that nondiversifiable risk is the primary dimension. As a practical matter, investments are considered to be comparable when they have identical nondiversifiable risk.

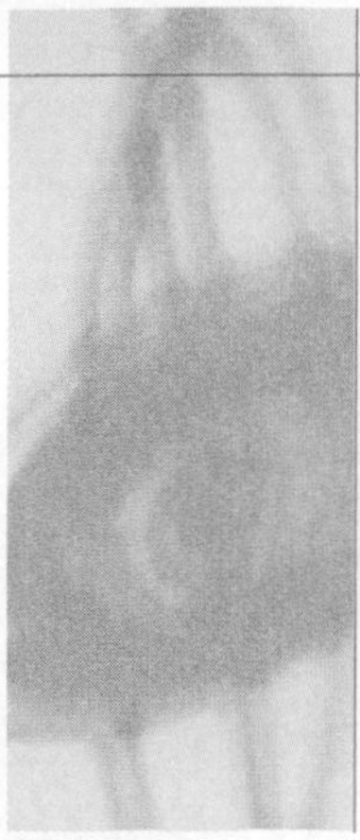

FOCUS ON PRINCIPLES

- *Risk-Return Trade-Off:* Consider the risk of the capital budgeting project when determining the project's cost of capital.
- *Time Value of Money:* The value that a capital budgeting project will create—its NPV—depends on its *cost of capital,* its required return.
- *Valuable Ideas:* Look for new ideas to use as a basis for capital budgeting projects that will create value.
- *Comparative Advantage:* Look for capital budgeting projects that use the firm's comparative advantage to add value.
- *Incremental Benefits:* Identify and estimate the incremental expected future cash flows for a capital budgeting project.
- *Options:* Recognize the value of options, such as the options to expand, postpone, or abandon a capital budgeting project.
- *Two-Sided Transactions:* Consider why others are willing to participate in a transaction.
- *Signaling:* Consider the actions and products of competitors.

11.1 THE COST OF CAPITAL

The term **cost of capital** is often misinterpreted. It is *not* the firm's historical cost of funds, such as coupon payments on existing bonds, that determines the cost of capital. The relevant cost is an *opportunity cost.* It is the rate at which investors would provide financing for the capital budgeting project under consideration *today.* If the firm's historical cost of capital is used to evaluate capital budgeting projects, the analysis will be wrong if market rates have changed.

Observing capital markets for just a short time will convince you that market rates are not constant. However, at any one time, there is only *one* expected/required return for a given risk level in an efficient capital market. Any differential in returns for comparable investments, or between a single investment's expected and required returns, will be eliminated quickly by arbitrage activity.

A second problem with the historical perspective involves risk differences. The cost of capital also is *not* the required return on the firm's existing (historical) operations. This is because the firm's current cost of capital reflects the average risk of *all* the firm's existing assets, but the new project's risk (the incremental project) may be very different from this average.

The cost of capital is the required return for a capital budgeting project. Any investment's required return is the minimum return investors must expect to earn in order to be willing to finance the investment today. When management acts in the shareholders' best interest, the cost of capital is the project's required return—that is, the return investors could earn today on comparable capital market securities that have the same risk.

Review

1. What is the cost of capital? Why is it *not* the firm's historical cost of funds?
2. Why is an investment's required return the minimum return investors must expect to earn in order to be willing to finance it today?

11.2 CORPORATE VALUATION

In a perfect capital market environment, a firm cannot affect its market value by changing the way it is financed. The firm's value depends only on the size of its expected future cash flows and the required return on those expected future cash flows. Firm value does not depend on how those cash flows must be divided between the debtholders and the shareholders. Therefore, a firm's capital structure—how the firm is financed—is irrelevant to the firm's value in a perfect capital market environment.

The Financing Decision

If the financing decision does not affect a firm's value, you might wonder why we are interested in it. There are at least three reasons. First, even if the financing decision does not affect the firm's value, it can provide us with important insight into how to estimate the cost of capital. Second, as a practical matter, even in an efficient capital market, mistakes can be made. It is important to understand the financing decision, if only to avoid making stupid mistakes in operating the firm. Finally, examining the financing decision in a perfect capital market environment provides a good foundation for understanding (later on) why and how certain capital market imperfections cause the financing decision to in fact affect firm value after all.

The value of a firm can be expressed as the value of the claims on its assets. That is, firm value equals the total market value of its liabilities plus the total market value of its owners' equity:

$$\text{Firm value} = \text{Equity} + \text{Debt} \qquad (11.1)$$

Although this may look suspiciously like the balance sheet equation, it is important to emphasize that it is given in *market values* rather than book values. Equity is the current value of all of the firm's outstanding shares of stock. This value is often estimated by multiplying the current market value per share times the number of outstanding shares.

For example, if Disney's stock is selling for \$21.60, and there are 2.0 billion shares outstanding, Disney's equity would be estimated to be worth \$43.2 billion (= [21.60]2.0). Similarly, debt is the market value of all of the firm's outstanding liabilities.

The Investment Decision

We can also express a firm's value in terms of its assets. That is, firm value is the sum of the market values of its assets, shown as $A_1, A_2, \ldots$:

$$\text{Firm value} = A_1 + A_2 + A_3 + \ldots$$

This representation is based on the market values of the assets on the left-hand side of the balance sheet, not their book values. Here, the firm's value is represented as a portfolio of its real assets.[2] The firm's investment decision consists of choosing which assets to add or remove from its portfolio. That choice is based on earning at least the required return on each asset.

This view of firm value as a portfolio of assets is important because it shows how each asset must "rest on its own bottom." That is, each asset (or group of interrelated assets) has its own unique value, required return, and expected return. Recall that a capital budgeting project's expected return is called its *internal rate of return (IRR).* An asset must be expected to earn at least its cost of capital (required return) to justify its inclusion in the firm's asset portfolio. In simple terms, the IRR must equal or exceed the cost of capital. Although this rule can break down in some situations, as shown in Chapter 6, the simple notion that the expected return must equal or exceed the required return provides us with important intuition about the concept of a cost of capital.

The Market Line for Capital Budgeting Projects

Our development of the capital-asset-pricing model (CAPM) in Chapter 10 is based on shares of common stock. However, the concept can be extended to include all real assets as well. We can

[2]Note that by equating these two expressions for firm value, we can see the "investment-pass-through" effect of the investment-vehicle model shown in Figure 1.4.

build on the idea of the security market line (SML) and create what might be called the capital budgeting project market line (PML). The cost of capital for capital budgeting project *j*, r_j, can then be expressed as a function of the nondiversifiable risk of the project, its beta:

$$r_j = r_f + \beta_j(r_M - r_f)$$

where r_f is the riskless return, β_j is the beta for project *j*, and r_M is the required return on the market portfolio. Capital budgeting projects are then evaluated on the basis of the PML in the same way securities are evaluated using the SML.

EXAMPLE Capital Budgeting for Wal-Mart

Wal-Mart is considering five capital budgeting projects. Undertaking any single project does not preclude, or require, undertaking any of the others. Each project costs an identical $1 million, has a unique beta (and therefore its own cost of capital), and promises a unique perpetual annual cash flow amount. The required return on the market portfolio is 15%, and the riskless return is 7%.

Table 11.1 shows the beta, cost of capital, annual cash flow, IRR, and NPV of each project. For example, the beta for project A is 1.30, and so its cost of capital is 17.4% (= 7 + 1.30[15 − 7]). Project A's annual cash flow is $200,000 making its IRR 20% (= 200,000/1,000,000). Finally, the NPV for project A is $149,430, which is the present value of the expected future cash flows, $1,149,430 (= 200,000/0.174), minus its initial cost of $1,000,000.

Figure 11.1 graphs the costs of capital and IRRs for the projects Wal-Mart is considering, along with the PML. The costs of capital fall on the PML, because they were determined by the PML equation. As with the SML, investments that are above the PML have a positive NPV. So projects A, B, and E have positive NPVs, whereas projects C and D have negative NPVs.

Review

1. True or false? A firm's capital structure does not affect its value in a perfect capital market environment.
2. Why should we be interested in how a firm finances itself?
3. Describe two ways to view the value of the firm.
4. What is the capital budgeting project market line (PML)? How is it like the security market line (SML)?

TABLE 11.1
Wal-Mart's capital budgeting projects.

PROJECT	BETA	COST OF CAPITAL	ANNUAL CASH FLOW	IRR	NPV
A	1.30	17.4%	$200,000	20%	$149,430
B	1.75	21.0	220,000	22	47,620
C	.95	14.6	140,000	14	−41,100
D	1.50	19.0	170,000	17	−105,260
E	.60	11.8	140,000	14	186,440

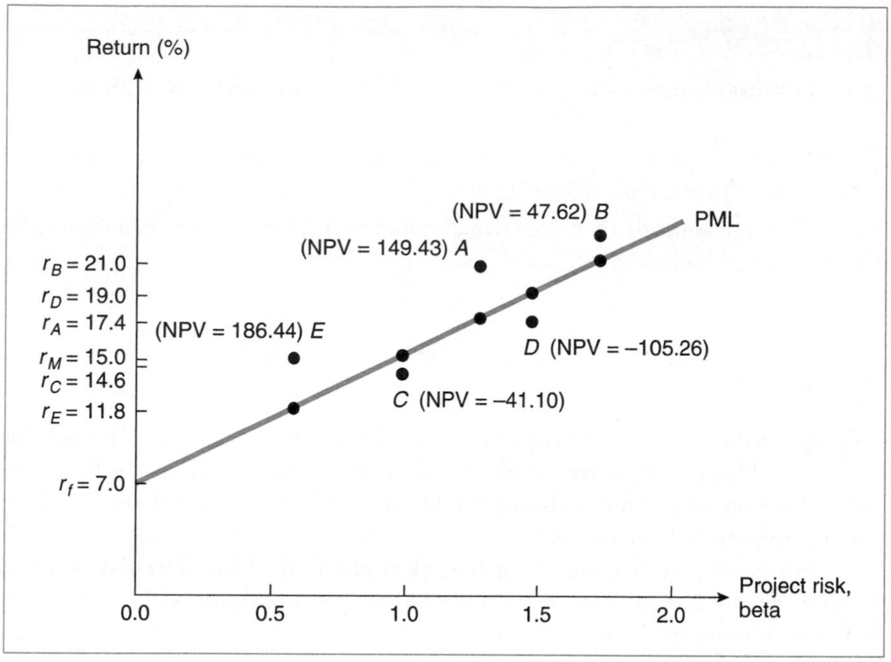

FIGURE 11.1 Wal-Mart's alternative capital budgeting projects and the PML (NPV in $ thousands).

11.3 VALUE AND THE RISK-RETURN TRADE-OFF

It is very important to keep in mind the relationship among the cost of capital, expected cash flows, and present value. Present value depends on both the cost of capital *and* the expected cash flows. When any one of these three things changes, at least one of the others must also change.

For example, if the cost of capital increases, present value will decrease if the expected cash flows do not also change. We have seen this with bonds and inflation. With constant coupon payments, the market value of a bond changes whenever market interest rates change.

Similarly, an increase in the expected cash flows will increase present value *if* the cost of capital (and therefore risk) has not changed. However, keep in mind that ***present value can remain constant even if there are changes in both the expected cash flows and the cost of capital (required return).*** The changes can exactly offset each other. This is precisely what the Principle of Risk-Return Trade-Off means. Present value can be constant, even if the required return and expected cash flows change. Consider the following simple example.

EXAMPLE A Pure Risk-Return Trade-Off

Suppose you have an asset that is expected to pay $50 per year forever. The asset's required return is 5%. So the asset's value is $1,000 (= 50/0.05). Now suppose you can exchange this asset for some other asset that is expected to pay an average of $100 per year forever, but, because of risk, its required return is 10%. The second asset's cash flow can be much smaller or larger than $100 per year. Should you make the exchange?

The value of the alternative asset is also $1,000 (= 100/0.1). Therefore, your choice depends *only* on your attitude toward risk. In other words, your choice represents a pure risk-return trade-off. Even though the other asset's expected cash flows are larger, *there is no difference in value.* Such is the case when an investor moves along the SML or a firm moves along the PML. Value is enhanced only when the increase (decrease) in expected cash flows exceeds (is less than) the increase (decrease) in risk.

Review

1. What happens to present value when the expected cash flows all increase and the cost of capital does not change?
2. What happens to present value when the cost of capital decreases and the expected cash flows do not change?
3. How can the present value remain constant if the expected cash flows and the cost of capital both change?

11.4 LEVERAGE

According to the CAPM, the required return depends only on the nondiversifiable risk of an investment. However, nondiversifiable risk borne by the shareholders can be further split into two parts. It is very important to distinguish between these two types of risk, because they affect required returns in different ways.

The main part of nondiversifiable risk is often called **business risk** or **operating risk.** Business risk is the inherent or fundamental risk of a business without regard to how it is financed. Business risk comes from operating the business; it is based on the firm's assets, the left-hand side of its balance sheet.

The secondary part of nondiversifiable risk is called **financial risk.** Financial risk comes from how the firm is financed; it is based on the firm's capital structure (its proportions of debt and equity), which is the firm's liabilities and owners' equity or right-hand side of its balance sheet.

In many cases, a firm cannot control its business risk. It is simply the inherent risk of an investment. By contrast, a firm's financial risk is determined by the amount of debt it has, its financial leverage, or simply **leverage.** More leverage increases financial risk.

The term *leverage* is derived from the mechanical lever that allows you to lift more weight than is possible by yourself. Financial leverage allows shareholders to control (lift, so to speak) more assets than is possible using only their own money. In addition to (financial) leverage there is a second type of leverage, called operating leverage. We now turn to this.

Operating Leverage

Operating leverage is the relative mix of fixed and variable costs required to produce a product or service. Multiple methods of producing a product or service may exist, whereby a firm spends more on fixed costs and less on variable costs, or vice versa. A decrease in the variable cost per unit creates an increase in the contribution margin (the selling price minus the variable cost). With a larger contribution margin, the firm's profit is more sensitive to changes in sales. That is, a small change in sales makes a large change in profit because the fixed costs are spent in either case.

By contrast, an increase in the variable cost per unit causes a decrease in the contribution margin. With a smaller contribution margin, the change in profit caused by a change in the sales level will not be as large. Therefore, lowering the variable cost per unit (by increasing fixed costs) increases the sensitivity of the firm's profit to changes in the level of sales. Such an increase in fixed cost is an increase in operating leverage.

EXAMPLE Eastern Mountain Apparel Ski Cap Production

Eastern Mountain Apparel will use one of two alternative production methods for manufacturing ski caps. Method A costs $30,000 to install and $6 to make one cap. Method B costs $54,000 to install and $4 to make one cap. Eastern sells caps for $11 apiece. Which production method should Eastern purchase?

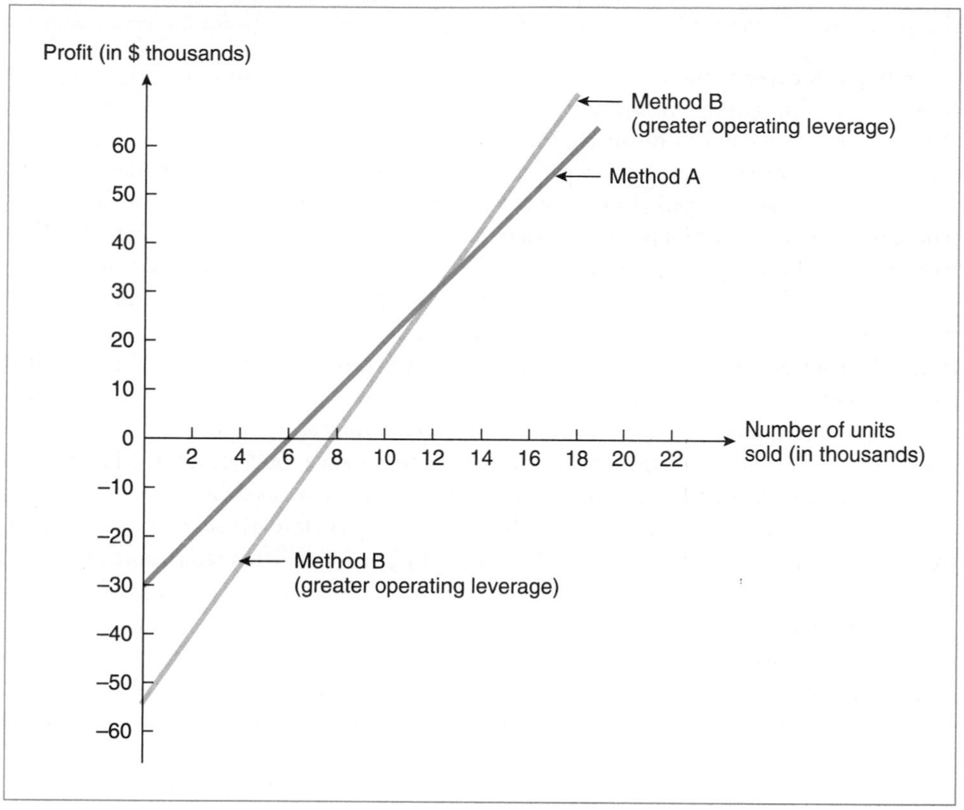

FIGURE 11.2 Eastern Mountain Apparel's operating leverage alternatives.

The answer, of course, depends on how many ski caps will be sold. For simplicity, let us ignore taxes and the time value of money. Profit will be the contribution margin times the number of caps sold, N, minus the fixed cost. The profit will be $5N − $30,000 for method A, and $7N − $54,000 for method B. Figure 11.2 illustrates Eastern's profit as a function of the number of ski caps sold for both methods.

As you might predict from our discussion above, method B with its higher operating leverage (larger fixed and smaller variable costs) will make Eastern's profit more sensitive to the number of units sold. The slope of the profit line for method B is steeper. If the number sold turns out to be more than 12,000 (the point where the profit functions are equal, $5N - 30{,}000 = 7N - 54{,}000$), then method B will have been the better choice. On the other hand, if sales turn out to be less than 12,000 units, then method A will have been the better choice. Of course, the best choice may not be obvious if the sales amount is highly variable or expected to be about 12,000.

Operating leverage is important because of its impact on the risk of the investment. However, a firm's choice of operating leverage is limited by the number of possible different methods of producing a product or service. In some cases, a firm has no choice because there is a single (or most efficient) method of production.

There are two important things to remember about operating leverage. First, operating leverage is generally unique for each investment rather than identical for all of the firm's investments. Second, operating leverage affects the total risk of the capital budgeting project, both diversifiable and nondiversifiable risk. Therefore, it also affects both the project's beta and its cost of capital.

Financial Leverage

Operating risk depends principally on the nature of the investment, and to a lesser extent on the firm's choice of operating leverage. In contrast, financial risk depends mostly on financial leverage. When a firm has some debt financing, that portion of its financing costs is fixed rather than variable. Although we would expect a larger return to shareholders than to debtholders, shareholder return can vary from one period to the next without affecting the operation of the firm. However, failure to make required debt payments can result in bankruptcy. We could say, then, that financial leverage substitutes fixed payments to debtholders for variable payments to shareholders.

Graphically, financial leverage looks similar to operating leverage. The realized return to the shareholders (owners) in an all-equity-financed firm is the same as the realized return to the firm. The realized return to the shareholders in a leveraged firm is the realized return *after* the fixed payment to the debtholders has been taken out. The shareholders are the *residual* owners.

Figure 11.3 illustrates the shareholders' realized return as a function of the firm's realized return with and without leverage. The leverage alternative assumes 50% debt financing. Figure 11.3 ignores taxes and assumes that the firm pays a 10% interest rate on its debt.

We have come across the concept of financial leverage before. Recall that investors in a perfect capital market should all invest in the same risky portfolio—the market portfolio. Investors set their risk and return levels by lending or borrowing. This kind of lending and borrowing is simply personal financial leverage.

There is a very important fact we learned about personal leverage: The choice of lending or borrowing (personal financial leverage) does not alter the *total* value of an investment. It is just like our example of a pure risk-return trade-off. Any change in the expected cash flows is exactly offset by a change in risk and required return.

So the choice of personal leverage is yet another pure risk-return trade-off. It is the investor's choice of personal capital structure that puts the investor at a particular point on the

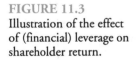

FIGURE 11.3
Illustration of the effect of (financial) leverage on shareholder return.

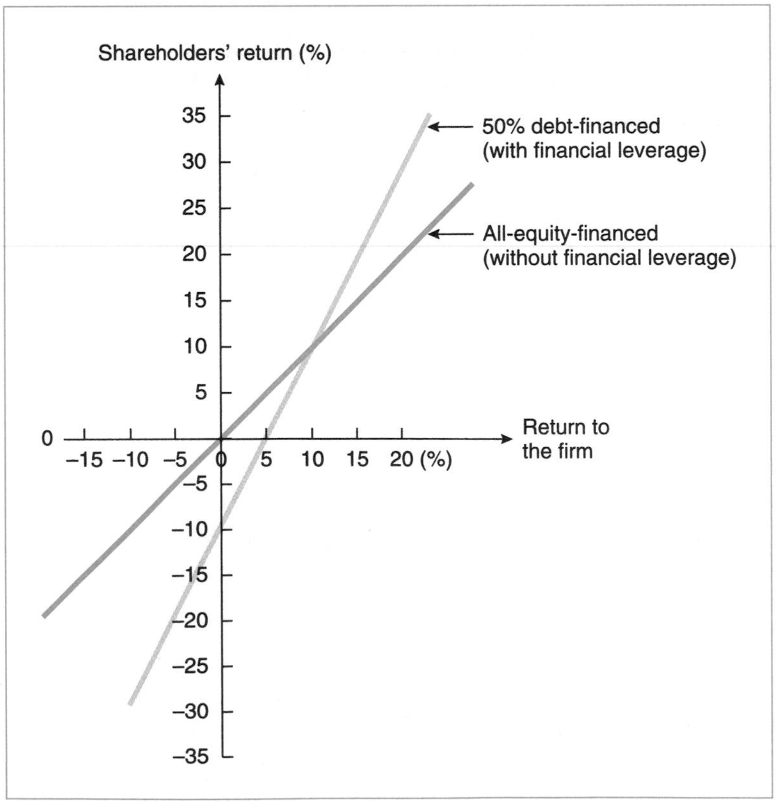

capital market line (CML). This same conclusion holds for a firm's choice of capital structure in a perfect capital market environment. Financial leverage is not a matter of value. It is a question of risk-return preference, subject to a market-determined risk-return trade-off.

Financial leverage has three important corresponding (and almost opposite) things to remember about it. First, a firm's choice of leverage is for the most part made for the entire firm rather than separately for each of the firm's investments. Second, leverage affects the risk borne by each class of investor (debt, equity, and so on), but does not affect the cost of capital for the investment in a perfect capital market environment. Third, within a very wide range, a firm can choose its amount of leverage.

Review

1. What are the two parts of nondiversifiable risk?
2. What is operating leverage? How does it differ from financial leverage? How is it similar?
3. How does a firm's choice of financial leverage affect its cost of capital in a perfect capital market environment?

11.5 LEVERAGE AND RISK BEARING

In a perfect capital market environment, leverage does not affect a firm's value or its cost of capital. However, even in a perfect capital market environment, leverage does affect the required returns for the debtholders and shareholders. This is because leverage affects how the risk of the firm is borne by each group. To see this, consider the following simple example.

EXAMPLE Leveraging Per-Pet, Inc.

Per-Pet, Inc. is financed only with equity. It has a perpetual expected cash inflow each year of \$150, which can be larger or smaller, but is never less than \$50 per year. Per-Pet's cost of capital is 15%, so Per-Pet is worth \$1,000 (= 150/0.15). Recently, the shareholders heard the old adage that "the way to get rich is to use someone else's money."

The manager agrees and has pointed out that the firm could borrow \$500 at 10% per year and give the \$500 to the shareholders. Then the shareholders' expected return on their remaining \$500 investment would increase to 20% per year. If \$500 of financing is converted into debt, the firm would be taking on leverage and have a capital structure that is half debt and half equity.

First of all, why would the debtholders accept a return of only 10% when the firm's cost of capital is 15%? The answer, of course, is the risk-return trade-off: The debtholders will get their 10% return *every* period without fail—their return is riskless. Because the shareholders are the *residual* claim holders, they get what is left after the debtholders have been paid. Their risk will increase with leverage.

When the firm is all-equity financed, the shareholders bear all the firm's risk, spread out over an investment of \$1,000. With the proposed 50% debt capital structure, the shareholders also bear all the firm's risk, but the risk is spread out over an investment of only \$500. Thus, the risk *per dollar invested* for the shareholders will be twice as large with the leverage as it is currently. So the shareholders "pay" for their increased expected return with an increase in risk.

What conclusions can we draw from the Per-Pet example? First, you can see once again that the expected operating income of \$150 coming into Per-Pet each year is not affected by how it must be paid out to those financing the firm. In other words, the return distribution for a capital budgeting project is not altered by a change in leverage in a perfect capital market environment.

Second, the shareholders' expected return increases with an increase in leverage, but so does their required return. The shareholders' increased risk from leverage exactly offsets their increase in expected return, so there is no change in the shareholders' collective wealth. Without leverage, shareholders have \$1,000 invested. Under the proposed leveraging, shareholders will have \$500 in cash to invest as they wish and \$500 of invested value (= 100/0.2) in Per-Pet stock, for an unchanged *total* value of \$1,000.

Finally, with the proposed leverage, debtholders provide \$500 in cash for promised future payments worth *exactly* \$500 (= 50/0.1).

This example also demonstrates that all investors do not bear the same amount of financial risk. As residual claimholders, the shareholders bear more risk per dollar invested than do the debtholders. At the same time, leverage does not affect the firm's cost of capital (required return). The cost of capital, when it is all-equity financed, is 15%. The weighted average required return from the proposed debt and equity financing is also 15% (= 0.5[0.2] + 0.5[0.1]). This is not a coincidence. This must hold in all cases in a perfect capital market environment.

EXAMPLE Leveraging Your Investment Returns

You have a chance to invest \$50,000 in a one-year investment. You can borrow \$30,000 of the money from a friend at a cost of 10% and use \$20,000 of your own money. There are no taxes. With this arrangement, you expect a return of 24% on your \$20,000 investment. What would your return be without the leverage? That is, what would your return be if the entire \$50,000 was your own money?

The total dollar return from the investment is expected to cover the interest cost of \$3,000 (= [0.10]30,000) plus provide you with \$4,800 (= [0.24]20,000). So the total dollar return is expected to be \$7,800, which is a return on the entire investment of 15.6% (= 7,800/50,000). If you put up the entire \$50,000, you would expect to earn 15.6% on it.

Another way to answer this question is to calculate the weighted average return; 60% of the money (\$30,000) is expected to earn 10%, and 40% of the money (\$20,000) is expected to earn 24%. So the weighted average is 15.6%:

$$(0.60)10\% + (0.40)24\% = 15.6\%$$

Review

1. As a firm's leverage increases, how will each of the following be affected in a perfect capital market environment: required return for debtholders, required return for shareholders, and cost of capital?
2. How does an increase in a firm's leverage affect its shareholders' collective wealth in a perfect capital market environment?

11.6 THE WEIGHTED AVERAGE COST OF CAPITAL

We always come back to opportunity cost. The **weighted average cost of capital (WACC)** can be described in terms of financing rates. Therefore, it can *always* be represented as the weighted average cost of the components of *any* financing package that will allow the project to be undertaken. For example, such a financing package could be 20% debt plus 80% equity, 55% debt plus 45% equity, and so on. Or it could be 30% 30-year debt, 10% 180-day debt, 10% preferred stock, 15% 20-year convertible debt, and 35% common stock.

The cost of capital is the return required by a group of investors to take on the risk of the project. But the investors can share the burden of that risk in any way they agree on. In a perfect capital market environment, each investor will require a fair return for the amount of risk borne. However, the *average* will always be the same—regardless of the components.

Certain capital market imperfections, such as asymmetric taxes, asymmetric information, and transaction costs, might cause the package to have an impact on the average cost, but we leave that part of the story for later. For now, it is most important to understand that the required return for each participant depends on the proportion of risk being borne by that participant.

Before proceeding, we need to say exactly what we mean by the components of a financing package. For simplicity, we will just use the proportions of financing provided by debt and equity. Let $L = D/(D + E)$ be the ratio of debt financing to total investment value. D is the market value of debt, E is the market value of equity, and $(D + E)$ is the firm's total market value (the market value of all its assets).

For example, suppose a project has a total present value of $10,000, and $4,000 of debt will be used to finance the project. Then $L = D/(D + E) = 0.4$. It is very important to note that L does not depend on the initial cost of the project; it depends on the total value of the project.

Suppose our example project has an initial cost of $8,000, and an NPV of $2,000, making up its present value of $10,000. Then the shareholders of this project will be putting up $4,000 and receiving $6,000 from the positive NPV. So the shareholders own 60% of the value, even though they will be putting up only 50% of the initial cost ($4,000 of the $8,000). The project is referred to as 40% debt financed and 60% equity financed because those proportions reflect the distribution of the *market* value of the project among the claimants. Proportions of the initial cost are not relevant because they disregard the project's NPV.

The Per-Pet example illustrates that the shareholders' required return depends on leverage. The same phenomenon occurs with respect to the debtholders' required return. It also depends on leverage. This might not be obvious because, as long as there is no chance of default, the debtholders' required return is the riskless return. However, when default is possible, the debtholders' required return must increase to reflect the risk that debtholders will not receive full payment.[3]

A Cost of Capital Formula

The WACC (weighted average cost of capital) can be expressed as the weighted average of the required return for equity, r_e, and the required return for debt, r_d, as we illustrated in the Per-Pet example. The weights are based on the market values of the firm's debt and equity.

$$\text{WACC} = \frac{E}{(D+E)} r_e + \frac{D}{(D+E)}(1-T)r_d = (1-L)r_e + L(1-T)r_d \tag{11.2}$$

where L is the market value proportion of debt financing, and T represents the marginal corporate tax rate on income from the project.

Note that the WACC is expressed as the after-corporate-tax return. Because the returns to equity investors are paid after corporate taxes, r_e is also an after-corporate-tax return (to equity). The return to debt, r_d, is a pretax return, and must be multiplied by $(1 - T)$ to convert it to an after-tax basis.[4]

---

[3]Note that full payment includes the time value of money. That is, late payments reduce the value debtholders receive.

[4]We first encountered this kind of adjustment in Chapter 3.

EXAMPLE General Patent's Cost of Capital

General Patent, Inc. makes innovative military equipment and has only long-term debt and common equity financing. Both securities are traded regularly on a securities exchange. What is the WACC for General Patent?

To begin, we gather the following information:

Current market value of General Patent's common stock (5 million shares outstanding)	\$33.25/share
Total market value of equity (= [5]33.25)	\$166.25 million
Next year's expected cash dividend	\$2.83/share
Expected constant annual dividend growth	6%
Current market value of General Patent's bonds (70,000 bonds outstanding, 7.10% coupon rate, maturing in 17 years)	\$800.00/bond
Yield to maturity on General Patent's bonds	9.5%
Total market value of debt (= [70,000]800)	\$56.00 million
Current total market value of General Patent (= 166.25 + 56.0)	\$222.25 million
General Patent's marginal corporate tax rate	34%

Based on this information, we can use the dividend growth model from Chapter 5 to estimate r_e. From Equation (5.5):

$$r_e = \frac{D_1}{P_0} + g = \frac{2.83}{33.25} + 0.06 = 0.145$$

The yield to maturity (YTM) on the long-term bonds, 9.5%, provides an approximation[5] of r_d. The proportion of debt financing, $L = D/(D + E)$, is 0.252 (= 56/222.25). From Equation (11.2), then, our estimate of General Patent's WACC is 12.43%:

$$\text{WACC} = (1 - L)r_e + L(1 - T)r_d = (0.748)(0.145) + (0.252)(0.66)(0.095) = 0.1243$$

The estimated 12.43% WACC in the General Patent example can be used as a cost of capital for capital budgeting projects that essentially duplicate (with respect to operating leverage and financing leverage) the firm's current operations. But how can we estimate a cost of capital for projects that are significantly different from the firm's current operations?

The firm's own securities are not appropriate because they reflect only the riskiness of the firm's existing asset mix. Conceptually, a firm could offer a financing package in the capital market to determine a project's cost of capital. However, this would be cumbersome to say the least. The transaction costs would almost certainly outweigh the benefits of this method.

In practice, a firm looks at existing market-traded securities of comparable risk to estimate a project's cost of capital. The estimate is derived from such market rates. We will get back to this later in the chapter.

[5]The yield to maturity is only an approximation because of tax considerations.

Review

1. What is the WACC? How is it calculated?
2. How is the ratio L calculated? Is it based on market or book values?
3. Suppose a project costs $10,000. Its NPV is $5,000. Shareholders put up $5,000, and debtholders lend $5,000. What is L in this case?
4. In the WACC formula, why do we multiply only r_d by $(1 - T)$?
5. Suppose a firm wanted to estimate the cost of capital for a project that differs from its current operations. Should the firm use its current WACC as the project's cost of capital? Explain.

11.7 A POTENTIAL MISUSE OF THE WEIGHTED AVERAGE COST OF CAPITAL

We have said that a project's cost of capital must reflect its own risk, not the risk of a firm's existing operations. But what happens if a firm incorrectly uses its weighted average cost of capital (WACC) for existing operations to evaluate all capital budgeting projects, regardless of risk? Figure 11.4 graphs the risk (beta) versus the IRR for some capital budgeting projects.

Assume the firm's existing operations have a risk equal to the average risk of the set of capital budgeting projects, and the rate w correctly reflects the WACC of the firm's current operations. The horizontal line wc in Figure 11.4 represents the use of the firm's WACC to evaluate the projects, where all projects with an IRR above w are accepted and all those below w are rejected.

If this decision rule is followed, the new projects undertaken will tend to be riskier than the firm's existing operations. This is because, taken as a group, the projects that would be accepted using this decision rule are riskier than the remaining set that would not be undertaken. (You can see this by visually estimating the center point of the groups, above and below wc, and comparing the two points.) Therefore, following such a decision rule will cause the risk of the firm to increase over time as new projects are undertaken. Of course, as a result, the firm's WACC will also increase to reflect the greater risk to investors.

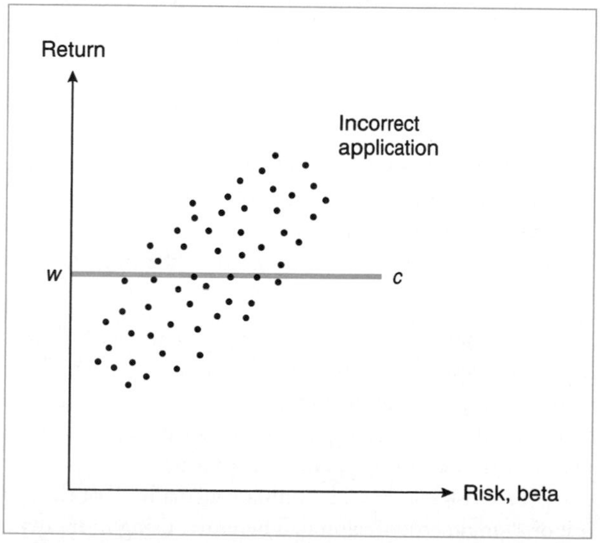

FIGURE 11.4
Misapplication of the WACC concept to capital budgeting project selection.

FIGURE 11.5
Proper capital budgeting project selection.

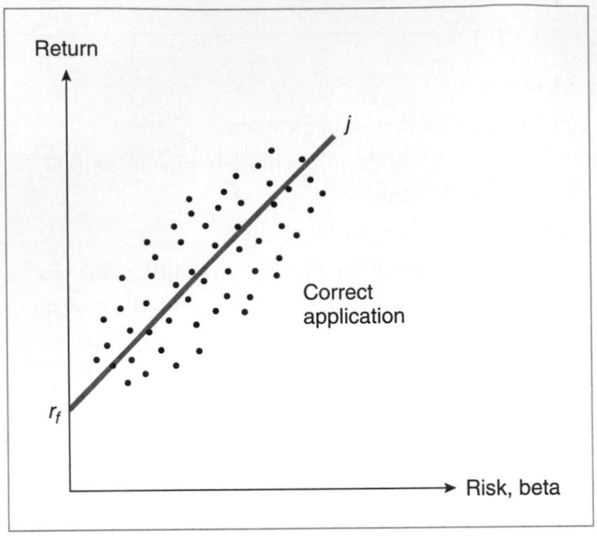

Taken to the extreme, misusing a firm's WACC to evaluate new projects could lead a firm with low operating risk, such as a utility, to take on high-risk projects, such as drilling exploratory oil wells. The incorrect low rate could make the project appear to be very desirable by incorrectly computing the project's NPV. Other firms that regularly undertake such projects would find the project to have a (correctly computed) negative NPV! Note also that in addition to undertaking bad projects, the firm would be incurring opportunity costs by passing up good projects.

Alternatively, consider what happens if a firm applies the PML concept and uses risk-adjusted costs of capital, such as those on the line connecting r_f and point *j* in Figure 11.5. As with the single cost of capital decision rule, projects above the line will be accepted, whereas projects falling below the line are rejected. In this case, the average risk of those above the line is approximately the same as those that are rejected. So the application of project-specific risk-adjusted costs of capital does not cause the risk of a firm to increase over time. Of course, in some cases, the total risk could change. However, a change in total risk will not matter as long as the firm earns the returns sufficient to compensate for the risk.

EXAMPLE Capital Budgeting at American Airlines

Suppose American Airlines has a beta of 1.3. It is considering issuing stock to raise money for a project that has a beta of 1.0. The project has an 18% IRR. The riskless return is 5%, and the expected return on the market is 10%. Should American go ahead with the project?

The project's cost of capital from the PML (project market line) is 10% (= 5 + 1.0[10 − 5]). Because the project's expected return, its IRR, of 18% is greater than its required return, its cost of capital, of 10%, American should go ahead with the project. Note that American's current beta of 1.3 is not relevant to the investment decision. Note also that how American will finance the project does not change the answer.

In practice, firms considering projects with differing risk levels often use a *set* of costs of capital to capture risk differences among capital budgeting projects. Each cost of capital corresponds to a particular **risk class.** For example, a firm might have a unique cost of capital for each of its divisions, or it might have a cost of capital for each of various types of projects, such as maintenance, expansion, and new products.

Five risk classes will eliminate virtually all of the problem of shifting risk created by the misuse of a single cost of capital. Therefore, using more than five risk classes is probably unnecessary and a waste of resources. However, using at least three different risk classes appears to be valuable.

EXAMPLE Using Risk Classes at Burch Trees, Inc.

Tim Burch, owner of Burch Trees, Inc. assigns capital budgeting proposals to one of three risk classes. Risk class A, typically modernization and equipment replacement proposals, is for the lowest risk projects. Risk class A projects are assigned a 12% required return. Risk class B projects, frequently expansions of existing lines of business, are riskier and have a 14% required return. Finally, risk class C projects, new products and new businesses, are given a 16% hurdle rate.

Seven capital budgeting proposals are briefly described in the table:

PROJECT NUMBER	PROJECT IRR	RISK CLASS	COST OF CAPITAL	DECISION
1412	15%	A	12%	Accept
1416	11	A	12	Reject
1429	13	B	14	Reject
1430	16	B	14	Accept
1431	19	B	14	Accept
1435	15	C	16	Reject
1436	26	C	16	Accept

A conventional investment project should be accepted whenever its IRR exceeds the required return for its risk class. As you can see in the table, this results in four projects being accepted and three being rejected. Assignment of a project to the appropriate risk class is crucial. Project 1412 would have been rejected if it were assigned to risk class C and project 1435 would have been accepted if it were in a lower risk class.

Review

1. What happens to the firm if it uses its (overall) WACC for existing operations to evaluate all capital budgeting projects?
2. Why does using the firm's WACC to evaluate all capital budgeting projects lead to incorrect investment decisions? Might the use cause the firm to accept some negative-NPV projects? Might it cause the firm to reject some positive-NPV projects?
3. Explain why applying the PML concept should lead to correct capital budgeting decisions.
4. How can a firm use risk classes to evaluate its capital budgeting projects? How many risk classes are usually sufficient?

11.8 FINANCIAL RISK

A firm's operating risk is determined by the characteristics of the individual assets in the firm's portfolio of assets. Therefore, as a portfolio, the betas of the individual assets combine to determine the operating risk of the entire firm.

In contrast to operating risk, financial risk depends on firm rather than individual asset characteristics. In some sense, an asset or new project undertaken by a firm has no financial risk; only the firm itself has financial risk. This is because financial risk is created by a firm's financial obligation.

If a firm is all-equity financed (no money owed at any time, no matter what), then the firm has no financial risk. Such a firm would not have even one creditor. All the risk of this hypothetical firm would be its operating risk, because the firm never owes anyone anything. In such a case there is no possibility of, or option to, default. In effect, the shareholders' limited liability has no effect on value.

Of course, such a firm could still go bust. But although the shareholders could lose everything they invested in the firm, no wealth can be transferred because no loss can ever be inflicted on anyone other than the shareholders. So although such shareholders still cannot lose more than they have invested in the firm, they also cannot benefit from limited liability and the default option.

Because financial risk depends on financial leverage, adjusting for the impact of financial risk must be done on the basis of whatever unit has responsibility for that financial obligation. Except in very special cases, the shareholders' obligation is not limited by the results of one capital budgeting project. Rather, the financial obligation extends to the entire firm.

In essence, the firm owns a portfolio of projects. When one project does poorly, the firm is still obligated to pay its debts from the proceeds of all its other projects. (Only when the firm's total performance from all its operations is inadequate to meet its promised obligations can the shareholders be relieved of their obligation—that is, exercise their option to default.)

Therefore, in marked contrast to considerations of operating risk, financing considerations cannot generally be accounted for on a project-by-project basis. Instead, because financial obligations are at the level of the firm, the impact of leverage on required returns is determined by the capital structure of the whole firm.

Another difference between financial risk and operating risk is the extent to which a firm can control each type of risk. A firm can control its financial risk to a reasonable extent (and typically at reasonable cost) by its choice of capital structure and the maturities of its financial obligations. As previously noted, in theory a firm could have zero financial risk if it was financed entirely with equity. By contrast, the firm's operating risk is not as easily controlled.

Although a firm's choice of assets affects its operating risk via operating leverage (commitments to fixed as opposed to variable costs), the choice of assets is often constrained in some way. Technological considerations may force a firm to use certain processes that have a large component of either fixed or variable expense. For example, some products can be produced by one method only. Thus, we point out again: Operating risk is not easily managed, whereas financial risk is controlled by the firm's financial policy.

Subsidiaries

Whenever a firm splits itself into separate legal units, with each unit having limited liability with respect to its financing, the capital structure of each unit becomes the relevant consideration for a cost of capital. Therefore, if a firm is considering a capital budgeting project where the financing will be obtained by creating a subsidiary for which the firm has limited liability, the project's cost of capital must reflect the subsidiary's capital structure.

How Leverage Affects the Cost of Capital

In a perfect capital market environment, capital structure (the choice of leverage) is a pure risk-return trade-off and does not affect value. We saw this in the Per-Pet example in section 11.5. This fact leads to important conclusions about the three required returns in Equation (11.2).

Most importantly, if capital structure is irrelevant, a project's value is not affected by how it is financed. This means that WACC *does not* vary with L; WACC is constant for *all* values of L because changes in L do not affect the total value of the project or its expected cash flows. If the present value and the expected cash flows are constant, the third parameter in the present value equation, WACC, must also be constant. Of course, as we saw in the Per-Pet example, changes in leverage alter how the risk of the project is borne by the debtholders and shareholders. Therefore, leverage *does* affect r_e and r_d, even in a perfect capital market environment.

Based on the fact that WACC is constant across all possible values of $L = D/(D + E)$, we can determine the values of r_e and r_d when L takes on either of its extreme possible values.[6] When

[6]We know of no firm that is literally all-debt financed ($L = 1.0$). Strictly speaking, L is always less than 1.0. For convenience, rather than continue to indicate that L is as close to 1.0 as possible, we will simply refer to $L = 1.0$.

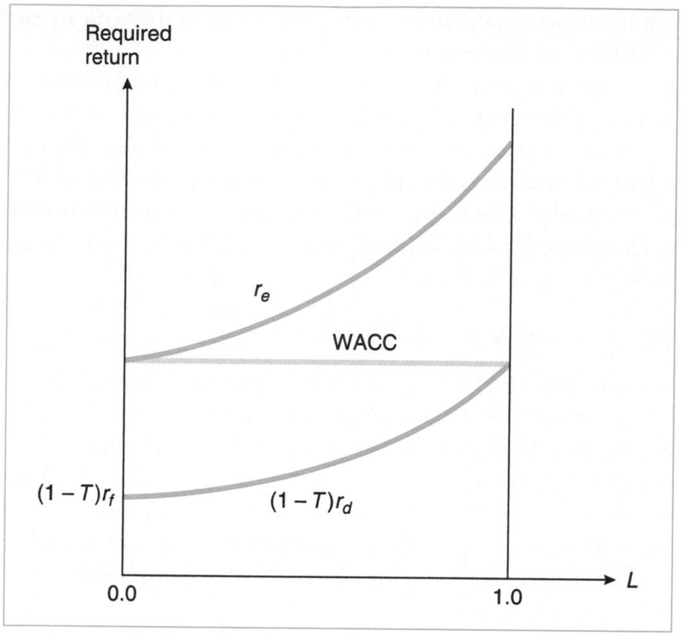

FIGURE 11.6
WACC (weighted average cost of capital), r_e (required return for equity), and r_d (required return for debt) as hypothetical functions of L (leverage ratio) in a perfect capital market environment.

the firm is all-equity financed, $L = 0.0$, the second term in Equation (11.2) drops out, so that WACC $= r_e$. At the other extreme, when the firm is all-debt financed, the first term drops out because $(1 - L) = 0.0$, and WACC $= (1 - T)r_d$.

The result that WACC $= r_e$ (with $L = 0.0$) and that WACC $= (1 - T)r_d$ (with $L = 1.0$) makes intuitive sense. The debtholders of a firm that is financed totally with debt would bear all of the firm's business risk. As such, the debtholders' risk would be the same as the risk borne by the shareholders if the firm were all-equity financed. Therefore, these two returns must be equal because the risks are equal. The only difference between the all-debt and all-equity alternatives would be in taxes—assuming an otherwise perfect capital market: An all-debt-financed firm that is just earning its required return would not pay any income taxes because interest would exactly offset its taxable income; the all-equity-financed firm would pay corporate income taxes because it would have no interest expense, and all its income would therefore be taxable.

A second implication to be drawn from a perfect capital market analysis involves the rate that debtholders will require for financing only an infinitesimal fraction of the investment—r_d when L is tiny. We established above that a firm that is truly 100% equity financed has no chance of default. Such a hypothetical firm can borrow a *very small* amount of money in our assumed environment at the riskless return. Of course, the amount of money such a firm could borrow at the riskless return may be only one cent for one minute. Still, conceptually, the required return on the first fraction of debt in a perfect capital market environment *must be* the required return for the riskless asset, r_f.

Based on these two implications from a perfect market analysis (and hypothetical functions for r_e and r_d), Figure 11.6 illustrates the relationships that can be established in a perfect capital market environment. There are a couple of ways to view taxes in a perfect market environment. One is to simply assume that there are no taxes. In that case, $T = 0$ in Figure 11.6. Alternately, symmetric taxes, where the market considers equity and debt income to be taxed equivalently, would also result in the relationship shown in the figure. Taxes and capital structure are discussed in detail in Chapter 15.

EXAMPLE Toshiba's Leveraged Investment

Toshiba is planning to invest \$1 million in a one-year capital budgeting project. The firm will borrow \$500,000 from a bank and put up \$500,000 in cash. The bank is charging 9% interest. Assume Toshiba pays no taxes and operates in a perfect capital market environment. With this arrangement, Toshiba expects a return of 16% on its equity investment. What would Toshiba's return be without the leverage?

Toshiba expects a dollar return (above its return of capital) of \$80,000 (= [0.16]500,000) after paying interest (above its repayment of capital) of \$45,000 (= [0.09]500,000). So the project is expected to have a total dollar return of \$125,000 (= 80,000 + 45,000). Without leverage, therefore, the project has an expected return of 12.5% (= 125,000/1,000,000).

Another way to answer the question is to calculate the weighted average of the returns. The project's 12.5% expected return = (0.5)16% + (0.5)9%.

How Leverage Affects Beta

We now know that leverage is a pure risk-return trade-off. But how does it affect beta?

An investor's risky portfolio, the market portfolio, is made up of individual stocks. Each has its own beta. Each stock contributes to the beta of the market portfolio. The investor then makes a choice about personal leverage (lending or borrowing). That leverage choice puts the investor's total investment at a specific point on the CML, and determines the investor's risk-return trade-off.

The process is similar for the firm's leverage, but actually occurs *before* an outside investor makes the personal leverage choice. So the stock's beta already has embedded in it the effect of the firm's leverage choice.

As we noted earlier, the firm can be viewed as a portfolio of assets. Therefore, the asset beta for the firm, β_A, is simply the weighted average of its asset betas, or

$$\beta_A = \sum_{j=1}^{J} w_j \beta_j \tag{11.3}$$

where J is the firm's total number of assets and w_j is the proportion of firm value invested in asset j ($j = 1, 2, \ldots, J$). The firm's WACC can then be expressed in terms of β_A as

$$\text{WACC} = r_f + \beta_A(r_M - r_f) \tag{11.4}$$

This expression is based on the asset (left-hand) side of our market value balance sheet view of the firm. In contrast, Equation (11.2) is based on the liabilities and owners' equity (right-hand) side of our market value balance sheet. Comparing the two expressions points out once again that the required return for equity, r_e, is not necessarily the WACC to use for measuring the NPV of a capital budgeting project, even if the risk of the project is identical to the risk of the firm as a whole. The difference is the firm's leverage. As shown in Figure 11.6, WACC and r_e are equal only if the firm has no leverage ($L = 0.0$).

Now we can draw the parallel between the firm's leverage and the shareholders' personal leverage. After choosing its assets, and therefore β_A, the firm then chooses its leverage, which determines the stock's beta, β.

What must be the relationship between the asset beta for the firm, β_A (which is a weighted average of asset betas), and the shareholders' beta? β_A can be thought of as the shareholders' beta if the firm were all-equity financed. But now we need to add the effect of debt. Just as there are equity betas and asset betas, there are debt betas.

A portfolio's beta is simply the weighted average of its component betas. Although the idea for a firm is the same, the equity and debt components are taxed in different ways. Corporate interest payments are tax deductible. Therefore, we must adjust the asset beta for this taxation difference, just as we did in other cases. The adjustment requires multiplying the asset beta by an adjustment factor that includes L and the corporate tax rate, T. The factor TL is simply adjusting for the tax deductibility of the interest on the proportion L of the project cost that is debt financed.

Equating the adjusted beta with the weighted average of the betas of the financing components, the debt and equity betas, we have:

$$(1 - TL)\beta_A = L\beta_d + (1 - L)\beta \tag{11.5}$$

where β_d is the debt beta for the given L, and β is the equity beta.[7] Equation (11.5) expresses β_A in terms of the liabilities and owners' equity (right-hand) side of our market value balance sheet, whereas Equation (11.3) expresses β_A in terms of the asset (left-hand) side of our market value balance sheet.

Review

1. True or false? Operating risk exists project by project. Financial risk exists for the firm as a whole.
2. How can a firm control its financial risk? Is operating risk easier to control?
3. Suppose a firm will finance a project through a subsidiary for which it will have only limited liability. Which capital structure should it use to calculate the WACC for the project?
4. True or false? A firm's asset beta, β_A, is simply the weighted average of its separate asset betas.
5. How is a firm's WACC related to its asset beta in a perfect capital market environment?

11.9 A PRACTICAL PRESCRIPTION FOR ESTIMATING A COST OF CAPITAL

When a firm takes on financial leverage, the risk borne by the debtholders is generally quite low.[8] If the debtholders bear no risk, β_d is zero. In such a case the debtholders will earn the riskless return, r_f. Even when the debtholders bear some of the firm's risk, the amount is typically small compared with other investment opportunities. As a practical matter, if we approximate β_d as zero, and solve for β_A, we can rewrite Equation (11.5) as

$$\beta_A = \frac{(1 - L)\beta}{(1 - TL)} \tag{11.6}$$

We can use this expression to approximate β_A.

EXAMPLE Calculating Officemate's β_A

Officemate Corporation is contemplating an expansion of its current operations. To evaluate the proposed expansion, the financial vice president has asked you to estimate the cost of capital for the project. How do you proceed?

First, you look in an investor's guide and find that the beta for shares of common stock in Officemate is estimated to be 1.25. Second, you note that the current market value of a share of Officemate is \$8.25 and that there are 2 million shares outstanding, so the market value of Officemate's equity is \$16.5 million (= [8.25]2 million). From Officemate's balance sheet you determine that the total book value of all of Officemate's liabilities is \$8.5 million.[9] For convenience, assume the market value of debt is close to the book value. Based on these

[7] Sometimes people add a subscript e to make it clear that it is the equity beta. In order to emphasize that it is the same β we used to develop the CAPM in Chapter 10, we have not added the subscript e.

[8] An exception to this is a so-called "junk" (or high-risk) bond.

[9] Theoretically, the market value of the liabilities should be used rather than the book value. In practice, the book value is often used. This conceptual violation is not significant when the difference between the two measures is not large, such as being less than 15%, which is often the case.

figures, L is approximately 0.34 (= 8.5/[8.5 + 16.5]). From Officemate's income statement, you estimate a marginal corporate tax rate of $T = 0.37$. Then, using Equation (11.6), β_A is about 0.981:

$$\beta_A = \frac{(1 - L)\beta}{(1 - TL)} = \frac{[1 - 0.34]1.30}{[1 - (0.37)(0.34)]} = 0.981$$

Finally, you estimate that r_f and r_M are 5% and 13%, respectively. Therefore, based on Equation (11.4), Officemate should use a cost of capital of about 12.85% for its expansion:

$$\text{WACC} = r_f + \beta_A(r_M - r_f) = 0.05 + 0.981(0.13 - 0.05) = 0.1285, \text{ or } 12.85\%$$

Estimating the Cost of Capital for a Capital Budgeting Project

In the Officemate example, the capital budgeting project was in the same risk class as the firm's overall current operations. Now let us consider how to estimate the cost of capital for a project that is significantly different from current operations and that has significantly different risk from the firm's average.

In the next example, we will show you how to use a group of firms as surrogates for estimating the project's risk. Because the leverage and tax rates of the surrogate firms vary from our firm and from each other, we cannot use these firms' stock betas directly. Instead, we must use equation (11.6) to find each firm's asset beta. The asset betas then provide a good estimate of our project's nondiversifiable operating risk.

EXAMPLE Expanding Medical Laser Production at Poly-brands

Poly-brands, Inc. is a multinational conglomerate with worldwide operations involving products and services that range from a ski resort in Vail, Colorado, to a high-tech ball-bearings manufacturing plant located in Bonn, Germany. The medical services division of Poly is considering an expansion of its medical laser manufacturing facilities located just outside of Tokyo. Poly needs to estimate the project's cost of capital.

Poly's stock and bonds are publicly traded on major exchanges and we can estimate Poly's WACC. However, in this case, Poly's WACC is not a good estimate of the project's cost of capital, because the manufacture of lasers has greater operating risk than the average risk of all of Poly's assets.

The steps for estimating the beta for this project are:

1. Obtain estimates of stock betas for a sample of surrogate firms whose primary business is the manufacture of medical equipment, especially cutting-edge technology such as lasers.
2. Estimate β_A for each of the firms in the manner illustrated in the Officemate example.
3. The average of all the firm betas is the estimate of beta for Poly's project.
4. Estimate the expected market return, r_M, and riskless return, r_f, as 13% and 5%, respectively.

Table 11.2 summarizes the beta estimation procedure. The estimate for the asset beta is 1.31. The cost of capital for Poly's project is then calculated using Equation (11.4):

$$\text{WACC} = 0.05 + 1.31(0.13 - 0.05) = 0.155, \text{ or } 15.5\%$$

TABLE 11.2
Estimating the beta of Poly-brands, Inc.'s capital budgeting project.

SAMPLE FIRM	β	L	T	$\frac{(1-L)\beta}{(1-TL)}$
A	1.70	0.29	0.42	1.37
B	1.85	0.45	0.31	1.18
C	1.95	0.37	0.34	1.41
D	1.90	0.43	0.28	1.23
E	2.00	0.42	0.34	1.35
F	1.60	0.35	0.38	1.20
G	1.65	0.26	0.42	1.37
H	1.80	0.34	0.37	1.36
			Average asset beta =	1.31

How Operating Leverage Affects Beta and the Cost of Capital

We said earlier that operating risk is the primary determinant of a project's cost of capital. We also noted that often a firm has little control over a project's operating leverage because of technological, efficiency, or other production considerations. However, for those projects where a firm has a choice of operating leverage, how does operating leverage affect the project's beta and cost of capital?

Unlike financial leverage, operating leverage affects β_A, and therefore affects the WACC. Its effect is similar to the effect of leverage on r_e—an increase in operating leverage increases β_A and the WACC. Changes in the WACC then in turn affect both r_e and r_d.

The Cost of Capital with a Choice of Operating Leverage

Because operating risk affects a project's beta, the estimation method outlined above must have one more condition added to it when there is a choice of operating leverage. If there are significant differences in operating risk among potential production methods, the sample of representative firms must be restricted to those firms that are using a set of assets and production methods that are approximately equivalent to those in the proposed project.

EXAMPLE Estimating the Cost of Capital with a Choice of Operating Leverage

Let us reexamine Poly-brands, Inc.'s capital budgeting project. A technological advance in the production process for manufacturing lasers has recently occurred. Poly's project will use this new process. Firms B, D, and F in Table 11.2 are using the new process. The other firms are more established and have not yet upgraded their production process. What cost of capital should Poly use?

In this case, the subsample of only firms B, D, and F are used to estimate beta. They have an average implied firm beta of about 1.20. So the estimated project beta would be 1.20, rather than the 1.31 average for all eight firms. This produces a slightly lower WACC of 14.6% (= 0.05 + 1.20[0.13 − 0.05]).

Review

1. Describe a four-step procedure for estimating the beta for a project whose risk differs from that of the firm considering it.
2. How does operating leverage affect a project's beta and its cost of capital?
3. How do differences in operating risk affect the choice of firms to use in estimating the beta for a project?

SUMMARY

The cost of capital—a capital budgeting project's required return—is based on the concept of an opportunity cost. It is estimated from the expected return on comparable publicly traded securities. The relevant question is: "What else can be done with the money?" In Chapter 15, we examine the effect of capital market imperfections such as asymmetric taxes, asymmetric information, and transaction costs on a firm's financing decision.

- The cost of capital is not the historical cost of funds. Market rates change regularly because of changes in expected inflation and in the supply and demand for money. Investment decisions must be based on the alternatives that are *currently* available.
- The cost of capital depends on a project's operating risk. Theoretically, each project has its own cost of capital. In practice, however, projects are typically categorized by risk classes, each of which has a different cost of capital.
- A project's cost of capital is the same as the cost of capital for the firm's current operations *only* if the nondiversifiable risk of the project is identical to the nondiversifiable risk of the existing firm taken as a whole.
- Present value is a function of both expected cash flows and the required return. With a pure risk-return trade-off, present value is constant, and changes in the other two parameters offset one another.
- Except for capital market imperfections, changes in financial leverage involve a pure risk-return trade-off. Therefore, a capital budgeting project's cost of capital does not vary as the degree of financial leverage changes—in a perfect capital market environment.
- A project's cost of capital does not equal either the required return on debt or the required return on leveraged equity. The cost of capital is the *weighted average* of the current required returns on debt and equity, where the weights are the market-value proportions of debt and equity in the firm's capital structure. In a perfect capital market environment, this weighted average is constant across alternative financing packages and is equal to the required return for an all-equity-financed firm.
- The leverage ratio, L, depends on the market values of the firm's debt and equity, not on the initial cost of the investment.
- The market value of an investment differs from its cost by the investment's NPV.
- Potential differences in the value of a project between one firm and another undertaking the project are reflected in the expected cash flows rather than the cost of capital.
- With riskless (or very low risk) debt, the relationship between the asset beta and the equity beta depends on the leverage ratio and marginal tax rate as given in Equation

(11.6). If debt is risky, the relationship between the asset beta and the equity beta is given by Equation (11.5).

- When a project's risk differs from the average risk of the firm's existing assets, its cost of capital can be estimated using the risk and cost of capital for other businesses (surrogate firms) with lines of business that resemble the project.

EQUATION SUMMARY

$$\text{Firm value} = \text{Equity} + \text{Debt} \tag{11.1}$$

$$\text{WACC} = \frac{E}{(D+E)} r_e + \frac{D}{(D+E)}(1-T)r_d = (1-L)r_e + L(1-T)r_d \tag{11.2}$$

$$\beta_A = \sum_{j=1}^{J} w_j \beta_j \tag{11.3}$$

$$\text{WACC} = r_f + \beta_A(r_M - r_f) \tag{11.4}$$

$$(1 - TL)\beta_A = L\beta_d + (1 - L)\beta \tag{11.5}$$

$$\beta_A = \frac{(1-L)\beta}{(1-TL)} \tag{11.6}$$

QUESTIONS

1. Define what we mean by the firm's financing decision and the firm's investment decision. What entities are on the "other side" of these decisions?
2. What is the NPV of a project that has an IRR exactly equal to its cost of capital?
3. What are the two factors on which present value depends?
4. Distinguish between operating leverage and financial leverage.
5. Give an example of a case where the expected future cash flows are increased but the present value of the flows remains unchanged.
6. A firm uses a single discount rate to compute the NPV of all its potential capital budgeting projects, even though the projects have a wide range of nondiversifiable risk. The firm then undertakes all those projects with positive NPVs. Briefly explain why such a firm would tend to become riskier over time.
7. What are the important differences in the way operating risk (versus financial risk) enters into the consideration of a capital budgeting project?
8. Describe how you would go about estimating a required return for computing the NPV of a project.

CHALLENGING QUESTIONS

9. The treasurer of a large firm is considering investing $50 million in 10-year Treasury notes that yield 8.5%. The firm's WACC is 15%. Is this a negative-NPV project? Explain.
10. Yukon Etiquette, Inc. has a beta of 1.85 and is deciding whether to issue stock to raise money for a capital budgeting project that has the same risk as the market and an IRR of 20%. If the riskless return is 10% and the expected return on the market is 15%, should the firm go ahead with the investment?
11. Assume that the value of a firm is not identical when it is computed using the left-hand versus right-hand sides of our market value balance sheet. In particular, suppose that the value of the assets ($A_1 + A_2 + \ldots$) is $10 million, whereas the value of the liabilities and owners' equity (Equity + Debt) is $8.5 million, both on the basis of market values in their respective markets. Assuming both values are correct, what transactions could you make to profit from this situation? Can you think of a second set of transactions you could use as an alternative way to profit from the situation?
12. A firm calculates its cost of debt and finds it to be 9.75%. It then calculates its cost of equity capital and finds it to be 16.25%. The firm's chairman tells the chief financial officer that the firm should issue debt because it is cheaper than equity. How should the chief financial officer respond to the chairman? (You may assume that the chief financial officer's job is secure!)

PROBLEMS

LEVEL A (BASIC)

A1. (Calculating the WACC) The required return on debt is 8%, the required return on equity is 14%, and the marginal tax rate is 40%. If the firm is financed 70% equity and 30% debt, what is the weighted average cost of capital?

A2. (Calculating the WACC) The required return on debt is 9%, the required return on equity is 16%, and the marginal tax rate is 35%. If the firm is financed 60% equity and 40% debt, what is the weighted average cost of capital?

A3. (Calculating the WACC) The following values apply to the Drop Corporation: $r_d = 7.5\%$, $r_e = 13\%$, $T = 38\%$, $D = \$100$, and $E = \$200$. What is the weighted average cost of capital?

A4. (Calculating the WACC) The following values apply to the Henry Corporation: $r_d = 5.5\%$, $r_e = 19\%$, $T = 40\%$, $D = \$200$, and $E = \$500$. What is the weighted average cost of capital?

A5. (Market versus book value weights) Prakesh Productions has 10,000 outstanding bonds that have a book value of $1,000 per bond and a market value of $1,050 per bond. Prakesh has 40,000 outstanding shares with a per-share book value of $20 and market value of $45. When estimating the weighted average cost of capital, what proportions of debt and equity capital should be used?

A6. (Market versus book value weights) Miami Distribution has 1,000 outstanding bonds that have a book value of $1,000 per bond and a market value of $1,200 per bond. Miami Distribution has 250,000 outstanding shares with a per-share book value of $40 and market value of $68. When estimating the weighted average cost of capital, what proportions of debt and equity capital should be used?

A7. (Estimating the WACC with three sources of capital) Eschevarria Research has the capital structure given here. If Eschevarria's tax rate is 30%, what is its weighted average cost of capital?

	BOOK VALUE	MARKET VALUE	BEFORE-TAX COST
Bonds	$1,000	$1,000	8%
Preferred stock	400	300	9%
Common stock	600	1,700	14%

A8. (Estimating the WACC with three sources of capital) NYM has the capital structure given here. If NYM's tax rate is 40%, what is its weighted average cost of capital?

	BOOK VALUE	MARKET VALUE	BEFORE-TAX COST
Bonds	$1,000	$1,000	10%
Preferred stock	800	1,200	15%
Common stock	2,000	2,200	12%

A9. (Calculating the WACC) Exxon Mobil's required return for equity, r_e, is 14%. Its required return for debt, r_d, is 8%, its debt-to-total-value ratio, L, is 35%, and its marginal tax rate, T, is 40%. Calculate Exxon Mobil's WACC.

A10. (Calculating the WACC) Getty's required return for equity, r_e, is 18%. Its required return for debt, r_d, is 6%, its debt-to-total-value ratio, L, is 45%, and its marginal tax rate, T, is 40%. Calculate Getty's WACC.

A11. (Finding NPVs with differing project risks) Assume the expected return on the market portfolio is 15% and the riskless return is 9%. Also assume that all of the projects listed here are perpetuities with annual cash flows (in $) and betas as indicated. None of the projects requires or precludes any of the other projects and each project costs $2,000.

a. What is the NPV of each project?

b. Which projects should the firm undertake?

PROJECT	A	B	C	D	E	F
Annual cash flow	310	500	435	270	385	450
Beta	1.00	2.25	2.22	0.65	1.37	2.36

A12. (Finding NPVs with differing project risks) Assume the expected return on the market portfolio is 14% and the riskless return is 7%. Also assume that all of the projects listed here are perpetuities with annual cash flows (in $) and betas as indicated. None of the projects requires or precludes any of the other projects and each project costs $1,000.

a. What is the NPV of each project?

b. Which projects should the firm undertake?

PROJECT	A	B	C	D	E	F
Annual cash flow	250	200	400	320	355	285
Beta	1.00	2.5	3.1	0.9	0.85	2.65

A13. (Asset and equity betas) Goh Travel, Inc. is a diversified conglomerate with six different business lines. The investments, their betas, and the proportion of the firm's value invested in each are given.

a. What is β_A for Goh Travel?

b. If Goh is 20% debt financed, what is Goh's equity beta, β? Ignore taxes for this problem.

BUSINESS LINES	A	B	C	D	E	F
Proportion of firm value	20%	10%	12%	10%	34%	14%
Beta	1.00	2.25	2.22	0.65	1.37	2.36

A14. (Asset and equity betas) Ultra Products, Inc. is a diversified corporation with six different divisions. The investments, their betas, and the proportion of the firm's value invested in each are given.

a. What is β_A for Ultra?

b. If Ultra is 20% debt financed, what is Ultra's equity beta, β? Ultra has a 40% tax rate.

DIVISION	A	B	C	D	E	F
Proportion of firm value	30%	15%	25%	10%	12%	8%
Beta	2.5	0.85	1.6	1.9	2.4	3.5

A15. (Asset and equity betas) If Goodyear has a debt-to-total-value ratio, L, of 43% and its common stock has a beta of 1.32, what is the approximate value of Goodyear's firm beta, β_A? Ignore taxes for this problem.

A16. (Asset and equity betas) If Michelin has a debt-to-total-value ratio, L, of 60% and its common stock has a beta of 1.1, what is the approximate value of Michelin's firm beta, β_A, if Michelin is taxed at the 40% rate?

LEVEL B

B1. (Cost of equity) The cost of capital is 10%, the after-tax cost of debt is 5%, and the firm is 50% debt financed. What is the cost of equity?

B2. (Cost of equity) The cost of capital is 15%, the after-tax cost of debt is 6%, and the firm is 30% debt financed. What is the cost of equity?

B3. (Cost of equity) The cost of capital is 11%, the before-tax cost of debt is 8%, and the marginal income tax rate is 40%. The market value of debt is \$40 million and the market value of equity is \$80 million. What is the cost of equity?

B4. (Cost of equity) The cost of capital is 15%, the before-tax cost of debt is 9%, and the marginal income tax rate is 40%. The market value of debt is \$50 million and the market value of equity is \$50 million. What is the cost of equity?

B5. (Capital structure weights) The cost of capital is 14%, the after-tax cost of debt is 6%, and the cost of equity is 16%. What proportions of the firm are financed with debt and equity?

B6. (Capital structure weights) The cost of capital is 13%, the after-tax cost of debt is 8%, and the cost of equity is 18%. What proportions of the firm are financed with debt and equity?

B7. (Capital structure weights) The required return on debt (before taxes) is 7.5%, the required return on equity is 15%, and the cost of capital is 10%. If the marginal income tax rate is 40%, what are the proportions of debt and equity financing?

B8. (Capital structure weights) The required return on debt (before taxes) is 7.6%, the required return on equity is 12%, and the cost of capital is 9%. If the marginal income tax rate is 40%, what are the proportions of debt and equity financing?

B9. (Evaluating investments with differing risks) You are considering three stocks for investment purposes. The required return on the market portfolio is 14%, and the riskless return is 9%. Based on the information given, in which (if any) of these stocks should you invest?

STOCK	BETA	CURRENT PRICE	LAST DIVIDEND	GROWTH RATE
A	1.3	$15	$1.20	5%
B	0.9	28	1.30	10
C	1.1	31	2.40	8

B10. (Evaluating investments with differing risks) You are considering three stocks for investment purposes. The required return on the market portfolio is 15%, and the riskless return is 6%. Based on the information given, in which (if any) of these stocks should you invest?

STOCK	BETA	CURRENT PRICE	LAST DIVIDEND	GROWTH RATE
A	1.6	$18	$1.50	2%
B	0.8	32	1.40	12
C	1.6	12	2.30	6

B11. (Finding the WACC) The information given here has been gathered about O'ryan Swim-Where, Ltd. Based on this information, estimate O'ryan's WACC.

Current market value of common shares (10 million outstanding)	$23.63/share
Next year's expected cash dividend	$1.92/share
Expected constant annual dividend growth rate	8%
Current market value of bonds	
(100,000 bonds outstanding, 8.5% coupon, maturing in 21 years)	$835.00/bond
Corporate tax rate	34%

B12. (Finding the WACC) The information given here has been gathered about Northern Outriggers, Inc. Based on this information, estimate Northern's WACC.

Current market value of common shares (2 million outstanding)	$14/share
Next year's expected cash dividend	$1.5/share
Expected constant annual dividend growth rate	3%
Current market value of bonds	
(10,000 bonds outstanding, 8.5% coupon, maturing in 10 years)	$950.00/bond
Corporate tax rate	40%

B13. (Graphing the cost of capital) The D. B. Spiess Finance Corporation is financed with 80% debt and 20% common equity. Its required return on equity is $r_e = 25\%$ and its pretax cost of debt is 10%. Its marginal ordinary income tax rate is 40%. The riskless return is 8% (pretax). Graph WACC, r_e, and $(1 - T)r_d$ for values of L between 0 and 1. What have you assumed in drawing these curves?

B14. (All-equity and leveraged returns) You plan to invest $10,000 in a security, borrowing $6,000 of the cost from a friend, thus putting up $4,000 of your own money. The cost of debt is 12%, and there are no taxes. With this arrangement, you expect a return of 20% on your equity investment. What would your return be without the leverage? That is, what would your return be if the entire $10,000 was your own money?

B15. (All-equity and leveraged returns) You plan to invest $100,000 in a security, borrowing $50,000 of the cost from a friend, thus putting up $50,000 of your own money. The cost of debt is 11%, and there are no taxes. With this arrangement, you expect a return of 18% on your equity investment. What would your return be without the leverage? That is, what would your return be if the entire $100,000 was your own money?

B16. (Estimating the WACC) Seitz Nails has 2,000 bonds outstanding with a $1,000 face value per bond, 7% annual coupon, 15-year maturity, and $950 market value. Seitz has 50,000 shares outstanding with a market value of $60 per share, expected dividend next year of $3.00, and a perpetual dividend growth rate of 6%. The marginal tax rate is 40%.

a. What is the after-tax cost of debt financing?

b. What is the after-tax cost of equity financing?

c. What is the weighted average cost of capital?

B17. (Estimating the WACC) Furst Cola has 5,000 bonds outstanding with a $1,000 face value per bond, 8% annual coupon, 20-year maturity, and $900 market value. Furst Cola has 50,000 shares outstanding with a market value of $85 per share, expected dividend next year of $5.00, and a perpetual dividend growth rate of 6%. The marginal tax rate is 40%.

a. What is the after-tax cost of debt financing?

b. What is the after-tax cost of equity financing?

c. What is the weighted average cost of capital?

B18. (Estimating the WACC) Latin Pollo has 10,000 bonds and 400,000 shares outstanding. The bonds have a 10% annual coupon, $1,000 face value, $1,050 market value, and 10-year maturity. The beta on the stock is 1.30 and its price per share is $40. The riskless return is 6%, the expected market return is 14%, and Latin Pollo's tax rate is 40%.

a. What is the after-tax cost of debt financing?

b. What is the after-tax cost of equity financing?

c. What is the weighted average cost of capital?

B19. (Estimating the WACC) Komishito has 100,000 bonds and 5,000,000 shares outstanding. The bonds have a 9% annual coupon, $1,000 face value, $1,100 market value, and 10-year maturity. The beta on the stock is 1.20 and its price per share is $50. The riskless return is 6%, the expected market return is 14%, and Komishito's tax rate is 40%.

a. What is the after-tax cost of debt financing?

b. What is the after-tax cost of equity financing?

c. What is the weighted average cost of capital?

B20. (Estimating the WACC from the asset structure) McCabe Interests has three major investments, which are given here. What should be McCabe's weighted average cost of capital?

INVESTMENT	MARKET VALUE	REQUIRED RETURN
Storage sheds	$35 million	12%
Ice rinks	15 million	17%
Office furniture sales	50 million	15%

B21. (Estimating the WACC from the asset structure) MBA Holdings has three major investments, which are given here. What should be MBA Holdings' weighted average cost of capital?

INVESTMENT	MARKET VALUE	REQUIRED RETURN
Vacuum cleaners	$10 million	16%
Computer rentals	30 million	18%
Accounting services	60 million	11%

B22. (Leveraged investment returns) You have a chance to make a $25,000 one-year investment. The investment is expected to earn 18%, and there are no taxes. If you borrow $10,000 at 10% and put up the other $15,000 with your own money, what would be your return on the $15,000?

B23. (Project market line) Parr's Poultry Place, Inc. is considering two mutually exclusive one-year capital budgeting projects, A and B. A costs \$100,000, and its expected payoff one year later is \$114,000. The standard deviation of its return is 25%. B costs \$50,000, and its expected payoff one year later is \$56,000. The standard deviation of its return is also 25%. The expected return and standard deviation of return on the market portfolio are 14% and 16%, respectively. The going rate on government bonds is 9%, and Parr has bonds outstanding with a current yield of 10.5%. The correlation coefficient, Corr, between the returns for A and the market is 0.8, whereas the correlation coefficient between the returns for B and the market is 0.32. Ignoring taxes and depreciation, determine what investment decision Parr should make concerning these projects.

B24. (Project market line) Suppose Texaco is considering two mutually exclusive one-year capital budgeting projects, A and B. A costs \$50,000, and its expected payoff one year later is \$57,000. The standard deviation of its return is 25%. B costs \$25,000, and its expected payoff one year later is \$28,000. The standard deviation of its return is also 25%. The expected return and standard deviation of return on the market portfolio are 14% and 16%, respectively. The going rate on government bonds is 9%, and Texaco has bonds outstanding with a current yield of 10.5%. The correlation coefficient, Corr, between the returns for A and the market is 0.8, whereas the correlation coefficient between the returns for B and the market is 0.32. Ignoring taxes and depreciation, determine what investment decision Texaco should make concerning these projects?

B25. (Excel: Capital structure in a perfect capital market) Graph the required return to equity, the after-tax required return to debt, and the WACC for Billett's Welcome Matt Corp, using a tax rate of 34%.

L	R_D	R_E
0.05	0.0710	0.1065
0.10	0.0731	0.1097
0.20	0.0777	0.1166
0.30	0.0830	0.1244
0.40	0.0889	0.1334
0.50	0.0959	0.1439
0.60	0.1040	0.1560
0.70	0.1135	0.1703
0.80	0.1250	0.1875
0.90	0.1391	0.2087
0.95	0.1475	0.2213
0.99	0.1550	0.2325

LEVEL C (ADVANCED)

C1. (Finding the WACC using surrogate firms) Eastern Chemical has an oil and gas subsidiary that is considering the purchase of \$100 million worth of proven oil and gas properties. Eastern's financial staff has compiled the following list of firms in the same business as the project under consideration. All eight firms as well as Eastern pay income tax at a 34% marginal rate. Eastern's target debt ratio is 0.40, and its oil and gas subsidiary's target debt ratio is 0.50.

a. Calculate an estimate of the unleveraged beta, β_A for the proven oil and gas project. Eastern's subsidiary has bonds outstanding with a yield to maturity of 15.15%.

b. Assuming a 10% riskless return and a 6% expected excess return on the market portfolio, calculate the required return on unleveraged equity, r_e, for the project.

c. Calculate the weighted average cost of capital, WACC.

FIRM	EQUITY BETA	DEBT RATIO, L
N.J. Chemical	1.35	0.35
Great Lakes Chemical	1.25	0.25
Johnson Chemical	1.50	0.45
Clark Chemical	1.40	0.40
Franklin Oil	1.40	0.50
Oscar Oil	1.45	0.50
VMB Oil & Gas	1.30	0.45
Peters Oil & Gas	1.55	0.60

C2. (Finding the WACC using surrogate firms) Pendleton Publishing has a magazine subsidiary that is considering the purchase of $5 million worth of publishing rights from a competing magazine. Pendleton's financial staff has compiled the following list of firms in the same business as the project under consideration. All five firms as well as Pendleton pay income tax at a 40% marginal rate. Pendleton's target debt ratio is 0.40, and its magazine subsidiary's target debt ratio is 0.50.

a. Calculate an estimate of the unleveraged beta, β_A for the magazine project. Pendleton's subsidiary has bonds outstanding with a yield to maturity of 11%.

b. Assuming a 9% riskless return and a 7% expected excess return on the market portfolio, calculate the required return on unleveraged equity, r_e, for the project.

c. Calculate the weighted average cost of capital, WACC.

FIRM	EQUITY BETA	DEBT RATIO, L
Florida Publishing	1.5	0.30
Norman Periodicals	1.2	0.45
Sherman Publishing	1.55	0.35
Frederick Publishing	1.35	0.25
B&Y Publishing	1.3	0.40

C3. (Estimating the WACC using a surrogate firm) Dyl Pickle is a new firm in the condiment business. Dyl has $25 million in debt and its equity is worth an estimated $50 million. Because Dyl is not publicly traded, it is unsure of its cost of capital and cost of equity. Dyl considers Mercado Products to be very similar to itself and will use Mercado as a surrogate firm to estimate its own WACC. Mercado's equity beta is 1.40, its leverage ratio is 40%, and its marginal tax rate is 34%. Dyl's tax rate is also 34%.

a. Estimate Mercado's and Dyl's asset beta.

b. Estimate Dyl's equity beta.

c. Assuming a riskless return of 6% and an expected return on the market of 14%, what should be Dyl Pickle's cost of capital and cost of equity?

C4. (Finding WACC using surrogate firms) A firm considering a capital budgeting project identifies five comparable firms and collects the information given here. The project should be one-third debt financed, and the firm's marginal tax rate is 34%.

a. Calculate the leveraged beta for the project.

b. The riskless interest rate is 9%, and the excess return on the market portfolio is 6%. Calculate the required return on project equity.

c. The cost of debt for the project (before taxes) is 11%. Calculate the cost of capital for the project.

FIRM	BETA	DEBT RATIO, L
A	1.10	0.25
B	1.20	0.30
C	1.15	0.20
D	1.30	0.50
E	1.25	0.25

C5. (Asset beta if debt is risky) Calimari Fisheries, Ltd. is financed with $L = 0.72$ proportion of debt that is so large that the beta of the firm's debt, β_d, is 0.32—too large to ignore. If the beta of Calimari's common stock is 3.1 and the tax rate is 34%, what is the beta for the firm's assets, β_A?

C6. (Asset beta if debt is risky) New Jersey Realtors is financed with $L = 0.65$ proportion of debt that is so large that the beta of the firm's debt, β_d, is 0.39—too large to ignore. If the beta of the firm's common stock is 2.8 and the tax rate is 40%, what is the beta for the firm's assets, β_A?

C7. (Excel: Equity and debt betas if debt is risky) DeFusco Corporation is 100% equity financed and has an equity beta of 1.20. The debt betas associated with the following amounts of debt financing are:

Debt financing	0%	10%	20%	30%	40%	50%	60%	70%	80%	90%	100%
Debt beta	0.00	0.00	0.00	0.02	0.05	0.10	0.20	0.35	0.55	0.80	1.20

a. Assume the tax rate is zero. What equity beta is associated with each of the amounts of leverage?

b. Assume the risk-free rate is 4.5% and the expected market return is 8.5%. What is the required return on debt, equity, and assets for each of the amounts of leverage?

MINICASE DIVISIONAL COST OF CAPITAL

A recent annual report for Diageo PLC explains that its investments are expected to generate cash returns that exceed its "long-term cost of capital," which Diageo estimated to be approximately 10%. Diageo has three main lines of business: food items, such as Haagen Dazs ice cream; alcoholic beverages, such as Seagrams; and restaurants, such as Burger King. Diageo did not report costs of capital separately for these three businesses. Information from the annual report is given here, followed by relevant market data.

Financial information:	
Cash and marketable securities	\$1,498 million (approximates market value)
Short-term debt	\$706 million (approximates market value)
Long-term debt	\$8,509 million (\$8,747 million market value)
Common shares outstanding	788 million
Year-end share price	\$55.875
Income tax rate	34%
Market data:	
Diageo's beta	1.00
Diageo's long-term borrowing rate	6.75%
Riskless returns:	
Short term	5.13%
Intermediate term	5.50
Long term	6.00
Market risk premium:	
Short term	8.40%
Intermediate term	7.40
Long term	7.00

The following table provides information concerning publicly traded restaurant firms.

FIRM	STOCK LISTED	BETA	TOTAL DEBT (\$ MILLIONS)	PREFERRED STOCK (\$ MILLIONS)	COMMON SHARES (MILLIONS)	CLOSING STOCK PRICE
Applebee's	NASDAQ	1.30	28.5	–	31.0	\$22.750
Bob Evans Farms	NASDAQ	0.95	54.7	–	42.3	19.000
Brinker International	NYSE	1.70	104.7	–	72.1	15.125
CKE Restaurants	NYSE	1.15	86.7	–	18.4	16.000
McDonald's	NYSE	1.00	4,820.1	411.1	694.0	45.125
NPC International	NASDAQ	0.80	81.4	–	24.5	7.250
Shoney's	NYSE	0.90	440.4	–	41.5	10.250
Wendy's International	NYSE	1.15	147.0	–	103.4	21.250

QUESTIONS

1. Diageo subtracts the value of its portfolio of short-term investments, which is held outside the United States and is not required to support day-to-day operations, from its total debt when calculating its "net debt ratio." Use Diageo's net debt ratio to calculate Diageo's overall WACC.
2. Should Diageo use its overall cost of capital to evaluate its restaurant investments? Under what circumstances would it be correct to do so?
3. Estimate the cost of capital for Diageo's restaurant businesses.
4. Explain why there is a difference between Diageo's overall cost of capital and the cost of capital for its restaurant businesses.

12

Risk, Return, and Contingent Outcomes

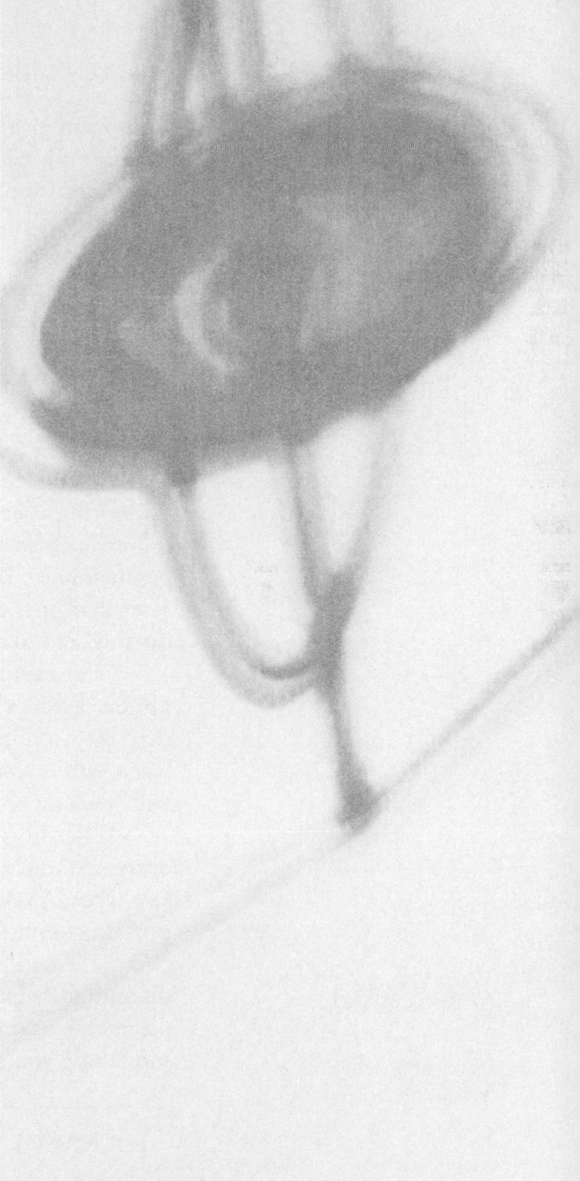

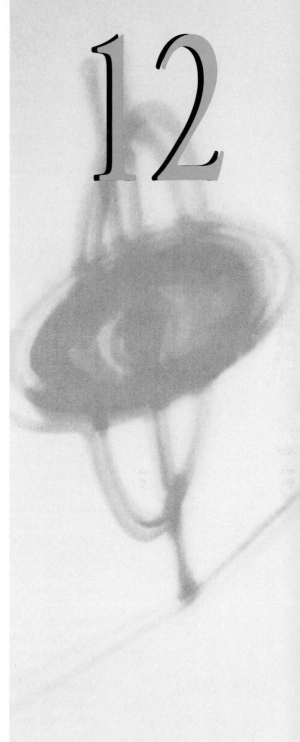

Options are everywhere. People often say *option* to refer to a choice or alternative. For example, someone might say they have a lot of options, or that they do not have any options. We all know the first situation is good, and the second is bad. That is because we understand the Options Principle: Options are valuable.

People like options. Options provide some amount of control over uncertain events. Insurance is an option you purchase for protection against bad events such as death or fire. At the heart of an option is a contingency—something that may happen but is not certain to. An option is a contingent claim to particular outcomes; it comes into play only when certain conditions occur, such as an accident or winning the lottery.

Of course, most options do not come with a "tag" attached that says "*option.*" Many of the options we focus on here are subtle or even difficult to recognize. They are implicit options inherent in a situation, such as the examples of "hidden" options we cited in our discussion of the Options Principle in Chapter 2.

Having told you that options are valuable, we must also say that options can be extremely complex. In some situations, measuring the exact value of an option can be very difficult. This can be the case even with obvious and explicit options, such as those traded in the capital markets.

This chapter explores what an option means in terms of participants' rights to a situation's possible outcomes. We identify and discuss both explicit and hidden options. We examine the factors that determine an option's value and how changes in those factors alter an option's value.

The purpose of this chapter is not to make you an expert at valuing options. Rather, we want to help you understand some important and very useful generalizations about options. These generalizations are powerful tools in our valuation skill set.

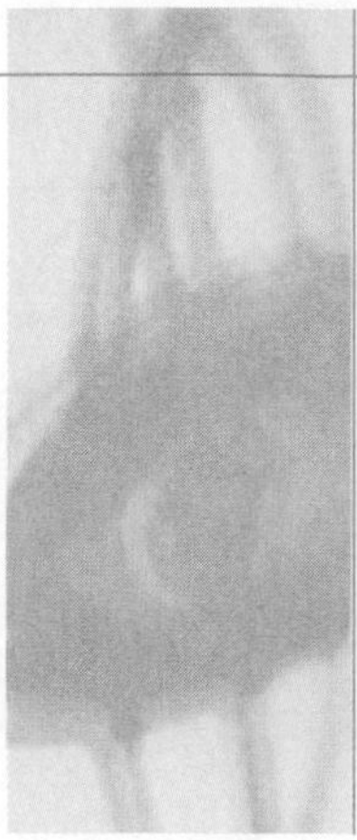

FOCUS ON PRINCIPLES

- *Options:* Look for options that significantly affect value.
- *Two-Sided Transactions:* Always consider both sides. The option buyer has the right, but the option seller has the obligation.
- *Incremental Benefits:* Measure the impact of options on an incremental basis.
- *Time Value of Money:* Include its impact on the value of an option.
- *Risk-Return Trade-Off:* An option splits the returns from an investment into pieces, altering risk and return for the buyers and sellers of the option.
- *Self-Interested Behavior:* People will exercise options when it benefits them. Options can be used to provide incentives to influence behavior.

12.1 OPTIONS

An **option** gives its holder the right to do something, without the obligation to do it. We use the term in its broadest sense: An option is *any* right that has no obligation attached to it. However, there are also specific types of options. A **call option** is the right to buy an asset. A **put option** is the right to sell an asset. In both cases the asset on which the option is written is known as the **underlying asset.** The **strike price** is the price at which the optionholder may buy or sell the underlying asset when the option is exercised. When you **exercise** an option, you make the exchange specified in the option contract.

When exercising an option would provide an advantage over buying or selling the underlying asset in the open market, the option is **in-the-money.** For example, an option to sell (put) an asset for $100 when its market value is only $80 is in-the-money. The option would allow the optionholder to sell the asset for $20 more than it is currently worth.

When exercising an option would *not* provide an advantage over buying or selling the underlying asset currently in the market, the option is **out-of-the-money.** For example, an option to buy (call) an asset at a strike price of $100, when you could buy it for $80 in the market, is out-of-the-money. By exercising the option contract, the optionholder would pay $20 more for the asset than it is currently worth. Out-of-the-money options are not exercised, but they are frequently sold to others who believe the option might become in-the-money in the future.

The **exercise value** (also called *intrinsic value*) is the amount of advantage an in-the-money option provides over buying or selling the underlying asset currently in the market. For example, the $20 just noted in the in-the-money example is its exercise value. An out-of-the-money option has a zero exercise value. After all, optionholders have the right without the obligation, so they will "walk away from the option" rather than exercise an out-of-the-money option.

Like most things, options do not live forever. An option's **expiration** is the point in time the option contract ceases to exist, the point at which the option expires or dies. Also, options are of two types. An **American option** is an option that can be exercised at any time prior to its expiration. In contrast, a **European option** can be exercised only at the end of the contract, not before.

The complexity of an option stems from its very nature. It is a contingent claim that has a discontinuity in the possible outcomes. The set of possible outcomes is cut off, or truncated, into pieces. Let us start by viewing an everyday item through "option glasses." Consider an example of something you might not think of as an option, a lottery ticket.

EXAMPLE An Option View of a Lottery Ticket

Suppose you bought a lottery ticket for $2.00. The first prize is $5,000 a week for life. There are five second prizes of $1,000 a week for life, and 20 third prizes of $250 a week for life. You, of course, would like to win the first prize. But you also understand that is not too likely;

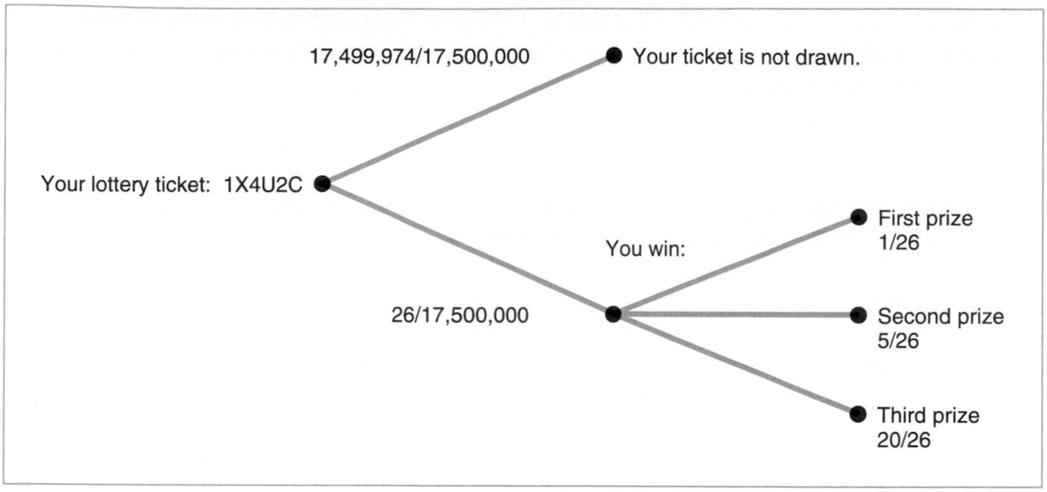

FIGURE 12.1
Lottery ticket outcomes.

17.5 million tickets will be sold. Upon reflection, the condition that it be *first prize* is not critical. You would rather win than not win—if you could choose. This is because the difference between winning one prize or another is relatively small compared to the difference between not winning and winning any of the prizes.

Your ticket is marked 1X4U2C. Watching the big drawing on TV, you see the 26 winning numbers. Your heart jumps, one of the second prizes is 1X4U2B. (None of the others are close.) Sooooo close! If only the last letter had been the next one in the alphabet. A small difference in the one drawn—a C rather than a B in that last place—would have made a *big* difference in your outcome. At the same time, a big difference in the one drawn—an outcome of 9A8B7C—would not have changed your outcome at all. You would still not have been a winner. This is what we mean by a discontinuity in the outcomes. The outcomes for your lottery ticket are shown in Figure 12.1.

Your lottery ticket is a contingent claim. A **contingent claim** can be made only if particular conditions occur. You can claim a prize only if your ticket is drawn a winner. In most cases (17,499,974 of the 17.5 million possible outcomes to be precise), your ticket is worthless and you get nothing. But if one of the 26 tickets that gets drawn happens to be yours, you can claim a prize in exchange for your lottery ticket. A contingent claim is an option in its broadest sense: the right without an obligation to do something.

Your lottery ticket is a European call option on a prize, which is the *underlying asset*. It is a *call option* because it gives you the right to "buy" the underlying asset for a *strike price* of zero. You will *exercise* your option by turning in your ticket if it has a winning number. It is a *European option* because you can do this only at its *expiration,* the end of the option's life just after the big drawing. Although you paid a $2 price for the ticket when you purchased it, your option had an *exercise value* of zero during its life because it gave zero advantage to claiming the prize before the drawing, so it was *out-of-the-money.* As it turned out, after the drawing, your option was still out-of-the-money when it *expired.*

A Call Option on an Asset

The lottery ticket example shows how something you do not think of as an option can implicitly be an option. Now let us look at an explicit call option on an asset.

Suppose Alice buys some land for $100,000 and immediately sells a *European call option* on the same piece of land with a *strike price* of $110,000 and *expiration* one year from today to Carl.

Both of their outcomes with respect to this land (the *underlying asset*) now include a contingency. At expiration, the most Alice can sell the land for is \$110,000; she might get less. The most Carl will have to pay for the land is \$110,000; he might be able to buy it for less. We can express this contingency for Alice as

$$\text{Alice's value} = \min\,[\text{market value; } 110{,}000]$$

The **min function** expresses the contingency in the situation mathematically. Its value is whichever is smaller, the market value *or* \$110,000.

Basic Option Value: The Exercise Value

The Principle of Two-Sided Transactions reminds us to consider the other side of the transaction. Carl's value is different from Alice's because he is on the other side of the transaction. We can show the "basic" value of Carl's call option, its *exercise value,* using the **max function,** which takes the largest of a set:

$$\text{Exercise value of Carl's call option} = \max[(\text{market value} - 110{,}000);\ 0]$$

We know Carl's option is never worth less than zero because an option cannot have a negative value. That is represented by the zero inside the max function. If the option is *out-of-the-money,* the exercise value is zero, and the option provides no advantage over an open market purchase. If the option is *in-the-money,* it would provide an advantage of (market value − 110,000) over an open market purchase.

Note that the strike price is a break point in the outcomes for both sides of the transaction. If the market value is below the strike price on a call option at expiration, it does not matter how much below, the option is worthless. Being just a little less is the same as being a great deal less. Whether the land's market value is \$109,000 or only \$1, the option is out-of-the-money and will not be *exercised.* But if the market value is above the strike price on a call option at expiration, the option is in-the-money and will be exercised. And the farther the market value is above the strike price, the larger the exercise value is.

The exercise value changes dollar for dollar with the market value whenever the market price is above the call option's strike price. This is shown in Figure 12.2, which graphs the exercise value of a call option against the market value of the underlying asset. The line going up from the strike price at a 45-degree angle shows the dollar-for-dollar relationship as the asset's market value

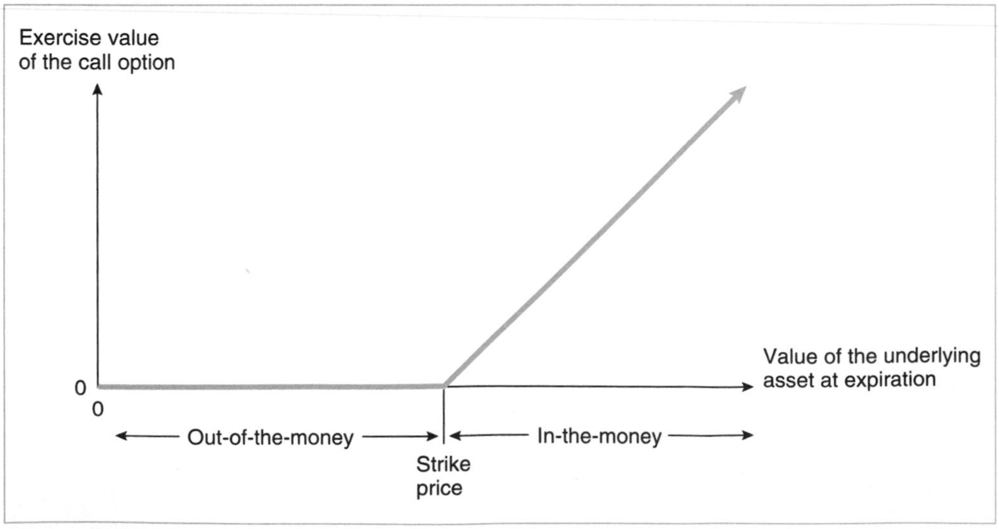

FIGURE 12.2
How the exercise value of a call option depends on the value of the underlying asset.

increases and the option becomes deeper in-the-money. The flat line shows how the exercise value is zero everywhere in the out-of-the-money area.

There is an important point to keep in mind when you look at a figure such as Figure 12.2. *There will be only one outcome.* At expiration, the underlying asset will have a single value, represented as one point on the horizontal axis. But before expiration, we do not know which point it will be. That is the nature of a risky—that is, uncertain—outcome. If we knew ahead of time what that outcome was going to be, we would know which side of the transaction was going to "win." And if we knew that, we would not need a complex analysis of option value. We would already know the exact value of the option!

Review

1. What is an option?
2. What is the difference between an American option and a European option?
3. What is the difference between a call option and a put option?
4. What does it mean to say that an option is in-the-money?

12.2 BUYING AND SELLING PARTS OF AN ASSET'S RETURN DISTRIBUTION

We can think of an asset as having a probability distribution of possible realized returns. Let us continue our example of Alice's land purchase. If she sells the land a year later for $126,000, she will have a realized return of 26% (= [126 − 100]/100). Now consider the impact of Carl's option on Alice's realized return.

A Call Option

Suppose Alice sold Carl the call option for $4,000. Figure 12.3 shows the net gain or loss to Alice and Carl a year later at the option's expiration, as a function of the market value of the land. Note once again that neither Alice nor Carl can choose the outcome. There will be only one value for the land a year later and they do not know what it will be.

Having sold the call option, a next-year market value outcome of $126,000 would give Alice a realized return of only about 14.6%.[1] Carl would exercise his option and buy the land for $110,000 (the strike price) because it is worth $126,000. As you can see, with any market value outcome greater than $110,000, Carl will exercise his option and Alice will have a realized return of 14.6% on her land investment and option sale. Carl has a claim on all of her possible realized returns above 14.6%.

When Alice sold the call option to Carl, she effectively sold him all her outcomes above a 14.6% realized return. So an option can be described as a claim to some of the possible realized returns on the underlying asset. Figure 12.4 presents the probability distribution of Alice's realized returns in terms of the sale value of the land.

We can divide the outcome distribution into two parts: one part above and the other part below $110,000. Alice would prefer the higher possible outcomes (those to the right of

[1]Alice spent $100,000 for the land and sold the option for $4,000, so her net investment is $96,000. She gains $14,000 because she must sell the land to Carl at $110,000. So her net gain of $14,000 provides a return of 14.6% (= 14/96).

Outcomes: Alice's Gain (Loss)	Alice's Return	Carl's Gain (Loss)	Carl's Return	Land value a year later ($)
$14,000	14.6%	$12,000	300%	126,000
14,000	14.6	8,000	200	122,000
14,000	14.6	4,000	100	118,000
14,000	14.6	0	0	114,000
14,000	14.6	−4,000	−100	110,000
10,000	10.4	−4,000	−100	106,000
6,000	6.3	−4,000	−100	102,000
0	0.0	−4,000	−100	96,000
−10,000	−10.4	−4,000	−100	86,000

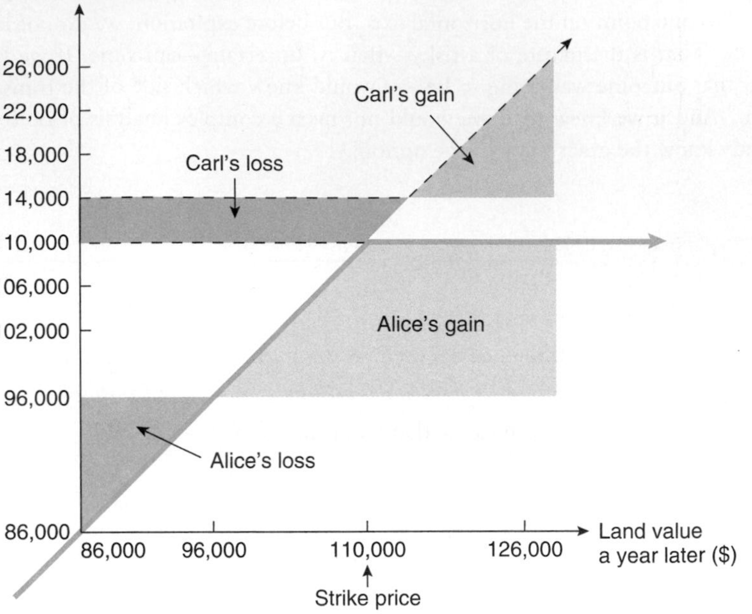

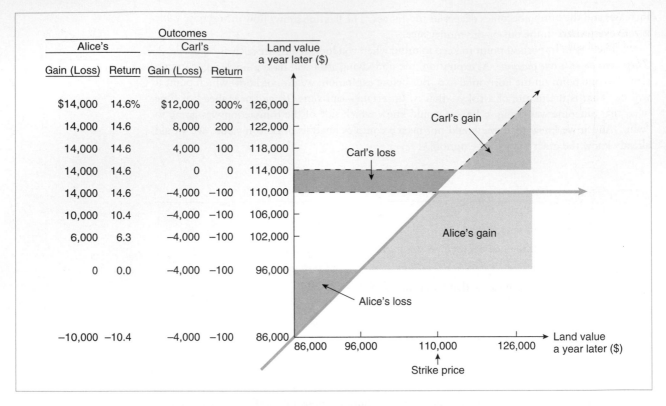

FIGURE 12.3
The gain or loss to Carl and Alice at the option's expiration, depending on the land's value. (Remember, there will be only one outcome for the land value (one point on the x-axis), which creates all of the y-axis outcomes. Alice's net investment is $96,000.)

FIGURE 12.4
The probability distribution of the future value of Alice's land.

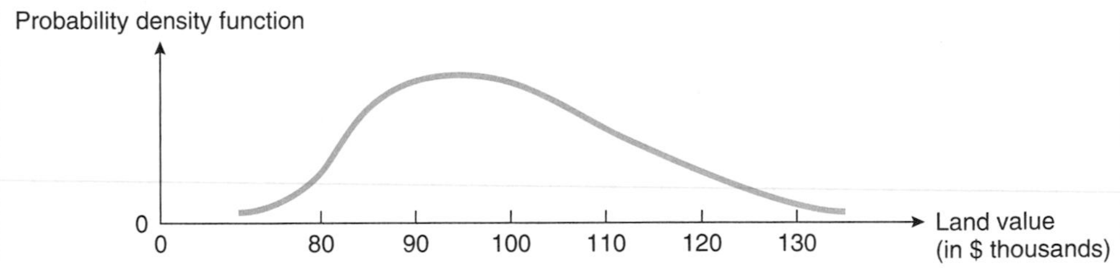

$110,000) over the lower possible outcomes (those to the left of $110,000). Of course, knowing that people prefer higher to lower return (Principle of Risk Aversion), this same statement can be made if we partition the distribution into two parts at *any* point. On this basis, we can view outcomes to the right of *any* split point as good outcomes, and those to the left as bad outcomes because all asset owners, like Alice, want the good outcomes but do not want the bad. As a result, asset owners must be paid to give up their claim to the good possible outcomes. This is why Carl had to pay Alice for his call option.

The split point between the good and bad outcomes is the strike price for the option. When an asset owner is paid for giving up good outcomes, the owner has sold a call option on the asset.

Figure 12.5 illustrates the claim portion of the return distribution for Carl's call option. A call option gives the optionholder the right to claim all of the good outcomes (the highlighted

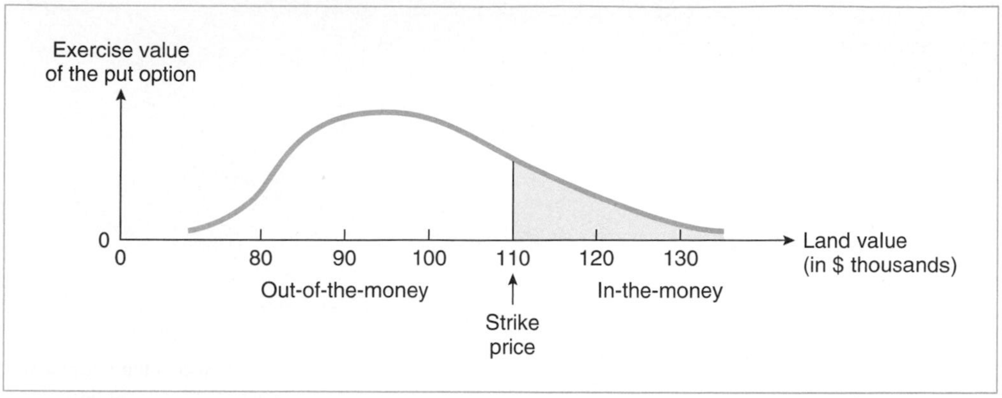

FIGURE 12.5
Carl's call option claim.

portion above the strike price) by exercising the option. Carl can avoid bad outcomes (those below the strike price) by simply not exercising his option. But if the outcome is more than $110,000, say $116,000, Carl can claim the return by buying the land from Alice for $110,000 and reselling it to someone else for $116,000, thereby gaining the $6,000 exercise value. You can see in Figure 12.3 that his net gain would then be $2,000 ($6,000 minus the $4,000 he paid for the call option).

EXAMPLE Computing Outcomes for a Call Option

Barb Wyre purchased a building in downtown San Francisco for $2.3 million. Right after this, she sold a one-year European call option on the building, with a strike price of $2.5 million, for $150,000 to Bob N. Weave. So Barb's net investment is $2.15 million. What are Barb's and Bob's outcomes, in terms of the land's possible value when the option expires?

They will be (in $ millions):

LAND VALUE	BARB'S GAIN (LOSS)	BARB'S RETURN	BOB'S GAIN (LOSS)	BOB'S RETURN
$3.00	$0.35	16.28%	$0.35	233.33%
2.75	0.35	16.28	0.10	66.67
2.50	0.35	16.28	−0.15	−100.00
2.25	0.10	4.65	−0.15	−100.00
2.00	−0.15	−6.98	−0.15	−100.00
1.75	−0.40	−18.60	−0.15	−100.00

A Put Option

Now consider the bad outcomes. Naturally, an asset owner like Alice would have to *pay* someone to get rid of the bad outcomes. When an asset owner pays someone else to take the bad outcomes, the asset owner has purchased a *put option* on the asset. The split point is again the (put) option's strike price. Figure 12.6 shows how exercise value of a put option (the savings from not having to keep the bad outcomes) depends on the value of the underlying asset.

If you look back at Figure 12.2, you can see how the exercise value of a put option is simply a mirror image of that for a call option. The 45-degree line, going up and to the left from the strike price, shows the one-for-one relationship between exercise value and asset value as the asset's market value decreases and the option becomes deeper in-the-money. The flat line shows how the exercise value is zero everywhere in the out-of-the-money area.

FIGURE 12.6
How the exercise value of a put option depends on the value of the underlying asset.

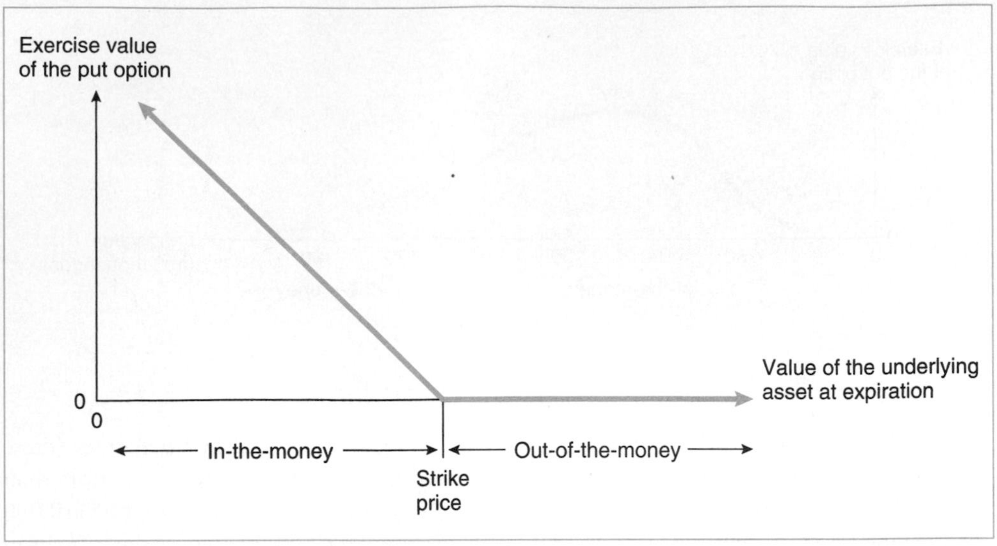

Buying a put option is like purchasing insurance on an asset. For example, automobile collision insurance is like a put option on a car, exercisable only in the event of an accident. In the event of an accident, the insurance company covers your loss (in an agreed-upon way, such as all but $100 if you have "$100 deductible" insurance). In effect, you had a bad outcome (an accident), so you "sell" the destroyed car to the insurance company for the strike price (typically, the car's market value before it was destroyed).

Let us return to Alice's land situation. Suppose for now that Alice has lost interest in selling a call option. However, she has just heard about put options and decided she does not want to have outcomes below $90,000. Because the outcomes below this $90,000 split point are bad outcomes, Alice would have to pay a person to take responsibility for them. In other words, Alice buys a put option from Paul (the put option writer) with a strike price of $90,000. The put option gives Alice the right to sell the land to Paul for $90,000.

Figure 12.7 illustrates Paul's put option obligation. The put option gives Alice the right to avoid all of the bad outcomes (the highlighted portion below the strike price) by exercising her option should one of them occur. Alice can claim the good outcomes by simply not exercising her put option. Therefore, if the land is worth more than $90,000, Alice will accept the outcome and let the put option expire without exercising it. With a land value less than $90,000, Alice will sell the land to Paul for $90,000, thereby gaining the exercise value of the put option—the difference between $90,000 and the market value of the land. Her net gain would then be the exercise value minus whatever she paid Paul for the option.

FIGURE 12.7
Paul's put option obligation (Alice's put option claim).

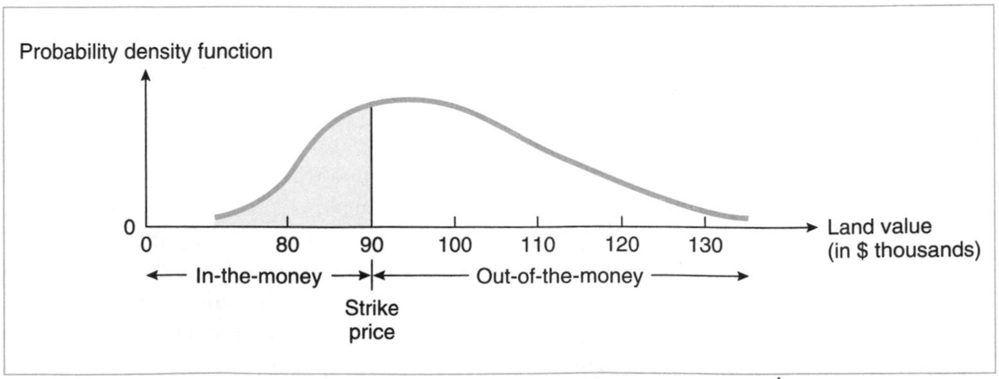

EXAMPLE Computing Outcomes for a Put Option

Barb Wyre purchased a building in downtown San Francisco for $2.3 million. Right after the purchase, she bought a one-year European put option on the building, with a strike price of $2.1 million, for $150,000 from Peter N. Da'Wolfe. So Barb's net investment is $2.45 million. What are Barb's and Peter's outcomes, in terms of the land's possible value when the option expires?

They will be (in $ millions):

LAND VALUE	BARB'S GAIN (LOSS)	BARB'S RETURN	PETER'S GAIN (LOSS)	PETER'S RETURN[2]
$3.00	$0.55	22.45%	$0.15	100.00%
2.75	0.30	12.24	0.15	100.00
2.50	0.05	2.04	0.15	100.00
2.25	−0.20	−8.16	0.15	100.00
2.00	−0.35	−14.29	0.05	33.33
1.75	−0.35	−14.29	−0.20	−133.33
1.50	−0.35	−14.29	−0.45	−300.00

Equivalent Claims, or Put-Call Parity

Sometimes the same claim can be structured in different ways. Suppose that instead of selling a call option to Carl, Alice buys a put option to sell her land to Paul with a strike price of $110,000. What will her payoff be like at expiration? If the land is worth less than $110,000, she will exercise her put and have $110,000. If the land is worth more than $110,000, she will have the value of the land.

Suppose that Carl wants a payoff identical to Alice's. If he invests in a bond that pays off $110,000 when the option expires and buys a call option with a strike price of $110,000, what will be his payoffs at expiration? If the land is worth less than $110,000, his call option is worthless, but his bond is worth $110,000. If the land is worth more than $110,000, he can use the $110,000 from the bond to exercise his call option, and he will have the value of the land.

The equivalence between the positions of Alice and Carl is called put-call parity. Alice owns the underlying asset and a put option. Carl owns a bond and a call option. **Put-call parity** expresses the relationship between the values of put and call options. Put-call parity is interesting. It means that there should be a unique relationship between the value of a call option and the value of a put option. But it also means: *Every situation that can be described in terms of a call option has a parallel description using a put option.* In this book, we try to use the description that seems easiest to see in a situation. However, because a situation can always be described in terms of *either* a call or a put option, we sometimes simply talk about the "optionality" in the situation.

Review

1. How does buying a call option let you benefit from the really good outcomes?
2. Why is buying a put option like purchasing insurance?
3. Suppose you do not want to sell a particular stock you own right now, because of tax reasons. But you are concerned its value might decline before you do sell it. Should you buy a call option or a put option?
4. What sort of relationship does put-call parity express?

[2]Peter's return is expressed as a percentage of the initial option value. Peter is taking risk, but he gets money at the start, rather than investing money. So his return is not "normal" in an economic sense.

12.3 VALUING AN OPTION

Thus far, we have not said much about the prices paid for options, except that Carl would have paid $4,000 for his call option. But where did that price come from? We referred to the exercise value of an option as the *basic* (or intrinsic) value of an option. But would Alice sell the call option to Carl for its exercise value? Of course not. In fact, the exercise value of Carl's call option is zero when he was to buy it—the option was out-of-the-money. The land is worth $100,000 (Alice just bought it for that price) and the strike price is $110,000. Alice would require more than the exercise value because she is taking on an obligation. Carl would have the right to buy the land for $110,000, because he would own the option (the right without the obligation). However, if Alice sold the option, she would have the obligation to sell the land for $110,000 if Carl decides to exercise his right. So there is more to an option's value than its exercise value.

Additional Option Value: The Time Premium

The **time premium of an option** (time premium for short) is the value of its "optionality." That is, the time premium is the extra value (above the exercise value) provided by having control. Control is the right without the obligation. It allows the optionholder to claim good outcomes and avoid bad ones. We call this part the time premium because it decreases as the option approaches expiration and becomes zero when the option is just about to expire. The time premium is determined by three factors: *time until expiration, risk of the underlying asset,* and market *riskless return.*

TIME UNTIL EXPIRATION It is easy to see why time is a determinant of option value. If you have a choice between two options where the only difference between them is their time until expiration, which option would you prefer to own? You can never be worse off with the option that has the longer time until expiration. Another way to think about this is to say that more time allows more chance for the option to be more in-the-money.[3]

RISK OF THE UNDERLYING ASSET Less obvious is how the *risk* (potential variation of the realized return) of the underlying asset affects the time premium. Figure 12.8 demonstrates the effect

FIGURE 12.8
The effect of risk on the value of a call option.

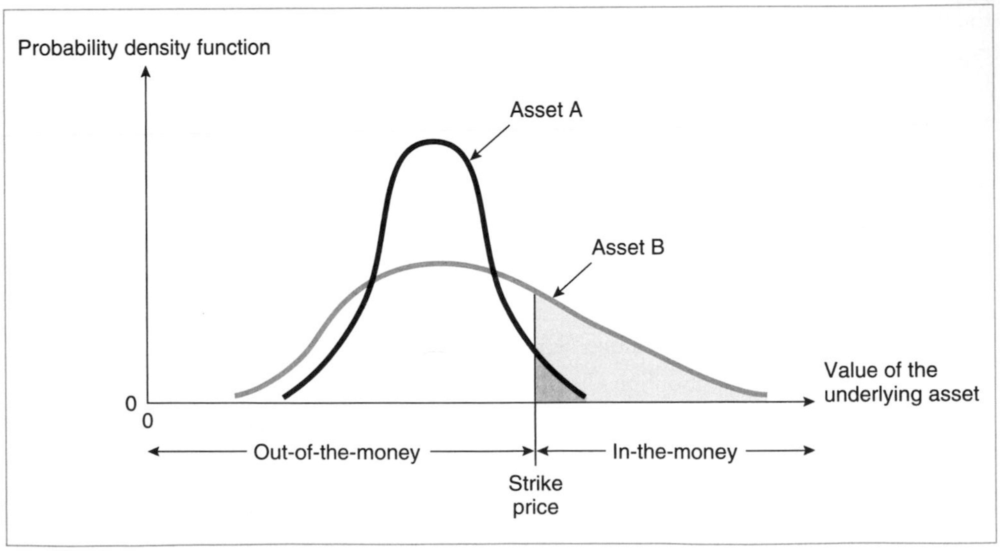

[3]Some cynics might point out that it also allows more chance to be more out-of-the-money. But remember, the optionholder can avoid bad outcomes—at least those beyond the strike price in the out-of-the-money direction.

of risk on a call option. It illustrates the claim portions for identical call options on assets with identical market values and strike prices but different risk levels. Asset A has an outcome distribution with a relatively small variation, whereas Asset B has an outcome distribution with a relatively large variation. As you can see, Asset B's claim portion is much larger. It has a much greater probability (the area under the curve) of having a good outcome than Asset A. Therefore, the call option for Asset B is worth more than the call option for Asset A. Although we illustrated this with a call option, the same concept holds for a put option. That is, greater asset risk also enlarges the value of a put option.

Here are two other ways to see the impact of asset risk on option value. First, the greater the risk, the more the underlying asset value can change in a given amount of time. And because the optionholder has control (claim the good outcomes, but leave the bad), if everything else is the same, the greater the possible change is, the more the option is worth.

Finally, note that an increase in risk (a flatter probability distribution) increases the number of outcomes at the extremes of the distribution. That means there are more extremely good outcomes to be claimed and also more extremely bad outcomes to be avoided. Again, with optionholder control, the more outcomes that are covered, the more valuable is the option.

RISKLESS RETURN The final determinant of the value of an option is the riskless return. It has opposite effects on call and put option values. We can think of the riskless return as the pure, or base, market required return. It is the basic, or benchmark, opportunity cost of money. The effect of the riskless return depends primarily on who has to pay the strike price if the option is exercised. The higher the riskless return is, the lower will be the present value of this payment, because the payment will not take place until the future when the option is exercised. A complexity of the riskless return is that its effect is reversed for call and put options. This is because the owner of a call option *pays* the strike price to obtain the underlying asset, whereas the owner of a put option *receives* the strike price to give the asset up.

As a result, an increase in the riskless return increases the value of a call option, but decreases the value of a put option.

Total Option Value

You can see now that an option's value has two parts: (1) its exercise (basic or intrinsic) value and (2) its time premium. We have just described the time premium. Let us review the option's exercise value. It contains the cutoff, or contingency, in the option. It is zero for an out-of-the-money option. For an in-the-money option, it is the difference between the strike price and the market value of the underlying asset. So the exercise value is itself determined by two factors: the *underlying asset's current market value* and the option's *strike price*. The larger the difference for an in-the-money option, the larger the exercise value and the more the option is worth. In other words, the deeper in-the-money an option is, the more it is worth.

MAXIMUM OPTION VALUE Although Alice may require Carl to pay more than the exercise value for the call option, there is a limit to what Carl will be willing to pay. In the extreme, that limit is the value of the land. After all, if he paid any more, he would be better off simply buying the land now. So the extreme upper limit on the value of a call option is the value of the underlying asset. In fact, except in the most extraordinary of situations, a call option's value would never even approach this limit.

We can now show you the boundaries of an option's value and what the total value of a typical call option looks like as a function of the value of the underlying asset. Figure 12.9 illustrates the value of two call options. As you can see, the options are worth more than their exercise values. The additional amount is the time premium. You can also see that one option is worth more than the other. Such a higher value can be due to a longer time until expiration, greater risk in the underlying asset, or an increase in the riskless return.

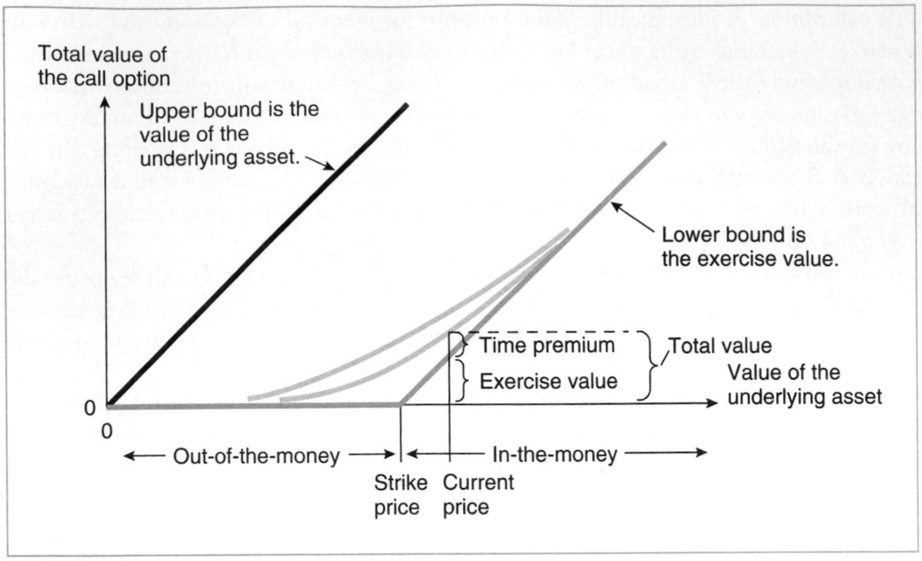

FIGURE 12.9
Total call option value as a function of underlying asset value.

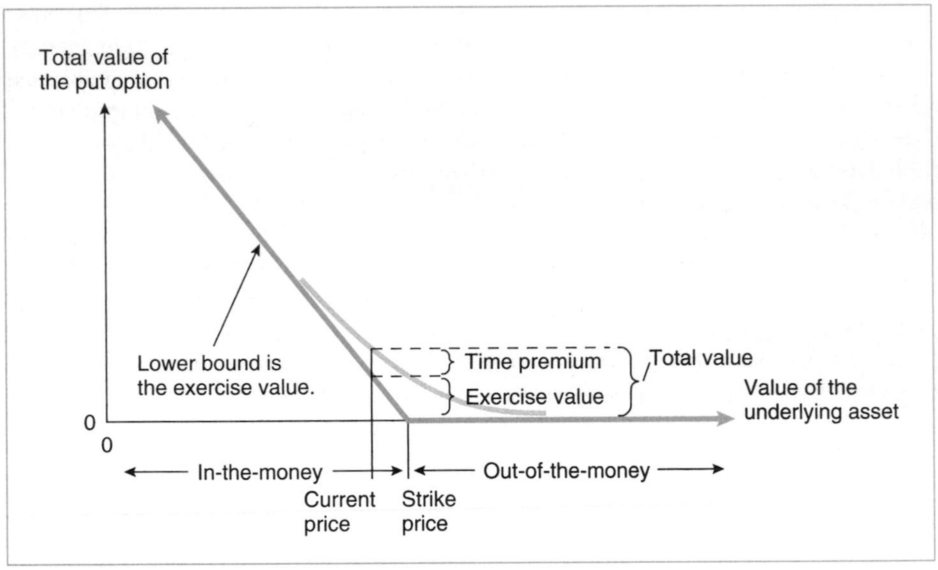

FIGURE 12.10
Total put option value as a function of underlying asset value.

Figure 12.10 illustrates the value of a put option as a function of underlying asset value. As with exercise value, you can see that total value of a put option increases when the stock price declines, whereas the call option's total value increases when the stock price increases.

Review

1. Why is there more to an option's value than its exercise value?
2. What is an option's time premium?
3. What three factors determine an option's time premium?
4. Why does greater asset risk increase the value of call options *and* put options?
5. What two factors determine an option's exercise value?

12.4 SOME IMPORTANT GENERALIZATIONS ABOUT OPTIONS

Using the determinants of an option's value, we can establish some generalizations about option valuation. These generalizations provide easy intuitions about the options, their values, and how the determinants affect value in a given situation. The generalizations are extremely important because they provide quick insights into many real world situations.

We start by looking at the determinants of option value. Table 12.1 summarizes these factors and indicates how an increase in each will affect the value of an option.

THE LARGEST TIME PREMIUM FOR AN OPTION OCCURS WHEN THE UNDERLYING ASSET'S VALUE EQUALS THE STRIKE PRICE You can see this for the options illustrated in Figure 12.9. The time premium is at its maximum here because the underlying asset's value could go either way. At the split point, when the underlying asset value exactly equals the strike price, the uncertainty is greatest about whether the option will expire in- or out-of-the-money.

AN OPTION'S TIME PREMIUM DECREASES AS THE OPTION BECOMES MORE IN- OR OUT-OF-THE-MONEY This phenomenon is also illustrated in Figure 12.9, and we note it in Table 12.1 as well. It occurs because there is less uncertainty about whether the option will expire in- or out-of-the-money when the underlying asset is *already* worth more or less than the strike price. Quite simply, an option that is already in- or out-of-the-money is more likely to stay that way than it is to change. (That is not to say it *cannot* change, but the likelihood is smaller. We are dealing with probabilities.)

AN AMERICAN OPTION IS NEVER WORTH LESS THAN A COMPARABLE EUROPEAN OPTION This is easy to understand. Essentially, there is more optionality in an American option. Consider two options that are comparable except that one is American and the other is European. The American option has everything the European option has, but in addition provides the added option of allowing exercise prior to expiration. Like any option, this added option cannot have a negative value. Therefore the American option is never worth less than the comparable European option. Of course, the added optionality has positive value in some situations, so in those cases the American option would be worth more than the comparable European option.

TABLE 12.1
The determinants of option value.

AN INCREASE IN THIS FACTOR	HAS THIS EFFECT ON THE OPTION'S VALUE
The option's exercise value	
depth in-the-money	increases it
depth out-of-the-money	has no effect on it
The option's time premium	
time until expiration	increases it
risk of the underlying asset	increases it
increase in riskless return	increases the value of a call option
increase in riskless return	decreases the value of a put option
depth in-the-money	decreases it
depth out-of-the-money	decreases it

AN OPTION'S TIME PREMIUM IS GENERALLY POSITIVE This always holds for an out-of-the-money option because an option cannot have a negative value. (This is our Corollary to the Options Principle.) For an in-the-money American option, if the time premium were negative, a person could buy and immediately exercise the option for an arbitrage profit. So market competition naturally enforces a positive time premium. This generalization does not hold strictly because in-the-money European options cannot be exercised during their life. It is therefore possible (although not frequent) to have a case where we know the asset's value is going down in the future, and the time premium becomes somewhat negative.

For example, consider a high-coupon bond that is currently selling above par value because of low interest rates. In the future, at maturity, the bond will be worth only its par value. Therefore, in such a case, we know the bond's value is going down in the future.

IT IS GENERALLY BETTER TO SELL RATHER THAN EXERCISE AN OPTION PRIOR TO ITS EXPIRATION Although this follows directly from the previous generalization, it is a very important insight. Quite simply, if you exercise an option before expiration, you give up its time premium. If you exercise the option, you get only its exercise value. If you sell the option, you get the exercise value *plus* the time premium. (This generalization also breaks down in the unlikely case of a negative time premium.)

THE FURTHER AN OPTION IS OUT-OF-THE-MONEY, THE LESS IT IS WORTH This generalization follows directly from two previous observations. First, an out-of-the-money option is worth only its time premium because its exercise value is zero. Second, the time premium decreases as the option gets further out-of-the-money.

But remember our lottery ticket example earlier. Even a very unlikely event *can* happen. Whenever one does, it can dramatically change things. When an option is far out-of-the-money, it is not worth very much and its existence seems insignificant. But if an unlikely event occurs and that option becomes in-the-money, the option's claim and value suddenly become very important. In Chapter 13, we show you how such things can happen with contingent stakeholder claims when a firm falls into financial distress.

Review

1. What underlying asset value produces the largest time premium for an option?
2. What happens to an option's time premium as the option becomes more in-the-money? What about when it becomes more out-of-the-money?
3. Can an American option ever be worth less than a comparable European option? Explain.
4. Is it generally better to sell or exercise an option prior to its expiration?

12.5 PLACES TO LOOK FOR OPTIONS

We said that options exist in *many* forms. The following sections show a number of places to look for options, to help you develop insight into their pervasive existence.

Easily Identified Options

Many options on financial securities have explicit terms and are easy to identify and understand.

INSURANCE As we noted earlier, in its simplest form, insurance is a put option. For complex insurance contracts, a put option is also the best starting point for understanding and valuing the insurance.

REAL ESTATE OPTIONS Options have been used for many years in real estate. For example, consider a person trying to develop a new shopping mall. The development depends on many things, such as buying several pieces of real estate, obtaining financing, and gaining commitments from retailers to lease shops. The development can proceed only if *all* the parts come together. Rather than invest in each piece of land sequentially, the developer can purchase call options from the landowners with agreed-upon strike prices. Then, *if* everything comes together, the developer has claim to the land for a particular price. Without the call option, the later landowners could hold out for extraordinary prices. Actually, the last landowner could require a price of almost the total positive NPV of the project.

To see this point, suppose the project's NPV is $5 million at the start of the development, based on estimates for purchasing all the pieces. Also assume that everything has happened exactly according to plan—so far. Only one last piece of land, which was expected to cost $100,000, remains to be purchased. Assuming the investment project *must* have this parcel of land to be completed, the owner of the land can refuse to sell for the expected $100,000 price. How much will the developer be willing to pay?

The developer will be better off as long as the price for the land is less than the $5 million in positive NPV. That, of course, is considerably more than what the land was worth before the project was this far along. Now, however, if the landowner sets a price of $4 million for the land, the developer will be $1 million ahead, even after paying the "inflated" price. A call option can keep the developer from being caught in the position of having to give up a substantial portion of the positive NPV of the project to a holdout.

CONVERTIBLES Convertible bonds and convertible preferred stock can be converted into shares of common stock at the securityholder's option. Such securities can be viewed as combinations of other securities. For example, a convertible bond can be seen as a "straight" corporate bond *plus* a call option on shares of the firm's common stock.

WARRANTS A **warrant** is a long-term call option on a stock. Warrants generally have very long lives when they are issued, such as 10 years or longer. They are issued by a firm on its own stock. Warrants differ from many other call options in that if they are exercised, the firm typically issues new shares of stock so that it actually creates new equity. Often, new warrants are issued together with new "straight" bonds. In effect, the package is like a convertible bond, except that the two parts are independent and can be bought and sold separately. Sometimes warrants are referred to as "sweeteners" that are added to the bond to make it more attractive to buy.[4]

EMPLOYEE STOCK OPTIONS Most American firms, and many European firms, grant employee stock options (ESOs). These give the employees the right to buy new shares of stock from the firm for a stated price for as long as 10 years. These warrants are an important part of employee compensation, particularly for smaller, newer firms with positive-NPV opportunities but limited cash and whose options can be very valuable. Both the firm and its employees can benefit from substituting ESOs for cash.

CALL PROVISIONS Many corporate bonds include a call provision that allows the *firm* to redeem the bond for a preset amount prior to maturity. A call provision is a call option. As with any option, it increases the firm's financial flexibility. More specifically, if interest rates decline, it allows the firm to save money: The firm can replace its high-interest-rate loan with a new low-interest-rate loan. So, in simple terms, this call option is a formal contract provision that says the

---

[4]It seems to us that the "sweetener" concept must have to do with a psychological marketing notion, like a rebate for buying a car. The rebate is simply a cut in the purchase price. Likewise, rather than adding the warrants, the bonds could have been offered for a lower price—the value of the warrants!

firm can pay off the money it owes sooner than was originally expected. Therefore, even the typical corporate bond is not a simple security. It is a combination of even more basic securities. The bondholder owns the asset (a "straight" bond) but also has written a call option on that asset. The firm is on the "other side of the transaction." It has sold the bond but also purchased a call option.

EXAMPLE The Option in Gibson Greetings's Treasury-Linked Swap

A number of years ago, Gibson Greetings, Inc. announced that it had lost approximately $20 million on a series of "swap" transactions with a major bank. One of them was a "Treasury-linked swap."

At the end of eight months, Gibson was to pay the bank $30 million in principal plus interest on that amount. Interest was to be charged at a well-known and regularly published variable market rate called LIBOR.[5] The "swap" (exchange) called for the bank to pay Gibson interest on $30 million at LIBOR *plus* 2%. (For example, if LIBOR turned out to be 8%, the bank would pay 10%.) In addition, the bank was to pay a principal amount of the smaller of either (1) $30.6 million or (2) a contingent amount P determined by a complex formula. P depended on future yields on two-year Treasury notes and 30-year Treasury bonds. The higher the yields, the lower P would be.[6]

Figure 12.11 shows the bank's savings on the principal amount (payoff) on the swap in terms of Treasury yields. The Treasury-linked swap contained an option. Compare Figures 12.6 and 12.11. In effect, Gibson had sold the bank a put option in exchange for the extra 2% interest. (The bank was paying Gibson 2% above LIBOR, whereas Gibson was paying the bank LIBOR.)

Unfortunately for Gibson, Treasury yields rose during the next 8 months. As they did, the contingent amount P fell farther and farther below the $30.6 million. This resulted in a large loss for Gibson. The bank, being on the other side of the transaction, did quite well, thank you, with an equally large gain.

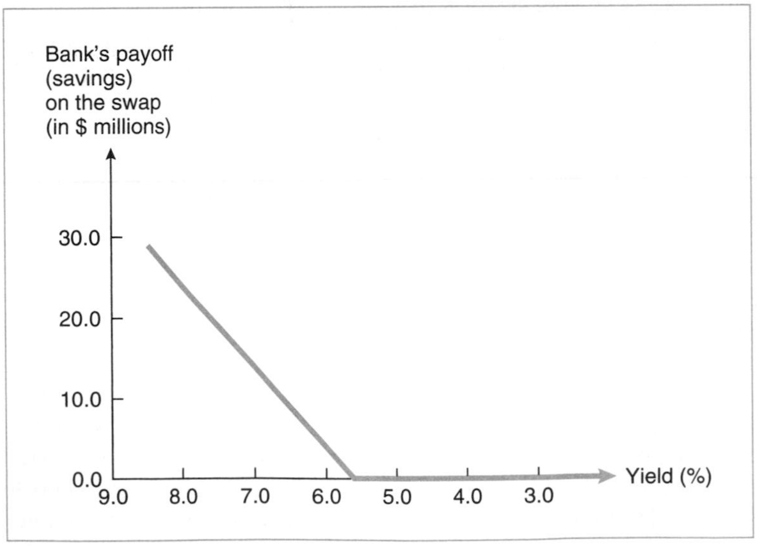

FIGURE 12.11
The bank's payoff on the treasury-linked swap.

[5]London Interbank Offer Rate.

[6]However, in the formula for P, the input variable representing the 30-year yield was the market *price* of the 30-year Treasury bond. This increased the complexity of the formula and apparently caused Gibson to misunderstand the deal.

PUBLICLY TRADED OPTIONS In addition to the Chicago Board Options Exchange, standardized puts and calls are also traded on the American and Philadelphia Stock Exchanges, among others. Warrants are also sometimes traded on the stock exchanges. Other publicly traded options, such as stock index options, interest rate options, commodity options, and currency options, are listed in the Money & Investing section (section C) of the *Wall Street Journal.*

"Hidden" Options

As we have noted before, the importance of options extends well beyond those cases where they can be easily identified. Many assets contain implicit, or "hidden," options. Whenever a claim is contingent upon particular outcomes, there is probably a hidden option involved. For example, being able to claim a tax loss on an asset requires that you sell the asset for a loss. So the "option" to claim the tax loss is contingent on having incurred the loss. Hidden options dramatically complicate the valuation process. This may seem to be an obvious statement because the option is hidden. However, even in cases that are known to contain an option, identifying it can pose a significant analytical puzzle. The difficulties are dramatically illustrated in the following examples.

Common Stock as an Option

In our overview of the Options Principle, we pointed out that *limited liability* creates the option to default and not fully repay a debt. When a debt contract is created, it is as though the debtholders have written the stockholders a sequence of European call options on the firm. Each required debt payment represents a strike price. Whenever *any* payment is due, interest or principal, the shareholders have, in effect, a decision whether they should "exercise" their call option.[7] If the firm is worth more than the payment that is due, the shareholders will exercise their option and "buy back" the firm from the debtholders by making the required payment. If the firm is ever worth less than the strike price (the required payment), the stockholders will simply refuse to exercise their call option, and the debtholders "keep" the firm. Therefore, when a firm has one or more debts, it is as though the shareholders have a call option on the firm.

We said earlier in our discussion of the concept of put-call parity that we would try to use the description that is easiest to see in a situation. Here is such a case where it might be easier to see this idea from the alternative viewpoint. So let us look at the optionality in this situation by trying on our "put option glasses."

The stockholders' option can also be viewed as a put option with a strike price of $0. If the stockholders do not want to make the required debt payment, they can "sell" the firm's assets to the debtholders for $0—and the debtholders have no choice but to accept the "sale." You might say the stockholders are "putting" it to the debtholders!

Although common stock can be described *exactly* as an option only under certain restrictive conditions, it is a very good approximation. More importantly, it can provide very important insights into a situation. For example, we show you in Chapter 13 how the stock-as-an-option view provides insights into stakeholder relationships and the practical management of a firm.

It is interesting to note that the hidden default option adds yet again to the complexity of the typical corporate bond. We pointed out that many corporate bonds include a call provision. Now you can see that they also include a hidden default option. So not only is the typical corporate bond not a simple security, but determining the makeup of its exact value is much more complex than it appeared to be in Chapter 5.

---

[7]Of course, the smaller the required payment, the less likely it is that the assets will not be worth the "strike price." So default is much more likely when a large payment is due.

Other "Hidden" Options

There are many other situations that contain hidden or implicit options that are not obvious. Here are a few.

PRINCIPAL-AGENT RELATIONSHIPS Chapter 13 applies our generalizations about option valuation to the contingent claims the firm's various stakeholders—such as the employees, stockholders, bondholders, and customers—have on the firm's assets and on each other.

REFUNDING A HOME MORTGAGE When a mortgage on a home permits prepayment of the loan (mortgage), if interest rates go down, the borrower can refinance the home loan at a lower interest rate. In effect, the right to refinance the loan involves a hidden call option; the homeowner can take out a new (lower-interest) loan and use the proceeds to prepay the original high-interest loan. The option to prepay the home mortgage loan is analogous to the call provision we noted on a corporate bond. Some banks charge the customer extra for prepaying a home mortgage. This additional charge can be viewed as a strike price for the hidden call option of prepayment. Of course, the larger such a charge is, the larger the interest savings would have to be to make refinancing attractive.

TAX-TIMING OPTIONS Tax laws include many contingencies. Some of them create valuable options. For example, one of them involves capital gains. Suppose a taxpayer purchased two stocks last year. Since then, one has increased and the other has decreased in value. So our taxpayer has earned "income" on one and lost "income" on the other. If this were regular income, the taxpayer would pay taxes on the gain and save taxes on the loss. But because this income is subject to capital gains tax rules, the taxes apply only when the taxpayer sells the stock, which is his "option." The taxpayer can use this option to his advantage: Keep the first stock, thereby continuing to postpone the tax liability; sell the second stock, thereby claiming the tax savings on the loss right away.

OPTIONS CONNECTED WITH CAPITAL INVESTMENTS In capital budgeting, we discuss options the firm has in connection with its capital investment projects. Such options include product price setting, as well as postponing, expanding, and abandoning an investment project. The values of these capital investment options are usually contingent upon some future prices or outcomes, such as the future price of gold or oil, future interest rates, government legislation, the bankruptcy of a competitor, the breakout of war, and many other economic events. These state-contingent capital investment options are often called real options (as opposed to financial options such as an option on IBM shares). Because of the importance of these future economic outcomes, options in capital budgeting can be very critical to a firm's future prosperity.

VARIABLE COST REDUCTION Operating leverage involves fixed versus variable costs. Firms sometimes have choices about these proportions. For example, firms have increased their use of robotic equipment in manufacturing as technology has advanced. Overall, firms determined that the robotic equipment would produce the product more cheaply. However, compared to human labor, robotic equipment has higher fixed cost (it is more costly to buy) and lower variable cost (it is cheaper to use). Consider what happens if production is temporarily suspended. Variable costs are no longer incurred, but fixed costs must still be paid. So if production is temporarily suspended, the firm would have the option of reducing its costs more if it had not invested in robotic equipment. Thus, a production process with relatively more variable cost and less fixed cost provides a hidden option to reduce total cost should production ever have to be temporarily suspended.

Review

1. What is the relationship between a convertible bond and a straight bond?
2. What is a warrant? How are warrants used as "sweeteners" in bond financing?
3. Why is a bond's call provision valuable to the firm that issued the bonds?
4. How can the common stock of a firm be described as an option on the firm's assets?
5. What type of option does the right to prepay a home mortgage involve?

12.6 A SIMPLE MODEL OF OPTION VALUATION

Determining the exact value of an option can be difficult. There are firms that sell complex mathematical models for valuing options. It is high tech. So, unfortunately, we are not going to be able to make you a whiz at valuing options in the space available here, but we will illustrate the basic relationships using a simplified valuation method. This model determines the value of an option by computing the present value of the option's expected outcomes. The model has four steps:

1. Compute the probabilities of possible price changes on the basis of what an investor can earn on the riskless asset.
2. Calculate the possible exercise values at expiration.
3. Determine the expected outcome as the probability-weighted average of the outcomes.
4. Compute the present value of the expected outcome by discounting at the riskless return.

EXAMPLE The Value of Carl's Call Option

Let us take a final look at Carl's call option on Alice's land. Suppose that Alice's land can have only one of two possible values next year, $120,000 or $94,138. In other words, the land can go up 20% or down 5.862% in value, from its current $100,000 price. Nothing else. Also assume that the riskless return is 5% per year. What is Carl's call option worth?

Our first step is to compute the probabilities of the two possible outcomes if the return on the land must equal the riskless return of 5%. Recall that the probabilities of all possible outcomes have to sum to 1.0. Since there are only two possible outcomes, the probability of a decrease is one minus the probability of an increase. Thus,

$$5\% = (\text{probability of an increase})(+20\%) + (1 - \text{probability of an increase})(-5.862\%)$$

Solving for the probability of an increase, we get 0.42, or 42%. The probability of a decrease is 1 minus this, so it is 0.58, or 58%.

We now move on to the second step, which is to compute the call option's possible exercise values at expiration. Recall that

$$\text{Exercise value of Carl's call option} = \max[(\text{market value} - 110{,}000); 0]$$

Because the land has only two possible values, Carl's call option can have only two possible exercise values as well. These are 0 or $10,000. (With the decrease, the out-of-the-money option has an exercise value of 0. With the increase, the exercise value is 120,000 − 110,000.)

Armed with the probabilities and exercise values, we can compute the expected value of Carl's outcome. It is simply the outcomes times their probabilities, or

$$(0.42)(10{,}000) + (0.58)(0) = \$4{,}200$$

Finally, the value of Carl's call option is the present value of the expected value of his outcome, or

$$(4{,}200)/(1.05) = \$4{,}000$$

So under these conditions, Carl's call option is worth $4,000.

Review

1. Why is it difficult to determine the exact value of an option?
2. What are the four steps in the simple option valuation model described in this section?

12.7 COMBINING OPTION VALUES

Another important problem is how option values combine. For traded options, this is straightforward: The value of owning multiple options is simply the sum of the values of the individual options. But it is not always this simple. In some cases, exercising one option can affect the value of another option. This is more likely when the options exist on the same asset. Such complex situations arise most often in connection with "hidden" options. This is because hidden options often do not require an incremental payment to create them. They occur naturally. Frequently, outside forces create them. In the case of the default option, it is part of our legal system.

Overlapping "Hidden" Options

Here is another useful generalization: **The value of two or more hidden options may be less than the sum of their individual option values.** This often occurs when the options provide "coverage" for some of the same outcomes.

Think about buying car insurance. Suppose you buy car insurance and then have an accident. Your "put option" (insurance) contract will require the insurance company to reimburse you for most, but not all, of your loss. Now consider buying car insurance from two different firms on the same car at the same time. If you did this and then had an accident, you could be reimbursed for all of your loss. However, you would not get more than your total loss. The firms would split the repair bill. Although you might get reimbursed more with two insurance policies than you would with one, the incremental cost for the second policy does not add enough value to be worth it. In short, if you are covered by one policy, the second policy does not add very much coverage.

EXAMPLE The Price-Setting and Production Quantity Options

Consider two hidden options a firm has in connection with the manufacture and sale of a product, the option to set the selling price and the option to choose the quantity produced. These options exist without action on the firm's part. They cannot be separated from the ownership of the underlying asset, the manufacturing process. Figure 12.12 is a Venn diagram of outcomes for price and production quantity choices. The circle marked A contains the "in-the-money outcomes" for the price-setting option. That is, the circle includes the price choices where the firm would make more money than it does now. (This can be a higher price if demand has been exceeding production, or a lower price with more sold if inventory has been accumulating.) The price-setting option is out-of-the-money for all other price choices, and its value is $12,000. The choices in the circle marked A, and option value, are based on the quantity the firm is currently producing.

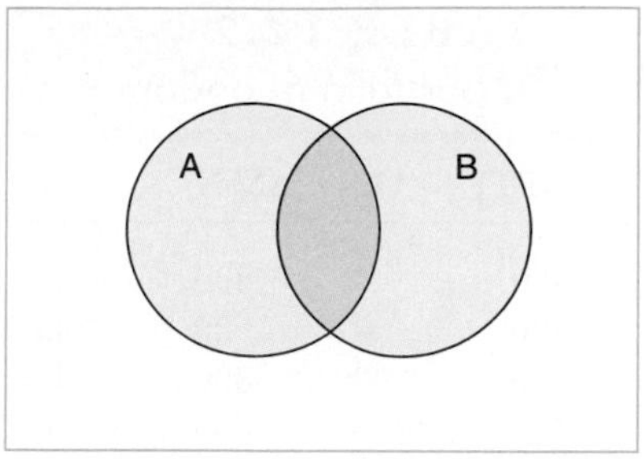

FIGURE 12.12
A Venn diagram of outcomes for price and production quantity choices.

Of course, the firm can choose a different production quantity. The circle marked B in Figure 12.12 contains the "in-the-money outcomes" for the production quantity option. That is, circle B includes the production quantity choices where the firm would make more money than it does now. (This can be a larger quantity if demand has been exceeding production, or a smaller quantity if inventory has been accumulating.) The production quantity option is out-of-the-money for all other quantity choices, and its value is \$10,000. Once again, these choices and values are based on current conditions, in this case including the price the firm is now charging.

Now look again at Figure 12.12. What additional value does the production quantity option offer, because the firm already has the price-setting option? The price-setting option "covers" the firm for all of the outcomes in circle A, and the production quantity option covers it for all of the outcomes in circle B. Because the firm owns the price-setting option, however, the production quantity option adds coverage *only* for those outcomes that are not also in circle A. In other words, the intersection of circles A and B is redundant, as long as the firm has either one of the options. If the firm is not selling all that it is producing, it can *either* lower its price *or* reduce the quantity it is producing. And even if it cannot do one of these, the other can take care of the problem.

Suppose the value of the overlap of the option coverage of outcomes is \$6,000. In this case, the combined value of the price-setting and production quantity options, V(A + B), is the sum of the values of the individual options, V(A) + V(B) = \$22,000 (= 12,000 + 10,000), *minus* the value of the intersection, $V(A \cap B)$ = \$6,000, or

$$V(A + B) = V(A) + V(B) - V(A \cap B) = 22{,}000 - 6{,}000 = \$16{,}000$$

So the value of having these two options is not equal to the sum of the separate values of the individual options. This lack of simple additivity is typically the case with overlapping hidden options.

A similar situation can occur when exercising one option affects the value of another option. The simplest case is where exercising one option eliminates another. Suppose a firm has an investment opportunity to build a new plant with a positive NPV. Just prior to starting, an alternative place to build becomes available. Building the plant on the newly discovered alternative spot is also a positive-NPV investment opportunity. In effect, the firm now has two options. But if the firm exercises one of the options, the other will become worthless. You may recognize this situation as an option view of an *opportunity cost:* Taking one action eliminates the possibility of taking other desirable actions. Although they can be difficult to determine accurately, such costs can be very significant. Therefore, it is important to include the lost value of options that are eliminated by exercising another option.

A Portfolio of Options

Consider two ways of holding options on a set of assets. You could buy a single option on the whole set of assets. For example, you could buy an "index option," which is an option on the

TABLE 12.2
A portfolio of options versus a single option on a portfolio of assets.

$ASSET_1$	O_1	$ASSET_2$	O_2	PORTFOLIO	O_P	$O_1 + O_2$	$(O_1 + O_2) - O_P$
400	0	400	0	800	0	0	0
400	0	600	100	1,000	0	100	100
400	0	800	300	1,200	200	300	100
600	100	400	0	1,000	0	100	100
600	100	600	100	1,200	200	200	0
600	100	800	300	1,400	400	400	0
800	300	400	0	1,200	200	300	100
800	300	600	100	1,400	400	400	0
800	300	800	300	1,600	600	600	0

value of an index, such as the S&P 100. Alternatively, you could buy an option on each asset individually, such as an option on each of the stocks in the S&P 100. In the first case, you would have a single option on a portfolio of assets. In the second case, you would have a portfolio of options. Would one way of holding options always be more valuable than the other? We just showed that sometimes an option does not add its entire stand-alone value. Still, options are valuable, and so an additional option cannot decrease your wealth.

The effects of diversification can help us understand the relative values of the two alternatives. An option is a claim on the good outcomes without the obligation to take the bad. So an option on each asset allows you to claim every good outcome and avoid every bad outcome among all the assets. In a portfolio of assets, good and bad outcomes are netted out by each. This is, after all, the basis for saying that diversification is beneficial. So a single option on the portfolio only allows you to claim the *net* of all the outcomes if the net is good and avoid claiming if it is bad.

So we have another important generalization about options: **The value of an option on a portfolio of assets is always less than or equal to the value of a portfolio of comparable options on the individual assets.**

EXAMPLE A Portfolio of Options

Suppose you can invest in two different assets using call options. Each asset can have a future value of \$400, \$600, or \$800. You can have either a single call option on a portfolio of the two assets with a strike price of \$1,000, or you can have two separate call options, one on each asset, each with a strike price of \$500. Which is worth more?

Table 12.2 shows the values of the assets, options, and combinations for each of the possible outcomes. As you can see, the portfolio of options has a higher value in four of the nine possible outcomes, and it has the same value as the single option on the portfolio of assets for all the other outcomes.

So the portfolio of options is worth more than the single option on the portfolio of assets.

Review

1. Can the value of two options ever be less than the sum of their separate option values?
2. Why is it that a firm's price-setting option may not add its entire stand-alone value when considered in addition to the firm's production quantity option?
3. What is the relationship between the value of an option on a portfolio of assets and the value of a portfolio of comparable options on the individual assets?

SUMMARY

Chapter 12 describes various types of options and shows how option contracts are a part of many business relationships. The factors that determine an option's value and how changes in those factors alter an option's value are examined. We explain several powerful and practical generalizations of options.

- An option gives its holder the right, but not the obligation, to do something. A call option is the right to buy an asset at the strike price, whereas a put option is the right to sell an asset at the strike price. An option is often referred to as a contingent claim because its value depends on some event.
- An option takes an asset's distribution of returns and divides it in some way between the buyer of the option and the seller of the option. An option can be viewed as a claim on a portion of an asset's return distribution.
- An option's value is the sum of its exercise value and its time premium.
- An option's exercise value is the difference between the underlying asset's market value and the strike price for in-the-money options. The exercise value is zero for out-of-the-money options.
- An option's time premium (1) increases with the option's time until expiration, (2) increases with the risk of the underlying asset, and (3) decreases with the option's depth in- or out-of-the-money (how far the underlying asset's value is from the strike price). A call (put) option's time premium (4) increases (decreases) with the market riskless return.
- It is generally better to sell, rather than exercise, an option prior to expiration because an option's value includes both the exercise value and a time premium. Exercising an option terminates its time premium.
- Options are found in many places. Options are inherent in insurance contracts, real estate contracts, bonds (callable bonds and convertible bonds), warrants, employee stock options, and publicly traded options.
- There are also many "hidden" options that can significantly affect the value of an asset. Tax-timing options, options in capital investments, and refunding mortgages are examples. The most important "hidden" option is that the firm's common stock can be considered to be a call option on the firm's assets.
- The chapter gives a simple option pricing model. More sophisticated models exist and are described in Chapter 21, which can be used to value options.
- The "optionality" in a situation can always be described in terms of either a put *or* a call option. This relationship is referred to as put-call parity.
- The value of two or more "hidden" options may be less than the sum of the values of the individual options.
- The value of a portfolio of options is greater than or equal to the value of a comparable single option on a portfolio of the assets.

QUESTIONS

1. Define the terms *option, call option,* and *put option.*
2. Define the terms *strike price, in-the-money, out-of-the-money, exercise value,* and *time value.*
3. Cite three situations involving "hidden" options.
4. In your own words, explain how limited liability makes shares of common stock like an option.
5. Explain how auto insurance can be viewed as a put option.

6. Why would an American call option traded in an efficient capital market never be worth less than its exercise value?
7. The value of an option includes its (a) exercise value and (b) the time premium. Name the parameters that determine each of these two parts and explain how each parameter affects the option's value.
8. Why is the time premium for an American option never negative?
9. Why is it generally better to sell rather than exercise an American option?
10. What is the relationship between the value of an American option and the value of a comparable European option? For example, is it always greater or less, or does the relationship depend on some parameter? Explain why the relationship is that way.
11. Explain why an option on a portfolio of assets is never worth more than a portfolio of comparable options on the individual assets.
12. Explain how shares of stock can be viewed as a put option on the firm's assets.

CHALLENGING QUESTIONS

13. Explain how shares of stock can be viewed as a call option on the firm's assets.
14. Consider the following statement: A call option is a great way to make money. If the asset goes up in value, you get the increase, but if the asset goes down in value, you do not exercise the option and do not lose any money. Therefore, everyone should invest in call options. Is this statement true, false, or partly true and partly false? Explain why.
15. Why does the maximum time premium for an option occur when the underlying asset's value equals the strike price? Why does the time premium decrease as the option becomes more in- or out-of-the-money?
16. Most stock options are not dividend protected. This means that if dividends are paid, the option terms are not adjusted to reflect the cash paid out and the accompanying reduction in the value of the stock. Assume that a large cash dividend reduces the stock price from $100 to $95 on October 18. A call option with an exercise price of $80 expires on October 20. What could the holder of an American call option do to protect the value of her option? What could the holder of a European call option do to protect the value of her option?
17. Why is an American put option worth more than a comparable European put option when the options are certain to be in-the-money during their entire remaining time until maturity?
18. We pointed out that common stock in a firm that has some debt can be viewed as a call option. Can common stock in a firm that has no debt also be viewed as a call option? If so, explain how. If not, explain why.

PROBLEMS

LEVEL A (BASIC)

A1. (Computing exercise values) What is the exercise value of the following options?

TYPE OF OPTION	STOCK PRICE	STRIKE PRICE	EXERCISE VALUE
call	$20	$25	_______
call	25	20	_______
put	20	25	_______
put	25	20	_______

A2. (Computing exercise values) What is the exercise value of the following options?

TYPE OF OPTION	STOCK PRICE	STRIKE PRICE	EXERCISE VALUE
call	$30	$35	______
call	35	30	______
put	30	35	______
put	35	30	______

A3. (Recognizing puts and calls) Indicate whether the stock price, strike price, and exercise value given here are for a call option or a put option.

STOCK PRICE	STRIKE PRICE	EXERCISE VALUE	TYPE OF OPTION PUT OR CALL?
$65	$ 60	$ 0	______
25	20	5	______
15	30	15	______
97	105	0	______

A4. (Recognizing puts and calls) Indicate whether the stock price, strike price, and exercise value given here are for a call option or a put option.

STOCK PRICE	STRIKE PRICE	EXERCISE VALUE	TYPE OF OPTION PUT OR CALL?
$44	$40	$ 0	______
25	20	5	______
5	50	45	______
34	40	0	______

A5. (Computing exercise values) You have a weird aunt who will give you your choice of one of the following options. They expire today, and each is an option on 100 shares. Which one is the most valuable? (a) A put option on Dell. The strike price is $30 and the stock price is $27.23. (b) A call option on General Electric. The strike price is $37.50 and the stock price is $32.60. (c) A call option on Tyco. The strike price is $40 and the stock price is $23.30. (d) A put option on Citigroup. The strike price is $50 and the stock price is $45.85.

A6. (Computing exercise values) Suppose you have a choice of one of the following options. They expire today, and each is an option on 100 shares. Which one is the most valuable? (a) A put option on Microsoft. The strike price is $60 and the stock price is $54.01. (b) A call option on IBM. The strike price is $85 and the stock price is $84.45. (c) A call option on Intel. The strike price is $27.50 and the stock price is $30.19. (d) A put option on Home Depot. The strike price is $60 and the stock price is $48.50.

A7. (Insurance as a put option) You own a $250,000 house and pay $1,000 for fire insurance.

a. What is the exercise value of the fire insurance put option if the house does not burn (and you have no claim)? What is the realized return on your investment in fire insurance?

b. What is the exercise value of the fire insurance put option if the house burns and you have $100,000 of damage? What is the realized return on your investment in fire insurance?

A8. (Insurance as a put option) You own a $100,000 house and pay $500 for fire insurance.

a. What is the exercise value of the fire insurance put option if the house does not burn (and you have no claim)? What is the realized rate of return on your investment in fire insurance?

b. What is the exercise value of the fire insurance put option if the house burns and you have $80,000 of damage? What is the realized rate of return on your investment in fire insurance?

A9. (Exercise value of executive stock options) In a few years, your employer announces a new compensation plan that includes stock options for the firm's managers. You are granted stock options on 10,000 shares with a strike price equal to the current stock price of $70. In five years when the options expire, what is the exercise value of your options if the stock price has risen to $135? What is the exercise value of your options if the stock price is $50?

A10. (Exercise value of executive stock options) In a few years, your employer announces a new compensation plan that includes stock options for the firm's managers. You are granted stock options on 5,000 shares with a strike price equal to the current stock price of $28. In five years when the options expire, what is the exercise value of your options if the stock price has risen to $36? What is the exercise value of your options if the stock price is $24?

A11. (Early exercise versus selling a call option) Joan Junkus owns IBM call options expiring in eight weeks. The strike price for her options is $80. The current stock price is $84.45 and the current market price for her option is $7.10. Would she be better off selling her options or exercising her options? Why?

A12. (Early exercise versus selling a call option) Bill owns Johnson & Johnson call options expiring in four weeks. The strike price for his options is $60. The current stock price is $60.45 and the current market price for his option is $2.05. Would he be better off selling his options or exercising his options? Why?

A13. (Exercise value and time premium) Find the missing option values:

TYPE OF OPTION	STOCK PRICE	STRIKE PRICE	EXERCISE VALUE	TIME PREMIUM OF OPTION	MARKET VALUE OF OPTION
call	$30	$20	______	$1.00	______
call	66	70	______	______	$2.50
put	42	40	______	1.50	______
put	24	30	______	______	8.00

A14. (Exercise value and time premium) Find the missing option values:

TYPE OF OPTION	STOCK PRICE	STRIKE PRICE	EXERCISE VALUE	TIME PREMIUM OF OPTION	MARKET VALUE OF OPTION
call	$25	$20	______	$1.00	______
call	90	93	______	______	$3.00
put	56	52	______	4.00	______
put	26	27	______	______	6.00

A15. (Exercise value and time premium) Exxon Mobil common stock is currently selling for $39.59. A call option expiring in 30 days with a strike price of 40 is selling for $0.85. A put option with the same strike price and expiration is selling for $1.20.

a. What is the exercise value and the time premium of the call option?

b. What is the exercise value and the time premium of the put option?

A16. (Exercise value and time premium) Ford common stock is currently selling for $16.73. A call option expiring in 30 days with a strike price of $15 is selling for $1.80. A put option with the same strike price and expiration is selling for $0.15.

a. What is the exercise value and the time premium of the call option?

b. What is the exercise value and the time premium of the put option?

A17. (Exercise value and time premium) Microsoft common stock is currently selling for \$54.01. A call option expiring in 60 days with a strike price of \$55 is selling for \$4.80. A put option with the same strike price and expiration is selling for \$5.70.

a. What is the exercise value and the time premium of the call option?

b. What is the exercise value and the time premium of the put option?

A18. (Exercise value and time premium) Philip Morris common stock is currently selling for \$54.34. A call option expiring in 30 days with a strike price of \$50 is selling for \$4.70. A put option with the same strike price and expiration is selling for \$0.20.

a. What is the exercise value and the time premium of the call option?

b. What is the exercise value and the time premium of the put option?

A19. (Graphing exercise values) Assume a strike price of \$50.

a. Show the exercise value of a call option as a function of the underlying stock price. Put the stock price on the horizontal axis and let it range from \$0 to \$100. Put the option value on the vertical axis.

b. On a similar graph, show the exercise value of a put option.

c. Increase the strike price to \$60 and redraw the value of a call option.

d. Increase the strike price to \$60 and redraw the value of a put option.

LEVEL B

B1. (Exercise value of a convertible bond) John Houston owns several convertible BIT Company bonds. Given their coupon, maturity, and riskiness, the bonds would have a straight bond value of \$850 each if they were nonconvertible. Each bond can be exchanged for 24 shares of BIT stock. The stock is currently selling for \$45 per share.

a. If John converts his bond, what is the conversion value of the 24 shares?

b. Consider the straight bond value to be the strike price. What is the exercise value of converting the bond to common stock?

c. Assume, instead, that the stock is selling for \$20 per share. What would be the exercise value at this price? Should John convert?

B2. (Exercise value of a convertible bond) Tom Sanders owns several convertible ABC Company bonds. Given their coupon, maturity, and riskiness, the bonds would have a straight bond value of \$925 each if they were nonconvertible. Each bond can be exchanged for 35 shares of ABC stock. The stock is currently selling for \$32 per share.

a. If Tom converts his bond, what is the conversion value of the 35 shares?

b. Consider the straight bond value to be the strike price. What is the exercise value of converting the bond to common stock?

c. Assume the stock is selling for \$28 per share. What would be the exercise value at this price? Should Tom convert?

B3. (Option values for both buyer and seller) Joan purchased a building in Chicago for \$75,000. Right after this, she sold a one-year European call option on the building, with a strike price of \$80,000, for \$3,000 to Bill. What are Joan's and Bill's outcomes for possible building values of \$70,000, 75,000, 80,000, 85,000, and 90,000 when the option expires?

B4. (Option values for both buyer and seller) Margaret purchased a building in Pittsburgh for \$100,000. Right after this, she bought a one-year European put option on the building, with a strike price of \$120,000, for \$20,000 from Wendy. What are Margaret's and Wendy's outcomes for possible building values of \$90,000, 110,000, 120,000, and 140,000 when the option expires?

B5. (Value of a call option) Suppose you can buy a call option on a business that is currently worth $10,000,000 but will be worth either 25% more or 15% less one year from today. The option's strike price is $11,000,000, and the riskless return is 6% per year. What is this call option worth today? Use the simple model of option valuation.

B6. (Value of a call option) Suppose you can buy a call option on a business that is currently worth $6,000,000 but will be worth either 20% more or 10% less one year from today. The option's strike price is $7,000,000, and the riskless return is 6.5% per year. What is this call option worth today? Use the simple model of option valuation.

B7. (Value of a call option) Suppose you can buy a call option on a parcel of land that is currently worth $200,000 but will be worth either 15% more or 8% less than this one year from today. The option's strike price is $215,000, and the riskless return is 7% per year. What is this call option worth today? Use the simple model of option valuation.

B8. (Value of a call option) Suppose you can buy a call option on a parcel of land that is currently worth $20,000 but will be worth either 30% more or 20% less than this one year from today. The option's strike price is $24,000, and the riskless return is 5% per year. What is this call option worth today? Use the simple model of option valuation.

B9. (The value of a portfolio of options versus the value of an option on a portfolio) Cheryl Jones has a call option on one share of Cytrans with a strike price of $20 and a call option on one share of Mallmax with a strike price of $30. Susan Parker has a call option on a portfolio that has one share of Cytrans and one share of Mallmax. The strike price on Susan's call option is $50. These options are all expiring today.

a. If Cytrans is selling for $40 and Mallmax for $25, what is the value of Cheryl's options? What is the value of Susan's option?

b. If Cytrans is selling for $15 and Mallmax for $35, what is the value of Cheryl's options? What is the value of Susan's option?

c. If Cytrans is selling for $40 and Mallmax for $35, what is the value of Cheryl's options? What is the value of Susan's option?

B10. (Value of a portfolio of options versus the value of an option on a portfolio) Sally has a call option on one share of Ultra with a strike price of $40 and a call option on one share of Boone with a strike price of $25. George has a call option on a portfolio that has one share of Ultra and one share of Boone. The strike price on George's call option is $65. These options are all expiring today.

a. If Ultra is selling for $50 and Boone for $15, what is the value of Sally's options? What is the value of George's option?

b. If Ultra is selling for $30 and Boone for $35, what is the value of Sally's options? What is the value of George's option?

c. If Ultra is selling for $45 and Boone for $35, what is the value of Sally's options? What is the value of George's option?

B11. (Excel: Option values for both buyer and seller) Tom Smith purchased a building in uptown Indianapolis for $50,000. Right after this, he sold a one-year European call option on the building, with a strike price of $54,000, for $2,200 to Sarah Smyth. What are Tom's and Sarah's outcomes for possible land values between $40,000 and 66,000 in $2,000 increments when the option expires?

B12. (Excel: Option values for both buyer and seller) Jenny Johnson purchased a building in New York's lower east side for $1.5 million. Right after this, she bought a one-year European put option on the building, with a strike price of $1.6 million, for $350,000 from Jimmy Johnsen. What are Jenny's and Jimmy's outcomes in terms of possible land values between $0.7 and $2.2 million in $0.1 increments when the option expires?

B13. (Excel: Value of a call option and value of a put option) For the options given, the current price is for today, and the high and low values are the only two possible values in one year. Calculate:

a. The probability of the high future value and the low future value
b. The exercise values in the high and low future states
c. The expected future payoff
d. The present value of the option.

Underlying asset values

	CURRENT PRICE	HIGH VALUE	LOW VALUE	STRIKE PRICE	INTEREST RATE
Call on share of stock	$100	$120	$95	$100	5%
Put on share of stock	$20	$24	$14	$21	10%
Call on gold mine	$2.1 bil	$3.0 bil	$1.5 bil	$2.5 bil	4%
Put on Harley cycle	$8,000	$10,000	$7,000	$9,000	6%
Call on office building	$250,000	$300,000	$210,000	$240,000	7%

B14. (Excel: Value of a call option for different strike prices) PH stock sells for $20 today and is expected to sell for either $16 or $25 in one year. The risk-free interest rate is 5%.

a. What is the probability of the high and low future stock price?
b. Assume that you have ten different one-year call options with strike prices of $16, $17, $18, $19, $20, $21, $22, $23, $24, and $25. For each call option, calculate the payoffs, expected payoff, and call option value.

LEVEL C (ADVANCED)

C1. (Put-call parity) The current stock value of Absteel Products is $19. At the end of the year, the price is equally likely to be either $24 or $16. The riskless rate of return is 5%.

a. What is the value of a one-year call option with a strike price of $20?
b. What is the value of a one-year put option with a strike price of $20?
c. Calculate the value of the call (calculated in part a.) plus the present value of the strike price ($20 discounted at 5% for one year) minus the current stock price.
d. Compare your answers to part b. and part c.

C2. (Put-call parity) The current stock value of Twin Cities Retail Products is $20. At the end of the year, the price is equally likely to be either $27 or $15. The riskless return is 6%.

a. What is the value of a one-year call option with a strike price of $22?
b. What is the value of a one-year put option with a strike price of $22?
c. Calculate the value of the call (calculated in part a.) plus the present value of the strike price ($22 discounted at 6% for one year) minus the current stock price.
d. Compare your answers to part b. and part c.

C3. (Put-call parity) Rick Dark purchased some stock from Roger Muns. As part of the transaction, Rick gave Roger a one-year call option with a strike price of $100 and received a one-year put option with a strike price of $100.

a. In one year, if the stock is worth more than $100, what cash should Rick receive?
b. In one year, if the stock is worth less than $100, what cash should Rick receive?
c. Assume that Rick's net investment (price of the stock − price of the call option + price of the put option) was $80. What rate of return should Rick earn on his investment?

C4. (Put-call parity) Larry Fauver purchased some stock from Bob Taggart. As part of the transaction, Larry gave Bob a one-year call option with a strike price of $1,000 and received a one-year put option with a strike price of $1,000.

a. In one year, if the stock is worth more than $1,000, what cash should Larry receive?

b. In one year, if the stock is worth less than $1,000, what cash should Larry receive?

c. Assume Larry's net investment (price of the stock − price of the call option + price of the put option) was $900. What return would Larry earn on his investment?

C5. (Describing an option) A particular type of bond that has actually been issued from time to time allows for the bond to be redeemed, at the option of the bondholder, at either of two future points in time. Suppose such a bond can be redeemed for its face value after either 10 or 20 years. That is, at the 10-year point, the bondholder makes a one-time decision to redeem or not. Clearly there is an option in this contract. Describe this complex bond in terms of one or more (a) option contracts and (b) bonds that are otherwise identical but do not have the two-points-of-redemption option.

C6. (Early exercise of an American put option) Assume that you hold an American put option on Netplus Communications. The option has a strike price of $50 and expires in one year. Netplus has utterly failed and its stock price has dropped to zero. It has no hope of recovering. The risk-free rate of return is 10%.

a. If you exercise your put in one year, what will be the payoff? What is the present value of this payoff?

b. If you exercise your put now, what will be your payoff? What is the present value of this payoff?

c. Consider your answers to a. and b. Should you exercise now or wait? It is generally considered unattractive to exercise an option prior to maturity. Is this an exception to this rule? Can you devise a rule for when it is favorable to exercise an American put option early?

d. Why is an American put option worth more than a comparable European put option?

C7. (Value of a call option) An investor is considering investing $5 million to acquire a thrift institution that currently has $1 billion of assets and zero net worth on its balance sheet. The thrift's liabilities consist principally of federally insured deposits. Its assets include principally real estate loans, which were recently written down to their supposed "fair market value" by the thrift's regulators to make it easier to sell the thrift. What does option theory tell you about how the investor should view the prospective $5 million investment?

C8. (Designing option contracts) Suppose you live in a state that has a usury law prohibiting interest charges above 9%. Current market interest rates are 18% for a project. You are a wealthy individual who wants to offer a one-year construction loan of $100,000 to Storage Partners to build a miniwarehouse.

a. If you lend the money at 9%, what will be your loan payoff in one year?

b. You want to receive a fair market return of 18%. Design a portfolio of contracts that will promise you a $118,000 payoff in one year.

MINICASE A MCDONALD'S HAPPY MEAL

A *Wall Street Journal* article once remarked that the professional managers of the McDonald's Corporation had recently digested the stock market equivalent of a "happy meal." In a two-month period, they had exercised options on 490,119 shares and sold 470,119 of them. For example, the chairman of McDonald's exercised and sold 135,000 shares, worth about $6.9 million. The profit represented nearly seven times his annual base salary.

According to McDonald's shareholder proxy that year, its board of directors believes the stock option program is "the best vehicle by which to link employees' interests with those of shareholders." The stock option program covers more than 22,000 employees. The number of options each employee is given depends on the individual's responsibilities and the "potential for influencing the firm's future results." The highest-level managers receive the greatest numbers of options.

The following table provides information from the shareholder proxy concerning compensation and stock options for McDonald's five highest-paid executives.

MANAGER	SALARY, BONUS, AND OTHER COMPENSATION	OPTIONS GRANTED	PERCENTAGE OF OPTIONS FIRM GRANTED	EXERCISE PRICE	EXPIRATION
Chairman & CEO	$2,115,930	350,000	2.6%	$30	10 years
President–USA	1,325,893	176,000	1.3	30	10
President–International	1,307,319	176,500	1.3	30	10
Vice Chairman & CFO	1,263,290	176,000	1.3	30	10
Senior Executive VP	855,273	72,600	0.5	30	10

QUESTIONS

1. Assuming the stock's market price was $30 when the options were granted, calculate each manager's option value at the end of 10 years assuming McDonald's share price grows at (i) 5% and (ii) 10% APY for 10 years.
2. Assuming a required return of 7.35% APY, calculate the present value of each manager's option value for (i) and (ii) in question 1, and the respective percentage they would be of each manager's total compensation for the year they were granted.
3. Why would you expect McDonald's stock option program to link the firm's professional managers' financial interests with those of the firm's shareholders?
4. The shareholder proxy noted that McDonald's stockholders' equity would increase by $13.2 billion over 10 years if its share price grows at 5% APY and would increase by $33.5 billion over 10 years if its share price grows at 10% APY. What proportion of the increase in stockholders' equity would each manager get from the 5% and 10% growth projections?
5. What are the options worth if McDonald's share price does not exceed $30 when the options are exercisable?

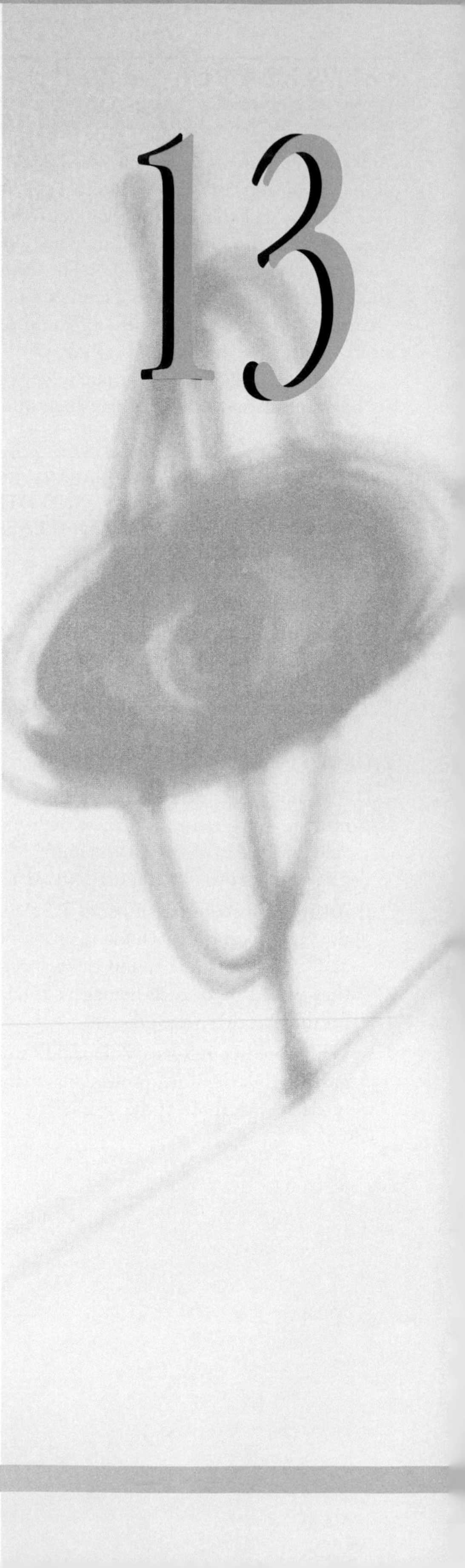

13

Risk, Return, and Agency Theory

The modern corporation is exceedingly complex. We touched on a little of that complexity in our fictionalized account of Henry Ford's car company in Chapter 1. A lot of the complexity occurs because there are so many implicit contractual relationships in addition to all the explicit ones.

Agency theory describes the business world in terms of *both* types of contracts, implicit and explicit. The purpose is to identify important practical considerations, such as the implicit aspects of the "stake," or contingent claims, the stakeholders each have in the firm.

The main issue in agency theory is how to minimize the costs of having someone else make decisions that affect you. This really refers to the cost of managing a situation in which you have a stake *through* other people. The answer lies in (1) creating incentives, constraints, and punishments; (2) having reasonable monitoring procedures; and (3) identifying and using contracts that minimize the *possibility* of conflicts of interest at the outset.

Costs associated with financial contracts (*agency costs*) occur throughout the business decision-making process and can be very significant. Therefore, these costs play an important role in many of the topics covered in this book.

FOCUS ON PRINCIPLES

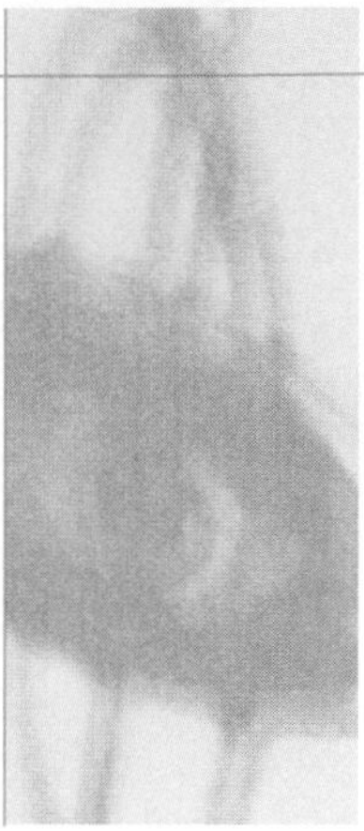

- *Self-Interested Behavior:* Look for the incentives that influence an agent's decision making.
- *Incremental Benefits:* Measure the incentives on an incremental basis.
- *Signaling:* Interpret the information contained in the actions of others. Recognize the incentive value of building and maintaining a good reputation.
- *Options:* Include all of the contingencies and their impact on incentives and value.
- *Two-Sided Transactions:* Consider every situation from both the principal's and the agent's points of view.

13.1 PRINCIPAL-AGENT RELATIONSHIPS

The **set-of-contracts model** of the firm highlights the complexity of the modern corporation. The model was developed using **agency theory,** which is the analysis of **principal-agent relationships.** Stakeholder relationships can be described as principal-agent relationships, where an **agent** is making decisions that affect a **principal.**

Some of the more visible examples of *explicit* principal-agent relationships include money managers, lawyers, and agents of real estate, travel, and insurance. Many other situations can be described in the principal-agent framework *as though* the two parties were principal and agent—even though one party is not literally an agent for the other. For example, even though most employees are not explicitly classified as agents for their employer, most act as agents at some point.

EXAMPLE A Principal-Agent Conflict

Seldon C. Fish is the CEO of a large financial firm. While looking over the firm's financial reports, he found that the latest quarter was great. A large change in interest rates provided a windfall for the firm. Although the extra income was not caused by anything the firm did, Sel was delighted. However, he knew competition would not allow his firm to have the same big margins next year, so the extra income was only a one-time bit of luck.

Now the firm must decide what to do with the extra income. Sel plans to make a recommendation on this matter to the firm's board of directors. He has narrowed it down to two possibilities: (1) extra-large employee bonuses as a reward for having such a successful year, or (2) a one-time "extra" cash dividend to the stockholders for getting lucky.

Suppose you are a stockholder (part owner) of this firm—but you are not also an employee. As a principal in this example, which alternative would you want Sel to recommend?

Now suppose you are an employee who gets part of the employee bonuses—but you are not also a stockholder. As an agent in this example, which alternative would you like Sel to recommend?

Finally, consider the CEO, Mr. Fish. He is both a stockholder (principal) and a bonus-earning employee (agent). How would he fare under each alternative? In other words, what are his incentives? To develop an opinion of which alternative you think he might like, here are some additional facts. The CEO will get 4% of this year's employee bonus money. If paid, the extra dividend would be split equally among the 9 million shares of the firm's stock. Sel owns 27,000 of these shares, so he would get 0.3% of the extra dividend. If you consider only these one-time financial incentives, what do you think Sel Fish is likely to recommend?

You can see that the CEO's incentives in this example favor the extra-large employee bonuses. Regardless of how much the extra distribution is, Sel Fish would get more of this one-time payment if it is paid out in employee bonuses (4% versus 0.3%). Note that for other bonus-earning employees who are stockholders, the employee bonus is also likely to be larger than their share of the dividend. Although they would get a smaller portion of the bonus, most own much less stock and would get less in dividends as well. Compared to other stockholders and employees, the CEO has a large stake. You might say he is a "big fish."

A potential conflict of interest between the agent and the principal creates an **agency problem.** Such conflicts can be as simple as the agent not putting forth "full effort." From the Principle of Self-Interested Behavior, we know that agents may be tempted to put their own self-interest ahead of those of the principal. As a result, an agent's decision making becomes suspect when the interests of the agent and principal diverge.

For example, is it okay for an employee (an agent), who is traveling on behalf of the firm, to take a side-trip vacation along the way? Answering this question can be difficult or even impossible. On the one hand, if travel is necessary for the employee to do the job, what's wrong with the employee getting a personal benefit from the trip? That is, if the employee benefits at no cost to the firm, why not allow the employee to take the side trip? The problem lies in making sure it is truly costless to the firm. It may be impossible to make sure the employee's travel decision was not influenced by a personal side benefit.

Agency problems occur because of asymmetric information. If the principal knows everything an agent does, the agent would never be able to take actions that were not in the best interest of the principal. Thus, if it were possible and not unreasonably costly for the principal to **monitor** the agent's actions perfectly, there would be no agency problems. Obviously, perfect monitoring, even if it were truly possible, is exorbitantly expensive. Therefore, contracts rarely have perfect monitoring, and the problem of **moral hazard** can arise. Moral hazard occurs whenever agents can take unobserved actions in their own interest, to the detriment of the principal.

The amount of monitoring is important with respect to efficient resource allocation. The more monitoring there is, the harder it is for an agent to misbehave—but the extra monitoring costs money. And because not all agents will take self-interested actions to the detriment of the principal, spending too much on monitoring agent behavior is wasteful. For any specific situation, there is a trade-off between the resources spent on monitoring and the possibility of agent misbehavior.

Alternatives to monitoring include constraints, incentives, and punishments that encourage an agent to act in the principal's best interest. An example of constraints is the legal regulation of insider trading. Managerial stock options, performance share plans, and sales commissions are examples of incentives. Getting fired would be a punishment.

If it were possible to create a contract that paid agents in perfect accord with the best interests of the principal, the need for monitoring would be eliminated. This is because when the agents act in their own best financial interest they would also be acting in the principal's best interest. But our world is not characterized by perfect accord or perfect information. Consequently, we need to search for better contracts, ones that minimize the *possibility* of conflicts of interest.

Review

1. What is a principal-agent relationship?
2. Why do principal-agent relationships give rise to agency problems?
3. How can monitoring reduce agency problems? Is there a cost involved?
4. What are some alternatives to monitoring an agent's behavior?

13.2 AGENCY COSTS

Monitoring, constraints, incentives, and punishments are designed to push agents to act in the principal's best interests, but they are costly. The costs of doing these things are called **agency costs.** Agency costs are the extra costs of having an agent act for a principal, those in excess of what it would cost the principals to "do it themselves." These costs are like friction in a machine—the more there is, the less efficient the machine, and the more energy that will be wasted.

Agency costs are defined in terms of the Principle of Incremental Benefits: The agency cost is the *incremental* cost of working *through* others, who serve as agents. In a perfect world, the agent would be paid exactly the fair amount without any waste. In our imperfect world, agency costs are a waste that is lost to the system.

Agency costs consist of three types:

1. Direct contracting costs, which include
   a. The transaction costs of setting up the contract, such as the selling commissions and legal fees of issuing bonds.
   b. The opportunity costs imposed by constraints that preclude otherwise optimal decisions (for example, an inability to undertake a positive-NPV investment because of a restrictive bond covenant).
   c. The incentive fees paid to the agent to encourage behavior consistent with the principal's goals, such as employee bonuses.
2. The costs to the principal of monitoring the agent (for example, auditing costs).
3. The loss of wealth the principal suffers as a result of misbehavior in spite of monitoring, such as unidentified excessive employee expense accounts or employees wasting time.

A major goal of agency theory is to find the optimal contract. The **optimal contract** minimizes the relationship's total agency costs. It transfers the decision-making authority in the most efficient way. It provides the smallest waste. Note that, in some cases, the cost of periodic misbehavior is less than the cost of monitoring. In most cases, the optimal contract entails some attention to each of the three component costs.

In our search for better contracts, it is important to identify those situations where conflicts of interest arise naturally. In the following sections, we examine several important relationships and conditions that are prone to such conflicts. Of course, no set of contracts can cover all possible contingencies. Therefore, it is impossible to eliminate all potential conflicts. This is an especially good reason to keep the Principles of Self-Interested Behavior and Two-Sided Transactions in your mind as you interact in the business world.

Review

1. What are agency costs, and how do they arise?
2. What are the three types of agency costs? Give an example of each.
3. What is a major goal of agency theory?

13.3 STOCKHOLDER-MANAGER CONFLICTS

The stockholder-manager relationship is created by separating ownership and control. In simple firms, the owners are the managers. In more complex firms, many stockholders have nothing to do with the daily operation of the firm. Still, in theory, the managers work for all the stockholders. If managers do not do a good job, the stockholders can fire them and hire new managers. But such a process is cumbersome and difficult to accomplish in practice.

Strictly speaking, the common stockholders of a publicly held corporation do not even own the firm; they own shares of common stock that entitle them to voting rights and certain other rights. Such corporations are operated by professional managers, who may or may not own shares themselves. The firm's board of directors hires the managers. Although the directors serve as the shareholders' elected representatives and have a legal responsibility to the shareholders, they are typically nominated for election by top management. You can see the problem right away. It seems almost circular if you ignore the obligation to the shareholders.

Managers, therefore, are the primary decision makers. They have considerable control over the firm and its assets. In some cases, managers have even been accused of using the firm's assets against the owners. So two important questions arise: Are the managers' interests different from the nonmanagement shareholders' interests? And if they are, whose interests are the managers really promoting?

How Stockholders' and Managers' Goals May Diverge

Based on the Principle of Self-Interested Behavior, the theory of finance holds that the goal of the stockholders is to maximize the present value of their investment.

Also on the basis of the Principle of Self-Interested Behavior, the theory of finance allows that managers' goals can differ from the stockholders' goal of maximizing stockholder wealth. Managers are alleged to favor growth and large size for a variety of reasons. Managers appear to value salary, power, and status, all of which are positively correlated with the size of the firm. Larger size, it is argued, provides management with (1) greater job security and (2) larger compensation. Faster growth creates more opportunities for the internal promotion of lower- and middle-level managers. Growth also creates opportunities to distinguish oneself as a productive member of the organization, one who is worthy of promotion. Other potential managerial objectives include greater prestige and discretionary expense accounts.

A Few Words about Ethics

The goal of stockholder wealth maximization should be pursued subject to a fundamental restriction: Corporate managers should take only steps that are legally and ethically sound.

You may encounter situations in your career that tempt you to "play it close to the edge" or even cross over the line that separates ethical from unethical behavior in order to enhance a firm's—and your own—position. But modest transgressions tend to lead to more serious transgressions and eventually to serious legal difficulties.

History offers many examples of price fixing, insider trading, market manipulation, dishonest accounting, and similar activities that people undertook after convincing themselves that it was somehow in their firms' best interests to do so. We explicitly exclude such behavior when we talk about maximizing stockholder wealth.

We have also said that managers may act in their own self-interest to the detriment of the stockholders. In some cases, these actions may not be illegal, or even explicitly prohibited, but they are not good for the corporation. Managers who abuse their positions set a bad example for everyone else. Still, as a practical matter, we must acknowledge that such behavior does exist.

Empirical evidence shows that the level of monitoring does make a difference in administrative costs (including management benefits). The most important benefit from monitoring is probably an increase in awareness by management. And such an awareness can help protect stockholders from unethical behavior.

Shareholder goals may conflict with those of lower-level employees, too. This is often a big issue in European countries where management and labor are appointed to supervising boards that set corporate policy. Recently, the Amsterdam Stock Exchange issued a report urging Dutch companies to pay more attention to shareholder value and to give shareholders a say in corporate decisions to issue shares or pay dividends. Holland's largest labor union responded that shareholder value should not take precedence over the interests of employees. In many European countries, the "Rhine" model of corporate governance, which emphasizes the larger interests of a company and its employees, is preferred over the "Anglo-Saxon" model, which awards top priority to shareholders.

Differences in the goals of stockholders and managers lead to several specific points of possible goal divergence, which we will now discuss. Note that, in this relationship, the stockholders are the principals who are trying to get the managers (agents) to act in their best interest.

Excessive Employee Perquisites and Compensation

One of the most obvious examples of moral hazard involves employee decisions that affect personal benefits, or **perquisites.** These include direct benefits, such as the use of a company car or an expense account for personal business, and also indirect benefits such as an up-to-date office decor. When excessive money is spent on such things, it is at the stockholders' expense.

Managers could also pay themselves excessive compensation if left unchecked. The Enron debacle is an extreme example, where tens of millions of dollars of income went to just one manager, which embarrassed the firm's board when it found out.

EXAMPLE Stockholder-Manager Conflict

Enron's chief financial officer set up and managed several partnerships that did business with Enron. Enron's board of directors waived the firm's conflict-of-interest rules to permit this. Bad accounting for the partnerships allowed Enron to keep billions of dollars of debt off its balance sheet and to hide hundreds of millions of losses. The partnerships paid Enron's CFO more than $30 million in addition to his regular compensation. Board members were shocked to discover this when they investigated the partnerships. And when the truth about Enron's true debt obligations was revealed, Enron went bankrupt. This is a good example of why it is important to have in place and to enforce rules barring conflicts of interest!

Employee Effort

Some employees would like to get paid without having to put forth any effort. It has been said that 20% of the people do 80% of the work.[1] The problem of an agent being neglectful or putting forth less than "full effort" is referred to as **shirking.**

The Nondiversifiability of Human Capital

The unique capabilities and expertise of individuals are referred to as **human capital.** Typically, human capital is tied to employment, and employees devote most of their efforts to a single firm. Therefore, employees cannot easily diversify their human capital. They become specialists in the

[1]Shareholders would of course like to have only "20%-type" employees, in which case—conceptually—the shareholders would need only one-quarter as many employees: X/100% = 20%/80% implies that X = 25%.

firm they serve and in the role they play. This creates a problem called the **nondiversifiability of human capital.**

Although we know about the benefits of diversification from the Principle of Diversification, it is extremely difficult to diversify human capital. Professionals, such as corporate managers, engineers, physicians, accountants, and lawyers, simply do not have the time to become proficient in several areas—and certainly not in a sufficient number to provide reasonable diversification. You would like to diversify across jobs, such as being an accountant, an engineer, a chemist, a salesman, a manager, and others. But you cannot. The value of one's work is also tied to the employing firm. If the firm fires you or goes bankrupt, much of your human capital dissolves. Professionals could diversify this risk by working for numerous firms, such as 5% for Firm 1, 3% for Firm 2, etc. That way, if one of the firms goes under, you have spread the risks across other firms that are still in business. Of course, this is impractical. The nondiversifiability of human capital leads to goal divergences between managers and stockholders.

CAPITAL INVESTMENT CHOICES The stockholders of large publicly traded corporations typically hold many different stocks in their financial investment portfolio. Therefore, they are not overly concerned with random fluctuations in the value of one particular firm. This is because the random fluctuations in the many different stock values tend to cancel each other out. In marked contrast, managers can be "wiped out" by a random fluctuation in the value of their firm. As a result, the stockholder and manager incentives for making investments can be quite different. But, of course, it is the managers who routinely make the firm's investment decisions.

To see this divergence of incentives, consider the impact of bankruptcy on a well-diversified stockholder versus its impact on an employee. Let us take the extreme bankruptcy case where the firm becomes worthless. Despite the lost stock value, the bankruptcy has no effect on the value of the stockholder's other investments, nor does it affect his job. Employees, however, can lose their jobs—even though their financial investments are unaffected. The important question is one of differential impact: Is the loss of a job worse than the loss of, say, 5% of one's financial investments? In the overwhelming majority of cases, job income is much larger than one's income from financial investments. Therefore, the impact of bankruptcy is much greater on the employee than it is on the stockholder.

This divergence of incentives results in an investment decision-making bias. Because employees have more to lose from really bad outcomes, they will have a bias against the firm making high-risk investments. And because the bias is based on risk (rather than return), it can still exist even if the investment has a large positive NPV.

ASSET UNIQUENESS Another impact of the nondiversifiability of human capital on agency costs involves the firm's products and services. If the products and/or services are unique (as opposed to generic), the employee's human capital may have low transferability to another employer. Highly specialized employees may be able to sell their special talents *only* to this firm, because no one else is in this exact business. In such cases, the stockholders will have to pay employees extra to compensate them for the extra risk they are taking. On the other hand, employees doing more generic work have options to work for other firms and would not have to be paid a risk premium.

The problems of capital investment choices and asset uniqueness impose their costs at different times. The agency cost with capital investment choices is the possibility of passing up positive-NPV investments. So this effect is on the choice of *new* investments. The agency cost of unique assets is the higher wages paid to employees to induce them to work for the firm. So this effect is on *existing* investments.

Review

1. How can stockholders' and managers' goals diverge?
2. What is shirking? Why is it an agency problem?
3. How does the nondiversifiability of human capital give rise to a stockholder-manager conflict?
4. How does asset uniqueness intensify the problem of the nondiversifiability of human capital?

13.4 DEBTHOLDER-STOCKHOLDER CONFLICTS

In a general sense, the stockholders can be viewed as having an option against the debtholders (bondholders): The stockholders have *limited liability,* the option to default. Consequently, there is always some possibility (even if extremely small) that the firm will not make the contractually required payments to corporate debtholders on or before the specified due dates. For this reason, the debt is called **risky debt.**

Incentive conflicts occur between the debtholders and the stockholders because the debt is risky. These conflicts lead to several specific problems we discuss in this section. First, let us get the roles straight. In the previous section, the stockholders are principals with respect to their corporate managers (agents). In this section, the stockholders reverse their role. Here, we are examining them in their role as agents in their relationship with debtholders (principals). The debtholders want to protect themselves against actions taken by the agent stockholders, who in turn make their decisions through the firm's managers.

The Asset Substitution Problem

Firms routinely make decisions that result in the substitution of assets. In the simplest and most common instance, cash is used to buy equipment or materials. In fact, for every investment, some assets are substituted for others. Prudent managers weigh the risks and returns of these investments. But with risky debt, stockholders may be motivated to substitute riskier assets for the firm's existing assets. The **asset substitution** problem occurs when riskier assets are substituted for the firm's existing assets, thereby expropriating value from the firm's debtholders.

Here is how the asset substitution problem happens. The total value of a firm is the market value of all its assets. The debtholders have a claim that is secured by this total value. The stockholders have a residual claim on the remaining firm value. Although the debtholders' claim is a fixed promised amount, the likelihood that they will actually get this amount can be changed. With the promised payment fixed, an increase in the risk of the assets decreases the value of the debtholders' claim. After all, with higher risk there is more chance the debtholders will not be repaid the promised amount. This lowers the expected value of the payment.

Table 13.1 gives a simple example of this. In Panel A, the firm's assets are worth \$1,200, with an equal chance of receiving \$1,600 and \$800. Because the firm's debt is \$1,000 and due immediately, the creditors receive \$1,000 when assets are high and \$800 when they are low. The payoffs for the stockholders are \$600 and \$0 in these two cases. The expected payoffs for debt and equity are \$900 and \$300, respectively. Now, suppose the managers sell some assets for new assets that have the same expected value, but a wider dispersion. Panel B of the table shows that if the riskier assets now pay off \$1,800 and \$600, the expected value of assets is still \$1,200, so that the new investments have an NPV of zero. However, the payoffs for debtholders are \$1,000 and \$600, with an expected value of \$800, and the payoffs for stockholders are \$800 and \$0, with an expected value of \$400. Note that the total value of the firm is unchanged, but debt has declined by \$100 and equity has increased by \$100.

TABLE 13.1
Asset substitution problem.

Panel A. Initial position: Promised debt payment = 1,000

PROBABILITY	ASSET VALUE	DEBT PAYMENT	EQUITY CLAIM
0.50	1,600	1,000	600
0.50	800	800	0
Expectation	1,200	900	300

Panel B. After asset substitution: NPV = 0 and promised debt payment = 1,000

PROBABILITY	ASSET VALUE	DEBT PAYMENT	EQUITY CLAIM
0.50	1,800	1,000	800
0.50	600	600	0
Expectation	1,200	800	400

Panel C. After asset substitution: NPV < 0 and promised debt payment = 1,000

PROBABILITY	ASSET VALUE	DEBT PAYMENT	EQUITY CLAIM
0.50	1,800	1,000	800
0.50	500	500	0
Expectation	1,150	750	400

The asset substitution problem arises because of the stockholders' valuable default option. So we can view the problem in terms of options (contingent claims). The value of an option increases and decreases with the risk of the underlying asset. In this case, the "underlying asset" is all of the firm's assets. Therefore, if the firm (that is, the stockholders) increases the risk of its assets through substitution, the value of this option goes up. This lowers the expected value of the debt payment, as we just noted. Expropriating this value from the debtholders distorts the stockholders' incentives. In fact, it can even cause a negative-NPV investment to actually *increase* stockholder wealth.

Consider the case where the asset substitution does not change the total value of the firm's assets. This is illustrated in Figure 13.1. With the same total value—the same-sized "pie"—and only the debtholders and stockholders as claimants, a decrease in the value of the debtholders' claim must cause an exactly offsetting increase in the value of the stockholders' claim. It is a zero-sum game between the debtholders and the stockholders. After making the risky asset substitution, the stockholders could sell their shares for more than before. If the debtholders sold their bonds, however, they would get equivalently less, because the marketplace would factor in the increased risk of default.

Figure 13.1 is a useful way of illustrating the debtholder-stockholder conflict. We use the same framework in Figures 13.2 through 13.7 to illustrate other aspects of this conflict. So it is "worth your while" to spend enough time with Figure 13.1 to understand and become comfortable with it.

The idea behind the asset substitution problem might seem puzzling at first. It *is* tricky. But examining its potentially dramatic implications in the following detailed example may help your intuition. Because it is so amazing, we want to stress that we did not make it up. It actually happened!

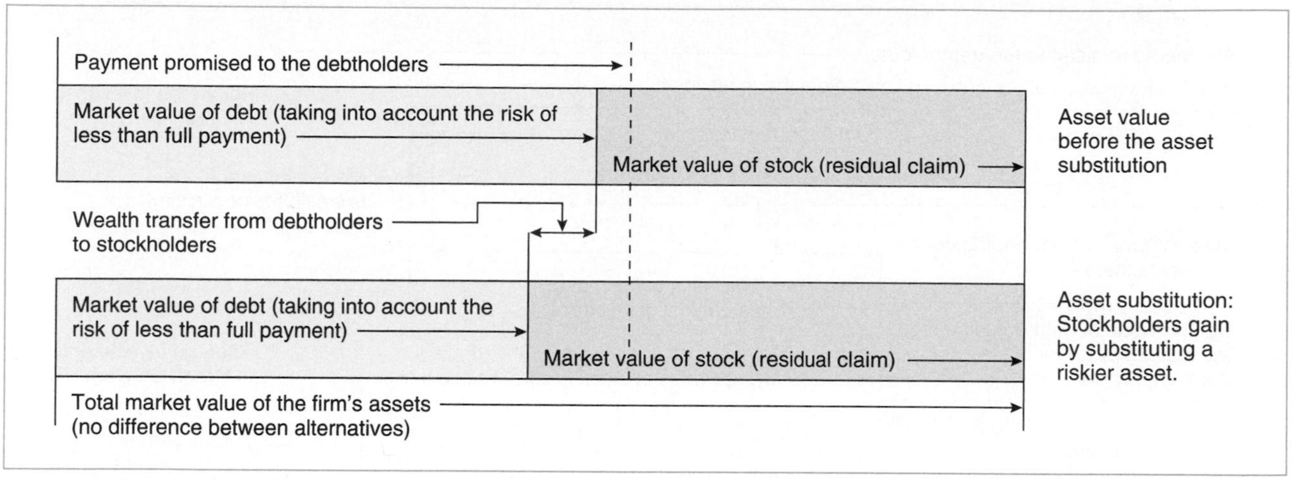

FIGURE 13.1
The asset substitution problem. (Stockholders gain at the expense of the debtholders.)

EXAMPLE The Green Canyon Project

The Hunt brothers' Green Canyon oil and gas drilling project illustrates the asset substitution problem. The three Hunt brothers of Dallas, sons of the legendary H.L. Hunt, owned Placid Oil Co., which defaulted on its bank loan agreement after a huge drop in oil prices. Placid filed for bankruptcy protection from its creditors, seeking to stretch out its loan payments to fund its Green Canyon project. Understandably, the banks wanted Placid to pay them off before undertaking new investments—especially highly risky ones.

The Hunt brothers had embarked on the highly risky $340 million Green Canyon project in the hope that a massive oil and gas discovery would save their business. (At one time, the Hunts contended that they might find a 70-million-barrel oil reserve worth upwards of $1 billion.) At that time, they apparently had debts they were unable to repay. These debts included Placid's debt, debts of Placid's sister firm Penrod Drilling Co., and personal debts that grew out of their unsuccessful, very expensive attempt to corner the world silver market.

The Green Canyon project entailed drilling for oil and gas in very deep water in the Gulf of Mexico. One well, drilled through 2,243 feet of water, set a world water-depth record for drilling. This is a very hostile operating environment. Hurricane gusts can reach 150 miles per hour. Also, they used an untested technology, a one-of-a-kind floating drilling and production system. The Hunts were "betting the ranch" on one of the world's riskiest ventures. Many industry experts questioned the project's economic viability. Understandably, the banks went to extraordinary lengths in their efforts to stop the project, arguing that if the project failed, there would be little left of Placid for them to collect toward their loans.

Consider the situation in terms of the "hidden" option where common stock is viewed as a call option on the firm's assets. When the firm's assets are worth less than its debt obligations, the stock is like an out-of-the-money call option. As such, the stock is not worth a whole lot. To risk such a relatively small equity value on an unlikely chance of the firm earning a lot of money is sort of like buying a lottery ticket: The stockholders have a lot to gain—but not much to lose. The asset substitution problem can be exacerbated in a financially distressed firm. Increasing the risk of the underlying asset (the firm's total assets), by using cash to invest in highly risky assets, increases the value of the call option (the firm's common stock). The gamble may not be very likely to pay off, but hey, you never know!

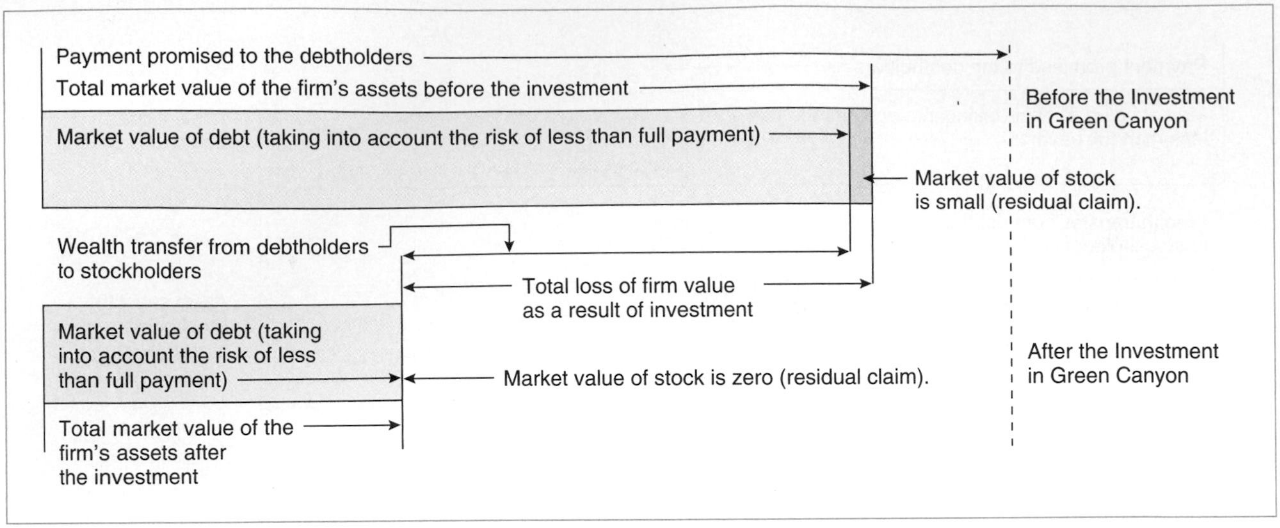

FIGURE 13.2
The effect of the Green Canyon Project on Placid Oil Co. (The debtholders bore the risk of the investment made by the stockholders.)

Afterward: Eventually, all three Hunt brothers' trusts and two of the Hunt brothers and their spouses wound up in bankruptcy as their financial woes mounted. The Green Canyon project did not pay off and Placid finally abandoned it. The banks did not do so badly after all. They got back their principal and some of the interest they were owed.

The effect of the Green Canyon project on Placid Oil Co. is illustrated in Figure 13.2. It is important to note that even though "everyone lost," it could have turned out differently. Winning this big gamble would have provided enough for everyone. The problem, of course, was that the debtholders put up all the money for the gamble—even though they did not want to. The stockholders chose the gamble, without putting up any additional money. Perhaps more of us would play the lottery if we could get other people to purchase the tickets for us!

Now let us consider a more general asset substitution situation where the increase in risk changes the total value of the firm. The change in assets may have either a positive or negative NPV. Let us look at the good investments first. Because the debt claim is fixed, the stockholders get the positive NPV (increase in "pie" size). If the value of the debtholders' claim is also reduced by the simultaneous increase in risk, the stockholders get that value as well. This is because it is a zero-sum game.

Panel C of Table 13.1 illustrates an asset substitution with a bad investment, a high risk investment with a negative NPV. The value of the firm, compared to Panel A, declines from \$1,200 to \$1,150, so the NPV is −\$50. The value of debt declines by \$150, whereas the value of equity increases by \$100. The stockholders gain \$150 at the debtholders expense, and, even though they lose \$50 from the negative-NPV investment, the stockholders have a net gain from this asset substitution.

What happens with bad investments like this? Even with a smaller-sized "pie" (a smaller firm value due to the negative NPV), if the decrease in the debtholders' claim value is *more* than the loss in the size of the pie, the value of the stockholders' claim *increases.* That is, if the wealth transfer dominates the negative NPV, the stockholders still gain. The debtholders suffer the entire negative NPV and then some.[2] The asset substitution problem is illustrated pictorially with a negative-NPV investment in Figure 13.3.

[2]You can see right away why the debtholders do not like this game!

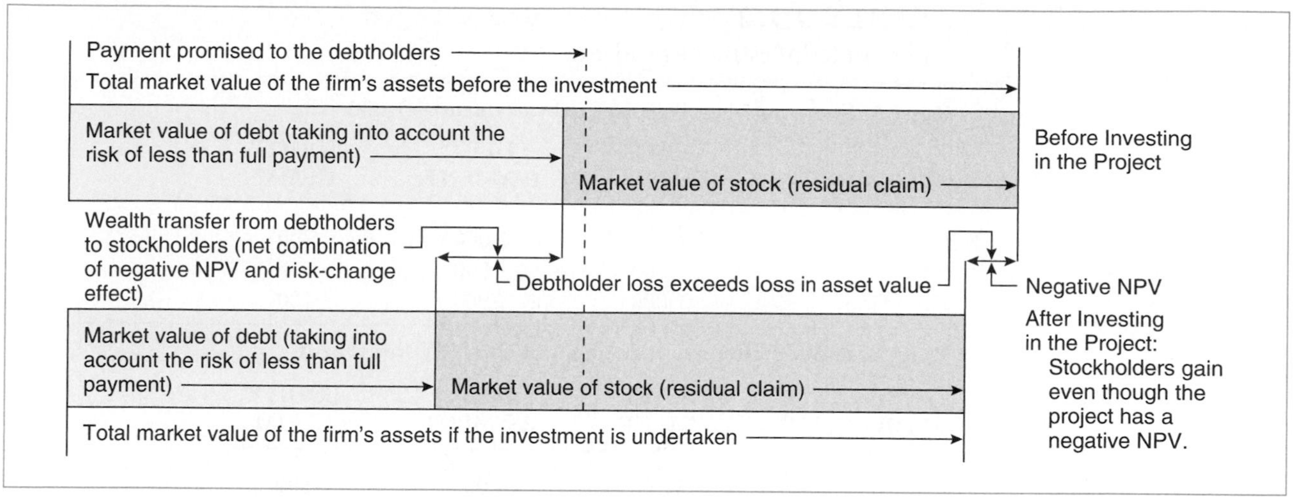

FIGURE 13.3
The problem of asset substitution with a negative-NPV investment. (The stockholders gain more in wealth transfer from the debtholders than they lose in negative NPV.)

Let us summarize. The asset substitution problem occurs when the stockholders substitute riskier assets for the firm's existing assets and expropriate value from the debtholders. This can be accomplished in the process of new investment (growth) or by selling some existing assets and purchasing new ones. Although the total value of the firm may stay the same, increase, or decrease, the value of the debtholders' claim goes down because of the greater chance of default. The decrease in debtholder value causes an exactly offsetting increase in stockholder value because of the zero-sum-game condition between the two claimants.

The Underinvestment Problem

Underinvestment is essentially the mirror image, or reverse, of the asset substitution problem. With risky debt outstanding, the stockholders may *lose* value if the firm makes a low-risk investment. And this can happen even if the investment has a positive NPV. As we saw in the asset substitution problem, with a neutral (zero-NPV) investment, the stockholders gain with an increase in risk. Logically, under the same conditions, the stockholders will lose with a decrease in risk. With asset substitution, stockholders may undertake a bad (negative-NPV), but high-risk, investment to expropriate wealth from the debtholders.

With underinvestment, stockholders refuse to undertake a good (positive-NPV), but low-risk, investment so as not to shift wealth away from themselves to the debtholders. Despite the loss from such a risk change, of course, stockholders can gain from an investment—if it has a sufficiently large positive NPV. However, if the decrease in stockholder value from lowering the asset risk outweighs the positive NPV of an investment, stockholders will refuse to undertake the investment. Table 13.2 gives an example of this. The firm is originally worth $1,000, with debt and equity worth $900 and $100, respectively. The managers have an opportunity to invest in a positive-NPV project, producing the values shown in Panel B. This project has a positive NPV of $25. But because the payoffs to debtholders are enhanced whereas those for stockholders are reduced, the value of debt increases by $75 and the value of equity declines by $50. Because stockholder wealth is diminished, managers will decline to invest in this project, even though it has a positive NPV. Figure 13.4 illustrates the underinvestment problem pictorially.

TABLE 13.2
The underinvestment problem.

Panel A. Initial position: Promised debt payment = 1,000

PROBABILITY	ASSET VALUE	DEBT PAYMENT	EQUITY CLAIM
0.50	1,200	1,000	200
0.50	800	800	0
Expectation	1,000	900	100

Panel B. Position after risk-reducing, positive-NPV investment

PROBABILITY	ASSET VALUE	DEBT PAYMENT	EQUITY CLAIM
0.50	1,100	1,000	100
0.50	950	950	0
Expectation	1,025	975	50

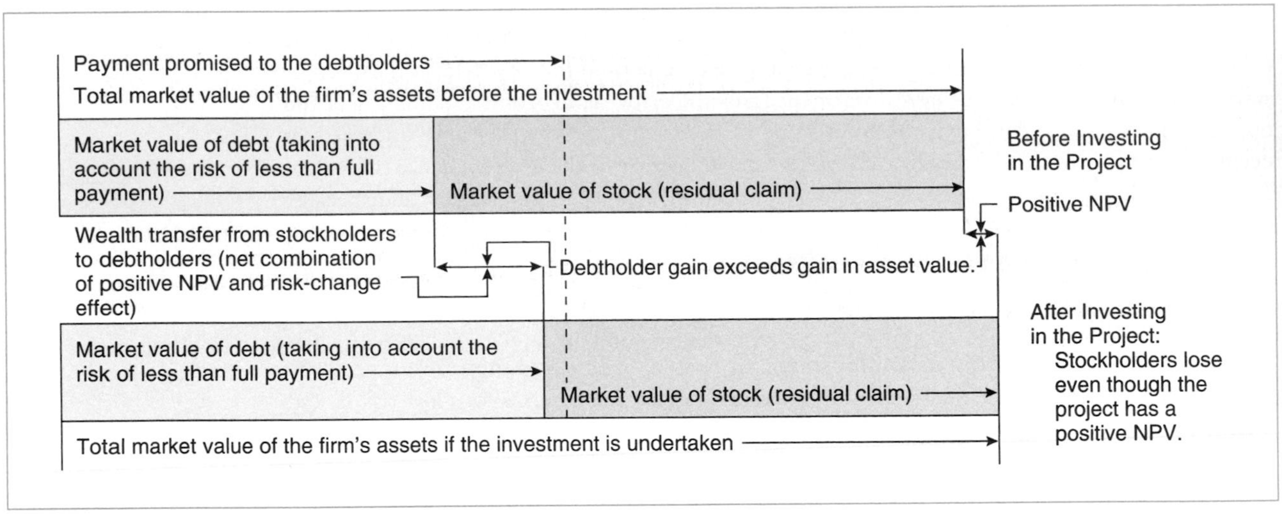

FIGURE 13.4
The underinvestment problem. (The stockholders would lose more in wealth to the debtholders than they would gain in positive NPV.)

Claim Dilution via Dividend Policy

Paying out a large cash dividend may dilute the existing debtholders' claim. The dividend simultaneously reduces the firm's cash and its owners' equity. The equity reduction enlarges the firm's proportion of debt financing, thereby increasing the risk of the debt and reducing the value of its claim. This process is illustrated in Panel A of Table 13.3. The firm has total assets of $500, financed with $300 of debt and $200 of equity. After paying a $100 cash dividend, assets and stockholders' equity decline by the $100, but the firm's debt obligations remain. There are now only $400 of assets supporting the debt. The proportion of the firm's assets financed with debt increased from 60% to 75%.

TABLE 13.3
Claim dilution via dividends or new debt.

Panel A. Claim dilution via dividends

BALANCE SHEET ACCOUNTS	BEFORE CASH DIVIDEND	AFTER $100 CASH DIVIDEND
Current assets	$300	$200
Fixed assets	200	200
Total assets	$500	$400
Current liabilities	$100	$100
Long-term debt	200	200
Stockholders' equity	200	100
Total liabilities and equity	$500	$400

Panel B. Claim dilution via new debt

BALANCE SHEET ACCOUNTS	BEFORE NEW DEBT	AFTER $300 NEW DEBT
Current assets	$300	$400
Fixed assets	200	400
Total assets	$500	$800
Current liabilities	$100	$200
Long-term debt	200	400
Stockholders' equity	200	200
Total liabilities and equity	$500	$800

This is simply a different form of asset substitution. The substituted assets are the same as the original assets, except for having a smaller amount of cash. Because cash is a riskless asset, removing some of it (paying it out to the stockholders) raises the average risk of the remaining assets. As you now know, the increase in risk will decrease the value of the firm's outstanding debt. Figure 13.5 illustrates the problem of claim dilution via dividend policy.

Claim dilution via dividend policy is why many bond issues (and virtually all "junk," or high-yield, issues) have some form of dividend restriction. Such a restriction typically limits cash dividends to a fraction of earnings or cash flow. When firms have a large portion of debt financing, the dividend restriction may prohibit the payment of cash dividends altogether until long-term debt is repaid to some specified level.

Claim Dilution via New Debt

A substantial increase in debt may also dilute the existing debtholders' claim on the firm's assets. Panel B of Table 13.3 gives an example. The firm borrows an additional $300, which is invested in new assets. This increases total assets and total debt (current and long-term) by the same amount. Before the expansion financed with new debt, the ratio of debt to assets was 60%. Afterwards, it increases to 75%. Although the book value of the old debt remains as before, its market value will decline because the firm is now riskier. Claim dilution will occur if the new debt increases the chance that the existing debtholders will not be repaid the promised amount. As with asset substitution, the increased risk decreases the value of the firm's outstanding debt. And once again, because of the nature of the zero-sum game and the contingent claim, the stockholders get the benefit of the debtholders' loss in value. Figure 13.6 illustrates the problem.

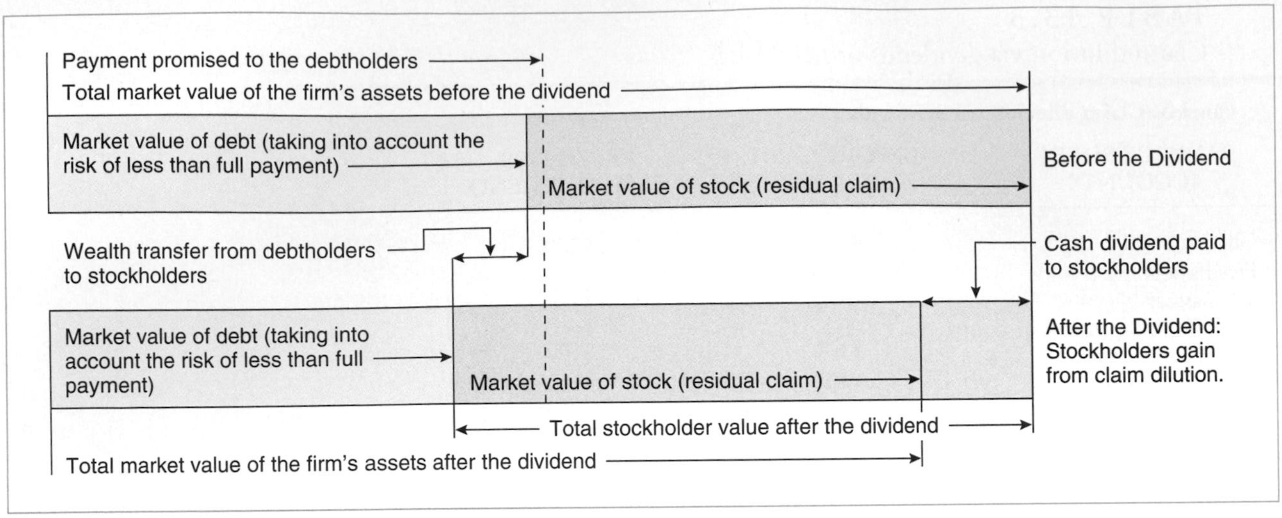

FIGURE 13.5
The problem of claim dilution via dividend policy. (Because cash is a riskless asset, paying it out to stockholders as a dividend increases the risk of the remaining assets. The value of the stock declines because of the drop in assets, but by less than the value of the dividend.)

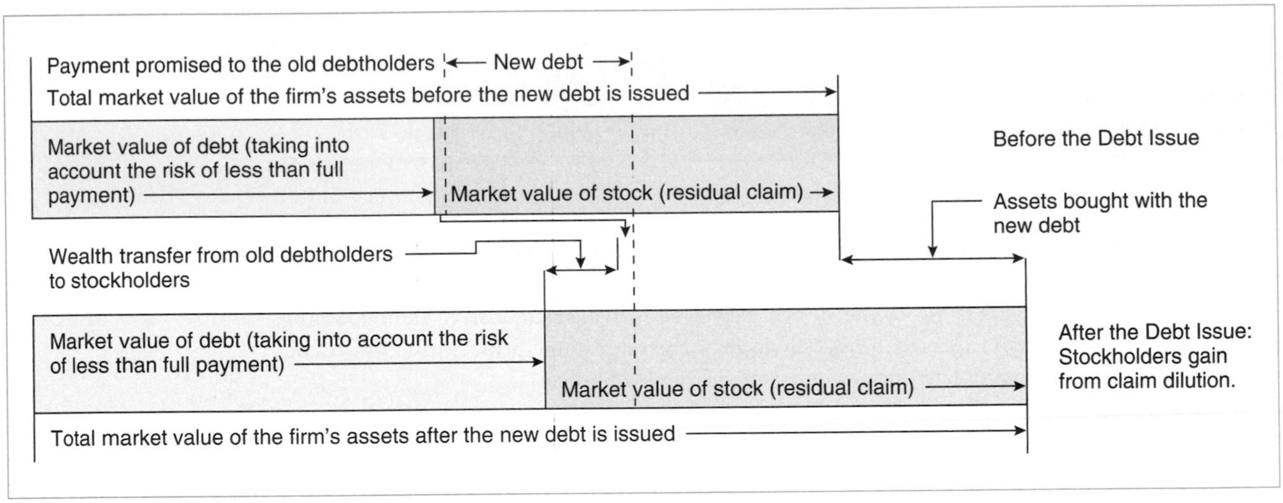

FIGURE 13.6
The problem of claim dilution via new debt. (The stockholders gain from a wealth transfer from the old debtholders.)

EXAMPLE RJR Nabisco's Leveraged Buyout

The leveraged buyout of RJR Nabisco, Inc. several years ago illustrates how claim dilution can be caused by new debt. The buyout increased the firm's outstanding debt from about \$5.7 billion to about \$23.2 billion. Following the announcement of the bid, existing RJR Nabisco bonds plunged roughly 20% in market value. The pre-existing debt did not have a legal restriction preventing a large amount of new debt. Existing bondholders had expected the firm to continue to use similar amounts of debt. But the bondholders were rudely confronted: Once the debt was issued, the firm constrained its actions *only* by the explicit legal debt contract.

Following the RJR Nabisco experience, there was near turmoil in the market for high-grade bonds issued by consumer products firms. After things settled down, many investors had learned a lesson from this incident. Since then, investors have required additional restrictions to try to prevent other firms from doing the same thing that RJR Nabisco did.

We have just explained how a firm may engage in claim dilution by paying a large dividend or by deliberately changing its *capital structure* (its mix of liabilities and owners' equity) by taking on a significant amount of new debt. A significant economic downturn can also cause claim dilution. This is because poor economic conditions increase the probability of default. In such cases, the claim dilution certainly may not have been the firm's choice!

Asset Uniqueness

In general, when a firm's assets are unique, as opposed to generic, there is more risk associated with the disposal of those assets, should that become necessary. So the collateral provided by the assets to the debtholders is of lower value. Although the assets might be highly sought after because of their uniqueness, they also might become worthless (or perhaps even costly to dispose of). Of course, this is the essence of a risk-return trade-off. Therefore, if everything else is equal, a firm with unique assets would have to pay a higher interest cost to compensate the debtholders for the increased risk.

EXAMPLE The Effect of Asset Uniqueness on Making a Loan

Imagine you are a banker considering two different loan applications. Each loan would enable its respective firm to build a business facility that would be almost entirely controlled by robotics equipment. The new facility would be the collateral for the loan. One is a storage facility that can be used for virtually anything that does not need specialized treatment such as refrigeration. The other is a facility for manufacturing a new kind of home entertainment product, such as a laser disc player. The cost of building the facilities would be identical. What would be the comparative risk of loaning money to these two firms?

The storage facility would be built by one firm for a specific use, but it could be easily used for something different at little extra cost. The manufacturing facility would also be built for a specific use, but using it for something else would require considerable additional cost. Therefore, if the second firm defaulted, it is likely that the facility would be worthless for its intended purpose. That is, if the product was unsuccessful, the robotics facility would require extensive and costly modifications to make it useful for another purpose. But if the first firm defaulted, the bank would stand a better chance of reselling the collateral to another business without having to spend much money to modify it.

As the banker, would you consider these loans equally risky? We would not. Even if the likelihood of default were identical, the bank's risk would be greater with the manufacturing facility because the value of the facility would be considerably less if it had to be used for something else. Therefore, for the manufacturing firm, we would either not loan as much money, or we would charge a higher interest rate on a loan of the same amount as the loan for the storage facility.

Just as the manager of a firm in a unique business would charge more for her labor, so a lender would charge the firm more. If the unique business defaults, the manager would need to become reeducated to recover the value of her human capital. The lender would have to reinvest to make the collateral assets equal their original value. When a firm heads for uncharted waters, the increased risk has its costs.

Review

1. Why is corporate debt risky?
2. What is the asset substitution problem, and how are debtholders hurt by it?
3. What is the underinvestment problem, and how are the debtholders hurt by it?
4. What does claim dilution mean? How does paying a cash dividend give rise to claim dilution? How does a new debt issue lead to claim dilution?
5. How does an asset's uniqueness affect its value as collateral for a loan?

13.5 CONSUMER-FIRM CONFLICTS

Many consumer-firm interactions can be viewed as principal-agent relationships. Of course, it is important to keep in mind who the players are. In the first situation we will discuss, the firm is the agent and the consumer is the principal. In the second situation, the firm is the principal and the consumer is the agent.

Guarantees and Service After the Sale

In its agent role, the firm promises future service, should it become necessary. The fundamental question is whether the consumer can "trust" the firm to fulfill its future obligations. If the consumer (principal) is confident the firm will live up to its promise, the firm can get full value for its products and services. The level of confidence is based on the firm's reputation. A good reputation is the assurance that promises will be fulfilled to the consumer's satisfaction. Needless to say, a firm in financial distress—even one with a great reputation—may not be able to provide adequate assurance of future service. When service is needed, the firm may be long gone!

EXAMPLE Consumer-Firm Conflicts and Chrysler's Financial Distress

Several years ago, Chrysler Corporation experienced financial distress. This led the federal government to provide more than $1.5 billion of loan guarantees. It stands as one of the few times the federal government has stepped in to "bail out" a private firm.

Warranties were a critical factor that compounded Chrysler's trouble. As Chrysler's financial woes mounted, consumers grew more concerned that Chrysler might not be around to honor its warranties and sell replacement parts. Sales plummeted, which led to greater losses. Even the cars that were sold had much lower prices compared to comparable competitor models. The federal government loan guarantees came just before Chrysler would have had to file for bankruptcy.

The Free-Rider Problem

What a customer does with a firm's product can in some cases significantly affect the firm. For example, a firm may be hurt by a customer who duplicates and sells the firm's products and/or services without proper agreement. (The "option" to do this is yet another hidden option.) As such, this relationship also can be viewed in a principal-agent framework. Recall the concept of a free rider, one who receives the benefit of someone else's expenditure (money, effort, or creativity) simply by imitation. The potential for consumers (the agents in this case) to duplicate and sell the firm's (the principal's) products and/or services without proper agreement is another example of the free-rider problem.

Consider the copying of books (photocopying or plagiarism), computer software, videotapes, audiotapes, and so on. Copyright laws make such misuse illegal. Similarly, patent laws make certain kinds of copying of a valuable idea illegal. The purpose of such laws is to provide incentives for people to be creative. In other words, our society has recognized the Principle of Valuable Ideas and encourages people to create value in this manner. In many cases these laws work very well. However, new products and technologies sometimes require the modification of existing laws. Such a modification was deemed necessary with respect to video-movie rentals. During the 1980s, royalties for movie rentals became mandated by law.

Another free-rider problem area involves international law. Making and enforcing copyright, patent, and royalty laws are important to international trade and relations. As markets become truly international, countries that do not recognize and enforce such laws become places where pirated material can be easily created. Alleged blatant violations are a major issue of contention in international talks, as they were recently in United States–China trade negotiations. Such pirated material can cause a significant loss to the creators.

How can the firm protect itself from unscrupulous consumers who exercise the hidden option to free ride? It is rumored that the Coca-Cola Company has employed people to order "Coke" in establishments that do not sell their product. If they failed to clarify that the drink served was not actually Coke, Coca-Cola is said to have sued the establishment for violation of its trademark. Although this may sound like a harsh measure, it may be one of the few methods available to protect a valuable trademark.[3]

Review

1. Describe two consumer-firm conflicts.
2. How does financial distress affect the consumer-firm conflict relating to promises of future service?
3. What is the free-rider problem, and how does it involve a hidden option?

13.6 WORKING IN CONTRACTUAL RELATIONSHIPS

There are a number of other practical considerations in ongoing explicit and implicit contractual relationships.

Financial Distress

Financial distress can intensify the problem of goal divergence. As an example, consider again the debtholder-stockholder relationship. After a debt contract has been made, stockholders make firm decisions (through the managers) within the constraints of the contract. The incentives to "push the edge of the contract" and engage in asset substitution and underinvestment increase dramatically if a firm becomes financially distressed. We saw this in practice in the Placid Oil Green Canyon project example.

In Figure 13.7, we illustrate two firms that are facing the same two alternative investments: a positive-NPV, low-risk investment; and a negative-NPV, high-risk investment. Firm A is financially healthy, but firm B is financially distressed. As you can see, the incentives differ for the two firms' stockholders. The stockholders of the financially distressed firm are better off engaging in asset substitution and underinvestment, taking the negative-NPV investment and leaving the

[3]Perhaps Coca-Cola has reason to worry. Many years ago, Bayer lost its trademark name, aspirin, after the term became commonly used to refer to the drug, regardless of the manufacturer.

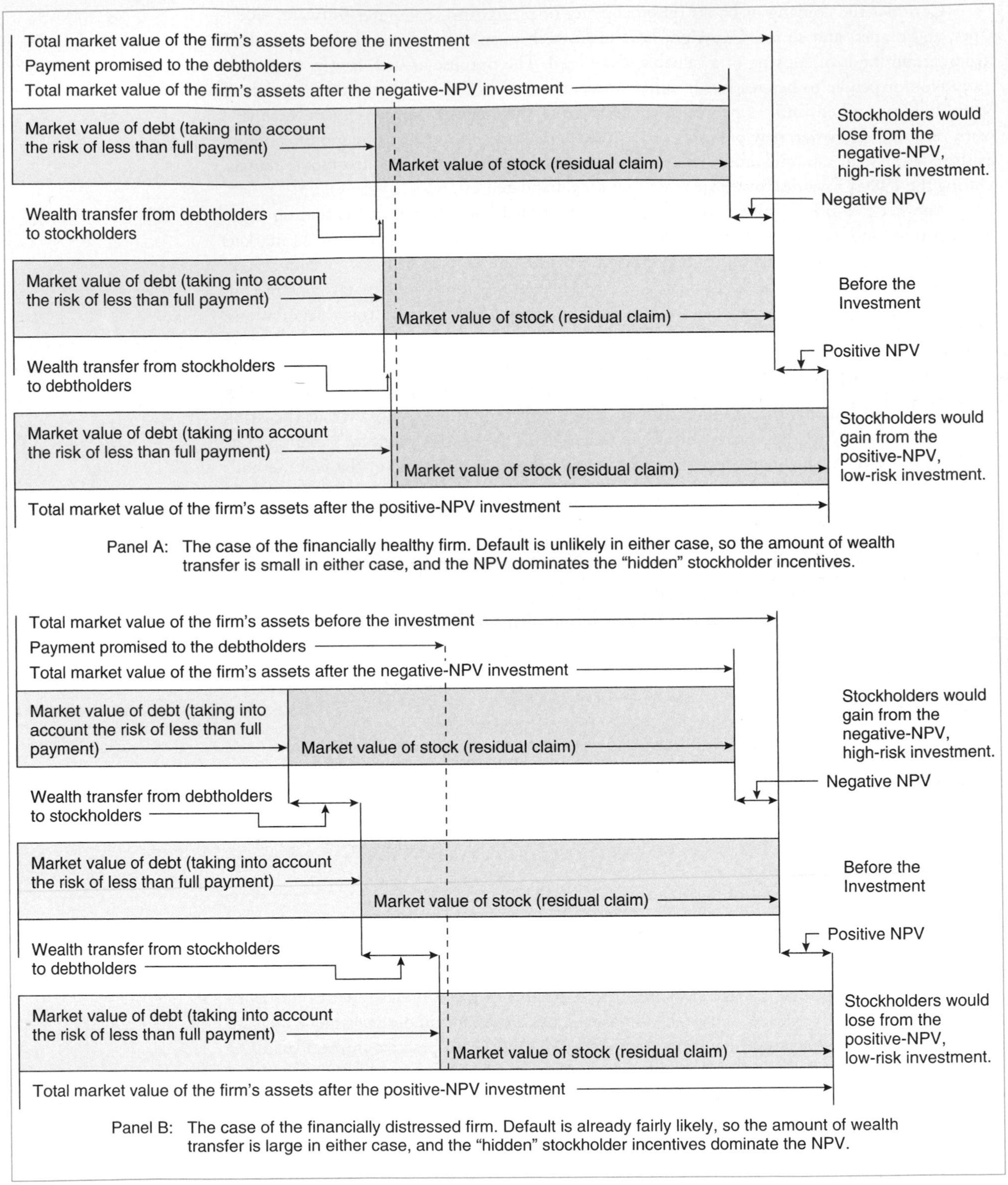

FIGURE 13.7
The potential effect of financial distress on investment choice.

positive-NPV investment. In contrast, the financially healthy firm has the incentives to take the positive-NPV investment and leave the negative-NPV one.

CLAIMANT COALITIONS Financial distress can distort other situations as well. It can create incentives for the firm's various claimants (stakeholders) to form coalitions and "gang up" on one another. For example, suppose a firm is in financial distress, and liquidation would produce the largest total value. Despite this, the managers might contract with a bank for a loan to continue operations.

Each claimant will favor or oppose liquidation on the basis of its own outcome, not on the basis of maximizing total firm value. The loan provides the managers with another chance to save their jobs (an option!), even though continuing hurts the stockholders. But the stockholders might support the loan, even though it hurts the debtholders. This can happen if the stockholders will get little from liquidation but stand to gain a lot if the firm recovers. If you ever played the board game Monopoly with several players until only one player is left, you probably saw, or even engaged in, a claimant coalition game. Of course, the play is considerably more intense when there is real money at stake!

A dramatic shift in incentives brought on by financial distress can occur when the contingent claim—the option—inherent in the situation falls out-of-the-money. At that point, the optionholder has little more to lose—perhaps only the time premium. The downside risk is limited because an option cannot have a negative value. At the same time, the option is worthless if it expires out-of-the-money, so the possibility of it coming back into the money can make it worth fighting to keep the option alive. You cannot lose much, but you might win. This combination can create powerful incentives to take risks and engage in protracted legal battles.

Information

A financial contract is complex because it involves imperfect information. In a perfect capital market, complete information is available to all participants at no cost. In a real capital market, you can apply the Signaling Principle to interpret actions. Although it would be nice if the meaning of all actions were absolutely clear, this is not the case. Interpretation can be complex and difficult. For example, when is a "sale" really a sale? Some retailers have essentially continuous sales. When is a sale or any other advertising claim credible?[4] This represents a significant and ongoing asymmetric information problem.

Even when the meaning of an action is clear, other problems can arise. For example, to avoid being taken advantage of one might choose to camouflage some actions. Suppose a firm always reduced its price on a model that was about to be discontinued. If you knew this, you would not think the sale was such a good deal. After all, the item might not be worth much after a new model comes out. So the firm faces the problem of adverse selection: Offering the reduced price is a negative signal indicating that the model is about to be discontinued. How can the firm reduce this problem?

One approach to this problem is to deliberately add uncertainty. Thus, the firm could occasionally (randomly) offer a lower price on items not being discontinued—a "real" sale. In that way, a reduced price can be a good deal rather than an obvious signal of a model discontinuation.

Incentives also play an important role. Ideally, an agent would have incentives to send accurate signals. But consider managers whose earnings depend on the firm's performance. Such managers might be tempted to mislead, or even falsely report better firm performance, unless they face penalties for being found out later. Properly structured, penalties lead to more credible signals by making it unattractive to mimic the activities of a "better" agent.

---

[4]You have probably wondered about particular advertising claims. Our own risk aversion toward lawsuits keeps us from citing specific examples.

AGENT REPUTATION There are many factors that determine an agent's incentives, such as rewards, punishments, ethical attitudes, the likelihood of being caught misbehaving, and the agent's reputation. As with firms, agents with good reputations can demand higher prices for their products or services.

An agent's good reputation carries with it an implicit guarantee of satisfactory performance. Therefore, building and maintaining a good reputation is valuable. Conversely, its loss would be costly. The opportunity cost of a lost good reputation increases the cost of being caught misbehaving. Therefore, an agent with a good reputation has a greater incentive to behave properly.

Management Contracts

Beyond the separation of ownership and control we noted earlier, stockholders can be a widely dispersed group. For example, AT&T and GM have more than 3.7 and 1.9 million common stockholders, respectively. This tremendous diffusion of ownership appears to intensify stockholder-manager conflicts. There are some who cite large executive salaries as evidence that the managers are winning the conflict, at least in the instances cited. However, empirical studies have reached conflicting conclusions about whether manager-controlled firms differ significantly from stockholder-controlled firms.

Even with widely diffused share ownership—and managerial control—stockholders possess several devices that help align managerial goals with their own. These devices include designing incentive compensation plans for managers, the right to sell their own shares, the right to replace managers, and the right to elect directors.

INCENTIVE COMPENSATION PLANS Management contracts often include stock options, performance shares, and bonuses. Because accounting measures can sometimes be manipulated, it is common to base bonuses on appreciation in the firm's share price.

EXAMPLE Lee Iacocca's First-Year Compensation Package

When Chrysler Corporation hired Lee Iacocca, he insisted on taking only one dollar in salary the first year. In place of the typical salary, he chose an incentive package that included options to purchase approximately 350,000 shares of Chrysler common stock. These options were far out-of-the-money. He argued that if he was successful in turning the firm around, he would be well paid; if he was not successful, he would appropriately get nothing.

Eight years later, Iacocca cashed in his options for a gain of roughly $20 million. Unfortunately, it was incorrectly reported that the $20 million was his pay for the single year in which he cashed in his options. Some people cite this and other evidence and argue that corporate executives are paid too much.

We will not take a position on the issue of whether executive compensation is fair. However, we believe the starting place for such a debate must be accurate facts and a complete understanding of the contract.

THE STOCKHOLDERS' RIGHT TO SELL THEIR SHARES Except in special cases, stockholders can sell the shares they own. This can create the threat of a takeover. If many stockholders offer to sell their shares, and the market price per share falls, others may buy up the shares and take over the firm if the price is low enough.

The right to tender shares to a prospective acquirer, or sell them in the market, is potentially the most effective (although last-resort) measure open to shareholders. However, many recently introduced antitakeover measures may have reduced the threat of takeover. So-called poison pills are an example of an antitakeover measure.

Poison pills typically take the form of an option to purchase shares in the target firm at a bargain price. The option becomes exercisable in the hands of the target firm's stockholders once an "unfriendly" suitor (one not approved by the firm's board of directors) acquires some specified percentage of the outstanding shares, often just 20%. The poison pill provision gets its name from the cyanide pill a spy is given to swallow when capture becomes imminent. Although such a poison pill prevents talking after being captured, it also has some other striking side effects!

EXAMPLE Chrysler's Poison Pill

A few years ago, Chrysler Corporation's largest stockholder, billionaire Kirk Kerkorian, demanded action from Chrysler. He owned about 9% of Chrysler's stock and felt it was undervalued. He wanted the firm to raise its dividend and buy back some of its shares.

At the time, Chrysler had a poison pill that prevented a shareholder from controlling 10% or more of Chrysler's shares without board approval. Kerkorian wanted to increase his ownership proportion to 15%. He asked Chrysler's board to modify the poison pill. Several large investors went even farther. They urged Chrysler to eliminate the poison pill.

Within a few weeks, Chrysler took action. The dividend was boosted 60% and a $1 billion stock buy-back program was announced. Finally, Chrysler modified its "shareholder-rights plan" to permit a shareholder to own up to 15% of the stock. Chrysler's board diluted the poison pill but did not discard it.

REPLACING MANAGERS Managers, like all agents, have significant incentives to build and maintain a good reputation. On average, executives who lose their jobs in connection with a financially distressed firm do not find comparable or better-paying jobs. In contrast, when a person is recruited away from an existing job into a higher-paying job, their past success is almost always cited as the basis for their being hired.[5]

EXAMPLE How Much Is an Executive Worth?

A few years ago, The Walt Disney Company hired Michael Ovitz as president and a director. Ovitz had cofounded Creative Artists Agency and was very highly regarded in Hollywood. It was rumored that MCA Inc. had tried to hire him just a few months before. To get Ovitz to leave Creative Artists, Disney offered 10-year options on 5 million of its shares. Compensation experts valued the option package at between $107 million and $140 million.

THE STOCKHOLDERS' ELECTION OF DIRECTORS Unhappy stockholders can elect new directors, or even mount a *proxy fight*.[6] However, this is difficult. Further, the recent practice of staggering directorships (such as electing one-third each year) makes winning a proxy fight even harder.

---

[5]Sadly, we must point out that there are also many people who are quite successful but never get hired away for "big bucks!"

[6]Sometimes one or more shareholders lead a takeover attempt by asking other shareholders to precommit to vote with them. This precommitment is called a *proxy*.

EXAMPLE Sallie Mae's Proxy Fight

The Student Loan Marketing Association (nicknamed Sallie Mae) buys and services student loans under federally sponsored student loan programs. At one point, a group of shareholders, led by former Sallie Mae chief operating officer Albert Lord, started a proxy fight. They said Sallie Mae was poorly managed and blamed current management for not paying enough attention to the firm's profit margin and stock price.[7] Earnings had slumped the prior year for the first time in the firm's history.

The proxy fight succeeded. At the next annual meeting, the dissidents elected eight new directors to the 21-member board. (Of the remaining 13, six were management candidates, and seven were appointed by President Clinton.) Management started a legal battle to keep the new directors from serving but gave up after a month. Meanwhile, Sallie Mae announced that it was considering changes in the way it ran its business.

Available empirical evidence indicates that, on average, there is general consistency between managers' and stockholders' interests. Still, we recommend the continued use of monitoring, because it may be a critical ingredient to this general consistency!

Debt Contracts

How do debtholders react to the risks of asset substitution, underinvestment, and claim dilution? They try to restrict the firm's ability to engage in these behaviors. For example, debt contracts may include specific limits on the firm's activities, such as restricting the firm from issuing new bonds without first paying off, or otherwise protecting, existing bonds. As we noted earlier, restrictions of this sort became much more widely used after the RJR Nabisco leveraged buyout. The debtholders may also start legal action with respect to an existing contract, as in the case of Placid Oil's Green Canyon project.

Despite all attempts at restriction, some possibility remains that stockholders will be able to expropriate wealth from the debtholders. The essential question is how large is the possibility. The larger it is, the higher the rate of interest the debtholders will require to compensate them for that risk. Such a higher rate is part of the agency costs borne by the stockholders. Also, contractual limitations may restrict more than just the targeted activities. Therefore, another part of agency costs is the reduced decision-making flexibility that might unintentionally prevent the firm from making a positive-NPV investment.

The legal contract for a publicly traded bond is called a *bond indenture.* The structure of this explicit contract affects the incentives by detailing responsibilities, constraints, punishments, and required monitoring. For example, such contracts specify the timing and amounts of all interest and principal payments. They also appoint a particular agent, called the *trustee,* who has a legal responsibility to look after the bondholders' interests.

Certain contractual provisions within a bond indenture are called **bond covenants.** These are designed to protect the interests of the bondholders. They are of two types. A **negative covenant** *prohibits* or *limits* certain actions, such as incurring more debt or paying dividends. A **positive covenant** *requires* certain actions, such as regularly making tax payments and providing periodic financial statements.

Bond covenants are a form of monitoring. They provide a warning system that is triggered when a firm fails to comply with a covenant. Of course, the warning system is activated only with a failure to comply. This can save resources because more complete monitoring—such as a monthly review of the firm's actions—is more costly and time consuming. Further, even when a

[7]Apparently, the market agreed. The firm's stock jumped 30% in value when the proxy fight was announced.

covenant is violated, corrective action can often be taken before the problem becomes more severe and the firm falls into financial distress. As such, a bond covenant can be an *early* warning device.

Bond covenants provide value by lowering the risk of the bonds. The bondholder gets increased protection against certain events, and therefore agrees to a lower interest rate. This benefits the firm. Of course, the value of a specific covenant depends on the particular situation. This is quite like the overlapping options problem discussed in Chapter 12.

With hidden options, the addition of an option may not add much value if the contingency it "covers" is already covered by other options. If the bondholder is protected in other ways, a covenant may not add much value. Generally, covenants are more valuable to bondholders in a higher-risk firm because the likelihood of running into a problem is greater.

However, bond covenants are also costly. They restrict the firm's operating flexibility and can eliminate positive-NPV investment opportunities. In short, they can eliminate valuable options for the firm. It is possible to solicit consent from the bondholders to relax a restrictive covenant. But such a process is cumbersome, time consuming, and often expensive. Bondholders normally demand some form of payment—either an immediate cash payment or an increase in the coupon rate—in exchange for their consent. Even when the firm does go to the trouble and cost of eliminating a covenant that is constraining, the lost time adds to the opportunity cost of that covenant. As with so many other things, there is a trade-off between the benefits and costs of bond covenants.

EXAMPLE Removing a Restrictive Covenant

A few years ago, the owners of the Seven-Up Company offered a group of its bondholders changes in the bond indenture: (1) an immediate one-time payment of $25 per $1,000 bond, (2) an increase in the coupon rate from 12-1/8% to 12-3/8% for the next two and a half years, and (3) a further increase in the coupon rate to 12-5/8% for the remaining five years of the bonds' life. At the same time, the Dr. Pepper Company offered a similar financial incentive to a group of its bondholders. The offers were in exchange for a consent to allow a leveraged buyout of each firm to form a single merged firm. The cost of the cash payment if all bondholders consented (a majority was required in each case) was $9.3 million. The increase in coupon rate, which would benefit every bondholder as long as a majority consented, amounted to $934,000 per year for the first increase and a further $934,000 per year for the second.

This is a particularly interesting example of managing *implicit* stakeholder claims. Both solicitation statements pointed out that the bondholder consents were not *legally* required for the planned leveraged buyout. Did this mean that the firm was paying something and getting nothing? Of course not. The firm offered a financial incentive in exchange for *explicit* consent to preempt potential legal action from the bondholders. This was important because even if all protesting bondholders lost their legal complaints, they could have caused a costly, or even disastrous, delay in the firm's plans.[8]

One alternative to an extensive array of restrictive bond covenants is the use of a conversion option to create a **convertible bond.** A convertible bond can be exchanged for a preset number of shares of the firm's common stock at the bondholder's option. The option in a convertible bond allows the securityholder to share in the upside if the firm is especially successful. Smaller, younger firms often issue convertible bonds, rather than bonds without the conversion option, for precisely this reason.

[8]This can be viewed as one more hidden option—the option to "make trouble" by suing, even though you do not expect to win!

Optimal Contracts

An optimal contract balances the three types of agency costs (contracting, monitoring, and misbehavior) against one another to minimize the total cost. In some cases, the optimal contract involves a fixed wage and some degree of monitoring, as is typically the case for employees. In other cases, the cost of monitoring is not worth it. When monitoring cost exceeds the expected cost of agent misbehavior, the optimal contract is a simple bonus based on the outcome. An example of such is a salesperson who earns only a commission, which is a percentage of sales.

Some of the decisions connected with the choice of a financial contract are similar to trade-offs an agent might make in an effort to earn a good reputation: Agents may forgo profiting from misbehaving in the short run to earn more in the long run. Demonstrating good behavior can increase the value of their services. Similarly, agents may agree to "severe" monitoring to earn more for their services. The principal agrees to the higher price because the severe monitoring reduces the chance of agent misbehavior. Again, it is a cost trade-off.

EXAMPLE Choosing the Best Contract

Let us say the Nintendo Corporation can choose one of four managerial contracts. The estimated annual total and component contracting costs (in millions of dollars) of these alternatives are given below. Which managerial contract should Nintendo choose?

	CONTRACTING	MONITORING	MISBEHAVIOR	TOTAL
Contract #1	1.4	0.0	5.0	6.5
Contract #2	1.1	2.4	0.1	3.6
Contract #3	2.2	0.4	0.4	3.0
Contract #4	2.6	0.1	0.7	3.4

Contract #3 is the best choice because it provides the lowest *total* costs among the alternatives. Based on the firm's estimates, it is the best game in town.

Unfortunately, a financial contract cannot cover every possible contingency; beforehand, you cannot conceive of everything that might go wrong. In any case, dealing with every possible situation would involve tremendous time and expense. Each party must take reasonable precautions, but must ultimately rely on the other parties to behave ethically and responsibly in those situations not explicitly covered by the agreement. If either party behaves unethically, the contractual provisions may not prove very effective anyway.

Review

1. Why does financial distress intensify the problem of goal divergence?
2. What devices do stockholders have for aligning managerial goals with their own?
3. What is a poison pill, and how does it help current management keep its jobs in the face of a takeover threat?
4. What is the purpose of bond covenants?
5. Describe an optimal contract in your own words.

13.7 MONITORING

A financial contract is complex because it involves imperfect information. Despite this complexity, there are a number of potentially cost-effective monitoring devices.

New External Financing

Whenever a firm seeks new external financing, it is exposed to special scrutiny, which is a form of monitoring. The firm must reveal new information. If the information is public, existing investors can look more closely at the firm. Even if the new information is not made public, the new investors provide a form of monitoring. They provide reassurance to existing investors by their willingness to invest their own money.

This reassurance concept is quite broad. Suppose a firm has a valuable new idea that would be damaged if it were made public, because of the free-rider problem. That is, others would copy the idea. In such cases, the firm may be able to issue new securities through investment bankers who underwrite the issue.

Here is how it works. The firm explains the idea to the investment bankers now, but does not make the idea public until it is marketed. With an underwritten issue, the investment bankers actually purchase the securities before reselling them to the public. Taking ownership, even for a short time, is much riskier than simply marketing the securities for a commission. Presumably, investment bankers would not take on this risk if they thought it was large. The investment bankers' purchase signals the market about the value of the new idea. As reputable middlemen, they can profit from the role as third-party monitor.

Other Monitoring Devices

Many elements of the financial environment serve as monitoring devices. People openly offer and seek information in the normal course of business. They also signal information through their actions. Information is revealed through government enforcement of laws and regulations. Even a firm's reputation and structure convey information. Common monitoring devices include the following:

- **Financial statements.** Audited accounting statements are a monitoring device for stockholder-manager, debtholder-stockholder, and consumer-firm relationships. They provide an early warning system.
- **Cash dividends.** Cash dividends can be a monitoring device in two ways. First, the failure to declare a cash dividend in the expected amount provides a warning. Although it may or may not be negative information, it prompts investors to look further. They must determine the meaning of the deviation. Second, paying cash dividends may force the firm to seek new external financing more frequently, the benefits of which we just noted.
- **Bond ratings.** Bond ratings by agencies such as Moody's or Standard & Poor's provide monitoring at issuance and, to a lesser extent, over the bonds' life.
- **Bond covenants.** Bond covenants provide a kind of warning system.
- **Government regulation.** Governments continue to evolve their monitoring devices in the public interest. For example, numerous federal agencies, such as the IRS, SEC, and FDA, monitor firms for various legal violations.
- **The entire legal system.** Theft, fraud, and many other forms of agent misbehavior are illegal. The legal system provides various forms of monitoring and punishment for everyone.
- **Reputation.** Reputation, and the general information it contains, is a form of monitoring. As we noted earlier, building and maintaining a good reputation is valuable. This creates incentives for providing accurate information, which also facilitates monitoring.

- **Multilevel organizations.** A firm that uses many levels of authority to review and evaluate decisions also provides a structural form of monitoring. Misbehavior is more difficult when you need a large number of people to do it. To get approval in such a firm, a plan must be widely discussed. Large groups are more likely to include honest people, braggarts, and blabbermouths. Not everyone can keep a secret.

Throughout the book we examine information from these and other sources to better understand the motivations contained in implicit and explicit financial contracts.

EXAMPLE The Barings Bankruptcy

Barings PLC was a venerable 233-year-old British investment bank. It had helped Britain reopen trade with the United States after the Revolutionary War. In 1803, it helped the United States double in size by financing the purchase of the Louisiana Territory from France. Despite a long and distinguished history, it took a single 28-year-old trader just a month of undetected trading to create a $1 billion loss, which caused the firm's demise.

Nicholas Leeson had been an arbitrage trader at Barings Securities. He was trading futures contracts in Singapore and Japan. He simultaneously bought in one market and sold the same contract in the other to exploit price differences. Profits were small but so were the risks.

One day, Leeson decided that "plain vanilla" arbitrage was too tame. So he changed tactics. He stopped matching buy and sell orders. He became a buyer who thought he knew which way Japanese stock prices and interest rates were headed. Without authorization, he bet big.

By the time Leeson's betting was finally discovered, he had bought stock futures contracts representing $7 billion worth of Japanese shares and interest rate futures contracts representing $22 billion worth of Japanese government bonds. (That is right, we said *billion.*) Unfortunately, Leeson did not know as much as he thought he did. He racked up about a $1 billion loss.

The regulators found there had been a "failure of control." Apparently, the firm did not really understand what Leeson was doing. It was reported that someone at a Barings risk committee meeting asked whether the high level of trading by Leeson was "safe." Barings' head of derivatives assured them it was. This is particularly surprising in light of press reports that Leeson's trading was large enough to generate comment throughout the Asian markets about his aggressive strategy.[9] As it turned out, the derivatives head's belief was based on reports filed by Leeson! Leeson's superiors thought he was trading on behalf of clients, rather than for the firm's own account.

Barings' lack of controls surprised Wall Street risk managers. Unlike most salesmen, Leeson was allowed to go to the trading floor to trade. Barings did not limit the size of Leeson's trading positions. In contrast to industry practice, he was both head derivatives trader and head of the back-office settlement department. He was therefore monitoring himself. This enabled him to withhold information from the head office and send in falsified reports. And that, of course, crippled the monitoring process.

It seems like the Barings' monitoring problem ought to be unique, but it is not! Kidder Peabody & Co. said its head government bond trader racked up $350 million in fake profits by entering false trades into its computer system. Daiwa Bank Ltd. suffered $1.1 billion of losses over an 11-year period due to questionable trading by a lone trader. Like Leeson, he headed a back-office department responsible for monitoring trading (including his own).

As these examples vividly illustrate, monitoring is not very effective when the individual being monitored is the one doing the monitoring!

[9] At one point, his trades accounted for *half* the outstanding positions on the Nikkei-225 futures contract.

Review

1. Describe three external monitoring devices.
2. How do investment bankers function as monitors when they underwrite a new issue of securities?
3. How do audited financial statements assist in monitoring?

SUMMARY

This chapter describes many of the problems that are revealed by a principal-agent framework in the set-of-contracts model of the firm. Figure 13.8 shows the contractual relationships we examined, each in a separate principal-agent framework.

Agency issues are everywhere. Agency theory has been used to an increasing extent to explain financial contracts that were not previously well understood. Several important concepts include:

- The modern corporation involves a large number of both explicit and implicit contracts.
- Both implicit and explicit contracts frequently involve contingent claims.
- The interests of principals and agents often diverge. For example, managers operate the firm but may own only a tiny fraction of it. Therefore, the firm's various stakeholders (such as managers, employees, stockholders, debtholders, and customers) may not have identical interests.

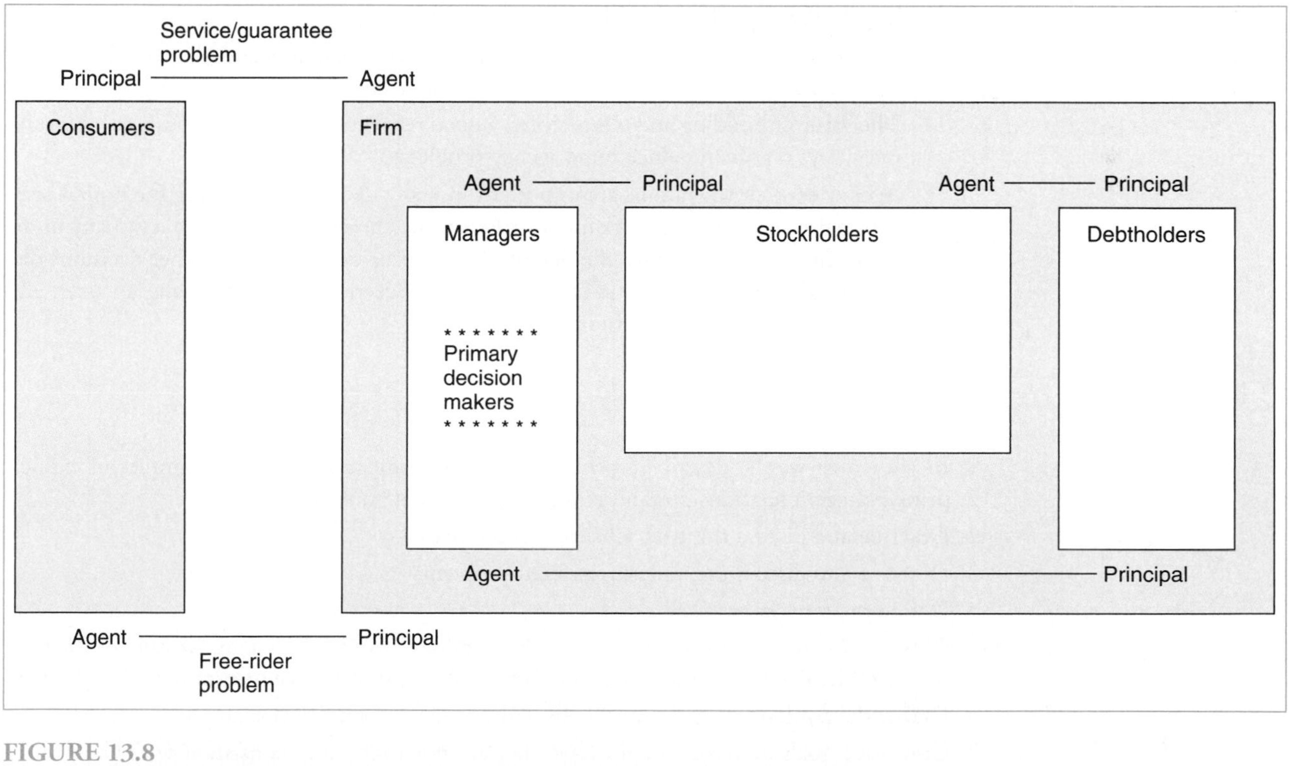

FIGURE 13.8
Important implicit principal-agent relationships connected with a firm.

- Incentives, constraints, punishments, and monitoring are necessary to ensure that an agent acts in the principal's best interest. Such devices impose agency costs. Agency problems and costs arise in many of the relationships that compose the set of contracts making up the modern corporation.
- An agency cost is the incremental cost of working through agents. The agency cost is the amount above whatever cost would be incurred in a perfect market environment.
- Financial distress complicates and intensifies many agency problems and costs.
- The existence of agency problems adds agency costs to the cost of doing business.
- An optimal financial contract minimizes the total agency cost, which is made up of direct contracting costs (transaction costs, opportunity costs, and incentive fees), monitoring costs, and misbehavior costs.
- Conflicts of interest can arise naturally between stockholders and managers because of employee perquisites, employee effort, and the nondiversifiability of an employee's human capital, among other things.
- Ultimately, if stockholders are dissatisfied, they can sell their shares. If the market value of a poorly run firm falls sufficiently, another firm or investor can purchase sufficient shares to gain control and fire inept managers.
- Conflicts of interest can arise naturally between debtholders and stockholders because of the possibility of asset substitution, underinvestment, and claim dilution, among other things.
- Debt contracts typically include provisions designed to control agency costs.
- The contingent-claim view of the firm's various stakeholders provides important insights into how the incentives can dramatically shift if the contingent claim (option) comes to be at or out-of-the-money. Because an option cannot have a negative value, the downside risk is limited. As such, it is kind of like a lottery ticket. The agent has little to lose, but the upside potential can be tremendous.
- Conflicts of interest can arise naturally between consumers and the firm because of guarantees and product imitation, among other things.
- The value of building and maintaining a good reputation provides important long-term incentives that help reduce some agency problems.
- Agency cost considerations are important in many decisions, including the capital budgeting process, the choice of capital structure, the choice of dividend policy, many of the firm's day-to-day decisions, the design of new securities issues, and other decisions discussed later in this book, such as the choice between leasing and buying an asset, and merger and acquisition decisions.

QUESTIONS

1. In your own words, describe a principal-agent relationship. Cite two examples of explicit principal-agent relationships and two examples that are not explicit.
2. Describe and discuss the asset substitution problem.
3. Describe and discuss the underinvestment problem.
4. Define the term *moral hazard.*
5. Define the term *free rider* and explain why it causes problems. Cite an example of the free-rider problem and a contract form that is typically used to reduce or eliminate the problem.
6. Define the concept of agency problems and cite three examples of such problems.
7. Cite three goals managers might have that are not necessarily consistent with the goal of maximizing shareholder wealth.

8. What is an agency cost? What are its three components? Cite an example of each one.
9. Cite and describe two ways that the uniqueness of assets creates agency costs for shareholders.
10. How can employee perquisites create a conflict between the shareholders and the employees?
11. How can product and service guarantees create an agency problem between the firm and its consumers?
12. Cite and briefly discuss four devices that naturally monitor agent behavior for the principal.
13. Define and explain in your own words the concept of an optimal contract.
14. Explain how covenants in a bond indenture help to reduce a firm's agency costs, thereby reducing the firm's cost of financing.
15. Explain why debtholders typically require covenants in the bond indenture that restrict the firm's ability to take on additional debt. Cite two such covenants that are common and relate them to your explanation.
16. Using the stock-as-an-option view, explain why stockholders might choose to undertake a high-risk investment, even if the NPV of the investment is negative. What group is on the other side of this transaction?
17. Using the stock-as-an-option view, explain why stockholders might choose not to undertake a low-risk investment, even if the expected NPV of the investment is positive. What group is on the other side of this transaction?
18. Using the stock-as-an-option view, describe the problem of claim dilution.
19. How does having a manager who is also a stockholder reduce potential conflicts of interest?
20. Explain the problem of the nondiversifiability of human capital.
21. How does the nondiversifiability of human capital cause a conflict of interest between the managers and the stockholders regarding the firm's choice of investments?
22. Explain how an agent's desire to maintain the ongoing value of a good reputation can facilitate shareholder monitoring of the agent.
23. Using a contingent-claim view, describe in your own words how financial distress can intensify conflicts of interest among the firm's claimants. Cite three specific examples of situations in which this can occur.
24. Explain why the stock price of a firm that is undergoing bankruptcy proceedings is virtually always positive and never negative.

CHALLENGING QUESTIONS

25. What methods do shareholders have at their disposal for aligning managers' goals with their goals?
26. Perfect monitoring in a perfect market environment always provides an optimal contract. Explain why monitoring is not always the best choice, even in a well-functioning market environment with low transaction costs.
27. Respond to the following statement: Because a firm can lower its interest cost by including more restrictive covenants in its bond indentures, a firm should use the most restrictive set of covenants it can in order to achieve the lowest interest cost. [Hint: The answer involves *two* different aspects, and the less obvious one has to do with options.]
28. Is it possible to have an agency problem if there is no asymmetric information? If so, cite an example; if not, explain why not.
29. In some bankruptcy settlements, the debtholders accept less than full payment on the claim and at the same time they agree to allow the stockholders to get a payment as well. Because the stockholders are only the *residual* claimants (after the debtholders get what they have been

promised), why do the debtholders agree to this? (Hint: Consider our example of the "unnecessary" payment the Seven-Up Company and Dr. Pepper Company made to their debtholders in exchange for their consent to the leveraged buyout—the hidden option to sue.)

30. Suppose you were a firm's debtholder. Would you be concerned about the firm's dividend policy? Explain why or why not.
31. How can employee perquisites create an agency problem between managers and the *debtholders?*
32. Explain in your own words how a complex multilevel organization provides a natural form of agent monitoring.
33. How does convertible debt help to reduce the agency problem between the shareholders and the debtholders?
34. We said that in cases of financial distress, various claimant coalitions can form. Is it possible to predict what those coalitions will be when the firm is healthy? If so, explain how. If not, explain why.

PROBLEMS

LEVEL A (BASIC)

A1. (Value of a managerial contract) John Hall is considering a new managerial contract for his firm. The contract will increase direct contracting costs (mostly cash incentive awards) by \$1.00 million. John estimates that the contract should save \$0.40 million in monitoring costs, such as accounting and oversight costs. It should also reduce misbehavior costs by \$0.95 million by reducing excessive perk consumption and managerial shirking. If his estimates are correct, what is the net cost or net benefit of Hall's proposed managerial contract?

A2. (Value of a managerial contract) Louise is considering a new managerial contract for her firm. The contract will increase direct contracting costs (mostly cash incentive awards) by \$500,000. Louise estimates that the contract should save \$100,000 in monitoring costs, such as accounting and oversight costs. It should also reduce misbehavior costs by \$600,000 by reducing excessive perk consumption and managerial shirking. If her estimates are correct, what is the net cost or net benefit of Louise's proposed managerial contract?

A3. (Optimal managerial contract) Estimates of the direct, monitoring, and misbehavior costs for three different managerial contracts are given here. Which of the contracts is optimal?

CONTRACT	CONTRACTING COSTS	MONITORING COSTS	MISBEHAVIOR COSTS
A	\$4.5	\$3.5	\$7.0
B	6.0	2.5	4.5
C	8.0	2.0	3.5

A4. (Optimal managerial contract) Estimates of the direct, monitoring, and misbehavior costs for three different managerial contracts are given here. Which of the contracts is optimal?

CONTRACT	CONTRACTING COSTS	MONITORING COSTS	MISBEHAVIOR COSTS
A	\$ 2.8	\$6.2	\$4.0
B	4.6	1.5	7.5
C	10.0	1.0	1.2

A5. (Optimal managerial contract) Because of excessive perk consumption, high salaries and compensation of executives, and a pattern of negligent and mediocre decision making, Michael Alderson has recommended that the firm restructure its managerial contracts. Michael expects that heightened monitoring will add \$750,000 of costs annually.

a. What decrease in direct costs and misbehavior costs is required to offset the additional monitoring costs?

b. If direct costs are reduced by \$250,000, what is the minimum reduction in misbehavior costs required to justify Michael's recommendation?

A6. (Optimal managerial contract) Because of excessive perk consumption, high salaries and compensation of executives, and a pattern of negligent and mediocre decision making, Frank has recommended that the firm restructure its managerial contracts. Frank expects that heightened monitoring will add \$675,000 of costs annually.

a. What decrease in direct costs and misbehavior costs is required to offset the additional monitoring costs?

b. If direct costs are reduced by \$100,000, what is the minimum reduction in misbehavior costs required to justify Frank's recommendation?

A7. (Effect of contracting costs on a lender) Frank Laatsch is considering a loan of \$500,000 to Regency Partners. Frank estimates that he will incur \$15,000 of costs per year to monitor this loan.

a. Regency is promising to pay 12% annually on the loan. After paying monitoring costs, what rate of return is Frank receiving?

b. If a fair rate of return on this loan is 10%, what is the minimum interest rate that Frank would require on this loan?

A8. (Effect of contracting costs on a lender) Laura is considering a loan of \$250,000 to Packard Holdings. Laura estimates that she will incur \$7,000 of costs per year to monitor this loan.

a. Packard is promising to pay 10% annually on the loan. After paying monitoring costs, what return is Laura receiving?

b. If a fair return on this loan is 9%, what is the minimum interest rate that Laura would require on this loan?

A9. (Claim dilution via dividend policy) Bosco Company purchased the common stock of Redux Insurance Company for \$10 million (1,000,000 shares at \$10 each). At the time of its acquisition, Redux had assets valued at \$90 million and liabilities of \$80 million.

a. What was the surplus of assets over obligations at the time of the purchase?

b. Immediately after the purchase, the Board of Directors of Redux, which Bosco now controlled, paid a \$18-per-share dividend to Bosco. After this transaction, what is the surplus of assets over obligations for Redux Insurance Company?

A10. (Claim dilution via dividend policy) Redline Company purchased the common stock of Tach Company for \$25 million (2,000,000 shares at \$12.50 each). At the time of its acquisition, Tach had assets valued at \$100 million and liabilities of \$75 million.

a. What was the surplus of assets over obligations at the time of the purchase?

b. Immediately after the purchase, the Board of Directors of Tach, which Redline now controlled, paid a \$15-per-share dividend to Redline. After this transaction, what is the surplus of assets over obligations for Tach Company?

A11. (Cost of a restrictive covenant) Peachtree Construction has a restrictive covenant in a loan contract that essentially prohibits the expansion of the firm into a new line of business that it is considering. The cost of this restriction is estimated to be $20 million. The debt can be called and paid off early by paying a $5 million penalty. What should Peachtree do?

A12. (Cost of a restrictive covenant) Johnson Refinishing has a restrictive covenant in a loan contract that essentially prohibits the expansion of the firm into a new line of business that it is considering. The cost of this restriction is estimated to be $30 million. The debt can be called and paid off early by paying a $15 million penalty. What should Johnson do?

A13. (Misbehavior costs)

a. Investors learn that the Chairman and CEO of the company lives in an $18,000,000 apartment given to her by the corporation and has a large art collection also financed by the company. When the information becomes public, the shares drop by $8.00. There are two billion shares outstanding. What is the total decline in the market value of the firm's stock?

b. The president of a company likes to dabble in the stocks of many of the companies where her friends have important executive positions. The president is under investigation for insider trading where she bought and sold shares based on insider information. The president's gains are estimated to be $200,000. However, news of this has hammered her company stock by $5 per share. With 800 million outstanding shares, what has been the loss in market value of her company's outstanding stock?

LEVEL B

B1. (Asset substitution) Michigan Mining and Manufacturing has a debt obligation of $100 million and assets with a value of $90 million. This debt must be paid off very shortly. When this happens, the value of the debt will be $90 million and the value of equity will be $0. Prior to paying off the debt, MMM has an opportunity to make a high-risk investment. MMM is considering an investment of $20 million (from existing assets) that will pay off $40 million or zero. The investment would have an NPV of either $20 million or −$20 million (NPV = the value of the payoff minus the investment) . The investment would be paid for with the firm's liquid cash holdings.

a. If the $40 million payoff (NPV = $20 million) occurs, what is the value of equity? What is the value of debt?

b. If the zero payoff (NPV = −$20 million) occurs, what is the value of equity? What is the value of debt?

c. Assume the probability of the high payoff is 0.25 and the probability of the low payoff is 0.75. What is the expected NPV of the investment? What is the expected value of the firm?

d. What is the expected value of equity? What is the expected value of debt?

e. How can stockholders benefit from a negative-NPV project?

B2. (Misbehavior costs) This has been a poor year for the firm. A little checking has revealed several questionable transactions that benefit the firm's president. (1) The firm purchased a condominium for $800,000 and gave the president an option to purchase it for $500,000. He exercised this option immediately. (2) He put his spouse on the payroll for a total cost of $150,000 annually. The wife's contributions were considered to have no value. (Luckily, they were not negative.) (3) He redecorated his office at a cost of $150,000. The office had been redecorated two years previously. (4) He has four club memberships costing $100,000 per year and has total travel and entertainment expenses of $120,000. A good guess is that half these are not justifiable. (5) He set up consulting contracts with his brother that cost $40,000 total. No tangible benefit from the contracts exists. (6) He made several decisions that violate labor, environmental, and securities laws that will expose the firm to future penalties. (7) His behavior causes many other executives and employees to engage in similar misbehavior. Several other employees have resigned from the firm because of their concerns about legal, ethical, and poor business practices. Ignoring items (6) and (7), which are not yet quantified, what do the other misbehavior costs sum to?

B3. (Misbehavior costs) This has been a poor year for the firm. A little checking has revealed several questionable transactions that benefit the firm's president. (1) The firm purchased a condominium for $500,000 and gave the president an option to purchase it for $450,000. She exercised this option immediately. (2) She put her spouse on the payroll for a total cost of $100,000 annually. The husband's contributions were considered to have a zero value. (Luckily, they were not negative.) (3) She redecorated her office at a cost of $75,000. The office had been redecorated two years previously. (4) She has four club memberships costing $75,000 per year and has total travel and entertainment expenses of $60,000. A good guess is that one-half of these are not justifiable. (5) She set up consulting contracts with her brother that cost $32,000 total. No tangible benefit from the contracts exists. (6) She made several decisions that violate labor, environmental, and securities laws that will expose the firm to future penalties. (7) Her behavior causes many other executives and employees to engage in similar misbehavior. Several other employees have resigned from the firm because of their concerns about legal, ethical, and poor business practices. Ignoring items (6) and (7), which are not yet quantified, what do the other misbehavior costs sum to?

B4. (Management incentives) The Board of Directors for Ettinger Manufacturing is considering a $.75-per-share dividend on its 4,000,000 shares. The board is also considering a $2,000,000 bonus payment to be shared by its top managers.

a. Sharon Conn, the firm controller, will receive 8% of the bonus pool and also owns 20,000 shares. How much will Sharon receive in dividends and bonus?

b. Marilyn Ettinger, the president and chief executive officer, will receive 15% of the bonus pool and owns 400,000 shares. What distributions will Marilyn receive?

c. One of the directors is advocating a shift of funds from the bonus pool to cash dividends. This plan would reduce the bonus pool to $1,000,000 and increase the dividend to $1.00 per share. Recalculate the distributions for Sharon and for Marilyn.

d. Which plan do you think Sharon and Marilyn would favor?

B5. (Management incentives) The Board of Directors for Delaware Manufacturing is considering a $1.50-per-share dividend on its 10,000,000 shares. The board is also considering a $5,000,000 bonus payment to be shared by its top managers.

a. Sally, the firm controller, will receive 6% of the bonus pool and also owns 15,000 shares. How much will Sally receive in dividends and bonus?

b. Thomas, the president and chief executive officer, will receive 9% of the bonus pool and owns 50,000 shares. What distributions will Thomas receive?

c. One of the directors is advocating a shift of funds from the bonus pool to cash dividends. This plan would reduce the bonus pool to $2,500,000 and increase the dividend to $1.75 per share. Recalculate the distributions for Sally and for Thomas.

d. Which plan do you think Sally and Thomas would favor?

B6. (Asset substitution) Your loan to Kansas City Construction Company (KCCC) is due at the end of the year. At that time, KCCC must pay you $500,000.

a. If the collateral for the loan is equally likely to be worth either $600,000 or $700,000, what payment would you expect from KCCC?

b. Assume that KCCC sells some of the collateral and replaces it with riskier assets. The value of the collateral at the end of the year is now equally likely to be either $350,000 or $950,000. What loan payments might you now expect from KCCC?

B7. (Asset substitution) Your loan to Sherman Landscaping Company is due at the end of the year. At that time, Sherman must pay you $200,000.

a. If the collateral for the loan is equally likely to be worth either $300,000 or $250,000, what payment would you expect from Sherman?

b. Assume Sherman sells some of the collateral and replaces it with riskier assets. The value of the collateral at the end of the year is now equally likely to be either $150,000 or $600,000. What loan payments might you now expect from Sherman?

B8. (Claim dilution via new debt) Your loan to Penguin Development is now due. Penguin has assets of $200, and your loan, the firm's only debt, has a $100 balance.

a. What loan payment do you expect from Penguin?

b. Penguin has taken on an additional $150 of debt, which has the same claim on assets as your debt. The firm still has $200 of assets. What loan payment do you now expect from Penguin?

B9. (Claim dilution via new debt) Your loan to Bill's Snow Removal is now due. Bill's has assets of $1,000, and your loan, the firm's only debt, has a $500 balance.

a. What loan payment do you expect from Bill's?

b. Bill's has taken on an additional $750 of debt, which has the same claim on assets as your debt. The firm still has $1,000 of assets. What loan payment do you now expect from Bill's?

B10. (Claim dilution) J & B Piano Company owes you $200,000. J & B sells all of the firm's assets for $100,000 cash. Then J & B pays a $40,000 cash dividend to its stockholders. Finally, J & B pays a $60,000 bonus to its managers. What is the value of your loan?

B11. (Claim dilution) Mohawk Valley Cement Company owes you $50,000. Mohawk Valley Cement sells all of the firm's assets for $95,000 cash. Then Mohawk Valley Cement pays a $55,000 cash dividend to its stockholders. Finally, Mohawk Valley Cement pays a $40,000 bonus to its managers. What is the value of your loan?

B12. (After-tax cost of compensation) Singh Financial Services has a handful of professionals, all of whom own stock in the firm. Singh is considering a year-end distribution to its professional staff. The marginal tax rate is 40%.

a. If Singh Financial Services pays $1,000,000 in cash dividends, what is the effect on taxable income, taxes due, and net income? What is the cash outlay on an after-tax basis?

b. If Singh pays $1,000,000 of salary bonuses, what is the effect on taxable income, taxes due, and net income? What is the cash outlay on an after-tax basis?

B13. (After-tax cost of compensation) McGregor Accounting Services has a handful of professionals, all of whom own stock in the firm. McGregor is considering a year-end distribution to its professional staff. The marginal tax rate is 40%.

a. If McGregor Accounting Services pays $500,000 in cash dividends, what is the effect on taxable income, taxes due, and net income? What is the cash outlay on an after-tax basis?

b. If McGregor pays $500,000 of salary bonuses, what is the effect on taxable income, taxes due, and net income? What is the cash outlay on an after-tax basis?

B14. (Excel: Asset substitution and underinvestment) Kim Corporation has $1,000 of debt due in one year. Kim's assets will either be $800 or $1,200 in one year. Each outcome has a 50% probability.

a. What is the expected value of assets, debt, and equity in one year?

b. Kim sells some of the assets and purchases others, resulting in asset values of $700 or $1,300, again equally likely. What is the NPV of the investment? What is the expected value of assets, debt, and equity?

c. Starting from the initial position again, Kim sells some of the assets and purchases others, resulting in asset values of $600 or $1,300, equally likely. What is the NPV of the investment? What is the expected value of assets, debt, and equity?

d. Starting from the initial position again, Kim can sell some of the assets and purchase others, resulting in asset values of $1,000 or $1,100, equally likely. What is the NPV of the investment? What is the expected value of debt and equity?

e. Starting from the initial position again, Kim can sell some of the assets and purchase others, resulting in asset values of $0 or $2,000. What is the minimum probability of the high outcome that could induce Kim to make the investment? With this probability, find the NPV, asset value, debt value, and equity value.

LEVEL C (ADVANCED)

C1. (Claim dilution via new debt) Assume that you work for Bank of North America and that you have made a large loan to Kinkus Publishing. At the end of the year, Kinkus must pay off the $20 million loan. Kinkus has undertaken a major expansion, and the value of its assets when the loan is due is expected to be either $25 million or $50 million. Let us call these two outcomes the "bad" and "good" scenarios.

a. Under these two scenarios, what loan repayment do you expect from Kinkus at the end of the year?

b. Assume now that Kinkus has issued some new debt to another party. Kinkus must pay $15 million to this other lender at the end of the year. Kinkus distributed the loan proceeds to its stockholders, so the assets of the firm are unaffected and the value of the firm's assets is still expected to be $25 or $50 million. If Kinkus is unable to pay its debts, your loan has the same priority as the new loan. If Kinkus cannot pay 100% of its debt, you will get the same percentage payoff as the other lender. What loan repayment do you now expect from Kinkus under the "bad" and "good" scenarios?

C2. (Claim dilution via new debt) Assume you work for Bank of South America and that you have made a large loan to GFD Simulation, which is GFD's only liability. At the end of the year, GFD must pay off the $14 million loan. GFD has undertaken a major expansion, and the value of its assets when the loan is due is expected to be either $16 million or $42 million. Let us call these two outcomes the "bad" and "good" scenarios.

a. Under these two scenarios, what loan repayment do you expect from GFD at the end of the year?

b. Assume now that GFD has issued some new debt to another party. GFD must pay $14 million to this other lender at the end of the year. GFD distributed the loan proceeds to its stockholders, so the assets of the firm are unaffected and the value of the firm's assets is still expected to be $16 or $42 million. If GFD is unable to pay its debts, your loan has the same priority as the new loan. If GFD cannot pay 100% of its debt, you will get the same percentage payoff as the other lender. What loan repayment do you now expect from GFD under the "bad" and "good" scenarios?

C3. (Asset substitution) Reconsider problem B1, for Michigan Mining and Manufacturing. Assume that the firm now has assets slightly more than its debts. MMM has a debt obligation of $100 million and assets with a value of $102 million. This debt must be paid off very shortly. When this happens, the value of the debt will be $100 million and the value of equity will be $2. Prior to paying off the debt, MMM has an opportunity to make a high-risk investment. MMM is considering an investment of $20 million that will pay off $40 million or zero. The investment would have an NPV of either $20 million or −$20 million (NPV = the value of the payoff minus the investment) . The investment would be paid for with the firm's liquid cash holdings.

a. If the $40 million payoff (NPV = $20 million) occurs, what is the value of equity? What is the value of debt?

b. If the zero payoff (NPV = −$20 million) occurs, what is the value of equity? What is the value of debt?

c. Assume the probability of the high payoff is 0.25 and the probability of the low payoff is 0.75. What is the expected NPV of the investment? What is the expected value of the firm.

d. What is the expected value of equity? What is the expected value of debt?

e. Do the stockholders benefit from the negative-NPV project?

C4. (Underinvestment) Assume that the value of the firm's assets is $1,000 and that the firm has debts of $750. If a catastrophe occurs, the assets are completely destroyed and have a value of $0. The probability of a catastrophe is 5%.

a. What is the value of debt and equity with no catastrophe? What is the value of debt and equity with a catastrophe? What is the expected value of debt and equity?

b. Assume that an insurance policy can be purchased for $60. It pays off $1,000 in the event of a catastrophe. Recompute the value of debt and equity with no catastrophe. Recompute the value of debt and equity with a catastrophe. (Remember to deduct the cost of the $60 insurance premium.)

c. This insurance policy has an NPV of −$10 because its cost of $60 exceeds the expected payoff of $50 (5% of $1,000). What was the impact of the investment in the insurance policy on the value of debt and equity? Who benefited from this insurance policy, stockholders or debtholders?

C5. (Underinvestment) Assume the value of the firm's assets is $10,000 and that the firm has debts of $6,000. If a catastrophe occurs, the assets are completely destroyed and have a value of $0. The probability of a catastrophe is 2%.

a. What is the value of debt and equity with no catastrophe? What is the value of debt and equity with a catastrophe? What is the expected value of debt and equity?

b. Assume an insurance policy can be purchased for $1,000. It pays off $10,000 in the event of a catastrophe. Recompute the value of debt and equity with no catastrophe. Recompute the value of debt and equity with a catastrophe. (Remember to deduct the cost of the $1,000 insurance premium.)

c. What would be the impact of the investment in the insurance policy on the value of debt and equity? Who would benefit from the insurance policy, stockholders or debtholders?

C6. (Contracting costs and the cost of borrowing) Uff Brothers Shipping is setting up a $200,000 loan. Uff Brothers make interest payments of $22,000 at the end of each year for four years and will repay the principal at the end of year 4.

a. Assuming no contracting costs, what is the effective cost of this loan to Uff Brothers?

b. Assume now that Uff Brothers incurs one-time setup costs of $10,000 at time 0 for legal and other contracting costs. In addition, Uff Brothers incurs another $1,000 of contracting costs at the end of each of the next four years. What is the effective annual cost of this loan including the contracting costs?

C7. (Contracting costs and the cost of borrowing) Upmann Retail is setting up a $75,000 loan. Upmann makes interest payments of $10,000 at the end of each year for five years and will repay the principal at the end of year 5.

a. Assuming no contracting costs, what is the APY cost of this loan to Upmann?

b. Assume now that Upmann incurs one-time setup costs of $3,000 at time 0 for legal and other contracting costs. In addition, Upmann incurs another $500 of contracting costs at the end of each of the next five years. What is the APY cost of this loan including the contracting costs?

MINICASE R.J. REYNOLDS BOND VALUE GOES UP IN SMOKE

A few years ago, RJR Nabisco, Inc. (RJRN) announced a bond-swap plan to restructure its debt. The swap was widely seen as a preliminary step in dividing RJRN's food and tobacco businesses into separate corporations. At the time, the firm had 32 issues of bonds with an aggregate principal amount of $8.5 billion.

Under the plan, Nabisco, Inc. (RJRN's food products subsidiary) would create 13 new debt issues, which would be identical in principal, coupon, and maturity to 13 outstanding issues of RJRN (the parent firm) debt. The Nabisco bonds would be offered in a one-for-one swap for the RJRN bonds. The 13 issues had an aggregate principal amount of $2.9 billion. The new debt would rank senior to the old debt with respect to the food business's assets and cash flow, have slightly less restrictive debt covenants than the old debt, and give RJRN's subsidiaries greater flexibility to borrow money.

The other 19 bond issues, with an aggregate principal amount of $5.6 billion, would remain with the parent. RJRN offered holders of the other 19 bond issues cash incentives for their *consents* to the swap: $2.50 per bond (0.25% of face amount) for the shortest maturities to $25.00 per bond (2.5% of face amount) for the longest maturity.

When the bond-swap plan was announced, RJRN, the parent, had a total market value of $31.4 billion and total debt of $11.1 billion. Nabisco, the subsidiary, represented $11.8 billion of the total value and $3.8 billion of the debt. The announcement of the swap offer affected the market values of RJRN's outstanding bonds—but not in identical ways. The following table provides four examples of its effect.

MATURITY (YEARS)	COUPON	OFFERED TO SWAP	YTM ONE DAY BEFORE	YTM ONE DAY AFTER	CONSENT FEE TO BE PAID
7	8.625%	no	8.840%	9.000%	$ 8.50
18	9.250	no	9.409	9.597	19.50
6	8.300	yes	8.905	8.324	0
22	8.625	yes	9.412	8.803	0

QUESTIONS

1. Calculate the change in bondholder value for each bond from one day before, to one day after, the announcement. Note that the consent fee would be paid to whomever owned the bond when consent later on had to be given. Therefore, it would transfer to any new owner.
2. Explain the bond price reactions in terms of claim dilution, considering that RJRN was likely to be broken into separately owned tobacco and food corporations (assume the breakup will be in the proportions of market value and total debt given), and there was substantial potential for additional future liability from tobacco litigation. (Hint: Consider the value of a portfolio of options on assets compared to the value of a comparable single option on the portfolio of assets. The options are the option to default.)
3. Following the announcement of the swap offer, holders of the bonds that would remain with RJRN argued that the consent fee should be three times what had been offered. Do you agree?
4. RJRN required the approval of a majority of holders of some issues and of at least two thirds of the other issues to complete the restructuring. That is, so long as the required (by the particular indentures) percentages of bondholders approved, all the bond indentures would be modified so as to permit the exchange offer to proceed. The changes would have the same effect on all holders of the 19 debt issues that would remain with RJRN. However, only those bondholders who had granted their consents would receive the cash incentive fees. How might this affect a bondholder's voting strategy?

PART IV

CAPITAL STRUCTURE AND DIVIDEND POLICY

Whether a firm's choice of *capital structure* (its mix of debt and equity) and dividend policy can affect its value—and if so, how it can—is controversial. Practitioners certainly behave as though these decisions are important. However, the significance of the factors involved continues to be debated. What we do know is that how a firm implements these policies can convey useful information to investors and thus affect the firm's value, even in an otherwise *efficient capital market.*

In an efficient capital market, the prices of securities reflect all available information and adjust fully and quickly to new information. Chapter 14 explains why it makes sense that active capital markets should be efficient. Competition to profit from new information lies at the heart of capital market efficiency. We also explain how three persistent *capital market imperfections* interfere with capital market efficiency.

Chapters 15 and 16 examine issues connected with capital structure. We show how capital market imperfections can cause a firm's capital structure to affect its value, and we outline a practical method of managing capital structure.

As with capital structure, there are conflicting viewpoints about dividend policy. Chapter 17 examines issues connected with dividends and outlines a practical method of managing dividend policy.

14

Capital Market Efficiency: Explanation and Implications

The prices of securities traded in *efficient* capital markets reflect all available information. Such prices adjust fully and quickly to new information. We first described the concept of capital market efficiency in Chapter 2. Here, we explain why it makes sense that active capital markets *should be* efficient. We also explain why inactive markets, in which securities seldom trade, may not be efficient. You will see how the Principle of Capital Market Efficiency is a by-product of many people applying other principles of finance to the capital market environment. We also explain the limitations of capital market efficiency and how three persistent *capital market imperfections* interfere with capital market efficiency.

The capital markets have evolved to perform several important functions. To explain capital market efficiency, we must first examine these functions and see how capital markets should operate. We can then understand how (1) new information becomes reflected in securities prices in active markets, (2) transaction costs can inhibit this process, and (3) information about differences in value can create opportunities for profit. The first person to recognize and take advantage of such an opportunity can indeed profit but will, at the same time, help eliminate the difference (*and* the opportunity). The competition to find and take advantage of such opportunities lies at the heart of capital market efficiency.

FOCUS ON PRINCIPLES

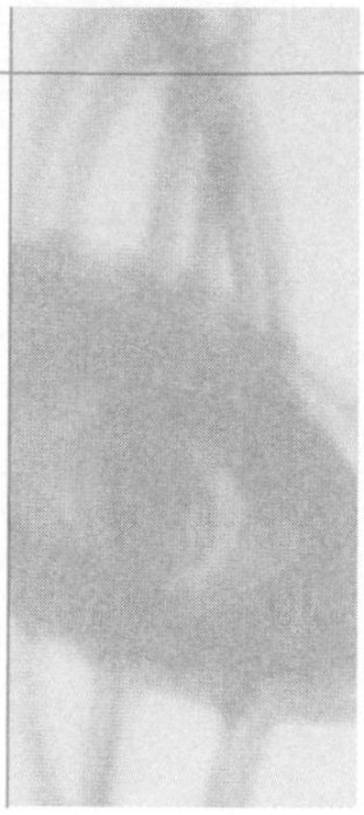

- *Self-Interested Behavior:* Self-interested capital market transactions push market prices toward being fair prices.
- *Two-Sided Transactions:* Intense capital market competition to get and use information to take advantage of arbitrage opportunities eliminates such opportunities.
- *Signaling:* Information in the transactions of others can be valuable, such as providing an accurate measure of current market value or information about expected future value.
- *Risk-Return Trade-Off:* Differences between financial assets are measured primarily in terms of risk and return. Investors choose the highest return for a given risk level.
- *Capital Market Efficiency:* The fact that people apply the Principles of Self-Interested Behavior, Two-Sided Transactions, and Signaling to an environment characterized by similar financial assets, low transaction costs, and intense competition leads to capital market efficiency.
- *Valuable Ideas:* New ideas can provide value when first introduced, even in an efficient capital market.
- *Comparative Advantage:* Capital market efficiency allows a firm to concentrate its primary efforts on its comparative advantage, rather than on its day-to-day financing.

14.1 EFFICIENCY

Thinking of capital markets as being *perfect* can be hard to accept at first. But it is the right place to start out. It provides several important insights. One is that investors cannot consistently earn abnormally high risk-adjusted returns, other than through extraordinarily good luck. This rather surprising implication has led to a great deal of criticism of the idea of perfect capital markets and to much doubt about the theory even though extensive evidence suggests that active capital markets are efficient. We hope the following analogy will help you see the logic of capital market efficiency.

Efficiency refers to the amount of wasted energy. Efficient machines do not waste much energy. Friction—the "stickiness" between things—is the main reason for the waste of energy in a machine. Lubricants, such as oil, are used to increase the efficiency of machines by reducing friction that wastes energy. The more efficient a machine is, the better it is. So too for capital markets.

A capital market is like a machine. In a capital market, **frictions** are the "stickiness" in making transactions. They are the total "hassle," including the time, effort, money, and associated tax effects of gathering information and making a transaction, such as buying stock or borrowing money. As with machines, efficiency is critical. Perfect efficiency represents an ideal, because unavoidable frictions keep a system (machine or market) from being perfectly efficient.

Conserving Energy

The physical law of energy conservation states that energy is neither created nor destroyed. Instead, energy is transformed from one form into another within a system. This law implies that no machine can be more than 100% efficient. So the energy output from a machine can never exceed the energy input to the machine. Simply stated, you cannot get something for nothing! In the financial world, schemes that seem to provide more output than input are known as scams. They are illegal, yet they persist. We will talk more about them later.

Our story uses refrigeration to illustrate the limits of efficiency. Suppose it is a hot summer day and you are a poor student who cannot afford the electric bills for running an air conditioner, let alone its initial cost. But on this particular day it is so hot you cannot stand it. You go into the kitchen and open the refrigerator door to feel a blast of cool, refreshing air across your face. Thinking you have solved the problem, you decide to stay in the kitchen with the refrigerator door open. What will happen?

Refrigerators work like air conditioners, so why shouldn't it be able to cool the kitchen? A refrigerator takes heat from inside itself and transfers that heat outside itself. But outside itself is still *inside* the kitchen, so the kitchen will not be cooled at all. In fact, because a refrigerator is substantially less than 100% efficient, energy escapes in the form of heat with each transfer. Thus, the kitchen will actually heat up if you leave the refrigerator door open!

Frictions in the Capital Markets: Transaction Costs

The analogy with the capital markets is that the transfer of assets from one party to another is like a transfer of heat from one area to another within the kitchen. The total wealth of the parties is like the temperature in the kitchen, with lower temperature corresponding to greater wealth. It makes no more sense to say that the total wealth of a group of people can be increased by the simple transfer of assets among them than it does to say that opening the refrigerator door can cool the kitchen! The only thing involved is a transfer from one to another.

You can, of course, make one individual better off at the expense of another individual, just as you can decrease the temperature inside the refrigerator by increasing the temperature outside it. So it is possible to make unbalanced transfers between people. (For example, we will not protest if you pay us $1,000 for an asset that is worth only $800.) But the wealth of the two individuals, taken together, cannot be increased by a transfer between them, any more than the kitchen can be cooled by a transfer of heat within its boundaries.

Pressing the analogy a little further, just as the kitchen will heat up as a result of wasted energy from many heat transfers, the total wealth of two parties will be wasted by many transfers of assets between them. The waste occurs because of factors that we classify as *transaction costs, asymmetric taxes,* or *asymmetric information.* **Transaction costs** are the time, effort, and money necessary to make a transaction, including such things as commission fees and the cost of physically moving an asset from seller to buyer. We will say a lot more about the other two later. These three factors are very much like friction: They slow down the process and waste resources (energy).

Review

1. True or false? Investors cannot consistently earn abnormally high risk-adjusted returns in an efficient capital market.
2. True or false? Transferring assets from one party to another cannot increase their combined wealth.
3. What are transaction costs? How can they reduce the combined wealth of the two parties to a transaction?

14.2 LIQUIDITY AND VALUE

The concept of **capital market efficiency** is linked to the concept of wasted wealth. An efficient capital market allows the transfer of assets with little loss of wealth. Capital market efficiency results from market prices reflecting all available information so that prices are *fair.* But what does it mean to reflect all available information?

There are three forms of capital market efficiency. The **strong form of capital market efficiency** requires that prices reflect *all* information that exists about the asset's value. This includes every bit of information known to anyone in the world that has any relevance whatsoever to the asset's value. The **semistrong form of capital market efficiency** requires only that prices fully

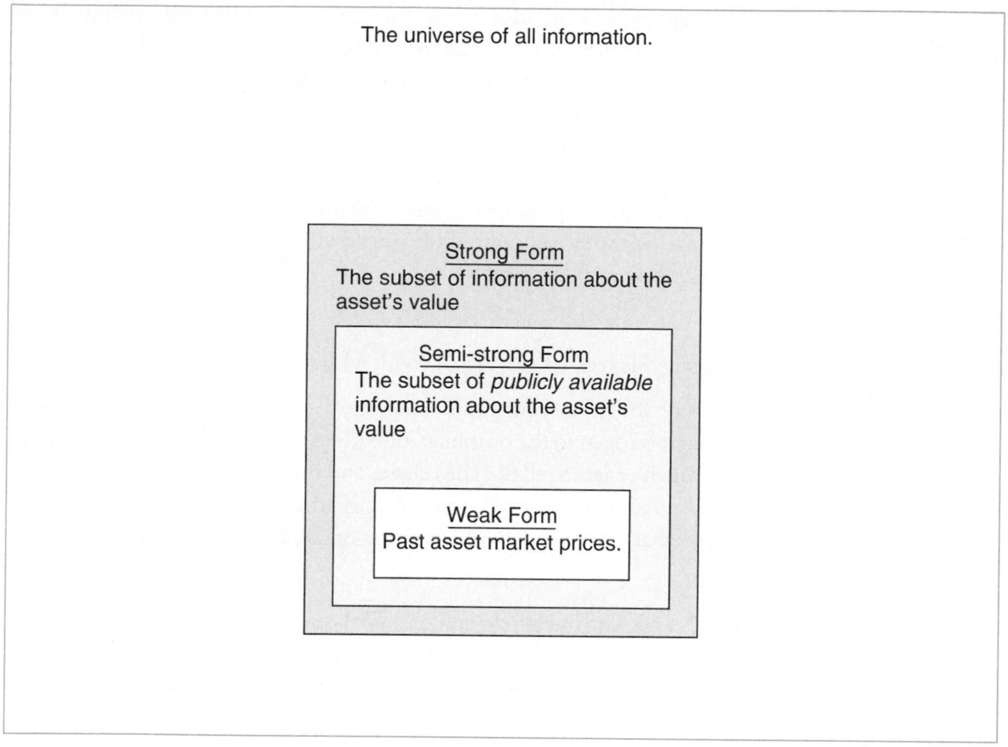

FIGURE 14.1
Information and the nested subsets of information about an asset's value pertaining to the strong, semi-strong, and weak forms of capital market efficiency.

reflect *publicly available* information. Publicly available information is a subset of all the information that exists about an asset's value. The **weak form of capital market efficiency** requires only that prices fully reflect the information *contained in past asset market prices,* the prices at which assets have been exchanged. Past asset prices are a small subset of the publicly available information about an asset's value. A market is **informationally efficient** if prices adjust very quickly and accurately to new information.

The relationships among various sets of information pertaining to the strong, semistrong, and weak forms of capital market efficiency can be seen in Figure 14.1. It shows how the information sets are nested, or contained within one another.

The Principle of Capital Market Efficiency refers to the semistrong form of capital market efficiency. So when we use the phrase *all available information,* we mean all publicly available information. Infamous *insider-trading* scandals clearly demonstrate that the capital markets are not efficient in the strong form sense. The available evidence indicates that actual capital markets are for the most part efficient. However, there are market segments where securities do not trade actively and there are anomalies like the tech stock bubble, which suggest that there are some important exceptions to this general statement.

The Reason for Capital Markets: Liquidity

Society has evolved by developing new ideas and procedures that facilitate life, retaining the best and discarding the rest. In ancient times, people met all their own needs. Over time, cooperative societies developed, and individuals specialized in certain tasks. This change embodied the initial recognition and application of the Principle of Comparative Advantage. A barter society then developed, in which individuals exchanged goods and services to meet their needs. Finally, money was used to *represent* the goods and services—to collect and store resources—because it is so easily exchanged. Money has proved so useful that today its logic is rarely questioned.

Money allows for an easier transfer of resources than barter, just like liquids can flow through a tube better than solids. The rate at which a liquid flows through a tube depends on how thick the liquid is. This analogy leads to the idea of asset *liquidity.* Liquidity reflects how easily assets are transferred without loss of value. Cash is the most liquid asset, because it is most easily transferred from one entity to another without loss of value. Real property, such as a building, is a less liquid type of asset. Considerable time, effort, and money can be spent in finding a buyer willing to pay a fair price for a building. Alternatively, a substantially reduced price may attract a buyer quickly. Either way, it can be costly.

Liquidity is the primary reason why money is used. Money enables us to exchange our efforts for another person's efforts without having to trade our services directly. Money also makes it possible to exchange one asset for another readily.

EXAMPLE Exchanging Shares of IBM for Wal-Mart Stock

Suppose you own 100 shares of IBM, but you would rather have your money invested in Wal-Mart stock. Although you might be open to the possibility of trading the IBM shares for Wal-Mart shares directly, it is generally much easier to sell the IBM shares and then buy the Wal-Mart shares. This saves your having to find a trading partner who wants exactly what you are offering (100 IBM shares) and who offers exactly what you want (Wal-Mart shares of corresponding value).

Stocks are very liquid because of the stock market. Without it, you would have to incur higher transaction costs—extra time, effort, and money. The stock market reduces the total transaction cost. In many markets, such as the New York Stock Exchange (NYSE), there is a *market maker* who increases liquidity by handling transactions in a particular asset. For example, when your orders to sell 100 IBM shares and buy Wal-Mart stock are carried out on the NYSE, a *specialist* (market maker) handling each stock, rather than another individual investor like yourself, may be on the other side of the transaction.

In fact, markets are generally set up specifically to increase liquidity by reducing the transaction costs of asset transfer. Think about what you would do if there were no stock market and you wanted to sell your IBM shares. One possibility is to consider the Principle of Valuable Ideas: Set up a stock market yourself, provide a service to other people, and earn money. If you were the first, you might earn a positive NPV. The developers of electronic marketplaces, such as eSpeed for bonds and Island ECN for stocks, have done just that. They gather and execute orders electronically, which reduces transaction costs.

Potential profit is exactly why capital markets exist. There are real benefits to the participants, which can be exploited for profit by those clever enough to do so.

An Unexpected Benefit: A Measure of Value

Even though markets are created in response to the need for liquidity, there is an additional benefit when market transactions are made public. Such transaction prices provide a measure of value that is visible to everyone.

EXAMPLE Pricing Intel Stock

What price would you have to pay for Intel stock? There are a couple of ways to establish a fair price. You could go online and get the latest trading price. Or you could look in the finance or business section of a newspaper, such as the *Wall Street Journal,* to find yesterday's closing price. Which price would likely be more accurate? The latest price is the more accurate one, because it reflects any new information that has come to light since yesterday's close. Of course, yesterday's closing price is generally a very good approximation of the security's current fair price in an efficient market.

Most capital market transactions are reported publicly, and the information is conveniently available shortly after the transactions take place. This means that fair market prices for thousands of securities are freely observable at any time.

So if you want a good estimate of what a share of Intel is worth, find out the most recent actual transaction price. After all, two parties actually transferred a share at that price. They did not just talk about it or *offer* to buy or sell it. Moreover, the price is not an average of many transactions from the last few weeks or months. The parties actually transferred shares within the last few minutes, and either one of them would have been willing for *you* to have been the other party in the transaction. (In most cases, they would not have known the difference if you had been!)

Therefore, even though liquidity is the main reason to create a market, a "spin-off" benefit of a public market is that it provides an inexpensive, fast, and accurate method of estimating fair prices: current market values.

Review

1. What are the strong form, semistrong form, and weak form of capital market efficiency? Which of these does the Principle of Capital Market Efficiency refer to? What is informational efficiency?
2. What is publicly available information? What is its importance to the three forms of capital market efficiency?
3. What relevance do the infamous insider-trading scandals have to the three forms of capital market efficiency?
4. What benefits do markets provide?
5. Suppose you wanted to know the most current value of Colgate-Palmolive common stock. What price would contain that information?

14.3 ARBITRAGE: STRIVING FOR EFFICIENCY

Now that we know why capital markets were created, let us turn to their operation. In this and the next section, we will present two concepts very important to the operation of the capital markets: *arbitrage* and *signaling*.

Getting Rich Quick?

Suppose the current price of a security in one market differs from the current price of that same security in a different market. Assume too that this information is available to one or more market participants. Someone who possesses this information can exploit it for profit by engaging in what is called arbitrage. **Arbitrage** refers to buying an asset in one market and immediately reselling it in another for a higher price.[1] Arbitrage is an important factor in the efficient operation of any market, but especially a capital market.

When people first learn about arbitrage, their usual reaction is to say that it sounds wonderful but that they are skeptical about the existence of such opportunities. Such skepticism is the intuition underlying capital market efficiency. Still, despite efficiency, market prices do sometimes differ between markets for short periods. For example, consider an asset that is traded in

[1]We start by using the dictionary definition of arbitrage, or what may be termed "riskless arbitrage." The term arbitrage is also used in the sense of "risk arbitrage" to describe the purchase of stock in firms that are expected to increase in value in the future for reasons such as becoming a takeover target. Such purchases involve a large element of speculation. We will distinguish arbitrage from speculation later.

two markets, such as shares of Exxon Mobil common stock. If Exxon Mobil shares were trading at a higher price on the Pacific Stock Exchange than on the NYSE, it would be possible to buy Exxon Mobil shares on the NYSE and resell them on the Pacific Stock Exchange for more than you paid for them.

Arbitrage is possible, whenever there is a price differential, by simply buying at the lower price and selling at the higher. The transactions, taken together, "lock in" a profit equal to the price differential multiplied by the number of shares simultaneously purchased and sold. This profit is "riskless," because the shares purchased and sold offset one another exactly. There are people who earn a living exploiting arbitrage opportunities that they observe while watching different capital markets that trade the same asset.

ONE DEFINITION OF A PERFECT MARKET Later on, we will list seven conditions that create a **perfect capital market.** But without getting into detail now, a convenient way to define a perfect capital market is simply to say that it is a market in which there are never any arbitrage opportunities.

Competition: If It Is That Easy . . .

Now that you know what arbitrage is and that opportunities for earning a riskless arbitrage profit sometimes exist, if you are like many of us, you may be considering applying the Principle of Self-Interested Behavior to participate in such a delightful process. You are not alone. Consequently, how often do you think trading price differences exist for the same asset between two markets? And when they exist, how large do you think the price differences are?

That is right—not very often, and not very large. And the larger the difference you are looking for, the less likely it is to occur. Rather than thinking this one through, we could have used a shortcut, the Principle of Capital Market Efficiency. Perhaps you were already applying it with your skepticism when we first told you about arbitrage.

There is an important implication of investor arbitrage. Suppose one investor discovers an arbitrage opportunity and trades securities to take advantage of it. When other investors become aware of this opportunity, the competition will eventually eliminate it. Consider the following example.

EXAMPLE Eliminating Arbitrage Opportunities

Edward O. Thorp, a "onetime university professor and mathematical whiz," developed arbitrage strategies for exploiting price discrepancies between a firm's common stock and securities that were convertible into its common stock. A few years ago, he closed his money management business, after more than 20 years in the business, and returned $200 million of his clients' money. Mr. Thorp had published some of his ideas in a book entitled *Beat the Market* and had set up a successful investment partnership that traded securities using his strategies. Mr. Thorp said he was withdrawing from the money management business because his ideas had become so widespread that only those investors with the lowest transaction costs could still use his arbitrage strategies profitably. His own success had helped to eliminate his arbitrage opportunities!

Competition among people engaged in arbitrage is actually an important contributing factor to capital market efficiency. The very existence of people, **arbitrageurs,** who are constantly looking for arbitrage opportunities ensures that prices for a particular asset will not differ very much among the various markets where the asset is traded. If it is easy to access both markets, then there is not much need for arbitrageurs. People making a transaction would buy or sell their assets for the best price provided by the two markets. When two markets are not easily accessed simultaneously, then it is worthwhile for arbitrageurs to incur the cost of accessing them, and in so doing to make transactions that push the two markets toward identical prices for a given asset.

Of course, in time, competition among arbitrageurs will drive their NPVs to zero. (Careful now—that does not mean the arbitrageur has a zero profit.)

When the NPV is zero, participants are getting exactly a fair return for the effort they are expending and an appropriate positive return for the risk they are taking on, and capital market efficiency is enforced.

Another important factor that contributes to the competitive environment of the capital markets is that financial assets are very similar. For example, consider a simple financial asset, a $10 bill. Would you exchange one $10 bill for another? Of course. Would you exchange a $10 bill for two $5 bills? Certainly. For the most part, people are indifferent to such exchanges. Forms of money are essentially equivalent. Almost any positive incentive (such as additional money or a polite request for change) will get people to exchange one form of money for another.

Similarity applies to securities as well as money. Let us say there are two securities that are exactly alike except for their expected return. The Principle of Risk-Return Trade-Off says that investors will choose the alternative with the higher expected return. Investors are fairly indifferent to owning shares in one firm versus another, except for differences in return and risk. For example, most people do not have strong feelings, beyond the financial considerations of return and risk, about owning shares of stock in Ford versus GM. Corporate bonds are also similar to government bonds, except that corporate bonds are riskier. For that matter, bonds are relatively similar to stocks, except that stocks are riskier.

When you think about it, you can see that financial assets are very similar to one another in comparison with physical assets such as houses. Because of this greater similarity, investors in financial assets can concentrate on the risk and return of an asset. When investors find two identical or even very similar investment opportunities, they will make transactions to increase the return on their investments, just as arbitrageurs do. Therefore, even though not all investors are primarily pursuing arbitrage opportunities, arbitrageurs must compete with the investing population as well as with each other.

Limits to Arbitrage: Transaction Costs

But how can arbitrage opportunities occur in efficient capital markets? How far apart do prices have to be for arbitrage opportunities to exist?

In theory, any price difference is an opportunity. In practice, however, transaction costs are not zero, and therefore if the difference between the prices is too small, arbitrageurs will not make a transaction because it will not be profitable. As you have probably already guessed, an arbitrage transaction is worth making only if the benefit exceeds the cost of the transaction.

Arbitrageurs have fixed and variable transaction costs. Variable transaction costs are specific to a particular arbitrage opportunity. For example, suppose a stock sells for $31.15 in London and $31.35 in New York, and that it will cost you $0.05 to buy in London, $0.05 to sell in New York, and $0.04 for transfer and communications costs. Consequently, it will cost you $0.14 to make $0.20. If you can buy and sell 1,000 shares, you make $60.00.

This sounds good. You will have more than covered your variable costs and earned a riskless arbitrage profit. But what about the cost of setting up your office and communication lines, educating yourself, and paying your support staff? These are fixed transaction costs, and they must be considered, too.

When two or more markets for the same asset exist, the differential between trading prices for the asset will exceed the variable cost of making a transaction only for a brief period. This period will be only as long as it takes arbitrageurs to buy and sell enough assets to reduce the price differential to less than the variable costs of making another transaction.

Because of arbitrage, *the price differential between markets is generally smaller than the variable transaction costs* for an asset traded in two markets.

How do variable transaction costs compare among different assets? How do the transaction costs of buying a used car in Los Angeles, taking it to Chicago, and selling it there compare with the costs of buying, transporting, and selling a share (or 1,000 shares) of stock? Unless you have someone who wants to drive across the United States from Los Angeles to Chicago, getting a car between those points can be costly in time (yours or someone you pay) as well as in gas and vehicle wear. In contrast, the stock ownership can be transferred quickly and easily via telecommunications, and all at a fairly low cost.

Transaction costs for buying and selling financial assets are low compared to transaction costs for physical assets, for several reasons. The most important reason is simply the physical difference. A few sheets of paper, or instructions typed at a computer keyboard, are much easier to transport than 3,000 pounds of automobile. A second important reason is market size. An enormous number of financial assets change hands every day. When many transactions take place, the fixed transaction costs are less on a per-transaction basis, because they can be spread over more transactions. So transaction volume is important. In an inactive market, the volume of trading may be so low that fixed transaction costs discourage arbitrageurs. This is the reason for a qualification: Active markets are efficient because arbitrage can achieve fair pricing.

Because transaction costs for financial assets are so low (in both relative and absolute terms), price differentials for financial assets in different markets are tiny compared with price differentials for physical assets in different markets. Even on a percentage basis, price differentials for financial assets are relatively small in active markets because of low transaction costs and high competition among arbitrageurs. The low price differentials among markets reflect capital market efficiency.

Arbitrage Versus Speculation

Let us return to our car example. Could we risklessly arbitrage used cars between areas of the country that have different market values for the same type of car?[2] Probably not, because the cars might need to be at both the purchase and sale points for careful inspection. This would eliminate the possibility of simultaneous purchase and sale. Literally speaking, a transaction that involves holding an asset for any length of time is not arbitrage.

We do not have a specific length of time that determines where riskless arbitrage leaves off and speculation begins. But when the asset is held for any positive time, risk is introduced. The longer the time between purchase and sale, the greater the risk. People who buy and sell a particular asset are not arbitrageurs but traders. **Traders** are people who engage in short-term speculation.

The continuum from arbitrage to speculation is important because, in many cases, traders anticipate price changes using less than perfect information. Traders are involved in "small gambles." But they are considered investments, because they average a positive return. After all, if the average return was not positive, the trader could not continue to do business while sustaining losses.

"Slightly" speculative transactions, which anticipate price changes, smooth the transition from one price level to another. New information does not generally occur in a complete and correct form. The first inkling of new information may come as a rumor. A trader's talent for determining more quickly than others which rumors are true and which are false is valuable, because facts can translate directly into price changes that can turn into profit.

Some talents cannot be taught, and interpreting information may be one of them. But we can point out that some actions carry with them subtle implications about a firm's current condition or its prospects for the future. This brings us to the topic of the next section.

---

[2]This is not a hypothetical example. Auto brokers are extensively involved in this process.

Review

1. What is arbitrage? How does it contribute to capital market efficiency?
2. How long do arbitrage opportunities exist in an efficient capital market?
3. What is a perfect capital market? How long do arbitrage opportunities exist in such a market?
4. For an asset traded in two markets, what is the relationship between the price differential and the variable transaction costs?
5. Which type of assets has smaller price differentials between markets, common stocks or used motor homes?
6. What is the difference between arbitrage and speculation?

14.4 SIGNALING AND INFORMATION GATHERING

There is a very important concept underlying the Principle of Capital Market Efficiency: Market participants react quickly to events that convey useful information. This quick reaction is due in part to the Signaling Principle, which states that actions convey information.

Recall that *signaling* refers to using actual behavior to infer things. Signaling involves asymmetric information. **Asymmetric information** is information that is known to some people but not to others. Actions convey the asymmetric information and in so doing eliminate it. Asymmetric information is a second imperfection, another one of the significant frictions in the capital markets.

In an efficient market, participants react to the information signals contained in such announcements by making buy and sell decisions. Executing the trades will cause securities prices to change. This is the mechanism by which the information content of the signals becomes reflected in securities prices.

What Is Signaling?

In our discussion of the Signaling Principle in Chapter 2, we introduced the concept of *adverse selection.* Adverse selection is when an offer implies negative information about a product or service. Adverse selection can discourage offering "good-quality" products or services, because doing so may give a seemingly negative signal. Consider the following example.

EXAMPLE Selling a Used Car

Suppose you decide to sell your car. The question for a buyer is *why* do you want to sell the car? One possibility is that it does not run well, and buyers would be foolish to buy it. If the car is in fact a good car, why would you be selling it?

This line of reasoning leads to the problem of adverse selection. Simply offering the car for sale can be a negative signal. How negative the signal is depends on how often sellers voluntarily sell good cars. And used-car prices will reflect this frequency.

If the only reason for selling a car is that it is not worth fixing, all used cars would be worthless. However, because there are reasons for selling a car other than its not being worth the trouble to repair, and because people have different levels of tolerance for car trouble, not all used cars are worthless. There is a chance that buying a used car will turn out well, and a chance it will turn out poorly. Many people who are not skilled at determining the quality of used cars always buy new cars to protect themselves from this problem. Others, skilled in evaluating the quality of a used car, put that skill to use and pay less for their dependable transportation. The savings represent the difficulty and cost—in time, effort, and money—of obtaining and using this valuable skill.

There have been many applications of the concept of signaling to financial transactions. Most applications are too technical to be detailed here, but it should be obvious that many daily events can be thought of as information signals. Firms make decisions nearly every day that provide an almost continuous flow of information about their current operations and intended future direction. For example, decisions about new equipment and raw materials, such as how much to buy and who to buy from, occur regularly. Other less frequent but telling information signals concern financing, such as decisions to issue new stock or bonds, or to change the dividend rate. Still other signals are not decisions made by the firm itself, but by people outside the firm, such as decisions to buy the firm's products. In addition, securities analysts gather and process information, which they provide in research reports. They help reduce information asymmetries. The market for a stock that is not followed by any analysts is less likely to be efficient than a stock that is actively followed by dozens of analysts.

Conditional Signals: Watching Management

Some information signals are sent intentionally and others inadvertently. Suppose you are listening to a chief executive officer (CEO) of a corporation speak about the firm's prospects for the future. The CEO paints a rosy picture, outlining plans for expanded production facilities to handle the projected increase in sales that will result in "big profits" for the next several years. The CEO is dynamic, enthusiastic, and persuasive.

But a week later, you find out the CEO sold 100,000 of the 150,000 shares she owned just three days after you heard the better-things-are-coming speech. How would it make you feel to learn that the CEO sold that stock? After hearing about the stock sale, what do you think the CEO really believed about the firm's prospects for the next several years?

It is possible that the CEO merely sold the 100,000 shares to pay for a new yacht, or that she exercised 200,000 stock options that were about to expire and sold 100,000 shares to pay the exercise price and taxes, and that the sale did not negatively reflect on the firm's prospects. However, most of us would consider it a negative signal if a person sells an asset while telling everyone else to buy it because of its investment value. Insider stock sales are often perceived as a signal of an upcoming fall in a firm's profitability.

Although this negative signal was fairly easy to read, many other signals can be positive or negative, depending on additional facts or decisions. For example, when a firm announces that it plans to borrow money, you would want to know why. Without any further information, that announcement could not be considered positive or negative. Borrowing can be a positive signal of new investment opportunities, a negative signal of low sales or poor management, or a neutral signal of replacing worn-out equipment.

Interpreting Signals: A Very Valuable Talent

Most information is easily and costlessly available if you just wait long enough. IBM's sales data for last year are easily obtained, but will not help you determine the future value of IBM's stock. Some information, like the number of shares owned by management and how much money a firm has borrowed, is published on a regular basis (every quarter or year), as required by the Securities and Exchange Commission (SEC). However, just like past sales, it is unlikely that the information can be profitably used *after* it is published.

Traders, as well as "speculators," who own stock for longer periods, are constantly searching for new information that will tell them if a stock price is going to increase or decrease in the future, so they will know whether to buy or sell the shares now. Competition is intense to obtain information before prices reflect that information. The more often a trader or speculator obtains valuable new information *first,* the more money she makes. (Such competition has lead some people to breach ethical and legal standards, creating insider-trading scandals.)

Of course, the more current that information is, the more difficult and costly it is to obtain. For example, a trader dealing in Wal-Mart's stock might pay someone to check local stores for the number of customers at various times and make statistical estimates of current sales, so that when Wal-Mart announces the latest sales figures, the trader has anticipated any stock price change that is due to higher- or lower-than-expected sales. Profits that a trader earns are the result of the cost—in time, effort, and money—of gathering information and using it to make informed trades.

When considering information like recent sales figures or amounts of borrowing, we are dealing with "hard facts." However, just as there is a continuum from arbitrage to speculation, there is a continuum for the quality of information. That continuum might be described, from one end to the other, as starting with hard information and moving to interpretive information, speculation, intuition, and finally to blind guesses.

We interpret information using inductive reasoning. Most of us are familiar with **deductive reasoning,** where a *general* fact provides accurate information about a *specific* situation. For example, if a friend tells you he just got a new cat, you can predict that the animal has four legs and a tail with a high probability of being correct.

In contrast, **inductive reasoning** attempts the reverse, to use a *specific* situation to make *general* conclusions. Therefore, accuracy depends on having sufficient information. For example, suppose a friend tells you he has just brought home an animal that has four legs and a tail. Without more information, making an accurate prediction of what kind of animal your friend got is virtually impossible. The pieces of information that are uncovered for use with inductive reasoning may be obvious—such as knowing that your friend had planned to visit a person whose cat recently had kittens. However, the missing pieces of information are often quite subtle, such as spotting a few cat hairs on your friend's knee.

Some information can be drawn from truly obscure facts, and interpreted in many different ways. Therefore, a person's talent for dealing with new or uncertain information is like any other talent a person might have, say in music, sports, or art. To some extent it is possible to teach people how to go about interpreting new or uncertain information. But as with other activities, there are differences in abilities among people despite identical training. Exceptional talent for dealing with new or uncertain information and interpreting information signals correctly has great value. For those of us who do not possess that unusual talent, it is still important to understand the process.

Review

1. What is *signaling?* How does the information that signaling conveys get reflected in security prices?
2. What is asymmetric information? How is signaling useful in eliminating asymmetric information?
3. Explain the concept of adverse selection.
4. Why is new information about a firm whose shares are actively traded unlikely to create profitable opportunities after it is published?

14.5 THE COLLECTIVE WISDOM

With many different ways to interpret new and uncertain information, and with so many people competing for information, could one person be consistently right? The answer is no. Yet, surprisingly, stock prices are good predictors of the future. How can this be? The information about the future is contained in the collective wisdom. The **collective wisdom** is the combination of all of the individual opinions about a stock's value. It is the *net* opinion that results from intense competition, and it is more accurate than any single assessment.

Information in Stock Price Movement

As you know, prices in efficient markets reflect all available information. A logical implication of this statement is that any transaction you make in an efficient market has a zero NPV (that is, the cost equals the value). So why bother to invest? The answer is that a zero NPV includes a profit that is appropriate for the risk of the investment. So the reason to invest, then, is to earn a profit (and perhaps a large profit, if you are willing to take on considerable risk).

This is another very important implication of market prices reflecting all available information: *Price movements are random in an efficient market.* If you think about it, this *must* be the case. If price movements could be predicted before new information arrived, the information would already be here! Instead, price movements take place only after someone can better assess an asset's value based on new information. Thus, because price movements depend on information arrival and information arrives randomly, price movements must reflect that randomness.

It is important to distinguish between *anticipated* and *unanticipated* new information. Some information, like earnings and dividend announcements, is available at regular intervals, such as quarterly. It is therefore anticipated by market participants, who will use whatever other information is available to formulate expectations, and may then enter into securities transactions in anticipation of the release of the new information.

If traders were skilled enough to anticipate the new information perfectly, market prices would actually reflect fully the new information even *before* the official announcement. When the new information is not perfectly anticipated—as when market participants expect an earnings increase, but instead there is a decrease—there can be price adjustments both before and after the announcement.

Other information cannot be anticipated. An example would be a fire that destroys a firm's production facilities or the discovery of a revolutionary product. The occurrence of such events is essentially random in nature. In such cases, the market can react only after the event occurs and is disclosed.

Information can arrive over time, which can cause the likelihood of a particular outcome to increase from unlikely to likely, and then from likely to an actual occurrence. Security analysts generate earnings forecasts and keep revising them up to the time of the actual earnings announcement. Although each security analyst may have perfectly valid reasons for each earnings forecast revision, the series of earnings forecasts and revisions taken collectively looks like a random process. With each tiny change in the likelihood of an outcome, the value of that stock changes. Because new information arrives almost continuously, and its interpretation goes on continuously, there will be many price changes, and they will be random. In fact, stock prices change almost constantly for precisely this reason.

The virtually constant movement of stock prices may appear, at first glance, to reflect uncertainty about what a stock is worth. At this point, however, we hope you can see that the movement in stock prices is the result of constantly *reassessing* what a stock is worth. Price changes are the result of competition in the ongoing interpretation of all available information, so random stock price movement can result from *rational* behavior.

The amount of time it normally takes for a market price to adjust to new information is a measure of capital market efficiency. As we have said, in an efficient market prices adjust quickly and fully (within minutes or hours) to new information. The process can be shown visually.

Three alternative price reactions to new information about a stock's value are shown in Figure 14.2: The perfect-market reaction, in which the price fully adjusts instantaneously; an overreaction, where the price drops too much and then increases during the adjustment period to the correct level; and an underreaction, where the price does not react immediately but declines

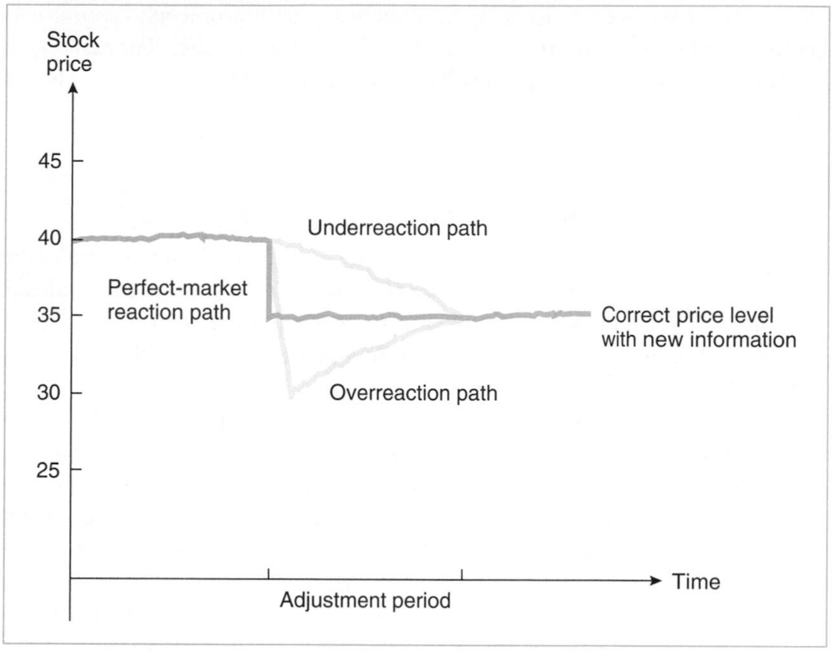

FIGURE 14.2
Alternative price reactions to new information indicating a stock is worth less than previously thought.

during the adjustment period to the correct level. The smaller the adjustment period, the more efficient the market.

The Stock Market as an Important Leading Economic Indicator

Random stock price movement implies that no single person can consistently predict future stock prices correctly. Traders use information that lies somewhere along the continuum ranging from hard facts to blind guesses. Still, most of their decisions are educated guesses.

A trader who has extraordinary talent in interpreting information and predicting future stock prices with great accuracy can amass a fortune very quickly. People observing this talent will value that trader's opinion more highly than the opinions of others. These people, then, by watching, would be interpreting the information available to them. They would have another signal to watch: the expert trader.

Thus far, no single trader, analyst, or firm has been consistently accurate enough to convince the rest of the world that he is *the* expert. Of course, some are more highly respected than others. As a group, however, their work and competition create prices that reflect the chances of future events more accurately than any single trader, analyst, or firm. In fact, stock prices are so accurate at assessing the probabilities of future events that stock market indexes such as the Standard & Poor's 500 Index of common stock prices are among the most accurate leading economic indicators.

Traders, or their representatives (who provide a valuable service for which traders are willing to pay), expend a lot of resources doing things like counting customers at Wal-Mart stores so they can translate those statistics into sales estimates, the sales into profit estimates, the profit into dividend estimates, the dividend estimates into predicted stock value, and finally, the predicted stock value into decisions to buy or sell.

The collective wisdom, as contained in a competitive price, generally provides a much more accurate assessment of value than any single assessment. Of course, it is always possible to find an assessment that at a particular point in time turns out to be more accurate than the market's assessment. However, we can establish this only after the fact. What has not yet been observed is an individual's assessment that is consistently, over a long period, more accurate than the market's competitive price.

There have been many temporary successes, with people who appear better than the market for a while. But even random guesses achieve some successes. For example, if you always pick heads when a coin is flipped, you will choose correctly 50% of the time. Think about the following example.

EXAMPLE Stock Market Prediction Experts

Suppose there are 4,096 market forecasters, and their predictions are evaluated quarterly. Every quarter each forecaster is just as likely to pick the stock market's direction correctly as incorrectly. With a 0.5 probability of being correct each time, we can use the binomial probability distribution to show that during an average year, 256 will be correct in every quarter ($[0.5]^4 = 6.25\%$; and 6.25% of 4,096 = 256).

Over a typical two-year period, 16 will have correctly predicted the stock market's movement each quarter. Even over a three-year period, on average, one of the forecasters will be exactly right *every* quarter. In spite of the equal likelihood of being right or wrong in any one quarter, one out of 4,096 prognosticators on average will make 12 correct predictions in a row ($2^{12} = 4{,}096$)—and a bunch will be right 10 or 11 out of 12 times.

From this you can see that a market forecaster can have a good run of luck, even if he does not possess any extraordinary predictive powers. Perhaps that is why an individual's duration as a market "guru" must be short-lived! And in fact, a review of the financial press reveals that some forecasters from time to time have appeared to be strikingly accurate.

But each one's period in the limelight has been limited. (Note that 4,096 is a very small number of forecasters compared to the actual number.) In any case, the competitive market price reflects the collective wisdom about the probabilities of all the possible outcomes, taking into account the cost of being wrong as well as the benefit of being right.

Review

1. Why bother to invest when any transaction you make in an efficient market has a zero NPV?
2. How do prices behave in an efficient market? Why must this be so?
3. Explain how random stock price movement results from rational investor behavior. When stock prices behave this way, can any single trader expect to be able to consistently predict future stock prices correctly?
4. Explain the stock market's role as an important leading economic indicator.
5. Why is a string of correct forecasts not necessarily proof that a particular forecaster is smarter than the collective wisdom.

14.6 VALUE CONSERVATION

Perfect markets—meaning entirely frictionless—are perfectly efficient. Another important, and startling, implication of perfect markets is the concept of value additivity. **Value additivity** means that the value of the whole (a group of assets) exactly equals the sum of the values of the parts (the individual assets). Value additivity holds in a perfect capital market. If this were not the case, there would be a profitable arbitrage opportunity. As discussed earlier, people would exploit this opportunity until further profits were no longer possible, at which point value additivity would have been restored.

The Law of Value Conservation

The law of value conservation in finance is like the law of energy conservation in physics. If value is conserved across transactions, as it is in a perfect market, value additivity will exist among assets. In the case of two assets, value additivity can be stated in this way: The value of two assets combined equals the sum of their two individual values. Algebraically, if V(A) stands for the value of A, V(B) stands for the value of B, and V(A + B) stands for their combined value, value additivity states that

$$V(A + B) = V(A) + V(B) \tag{14.1}$$

Note that this equation describes the process of separating assets as well as combining them. Also note that the equation can easily be generalized to more than two assets.

The two people most responsible for introducing the concept of value conservation into finance are Franco Modigliani and Merton Miller, commonly referred to as MM (pronounced "M 'n' M"). Both are Nobel Prize winners for their work because they changed the way people think about finance.

Recall that a zero-sum game is where one side's gain (loss) is the other side's loss (gain). Without new information, an efficient market is a *zero-sum game* at each point in time. Value additivity results from competition within that environment, that is, from the combination of capital market efficiency and two-sided transactions.

It sounds simple to say that value is neither created nor destroyed when assets are exchanged, and yet extraordinary time and effort have gone into debating this issue. The fundamental question is whether an asset can be worth different amounts, depending upon whether it is attached to another asset. The Principle of Valuable Ideas says, in effect, that it may be possible to combine assets in value-increasing ways. But the Principle of Capital Market Efficiency says it is not possible if people are already aware of the value-increasing possibility. How do we resolve this apparent contradiction?

RECONCILING VALUABLE NEW IDEAS WITH CAPITAL MARKET EFFICIENCY A financial asset is really only a set of expected cash flows. If we combine cash flows from various sources, can they be worth more in total after they are combined than before? *They are, only if we are the first ones to think of making this valuable combination.* If the owners of the separate cash flow streams know that the cash flows are worth more when combined, they will either make the combination themselves, or charge us the equivalent combined value for the assets because they *could* combine the cash flows themselves.

We could also ask the opposite question: Can cash flows be worth more if they are split up? Again, they are, only if we are the first ones to think of a value-increasing breakup.

To appreciate the concept underlying the law of value additivity, recall our example of that simple financial asset, a $10 bill. Would you exchange a $10 bill for nine $1 bills? Of course not. But how about exchanging it for 11 of them? More interested? Value additivity says that breaking a $10 bill into several smaller assets does not change the total value—you will still have $10 worth of assets.

Similarly, suppose you have two $5 bills. Can combining the two bills by exchanging them for one $10 bill make the total worth more than the sum of the two taken separately? No. Consider the following example.

EXAMPLE Dismembering a $10 Bill

What if a $10 bill has been torn into four equal pieces, with each piece given to a different person. Individually, the pieces are all worthless—or are they? Suppose you know the four people who each hold a piece. You point out to each individual that the piece is worthless, but that you will be happy to take it off their hands at no cost to them. If everyone gives you their pieces, you will have an asset worth $10. Assuming each person knows that the other three pieces are obtainable, however, the holders are not likely to *give* their pieces to you. The holders would be willing to *sell* their pieces to you for $2.50 each, but then there would be no reason for you to bother with the transaction, because it would cost you $10 for an asset worth $10. If the four individuals did not want to bother spending the time, effort, and money to get together and make the deal themselves, however, you might get them to sell their pieces for less than $2.50 each. If they sold you the pieces for $2 each, you would make a "commission" of $2 on the transaction, and they would be paying a transaction cost of 50 cents each.[3]

The capital markets are just a more sophisticated application of this $10-bill example. Value additivity holds exactly when all the parts are included. That is, when the loss due to frictions is included, there is perfect conservation of value. More importantly, however, value additivity is the best approximation of a situation with relatively low transaction costs. And this is the case with active capital markets.

A Chance for a Bigger Pie to Split: Lowering Your Taxes

Taxes can create a situation that is not a zero-sum game. This can happen when two parties pay taxes at different rates. When one records a dollar of revenue and the other records a dollar of expense in a single transaction, an asymmetry in taxes occurs if the two parties pay taxes at different rates. The revenue increases taxes collected, and the expense decreases taxes collected. But because of the different rates, the tax amounts are not equal. So the government may collect more or less taxes on the revenue than it gives up on the expense. This means there can be an advantage if the transaction reduces their combined tax bill. Such a situation is called a **tax asymmetry.**

Because people understand the phenomenon, the government generally collects fewer tax dollars when such tax asymmetries occur. Of course, in many of these cases people are doing exactly what the government is encouraging them to do. For example, the government uses the tax code to encourage saving for retirement. It creates special advantages for retirement accounts. The goal is to reduce the future burden on social programs.

EXAMPLE The Tax Treatment of Zero-Coupon Bonds

A tax asymmetry Congress may not have intended involves zero-coupon bonds. A zero-coupon bond makes only one payment when it matures. Such a bond might be sold for $100 when issued and pay $1,000 twenty years later. The interest compounds over the life of the bond. That is, the discount ($900 in the example) is the total amount of interest over the bond's entire life.

The Internal Revenue Code, at one time, permitted the issuer and the holders to allocate equal amounts of the discount to each year of the bond's existence, rather than allocate the discount on the basis of how interest truly compounds. By using the straight-line allocation of interest expense, the firm lowers its present value cost of taxes because it claims the interest sooner, even though the total amount claimed over the life of the security is the same.

---

[3]Note that an interesting sunk-cost problem could arise. If you bought three of the pieces for $2.50 each and the holder of the fourth piece discovers that information, he could bargain for a higher price. How much higher? The $7.50 you have already paid is a sunk cost. If your three pieces are not worth anything without the fourth piece, the fourth person can demand up to $9.99, and you would be better off making the transaction, in spite of the $7.50 you already spent! (Of course, you might take nothing rather than let the fourth person "fleece" you. Acting out of frustration would be due to emotional rather than financial considerations.) To avoid this problem, you could bargain with each person separately and purchase options from them before making any transactions. Although the options would complicate the valuation problem by creating more "pieces," the whole would still be worth exactly $10.

Continuing our example, interest would be allocated as $45 for each of the 20 years (= 900/20). This amount was both claimed by the firm as an expense and recorded as income by each bondholder. As we know, the amount of interest actually compounds slowly at first but increases over time. The actual interest accrued is $12.20 in the first year and $108.75 in the last year. Thus, the firm is overstating its interest expense for tax purposes in the early years ($45 versus $12.20 in the first year), and understating its interest expense in the later years.

This "incorrect" allocation of the interest expense causes a shift in the firm's tax payments: Lower taxes are paid in the early years, and higher taxes are paid in the later years, than would be paid under the "correct" allocation. Although the total underpayment in the early years exactly equals the total overpayment in the later years, this shift is valuable to the firm because of the time value of money. The firm can invest the tax underpayments in the early years so that it will have more than enough money to cover the added cost of the tax overpayments in the later years.

The shift in tax payments is good for the firm, but the Principle of Two-Sided Transactions reminds us to look at the other side of the transaction—the bondholders' position in the scheme of things. Sure enough, the shift in tax payments would seem bad for the bondholders. However, several billion dollars worth of zero-coupon bonds were issued. The buyers were primarily tax-exempt investors, such as pension funds, who are not affected by taxes. The decrease in taxes from the issuing corporations was not offset by an increase in taxes from the bondholders.

As more firms learned about this opportunity, the number of new zero-coupon bonds being issued began to dramatically increase. When the IRS realized that this tax asymmetry was occurring on a large scale and significantly affecting the taxes being collected, it asked Congress to change the tax law. Congress agreed, and the rule for allocating interest expense/income for a zero-coupon bond was changed to how it actually compounds, to accurately reflect each year's interest cost.

Zero-coupon bonds are only one example of many tax asymmetries that have occurred, or that still exist. A lot of attention has been given to tax asymmetries connected with leasing. For example, a significant reduction in the tax deductibility of personal interest at one point substantially increased the attractiveness of leasing to many individuals, and dramatically increased the car-leasing market. Although most tax asymmetries exist by Congressional design, many people spend considerable effort looking for others to exploit for profit.

Apparent Exceptions to Value Additivity

People are often reluctant to believe that value conservation is the best approximation of the valuation of assets traded in actual capital markets. To some extent, this skepticism may rest on the hope for an easy way to riches, or on what people perceive as exceptions to the conservation of value. Our next two examples examine two such seeming exceptions.

EXAMPLE Going Public

Consider the owners of a privately held firm who have decided they want to sell shares of stock in their firm. The first step in the process is to find potential buyers for the stock. It can take substantial time, anxiety, and money to locate buyers. In many markets there are specialists paid to *search* for potential buyers. After locating one or more potential buyers, each of the parties (the firm and each buyer) must assess the value of the firm. This is a second task that takes time, effort, and money. After valuing the firm, negotiations are necessary to reach agreement for any sale.

When potential buyers are thinking about buying stock, they must consider resale, especially due to unforeseen future events. Purchasers in a private transaction face significant restrictions on their ability to resell their stock unless the firm registers it under the U.S. securities laws.

Assume for the moment that the stock in question is unregistered. What would happen if it becomes necessary to resell shares? Who would buy them? Realistically, "sophisticated purchasers" (high-net-worth individuals and financial institutions) would be the only potential buyers for the unregistered shares, unless the holder could convince the firm to go to the time, trouble, and expense of registering the stock before the resale.

What would these *other* investors be willing to pay for the shares? They would have an awareness of the resources used to get this far in the negotiations for *this* sale. These contingencies increase the buyer's risk. Because of the higher risk, the Principle of Risk-Return Trade-Off tells us that buyers will lower the price they are willing to pay in order to raise their expected return to compensate for the higher risk.

Now consider the same scenario but with the resources that the current owners put into finding potential buyers instead going into registration for public sale. In this second case, when potential buyers consider the purchase of shares, one aspect of risk and transaction costs has been removed. With the stock registered for public sale, there is a much higher likelihood that a resale could be transacted quickly and at low cost. Shareholders can sell in the public market. They are not restricted to selling to sophisticated investors, as they are in the case of a private transaction. (Of course, registration does nothing to guarantee the resale price.)

The process of going public appears to add value to the firm. However, we hope you can see that value has not actually been *created*. Rather, transaction costs have been reduced: There is a broader market, so the time and cost of locating buyers have been reduced. Investment risk has also been reduced, because of increased liquidity and the greater valuation accuracy that comes from public prices and more people valuing the firm. Finally, the costs of transferring ownership have been reduced. In short, the increased liquidity of the shares, due to their public registration and their being traded in the stock market, is valuable.

EXAMPLE Pyramid Schemes

The **pyramid scheme** is a scam in which a con artist tells victims that they can earn an extraordinary return on their money, such as 10% per quarter, with no risk. The con artist takes the money, then returns the investment with the promised interest one quarter later, and inquires about reinvesting. The soon-to-be victim is pleased because he has gotten the money back with tremendous interest, as promised. Usually people reinvest their money and can be called upon to cajole some friends into investing, too.

The con artist takes in the invested money, using the new money coming in to pay off any investors who want to quit. Of course, most people want to keep their money invested in such a great investment, so the outflow for "quitters" is small for quite a while. In the meantime, a lot of money comes in.

From the start, the amount of promised money exceeds the amount of money actually held by the con artist, and over time the difference between promised returns and funds available grows and eventually becomes enormous. At some point, the con artist disappears, along with whatever money actually remains.

This may seem to be an unlikely scenario because of the difficulty of pulling it off. The scheme is illegal, and there are many checks in the system to prevent its occurrence. However, about every decade there seems to be one or more pyramid schemes that have been at least partially successful for the con artist. For example, Bennett Fund Group bilked about 12,000 investors out of about $700 million by selling securities based on phony office-equipment leases. This ranks as one of the biggest pyramid schemes of all time.[4] In another case, the col-

[4]The mastermind was convicted of 42 counts of fraud and money laundering.

lapse of widespread pyramid schemes in which many investors lost all their savings led to a rebellion that forced the Albanian government to impose a nationwide state of emergency.

The pyramid scheme is not an exception to value additivity, because the cash to pay interest to those who wish to withdraw is obtained from others who have been sucked in. Value is not created; it is simply transferred from one group of participants to another, with a sizable "commission" being taken by the promoter.

Review

1. What is value additivity? What does it imply about the relationship between the value of two assets X and Y and their combined value? Must value additivity hold in a perfect capital market?
2. How can a tax asymmetry benefit both parties to a transaction?
3. True or false? Value conservation is a good approximation of the valuation of assets traded in efficient capital markets.
4. Is the increase in value of the shares of a firm that goes public an exception to value conservation? Why or why not?
5. Why are pyramid schemes not an exception to value additivity?

14.7 PERFECT CAPITAL MARKETS

Earlier, we noted that certain market imperfections such as transaction costs can limit market efficiency, chiefly by interfering with the arbitrage process. We also defined a perfect capital market simply as a market in which there are never any arbitrage opportunities. More formally, a perfect capital market is one in which:

1. There are no barriers to entry that would keep any potential suppliers or users of funds out of the market.
2. There is perfect competition—that is, each participant is sufficiently small that its actions cannot affect prices.
3. Financial assets are infinitely divisible.
4. There are no transaction costs, including no bankruptcy costs.
5. All existing information is fully available to every capital market participant without cost.
6. There are no tax asymmetries.
7. There are no government or other restrictions on trading.

Do these perfect market conditions describe existing capital markets? The answer is not *perfectly* (pun intended). How far a market deviates from these seven conditions determines how "imperfect" the market is. For example, if there are few participants in the market for a stock and if the flow of information to investors is very poor because there are no security analysts who monitor the stock and prepare research reports on it, the market for the stock may not always behave efficiently.

Despite their lack of perfection, the idea of a perfect market is still an excellent starting point for analysis. The Principle of Capital Market Efficiency states that the capital markets are efficient—but how far is "efficient" from perfect? We do not have a precise way of separating the two concepts, but our seven conditions provide us with guidance in looking for important exceptions to a perfect capital market. If you think about it, you might see that we have already told you how the capital markets are imperfect. We have identified three significant frictions in the capital markets, three persistent capital market imperfections. Let us summarize.

Asymmetric Taxes

Asymmetric taxes are one significant type of market imperfection. Because tax laws change frequently, we refrain from getting into too much detail about them in this book. At various points, we describe some tax asymmetries that have existed for quite awhile and are relevant to major corporate decisions. However, even those tax asymmetries might be changed by Congress. It is important to remember to check for tax asymmetries as a potential explanation for transactions that otherwise would appear to be a zero-sum game.

Asymmetric Information

A second type of significant market imperfection concerns the availability of information. In our discussion on speculation, we pointed out the importance and cost of obtaining information. New information relevant to pricing a security is not costless and available to everyone. However, because competition puts new information into prices so quickly and information is published almost as quickly, it is a good approximation of the environment to say that information is freely available to everyone. The securities laws promote this. For example, the SEC approved Regulation FD (Fair Disclosure) with the intent of making important corporate information available to all investors at the same time. Signaling is an important component of the flow and interpretation of information. As with tax asymmetries, information flow—sending signals—is a potential explanation for transactions that otherwise would appear to be a zero-sum game.

Transaction Costs

Transaction costs are a third imperfection we discussed. Unbelievable as this may sound, transaction costs may be less important than asymmetric taxes and asymmetric information. Transaction costs affect transactions in a way that is fundamentally different from the effects of asymmetric taxes and asymmetric information. Transaction costs are usually symmetrical. Although they may inhibit arbitrageurs, traders, and speculators from making transactions, transaction costs do not *bias* prices upward or downward, nor do they provide an incentive for making a transaction. That is, they do not create profit in and of themselves, except for the financial intermediary collecting a commission or finding a way to structure a transaction that reduces transaction costs.

The significant effect that transaction costs can have is to favor one *type* of transaction over another. For example, the existence of fixed transaction costs favors less frequent larger transactions over more frequent smaller ones. Note that price discounts because of a lack of liquidity are transaction costs.

Despite the existence of these three imperfections, perfect is a very good approximation for most segments of the capital markets. Value conservation—value is neither created nor destroyed through splitting or combining cash flows—is the best *starting* point for financial analysis. This is why we so often use this "starting-with-a-clean-slate" approach in our analyses.

Review

1. Cite the seven characteristics of a perfect capital market.
2. Describe three significant capital market imperfections.
3. Are transaction costs likely to be more, or less, important than asymmetric taxes and asymmetric information in inhibiting capital market efficiency?
4. Why does a perfect capital market serve as the best starting point from which to analyze capital market transactions?

SUMMARY

The Principles of Self-Interested Behavior, Two-Sided Transactions, Signaling, and Risk-Return Trade-Off combine with the similarity of financial assets, low transaction costs, and large size in a very competitive market environment and lead us to the Principle of Capital Market Efficiency.

- Transaction costs are the time, effort, and money necessary to make a transaction.
- Capital market efficiency states that, at any point in time, capital market prices reflect all available information and adjust fully and quickly to new information. Although disparities in valuation can occur, these will prove temporary when transaction costs are low, because arbitrage activity will tend to eliminate them quickly and restore efficient pricing.
- The strong form of capital market efficiency requires that market prices reflect *all* information that exists about the asset's value. The semistrong form of capital market efficiency requires that market prices reflect all *publicly available* information. The weak form of capital market efficiency requires that prices fully reflect the information *contained in past asset market prices. Informational efficiency* requires that prices adjust quickly and accurately to new information.
- Price movements in an efficient market are random because market participants will react to each new piece of information, and the events that generate this new information occur randomly.
- Market prices at any point in time will reflect the up-to-date collective wisdom of the market participants about the "correct" value of each asset.
- Arbitrage is the act of buying and selling an asset simultaneously, where the sale price is more than the purchase price, providing a riskless profit.
- Market participants will interpret each new event and respond with buy and sell decisions—or do nothing. This involves the interpretation of many events, such as dividend or new product announcements, as *signals* regarding possible changes in the firm's financial condition or prospects.
- A perfect market is a market where there are never any arbitrage opportunities. A perfect market is one in which:
    1. There are no barriers to entry.
    2. There is perfect competition.
    3. Financial assets are infinitely divisible.
    4. There are no transaction costs, including no bankruptcy costs.
    5. All information is fully available to everyone without cost.
    6. There are no tax asymmetries.
    7. There are no restrictions on trading.
- Conservation of value across transactions leads to value additivity. In the special case of a perfect capital market, where there are no frictions such as asymmetric taxation or transaction costs and information is fully and costlessly available to everyone, the value of combined assets exactly equals the sum of their individual values. As a result, the law of value conservation holds: Value is neither created nor destroyed when assets are combined or separated. Transaction costs appear to cause only minor departures from value additivity because they are not biased. That is, both parties to a transaction tend to pay approximately equivalent transaction costs.
- Asymmetric taxes can cause the capital markets to deviate from being a zero-sum-game environment. So tax-related factors might be responsible for transactions that would otherwise seem to be zero-sum games. In practice, tax-related factors are often the driving force behind a transaction.

- Asymmetric information is an important capital market imperfection and a frequent reason for making transactions. Such transactions can be the method by which the asymmetric information is eliminated and put into security prices.
- Transaction costs do not generally cause a bias in prices. However, as we show later, transaction costs can have important effects on decisions.
- In spite of capital market imperfections, the assumption of a perfect capital market usually serves as the best starting point from which to analyze capital market transactions.

EQUATION SUMMARY

$$V(A + B) = V(A) + V(B) \tag{14.1}$$

QUESTIONS

1. Explain how public securities prices provide a measure of value.
2. Define the term *riskless arbitrage.*
3. How can arbitrage be used to define a perfect market?
4. What conditions must hold for a perfect market to exist?
5. Respond to the following: "Why should I invest in the capital markets when I do not earn any money—that is, when I get a zero NPV?"
6. What do we mean when we say that financial assets are very similar?
7. What does the term *collective wisdom* mean?
8. Why is it important to distinguish between anticipated and unanticipated new information?
9. What is value additivity?
10. Describe what we mean by the term *asymmetric taxes.*
11. What is asymmetric information?
12. Cite and briefly discuss three types of capital market imperfections that may affect corporate decision making.
13. Capital markets were created to bring users and suppliers of capital together. In addition to this important purpose, we now find that there are important side benefits. Cite and discuss three benefits that capital markets provide for society.
14. Explain the importance of arbitrage to the efficiency of the capital markets.
15. Is the following statement true or false? Because arbitrageurs sell assets for more than they paid for them, arbitrageurs must make a lot of money. Justify your answer.
16. Explain how an increase in the liquidity of a financial security can appear to be a violation of value additivity.
17. Explain how the similarity of assets contributes to the efficiency of the capital markets.
18. Describe the problem of adverse selection in your own words.
19. Describe the law of value conservation in your own words.
20. For what reason were capital markets originally created?

CHALLENGING QUESTIONS

21. Using the Principles of Finance, explain why a market return is often referred to as an opportunity cost of capital (or an opportunity cost discount rate).

22. Applying the Signaling Principle involves inductive reasoning. Cite an important aspect of inductive reasoning that can make some applications of this principle extremely difficult.
23. Evaluate the following statement: As the evidence seems to suggest, price movements are random; this clearly implies that the capital markets are not functioning well.
24. Rank the following assets from the most liquid to the least: (a) 400 shares of McDonalds' Corporation; (b) one of Chagal's lesser-known paintings; (c) a two-year old Ford Taurus; (d) cash
25. In each of the following situations, indicate whether the strategy is a violation of the weak form of market efficiency, the semistrong form of market efficiency, or the strong form of market efficiency. Each person expects to earn an abnormally high return from his/her decision. (a) Michael buys 100 shares of ABBA Corp. because it had an extraordinary total return exceeding 100% last year. (b) Sheila buys stock in the Utah Gaming Company because it has a high ratio of the market value of the stock to book value. (c) Edward has been selling cocaine to Charles, an employee of an auditing firm. Edward has decided to invest in Memphis Multimedia because Charles has confided in him that the firm is about to report quarterly earnings that are substantially above analyst expectations. (d) Susan is buying a pharmaceutical stock because the Food and Drug Administration announced approval of an important new drug that the firm will market in the U.S.
26. Two firms both announce 20% earnings increases. One firm's stock increases substantially and the other firm's stock is basically unchanged. Why did the market react differently to these announcements?
27. Explain how the effect of transaction costs on market prices is fundamentally different from the effects of asymmetric taxes and asymmetric information.
28. Comment on the following statement: If *all* markets were perfect, it would be both a blessing and a curse.
29. Both fixed and variable transaction costs for arbitrageurs inhibit capital market efficiency. How would the effect of relatively large fixed and small variable transaction costs differ from that of relatively small fixed and large variable transaction costs?
30. The Internet has made all types of information more available and at lower cost. Why would you expect this to increase capital market efficiency?
31. Some would view the sharp runup in technology stock prices during the dot-com frenzy, and their subsequent very sharp price decline, as a stock price bubble that burst. Explain why a price bubble should not occur in an efficient market.
32. Transaction costs are often cited as definite proof that capital markets are not perfect.
    a. Explain why although this is literally true, transaction costs do not generally cause actual capital market prices to be a bad approximation of perfect capital market prices.
    b. Explain how the magnitude of the bid-ask spread (the difference between the share price a dealer is willing to pay to buy a stock and the price that a dealer is willing to sell the same stock for) and the proportionate transaction costs purchasers and sellers must pay affect your answer to part a.
33. Explain how the Behavioral Principle is related to the Principle of Capital Market Efficiency.

PROBLEMS

LEVEL A (BASIC)

A1. (Arbitrage opportunities) Which of the following transactions would allow you to make arbitrage profits?

a. You can buy 15,000 shares of Denver Crude Drilling Company for \$2.125 per share in New York and sell them for \$2.625 in Atlanta. Transaction costs will be \$0.25.

b. You can buy a used single-engine plane in Phoenix for $135,000 and fly it to Vancouver and sell it for $148,000. Transaction, licensing, and shipping costs total $18,000.

c. You can buy a Tuscarora General Obligation bond for $1,050 from an acquaintance and sell it for $1,065 to a municipal bond dealer. Commissions will be $20.

A2. (Arbitrage opportunities) Which of the following transactions would allow you to make arbitrage profits?

a. You can buy 1,000 shares of Benet Bancorporation for $61.25 per share in Toronto and sell them for $61.50 in Seattle. Transaction costs will be $0.50.

b. You can buy a used diesel engine in Phoenix for $4,500 and ship it to St. Louis and sell it for $5,700. Transaction and shipping costs total $700.

c. You can buy a Richmond Utility bond for $700 from a small Georgia bank and sell it for $730 to a Baltimore bond dealer. Commissions will be $40.

A3. (Arbitrage opportunities) Which of the following transactions would allow you to make arbitrage profits?

a. You can buy 5,000 shares of IBM for $67.25 per share in New York and sell them for $67.45 in Atlanta. Transaction costs will be $0.25 per share.

b. You can buy an antique Chevrolet Corvette in California for $35,000 and drive it to New York and sell it for $48,000. Transaction, licensing, and shipping costs total $15,000.

c. You can buy an Intel bond for $975 in Hong Kong and sell it for $990 in London. Commissions will be $18.

A4. (Arbitrage) You can purchase Nestle stock in London for $35 per share and sell it in New York for $35.875 per share.

a. If transaction costs are $0.50 per share, can you earn an arbitrage profit on trading Nestle shares?

b. What is the largest transaction cost you could absorb with these Nestle share prices and still make a profit?

A5. (Arbitrage) You can purchase gold bullion in Zurich for $302.50 per ounce and sell it in London for $304.75 per ounce.

a. If transaction costs are $3.50 per ounce, can you earn an arbitrage profit on trading gold?

b. What is the largest transaction cost you could absorb with these gold prices and still make a profit?

LEVEL B

B1. (Transaction costs) Steve Bolten sold his sailboat for $225,000. He paid a sales commission of 10% ($22,500) to the boat brokers, had legal fees of $500, and had additional selling costs of $1,000.

a. What are Steve's total transaction costs?

b. What are his transaction costs as a percent of the gross selling price?

c. What are his transaction costs as a percent of his net proceeds?

B2. (Transaction costs) Jackie Dunn sold her condo for $150,000. She paid a sales commission of 6% ($9,000) to the real estate brokers, had legal fees of $750, and had additional selling costs of $1,250.

a. What are Jackie's total transaction costs?

b. What are her transaction costs as a percentage of the gross selling price?

c. What are her transaction costs as a percentage of her net proceeds?

B3. (Arbitrage) A large investor wants your firm to help him sell a large block of 100,000 shares of a stock. The current market price of the stock is $28.00 per share. When this block of stock hits the market, it should depress prices from their current level. Consequently, this investor is willing to sell to your firm at a price of $25.00 per share.

a. If transaction costs are $0.30 per share and the market price does not move, what profit would your firm make with this deal?

b. If the market price drops to $22.00 per share, what profit would your firm make?

c. What is the largest price drop that would still enable your firm to make a profit?

B4. (Arbitrage and put-call parity) Arbitrage not only tends to equalize the price of identical securities across markets, but it also forces the prices of securities and derivative securities to have predictable relationships among themselves. One such relationship is put-call parity, where the price of a call option minus the price of a put option should equal the stock price minus the present value of the exercise price. Docent shares are selling for $124.25, the present value of the $120 exercise price is $119.25, and the value of a call option (with the $120 exercise price) is $7.25. What should be the price of a put option with a $120 exercise price?

B5. (Arbitrage) A large investor wants your firm to help him sell a large block of 50,000 shares of a stock. The current market price of the stock is $36.00 per share. When this block of stock hits the market, it should depress prices from their current level. Consequently, this investor is willing to sell to your firm at a price of $34.00 per share.

a. If transaction costs are $0.40 per share and the market price does not move, what profit would your firm make with this deal?

b. If the market price drops to $33.00 per share, what profit would your firm make?

c. What is the largest price drop that would still enable your firm to make a profit?

B6. (Transaction costs) George Miller sold his house for $97,500. He paid a sales commission of 6% ($5,850) to the real estate brokers, had legal fees of $750, and had additional selling costs of $2,000.

a. What are George's total transaction costs?

b. What are his transaction costs as a percent of the gross selling price?

c. What are his transaction costs as a percent of his net proceeds?

B7. (Tax asymmetry) A 20-year zero-coupon bond with a maturity value of $1,000 currently sells for $100. Show that the first and last year's implied interest for this zero-coupon bond example are in fact $12.20 and $108.75, respectively.

MINICASE PICKING WINNERS AND LOSERS

There are numerous daily business reports, weekly TV-show commentators, and regular opinion columns in newspapers and magazines providing information and recommendations about business conditions, corporate performance, and future stock prices. There are entire cable stations devoted to this endeavor. How well do you think they do? Let us do some empirical research, and form our own conclusions.

After your professor has specified a time period over which to conduct our experiment, gather information from these sources over a few days. Based on this information, place hypothetical purchase orders for three stocks that are expected to increase in value over the next time period (expected winners), and hypothetical sell orders for three stocks that are expected to decrease in value over the next time period (expected losers).

QUESTIONS

1. At the end of the time period, place hypothetical sell orders for the three stocks you purchased at the start, and hypothetical buy orders for the stocks you sold at the start. Calculate your realized holding period APY for each of the six stocks, using the procedure developed in Chapter 9 and applied in problems C4 and C5 in Chapter 9. Compute and compare the average realized APY for the three expected winners with that of the three expected losers. How did you do?
2. Collect the results from everyone in the class. Calculate the proportion of those whose expected winners outperformed their expected losers. Calculate the average realized APY for all the expected winners and compare it to that of all the expected losers. How did the class members do over all?

15

CAPITAL STRUCTURE POLICY

A firm's mix of financing methods is called its **capital structure.** In simple terms, capital structure is the proportion of firm value financed with debt, the leverage ratio. The leverage ratio was represented by L in Equation (11.2). In Chapter 11, we said that capital structure does not affect firm value—*in a perfect capital market environment.* Capital structure choice is a pure risk-return trade-off. We then showed that this is equivalent to saying that leverage does not affect the cost of capital—in a perfect capital market environment.

The question of whether capital structure affects firm value in real capital markets has been called the *capital structure puzzle.* Puzzle is a particularly appropriate term because our understanding has evolved in much the same way that a puzzle is pieced together. Currently, pieces are still being added, and we still do not have the complete picture.

Capital structure matters in practice if for no other reason than that firms actually behave as though it does. The empirical evidence shows consistent patterns of leverage ratios, as though there are definite reasons for following certain policies. Some argue that firms are simply following the Behavioral Principle of Finance—just copying each other—and that these patterns continue from habit and imitation even though they do not affect firm value. We believe this is too simplistic.

We have found that firms manage their capital structures carefully. The factors involved with choosing a capital structure are complex, and the impact of each factor on the value of the firm is not clear cut. However, we can describe such factors using the three persistent capital market imperfections identified in Chapter 14: asymmetric taxes, asymmetric information, and transaction costs.

In principle, a firm should balance the incremental advantage of more financial leverage against the incremental costs. Unfortunately, we cannot precisely measure all the factors.

A number of methods exist for analyzing the impact of alternative capital structures, but in the end, the choice of capital structure requires expert judgment. The analytical models give us a range of reasonable capital structures, rather than pinpointing the absolute best. In this chapter, we show you how a firm can take into account the various relevant factors to select an appropriate capital structure. The next chapter describes a practical method for managing capital structure.

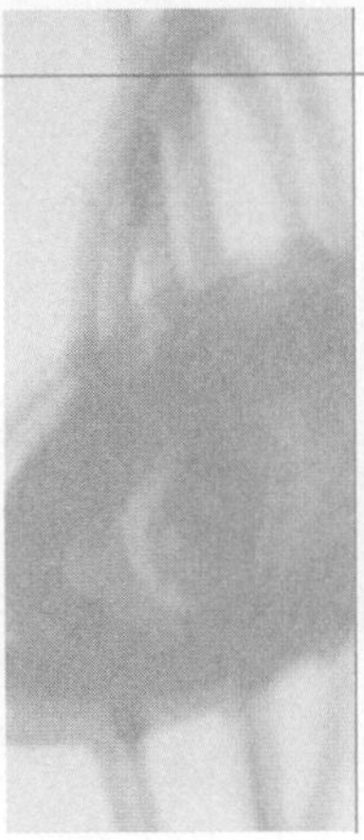

FOCUS ON PRINCIPLES

- *Incremental Benefits:* Consider the possible ways to minimize the value lost to capital market imperfections, such as asymmetric taxes, asymmetric information, and transaction costs. At the same time, be sure to include all of the transaction costs of making potentially beneficial financing transactions, because they reduce the *net* benefit from such transactions.
- *Capital Market Efficiency:* Recognize that the potential to increase firm value through capital structure is smaller than the potential to increase firm value through the introduction of *valuable new ideas* and wise use of the firm's *comparative advantages.*
- *Signaling:* Consider any possible change in capital structure carefully, because financing transactions and capital structure changes convey information to outsiders and can be misunderstood.
- *Time Value of Money:* Include any time-value-of-money tax benefits from capital structure choices.
- *Valuable Ideas:* Look for opportunities to create value by issuing securities that are in short supply, perhaps resulting from changes in tax laws.
- *Behavioral:* Look to the information contained in the capital structure decisions and financing transactions of other firms for guidance in choosing a capital structure.
- *Risk-Return Trade-Off:* Recognize that capital structure changes made at fair market security prices also change equity-debt risk bearing, and they are simply a risk-return trade-off. Such transactions do not affect firm value (except for possible signaling effects).

15.1 DOES CAPITAL STRUCTURE MATTER?

Chapter 11 showed that capital structure does not affect a firm's value in a perfect capital market environment. Our Per-Pet example demonstrates that leverage is a pure risk-return trade-off in such an environment. This result is called the **perfect market view of capital structure.** Firm value depends only on its expected future operating cash flows and the cost of capital, not on how those cash flows are divided between the debtholders and the shareholders. Chapter 14 described the fundamental concept underlying the perfect market view: value conservation.

Let us review our Per-Pet example. With or without leverage, the total value of the firm is \$1,000. With leverage, the shareholders get \$500 in exchange for half their claim on the firm. Figure 15.1 illustrates these cases in terms of "pies." The total size of the pie is the same whether the firm is leveraged or all-equity financed. The only difference is in the claims on that pie. Figure 15.1 expresses the perfect market view in terms of total firm value, the present value of the expected future cash flows.

Figure 15.2 is a reproduction of Figure 11.6. Figure 15.2 also illustrates the perfect market view, but it does so in terms of the cost of capital, WACC, and the required returns on the expected future cash flows.

Recall that present value depends on both the cost of capital and the expected cash flows. If the cash flows do not change and the cost of capital does not change, then the present value must also remain constant. However, also recall that even though the leverage ratio L (the market-value proportion of debt financing—$D/[D + E]$) does not affect WACC, it does affect how the risk of the firm is borne by the shareholders and debtholders. Therefore, the required returns on equity and debt (r_e and r_d, respectively) depend on L.

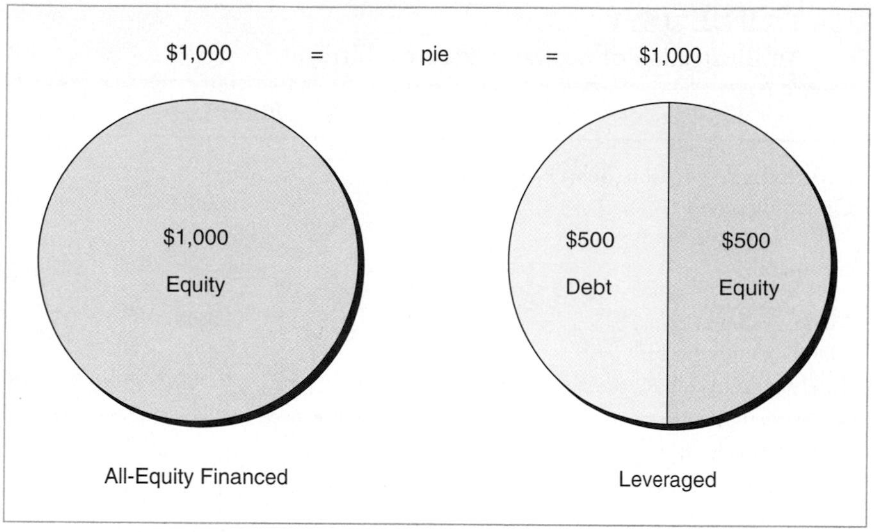

FIGURE 15.1
A "pie" representation of the perfect market view of capital structure.

Finally, recall that the WACC can always be expressed as the weighted average cost of any financing package. With only equity and debt, the WACC is the weighted average of r_e and r_d adjusted for taxes,[1] or

$$\text{WACC} = (1 - L)r_e + L(1 - T)r_d \tag{15.1}$$

Note how the weight shifts from the higher return r_e to the lower return r_d as L increases and $(1 - L)$ decreases, leaving WACC unchanged.

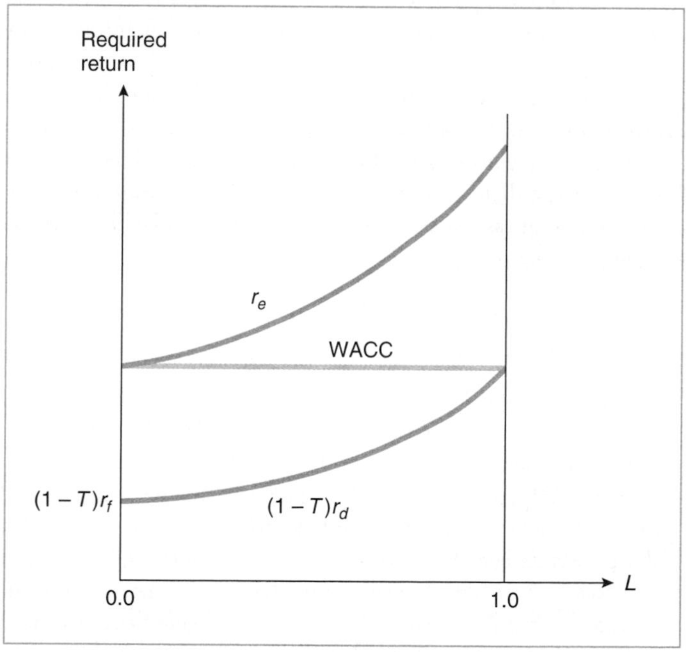

FIGURE 15.2
WACC (weighted average cost of capital), r_e (required return for equity), and r_d (required return for debt), as hypothetical functions of L (the leverage ratio) under the perfect market view of capital structure.

[1]The tax adjustment is necessary because interest payments are paid out *before* corporate taxes are levied on the firm's income, but dividends are not paid out until after. See Figure 15.6 for a visual representation of this process that includes personal taxes.

TABLE 15.1
An illustration of capital structure arbitrage.

	FIRM L	FIRM U
Leverage ratio [= debt/(debt + equity)]	50%	0
Operating income	$10,000,000	$10,000,000
— Interest expense[a]	3,600,000	0
Net income	$ 6,400,000	$10,000,000
Market value of equity	$30,000,000	$50,000,000
Market value of debt	30,000,000	0
Total market value	$60,000,000	$50,000,000

[a]At a 12% interest rate.

Another way of illustrating capital structure irrelevance is with an arbitrage argument. We show below that if two firms have identical operating profitability but different capital structures, arbitrage among investors will ensure that the two firms have equal market values.

An Arbitrage Argument

Consider two firms operating in a perfect capital market environment. Each will generate $10,000,000 of operating income. They are identical in every other respect except for their capital structures. Firm L is leveraged and has debt in its capital structure. Firm U is unleveraged; it has an all-equity capital structure. The two firms have the market values shown in Table 15.1. Firm L has a higher market value, supposedly because of its leverage.

According to the perfect market view, the situation shown in Table 15.1 cannot persist because of a profitable arbitrage opportunity. Shareholders of firm L can realize a greater return on their investment, with no increase in either their investment risk or the amount of funds they have invested, by making the following transactions. First, sell their shares of firm L. Second, borrow and create their own personal 50% leverage to duplicate firm L's capital structure. Third, use all the resulting cash to purchase shares of firm U. To illustrate this opportunity, consider the following example.

EXAMPLE Arbitraging Leverage Valuation Differences

An investor owns 1% of the shares of firm L. The first step in the arbitrage process is to sell these shares at their market value of $300,000 (1% of $30,000,000). The second step is to borrow an identical amount, $300,000, at an interest rate of 12% per year. This creates a personal capital structure that is 50% debt and 50% equity, exactly firm L's capital structure. The final step is to use the total funds to purchase $600,000 (= 300,000 + 300,000) of firm U shares, which happens to be 1.20% (= 600,000/50,000,000) of firm U.

Now let us compare the return before and after. Before the three-step transaction, the investor's return per year is 1% of firm L's expected net income, $64,000. After, the return per year is $120,000 (1.20% of firm U's expected net income) minus an interest charge of $36,000 (12% of $300,000), or $84,000. Thus, without adding any funds, our investor has an investment with an identical amount of leverage (and therefore identical risk) that earns $20,000 (84,000 − 64,000) per year more after completing the arbitrage transaction.

With self-interested arbitrage activity, investors continue to sell firm L and buy firm U until their total market values (debt plus equity) are equal. Only when the total firm values are equal will there be no further profitable arbitrage opportunity.

Capital Market Imperfections

In our chapter introduction, we mentioned three persistent capital market imperfections: tax asymmetries, information asymmetries, and transaction costs. So an important place to look for value-changing market imperfections is in the tax code. Whenever tax rates differ for the two sides of a transaction, there is a tax asymmetry that might be used to enhance firm value. We will do this in the next section.

Review

1. What is the perfect market view of capital structure?
2. What is the formula for the WACC? Explain each variable and how it contributes to the WACC.
3. What is the shape of the WACC curve according to the perfect market view?

15.2 THE ROLE OF INCOME TAXES

We have pointed out numerous times that interest payments are tax deductible to the firm, whereas dividend payments are not. This tax asymmetry gives rise to the **corporate tax view of capital structure.** In this view, corporate taxes cause debt to be cheaper than equity. The corporate tax view concludes that the maximum firm value results from being essentially all-*debt* financed.

Corporate Income Taxes

We will illustrate the corporate tax view by extending our Per-Pet example.

EXAMPLE Corporate Taxes at Per-Pet, Inc.

As in our Chapter 11 example, we will start with an all-equity firm and examine the effect of leverage on firm value. We assume that Per-Pet must pay corporate taxes on its net income at the rate of 37.5%, but operates in an otherwise perfect capital market environment. What is Per-Pet worth if it is all-equity financed, and what is it worth with leverage?

Per-Pet has a perpetual expected cash inflow each year of $150, which can be larger or smaller, but is never less than $50 per year. Therefore, its expected after-tax net income is $93.75 per year (= [1 − 0.375]150). Per-Pet's cost of capital is 15%, so Per-Pet is worth $625 (= 93.75/0.15), compared to a $1,000 value without corporate taxes.

Now suppose the firm borrows $500 at 10% per year and gives the $500 to the shareholders. This debt will require $50 per year in interest payments. Because the interest payments are made *before* corporate taxes are assessed, they cost only $31.25 (= [1 − 0.375]50) in after-tax cash flow. After the capital structure change, then, the residual expected future cash flow to be paid out to shareholders each year is $62.50 (= $93.75 − 31.25).[2] Once

[2]This amount can also be computed starting with the firm's expected income of $150 per year: Subtract the $50 interest payment and apply the corporate tax rate so that (1 − 0.375)(150 − 50) = $62.50.

again, the leverage would increase the shareholders' required return to 20%. Therefore, under the proposed leveraging, shareholders would get \$500 from the debtholders in cash to invest as they wish and have a remaining investment worth \$312.50 (= \$62.50/0.20), for a total value of \$812.50. Thus, in this environment, the proposed leveraging increases shareholder value by \$187.50 (= 812.50 − 625.00).

Simultaneously, the total value of Per-Pet would also increase by the same \$187.50 amount. With no leverage, the firm is worth \$625.00 (= 93.75/0.15). Under the proposed leveraging, total firm value is the value of the debt (\$500) plus the value of the equity (\$312.50), for a total value of \$812.50.

The extra value for the Per-Pet shareholders can be traced directly to the tax asymmetry. The expected after-tax cash flows to investors increase because the government collects fewer tax dollars from the leveraged firm. Specifically, with the all-equity capital structure, the firm pays an average tax of \$56.25 (= [0.375]150) per year. It pays an average tax of only \$37.50 (= [0.375][150 − 50]) per year with the leveraged capital structure.

Figure 15.3 illustrates the corporate tax view of capital structure, showing the Per-Pet alternatives in terms of "pies." Once again, the total size of the pie is the same whether the firm is leveraged or all-equity financed, \$1,000. The only difference is in the claims on the pie. However, this time, under the corporate tax view, there are three claimants: shareholders, debtholders, and the government. By selling part of the cash flow to the debtholders, the government collects less in taxes. This shrinks the government claim and leaves more for investors. Leverage increases the total after-tax firm value from \$625 to \$812.50.

The Cost of Capital with Corporate Income Taxes

Although leverage actually changes the after-tax cash flows, the effect can be equivalently accounted for by adjusting the cost of capital. Let $\overline{I}$ represent the expected perpetual cash inflow per year. Then the unleveraged firm pays taxes of $T\overline{I}$ each year, and the shareholders get

FIGURE 15.3
A "pie" representation of the corporate tax view of capital structure.

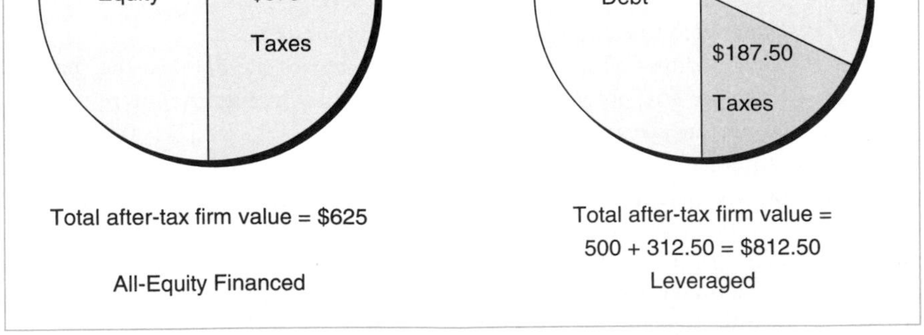

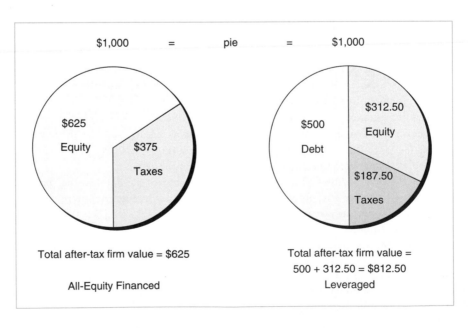

the rest, an expected yearly after-tax cash flow $\bar{I}(1 - T)$. The value of the unleveraged firm, V_U, is then

$$V_U = \frac{\bar{I}(1-T)}{r} \tag{15.2}$$

where r is the unleveraged cost of capital (15% in the Per-Pet example).

In the Per-Pet example, we adjusted the after-tax cash flows and the required returns for equity (20%) and debt (10%) to find the value of the leveraged firm. Alternatively, we can represent the value of the leveraged firm, V_L, in terms of the "basic" after-tax cash flow to the firm and an appropriately adjusted cost of capital. The "basic" cash flow is the cash flow to the shareholders if the firm were unleveraged, $\bar{I}(1 - T)$. This cash flow is what we called CFAT in capital budgeting (see Chapter 7). Then

$$V_L = \frac{\bar{I}(1-T)}{\text{WACC}} \tag{15.3}$$

where WACC is the weighted average cost of capital, which has been adjusted for the effect of corporate taxes. Now we need to determine just what that adjustment is.

The firm uses an amount of debt, $D = LV_L$, with interest payments of $r_d D$, the interest rate times the amount of debt. The debtholders earn a *risky* (rather than riskless) amount each period, which has an expected payment of $r_d D$.

The firm pays taxes on all its income that is not paid out as interest. So the firm's annual taxes are expected to be

$$T(\bar{I} - r_d D)$$

The combined after-tax cash flow expected to be paid out to debtholders and shareholders is a yearly perpetuity of

$$\bar{I} - T(\bar{I} - r_d D) = \bar{I}(1 - T) + Tr_d D$$

The cash flows in this equation do not all have the same risk. The tax savings due to interest ($Tr_d D$) have exactly the same riskiness as the debt (because they are strictly proportional to the debt), and so the tax savings are discounted at r_d. The "basic" after-tax cash flow to equity is discounted at r, because the equity cash flow is riskier than the debt payments. The value of the leveraged firm is then the present value of these two cash flow streams:

$$V_L = \frac{\bar{I}(1-T)}{r} + \frac{Tr_d D}{r_d} = \frac{\bar{I}(1-T)}{r} + TD \tag{15.4}$$

Because $\bar{I}(1 - T)/r$ is equal to the value of the unleveraged firm, Equation (15.2):

$$V_L = V_U + TD \tag{15.5}$$

This is the most common way of mathematically expressing the corporate tax view. The value of the leveraged firm is equal to the value of the unleveraged firm plus the tax rate times the amount of debt.

We can build on this result. A value for WACC can be derived by setting Equations (15.3) and (15.4) equal to each other and solving for WACC. We will spare you the details, and just give you the result:

$$\text{WACC} = r(1 - TL) \tag{15.6}$$

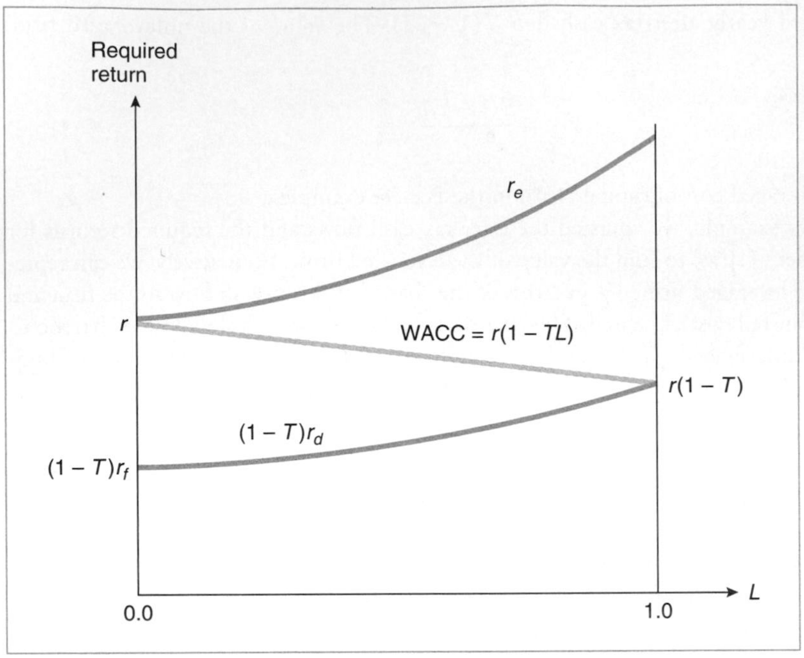

FIGURE 15.4 WACC (weighted average cost of capital), r_e (required return for equity), and r_d (required return for debt), as hypothetical functions of L (the leverage ratio) under the corporate tax view of capital structure.

Figure 15.4 illustrates the corporate tax view of capital structure in terms of the WACC and hypothetical functions for the required returns on equity and debt. Note that the function for WACC is a straight line. WACC decreases as leverage increases. The lowest value for WACC, $r(1 - TL)$ occurs when the firm is financed entirely with debt, that is, when $L = D/(D + E) = 1.0$. Under the corporate tax view, the optimal capital structure—the one that creates the most valuable firm—is the one that contains as much debt as possible.

EXAMPLE The Cost of Capital at Per-Pet, Inc.

Now we can check our work by applying the adjusted cost of capital given in Equation (15.6) to our Per-Pet example with corporate taxes. Under the proposed leveraging, the firm borrows \$500, and leveraged firm value is \$812.50. This means that Per-Pet's leveraged capital structure would be $L = D/(D + E) = 0.61538$ (= 500/812.50). (Remember, the leverage ratio is based on market values.) What is Per-Pet's cost of capital under the proposed leveraging?

From Equation (15.6), we have

$$\text{WACC} = r(1 - TL) = (0.15)[1 - (0.375)(0.61538)] = 0.115385 = 11.5385\%$$

Alternatively, we can also find the WACC using Equation (15.1):

$$\begin{aligned}\text{WACC} &= (1 - L)r_e + L(1 - T)r_d \\ &= (0.38462)(0.20) + (0.61538)(1 - 0.375)(0.10) = 0.115385 = 11.5385\%\end{aligned}$$

We can also verify that our adjustment produces the correct value for V_L using this WACC and Per-Pet's CFAT of \$93.75 in Equation (15.3):

$$V_L = \frac{\bar{I}(1 - T)}{\text{WACC}} = \frac{93.75}{0.115385} = \$812.50$$

Before moving on, we want to emphasize the equivalence between (1) adjusting the WACC and (2) adjusting the after-tax cash flows and required returns on equity and debt. The first method, adjusting the WACC, is more commonly used, probably because of convenience. It involves only a single adjustment.

Also, it is important to reemphasize that *the leverage ratio is based on market values.*

Review

1. What is the corporate tax view of capital structure?
2. Why does the U.S. corporate tax system seem to favor debt financing over equity financing?
3. According to the corporate tax view, what is the relationship between the leveraged value of the firm V_L and its unleveraged value V_U?
4. What is the shape of the WACC curve according to the corporate tax view?

Personal Income Taxes

From an income tax perspective, our Per-Pet corporate tax example is incomplete. There are other significant taxes besides corporate income taxes. The firm pays taxes on its income, but investors then pay personal income taxes on their income from the firm. And the rates investors pay are not all the same. The rates depend on the form of the investment, in particular whether it is equity or debt.

Interest and dividends are taxed when they are received, but capital gains are not taxed until the asset is sold. Therefore, a shareholder can postpone the tax on a gain by not selling the shares. At the same time, there is a mirror image treatment of losses. The shareholder can claim the tax shield resulting from a loss right away by selling the asset. This creates the valuable tax-timing option we first described in Chapter 3. The capital gain tax-timing option lowers the effective tax rate on shareholder income. In turn, this lower effective rate leads to the **personal tax view of capital structure.** According to this view, the firm is still operating in a perfect capital market environment, except for corporate *and* personal income taxes.

The personal tax view concludes that the differential between tax rates on personal income from equity and from debt cancels out the corporate tax asymmetry. The outcome is that leverage has no effect on firm value in this environment and, once again, capital structure is irrelevant.

To illustrate the personal tax view of capital structure, let us extend our Per-Pet example one more time.

EXAMPLE Personal Taxes at Per-Pet, Inc.

Once again, we will start with an all-equity firm and examine the effect of leverage on firm value. Suppose Per-Pet's debtholders' tax rate is 50%, whereas the shareholders' rate is 20%. Per-Pet's corporate tax rate is the same 37.5%, and it operates in an otherwise perfect capital market environment. What is Per-Pet worth if it is all-equity financed, and what is it worth with leverage?

After paying 20% in personal taxes, the shareholders get to keep 80% (= 1.0 − 0.20) of their cash flow from the firm, which after corporate taxes is expected to be $93.75 (= [1 − 0.375]150). With an all-equity capital structure, then, the shareholders' expected cash flow after corporate *and* personal taxes is $75.00 (= [0.8]93.75). On the basis of Per-Pet's 15% unleveraged cost of capital, Per-Pet is worth $500 (= 75.00/0.15).

Now suppose the firm borrows $250 at an after-personal-taxes required return of 10%. So the debtholders must receive 10% of $250, or $25 after taxes. Therefore, the interest payment from the firm must be \$50 (= 25/[1 − 0.5]) per year. After the interest payment and corporate taxes the shareholders have an expected income of \$62.50 (= [1 − 0.375][150 − 50]), on which they must pay personal taxes. Therefore, under the proposed leveraging, the shareholders have an expected annual cash flow after corporate and personal taxes of \$50 (= [1 − 0.2]62.50). Again, the leverage would increase the shareholders' required return to 20%. Under the proposed leveraging, then, shareholders would get \$250 from the debtholders in cash to invest as they wish and have a remaining investment in Per-Pet worth \$250 (= 50/0.20). Thus, shareholders will have the same total value of \$500 whether or not the firm is leveraged.

The total value of Per-Pet is not changed, and capital structure is irrelevant in this environment. In both cases, the firm is worth \$500—either \$500 worth of equity, or \$250 worth of equity plus \$250 worth of debt.

Figure 15.5 illustrates the personal tax view of capital structure, showing the alternatives in our Per-Pet example with personal taxes in terms of "pies." In this case, the total size of the pie is the same and the total taxes paid are the same. The only difference is the amounts paid of each type of tax. With all-equity financing, more corporate taxes and less personal taxes are paid than under the proposed leveraging. So in this case the total after-tax value is \$500 either way.

If it occurs to you that the results illustrated in Figure 15.5 depend on the personal tax rates we use, you are right. The critical issue is the amount that reaches the investor after corporate and personal taxes. Let T_d, T_e, and T represent the tax rates for debtholders, equityholders, and the corporation, respectively. The difference in equity and debt personal taxes exactly cancels out the corporate tax asymmetry *only* when

$$(1 - T_d) = (1 - T_e)(1 - T) \tag{15.7}$$

When this condition holds, the effective tax rates are the same and the after-corporate-and-personal-taxes portion of the firm's cash flow that "reaches" an investor is the same, whether the investor has an equity or debt claim. That is, a before-tax dollar singly taxed at T_d provides the same net amount to an investor as a before-tax dollar taxed at T and then taxed again at T_e.

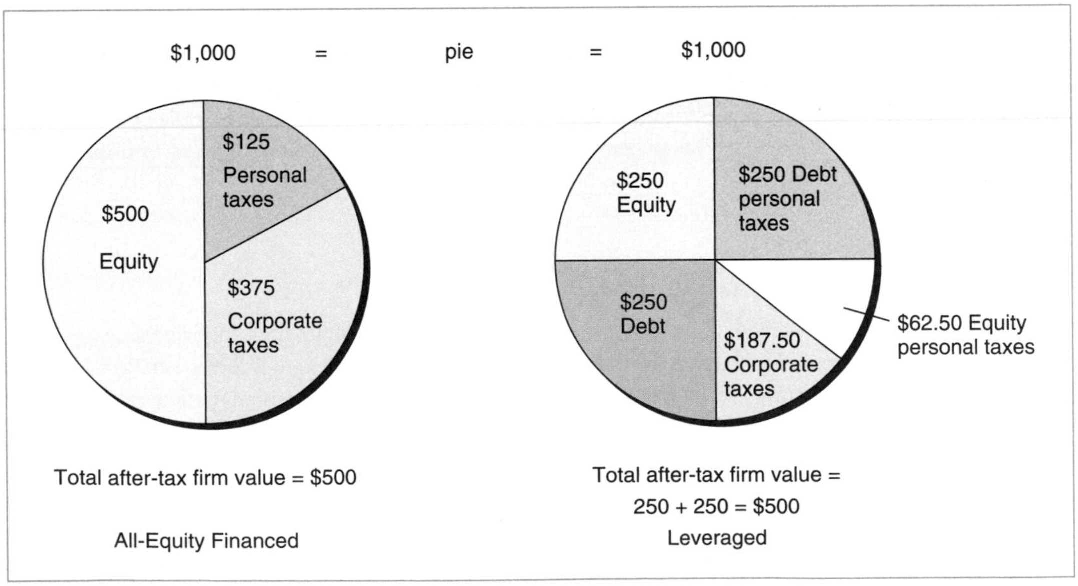

FIGURE 15.5
A "pie" representation of the personal tax view of capital structure.

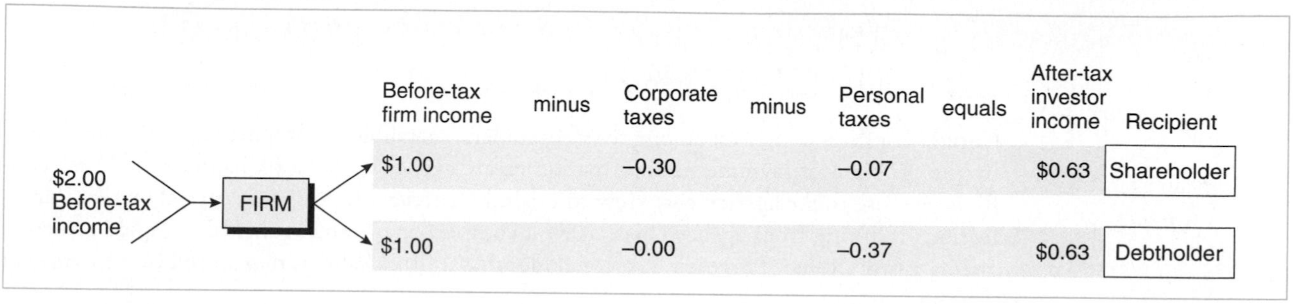

FIGURE 15.6
An example of corporate and personal taxation of cash flows going to shareholders and debtholders.

EXAMPLE Neutral Tax Rates

If $T_e = 10\%$, $T = 30\%$, and $T_d = 37\%$, then Equation (15.7) is satisfied:

$$(1 - 0.37) = (1 - 0.1)(1 - 0.3) = 0.63$$

Figure 15.6 illustrates the tax process using these tax rates. Note once again how the cash flows to the shareholders are taxed twice, whereas those going to the debtholders are taxed only once, but at a higher rate.

It is important to understand that the personal tax view that capital structure is irrelevant depends on having tax rates that satisfy Equation (15.7).

Combined Effect of Corporate and Personal Income Taxes

Suppose tax rates are such that (1) personal taxes do not *exactly* cancel out the corporate tax asymmetry and (2) the single tax rate on debt income is smaller than the combined tax rate on corporate income and equity returns. Then the conclusion of the corporate tax view of capital structure still holds—more leverage increases firm value by reducing the net loss to taxes. But the benefit to leverage is significantly less than if we ignore personal taxes. Therefore, even if personal taxes do not eliminate the corporate tax asymmetry, they significantly reduce it, along with the net benefit to leverage.

We believe—as do most of our colleagues in the finance profession—that there is a net tax benefit to leverage. If so, why don't firms employ 100% leverage? We explore reasons for this in the next three sections of the chapter.

Review

1. What is the personal tax view of capital structure?
2. If $T = 0.3$ and $T_d = 0.35$, what tax rate on equity income T_e leads Equation (15.7) to hold?
3. How can the personal tax view reach the same conclusion as the perfect market view concerning the irrelevance of capital structure?
4. How do personal taxes modify the conclusion of the corporate tax view of capital structure?
5. Explain how the capital gains tax law creates a tax-timing option.

15.3 THE ROLE OF AGENCY COSTS AND FINANCIAL DISTRESS COSTS

Certain conflicts of interest among the debtholders, shareholders, and managers that are caused by the problem of asymmetric information create agency costs (see Chapter 13). These conflicts give rise to the **agency cost view of capital structure.** In this view, capital market imperfections resulting from agency costs create a complex environment in which capital structure affects a firm's value. This view also concludes that a firm's value is maximized by a mixture of debt and equity.

Agency Costs of Debt

A major conflict that arises from the use of debt financing is the possibility that shareholders will expropriate wealth from the debtholders through *asset substitution.* Suppose that debtholders loan money to the firm assuming that the firm will invest in a low-risk project, and therefore they agree to a low interest rate on the loan. If the firm then invests in a (substitute) high-risk project, the risk of the loan will increase. This increases the required return on the loan and lowers the present value of the loan.

As a second example, consider the problem of *claim dilution.* Assume the firm has existing debt and the firm's managers do a leveraged buyout. That is, they take over ownership of the firm with a very small amount of equity financing and a tremendous amount of debt. What happens to the value of the original debt? Because of the higher risk, the present value of the original debt decreases, and the decrease is lost by those debtholders, but gained by the shareholders.[3]

However, the asset substitution and claim dilution agency costs may not be significant for low levels of leverage. Furthermore, the use of leverage may provide some benefits to shareholders. The bondholders will provide some monitoring of management activities that may benefit shareholders. The bond restrictive covenants in bond contracts may also protect shareholders from managerial abuse in addition to protecting bondholders. Small amounts of debt may actually benefit the corporation. Of course, at higher debt levels, the effects of asset substitution and claim dilution could more than offset the agency benefits of debt financing.

Agency conflicts among the firm's various claimants must be resolved in some way. When possible, contracts that eliminate these conflicts are created. For example, restrictive covenants, such as a restriction on leverage, are used to limit potential conflicts. The agency costs of debt tend to increase with leverage. These costs limit how much leverage is beneficial to shareholders.

The trade-off among the agency costs of all the firm's various claimants (stakeholders) leads to the agency cost view. This view holds that the optimal capital structure is a mix of multiple types of securities, rather than simply all debt or all equity. A financing mix reduces the firm's *total* agency costs.

There is also an aspect of debt financing that reduces the firm's agency costs: the costs of the debtholders monitoring the shareholders, and of the shareholders monitoring the managers. Whenever the firm issues new debt, prospective debtholders will analyze the firm very carefully to determine a fair price to offer for the debt. Each time new debt is issued, then, existing debtholders and shareholders are provided with a free outside "audit" of the firm. This outside audit reduces the cost of monitoring to ensure that agents (managers) are acting responsibly.

---

[3]Other debtholder-stockholder conflicts that are relevant to a firm's capital structure include the underinvestment problem and the effect of asset uniqueness.

Debt can also reduce problems of asymmetric information. For example, a sinking fund provides monitoring. With a sinking fund, the firm must be able to meet the periodic required payments in addition to the interest payments. Difficulty in doing so can provide a relatively early warning that the firm is in trouble. Inability to make the required sinking fund payments can trigger default. Obviously, this monitoring function is beneficial for debtholders, but it also provides further monitoring of the managers for the benefit of the shareholders.

Securing debt by using specific tangible assets as collateral can play a role in reducing the agency costs of debt. Secured debt limits the potential for debtholder loss in case of bankruptcy, thereby limiting the amount of wealth shareholders can expropriate from the debtholders. Assets securing a debt instrument cannot be sold without the permission of the debtholders or the bankruptcy court.

Review

1. What is the agency cost view of capital structure?
2. How does increased leverage provide incentives for asset substitution?
3. How does increased leverage lead to claim dilution?

Financial Distress and Bankruptcy Costs

With debt in its capital structure, a firm has an expected cost of bankruptcy. This gives rise to the **bankruptcy cost view of capital structure.** In this view, capital market imperfections associated with financial distress and bankruptcy offset the net benefits from leverage due to taxes and agency costs.

IT IS AN EXPECTED COST Financial distress or bankruptcy costs occur only if financial distress or bankruptcy actually occurs. Therefore, it is important to note that with an ongoing firm that is not in financial distress, the cost is a mathematical expectation. This expected value is considerably less than the actual cost when there is only a small chance of bankruptcy.

The expected cost of financial distress and bankruptcy includes *indirect costs* and *direct costs,* such as notification costs, court costs, and legal fees. Somewhat surprisingly, the direct costs are relatively small when compared to the firm's value or the indirect costs of bankruptcy.

The indirect costs of financial distress and bankruptcy can involve virtually every aspect of the firm. It can be very costly to have management's attention diverted from the day-to-day operation of the business in order to deal with the financial distress and bankruptcy process. After filing for bankruptcy, every major decision a firm makes may require approval by the bankruptcy court. When financial distress occurs, suppliers may refuse to ship goods other than on a COD basis, or even refuse to ship altogether. For example, at one point, K-Mart experienced financial difficulties that led many suppliers to halt shipments of goods.

A firm may lose tax shields during periods of financial distress. This is another tax asymmetry that can affect a firm's value.[4] Loss carryforwards and loss carrybacks are sometimes limited. As a result, some of the corporate tax shields due to leverage may be lost during a period of financial distress. And even if all current losses can be fully carried forward and eventually deducted from future income, the firm still loses the time value of money on the tax shields. So the possibility of lost tax shield value limits the net tax benefits of leverage and makes "too much" leverage undesirable.

The most significant potential cost of financial distress and bankruptcy is an indirect cost that can be difficult to measure but should not be underestimated. It arises because of the possibility that

[4]This loss includes lost tax deductions and lost tax credits. Tax credits are the more valuable of the two. Tax credits offset taxes owed dollar for dollar. Tax deductions reduce taxable income; their value equals the tax rate times the reduction in the amount of taxable income.

the firm will not continue as a going concern. This likelihood is important, because it can dramatically affect the value of the firm's products. Consider the case where consumers believe the firm may not be able to honor warranties, provide service, or even supply replacement parts in the future.[5] Such a belief can dramatically hurt sales, as it once did for a U.S. car manufacturer in financial distress.[6]

When potential customers fear product discontinuation, they will force the firm to sell its product for a lower price than what it would otherwise be worth. The lower price reduces and can easily eliminate the manufacturer's profit margin on the product. This forgone profit can be very substantial. In fact, even though it is an opportunity cost that is difficult to measure, *this loss is the largest of the financial distress and bankruptcy costs by a wide margin.*

EFFECT OF LEVERAGE The expected costs of financial distress and bankruptcy depend in part on the uniqueness, or degree of specialization, of the firm's assets. The higher the degree of specialization, the lower the degree of liquidity and the greater the sales transaction costs. In the extreme case, a specially designed piece of equipment that is unique to just one firm's production process might be worth only its scrap value if the firm goes bankrupt.

An argument similar to the argument concerning specialized assets also applies to a firm's type of assets: A firm with primarily tangible assets can borrow more than an otherwise comparable firm with primarily intangible assets (such as patents and trademarks). Intangible assets are less liquid and have higher sales transaction costs than tangible assets, and their value may be more firm specific. The values of patents and trademarks depend on how they are used and on past conditions. Another firm may not be able to realize as much value from them. For example, the good-service reputation of a trademark product may be damaged or even destroyed by bad service resulting from otherwise unrelated financial distress problems. As a consequence, firms with more intangible assets have larger expected bankruptcy costs.

The effect on capital structure of possible financial distress and bankruptcy costs is as follows. Suppose all other factors—such as personal and corporate taxes, agency costs, and other transaction costs—combined create a net value benefit to leverage, thereby making leverage desirable. But leverage will be desirable only up to a certain point because, as the firm increases its debt financing, expected bankruptcy costs also increase and offset that benefit. So bankruptcy costs reduce the net value benefit of leverage and make "too much" leverage undesirable. (Of course, if there were no net benefit to leverage from all the other factors combined, expected bankruptcy costs would make it so that even the first dollar of leverage would reduce a firm's value and therefore be undesirable.)

The bankruptcy effect produces an "optimal" capital structure that balances the expected bankruptcy cost off against the other benefits. This is similar to the net effect of the various agency costs. Also like agency costs, a solution is hard to quantify. The bankruptcy view, however, is more realistic than the corporate tax view, because it does not call for the extreme of 100% debt financing.

Review

1. What is the bankruptcy cost view of capital structure?
2. Describe the difference between the direct and indirect costs of financial distress and bankruptcy. Which is more significant?
3. Explain why "too much" leverage is undesirable if the firm may lose tax shields.
4. Why do tangible assets support higher leverage than intangible assets?

---

[5]Additional coverage of consumer-firm conflicts is contained in Chapter 13.

[6]This possibility helped convince the U.S. Congress to provide loan guarantees for the Chrysler Corporation when it was in financial distress. The loan guarantees made Chrysler's warranties and promises of future service and parts availability believable.

15.4 EXTERNAL FINANCING TRANSACTION COSTS

The transaction costs associated with obtaining new external financing can play an important role in a firm's capital structure decisions. As in the case of bankruptcy, there are both direct and indirect costs. These costs lead to the **pecking order view of capital structure.** In the pecking order view, firms use internally generated funds as much as possible for financing new projects. New debt is less preferred than internal funds, but more preferable than other sources of financing. Debt-equity combinations, such as convertible debt, are third in the pecking order, with securities that have smaller proportions of equity being preferred to those with larger proportions of equity. Last in the pecking order is new external equity.

The cost of obtaining new financing affects the firm's management of its capital structure. These costs affect the firm's capital structure decisions over time in a dynamic way. We touched on this dynamic dimension in Chapter 8 when we said that the transaction costs connected with additional financing are a legitimate reason for capital rationing.

The transaction costs associated with obtaining new external financing make it much more costly for a firm to sell a series of small issues compared to issuing a single large amount when it needs to obtain additional external funds. So the firm should sell larger issues, less often, to reduce the net transaction costs of new external financing.

The idea of issuing a relatively large amount of a security when the firm obtains new external financing does not imply a preference for any particular method of financing. However, it does imply that the dynamic management of the firm's capital structure is important to the value of the firm. A firm can waste resources on issuance expenses if it does not manage its capital structure carefully.

Concerning particular methods, the total cost of new debt (negotiating private debt or the combination of the underwriting spread and direct issuance expenses connected with public debt) is typically lower than the total cost of obtaining other new external financing. Therefore, whether or not other factors create a net value benefit to leverage, debt is generally attractive *relative* to equity when a firm has already decided that it is going to obtain additional outside financing.

Signaling and the Choice of Financing Method

A firm's decision of how to finance a project reflects its choice of capital structure. It may also convey information about the project and about how the firm's managers view its current market value.

Consider two examples. The first illustrates how the choice between internal (equity) and external financing can convey information about project value. The second illustrates how the debt-equity choice can convey information about any perceived under- or overvaluation of the firm's shares.

EXAMPLE Internal Financing Versus Issuing Securities

Two firms, G and N, are identical except for new projects they are about to undertake. G has a good project that has a large positive NPV, whereas N has a neutral project that has a zero NPV. The owners of G are eager to provide the financing for the new project themselves, using personal funds so that they alone will earn the large expected NPV. In contrast, the owners of N are indifferent to allowing outside investors to invest in the new project because it has a zero NPV. Generalizing the argument, then, the percentage of owner financing may provide a signal of the owners' opinion of investment opportunities.

EXAMPLE Debt Versus Equity Financing

Suppose the shareholders know the firm is currently overvalued. They would like to have partners to share in the decline in market value that will take place in the future when others realize the firm is overvalued. Suppose instead they know the firm is currently undervalued. Then they would not want to have new partners who will get a share of the increase in market value that will take place in the future when others realize the firm is undervalued. Shareholders of properly valued firms would be indifferent to having new partners.

This leads to the idea that if additional financing is needed, the firm will choose debt or equity depending on whether or not they want new partners. That is, undervalued firms will issue new debt, whereas overvalued firms will issue new equity. Of course, in this simple world we have just described, shareholders of overvalued firms may not want to be identified as such. Therefore, they may try to imitate undervalued firms by issuing debt instead of equity. Situations such as this will require other information to allow investors to interpret the firm's actions.

Sometimes firms with existing publicly traded stock issue additional new shares. Apparently, therefore, there are cases where managers believe a new project is sufficiently good to justify the potential loss connected with issuing new equity.

One way in which firms may try to overcome the negative impression of issuing additional new shares is to use underwriters, rather than selling securities themselves. This can be especially useful if there is a need to protect trade secrets. The underwriter may be able to "certify" the value of the firm and its new projects by standing ready to purchase all the new shares without revealing (and therefore destroying the value of) certain types of private information.

Changes in Capital Structure

Evidence indicates that the stock market reacts favorably to increases in leverage and negatively to decreases in leverage. Investors apparently interpret an increase in leverage as a signal that the firm's prospects have improved. Its future cash flow will support greater leverage. A decrease in leverage signals the opposite. Weaker prospects reduce the firm's ability to service debt.

Review

1. Why do transaction costs make it more costly to sell a series of small issues as compared to a single large issue?
2. Based on the transaction costs of obtaining funds, what is the pecking order among internally generated funds, external debt financing, external debt-equity financing (such as convertible debt), and external equity?
3. Why is internal financing often a more positive signal about the firm than external financing?
4. Why is debt financing often a more positive signal about the firm than equity financing?
5. Explain how using underwriters might help a firm to reduce the negative impression connected with issuing additional new shares.

15.5 FINANCIAL LEVERAGE CLIENTELES

Both personal tax and corporate tax considerations affect the desirability of a particular capital structure. Investors will take their own tax situations into account in deciding whether to invest in a particular firm. The idea that investors "sort" themselves into groups, where each group prefers the firms it invests in to follow a certain type of policy, is called the **clientele effect.**

How the Clientele Effect Works

When applied to financial leverage, the clientele effect refers to those investors who prefer a particular type of security or capital structure. A similar concept in marketing is called *market segmentation.* A market segment is an identifiable group of consumers who purchase a product with particular attributes distinct from the attributes of alternative products. An example would be a market segment that buys luxury cars versus one that buys economy cars.

The existence of various leverage clienteles mitigates some, but not all, of the arguments in favor of capital structure relevance. With respect to taxes, some securities may be a more or less attractive investment for certain investors. For example, investors with a high marginal income tax rate may find debt securities less attractive, whereas tax-exempt investors may find debt securities relatively more attractive. Similarly, investors with a low marginal income tax rate may prefer firm leverage to personal leverage because of the higher corporate tax rate. The interest expenses generate more tax savings for the corporation than they would for an individual if the corporation has the higher tax rate. Investors can increase their risk and lower combined corporate and personal taxes (and avoid transaction costs of personal leverage) by simply investing in a firm that already has their preferred amount of leverage.

Taxes and transaction costs reduce the return to shareholders. Therefore, investors should, and do, invest in securities that minimize their aggregate taxes and transaction costs for any particular combination of risk and return. The result of taking taxes and transaction costs into account is that a particular clientele group may pay a premium for a certain type of security. (Note that the premium is measured relative to the prices of securities that are equivalent.) Such a premium gives firms an incentive to follow particular policies that appeal to various clientele groups. Of course, this is simply another application of the Principle of Valuable Ideas: Being the first to have the idea has the potential to create value.

The result is that it may be possible to earn a premium for supplying a security or capital structure policy that is in short supply. (Note that this gain must be weighed against the transaction costs of investors' rearranging their security holdings.) Whenever a law is changed that affects the taxes and transaction costs for a particular financial leverage clientele, opportunities may arise for a firm to earn a positive NPV by changing its capital structure.

Practical Limitations

Opportunities to profit from capital structure changes have natural limitations. First, direct transaction costs to the firm reduce the potential benefit from a change in capital structure. Second, shareholder transaction costs make it expensive for investors to buy and sell shares, and this can affect the market price of the firm's stock.

These factors make sudden or frequent shifts in a firm's capital structure generally undesirable. A sudden shift may be disruptive to the firm's stock price in the near term, and frequent major shifts may be disruptive over the longer term.

In practice, most firms maintain a stable capital structure. It appears, then, that firms depart from a stable capital structure only when the managers believe there are valid reasons to do so. These reasons include significant changes in the firm's investment opportunities, its earnings, or its own or its shareholders' tax position.

Review

1. Explain what is meant by the clientele effect.
2. According to the clientele effect, investors with low marginal income tax rates should prefer to invest in firms with high leverage. Do you agree? Explain.
3. How might a firm profit when a change in tax law causes a particular financial leverage clientele to change its investment preferences?

15.6 THE CAPITAL MARKET IMPERFECTIONS VIEW OF CAPITAL STRUCTURE

Taken in total, the view that emerges from the various factors we have discussed can be characterized as a dynamic process that involves various trade-offs and results in a general preference order among a firm's financing alternatives. We call this the **capital market imperfections view of capital structure.** In this view, debt is generally valuable.

With a low amount of leverage, there is little chance of incurring financial distress, so the *expected* value of the costs of financial distress is low. Therefore, an increase in leverage at lower levels offers benefits from taxes and agency considerations (monitoring and reducing asymmetric information problems). At lower levels of leverage, these benefits dominate the combination of agency costs (misbehavior) and expected costs of financial distress. At some point, the set of costs overcome the set of benefits. Along the way, dynamic considerations involving transaction costs, asymmetric information considerations, and monitoring benefits also affect the attractiveness of the various alternative types of financing at particular points in time.

The firm's choice of capital structure, then, is a dynamic process that involves all these various considerations in conjunction with its investment opportunities and the amount of internal funds it is able to generate. The firm "factors them all in" when deciding on the type, amount, and timing of new external financing.

Total Market Value and Market Imperfections

The optimal capital structure is the one that maximizes the firm's total value. Figure 15.7 is a conceptual picture of the effect on firm value of all the various factors we have examined. It is not as complicated as it looks. Let's walk through it. In the figure, V_T is the value of the unleveraged firm plus the net tax benefits. V_A is the agency cost of debt. V_A is initially positive, because of the benefits from monitoring and reducing problems of asymmetric information, and shows that leverage can actually be beneficial to the firm. At higher amounts of leverage, this benefit begins declining and becomes negative because of conflicts of interest. V_B is the expected financial distress and bankruptcy costs, which are zero for low amounts of leverage, but ever-increasingly negative for the firm when leverage increases. Finally, V_L is the total value of the leveraged firm, including the effects of taxes, agency costs, and financial distress costs.

Let's summarize. For low amounts of leverage, the tax benefit and the agency considerations lead to increases in the total value of the firm. Eventually, however, the negative effects consisting of the expected costs of financial distress, bankruptcy, and agency considerations offset the benefits, resulting in an optimal capital structure at the point in the figure where the total value of the firm is at its maximum.

It is important to understand that Figure 15.7 is only a "snapshot"; it cannot include the dynamic considerations that transaction costs, asymmetric information considerations, and monitoring benefits connected with external financing introduce into the picture. These managerial considerations mean that the "optimal" capital structure is not a simple fixed proportion of debt financing.

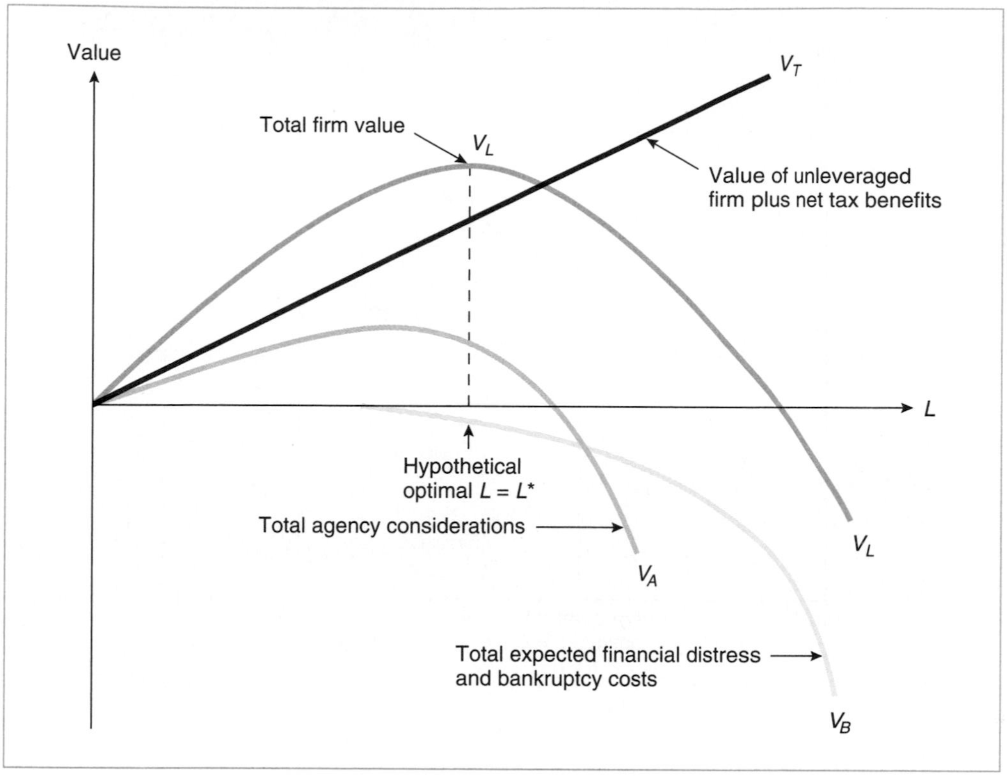

FIGURE 15.7
The capital market imperfections view of capital structure.

The Cost of Capital and Market Imperfections

Figure 15.7 illustrates the capital market imperfections view in terms of a firm's total value. Once again, the view can be represented in a corresponding way in terms of the firm's WACC, its weighted average cost of capital. The optimal capital structure is the point where firm value reaches its maximum by minimizing the firm's WACC.

Figure 15.8 illustrates the capital market imperfections view of capital structure that takes into account all of the factors we have discussed. In Figure 15.8, WACC is expressed in terms of hypothetical functions of r_d and r_e.

Figure 15.8 is a "snapshot" like Figure 15.7. So the firm's optimal capital structure is in truth more complex than these figures indicate. Although Figure 15.8 provides a visual aid to understanding the impact of capital structure on the WACC, we need an equation for WACC to determine more precise values.

The Net Benefit to Leverage

To capture the impact of *all* the relevant dimensions connected with debt financing, define T^* as the **net-benefit-to-leverage factor.** T^* is assumed to be derived from a linear approximation to the actual net-benefit-to-leverage relationship over some relevant range of values for the leverage ratio L. T^* allows us to operationalize the total impact of leverage on firm value in the capital market imperfections view. We can use the same sort of mathematics we used with the corporate tax view to adjust the WACC for all of the relevant factors. In this more general case, we can express the value of the leveraged firm as

$$V_L = V_U + T^*D = \frac{\overline{I}(1-T)}{r} + \frac{T^* r_d D}{r_d} \qquad (15.8)$$

which is a generalization of Equation (15.5).

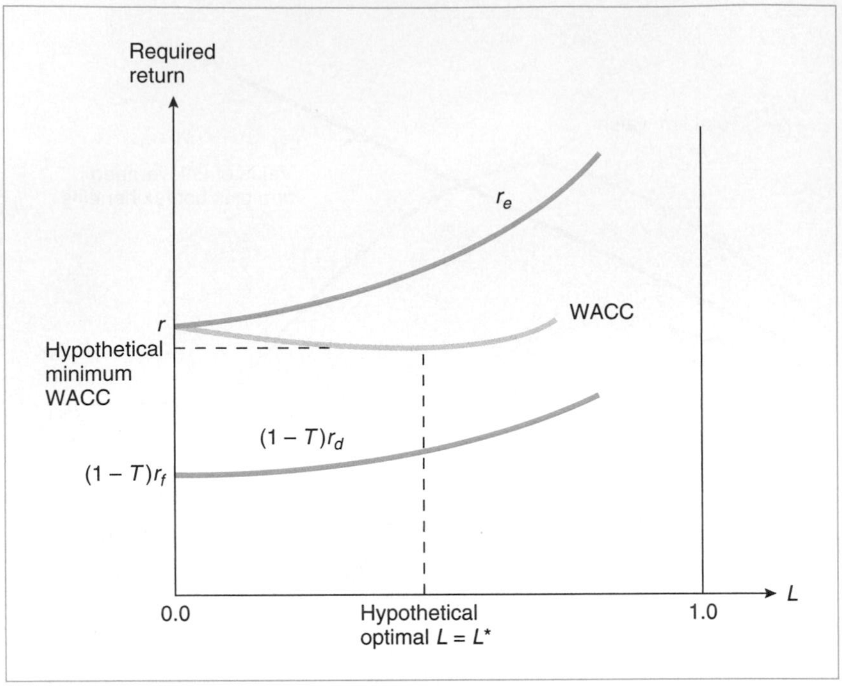

FIGURE 15.8 WACC (weighted average cost of capital), r_e (required return for equity), and r_d (required return for debt), as hypothetical functions of L (the leverage ratio) under the capital market imperfections view of capital structure.

Once again, V_L can be viewed as being made up of two components. The first component is the basic value of the firm if it is unleveraged, V_U. The second component is the net benefit to leverage. Each component represents the present value of a stream of expected future cash flows. The first stream is $\bar{I}(1 - T)$, the firm's after-tax income each period, its CFAT. The second stream is the net benefit from maintaining an amount D of debt. This net benefit can be expressed as T^* times the interest payment each period, or $T^* r_d D$.

For the perpetuity case, the present value is simply these cash flow streams divided by their required returns. The required return for the firm's (unleveraged) after-tax income stream, its CFAT, is r. Because of lower risk, the required return for the net-benefit-to-leverage stream is r_d, which is lower than r.

Finally, the parallel is completed by expressing the impact on firm value in terms of the firm's WACC (its required return). As before, we will not prove it, but the result is

$$\text{WACC} = r(1 - T^* L) \tag{15.9}$$

The usefulness of Equation (15.9) is based on how easily it fits into our framework for making capital budgeting decisions. It is simply an adjustment made to the project's cost of capital, which accounts for the effect of leverage on project value. The adjusted rate is then used to compute the present value of the project's CFATs, its NPV.

Total Firm Value and Capital Market Imperfections

There is one final point we want to make. All of the views of capital structure, beyond that of a perfect capital market, are based on minimizing the value lost to one or more imperfections. Therefore, even though we talk about using leverage to increase firm value, in fact we are actually describing ways to use leverage to *reduce the loss* connected with various imperfections. What this means is that the total value of the firm is never more than what it would be in a

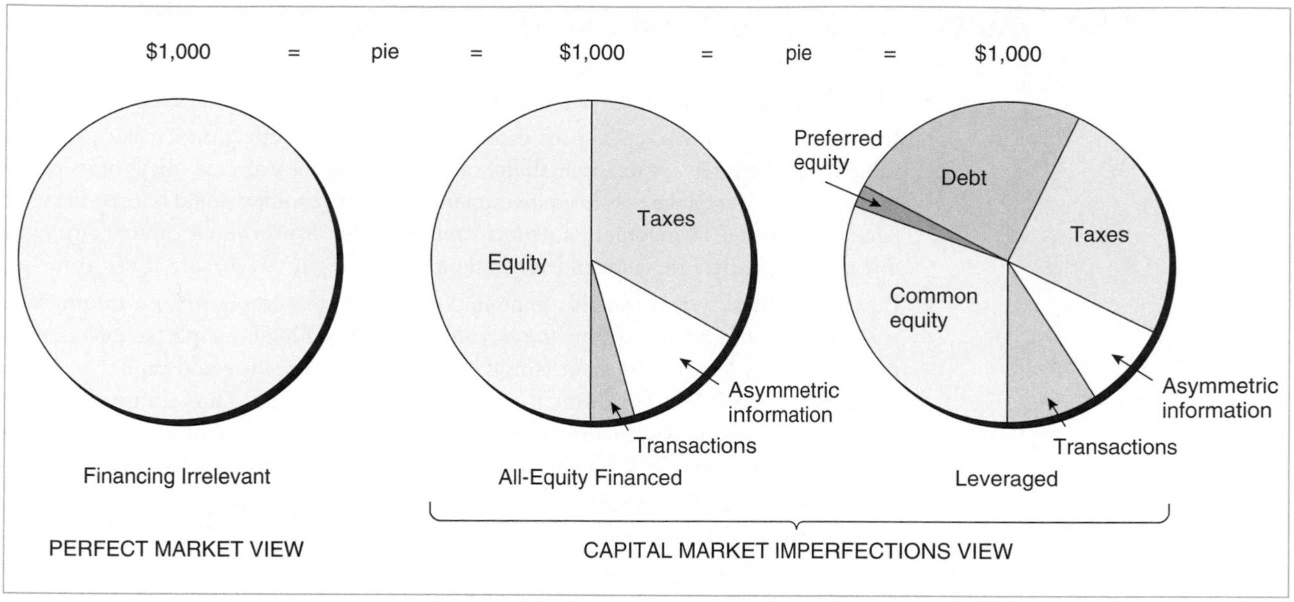

FIGURE 15.9
These three "pie" views of capital structure illustrate the loss of firm value from all the various capital market imperfections and the minimization of that loss through the choice of capital structure.

perfect capital market. We illustrate this point in Figure 15.9 by using three "pie" views of a $1,000 firm.

In Figure 15.9 the far-left "pie" shows the perfect market view. In it, there is no loss in value from imperfections. A firm's value does not depend on its capital structure. The other two pies reflect the capital market imperfections view of capital structure. In them, a dynamic optimal capital structure minimizes the total loss from all the various imperfections. In the middle pie, the firm is all-equity financed. In the far-right pie, the firm has multiple types and amounts of financing that might typically be found in the practice of financial management.

The net benefit to leverage can be seen in Figure 15.9. It is the difference between the value of the firm on the far right (the combined values of common equity, preferred equity, and debt) and the value of the firm in the middle pie (the equity value). However, despite this positive net benefit to leverage, the total value of the firm on the far right is substantially less than the firm value would be in a perfect capital market. This is because of losses to capital market imperfections.

Review

1. What is the capital market imperfections view of capital structure?
2. What is the shape of the WACC curve according to the capital market imperfections view?
3. What is the net-benefit-to-leverage factor?
4. Suppose the net-benefit-to-leverage factor is $T^* = 0.20$. How would you interpret this value?

SUMMARY

- The critical issue concerning capital structure is whether it affects the value of the firm.
- In a perfect capital market, a firm's capital structure has no effect on its value. A firm's value is based entirely on the profitability of its assets and the expected NPVs of its future projects. Even if leverage enhanced investment value, shareholders could borrow to create personal leverage. Therefore, in a perfect capital market, firms cannot capture any value due to leverage, because shareholders can do it themselves just as cheaply as the firm.
- But our financial system contains some important persistent imperfections. Information is not costless and freely available to everyone, so the Signaling Principle (actions contain information) is a very important consideration. Capital structure and capital structure changes may provide information about the firm to the public. Thus, a firm should be careful to choose the best method of financing, taking all costs into account—including the information investors will infer from the firm's financing transactions.
- There are other market imperfections. The system of corporate income taxation imposes a bias in favor of debt over equity, as do issuance costs.
- However, the system of individual income taxation, as well as direct and indirect financial distress/bankruptcy costs, have an opposite bias.
- Aggregate agency costs and tax-timing options both favor a mix of debt and equity rather than using one or the other exclusively. Taken together, these market imperfections lead to a view that there is some dynamic optimal capital structure that maximizes the value of a firm.
- The clientele effect, where individuals make investments in firms that have capital structures that are best for the individuals, may mitigate some of these considerations. Changes in laws, particularly the tax code, sometimes create a demand for new types of securities or alter the demand for existing ones. Such changes in demand may in turn create profitable opportunities for a firm to supply a particular type of security to satisfy this new demand.
- Firms manage their capital structures carefully. Choosing an appropriate capital structure balances the net tax advantage against the (1) agency costs, (2) larger expected cost of financial distress, and (3) cost of reduced financial flexibility from additional debt. Simultaneously, transaction costs and information effects must also be considered. Unfortunately, these costs cannot be measured precisely. As a result, the "best" capital structure cannot be precisely determined.

EQUATION SUMMARY

$$\text{WACC} = (1 - L)r_e + L(1 - T)r_d \tag{15.1}$$

$$V_U = \frac{\bar{I}(1 - T)}{r} \tag{15.2}$$

$$V_L = \frac{\bar{I}(1 - T)}{\text{WACC}} \tag{15.3}$$

$$V_L = \frac{\bar{I}(1 - T)}{r} + \frac{Tr_d D}{r_d} = \frac{\bar{I}(1 - T)}{r} + TD \tag{15.4}$$

$$V_L = V_U + TD \tag{15.5}$$

$$\text{WACC} = r(1 - TL) \tag{15.6}$$

$$(1 - T_d) = (1 - T_e)(1 - T) \tag{15.7}$$

$$V_L = V_U + T^* D = \frac{\bar{I}(1 - T)}{r} + \frac{T^* r_d D}{r_d} \tag{15.8}$$

$$\text{WACC} = r(1 - T^* L) \tag{15.9}$$

QUESTIONS

1. Briefly explain the corporate tax view of capital structure.
2. Give an example of a tax-timing option and explain why it is valuable.
3. Cite an example of how transaction costs might affect a firm's choice of financing.
4. Define the term *leverage clientele.*
5. Briefly explain in your own words why taxes would not be asymmetric if Equation (15.7) holds.
6. What is the shape of the WACC curve according to the perfect market view?
7. What is the shape of the WACC curve according to the capital market imperfections view?
8. Briefly explain how the personal tax view of capital structure mitigates the corporate tax view.
9. True or false: The *direct* costs connected with financial distress and bankruptcy are large as a proportion of the value of the firm.
10. True or false: The *direct* costs connected with financial distress and bankruptcy are much larger than the indirect, implicit opportunity costs such as lost sales, depressed product price, and lost tax credits.
11. Why might potential new equity investors in a firm be leery of buying newly issued stock in a firm?
12. Why should a firm's ability to use tax credits affect its capital structure?
13. Describe the capital market imperfections view of capital structure.

CHALLENGING QUESTIONS

14. Explain how financial distress can affect the value of the firm through its tax credits, even when a firm is able to use completely all tax credits via loss carryforwards.
15. Suppose that a firm is operating with neutral corporate and personal taxes in an otherwise perfect capital market and Equation (15.7) currently holds. In such a world, a firm would never take on any risky debt. Why not? (*Hint:* Consider what would happen in financial distress.)
16. Leverage increases the risk (and therefore the required return) of equityholders. Above some point, an increase in leverage also increases the risk (and required return) of debtholders. How is it possible, then, that in a perfect capital market environment, the weighted average of the two is constant because both required returns are increasing?
17. How can restrictive debt covenants reduce agency costs?
18. Why might a firm that manufactures a unique product using specialized employee expertise tend to finance with less debt than an otherwise identical firm that manufactures a generic product?
19. What is the basis for the view that a firm's total market value is invariant to its choice of capital structure? Cite three broad types of capital market imperfections that can cause the capital structure of a firm to have an effect on the value of that firm. Give three examples (one for each type) where such an imperfection would cause a firm's capital structure to have an effect on the value of that firm. Explain *how* each of the three examples you gave would cause a firm's capital structure to have an effect on the value of that firm.

20. A journalist once commented that the trouble with U.S. corporations was obvious from reading their balance sheets: They owed more money than they had! His conclusion was based on the firm's debt being larger than its equity. How would you respond to such a comment? (Think about it before responding.)
21. The good fairy has decided to smile upon you and has offered you a choice between two "great" outcomes. The alternatives concern an investment that has the same risk as the market portfolio and requires an initial investment of $10 million. The alternatives are: (1) the cost of financing for the investment will be three standard deviations less than the current average market required return for financing such investments, but the investment will have an otherwise zero NPV or (2) the expected future cash inflows from the investment will be three standard deviations larger than those that would make the investment have a zero NPV, but the cost of financing for the investment will be at the current average market required return for financing such investments. Therefore, either alternative will provide you with a positive-NPV investment. Alternative 1 does so by virtue of "great" financing, whereas alternative 2 does so by virtue of "great" investing. Which alternative should you choose, and why?

PROBLEMS

LEVEL A (BASIC)

A1. (Calculating a leverage ratio) William Bates is contemplating starting a new firm that will provide background music for elevators, dentist offices, and the like. He estimates a positive NPV of $270,000 for the investment. Mr. Bates plans to call the firm Tarry-Tune, Unlimited. He estimates that the initial investment needed to start Tarry-Tune is $325,000. He plans to borrow $200,000 of the initial investment. What is the expected leverage ratio, L, for Tarry-Tune?

A2. (Calculating a leverage ratio) Jane Guydosh is contemplating starting a new firm that will provide carpet cleaning services for the downtown metropolitan area. She estimates a positive NPV of $150,000 for the investment. Ms. Guydosh plans to call the firm Jane's Carpet Cleaning Co. She estimates that the initial investment needed to start Jane's Carpet Cleaning Co. is $120,000. She plans to borrow $80,000 of the initial investment. What is the expected leverage ratio, L, for Jane's Carpet Cleaning Co.?

A3. (Taxes, leverage, and WACC) Suppose a firm is unleveraged and has an unleveraged required return, $r = 15\%$. The firm borrows 30% of the value of the firm at $r_d = 8\%$. Because of the financial leverage, r_e becomes 18%. What is the firm's WACC:

a. Assuming the firm is operating in a perfect capital market (including no taxes)?

b. Assuming there are only corporate taxes at a rate of 35% in an otherwise perfect capital market?

A4. (Taxes, leverage, and WACC) Suppose a firm is unleveraged and has an unleveraged required return of $r = 15\%$. The firm borrows 40% of the value of the firm at $r_d = 9\%$. Because of the financial leverage, r_e becomes 19%. What is the firm's WACC:

a. Assuming the firm is operating in a perfect capital market (including no taxes)?

b. Assuming there are only corporate taxes at a rate of 40% in an otherwise perfect capital market?

A5. (Value of firm and WACC) Suppose a firm currently has an unleveraged required return of 13% and perpetual unleveraged after-tax income of $100,000 per year. The firm has come up with an investment opportunity that would alter the firm's asset makeup so that it would increase its perpetual unleveraged after-tax income to $120,000 per year. Because the new asset mix is riskier, the firm's unleveraged required return would also increase to 15%. Should the firm undertake this investment opportunity?

A6. (Corporate taxes and firm value) Jahera Mines issues $50,000,000 of perpetual new debt paying 9% interest. Jahera is in the 40% marginal income tax bracket. Assume no market imperfections except corporate taxes.

a. What are the annual tax savings that result from the debt financing?

b. What is the increase in the value of Jahera Mines that results from this debt issue?

A7. (Corporate taxes and firm value) Radguard issues $100,000,000 of perpetual new debt paying 8% interest. Radguard is in the 40% marginal income tax bracket. Assume no market imperfections except corporate taxes.

a. What are the annual tax savings that result from the debt financing?

b. What is the increase in the value of Radguard that results from this debt issue?

A8. (Corporate taxes and leverage) Caples Communications is evaluating how to finance the firm. Caples expects to have a perpetual operating cash flow of $1,000 and a marginal tax rate of 40%. As an unleveraged firm, Caples will have a cost of capital of 12%. As a leveraged firm, Caples will issue $3,000 of perpetual debt paying 8% interest.

a. Assume that Caples chooses to be an all-equity (unleveraged) firm. What is the after-tax cash flow to stockholders? What is the value of Caples as an unleveraged firm?

b. Assume that Caples chooses the leveraged capital structure. What is the after-tax cash flow to stockholders and bondholders of the leveraged firm? What is the value of the unleveraged firm? What is the leveraged firm's cost of capital?

c. What accounts for the difference in the value of the two firms?

A9. (Corporate taxes and leverage) WRIT is evaluating how to finance the firm. WRIT expects to have a perpetual operating cash flow of $2,000 and a marginal tax rate of 40%. As an unleveraged firm, WRIT will have a cost of capital of 14%. As a leveraged firm, WRIT will issue $2,500 of perpetual debt paying 8% interest.

a. Assume WRIT chooses to be an all-equity (unleveraged) firm. What is the after-tax cash flow to stockholders? What is the value of WRIT as an unleveraged firm?

b. Assume WRIT chooses the leveraged capital structure. What is the after-tax cash flow to stockholders and bondholders of the leveraged firm? What is the value of the unleveraged firm? What is the leveraged firm's cost of capital?

c. What accounts for the difference in the value of the two companies?

A10. (Corporate taxes and leverage) An unleveraged firm has a perpetual operating cash flow of $100, a marginal tax rate of 40%, and an unleveraged cost of capital of 10%. An otherwise identical firm is leveraged with $400 of perpetual debt paying 8% interest.

a. What is the after-tax cash flow to stockholders of the unleveraged firm? What is the value of the unleveraged firm?

b. What is the after-tax cash flow to stockholders and bondholders of the leveraged firm? What is the value of the unleveraged firm? What is the leveraged firm's cost of capital?

c. What accounts for the difference in the value of the two firms?

A11. (Corporate and personal taxes) Sarin Software Corporation has a corporate tax rate of 30%, its bondholders have a personal tax rate of 30%, and the effective tax rate that its stockholders pay is 20%.

a. Sarin has $100 of before-tax cash flows, which it pays as interest to its bondholders. What is the total corporate and personal tax on this cash flow? What is after-tax bondholder income?

b. Sarin has $100 of before-tax cash flows. After corporate taxes, it is distributing the balance to stockholders. What is the total corporate and personal tax on this cash flow? What is after-tax stockholder income?

c. Are these tax rates neutral? Which form of financing is favored, debt or equity financing?

A12. (Corporate and personal taxes) RST Inc. has a corporate tax rate of 40%, its bondholders have a personal tax rate of 30%, and the effective tax rate that its stockholders pay is 25%.

a. RST has $500 of before-tax cash flows, which it pays as interest to its bondholders. What is the total corporate and personal tax on this cash flow? What is after-tax bondholder income?

b. RST has $500 of before-tax cash flows. After corporate taxes, it distributes the balance to stockholders. What is the total corporate and personal tax on this cash flow? What is after-tax stockholder income?

c. Are these tax rates neutral? Which form of financing is favored, debt or equity financing?

A13. (Corporate and personal taxes) LaPlante Corporation has a corporate tax rate of 30%, its bondholders have a personal tax rate of 44%, and the effective tax rate that its stockholders pay is 20%.

a. LaPlante has $100 of before-tax cash flows, which it pays as interest to its bondholders. What is the total corporate and personal tax on this cash flow? What is after-tax bondholder income?

b. LaPlante has $100 of before-tax cash flows. After corporate taxes, it distributes the balance to stockholders. What is the total corporate and personal tax on this cash flow? What is after-tax stockholder income?

c. Are these tax rates neutral? Which form of financing is favored, debt or equity financing?

A14. (Excel: WACC) The managers of Dadalt Company expect the before-tax costs of debt and equity as a function of the firm's capital structure that are shown here. Dadalt's tax rate is 25%.

a. Calculate the WACC for each amount of leverage.

b. Plot the after-tax costs of debt and equity and the WACC as a function of L.

c. What is Dadalt's optimal capital strucure?

DEBT (L)	**0.0**	**0.1**	**0.2**	**0.3**	**0.4**	**0.5**	**0.6**	**0.7**	**0.8**
r_d (%)	—	8.0	8.1	8.3	8.5	8.8	9.1	9.5	10.0
r_e (%)	12.0	12.1	12.2	12.5	13.0	13.5	14.2	15.6	17.0

LEVEL B

B1. (Leveraged and unleveraged returns) You invest $12,000 in Joe's Garage, Inc., borrowing $5,000 of the money at 10%. If you expect to earn 24% on your investment under this arrangement, what would you expect to earn if you put up the entire $12,000 from your own money? Ignore taxes.

B2. (Leveraged and unleveraged returns) You invest $50,000 in George's House Painting Inc., borrowing $30,000 of the money at 9%. If you expect to earn 20% on your investment under this arrangement, what would you expect to earn if you put up the entire $50,000 from your own money? Ignore taxes.

B3. (Capital structure arbitrage) Consider two firms operating in a perfect capital market environment. Each will generate $10 million of operating income, and they are identical in every other respect, except that firm L has debt in its capital structure and firm U has an all-equity capital structure. Suppose that investors currently value L as indicated in Table 15.1, but the market value of the equity in U is $65 million. According to the perfect market view, this situation cannot persist. Suppose an investor owns 1% of the shares of U. Show how this owner can profit from arbitrage.

B4. (Capital structure arbitrage) Miles's Manor, an unassuming resort in midstate Pennsylvania, currently has an all-equity capital structure. Miles's Manor has an expected income of \$10,000 per year forever and a required return to equity of 16%. There are no personal taxes, but Miles's pays corporate taxes at the rate of 35%. All transactions take place in an otherwise perfect capital market.

a. What is Miles's Manor worth?

b. How much will the value of the firm increase if Miles's Manor leverages the firm by borrowing half the value of the unleveraged firm at an interest rate of 10% and the leverage causes the required return on equity to increase to 18.89%?

B5. (Corporate and personal taxes) Dick's Pet-Way Corporation (DPC) is a chain of pet stores that has an expected cash inflow of \$1,000 each year forever. DPC's required return is 20% per year. Assume all of DPC's income is paid out to the firm's investors.

a. If DPC is all-equity financed and there are no taxes, what would DPC be worth in a perfect capital market?

Now suppose DPC's corporate tax rate is 30%.

b. If DPC is all-equity financed and there are no personal taxes, what would DPC be worth in an otherwise perfect capital market?

In addition to corporate taxes, suppose DPC borrows \$1,400 at a required return on the debt of 10%. (Note: Because of risk, the required return on equity increases to 23.89%.)

c. If there are no personal taxes, what would DPC be worth in an otherwise perfect capital market? What would be DPC's leverage ratio, L?

d. If there are personal taxes on debt income at a rate of 37%, and personal taxes on equity income at a rate of 10%, what would DPC be worth in an otherwise perfect capital market?

e. If there are personal taxes on debt income at a rate of 25%, and personal taxes on equity income at a rate of 10%, what would DPC be worth in an otherwise perfect capital market?

f. Finally, compute the value of DPC as a 35.7% leveraged firm, with a 10% interest rate on the debt when there are no taxes at all in a perfect capital market.

B6. (Cost of capital) The Query Company has identified two alternative capital structures. If the firm borrows 15% of the value of the firm, it can borrow the money at $r_d = 10\%$, and the shareholders will have a required return of $r_e = 18\%$. If the firm borrows 45% of the value of the firm, it can borrow the money at $r_d = 12\%$, and the shareholders will have a required return of $r_e = 23.21\%$. Query pays corporate taxes at the rate of 35%. Which capital structure should Query adopt? If Query is operating in an essentially perfect capital market except for taxes, are the taxes approximately symmetric, or are they asymmetric?

B7. (Cost of capital) ACE Corp. has identified two alternative capital structures. If the firm borrows 25% of the value of the firm, it can borrow the money at $r_d = 9\%$, and the shareholders will have a required return of $r_e = 17\%$. If the firm borrows 50% of the value of the firm, it can borrow the money at $r_d = 11\%$, and the shareholders will have a required return of $r_e = 21.6\%$. ACE pays corporate taxes at the rate of 40%. Which capital structure should ACE adopt? If ACE is operating in an essentially perfect capital market except for taxes, are the taxes approximately symmetric, or are they asymmetric?

B8. (Excel: Leverage, taxes, and WACC) The RTE Corporation expects to pay a dividend next year of \$2.22. It expects its cash dividends to grow 5% per year forever. RTE has a debt ratio of $L = 35\%$. Its borrowing rate is $r_d = 9\%$. RTE pays corporate taxes at the rate of 30%. If $r_f = 6\%$, $r_M = 12\%$, and RTE's common stock is currently selling for \$20 per share:

a. What is the current (leveraged) required return, r_e, on RTE's common stock?

b. What is RTE's WACC?

c. What is RTE's unleveraged required return, r?

d. What unleveraged beta is implied by r?

B9. (Excel: Leverage, taxes, and WACC) The LPE Corporation expects to pay a dividend next year of $1.50. It expects its cash dividends to grow 6% per year forever. LPE has a debt ratio of $L = 20\%$. Its borrowing rate is $r_d = 6\%$. LPE pays corporate taxes at the rate of 25%. If $r_f = 4\%$, $r_M = 10\%$, and LPE's common stock is currently selling for $17 per share:

a. What is the current (leveraged) required return, r_e, on LPE's common stock?

b. What is LPE's WACC?

c. What is LPE's unleveraged required return, r?

d. What unleveraged beta is implied by r?

■ LEVEL C (ADVANCED)

C1. (Capital structure arbitrage) Firms A and B are identical except for their capital structures. A has a debt ratio of 25%. B has a debt ratio of 33.33%. Suppose that the interest rate on both firms' debt is 10% and that investors can also borrow at a 10% interest rate.

a. An investor owns 5% of the common stock of firm A, half of which is financed through borrowings. What investment-loan package involving B will produce identical returns?

b. An investor owns 10% of the common stock of B, none of which is financed through borrowings. What investment-loan combination involving A will produce identical returns?

C2. (WACC and net benefit to leverage) Both the common stock and long-term bonds of Crib-Tick, Inc., makers of baby furniture, are traded publicly on the NYSE. Currently, the market value of Crib-Tick common stock is $14 per share, and there are 4 million shares outstanding. Crib-Tick's latest earnings were $2.09 per share, and next year's dividend is expected to be $1.02 per share. Five years ago, Crib-Tick paid a dividend of $0.72 per share. Crib-Tick has long-term bonds with a total market value of $30 million. The bonds mature in 11 years and have an 8% coupon. They are currently selling for $880. (Assume the bonds have 22 more coupon payments until maturity.) In addition to long-term bonds, Crib-Tick has $5 million in notes payable and $10 million in other current liabilities. Current market conditions are $r_f = 6\%$ and $r_M = 13.75\%$. Crib-Tick has a beta of 1.1, and it pays corporate taxes at a rate of 30%. It has estimated $T^* = 0.18$. Estimate Crib-Tick's WACC.

C3. (Financing-investment puzzle) The Ida Rather Knot Corporation, a modest rope manufacturing firm in the northeast corner of the Yukon, has been contacted by Wile E. Coyote and offered an investment opportunity that will pay her $2,500 per month for 60 months. Ida must invest $10,000 now and borrow $90,000 from Wile E. at 16% APR, for a total initial investment of $100,000. The entire loan must be paid back at the end of the 60 months (principal and interest will total $199,242.62). There are no taxes. Assume that this investment is riskless, as Wile E. Coyote has claimed. Under what conditions would you recommend that Ida undertake this investment?

C4. (Financing-investment puzzle) Suppose you have been offered an investment opportunity that will pay you $2,200 per month for 60 months. However, you must invest $10,000 now and borrow $90,000 from a specified institution at 16% APR, for a total initial investment of $100,000. The entire loan must be paid back at the end of the 60 months (principal and interest will total $199,242.62). There are no taxes. Assume this investment is riskless. Under what conditions would you want to undertake this investment?

MINICASE PEPSICO'S CAPITAL STRUCTURE CHOICE

PepsiCo, the soft drink and snacks company, has established a long-term target range of 20% to 25% for what it calls its "net debt ratio." PepsiCo measures its net debt ratio on a market-value basis. Net debt equals total debt, including the present value of its operating lease commitments, minus the cash and marketable securities it holds outside the United States (it does so mainly for tax reasons). The net debt ratio is defined as

$$L^* = \frac{D + \text{PVOL} - \text{CMS}}{(N)(P) + D + \text{PVOL} - \text{CMS}}$$

where D is the total market value of debt, PVOL is the present value of operating lease commitments, CMS is cash and marketable securities (net of the cost of remitting these funds to the United States), N is the number of common shares, and P is the common stock price. PepsiCo's annual report shows that the firm had 788 million shares of common stock outstanding, and the stock price closed at $55.875.

The table below provides information regarding comparable firms.

FIRM	DEBT RATINGS (MOODY'S/ S&P)	ANNUAL EBIT	ANNUAL RENTAL EXPENSE	ANNUAL INTEREST	CASH AND MARKETABLE SECURITIES	MARKET VALUE OF LONG-TERM DEBT	MARKET VALUE OF TOTAL DEBT	ANNUAL CASH FLOW
PepsiCo	A1/A	$3,114	$479	$682	$1,498	$8,747	$9,453	$3,742
Cadbury Schweppes	A2/A	661	25	135	129	864	1,490	492
Coca-Cola	Aa3/AA	4,600	—	272	1315	1,141	1,693	3,115
Coca-Cola Enterprises	A3/AA—	471	31	326	8	4,138	4,201	644
McDonald's	Aa2/AA	2,509	498	340	335	4,258	4,836	2,296

QUESTIONS

1. Calculate PepsiCo's net debt ratio, assuming the present value of operating leases is five times the annual rental expense and that remitting the cash and marketable securities to the United States reduces them by 25% due to taxes and transaction costs.
2. For each firm in the table, calculate the interest coverage ratio, the fixed charge coverage ratio, the long-term debt ratio, the total debt to adjusted total capitalization (recall that adjusted capitalization includes short-term debt), the ratio of cash flow to long-term debt, and the ratio of cash flow to total debt.
3. (Supplemental question based on Chapter 16) Suppose PepsiCo's real objective is to maintain a single-A senior debt rating. Does its net debt ratio target seem reasonable, or would you recommend a different target?

Managing Capital Structure

16

Corporations manage their capital structure carefully. As we described in the preceding chapter, the factors involved with choosing a capital structure are complex, and the impact of each factor on the value of the firm is not clear cut. In principle, a firm should balance the incremental advantage of more financial leverage against the incremental costs. Unfortunately, we do not have methods to precisely measure such things as the expected costs of financial distress, agency costs, and the cost of reduced financing flexibility.

A number of methods exist for analyzing the impact of alternative capital structures but, in the end, the choice of capital structure requires expert judgment. The analytical models give us a range of reasonable capital structures, rather than pinpointing the absolute best.

In this chapter, we describe how a firm can take into account the various relevant factors to select an appropriate capital structure. We then show how to incorporate the effect of that capital structure choice on the cost of capital for a firm or one of its capital budgeting projects. The method is very practical because it simply adjusts the WACC (weighted average cost of capital), which is then used in a "standard" NPV calculation without any other changes.

FOCUS ON PRINCIPLES

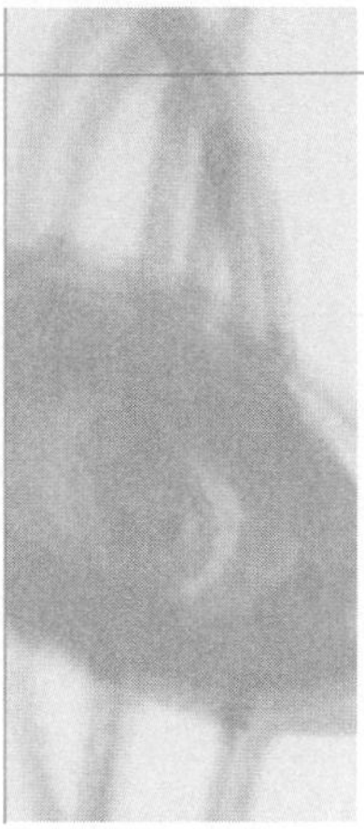

- *Behavioral:* Look to the information contained in the capital structure decisions and financing transactions of other firms for guidance in choosing a capital structure.
- *Risk-Return Trade-Off:* Recognize that capital structure changes made at fair market security prices are simply a risk-return trade-off. Such transactions do not affect firm value (except for possible signaling effects), although they change equity-debt risk sharing.
- *Incremental Benefits:* Consider the possible ways to minimize the value lost to capital market imperfections, such as asymmetric taxes, asymmetric information, and transaction costs. At the same time, be sure to include all of the transaction costs of making potentially beneficial financing transactions, because they reduce the *net* benefit from such transactions.
- *Valuable Ideas:* Look for opportunities to create value by issuing securities that are in short supply, perhaps resulting from changes in tax law.
- *Signaling:* Consider any possible change in capital structure carefully, because financing transactions and capital structure changes convey information to outsiders and can be misunderstood.
- *Time Value of Money:* Include any time-value-of-money tax benefits from capital structure choices.
- *Capital Market Efficiency:* Recognize that the potential to increase firm value through capital structure is smaller than the potential to increase firm value through the introduction of *valuable new ideas* and wise use of the firm's *comparative advantages.*

16.1 INDUSTRY EFFECTS

We have a pretty good understanding of the main factors that affect a firm's choice of capital structure. But financial theory does not tell us *precisely* how they determine a firm's *optimal* capital structure. In practice, firms usually apply the Behavioral Principle to select an *appropriate* capital structure. They look to the capital structure choices of comparable firms for guidance about their choice of capital structure.

Studies show systematic differences in capital structures across industries. These are due mostly to differences in:

1. The degree of operating risk
2. Availability of tax shelters provided by things other than debt, such as accelerated depreciation, investment tax credit, and operating tax loss carryforwards
3. The ability of assets to support borrowing
4. Management's attitude toward the risk created by financial leverage

Debt Ratings

Differences among average industry capital structures, however, are only part of the story. A firm cannot simply adopt the industry average debt ratio because differences exist among firms in any particular industry with respect to tax position, size, competitive position, operating risk, business prospects, and other factors. Firms also differ in their willingness to bear financial risk and in their desire to maintain access to the capital markets.

In practice, a firm's bond rating has important implications concerning the choice of capital structure. Table 16.1 shows the debt rating definitions of two major rating agencies, Moody's Investors Service and Standard & Poor's. The highest four rating categories are known as **investment-grade ratings.** For Moody's, the investment-grade ratings are Aaa, Aa, A, and Baa. For Standard & Poor's, investment-grade ratings are AAA, AA, A, and BBB. Ratings lower than investment-grade are called **speculative-grade ratings.**

Each agency distinguishes different levels of credit quality within each rating category below triple A. Moody's attaches the numbers 1 (high), 2 (medium), and 3 (low). Standard & Poor's attaches a plus sign for the highest and a minus sign for the lowest. For example, a medium-grade single-A credit would be rated A2 by Moody's and A by Standard & Poor's, and would be somewhat higher in quality than one rated A3 by Moody's or A− by Standard & Poor's.

TABLE 16.1
Bond rating definitions.

MOODY'S INVESTORS SERVICE[a]	STANDARD & POOR'S[b]
Investment-Grade Ratings	
Aaa Bonds and preferred stock which are rated Aaa are judged to be of the best quality. They carry the smallest degree of investment risk and are generally referred to as "gilt edged." Interest payments are protected by a large or by an exceptionally stable margin, and principal is secure. While the various protective elements are likely to change, such changes as can be visualized are most unlikely to impair the fundamentally strong position of such issues.	**AAA** Debt rated AAA has the highest rating assigned by Standard & Poor's. Capacity to pay interest and repay principal is extremely strong.
Aa Bonds and preferred stock which are rated Aa are judged to be of high quality by all standards. Together with the Aaa group, they comprise what are generally known as high-grade bonds. They are rated lower than the best bonds because margins of protection may not be as large as in Aaa securities, fluctuation of protective elements may be of greater amplitude, or there may be other elements present that make the long-term risk appear somewhat larger than the Aaa securities.	**AA** Debt rated AA has a very strong capacity to pay interest and repay principal and differs from the higher-rated issues only in small degree.
A Bonds and preferred stock which are rated A possess many favorable investment attributes and are to be considered as upper-medium-grade obligations. Factors giving security to principal and interest are considered adequate, but elements may be present that suggest a susceptibility to impairment some time in the future.	**A** Debt rated A has a strong capacity to pay interest and repay principal, although it is somewhat more susceptible to the adverse effects of changes in circumstances and economic conditions than debt in higher-rated categories.
Baa Bonds and preferred stock which are rated Baa are considered medium-grade obligations (they are neither highly protected nor poorly secured). Interest payments and principal security appear adequate for the present, but certain protective elements may be lacking or may be characteristically unreliable over any great length of time. Such bonds lack outstanding investment characteristics and in fact have speculative characteristics as well.	**BBB** Debt rated BBB is regarded as having an adequate capacity to pay interest and repay principal. Whereas it normally exhibits adequate protection parameters, adverse economic conditions or changing circumstances are more likely to lead to a weakened capacity to pay interest and repay principal for debt in this category than in higher-rated categories.

TABLE 16.1
Continued

MOODY'S INVESTORS SERVICE[a]	STANDARD & POOR'S[b]
Speculative-Grade Ratings	
Ba Bonds and preferred stock which are rated Ba are judged to have speculative elements; their future cannot be considered as well-assured. Often the protection of interest and principal payments may be very moderate, and thereby not well safeguarded during both good and bad times over the future. Uncertainty of position characterizes bonds in this class.	**BB** Debt rated BB has less near-term vulnerability to default than other speculative issues. However, it faces major ongoing uncertainties or exposure to adverse business, financial, or economic conditions that could lead to inadequate capacity to meet timely interest and principal payments. The BB rating category is also used for debt subordinated to senior debts that is assigned an actual or implied BBB– rating.
B Bonds and preferred stock which are rated B generally lack characteristics of the desirable investment. Assurance of interest and principal payments or of maintenance of other terms of the contract over any long period of time may be small.	**B** Debt rated B has a greater vulnerability to default but currently has the capacity to meet interest payments and principal repayments. Adverse business, financial, or economic conditions will likely impair capacity or willingness to pay interest and repay principal. The B rating category is also used for debt subordinated to senior debt that is assigned an actual or implied BB or BB– rating.
Caa Bonds and preferred stock which are rated Caa are of poor standing. Such issues may be in default, or there may be present elements of danger with respect to principal or interest.	**CCC** Debt rated CCC has a currently identifiable vulnerability to default and is dependent upon favorable business, financial, and economic conditions to meet the requirements of timely payment of interest and repayment of principal. In the event of adverse business, financial, or economic conditions, it is not likely to have the capacity to pay interest and repay principal. The CCC rating category is also used for debt subordinated to senior debt that is assigned an actual or implied B or B– rating.
Ca Bonds and preferred stock which are rated Ca represent obligations that are speculative in a high degree. Such issues are often in default or have other marked shortcomings.	**CC** The rating CC is typically applied to debt subordinated to senior debt that is assigned an actual or implied CCC rating.
C Bonds and preferred stock which are rated C are the lowest-rated class of bonds, and issues so rated can be regarded as having extremely poor prospects of ever attaining any real investment standing.	**C** The rating C is typically applied to debt subordinated to senior debt that is assigned an actual or implied CCC– rating. The C rating may be used to cover a situation where a bankruptcy petition has been filed but debt-service payments are continued.
	CI The rating CI is reserved for income bonds on which no interest is being paid.
	D Debt rated D is in payment default. The D rating category is used when interest payments or principal payments are not made on the date due even if the applicable grace period has not expired, unless S&P believes that such payments will be made during such grace period. The D rating also is used upon the filing of a bankruptcy petition if debt-service payments are jeopardized.

[a]Moody's applies numerical modifiers 1, 2, and 3 in each generic rating classification from Aa through Caa. The modifier 1 indicates that the obligation ranks in the higher end of its generic rating category; the modifier 2 indicates a mid-range ranking; and the modifier 3 indicates a ranking in the lower end of that generic rating category.
[b]The ratings from "AA" to "CCC" may be modified by the addition of a plus or minus sign to show relative standing within the major rating categories.
Sources: Reprinted by permission of Moody's Investors Service and reprinted by permission of Standard & Poor's.

As you can see by reading Table 16.1, the ratings are indicators of the likelihood of financial distress, as judged by the rating agencies. Bonds in the top three investment-grade categories are judged from "favorable" to "gilt edged" (edged with gold). They have a capacity to pay interest that ranges from "strong" to "extremely strong." Bonds rated in the lowest category (Baa or BBB) offer investors less protection than higher-rated bonds. The risk of financial distress is greater for lower-rated bonds.

The distinction between investment-grade and speculative-grade ratings is important because of institutional investment restrictions. To qualify as *legal investments* for commercial banks, bonds must usually be investment grade. In addition, various state laws impose minimum rating standards and other restrictions for bonds to qualify as legal investments for savings banks, trust companies, public pension funds, and insurance companies. Bonds rated speculative grade fail to qualify as legal investments for many financial institutions. Consequently, a firm's bond rating is very important for maintaining access to capital markets on acceptable terms.

The National Association of Insurance Commissioners (NAIC) has established six bond rating categories. The amount of reserves an insurance company must maintain for each bond investment depends on the bond's rating. Bonds rated NAIC-3 or below are speculative grade. They require significantly more capital.[1] With the introduction of this new rating system and capital-maintenance standards, speculative-grade bonds have become much less attractive to insurance companies. And of course, the yields that insurance companies require from speculative-grade bonds are significantly higher to compensate for the greater amount of capital they must maintain.

Choosing a Bond Rating Objective

A firm can choose a bond rating objective. Such a choice involves a decision about (1) the chance of future financial distress and (2) the desire to maintain access to the capital markets. When it looks like a firm could gain value from raising its proportion of debt financing, but the firm chooses not to (because it has a higher bond rating objective), the value that is missed can be viewed as a "margin of safety." The desired margin of safety is determined by how much risk of future financial distress, or restricted market access, the firm is willing to bear. A single-A rating would seem to be a reasonable rating target, but some firms are more or less risk averse than this standard implies.

Bond Ratings and Financial Ratios

Once a firm has chosen its rating target, what financial steps should the firm take to hit the target? The rating agencies use many criteria to rate a bond. For example, in the case of industrial firms, Standard & Poor's evaluates (1) operating risk, (2) competitive position, (3) size and diversification, (4) margins and other measures of profitability, (5) management quality, (6) conservatism of accounting policies, (7) fixed charge coverage, (8) financial policies, (9) leverage (including off-balance-sheet debt) compared to the liquidation value of assets, (10) adequacy of cash flow to meet future debt service obligations, (11) need for outside capital, and (12) future financial flexibility in light of future debt service obligations and planned capital expenditure requirements.

Each factor bears on the risk of future financial distress. When the rating agencies weigh the relevant factors in order to assign a bond rating, there is no all-purpose formula. In fact, several factors are difficult to quantify. Nevertheless, certain key credit statistics for comparable firms whose debt carries the target rating offer useful guidance.

---

[1]NAIC-2 corresponds to Moody's Baa (and to Standard & Poor's BBB). NAIC-3 corresponds to Moody's Ba (and to Standard & Poor's BB). Life insurance companies' reserve requirements for NAIC-3 bonds are more than three times as high as for NAIC-2 bonds. Property and casualty insurance companies can account for bonds rated NAIC-3 or higher based on their historical cost but must account for bonds rated NAIC-4 or lower based on their current market value.

TABLE 16.2
Senior debt ratings as indicators of credit quality.

	KEY FINANCIAL RATIOS[1]						
SENIOR DEBT RATING[2]	AAA	AA	A	BBB	BB	B	CCC
EBIT Interest coverage ratio[3]	21.4	10.1	6.1	3.7	2.1	0.8	0.1
EBITDA/Interest[4]	26.5	12.9	9.1	5.8	3.4	1.8	1.3
Free operating cash flow/Total debt	84.2	25.2	15.0	8.5	2.6	−3.2	−12.9
Funds from operations/Total debt	128.8	55.4	43.2	30.8	18.8	7.8	1.6
Pretax return on permanent capital	34.9	21.7	19.4	13.6	11.6	6.6	1.0
Operating income/Sales	27.0	22.1	18.6	15.4	15.9	11.9	11.9
Long-term debt/Capitalization	13.3	28.2	33.9	42.5	57.2	69.7	68.8
Total debt/Adjusted capitalization (including short-term debt)	22.9	37.7	42.5	48.2	62.6	74.8	87.7
Companies	8	29	136	218	273	281	22

[1]Median of the three-year simple arithmetic averages for the period 1998 to 2000 for firms whose senior debt had the indicated rating.
[2]As assigned by Standard & Poor's.
[3]EBIT = Earnings before interest and taxes.
[4]EBITDA = Earnings before interest, taxes, depreciation, and amortization.
Source: Reprinted by permission of Standard & Poor's.

Table 16.2 shows how the values of eight key credit statistics vary across the six highest rating categories assigned by Standard & Poor's. Note how all the ratios are progressively better, the higher the firm's senior debt rating. Taken together, they go a long way toward distinguishing a stronger credit rating from a weaker one.

Having selected a rating target, a firm can use the values of the key credit statistics of comparable firms with that target rating as a rough guide to the ratio targets it should set for itself. We show how to do this later in the chapter. For now, four points of caution should be emphasized:

1. Quantitative factors are not the entire story. A deteriorating market position, or perceived weaknesses in management, will negatively affect the credit rating.
2. Achieving an improved credit rating requires a proven track record. Simply improving credit statistics will not guarantee a higher credit rating unless the firm demonstrates that it can maintain the statistics.
3. The averages may change over time.
4. Cyclical industries, such as mining and chemicals, exhibit substantial swings in credit statistics over the industry cycle. This makes it very important to compare firms in the same industry.

Review

1. What four factors might explain the systematic differences in capital structures across industries?
2. What are investment-grade ratings, and what are speculative-grade ratings? Why is this distinction important?
3. Cite three factors Standard & Poor's evaluates to determine a bond rating for an industrial firm.
4. What do bond ratings indicate regarding the likelihood of default?

16.2 FACTORS AFFECTING A FIRM'S CHOICE OF CAPITAL STRUCTURE

There are five basic considerations involved in a firm's choice of capital structure: (1) Ability to service debt; (2) Ability to use interest tax shields fully; (3) Ability of assets to support debt (protection against illiquidity); (4) Desired degree of access to capital markets; (5) Dynamic factors and debt management over time. Let us look at each of these factors in turn.

Ability to Service Debt

A careful financial manager will not recommend that a firm take on more debt unless she is confident the firm will be able to service the debt, that is, be able to make the contractually required payments on time, even under adverse conditions. Many firms appear to maintain a margin of safety, or unused debt capacity, to control the risk of financial distress and maintain access to the capital markets.

There are various measures of debt-servicing capacity. One is the **interest coverage ratio:**

$$\text{Interest coverage ratio} = \frac{\text{EBIT}}{\text{Interest expense}} \tag{16.1}$$

where EBIT denotes earnings before interest and income taxes. Rental (including lease) payments include an interest component. Fixed charges, which include interest expense and one-third of rental expense, represent a better indicator of true interest expense. To take these factors into account, we can calculate a **fixed charge coverage ratio:**[2]

$$\text{Fixed charge coverage ratio} = \frac{\text{EBIT} + 1/3 \text{ Rentals}}{\text{Interest expense} + 1/3 \text{ Rentals}} \tag{16.2}$$

The one-third rentals is an attempt to approximate the interest component of rental expense.

To avoid default, a firm must meet its principal repayment obligations as well as its interest obligations on schedule. A more comprehensive measure of a firm's ability to service its debt obligations is its **debt service coverage ratio:**

$$\text{Debt service coverage ratio} = \frac{\text{EBIT} + 1/3 \text{ Rentals}}{\text{Interest expense} + 1/3 \text{ Rentals} + \dfrac{\text{Principal repayments}}{1 - \text{Tax rate}}} \tag{16.3}$$

The amount of principal repayments is divided by 1 minus the tax rate because principal repayments are not tax deductible. They are paid with after-tax dollars, whereas interest expense and rental expense are tax deductible.

The coverage ratios can be used in pro forma analysis to gauge the impact of a new issue.

EXAMPLE Pro Forma Credit Analysis

A firm has EBIT of $25 million and interest expense of $10 million. It is considering issuing $50 million of 10% debt. Calculate its pro forma interest coverage ratio assuming the entire proceeds are invested in a plant under construction. Recalculate it assuming the investment produces additional EBIT of $10 million per year.

---

[2]The fixed charge coverage ratio in Equation (16.2) is the one specified by the Securities and Exchange Commission. However, some analysts prefer to use total rentals rather than one-third this amount.

In the first case,

$$\text{Interest coverage ratio} = \frac{25}{10 + (50)(0.1)} = 1.67x$$

In the second case,

$$\text{Interest coverage ratio} = \frac{25 + 10}{10 + 5} = 2.33x$$

A firm can evaluate the impact of alternative capital structures using *sensitivity analysis.* The firm calculates the interest coverage ratio, fixed charge coverage ratio, and debt service coverage ratio for each capital structure under a variety of projected business scenarios. Then the calculated values are compared with benchmarks that reflect the firm's desired credit rating. Table 16.2 suggests the following rough benchmarks. If a firm's industry has average operating risk, and the firm wishes to meet minimum investment-grade standards (a BBB rating), it should strive for an annual interest coverage ratio of at least 3.7 under reasonably conservative "expected case" assumptions. It should strive for a debt service coverage ratio of at least 1.00 under pessimistic assumptions.[3]

A firm in a highly cyclical industry should set higher interest coverage and fixed charge coverage ratio standards to compensate for the greater operating risk, whereas a firm in a noncyclical industry can safely set lower standards. For example, an electric utility can set lower coverage ratio standards than a manufacturer of rollerblades.

A firm that wishes to maintain single-A-type ratios would aim toward an interest coverage ratio of at least 6.1 if it is in an industry of average operating risk. Higher (or lower) standards would be appropriate for firms in industries that have more (or less) operating risk. You could obtain more precise benchmarks by calculating ratios for firms in the same industry that have the target rating.

Ability to Use Interest Tax Shields Fully

Firms using debt financing must generate sufficient income from operations to claim the interest deductions. A firm that does not pay income taxes and does not expect to become a taxpayer has less incentive to incur additional debt. The tax shields would go unused. That would raise the after-tax cost of debt, and the additional debt would also increase the risk of financial distress. A firm can carry tax losses forward. The added debt will be beneficial only if the expected present value of the tax shields exceeds the expected present value of the costs of financial distress plus the expected present value of the increase in agency costs.

A firm's capital structure should probably contain no more debt than its future tax position will let it use. For example, firms in industries with other substantial tax shelter opportunities, such as oil and gas companies (with their depletion allowances) and steel makers (with their depreciation and loss carryforwards), should have lower leverage ratios than firms in other industries.

As we have said before, there are frequent changes to the tax code. These changes complicate this analysis, and can cause the firm's target capital structure to change over time.

Ability of Assets to Support Debt

A firm should not incur additional debt if doing so would involve a significant chance of insolvency. The risk of insolvency depends not only on the projected debt service coverage, but also on the firm's ability to generate cash through additional borrowing, the sale of equity securities, or the sale of assets.

[3]The particular minimum chosen for the debt service coverage ratio depends, to a certain extent, on the firm's confidence in its ability to refinance its debt.

Assets vary in their ability to support debt. Lower-risk assets with more stable market values provide better collateral for debt. This allows a firm to borrow a larger proportion of such assets' market values. For example, a real estate firm or a credit company can generally support a relatively large amount of leverage.

EXAMPLE Leverage and Discovering Oil

Imagine you bought 200 acres of land in order to create a catfish ranch. You paid \$100,000 for the land and have an \$80,000 mortgage on it. You plan to use an additional \$60,000 of your own money to develop the ranch. You figure the project has an NPV of \$40,000, so the total value of the project is \$200,000 (= 100 + 60 + 40) at a cost of \$160,000. Therefore, your ranch project has a 40% leverage ratio (its proportion of debt financing is $L = 80/200$).

In the process of digging a pond for the catfish, you discover oil on your land. An analysis of the discovery puts the new value of your land at \$15.25 million. Now your project is only about $L = 0.5\%$ debt financed! But not to worry. You can, of course, increase your leverage by borrowing against the increased market value of your land.

Desired Degree of Access to Capital Markets

A firm planning a substantial capital expenditure program will want to maintain access to the capital markets on acceptable terms. This requires adequate credit strength. Historically, a firm large enough to sell debt publicly could be reasonably confident of maintaining such access if it had a senior debt rating of single-A or better. In 1983, the "junk bond" market expanded rapidly and appeared to lessen the need to have such a high credit standing for maintaining market access. In 1990, however, the junk bond market all but collapsed, emphasizing the risk inherent in increasing leverage to such an extent that a firm's debt rating falls below investment grade.

Dynamic Factors and Debt Management over Time

The four factors just discussed all affect a firm's capital structure target. The capital market imperfections view of capital structure also plays a role. A firm might appear to deviate from the normal financing preference order. This could be, for example, because one large issue has proportionally lower transaction costs than two or more smaller issues. Similarly, a firm that needs only a relatively small amount of external funds would tend to use bank lines of credit rather than issue securities, even if issuing securities would appear to be better.

The dynamic process can even make it appear that a firm has *no* target capital structure. For example, if a firm takes advantage of an attractive but temporary financing opportunity (say, the opportunity to issue tax-exempt securities prior to the date the authority to issue such securities expires), its capital structure may move away from its "target." Such apparent deviations in a firm's capital structure policy can simply reflect the dynamic nature of an optimal capital structure.

Review

1. What are the five basic considerations involved in a firm's choice of capital structure?
2. What are coverage ratios? What do they measure? Why should a firm and its investors be concerned with the values of the firm's coverage ratios?
3. How would a firm in a highly cyclical industry compensate for that in selecting its financial ratio targets?
4. Explain why some assets provide better collateral value than others.

16.3 CHOOSING AN APPROPRIATE CAPITAL STRUCTURE

In this section we will tie together the considerations just discussed into a single framework for determining an appropriate capital structure. To do this, we will use comparative credit analysis and pro forma capital structure analysis. A *comparative credit analysis* suggests a range of target capital structures that might be appropriate. A *pro forma capital structure analysis* shows the impact of the alternatives within the target range on the firm's credit statistics and reported financial results, and indicates whether the firm will be able to fully use tax shield benefits. This enables the firm to select a specific target capital structure.

Comparative Credit Analysis

In practice, a comparative credit analysis is the most widely used technique for selecting an appropriate capital structure. This approach is an application of the Behavioral Principle. It involves the following steps:

1. Select the desired rating objective.
2. Identify a set of comparable firms that also have the target senior debt rating.
3. Perform a comparative credit analysis of these firms to define the capital structure (or range of capital structures) most consistent with this rating objective.

Earlier, we discussed five considerations that enter into the capital structure decision. Choosing a target debt rating actually encompasses three of the five. The only two not covered are the ability to use tax benefits and debt management considerations (such as issuance expenses) that affect the immediate preference order of the various sources of funds. We must evaluate these two factors separately.

As we said earlier, a single-A rating provides a compromise between maintaining capital market access and getting more tax savings from additional leverage. However, more conservative firms, and firms with very heavy future financing programs, might strive for a higher rating. Other firms that are willing to bear greater financial risk might set a lower rating target.

EXAMPLE Comparative Credit Analysis

Table 16.3 illustrates a comparative credit analysis of specialty chemicals firms that are comparable to the firm being analyzed, Washington Chemical Corporation. There are six specialty chemicals firms with rated debt. The senior debt ratings (Moody's/Standard & Poor's) range from a low of Ba1/BB to a high of A2/A.

Washington Chemical has decided on a target senior debt rating "comfortably within" the single-A range. Three of the firms in Table 16.3 have at least one senior debt rating in the single-A category, and Johnson Chemical and Wilson Chemical are rated in the middle of the single-A category by both agencies.

Washington Chemical is significantly more profitable than one of the A2/A issuers and only slightly less profitable than the other. Washington Chemical's debt-to-capitalization, funds-from-operations-to-debt, and fixed charge coverage ratios fall between the higher and lower of the two values for each ratio exhibited by the two A2/A specialty chemicals firms. Washington Chemical's ratios are substantially better than those of Myers Chemicals, which is a borderline triple-B-single-A. Washington Chemical concluded from this analysis that its financial condition is of medium-grade single-A quality.

TABLE 16.3

A comparative credit analysis of specialty chemicals firms.

	WASHINGTON CHEMICAL CORPORATION	MYERS CHEMICALS CORP.	NORTHWEST CHEMICALS INC.	DELAWARE CHEMICALS CORP.	WESTERN INDUSTRIES	JOHNSON CHEMICAL INC.	WILSON CHEMICAL CORP.
Senior debt rating (Moody's/Standard & Poor's)	—	A3/BBB+	Ba1/BBB−	Baa2/BBB−	Ba1/BB	A2/A	A2/A
Profitability							
Operating profit margin	7.4%	5.9%	1.9%	4.5%	8.9%	4.1%	9.2%
Net profit margin	3.9	2.6	1.0	2.3	2.2	2.3	4.1
Return on assets	4.8	3.2	2.2	4.9	2.8	4.3	4.9
Return on common equity	10.3	9.2	5.0	13.9	8.8	10.8	10.0
Capitalization							
Short-term debt	$ 16	$ 60	$ 10	$ 10	$ 16	$ 8	$ 36
Senior long-term debt	$158	$144	$ 49	$163	$110	$140	$245
Capitalized lease obligations	—	22	10	20	—	—	1
Subordinated long-term debt	—	—	—	13	80	8	—
Total long-term debt	158	166	59	196	190	148	246
Minority interest	—	—	3	2	—	—	—
Preferred equity	—	2	35	5	—	—	—
Common equity	321	253	165	334	162	278	659
Total capitalization	$479	$421	$262	$537	$352	$426	$905
Long-term debt ratio	33%	39%	23%	36%	54%	35%	27%
Total-debt-to-adjusted-capitalization ratio	35	47	25	38	56	36	30
Funds-from-operations-to-long-term-debt ratio	60	42	45	35	27	51	63
Funds-from-operations-to-total-debt ratio	55	31	39	33	25	49	55
Liquidity							
Current ratio	2.4*x*	1.9*x*	2.7*x*	2.1*x*	1.9*x*	2.2*x*	2.6*x*
Fixed Charge Coverage Ratio							
Last 12 months	3.5*x*	2.3*x*	2.4*x*	3.3*x*	2.0*x*	3.3*x*	3.7*x*
Latest fiscal year	4.3	4.0	3.8	2.9	2.3	4.4	4.2
One year prior	5.6	3.0	3.2	2.7	2.8	5.4	5.7
Two years prior	6.3	4.0	2.8	2.2	3.8	7.9	4.9

We need to clarify one point regarding this example. We have emphasized the importance of basing financial decisions on market values, but the financial ratios in Table 16.3 contain some book value items. This is because it is simply not practical to include current market values in every case. The rating agencies consider the market value of a firm's assets in assessing its leverage. But they value these assets conservatively, assuming they could be sold in fair market value transactions.

The actual debt-to-capitalization ratio should value the common equity component on the basis of the liquidation value of the assets rather than on the basis of the firm's prevailing share price (which reflects the value of the firm on a going-concern basis). Assets such as proven oil and gas reserves, which are relatively liquid, will support a higher degree of leverage than less liquid assets. New plant and equipment will tend to support greater leverage than an equal book value amount of old plant and equipment. But determining these liquidating values is necessarily subjective, because there are no liquid markets for fixed assets, and appraisals generally are not available. Still, the quality of assets will vary systematically from one industry to another. Thus, for a particular rating category, the debt-to-capitalization ratios for firms in one industry, when compared to the debt-to-capitalization ratios for firms in another industry whose debt bears the same rating, will reflect interindustry differences in liquidating asset value.

An analysis like the one in Table 16.3 is necessarily imperfect. But if comparable firms are chosen carefully, and if differences between the comparable firms and the firm being analyzed are carefully weighed, the comparative credit analysis can produce useful guidelines.

EXAMPLE Comparative Credit Analysis (continued)

As we said, in the final analysis the choice of capital structure requires judgment. Before reaching a decision, Washington Chemical evaluated its expected profitability. Washington Chemical believed that its profitability would exceed that of its single-A competitors. Based on its careful consideration of all these factors, Washington Chemical decided to try to stay within the following ranges:

Annual fixed charge coverage ratio: 3.50*x* to 4.00*x*
Annual funds-from-operations-to-total-debt ratio: 40% to 50%
Long-term debt ratio: 30% to 35%

Before deciding where to aim within each of these ranges, Washington Chemical decided to (1) confirm its ability to fully use the estimated tax shield benefits, particularly under somewhat adverse conditions, and (2) assess the impact of these obligations on its future financing requirements. Table 16.4 contains a pro forma capital structure analysis.

In its evaluation, Washington Chemical realized the importance of considering a reasonably pessimistic case as well as its expected case. Consequently, there are four cases considered in Table 16.4. They correspond to two degrees of leverage (long-term debt ratio of 30% and 35%) and two operating scenarios (10% growth and 5% growth).

It is evident from cases l and 2 that Washington Chemical could justify a 35% long-term debt ratio in the expected case. Both the fixed charge coverage and funds-from-operations-to-total-debt ratios increase steadily and remain comfortably within their target ranges. Moreover, Washington Chemical could fully use the tax benefits of ownership and fully claim all interest deductions.

Under a more pessimistic scenario, cases 3 and 4 show that Washington Chemical's fixed charge coverage and funds-from-operations-to-total-debt ratios would eventually fall below their target ranges. The deterioration is less severe in case 4, because the long-term debt ratio is only 30%. However, the external equity financing requirement is greater. Washington Chemical decided to finance itself with a leverage ratio of 1/3.

TABLE 16.4
A pro forma capital structure analysis (p. 1).

		PROJECTED AHEAD				
	Initial	1 Year	2 Years	3 Years	4 Years	5 Years
Case 1: Leverage at upper end of range/expected case operating results						
Pre-interest taxable income[a]	$ 61	$ 67	$ 74	$ 81	$ 89	$ 98
Interest	18	20	22	24	26	28
Surplus (Deficit)[b]	$ 43	$ 47	$ 52	$ 57	$ 63	$ 70
Earnings before fixed charges and income taxes[c]	$ 70	$ 77	$ 85	$ 93	$102	$113
Fixed charges[d]	20	22	24	26	28	30
Fixed charge coverage	3.5*x*	3.5*x*	3.5*x*	3.6*x*	3.6*x*	3.8*x*
Net income	$ 30	$ 33	$ 36	$ 42	$ 45	$ 51
Noncash expenses	65	72	79	84	94	102
Funds from operations[c]	95	105	115	126	139	153
Dividends	(10)	(11)	(12)	(14)	(15)	(17)
Internal cash generation	85	94	103	112	124	136
Capital expenditures	(125)	(125)	(125)	(135)	(150)	(160)
Cash required	$ 40	$ 31	$ 22	$ 23	$ 26	$ 24
External debt requirement	$ 20	$ 17	$ 14	$ 15	$ 17	$ 17
External equity requirement[e]	$ 20	$ 14	$ 8	$ 8	$ 9	$ 7
Funds from operations to total debt[f]	55%	55%	56%	57%	59%	60%
Case 2: Leverage at lower end of range/expected case operating results						
Pre-interest taxable income[a]	$ 61	$ 67	$ 74	$ 81	$ 89	$ 98
Interest	18	19	21	23	25	26
Surplus (Deficit)[b]	$ 43	$ 48	$ 53	$ 58	$ 64	$ 72
Earnings before fixed charges and income taxes[c]	$ 70	$ 77	$ 85	$ 93	$102	$113
Fixed charges[d]	20	21	23	25	27	28
Fixed charge coverage	3.5*x*	3.7*x*	3.7*x*	3.7*x*	3.8*x*	4.0*x*
Net income	$ 30	$ 33	$ 36	$ 42	$ 45	$ 51
Noncash expenses	65	72	79	84	94	102
Funds from operations[c]	95	105	115	126	139	153
Dividends	(10)	(11)	(12)	(14)	(15)	(17)
Internal cash generation	85	94	103	112	124	136
Capital expenditures	(125)	(125)	(125)	(135)	(150)	(160)
Cash required	$ 40	$ 31	$ 22	$ 23	$ 26	$ 24
External debt requirement[g]	$ 17	$ 15	$ 12	$ 13	$ 15	$ 15
External equity requirement[g]	$ 23	$ 16	$ 10	$ 10	$ 11	$ 9
Funds from operations to total debt[f]	55%	56%	57%	59%	61%	63%

Other Aspects of the Capital Structure Decision

Washington Chemical's target capital structure contains only long-term debt and common equity. Firms often adopt more complex capital structures that include one or more layers of subordinated debt, convertible debt, capitalized lease obligations, or preferred equity. Let us take a quick look at each of these.

SUBORDINATED DEBT Subordinated debt ranks below senior debt in case of default. If strict priority was preserved in bankruptcy, a layer of subordinated debt would be just as beneficial to

TABLE 16.4
Continued

		PROJECTED AHEAD				
	Initial	1 Year	2 Years	3 Years	4 Years	5 Years
Case 3: Leverage at upper end of range/pessimistic case operating results						
Pre-interest taxable income[a]	$ 61	$ 64	$ 67	$ 71	$ 74	$ 78
Interest	18	20	22	24	27	30
Surplus (Deficit)[b]	$ 43	$ 44	$ 45	$ 47	$ 47	$ 48
Earnings before fixed charges and income taxes[c]	$ 70	$ 74	$ 78	$ 82	$ 86	$ 90
Fixed charges[d]	20	22	24	26	29	32
Fixed charge coverage	3.5*x*	3.4*x*	3.3*x*	3.2*x*	3.0*x*	2.8*x*
Net income	$ 30	$ 30	$ 33	$ 33	$ 33	$ 33
Noncash expenses	65	70	72	77	82	88
Funds from operations[c]	95	100	105	110	115	121
Dividends	(10)	(10)	(11)	(11)	(11)	(11)
Internal cash generation	85	90	94	99	104	110
Capital expenditures	(125)	(125)	(125)	(135)	(150)	(160)
Cash required	$ 40	$ 35	$ 31	$ 36	$ 46	$ 50
External debt requirement	$ 20	$ 18	$ 17	$ 19	$ 23	$ 25
External equity requirement[e]	$ 20	$ 17	$ 14	$ 17	$ 23	$ 25
Funds from operations to total debt[f]	55%	52%	50%	48%	46%	44%
Case 4: Leverage at lower end of range/pessimistic case operating results						
Pre-interest taxable income[a]	$ 61	$ 64	$ 67	$ 71	$ 74	$ 78
Interest	18	19	21	23	26	28
Surplus (Deficit)[b]	$ 43	$ 45	$ 46	$ 48	$ 48	$ 50
Earnings before fixed charges and income taxes[c]	$ 70	$ 74	$ 78	$ 82	$ 86	$ 90
Fixed charges[d]	20	21	23	25	28	30
Fixed charge coverage	3.5*x*	3.5*x*	3.4*x*	3.3*x*	3.1*x*	3.0*x*
Net income	$ 30	$ 30	$ 33	$ 33	$ 33	$ 33
Noncash expenses	65	70	72	77	82	88
Funds from operations[c]	95	100	105	110	115	121
Dividends	(10)	(10)	(11)	(11)	(11)	(11)
Internal cash generation	85	90	94	99	104	110
Capital expenditures	(125)	(125)	(125)	(135)	(150)	(160)
Cash required	$ 40	$ 35	$ 31	$ 36	$ 46	$ 50
External debt requirement[g]	$ 17	$ 16	$ 15	$ 17	$ 20	$ 22
External equity requirement[g]	$ 23	$ 19	$ 16	$ 19	$ 26	$ 28
Funds from operations to total debt[f]	55%	53%	51%	50%	48%	46%

[a]As computed for federal income tax purposes. Estimated to grow at 10% per annum in the "expected case" and 5% per annum in the "pessimistic case."
[b]Calculated as pre-interest taxable income minus interest.
[c]Estimated to grow at 10% per annum in the "expected case" and 5% per annum in the "pessimistic case."
[d]Assumes rental expense of $6 million per year. Under the SEC method, one-third of this amount is included in fixed charges.
[e]Calculated to preserve a ratio of 35% long-term debt financing to 65% additional common equity.
[f]The amount of total debt at the end of the initial year is $174 (= 16 + 158 from Table 16.3). The debt level for any single year projected ahead is the initial amount plus the sum of the annual external debt requirements up to the year in question. The debt level projected ahead 2 years is $205 (= $174 + 17 + 14) so that funds from operations to total debt equals 56% (= 115/205) in Case 1. Similar calculations apply in the other three cases.
[g]Calculated to preserve a ratio of 30% long-term debt financing to 70% additional common equity.

senior debtholders as more equity. In addition, the interest payments to subordinated debtholders are tax deductible, whereas payments to shareholders are not, which benefits the issuer. However, interest payments and principal repayments must be made in a timely fashion on subordinated debt as well as on senior debt for the issuer to avoid default.

In view of the greater exposure to default risk, the rating agencies usually rate subordinated debt one step below senior debt if the senior debt is rated investment grade, and two steps below if the senior debt is rated speculative grade.[4] The rating differential increases the cost of a new debt issue (consistent with the Principle of Risk-Return Trade-Off). Moreover, because strict priority is not always preserved in bankruptcy, the rating agencies will generally add nonconvertible subordinated debt to senior debt for purposes of their ratio calculations. In view of the higher interest cost, $1 of subordinated debt has a more severe impact than $1 of senior debt on a firm's coverage and funds-from-operations-to-debt ratios. Consequently, investment-grade manufacturing firms seldom find it attractive to issue nonconvertible subordinated debt.

Finance firms, on the other hand, often do issue subordinated debt. Because of the comparatively close matching of the maturity structures of their assets and their liabilities, credit firms can support a high degree of leverage. The bulk of their business consists of lending funds at a favorable spread over their funding costs. So a well-run finance firm will have the capacity to fully use the interest tax shields, even when it is very highly leveraged. The subordinated debt, like equity, will provide comfort to senior lenders and tax deductions to the issuer, which equity would not provide.

CONVERTIBLE DEBT Firms usually issue convertible debt on a subordinated basis. Both issuers and investors expect the issue to be converted into common equity within a few years. It is thus appropriate that convertible debt be junior to nonconvertible debt with respect to bankruptcy priority.

CAPITALIZED LEASE OBLIGATIONS Firms that cannot fully use the tax benefits of ownership often find it attractive to lease assets from entities that can claim these tax deductions and are willing to pass on part of the tax benefits in the form of reduced lease payments. But failure to make a timely lease payment places a firm in default under the lease agreement. Consequently, leases are really a form of secured debt. Rating agencies customarily include capitalized leases, which are reported on the face of the balance sheet, in long-term debt. The decision whether to take on capitalized leases or conventional debt thus hinges principally on tax considerations.

PREFERRED EQUITY Preferred stock is a hybrid security. It incorporates certain debt features and certain equity features. Failure to make a timely preferred dividend or preferred sinking fund payment will not put the issuer into default. Consequently, substituting preferred stock for a portion of a firm's debt will enhance the position of debtholders in case of default. However, firms normally treat their preferred stock payment obligations as though they were fixed. If a firm issues a significant amount of preferred stock, particularly if it contains a sinking fund, these payment obligations can impair the credit standing of the firm's debt securities.

The rating agencies give greater equity weight to preferred stock the longer its remaining maturity. Mandatory convertibles (into common stock) are given more equity weight than standard convertibles, which are given more weight than nonconvertible preferred.

---

[4]For example, a senior debt rating of A2/A would imply a subordinated debt rating of A3/A−. Conversely, a senior debt rating can be inferred from a subordinated debt rating when a firm has only rated subordinated debt outstanding. For example, Western Industries has convertible subordinated debt outstanding, which is rated Ba3/B+. This implies the senior debt rating of Ba1/BB (i.e., up two notches because it is speculative grade), as indicated in Table 16.3.

Making a Capital Structure Change

When a firm finds that its desired capital structure differs significantly from its current capital structure, what should it do? There are two basic choices: change its capital structure slowly, or change it quickly. A firm can alter its capital structure slowly by adjusting its future financing mix appropriately.

For example, suppose a firm's target capital structure consists of 35% long-term debt and 65% common equity, and its current capital structure contains 25% long-term debt and 75% common equity. The firm could cure this underleveraged condition by using long-term debt for all new external financing until the long-term debt ratio reaches 35%. However, this means that the firm's capital structure would continue to be "suboptimal" while the firm changes it over time.

Alternatively, the firm could change its capital structure quickly through an exchange offer, recapitalization offer, debt or share repurchase, or stock-for-debt swap. This would enable the firm to begin immediately employing a mix of financing that conforms to its desired capital structure. Of course, this approach is not without cost either. The firm will incur transaction costs. Also, there will be signaling effects associated with the capital structure change.

If the distance of a firm's capital structure from its target corresponds to one full rating category or more, some type of one-time transaction to make an immediate change in capital structure is probably warranted. A leverage increase for a significantly underleveraged firm is likely to increase the firm's share price. If the firm is less than one full category away from its rating objective (for example, it is a weak single-A and wants to become a strong single-A), altering its retention ratio and its external financing mix is probably more cost effective.

Review

1. What are the three steps in a comparative credit analysis?
2. How can a firm select an appropriate rating objective?
3. Why is it useful to consider different economic scenarios when conducting a pro forma capital structure analysis?
4. What is subordinated debt? Why do firms usually issue convertible bonds in that form rather than as senior debt?
5. Suppose a firm's capital structure is different from its target capital structure. Explain how it could bring its capital structure back into line with the target? How might it do so quickly?

16.4 ADJUSTING PRESENT VALUE AND REQUIRED RETURNS FOR CAPITAL STRUCTURE EFFECTS

In Chapter 11, we described a basic method of estimating a cost of capital. We treated the investment and financing decisions independently of one another. But in Chapter 15, we saw that capital structure can affect a firm's value and, therefore, the value of an investment it undertakes. Because of this interaction, the investment and financing decisions cannot be completely separated. In the balance of this chapter, we will show you how to account for the valuation impact of capital structure.

In practice, the cost of capital, WACC, is simply adjusted to reflect the capital structure impact on firm value. In many cases, the adjustment is only an estimate of a complex process. Yet this method is particularly useful. After adjusting WACC, we can use it directly in our valuation procedure without any other changes. The only difference is that the (adjusted) WACC reflects the firm's capital structure *in addition* to the project's risk.

A Capital Budgeting Project's Cost of Capital

Before going any further, we will review a few things. First, recall that the required return is an *opportunity cost of capital.* It is not a historical cost of funds. The required return is the rate at which investors would provide financing for the project under consideration *today.* Theoretically, each project has its own cost of capital. Second, remember that value is a function of both expected future cash flows and the required return. Value can remain unchanged even though both the expected future cash flows and the required return change, if the changes exactly offset each other. Third, because of the risk-return trade-off, there is a single return for each level of risk in an efficient capital market.

Recall that a firm's weighted average cost of capital, WACC, can always be described in terms of financing rates. This also holds for a capital budgeting project's cost of capital. We can think of the project as a "mini" firm. Therefore, a project's WACC can also always be represented as the weighted average of the market value proportions of any debt and equity financing package that will allow the project to be undertaken:

$$\text{WACC} = (1 - L)r_e + L(1 - T)r_d \tag{16.4}$$

where L is the market value proportion of debt financing, T is the relevant corporate tax rate, r_d is the required return on debt, and r_e is the required return on equity. Both r_d and r_e are specific to the project. You may recognize that Equation (16.4) is identical to both Equation (15.1) and Equation (11.2).

As we have said, this equation is always correct. However, it can be difficult to apply in some situations. As we saw in Chapter 15, r_e and r_d depend upon tax laws, asymmetric information considerations, and transaction costs associated with a given capital structure. If accurate functions for r_e and r_d did exist, they could simply be substituted into Equation (16.4), and our job would be done. Unfortunately, we cannot do this without making assumptions that only approximate the circumstances of the firm and the world in which it operates.

The Basis for Adjusting for Capital Structure Effects

The effect of capital structure on value is based on the entire firm's financing. Therefore, the project's cost of capital must be adjusted on the same basis. This means that adjusting the project's cost of capital is fundamentally different from the adjustment for risk. In a sense, a project undertaken by an ongoing firm has no financial risk. Still, the firm itself does have financial risk. Financial risk is created by issuing financial obligations, such as long-term debt. The shareholders' obligation is not limited by the results of one investment. Rather, the financial obligation extends to the results of the whole firm. When one investment does poorly, the firm must still pay whatever debts come due from the proceeds of all its other investments. Thus, financing considerations cannot be accounted for on a project-by-project basis. Instead, the impact of financing on the project's cost of capital is determined by the capital structure of the whole firm.

In the event that a firm finances an investment through a separate corporate subsidiary, the parent firm has no direct liability for any of the subsidiary's financial obligations. The parent is a shareholder. The corporate firm thus limits its liability to what it has invested in the subsidiary. In that case, the subsidiary's capital structure is the relevant one on which to base the project's cost of capital.

When Capital Structure Effects Are Important

There are two situations in which it is particularly important to adjust explicitly for capital structure effects. The first is when the repayment of a loan is tied to one or more specific assets. Leverage will change as the loan is repaid, and as the asset is used up and its value declines.[5] This planned reduction in leverage makes it *both* inappropriate to assume a constant debt ratio (as the procedure devel-

[5]An example is a leveraged buyout, which is discussed in Chapter 25. It involves an asset-specific capital structure. By design, the leverage will decrease over time. Cash flows from asset sales and operations are dedicated to repay debt. The owners of the firm intend to restore its capital structure to one that is more 'normal,' typically within five to seven years.

oped in Chapter 11 assumes) and impractical to assume some sort of time-weighted average debt ratio. The *adjusted-present-value (APV)* approach discussed in this chapter can handle this situation.

The second case occurs in practice when firms adjust their capital structures to coincide with their target capital structures. A firm's total amount of debt (as distinguished from the proportion, L) at any point in time therefore depends on the firm's profitability. More profitable firms accumulate retained earnings more quickly and can add debt faster. The reverse is true for less profitable firms. Capital structure rebalancing thus adds an element of risk to the firm's financial situation, which affects its cost of capital. Later in the chapter we will explain how to incorporate this factor into a firm's cost of capital calculation.

Review

1. Explain why each capital investment project has its own cost of capital.
2. Describe two situations where it is important to adjust the cost of capital for capital structure effects.

16.5 ADJUSTED PRESENT VALUE

The value of a leveraged firm, or any investment, is given by Equation (15.8):

$$V_L = V_U + T^*D = \frac{\bar{I}(1-T)}{r} + \frac{T^*r_dD}{r_d} \tag{15.8}$$

The right-hand side expresses the total present value as the present value of two perpetuities (the cash flow divided by the discount rate). The first is the present value of the firm's operating cash flow stream, calculated as though the firm had no debt. The second is the present value of the stream of interest tax shields. Equation (15.8) implies the required return given by Equation (15.9):

$$\text{WACC} = r(1 - T^*L) \tag{15.9}$$

which is appropriate for investments that are level perpetuities.[6] But most investments are not level perpetuities. We could still use Equation (15.9) as a less-accurate estimate, but more accurate ones are available.

Suppose a firm's loan is tied to one or more specific assets by an agreement such as a mortgage or lease. In such cases, the interest and principal payments are prespecified to occur within the asset's life. Over that payment period, the value of the asset declines with its use because the project (asset) has a finite life. Finite life projects with contractually specified debt payment schedules are fundamentally different from perpetual investments. In these cases, we know at the start of the project what the exact pattern of the "capital structure" will be (the remaining debt at any point), because of the repayment contract. Such a project's cost of capital can then be adjusted for the effects of this capital structure over the project's life. **Adjusted present value (APV)** is a method that can account for such patterns.

Equation (15.8) expresses the firm's value as the sum of two components. We can rewrite this equation to approximate a project's value as the sum of two components, each of which is the present value of a *finite* cash flow stream. The first is the "basic" project income, its CFATs, and the other is the net benefits from debt financing. So the value of the project, its APV, is

$$\text{APV}_0 = \sum_{t=1}^{n} \frac{\text{CFAT}_t}{(1+r)^t} + \sum_{t=1}^{n} \frac{T^*\text{INT}_t}{[1+r_d]^t} \tag{16.5}$$

[6] We say *level* perpetuity to emphasize that the cash flow is constant, and to distinguish it from a *growing* perpetuity. We first encountered growing perpetuities in Chapter 5 in the dividend growth model.

TABLE 16.5
Loan amortization schedule for SBP (dollar amounts in millions).

YEAR	0	1	2	3	4	5	6
(a) Loan balance at start of period	0	2.5000	2.3000	2.1000	1.9000	1.7000	1.5000
(b) Interest for the period (13.2% of loan balance)	0	0.3300	0.3036	0.2772	0.2508	0.2244	0.1980
(c) Principal repayment	0	0.2000	0.2000	0.2000	0.2000	0.2000	1.5000
(d) Loan balance at end of period, (a)–(c)	2.5000	2.3000	2.1000	1.9000	1.7000	1.5000	0

where n is the number of periods in the life of the project and INT_t is the interest payment in period t. Each sum is the present value of finite stream, which corresponds to the present value of a perpetuity in Equation (15.8).

EXAMPLE Calculating an APV at Borden

Borden is evaluating an investment in a new type of soybean processing plant. The investment would be set up as a wholly owned subsidiary, called SBP. SBP would be financed with $2.5 million of debt and $1.5 million of cash, provided by Borden as equity. The (unleveraged) after-tax cash flows, the CFATs, expected to result from SBP are $1 million per year for six years. After that time, the project is expected to be sold off for a net after-tax $2 million in cash. SBP will have six-year debt at an interest rate of 13.2% per year. Principal repayments will be $200,000 per year for five years, and $1.5 million at the end of year 6. Suppose the net-benefit-to-leverage factor, T^*, for this investment is 0.25 and the (unleveraged) required return for the project, r, is 20%. What is the value of the project to Borden? In other words, what is the project's *net* APV?

Table 16.5 gives an amortization schedule for SBP's loan. It identifies the interest payments that SBP must make over the life of the loan. From Equation (16.5), we have

$$APV_0 = \sum_{t=1}^{6} \frac{1.0}{(1.2)^t} + \frac{2.0}{(1.2)^6} +$$

$$\left[\frac{0.3300}{1.132} + \frac{0.3036}{(1.132)^2} + \frac{0.2772}{(1.132)^3} + \frac{0.2508}{(1.132)^4} + \frac{0.2244}{(1.132)^5} + \frac{0.1980}{(1.132)^6}\right][0.25]$$

$$APV_0 = 3.325510 + 0.941571 = \$4.267 \text{ million}$$

The net APV (APV_0 minus the initial cost) is then $0.267 million (= 4.267 − 4.0).

Review

1. What are the two components of the adjusted present value of a project?
2. Explain why Equation (16.5) for a particular project is analogous to Equation (15.8) for the whole firm.
3. What is the difference between the APV and the net APV?

16.6 MANAGING CAPITAL STRUCTURE AND ITS IMPACT ON FIRM VALUE

APV is very useful in situations where the financing and investment are tied together, such as leases and leveraged buyouts.[7] However, capital budgeting decisions usually do not involve financing that is tied to the project. Nevertheless, even if the firm's financing decisions are separate from its capital budgeting decisions, if T^* is positive, capital structure affects the value of the firm's investments. To include that value effect, we must know the *pattern* of debt payments.

Leverage Rebalancing

A firm generally establishes a capital structure policy that involves a target debt ratio, L^*. The firm's actual debt ratio, L, might be above or below L^* at any point in time. Although the firm does not maintain $L = L^*$ at all times, periodically the firm adjusts its capital structure back to $L = L^*$. Such adjustments are especially common when a firm has additional reasons for making a major financial transaction, such as issuing new bonds or paying off old ones. When a firm adjusts its capital structure back to L^*, it is referred to as **leverage rebalancing.**

Unintended changes in a firm's capital structure may necessitate leverage rebalancing. These unintended changes can occur for a number of reasons. Most often such changes occur because new information arrives. For example, an innovation in technology can cause an increase or decrease in the value of a firm. Because L is the ratio of debt to the *total market value* of the firm, a change in the firm's value causes L to change.

A General Pattern for Debt Payments

Suppose a firm has a target leverage ratio, and it periodically rebalances its leverage to that target. In particular, suppose leverage is rebalanced each period on the basis of the project's realized market value. This sounds much more complex than it turns out. Under such a policy, there is a simple adjustment to the unleveraged required return, r, to get the cost of capital for correctly computing the value of an investment. And this works even when the project's CFAT stream is not a level perpetuity.

When leverage is rebalanced each period on the basis of the realized market value, the net benefit to leverage in future periods will vary with the value of the project. So the net benefit to leverage in future periods is riskier with leverage rebalancing than it is with a fixed debt payment schedule. In fact, the actual debt pattern will vary in the same way project value varies.

With leverage rebalancing, the present value of the net benefits to leverage is not determined by r_d. Only the net benefit from the first period is discounted at r_d, because only the first period's debt is known at the start ($t = 0$). The net benefit to leverage in later periods must be discounted at r, the project's unleveraged required return, because this net benefit will vary as the project value varies in future periods.

Adjusting WACC for Capital Structure Valuation Effects

We will derive the adjustment to r that gives the project's correct cost of capital assuming income that is a level perpetuity, because it is easier to understand. However, the answer also applies to projects that have finite lives.

With level perpetual income, there is a "basic" expected after-tax cash flow, CFAT, of $\bar{I}(1 - T)$ each period. There is also an expected (mathematical expectation) net benefit to leverage each period of $T^* L r_d \mathrm{E}[V_L]$, where $\mathrm{E}[V_L]$ is the expected value of the project. Note that the actual value of the project at each future time is a *realization*. It will almost surely differ from the expectation, just as the realized return differs from the expected return.

---

[7]Leasing is covered in Chapter 20 and leveraged buyouts in Chapter 25.

FIGURE 16.1
Present value calculation for the net benefit to leverage.

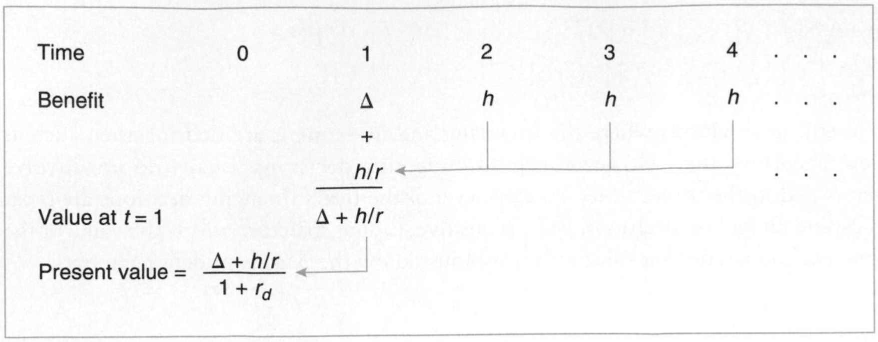

According to Equation (15.8), the total value of the investment is the sum of the two present values. However, to compute these present values, we need to know the required return for each income stream. The required return for the first stream is straightforward. It is the unleveraged required return, *r*. Thus, the present value, V_U is:

$$V_U = \frac{\bar{I}(1-T)}{r} \tag{15.2}$$

Determining the required return for the second stream is more complex. V_L is the value of the project at $t = 0$. The net benefit to leverage in the first period is $T^* L r_d V_L$, because the debt level is LV_L. This amount has the same risk as the debt. However, the net benefits to leverage in later periods are based on the expected value, $E(V_L)$. They are therefore riskier. The amount of debt in each future period depends on what the project's value turns out to be at that time. The risk of those tax benefits is therefore comparable to the risk of the unleveraged cash flows.

Let the net benefit to leverage in the first period be $\Delta = T^* L r_d V_L$. Let the expected net benefit to leverage in all periods after the first be $h = T^* L r_d E(V_L)$. The stream of net benefits to leverage and the present value calculation for them are illustrated in Figure 16.1.

At time $t = 1$, the stream of future net benefits to leverage is a level perpetuity with an expected value of h each period. So the value, at $t = 1$, of future benefits in periods 2, 3, 4, . . . is simply h/r—the present value of a perpetuity. The total value attributable to leverage, at $t = 1$, equals $\Delta + h/r$. To get the total value at $t = 0$, we must discount the value at $t = 1$ back one period. We discount it at r_d because it belongs to the same risk class as the debt itself. The present value of all the net benefits to leverage over the life of the project is then

$$\text{PV (net benefit to leverage)} = \frac{\Delta + h/r}{1 + r_d} \tag{16.6}$$

The total value of the leveraged investment, V_L, equals the sum of V_U and the PV (net benefit to leverage):

$$V_L = \frac{\bar{I}(1-T)}{r} + \frac{\Delta + h/r}{1 + r_d} \tag{16.7}$$

$\bar{I}$ is a level expected perpetuity. Its expected value at any future point in time is the same as its current expected value. Therefore $E(V_L) = V_L$ and $h = \Delta$. Thus, we can substitute $T^* L r_d V_L$ for both Δ and h in Equation (16.7). Making these substitutions and rearranging terms (which we will not drag out here) gives the following expression for the total value of the leveraged investment:

$$V_L = \frac{\bar{I}(1-T)}{r - T^* L r_d \left[\dfrac{1+r}{1+r_d}\right]} \tag{16.8}$$

Equation (16.8) expresses V_L as the present value of a perpetuity consisting of CFAT = $\bar{I}(1 - T)$. Therefore, the denominator must be the required return for this perpetuity. Therefore

$$\text{WACC} = r - T^* L r_d \left[\frac{1 + r}{1 + r_d}\right] \tag{16.9}$$

Equation (16.9) shows a firm's or project's (weighted average) cost of capital, assuming the firm follows a policy of leverage rebalancing each period based on the investment's realized market value.

EXAMPLE Calculating Bausch & Lomb's WACC

Let us say the unleveraged required return, r, for Bausch & Lomb's entire portfolio of assets is 18%. Suppose $T^* = 0.25$ and Bausch & Lomb rebalances its capital structure each year to a target of $L = 0.35$. Bausch & Lomb can borrow currently at a rate of $r_d = 11.5\%$. What is Bausch & Lomb's WACC?

From Equation (16.9) we have

$$\text{WACC} = 0.18 - 0.25(0.35)(0.115)\left[\frac{1.18}{1.115}\right] = 0.1694, \text{ or } 16.94\%$$

Estimating the Unleveraged Required Return

Equation (16.9) shows the WACC for a firm or project based on the unleveraged required return, r. Often we need to reverse this process and estimate r based on the WACC.

We know that Equation (16.4) is always correct. And we have said that the debt management pattern assumed in Equation (16.9) represents typical corporate policy quite well. Therefore, we can use Equation (16.4) to estimate the WACC and use that value to calculate r. To simplify the notation (if you can imagine it), we will use a variable, H:

$$H = \frac{T^* L r_d}{1 + r_d} \tag{16.10}$$

Then, expressing Equation (16.9) in terms of H and solving for r gives the following expression for the unleveraged required return:[8]

$$r = \frac{\text{WACC} + H}{1 - H} \tag{16.11}$$

EXAMPLE Estimating Conoco's Unleveraged Required Return

Suppose Conoco wants to estimate the unleveraged required return for a project it is considering. Conoco's finance staff has identified Prairie Oil and Gas, a publicly traded firm in the same business as the Conoco project. Prairie's operating risk profile should therefore be similar to that of the project. Prairie's leverage ratio is $L = 0.40$. They estimate that Prairie's new

[8]Equation (16.9) becomes WACC = $r - (1 + r)H$. Then solving for r we get Equation (16.11).

issue debt rate is $r_d = 12\%$, and calculate Prairie's WACC = 15%. They also estimate $T^* = 0.25$. What is the project's unleveraged required return?

Substituting into Equation (16.10),

$$H = \frac{(0.25)(0.40)(0.12)}{1.12} = 0.01071$$

Substituting into Equation (16.11),

$$r = \frac{0.15 + 0.01071}{1 - 0.01071} = 0.1625$$

So the unleveraged required return for the Conoco project is estimated to be 16.25%.

Review

1. What does it mean to say that a firm follows a capital structure policy of periodically rebalancing its debt level?
2. Explain why r, and not r_d, is the appropriate discount rate for calculating the present value of the future interest tax shields when the firm regularly rebalances its debt level.
3. As long as T^* can never be negative, explain why the WACC can never exceed the unleveraged required return, r.

16.7 ESTIMATING THE WACC FOR A CAPITAL BUDGETING PROJECT

Now let us see how to calculate the WACC for a project when the firm regularly rebalances its capital structure. We will combine the procedure outlined in the previous section with the other basic steps discussed previously. That will give you the complete set of steps you need to follow.

The process for estimating a WACC can be outlined as follows:

1. Choose one or more comparable firms (with publicly traded securities) that have similar risk and industry characteristics as that of the project.
2. For each comparable firm:
   a. Estimate L. L is the market value of all the firm's debt (total liabilities) divided by the sum of the total market values of the firm's debt and equity. Sometimes the book value of debt approximates the market value of debt pretty well.
   b. Estimate r_d. r_d can be estimated as the yield to maturity on the firm's outstanding debt.
   c. Estimate r_e. Estimating r_e is more difficult and requires professional judgement. The dividend growth model (Chapter 5), or the capital-asset-pricing model (Chapter 10),[9] can be used to estimate r_e.
   d. Estimate the firm's marginal tax rate, T, using publicly reported data.
   e. Estimate the net-benefit-to-leverage factor for the firm, T^*. T^* is the most difficult parameter to estimate. Estimating T^* involves considering the firm's marginal tax rate, the uniqueness of its products, and the amount of nondebt tax shields, among

[9] If you do not have enough information to use one of these analytical methods, Emery's rule says that r_e is normally about 1.5 times r_d.

other factors discussed in Chapter 15. The estimate of T^* is ultimately based on subjective professional judgment. Based on empirical research, we would expect most estimates for a healthy firm to fall somewhere between 0.10 and 0.25.

3. For each comparable firm, use the parameter estimates from point 2 above to estimate H using Equation (16.10) and the WACC using Equation (16.4). Then use Equation (16.11) to estimate r.
4. Based on the set of one or more estimates of r from comparable firms, make a single estimate of r. Usually an average can be used. However, judgment is necessary when the variation in the estimates is large or some of the estimates are very different from each other. r must reflect the project's business risk.
5. The estimate of the project's WACC (which includes both business risk and the effects of capital structure) can now be computed using Equation (16.9), the single estimate of r derived above, and estimates for the firm considering the investment:
   a. the firm's target capital structure, L^*, which the firm plans to maintain;
   b. the firm's current r_d based on L^*; and
   c. the firm's net-benefit-to-leverage factor, T^*.

EXAMPLE Estimating a Project's WACC for PepsiCo

Suppose PepsiCo is considering an investment opportunity in laser printers, an area in which it has no previous experience. PepsiCo has identified several firms that are primarily in this business. One of these firms is H-P, whose common stock and bonds are traded publicly on the NYSE. Suppose the market value of H-P common stock is \$27 per share. H-P has 10 million shares outstanding. H-P's latest earnings were \$3.40 per share. Next year's dividend is expected to be \$1.60 per share. Five years ago, H-P paid a dividend of \$0.73 per share. H-P has long-term bonds with a total market value of \$120 million. Its 9% coupon bonds maturing in 18 years are currently selling for \$860. In addition to long-term bonds, H-P has \$20 million in notes payable and \$40 million in other current liabilities.

H-P has total liabilities of \$180 million consisting of long-term bonds and current liabilities (= 120 + 20 + 40). Current liabilities mature soon enough that the book and market values are sufficiently close to ignore the difference and simply use the book value in our calculations. Total equity is \$270 million (= [27]10 million). The total market value of H-P is \$450 million (= 120 + 60 + 270), and $L = 0.40$ (= 180/450). H-P's 9% coupon bonds have a 10.8% yield to maturity, and an 11.09% APY.

CALCULATOR SOLUTION

Data Input	Function Key
36	N
860	PV
45 (=90/2)	PMT
1,000	FV
5.4%	I

Because the bonds are selling at a discount and will incur lower taxes due to capital gains tax deferral, we estimate that new debt for H-P has a required return that is slightly higher than the 11.09% APY. We estimate r_d to be 11.25% APY.

Lasser Financial Services estimates that H-P's beta is 1.25. Short-term U.S. government securities are currently earning 7%, so we estimate the riskless rate, r_f, to be 7%. The required return on the market portfolio, r_M, is estimated to be 15%. The CAPM estimate of H-P's required return on equity is $r_e = 0.07 + 1.25(0.15 - 0.07) = 0.17$, or 17%. During the six-year period from five years ago until next year, H-P's cash dividend grew from \$0.73 to \$1.60, which represents an annual growth rate of $g = 14\%$. The current market value is $P_0 = \$27$, and next year's expected dividend is $D_1 = \$1.60$. The dividend growth model estimate of the required return for equity is $r_e = (1.6/27) + 0.14 = 0.20$, or 20%.

The estimate obtained from the dividend growth model is based on a growth rate that is almost as large as the return to the market portfolio, and is considerably larger than the return on the riskless asset. It is unlikely that growth of this magnitude could be maintained indefinitely. Thus, the dividend growth model estimate of r_e is probably too large. However, it is plausibly close to the CAPM estimate. Therefore, the two estimates do not appear to significantly contradict one another. Because the CAPM estimate is more reliable, we will use it as our estimate of H-P's required return on equity.

PepsiCo's financial staff estimates that H-P's net-benefit-to-leverage factor is $T^* = 0.2$. Applying Equation (16.10), with $T^* = 0.20$, $L = 0.40$, and $r_d = 11.25\%$,

$$H = \frac{T^* L r_d}{1 + r_d} = \frac{(0.2)(0.4)(0.1125)}{1.1125} = 0.00809$$

The relevant marginal tax rate is estimated as $T = 35\%$. Therefore, with $r_e = 17\%$, applying Equation (16.4) we get

$$\text{WACC} = (1 - L)r_e + L(1 - T)r_d = 0.6(0.17) + 0.4(0.65)(0.1125) = 0.13125$$

Finally, putting $H = 0.00809$ and WACC = 13.125% into Equation (16.11), we have

$$r = \frac{\text{WACC} + H}{1 - H} = \frac{(0.13125 + 0.00809)}{(1 - 0.00809)} = 0.1405$$

Assume that the above procedure was followed for other comparable firms in addition to H-P, and the single estimate of r based on the set of comparable firms is 14%. We can now estimate WACC for the project based on this "best" estimate of r and the following estimates of PepsiCo's financial parameters: $r_d = 11\%$, $L^* = 0.3$, and (because of its unique tax situation) $T^* = 0.15$. From Equation (16.9),

$$\text{WACC} = r - T^* L r_d \left[\frac{1 + r}{1 + r_d}\right] = 0.14 - (0.15)(0.3)(0.11)\left[\frac{1.14}{1.11}\right] = 0.135, \text{ or } 13.5\%$$

Thus, PepsiCo should use a 13.5% WACC to compute the NPV of its proposed investment in laser printers.

Review

1. List the steps in the five-step process for estimating the WACC for a capital budgeting project.
2. Explain why the estimate of r calculated at step 4 reflects the operating risk of the project under consideration *and does not* reflect any financial risk.
3. Explain how step 5 adjusts for financial risk based on the project sponsor's capital structure.
4. Which factor is most difficult to estimate, r, T^*, L, or r_d? Why?

SUMMARY

The following procedure is useful for choosing and managing capital structure:

- Determine the *rating objective.* It reflects the desired margin of safety for the risk of financial distress and for maintaining access to the capital markets.
- Conduct a *comparative credit analysis* of comparable firms to determine the capital structure that is consistent with the chosen rating. It is particularly important to select

firms with similar asset portfolios, because asset type affects the costs of financial distress and the amount of leverage for a particular rating. It is also important to select firms that are comparable in size, because other things being equal, the larger a firm, the greater the amount of debt the rating agencies will tolerate for a given rating.

- Determine the values of the *key financial ratios that characterize leverage.* Three such ratios that are particularly meaningful are annual fixed charge coverage ratio, annual funds-from-operations-to-total-debt ratio, and long-term debt ratio. However, three simple ratios usually do not tell the whole story. So many analysts use additional ratios to define the target capital structure.
- Conduct a *pro forma financial analysis* to test the firm's ability to use fully both the tax benefits of ownership under its planned capital expenditure program and the interest tax shields if it finances in accordance with its target capital structure. Also test the impact on financial ratios of different future operating scenarios to determine what adjustment to the target capital structure is appropriate in light of the firm's expected future operating environment.
- Determine the need for and desirability of a *share repurchase or other form of transaction* to adjust capital structure quickly.
- APV (adjusted present value) is a method for including the effect of capital structure on investment value, using the unleveraged value V_U and "adjusting" that basic value by adding the value obtained from leverage.
- With APV, the added value from leverage is the present value of a series of cash flow adjustments stemming from a fixed debt payment pattern, such as with leases or a leveraged buyout, or any unique debt pattern.
- A more general form of APV adjusts the WACC, using an approximation of leverage rebalancing on the basis of realized market value. Although the adjustment is only an estimate of a more complex process, this method is widely used in practice and is particularly useful because it simply modifies the rate used in an otherwise "standard NPV calculation."

EQUATION SUMMARY

$$\text{Interest coverage ratio} = \frac{\text{EBIT}}{\text{Interest expense}} \tag{16.1}$$

$$\text{Fixed charge coverage ratio} = \frac{\text{EBIT} + 1/3 \text{ Rentals}}{\text{Interest expense} + 1/3 \text{ Rentals}} \tag{16.2}$$

$$\text{Debt service coverage ratio} = \frac{\text{EBIT} + 1/3 \text{ Rentals}}{\text{Interest expense} + 1/3 \text{ Rentals} + \dfrac{\text{Principal repayments}}{1 - \text{Tax rate}}} \tag{16.3}$$

$$\text{WACC} = (1 - L)r_e + L(1 - T)r_d \tag{16.4}$$

$$\text{APV}_0 = \sum_{t=1}^{n} \frac{\text{CFAT}_t}{(1 + r)^t} + \sum_{t=1}^{n} \frac{T^*\text{INT}_t}{[1 + r_d]^t} \tag{16.5}$$

$$\text{PV (net benefit to leverage)} = \frac{\Delta + h/r}{1 + r_d} \tag{16.6}$$

$$V_L = \frac{\bar{I}(1-T)}{r} + \frac{\Delta + h/r}{1+r_d} \tag{16.7}$$

$$V_L = \frac{\bar{I}(1-T)}{r - T^* L r_d \left[\dfrac{1+r}{1+r_d}\right]} \tag{16.8}$$

$$\text{WACC} = r - T^* L r_d \left[\frac{1+r}{1+r_d}\right] \tag{16.9}$$

$$H = \frac{T^* L r_d}{1+r_d} \tag{16.10}$$

$$r = \frac{\text{WACC} + H}{1-H} \tag{16.11}$$

QUESTIONS

1. Why is a pro forma analysis an important prerequisite to choosing a capital structure?
2. What is the major reason that subordinated debt is typically rated lower than senior debt?
3. Explain why selecting a target senior debt rating is a reasonable approach to choosing a capital structure. Explain why a target senior debt rating of single-A is a prudent objective when there is only a very limited new issue market for non-investment-grade debt, and when investor willingness to purchase triple-B-rated debt is likely to be highly sensitive to the state of the economy.
4. A firm's capital structure consists solely of debt and common equity. What form would an exchange offer take if the firm believes it is (a) Overleveraged? (b) Underleveraged?
5. Because the weighted average given in Equation (16.4) is always a correct measure of a required return, why do firms not create securities to finance each project and offer them in the capital market in order to accurately determine the required return for the project?
6. Why should a firm's ability to use tax credits affect its capital structure?
7. How does a firm's size (as measured by total assets or total sales, for example) affect its choice of capital structure under the comparable-firms approach?
8. Why would lenders be willing to lend a larger proportion of the market value of tangible assets such as plant and equipment than of the market value of intangible assets such as "special" formulas and goodwill?
9. Suppose that a firm wishes to maintain a capital structure that is consistent with an A senior debt rating. Under what circumstances would the firm maintain a lower degree of leverage than a cross section of single-A-rated firms?

CHALLENGING QUESTIONS

10. Why is it so important to note that the required return is not a historical cost of funds? Cite two factors that can render the use of a firm's historical cost of funds (to evaluate a new investment) to be potentially damaging to the firm.
11. In what sense is subordinated debt advantageous to senior debtholders, and in what sense is it disadvantageous to them?

12. Explain in your own words why you might expect to observe a negative correlation between financial leverage and operating leverage.
13. Using agency theory concepts, explain how restrictive covenants that forbid leases and liens on a firm's assets might cause the firm to achieve a higher rating on its bonds than would be possible without such covenants.
14. The development of the new issue junk bond market had important implications for capital structure choice. The existence of a viable junk bond market means that firms can comfortably maintain higher degrees of leverage than they could prior to the development of this market. Do you agree or disagree? Justify your answer.
15. A balance sheet sometimes has something called minority interest, which appears below long-term debt and above preferred stock. Discuss whether minority interest should be treated as debt or equity, assuming
    a. It consists of outstanding common stock of a subsidiary, and the parent firm has no intention of repurchasing or otherwise retiring that common stock.
    b. It consists of redeemable preferred stock of a subsidiary, which the firm is obligated to redeem in equal annual amounts over the next five years.
    c. What is your conclusion regarding whether minority interest is really debt or equity?

PROBLEMS

LEVEL A (BASIC)

A1. (Coverage ratio) A firm's latest 12 months' EBIT is $30 million, and its interest expense for the same period is $10 million. Calculate the interest coverage ratio.

A2. (Coverage ratio) The firm in the preceding problem also had $15 million of rental expense during the latest 12 months. Calculate the firm's fixed charge coverage ratio.

A3. (Coverage ratio) The firm in the two preceding problems also had $6 million of principal repayments during the latest 12 months. Its marginal tax rate is 40%. Calculate the debt service coverage ratio.

A4. (WACC with rebalancing) Nathan's Catering is a gourmet catering service located in Southampton, NY. It has an unleveraged required return of $r = 43\%$. Nathan's rebalances its capital structure each year to a target of $L = 0.52$. $T^* = 0.20$. Nathan's can borrow currently at a rate of $r_d = 26\%$. What is Nathan's WACC?

A5. (Unleveraging the cost of equity) Maxicomputer Corporation is considering building a new manufacturing facility in Taiwan. Maxicomputer's debt ratio is $L = 0.5$. Maxicomputer's cost of debt is $r_d = 10\%$. Maxicomputer estimates that the leveraged cost of equity capital for the project is $r_e = 16\%$. $T^* = 0.25$. Maxicomputer's marginal ordinary income tax rate is 40%. Calculate the project's unleveraged required return, r.

A6. (Estimating a project's WACC) Reconsider the PepsiCo example. PepsiCo has identified a second firm that is closely comparable to H-P. Epson has a debt ratio of $L = 0.60$, a cost of debt of $r_d = 12\%$, a leveraged required return to equity of $r_e = 20\%$, a 40% marginal tax rate, and a net-benefit-to-leverage factor of $T^* = 0.20$.
    a. Calculate Epson's unleveraged required return, r.
    b. Recalculate the estimate of r for PepsiCo to use by averaging H-P's and Epson's unleveraged required returns.
    c. What is the required return that PepsiCo should use to compute the (adjusted) NPV of the capital budgeting project?

A7. (NPV of a risky project) Suppose a firm currently has an unleveraged required return of 10% and perpetual unleveraged after-tax income of $140,301 per year. The firm has come up with an investment opportunity that would alter the firm's asset makeup so that it would increase its perpetual unleveraged after-tax income to $170,650 per year. Because the new asset mix is riskier, the firm's unleveraged required return would also increase to 12.165%. Should the firm undertake this investment opportunity?

LEVEL B

B1. (Choosing financial targets) Bixton Company's new chief financial officer is evaluating Bixton's capital structure. She is concerned that the firm might be underleveraged, even though the firm has larger-than-average research and development and foreign tax credits when compared to other firms in its industry. Her staff prepared the industry comparison shown here.

a. Bixton's objective is to achieve a credit standing that falls, in the words of the chief financial officer, "comfortably within the 'A' range." What target range would you recommend for each of the three credit measures?

b. Before settling on these target ranges, what other factors should Bixton's chief financial officer consider?

c. Before deciding whether the target ranges are really appropriate for Bixton in its current financial situation, what key issues specific to Bixton must the chief financial officer resolve?

RATING CATEGORY	FIXED CHARGE COVERAGE	FUNDS FROM OPERATIONS/ TOTAL DEBT	LONG-TERM DEBT/ CAPITALIZATION
Aa	4.00–5.25*x*	60–80%	17–23%
A	3.00–4.30	45–65	22–32
Baa	1.95–3.40	35–55	30–41

B2. (Choosing financial targets) Sanderson Manufacturing Company would like to achieve a capital structure consistent with a Baa2/BBB senior debt rating. Sanderson has identified six comparable firms and calculated the credit statistics shown here.

a. Sanderson's return on assets is 5.3%. It has a total capitalization of $600 million. What are reasonable targets for long-term debt/cap, funds from operations/LT debt, and fixed charge coverage?

b. Are there any firms among the six who are particularly good or bad comparables? Explain.

c. Suppose Sanderson's current ratio of long-term debt to total cap is 60% but its fixed charge coverage is 3.00. What would you recommend?

FIRM	A	B	C	D	E	F
Senior debt rating	Baa2/BBB	Baa3/BBB−	Baa2/BBB	Baa1/A−	Baa1/BBB−	Baa2/BBB+
Return on assets	5.2%	5.0%	5.4%	5.7%	5.2%	5.3%
Long-term debt/cap	38%	41%	45%	40%	25%	43%
Total cap ($MM)	425	575	525	650	210	375
Funds from operations/LT debt	39%	43%	28%	46%	57%	43%
Fixed charge cov	2.57	2.83	2.75	2.38	3.59	2.15

B3. (Coverage ratios) Show that of the interest coverage ratio, fixed charge coverage ratio, and debt service coverage ratio, (1) the interest coverage ratio will always have the greatest value and (2) the debt service coverage ratio will always have the smallest value, as long as interest coverage exceeds 1. Under what circumstances will all three ratios have the same value?

B4. (Coverage ratios) Mi Furst, Inc. has \$100 million of earnings before interest and taxes and \$40 million of interest expense.

a. Calculate Mi Furst's interest coverage ratio.

b. Calculate the pro forma interest coverage ratio assuming the issuance of \$100 million of 10% debt with the issue proceeds to be invested fully in a plant under construction.

c. Calculate the pro forma interest coverage ratio assuming the issuance of \$100 million of 10% debt with the proceeds to be invested temporarily in commercial paper that yields 8%.

B5. (APV) Suppose a firm is evaluating a potential new investment. The investment will be financed with \$100,000 of debt and \$100,000 of equity. The (unleveraged) after-tax cash flows, the CFATs, expected to result from the investment are \$150,000 per year for four years. At that time the firm expects to be able to sell the project for a net after-tax \$100,000 in cash. The debt financing will be four-year debt with interest payments of 14% per year on the remaining balance. Principal payments will be zero in year 1, \$20,000 in year 2, \$30,000 in year 3, and a final principal payment of \$50,000 at the end of year 4. The net-benefit-to-leverage factor, T^*, is 0.20. The (unleveraged) required return for the project is 20%. What is the project's net APV?

B6. (WACC, leverage, beta) Rusty-Sell, Inc., a midstate Pennsylvania recycling facility, is $L = 27\%$ debt financed. It pays corporate taxes at the rate of 35%. The firm's (leveraged) beta is 1.45. $T^* = 0.21$, $r_d = 12\%$, $r_f = 8\%$, and $r_M = 15\%$. Assume annual capital structure rebalancing.

a. What is Rusty-Sell's required return to (leveraged) equity, r_e?

b. What is Rusty-Sell's WACC?

c. What is Rusty-Sell's unleveraged required return, r?

d. What unleveraged beta is implied by r?

B7. (Cost of capital estimation) Managers of the Stan Lee Martin Corporation are considering a capital budgeting project that is unrelated to their current investments. The proposed project will be 40% debt financed at $r_d = 11.25\%$. They have identified three firms that they believe are basically comparable to the capital budgeting project under consideration, and they have collected the information about those comparable firms as shown below. Assume the following hold for all firms: (1) $r_M = 15\%$, (2) $r_f = 7\%$, (3) $T = 0.35$, (4) $T^* = 0.2$, and (5) the total debt is the number of bonds indicated, each with a par value of \$1,000 and 10 years to maturity. What cost of capital would you recommend the managers of Stan Lee Martin Corporation use to evaluate the proposed capital budgeting project?

FIRM	STOCK BETA	STOCK PRICE	# SHARES	BOND PRICE	COUPON	# BONDS
A	1.10	\$25	1 million	\$1,100	12%	10,700
B	1.20	\$30	2 million	\$900	10%	67,000
C	1.15	\$22	5 million	\$850	8%	32,350

B8. (Review, CAPM) The riskless return is 8%. The expected return on the market portfolio is 16%. A stock's beta is 1.5. Calculate the cost of equity capital.

B9. (Review, dividend growth model) A stock's current market price is \$25. The expected annual cash dividend is \$1 per share. In addition, investors expect the firm to pay a 4% dividend in common stock. The expected growth rate of the cash dividend is 10% per year.

a. Calculate the cost of retained earnings.

b. If a new share issue would require 5% flotation costs, what is the cost of the new issue?

B10. (Review, CAPM) The riskless return is 6%. The expected excess return on the market portfolio is 8%. A stock's beta is 1.35. Calculate the cost of equity capital.

B11. (Review from Chapter 11.) A stock's unleveraged beta is 0.8. The firm's debt ratio is $L = 0.4$. The riskless return is 5%, the tax rate is 30%, and the expected return on the market portfolio is 15%. What is the firm's cost of equity capital?

B12. (Review from Chapter 5.) A perpetual preferred stock issue can be sold for $25 per share. It would require a quarterly dividend rate of $0.50 per share. The underwriting fees and out-of-pocket expenses amount to 1.75% of the public offering price. What is the cost of preferred stock?

B13. (Excel: APV and WACC) Cans-R-Us, Inc (CRU) is a recycling firm located in the suburbs of Missouri City, Kansas. CRU is currently evaluating a potential new investment. The investment will be financed with $700,000 of debt and $1,200,000 of equity. The (unleveraged) after-tax cash flows, the CFATs, expected to result from the investment are $1 million per year for three years, after which time the project is expected to be sold off for a net after-tax $1 million in cash. The debt financing will take the form of three-year debt with interest payments of 15% per year on the remaining balance. Principal payments will be $100,000 in year 1, $200,000 in year 2, and $400,000 at the end of year 3. The net-benefit-to-leverage factor, T^*, is 0.25 for this investment. The (unleveraged) required return for the project is 25%. The corporate tax rate is 30%.

a. What is the project's net APV?

b. Based on the net APV computed in part a, what is L for this project?

c. Also based on the net APV computed in part a, what is the project's WACC? (*Hint:* You will need to use trial and error to solve for WACC.)

d. Based on the WACC computed in part c, what is the unleveraged required return, r, for this project?

LEVEL C (ADVANCED)

C1. (Excel: APV and WACC) Alpha Manufacturing is considering building a new distribution center that would cost $1 million. Alpha would finance the investment with $250,000 of equity and $750,000 of debt. The (unleveraged) after-tax cash flows, the CFATs, expected to result from the investment are $400,000 per year for 10 years, after which the distribution center will be sold off for a net after-tax amount of $200,000 cash. The loan will bear interest at a rate of 12% payable annually. It will be repaid in equal annual installments of $75,000, beginning at the end of year 1. The corporate tax rate is 35%, $T^* = 0.30$, and the unleveraged cost of equity for the project is 17%.

a. Calculate the project's net APV.

b. Calculate the WACC and the leveraged required return to equity, r_e, for the project.

c. Calculate the (adjusted) NPV of the project.

d. Reconcile your answers to parts a and c.

MINICASE DEBT-FOR-EQUITY EXCHANGE AT AMERICAN AIRLINES

AMR Corporation (AMR), the parent firm of American Airlines, found that its profitability had improved a few years ago. Several years prior, AMR had issued privately about $1.1 billion of convertible preferred stock. As you know, interest is tax deductible whereas dividends are not. AMR decided to offer the preferred stockholders the chance to exchange their shares for a new issue of convertible Quarterly Income Capital Securities ("QUICS"). AMR offered to exchange $1,000 face amount of 6.125% convertible QUICS for $1,000 face amount of 6% convertible preferred stock. All $1.1 billion of preferred stock could be exchanged at the holder's option.

The QUICS would carry a slightly higher yield and would rank senior to the preferred stock. But QUICS include an interest-deferral feature: AMR can defer interest payments from time to time for up to 20 consecutive quarters. It was reported that because of this feature, the rating agencies view QUICS as "virtually identical to the preferred."

AMR's main purpose in offering to exchange convertible QUICS for convertible preferred was to improve the firm's after-tax cash flow because of the tax deductibility of interest. The table below compares the QUICS and the preferred stock.

Just prior to the exchange offer, AMR's capitalization was (dollar amounts in millions):

Long term debt:	
Current maturities	$ 189
Long-term debt, less current maturities	7,710
QUICS	0
Total long-term debt	7,899
Convertible preferred stock	1,081
Common stock	3,318
Total stockholders' equity	4,399
Total capitalization	$12,298

	QUICS	PREFERRED
Interest/Dividend Rate	6⅛% APR; payable quarterly; interest payments can be deferred for up to 20 calendar quarters; at the end of the deferral period, all accrued and unpaid interest must be repaid, together with interest on the unpaid amount compounded quarterly at the 6⅛% APR.	6% APR; payable quarterly out of funds legally available therefore.
Conversion	At $79.00 per common share.	At $78.75 per common share.
Subordination	Subordinated to all existing and future senior debt of AMR and its subsidiaries but senior to AMR's preferred stock.	Subordinated to all debt of AMR.
Market	Registered for public trading; listed on the New York Stock Exchange.	Privately placed; not registered for public trading.

QUESTIONS

1. Describe the QUICS. Are they debt, or are they equity? How do they differ from the convertible preferred stock?
2. Recalculate AMR's capitalization if holders of (i) 50% and (ii) 100% of the convertible preferred stock exchanged them for QUICS.
3. Calculate the increase in net income available for common stock that would result from (i) 50% and (ii) 100% of the convertible preferred stock being exchanged for QUICS.
4. Why does this debt-for-equity exchange increase the risk of the common stock? How does the interest-deferral feature affect your interpretation of the QUICS? The risk of the common stock?
5. What trade-off did AMR have to evaluate as it considered whether to proceed with the exchange offer?

17

DIVIDEND POLICY

A firm's **dividend policy** is an established guide for the firm to determine the amount of money it will pay out as dividends. Don't you think it is reasonable that a firm should give its owners part of the profit? Why not share the wealth? But suppose the firm has positive-NPV projects it can invest the money in. Might the shareholders be better off if the firm retains and reinvests the money? Of course, if the firm paid the dividends, it could issue new debt or equity to get the money to invest in the positive-NPV projects, which could change its capital structure.

A dividend policy, then, involves a trade-off among cash dividends, capital budgeting, and capital structure. We are interested in whether this dividend policy trade-off affects the value of the firm. Just like capital structure, dividend policy does not matter in a perfect capital market environment. However, the same three groups of persistent capital market imperfections—asymmetric information, asymmetric taxes, and transaction costs—that cause capital structure to affect a firm's value also cause dividend policy to affect its value, but to a lesser extent.

As with capital structure, there are conflicting viewpoints about dividend policy. And just like capital structure, dividend policy is relevant in practice, because firms certainly behave as though it matters. The empirical evidence shows consistent patterns of dividend policy, and it shows significant average stock price reactions to dividend changes. This evidence suggests there are definite reasons for following certain policies, that some policies are superior to others. You might think firms are all following the Behavioral Principle and just copying each other. We think this is too simplistic. We will explain why in this chapter.

FOCUS ON PRINCIPLES

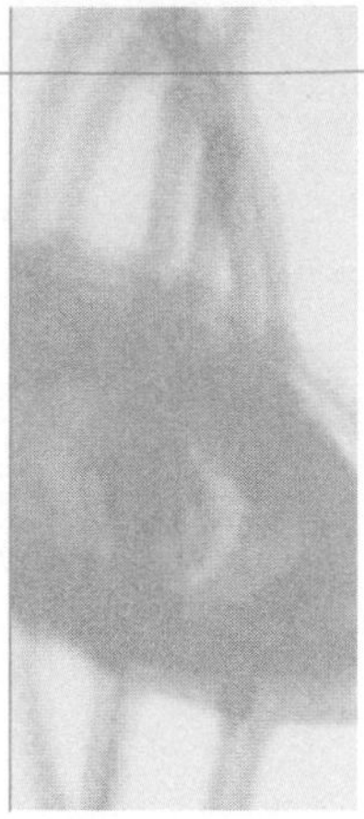

- *Capital Market Efficiency:* Recognize that the potential to increase firm value through dividend policy is smaller than the potential to increase firm value through the introduction of *valuable new ideas* and wise use of the firm's *comparative advantages.* The potential value differential is also smaller for dividend policy than it is for capital structure policy.
- *Risk-Return Trade-Off:* Recognize that the difference between receiving the dividend now and getting it later is risk and the time value of money. It is a risk-return trade-off that does not affect the value of the firm.
- *Signaling:* Consider any possible change in dividend policy carefully because dividend changes convey information to outsiders and can be misunderstood.
- *Behavioral:* Use the information contained in the dividend decisions of other firms.
- *Two-Sided Transactions:* Repurchasing shares from a takeover raider at a premium to their fair market value transfers wealth away from the other stockholders.
- *Valuable Ideas:* Look for opportunities to create value by supplying a dividend policy that is in short supply, perhaps resulting from changes in tax law.
- *Time Value of Money:* Include any time-value-of-money tax benefits from dividend choices.
- *Options:* Recognize the value of transferable put rights (options).

17.1 DIVIDEND POLICY IN PRACTICE

Thus far, for simplicity, we have characterized a dividend policy simply as a *payout ratio,* the ratio of dividends paid to earnings (see Chapter 5). However, it is more complex than this. A firm's payout ratio typically varies over time. For example, a small and rapidly growing firm may retain all its earnings for many years to help finance its growth. As a firm matures, typically it begins to pay dividends at some point and then, over time, increases the proportion of its earnings that are paid out in dividends. About 50% of the earnings of all U.S. corporations over the past half century have been paid out as dividends. The actual dividend policies of firms provide a useful backdrop for our discussion of dividend policy.

Characteristics of Corporate Dividend Policies

In practice, publicly traded firms prefer to (1) pay at least some minimum level of dividends on a regular basis, (2) maintain a stable payout ratio and dividend rate, (3) make orderly changes in the dividend rate, and (4) avoid cutting an established dividend rate.

SHARING THE PROFITS Smaller and younger firms generally do not pay cash dividends. At some point in its life cycle, a firm decides that it is sufficiently "mature" to share the profits. This may be due to a desire to demonstrate the firm's stability or a decline in profitable investment opportunities. It could also result in part from investor desires for at least some minimal level of cash distributions, an effort to broaden the market for the firm's stock to include investors who are prohibited from buying non-dividend-paying stocks, or other factors. Among New York Stock Exchange-listed common stocks, for example, in any given year between 75% and 90% pay cash dividends.

EXAMPLE Initiating a Dividend at FedEx

After 31 years in business, FedEx Corp. announced it would pay its first cash dividend—five cents per share per quarter. FedEx noted that it would need less capital than in the past to expand its global delivery network and expected to have a growing stream of free cash flow. FedEx's CFO commented that the dividend "sends a very strong signal . . . that FedEx has a sustainable, strong, positive cash flow for the foreseeable future."

DIVIDENDS ARE MORE STABLE THAN EARNINGS Figure 17.1 illustrates the pattern of corporate earnings and dividends from World War II to the present. Dividends are more stable than earnings. This is also true for most individual firms, as illustrated in Figure 17.2 for Exxon Mobil Corporation.

REGULAR PAYMENT AND REGULAR CHANGES Dividend-paying firms usually make quarterly payments. Once they begin paying dividends, firms strive to continue making regular payments. In fact, firms frequently highlight the length of their uninterrupted dividend records each quarter they declare another dividend. Furthermore, most firms review their dividend policies at least once annually, often during the same quarter each year. Many firms increase the quarterly dividend each year.

RELUCTANCE TO CUT THE DIVIDEND Firms exhibit a strong aversion to cutting an established *dividend rate* (i.e., a total dollar amount per period). This is probably because a dividend cut is viewed by the market as a negative signal.

FIGURE 17.1
Corporate dividends and earnings from World War II to the present.

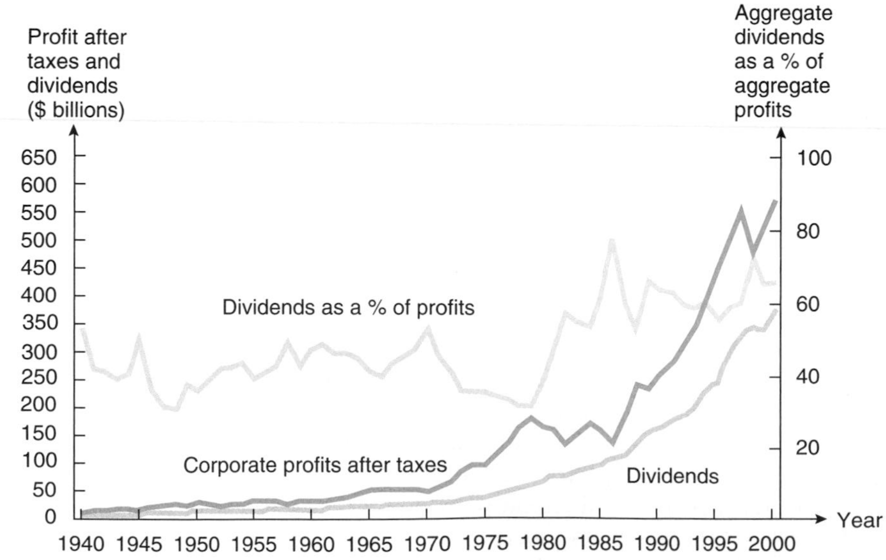

Source: Bureau of Economic Analysis, *www.bea.gov.*

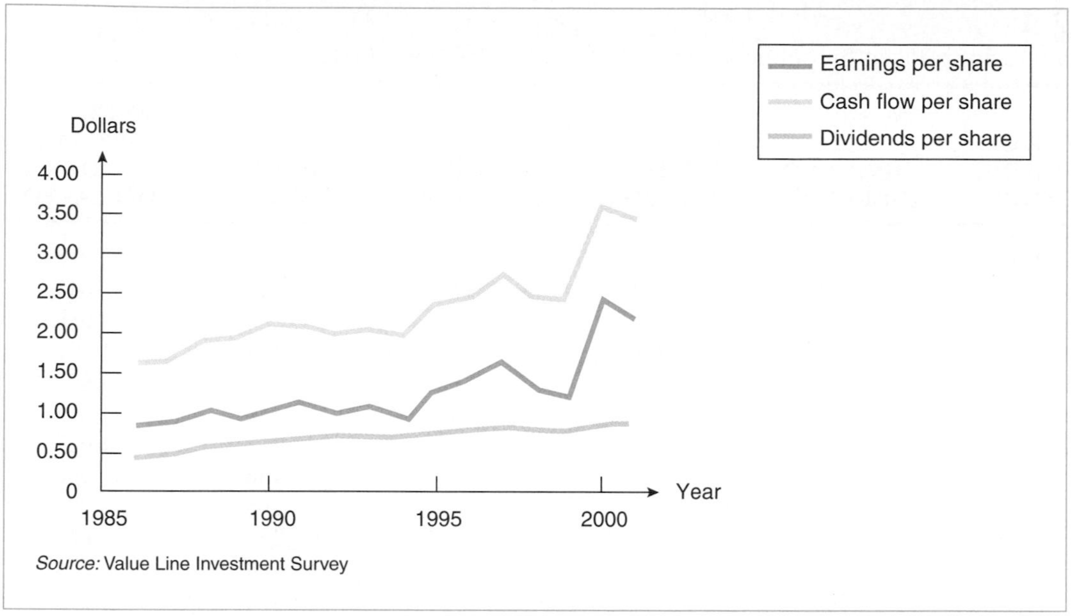

FIGURE 17.2
Earnings, cash flow, and dividends per share for Exxon Mobil Corporation, 1986 to 2001.

Table 17.1 summarizes the dividend changes U.S. firms announced during the period 1970 to 2001. Fewer than 9% of the dividend actions taken during the period involved either dividend decreases or *dividend omissions* (reducing the dividend rate to zero). Dividend increases and *dividend resumptions* (paying dividends once again after having previously cut the dividend rate to zero) outnumbered decreases and omissions by almost 8 to 1. Lack of changes in the dividend rate outnumbered decreases and omissions by more than 30 to 1.

You can see that the numbers of dividend decreases and omissions increased sharply—and the numbers of dividend increases and resumptions decreased sharply—during the recession periods 1974 to 1975, 1980 to 1982, 1990 to 1991, and 2001 to 2002. Investors generally interpret dividend reductions as a signal that the firm's earnings prospects have worsened. This can adversely affect a firm's share price and, in some cases, the share prices of other firms in the same industry.

EXTRA AND SPECIAL DIVIDENDS Table 17.1 also indicates that a minority of firms declared *extra dividends* or *special dividends*. An **extra dividend** is paid in addition to a "regular" quarterly dividend, to distribute unusual—and unsustainable—earnings. They tend to be considerably more variable in amount than "regular" dividend payments. Extra dividends usually occur near the end of the fiscal year (the October–December quarter for most firms), as in the example below. How would you interpret this? Firms appear to pay extra dividends when the year-end review reveals unusually high earnings, and it wishes to pay out its target percentage of earnings, without falsely signaling a higher sustainable level of earnings. Many firms in cyclical businesses declare extra dividends when earnings are at a cyclical peak. They increase the regular dividend rate only when they believe they have reached a higher level of sustainable earnings.

Special dividends are often declared when a firm finds itself with substantial excess cash it wishes to distribute to its shareholders. For special dividends, this excess cash usually comes from sources beyond normal operating results, such as the sale of a subsidiary or a decision to liquidate the firm. Both extra and special dividends are less effective devices for signaling a change in a firm's earnings prospects than changes in the regular dividend.

TABLE 17.1
Dividend changes announced by publicly owned U.S. firms, 1970 to 2001.

YEAR	NUMBER OF FIRMS PAYING DIVIDENDS	DIVIDEND INCREASED	DIVIDEND RESUMED	DIVIDEND DECREASED	DIVIDEND OMITTED	EXTRA OR SPECIAL DIVIDEND DECLARED
1970	About 9,800	828	75	201	284	910
1971	About 9,800	885	111	154	213	841
1972	About 9,800	1,563	107	73	103	980
1973	About 9,800	2,197	116	37	114	1,105
1974	About 9,800	2,120	139	86	228	1,097
1975	About 9,800	1,648	129	186	266	1,013
1976	About 9,800	2,624	137	74	117	1,047
1977	Over 10,000	2,984	120	68	138	968
1978	Over 10,000	3,211	105	46	105	997
1979	Over 10,000	2,968	71	46	131	829
1980	Over 10,000	2,445	51	88	160	719
1981	Over 10,000	2,160	45	103	198	640
1982	Over 10,000	1,590	46	258	315	515
1983	Over 10,000	1,833	66	106	126	480
1984	Over 10,000	1,774	58	65	116	435
1985	Over 10,000	1,560	35	68	139	428
1986	Over 10,000	1,513	46	96	189	359
1987	Over 10,000	1,590	54	74	104	403
1988	Over 10,000	1,705	38	62	117	501
1989	Over 10,000	1,658	41	85	160	524
1990	Over 10,000	1,263	39	143	266	385
1991	Over 10,000	1,086	50	187	250	322
1992	Over 10,000	1,333	53	131	146	317
1993	Over 10,000	1,635	75	87	106	368
1994	Over 10,000	1,826	52	59	77	384
1995	Over 10,000	1,882	51	49	73	358
1996	Over 10,000	2,171	37	50	80	444
1997	Over 10,000	2,139	24	46	49	439
1998	Over 10,000	2,047	17	84	61	425
1999	Over 10,000	1,701	38	62	83	385
2000	Over 10,000	1,438	32	69	75	327
2001	Over 10,000	1,244	17	117	70	282
Total	Over 308,600	58,621	2,075	3,060	4,659	19,227

Source: Reprinted by permission of Standard & Poor's.

EXAMPLE Alcoa's Extra Dividends

A few years ago, Aluminum Company of America (Alcoa), the world's largest aluminum producer, declared regular cash dividends of \$0.20 in each quarter for two consecutive years. Alcoa earned \$5.34 per share in the first year and then declared an extra dividend of \$0.70 per share on January 19 of the second year. Because the extra dividend came so close to

Alcoa's December 31 year-end, we will add it to the regular cash dividends in calculating the payout ratio for the first year:

$$\text{Payout ratio} = \frac{4(0.20) + 0.70}{5.34} = 28\%$$

In the second year, Alcoa earned \$3.30 per share. Again, it declared an extra dividend, this time of \$.09 per share on January 18. The implied payout ratio for the second year is then:

$$\text{Payout ratio} = \frac{4(0.20) + 0.09}{3.30} = 27\%$$

In the following three years, Alcoa's earnings per share varied between \$0.40 and \$1.64, and Alcoa did not declare any extra dividends subsequent to those year-ends. However, it continued to pay \$0.20 per quarter in regular cash dividends.

Industry Differences

Payout ratios vary systematically across industries. What might explain this? We suspect it is due, at least in part, to the similar investment opportunities that firms within a particular industry face. These differences may be industry-related.

Table 17.2 summarizes differences in average industry payout ratios. The electric utility industry has had the highest payout ratios. The drugs and health care, metals and mining, and aerospace and aircraft industries generally have had the lowest payout ratios. The paper and paper products industry's five-year average payout ratio varied more than the others.

TABLE 17.2
Industry differences in payout ratio.

	FIVE-YEAR INDUSTRY AVERAGE				
INDUSTRY	**1981–1985**	**1986–1990**	**1991–1995**	**1996–2000**	**OVERALL 1981–2000**
Drugs and Health Care	11.9%	8.7%	5.9%	4.7%	7.8%
Metals and Mining	10.4	10.8	18.7	24.0	16.0
Aerospace and Aircraft	24.8	16.8	17.7	8.1	16.8
Textiles	26.3	17.0	15.6	14.2	18.3
Building Materials	29.6	26.0	17.9	13.1	21.7
Business Equipment	20.6	23.7	25.6	18.6	22.1
Oil	21.9	25.7	26.0	14.8	22.1
Life Insurance	34.7	35.6	16.7	24.1	27.8
Foods	26.8	32.0	27.5	26.9	28.3
Steel	26.1	45.0	22.6	24.0	29.4
Chemicals	26.1	29.4	32.9	37.7	31.5
Paper and Paper Products	52.9	27.0	30.9	29.1	35.0
Electric Utilities	69.7	72.7	78.5	76.2	74.3
Average	29.4%	28.5%	25.9%	24.3%	27.0%

Source: Compustat.

Declaration of Dividends

A dividend must be declared by the firm's board of directors.[1] When the board declares a dividend, it specifies a **record date** and a **payment date.** Each *shareholder of record* (i.e., owner of shares according to the firm's stock ownership record) as of the close of business on the record date will receive a check dated on the payment date for the dividends declared on the shares owned. Currently, stock transactions must be settled by the third business day following the transaction. Consequently, the major stock exchanges and securities dealers (in the over-the-counter market) establish an **ex-dividend date** two business days prior to the record date. On that date, the shares begin trading *ex-dividend,* that is, without dividend rights. Consequently, a stock normally opens for trading on the ex-dividend date at approximately the preceding day's closing price less the amount of the dividend per share.

EXAMPLE Dividend-Related Events for GE

During a recent year, GE established the following declaration, ex-dividend, record, and payment dates for its dividends. At the time, stock transactions had to be settled by the third business day following the transaction:

QUARTER	DECLARATION DATE	EX-DIVIDEND DATE	RECORD DATE	PAYMENT DATE	DIVIDEND PER SHARE
1	12/15	12/27	12/29	1/25	$0.16
2	2/9	3/5	3/7	4/25	0.16
3	6/22	7/5	7/9	7/25	0.16
4	9/7	9/26	9/28	10/25	0.16

Note the regularity in the pattern of dates and payments.

The time line presented in Figure 17.3 shows the relative timing of the key dividend-related dates for GE's second quarter dividend.

Legal Limitations on Dividend Payments

Two forms of legal restrictions on dividend payments are important. To start with, most bond indentures, loan agreements, and preferred stock agreements usually contain restrictions on the amount of common dividends a firm can pay. These limitations are designed to minimize the firm's agency costs.

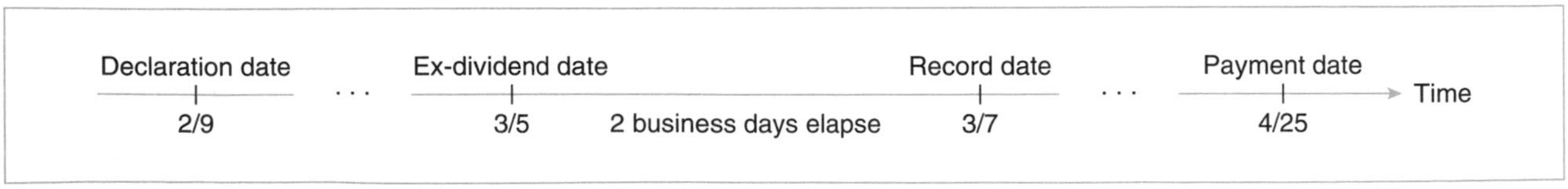

FIGURE 17.3
A time line for GE's second quarter dividend-related events.

[1]Legal restrictions on dividend payments are discussed below.

State laws also impose restrictions. They are designed to prevent excessive cash distributions. Most states prohibit a firm from paying dividends if doing so would render it insolvent. Many also prohibit firms from making dividend payments out of accounts that fall outside a legally defined "surplus." In some cases, this surplus includes only retained earnings; in others it also includes paid-in capital. In some states, a firm can distribute current earnings, even though prior losses had eliminated its surplus.

These limitations are seldom troublesome to a healthy firm. They help prevent unhealthy firms from expropriating wealth from lenders and other creditors.

Review

1. List four characteristics of corporate dividend policies.
2. Which are more stable, dividends or earnings?
3. Why are firms reluctant to cut their dividend?
4. What are extra dividends, and when do firms pay them?
5. What happens on the ex-dividend date?

17.2 DOES DIVIDEND POLICY MATTER?

As we have said, a firm's choice of dividend policy does not affect its value in a perfect capital market environment. The perfect capital market environment is the place to start the analysis of financial policy. Of course, actual capital markets are not perfect, and capital market imperfections affect our conclusions about dividend policy. However, because the capital markets are so efficient, a firm's value is less affected by its dividend policy than by its capital budgeting decisions and capital structure policy. Despite this, a firm should use its dividend policy to whatever extent possible to maximize shareholder wealth.

After demonstrating dividend irrelevance in a perfect capital market environment, we will relax our assumptions and see how that affects dividend policy.

What Is Dividend Policy?

Although we have characterized dividend policy as simply a payout ratio, it is more than that. Dividend payments are generally made in cash, and a firm has alternative uses for its cash. As a result, there is confusion sometimes among a firm's dividend, capital budgeting, and capital structure policies. For example, if making a capital expenditure will reduce the firm's cash dividends by the amount of the expenditure, then the dividend decision would simply be the result of the investment decision. We could not distinguish the valuation effect of a dividend change from that of a change in capital budget. The two policies would simply mirror each other. Similarly, if the capital budget is held constant, and the firm issues debt to finance the dividend, dividend policy would simply be a result of the capital structure policy.

If we maintain constant capital budgeting and capital structure policies, we may have too little or too much cash for dividends. In a strict sense, then, a pure dividend policy decision involves only a trade-off between retaining earnings on the one hand and selling new shares to obtain the cash to pay dividends on the other. Although some firms (mostly utilities) have maintained a high payout ratio of regular quarterly cash dividends and simultaneously sold new issues of common stock, they are not typical.

To understand the role of dividends, then, we must isolate the effect of a change in cash dividends from the firm's choices of investments and capital structure. Otherwise, we would not be analyzing dividend policy exclusively.

Another complication is the method of payment. There are different ways to distribute cash to shareholders. A firm can make regular payments (say, quarterly) or it can make larger irregular payments of "special" dividends. Or instead of paying any dividends, it can use the cash to repurchase shares, which may have tax advantages.

Dividends in a Perfect Capital Market Environment

The crux of the dividend irrelevance argument is that fair market transactions are neutral and do not transfer wealth. Let's look at the transactions involved with a dividend and examine how it is financed.

When a firm pays a dividend, money is simply transferred from one form to another. Before payment of the dividend, the money is in the form of a shareholder claim on the firm's assets. After payment of the dividend, the shareholder has cash. But as long as the transfer is a fair market transaction in a perfect capital market environment, the value is the same.

Another transaction we need to consider is selling new shares. Again, this is simply a transfer of money from one form to another. Before the transaction, the new investors have cash. After exchanging the cash for new shares, the new investors have an equal-value claim on the firm's assets. And again, as long as the transfer is a fair market transaction in a perfect capital market environment, the value is the same.

Now let us consider a dividend under three different cases. In the first case, the firm has the necessary cash and simply reduces its cash account to pay the dividend. The "offsetting" amount in the double-entry system is an equal reduction in the shareholder equity account. This is the transfer of money from one form, a claim on the firm, to another form, cash in the shareholder's "hand."

In the second case, the firm does not have the cash to pay the dividend, so it issues new shares in exchange for cash, which temporarily increases the total value of the firm. Then the firm makes the dividend payment, which reduces total firm value back to its pre-new-share value. Because both transactions are simply fair market transactions that transfer money from one form to another, each party's value is the same, and after both transactions, firm value is unchanged.

Figure 17.4 illustrates the second case. The firm pays out 20% of its value as a cash dividend. It then raises an equal amount of cash by selling new shares. The new shareholders own 20% of the firm.

Think about what happened in this second case. In effect, existing shareholders—through the firm's transactions—sold part of their claim on the firm to the new investors.

In our third case, a shareholder wants a cash dividend and thus wants the firm to make the transactions in Figure 17.4. But the firm has decided not to pay the dividend because it does not want to go to the trouble of making the two transactions. The existing shareholder can go out and find a new investor and sell some shares directly to that new investor in exchange for cash. The net effect of this direct sale is the same as the firm's two transactions in the second case. Part of the existing shareholder's claim would go to the new investor in exchange for cash. And as long as it is a fair market transaction in a perfect market environment, neither party gains nor loses value. This direct transaction—a shareholder selling some shares to get cash—is called a **homemade dividend.**

Figure 17.5 illustrates a homemade dividend. Let us compare the alternatives. When the firm pays a cash dividend and sells additional shares to pay for it, total value is unchanged. But the number of shares outstanding increases, and the value per share (the stock price) declines. The original shareholders are just as well off, because even though their shares are worth less and they have the same number of shares, they have cash that is equal to their decline in share value. With a homemade dividend, the original stockholders sell some of their shares, and the number of outstanding shares does not change, so the stock price does not change. The original stockholders are

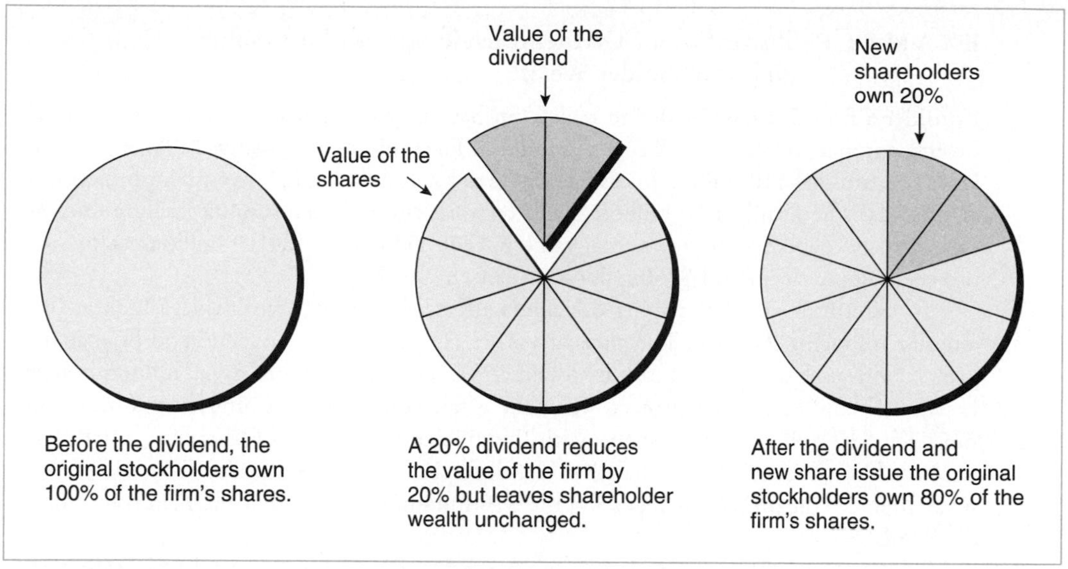

FIGURE 17.4
The transfer of value when a firm pays a cash dividend and finances it with a new share issue.

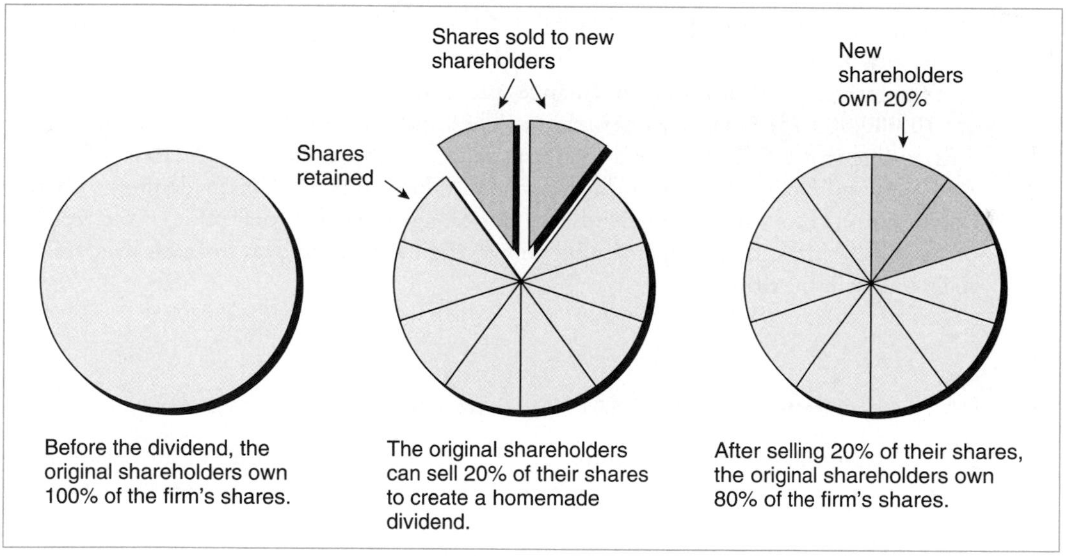

FIGURE 17.5
The transfer of value when the original shareholders sell some of their shares to create a homemade dividend.

just as well off, because even though they have fewer shares worth the same per share, they have cash that is equal to their decline in share value.[2]

Therefore, despite the differences in the number of shares outstanding and stock (per-share) price, value is maintained. The two alternatives leave the original shareholders equally well off. Thus, dividend policy (choosing whether to pay a dividend and, if so, how much) is irrelevant—in a perfect capital market environment.

---

[2]The original shareholders sell 20% of their holdings (which corresponds to 2 of the 10 slices in the pie chart). Problem B1 at the end of the chapter provides a numerical example consistent with the pie charts in Figures 17.4 and 17.5.

EXAMPLE Illustration of Dividend Irrelevance to Firm Value and Stockholder Wealth

Consider a firm that has decided to make, but has not yet announced, a major new capital investment in a project that will cost \$10 million. The project has a positive NPV of \$20 million. The firm has \$10 million in cash available to finance the capital investment project if it so chooses. The firm has 10 million shares of stock currently outstanding, selling for \$24 each, and no debt. So the firm's total value is \$240 million (= [24]10 million) before the project announcement and \$260 million (= 240 + 20) after.

To determine whether paying dividends affects shareholder wealth, let's look at two alternatives facing the firm. The alternatives are (1) pay no cash dividend and finance the project with cash or (2) pay a cash dividend of \$1 per share and obtain \$10 million in new external financing for the project. To make a fair comparison of alternatives, the firm must sell \$10 million in new shares with the dividend alternative. Otherwise, any difference could be due to factors other than the difference in dividend policy. The sale of new stock finances the project by replacing the \$10 million in equity that the firm pays out as dividends.

With no dividend, the firm simply uses the cash to finance the project. In that case, each share would be worth \$26 (= 260/10). If all the shareholders want the \$10 million dividend, they can sell 384,615 (= 10,000,000/26) of their shares to get it.

With a dividend, the firm pays out \$10 million cash and sells \$10 million worth of new shares. After payment of the dividend, each share will be worth the predividend share price (\$26) minus the dividend (\$1), or \$25. Note that paying the dividend does not affect shareholder wealth; it is \$26 before and 25 + 1 = \$26 after.

To get the \$10 million to finance the project, the firm must sell 400,000 (= 10,000,000/25) fair-priced new shares. Then the firm will have 10.4 million shares outstanding worth \$25 each, for a total firm value of \$260 million (= [25]10.4 million). And \$260 million is exactly what the firm's total value was before the dividend-new-share transactions. Therefore, the dividend does not change the firm's total value or the wealth of its shareholders. In effect, it simply allows original shareholders to "cash in" part of their equity in the firm.

But Are Capital Gains Riskier than Dividends?

Dividends represent cash in hand. Reinvesting that cash in the hope of realizing greater dividends and/or additional capital gain sometime in the future represents a risky prospect. So are shareholders better off getting a dividend?

At this point, we hope you recognize an opportunity to apply the Principle of Risk-Return Trade-Off and answer, "No, not necessarily." The difference between the dividend now and later is, of course, risk and the time value of money. Therefore, if we want the dividend now, we must accept a lower return on the investment in those shares. The issue is whether the existing shareholders or some "new" shareholders are going to invest the \$10 million in the new project.

Shareholders who decide that future dividends and capital gains are excessively risky (as opposed to being in accordance with the risk-return trade-off) can sell some of their shares. This involves transaction costs, but it does enable shareholders to satisfy individual risk-return objectives. Moreover, by holding the firm's capital investment program and capital structure fixed, paying a dividend does not alter the firm's or its shareholders' risk profile. Therefore, the uncertainty of future dividends and capital gains does not invalidate the dividend irrelevance argument.

Shareholder Preference for Current Income

Suppose shareholders want a regular flow of income. Would they prefer the firm to pay dividends rather than reinvest the cash? Not in a perfect market. As we have already explained, shareholders can sell shares on a regular basis to generate income. In a perfect market, a preference for current income does not alter the conclusion that dividend policy is irrelevant. Dividend policy would not affect firm value or stockholder wealth, regardless of individual stockholders' preferences regarding liquidity or risk. Why, then, do rational market participants act as if it does matter?

Capital Market Imperfections

Of course, the perfect market view leaves out taxes, transaction costs, and information asymmetries. If capital gains are taxed at a lower rate than dividends, shareholders paying taxes on both types of income should prefer getting the income as capital gains rather than as dividends.

There are also psychological theories that provide a rationale for some individuals' preferring cash dividends over capital gains. These theories argue that for psychological reasons, dividends and capital gains are not perfect substitutes for one another. For example, a lack of self-control provides a reason for an investor to prefer regular cash dividends. If the investor had to sell stock to get income, he might sell more and spend too much, thereby using up his capital too quickly for his own good. These psychological reasons are additional capital market imperfections that can make dividend policy relevant.

Finally, it may be that dividend policy can be used, less expensively than other methods, to convey information to the public.

All of these concerns are valid. Capital market imperfections, including asymmetric information considerations, contribute to the relevance of dividend policy.

Review

1. What does the term *dividend policy* mean?
2. What is a homemade dividend?
3. Why are homemade dividends and cash dividends perfect substitutes in a perfect capital market?

17.3 THE ROLE OF INCOME TAXES

Tax laws change with some regularity. As in the case of capital budgeting projects, you must know the relevant tax laws before making decisions on dividend policy. Currently, personal taxes are higher on dividends than on capital gains. The maximum tax rate on long-term capital gains is 20% versus 39.1% in the top bracket for ordinary income.[3] In addition, there is the valuable capital gains tax-timing option—postpone the tax on a gain, and claim the tax reduction on a loss.[4] The capital gains tax-timing option further lowers the *effective* tax rate on capital gains. Previous versions of the Internal Revenue Code have also included such a tax differential.

From a tax viewpoint, then, shareholders prefer capital gains over dividends, and hence low payout ratios, because capital gains are effectively taxed at a lower rate than dividends. Therefore, shareholders who are paying taxes on both types of income may prefer capital gains rather than dividends.

[3]This is the rate for 2001. The peak tax rate is scheduled to drop slightly in 2002.

[4]Recall that capital gains are taxed at the time of the sale of the asset, not as they accrue. So the tax liability for a capital gain is reinvested and earns the time value of money until the tax payment is actually made.

But transaction costs to create a homemade dividend offset the tax gain. Thus, other shareholders who want liquidity and face large enough transaction costs can still be better off with the dividend. And even if transaction costs to create a homemade dividend are not very high, tax-exempt shareholders who want liquidity will prefer dividends as long as transactions are not costless. This is because they can save the transaction costs, but they cannot save taxes because they do not pay taxes.

Corporate shareholders actually have a "reversed" tax preference. Currently, corporate shareholders pay income tax at a 35% maximum marginal rate and are not taxed on 70% of the dividends received (see Chapter 3). A corporate shareholder would therefore pay tax on dividend income at a rate no greater than 10.5% (= [1 − 0.70]0.35), because only 30% of the dividends it receives are taxable. In contrast, corporate shareholders pay tax on long-term capital gains at rates up to 35%. Thus, corporate investors may prefer dividends over capital gains from the tax perspective.

EXAMPLE The Effect of Personal Taxes on Firm Value

Suppose dividends are taxed at a 36% rate and capital gains are not taxed. We can show that a dividend-paying firm will have a lower value than an otherwise identical non-dividend-paying firm.

Firm A has a \$50 share price. It pays no dividend. Investors expect its share price to be \$57.50 after one year. Shareholders thus expect a capital gain of \$7.50 per share. The expected return is 15% (= 7.50/50) both pretax and after tax.

Firm B is identical except that it will pay a \$5 dividend per share at the end of the year. The ex-dividend price will be \$52.50 (= 57.50 − 5.00). Its shares and those of firm A are equally risky. So firm B's shares must also provide a 15% after-tax return.

What is firm B's share price? The tax on the dividend is \$1.80 (= [0.36]5.00). The after-tax dividend is \$3.20 (= 5.00 − 1.80). An investor will have \$55.70 (= 52.50 + 3.20) per firm B share. To provide a 15% return, each share of firm B must be worth, today, the present value of its expected future value. That is,

$$\text{Share price} = \frac{55.70}{1.15} = \$48.43$$

What is the pretax return on firm B's shares? It is

$$\text{Pretax return} = \frac{57.50 - 48.43}{48.43} = 18.73\%$$

Therefore, firm B's shares must provide a higher expected pretax return (18.73% versus 15%). This higher return is to compensate for the tax liability.

Tax Clienteles

The *clientele effect* (discussed in Chapter 15) is also important in the study of dividend relevance. The clientele effect refers to investors "sorting" themselves into groups, each of which prefers the firms it invests in to follow a particular type of policy. When applied to dividend policy, the clientele effect refers to those investors who prefer one dividend policy over another for a particular reason.

The clientele effect lessens, and may even eliminate, the rationale for the tax differential view of dividend policy. As you might guess from our foregoing discussion, there are natural clienteles for high-cash-dividend stocks and low-cash-dividend stocks. Extensive empirical evidence identifies investor clienteles. On the basis of their tax positions, investors choose stocks with high or low cash dividends. A firm's dividend policy simply appeals to different tax clienteles. Each tax clientele can invest in the shares of firms whose dividend policies best suit that clientele's tax posture. As long as there is a sufficient supply of investment opportunities for each group, no premium is needed to buy a preferred investment instrument. With no premium, dividend policy would again be irrelevant—in spite of the apparent tax asymmetry.

Where does this leave us concerning taxes? Income taxes can affect the sort of dividend policy shareholders want. But the clientele effect reduces the importance of taxes. Changes in the tax system are probably more important than the level of taxes at any particular time. They can create profitable opportunities for a firm to offer a dividend policy that is in short supply and becomes attractive because of a tax law change. However, such opportunities are limited. And although an optimal dividend policy can contribute to the profitability of a firm, the possibility of extraordinary success rests primarily on the firm's real investment decisions.

Review

1. On the basis of taxes only, would a U.S. tax-paying stockholder prefer the firm favor dividends or capital gains?
2. How does the existence of tax clienteles affect our conclusion that the differential taxation of dividends and capital gains can affect dividend policy?

17.4 TRANSACTION COSTS

Transaction costs can also cause dividend policy to matter. There are two types: flotation costs and commission charges, and legal and policy restrictions.

Flotation Costs and Brokerage Commissions

Flotation costs and brokerage commissions vary inversely with the size of the transaction. This makes it cheaper for a firm to sell a large block of shares than for individual shareholders to make small purchases to reinvest their dividends. Likewise, it is cheaper for a firm to pay a cash dividend than it is for individual shareholders to make small sales to create a homemade dividend. Therefore, the effect of such transaction costs depends on shareholder preferences and reinforces the clientele effect.

In recent years the growth of the discount brokerage industry has reduced commissions. However, the greatest commission reductions have occurred in connection with larger share transactions, so these frictions still tend to favor a clientele effect.

Dividend Reinvestment Plans

Dividend reinvestment plans offer shareholders the option to reinvest their dividends with little or no brokerage commission. This reduces the transaction-cost penalty a high-dividend-payout policy would otherwise impose on shareholders who wish their dividends to be reinvested. These plans also have permitted firms to reduce issuance costs substantially, perhaps to as little as 2% (versus 4% to 5% for normal-size public offerings). They do not, however, eliminate the tax bias in favor of capital gains because shareholders must recognize the reinvested dividends as income. Nevertheless, by reducing flotation costs, dividend reinvestment plans may have led to increased payout ratios for those firms, such as electric utility firms, whose investor clienteles desire a relatively high level of dividend income.

Legal and Policy Restrictions

Certain institutions are prohibited, by law or policy, from investing in the common stocks of firms that do not have an established history of regular dividend payments. Others, such as many trust and endowment funds, can use only dividend income as a matter of policy. These investors prefer at least some minimum level of regular dividend income to maintain institutional decision-making flexibility. Legal and policy restrictions create indirect transaction costs.

Net Effect of Transaction Costs

We believe the tax bias in favoring capital gains exerts a stronger influence than transaction costs on what a firm's dividend policy ought to be. We think the majority of our colleagues in the finance profession would agree. Consequently, the combined effect of taxes and transaction costs favors retentions over dividends to some degree.

Review

1. How do brokerage commissions affect the choice between homemade dividends and true dividends?
2. What sort of legal and policy restrictions give firms an incentive to pay at least a small dividend?
3. What is the net effect of taxes and transaction costs on dividend policy?

17.5 SIGNALING AND THE DIVIDEND ADJUSTMENT MODEL

Dividend changes can affect a stock's market value if investors believe such changes convey useful information. For example, suppose a firm has rarely changed its dividend rate, and each time the rate was changed, the firm's earnings also subsequently changed in the same direction. Investors would then interpret future changes in the dividend rate as a signal that management believes the firm's earnings prospects have changed. A dividend increase would be a positive signal of greater future earnings. A dividend decrease would be a negative signal of lower future earnings.

Because of the informational content of dividend changes, simply paying out residual cash flow on a year-by-year basis may not be in the shareholders' best interest. Such a policy would lead to a dividend level and a payout ratio that could fluctuate wildly, depending on year-to-year changes in the availability of attractive investment projects. In fact, most firms seek slow changes in dividends. Look back at Figure 17.1 and notice that yearly payout ratios varied inversely with earnings to produce a fairly smooth curve of growing dividends. This is no coincidence.

Research based on interviews with corporate executives shows that managers think a firm should aim toward a long-term **target payout ratio** to give shareholders a "fair share" of the firm's earnings. The following model was created to explain dividend changes:

$$DPS_1 - DPS_0 = ADJ[POR(EPS_1) - DPS_0] \tag{17.1}$$

Currently the firm's dividends are DPS_0 per share. It has a target payout ratio of POR. It will adjust (ADJ) its dividend rate, but less than fully, as its earnings per share (EPS) change. If the firm always paid out its target ratio, then its next-period dividend per share would be $POR(EPS_1)$. But firms "manage" their dividend payments so as to produce a smooth progression in dividends, so $ADJ < 1$. Dividends progress toward the target level over several periods rather than all at once. This, of course, reduces the likelihood that a dividend increase will have to be "rolled back" in the future. Because of this "stickiness," dividend changes serve as a signaling device. A firm will not increase its dividend rate unless it believes the increase is sustainable because of a higher sustainable level of earnings.

EXAMPLE Adjusting Dividends for EPS Changes at Snapple

Snapple Corporation has historically paid out 40% of its earnings as dividends. Snapple's treasurer believes it is appropriate to adjust the dividend rate in a gradual manner. She applies the dividend adjustment model (17.1) with ADJ = 2/3. Snapple earned $5.00 per share last year and paid dividends of $0.50 per quarter, or $2.00 per year. She believes earnings will reach $6.00 per share this year and stay at that level into the foreseeable future. According to Equation (17.1), how would the dividend rate change this year and the next four?

Using (17.1), the first year dividend is

$$DPS_1 - DPS_0 = ADJ[POR(EPS_1) - DPS_0]$$
$$DPS_1 - 2.00 = (2/3)[0.4(6.00) - 2.00]$$
$$DPS_1 = 2.266667 \cong 2.27$$

The next year, the dividend becomes

$$DPS_1 - 2.266667 = (2/3)[0.4(6.00) - 2.266667]$$
$$DPS_1 = 2.355556 \cong 2.36$$

Figure 17.6 shows the pattern of dividend changes. The dividend rate moves to the steady-state dividend rate of $2.40 per year [= 0.4(6.00)], each year closing two-thirds of the remaining gap.

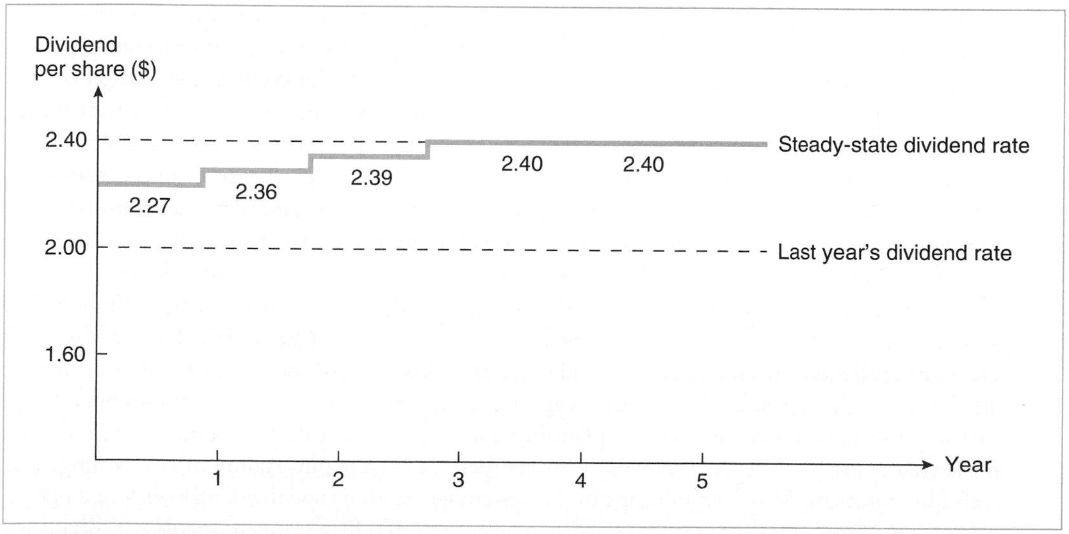

FIGURE 17.6
The adjustment of the dividend rate to a change in earnings per share.

Review

1. How do investors usually interpret a dividend increase? A dividend decrease?
2. How do stock prices usually react to a dividend increase? A dividend decrease? Why?
3. Explain the dividend adjustment model in your own words.

17.6 DIVIDEND POLICY GUIDELINES

Establishing a firm's dividend policy involves a variety of conflicting and sometimes confusing considerations. Almost any dividend decision of a firm with a diversified shareholder mix will disappoint at least some of its shareholders.

Determining an appropriate dividend policy for a firm involves a three-step approach. The firm must (1) estimate its future residual funds, (2) determine an appropriate target payout ratio, and (3) decide on the quarterly dividend.

Step 1: Estimate Future Residual Funds

Start with the firm's earnings and cash flow projections over a reasonable time horizon. Five years is typical. At a minimum, a firm should pay out cash that it cannot invest in positive-NPV projects. After considering investor-related factors, it might decide to pay out more than this minimum. However, because of flotation costs, it is usually unwise for a firm to pay out so much more than the minimum as to trigger the need for new equity.

Many factors complicate this analysis. Capital budgeting projects often come in large units, and they are subject to substantial deviation from their projected timing and cost. As economic and business conditions change, so will the desired portfolio of capital expenditure projects. Similarly, future operating cash flow is not entirely predictable. Thus, analyzing even the most carefully prepared cash flow projections will suggest a range of distributable amounts, a range of funds needs, and hence a range of *feasible target payout ratios.*

Step 2: Determine an Appropriate Target Payout Ratio

Applying the Behavioral Principle provides a good starting point for establishing a target payout range. The payout ratios of comparable firms—essentially those in the same industry, of nearly the same size, and with similar product mix and other operating characteristics—will suggest a range of *customary payout ratios* for that industry or industry segment. A firm should consider the range of feasible target payout ratios together with the range of customary payout ratios and any special shareholder mix considerations in setting its long-term target payout ratio.

Step 3: Set the Quarterly Dividend Rate

Given its target payout ratio and its earnings and cash flow projections, a firm should establish its quarterly dividend rate at the highest *comfortably sustainable* level. That is, the dividend rate should be sustainable at least over the planning horizon. Prudence dictates setting the actual rate somewhat below the expected maximum to compensate for the uncertainty of the earnings and cash flow forecasts. Most corporations find it advantageous to review dividend policy in a particular quarter each year, thus creating a predictable pattern. If a firm wants to increase its dividend, it may be better to make one significant increase per year than tiny ones each quarter.

Review

1. What are the three steps in the recommended approach to setting dividend policy?
2. How can you use comparable firms to determine an appropriate target payout ratio?

17.7 APPLYING THE DIVIDEND POLICY GUIDELINES

The board of directors of Major Pharmaceutical Company is considering whether to change the dividend. Major's Financial Planning Group has prepared a five-year plan, which the board has tentatively approved. Table 17.3 provides the projected values of certain financial variables drawn from the five-year plan.

Estimated Future Residual Funds

Major's board has tentatively approved a five-year capital expenditure plan. It calls for expenditures of $335 million on positive-NPV projects. The plan provides for capital investment amounting to $45.0 million in year 1, $54.0 million in year 2, $74.0 million in year 3, $72.0 million in year 4, and $90.0 million in year 5. Over the five-year period, Major projects aggregate residual funds of $115.0 million.

Target Payout Ratio

The projected residual funds of $115.0 million represent 31% of projected earnings available for common. Earnings are estimated to be $367.0 million for the five-year period. A detailed analysis of Major's shareholder group would be expensive and time consuming. However, Major's treasurer realizes that as long as their dividend policies are clearly articulated and stable, particular industries and particular firms tend to attract certain shareholder clienteles.

Major's payout ratio has averaged 33.5% over the past 10 years and 32.2% over the past five. Major's financial staff has also analyzed the payout policies of Major's closest 10 competitors in the ethical drug segment of the pharmaceutical industry. Major derives more than 90% of its sales revenue and operating income from this industry segment. The average payout ratio for these firms for the preceding year was 36.6%. The range of payout ratios was 18.6% to 53.7%. Major's treasurer concluded that a payout ratio from 30% to 40% would be appropriate. Major projects heavy capital expenditure requirements beginning in year 3. She therefore feels that Major's payout ratio will remain below the industry average.

Analyzing the Impact of Alternative Dividend Policies

Table 17.3 also illustrates how to evaluate alternative dividend policies. A firm would normally examine several such alternatives before deciding on a particular dividend action.

The current indicated annual dividend rate is $1.44 per share. Suppose Major maintains this dividend rate through year 5. Its payout ratio trends steadily downward. Major would retain substantial residual funds.

Two alternative policies are considered. Under both alternatives, Major would pay out all the estimated residual funds to shareholders. Alternative B provides for increases each year. It avoids the very large increases in years 4 and 5 that alternative A calls for. Also, the payout ratio is less variable and closer to the long-run target under alternative B.

Major reassesses its dividend policy each year. Major is therefore more concerned about year 1 than the later years. It appears that Major can sustain a 24-cent increase in its dividend rate

TABLE 17.3
Projecting dividends for major pharmaceutical company.

	INITIAL	PROJECTIONS: YEAR 1	YEAR 2	YEAR 3	YEAR 4	YEAR 5	TOTALS
Earnings per common share	$4.25	$ 5.00	$ 6.00	$ 7.20	$ 8.50	$ 10.00	
Number of common shares (millions)		× 10	× 10	× 10	× 10	× 10	
Earnings available for common		$50.0	$60.0	$72.0	$ 85.0	$100.0	$367.0
Depreciation and other noncash charges		12.0	14.0	16.0	19.0	22.0	83.0
Funds from operations available for reinvestment or dividends		62.0	74.0	88.0	104.0	122.0	450.0
Capital investment requirement		45.0	54.0	74.0	72.0	90.0	335.0
Residual funds		$17.0	$20.0	$14.0	$ 32.0	$ 32.0	$115.0
Assuming No Change in the Dividend							
Dividend per share	$1.44	$ 1.44	$ 1.44	$ 1.44	$ 1.44	$ 1.44	
Payout ratio	33%	29%	24%	20%	17%	14%	
Residual funds		$17.0	$20.0	$14.0	$ 32.0	$ 32.0	$115.0
Dividend requirements		14.4	14.4	14.4	14.4	14.4	72.0
Surplus (deficit)		$ 2.6	$ 5.6	$ (0.4)	$ 17.6	$ 17.6	$ 43.0
One Possible Dividend Policy Alternative A							
Dividend per share	$1.44	$ 1.70	$ 1.70	$ 1.70	$ 2.70	$ 3.70	
Payout ratio	33%	34%	28%	24%	32%	37%	
Residual funds		$17.0	$20.0	$14.0	$ 32.0	$ 32.0	$115.0
Dividend requirements		17.0	17.0	17.0	27.0	37.0	115.0
Surplus (deficit)		—	$ 3.0	$ (3.0)	$ 5.0	$ (5.0)	$ 0.0
Another Possible Dividend Policy Alternative B							
Dividend per share	$1.44	$ 1.68	$ 1.88	$ 2.00	$ 2.64	$ 3.30	
Payout ratio	33%	34%	31%	28%	31%	33%	
Residual funds		$17.0	$20.0	$14.0	$ 32.0	$ 32.0	$115.0
Dividend requirements		16.8	18.8	20.0	26.4	33.0	115.0
Surplus (deficit)		$ 0.2	$ 1.2	$ (6.0)	$ 5.6	$ (1.0)	$ 0.0

to $1.68 per share per year. Such an increase seems appropriate in light of Major's improved earnings prospects. Of course, other considerations might indicate that a dividend rate different from $1.68 is more appropriate. But the analysis of Major's estimated residual funds position is the best starting place for such an analysis.

What about years 4 and 5? Alternative B suggests very large dividend increases. They will necessarily be reconsidered in the future. Major would implement them only if it continues to find them sustainable.

Special Considerations for the Privately Held Firm

The preceding example applies only to *publicly traded firms.* In most cases, *privately held* firms do not have informational effects to worry about. However, tax considerations and the owners' liquidity needs are of great importance.

Because of taxes, the owners of a privately held firm can normally benefit more from capital gains than from dividends. Double taxation is avoided. If the firm is sold, the reinvested earnings will have benefitted from tax deferral, and will be taxed at capital gains rates, which might be lower than ordinary income tax rates. For this reason, Internal Revenue Service regulations prohibit excessive earnings retention. But the definition of "excessive" is not clear. Privately held firms are usually smaller than publicly traded firms. They consequently have less financial flexibility and somewhat more variable liquidity requirements. Greater retentions are therefore warranted to compensate for the higher liquidity risks they face. Minimizing dividend payouts—especially until a surplus has been built up—may therefore be financially prudent as well as beneficial from a tax standpoint.

Review

1. Why is it useful to consider more than one dividend policy alternative?
2. What special dividend policy considerations apply to privately held firms?

17.8 SHARE REPURCHASES

Firms that want to distribute cash to their shareholders usually do so by declaring cash dividends. A **share repurchase** is an alternative to a cash dividend. The firm spends the cash on repurchasing shares of its common stock. For example, IBM once offered to buy up to 4 million shares of its common stock. At the time, IBM had more than $6 billion in cash and marketable securities on its balance sheet. IBM actually bought 2,546,000 shares at a cost of $280 per share, for a total cost of about $713 million.

Share Repurchase Versus Dividends

We showed that if a firm is expanding, shareholders are indifferent between (1) dividend payout with the issuance of new shares and (2) retention of earnings—in a perfect capital market environment. Similarly, in a perfect capital market environment, if a firm is contracting (the mirror image of expanding), shareholders are indifferent between cash dividends and repurchasing shares. Our next example illustrates this point.

EXAMPLE Illustration of Equivalence of Dividends and Share Repurchases

International Paper (IP) has decided to distribute $50 million cash. IP has 10 million shares outstanding. It expects to earn $2.50 per share; the current market value per share is $25. IP could pay a cash dividend of $5 per share, implying an ex-dividend value of $20 per share. Alternatively, it could use the $50 million to repurchase 2,000,000 (= 50,000,000/25) shares. After the share repurchase, each share would be worth

$$\frac{10{,}000{,}000(25) - \$50{,}000{,}000}{10{,}000{,}000 - 2{,}000{,}000} = \$25$$

Therefore, as long as IP repurchases shares at the current market price of $25, a shareholder who does not sell will have the same wealth per share as a shareholder who does sell, namely $25 per share. The only difference is that one person has the wealth in the form of cash and the other has it in the form of stock. Similarly, if IP pays the $5 dividend, each shareholder would have an identical $25 per share value in the form of $5 in cash plus a share of stock worth $20.

Note that to the extent IP pays a repurchase price in excess of the market price, there is a *transfer of wealth* to the shareholders who sell from those who do not.

EXAMPLE Greenmail: Wealth Transfer through Share Repurchases

Let's continue our IP example. IP decides to spend $50 million to buy shares for $30 each from one of its shareholders. IP can purchase 1,666,667 (= 50,000,000/30) shares. Following the share repurchase, each share will be worth

$$\frac{10{,}000{,}000(25) - 50{,}000{,}000}{10{,}000{,}000 - 1{,}666{,}667} = \$24$$

There is a transfer of wealth *to* the selling shareholder amounting to $8,333,333 (= [30 − 25]1,666,667), and there is a transfer of wealth *from* the remaining shareholders amounting to the same $8,333,333 (= [25 − 24]10,000,000 − 1,666,667). In the past, many firms have paid premiums to buy back shares from a takeover raider. When they do, the takeover raider effectively expropriates a portion of the other shareholders' collective wealth. This expropriation of wealth has come to be known by the colorful name **greenmail.**

EPS Impact

Less sophisticated market participants often misunderstand how a share repurchase affects shareholder wealth. They judge its impact in terms of earnings per share (EPS). In the first example, before the cash distribution, IP had a price-earnings ratio (P/E) of 10 (= 25/2.50). After the cash distribution, IP should have a P/E of 8 (= 20/2.50). But this is true regardless of whether the cash is distributed as a dividend or through share repurchase. Neither IP's capital structure nor its capital investment policies is affected by the method of cash distribution. The share repurchase alternative would result in a projected EPS of

$$\frac{2.50(10{,}000{,}000)}{8{,}000{,}000} = \$3.125$$

However, although the EPS is higher with the share repurchase, each share would still be worth

$$3.125(8) = \$25$$

The increase in projected EPS is just offset by the decline in the P/E (from 10 to 8).

The confusion over the impact of share repurchases results from the mistaken belief that share repurchase will not alter the P/E. But if the P/E remained unchanged, the risk-return relationship would differ between the alternatives. This would be inconsistent with the Principles of Capital Market Efficiency and Risk-Return Trade-Off.

Advantages of Repurchasing Shares

In the first IP example, the share repurchase program did not affect shareholder wealth. But this conclusion depends on our assumption of a perfect capital market. Asymmetric taxes can change this conclusion. Because of lower effective taxes on capital gains, taxable individual shareholders in the United States generally prefer a share repurchase to a cash dividend.

Suppose dividends are taxed at a 50% rate and capital gains at a 20% rate. Shareholders would have to pay $25,000,000 (= [0.5]50,000,000) in total taxes on the dividend distribution, but no more than $10,000,000 (= [0.2]50,000,000) in total taxes on the share repurchase (depending on the tax basis of the shares).

On the other hand, dividends paid to other corporations are taxed at a lower rate than capital gains because of the 70% dividends-received deduction. Consequently, corporate shareholders usually prefer dividends over capital gains. The overall net tax advantage (or disadvantage) of share repurchase versus dividends thus depends on the shareholder mix.

EXAMPLE Share Buybacks in Japan

A couple of years ago, several large Japanese firms announced share repurchase plans, including Honda and Toyota, whose shares are widely held in the United States. Analysts and investors welcomed this as a sign that Japanese firms were finally becoming more shareholder friendly.

Taxation can affect the choice between repurchases and dividends in other countries, too.

EXAMPLE Unilever's $8 Billion Dividend

Uniliver, the Anglo-Dutch consumer-goods giant, declared an $8 billion special dividend a few years ago to give shareholders cash it had raised from asset sales. It decided on a dividend rather than a buyback because Dutch tax regulations favored the dividend.

Implementing a Share Repurchase Program

Once a firm decides to undertake a share repurchase program, it must choose a method of doing it. There are five basic methods to repurchase shares: open market purchases, cash tender offers, transferable put rights, privately negotiated block purchases, and exchange offers. We will discuss each in turn.

OPEN MARKET PURCHASES A firm can repurchase shares of its common stock in market transactions at current market prices. An *open market repurchase program* averages the firm's repurchase prices during the repurchase period. Approximately two-thirds of the shares repurchased in the United States are bought in open market purchases. Firms typically use such programs to satisfy their needs for shares—for example, for stock option and other employee benefit programs and to have them available upon conversion of convertible securities. Open market repurchases are subject to SEC regulations governing the timing, price, volume, and coordination of share purchases. These rules are designed to minimize the impact of the share repurchase program on the firm's share price.

CASH TENDER OFFERS The offer can be either an offer to purchase a stated number of shares at a fixed price or a Dutch auction. To repurchase a relatively large number of its shares quickly, a firm can announce a **fixed-price tender offer.** It specifies the number of shares it seeks and the price it is willing to pay. Such an offer has the advantage of giving all shareholders an equal opportunity to sell their shares back to the firm. However, transaction costs for tender offers are generally higher than for other types of share repurchase programs (in particular, premiums paid to induce tendering). At the same time, perhaps because of their higher cost, tender offers are generally a more positive signal than open market purchase programs.

The **Dutch auction tender offer** is a variation that gives a firm greater flexibility in determining the price at which it repurchases the shares. A Dutch auction "reverses" the tender process. Shareholders can offer to sell shares at prices with a specified range.

EXAMPLE Holiday Inns, Inc.'s Dutch Auction Tender Offer

Holiday Inns, Inc. used a Dutch auction tender offer to buy up to 8 million shares. Table 17.4 shows the details: A minimum of 2.5 million and maximum of 8 million shares, at a minimum of \$46 and maximum of \$49 price. Shareholders specified the minimum price (within the range) they were willing to accept. If less than 2.5 million shares were tendered (offered to sell back), the firm would pay \$49 per share. Otherwise, the firm would pay a price within the specified range, and buy all shares tendered at that or a lower price (up to the stated maximum).

Holiday Inns purchased all of the 6.3 million shares that were tendered at \$49 per share. Note that if a firm is willing to pay the maximum price in a fixed-price tender offer, the Dutch auction provides the chance that the firm might get the shares at a lower price.

There are two important considerations with a tender offer: (1) how to set the **tender offer premium** and (2) whether to use one or more soliciting dealers. The tender offer premium is the amount offered above the current market price. In general, the premium should be just large enough to attract the desired number of shares. In most cases, the tender offer premium is between 10% and 25%. A smaller premium (perhaps 5% or less) is possible if a block[5] holder wants to sell shares anyway. On the other hand, a larger premium (perhaps 20% or greater) would normally be needed for a low-trading-volume, widely held, stock.

On the second question, it is usually beneficial to use dealers. Without their solicitation efforts, a larger tender premium would normally be required.

TRANSFERABLE PUT RIGHTS A fixed-price tender offer conveys to shareholders nondetachable put options. Shareholders can get the value of their options only by tendering shares to the firm, which might create a tax liability. Instead, a firm can issue **transferable put rights** to its shareholders. Those who do not want to sell shares can sell the put rights. Put rights are thus more "tax efficient" than a fixed-price tender offer. Also, there is no risk of oversubscription because the number of puts issued limits the number of shares that shareholders can tender. Transferable put rights are described and discussed in detail in the next section.

---

[5]A *block* is generally defined in terms of some minimum number of shares or some minimum market value. The NYSE defines a block (of shares sold in a single transaction) as consisting of the lesser of (a) 10,000 (or more) shares or (b) shares (regardless of the number) with a market value of \$200,000 or more.

TABLE 17.4
Holiday Inns, Inc.'s tender offer for up to 8 million shares of its common stock.

Length of tender period	17 days
Tender method	Dutch auction
Purpose for the offer	The firm's board believes the firm's stock represents an "attractive investment."
Number of shares sought	
Maximum:	8,000,000 (The firm reserved the right to increase the maximum to 10,000,000 shares.)
Minimum:	2,500,000
Number of shares outstanding	34,786,931
Percentage of shares sought	
Maximum:	23.0% (up to 28.7% if the maximum is increased)
Minimum:	7.2
Pre-tender closing share price	$44.00
Tender offer price	
Maximum:	$49.00
Minimum:	46.00
Tender offer premium	
Maximum:	11.4%
Minimum:	4.5
Dollar value of tender	
At maximum price:	$392 million ($490 million if maximum increased)
At minimum price:	368 million ($460 million if maximum increased)
Number of shares tendered	6,300,000
% of outstanding tendered	18.1%
Success ratio	78.8%
Source of funds	$500 million bank credit agreement
Expenses	
Dealer/manager fee:	$0.15 per share purchased
Soliciting dealer fee:	None

PRIVATELY NEGOTIATED BLOCK PURCHASES Privately negotiated block purchases are most often made in connection with, rather than as a substitute for, an open market purchase program. Large blocks can often be purchased for less than the current market price, particularly when the transaction is initiated by the seller. As with greenmail, firms sometimes purchase large blocks, often at substantial premiums, from troublesome or potentially threatening minority shareholders. As noted earlier, there are agency problems associated with such repurchases, so it is not clear that the repurchases are always in the *collective* shareholders' best interest.

EXCHANGE OFFERS Instead of offering cash to repurchase shares, a firm might offer bonds or preferred stock in an **exchange offer.** One problem with an exchange offer is the difference in liquidity of the two securities. A larger premium might be necessary to compensate for the lower liquidity of the replacement security. Probably for this reason, most common stock repurchase programs involve cash purchases.

Table 17.5 summarizes the advantages and disadvantages of the five repurchase methods. Regardless of the method chosen, a publicly traded firm must comply with SEC regulations. These involve certain disclosure requirements and restrictions on a firm's simultaneously engaging in both a share repurchase program and a sale or other distribution of its common stock or securities that are convertible into its common stock.

TABLE 17.5
Summary comparison of share repurchase methods.

ADVANTAGES	DISADVANTAGES
Open Market Purchases	
• No premium over market price • Can extend over long period, thereby providing long-term support to the market • Holders who desire liquidity receive cash • Less market impact than tender offer or exchange offer if program is not completed successfully	• If blocks do not materialize, daily volume limitations make it difficult to complete program quickly • Risk that market price can appreciate independent of the repurchase program before the program is completed • Danger that buying can drive up market price, leading to a de facto premium
Private Block Purchases	
• Blocks can often be purchased at a discount from market price • Attracts less attention than other methods	• Success of program dependent on locating blocks (private block purchases are therefore normally used to supplement open market purchase program) • May provide less long-term support to the market • Preferential treatment toward the selling shareholders may become an issue with other shareholders if blocks are purchased at a significant premium
Tender Offer	
• Allows repurchase of significant number of shares quickly at a (maximum) price fixed at the outset of the program • Provides an equal opportunity to all shareholders to sell their shares • Evidence indicates that tender offers have more positive market impact after repurchase program is completed than open market purchase program • More effective than open market purchase at drawing out "loose" shares • Provides means of eliminating small holdings • Holders who desire liquidity receive cash	• Normally requires premium of 10% to 25% over market price (Dutch auction may reduce this) • Higher transactions costs than open market purchase program • Oversubscription or undersubscription can embarrass firm • Oversubscription may indicate vulnerability to hostile takeover
Transferable Put Rights	
• Allows repurchase of significant number of shares quickly at a (maximum) price fixed at the outset of the program • Reduces agency costs by providing an equal opportunity to all stockholders to sell their shares • More effective than open market purchase at drawing out "loose" shares • Holders who desire liquidity receive cash • Transferability enables nontendering shareholders to receive value for their rights • More tax efficient than a tender offer • No risk of oversubscription • Relatively low-tax-basis shareholders retain their shares, which will make the firm more costly to a takeover raider	• Higher transaction costs than open market purchase program and than tender offer (for example, if fees are paid to list the put rights for trading on a stock exchange) • Put rights taxed as a dividend upon distribution but give rise to a short-term capital loss if they expire worthless; a variety of additional tax consequences that are complex
Exchange Offer	
• If preferred stock is offered in the exchange, there is a tax advantage to shareholders who exchange and hold the preferred • Transaction cost savings to shareholders who exchange and hold	• Higher transaction costs than open market purchase program • Shareholders are offered a less liquid security that they may not wish to hold; therefore, an exchange offer may require a larger premium than a tender offer • Oversubscription or undersubscription can embarrass firm

Review

1. What is a share repurchase?
2. Why is a share repurchase a substitute for a dividend?
3. How does a share repurchase affect projected EPS? Does that mean the share price will rise?
4. Describe five methods of repurchasing shares.
5. Which method usually conveys a more favorable signal, announcing an open market purchase program or announcing a tender offer?

17.9 TRANSFERABLE PUT RIGHTS

A firm cannot force its shareholders to sell their shares. It can only offer to repurchase them. In the typical tender offer, the firm sets a maximum number of shares it is willing to repurchase at the tender price. Each shareholder is free to tender their shares (accept the offer and sell shares to the firm) or reject the offer (and keep the shares). If the aggregate number of shares tendered exceeds the maximum, the firm can repurchase a prorated (a proportionately reduced) number of shares from each shareholder. So shareholders may sell fewer shares than they had intended.

A fixed-price tender offer gives shareholders a put option. The tender price is the strike price. When the tender price exceeds the market price, the put option is in-the-money. We know from the Options Principle that this option is valuable. But shareholders cannot sell this option separately from their shares. They can get the option's value only by exercising it.

If shareholders do not exercise the option, it expires and they get nothing for it. Also, the premium paid over market price transfers wealth from the shareholders who do not tender to those who do. But because of taxes, the *net* value of this put option is not the same for all shareholders.

Shareholders with a low tax basis in their shares would trigger a large capital gains tax liability if they tender the shares. Tendering would eliminate their tax-timing option to continue to postpone the tax on their capital gain. Triggering this tax liability then reduces the incentive for low-tax-basis shareholders to sell their shares. Higher-tax-basis shareholders do not face this problem. Therefore, if the tender offer is open to all shareholders (as the law requires), there is a tax inefficiency: Some investors with low tax bases, and hence greater tax liabilities as a result of tendering, will not sell shares, whereas investors with higher tax bases, and hence smaller potential tax liabilities, will sell all their shares.

Transferable put rights are designed to minimize these inefficiencies. A transferable put right is the right to sell the firm one share of its common stock at a fixed price (the strike price) within a stated period (the time to maturity). This security gets its name "transferable" because, after being created, it is separated from its "birth" share (our analysis assumes one put right is attached to each share). After being separated, it becomes transferable. The put right can be bought and sold in the capital markets. In this way, shareholders can get the option value by selling the put right if they do not want to exercise it (perhaps because of a capital gains tax liability).

In Chapter 18, we discuss rights offerings, which distribute call options to a firm's shareholders. Such call options give the right to buy (from the firm) one share of the firm's common stock at a fixed price within a stated period. Transferable put rights and a rights offering are symmetrical: the former provides the right to sell shares, whereas the latter provides the right to buy shares. Exercising a transferable put right is a share repurchase that shrinks the firm's total amount of equity in the same way as a dividend. On the other hand, conducting a rights offering creates new shares that grow the firm's total amount of equity.

EXAMPLE Gillette's Transferable Put Rights Offering

The Gillette Company issued one transferable put right for each seven shares held as of three days earlier. Each put right entitled the holder to sell one share of stock to the firm anytime in the next 35 days at a price of \$45, a significant premium above the market price of \$34.875. Gillette had 112,100,227 shares outstanding, and would repurchase 16,014,318 shares (one-seventh of the shares outstanding) at a cost of approximately \$721 million (= [45]16,014,318) if all the put rights were exercised.

Valuing Transferable Put Rights

As explained in Chapter 12, the value of an option, and therefore a put right, is a function of the (1) strike price, (2) value of the underlying asset, (3) time to expiration, (4) variance of the return on the underlying asset, and (5) riskless return. In addition, the value of a put right depends on the decrease in the number of shares outstanding.

Put rights are usually issued significantly in-the-money to encourage shareholders to exercise them, as Gillette did. That is, the issuer sets a positive exercise value by setting the repurchase (strike) price above the stock's current market price. Because of the short time to expiration, the option's time premium is typically small and therefore a relatively insignificant determinant of the value of the put right. For convenience, we ignore it.

The initial value of a put right just after the offering is announced, and while the put right is still attached to the share, is approximately:

$$R_P = \frac{S - P_R}{N - 1} \tag{17.2}$$

where R_P is the value of one put right, P_R is the market value of a share with the put right attached, S is the strike price, and N is the number of rights to sell one share (assuming one put right is created for each outstanding share).

EXAMPLE Gillette's Transferable Put Rights Offering (continued)

The initial value of one of Gillette's transferable put rights, on a per-share basis, was approximately:

$$R_P = \frac{45.00 - 34.875}{7 - 1} = \$1.6875$$

Because Gillette issued one put right per seven common shares, the value on a per-put-right basis is seven times the per-share value, \$11.8125 (= [7]1.6875).

After the put right is separated from the stock, the share price decreases by the value of the right. Therefore, P_E, the share price alone (after separation), is

$$P_E = P_R - R_P \tag{17.3}$$

Thereafter, the value of the put right varies with the price of the firm's shares:

$$R_P = \frac{S - P_E}{N} \tag{17.4}$$

EXAMPLE Gillette's Transferable Put Rights Offering (continued)

The closing price for put rights on the day trading began was $10.625, and the stock closed at $33.75 per share. Substituting into Equation (17.4), the value of each put right, on a per-share basis, would be

$$R_P = \frac{45.00 - 33.75}{7} = \$1.6071$$

Because Gillette issued one put right per seven common shares, the value on a per-put-right basis is seven times the per share value, $11.2497 (= [7]1.6071). This is more than the market price. Surprised?

Taxes

One additional factor that can affect the value of a put right is not in Equations (17.2) and (17.4): taxes. Put rights enable low-tax-basis shareholders to get the value of the option by selling the put right, thereby avoiding the capital gains tax they would incur if they sold their shares. Avoiding (or at least deferring) this tax liability is valuable. Depending upon the supply of put rights offered by low-tax-basis shareholders and the demand for put rights by high-tax-basis shareholders, the put price can be bid up above the sum of its exercise value plus its time value. To the extent that it is bid up above the sum of these values, low-tax-basis shareholders effectively get a greater proportion of the value of the tax savings relative to a fixed-price tender offer.

The following generalized version of Equation (17.4) reflects these tax considerations:

$$R_P = \frac{(1 - T_g)S + T_g B - P_E}{(1 - T_g)N} \tag{17.5}$$

where T_g stands for the capital gains tax rate, and B is the tax basis of the marginal purchaser of put rights.

EXAMPLE Gillette's Transferable Put Rights Offering (concluded)

Here we conclude the Gillette example. Suppose the marginal purchaser had a tax rate of 18% and a tax basis of $30 per share. Then the value of the Gillette transferable put rights, on a per-share basis, is

$$R_P = \frac{(1 - 0.18)45.00 + (0.18)30.00 - 33.75}{(1 - 0.18)7} = 1.4895$$

which is $10.4265 on a per-put-right basis (= [7]1.4895). This implies a time premium of $0.1985 (= market value minus exercise value = 10.625 − 10.4265) for the put right (with the assumed tax rate and tax basis). This example shows clearly that tax factors can affect option valuation.

Advantages of Transferable Put Rights

Transferable put rights offer at least three potentially significant advantages over a fixed-price tender offer:

1. Low-tax-basis shareholders are able to get the value for their rights without having to incur the tax liability that the sale of their shares would trigger.

2. There is no risk of oversubscription.
3. There is a "tax-efficiency" gain (at the expense of the U.S. Treasury) because low-tax-basis shareholders sell their rights rather than their shares.

Transferable put rights are an innovative share repurchase strategy. The only potential drawback we can see is that because of tax law complexity, shareholders may be forced to incur significant transaction costs in the form of effort (or cost of tax advice) necessary to determine the correct tax treatment of the receipt and exercise of the put rights. This problem should prove relatively minor in the long run, as investors become more familiar with put rights, and we expect that transferable put rights will become more widely used in the future because of their inherent advantages.

Review

1. What are transferable put rights?
2. What are the advantages to shareholders of a transferable put rights offering as compared to a fixed-price tender offer?

17.10 STOCK DIVIDENDS AND STOCK SPLITS

Firms do not always pay dividends in cash. Frequently firms pay **stock dividends.** For example, suppose a firm declares a 5% stock dividend. Then a shareholder will receive five new shares for each 100 shares owned.

A firm can achieve much the same financial effect through a **stock split.** Although there is a technical difference between the two, stock dividends and stock splits represent alternative ways to rearrange a firm's capital accounts on its balance sheet. Neither affects the net worth of the firm, or the proportion of ownership interest of any of its shareholders. Stock dividends and stock splits, however, may send a signal to the market.

Accounting for Stock Dividends and Stock Splits

A stock dividend proportionally increases the number of shares each shareholder owns. The accounting treatment of "small" and "large" stock dividends is different. A "small" stock dividend is one that is less than 25% of the previously outstanding shares. The two accounting treatments are:

For a small stock dividend: The *fair market value* of the shares distributed in the stock dividend is transferred from the retained earnings account to the *paid-in capital* and *capital contributed in excess of par value* accounts on the firm's balance sheet.

For a large stock dividend: The *par value* of the shares distributed in the stock dividend is transferred from the retained earnings account to the *paid-in capital* account on the firm's balance sheet.

A stock dividend is a transaction that reallocates part of the firm's retained earnings into either the paid-in capital or the capital contributed in excess of par value accounts. For a small stock dividend, the accounting treatment is like a cash dividend (which reduces retained earnings) and sale of new shares at their fair market value (which increases the paid-in capital and capital contributed in excess of par value accounts by the amount that retained earnings were reduced). Because of certain problems,[6] large stock dividends are treated differently. For this case, only the par value of the new shares is moved from retained earnings to paid-in capital.

---

[6]For example, the fair market value of the new shares distributed could exceed the total value of retained earnings.

The accounting treatment for a stock split is simpler:

> For a stock split, no change is made in the dollar amounts of the paid-in capital, capital contributed in excess of par value, or retained earnings accounts. The number of shares and par value per share are adjusted for the new shares that are distributed.

For a 2-for-1 stock split, the number of shares is doubled and the par value per share is cut in half. If the firm implements a 3-for-2 split, the number of shares increases by 50% and the par value per share decreases by one-third. The following example illustrates the mechanics of the accounting for a small stock dividend, large stock dividend, and a stock split.

EXAMPLE A 10% Stock Dividend, a 100% Stock Dividend, and a 2-for-1 Stock Split

Table 17.6 illustrates the balance sheet impact of a 10% stock dividend, a 100% stock dividend, and a 2-for-1 stock split for a firm whose shares are selling at $30.

For the 10% stock dividend, 100,000 new shares are distributed. This is treated as a small stock dividend. The $3 million *fair market value* of these shares is taken out of retained earnings, with $1 million added to paid-in capital account at par value (because the par value is $10 per share) and the balance, $2 million, is added to the capital contributed in excess of par value account.

For a 100% stock dividend, 1,000,000 new shares are distributed. This is treated as a large stock dividend because the distribution is at least 25% of the previously outstanding shares. For a large stock dividend, only the par value of the new shares is taken from retained

TABLE 17.6
Comparison of the balance sheet impact of a 10% stock dividend, a 100% stock dividend, and a 2-for-1 stock split.

Common Stockholders' Equity Initially	
Paid-in capital ($10 par value; 1,000,000 shares)	$ 10,000,000
Capital contributed in excess of par value	20,000,000
Retained earnings	70,000,000
Common stockholders' equity	$100,000,000
Common Stockholders' Equity Following 10% Stock Dividend	
Paid-in capital ($10 par value; 1,100,000 shares)	$ 11,000,000
Capital contributed in excess of par value	22,000,000
Retained earnings	67,000,000
Common stockholders' equity	$100,000,000
Common Stockholders' Equity Following 100% Stock Dividend	
Paid-in capital ($10 par value; 2,000,000 shares)	$ 20,000,000
Capital contributed in excess of par value	20,000,000
Retained earnings	60,000,000
Common stockholders' equity	$100,000,000
Common Stockholders' Equity Following 2-for-1 Stock Split	
Paid-in capital ($5 par value; 2,000,000 shares)	$ 10,000,000
Capital contributed in excess of par value	20,000,000
Retained earnings	70,000,000
Common stockholders' equity	$100,000,000

earnings and put into the paid-in capital account. As you can see in Table 17.6, $10 million (= [10]1,000,000) is moved from retained earnings to paid-in capital.

For the 2-for-1 stock split, 1,000,000 new shares are distributed. The only change in the balance sheet accounts is the notation that outstanding shares are now 2,000,000 and the par value is reduced from $10 per share to $5.

In all cases, the firm's net worth remains $100 million.

EXAMPLE GE's Stock Split

A few years ago, GE announced a 2-for-1 stock split. Holders of record got one additional share for each share held. (Sounds a lot like a stock dividend, doesn't it?) Prior to the stock split, GE had approximately 926,564,000 shares outstanding. Following the split, it had approximately 1,853,128,000 shares outstanding. Typically, a firm makes a dividend adjustment simultaneously, but GE maintained the per-share dividend rate of $0.36. Thus, the action doubled the dividend payout. An owner of 100 shares before the split got a $36.00 dividend per quarter. After the split, that same shareholder owned 200 shares and got a $72.00 dividend per quarter.

Stock Dividends Versus Stock Splits

Firms generally use stock dividends when they are making relatively small stock distributions, and use stock splits for larger ones. For example, the rules of the New York Stock Exchange prescribe that firms should make share distributions of less than 25% through stock dividends rather than stock splits.

Another difference between stock splits and stock dividends is based on state laws where a corporation is chartered. Some states allow dividends to be paid from retained earnings (or from retained earnings and capital contributed in excess of par value). By reducing retained earnings and by increasing par values, a stock dividend can reduce the ability of a corporation to pay cash dividends. A stock split would have no such effect. In practice, this possible effect on the ability to pay cash dividends is rarely ever significant.

Financial Impact of Stock Dividends and Stock Splits

Both the 100% stock dividend and 2-for-1 stock split each doubled the number of shares outstanding. But they did not affect the firm's liquidity position, capital budget, leverage, or any operating variable. Consequently, barring any informational effects, a stock dividend or a stock split should leave the stock market value of a firm unchanged. Hence, a proportional reduction in the firm's share price should occur:

$$\text{Price}_{\text{After}} = \frac{\text{Price}_{\text{Before}}}{1 + \%\text{ stock dividend}} = \frac{\text{Price}_{\text{Before}}}{\text{Stock split factor}} \tag{17.6}$$

For example, if the price per share is $60 before a 100% stock dividend or a 2-for-1 split, it should be $30 afterwards.

So what is the value of a stock dividend or a stock split?

According to the Signaling Principle, actions convey information. The principal benefit of a stock dividend or stock split is probably the information it conveys. About half the shares listed on the New York Stock Exchange, for example, tend to trade in the range between $10 and $30 per share in any particular year, as illustrated in Table 17.7.

Stock dividends and stock splits are usually associated with firms that have (or at least believe they have) excellent growth prospects. A stock split, in particular, may signal management's expectation that

TABLE 17.7
Distribution of New York Stock Exchange-listed common stocks, 1967 to 2001.

	AS OF JANUARY 6, 1967		AS OF JANUARY 7, 1972		AS OF FEBRUARY 3, 1978		AS OF JANUARY 31, 1984		AS OF DECEMBER 31, 1990		AS OF DECEMBER 30, 1994		AS OF DECEMBER 31, 1998		AS OF DECEMBER 31, 2001	
PRICE GROUP	Number of Firms	Percentage of Total	Number of Firms	Percentage of Total	Number of Firms	Percentage of Total	Number of Firms	Percentage of Total	Number of Firms	Percentage of Total	Number of Firms	Percentage of Total	Number of Firms	Percentage of Total	Number of Firms	Percentage of Total
Under $10.00	77	6.1%	105	7.4%	283	18.0%	219	14.5%	604	35.6%	487	28.1%	606	20.9%	578	22.5%
$10.00–19.99	282	22.3	350	24.8	561	35.7	448	29.6	589	34.7	704	40.7	949	32.7	796	31.0
$20.00–29.99	327	25.8	355	25.2	457	29.0	384	25.3	283	16.7	51	2.9	624	21.5	491	19.1
$30.00–39.99	251	19.9	241	17.0	163	10.4	238	15.7	111	6.6	258	14.9	337	11.6	311	12.1
$40.00–49.99	139	10.9	173	12.3	64	4.1	112	7.4	56	3.3	102	5.9	190	6.5	182	7.1
$50.00–59.99	73	5.8	71	5.1	22	1.4	56	3.7	26	1.5	67	3.9	99	3.4	97	3.8
$60.00–99.99	102	8.0	91	6.5	18	1.1	50	3.3	21	1.2	52	3.0	84	2.9	97	3.8
$100.00 and over	14	1.2	25	1.7	4	0.3	8	0.5	7	0.4	11	0.6	14	0.5	16	0.6
Total	1,265	100.0%	1,411	100.0%	1,572	100.0%	1,515	100.0%	1,697	100.0%	1,732	100.0%	2,901	100.0%	2,568	100.0%
Closing value of Dow Jones Industrial Average	808.74		910.37		770.96		1,211.57		2,633.66		3,834.44		9,181.43		10,021.5	

the firm's share price would, in the absence of the split, move further away from this customary trading range. If so, investors ought to react favorably to the news of an impending stock split.

In connection with a stock split, firms frequently announce their desire to reduce the price of a share to a more popular trading range. More important, there is evidence that investors react positively to this signal. A stock split, normally involving a greater reduction in share price than a stock dividend, is likely to have the greater informational content of the two.

Following a stock dividend, firms often maintain the cash dividend per share. Following a stock split, firms typically either reduce the per-share cash dividend less than proportionally, or else maintain it, as GE did. These actions increase the cash dividend payout. Such increases are generally interpreted as positive signals.

By reducing the share price to a more popular trading range, a stock split—and to a lesser degree, a stock dividend—may increase trading activity in a stock and thus improve its liquidity. By increasing the number of shares outstanding (and increasing the volume of trading activity), a stock split—and to a lesser degree, a stock dividend—may broaden the ownership of a firm's shares. However, the evidence on both points is not conclusive.

Stock Dividend Versus Cash Dividend

Firms sometimes declare a stock dividend in lieu of a cash dividend to conserve cash and yet convey information. Do you think investors miss the significance of the switch? When a firm substitutes a stock dividend for a cash dividend because of financial difficulty, investors will probably view this as negative rather than positive information.

Review

1. What is a stock dividend, and what is a stock split? How do they differ?
2. How does a stock dividend work?
3. What is the value to shareholders of a stock dividend or a stock split?

SUMMARY

- Publicly traded firms have historically paid dividends on a regular basis, maintained both a stable payout ratio and dividend rate, made orderly changes in the dividend rate, and avoided whenever possible cutting the dividend rate. There are systematic industry differences in payout policies.
- Dividend policy is irrelevant in a perfect capital market environment.
- Asymmetric information, asymmetric taxes, and transaction costs are persistent capital market imperfections that can cause dividend policy to affect a firm's value.
- A firm should use its dividend policy to whatever extent possible to maximize shareholder wealth. Its payout policy should be determined chiefly in keeping with its investment opportunities and internal funds needs.
- But also important are
  1. market reactions to the firm's changes, *or* lack of changes, in its dividend policy;
  2. changes in laws that create a demand for innovative dividend policies that might be valuable;
  3. shareholder preferences for capital gains and dividends;
  4. shareholder preferences for liquidity;

5. the relative transaction costs of selling shares for the firm versus the shareholders selling them; and
6. any legal or policy restrictions on the firm and its shareholders concerning dividend policy.

- The individual tax system imposes a bias in favor of capital gains and against dividends. The system of corporate taxation does just the opposite for corporate investors. Depending upon the circumstances, tax-exempt pension funds may have preferences in either direction. As a result, high-income individual investors appear to gravitate toward low-payout firms, and corporate investors prefer high-payout firms.
- Transaction costs for the firm impose a bias in favor of retained earnings over new share issues. However, transaction costs for investors impose at least some bias in favor of dividends over retained earnings for investors who want some minimum level of dividend income.
- The clientele effect, which involves investors investing in firms that have adopted dividend policies that are best for them, reduces or even eliminates tax and transaction cost considerations.
- Dividend policy may act as a signaling device. Simply paying out residual earnings year by year is unwise because it could cause the dividend rate to fluctuate wildly. This would reduce the information value of dividends.
- The chapter outlined and illustrated the application of a three-step set of dividend policy guidelines.
  1. The appropriate dividend action depends on the firm's future earnings and cash flow prospects and anticipated fund requirements. A firm should determine what percentage of its earnings it expects to have available for distribution over its planning horizon (typically five years). This percentage depends on its earnings and cash flow prospects, the availability of attractive investment opportunities, and the firm's chosen capital structure policy.
  2. Having determined how much cash is available for distribution, the second step involves deciding on an appropriate target payout ratio. A firm should determine whether a higher or a lower payout ratio is warranted in view of the firm's particular shareholder mix but should avoid setting the target payout ratio at a level that would trigger the need for an additional equity issue. The payout ratios of comparable firms provide a useful guide in this regard. Generally, a shareholder mix dominated by upper-income individual shareholders would argue for a payout ratio somewhat below that justified solely on the basis of residual earnings considerations, whereas a shareholder mix dominated by corporate shareholders, retired individuals, and tax-exempt institutions would argue for the opposite.
  3. Decide on quarterly dividends that are comfortably sustainable.
- Firms can repurchase shares in lieu of distributing cash dividends. Share repurchases are usually more beneficial from a tax standpoint to individual shareholders. Nontaxable institutional shareholders may prefer, and corporate shareholders usually will prefer, a dividend distribution. A firm's shareholder mix helps determine whether a share repurchase program is preferable to a dividend distribution—or whether the firm should use some combination of the two.
- If a firm has decided to repurchase shares, it should consider doing so through a transferable put rights offering.
- Although there are some accounting differences between stock dividends and stock splits, their financial significance depends on signals affirming the action, such as the positive signal from an increase in cash dividends.

EQUATION SUMMARY

$$\text{DPS}_1 - \text{DPS}_0 = \text{ADJ}[\text{POR}(\text{EPS}_1) - \text{DPS}_0] \tag{17.1}$$

$$R_P = \frac{S - P_R}{N - 1} \tag{17.2}$$

$$P_E = P_R - R_P \tag{17.3}$$

$$R_P = \frac{S - P_E}{N} \tag{17.4}$$

$$R_P = \frac{(1 - T_g)S + T_g B - P_E}{(1 - T_g)N} \tag{17.5}$$

$$\text{Price}_{\text{After}} = \frac{\text{Price}_{\text{Before}}}{1 + \%\ \text{stock dividend}} = \frac{\text{Price}_{\text{Before}}}{\text{Stock split factor}} \tag{17.6}$$

QUESTIONS

1. Consider the following four dates: April 10, April 24, April 27, and May 5. Which is the: (a) Ex-dividend date, (b) Record date, (c) Payment date, (d) Declaration date?
2. Among the following alternatives, which is the most common pattern of dividend policy? (a) A stable payout ratio where dividend payments vary with earnings. (b) A stable payment rate per share where dividend payments are more stable than earnings. (c) Dividend payments that vary each year according to the firm's capital investment opportunities. (d) A stable payment rate per share with a once-a-year "extra payment" based on the firm's earnings so that dividend payments are more stable than earnings.
3. Explain briefly why dividend policy is irrelevant in a perfect capital market environment.
4. Briefly explain why the signal of paying a dividend can cause dividend policy to affect a firm's value.
5. Explain what we mean by the term *dividend clientele.* How does the existence of dividend clienteles lessen or even eliminate the tax differential view of dividend policy in a perfect market?
6. True or False:
   a. Evidence shows that on average, a dividend decrease affects the firm's stock price negatively but a dividend increase has no effect on the firm's stock price.
   b. A large majority of firms follow a dividend policy that specifies a fixed payout ratio, so that the dollar amount each quarter fluctuates according to the firm's earnings.
   c. Typically, a firm has a target payout ratio that it aims for over time, but the payout ratio for any particular quarter can be substantially different from this target.
   d. To pay a cash dividend, it is necessary only for the firm to have sufficient retained earnings to afford the dividend payment. (If false, cite two factors that could preclude a firm from paying a dividend.)
   e. Dividends are normally paid quarterly, whereas bond interest payments are normally made semiannually.
7. Cite two examples of how transaction costs might affect a firm's choice of dividend policy.
8. Briefly describe our three-step approach to the dividend decision.

9. What is the difference between a stock dividend and a stock split, and what conditions make one more likely to be used than the other?
10. In what sense are share repurchases and dividend payments substitutes for one another? Under what circumstances, if any, are they perfect substitutes?
11. What are the major advantages of a share repurchase over a cash dividend?
12. Explain why a firm's share price falls on the ex-dividend date. By how much would you expect it to fall? Does it matter whether the dividend is paid in cash or additional stock?
13. Can it *ever* happen that a person owns shares of stock but does not receive the same cash dividend per share paid to other shareholders, or that a person no longer owns shares of stock but does receive a cash dividend?
14. How might the cost of issuing new stock affect a firm's choice of dividend policy?
15. Describe how a Dutch auction tender offer works and how it differs from a fixed-price tender offer.
16. What are the principal advantages of the transferable put rights method of share repurchase relative to the fixed-price tender offer method?

CHALLENGING QUESTIONS

17. Illustrate how a firm's repurchasing its own shares will increase the firm's leverage. Ignore taxes and assume a perfect capital market environment.
18. Describe conditions under which a firm might find it advantageous to substitute a stock dividend for an increase in its cash dividend.
19. What is the basis for the view that a firm's total market value is invariant to its choice of dividend policy? Cite three broad types of capital market imperfections that might cause the dividend policy of a firm to have an effect on the value of that firm. Give three examples (one for each type) where such an imperfection would cause a firm's dividend policy to have an effect on the value of that firm. Explain *how* each of the three examples you gave would cause a firm's dividend policy to have an effect on the value of that firm.
20. Several years ago, Allegis Corporation (now UAL Corp.) announced that it expected to declare a special dividend of not less than $50 per share to be paid out of the after-tax proceeds from the sale of its Hilton International and Westin Hotels & Resorts hotel subsidiaries and Hertz Corp. car rental subsidiary. Its quarterly common dividend rate at the time was $0.25 per share.
    a. What does the special dividend announcement tell you about Allegis Corporation's ability to reinvest profitably the after-tax proceeds from the sale of its subsidiaries?
    b. Why do you suppose Allegis Corporation planned to pay a special dividend, rather than increase the regular dividend?
    c. Allegis Corporation eventually used the after-tax proceeds to repurchase approximately $3 billion worth of its common stock. It acted at the behest of at least one large shareholder. What does the large shareholder's preference for a share repurchase rather than a special dividend seem to indicate about that shareholder's tax position?
21. Mega Electric Company has been denied its request for an electricity rate increase. Mega has continued to pay $2 per share per year in cash dividends in anticipation of receiving permission to increase electric rates. As a result of the denial, Mega's payout ratio will go over 100% within 12 months unless something is done quickly.
    a. Mega Electric's chairman asks you, as the utility's chief financial officer, to study the advisability of paying a $1 cash dividend and a $1 common stock dividend in order to

"preserve the dividend and not send a negative signal to the market." How would you respond to the chairman?

b. Mega Electric's president comes to you with a "better idea." She suggests paying a $1 cash dividend and distributing the "rest" of the dividend as a $1 face amount of a new 12% debenture. (Assume the 12% interest rate would make the debenture worth its par value.) How would you respond to the president?

22. If the price of a share of common stock can be expressed as the present value of the future dividend stream, how could it be that dividend policy is irrelevant?
23. Why might transaction costs cause a firm to find it advantageous to repurchase small shareholdings that are outstanding?
24. Suppose a firm is facing the possibility of a necessary dividend rate cut because of poor economic conditions. Suppose further that you are a member of the firm's board of directors. How would you respond to the argument of another board member that the firm should publicly deny the possibility of such a cut until the board has decided that the cut is an unavoidable necessity? The other member's argument is that unless the firm denies the possibility of a dividend cut, its stock price will drop. If the cut can be avoided, the drop will have been unnecessary, and the firm's stockholders will have suffered needlessly.
25. Our discussion in this chapter leads to a less-than-completely-satisfying conclusion. Specifically, we do not provide a prescription that specifies *exactly* how to maximize shareholder wealth through dividend policy. If you will recall, our prescription concerning capital structure was somewhat similar. Now the question: Suppose the good fairy can tell you exactly how to optimize both your firm's capital structure policy and your firm's dividend policy. Although the good fairy wants to be good to you, he does not want to be too good to you and has offered to provide you with the optimal prescription for your firm's capital structure policy *or* your firm's dividend policy, but not both. Based on what you now know of the potential gains to be had from each policy, which one would you choose to optimize? Explain your reasoning.
26. It has been argued by a journalist that electric companies should not be allowed to pay cash dividends because such a prohibition would (a) reduce their need to raise external capital, thus (b) reducing their transaction costs, so that (c) they would have a lower cost of capital, and consequently (d) lower utility rates, and (e) make customers better off. Utility stockholders would receive capital gains instead of dividends, which (because of lower tax rates or tax deferral) would lower their taxes. Do you think a legal restriction preventing utilities from ever paying a cash dividend would result in this chain of events? If not, where does the logic break down?

PROBLEMS

LEVEL A (BASIC)

A1. (Extra dividend) Escarraz Soy Products has the following quarterly earnings per share and has paid a regular quarterly dividend of $.30.

QUARTER	1	2	3	4	TOTAL
Earnings per share	$.60	$1.10	$1.20	$.90	$3.80
Dividends per share	.30	.30	.30	.30	1.20

Escarraz wants the annual payout to be 40% of earnings. What extra dividend in the fourth quarter would give the firm its planned payout?

A2. (Extra dividend) Alonzo, Inc. has the following quarterly earnings per share and has paid a regular quarterly dividend of $.70.

QUARTER	1	2	3	4	TOTAL
Earnings per share	$1.00	$1.50	$1.25	$2.10	$5.85
Dividends per share	.70	.70	.70	.70	2.80

Alonzo wants the annual payout to be 60% of earnings. What extra dividend in the fourth quarter would give the firm its planned payout?

A3. (Extra dividend) Sensor Technologies pays a regular dividend of $.10 per quarter plus an extra dividend in the fourth quarter equal to 40% of the amount that annual earnings per share exceeds $2.00.

a. If annual earnings per share are $2.80, what is the fourth quarter extra dividend?

b. If annual earnings per share are $1.75, what is the fourth quarter extra dividend?

A4. (Extra dividend) C-Tech, Inc. pays a regular dividend of $0.20 per quarter plus an extra dividend in the fourth quarter equal to 50% of the amount that annual earnings per share exceeds $5.00.

a. If annual earnings per share are $5.75, what is the fourth quarter extra dividend?

b. If annual earnings per share are $4.25, what is the fourth quarter extra dividend?

A5. (Taxes on cash dividends versus repurchased shares) The board of directors of General Motors is debating the payment of an extra $500 million in cash dividends on common stock versus repurchasing $500 million of common shares.

a. Assume that GM pays a cash dividend of $500 million and that the marginal tax rate of its investors is 40%. What is the tax liability?

b. Assume that GM repurchases $500 million of common shares. The cost of these shares for the selling shareholders is $300 million. Assuming a 40% tax rate, what is the tax liability on the capital gain?

A6. (Taxes on cash dividends versus repurchased shares) The board of directors at Microsoft is debating paying an extra $200 million in cash dividends on common stock versus repurchasing $200 million of common shares.

a. Assume Microsoft pays a cash dividend of $200 million and that the marginal tax rate of its investors is 35%. What is the tax liability?

b. Assume Microsoft repurchases $200 million of common shares. The cost of these shares for the selling shareholders is $75 million. Assuming a 35% tax rate, what is the tax liability on the capital gain?

A7. (Accounting for a stock dividend) Deryl Martin Interests has the common stock accounts as shown. The stock has a $22 per share market value. If Deryl Martin pays a 5% stock dividend, show the revised common stock accounts.

Paid-in capital ($.42 par value, 1,000,000 shares)	$ 420,000
Capital contributed in excess of par value	4,720,000
Retained earnings	8,200,000
Common stockholders' equity	$13,340,000

A8. (Accounting for a stock dividend) Epson, Inc. has the common stock accounts as shown. The stock has a $38 per share market value. If Epson pays a 10% stock dividend, show the revised common stock accounts.

Paid-in capital ($0.50 par value, 10,000,000 shares)	$ 5,000,000
Capital contributed in excess of par value	13,000,000
Retained earnings	60,000,000
Common stockholders' equity	$78,000,000

A9. (Accounting for a stock split) Bendeck Brake has the common stock accounts as shown. Bendeck stock is selling for $21.00 per share. If Bendeck has a 2-for-1 stock split, what will be the revised common stock accounts for the firm?

Paid-in capital ($.42 par value, 1,000,000 shares)	$ 420,000
Capital contributed in excess of par value	4,720,000
Retained earnings	8,200,000
Total common stockholders' equity	$13,340,000

A10. (Accounting for a stock split) Cannon has the common stock accounts as shown. Cannon stock is selling for $25.00 per share. If Cannon has a 2-for-1 stock split, what will be the revised common stock accounts for the firm?

Paid-in capital ($0.50 par value, 10,000,000 shares)	$ 5,000,000
Capital contributed in excess of par value	13,000,000
Retained earnings	60,000,000
Total common stockholders' equity	$78,000,000

A11. (Market prices following a stock split or stock dividend) Assume that IBM is selling for $180 per share. IBM implements one of the following stock dividends or stock splits, and no other change in the value of the firm occurs. What is the value of one share for each of the following?

a. An 8% stock dividend.

b. A 50% stock dividend.

c. A 3-for-2 stock split.

d. A 2-for-1 stock split.

A12. (Market prices following a stock split or stock dividend) Assume GMC is selling for $95 per share. GMC implements one of the following stock dividends or stock splits, and no other change in the value of the firm occurs. What is the value of one share for each of the following?

a. A 10% stock dividend.

b. A 40% stock dividend.

c. A 3-for-2 stock split.

d. A 2-for-1 stock split

A13. (Market prices following a stock split) General Electric is selling for $90 per share. The board of directors declares a 3-for-2 stock split.

a. What is the market price per share after the split if there is no further information to cause investors to revalue the firm?

b. Suppose that the board of directors increases cash dividends substantially and investors increase the value of General Electric by 10%. What should be the market price per share reflecting the split and the new information?

A14. (Market prices following a stock split) Boston Utility is selling for $65 per share. The board of directors declares a 3-for-2 stock split.

a. What is the market price per share after the split if there is no further information to cause investors to revalue the firm?

b. Suppose that the board of directors increases cash dividends substantially and investors increase the value of Boston Utility by 10%. What should be the market price per share reflecting the split and the new information?

A15. (Accounting for stock dividends and stock splits) Shore Electronics Corporation's common stock is selling for $44 per share and its common stockholders' equity is shown below.

a. Show the impact of a 50% stock dividend. (Hint: This is a large stock dividend, not a small one.)

b. Show the impact of a 3-for-2 stock split.

c. Describe how the stock market would react to each event. How would you explain the difference in reaction?

Paid-in capital ($4 par value; 5,000,000 shares)	$ 20,000,000
Capital contributed in excess of par value	30,000,000
Retained earnings	50,000,000
Common stockholders' equity	$100,000,000

A16. (Accounting for a stock dividend and a stock split) Ligon Diagnostics common stock is selling for $35 per share and its common stockholders' equity is shown below.

a. Show the capital accounts for a 25% stock dividend.

b. Show the capital accounts for a 5-for-4 stock split.

Paid-in capital ($1 par value, 5,000,000 shares)	$ 5,000,000
Capital contributed in excess of par value	45,000,000
Retained earnings	100,000,000
Common stockholders' equity	$150,000,000

A17. (Accounting for stock dividends and stock splits) Grantel's common stock is selling for $78 per share and its common stockholders' equity is shown below.

a. Show the impact of a 50% stock dividend.

b. Show the impact of a 5-for-4 stock split.

c. Describe how the stock market would react to each event. How would you explain the difference in reaction?

Paid-in capital ($5 par value, 30,000,000 shares)	$150,000,000
Capital contributed in excess of par value	78,000,000
Retained earnings	350,000,000
Common stockholders' equity	$578,000,000

A18. (Transferable put rights) Common stock of the I.M. Wright Corp. has a current market value of $47. Suppose Wright issues transferable put rights to its shareholders, and five put rights are required to sell one share back to the firm for $55. What would you expect a put right to be worth, ignoring taxes?

A19. (Dividend adjustment model) Regional Software has made a bundle selling spreadsheet software and has begun paying cash dividends. The firm's chief financial officer would like the firm to distribute 25% of its annual earnings (POR = 0.25) and adjust the dividend rate to changes in earnings per share at the rate ADJ = 0.75. Regional paid $1.00 per share in dividends last year. It will earn at least $8.00 per share this year and each year in the foreseeable future. Use the dividend adjustment model, Equation (17.1), to calculate projected dividends per share for this year and the next four.

A20. (Dividend adjustment model) Last year's dividend for Woolridge Outfitters was $1.00. This year's earnings per share are $4.00, and Woolridge's target payout ratio is 40%. Using the dividend adjustment model, Equation (17.1), what would be this year's dividend with each of the following adjustment factors?

a. 70%

b. 0%

c. 100%

A21. (Dividend adjustment model) KLH Recording Studios has made a large profit from a new recording contract and has begun paying cash dividends. The firm's chief financial officer would like the firm to distribute 30% of its annual earnings (POR = 0.30) and adjust the dividend rate to changes in earnings per share at the rate ADJ = 0.60. KLH Recording Studios paid $2.00 per share in dividends last year. It will earn at least $10.00 per share this year and each year in the foreseeable future. Use the dividend adjustment model, Equation (17.1), to calculate projected dividends per share for this year and the next four.

LEVEL B

B1. (Cash versus homemade dividends) Refer to Figures 17.4 and 17.5. A firm currently has 8,000 shares outstanding that are worth \$100 each. The firm's shareholders desire a dividend of \$20 per share. Assume a perfect capital market.

a. Suppose the firm pays a dividend of \$20 per share and sells new shares to raise \$160,000 to replace the cash it paid out. Show that these steps do not alter the wealth of the original shareholders. What percentage of the firm do the original shareholders end up owning?

b. Suppose instead the shareholders raise \$160,000 by selling some of their own shares. How many shares must they sell? Show that the two dividend alternatives leave them equally well-off.

B2. (Dividend policy) A firm has 20 million common shares outstanding. It currently pays out \$1.50 per share per year in cash dividends on its common stock. Historically, its payout ratio has ranged from 30% to 35%. Over the next five years it expects the earnings and discretionary cash flow shown below.

a. Over the five-year period, what is the maximum overall payout ratio the firm could achieve without triggering a securities issue?

b. Recommend a reasonable dividend policy for paying out discretionary cash flow in years 1 through 5.

	1	2	3	4	5	THEREAFTER
Earnings	100	125	150	120	140	150+ per year
Discretionary cash flow	50	70	60	20	15	50+ per year

B3. (Cash dividend versus share repurchase) Consider a firm that has decided to make, but has not yet announced, a large "bonus" cash dividend amounting in the aggregate to \$5 million. The firm has 1 million shares outstanding that sell for \$20 each. The firm has no debt; there are no taxes; and all transactions take place in a perfect capital market. Using calculations like those in the illustration of dividend irrelevance in a perfect capital market, show that shareholders will be indifferent between whether the firm pays out the "bonus" as a dividend or uses the money to buy back \$5 million of its shares.

B4. (Dividend change after a stock split) A few years ago, International Paper Co. announced a 2-for-1 stock split. At the same time, it announced that the quarterly dividend rate, which had been 42 cents per pre-split share, would become 25 cents a share after the stock split.

a. Did International Paper increase its dividend rate? Explain.

b. How would you expect the market to react to this dual announcement?

B5. (Dividend change after a stock split) InfoNet Co. has announced a 2-for-1 stock split. At the same time, it announced that the quarterly dividend rate, which had been 38 cents per pre-split share, would become 25 cents a share after the stock split.

a. Did InfoNet increase its dividend rate? Explain.

b. How would you expect the market to react to this dual announcement?

B6. (Share repurchase) A firm's common stock is trading at a P/E ratio of 12. Its projected earnings per share are \$2.00, and its share price is \$24. All its shareholders are tax exempt. An open market purchase would result in projected earnings per share of \$2.30. How would you expect the announcement of the share repurchase program to affect the firm's share price?

B7. (Share repurchase) A firm's common stock is trading at a P/E of 20. Its projected earnings per share are \$2.00, and its share price is \$40. All its shareholders are tax exempt. An open market purchase would result in projected earnings per share of \$2.70. How would you expect the announcement of the share repurchase program to affect the firm's share price?

B8. (Extra dividends) Alcoa recently announced a new dividend policy. The firm said it would pay a base cash dividend of 40 cents per common share each quarter. In addition, the firm said it would pay 30% of any excess in annual earnings per share above \$6.00 as an extra year-end dividend.

a. If Alcoa earns \$7.50 per share next year, what percentage of next year's earnings would it pay out as cash dividends under the new policy?

b. For what types of firms would Alcoa's new dividend policy be appropriate? Explain.

B9. (Extra dividends) Borland recently announced a new dividend policy. The firm said it would pay a base cash dividend of 60 cents per common share each quarter. In addition, the firm said it would pay 25% of any excess in annual earnings per share above \$5.00 as an extra year-end dividend.

a. If Borland earns \$8.00 per share next year, what percentage of next year's earnings would it pay out as cash dividends under the new policy?

b. For what types of firms would Borland's new dividend policy be appropriate? Explain.

B10. (Dividend policy) Gotham Manufacturing Corporation (GMC) pays quarterly cash dividends on its common stock. Suppose GMC forecasts earnings per share of \$3.00 this year and \$2.70, \$3.30, \$3.90, and \$3.60 over the following four years, respectively, and believes it can maintain a long-term payout ratio of 1/3. GMC revises its dividends once per year, and the quarterly dividend is one-fourth of the annual dividend. Which of the following annual dividend patterns would you recommend?

1. \$1.00, \$1.00, \$1.00, \$1.30, \$1.20
2. \$1.00, \$0.90, \$1.10, \$1.30, \$1.20
3. \$1.00, \$1.00, \$1.10, \$1.20, \$1.20
4. \$1.00, \$0.90, \$1.20, \$1.20, \$1.20

B11. (Dividend policy) 3M pays quarterly cash dividends on its common stock. Suppose 3M forecasts earnings per share of \$4.00 this year and \$3.80, \$3.20, \$4.80, and \$4.08 over the following four years, respectively, and believes it can maintain a long-term payout ratio of 1/4. 3M revises its dividends once per year, and the quarterly dividend is one-fourth of the annual dividend. Which of the following annual dividend patterns would you recommend?

1. \$2.00, \$1.05, \$0.85, \$1.45, \$1.25
2. \$1.20, \$1.00, \$0.75, \$0.95, \$1.40
3. \$1.00, \$0.95, \$0.80, \$1.20, \$1.02
4. \$0.80, \$0.80, \$0.95, \$1.00, \$1.05

B12. (Greenmail) The common stock of Trans-World-Dilemma (TWD) has a current price of \$30 per share. If TWD has 10 million shares outstanding and it buys back 1 million shares from Karl I. Can, paying Karl \$35 per share for the block of shares:

a. What should be the firm's share price immediately following the buyback?

b. How has the payment of greenmail affected the holders of the other 9 million shares?

B13. (Greenmail) The common stock of Ultra has a current price of \$24 per share. If Ultra has 5 million shares outstanding and it buys back 1 million shares from an investor, paying \$30 per share for the block of shares, and assuming perfect capital market transactions:

a. What should be the firm's share price immediately following the buyback?

b. How has the payment of greenmail affected the holders of the other 4 million shares?

B14. (Greenmail) Easy Mark, Inc. has a pain-in-the-neck minority shareholder who owns 10% of the firm's 50 million outstanding shares. Easy Mark's share price is \$12 per share, but the minority shareholder wants the firm to repurchase her shares for $15 each. Assume all transactions take place in a perfect capital market (including no taxes).

a. How would such a repurchase affect the minority shareholder's wealth?
b. How would such a repurchase affect Easy Mark's share price?
c. How would such a repurchase affect the wealth of Easy Mark's other shareholders?
d. What do you conclude regarding the impact of greenmail on shareholder wealth?

B15. (Greenmail) Carnival Inc. has an obnoxious minority shareholder who owns 10% of the firm's 2 million outstanding shares. Carnival's share price is $20 per share, but the minority shareholder wants the firm to repurchase her shares for $25 each. Assume all transactions take place in a perfect capital market (including no taxes).

a. How would such a repurchase affect the minority shareholder's wealth?
b. How would such a repurchase affect Carnival's share price?
c. How would such a repurchase affect the wealth of Carnival's other shareholders?
d. What do you conclude regarding the impact of greenmail on shareholder wealth?

B16. (Transferable put rights) Common stock of TarHeals Medicinal Products, Ltd. has a current market value of $23. TarHeals is planning to issue transferable put rights to its shareholders, with four put rights required to sell one share back to the firm for $30. I.M. Confused has a tax basis of $17.50 per share for his shares in TarHeals. If I.M.'s capital gains tax rate is 14%, what would you expect a put right to be worth to him?

B17. (Transferable put rights) Common stock of Robbing Hood's Protection Service, Inc. has a current market value of $47. Rob is planning to issue transferable put rights to its shareholders, with five put rights required to sell one share back to the firm for $55. I.B. Sharpe has a tax basis of $25.25 per share for her shares in Rob's. If I.B.'s capital gains tax rate is 20%, what would you expect a put right to be worth to her?

LEVEL C (ADVANCED)

C1. (Dividends, share repurchases, and taxes) Cardinal Computer Corporation has developed a phenomenally successful software package that makes it very easy to combine spreadsheet modeling and basic financial calculations. As a result, Cardinal has $20 million of excess cash that is available for distribution to its shareholders. All of Cardinal's shareholders invested at the firm's inception and consequently have a negligible tax (cost) basis in their Cardinal shares. Cardinal has 10 million shares outstanding.

a. Assuming dividend income is taxed at a 40% rate and capital gains income is taxed at a 20% rate, calculate the impact on shareholder wealth of a $20 million cash dividend distribution and a $20 million share repurchase.
b. Under what circumstances, if any, would Cardinal's shareholders be better off having Cardinal retain and reinvest the cash in short-term financial instruments rather than pay it out to shareholders?

C2. (Dividends, share repurchases, and taxes) America Online has $30 million of excess cash that is available for distribution to its shareholders. All of America Online's shareholders invested at the firm's inception and consequently have a negligible tax (cost) basis in their shares. America Online has 20 million shares outstanding.

a. Assuming dividend income is taxed at a 40% rate and capital gains income is taxed at a 20% rate, calculate the impact on shareholder wealth of a $30 million cash dividend distribution and a $30 million share repurchase.
b. Under what circumstances, if any, would America Online's shareholders be better off having America Online retain and reinvest the cash in short-term financial instruments rather than pay it out to shareholders?

MINICASE CBS'S SHARE REPURCHASE

Several years ago, CBS, Inc. had generated substantial free cash flow and accumulated nearly $1.6 billion of cash and marketable securities. CBS then offered to purchase 3,500,000 shares of its common stock for $325 cash per share. CBS's common stock had closed the previous day on the New York Stock Exchange at $309.25 per share. Shareholders could sell their shares to CBS under the terms of the offer anytime within the next 20 business days. If shareholders offered to sell more than 3,500,000 shares, CBS would purchase shares in the following order: (1) all the shares owned by any holder of 25 or fewer shares who offered to sell his/her entire CBS shareholding and (2) shares from all other shareholders on a pro-rata basis so as to bring its aggregate share repurchases to 3,500,000.

At the time of the offer, Laurence A. Tisch was CBS's chairman and chief executive, CBS had approximately 15.6 million shares outstanding, and Loews Corp. owned 19.4% of those shares through a subsidiary called L.T. Holding Corp. In response to the CBS repurchase offer, L.T. Holding Corp. announced that it intended to sell at least 2 million, and possibly all 3.03 million of its CBS shares. Oh, by the way, Laurence A. Tisch coincidentally also controlled Loews Corp.

The table below provides summary financial statements for CBS for the 12 months prior to the share repurchase announcement.

CBS SUMMARY BALANCE SHEET ($ millions)

Cash and cash equivalents	$ 799.4
Other current assets	963.4
Total current assets	1,762.8
Marketable securities	797.4
Other long-term assets	919.1
Total assets	$3,479.3
Current liabilities	$1,017.6
Long-term debt	590.2
Other liabilities	544.5
Preferred stock subject to redemption	117.8
Stockholders' equity	1,209.2
Total liabilities and equity	$3,479.3

CBS SUMMARY INCOME STATEMENT ($ millions)

Net sales	$3,878.3
Costs and expenses	(3,477.9)
Other income, net	50.6
Operating income	451.0
Investment income	96.8
Interest expense	(39.9)
Earnings before interest and taxes	507.9
Income taxes	(166.6)
Preferred stock dividends	(12.3)
Net income available for common	$ 329.0

QUESTIONS

1. What type of share repurchase program did CBS announce? What are the main advantages of this method versus the alternative share repurchase methods? What are the benefits from repurchasing all the shares from holders of 25 or fewer shares?
2. What percentage of its outstanding shares did CBS offer to purchase, and what was the potential aggregate cost? What was the tender offer premium, and why should CBS offer shareholders a premium?
3. Show the pro forma effect on CBS's balance sheet and income statement of repurchasing (i) 1,750,000 and (ii) 3,500,000 shares, assuming cash and marketable securities both earn interest at an 8% APR and that CBS's income tax rate is 40%.
4. If 5,000,000 shares are tendered, how many shares would CBS repurchase from a holder of (i) 20 shares who tenders all his shares, and (ii) 10,000 shares who tenders 2,000 of them?
5. How would you expect the stock market to react to the share repurchase announcement without knowledge of L.T. Holding's announcement? How would you expect L.T. Holding's announcement to affect the market's reaction?

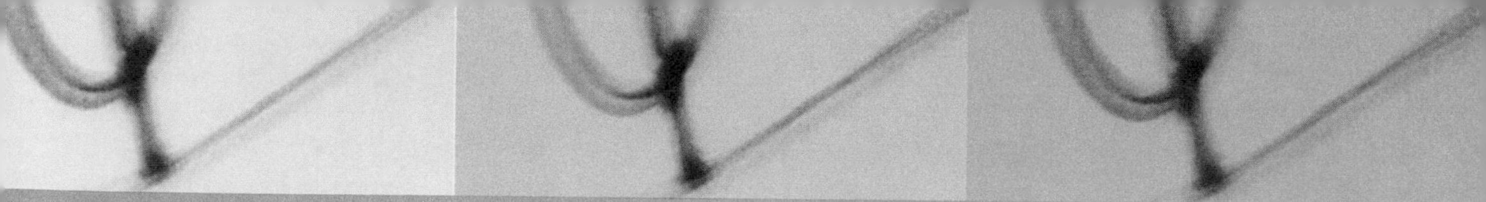

PART V

LONG-TERM FINANCING

Firms require financing if they are going to undertake capital budgeting projects, such as those analyzed in Part III. Part IV examined capital structure, a firm's mix of financing. In Part V, we look at how firms access the various sources of long-term funds, such as common stock, preferred stock, debt, leases, and options.

A firm can sell securities to investors at large in a *general cash offer.* It can make *private placements* with large financial institutions. Common stock can be sold to existing investors through a *rights offering.* Rights are call options. We describe the features, advantages, and disadvantages of each method.

Firms also must choose among alternative security design features, which we describe. A call option is a potential long-term bond feature. As we said in Chapter 5, firms often include the option to call bonds and redeem them before the maturity date. We explain and illustrate alternative types of call options and how firms can best use these valuable options. We also discuss a special form of debt financing called *leasing* and show why leasing can be a tax-efficient debt alternative.

A *derivative* gets (derives) its value from another asset. An option is one type of derivative. Derivatives have a wide variety of uses in corporate financial management, particularly in managing the firm's risk through what is called *hedging.* We describe the basic types of derivatives, explain how to value them, and show how firms use them to obtain financing and hedge risks.

18

Issuing Securities and the Role of Investment Banking

A healthy firm needs capital to maintain its assets, as well as to grow and acquire additional assets. Firms usually finance the purchase of long-term assets with long-term capital. Retained earnings are the major internal source of long-term capital. But when capital requirements exceed the firm's ability to generate cash internally, it must raise funds externally.

In this chapter, we examine external sources of long-term capital. Our focus here is on how firms go about obtaining the financing they have decided they need. In particular, we look at how firms issue securities (as opposed to borrowing money from banks) and the markets in which they issue them. We explore the investment banking process and consider how investment bankers can help firms obtain additional external financing, and at what cost.

Sometimes firms issue securities directly to private investors. Private placement eliminates certain requirements but, at the same time, reduces the liquidity of the securities.

Finally, we consider the benefits and costs of a private firm going public, and of a public firm going private.

FOCUS ON PRINCIPLES

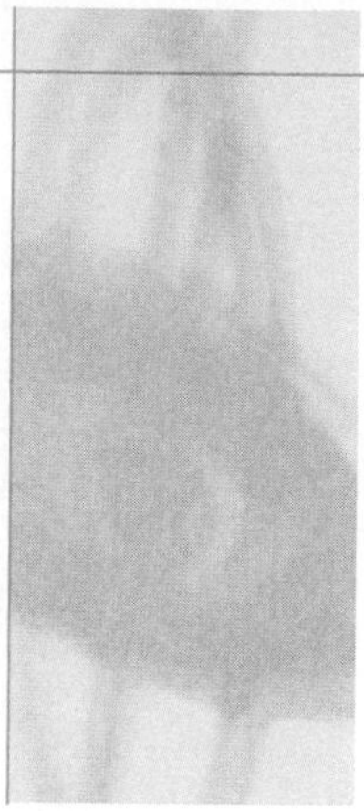

- *Two-Sided Transactions:* When issuing securities, set a price and other terms that investors will find acceptable.
- *Signaling:* Recognize that announcing a seasoned public offering of common stock usually leads to a negative stock market reaction because it suggests that the firm's managers think the firm's stock is overvalued.
- *Valuable Ideas:* Look for opportunities to develop new securities that reduce issuers' funding costs and raise investors' risk-adjusted after-tax return.
- *Options:* Value the rights distributed to shareholders and any options connected with bonds just as you would any other option.
- *Comparative Advantage:* Contract with underwriters to bear the risk in issuing securities—if they can bear that risk more cheaply.
- *Risk-Return Trade-Off:* Look for innovative securities that reduce the investors' risk, which will enable you to pay a lower interest rate than an otherwise identical conventional security would require.
- *Capital Market Efficiency:* Use the market price at which a firm's common shares are actively trading as the best measure of their value.

18.1 THE LONG-TERM FINANCING MENU

Every time a firm raises funds externally, it must decide which type or types of securities to issue. Transaction costs play a role, because they are proportionately smaller for larger issues. The fixed cost is spread out over a larger number of shares. The variable costs are also greater for relatively smaller issues.

Debt, common stock, and preferred stock are the main sources of external long-term corporate financing. Table 18.1 shows the relative proportions of funds U.S. firms raised by issuing common stock, preferred stock, and long-term debt between 1980 and 2000. Over that 21-year period, common stock, preferred stock, and long-term debt accounted for 9.7%, 2.4%, and 87.9%, respectively, of the funds raised.

The total amount of common stock issued at any time is sensitive to stock market conditions. Firms try to take advantage of rising markets when the demand for common stock is relatively strong. New-issue activity tends to increase during periods of rising share prices. Correspondingly, firms are usually reluctant to sell new issues of common stock when the share price is low by historical standards.

Similarly, the volume of fixed-income security issues (preferred stock and debt) tends to vary inversely with the level of long-term interest rates. During periods of rising long-term interest rates, firms tend to favor short-term borrowing. Then, if and when long-term interest rates fall, many firms start replacing the short-term debt with long-term fixed-income securities.

Review

1. Among debt, common stock, and preferred stock, which provides the largest proportion of external financing by firms? Which accounts for the smallest?
2. Why are the volumes of common stock and debt financing sensitive to market conditions?

TABLE 18.1
The main sources of domestic external long-term financing by U.S. firms, 1980 to 2001 (dollar amounts in millions).

		PERCENTAGE REPRESENTED BY									
		COMMON STOCK				DEBT[c]					
YEAR	AGGREGATE DOMESTIC EXTERNAL FINANCING[a]	Seasoned	IPO	Total	PREFERRED STOCK[b]	Investment-Grade	Speculative-Grade	Total	PERCENT CHANGE IN S&P 500 INDEX DURING YEAR	MOODY'S AVERAGE OF YIELDS ON Aa-RATED CORPORATE BONDS
1980	$ 57.6	19.8%	2.4%	22.2%	5.6%	69.8%	2.4%	72.2%	25.80%	12.50%
1981	55.9	19.3	5.5	24.9	3.0	69.9	2.1	72.1	−9.70	14.75
1982	63.2	20.1	2.1	22.2	8.5	65.3	4.0	69.3	14.80	14.41
1983	97.4	25.2	12.8	38.0	8.7	45.7	7.6	53.3	17.30	12.42
1984	82.6	6.4	4.7	11.1	4.8	67.1	16.9	84.0	1.40	13.31
1985	138.0	11.7	6.2	17.9	6.2	65.6	10.3	75.9	26.30	11.82
1986	284.8	7.3	7.8	15.2	4.9	68.8	11.2	80.0	14.60	9.47
1987	272.3	6.4	8.8	15.2	4.2	70.3	10.3	80.6	2.00	9.68
1988	274.5	2.2	8.6	10.8	2.8	76.3	10.1	86.4	12.40	9.94
1989	305.5	3.0	4.5	7.5	2.5	81.7	8.3	90.0	27.30	9.46
1990	312.3	2.9	3.2	6.1	1.5	91.9	0.4	92.3	−6.60	9.56
1991	587.4	5.3	4.3	9.5	3.4	85.4	1.7	87.1	26.30	9.05
1992	855.6	3.8	4.6	8.5	3.4	83.7	4.4	88.1	4.50	8.46
1993	1,063.3	4.2	5.4	9.6	2.7	82.5	5.2	87.7	7.10	7.04
1994	716.4	3.9	4.7	8.6	2.2	84.6	4.6	89.3	−1.50	8.15
1995	722.4	7.2	4.2	11.4	2.1	82.6	4.0	86.6	34.10	7.72
1996	978.9	6.7	5.1	11.8	3.7	80.7	3.8	84.5	20.30	7.55
1997	1,317.3	5.8	3.4	9.1	2.5	86.0	2.4	88.4	31.00	7.47
1998	1,868.3	3.8	2.3	6.2	2.0	89.5	2.3	91.8	26.70	6.80
1999	1,959.7	5.0	3.4	8.4	1.4	88.4	1.9	90.2	19.50	7.35
2000	1,851.1	6.1	4.1	10.2	0.8	87.6	1.4	89.0	−10.10	7.83
Total	$13,864.5	5.4%	4.3%	9.7%	2.4%	84.3%	3.6%	87.9%		

[a]Aggregate amount raised through issuance of common stock, nonconvertible preferred stock, nonconvertible debt, and convertible securities.
[b]Includes convertible preferred and preference stock.
[c]Includes convertible debt.
Sources: 2001 Securities Industry Fact Book (New York, 2001), *Moody's Bond Record* (New York, 1997), and *Mergent Bond Record* (New York, 2002).

18.2 COMMON STOCK

Large firms usually get most of their new common equity internally from retained earnings. But smaller or rapidly growing firms usually also issue new common stock. Even large firms sometimes issue new common stock. In addition, many firms have instituted dividend reinvestment or employee stock purchase plans that also generate common equity.

Main Features of Common Stock

Common stock is a perpetual security that is not redeemable by the issuer. All the issuer can do is offer to repurchase shares. Common stockholders are entitled to get any dividends the firm's board of directors declares, but the board is not contractually obligated to declare any.

A firm's corporate charter specifies the features of its common stock. Many of these features are determined by the corporate laws of the state in which the firm is incorporated.

Rights and Privileges of Common Stock

The rights and privileges fall into four categories: voting rights, dividend rights, liquidation rights, and preemptive rights. These are the same rights of ownership we discussed in Chapter 1. Let's take a quick look at each.

VOTING RIGHTS Voting may be either cumulative or noncumulative. *Cumulative voting* allows a shareholder to target votes to a subset of the directors up for reelection. For example, a holder of 100 shares could cast all 100 votes for a single director. State law usually requires an annual election of directors but many permit staggered elections. A popular structure is to have directors serve three-year terms, with one-third standing for reelection each year.

Shareholders can vote in person or can transfer that vote to a second party who can vote it by proxy. A *proxy* conveys the right to vote your shares to someone else. Management solicits shareholder proxies and usually secures sufficient proxies to assure the election of its nominated slate. However, dissident shareholders can also solicit proxies to mount a **proxy contest** for control. Although the odds of succeeding are long, dissidents have won some battles.

DIVIDEND RIGHTS State laws usually require that all shares belonging to a single class of common stock must share pro rata in any distributions of dividends to that class of shares. Although it is not typical in the United States, some firms have two or more classes of common stock with different dividend rights.

LIQUIDATION RIGHTS Common stockholders are entitled to share pro rata in any distributions of assets by a firm when it winds up its affairs and liquidates.

PREEMPTIVE RIGHTS When common stockholders have *preemptive rights,* the firm must offer any new issue of common stock—or a new issue of any securities that are convertible into common stock—to existing shareholders before it can offer them to any other prospective investors.

Classification of Shares

A firm's corporate charter limits the number of *authorized shares* of common stock. A firm cannot issue shares unless it has authorized shares available. Increasing the number of authorized shares is usually noncontroversial, but it does require a shareholder vote.

Shares become *issued shares* when a firm sells them to investors. Issued shares consist of *outstanding shares* and *treasury shares.* Outstanding shares are held by investors. Treasury shares are those that the firm has repurchased from investors. Earnings per share and book value per share calculations are based on the number of outstanding shares.

TABLE 18.2
Shareholders' equity and EPS of E.I. du Pont de Nemours and Company (dollar amounts in millions except for per-share amounts).

Preferred stock, without par value:		
$4.50 Series—1,672,594 shares	$	167
$3.50 Series— 700,000 shares		70
Total preferred stock		237
Common stock, $0.30 par value:		
1,800,000,000 shares authorized;		
1,088,994,789 shares issued		327
Additional paid-in capital		7,371
Reinvested earnings		13,517
Accumulated other comprehensive income (loss)		(273)
Treasury stock		(6,727)
Common stockholders' equity		14,215
Total stockholders' equity	$	14,452
Net income	$	4,339
Preferred dividends		10
Available for common	$	4,329
Average common shares outstanding		1,035,992,748
Earnings per common share		$ 4.18

Source: E.I. du Pont de Nemours and Company, *Annual Report to Shareholders*.

Table 18.2 shows a recent shareholders' equity section of the balance sheet and the EPS (earnings per share) for E. I. du Pont de Nemours and Company. At the time, the firm had 1.8 billion shares of common stock authorized, 1,088,994,789 of which were issued, and there were 87 million shares in the treasury. Du Pont had an average of 1,035,992,748 common shares outstanding and earned $4.18 per average outstanding share.

Shares of common stock are issued with or without par value. Because some states do not permit firms to sell shares at a price below par value, par values are generally very small. Par value therefore has little real significance.

Book Value per Common Share

Book value per common share is the ratio of (1) common stockholders' equity, adjusted for any liquidation premium on any preferred or preference stock the firm may have outstanding, to (2) the number of common shares outstanding on that date:

$$\text{Book value per common share} = \frac{\text{Common stockholders' equity}}{\text{Number of common shares outstanding}} \tag{18.1}$$

For example, DuPont's book value per common share was $14.19 (= 14,215/1,002).[1]

[1]Du Pont's preferred stock does not carry any *liquidation premium*. But to illustrate how a liquidation premium affects the book value per common share calculation, suppose that the liquidation premium is 5%. Thus, the liquidation value of the preferred stock would be $249 million, or $12 million greater than its face amount. Reducing common stockholders' equity by this amount leads to

$$\begin{array}{l}\text{Book value per common share adjusted}\\ \text{for preferred stock liquidation premium}\end{array} = \frac{14,203}{1,002} = \$14.17$$

Book value per common share is the value per share if the firm's assets are sold and liabilities are paid off at the amounts shown on the balance sheet, including preferred stock paid off at its involuntary liquidation value. Of course, book values generally bear no direct relation to the true liquidation values of a firm's assets because, as we explained in Chapter 3, book value is based on historical cost and accounting measures of depreciation.

Review

1. What are the rights of common stockholders?
2. What is cumulative voting?
3. What is the difference between authorized shares, outstanding shares, and treasury shares?
4. What is the book value per share of common stock? How is it related to the market price per share?

18.3 ISSUING SECURITIES

Just as there are various financing alternatives, there is a choice of issue methods. Larger firms usually make a **general cash offer,** also referred to as a *registered public offering.* The procedure is much the same for debt and equity. The issuer must satisfy the securities laws, which are enforced by the Securities and Exchange Commission (SEC). In particular, securities sold in a public offering must be registered with the SEC. The firm can then offer the securities to investors at large, usually with the help of **underwriters.** Underwriters are middlemen who buy securities from the issuing firms and sell them to others. In most cases, they also guarantee the price the issuer will receive.

A firm can also offer new common stock directly to existing holders. This procedure is called a **rights issue** (or *rights offering*), which is different from a general cash offer in several ways, including lower issuance costs. Interestingly, rights issues are rare in the United States, but common elsewhere, for reasons we will explain.

Many firms, particularly smaller ones, issue debt securities directly to investors through a **private placement.** Any type of security can be privately placed, but most private placements involve debt. Privately placed securities are not registered for sale to the public. Private placements must satisfy the requirements for exemption from registration under the Securities Act of 1933. These requirements limit the investors to whom unregistered securities may be offered for sale. There are also significant restrictions on resale to other investors, which makes such securities less liquid. As a result, a private placement tends to be more expensive than a general cash offer because investors demand a premium for the lack of liquidity.

There are foreign markets for securities, too. The **Eurodollar bond market** is the market outside the United States for U.S. dollar-denominated bonds. At times, the Eurodollar bond market provides more attractive new issue terms than the U.S. market. It therefore pays a prospective bond issuer to keep an eye on the Eurodollar bond market.

General Cash Offers

When a firm issues securities in a general cash offer, it must register them with the SEC.[2] A general cash offer involves the following steps.

---

[2]The Securities Act of 1933 (the 1933 Act) and its related rules regulate interstate issues of securities. All the states have their own laws to regulate intrastate securities issues. An offering for no more than $1,000,000 that is limited to one state only is registered with the state securities department, rather than the SEC. In addition, each state's "blue sky" laws regulate the sale of any securities (including SEC registered) within that state.

WHAT TO ISSUE? Managers must first decide how much they need to raise and what type of security to issue. The firm's target capital structure will affect the decision. But other considerations, such as the specific terms available and management's view of how its common stock is priced, also play a role. Recall from Chapter 2 that a firm issuing shares of common stock to the public for the first time is called an *initial public offering,* whereas if the firm already has publicly trading shares outstanding, issuing additional shares is called a *seasoned offering.*

Management must obtain board approval to issue new securities. Shareholder approval is required if the firm needs to increase the number of authorized shares of common or preferred stock.

REGISTRATION STATEMENT The prospective issuer must prepare and file a **registration statement** with the SEC.[3] The registration statement contains a *preliminary* **prospectus.** A preliminary prospectus is also called a *red herring* because of a warning legend that must be printed on its cover in bold red letters. A prospectus gives the information about the issuer and the proposed issue that investors need to make their decision to invest. A few years ago, the SEC issued new 'plain English' rules designed to make the prospectus easier to read. For example, they discourage the use of legal and highly technical terms and encourage the use of descriptive headings, short sentences, and clear explanations.

The SEC reviews the registration statement and makes comments. Once this review process is complete, the issuer and the underwriters can agree on the pricing terms for the new issue.

PRICING The issuer and underwriters negotiate the terms of the offering and the underwriters' compensation. The issuer then files the final amendment to the registration statement, which contains the *final prospectus.* Figures 18.1 and 18.2 show the cover and summary pages from a typical prospectus. After registration, the securities can be traded freely by investors.

CLOSING The offering *closes* three business days later. Corporate securities transactions customarily settle, or close, in the United States on the third business day following the transaction date. At the closing, the issuer delivers the securities. The underwriters simultaneously deliver payment, net of their fees. The underwriters then deliver the securities to investors in return for payment.

EXAMPLE GM's General Cash (Seasoned) Offer of Common Stock

Several years ago, General Motors Corporation reported net losses of $2.0 and $4.5 billion in back-to-back years and forecast another operating loss for the next year. In addition, GM had adopted Financial Accounting Standards Board Statement No. 106, *Employers' Accounting for Postretirement Benefits Other Than Pensions* (primarily postretirement medical, dental, vision, and life insurance benefits). This accounting change reduced GM's stockholders' equity by $20.6 billion.

GM decided to make a seasoned offering (sell new shares of common stock) as one step in rebuilding its stockholders' equity. GM chose the general cash offer method and filed a registration statement with the SEC. After receiving the SEC's comments, GM filed an amended registration statement with the SEC and sold 57 million shares of its $1 2/3 par value common stock at $39 per share, and realized net proceeds of $2.2 billion.

[3]There are some exemptions from this requirement. Footnote 2 mentioned the intrastate exemption. There is a commercial paper exemption for notes that will mature within 270 days of issue. There is also a small-issue exemption. Regulation A under the 1933 Act provides for an abbreviated offering statement when the issue will raise no more than $5 million.

3,500,000 Shares

eBay Inc.

Common Stock
(par value $.001 per share)

Of the 3,500,000 shares of Common Stock offered hereby, 3,489,275 shares are being sold by eBay Inc. and 10,725 shares are being sold by a Selling Stockholder on behalf of a charitable foundation established by the Company. See "Principal and Selling Stockholders". The Company will not receive any of the proceeds from the sale of the shares being sold by the Selling Stockholder. Prior to the offering, there has been no public market for the Common Stock of the Company. For factors considered in determining the initial public offering price, see "Underwriting".

See "Risk Factors" on page 6 for material risks relevant to an investment in the Common Stock.

The shares of Common Stock have been approved for quotation on the Nasdaq National Market under the symbol "EBAY," subject to official notice of issuance.

THESE SECURITIES HAVE NOT BEEN APPROVED OR DISAPPROVED BY THE SECURITIES AND EXCHANGE COMMISSION OR ANY STATE SECURITIES COMMISSION NOR HAS THE SECURITIES AND EXCHANGE COMMISSION OR ANY STATE SECURITIES COMMISSION PASSED UPON THE ACCURACY OR ADEQUACY OF THIS PROSPECTUS. ANY REPRESENTATION TO THE CONTRARY IS A CRIMINAL OFFENSE.

	Initial Public Offering Price	Underwriting Discount (1)	Proceeds to Company (2)	Proceeds to Selling Stockholder
Per Share	$18.00	$1.26	$16.74	$16.74
Total (3)	$63,000,000	$4,410,000	$58,410,463	$179,537

(1) The Company and the Selling Stockholder have agreed to indemnify the Underwriters against certain liabilities, including liabilities under the Securities Act of 1933, as amended. See "Underwriting."
(2) Before deducting estimated expenses of $975,000 payable by the Company.
(3) The Company has granted the Underwriters an option for 30 days to purchase up to an additional 525,000 shares at the initial public offering price per share, less the underwriting discount, solely to cover over-allotments. If such option is exercised in full, the total initial public offering price, underwriting discount and proceeds to Company will be $72,450,000, $5,071,500 and $67,198,963, respectively. See "Underwriting".

The shares offered hereby are offered severally by the Underwriters, as specified herein, subject to receipt and acceptance by them and subject to their right to reject any order in whole or in part. It is expected that the shares will be ready for delivery in New York, New York on or about September 29, 1998, against payment therefor in immediately available funds.

Goldman, Sachs & Co.
Donaldson, Lufkin & Jenrette
BancBoston Robertson Stephens
BT Alex. Brown

The date of this Prospectus is September 24, 1998.

FIGURE 18.1
Prospectus cover page.

The Offering

Common Stock offered by the Company	3,489,275 shares
Common Stock offered by the Selling Stockholder on behalf of the eBay Foundation	10,725 shares
Common Stock to be outstanding after this offering	39,739,073 shares(1)
Use of proceeds	For capital expenditures, to repay indebtedness and for general corporate purposes, including working capital. See "Use of Proceeds."
Proposed Nasdaq National Market symbol	"EBAY"

Summary Financial Information
(in thousands, except per share data)

	Year Ended December 31,		Six Months Ended June 30,	
	1996	**1997**	**1997**	**1998**
Statement of Income Data:				
Net revenues	$ 372	$ 5,744	$ 1,658	$ 14,922
Gross profit	358	4,998	1,498	13,186
Income from operations	253	1,487	844	2,691
Net income	148	874	486	215
Net income per share(2):				
Basic	$ 0.07	$ 0.11	$ 0.08	$ 0.02
Weighted average shares—basic	2,125	7,438	6,163	10,711
Diluted	$ 0.01	$ 0.03	$ 0.02	$ 0.01
Weighted average shares—diluted	14,315	27,553	25,811	34,231
Pro forma net income per share(3):				
Basic		$ 0.06		$ 0.01
Weighted average shares—basic		14,591		19,145
Diluted		$ 0.03		$ 0.01
Weighted average shares—diluted		27,553		34,231
Supplemental Operating Data:				
Number of registered users at end of period	41	341	150	851
Gross merchandise sales(4)	$ 7,279	$95,271	$26,967	$243,746
Number of auctions listed	289	4,394	1,237	10,793

	June 30, 1998		
	Actual	**Pro Forma(5)**	**Pro Forma As Adjusted(5)(6)**
Balance Sheet Data:			
Cash and cash equivalents	$10,716	$10,716	$67,720
Working capital	8,803	8,803	66,079
Total assets	19,815	19,815	76,819
Debt and leases, long-term portion	167	167	8
Series B Mandatorily Redeemable Convertible Preferred Stock	5,157	—	—
Total stockholders' equity	9,122	14,279	71,714

(1) Based on shares of Common Stock outstanding as of June 30, 1998. Excludes (i) 1,071,162 shares of Common Stock issuable upon the exercise of stock options outstanding as of June 30, 1998, at a weighted average per share exercise price of $3.52, under the Company's 1996 Stock Option Plan (the "1996 Plan"), the Company's 1997 Stock Option Plan (the "1997 Plan") and option grants outside of the 1996 Plan and 1997 Plan, (ii) 961,500 shares of Common Stock available for future grant as of June 30, 1998 under the 1997 Plan, (iii) an additional 4,700,000 shares available for future grant or issuance under the Company's 1998 Equity Incentive Plan (the "Equity Incentive Plan") and 1998 Directors Stock Option Plan (the "Directors Plan") and (iv) 300,000 shares available for issuance under the Company's 1998 Employee Stock Purchase Plan (the "Purchase Plan"), which number is subject to automatic annual increases up to a maximum of an aggregate 1,500,000 shares during the term of the Purchase Plan. Subsequent to June 30, 1998, the Company increased the number of shares reserved under the 1997 Plan by 500,000 and granted options to purchase an additional 2,053,752 shares of Common Stock. These grants included all of the 961,500 shares available for future grant at June 30, 1998, and 600,000 shares issued outside the plans. An aggregate of 5,007,748 shares are available for future grant or issuance under the Company's various benefit plans. See "Capitalization," "Management—Director Compensation," "Management—Employee Benefit Plans," "Description of Capital Stock" and Notes 8, 9, 10 and 11 of Notes to Consolidated Financial Statements.

(2) See Note 1 of Notes to Consolidated Financial Statements for a description of the method used to compute basic and diluted net income per share.

(3) Pro forma net income per share gives effect to the conversion of all outstanding shares of the Company's Series A Convertible Preferred Stock and Series B Mandatorily Redeemable Convertible Preferred Stock into Common Stock upon the closing of this offering as if such conversion had occurred on January 1, 1997, or the date of original issuance, if later. See Note 1 of Notes to Consolidated Financial Statements for a description of the method used to compute pro forma basic and diluted net income per share.

(4) Represents the aggregate sales prices of all goods for which an auction was successfully concluded (i.e., there was at least one bid above the seller's specified minimum price or reserve price, whichever was higher).

(5) Gives effect to the conversion of all outstanding shares of the Company's Series A Convertible Preferred Stock and Series B Mandatorily Redeemable Convertible Preferred Stock into Common Stock upon the closing of this offering. See "Capitalization."

(6) Adjusted to give effect to the sale of the 3,489,275 shares of Common Stock offered by the Company hereby, after deducting the underwriting discount and estimated offering expenses, and the application of the net proceeds therefrom. See "Use of Proceeds" and "Capitalization."

FIGURE 18.2
Prospectus summary page.

PRIMARY VERSUS SECONDARY OFFERINGS The GM common stock offering was a **primary offering.** In a primary offering, a firm sells newly issued securities to investors. Sometimes insiders or large institutional shareholders sell securities they hold in a registered public offering. Such an offering is known as a **secondary offering.** Shareholders sell previously issued securities that they purchased from the firm or other investors.

EXAMPLE GM Pension Funds' Secondary Offering

Firms sometimes find it advantageous to issue common shares to their pension funds in lieu of making cash contributions. The share issue augments the stockholders' equity without the stockholders having to pay the flotation costs they would incur in a public offering. At some point, the pension funds might decide to sell some or all of these shares for diversification purposes. A couple years after its seasoned offering, GM contributed 173,163,187 shares of GM Class E Common Stock to its pension plans.

The GM pension plans subsequently decided to sell 42,550,000 of these shares in a registered secondary offering. The pension plans sold the shares in a global offering for $42.375 each, realizing net proceeds of $1.75 billion.

With a public offering, underwriters usually publish advertisements like the one in Figure 18.3 to advertise their role. These are called *tombstone advertisements* because of their appearance.

The ad in Figure 18.3 lists two groups, called **syndicates,** of underwriters. The first is a group of U.S. underwriters (306 million shares). The second is a group of international underwriters (54 million shares). Goldman, Sachs & Co., Merrill Lynch & Co., and Salomon Smith Barney acted as joint global coordinators, coordinating the selling activity of the two syndicates and redistributing shares from one to another according to the demand for the offering.

Review

1. What is the difference between a general cash offer and a rights issue?
2. What are the steps involved in a general cash offer?
3. What is an underwriter? A private placement?
4. What is the difference between a primary offering and a secondary offering?

18.4 INVESTMENT BANKING AND THE COST OF ISSUING SECURITIES

A firm can market its securities itself (as the U.S. government does), but most use investment bankers because of their expertise and experience. Table 18.3 shows the ranking of the 15 leading securities underwriters in the United States and outside it during 2001. Note that the five largest firms accounted for nearly 50% of all underwritten securities offerings in the United States.

Investment Bankers

The **investment banker** serves as an intermediary between the issuer and the purchasers. Investment bankers usually provide advice regarding the type and terms of the security to issue, and the market that provides the most advantages. They also help prepare the documentation (such as the prospectus) and underwrite and price the new issue.

THE WALL STREET JOURNAL THURSDAY, JUNE 15, 2000

This announcement is under no circumstances to be construed as an offer to sell or as a solicitation of an offer to buy any of these securities.
The offering is made only by the Prospectus.

New Issue | April 26, 2000

$10,620,000,000

AT&T

AT&T Wireless Group Tracking Stock

360,000,000 Shares

Price $29.50 Per Share

The New York Stock Exchange symbol is AWE

Global Coordinators and Joint Book-Running Managers

Goldman, Sachs & Co. | Merrill Lynch & Co. | Salomon Smith Barney

Copies of the Prospectus may be obtained in any State or jurisdiction in which this announcement is circulated from only such of the undersigned or other dealers or brokers as may lawfully offer these securities in such State or jurisdiction.

306,000,000 Shares

The above shares were underwritten by the following group of U.S. Underwriters.

Goldman, Sachs & Co. | Merrill Lynch & Co. | Salomon Smith Barney
Credit Suisse First Boston | Lehman Brothers | Morgan Stanley Dean Witter
Banc of America Securities LLC | M.R. Beal & Company | Bear, Stearns & Co. Inc.
Chase H&Q | Deutsche Banc Alex. Brown | Donaldson, Lufkin & Jenrette
J.P. Morgan & Co. | PaineWebber Incorporated | Prudential Volpe Technology Group (A unit of Prudential Securities)
Sanford C. Bernstein & Co., Inc. | Thomas Weisel Partners

Ameritrade | Allen & Company Incorporated | BMO Nesbitt Burns Corp. | Blaylock & Partners, L.P. | CIBC World Markets
A.G. Edwards & Sons, Inc. | Fidelity Capital Markets (A Division of National Financial Services Corp.) | First Union Securities, Inc. | Guzman & Company
Edward D. Jones & Co., L.P. | Lazard Frères & Co. LLC | RBC Dominion Securities Corporation | Robertson Stephens | SG Cowen
Muriel Siebert & Co., Inc. | Utendahl Capital Partners, L.P. | Wasserstein Perella Securities, Inc. | Wit SoundView
Advest, Inc. | Robert W. Baird & Co. Incorporated | William Blair & Company | J. C. Bradford & Co. | Chatsworth Securities LLC | Dain Rauscher Wessels | Fahnestock & Co. Inc.
Friedman Billings Ramsey | Gerard Klauer Mattison & Co., Inc. | J. J. B. Hilliard, W. L. Lyons, Inc. | Janney Montgomery Scott LLC | C. L. King & Associates, Inc.
Legg Mason Wood Walker Incorporated | McDonald Investments Inc. | Morgan Keegan & Company, Inc. | Needham & Company, Inc. | Neuberger Berman, LLC | Ormes Capital Markets, Inc.
Pryor, McClendon, Counts & Co., Inc. | Ragen MacKenzie Incorporated | Ramirez & Co., Inc. | Raymond James & Associates, Inc. | The Robinson-Humphrey Company
Scott & Stringfellow, Inc. | Stephens Inc. | Stifel, Nicolaus & Company Incorporated | SunTrust Equitable Securities | Sutro & Co. Incorporated | Tucker Anthony Cleary Gull
C.E. Unterberg, Towbin | U.S. Bancorp Piper Jaffray | Wachovia Securities, Inc. | The Williams Capital Group, L.P.
Adams, Harkness & Hill, Inc. | Arnhold and S. Bleichroeder, Inc. | George K. Baum & Company | Brean Murray & Co., Inc. | Burnham Securities Inc. | The Chapman Company
Crowell, Weedon & Co. | Davenport & Company LLC | D. A. Davidson & Co. | Doft & Co., Inc. | Doley Securities, Inc. | E*OFFERING Corp. | Gabelli & Company, Inc.
Gardner Rich & Co. , Inc. | Gruntal & Co., L.L.C. | Jackson Securities Incorporated | Janco Partners, Inc. | Jefferies & Company, Inc. | Josephthal & Co. Inc.
Kaufman Bros., L.P. | Loop Capital Markets | May Davis Group Inc. | Mellon Financial Markets LLC | Melvin Securities Corporation L.L.C. | Parker/Hunter Incorporated | Brad Peery Inc.
Pennsylvania Merchant Group | Pittsburg Institutional Inc. | Redwood Securities Group, Inc. | SBK Brooks Investment Corp. | Sanders Morris Harris
Sands Brothers & Co., Ltd. | The Seidler Companies Incorporated | Sturdivant & Co., Inc. | B. C. Wainwright & Co., Inc. | Wedbush Morgan Securities

54,000,000 Shares

The above shares were underwritten by the following group of International Managers.

Goldman Sachs International | Merrill Lynch International | Salomon Smith Barney International
ABN AMRO Rothschild | Credit Suisse First Boston | Deutsche Bank | Warburg Dillon Read
BANCA IMI | BNP Paribas Group | Cazenove & Co. | Daiwa SBCM Europe | HSBC | ING Barings Limited

FIGURE 18.3
Tombstone advertisement for AT&T Wireless Group's public common stock offering.
Source: Reprinted by permission of Goldman Sachs & Company.

TABLE 18.3
Leading managing underwriters of general cash offers in 2001.

ALL DOMESTIC ISSUES[a]
(FULL CREDIT TO LEAD MANAGER)
JANUARY 1, 2001–DECEMBER 31, 2001

RANK	MANAGER	AMOUNT ($ THOUSANDS)	%	ISSUES
1	J.P. Morgan	704,107,097	16	3,078
2	Bank of America	526,517,078	12	4,398
3	Salomon Smith Barney	447,662,206	10	3,189
4	Credit Suisse First Boston	274,005,673	6	4,087
5	Goldman Sachs & Co.	222,093,063	5	1,844
6	Lehman Brothers	220,391,454	5	2,810
7	Merrill Lynch & Co.	198,346,674	5	2,149
8	UBS Warburg	167,323,574	4	3,418
9	Citibank	165,860,131	4	679
10	Bear Stearns & Co. Inc.	147,322,461	3	2,653
11	Deutsche Bank AG	137,310,407	3	1,155
12	Morgan Stanley	127,493,196	3	944
13	Bank One	114,658,256	3	991
14	Fleet Boston Corp.	77,043,752	2	777
15	Wachovia Corp.	75,496,631	2	928

[a]Full credit is given to the lead managing underwriter.
Source: Bloomberg L.P.

OFFERINGS OUTSIDE THE UNITED STATES[a]
(ALL DEBT AND EQUITY)
JANUARY 1, 2001–DECEMBER 31, 2001

RANK	MANAGER	AMOUNT ($ THOUSANDS)	%	ISSUES
1	J.P. Morgan	105,429,059	14	192
2	Salomon Smith Barney	100,536,697	13	189
3	Deutsche Bank AG	73,041,792	9	112
4	Morgan Stanley	66,343,342	9	102
5	Merrill Lynch & Co.	66,181,996	9	117
6	Lehman Brothers	54,148,261	7	88
7	Credit Suisse First Boston	51,307,704	7	99
8	Goldman Sachs & Co.	48,719,566	6	74
9	UBS Warburg	44,355,816	6	78
10	Bank of America	29,864,120	4	100
11	ABN Amro	21,077,256	3	42
12	Bear Stearns & Co. Inc.	17,606,475	2	42
13	Barclays Capital	14,309,476	2	29
14	HSBC	12,125,682	2	34
15	Citibank	11,478,857	1	27

[a]Full credit is given to the lead managing underwriter.
Source: Bloomberg L.P.

Investment bankers also devote much time and energy to designing new securities. They try to develop new securities that will reduce issuers' funding costs and increase investors' after-tax risk-adjusted rates of return. In keeping with the Principle of Valuable Ideas, they do so to generate profitable securities marketing opportunities.

Underwriting

There are two types of underwriting: (1) purchase and sale and (2) best efforts. A true underwriting agreement involves a *purchase and sale,* in which an investment bank purchases the securities from the issuer at a fixed price and agrees to reoffer them to investors at a specified price less a specified commission. The securities firm bears the risk that the entire issue may not be able to be sold at the initial offering price. If it is not, the securities firm will sell the securities at the market clearing price and bear the loss. A purchase-and-sale underwriting thus involves a form of insurance for the issuing firm.

In a *syndicated public offering,* an underwriting group, or syndicate, is formed to purchase the securities from the issuer and reoffer them to investors. The lead managing underwriter assembles a syndicate consisting of those securities firms it believes can best market the issue successfully.

Nonunderwritten Offerings

Securities issues sold through investment bankers are not always underwritten. In a *best-efforts* arrangement, an investment bank commits to use its best efforts to market the securities to investors. There is no commitment to purchase, and therefore there is little financial risk to the investment banker. Informally, the securities firm may be called a *best-efforts underwriter,* even though it never owns the securities. Public offerings of the securities of smaller, lesser-known firms are often handled on a best-efforts basis. This may be due to the risk involved: The issuer is unable to find a securities firm willing to enter into a purchase-and-sale commitment (at least at an acceptable price).

In connection with private placements, securities firms customarily serve as *agent* for the issuer. The issuer sells the securities directly to investors. Securities firms help negotiate the terms of sale but do not underwrite the issue. Such offerings are sold on a best-efforts basis.

Some firms, including finance companies, may bypass the investment banks altogether and issue securities directly to investors. This reduces issuance expenses. The strategy can be cost effective when the issuer has a natural market it can exploit, such as current security holders.

In most cases, however, the investment banker has superior access to market information and to the channels of distribution. These advantages result from the investment banker's day-to-day interaction with prospective investors. Normally it is more economical for an issuer to sell securities through an investment banker.

Underwriters' Compensation

For their services in an underwritten public offering, underwriters charge a **gross underwriting spread.** It is calculated as a percentage of the public offering price of the issue. This spread has three components. The *management fee,* usually 15% to 20% of the total, compensates the managing underwriters for their assistance in designing the issue, preparing the documentation, forming the syndicate, and directing the offering process. The *underwriting fee,* usually 15% to 20% of the total, compensates for the underwriting risk. The *selling concession,* generally 60% to 70% of the total, compensates for the selling effort.

Underwriters' compensation represents a significant portion of the flotation expense. Table 18.4 provides a flotation expense breakdown for public offerings of various types and sizes during the period 1977 to 2001. It is generally most expensive to float a common stock issue and least expensive to float an issue of (nonconvertible) bonds. This reflects differences in underwriting risks. It is also due to the higher selling commissions required to distribute common

TABLE 18.4

Average gross underwriting spread and out-of-pocket expenses as percentage of principal amount for registered domestic public offerings, 1977 to 2001.[a]

	COMMON STOCK			PREFERRED STOCK			CONVERTIBLE PREFERRED STOCK AND CONVERTIBLE DEBT			BONDS		
PRINCIPAL AMOUNT ($ MILLIONS)	Gross Under-writing Spread (%)	Out-of-Pocket Expenses (%)	Total (%)	Gross Under-writing Spread (%)	Out-of-Pocket Expenses (%)	Total (%)	Gross Under-writing Spread (%)	Out-of-Pocket Expenses (%)	Total (%)	Gross Under-writing Spread (%)	Out-of-Pocket Expenses (%)	Total (%)
0.0–9.9	7.69	5.94	13.63	4.69	3.65	8.34	8.51	6.15	14.66	2.04	1.91	3.95
10.0–24.9	5.99	2.70	8.69	3.05	1.24	4.29	4.55	1.94	6.49	1.29	1.11	2.40
25.0–49.9	5.52	1.57	7.09	2.33	0.57	2.90	3.42	0.98	4.40	0.95	0.68	1.63
50.0–99.9	5.13	0.89	6.02	2.06	0.28	2.34	2.63	0.55	3.18	0.96	0.43	1.39
100.0–199.9	4.68	0.59	5.27	2.76	0.28	3.04	2.40	0.39	2.79	0.90	0.30	1.20
200.0–499.9	4.16	0.41	4.57	2.63	0.17	2.80	2.17	0.19	2.36	0.84	0.16	1.00
500.0 and over	3.49	0.14	3.63	2.62	0.10	2.72	1.57	0.09	1.66	0.57	0.08	0.65

[a]Excludes rights issues, issues callable or putable in under one year, and issues which are not underwritten.
Source: Reprinted by permission of Thomson Financial

stock issues, large portions of which are usually marketed very broadly to individual investors. Note the significant economies of scale in issuing securities.

Negotiated Versus Competitive Offerings

A firm can offer securities publicly using either competitive bidding or a negotiated offering. Under **competitive bidding,** the issuer specifies the type of securities it wishes to sell and invites securities firms to bid for the issue. It puts the securities up for bid, and the bidding process determines which investment bankers will market the issue and at what price.

In a **negotiated offering,** the issuer selects one or more securities firms to manage the offering and works closely with them to design the terms of the issue and determine the appropriate time to issue the securities. Currently, registered public utility holding companies are required to offer securities competitively, but other firms are free to choose the offering technique. Other electric utilities tend to offer debt and preferred stock by competitive bid (except during periods of heightened market volatility) but generally sell common stock on a negotiated basis. Railroads frequently sell equipment trust certificates through competitive bidding.

Are Competitive Offerings Cheaper?

Which offering method costs less? The question has been hotly debated, and the evidence is inconclusive. However, recent studies suggest that the competitive process usually does not lead to significant cost savings, except perhaps during stable market periods when strong competition among bidding groups results in lower costs. Competitive bidding generally results in lower underwriting spreads, but competitive underwritings may involve greater underwriting spreads than negotiated underwritings during periods of great market uncertainty.

Moreover, the negotiated offering process offers greater flexibility in the design of the securities and the timing of the issue. The issuer has not committed in advance to a specific set of terms (for example, maturity and redemption terms) or to a particular offering date (in competitive bidding, the date bids are to be received).

A negotiated offering also gives securities firms the opportunity to form the most effective selling group for the issue. Rather than splitting them into competing bidding groups, the negotiation process provides a stronger incentive for securities firms to assess the demand for, and stimulate interest in, the issue prior to pricing. Because they know that they will have the securities to sell, they will not hesitate to begin marketing activities. Competitive bidders, in contrast, lose their marketing investment if they are not selected.

Shelf Registration

The Securities and Exchange Commission's Rule 415 is commonly known as **shelf registration.** Rule 415 allows a firm to register an inventory of securities of a particular type sufficient to cover its financing requirements for up to two years and sell the securities whenever it chooses. The securities remain "on the shelf" until the issuer finds market conditions sufficiently attractive to sell them.

Shelf registration has improved firms' financing flexibility. A firm does not have to file a new registration statement each time it offers securities, which reduces flotation costs. Securities can be sold within minutes. Also, a single shelf registration statement can cover many types of securities. This permits issuers to design the security at the time they sell it to exploit any special investor preferences and minimize their cost of funds.

Rule 415 has effectively extended competitive bidding to issues of securities by the roughly 2,000 large firms that qualify to use shelf registration. Securities firms and institutional investors can bid for securities that a firm has on the shelf. But the evidence is mixed on whether Rule 415 has had any impact on transaction costs.

Other Costs of Issuing Securities

In addition to the gross underwriting spread, there are out-of-pocket expenses, such as lawyers' and accountants' fees, and engraving, printing, and mailing costs. Out-of-pocket expenses tend to be fixed expenses and are therefore a significant cost factor only in connection with small offerings.

Any market price decline associated with the announcement of the offering and subsequent marketing activity is also a cost. This last cost is most significant in connection with public common stock offerings.

MARKET IMPACT OF A STOCK ISSUE A firm's share price often declines upon the announcement of a public common stock offering. This may seem puzzling. If the corporation intends to invest the issue proceeds in positive-NPV projects, the share price should increase. But evidence indicates that the Signaling Principle is at work.

The share price falls because the offering apparently sends a negative signal to investors. This reaction has been explained in terms of asymmetric information. If management acts in its shareholders' best interest, it will refrain from issuing shares when it believes the firm's stock is relatively undervalued in the market, and it will choose to sell new shares when it believes the firm's shares are relatively overvalued. Accordingly, the announcement of the new issue may signal overvaluation and lead to a negative market reaction. Taking this line of reasoning a step further, the larger the size of the offering, the more the share price should decrease.

Review

1. Explain the difference between a negotiated and a competitive offering.
2. Distinguish between an underwritten and a best-efforts offering.
3. What is the role of the underwriters in a general cash offer? What are the three components of the gross underwriting spread?
4. What is a shelf registration?
5. Why might a firm's stock price decline when the firm announces a public offering of new common shares?

18.5 PRIVATE PLACEMENTS

Instead of selling securities to the general investing public, firms can sell securities directly to institutional investors through a private placement.

Features of Privately Placed Securities

Privately placed securities are not registered and, therefore, are not freely tradable. For this reason, securities regulations require firms to offer securities privately only to investors sophisticated enough to make an independent determination of their investment merits. The largest group of such investors by far is life insurance companies. Others include foreign banks, U.S. commercial banks, pension and trust funds, property and casualty insurance companies, finance companies, mutual funds, and wealthy individuals. Table 18.5 lists 25 of the largest private placement buyers.

Advantages of a Private Placement

A private placement offers the following advantages in comparison with a public offering:

- *Lower issuance costs* for smaller issues. A private placement avoids the costs of registering the securities, printing prospectuses, and obtaining credit ratings. Also, the private placement agent's fee is generally a lot less than the underwriting expenses for a comparable public offering, and can be avoided altogether if the issuer negotiates directly with investors.
- *Issues can be placed more quickly* for firms that do not qualify for shelf registration. Registering securities requires time to prepare the registration statement and have the SEC review it.
- *Greater flexibility of issue size.* The private market is more receptive to smaller issues. Issues of only a few million dollars each are not uncommon. Public debt and preferred stock issues of less than $50 million principal amount are usually more costly, because their small size decreases their liquidity and thus lessens their attractiveness to investors.
- *Greater flexibility of security arrangements* and other terms. Private investors are capable of analyzing complex security arrangements, and it is easier to tailor the terms of an issue to suit both sides of the transaction. It is also easier to obtain lenders' consents to a change in terms should the firm's circumstances change both because the debtholders are sophisticated and also because there are fewer of them.

TABLE 18.5
Twenty-five of the largest buyers of private placements in the United States.

John Hancock Life Insurance	Nationwide Insurance Companies
Teachers Insurance & Annuity Association	Lincoln Investment Management Inc.
Prudential Insurance Company of America	Guardian Life Insurance Company of America
Hartford Investment Management Company	Mutual of Omaha Companies
Metropolitan Life	Jefferson-Pilot Life Insurance Company
Citigroup Global Investments	State of Wisconsin Investment Board
American General Investment Management	Mony Life Insurance
New York Life Investment Management	Sun Life Financial
AIG/SunAmerica Investments	Advantus Capital Management
Principal Capital Management	Lutheran Brotherhood
Cigna Investment Management	AmerUs Capital Management
ING Investment Management	American United Life Insurance Company
Provident Investment Management LLC	

- *Lower cost of resolving financial distress.* Private debt tends to be easier than public debt to restructure, because it will generally involve fewer and more sophisticated investors. Empirical research has found that financial distress is more likely to be resolved outside bankruptcy when more of the firm's debt is owed to banks, but is less likely to be resolved outside bankruptcy when the firm has more than one public debt issue outstanding.
- *More favorable share price reaction than a public offering.* Studies have found that the stock market generally reacts positively to the announcement of private placements of debt, convertible debt, and equity. The larger private placements of debt have tended to elicit the most positive market response, and the positive impact tends to be especially large for firms that have never issued debt publicly. These results are consistent with the notion that private placement leads to reduced information asymmetries, increased monitoring, and certification.

In connection with a public offering, the investment banks investigate the affairs of the issuer on behalf of the investing public (the process is referred to as *due diligence*). In a private placement, the institutional investors conduct their own investigation. Private placement may therefore allow investors access to information about a firm that is not available to the general investing public. With respect to monitoring, privately placed debt issues usually have more restrictive covenants than comparable public debt issues. The tighter covenants improve monitoring efficiency. Finally, the purchasers—because they tend to be large sophisticated institutional investors—are making a comment about the firm's quality in their willingness to purchase and hold the firm's securities. A larger private placement, because of the accompanying increased commitment of funds, may intensify all of these considerations, thereby communicating greater confidence in the firm's quality.

Disadvantages of a Private Placement

A private placement has the following disadvantages relative to a public offering:

- *Higher yield.* To compensate for the lack of liquidity, purchasers of privately placed securities require a yield premium relative to publicly traded securities. Purchasers of privately placed common stock require a substantial discount to the price at which the shares would trade in a liquid secondary market.
- *More stringent covenants and more restrictive terms.* Private issuers are often not public firms and thus not subject to the SEC's reporting requirements. Private purchasers insist on tighter covenant restrictions to compensate for the greater agency costs due to greater asymmetric information. The covenants alert investors when something has "gone wrong," such as a sharp reduction in net worth. Private lenders have also insisted on tighter protection against *event risk,* the risk that stockholders might initiate events such as a leveraged buyout that could expropriate bondholder wealth. These covenants can limit a firm's operating flexibility, possibly forcing it to pass up profitable investment opportunities.

RULE 144A PRIVATE PLACEMENTS SEC Rule 144A has broadened the market for private-placement financing in the United States, especially for foreign issuers. In a **Rule 144A private placement,** the issuer sells its unregistered securities to one or more investment banks, which then resell the securities to "qualified institutional buyers" (QIBs).[4] This process is much like an underwritten public offering.

[4]A QIB generally is defined as a financial institution that invests on a discretionary basis at least $100 million in money market instruments, publicly traded corporate securities of unaffiliated firms, or Treasury securities. QIBs can trade freely with each other in securities that have not been registered with the SEC.

Review

1. Who are the main purchasers of privately placed securities?
2. What are the advantages and disadvantages of a private placement as compared to a general cash offer?
3. What is a Rule 144A private placement?

18.6 RIGHTS ISSUES

Instead of offering common stock directly to the general public, a firm may offer new stock to its current shareholders on a privileged-subscription basis. This is called a rights offering, because the firm distributes to its shareholders *rights* to subscribe for additional shares at a specified price.

From World War II to the 1960s, roughly two-thirds of all common stock issues were rights issues. But beginning in the late 1960s, virtually all large U.S. firms, which tend to have widely dispersed shareholdings, obtained shareholder approval to eliminate preemptive rights. However, firms outside the United States tend to rely heavily on rights offerings to raise additional equity capital. For example, the London Stock Exchange changed its rules in 1975 to allow general cash offers. Nevertheless, rights issues continue to be the predominant method of external equity financing there. In some countries, firms are required by law to sell new share issues through rights offerings.

EXAMPLE Eurotunnel's Two Rights Issues

The Eurotunnel project involved the construction of twin-bore rail tunnels beneath the English Channel to link the rail systems of France and the United Kingdom. When cost overruns made it necessary to raise additional common equity, Eurotunnel conducted an underwritten rights issue that raised £532 million (net of expenses).

Further cost overruns necessitated another equity offering. The second time, Eurotunnel raised £816 million (net of expenses) through an underwritten rights offering.

How a Rights Offering Works

In a rights offering, the firm distributes to each shareholder one right for each share the holder owns as of the specified *record date* for the offering. Rights are call options on newly issued shares. The firm will indicate the number of rights required to purchase one new share of stock. For instance, stockholders may be given rights to buy one new share for every three shares already owned. As with other market-traded options, a right has a time until expiration and a strike price. The time until expiration is called the *subscription period.* The strike price to purchase each new share is called the *subscription price.*

Shareholders can either (1) exercise the rights and subscribe for shares or (2) sell the rights if they are transferable (they usually are). If the shareholders do neither, the rights expire, worthless, at the close of business on the expiration date. If shareholders wish to purchase extra shares, they can purchase additional rights from other shareholders who choose to sell their rights. Or if the firm gives shareholders an *oversubscription privilege* to purchase the shares for which other shareholders fail to subscribe, they can buy them from the issuer to the extent that they are available.

Value of Rights

The Options Principle states that options are valuable. Because a right is a call option, it will always have a positive value prior to its expiration. We show in Chapter 12 that the value of an option, and therefore of a right, is a function of (1) the strike price, (2) the value of the underlying stock, (3) the time until expiration, (4) the variance of the underlying stock's return, and (5) the riskless return. In addition, the value of a right depends on its dilutive effect, which is caused by its creation of new equity. Loosely speaking, the dilutive effect is the difference between the strike price (the new equity) and the market value (existing equity). Recall that when the value of the underlying stock is more than the strike price, a call option is in-the-money. The smaller the strike price relative to the share price, the more valuable the call option.

To encourage subscription, rights are issued in-the-money. That is, the issuer sets the subscription price at less than the market price of its stock on the record date. Because of the short time to expiration, the exercise value—which is the difference between the strike price and share price—is the main factor that determines the value of a right. With a very short life, the time premium of the in-the-money option is small. For simplicity, we ignore the time premium on the right, but if the life is more than a month and only a little in-the-money, the time premium can be significant.

The initial value of each right just after the offering is announced, and when the stock is trading *rights-on* (that is, the rights are still attached to the stock), is approximately

$$R = \frac{P_R - S}{N + 1} \tag{18.2}$$

where R is the value of the right, P_R is the market value of a share trading rights-on, S is the strike price, and N is the number of rights to purchase one new share.

EXAMPLE The Long Island Lighting Company Rights Offering

A number of years ago, the Long Island Lighting Company offered 6,402,515 additional shares of its common stock to its current shareholders on the basis of one new share for seven rights (that is, each seven shares already owned), plus a subscription price of $17.15 per new share during the 18-day subscription period. At the time, shares were trading at $18.375. What was the approximate value of each right?

Using Equation (18.2), the initial value of each right was

$$R = \frac{18.375 - 17.15}{7 + 1} = \$0.1531$$

After the ex-date, the stock is said to trade *ex-rights* because the purchaser of the shares is not entitled to receive the rights. On the ex-date, the share price decreases by the value of the right, which is no longer attached to it. Therefore, the share price ex-rights, P_E, is

$$P_E = P_R - R \tag{18.3}$$

In the case of the Long Island Lighting rights offering,

$$P_E = \$18.375 - \$0.1531 = \$18.2219$$

Immediately after the ex-date, the market value of each right will vary with the price of the firm's common stock:

$$R = \frac{P_E - S}{N} \tag{18.4}$$

In this equation we divide by N, rather than $N + 1$, because the rights have separated from the shares.

Underwritten Rights Offering

Firms would generally prefer to have an investment banker stand ready to purchase unsubscribed shares on an underwritten basis rather than have to reduce the subscription price to ensure a successful offering, which occurred in the Eurotunnel rights offerings. The underwriters are paid a standby fee for each share offered for subscription, plus a take-up fee payable on shares acquired by the underwriters through the exercise of rights during the subscription period and on shares remaining unsubscribed at the end of the period.

Advantages and Disadvantages of a Rights Offering

The fundamental idea underlying a rights offering is to provide shareholders with the option to retain their proportionate ownership in a firm when it sells additional common shares. However, because of the separation of ownership and control, this probably benefits only shareholders with large holdings.

It is often argued that a rights offering is beneficial to shareholders because they can buy shares at a bargain price or because they perceive the rights as a kind of dividend. But a stockholder receives no benefits from the rights other than the option of retaining proportionate ownership. The firm's share price falls on the ex-date, and the decrease in price offsets the value of a right, as in the case of a stock dividend. The shareholder is just as well off after the rights offering as before it, provided that he either sells the rights or exercises them.

The main benefit of a rights offering is that it protects existing shareholders from a potential loss of wealth that can result from a public offering. To induce sales, shares are offered at a price below the current market value. In a public offering, this inducement transfers wealth from existing shareholders to the purchasers of the newly created shares. The rights offering avoids this wealth transfer. It gives the inducement to existing shareholders, so long as they sell or exercise their rights.

A rights offering may also be more beneficial than a public offering to a firm that does not have broad market appeal or a firm that has concentrated stock ownership, because it enables the selling effort to be focused on investors who already own shares and are therefore familiar with the firm. In addition, common stock issued in a rights offering can be purchased on margin, whereas common stock issued in a public offering cannot.

On the other hand, there are two principal disadvantages to a rights offering: It generally takes longer to complete, and it eliminates the possible transaction cost savings of selling large blocks of shares to institutions that do not currently own the stock.

Dividend Reinvestment Plans

Many firms sponsor dividend reinvestment plans. A **dividend reinvestment plan (DRIP)** allows each common stockholder to use dividends to purchase shares of the firm's common stock. In a *new-issue DRIP,* the firm sells newly issued shares to its shareholders. The price is often slightly (up to 5%) below the stock's current market price. New-issue DRIPs resemble rights offerings; in effect, the firm offers new shares pro rata to existing shareholders. An *open-market DRIP* is different. In such a plan, the firm uses the reinvested dividends to repurchase shares on behalf of shareholders. A new-issue DRIP is a source of new capital; an open-market DRIP is not.

Review

1. Is a right a call option or a put option? What are the primary determinants of the value of a right?
2. What is the difference between a share trading rights-on and a share trading ex-rights?
3. What are the advantages and disadvantages of a rights offering as compared to a general cash offer?
4. What is a dividend reinvestment plan (DRIP)?

18.7 DILUTION

Practitioners often worry about possible dilution when a firm sells additional common shares. **Dilution** refers to a decrease in equity value per common share. The term has at least three different meanings:

1. Dilution in percentage ownership
2. Dilution in price (a market value change)
3. Dilution in book value or earnings per share (a book value change)

Can you see why the three are not identical? The three meanings create confusion. Worse, it also leads to misconceptions about the impact of accounting dilution. The real issue is whether there is a loss of shareholder wealth. As we have said many times, it is market value that matters!

Dilution in Percentage Ownership

Dilution in percentage ownership occurs whenever a firm sells additional shares and a shareholder's percentage voting interest falls. The following example illustrates that no change in shareholder wealth need occur.

EXAMPLE Dilution in Percentage Ownership

Let's say you own 10,000 shares of Reliable Fabric Corp., a firm your father founded. (He gave you the shares as a graduation gift!) There are 200,000 shares outstanding, so you own 5% (= 10,000/200,000) of the firm. You get 5% of the dividends and cast 5% of the votes.

Suppose Reliable needs to sell 50,000 shares to finance expansion. It sells the shares in a general cash offer. You do not buy any. Your percentage ownership falls to 4% (= 10,000/250,000). Your ownership has been diluted. But has your wealth been affected? Not necessarily. Suppose your shares were worth $12 each before the offering and Reliable issued the new shares for $12 each. Prior to the new issue, Reliable was worth $2.4 million (= [12]200,000). You owned 5%, worth $120,000 (= [0.05]2.4 million). After the new issue, you own 4%, also worth $120,000 (= [0.04]3.0 million). So the decrease in percentage ownership has not changed your wealth.

A rights issue would let you maintain your percentage ownership. If this is important to you and your fellow shareholders, a rights offering may be the way to go.

Dilution in Value

Let us tackle the next two forms of dilution at the same time. The following example illustrates how dilution in book value can occur without any dilution in market value.

EXAMPLE Dilution in Value: Market Value Versus Book Value

International Nickel Corp. plans to build a new nickel smelter, which will cost $36 million. Table 18.6 shows that the firm currently has 10 million shares outstanding but no debt. Its

TABLE 18.6
The impact of International Nickel's equity offering.

	PRIOR TO THE OFFERING	NEW PROJECT HAS POSITIVE NPV	NEW PROJECT HAS NEGATIVE NPV
Number of common shares	10,000,000	13,000,000	14,000,000
Share price	\$10.00	\$12.00	\$9.00
Aggregate market value	\$100 million	\$156 million	\$126 million
Aggregate book value	\$140 million	\$176 million	\$176 million
Book value per share	\$14.00	\$13.54	\$12.57
Market/Book	0.71	0.89	0.72
Return on book equity	12%	12%	12%
Return on new equity		13	12
Earnings	\$16,800,000	\$21,480,000	\$21,120,000
Earnings per share	\$1.68	\$1.65	\$1.51
Project NPV		\$20 million	−\$10 million

share price is \$10, giving International Nickel equity with a market value of \$100 million. The firm's equity has a book value of \$14 per share.

Let's consider two possibilities. First, suppose the project NPV is \$20 million. Announcing the project causes the share price to rise by \$2 (= 20/10) to \$12. (The prospectus for the offering contains enough information for investors to gauge the project's NPV.) International Nickel will have to sell 3 million (= 36 million/12) new shares to raise the \$36 million project cost. Its aggregate market value rises to \$156 million (= [12]13 million). Its aggregate book value rises to \$176 million (= 140 + 36), whereas its book value per share falls to \$13.54 (= 176/13). The NPV is positive, and International Nickel should undertake the project, despite the dilution in book value per share.

Suppose instead the project's NPV is −\$10 million. Announcing the project would cause the share price to fall by \$1 (= 10/10) to \$9. International Nickel would have to sell 4 million (= 36 million/9) new shares. Its aggregate market value would be \$126 million (= [9]14 million). Its aggregate book value would again be \$176 million, whereas its book value per share would fall to \$12.57 (= 176/14). Once again book value per share falls, but by more than in the case of a positive-NPV project.

Book value per share falls in both cases. This *always* happens when the market-to-book ratio is less than one. But market value, not book value, is what matters. The firm should undertake the project if its NPV is positive—even though book value per share suffers dilution. Market value per share sends the right signal. The negative-NPV project dilutes market value per share (to \$9 from \$10). The positive-NPV project has the opposite effect.

Some practitioners worry instead about dilution in earnings per share. But it can be just as misleading as dilution in book value. For example, EPS might be higher or lower whether the project NPV is positive or negative. In Table 18.6, financing the project with equity dilutes EPS, but more so in the negative-NPV case.[5]

[5]Problem B13 asks you to verify the EPS calculations.

Review

1. What are the three types of dilution? Which one should be of paramount concern to stockholders?
2. True or False?
   a. If new shares are sold for more than the current book value per share, the book value per share will increase.
   b. If new shares are sold for more than the current book value per share, the market value per share will increase.
   c. The firm announces a positive-NPV project that will be financed by issuing new shares. Assume no issuing costs or signaling. The market price per share should increase.

18.8 GOING PUBLIC AND GOING PRIVATE

When a firm's common stock is not registered for listing on an exchange or for trading in the over-the-counter market, it is said to be privately held. Privately held firms normally do not have to file regular quarterly financial reports with the SEC. Therefore, they are also private in the sense that much of the information concerning them is not public.

When a firm first sells its common stock to the investing public in an **initial public offering (IPO),** it becomes publicly held. It also becomes subject to the regular reporting requirements of the securities laws. On the other hand, when a small group of investors (usually including the firm's managers) buys up all the common stock, the firm is said to *go private* because it becomes privately held.

Going Public

Firms go public through an IPO. It is a watershed event in the life of a firm. The decision to go public depends on a number of factors. The key stockholders must conclude that the advantages outweigh the disadvantages.

To make a successful IPO, a firm must (1) find capable underwriters to sponsor and assist it and (2) complete its offering at an acceptable price. Its ability to achieve these goals will depend largely on its profitability and future prospects. A firm that wishes to go public normally tries to do so when it believes the stock market is most receptive.

Table 18.7 shows how the volume of IPOs varied from 1975 to 2001. The receptivity of investors depends to a great extent on the overall prospect for capital gains, which depends on the tone of the stock market and on how investors expect these capital gains to be taxed. The new-issues boom of 1980 to 1983 coincided with a major stock market rally, when the S&P 500 index increased by nearly 50% between 1979 and 1983. It also began soon after the 1978 reduction in the capital gains tax rate and was enhanced by another reduction in 1981. A second new-issues boom from 1992 to 1999 coincided with a tripling in the S&P 500 index.

PREPARING THE FIRM TO GO PUBLIC Before going public, firms may have to modify some of their practices and put dealings with insiders on an arm's-length basis. Individuals from outside the firm usually have to be added to the board of directors to monitor the firm's performance on behalf of public investors. The firm will have to change its accounting procedures to conform to generally accepted accounting principles, including regular audits, if they do not conform already.

PRICING THE OFFERING Underwriters generally try to price an IPO 10% to 15% below the expected trading price. In some cases it is substantially more than 15% "underpriced."

TABLE 18.7
Volume of initial public offerings, 1975 to 2001.

	INITIAL PUBLIC OFFERINGS*			S&P 500 INDEX	
YEAR	Number	Aggregate Value	Average Size	Beginning of Year	Change During Year
1975	5	$ 176	$ 35.3	68.6	31.5%
1976	40	337	8.4	90.2	19.2
1977	31	221	7.1	107.5	−11.5
1978	38	225	5.9	95.1	1.1
1979	62	398	6.4	96.1	12.3
1980	148	1,327	9.0	107.9	25.9
1981	347	3,055	8.8	135.8	−9.7
1982	121	1,425	11.8	122.6	14.7
1983	679	13,298	19.6	140.6	17.3
1984	354	4,011	11.3	164.9	1.4
1985	306	7,974	26.1	167.2	26.4
1986	699	19,671	28.1	211.3	14.6
1987	519	15,186	29.3	242.2	2.0
1988	228	6,387	28.0	247.1	12.4
1989	208	6,464	31.1	277.7	27.3
1990	173	4,734	27.4	353.4	−6.6
1991	368	17,256	46.9	330.2	26.3
1992	521	26,116	50.1	417.1	4.5
1993	712	44,753	62.9	435.7	7.1
1994	631	31,973	50.7	466.5	−1.5
1995	582	33,631	57.8	459.2	34.2
1996	870	54,794	63.0	615.9	19.3
1997	622	45,947	73.9	740.7	31.7
1998	372	40,316	108.4	970.4	26.1
1999	516	62,227	120.6	1229.2	19.6
2000	390	59,869	153.5	1469.3	−9.3
2001	108	37,502	347.2	1320.3	−10.5

*Excludes rights issues, closed end-funds, and issues not underwritten.
Source: Reprinted by permission of Thomson Financial

Underwriters apparently underprice IPOs to increase their attractiveness and the likelihood that the shares will perform well in the aftermarket. However, research shows that IPOs generally underperform the market for up to three years after the initial price surge following their issuance.

Advantages of Going Public

There are several advantages to going public.

RAISE NEW CAPITAL Going public enables a firm to raise additional capital. Also, shares generally bring a higher price in the public market than in the venture capital or private placement markets.

ACHIEVE LIQUIDITY AND DIVERSIFICATION FOR CURRENT SHAREHOLDERS Existing shareholders usually sell portions of their shares as part of the IPO. This gives them a cash return on their investment and allows them to diversify their investment portfolios.

CREATE A NEGOTIABLE INSTRUMENT Going public makes the common stock negotiable and creates a visible market value. After going public, the firm usually finds it easier to acquire other firms in exchange for shares of its stock. If all else is equal, marketable securities are worth more because of their greater liquidity.

INCREASE THE FIRM'S EQUITY FINANCING FLEXIBILITY A publicly traded firm is able to raise additional equity more quickly and more cheaply than it could were it not public.

ENHANCE THE FIRM'S IMAGE Because of the standards investment bankers apply before agreeing to take a firm public, going public represents a milestone in a firm's development.

Disadvantages of Going Public

Going public is not without disadvantages, however.

EXPENSE OF GOING PUBLIC Going public involves significant expenses—generally from 6 to 13% of the amount of the offering, and even more for very small offerings. Going public can also take a substantial amount of valuable management time.

HIGHER ESTATE VALUATION Negotiability increases a stock's value because of liquidity. Estate tax obligations are consequently greater when a stock is publicly traded. On the other hand, a public market provides a way of selling shares to get cash to pay the tax.

DILUTION OF OWNERSHIP INTEREST Existing shareholders lose a portion of their ownership interest to public shareholders. This can be a significant change, and existing shareholders can even lose voting control.

DISCLOSURE REQUIREMENTS A public firm is subject to regulations governing regular reporting to shareholders, proxy solicitation and insider trading, and to other regulations. A public firm must publicly report on a regular basis information regarding its operating results, financial condition, significant business developments, and other sensitive matters, such as officers' compensation and transactions between the firm and its management.

ACCOUNTABILITY TO PUBLIC SHAREHOLDERS AND PRESSURE FOR SHORT-TERM PERFORMANCE As a result of information asymmetries, the managers of a publicly held firm might make decisions that look good in the short run but are significantly inferior in the long run. "Managing" quarter-to-quarter earnings can also hamper a firm's operating flexibility.

PRESSURE TO PAY DIVIDENDS Public shareholders expect the firm to begin paying dividends eventually. This may not be best if the firm is able to reinvest the funds in positive-NPV projects.

Decision to List the Shares on an Exchange

When a firm goes public, it must decide where its shares will trade. Each of the exchanges and NASDAQ have established minimum listing requirements (net income, shares held by investors other than insiders, etc.) and reporting requirements. The NYSE's minimum requirements for listing are the most demanding. In order to have its stock listed on an exchange or quoted in the NASDAQ, a firm that meets the listing/quotation criteria files an application, pays a modest fee, and agrees to abide by the disclosure requirements and other rules.

Are there benefits to listing the stock on the NYSE or some other exchange rather than having it quoted on NASDAQ? An exchange appoints a single market maker for each stock it lists.

The market maker commits its capital to maintain an orderly market and must adhere to the rules of the exchange. In contrast, there is no central market and no unique market maker committed to a NASDAQ stock. Many firms feel that prestige is associated with their stock being exchange listed. Research shows that exchange markets have lower transaction costs. However, they are not necessarily more liquid than the NASDAQ market. And many prestigious firms, including Apple Computer, Intel, and Microsoft, have remained with NASDAQ even though they could qualify for exchange listing.

Going Private

Going private is the reverse of going public. When a small group of investors (usually in conjunction with members of senior management) purchases the entire common equity of a publicly traded firm, the firm becomes privately held. It is no longer subject to the financial reporting requirements of a public firm. If the disadvantages of being publicly owned outweigh the advantages, it is possible to revert to private ownership. Because going public and going private each involve substantial transaction costs, we do not observe firms frequently switching back and forth.

Review

1. What are the advantages of going public?
2. What are the disadvantages of going public?

18.9 PREFERRED STOCK

Preferred stock and *preference stock* are hybrid securities. They combine features of common stock and features of debt. They rank senior to common stock, and junior to debt, in claims on the firm's operating income and on the firm's assets in the event of liquidation. The only significant difference between preferred stock and preference stock is that preferred stock is senior. Dividends must be paid in full on the preferred stock before the firm can pay dividends on its preference stock. Firms normally issue preference stock only when charter limitations prevent them from issuing additional preferred stock. Because of the basic similarity between the two, the balance of this section will refer simply to preferred stock.

Main Features of Preferred Stock

Preferred stock has the following key features:

- A *par value* or *stated value,* generally \$25, \$50, or \$100 per share. Issues that are to be sold mainly to institutional investors are usually given a \$100 par value. Issues targeted to individual investors are usually given a \$25 par value, so that a round lot (100 shares) would cost only \$2,500.
- A stated *dividend rate.* Preferred stock pays dividends quarterly, like common stock, but at a stated rate, like debt. The dividends are not deductible for tax purposes. Also, preferred stock issues usually have a *cumulative dividend feature.* That is, missed dividends are accumulated. This cumulative amount must be paid in full before any cash dividends can be paid on common stock.
- An *optional redemption provision.* Preferred stock usually has optional redemption provisions similar to those found in debt issues that allow the firm to retire the securities.
- *Redeemability.* Preferred stock may be redeemable or nonredeemable. *Redeemable preferred stock* contains sinking-fund provisions similar to those found in sinking-fund debentures. *Nonredeemable preferred stock* is perpetual, like common stock. In general, the shorter the average life of the preferred stock issue, the more debtlike it is.

Financing with Preferred Stock

Why do firms issue preferred stock? Sinking-fund preferred stock is like debt except that the dividend payments are not tax deductible. However, missing a scheduled dividend payment will not force the issuer into default.

Preferred stock dividends qualify for the 70% dividends-received deduction when the preferred stockholder is a corporation. Because of this, preferred stock yields are usually lower than the yields of comparable debt instruments. If a corporation does not have taxable income, because it is carrying forward tax losses from prior years or because of other substantial expenses, it could cost the firm less than issuing tax-deductible debt. Thrift and commercial banks have been the heaviest issuers of adjustable-rate preferred stock.

There is another rationale for issuing preferred stock. Utility companies have been the heaviest issuers of fixed-dividend-rate preferred stock. Preferred stock generally represents 5% or more of an electric utility firm's capitalization. Regulated utilities can pass the cost of preferred dividends through to their customers.

Review

1. What is preferred stock? What are the main features of preferred stock?
2. What is the tax treatment of preferred dividends to (a) the issuing corporation, (b) dividend-receiving corporations, and (c) dividend-receiving individuals?

SUMMARY

There are many alternative ways to issue securities, including through investment bankers. In a given situation, a firm must weigh the costs and benefits and choose its best alternative.

- Many different types of financial securities make up the long-term financing menu. For example, securities may be equity, debt, or some combination. Securities may also be domestic or international.
- The main source of new equity capital is retained earnings.
- The rights of stockholders include voting rights, dividend rights, liquidation rights, and the preemptive right.
- A firm that needs to raise external capital can sell securities in the public market or in the private market. It can sell them directly to investors or engage a securities firm to assist it.
- The bulk of the securities issued by U.S. firms are sold in the domestic market in negotiated underwritten offerings.
- The initial decision involves what type of security to sell. Most important, the firm must decide in light of its capital structure objectives and its current financial condition whether to sell debt or equity securities. Economies of scale involved in issuing securities make it impractical for a firm to sell debt and equity securities each time it needs funds in the exact debt and equity proportions embodied in the firm's target capital structure.
- After deciding what type of security to sell, the firm must determine which market offers the most attractive terms. The private market offers some advantages but also suffers some disadvantages relative to the public market. The private market is generally more attractive than the public market for small debt issues or for debt issues backed by complex security arrangements. The Eurobond market is another alternative.

- There are a number of sources of additional common equity capital: retained earnings, public offerings of new shares, rights offerings of new shares to current shareholders, private placement of new shares, sale of new shares through a dividend reinvestment or employee stock plan, or a contribution of shares in lieu of cash to the firm's pension plan. Public offerings account for most of the new common equity capital firms raise from external sources.
- New securities can be marketed in a variety of ways. For example, they may be underwritten by one or more investment banking firms, sold on a best-efforts basis by one or more investment banking firms, sold directly to the public by the firm or, in the case of common stock, sold through either a rights offering or a dividend reinvestment plan to current shareholders.
- Issuance costs are proportionately lower for larger issues.
- Bonds have lower explicit issuance costs than common stock for comparable dollar amounts.
- Common stock is most often issued through a general cash offer on a negotiated basis. Rights offerings are rare in the United States but are the typical method of offering additional common stock in many other countries.
- Dilution is the reduction in the market value per equity share that accompanies the issue of new shares. The term dilution is also applied to a reduction in the percentage of shares owned or a reduction in earnings per share.
- Going public enables a firm to raise capital and creates a negotiable instrument for use in acquisitions or for other purposes, but obligates a firm to make regular financial disclosures and to deal with a new constituency, its public shareholders. A firm should go public only if it has determined that the advantages outweigh the disadvantages of being publicly held.
- Preferred stock has a *par value* or *stated value* and stated *dividend rate.* It pays dividends quarterly. If a preferred stock issue has a *cumulative dividend feature,* any missed dividends are accumulated and must be paid in full before any cash dividends can be paid on common stock. Preferred stock usually has optional redemption provisions similar to those found in debt issues. Preferred stock may be redeemable or nonredeemable. *Redeemable preferred stock* contains sinking-fund provisions similar to those found in sinking-fund debentures. *Nonredeemable preferred stock* is perpetual, like common stock.
- Preferred stock is a hybrid financial instrument. Adjustable-rate preferred stock, which has undergone a number of refinements, gives rise to a potential tax benefit when the issuer is nontaxpaying and the investors are corporations that can use the 70% dividends-received deduction.

EQUATION SUMMARY

$$\text{Book value per common share} = \frac{\text{Common stockholders' equity}}{\text{Number of common shares outstanding}} \tag{18.1}$$

$$R = \frac{P_R - S}{N + 1} \tag{18.2}$$

$$P_E = P_R - R \tag{18.3}$$

$$R = \frac{P_E - S}{N} \tag{18.4}$$

QUESTIONS

1. How do public and private financing differ?
2. Cite three advantages and the major disadvantage of private financing.
3. What are the three meanings of the term *dilution?* Why are they different? Which ones are important to shareholders?
4. What are the principal features of common stock? How are the principal features of common stock and preferred stock different?
5. Why does the par value of common stock have little real significance?
6. What is by far the largest source of new external financing?
7. What is by far the largest source of new equity financing?
8. Why would you expect debt securities sold in a Rule 144A private placement to offer a lower yield than the same securities sold in a traditional private placement?
9. Name the three explicit transaction cost components of the gross underwriting spread in an underwritten public offering.
10. Explain why the real transaction cost of an issue consists of the market impact as well as the gross spread.
11. What is a rights offering?
12. How can a dividend reinvestment plan raise new equity capital?
13. Explain the difference between a negotiated and a competitive offering.
14. Why is preferred stock viewed as a "hybrid" security?
15. Explain why the announcement of a public offering of common stock generally has a negative impact on the firm's share price.
16. Describe the major advantages and disadvantages of going public.
17. Explain each of the following rights and privileges associated with common stock: (a) dividend rights, (b) liquidation rights, (c) preemptive rights, (d) voting rights.

CHALLENGING QUESTIONS

18. A firm announces a new issue of common stock.
    a. How would you expect the stock market to react? Why?
    b. Would it make a difference if the firm announced that it would place the shares privately with three of the largest life insurance companies in the United States?
19. How is stockholders' wealth affected when a firm sells new shares of common stock for a price:
    a. Greater than its book value?
    b. Less than its book value?
20. Explain why a firm making a new securities issue, especially one that includes some component of equity, must be concerned with more than simply the explicit transaction costs such as underwriter fees.
21. Explain why a preferred stock issue that contains a sinking-fund provision is similar to debt. How does the design of this feature affect how debtlike the preferred stock is?
22. In what sense is preferred stock: (a) "expensive" debt? (b) "cheap" equity?
23. Venture capitalists invest funds that enable firms to start up. They also finance the early stages of development before the firm goes public. They usually ask for preemptive rights, at least at the time of their initial investment. What is their rationale?

24. In the case of many European firms, a few large institutions or wealthy individuals are the dominant shareholders. Why would you expect such firms to use rights offerings rather than general cash offers to raise additional common equity?
25. Suppose a firm has 100 million shares outstanding that are worth $20 each. It has 1 million shareholders who each own 100 shares. The firm wants to sell $50 million of common stock.
    a. State an argument in favor of a rights offering.
    b. State the arguments in favor of a general cash offer.
26. Suppose GM has decided it needs to raise additional equity. Its investment bankers recommend that GM issue preferred stock because a recent change in tax law has increased the dividends-received deduction. How can GM design the preferred stock issue to be as much like common stock as possible?
27. Explain why the shelf registration process might lead to a more efficient capital market.
28. A rights offering involves the distribution of call options to a firm's shareholders. A transferable put rights offering, discussed in Chapter 17, involves the distribution of put options to shareholders. In what sense are these transactions "mirror images" of one another?

PROBLEMS

LEVEL A (BASIC)

A1. (Book value per share) According to a Microsoft annual report, the firm had $5,333 million of total stockholders' equity, and 588 million common shares outstanding. Calculate Microsoft's book value per common share.

A2. (Book value per share) Portland Trust has a book value of common stockholders' equity of $55,000,000. The firm's financial statements show 2,000,000 authorized shares, 1,000,000 outstanding shares, and 200,000 treasury shares. What is the book value per share?

A3. (Underwriting costs) Green Shoe Company needs to raise $20 million for a new project.

a. It can sell new stock for an estimated price of $24. If the underwriting spread and out-of-pocket expenses will total 9% of the offering price, what will be the net proceeds per share to Green Shoe? How many shares will Green Shoe need to sell to raise its needed funds?

b. It can sell new bonds for an estimated price of $1,010. If the underwriting spread and out-of-pocket expenses will total 3.5% of the offering price, what will be the net proceeds per bond to Green Shoe? How many bonds will Green Shoe need to sell to raise its needed funds?

A4. (Underwriting costs) Eurosport Spas is issuing 1,200,000 shares at an offering price of $20 per share. The management fee is $.25 per share, the underwriting fee is $.25 per share, and the selling concession is $.75 per share.

a. What is the gross underwriting spread per share? What is the total dollar amount of the underwriting costs?

b. What are the gross underwriting costs as a percentage of the offering price?

A5. (Underwriting costs) Suppose RST needs to raise $50 million for a new project.

a. It can sell new stock for an estimated price of $45. If the underwriting spread and out-of-pocket expenses will total 10% of the offering price, what will be the net proceeds per share to RST? How many shares will RST need to sell to raise its needed funds?

b. It can sell new bonds for an estimated price of $1,100. If the underwriting spread and out-of-pocket expenses will total 4% of the offering price, what will be the net proceeds per bond to RST? How many bonds will RST need to sell to raise its needed funds?

A6. (Underwriting costs) Newmart is issuing 1,000,000 shares at an offering price of $40 per share. The management fee is $0.35 per share, the underwriting fee is $0.25 per share, and the selling concession is $0.65 per share.

a. What is the gross underwriting spread per share? What is the total dollar amount of the underwriting costs?

b. What are the gross underwriting costs as a percentage of the offering price?

A7. (Issuing costs) A firm's share price is $30. It has 5 million shares outstanding. When it announces a public offering of 1 million shares of its common stock, its share price falls to $29.

a. Compute the reduction in shareholder wealth that results from the announcement.

b. The firm issues the shares at $29 each. Express the reduction in wealth as a percentage of the gross proceeds of the issue.

c. The gross underwriting spread is 5%. Which factor, the impact of the announcement or the flotation expense, had the greater effect on shareholder wealth?

A8. (Rights issue) Upton Signal Co. has 600,000 outstanding shares with a market value of $40 per share. Upton has announced a rights offering of 200,000 new shares with a subscription price of $30 each.

a. What is the total market value of the firm before the rights offering? What should be the total market value of the firm after the rights issue?

b. How many rights will be needed to purchase a new share?

c. What is the value of one right?

d. What should be the ex-rights price of Upton Signal stock?

A9. (Rights issue) Lowell Corporation has 500,000 outstanding shares with a market value of $50 per share. Lowell has announced a rights offering of 100,000 new shares with a subscription price of $40 each.

a. What is the total market value of the firm before the rights offering? What should be the total market value of the firm after the rights issue?

b. How many rights will be needed to purchase a new share?

c. What is the value of one right?

d. What should be the ex-rights price of Lowell stock?

A10. (Value of a right) Rollins Company common stock is selling for $33.50 per share. Rollins has announced an offer of additional shares of its common stock to current shareholders on the basis of one new share for five rights plus a subscription price of $27.50 per new share.

a. What is the value of one right?

b. What should happen to the stock price when it goes ex-rights?

A11. (Value of a right) When Mammalcloners Company goes ex-rights, the market price per share is expected to drop from $44.50 to $43.25. What is the value of one right?

A12. (Value of a right) When Marble Company goes ex-rights, the market price per share is expected to drop from $33.25 to $32.50. What is the value of one right?

A13. (Cost of private placement versus public offering) Base Metal Company is considering the two debt financing alternatives shown below. What is the cost of funds from each source? (Calculate the yield to maturity assuming semiannual compounding.)

Private placement: 20-year maturity, 8.20% coupon paid semiannually, offering price = 100% of face value, and issuing costs = 1.5% of the offering price.

Public offering: 20-year maturity, 8.00% coupon paid semiannually, offering price = 100% of face value, and issuing costs = 4.0% of the offering price.

A14. (Cost of private placement versus public offering) PlastiCo. is considering the two debt financing alternatives shown below. What is the cost of funds from each source? (Calculate the yield to maturity assuming semiannual compounding.)

Private placement: 15-year maturity, 8% coupon paid semiannually, offering price = 100% of face value, and issuing costs = 2.0% of the offering price.

Public offering: 15-year maturity, 7.25% coupon paid semiannually, offering price = 100% of face value, and issuing costs = 5.0% of the offering price.

LEVEL B

B1. (Flotation costs and cost of preferred stock) A firm is considering issuing preferred stock that bears an 8% dividend rate (payable quarterly). The issue is perpetual. Issuance expenses are 1%.

a. What is the cost of this preferred stock?

b. How does your answer to part a. change if the preferred stock matures in one lump sum after 10 years?

c. How does your answer to part b. change if the issue has a sinking fund calling for equal payments in years 9 and 10?

B2. (Flotation costs and cost of preferred stock) A firm is considering issuing preferred stock that bears a 10% APR dividend rate (payable quarterly). The issue is perpetual. Issuance expenses are 2%.

a. What is the cost of this preferred stock?

b. How does your answer to part a. change if the preferred stock matures in one lump sum after eight years?

c. How does your answer to part b. change if the issue has a sinking fund calling for equal payments in years 7 and 8?

B3. (Book value of equity) Your friend has asked your help in calculating book value per common share. The balance sheet contains the information shown below. There is a 3% preferred stock liquidation premium. Compute the book value per common share.

Total shareholders' equity	$37.415 billion
Preferred stock	$554 million
Authorized common shares	2 billion
Issued common shares	1.813 billion
Treasury shares	571 million

B4. (Public offering versus rights issue) Consider a firm about to make a new equity issue. The firm feels it can make either a public offering or a rights issue to all existing shareholders. The firm wants to raise $14.4 million, net new equity capital. The current share price is $30, with 3 million shares outstanding. Under plan I, a public offering would be made as follows: 576,000 new shares would be underwritten at a market price of $26 per share and a net price to the firm of $25 per share. Theoretically, after the issue is completed, the market price per share will be $29.195. Under plan II, a rights offering (one right per share issued to each current shareholder) would be made with the following features: 1 million new shares would be sold at $15 each, and three rights would be necessary to buy each share. Total flotation costs would be $600,000 for plan II. Theoretically, after the issue is completed, the market price per share should be $26.10. Assuming that the firm's actual goal is to maximize shareholder wealth, which of these plans would be better, and why?

B5. (Rights issue) The A.B. Sea Company wishes to raise \$100 million through a rights offering. It has 70 million shares outstanding, trading at \$25 per share. It wishes each right to be worth at least \$0.20 initially.

a. Find the subscription price and subscription ratio.

b. After the offering commences, the shares trade at a price of \$23 per share. What is the value of one right?

c. In what situations is a rights offering more appropriate than a general public offering?

d. What is the principal drawback to a rights offering?

B6. (Cost of new equity) A stock's current market price is \$40. The expected annual cash dividend is \$2 per share. In addition, investors expect the firm to pay a 6% dividend in common stock. The expected growth rate of the cash dividend is 5% per year.

a. Calculate the cost of retained earnings.

b. If a new share issue would require 7% flotation costs, what is the cost of the new issue?

B7. (Cost of preferred stock) A perpetual preferred stock issue can be sold for \$35 per share. It would require a quarterly dividend rate of \$0.60 per share. The underwriting fees and out-of-pocket expenses amount to 3% of the public offering price. What is the cost of preferred stock?

B8. (Review, leveraged cost of equity) A stock's unleveraged beta is 0.8. The firm's debt ratio is $L = D/(D + E) = 0.4$. The riskless return is 5%, and the expected return on the market portfolio is 15%. What is the firm's cost of equity capital?

B9. (Dilution) Consider again the dilution in percentage ownership example, the Reliable Fabrics example in the section on dilution. Suppose Reliable needs to raise \$650,000 to finance a project with an NPV of \$200,000.

a. How will the announcement of the project affect Reliable's share price?

b. How many shares will Reliable have to sell to raise \$650,000?

c. What has happened to your wealth?

d. Is there a direct connection between the change in percentage ownership and the change in shareholder wealth?

B10. (Dilution) Consider again the dilution in percentage ownership example, the Reliable Fabrics example in the section on dilution. Suppose Reliable will invest the new issue proceeds in a project with a zero NPV. But in order to sell the shares, Reliable will have to offer them at \$10 each.

a. How will the announcement of the new issue affect Reliable's share price?

b. How will the new issue affect your wealth?

c. What conclusion can you draw about the effect on shareholder wealth of selling shares for less than their market value? Is this conclusion related to the change in percentage ownership?

B11. (Dilution) A common stockholder owns 30% of a firm's 1 million outstanding shares. The firm plans to sell 200,000 new shares.

a. By how much is the stockholder's percentage ownership diluted if the firm sells all the shares to new investors?

b. How should the stockholder maintain her 30% ownership interest?

B12. (Cost of preferred stock) A perpetual preferred stock issue can be sold for \$25 per share. It would require a quarterly dividend rate of \$0.50 per share. The underwriting fees and out-of-pocket expenses amount to 1.75% of the public offering price. What is the cost of preferred stock?

B13. (Dilution) Look back at Table 18.6. Suppose International Nickel instead earns a 14% rate of return on book equity.

a. Calculate the firm's earnings and EPS.

b. Suppose the project has a positive NPV, and the firm earns a 16% rate of return on the equity it invests in the project. Calculate earnings and EPS.

c. Suppose the project has a negative NPV, and the firms earns a 12% rate of return on the project equity. Calculate earnings and EPS.

B14. (Dilution) Public Service Company of New York has 20,000,000 common shares outstanding. Its share price is $30. Book value per share is $50. Public Service plans to raise an additional $100 million by selling shares. It will invest the proceeds in a new electric generating plant. Its regulators allow Public Service to earn a 10% rate of return on equity.

a. Suppose the project has a $10 million NPV. Investors are aware of this at the time of the offering. What happens to market value per share, book value per share, and EPS?

b. Redo part a. assuming project NPV is −$20 million.

c. Public Service currently has 10,000 shareholders who own equal numbers of shares. All the additional shares will be sold to new investors. Calculate the dilution in percentage ownership in parts a. and b.

d. Which measure of dilution, if any, indicates a change in shareholder wealth?

LEVEL C (ADVANCED)

C1. (Rights offering) Several years ago, Time Warner Inc. announced an innovative rights offering, which proved controversial among the firm's shareholders. Time Warner stated that it would distribute transferable rights to purchase approximately 34,450,000 shares. Each Time Warner shareholder would receive 0.6 right for each Time Warner share held. Each full right would entitle the holder to purchase one Time Warner share at a subscription price of $105. Any shares unsubscribed for when the offering terminated would be distributed pro rata among subscribers at no additional cost to them. However, Time Warner would complete the offering only if at least 60% of the rights were exercised (and the shares purchased for cash).

a. If only 60% of the shares were purchased for cash, and the rest distributed for free, what would be the effective subscription price?

b. Express the share price ex-rights (P_E) in terms of the share price rights-on (P_R), the fraction of a right distributed for each share (F), and the exercise value of one right (R).

c. If the fraction of rights that will be exercised (G) is known with certainty, express the share price ex-rights in terms of the share price rights-on, the subscription price (S), the fraction F, and the fraction G.

d. Use the expressions in parts b. and c. to obtain an expression for the intrinsic value of one right.

e. Some institutional investors said they found the structure of the offering a "brilliant coercive measure." How would you explain this reaction?

MINICASE LUCENT TECHNOLOGIES' IPO

When AT&T Corp. announced that it intended to separate into three firms—telecommunications services, telecommunications equipment, and computers—it also announced its plan to create a new firm, Lucent Technologies Inc., which would operate AT&T's former telecommunications equipment business. Lucent would design, develop, and manufacture a wide range of communications networks and software, consumer and business telephone systems, and microelectronic components. AT&T planned to take Lucent public within the coming year and then distribute the remaining shares of Lucent to its own stockholders through a tax-free spin-off later in the year.

Subsequently, AT&T announced it would offer for sale 112 million shares (about 18%) of Lucent's stock. AT&T projected an offering price from $22 to $25 per share. At $23.50 per share, the Lucent IPO would raise $2.6 billion and become the largest IPO ever in the United States.

Pricing the IPO would be difficult because Lucent was at the beginning of a potentially stressful period. It had taken a $2.8 billion pretax restructuring charge in its first year, which resulted in a loss of $867 million. The restructuring would cut 23,000 jobs. Also, the spin-off would sever the umbilical cord to its financially stronger parent. Finally, Lucent's business was becoming increasingly competitive.

The table below provides financial information about Lucent, AT&T, and three comparable publicly traded firms at the time of the offering, which securities underwriters might use to price an IPO.

				MARKET VALUE			LATEST 12 MONTHS				
FIRM	STOCK LISTED	NUMBER OF SHARES OUTSTANDING	CLOSING PRICE	Common Equity	Preferred Equity	Long-Term Debt	Earnings Per Share	EBITDA[a]	PROJECTED ANNUAL EARNINGS PER SHARE	BOOK VALUE OF EQUITY	INDICATED ANNUAL DIVIDEND RATE[b]
Lucent Technologies	NYSE[c]	637	—	—	—	$ 3,965	$1.56[d]	$3,457	$1.62	$ 2,329	$0.30[c]
AT&T	NYSE	1,596	$64.125	$102,344	—	11,635	2.71[e]	6,060	3.71	18,001	1.32
British Telecommunications[f]	NYSE	623	57.00	35,511	—	5,330	5.00	8,445	4.97	20,170	3.95
Cable & Wireless[g]	NYSE	733	24.25	17,775	—	1,362	1.30	2,319	1.19	6,025	0.70
Northern Telecom	NYSE	256	49.75	12,736	$73	1,236	1.93	277	2.43	4,454	0.44

[a]EBITDA = Earnings Before Interest, Taxes, Depreciation, and Amortization.
[b]Calculated by multiplying the latest quarterly dividend rate by 4 or the latest semiannual rate by 2.
[c]Planned.
[d]Before a $1.85 billion after-tax restructuring charge.
[e]Before a $4.18 billion after-tax restructuring charge.
[f]Per-share amounts are expressed in terms of American Depository Receipts (ADRs) (1 ADR = 10 shares).
[g]Per-share amounts are expressed in terms of ADRs (1 ADR = 3 shares).
Sources: Bloomberg, L. P., and *Value Line Investment Survey.*

QUESTIONS

1. For each of the comparable firms, calculate the
   a. price/earnings ratio based on the latest 12 months earnings per share
   b. price/earnings ratio based on the projected annual earnings per share
   c. ratio of total market value (equity plus debt) to EBITDA
   d. book value per share, market-to-book ratio, and annual dividend yield
2. Make each of the requested calculations in question 1 for Lucent, assuming a share price of (i) $20, (ii) $25, and (iii) $30.
3. Which price/earnings ratio do you think is more meaningful in an efficient market, one based on the latest 12 months earnings per share, or one based on projected annual earnings per share? Explain.
4. Underwriters say they attempt to price an IPO 10% to 15% below the expected trading price. Based on this and the calculations you made in questions 1 and 2, estimate a price for Lucent's IPO.

APPENDIX
EVALUATING THE MERITS OF INNOVATIVE FINANCING

Investment bankers spend considerable time and effort trying to come up with valuable new securities ideas. As you may know, when investment bankers develop new securities, they generally give them cute names (built on an acronym). The list includes LYONs, TIGRs, PRIDES, PERCS, SPINs, DECS, SABRES, SIGNs, and many more.

The rapid pace of securities innovation has produced an almost overwhelming number of financing instruments. Some of these new instruments include complex and difficult-to-evaluate options structures. Confronted with the choice among existing financing alternatives and yet another innovative security, managers must try to strip away the veneer and determine whether the bankers' claim that the new security is valuable is valid.

In addition to pursuing valuable ideas, two important developments account for the revolution in securities innovation. First, the investment banking business has become more competitive. Developing an innovative security provides an opportunity for the developer to solicit business from firms that have been using other investment bankers. It usually also enables the innovator to obtain the mandate to market the new security on a negotiated basis, rather than having to bid for securities.

Second, inflation rates and interest rates have become more volatile, tax changes have become more frequent, and regulatory changes have become more profound as a result of deregulation. Financial innovation is, at least in part, a response to the changing economic and financial environment. For example, increased interest rate volatility led to the development of adjustable-rate preferred stock—and a series of refinements—designed to eliminate the exposure of the securityholder's principal to interest rate changes.

A new security is truly valuable only if it enables an investor to realize a higher after-tax risk-adjusted return, or an issuer a lower after-tax required return, than with previously existing securities. Just being different is not enough. There must be real value to the issuing firm's shareholders. A new security could accomplish this by creating a pattern of risk-return combinations that investors could not have achieved previously, thereby making the financial markets more *complete.* A new security could also reduce taxes, reduce transaction costs, or resolve information asymmetries, thereby lessening the valuation impact of market imperfections.

Sources of Value Added

A new security can enhance shareholder value in any of the following ways:

1. The lower the after-tax required return is, compared to that for conventional securities, the greater the value to the firm. The lower the required return is, the higher is the price the firm can get for the security.

   If a firm can repackage a payment stream—create a new type of security—so that it either involves less risk, or reallocates risk from one class of investors to another that is less risk sensitive, shareholder value will be enhanced because the firm will pay a smaller risk premium. Collateralized mortgage obligations (CMOs) are an example. CMOs include multiple classes of claims against a pool of mortgages. The different classes of securities that make up the CMO package are prioritized with respect to their right to receive principal payments from the underlying mortgage portfolio. For example, class A might get the first priority, giving it a very short average life, and class Z might have the lowest priority, giving it a very long average life (because all prior classes have to be paid off before class Z holders receive anything).
2. The smaller the percentage underwriting commissions and other expenses, the greater the value to the firm. Lower transaction costs increase the *net* proceeds the firm gets. If

a firm can structure a new issue so that underwriting commissions are reduced, shareholder value will be enhanced. Extendible notes are an example. Their maturity can be extended by mutual agreement of issuer and investors, effectively rolling over the notes without additional underwriting commissions.

3. The lower the agency costs associated with a particular security, the greater the market value of the firm, if all else is equal. If a firm can structure a new security to reduce agency costs, shareholder wealth can be enhanced. For example, interest rate reset notes protect bondholders against a deterioration in the issuer's credit standing prior to the reset date. The interest rate is reset automatically if the rating agencies reduce the rating they assign to the notes. Under the Principle of Capital Market Efficiency, without such protection we would expect bondholders to increase their required return to compensate for this risk. Due to asymmetric information, they might charge a significant risk premium even if management has no intention of engaging in such things as *asset substitution.* Interest rate reset notes would be mutually advantageous in that case.
4. The smaller the holders' tax liability associated with the new security, the greater the value to the firm. If a firm can structure a new security to reduce investor taxes without increasing corporate income taxes, shareholder value will be enhanced as a result of this tax arbitrage. For example, a firm that is currently not a taxpayer can create such an arbitrage by issuing adjustable-rate preferred stock in lieu of commercial paper. Industrial firms and banking institutions that have large tax loss carryforwards have accounted for a high percentage of adjustable-rate preferred stock issues. Both adjustable-rate preferred stock and commercial paper are purchased by corporate money managers, but preferred stock dividends are more valuable to a corporation than interest payments because the corporation is tax exempt on 70% of the dividends it receives. Consequently, adjustable-rate preferred stock carries a lower pretax yield than similarly rated commercial paper.
5. The greater the corporate tax shield, all else equal, the greater the market value of the firm. If a firm can structure a new security to increase the present value of tax shields available to the issuer or to reduce the issuer's income tax liability without simultaneously increasing the investors' tax liabilities, shareholder value will again be enhanced through tax arbitrage. For example, selling zero-coupon bonds to tax-exempt investors before the Tax Equity and Fiscal Responsibility Act of 1982 (TEFRA) resulted in such an arbitrage because the issuer could deduct the original issue discount on a straight-line basis, that is, faster than interest on the notes implicitly compounded. TEFRA changed the method of amortization to the scientific interest method, as interest implicitly compounds, and eliminated this arbitrage opportunity.

Other reasons are often given to explain securities innovations. Examples include a desire to achieve a particular accounting treatment or a particular regulatory treatment. The value added by innovations introduced only for their accounting advantages is highly suspect. An efficient capital market can see through accounting transformations to determine the true financial benefits, if any, arising out of a new financial instrument.

The Evolution of Adjustable-Rate Preferred Stock

As we just noted, corporate cash managers have a tax incentive to purchase preferred stock rather than commercial paper or other short-term debt instruments. Nontaxable corporate issuers find preferred stock cheaper than debt because corporate investors are willing to pass back part of the value of the tax arbitrage by accepting a lower dividend rate.

Purchasing long-term, fixed-dividend-rate preferred stock, however, exposes the purchaser to interest rate risk. A variety of preferred stock instruments have been designed to deal with this problem.

Adjustable-rate preferred stock was designed to reduce interest rate risk by adjusting the dividend rate as interest rates change. The dividend rate adjusts according to a formula specifying a fixed margin over the maximum of three specified Treasury yields.[6] Despite the dividend adjustment, other risk continued to cause significant deviations in value of the security.

Convertible adjustable preferred stock (CAPS) was designed to eliminate this deficiency by making the security convertible on each dividend payment date into enough shares of common stock (or the equivalent value in cash) to make the security worth its par value. Although CAPS generally traded closer to their respective face amounts than adjustable-rate preferred stocks, there have been few such issues. Issuer reluctance may have stemmed from the security's conversion feature, which could force the issuer to issue common stock or raise a large amount of cash on short notice.

Auction-rate preferred stock carried the evolutionary process a step further. The dividend rate is reset by Dutch auction every seven weeks, which represents just enough time to meet the 46-day holding period required to qualify for the 70% dividends-received deduction. There are various versions of auction-rate preferred stock that are sold under different acronyms, such as MMP (Money Market Preferred) and AMPS (Auction Market Preferred Stock), coined by the different securities firms that offer the product. Although the names differ, the securities are the same.

In an effort to further refine the adjustable-rate preferred stock, there have been at least two attempts to design a superior security, but only one was successful. *Single-point adjustable-rate stock* (SPARS) has a dividend rate that adjusts automatically every 49 days to a specified percentage of the 60-day high-grade commercial paper rate. The security is designed so as to afford the same degree of liquidity as auction-rate preferred stock, but with lower transaction costs because no auction need be held. The problem with SPARS, however, is that the fixed-dividend-rate formula involves a potential agency cost that auction-rate preferred stock does not. Because the dividend formula is fixed, investors will suffer a loss if the issuer's credit standing falls. Primarily for this reason, there have been only two SPARS issues.

Remarketed preferred stock, by contrast, pays a dividend that is reset at the end of each dividend period to a dividend rate that a specified remarketing agent determines will make the preferred stock worth par. Such issues permit the issuer considerable flexibility in selecting the length of the dividend period (it can be as short as one day). Remarketed preferred also offers greater flexibility in selecting the other terms of the issue. In fact, each share of an issue could have a different maturity, dividend rate, or other terms, provided the issuer and holders so agree. Remarketed preferred has not proven as popular with issuers as auction-rate preferred stock, but that could change due to the greater flexibility remarketed preferred affords.

Variable cumulative preferred stock was born out of the controversy over whether auction-rate preferred stock or remarketed preferred stock results in more equitable pricing. This variation effectively allows the issuer to decide at the beginning of each dividend period which of the two reset methods will determine the dividend rate at the beginning of the next dividend period.

QUESTIONS

1. When is a new security truly valuable to the issuer's shareholders?
2. What is the difference between adjustable-rate preferred stock and auction-rate preferred stock?
3. What are the relative advantages of auction-rate preferred stock and remarketed preferred stock?
4. What is the principal drawback to convertible adjustable preferred stock?
5. What are the primary incentives for financial innovation?

---

[6]There is a short-term Treasury yield (usually the three-month bill yield), an intermediate-term yield (usually the 10-year yield), and a long-term bond yield (generally the 30-year yield).

LEVEL B PROBLEMS

1. (Adjustable-rate preferred stock dividends) An issue of adjustable-rate preferred stock pays a dividend rate per annum equal to 100 basis points plus the greatest of (1) the three-month Treasury bill yield, (2) the 10-year Treasury yield, and (3) the 30-year Treasury bond yield.
   a. The three-month Treasury bill yield is 8.00% (on a bond-equivalent-yield basis); the 10-year Treasury yield is 8.50%; and the 30-year Treasury yield is 8.70%. What is the annual dividend rate?
   b. The issue pays dividends quarterly. The par value is $100 per share. What is the quarterly dividend for the next quarter?
2. (Zero-coupon debt) Suppose GE sells a five-year zero-coupon debt issue. The principal amount is $1,000 per bond. The yield to maturity is 12% (annual).
   a. Compute the annual interest deductions for tax purposes. [Hint: interest compounds annually.]
   b. Compute the annual interest deductions assuming GE can deduct the original issue discount on a straight-line basis.
   c. Why is the straight-line method more valuable to GE? Can you quantify the value of the straight-line method? What is the source of this value?

LONG-TERM DEBT

19

No doubt you have borrowed money before. If you have a credit card, you borrow money each time you use it. The card issuer pays the merchant, and you must repay the card issuer. If you always pay when you are billed, the loans are *interest free*. You simply repay the amount you borrowed; no interest is charged. If you do not pay right away, however, you begin to owe interest.

Credit card loans are easy to arrange. (Maybe that is why there is so much credit card debt in the United States![1]) You do not have to sign a new loan agreement each time you use the card. But you did enter into a form of loan agreement when your application was approved. The agreement has a lot of fine print, which spells out the loan terms. (Have you ever read it?) For example, it tells you the interest rate and how interest is calculated.

You may have also entered into more formal, longer-term loan arrangements. Do you have student loans to pay part of the cost of your education? Have you borrowed to buy a car? Perhaps you have, or soon will take out, a mortgage loan to buy a house. Borrowing money is something individuals normally do. So do firms.

When a firm decides to borrow, it must decide several things. Should the debt have a fixed or a variable interest rate? When should it mature? Should it include a sinking fund that will retire it in installments? Should the firm retain a call option so that it can call in the debt and refund it if interest rates drop? Would international debt financing be better than domestic debt? These are a few of the points we discuss in this chapter.

---

[1]About $700 billion recently, according to the Federal Reserve Board.

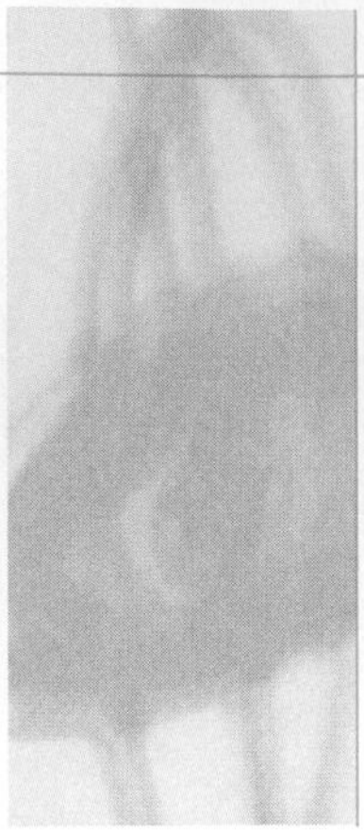

FOCUS ON PRINCIPLES

- *Self-Interested Behavior:* Look for the most advantageous ways to finance the firm, such as the lowest-cost debt alternative.
- *Two-Sided Transactions:* Set a price and other terms that investors will find acceptable when issuing securities.
- *Signaling:* Recognize that announcing the firm's decision to issue securities conveys information about the firm.
- *Risk-Return Trade-Off:* Recognize that riskier securities must offer investors a higher expected return.
- *Capital Market Efficiency:* Use the market value of a firm's securities as the best measure of their value.
- *Options:* Recognize the value of a bond's call option. It is valuable because it enables the issuing firm to redeem the debt and replace it at a lower cost if interest rates drop. Bond put options are valuable to the bondholder.
- *Valuable Ideas:* Look for ways to reduce financing costs by creating innovative securities that reduce issuing costs and/or raise investors' risk-adjusted after-tax returns.
- *Comparative Advantage:* Contract with underwriters to bear the risk in issuing securities if they can bear that risk more cheaply.
- *Incremental Benefits:* Calculate the net advantage of leasing versus borrowing and buying, as well as the net advantage to refunding a bond, on the basis of the incremental after-tax benefits the transaction will produce.
- *Time Value of Money:* Use discounted cash flow analysis to compare the costs and benefits of financing decisions, such as alternative securities to sell, lease versus borrow and buy, and bond refunding.

19.1 TYPES OF LONG-TERM DEBT

There are four main classes of long-term corporate debt: secured, unsecured, tax-exempt, and convertible. We will cover the first three here. The fourth class, convertible debt, is discussed in Chapter 21, Derivatives and Hedging.

Secured Debt

Secured debt is backed by specific assets. This backing reduces the lenders' risk and, therefore, the bonds' required return. Mortgage bonds, collateral trust bonds, equipment trust certificates, and conditional sales contracts are the most common types of secured debt.

MORTGAGE BONDS **Mortgage bonds** are secured by a lien on specific assets of the issuer. The assets are described in detail in the legal document, called a *mortgage,* that grants the lien. If the issuer defaults—fails to make a required payment—or fails to perform some other provision of the loan contract, lenders can seize the assets that secure the mortgage bonds and sell them to pay off the debt obligation. The extra protection the mortgage provides lowers the risk and, in turn, lowers the required return. But the issuer sacrifices flexibility in selling assets. The assets can be sold only with the mortgage bondholders' permission or with suitable replacement collateral.

COLLATERAL TRUST BONDS Collateral trust bonds are similar to mortgage bonds except that the lien is against securities, such as common shares of one of the issuer's subsidiaries, rather than against real property such as plant and equipment.

EQUIPMENT TRUST CERTIFICATES AND CONDITIONAL SALES CONTRACTS Equipment trust certificates and conditional sales contracts are frequently issued to finance the purchase of aircraft or railroad engines and cars. The two financing mechanisms are similar. The borrower obtains title to the assets only after it fully repays the debt.

Unsecured Debt

Unsecured long-term debt consists of notes and debentures. By the securities industry convention, **notes** are unsecured debt with an original maturity of 10 years or less. **Debentures** are unsecured debt with an original maturity greater than 10 years. Notes and debentures are issued on the strength of the issuer's general credit. A financial contract (the bond indenture) specifies their terms. They are not secured by specific property. If the issuer goes bankrupt, noteholders and debentureholders are classified as general creditors.

Debentures may have different levels of seniority. *Subordinated debentures* rank behind more *senior debentures* in payment of interest and principal, and in claims on the firm's assets in the event of bankruptcy. This subordinated position exposes lenders to greater risk. Subordinated debentures therefore have a higher required return than senior debt of the same firm.

Tax-Exempt Corporate Debt

Under the Internal Revenue Code, firms can issue tax-exempt bonds for specified purposes. Congress grants tax-exempt bonding authority from time to time to encourage investment in specified types of projects that are in the public interest. The Tax Reform Act of 1986 sharply reduced the list of activities that qualify for tax-exempt financing. Activities that still qualified following that act include solid waste disposal and hazardous waste disposal facilities.

When a project qualifies for tax-exempt financing, holders of the tax-exempt bonds do not have to pay federal income tax on the interest payments they receive. Consequently, they are willing to accept a lower interest rate than on taxable debt. This creates a tax asymmetry. As a general rule, if a firm plans to construct facilities that qualify for tax-exempt financing, it should use such financing to the maximum extent.

Review

1. What are the four main classes of long-term corporate debt?
2. What is the difference between secured and unsecured debt?
3. Why is issuing tax-exempt debt beneficial to a firm (when a project qualifies for it)?

19.2 MAIN FEATURES OF LONG-TERM DEBT

Long-term debt issues (initial maturity of one year or greater) have several common features:

- *Stated maturity.* This is the date the borrower must repay the money it borrowed.
- *Stated principal amount.* This is the amount the borrower must repay.
- *Stated coupon rate of interest.* The interest rate is usually a fixed rate, but it can be a variable rate that is adjusted according to a specified formula.
- *Mandatory redemption* (or *sinking fund*) *schedule.* Some bonds contain a sinking fund, whereas others are repaid in a single sum at maturity. A sinking fund involves a sequence of principal repayments prior to the maturity date. Bonds are redeemed in cash at their face amount or else

through capital market purchases.[2] The purpose of a sinking fund is to spread out the redemption of the bond over time to decrease the likelihood of default.

- *Optional redemption provision.* The issuer has the right to call the issue (or some portion of it) for early redemption. A schedule of optional redemption prices is specified at the time of issue. Callable bonds usually provide for a grace period immediately following issuance. Bonds are *noncallable* during this period. Many long-term issues contain a weaker provision. The bonds are only *nonrefundable.* This means that the issuer can call and redeem the bonds for cash or the proceeds from an equity issue (or in some cases, out of the proceeds of a junior debt issue). However, during the nonrefundable period, the issuer cannot use the proceeds from a new debt issue that ranks senior to, or on a par with, the outstanding debt to refund the issue.

Protective Covenants

Debt issues contain **covenants** that impose restrictions on the long-term bond issuer. They are contained in a financial contract that is designed to protect the bondholders. For public debt issues, this contract is called a *bond indenture.* A trustee acts as agent for the bondholders and monitors the issuer's compliance with the provisions of the indenture. For a private issue, the contract is called a *bond agreement* or *note agreement.* These contracts specify the maturity, interest rate, and other terms mentioned earlier. In many cases they include a number of restrictive covenants. The covenants often spell out financial tests that must be met before the borrower can (1) incur additional indebtedness (*debt limitation*), (2) use cash to pay dividends or make share repurchases (*dividend limitation*), (3) mortgage assets (*limitation on liens* and/or a *negative pledge clause*), (4) borrow through one of its subsidiaries (*limitation on subsidiary borrowing*), (5) sell major assets (*limitation on asset dispositions*), (6) merge with another firm or sell substantially all its assets to another firm (*limitation on merger, consolidation,* or *sale*), or (7) sell assets and lease them back (*limitation on sale and leaseback*).

EXAMPLE Debt Covenants

A debt limitation covenant prohibits a borrower from issuing additional long-term debt if it would cause the issuer's interest coverage ratio (EBIT to total interest) to fall below 3.00 times (an *interest coverage test*), or if it would cause its ratio of tangible assets to long-term debt to fall below 1.50 times (an *asset coverage test*). A dividend covenant restricts cash dividends or share repurchases to $10,000,000 plus 50% of cumulative earnings (less the cumulative amount already used for this purpose) since the date of issuance of the bonds.[3]

Any covenant can restrict the firm's flexibility. For example, the interest coverage test can restrict its ability to issue new debt. Suppose the firm's earnings before interest and taxes (EBIT) are $39 million, and interest is $10 million. How much additional 6% debt can the firm incur without reducing the interest coverage ratio to below 3.00?

If interest expense rises to $13 million, interest coverage will be 3.00 times (= 39/13). The extra $3 million (= 13 − 10) of interest will allow the firm to issue $50 million (= 3/0.06) of debt.

---

[2]If the bonds are selling at or above par value, the firm will call individual bonds that have been chosen randomly and pay the owner the par value. If the bonds are selling below par value, the indenture usually permits the firm to repurchase bonds in the open market to satisfy the sinking fund requirement.

[3]See Chapter 13 for a discussion of the use of bond covenants to control agency costs.

Events of Default

Bond indentures and bond agreements also specify **events of default.** If the issuer fails to pay interest or repay principal promptly, defaults on another debt issue, or fails to adhere to one of the covenants, the lenders can demand immediate repayment of the debt. Often, however, bondholders will try to negotiate before pursuing default proceedings, because they usually do not want to take ownership of the firm.

Review

1. What are the main features of long-term debt instruments?
2. What is a sinking fund schedule? What is its main purpose?
3. What is an optional redemption schedule? Why is it valuable to a firm?
4. What are bond covenants? What is their main purpose?

19.3 DESIGNING A LONG-TERM DEBT ISSUE

Firms that wish to borrow must offer attractive debt opportunities to potential lenders. Borrowers design the terms of their long-term debt. The Principle of Two-Sided Transactions applies here. The issuer's choices are guided by how much compensation investors will require for the package of features selected.

Choice of Debt Maturity

Ideally, a firm would choose a debt maturity that causes its outflow obligations to be in line with its expected inflows. This would bring the total debt service stream into line with its projected total operating cash flow stream. A debt repayment schedule that bunches the firm's debt repayment obligations within a few brief periods involves greater insolvency risk than a debt repayment schedule that spreads these repayment obligations over a longer period. But the matching does not have to be exact. For example, if the firm is rapidly growing or changing in significant ways (such as improving profitability), issuing shorter-maturity debt will allow it to renegotiate its debt contract in the future after its financial condition has improved.

SIGNIFICANCE OF INCLUDING A SINKING FUND A sinking fund requires the firm to repay the debt in installments, rather than in a lump sum. It has two important consequences. First, the need to make principal repayments creates a monitoring device. Second, a sinking fund shortens the bond issue's effective maturity from its stated maturity. The firm is not borrowing all the money for the entire life of the issue.

For example, suppose a debt issue that matures in 10 years requires equal sinking fund payments at the end of years 6 through 10. Therefore, only one fifth of the issue is actually borrowed for the entire 10 years. One fifth is borrowed for only six years. This issue has what might be thought of as an effective maturity of eight years. On a time-weighted basis, the debt will be repaid in an average of eight years. This effective maturity is called **average life.** The formula for average life is

$$\text{Average life} = \frac{\sum_{t=1}^{N} tA_t}{\sum_{t=1}^{N} A_t} \tag{19.1}$$

where A_t is the sinking fund payment due t periods from the date of issue.

Average life uses the sinking fund payments as weights in its weighted average. Many professionals make two adjustments to this calculation. They use the total cash flow (principal *plus* interest), and they calculate the present value of each payment and use these present values as the weights. The result is called the bond's **duration.** The formula for duration is

$$\text{Duration} = \frac{1}{P}\sum_{t=1}^{N}\frac{t\,CF_t}{(1+y)^t} \tag{19.2}$$

where P is the bond's price, CF_t is the total cash flow from the bond at t (principal plus interest), and y is the yield per time period. The t in the numerator measures the length of time (number of periods) until CF_t will be received. Duration is the present-value-weighted average number of interest periods until the bond "matures." For a bond that pays semiannual interest, divide the APR yield by 2, and also divide the duration calculated in Equation (19.2) by 2 to express it in years.

EXAMPLE Calculating Duration

A bond pays semiannual interest at 10% APR. It has a sinking fund that repays $50 million each at the end of years 4 and 5. Total principal is $100 million. The bond's yield to maturity is 9% APR. Calculate the bond's duration.

First calculate the cash flows. There are 10 interest periods. For the first seven periods, the bond pays interest only. Thus $CF_1 = CF_2 = \ldots. = CF_7 = \$5.0$ million [= 100(0.10/2)]. The bond pays principal at the end of period 8, so $CF_8 = \$55.0$ million. That leaves $50 million of principal remaining, so $CF_9 = \$2.5$ million [= 50(0.10/2)], and $CF_{10} = \$52.5$ million. Using the yield to maturity, the bond's price is

$$P = \sum_{t=1}^{10}\frac{CF_t}{(1.045)^t} = \$103.63 \text{ million}$$

Using Equation (19.2), the bond's duration is

$$\begin{aligned}
\text{Duration} &= \frac{1}{103.63}\sum_{t=1}^{10}\frac{t\,CF_t}{(1+y)^t} \\
&= \frac{1}{103.63}\left[\frac{5}{(1.045)^1}+\frac{10}{(1.045)^2}+\frac{15}{(1.045)^3}+\frac{20}{(1.045)^4}+\frac{25}{(1.045)^5}\right] \\
&\quad + \frac{1}{103.63}\left[\frac{30}{(1.045)^6}+\frac{35}{(1.045)^7}+\frac{440}{(1.045)^8}+\frac{22.5}{(1.045)^9}+\frac{525}{(1.045)^{10}}\right] \\
&= 7.48 \text{ periods}
\end{aligned}$$

With six-month periods, the duration is 3.74 years [= 7.48/2]. Note that the average life of the issue is 4.5 years. Duration is a better measure of the average timing of the bond's total cash flows.

MAXIMUM MATURITY Maturities can vary widely and have gotten longer within the past few years. Some firms have issued debt with 40- and 50-year maturities. The Coca-Cola Company even issued 100-year debentures.

Setting the Coupon Rate

Most debt issuers select a coupon rate that will make the bonds worth par. However, at times tax or other factors can make it advantageous either to set the coupon rate below the prevailing market rate or to let the interest rate float according to some specified formula.

DEEP-DISCOUNT BONDS When interest rates were very high by historical standards, many firms issued *deep-discount bonds.* These bonds carried very low interest rates and were sold at prices well below their principal amounts. For example, Du Pont sold $600 million principal amount of 6% 20-year debentures at a price of 46.852% ($468.52 per $1,000 bond). Because *zero-coupon bonds* make only a single payment at maturity, they are the deepest-discount bonds possible. For example, Beatrice Foods sold $250 million principal amount of 10-year zero-coupon notes at a price of 25.50%.

Some investors, particularly pension funds, found the deep-discount bonds and zero-coupon bonds attractive. The bonds generally have a call price equal to their par value. Unless the bonds have a call price schedule well below their par value, it is unlikely that a firm would ever exercise its call option. Although a reduced risk of a call benefits the bondholders, it is of course at the expense of the issuer's refunding flexibility.

The discount also reduces the lender's reinvestment risk. In the case of a zero-coupon bond, the investor's "income" each period is effectively reinvested at the issue's yield to maturity, regardless of what interest rates are at the time. This protects the investor's total return from interest rate movements between the dates of issuance and maturity. The absence of reinvestment risk also enables investors such as pension funds to match their investment income against future liabilities more closely than they could with alternative investments. This feature is more valuable at higher interest rates.

Issuers also found the deep-discount bonds and zero-coupon bonds attractive because of a tax asymmetry. At one time, issuers were permitted to deduct an equal portion of the discount (the difference between par value and the issue price) each period. Thus, interest could be deducted at a faster rate than it accrued. This feature is more valuable at higher bond yields. It substantially reduced the effective after-tax cost of the debt. Because most purchasers of zero-coupon bonds were tax exempt, the manner of amortizing the discount did not affect them.

FIXING THE COUPON RATE OR LETTING IT FLOAT Banks and finance firms earn returns on assets that fluctuate with interest rate movements. They often find it best to issue floating-rate long-term debt.

Most other firms choose to fix the interest rate on long-term debt issues. They adjust the mix of fixed- and floating-rate debt by altering the mix of short-term bank debt and commercial paper on the one hand, and fixed-rate longer-term debt on the other. Before deciding whether to issue floating-rate intermediate- or long-term debt, a firm should at least compare the prospective terms for such an issue against the following alternatives:

- Issuing a sequence of shorter-term issues, whose successive maturities match the successive interest rate adjustment dates
- Issuing fixed-rate debt that matures the day the floating-rate issue does

In the first case, the sequence of shorter-term issues will involve roughly the same degree of interest-rate risk as the longer-term floating-rate issue. The sequence of shorter-term issues will involve greater issuance expenses than the longer-term floating-rate issue. In the second case, the floating-rate issue exposes the issuer to the risk that interest rates will change. Because of this, it is not surprising that industrial firms generally borrow long term on a fixed-rate basis to fund investments in fixed assets. By contrast, when the issuer's revenues are sensitive to movements in interest rates, borrowing on a floating-rate basis may actually reduce the firm's financial risk by aligning the fluctuations in revenues and interest expense.

Setting the Optional Redemption Provisions

The optional redemption provision is a call option that gives the issuer the right to buy back the issue. Setting the optional redemption provisions involves two questions: Should the issue include a call option? If so, what form should it take? In a perfect capital market environment, an issuer would not derive any net benefit from including a call provision, because lenders would require a yield premium sufficient to compensate them fully for the risk of a call. However, market imperfections might make a call provision advantageous in some situations. **Bond refunding** is replacing an outstanding bond before its maturity with a new bond. When current interest rates are below the fixed interest rate on the outstanding bond, refunding may be profitable.

DESIGN OF CALL PROVISIONS The call provision included in corporate debt issues has become highly standardized. The first year's call price is normally equal to the public offering price plus the coupon rate. Thereafter, the annual call prices decrease by equal amounts to par, at which price the bonds are callable over the remaining years to maturity. Usually the call provision also imposes limits on the issuer's ability to exercise the option. In the public market, long-term electric utility debt issues are nonrefundable for five years, and long-term telephone utility debt issues are noncallable (for any reason) for five years.

EXAMPLE An Optional Redemption Price Schedule for a Long-Term Bond

Table 19.1 contains an optional redemption price schedule for a long-term bond. The bond has a 25-year maturity. It bears a 10% coupon. Its issue price is 95 (95% of par, or $950 per $1,000 principal amount). The initial year's redemption price equals the offering price plus the coupon, 95 + 10 = 105. The bond is callable at par during the last five years. The call price steps down annually by equal amounts. There are 20 steps. What is the size of each step?

Each step is $0.25 (= [105 − 100]/20).

BOND PUT OPTIONS Interestingly, within the past few years, some corporate issuers have begun to include *put* options in their debt issues. The put option represents a mechanism for reducing agency costs. It limits the possibility of *claim dilution,* such as the loss in value that would result if a firm effected a leveraged buyout. The put option limits this loss by permitting holders to force early redemption.

TABLE 19.1
Optional redemption price schedule.

YEAR	CALL PRICE	YEAR	CALL PRICE	YEAR	CALL PRICE
1	105.00[a]	8	103.25	15	101.50
2	104.75[a]	9	103.00	16	101.25
3	104.50[a]	10	102.75	17	101.00
4	104.25[a]	11	102.50	18	100.75
5	104.00[a]	12	102.25	19	100.50
6	103.75	13	102.00	20	100.25
7	103.50	14	101.75	21–25	100.00

[a]Bond is not refundable out of the proceeds of a debt issue that ranks senior to, or on a par with, this bond.

Frequency and Timing of Debt Issues

Economies of scale make larger issues relatively more attractive. Larger issues also help promote a relatively liquid secondary market for the bonds. Consequently, firms issue long-term debt in larger amounts less often, planning their debt issues carefully. Because of capital market efficiency, it is unlikely that any single firm will be able to gain by speculating on interest rate movements.

When a firm plans to issue debt, it may be possible to obtain a modest reduction in the total cost of the transaction with short-term debt management. A firm should not issue debt when conditions look volatile or temporarily bad. For example, the supply of funds for non-investment-grade bonds tends to shrink during periods of tight money or particularly volatile interest rates. Also, a large U.S. Treasury financing can temporarily depress the debt market. Therefore, issuers should remain flexible with respect to timing in order to prevent temporary factors from adversely affecting their cost of borrowing.

Review

1. What does the average life of a debt issue measure?
2. What is a deep-discount bond? What is a zero-coupon bond?
3. What types of firms prefer fixed-interest-rate bonds? What types prefer floating-rate debt?
4. What does the optional redemption price schedule for a long-term bond usually look like?

19.4 RECENT INNOVATIONS IN THE BOND MARKET

Debt contracts are designed to meet the needs of both borrowers and lenders. Most debt innovations involve some form of risk reallocation as compared to conventional debt instruments. Risk reallocation adds value by transferring risks away from issuers or investors to others better able to bear them. Risk reallocation may also be beneficial if a firm can design a security that better suits the risk-return preferences of a particular class of investors. Investors with a comparative advantage in bearing some types of risks will pay more for innovative securities that allow them to specialize in bearing such risks. This section describes five recent debt innovations: commodity-linked bonds, collateralized mortgage obligations, floating-rate notes, credit-sensitive notes, and extendible notes.

Commodity-Linked Bonds

Commodity-linked bonds were developed in response to rising and increasingly volatile commodity prices. The principal repayment, and in some cases the coupon payments, are tied to the price of a particular commodity, such as oil or silver, or a specified commodity price index. Such bonds are often structured to enable the producer of a commodity to hedge its exposure to a sharp decline in commodity prices and thus in its revenues. Such securities effectively increase a firm's debt capacity by shifting the debt service burden from times when the commodity producer is least able to pay to periods when it is most able to do so. Commodity-linked bonds are analogous to variable-rate loans indexed to some measure of current interest rates.

EXAMPLE An Oil-Indexed Debt Issue

An oil producer could design an "oil-indexed" debt issue with interest payments that rise and fall with oil prices. Investors might be willing to accept significantly lower yields for two reasons. First, the firm's cash flows after it pays interest would be more stable than in the case of a straight, fixed-rate debt issue, because when cash flows are down (up), interest costs go down (up). This reduces default risk because the firm pays higher interest cost when it is most able to, and gets a "break" on interest cost when it needs it. Second, some investors may be seeking a "play" on oil prices not otherwise available in the commodity futures or options market. In this latter sense, many securities innovations that reallocate risk also add value by "completing the market."

Collateralized Mortgage Obligations

Collateralized mortgage obligations (CMOs) address a somewhat different kind of "reinvestment risk"—one that investors in mortgage pass-through certificates find troublesome.[4] Most mortgages are prepayable at par at the option of the mortgagor after some brief period. The fact that many mortgages will be paid off if interest rates decline creates a significant "prepayment" risk for investors. If their principal is returned prematurely, they will have to reinvest at lower rates.

To address this prepayment risk, CMOs repackage the mortgage payment stream from a portfolio of mortgages into several series of debt instruments. They are prioritized in terms of their right to receive principal payments. In the simplest form, each series must be repaid in full before any principal payments can be made to the holders of the next series. In this way, a CMO effectively shifts most of the mortgage prepayment risk to the lower priority class(es). The higher priority class(es) benefit from a significant reduction in the uncertainty as to when the debt obligation will be fully repaid.

Floating-Rate Notes

Floating-rate notes are one of the innovative securities developed in response to rising and increasingly volatile interest rates. They adjust interest payments to correspond to changes in market interest rates. Floating-rate notes thus reduce the lender's principal risk by transferring interest rate risk to the borrower. Of course, this transfer exposes the *issuer* to floating interest-rate risk. But such a reallocation of interest-rate risk can be of mutual benefit to issuers with assets whose values are directly correlated with interest rate changes. For this reason, banks and finance firms are prominent among issuers of these securities.

Credit-Sensitive Notes

A new security can increase shareholder value by reducing agency costs. These costs arise out of the inherent conflicts of interest among professional corporate managers, stockholders, and bondholders. For example, managers can increase shareholder value at the expense of bondholders by leveraging up the firm. *Credit-sensitive notes* bear a coupon rate that varies inversely with the issuer's credit standing. The coupon increases if the issuer's credit standing falls.

These securities, however, have a potentially serious risk to the issuer: The interest rate adjustment mechanism will tend to increase the issuer's debt service burden just when it can least afford it. For instance, if operating cash flows diminish because of a recession, the firm's credit rating could fall. The credit-sensitive notes would reduce after-paying-interest cash flows even further.

---

[4]Mortgage pass-through certificates consist of ownership interests in a portfolio of mortgages. Principal and interest payments are passed through pro rata to certificate holders.

Extendible Notes

Extendible notes increase stockholder value by reducing the underwriting commissions and other transaction costs associated with raising capital. They give the issuer or investor the option to extend the security's maturity. For example, extendible notes generally provide for an interest rate adjustment every two or three years. They thus represent an alternative to rolling over two- or three-year note issues without incurring additional issuance expenses.

Review

1. What is a commodity-linked bond, and what types of firms might find it attractive to issue such bonds?
2. What are collateralized mortgage obligations (CMOs)? How do they reallocate mortgage prepayment risk?
3. Why do banks often issue floating-rate notes?
4. What are credit-sensitive notes?
5. What are extendible notes?

19.5 INTERNATIONAL DEBT FINANCING

A firm can sell U.S.-dollar-denominated bonds to U.S. investors in the domestic bond market, or to foreign investors in the Eurobond market. Alternatively, a firm can sell bonds denominated in a foreign currency. However, issuing bonds denominated in a foreign currency involves a foreign exchange risk. The issuer must either realize foreign currency from its operations or purchase foreign currency to meet its future debt service obligations. We consider this possibility in Chapter 27.

Dollar-Denominated Borrowing in the Eurobond Market

A **Eurobond** is a bond issued outside the country in whose currency it is denominated. Firms headquartered in the United States issue dollar-denominated Eurobonds to investors in Europe (hence the prefix *Euro*) and other areas outside the United States. Eurobonds denominated in other currencies are also issued, but U.S.-dollar-denominated bonds often represent more than half the total Eurobond market.

The Eurobond market developed during the 1960s when the U.S. government levied an interest equalization tax on the purchase of foreign securities by U.S. investors and imposed restrictions on capital exports by American firms. Large U.S. balance of payments deficits continued the outflow of dollar funds. The U.S.-imposed withholding tax on interest payments by domestic firms to foreign investors discouraged foreign investment of these funds in domestic bond issues for many years. Instead, foreign investors avoided this withholding tax by purchasing Eurobonds issued by special-purpose subsidiaries of U.S. firms established in the Netherlands Antilles, which enjoyed a special status as a result of its tax treaty with the United States. The 30% withholding tax was eliminated in 1984, permitting U.S. firms to sell debt directly to foreign investors free of this tax. Nevertheless, the Eurobond market continues to thrive.

Characteristics of Eurobonds

Dollar-denominated Eurobond issues are as varied as domestic bond issues. Most are straight debt issues, but convertible Eurobonds and Eurobonds with warrants are not uncommon.

Nevertheless, there are important differences between the domestic bond market and the Eurobond market:

- The Eurobond market is essentially unregulated. It is a truly international market. Hence, Eurobond yields are somewhat less susceptible to government influence than domestic bond yields. Nevertheless, arbitrage activity ensures that Eurobond yields normally track domestic bond yields fairly closely.
- Eurobond investors usually own assets denominated in several currencies. The relative attractiveness of dollar-denominated Eurobonds, and hence the relationship between bond yields in the domestic bond market and the dollar-denominated Eurobond market, depends on U.S. dollar exchange rates. When the U.S. dollar is appreciating relative to the other major currencies, Eurobond investors tend to increase their purchasing of dollar-denominated Eurobonds (as well as other dollar-denominated assets). This activity can drive Eurobond yields below domestic bond yields and create an attractive borrowing opportunity for U.S. firms. This gives rise to a so-called *Eurobond market window.*
- Because of investors' exchange rate sensitivity, Eurobond maturities are usually shorter, and issue sizes generally smaller, than in the domestic market.
- Eurobonds are generally *bearer bonds.* Issuing bonds in bearer form (payable on demand, there is no ownership record) makes it more difficult to refund them prior to maturity, because communication with most buyers is only when they come to the paying agent to claim their interest payments.
- Eurobonds usually pay interest *annually.* Domestic bonds generally pay interest semi-annually, therefore, domestic and Eurobonds must be compared by their APYs.

EXAMPLE Comparing Domestic and Eurobond Borrowing Costs

A firm can issue a 10-year public debt issue at par bearing a 12% coupon in the domestic market. It can also issue 12-1/8% Eurobonds. The total issuance expenses are identical for both issues. We can use the coupon rates to compare the borrowing costs. From Equation (4.11), the APY for the domestic bond is $(1.06)^2 - 1 = 12.36\%$. For the Eurobond issue it is 12.125%. Therefore, the Eurobond issue is slightly cheaper in spite of its higher coupon rate.

The Eurobond market is an alternative to borrowing domestically. Table 19.2 presents the mix of domestic and international bond financing by U.S. firms from 1984 to 2001. The volume of Eurobond financing picked up sharply in 1985 and 1996–1997, when the strength of the U.S. dollar and other factors lead to a sharp increase in foreign demand for dollar-denominated bonds.

Review

1. What is a Eurobond? How did the Eurobond market develop?
2. How do dollar-denominated Eurobonds differ from U.S. domestic bonds?
3. What adjustment do you usually have to make in order to compare the cost of issuing Eurobonds with the cost of issuing domestic bonds?

TABLE 19.2
Volume of domestic and international bond financing by U.S. firms, 1984 to 2001 (dollar amounts in millions).

YEAR	DOMESTIC[a]	INTERNATIONAL[a]	TOTAL[a]	PERCENT DOMESTIC	TRADE-WEIGHTED DOLLAR EXCHANGE RATE[b]
1984	$ 81,467	$ 19,970	$ 101,437	80.3%	125.85
1985	79,687	43,502	123,189	64.7	130.58
1986	145,461	51,357	196,818	73.9	107.26
1987	125,131	28,564	153,695	81.4	94.86
1988	115,341	22,820	138,161	83.5	88.17
1989	138,771	25,723	164,494	84.4	91.81
1990	105,507	23,208	128,715	82.0	87.82
1991	201,215	29,311	230,526	87.3	86.37
1992	303,678	29,287	332,965	91.2	84.89
1993	415,058	40,326	455,384	91.1	87.15
1994	346,074	53,457	399,531	86.6	85.63
1995	439,357	60,260	499,617	87.9	80.80
1996	502,496	98,711	601,207	83.6	84.60
1997	740,091	131,294	871,385	84.9	91.23
1998	1,078,653	132,523	1,211,176	89.1	95.75
1999	1,198,728	137,358	1,336,086	89.7	94.02
2000	1,089,254	131,433	1,220,687	89.2	98.31
2001	1,351,843	97,613	1,449,456	93.3	104.30
Total	$8,457,812	$1,156,717	$9,614,529	88.0	

[a]Includes convertible debt.
[b]Index for which March of 1973 = 100.
Source: Reprinted by permission of Thomson Financial.

19.6 BOND REFUNDING[5]

A bond's optional redemption provision is a valuable call option. It gives the issuer the right to redeem the bond prior to maturity. If interest rates rise throughout the life of the issue, the call option will expire worthless. But if interest rates fall sufficiently, the issuer can call the bond and replace it with lower-cost debt.

Replacing an outstanding bond with a new bond before its scheduled maturity is referred to as *refunding.* A well-managed firm will look for opportunities to refund its debt at a profit. We will show you how a firm can evaluate a bond refunding opportunity to decide whether it is in the shareholders' interest to refund.

A call provision is not free. Consider the other side of the transaction, the bondholders' viewpoint. If interest rates fall and the issuer calls the bond, the bondholders will have to reinvest their funds at a lower interest rate. A higher required return is needed to compensate them. Therefore, the firm must decide whether including a call feature is worth the price.

[5]See *Debt Management, a practitioner's guide* by Finnerty and Emery (Harvard Business School Press: 2001) for an in-depth discussion of this topic and issues related to it.

What Gives Rise to Profitable Bond Refunding Opportunities?

Volatile interest rates create profitable bond refunding opportunities. Figure 19.1 illustrates that between 1985 and 1987, and again between 1993 and 1998, interest rates on corporate bonds decreased sharply. These decreases gave rise to profitable refunding opportunities.

Debt Service Parity

When a firm refunds debt, its capital structure may change. It is important to calculate the net benefit to shareholders of a refunding exclusive of these side effects. One method of neutralizing them is called the *debt service parity (DSP) approach.* The basic idea is simple.

Construct a replacement debt obligation that has the same after-tax payments, period by period, as the outstanding debt obligation. If this stream of after-tax debt service payments will support sufficient new debt to cover the cost of retiring the outstanding issue *and* cover all transaction costs, then refinancing will provide a net benefit to the firm's shareholders. The DSP approach values the incremental after-tax cash flows by computing their present value at the after-tax cost of the new debt issue.

The DSP principle extends beyond cash flows. Parity implies that all rights and obligations of the old issue must also be maintained in the new. Therefore, the sinking fund schedule and maturity of the hypothetical new issue must be identical to those remaining on the old issue.

For example, consider a debt issue with a remaining life of six years and required after-tax interest and principal payments of $9.2 million per year for the next five years and $19.2 million in the last year. An evaluation for refunding this issue would be against a hypothetical six-year refunding issue with exactly the same cash flows. Note that if the refunding were undertaken, the actual new issue might have a maturity other than six years and/or a different cash flow pattern. The maturity and cash flow pattern of the actual new issue are separate decisions. The firm should choose the features of the new debt only after it has determined that refunding is advantageous.

FIGURE 19.1
Average yield on AA-rated long-term corporate bonds, 1980–2001.

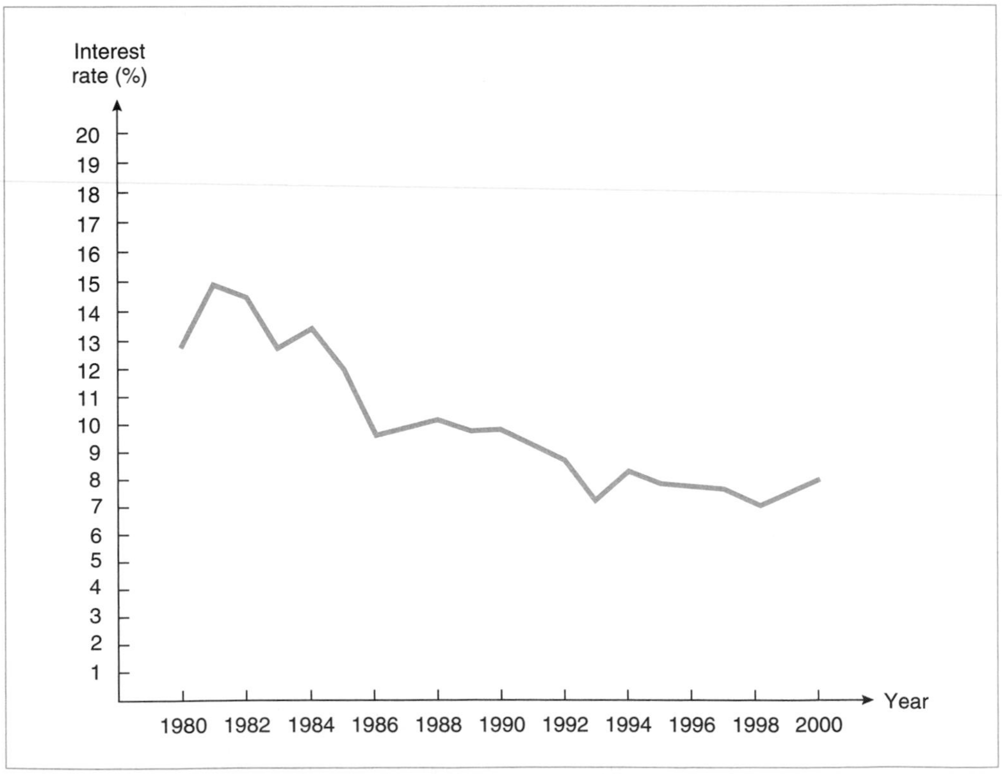

Review

1. What does it mean to refund a bond issue?
2. What gives rise to profitable bond refunding opportunities?
3. Briefly describe the debt service parity approach to bond refunding analysis.

Tax Considerations

As with other financial decisions, the refunding decision must reflect the related tax consequences. This involves adjusting the cash flows and the discount rate appropriately. As we have said, tax laws change, so the current tax treatment must be used.

All of the expenses connected with a refunding are tax deductible, some during the year of the refunding and the others over the life of the new issue. The basic rules are: (1) expenses connected with retiring the old issue may be deducted in the year of the refunding, and (2) expenses connected with the new issue (including any discount or premium) must be amortized over its life.

Those expenses that are deductible in the year the refunding occurs include:

- The call premium—the difference between the call price and par value.
- The unamortized balance of issuance expenses on the old debt.
- Transaction costs, such as legal fees, printing costs, fees paid to the trustee for canceling the old bonds, and any overlapping interest cost.[6]

The Net Advantage of Refunding

A firm should undertake a refunding only if it will increase shareholder wealth. The *net advantage of refunding* (NA) equals the present value savings (PVS) minus the total cost (Cost) of the refunding:

$$\text{NA} = \text{PVS} - \text{Cost} \tag{19.3}$$

Both PVS and Cost are computed on a present-value after-tax basis. If the present value of the savings exceeds the total cost, NA is positive and the refunding is attractive.

Transaction costs can affect the refunding decision. We will include their effect on the decision, but will not explain the details of calculating the after-tax transaction costs of refunding. Problem C2 at the end of the chapter explores this topic.

Under the debt service parity approach, PVS equals the present value of the after-tax interest savings. The discount rate is the after-tax cost of the new debt issue.

The net advantage of refunding high-coupon debt that has a bullet maturity is

$$\text{NA} = \sum_{n=1}^{N} \frac{(1-T)(r-r')D}{[1+(1-T)r']^n} - (1-T)(P-D) - \text{Trans} \tag{19.4}$$

where the variables are defined as

D = par value of the old debt
N = number of periods until the old debt is scheduled to mature
P = call (strike) price of the old debt (excluding accrued interest)
r = coupon rate on the old debt
r' = coupon rate on a new debt issue sold at par
T = issuer's marginal ordinary income tax rate
Trans = after-tax transaction costs of refunding

[6]Overlapping interest arises because the new bonds are typically sold before the old ones are retired. In such cases, the difference between the interest cost of, and the investment return on, the surplus funds during the overlap period is tax deductible (or taxable if the investment return exceeds the interest cost).

The first term in Equation (19.4) represents the present value of the after-tax savings from replacing the old debt at the new interest rate. The second term represents the after-tax cost of buying back the debt (the call premium).

EXAMPLE Analyzing a High-Coupon Bond Refunding Opportunity

Palo Alto Refinancing (PAR) specializes in helping consumers refinance their personal debt. PAR's managers have decided that charity begins at home. The firm has a $100 million bond issue outstanding, which is scheduled to mature in a single lump sum 15 years from today. This issue has a 12% coupon rate (6% semiannual). PAR can call the bonds at a strike price of $1,050 each. PAR can issue new 15-year noncallable debt at par value if it has a 10.40% coupon rate (5.20% semiannual). After-tax transaction costs to refund will be $2 million. The other terms of the new bonds are identical to those of the old bonds. PAR's marginal income tax rate is 34%. Table 19.3 shows the calculation of the net advantage of refunding the 12% issue.

The after-tax interest savings per period amount to

$$(1 - T)(r - r')D = (1 - 0.34)(0.06 - 0.052)100{,}000{,}000 = \$528{,}000$$

The discount rate is the semiannual after-tax cost of the new debt, 3.432% (= [1 − 0.34]5.20). The present value of the stream of savings is

$$\sum_{n=1}^{30} \frac{528{,}000}{(1.03432)^n} = \$9{,}794{,}266$$

TABLE 19.3
The net advantage of refunding PAR's outstanding 12% bonds.

	OLD ISSUE	NEW ISSUE
I. Conditions		
Principal amount	$100,000,000	$100,000,000
Coupon	12%	10.40%
Maturity	15 years	15 years
	BEFORE TAXES	**AFTER TAXES**
II. Interest Savings		
Interest on old bonds per period	$ 6,000,000	$ 3,960,000
Interest on new bonds per period	5,200,000	3,432,000
Interest savings per period	800,000	528,000
Present value savings[a]		$ 9,794,266
III. Total Cost		
Redemption premium	$ 5,000,000	$ 3,300,000
After-tax transaction cost		2,000,000
		$ 5,300,000
IV. Net Advantage		
Present value savings		$ 9,794,266
Total cost		5,300,000
Net advantage of refunding		$ 4,494,266

[a]The discount rate is 3.432% per semiannual period (= [1 − 0.34]5.2).

The call price exceeds the par value by \$50 per bond. There are 100,000 bonds (= 100,000,000/1,000) outstanding. PAR will incur an after-tax redemption cost of \$3,300,000 (= [1 − 0.34][50]100,000). With transaction costs, the net advantage of refunding is

$$NA = 9{,}794{,}266 - 3{,}300{,}000 - 2{,}000{,}000 = \$4{,}494{,}266$$

Why Firms Issue Callable Bonds

Thus far, we have been discussing a *fixed-price* call provision. In recent years, a large proportion of investment-grade bonds have instead included a *make-whole call provision.* The make-whole call provision specifies a formula (based on a published interest rate index) for estimating the bond's market value. (Typically, the formula is somewhat favorable to the bondholder.) The provision allows the firm to call the bonds at its discretion by paying the formula-specified bond value. In concept, the bondholder gets full value for the bond, but the firm retains the flexibility to pay off the bond.

In a perfect capital market environment, including any type of call provision is a zero-sum game. Any gain to the party on one side of the transaction would be exactly offset by a loss to the party on the other side of the transaction. (Recall the Principle of Two-Sided Transactions.) A fairly priced call provision does not provide a value advantage to either side of the transaction. At the same time, if interest rates are relatively high, a fixed-price call provision provides insurance for the firm against a drop in interest rates. To compensate the bondholders for this insurance, the bond's coupon rate is higher than if there were no call provision.

The make-whole call provision does not provide insurance against a drop in interest rates, so that investors do not need to be compensated for the insurance, and the provision is much less costly. With relatively low interest rates in recent years, many corporate managers have felt that protection against lower interest rates was not important, and they have not included a fixed-price call provision. However, many have included a make-whole call provision. We believe that the three persistent capital market imperfections we have identified offer reasons why firms often include some type of call provision in bonds they issue.

ASYMMETRIC INFORMATION When a firm borrows, debtholders may require a higher rate of interest because of the possibility of asset substitution. Later on, when a firm has not engaged in asset substitution, the debt can increase in value. The firm may be able to recoup this increase in value from the debtholders by exercising its call option. In this way, the fixed-price call option offers a bonus for firms that forego their asset substitution option. In other situations, a firm may have information about future investment opportunities it cannot reveal now for competitive reasons. Without knowing that favorable information, suppose the market requires restrictive bond covenants of some sort that will make it difficult for the firm to take advantage of its future investment opportunities. Suppose further that the firm issues bonds now with those restrictive covenants, but also with a make-whole call provision. In the future, if the firm does get the opportunities it hoped for, it can call and retire these bonds so that it can undertake the opportunities. In the meantime, the firm does not pay for insurance against a drop in interest rates.

TAXES A firm can benefit from including a fixed-price call option when it is taxed at a higher marginal rate than bondholders. When this is so, the call option is worth more to the issuer than the after-tax cost of the interest rate premium it must pay bondholders to obtain this privilege. This is another example of how a tax asymmetry can create a non-zero-sum game.

TRANSACTION COSTS Lower transaction costs provide an incentive to include a call provision. Calling bonds involves lower transaction costs than repurchasing them in the open market. If a firm believes there is a chance it will need to eliminate a bond issue in the future because of, for example, restrictive covenants, a make-whole call provision can be a lower-cost alternative to future open-market purchases. In other situations, a firm might expect its credit standing to improve prior to the debt's maturity. It could then refund the debt profitably if it included a fixed-price call provision. It is for this reason that speculative-grade bond issues rarely include a make-whole call provision but often include a fixed-price call provision.

Timing Considerations

Suppose a firm determines that refunding a debt issue would be profitable. It should also consider that it might be more profitable to postpone the refunding. If the call price exceeds the market price of the bonds, then calling the bonds immediately involves a transfer of wealth from the shareholders to the bondholders. It equals the difference between the aggregate redemption price for the bonds and their aggregate market value immediately prior to the announcement of the call.

If capital markets were perfect, this transfer of wealth could be avoided by following a simple decision rule: Call a (nonconvertible) bond issue only when the market price of the bonds (including accrued interest) reaches the *effective call price,* that is, the stated call price plus accrued interest. However, because transaction costs are not zero, the timing issue is not so simply resolved.

In practice, firms often call their high-coupon bond issues for redemption before their market value reaches the call price. Issuers thus face a call-or-wait decision. Even if immediate refunding is (apparently) profitable, a greater value might be possible if the firm postpones the refunding. Making the refund-or-wait decision requires the assessment of the relative likelihood of favorable changes in future interest rates.[7]

Review

1. What does it mean to say that the net advantage of refunding a bond issue is positive?
2. True or false? Discounting the change in the after-tax debt service payment stream at the after-tax cost of the new issue is consistent with the debt service parity (DSP) approach.
3. How do taxes affect the profitability of a refunding?
4. Why do firms issue callable bonds?

SUMMARY

- Many different types of debt securities make up the long-term debt financing menu. For example, debt may be secured or unsecured, taxable or tax-exempt, and domestic or international.
- There are four main classes of long-term corporate debt: secured, unsecured, tax-exempt, and convertible debt.
- Mortgage bonds, collateral trust bonds, and equipment trust certificates are common forms of secured debt. Notes and debentures are unsecured debt.

---

[7]See *Debt Management, a practitioner's guide* by Finnerty and Emery (Harvard Business School Press: 2001) for ways to handle the timing problem.

- Debt instruments have a stated maturity, stated principal amount, stated coupon rate of interest (or interest rate formula in the case of floating-rate debt), mandatory redemption schedule, optional redemption provision, and covenant restrictions designed to protect bondholders.
- The terms of a debt issue will affect the interest rate investors require. Provisions such as the covenants contained in an indenture should be carefully examined. Contractual agreements may be able to reduce agency costs, but such provisions are not costless. For example, restrictive covenants may reduce a firm's interest cost, but may also reduce operating flexibility.
- Recent innovations in the bond market include commodity-linked bonds, collateralized mortgage obligations, floating-rate notes, credit-sensitive notes, and extendible notes.
- The exact debt repayment schedule can affect a firm's cost of financing. A sinking fund reduces the effective maturity of the issue. Therefore, a sinking fund may affect the cost of an issue because of differences in the term structure of interest rates.
- A firm should refund outstanding bonds only if it will increase shareholder wealth. Discount the change in after-tax debt service payments at the after-tax cost of money for the new issue, and then subtract the after-tax costs and expenses associated with the refunding. A high-coupon debt issue should be called for optional redemption when its market value reaches its redemption value (or call price).

EQUATION SUMMARY

$$\text{Average life} = \frac{\sum_{t=1}^{N} tA_t}{\sum_{t=1}^{N} A_t} \tag{19.1}$$

$$\text{Duration} = \frac{1}{P}\sum_{t=1}^{N} \frac{t\,\text{CF}_t}{(1+y)^t} \tag{19.2}$$

$$\text{NA} = \text{PVS} - \text{Cost} \tag{19.3}$$

$$\text{NA} = \sum_{n=1}^{N} \frac{(1-T)(r-r')D}{[1+(1-T)r']^n} - (1-T)(P-D) - \text{Trans} \tag{19.4}$$

QUESTIONS

1. Describe the difference between secured and unsecured debt.
2. Explain the role of debt covenants, and cite three examples.
3. On what basis would a firm ideally choose the maturity of its debt?
4. Explain how the presence of a sinking fund affects the effective maturity of a debt issue.
5. What are deep-discount bonds?
6. Explain the reasons for including a call option in a corporate bond issue.
7. What are commodity-linked bonds?

8. What are floating-rate notes?
9. What is a Eurobond?
10. What is a high-coupon bond refunding?

CHALLENGING QUESTIONS

11. Explain briefly the debt service parity approach (DSP) to evaluating the net advantage of a proposed bond refunding.
12. Explain why a firm should not necessarily refund an outstanding debt issue the instant the net advantage becomes positive.
13. Who benefits from a call provision, and how does it affect the bond's coupon rate?
14. Who benefits from a bond put option, and how does it affect the bond's coupon rate?
15. What is the difference between average life and duration?
16. Explain why zero-coupon bonds have a longer duration than coupon bonds of equivalent maturity and yield.

PROBLEMS

LEVEL A (BASIC)

A1. (Bond covenants) Montgomery Business Products has a large bond issue whose covenants require: (1) that Montgomery's interest coverage ratio exceeds 5.0; (2) that its ratio of tangible assets to long-term debt exceeds 2.0; and (3) that cumulative dividends and share repurchases not exceed 50% of cumulative earnings since the date of the issuance of the bonds. Montgomery has earnings before interest and taxes of $90 million and interest expense of $20 million. Tangible assets are $500 million and long-term debt is $210 million. Since the bonds were issued, Montgomery has earned $150 million, paid dividends of $60 million, and repurchased $2 million of common stock. Is Montgomery Business Products in compliance with its bond covenants?

A2. (Bond covenants) Dallas Instruments has a large bond issue whose covenants require: (1) that DI's interest coverage ratio exceeds 4.0; (2) that DI's ratio of tangible assets to long-term debt exceeds 1.50; and (3) that cumulative dividends and share repurchases not exceed 60% of cumulative earnings since the date of the issuance of the bonds. DI has earnings before interest and taxes of $70 million and interest expense of $14 million. Tangible assets are $400 million and long-term debt is $175 million. Since the bonds were issued, DI has earned $200 million, paid dividends of $40 million, and repurchased $40 million of common stock. Is DI in compliance with its bond covenants?

A3. (Comparing borrowing costs) Stephens Security has two financing alternatives: (1) A publicly placed $50 million bond issue. Issuance costs are $1 million, the bond has a 9% coupon paid semiannually, and the bond has a 20-year life. (2) A $50 million private placement with a large pension fund. Issuance costs are $500,000, the bond has a 9.25% annual coupon, and the bond has a 20-year life. Which alternative has the lower cost (annual percentage yield)?

A4. (Comparing borrowing costs) Mitchell Automotive is considering two financing alternatives: (1) A publicly placed $75 million bond issue. Issuance costs are $1 million, the bond has an 8% coupon paid semiannually, and the bond has a 20-year life. (2) A $75 million private placement with Pearce Investment Partners, a large money management firm. Issuance costs are $500,000, the bond has an 8.125% annual coupon, and the bond has a 20-year life. Which alternative has the lower cost (annual percentage yield)?

A5. (Average life of a bond) A debt issue repays principal in seven equal installments at the end of years 14 through 20. What is its average life?

A6. (Floating-rate bond) Maberly Marina has a $1 million floating-rate mortgage bond outstanding. The interest rate will float with the one-year Treasury rate plus 3%. The principal of the loan will remain unchanged for the next few years.

a. What will Maberly's annual interest expense be if the Treasury rate is 5%, 6%, 9%, 7%, and 7% for the next five years?

b. Suppose that Maberly has a floating-rate bond that charges the one-year Treasury rate plus 3.25%, but that the rate is capped at 9%. This means that if the formula requires a rate above 9%, Maberly pays only 9%. What would Maberly's annual interest expense be for the next five years if interest rates are 5%, 6%, 9%, 7%, and 7%?

A7. (Debt covenants) Detroit Auto Supplies issued bonds with covenants preventing the interest coverage ratio from falling below 2.5. Suppose Detroit's EBIT is $25 million and its current interest expense is $7 million. How much 8% debt could Detroit issue without violating its debt covenant?

A8. (Debt covenants) United Packing Service has outstanding bonds with covenants preventing the interest coverage ratio from falling below 2.0. Suppose United's EBIT is $40 million and its current interest expense is $15 million. How much 10% debt could United issue without violating its debt covenant?

A9. (Duration) A bond pays semiannual interest at 9% APR. It has a sinking fund that repays $20 million at the end of each of years 5 and 6. The bond's yield to maturity is 8.5%. What is the bond's duration if the total principal amount is $40 million?

A10. (Duration) A bond pays semiannual interest at 8% APR. It has a sinking fund paying $75 million at the end of each of years 3 and 4. Total principal is $150 million. If the bond's yield to maturity is 10%, what is the bond's duration?

A11. (Excel: Optional redemption schedule) A callable bond has a 15-year maturity, and has a 10% coupon rate. Its issue price is $1,000. The initial year's redemption price is par plus one year's coupon. The bond is callable at par during its last five years. The call price steps down in equal amounts. Create a schedule of call prices over the bond's life.

A12. (Domestic versus Eurobond borrowing costs) A firm can issue an eight-year public debt issue at par with an 11% coupon in the domestic market. It can also issue 11.25% Eurobonds. If all other expenses are equal, which issue offers the firm the lower borrowing cost?

LEVEL B

B1. (Cost of a bond with a sinking fund) A debt issue bears a 10% coupon and has a sinking fund that makes equal payments at the end of years 4 and 5. Interest is paid semiannually at the end of each period.

a. What are the bonds' cash flows for interest payments and repayment of principal?

b. If the issuing firm nets a price equal to 95% of the face amount of the debt, what is the pretax APY cost of the debt?

B2. (Taxes and the cost of borrowing) A new debt issue bearing a 12% coupon and maturing in one lump sum at the end of 10 years involves issuance expenses equal to 2% of the gross proceeds.

a. Assume the issuing firm pays tax at a 50% marginal rate. What is the after-tax cost of debt?

b. Suppose instead the firm is not a taxpayer and expects never to be. What is the after-tax cost of debt?

c. Explain how your answer to part b would change if the firm expected to pay taxes at a 50% rate after five years.

B3. (Cost of floating-rate debt) A new floating-rate debt issue pays interest annually based on the one-year Treasury bill rate. Assume zero issuance cost. The issue matures in five years. The current one-year Treasury bill rate is 9%, and the forecast one-year rates over the next four years are 9.25%, 9.5%, 9.75%, and 10%. The coupon equals the beginning-of-period Treasury rate plus 100 basis points. There is no sinking fund.

a. Project the debt service payment stream.

b. Calculate the pretax cost of debt.

c. Calculate the after-tax cost of debt, assuming a 34% tax rate.

B4. (Average life) A long-term debt issue in the amount of $100 million calls for mandatory redemption payments of $20 million each at the end of years 7, 8, and 9, and repayment of the remaining balance (called the *balloon*) at the end of year 10. Calculate the issue's average life.

B5. (Cost of borrowing alternatives) General Aviation Corporation has decided to issue $100 million of 10-year debt. It has three alternatives. A U.S. public offering would require a 9% coupon with interest payable semiannually and $1 million of flotation expense. A U.S. private placement would require a 9-1/8% coupon with interest payable semiannually and $750,000 of flotation expense. A Eurobond offering would require a 9-1/8% coupon with interest payable annually and $1,250,000 of flotation expense.

a. Calculate the cost of borrowing for each alternative.

b. Which alternative has the lowest cost of borrowing?

c. What other factors should General Aviation consider before it decides how to raise $100 million?

B6. (Cost of borrowing alternatives) Exxon Mobil has a 34% tax rate and has decided to issue $100 million of seven-year debt. It has three alternatives. A U.S. public offering would require an 8% coupon with interest payable semiannually and $900,000 of flotation expense. A U.S. private placement would require an 8-3/8% coupon with interest payable semiannually and $500,000 of flotation expense. A Eurobond offering would require an 8-1/8% coupon with interest payable annually and $1,100,000 of floatation expense.

a. Calculate the after-tax cost of borrowing for each alternative.

b. Which alternative has the lowest cost of borrowing?

B7. (Bond covenant) A debt issue contains a dividend limitation. Cumulative dividends cannot exceed the sum of $25 million and 60% of cumulative net income since the debt was issued three years ago. The firm earned $50 million net income in each of those years. It paid total dividends of $15 million and $20 million the past two years and $25 million so far this year. How large a dividend could the firm pay at the end of the third year without violating the dividend limitation?

B8. (Bond covenant) A debt issue contains a coverage test that prohibits a firm from issuing additional debt if doing so would reduce its interest coverage below 2.50 times. Its earnings before interest and taxes are currently $100 million. Its interest expense is currently $25 million. How much additional 10% debt could the firm incur under this test?

B9. (Bond covenant) An asset coverage test prohibits a firm from issuing additional long-term debt if doing so would reduce the ratio of tangible assets to long-term debt below 1.50 times. A firm currently has $1 billion of tangible assets and $400 million of long-term debt. How much additional long-term debt could it issue if it invests the entire proceeds in tangible assets?

B10. (Average life) A debt issue repays 10% of the principal at the end of years 14 through 19. The remaining 40% is repaid at the end of year 20. What is its average life?

B11. (Duration) A long-term debt issue in the amount of $200 million calls for mandatory redemption payments of $30 million each at the end of years 7, 8, and 9, and repayment of the remaining balance (called the *balloon*) at the end of year 10. Calculate the issue's duration.

B12. (Duration) A bond pays interest semiannually at a 7% APR. The bond has a sinking fund that makes equal payments of $20 million at the end of years 6, 7, and 8. The total principal is $60 million. The bond's yield to maturity is 6% APR.

a. Calculate the bond's price.

b. Calculate the bond's average life.

c. Calculate the bond's duration.

d. Which of the figures calculated in parts b and c is the better measure of the average timing of the bond issue's total cash flow?

B13. (Duration) A bond pays interest semiannually at a 10% APR. The bond has a sinking fund that makes equal payments at the end of years 8, 9, and 10. The bond's price is 105% of its face amount.

a. Calculate the bond's yield to maturity.

b. Calculate the bond's average life.

c. Calculate the bond's duration.

B14. (Net advantage of refunding) A firm has a $50 million debt issue outstanding that bears a 15% coupon (7.5% semiannual). It matures in a lump sum at the end of 10 years. The call price is $1,100 per bond. A new 10-year debt issue would require a 12.5% coupon (6.25% semiannual). The firm's marginal income tax rate is 40%.

a. Calculate the semiannual after-tax savings that would result if the firm issued $50 million of 12.5% debt.

b. Calculate the net advantage of refunding the 15% debt issue.

B15. (Net advantage of refunding) RST, Inc. has $70 million of 12% bonds outstanding. It can call the bonds at a price of $1,100 per bond. The bonds have a remaining life of 10 years. RST is considering refunding the issue with a new $70 million issue of 11% bonds. RST's tax rate is 40%. What is RST's net advantage of refunding the outstanding bonds?

B16. (Net advantage of refunding) The Radguard Corporation sold $50 million of 25-year, 10% bonds during a period of very high interest rates 10 years ago. Radguard can now refund that bond issue with 15-year, 8% bonds, which would sell at par value. There is a 5% call premium. Radguard's tax rate is 40%. What is Radguard's NA of refunding the outstanding bonds?

B17. (Excel: bond duration) Consider the following four bonds:

Bond A. Three-year bond with 8% coupon (paid semiannually)
Bond B. Twenty-year bond with 8% coupon (paid semiannually)
Bond C. Twenty-year bond with 6% coupon (paid semiannually)
Bond D. Twenty-year zero-coupon bond

a. Calculate the duration of the four bonds assuming a yield-to-maturity of 9% compounded semiannually.

b. Calculate the percentage increase in the value of each bond if the yield to maturity decreases from 9% to 8.8%.

c. How do the percentage increases in part b compare to the durations in part a?

B18. (Excel: net advantage of refunding) Guo Corp. has $60 million of 10% bonds outstanding with a remaining life of 15 years. Guo Corp. can call the bonds at a price of $1,080 per bond. The bonds could be replaced with a new bond issue of 8.2% bonds. The marginal tax rate is 35%.

a. Calculate the net advantage of refunding the 10% debt issue.

b. What is the interest rate on the new debt necessary to break even on refunding the 10% debt issue?

LEVEL C (ADVANCED)

C1. (Cost of borrowing) A firm issues a 10-year debt obligation that bears a 12% coupon rate and gives the investor the right to put the bond back to the issuer at the end of the fifth year at 103% of its face amount. The issue has no sinking fund. Interest is paid semiannually. The issuer's tax rate is 34%.

a. Calculate the after-tax cost of debt, assuming the debt remains outstanding until maturity.

b. Calculate the after-tax cost of debt, assuming investors put the bond back to the firm at the end of the fifth year. (*Note:* Any unamortized issuance expenses and any redemption premium can be deducted for tax purposes in the year of redemption.)

C2. (Including detailed transactions cost in the net advantage of refunding) The net advantage of refunding high-coupon debt can be expressed as

$$\text{NA} = \sum_{n=1}^{N} \frac{(1-T)(r-r')D + T([E-U]/N)}{[1+(1-T)r']^n}$$
$$-(1-T)(P-D) - [E + (1-T)F - TU] - (P-B)$$

where D, N, P, r, r', and T are defined as in Equation (19.4) and

B is the market price of the old debt issue (excluding accrued interest);
E is the underwriting commissions and other expenses associated with the new debt issue;
F is the tax-deductible, out-of-pocket expenses associated with the refunding; and
U is the unamortized balance of issuance expenses on the old debt.

a. Issuance expenses are tax deductible over the life of the debt issue on a straight-line basis. Interpret the term $T([E-U]/N)$.

b. The unamortized balance of issuance expenses on the old debt can be written off for tax purposes in the year of refunding. Interpret the term TU.

c. Suppose bonds are redeemed at a price that exceeds their market value. Bondholders benefit at the expense of shareholders. Interpret the term $P-B$. Why is it subtracted?

d. Explain how the tax treatment of issuance expenses in bond refunding is like the tax treatment of equipment cost in capital budgeting.

C3. (Net advantage of refunding with detailed transaction costs) Northern Gas Company has outstanding $100 million principal amount of 12% debentures (6% payable semiannually) that mature in a lump sum at the end of 20 years. The unamortized balance of issuance expenses is $500,000. A par-value $100 million noncallable refunding issue would require a 10% coupon (5% semiannual) and $750,000 of issuance expenses. The 12% issue is callable at a price of $1,020 per bond (pretax), and miscellaneous debt retirement costs amount to $3.00 per bond. Northern Gas's marginal income tax rate is 40%.

a. Calculate the net advantage of refunding assuming the bonds had a market value of $1,020 each.

b. How would your answer to part a change if the 12% debentures were selling at a market price of $1,017 per bond?

MINICASE DISNEY'S 100-YEAR BONDS

The Walt Disney Company (Disney) is known to all, with its theme parks, resorts, and media holdings. Several years ago, Disney decided to issue additional long-term debt. Its investment bankers advised that a 100-year debt issue might be possible. Disney was conservatively capitalized. Its long-term debt was rated A1 by Moody's Investors Service and AA− by Standard & Poor's. At the time, its capitalization and interest coverage for the previous 12 months were:

BOOK VALUE CAPITALIZATION (Dollar amounts in millions)	
Long-term debt	$1,455.5
Stockholders' equity	5,169.1
Long-term capitalization	$6,624.6
Short-term debt	503.7
Total capitalization	$7,128.3

INTEREST COVERAGE (Dollar amounts in millions)	
Earnings before interest and taxes	$1,640.5
Interest expense	122.4
Interest coverage ratio	13.4x

Interest rates had decreased for the previous few years, which made long-term debt an attractive financing alternative. At the same time, many investors in long-term fixed-rate debt had come to believe that the United States had inflation under control and that long-term interest rates were unlikely to return to the very high levels experienced a number of years ago. They thought that long-term interest rates might even decline further because the gap between long-term Treasury yields (6.40% for the 30-year bond) and the projected inflation rate (3%) was relatively high by historical standards. Thus, a 100-year maturity, almost unthinkable just a few years before this time, was now possible according to Disney's investment bankers at Morgan Stanley & Co.

Disney could issue noncallable semiannual bonds at the following rates/maturities:

Maturity (years):	3	5	7	10	20	30	100
Offering yield (% APR):	5.15	5.85	6.25	6.60	7.25	7.35	7.35

If it issued 100-year bonds, Disney wanted to preserve some flexibility to retire it before its maturity. Morgan Stanley advised Disney that it could issue $300 million principal amount of 100-year debt that was callable beginning 30 years from the issue date at an interest cost of 7.55% APR. The initial call price would be 103.02. The call price would become 100.00 beginning 50 years after the issue date.

QUESTIONS

1. Estimate the cost of the call option to Disney by calculating the present value of the difference in payments Disney would have to make, assuming it called the bonds after 30 years. Explain what Disney would get in exchange for this cost.
2. Calculate the duration of the 5-, 10-, 30-, and 100-year bonds bearing the interest rates indicated above. Do you see any pattern between duration and offering yield?
3. Show the pro forma impact on Disney's capitalization and interest coverage from issuing $300 million principal amount of 30-, noncallable 100-, and callable 100-year bonds.
4. Consider the 30-year and 100-year bonds. If Disney issues 30-year bonds now and refunds them with 70-year bonds 30 years from now, what interest rate on the subsequently issued 70-year bonds would make Disney just as well off as if it issued noncallable 100-year bonds today?
5. Consider the callable and noncallable 100-year bonds. If Disney issues callable 100-year bonds now and refunds them at the end of the 30th year with 70-year bonds, what interest rate on the subsequently issued 70-year bonds would make Disney just as well off as if it had issued noncallable 100-year bonds instead?
6. Do you think Disney should issue callable 100-year bonds or one of the other alternatives? Explain.

LEASING AND OTHER ASSET-BASED FINANCING

20

You have probably rented a car, a bike, or some other item. Maybe you rented a trailer to take all your belongings to school. Did you consider buying instead? Not if you needed the item only for a few days. Rentals are typically for short periods, but firms often rent equipment and real estate for much longer periods. Sometimes they even rent entire plants.

We discussed the traditional methods of raising funds in Chapters 18 and 19. Firms can retain earnings or they can sell new issues of bonds, common stock, or preferred stock. They raise those funds on the strength of their general promise to pay and overall profitability. Investors look to the cash flow from the firm's entire asset portfolio to provide the return on their investments.

Asset-based financing is different. The investors involved in **asset-based financing** must look to the cash flow from a specific asset for the return on their investment. In many cases, the lenders involved in asset-based financing lend on a nonrecourse basis. They look exclusively to a specific pool of assets for the cash flow to service their loans.

There are many types of asset-based financing, including lease financing, project financing, limited partnership financing, and corporate real estate mortgage financing. Lease financing is the most important. There are a variety of models for analyzing lease financing. The key to proper leasing analysis is making sure that the alternatives are comparable. We do this by applying the concept of debt service parity (DSP): Each alternative must have the same after-tax payment schedule. Toward the end of the chapter, after we discuss leasing, we take a quick look at project financing and limited partnership financing.

FOCUS ON PRINCIPLES

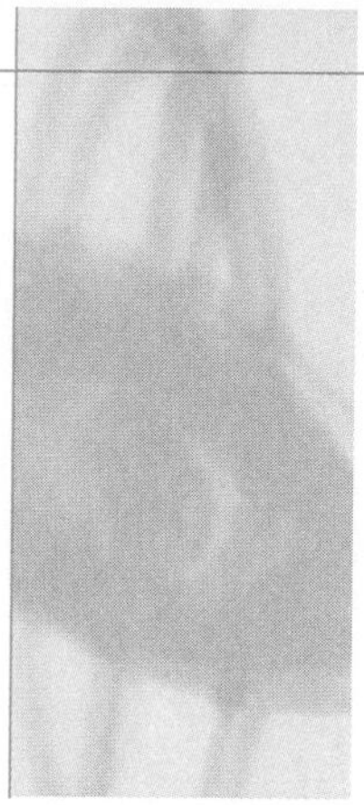

- *Self-Interested Behavior:* Look for profitable opportunities to lease (or rent) an asset, rather than borrow and buy it. Also look for profitable opportunities to arrange project financing or limit partnership financing for an asset you wish to purchase.
- *Incremental Benefits:* Calculate the net advantage to leasing based on the incremental after-tax benefits that leasing will provide.
- *Time Value of Money:* Use discounted cash flow analysis to compare the costs and benefits of leasing, relative to the alternative of borrowing and buying.
- *Two-Sided Transactions:* Leasing transfers the tax benefits of ownership from the lessee to the lessor.
- *Comparative Advantage:* Transfer the tax benefits of ownership to other parties if they are willing to pay for benefits your firm cannot use.
- *Valuable Ideas:* Look for opportunities to develop asset-based financing arrangements that offer new positive-NPV financing mechanisms.
- *Options:* Recognize that options in a lease, such as those to buy, extend, and cancel, are valuable to the lessee.
- *Capital Market Efficiency:* Use the lease information disclosed in the footnotes to a firm's financial statements to gauge the true financial impact of any leasing or rental agreements that do not appear on the face of the balance sheet.

20.1 LEASE FINANCING

Leasing is not new. We know that leasing originated at least 3,000 years ago, because records show that the ancient Phoenicians chartered ships. Since that time, chartering, a form of ship leasing, has played a major role in financing maritime activities. Lease financing has also expanded to cover just about any type of capital equipment. Its use has grown very rapidly in recent decades. This is partly because capital equipment has become increasingly complex and costly, and quickly obsolete. Leasing offers a means of efficiently transferring the risk of obsolescence. More importantly, firms in capital-intensive industries, such as railroads, airlines, and utilities, have been unable to make full use of the tax deductions that result from asset ownership. Lease financing provides a way to effectively transfer tax deductions from those who can not use them to those who can.

What Is a Lease?

A **lease** is a rental agreement that extends for one year or longer. Under a lease agreement, the owner of an asset (the **lessor**) grants another party (the **lessee**) the exclusive right to use the asset during the specified term of the lease in return for a specified series of payments, typically an annuity. In this way a lease resembles a secured loan.

Payments are typically made monthly, quarterly, or semiannually. The first lease payment is usually due when the lease agreement is signed. Payments are normally equal, like a mortgage or car payment. However, this time pattern can be altered, for example, to provide for lower payments during the early years before the asset reaches its full potential to generate cash flow.

Often lease agreements also give the lessee the option to renew the lease or purchase the asset. Sometimes the purchase option specifies a fixed price, but usually it is the asset's fair market value at the date the lessee exercises the option. If the purchase option is not exercised, the leased asset continues to belong to the lessor.

TYPES OF LEASES With *a full-service lease,* the lessor (owner) is responsible for maintaining and insuring the assets and paying any property taxes due on them. With a *net lease,* the lessee is responsible for these costs. **Operating leases** are short term and are generally cancelable at the lessee's option before the end of the lease term. **Financial leases** (or capital leases) are long term. They generally extend over most of the estimated useful economic life of the asset. Usually they cannot be canceled by the lessee before the end of the lease period. Those financial leases that *can* be canceled generally require the lessee to reimburse the lessor for any losses the cancellation causes.

FINANCIAL LEASES Financial leases represent an important source of long-term financing. Entering into a financial lease is like entering into a loan agreement. The lessee receives an immediate inflow equal to the value of the asset. The lessee realizes this value as if it were cash, because it gets the exclusive use of the asset without having to purchase it. The firm also realizes the same stream of economic benefits (other than tax deductions) that it would have if it had purchased the asset.

On the other hand, the lease agreement calls for specified periodic payments, just like a loan agreement. Moreover, if the lessee fails to make timely lease payments, the lessee runs the risk of bankruptcy, just as it would if it missed an interest payment or principal repayment on a loan. Therefore, a lease is very much like a secured loan.

Lease Financing Alternatives

Most financial leases fall into one of three categories: direct leases, sale-and-lease-back arrangements, or leveraged leases (Figure 20.1).

FIGURE 20.1
Illustration of the types of lease financing.

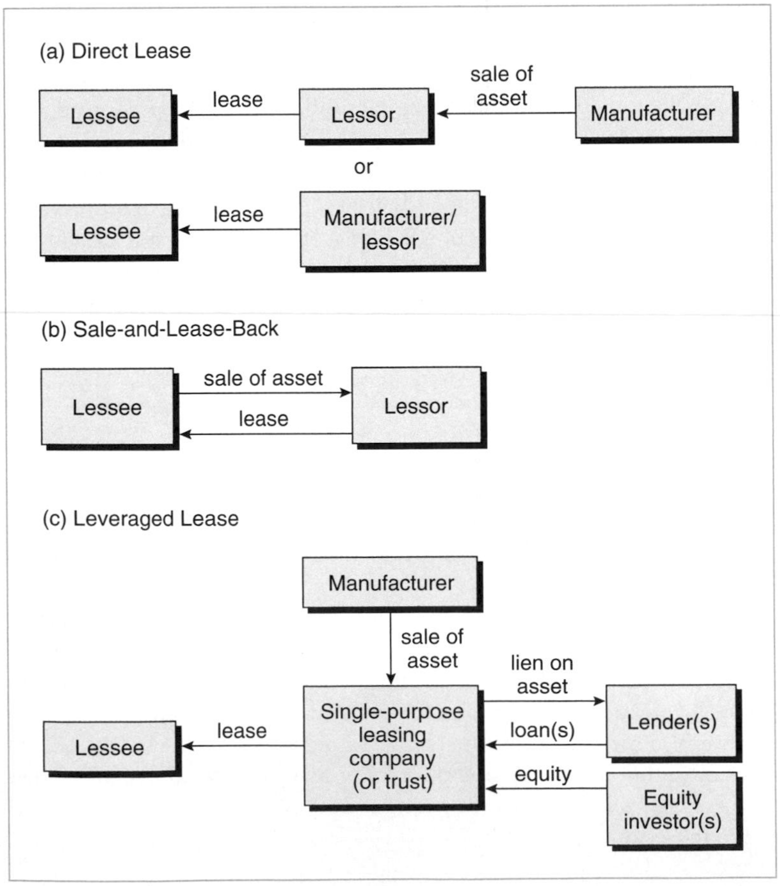

DIRECT LEASES Assets covered by financial leases are generally new. Under a direct lease, the lessee identifies the asset it requires. Then it either leases it directly from the manufacturer or arranges for some other lessor to buy it from the manufacturer and lease it to the lessee.

SALE-AND-LEASE-BACK ARRANGEMENTS A firm may sell an asset it already owns and lease it back from the purchaser. Such arrangements are common in real estate. Under a **sale-and-lease-back** arrangement, the owner of an asset sells it, usually at market value, for cash. The purchaser assumes legal ownership, and thereby the right to the tax deductions associated with ownership and to the residual value. The seller gets the exclusive right to use the asset during the basic lease period in return for periodic lease payments.

LEVERAGED LEASES A lessor who provides lease financing for an expensive piece of equipment, such as an aircraft, may wish to borrow a portion of the funds to make that investment. Under a **leveraged lease,** the lessor borrows a substantial portion of the purchase price of the asset, generally up to 80%. The lessor provides the balance of the purchase price in the form of equity. To secure the loan, the lessor grants the long-term lender(s) a mortgage on the asset, and assigns the lease contract to the lender(s). So lenders have a prior claim on the lease payments, as well as what is called a perfected first lien on the asset. Under such a lien, if the lessee fails to make timely lease payments, the lenders are entitled to seize the asset.

Advantages of Leasing

Leasing offers a number of legitimate advantages.

- *More efficient use of tax deductions and tax credits of ownership.* The main reason to choose lease financing is the lessor's ability to use the tax deductions and tax credits associated with asset ownership more efficiently than the lessee can.
- *Reduced risk.* Short-term operating leases, in particular, provide a convenient way to use an asset for a relatively short period of time. Cancelable operating leases, such as computer leases, relieve the lessee of the risk of product obsolescence. This risk shifting is efficient. The lessor, such as the equipment manufacturer, is usually in a better position to assume the risk. This motivation for leasing reflects the Options Principle: The cancellation option is valuable.
- *Reduced cost of borrowing.* Lessors of assets that can be sold readily, such as vehicles, generally do not have to perform credit analyses quite as detailed as those conducted by general lenders. They are also more likely to be able to use "standardized" lease documentation. Both factors reduce transaction costs, and thus result in a lower cost of borrowing for the lessee. This can especially benefit a smaller firm that may face restricted access to conventional sources of funds.
- *Bankruptcy considerations.* In the case of aircraft and vessels, special provisions of the bankruptcy law give a lessor greater flexibility than that of a secured lender to seize the asset in the event of bankruptcy because the lessor owns the asset. Suppliers of capital to smaller or less creditworthy firms, for which the risk of financial distress is greater, often prefer to advance funds through a lease rather than a loan. Because the lessor retains ownership of the asset, it can seize it if the lessee defaults.
- *An alternative source of financing.* Lease financing may permit a lessee to access a new source of funds. For example, a finance company might not purchase the lessee's securities, but might offer a lease. The new source is beneficial, of course, only if it results in a truly lower cost of borrowing.

Leasing also offers opportunities to circumvent restrictions.

- *Circumventing restrictive debt covenants or other restrictions.* A firm might be able to borrow funds through lease financing even when conventional debt financing is prohibited by its debt covenants.[1] The leases represent a disguised form of debt financing, and so may affect the

[1]In a notorious leasing arrangement, the U.S. Navy leased a fleet of oil tankers instead of seeking Congressional appropriations to finance the purchase of the vessels.

lessee's agency costs. However, recently drafted indentures and loan agreements usually contain limitations on leasing that close this loophole.

- *Off-balance-sheet financing.* Firms often go to great lengths to design leases that achieve off-balance-sheet treatment. Many firms also try to keep lease payments as low as possible during the early years of the lease term, in order to minimize the impact on reported earnings per share. Based on the Principle of Capital Market Efficiency, however, you would expect the leasing information disclosed in the footnotes to the firm's financial statements to enable market participants to gauge the true financial impact of the leasing arrangements. In fact, evidence shows that investors correctly evaluate the financial impact of firms' financial lease obligations. So the apparent income statement and balance-sheet benefits are of highly dubious value.

Of course, as you might also expect, a market imperfection can cause the accounting treatment to affect value. Off-balance-sheet treatment can prove beneficial to a regulated firm, such as a bank, in certain situations. Banks are required to maintain a minimum ratio of capital to total assets based on balance sheet figures. Given any particular amount of capital, the minimum required capital-to-assets ratio determines the maximum amount of assets, as reported in the bank's balance sheet. But by leasing assets off balance sheet, a bank can increase its assets above the constrained amount. When a bank's assets are already at the permitted maximum, the incremental after-tax cash flow the bank will realize by employing the leased assets in its business should be included in calculating the benefits of leasing.

EXAMPLE Synthetic Leases

Firms have used synthetic leases to get the use of assets but keep the debt off their balance sheet. An unrelated financial institution invests some equity and sets up a special-purpose entity (SPE) that borrows money, buys or constructs an asset the firm/lessee needs, and leases it to the firm under an operating lease. The firm/lessee owns the SPE for tax purposes. So the firm/lessee has the best of both worlds: It gets the depreciation and interest tax credits but the debt stays off its balance sheet. Firms have used synthetic leases to finance office buildings and plants. However, since the Enron bankruptcy put the spotlight on SPEs that hide corporate debt, firms have been much more reluctant to use synthetic leases.

Disadvantages of Leasing

There are two main disadvantages to leasing. First, the lessee forfeits the tax deductions associated with asset ownership. Second, the lessee must usually forgo residual value. A prospective lessee should evaluate carefully the cost of losing these benefits. Only then can it be decided if leasing is really cheaper than the alternative of borrowing and buying.

Bear in mind the Principle of Two-Sided Transactions. The tax benefits of leasing to the lessor are offset to some extent by certain tax detriments. The lessor must recognize the full amount of each lease payment as taxable income. As we have pointed out, a lease is like a loan. However, it is a loan in which the entire debt service payment is tax deductible to the borrower/lessee and taxable to the lender/lessor. Leasing is only beneficial when the present value of the benefits of leasing exceeds the present value of the costs of leasing.

Review

1. What is a lease? What is a leveraged lease?
2. How is a financial lease different from an operating lease?
3. What are the main advantages of leasing as compared to conventional debt financing?
4. What are the two main disadvantages to leasing?

20.2 TAX AND ACCOUNTING TREATMENT OF FINANCIAL LEASES

There are special tax and accounting provisions that relate to financial leases. It is important for you to understand them, particularly the tax provisions, if you are going to be involved in a leasing transaction.

Tax Treatment of Financial Leases

The Internal Revenue Service (IRS) has established guidelines to distinguish true leases from installment sales agreements and secured loans. If the terms of the leasing arrangement satisfy the guidelines, the lessee can deduct for tax purposes the full amount of each lease payment, and the lessor is entitled to the tax deductions and tax credits of asset ownership. Here are the main guidelines:

- The term of the lease cannot exceed 80% of the useful life of the asset. The term includes all renewal or extension periods other than renewals or extensions that are (1) at the option of the lessee and (2) at the fair market rental prevailing at the time of renewal or extension.
- The lessor must maintain a minimum equity investment in the asset of no less than 10% of the asset's original cost throughout the term of the lease.
- The lessor can grant the lessee a purchase option. However, the exercise price must equal the asset's fair market value at the time the purchase option is exercised. Certain lease transactions do take place with a purchase option that provides for a fixed price equal to the estimated future fair market value, but such a lease in that case does *not* conform to the guidelines and therefore does not qualify for an advance IRS ruling that it is a valid lease for tax purposes.
- The lessee does not pay any portion of the purchase price of the asset. In addition, if the lease is a leveraged lease, the lessee does not lend the lessor funds with which to purchase the leased asset or guarantee loans from others to the lessor for this purpose.
- The lessor must hold title to the property, and it must demonstrate that it expects to earn a pretax profit from the lease transaction—that is, profit apart from any tax deductions and tax credits it will realize.

These and the other requirements the IRS establishes are subject to change from time to time. As we have said several times, it is important to review the applicable tax rules. It is important to verify that a proposed lease arrangement would qualify as a true lease and to confirm that it is advantageous to lease.

Accounting Treatment of Financial Leases

The accounting treatment accorded leases has undergone significant changes in recent decades. At one time, leases represented off-balance-sheet financing. That is, neither the leased asset nor the associated lease obligations were recorded on the face of the lessee's balance sheet. However, generally accepted accounting principles did require a lessee to disclose certain details regarding lease transactions in the footnotes to the lessee's financial statements.

Financial Accounting Standards Board Statement No. 13 (FASB 13) requires lessees to capitalize on their balance sheets all leases entered into on or after that date that meet any one of the following requirements:

- The lease transfers ownership of the asset to the lessee before the lease expires.
- The lease agreement grants the lessee the option to purchase the asset at a bargain price.
- The term of the lease equals or exceeds 75% of the estimated useful economic life of the asset.
- The present value of the minimum lease payments, discounted to the beginning of the lease period at the smaller of (1) the lessee's incremental borrowing rate or (2) the interest rate implicit in the lease payment stream (the *lease rate*) equals or exceeds 90% of the asset's value (net of any investment tax credit claimed by the lessor).

Leases that "fail" all four tests are operating leases from an accounting standpoint, and they do not have to be capitalized on the face of the balance sheet.

FASB 13 assumes that if one of the four conditions is met, the lease arrangement is like purchasing the asset with borrowed funds. Accordingly, FASB 13 requires the lessee to report the present value of the lease payments under capital leases next to long-term debt on the right-hand side of the balance sheet, with a corresponding amount reported as an asset on the left-hand side of the balance sheet. The lessee amortizes the leased asset over the term of the lease. Correspondingly, under the "interest" method, the lessee separates each lease payment into an interest component and a principal repayment component. The amortization amount and the interest component of the lease payment are deducted from income for financial reporting purposes. The principal repayment component reduces the amount of the capitalized lease obligation reported on the lessee's balance sheet.

Review

1. Why does a lessor want to be sure that a lease qualifies as a lease for tax purposes?
2. What are the guidelines a lease must satisfy to qualify as a lease for tax purposes?
3. Are there any advantages to getting a lease off balance sheet? Suppose the lessee must provide the details of the lease in the footnotes to its financial statements.

20.3 VALUING A FINANCIAL LEASE

Leasing analysis can be complex. A lease financing normally affects a firm's capital structure. Because of its complexity, leasing analysis is one of the more controversial issues in financial management. In the past, there was considerable debate over the correct discount rate. However, the past controversy has been essentially resolved. Therefore, we focus our discussion on the generally accepted methods of leasing analysis.

Leasing involves an investment-financing interaction. That interaction can affect the decision to lease or to borrow and buy. It is even possible that the net present value of a capital investment project is negative when it is financed on a conventional basis, but positive when the asset is leased. Therefore, you should not limit your lease-versus-buy analysis just to those projects that can be justified on a purchase basis.

Leasing Displaces Borrowing

Lease analysis is similar to bond refunding analysis (Chapter 19). Just as one bond issue displaces another, so lease financing displaces debt. A firm that leases a piece of equipment reduces its borrowing capacity because it must meet its lease payment obligations on time in order to have uninterrupted use of the leased asset. If the lessee misses a lease payment, the lessor can reclaim the asset (which it legally owns) and sue the lessee for the missed lease payment. The consequences of failing to make a lease payment are the same as the consequences of failing to pay interest or repay principal on outstanding debt. The lessor becomes a creditor who can force the lessee into bankruptcy. Consequently, for purposes of financial analysis, a firm's lease payment obligations belong in the same risk category as the firm's interest and principal repayment obligations.

EXAMPLE Leasing Is an Alternative to Borrowing

North American Coal Company (NACCO) has a coal mine project under consideration. The project would cost $100 million. Among the required equipment, NACCO needs an electric shovel that costs $10 million. NACCO would use the electric shovel for 10 years before selling it. NACCO expects the shovel to be worth $500,000 after 10 years. The firm

TABLE 20.1
A financial lease displaces conventional debt.

	INITIAL CAPITALIZATION	CONVENTIONAL FINANCING	LEASE FINANCING	TARGET DEBT RATIO RESTORED
Long-term debt:				
Conventional debt	$100	$105	$100	$ 95
Financial lease obligations	—	—	10	10
Total long-term debt	100	105	110	105
Stockholders' equity	100	105	100	105
Net assets	$200	$210	$210	$210
Debt ratio	50%	50%	52.4%	50%

can depreciate the electric shovel on a straight-line basis over 10 years for tax purposes. A finance company has offered to lease the shovel to NACCO. The lease would require annual payments of $1.745 million (payable at the end of each year) for 10 years.

Table 20.1 illustrates the interrelatedness of leasing and borrowing. Suppose NACCO currently has net assets worth $200 million and a debt ratio of 50%. If NACCO financed the $10 million electric shovel on a conventional basis without altering its capital structure, then it would borrow $5 million and raise $5 million of equity funds. That would leave the firm with $105 million of debt and $105 million of equity. Suppose instead that NACCO leased the electric shovel, and that the associated lease obligations have a present value of $10 million. NACCO's debt—including this lease obligation—increases to $110 million. No equity funds are required. The lease provides what practitioners like to refer to as "100% financing." However, you can see that leasing has changed the firm's capital structure. NACCO's debt ratio increases from 50% to 52.4% (= 110/210). So the two alternatives are not comparable, because they do not leave the firm with identical capital structures.

NACCO can restore its capital structure to 50% debt only if it issues $5 million of equity and reduces its other borrowing by $5 million. In that case, its debt would consist of $95 million of preexisting debt plus the $10 million new lease obligation. Under both alternatives, NACCO has total debt of $105 million. However, under the leasing alternative, $10 million of that total consists of the new lease obligation. It is in this sense that a financial lease displaces conventional debt dollar for dollar.

Only when the alternatives of leasing, or borrowing and buying, are placed on a comparable basis can we make an accurate choice. Such a comparable basis includes the firm's capital structure. Whether the firm will in fact have identical capital structures after implementation of either alternative is a separate decision and should be evaluated on its own merits. The important point is to isolate the decision under consideration and not to confuse a lease versus borrow-and-buy decision with a capital structure decision.

Basic Analytic Framework

We have pointed out how the cash flow stream associated with a financial lease is similar in financial effect to the cash flow stream of a secured loan. This suggests an appropriate starting point for analyzing a financial lease: Compare it to the alternative of borrowing to finance the purchase price of the asset and repaying this loan over the lease term.

TABLE 20.2
Direct cash flow consequences to NACCO of lease financing an electric shovel.

YEAR	0	1	2	3	4	5	6	7	8	9	10
Benefits of Leasing:											
Initial outlay (avoided)	+10,000										
Costs of Leasing:											
Lease payments[a]		−1,745	−1,745	−1,745	−1,745	−1,745	−1,745	−1,745	−1,745	−1,745	−1,745
Lease payment tax credit[b]		+698	+698	+698	+698	+698	+698	+698	+ 698	+698	+698
Depreciation tax credits forgone[c]		−380	−380	−380	−380	−380	−380	−380	−380	−380	−380
Salvage value forgone											−500
Net cash flow to leasee	+10,000	−1,427	−1,427	−1,427	−1,427	−1,427	−1,427	−1,427	−1,427	−1,427	−1,927

[a]Lease payments made annually in arrears.
[b]Assumes the lessee's marginal income tax rate is 40%.
[c]Assumes straight-line depreciation to a $500,000 terminal book value for tax purposes.

EXAMPLE A Financial Lease Is Similar to a Secured Loan

Let's consider further our NACCO example. What are NACCO's direct cash flows for leasing versus buying an electric shovel?

Table 20.2 shows the firm's direct cash flow consequences of lease financing an electric shovel. The firm does not have to spend $10 million to purchase the shovel. The effect is equivalent to a cash inflow of $10 million. However, NACCO must make periodic lease payments. These are tax deductible. Therefore, assuming a 40% tax rate, a lease payment of $1,745,000 gives rise to a tax deduction worth $698,000 (= [0.4]1,745,000). It must also forgo the depreciation tax deductions and residual value of ownership. Each electric shovel is depreciated to a salvage value of $500,000. Depreciation is straight line. Each year's deduction is $950,000 (= [10,000,000 − 500,000] ÷ 10). The after-tax value of each year's deduction is $380,000 (= [0.4] 950,000). Putting all these factors together, there is an effective initial net cash inflow of $10.0 million. It is followed by effective net cash outflows of $1.427 million in each of years 1 through 9 and $1.927 million in year 10.

Note that a different tax rate would change the cash flows. So, for example, if the firm did not expect to pay income taxes during the lease, the value of the depreciation tax deductions forgone would be zero.

Note also that in addition to the direct cash flows, leasing causes NACCO to forgo the tax deductions associated with asset ownership. We incorporate this effect later when we calculate the net advantage to leasing using the incremental cash flows.

Using Debt Service Parity

The debt service parity (DSP) approach is useful for this purpose. It applies to leasing analysis much as it does to bond refunding. As we have said, the principal tenet of the DSP approach is that the two alternatives must be evaluated as though the firm's total after-tax obligation (either lease payments or debt service payments) will be exactly the same under either alternative. Maintaining such parity is important. Evaluating the lease-versus-borrow-and-buy decision must avoid the complications associated with other possible simultaneous decisions. These complications could bias the calculation of the net advantage to leasing.

When you apply the DSP approach, you ask the question, "How much money can I raise today by selling the debt stream promised by the lease?" If this amount is greater than the purchase price of the financed asset, then the lease will not increase shareholder wealth. You could buy the asset more economically using borrowed funds.

First, we must determine the amount of debt the firm can issue today, if the obligation connected with the after-tax period-by-period debt service payments for the borrow-and-buy alternative is exactly the same as that of the lease alternative. Here is how you might view the amount of debt the firm could issue today. Think of the after-tax lease payments as a set of promised future cash flows that could be "auctioned off" in the capital market. The amount of debt the firm can issue today is then the amount it would receive in exchange for that set of promised future cash flows. If the proceeds of the debt are not enough to purchase the equipment, then the leasing alternative has a positive NPV and should be undertaken. Of course, if the debt proceeds are greater than the cost of purchasing the equipment, then leasing would decrease shareholder wealth and should not be undertaken.

THE NET ADVANTAGE TO LEASING The **net advantage to leasing** equals the purchase price minus the present value of the incremental after-tax cash flows, the CFATs, associated with the lease. The net advantage to leasing (NAL) can be expressed in equation form as:

$$\text{NAL} = P - \text{PV(CFATs)} \tag{20.1}$$

where P is the purchase price and PV(CFATs) is the present value of the CFATs.

What is the appropriate discount rate for determining the present value of the lease payments, any after-tax change in operating or other expenses (due to the lessor becoming responsible for paying them under the terms of the lease), and depreciation tax deductions? They should all be discounted at the lessee's after-tax cost of similarly secured debt (assuming 100% debt financing for the asset). In Chapter 19, we saw that secured debt is debt that provides lenders with a lien on certain assets. This is also the required return for the lease payments. This is true because a firm's lease payments belong to the same risk class as the firm's debt payments. In addition, the lease obligation is secured because the lessor retains ownership of the asset. However, the lessee is effectively borrowing 100% of the purchase price. So the financial lease obligation is not overcollateralized, as is typically the case with conventional secured debt financing.[2] Accordingly, the secured debt rate used in the financial lease valuation should reflect the absence of overcollateralization. Typically, it will be a weighted average of the cost of fully secured debt and the cost of unsecured debt.

The present value of the expected residual value of the asset—the salvage value—is determined by discounting at a higher required return to reflect its greater riskiness. Residual value is more closely related to overall project economic risk than to financing risk. Therefore, the required return for the project is used to determine the present value of the expected residual value.

The relevant incremental cash flows associated with a lease-versus-borrow-and-buy decision include (1) cost of the asset (savings), (2) lease payments (cost), (3) incremental differences in operating or other expenses between the leasing and buying alternatives (cost or savings), (4) depreciation tax deductions (forgone benefit), (5) expected net residual value (forgone benefit),[3] and (6) investment tax credit or other tax credits (forgone benefit).

The net advantage to leasing can be rewritten as

$$\text{NAL} = P - \sum_{t=1}^{N} \frac{(1-T)(\text{CF}_t - \Delta E_t) + TD_t}{[1+(1-T)r']^t} - \frac{\text{SAL}}{[1+r]^N} - \text{ITC} \tag{20.2}$$

[2]An asset's value can decrease. So secured loans are overcollateralized to protect lenders. For example, lenders may require 25% overcollateralization before they will treat a loan as "fully secured" and lend at the lower fully secured debt rate. In that case, a firm that pledges $100 million of assets can borrow up to $80 million at the secured debt rate.

[3]The asset's residual value at the end of the lease term is also important for tax reasons. If the asset's residual value is expected to be insignificant, the Internal Revenue Service may take the position that the lease is not a true lease. It would then deny the tax deductibility of the portion of the lessee's lease payments that effectively represents principal repayments.

where

D_t = the depreciation deduction (for tax purposes, not financial reporting purposes) in year t
ΔE_t = the total incremental difference in operating or other expenses in year t between the leasing and buying alternatives
ITC = investment tax credit, if available
CF_t = lease payment in year t
N = the number of periods in the life of the lease
NAL = the net advantage to leasing
P = the purchase price of the asset
r = the required return for the asset (its after-tax weighted average cost of capital)
r' = the pre-tax cost of debt, assuming 100% debt financing for the asset (typically, this will be a weighted average of the fully secured and unsecured debt rates)
SAL = salvage value of the asset (the expected residual value of the asset at the end of the lease)
T = the lessee's (asset user's) marginal ordinary income tax rate

Equation (20.2) assumes the lease payments are made in arrears (that is, at the end of each period), not in advance (at the beginning of each period). Lease agreements often provide for lease payments to be made in advance. In such cases, adjust Equation (20.2), and the other equations presented in this section, appropriately to reflect properly the exact timing of the lease payments. The equation also assumes that the lessor claims any investment tax credit (ITC). Lease agreements sometimes permit the lessee to claim it instead. Before performing a leasing analysis, check the proposed lease terms to determine the timing of the lease payments and who is entitled to claim any available ITC.

Analyzing a Lease-or-Buy Decision

Let us apply the DSP approach to NACCO's lease-or-buy decision. First, we must specify current capital market conditions. NACCO can borrow 10-year secured installment debt in the amount of 80% of the value of each electric shovel at a pretax interest rate of 11.5% per year. NACCO can borrow unsecured installment debt in the amount of the remaining 20% of the value of each electric shovel at a pretax interest rate of 14.0% per year. Finally, the after-tax required return (weighted average cost of capital) for this project is 15% per year. NACCO's marginal tax rate is 40%.

EXAMPLE NACCO's Net Advantage to Leasing

NACCO's cost of debt, assuming 100% debt financing with 80% secured and 20% unsecured, is 12.0% (= [0.8]11.5% + [0.2]14.0%) before tax and 7.2% after tax (= [1 − 0.4]12.0%). The lease payments are $1,745,000 at the end of each year for 10 years. They are tax deductible. The amount of the depreciation tax deductions forgone is $950,000 per year (= [10,000,000 − 500,000]/10). The related tax savings forgone is $380,000 per year (= [0.4]950,000). The salvage value is $500,000. There is no ITC. Therefore, applying Equation (20.2), the net advantage to leasing for NACCO is:

$$\begin{aligned}\text{NAL} &= 10,000,000 - \sum_{t=1}^{10} \frac{(1-0.40)1,745,000 + 380,000}{(1.072)^t} - \frac{500,000}{(1.15)^{10}} - 0 \\ &= 10,000,000 - 9,930,644 - 123,592 = -\$54,236\end{aligned}$$

The net advantage to leasing is negative. The firm should borrow and buy rather than lease the shovel. We will show you later that NACCO's ability to fully use the tax deductions associated with asset ownership itself is largely responsible for this negative value.

Leasing and Capital Budgeting

As we saw in the case of capital structure, taxes affect asset value. Lease financing can affect the value of an investment by enabling a lessee to take advantage of any potential tax asymmetry. It is possible for a project that would have a negative NPV, if the firm financed it on a conventional basis, to have a positive NPV if it is lease financed. If the lessor can benefit from tax deductions and credits and their timing but the lessee cannot, leasing can increase the investment value.

EXAMPLE Lease Financing Can Affect the Value of an Investment Project

The top panel of Table 20.3 illustrates the cash flow streams for an electric power project. The project's owner can lease the power generation equipment. The firm will never be able to claim the tax deductions associated with asset ownership. The firm has determined that debt financing is of no benefit because it is unable to claim the interest tax deductions. The firm's investments require a 15% return (zero leverage). The NPV of the project is −$1,907,113. The project would therefore be unprofitable if it were financed on a conventional basis.

Suppose instead that the project is lease financed. The middle panel of Table 20.3 shows the associated cash flows. The lease arrangement calls for lease payments of $10,300,000 at the end of each year. The net advantage to leasing in $2,241,434.

TABLE 20.3
Illustration of how lease financing can turn a project profitable.

NPV (CONVENTIONALLY FINANCED)

Time	Item	CFBT	CFAT	PV at 15%
0	Initial outlay	−50,000,000	−50,000,000	−50,000,000
1–7	ΔRev − ΔExp.	11,378,903	11,378,903	47,341,013
7	Residual value	2,000,000	2,000,000	751,874
			NPV =	−$1,907,113

NET ADVANTAGE TO LEASING

Time	Item	CFBT	CFAT	PV at 12%[a] (15% for residual value)
0	Initial outlay	50,000,000	50,000,000	50,000,000
1–7	Lease payments	−10,300,000	−10,300,000	−47,006,692
7	Residual value	−2,000,000	−2,000,000	−751,874
			NAL =	$2,241,434

TOTAL NET PRESENT VALUE

Total net present value = −$1,907,113 + 2,241,434 = $334,321

[a]Assumes a new issue rate of 12.00% for the firm's debt.

By combining the NPV of the conventionally financed project with the net advantage to leasing (NAL), we get the total NPV of the project lease financed, shown in the bottom panel of Table 20.3:

$$\begin{aligned} \text{NPV(leased)} &= \text{NPV(conventional)} + \text{NAL} \\ &= -1{,}907{,}113 + 2{,}241{,}434 = \$334{,}321 \end{aligned} \tag{20.3}$$

The lease rate is low enough that the net advantage to leasing outweighs the negative net present value of the project when it is financed on a conventional basis. In effect, the lessor is willing to pay enough for the tax deductions to make the project profitable. Thus, the project is profitable when lease financed but unprofitable otherwise.

Note that the project's residual value could also play an important role in the economics of leasing. Suppose the residual value in the example just given were, say, \$10 million. The net present value of the project when financed on a conventional basis would be \$1.10 million, and the net advantage to leasing would be −\$0.77 million. The sponsor should finance the project in that case on a conventional basis even though it does not expect to be able to use any of the tax deductions associated with asset ownership.

When Is Lease Financing Advantageous?

As you would expect, leasing would be a zero-sum game between lessor and lessee in a perfect capital market environment. Even with taxes, in an otherwise perfect capital market environment, it will be a zero-sum game if both parties have the same marginal tax rate.

Of course, in an imperfect capital market environment, there is a possibility that a tax asymmetry, information asymmetries, or transaction costs may cause leasing to be favorable for both lessor and lessee. Therefore, if the lessor and the lessee have different marginal income tax rates, the CFATs can have different present values to the two parties. Leasing may also offer a better way to allocate the risk connected with an asset. Certain parties may have a comparative advantage in dealing with certain kinds of uncertainty. Finally, still other parties may have a comparative advantage in dealing with particular transaction costs connected with an asset.

BAD REASONS FOR LEASING Managers are sometimes tempted to play accounting "games" to try to fool investors. Such games are not likely to be successful, but more important, they can lead to negative-NPV decisions. Earlier, we noted that it appears to some people that leasing provides "100% financing," whereas debt provides less. This is sometimes given as a reason for leasing, but we hope you can see that is false. Finally, we also noted that leasing may offer an opportunity to circumvent one or more restrictions. If this is the purpose of the lease, you should consider very carefully whether leasing is wise. Regulations and restrictions may exist for good reasons.

Review

1. How does a lease displace conventional debt?
2. What is the net advantage to leasing?
3. How is the debt service parity approach applied to leasing?
4. Why is the discount rate applied to the expected residual value different from the discount rate applied to the lease payments?
5. How can lease financing enhance the NPV of a project when the firm that develops it does not pay income taxes?

20.4 PROJECT FINANCING

Firms often find it advantageous to finance large capital investment projects that involve discrete assets on a project, or stand-alone, basis. **Project financing** is generally possible when a project possesses the following two characteristics:

1. The project consists of a discrete asset or a discrete set of assets capable of standing alone as an independent economic unit.
2. The economic prospects of the project, combined with commitments from the sponsors or from third parties, assure that it will generate sufficient revenue net of operating costs to service project debt.

Mines, mineral processing facilities, electric generating facilities, pipelines, dock facilities, paper mills, oil refineries, and chemical plants are examples of assets that firms have financed on a project basis. In each case, the project's assets and the related debt obligations are separated from the sponsoring firms' other assets and liabilities, and the project is analyzed as a separate (though not necessarily independent) unit.

Project Structure

Each project is unique in some respects, and the financing arrangements are designed to suit the project's special characteristics and to resolve potential agency problems.

EXAMPLE Project Financing Versus Conventional Financing

Suppose that NACCO wishes to develop the coal mine project discussed previously in order to obtain coal to sell to Electric Generating Company. NACCO could finance the mine on its general credit by selling equity securities or debentures and investing the proceeds in the project. Suppose, however, that in return for an assured source of coal supply, Electric Generating is willing to enter into a long-term coal purchase contract with NACCO. The mine will cost $100 million, which NACCO would like to borrow. The terms of the coal purchase contract can be drawn in such a way that the contract will provide support for the loans. NACCO will arrange to finance development of the mine and minimize potential agency costs. In the extreme case, the loans may be nonrecourse to NACCO. In that case, lenders will look solely to payments under the coal purchase contract for the payment of interest and the repayment of principal on their loans. The loans would then be designed to be self-liquidating from the revenues to be derived from coal sales to Electric, and the project financing would have little impact on NACCO's borrowing capacity.

The coal mine is capable of standing alone as an independent economic unit because of the long-term coal purchase contract, which will guarantee a market for its output. Normally, the project sponsor would have to make additional commitments (described next) to lenders as a condition for their agreeing to lend to the project.

Project Financing

Financial engineering is crucial in project financing. It is necessary to design contractual arrangements to allocate project risks among the entities involved with the project, allocate the economic rewards among them, convey the credit strength of creditworthy firms to support project debt, and minimize total agency costs. Typical credit support arrangements include the following:

- *Completion undertaking.* Such an undertaking obligates the sponsors or other creditworthy entities either (1) to assure that the project will pass certain performance tests by some specified date, or (2) to repay the debt. As an example of the former, the coal mine mentioned earlier might be required to produce a certain number of tons of coal per month for a certain specified number of months prior to some specified date. Completion undertakings are designed to control the equityholders' tendency to pursue high-risk projects at the expense of lenders. They also prevent the equityholders from abandoning a project without fully compensating lenders if a project becomes unprofitable.

- *Purchase, throughput, or tolling agreements.* These obligate one or more creditworthy entities to purchase the project's output or use its facilities. Purchase agreements that are capable of supporting project financing take the form of take-or-pay contracts or hell-or-high-water contracts. Take-or-pay contracts obligate the purchaser to take the project's output or else pay for it if the product is offered for delivery (but normally only if the product is available for delivery). Hell-or-high-water contracts obligate the purchaser to pay in all events, that is, whether or not any output is available for delivery. The latter is, of course, stronger and therefore provides greater credit support. Throughput agreements are often used in pipeline financing. They require shippers to put some specified minimum amount of a product (for example, oil) through the pipeline each month (or interest period) in order to enable the pipeline to generate sufficient cash to cover its operating expenses and debt service requirements. They can take the form of either ship-or-pay (similar to take-or-pay obligations) or hell-or-high-water undertakings. Tolling agreements are often used in financing processing facilities, such as an aluminum smelter, where the user retains ownership of the item throughout the production process. Such arrangements require users to process a certain specified minimum amount of raw material each month (or interest period).
- *Cash deficiency agreements.* Unless the purchase, throughput, or tolling agreement is of the hell-or-high-water variety, interruptions in availability or deliverability can result in the project realizing insufficient cash to meet its debt service obligations. Sponsors may therefore have to provide supplemental credit support in the form of a cash deficiency agreement. It obligates the sponsor to invest additional cash as required by the project to meet its debt service obligations.

Advantages of Project Financing

Project financing can provide significant advantages in certain situations.

- *Risk sharing.* A sponsor can enlist one or more joint venture partners to share the equity risk. Such risk sharing is beneficial in the presence of significant costs of financial distress. It should be considered whenever a capital investment project is so large relative to a firm's existing asset portfolio that pursuing it alone would increase the firm's risk of bankruptcy to an unacceptable level. Under some circumstances, a project sponsor can transfer risks to suppliers, purchasers, and, to a limited degree, lenders through contractual arrangements like those just discussed. Risks can be allocated to parties who are willing to bear them at the lowest cost.
- *Expanded debt capacity.* By financing on a project basis rather than on its general credit, a firm may be able to achieve a higher degree of leverage than would be consistent with its senior debt rating objective if it financed the project entirely on its own. Project-related contractual arrangements transfer portions of the business and financial risk to others. This permits greater leverage.
- *Lower cost of debt.* Suppose the purchasers of the project's output have a higher credit standing than project sponsors. In that case, financing on the purchasers' credit rather than on the sponsors' credit can lead to a lower cost of debt. This benefit is more likely to occur when the output of the project will create a positive NPV for the purchaser that can be realized only if the sponsor undertakes the project. The project sponsor is effectively realizing a portion of the purchaser's positive NPV through the lower cost of borrowing it achieves.

Disadvantages of Project Financing

Project financing can involve significant transaction costs. The contractual arrangements mentioned earlier are often complex. Consequently, arranging project financing usually involves significant legal fees. In addition, lenders generally require a yield premium in return for accepting credit support in the form of contractual undertakings rather than a firm's direct promise to pay because of the higher agency costs.

When to Use Project Financing

A project should be financed on a project basis only if that method of financing maximizes shareholder wealth. This will generally be the case when (1) project financing facilitates a higher degree of leverage than conventional financing and (2) the tax effects owing to the higher degree of leverage exceed the sum of the costs associated with the yield premium lenders require plus the higher after-tax transaction costs.

Review

1. When might project financing be a feasible financing alternative?
2. What are the contractual arrangements in a project financing designed to accomplish?
3. What is a completion undertaking?
4. What are the main advantages and disadvantages of project financing?

20.5 LIMITED PARTNERSHIP FINANCING

We said earlier in this chapter that leveraged lease financing represents a cost-effective alternative to debt financing when the lessee is unable to fully use the tax benefits of asset ownership. Limited partnership financing represents another form of tax-oriented financing. But unlike leasing, the sale of limited partnership units represents a form of equity financing.

Limited partnerships have been formed to finance real estate projects, oil and gas exploration, film making, research and development projects, the construction of cable television systems, Broadway shows, Hard Rock Cafe restaurants, and various other ventures.

Characteristics of Limited Partnerships

A **limited partnership** is a special form of partnership. Certain partners, called limited partners, enjoy limited liability. They are passive investors like the stockholders of a corporation. But a limited partnership, like partnerships generally, does not pay income taxes. Income or loss for tax purposes is passed through to the partners. So suppose a firm plans a capital-intensive investment, such as oil and gas drilling, but believes it will not have sufficient taxable income to fully use the tax deductions and tax credits of the venture. It could form a limited partnership in order to direct the tax benefits through to the investors.[4] Particularly in risky projects like oil exploration, these tax benefits can offer a substantial inducement to individual investors to share the investment risks inherent in such projects.

[4]The tax advantages of a limited partnership (as compared to the corporate form of organization) are greatest for firms with high tax rates and low retention rates (that is, those in "mature" industries). Very rapidly growing firms that need to reinvest all their earnings and have low corporate tax rates are unlikely to find a limited partnership structure beneficial for tax purposes.

The limited partnership is operated by a general partner. The general partner is responsible for the liabilities of the limited partnership (except for those liabilities specifically assumed or guaranteed by the limited partners). Income, losses, tax credits, and distributions are allocated among the partners in accordance with a sharing formula specified at the time the limited partnership is formed.

EXAMPLE The Cinema Group Partners Limited Partnership

Cinema Group Partners was formed some years ago. The general partner contributed 10% of the partnership capital. The limited partners were promised 98% of profits, losses, tax credits, and cash distributions until they recovered their investment. Thereafter, they were promised 80% until they received cash representing in the aggregate 200% of their investment. After that, they were promised 70% until they received cash representing in the aggregate 300% of their investment, and 60% of any subsequent cash distributions. In addition, the general partner receives a management fee equal to 4% of the limited partnership's net worth.

Measuring the Cost of Limited Partner Capital

A firm that sets up a limited partnership and serves as general partner effectively experiences the following cash flow benefits and costs:

- Initial cash inflow equal to the net proceeds from the sale of units of limited partnership interest
- Annual cash inflows equal to the taxes payable on the portion of partnership taxable income allocated to the limited partners
- Initial cash outflow equal to the amount of the investment tax credit, if any, allocated to the limited partners
- Annual cash outflows equal to (1) the cash distributions to the limited partners plus (2) the tax shields resulting from the portion of partnership losses for tax purposes allocated to the limited partners
- Terminal cash outflow equal to the residual value of the limited partnership's assets allocated to the limited partners

EXAMPLE Calculating the Cost of Limited Partner Capital

Table 20.4 provides the incremental cash flows associated with financing a new cable television system through a limited partnership that the general partner intends to terminate after 10 years. The financing involves the sale of $50 million of units of limited partnership interest that raises $45 million net of issuance expenses. The general partner will invest $5 million for a 10% ownership interest. The limited partnership agreement calls for the limited partners to pay all the issuance expenses and contribute 90% of partnership capital. The limited partners will also receive 90% of partnership income, losses, tax credits (if any), and cash distributions until they have received aggregate cash distributions equal to their original $50 million investment. After that, the limited partners will receive 50% of partnership income, losses, tax credits (if any), and cash distributions. The sponsor's marginal ordinary income tax rate is 40%.

The initial cash flow is the $45 million inflow, representing the net proceeds from the sale of the units of limited partnership interest (column 1). Each annual cash flow thereafter (column 7) except the last year's is equal to the amount of income taxes saved (tax credits lost) on the portion of partnership income (loss) allocated to the limited partners (column 5) less the cash distributions to limited partners (column 4). Note that in year 8 the limited partners reach $50 million in aggregate cash distributions after the payment of $4.1 million that year. The $4.1 million payment represents 90% of $4.56 million. The remaining $11.44 million of year 8's operating cash flow is divided equally between the general and limited partners, giving the limited partners total

TABLE 20.4
Calculation of cost of limited partner capital.

END OF YEAR	(1) NET PROCEEDS OF FINANCING[a]	(2) PARTNERSHIP OPERATING CASH FLOW[b]	(3) PARTNERSHIP TAXABLE INCOME[c]	(4) DISTRIBUTION TO LIMITED PARTNERS[d]	(5) TAX ON INCOME (LOSS) FORGONE[e]	(6) RESIDUAL VALUE FORGONE[f]	(7) NET CASH FLOW TO SPONSOR[g]
0	$45.0	—	—	—	—	—	$45.00
1	—	$1.5	−$3.5	$1.35	−$1.26	—	−2.61
2	—	3.0	−2.0	2.70	−0.72	—	−3.42
3	—	3.5	−1.5	3.15	−0.54	—	−3.69
4	—	7.0	2.0	6.30	0.72	—	−5.58
5	—	10.0	5.0	9.00	1.80	—	−7.20
6	—	12.0	7.0	10.80	2.52	—	−8.28
7	—	14.0	9.0	12.60	3.24	—	−9.36
8	—	16.0	11.0	9.82	2.70	—	−7.12
9	—	17.5	12.5	8.75	2.50	—	−6.25
10	—	19.0	14.0	9.50	2.80	$51.30	−58.00
						Cost of limited partner capital[h] =	12.88%

[a]Calculated as gross proceeds of $50 million less 10% issuance expenses.
[b]As projected by the general partner.
[c]Calculated as operating cash flow less straight-line depreciation amounting to $5 million per year.
[d]Calculated as 90% of operating cash flow until limited partners recover their $50 million investment (during year 8) and as 50% of operating cash flow thereafter.
[e]Taxes payable (credit) by the general partner if the income allocated to the limited partners had instead been included in its income. Limited partners are allocated the same percentage of partnership taxable income as their percentage of partnership operating cash flow. Amount is calculated by multiplying column 3 by the allocation percentage and by the tax rate: for year 3, $-1.5 \times 0.9 \times 0.4 = -0.54$.
[f]Assumes the cable television system is sold for 9 times year 10 operating cash flow, or $171.0 million. Residual value is net of taxes (at a 40% marginal rate) on the half of terminal value that is forgone. Note that the $50 million project is fully depreciated to 0.
[g]Calculated as the net proceeds of financing plus tax on income (loss) forgone less distribution to limited partners less also residual value forgone.
[h]Calculated as the internal rate of return of the net cash flow to sponsor.

cash distributions of $9.82 (= 4.1 + 5.72) million for the year. Table 20.4 assumes that the limited partnership sells the cable television system for nine times the last year's operating cash flow, or $171 million, half of which it must distribute to the limited partners. The general partner forgoes $85.5 million. Because the cable television system has been fully depreciated, there is a $171 million gain on the transaction, half of which is borne by the limited partners. After-tax residual value forgone (column 6) is therefore $51.3 million (= [0.6]85.5).

The **cost of limited partner capital** (that is, capital raised from the limited partners, CLPC in the following equation) is just the discount rate that equates the present value of the net cash outflows from the sponsor in Table 20.4 to the $45 million net proceeds of financing:

$$\text{NP} = \sum_{t=1}^{T} \frac{\text{CFAT}_t}{(1 + \text{CLPC})^t} \tag{20.4}$$

$$= \$45.0 \text{ million} \quad \text{CLPC} = 12.88\%$$

NP is the net proceeds from the limited partnership financing. CFAT_t is the net after-tax cash flow in year t. CLPC is the cost of limited partner capital, and T is the term of the limited partnership.

Limited partnership financing in this case represents an alternative to all-equity financing.[5] The cost of limited partner capital in Equation (20.4) should therefore be compared with the unleveraged required return for the project (because this limited

[5]The limited partnership has no debt. If it did, CLPC would have to be compared to the required return for a conventionally financed and identically leveraged project.

partnership has no debt). Suppose the capital investment project has a 15% unleveraged required return. Then limited partnership financing is cheaper than conventional all-equity financing.

The cost of limited partner capital depends importantly on the limited partners' tax position and on the asset's residual value. The higher the tax rate on the limited partners' income, the greater the value of the tax credits transferred to them. Hence, the lower is likely to be the firm's cost of raising funds through limited partnership financing. In addition, the lower the portion of residual value that needs to be allocated to limited partners, the lower the cost of funds, as was the case with lease financing.

Advantages and Disadvantages of Limited Partnership Financing

Limited partnership financing provides an alternative means of "selling" the tax deductions and tax credits associated with asset ownership. As in the case of lease financing, limited partnership financing can be mutually beneficial to the firm and to the investor when the investor pays income tax at a higher marginal rate than the firm.

Also as in the case of lease financing, the firm must sacrifice a portion of the asset's residual value. When the forgone residual value is taken into account, limited partnership financing may prove to be more expensive than conventional equity financing.

In contrast to lease financing, limited partnership financing can also be advantageous to profitable firms. A partnership is nontaxable. Organizing a project (or a business) as a limited partnership, rather than having a corporation own it, eliminates a layer of taxation.

Review

1. What is a limited partnership? How do the liabilities of general partners and limited partners differ?
2. How is limited partnership financing similar to lease financing? How is it different?
3. What is the cost of limited partner capital?
4. What are the main advantages and disadvantages of limited partnership financing?

SUMMARY

- A firm can finance a project on the strength of its general promise to pay and overall profitability by promising investors and/or lenders a share of the future cash flow from its entire portfolio of assets. Alternatively, it can use asset-based financing. In that case, the amount providers of capital are paid is tied to the firm's use of a particular asset.
- Asset-based financing techniques include leasing, various forms of project financing, and limited partnership financing.
- Asset-based financing should be employed only if it increases shareholder wealth.
- Lease financing is equivalent to borrowing to buy the asset. The decision whether to lease must therefore be evaluated relative to the borrow-and-buy alternative, while neutralizing the capital structure side effects. Use the DSP approach.

- Lease financing can be cheaper than conventional secured debt financing for a firm due to a potential tax asymmetry. Lease financing will have a positive net advantage only if the net present value of the net cash flows to the lessee is positive, or equivalently, only if the lease financing provides a greater amount of funds to the lessee than an equivalent loan.
- Lease financing may be beneficial when the lessor is better able to bear the risks of technical obsolescence than the lessee, as may be the case with lessor/manufacturers of high-technology assets such as computers.
- Project financing should be considered whenever a capital investment project (1) consists of a discrete asset (or set of assets), (2) has a positive expected net present value, and (3) is so large relative to the sponsor's existing asset portfolio that pursuing it alone would increase the sponsor's risk of bankruptcy to an unacceptable level.
- Project financing should also be considered whenever there is a readily identifiable set of purchasers for the project's output who would be willing to enter into contractual commitments against which the sponsor could borrow funds for the project on a nonrecourse basis.
- Limited partnership financing can be cheaper than conventional equity financing for a firm that cannot fully use the tax benefits of asset ownership, or for a profitable firm that can operate a portion of its business in a separate partnership entity and thereby eliminate corporate taxation of the separate entity's income. Limited partnership financing will have a positive net advantage to a firm only if the cost of limited partner capital is less than the firm's cost of capital for equivalent conventional financing.

EQUATION SUMMARY

$$\text{NAL} = P - \text{PV(CFATs)} \tag{20.1}$$

$$\text{NAL} = P - \sum_{t=1}^{N} \frac{(1-T)(\text{CF}_t - \Delta E_t) + TD_t}{[1+(1-T)r']^t} - \frac{\text{SAL}}{[1+r]^N} - \text{ITC} \tag{20.2}$$

$$\text{NPV(leased)} = \text{NPV(conventional)} + \text{NAL} \tag{20.3}$$

$$\text{NP} = \sum_{t=1}^{T} \frac{\text{CFAT}_t}{(1+\text{CLPC})^t} \tag{20.4}$$

QUESTIONS

1. Define the terms *lease, lessor,* and *lessee.* What is the relationship between a lessor and a lessee?
2. Explain the principal differences between a direct lease, a sale-and-lease-back, and a leveraged lease.
3. What are the principal advantages and principal disadvantages of lease financing? Which of the purported advantages are really of dubious value?
4. Explain why a dollar of lease financing displaces a dollar of conventional debt financing.
5. What are the principal tax benefits associated with asset ownership?
6. What requirements must a lease satisfy to qualify as a true lease for tax purposes?
7. Describe how the net advantage to leasing is measured.

8. What is the appropriate discount rate to use in calculating the present value of the incremental after-tax cash flows associated with a lease financing? Why is the expected residual value of the asset discounted at a higher rate?
9. Define the term *project financing*. Under what circumstances is project financing an appropriate method of financing a capital investment project?
10. Explain how the contractual arrangements in a project financing can be designed so as to cover the following contingencies: (a) completion risk; (b) technological risk; (c) economic risk
11. What are the principal advantages and disadvantages of project financing?
12. What do lease financing and limited partnership financing have in common?
13. Secured debt is overcollateralized whereas a lease is not. How do we account for this difference in determining the net advantage to leasing?

CHALLENGING QUESTIONS

14. Leasing enables a firm to acquire the use of an asset just as a cash purchase would. So should the asset acquisition/lease decision be evaluated by using the lessee's required return for the asset as the discount rate? But lease financing displaces conventional debt financing. So should the asset acquisition/lease decision be evaluated by using the lessee's cost of secured debt as the discount rate? How would you resolve these apparently contradictory arguments?
15. A lessor purchases an asset and immediately enters into an agreement to lease the asset to another firm. The lease obligation is a form of secured debt obligation. So should the lessee's cost of secured debt (as determined in the capital market) be used in the analysis of the net advantage to the lessor of entering into the lease? Alternatively, the lessor must finance its purchase of the asset somehow. So should the lessor instead use its own cost of capital in evaluating the net advantage to the lessor of entering into the lease? How would you resolve these apparently contradictory arguments?
16. Suppose a limited partnership has debt.
    a. How would you interpret the cost of limited partner capital?
    b. How would you compare the cost of limited partner capital in that case to the cost of conventional financing?
17. A copper mining firm would like to finance the construction of a copper mine on a nonrecourse project basis. It will set up a separate corporation to finance, build, own, and operate the mine. It will also agree to purchase all the mine's output on terms that will be spelled out in a copper purchase agreement. The separate corporation will pledge the copper purchase agreement as security for a bank loan.
    a. Describe the agency costs involved in this arrangement.
    b. Why would the bank charge a higher interest rate on this loan than it would on an otherwise identical loan directly to the mining firm?
18. Suppose the copper mining firm in question 17 has outstanding debt that is rated single-B. Suppose also that it can arrange to sell the entire output of the new copper mine to a triple-A-rated Japanese firm under a hell-or-high-water contract. Explain how this contract could reduce the mining firm's cost of capital for the new mine project.

PROBLEMS

LEVEL A (BASIC)

A1. (Net advantage to leasing) Arkansas Instruments (AI) can purchase a sonic cleaner for \$1,000,000. The machine has a five-year life and would be depreciated straight line to a

$100,000 salvage value. Hibernia Leasing will lease the same machine to AI for five annual $300,000 lease payments paid in arrears (at the end of each year). AI is in the 40% tax bracket. The before-tax cost of borrowing is 10%, and the after-tax cost of capital for the project would be 12%.

a. What cash flows does AI realize if it leases the machine instead of buying it?

b. What is the net advantage to leasing (NAL)?

A2. (Net advantage to leasing) Look back at the NACCO example in the chapter. Suppose the lease rate is $1.7 million payable annually in arrears, and the cost of secured debt is 11%. The required return for the project is 14% assuming NACCO's tax rate is 40% and 17% assuming its tax rate is zero. The depreciation schedule and residual value are unchanged.

a. Calculate the net advantage to leasing assuming NACCO's tax rate is 40%. Should NACCO lease, or borrow and buy?

b. Calculate the net advantage to leasing assuming NACCO will never be able to use the tax deductions associated with asset ownership. Should the firm lease, or borrow and buy?

A3. (Net advantage to leasing) Allied Metals Inc. is considering leasing $1 million worth of manufacturing equipment under a lease that would require annual lease payments in arrears for five years. The net cash flows to lessee over the term of the lease (with zero residual value) are given below. Allied's cost of secured debt is 12%, and its cost of capital is 16%. Allied pays taxes at a 34% marginal rate.

a. Calculate the net advantage to leasing.

b. Should Allied lease, or borrow and buy?

Year	0	1	2	3	4	5
Net cash flow ($000)	1,000	−300	−275	−250	−225	−200

A4. (Net advantage to leasing) A firm is considering leasing a computer system that costs $1,000,000 new. The lease requires annual payments of $135,000 in arrears for 10 years. The lessee pays income taxes at a 35% marginal rate. If it purchased the computer system, it could depreciate it to its expected residual value over 10 years. The lessee's cost of similarly secured debt is 10% and its WACC is 15%.

a. Calculate the net advantage to leasing assuming zero residual value. Should the firm lease the computer system?

b. Calculate the net advantage to leasing assuming $250,000 residual value. Should the firm lease the computer system?

A5. (Net advantage to leasing) Suppose you are considering leasing an entertainment center. It would cost $5,000 new. You can lease it for five years for $100.00 per month payable on the last day of each month and then buy it for $1 at the end of the five years. Your mother is willing to lend you the $5,000 at 8% interest. The tax code does not permit you to deduct depreciation or personal interest from your (meager) income. Should you lease the center, or borrow from your mother and buy it?

A6. (Net advantage of leasing) Hyland Music Company is planning to purchase a new computer system costing $90,000. The computer has a five-year life and would be depreciated straight line to a $10,000 salvage value. Stolz Leasing will lease the computer to Hyland for five annual $30,000 lease payments paid in arrears (at the end of each year). Hyland is in the 40% tax bracket. The before-tax cost of borrowing is 10%, and the after-tax cost of capital for the project would be 14%.

a. What cash flows does Hyland realize if it leases the machine instead of buying it?

b. What is the net advantage to leasing (NAL)?

A7. (Cost of limited partner capital) Suppose the cable television limited partnership example in the text instead enabled the limited partners to receive 90% of partnership income, losses, tax credits, and cash distributions for the life of the limited partnership. Calculate the cost of limited partner capital.

A8. (Cost of limited partner capital) What is the cost of limited partner capital if a limited partner invests $50 million at time zero and receives net distributions of $8 million for the next 10 years?

A9. (Cost of limited partner capital) What is the cost of limited partner capital if a limited partner invests $75 million at time zero and receives net distributions of $16 million for the next seven years?

A10. (Calculating a lease discount rate) U.S. Aluminum overcollateralizes its secured debt by 25%. If U.S. Aluminum's secured borrowing rate is 9%, and its unsecured borrowing rate is 11%, what is the proper discount rate to use when computing the net advantage to leasing?

A11. (Calculating a lease discount rate) New Technologies wants to lease the latest generation of equipment. Its bank said a secured loan would require 50% overcollateralization because the equipment will lose value very quickly. If New Tech's secured borrowing rate is 11%, and its unsecured borrowing rate is 13%, what discount rate should New Tech use to evaluate a lease agreement for the new equipment?

A12. (Net advantage to leasing) You want to lease a car that costs $25,000 new. You can lease it with zero down for $500 per month at the start of each month for the next five years, and then buy the car for $8,000 at the end of the lease. Your rich uncle thinks leases are a bad deal and offers to loan you the $25,000 at a 9% APR interest rate. You cannot deduct interest expense or car depreciation on your tax return. What do you tell your uncle?

LEVEL B

B1. (Time value of money) Show how to modify Equation (20.2) to reflect the timing of lease payments when the lease calls for payments *at the beginning* of each year.

B2. (Net advantage to leasing) New Horizon Natural Foods is considering whether to lease a delivery truck. A leasing company has offered to lease the truck. It costs $35,000. New Horizon has proposed a five-year lease that calls for annual payments of $7,850 *at the beginning* of each year. New Horizon could depreciate the truck to $5,000 at the end of five years on a straight-line basis and claim depreciation tax deductions at the beginning of each year. Its marginal tax rate is 34%, its cost of five-year secured debt is 10%, and its required return for the project is 12% after tax and 16% pretax.

a. Should New Horizon lease the truck, or borrow and buy?

b. Suppose instead that New Horizon does not expect to pay income taxes in the foreseeable future. Should New Horizon lease the truck, or borrow and buy?

B3. (Net advantage to leasing) Neighborhood Savings Bank is considering leasing $100,000 worth of computer equipment. A four-year lease would require payments in advance of $22,000 per year. The bank does not currently pay income taxes and does not expect to have to pay income taxes in the foreseeable future. If the bank purchased the computer equipment, it would depreciate the equipment on a straight-line basis down to an estimated salvage value of $20,000 at the end of the fourth year. The bank's cost of secured debt is 14%, and its cost of capital is 20%. Calculate the net advantage to leasing.

B4. (Net advantage to leasing) Brown Toyota is considering leasing $120,000 worth of computer equipment. A four-year lease would require payments in advance of $33,000 per year. Brown does not currently pay income taxes and does not expect to have to pay income taxes in the foreseeable future. If Brown purchased the computer equipment, it would depreciate the equipment on a straight-line basis down to an estimated salvage value of $30,000 at the end of the fourth year. Brown's cost of secured debt is 14%, and its cost of capital is 20%. Calculate the net advantage to leasing.

B5. (Net advantage to leasing) Rashid Singh, the president of Surf-side Beer Distributors of Salina, Kansas, has decided that his firm must acquire a new machine that costs $800,000. The firm's corporate borrowing rate is 12%. The machine can be leased for $110,000 per year for its 10-year life. If the firm leases, it gets no salvage value. If it owns, the expected salvage value is $50,000. Maintenance costs will be the same whether Surf-side leases or buys. The firm uses straight-line depreciation (to the salvage value), and its tax rate is 40%. Can you demonstrate which would be better for Rashid, leasing or buying?

B6. (Net advantage to leasing) Empire Excavation Corporation plans to acquire a fleet of 10 dump trucks. Each truck costs $75,000. Empire can borrow $750,000 on a secured basis at a pretax cost of 14%. The dump trucks can be depreciated for tax purposes on a straight-line basis to zero over a five-year useful life. Truck Leasing Corp. has offered to lease the fleet of trucks to Empire under a five-year lease that calls for lease payments of $190,000 at the end of each year. Empire estimates that forgone residual value would be $10,000 per truck (net of taxes). Empire's tax rate is 34%. Its cost of capital is 16%.

a. Calculate the stream of net cash flows to Empire under the lease financing.

b. Calculate the net advantage to leasing.

B7. (Net advantage to leasing) A three-year lease entails the following stream of net cash flows (in millions of dollars) to the lessee: $10.5, −$3.0, −$5.0, −$5.0. The lessee's pretax cost of secured debt is 13%. The lessee does not pay taxes, and it does not expect to become a taxpayer in the near future. The item will have zero residual value at the end of the lease term. Calculate the net advantage to leasing.

B8. (Net advantage to leasing) Carrion Luggage, Ltd. is considering leasing $50 million worth of warehousing equipment under a lease that would require annual lease payments in arrears for five years. The net cash flows to the lessee over the term of the lease (with zero residual value) are given below. Carrion's cost of secured debt is 11%, and its cost of capital is 14%. Carrion pays taxes at a 40% marginal rate.

a. Calculate the net advantage to leasing.

b. Calculate the IRR for the lease.

c. Should Carrion lease, or borrow and buy?

Year	0	1	2	3	4	5
Net cash flow ($ millions)	50	−15	−15	−15	−15	−15

B9. (Net advantage to leasing) Lake Trolley Company is considering whether to lease or buy a new trolley that costs $25,000. The trolley can be depreciated straight line over an eight-year period to an estimated residual value of $5,000. Lake Trolley's cost of eight-year secured debt is 12%. Its required return for the project is 16% after tax and 20% pretax. National Trolley Leasing Corporation has offered to lease the trolley to Lake Trolley in return for annual payments of $5,000 payable at the end of each year.

a. Specify the incremental cash flow stream associated with the lease, assuming Lake Trolley's marginal income tax rate is 40%.

b. Calculate the net advantage to leasing, assuming Lake Trolley's tax rate is 40%. Should Lake Trolley lease, or borrow and buy?

c. Calculate the net advantage to leasing, assuming Lake Trolley's tax rate is zero. Should Lake Trolley lease, or borrow and buy?

d. How would your answers to parts b and c change if the residual value at the end of eight years is $500, but the trolley is depreciated to $5,000?

B10. (Net advantage to leasing) A lease calls for payments of $1 million at the end of each of the next five years and payments of $2 million at the end of each of the following five years. The asset to be leased costs $10 million. The 10-year depreciation schedule to a residual value of $500,000 at the end of the lease term is given below. The lessee's marginal income tax rate is currently 40%. Its cost of 10-year secured debt is 12.5%. Its required return for the project is 15% after tax and 17.5% pretax.

a. Calculate the net advantage to leasing.

b. How would your answer to part a change if the lessee did not expect to pay any income taxes for the next three years but to pay income taxes each year thereafter at a 40% rate? (*Hint:* Any tax losses in years 1 to 3 can be carried forward and realized in year 4.)

Year	1	2	3	4	5	6	7	8	9	10
Depreciation ($000)	2,000	1,750	1,500	1,250	1,000	400	400	400	400	400

B11. (Negotiating a lease rate) Amalgamated Leasing Corp. would like to submit a leasing proposal to the Sandoval Hardware Manufacturing Company. Sandoval has asked to lease $5 million worth of equipment under a six-year lease. Amalgamated can depreciate the equipment for tax purposes on a straight-line basis over the six-year term to an estimated residual value of $250,000. The leasing firm's income tax rate is 40%. Amalgamated has estimated Sandoval's six-year cost of funds to be 10% for secured debt (83.33% financing) and 12% for unsecured debt. It has also estimated the required after-tax return for an investment in the assets to be 15%.

a. At what lease rate would Amalgamated be indifferent to making the lease?

b. Assume Sandoval pays income taxes at a 30% rate. Calculate Sandoval's net advantage to leasing at Amalgamated's indifference lease rate.

c. At what lease rate would Sandoval be indifferent.

d. Is it possible for Amalgamated and Sandoval to find a mutually beneficial lease rate?

B12. (Cost of limited partner capital) A limited partnership would expect the net cash flows given here from a project.

a. Calculate the cost of limited partner capital.

b. Suppose the firm's unleveraged cost of equity is 15%, and the limited partnership has no debt. Should the firm employ limited partnership financing?

Year	0	1	2	3	4	5	6	7
Net cash flow ($ millions)	125.0	−10.5	−12.0	−14.5	−16.5	−19.5	−22.5	−112.5

B13. (Cost of limited partner capital) The Light Rock Cafe plans to raise capital to finance a new restaurant through the sale of limited partnership interests. The firm, as general partner, plans to raise $5.25 million. Of this amount, $5 million will be invested in the restaurant, and the balance will be used to pay issuance expenses. The assets can be depreciated to zero over eight years on a straight-line basis. The partnership will be terminated at the end of eight years. Upon termination, the general partner will buy out the limited partners at a price equal to seven times the last year's operating cash flow. The projected operating cash flow stream for the partnership is:

Year	1	2	3	4	5	6	7	8
Cash flow ($000)	250	1,000	1,500	2,000	2,250	2,500	2,750	3,000

The limited partners will be entitled to receive 75% of each year's partnership income, losses, tax credits (if any), and cash distributions. They will also be entitled to receive 75% of the residual value. The Light Rock Cafe will not invest cash but will contribute its name and "know-how" (that is, its experience) to the project in return for a 25% ownership interest. Assume the general partner's marginal ordinary income tax rate is 40%. Calculate the cost of limited partner capital.

B14. (Lease versus buy) Suppose you can either purchase a new Honda Civic for $20,000 cash or lease it from Honda for $2,000 down and $360 per month for 48 months. At the end of the lease, you will be able to purchase the car for $6,000, which is your estimate of its residual value. Your cost of borrowing the funds to buy the car is 12% APR.

a. You cannot depreciate the car for tax purposes. Nor can you deduct the lease payments or interest expense. Should you lease the car, or borrow to buy it?

b. Honda can depreciate the car straight line to $6,000 over four years. Honda's required return on the lease is 12% pretax APR. Honda's marginal income tax rate is 40%. Is leasing advantageous to Honda?

c. Explain why leasing a car can be mutually advantageous to the manufacturer and the customer.

B15. (Excel: net advantage to leasing) Brown Storage Technology is planning to buy a propane-fueled truck for $100,000. Brown expects to use the truck for eight years after which it has an expected salvage value of $8,000. Brown's before-tax cost of borrowing is estimated to be 8.0% and its marginal tax rate is 40%. McLeavey Leasing will lease this same truck to Brown for eight beginning-of-year lease payments of $16,000. The tax savings from depreciation occur at the end of the year and the tax savings from the lease payments occur at the time they are paid.

a. Assuming that the truck is depreciated straight-line to a zero salvage value over eight years, what is Brown's net advantage to leasing?

b. Assuming that the truck is depreciated as five-year property under MACRS, what is the net advantage to leasing? (Refer to Table 7.8 for the MACRS depreciation schedule.) Why does your answer differ from part a?

c. Still using the five-year MACRS depreciation schedule, what is the maximum lease payment that McLeavey could charge Brown? I.e., what lease payment would result in a zero net advantage to leasing?

B16. (Excel: net advantage to leasing) Purdue Systems can purchase a commercial DVD burner for $3,000,000. The equipment will be depreciated as three-year MACRS property (refer back to Table 7.8 for the MACRS depreciation schedule). The depreciation tax savings will be realized at the end of each year. The equipment will have a five-year life and will have a before-tax salvage value of $700,000. Purdue Systems has a before-tax cost of debt of 9% and a cost of capital of 12%. Lafayette Leasing will purchase this DVD burner and lease it to Purdue Systems for five years, charging a lease payment of $550,000 payable at the beginning of each year. The tax saving on a lease payment is realized at the time the payment is made. Purdue will have no rights to purchase or use the equipment at the end of the five-year lease period. Purdue has a 30% marginal tax rate. What is the net advantage to leasing for Purdue Systems?

LEVEL C (ADVANCED)

C1. (Excel: Break-even lease payment) The break-even tax rate is the income tax rate for the lessee that would make the lessee indifferent between leasing an asset on the one hand and borrowing and buying it on the other. Calculate the break-even lease payment for Lake Trolley in problem B9 under the assumption that the residual value is $500.

C2. (Leasing, taxes, and the time value of money) The lessor can claim the tax deductions associated with asset ownership and realize the leased asset's residual value. In return, the lessor must pay tax on the rental income.

a. Explain why a financial lease represents a secured loan in which the lender's entire debt service stream is taxable as ordinary income to the lessor/lender.

b. In view of this tax cost, what tax condition must hold in order for a financial lease transaction to generate positive net-present-value tax benefits for both the lessor and lessee?

c. Suppose the lease payments in Table 20.2 must be made in advance, not arrears. (Assume that the timing of the lease payment tax deductions/obligations changes accordingly but the timing of the depreciation tax deductions does not change). Show that the net advantage to leasing for NACCO must decrease as a result. Explain why this reduction occurs.

d. Show that if NACCO is nontaxable, the net advantage to leasing is negative and greater in absolute value than the net advantage of the lease to the lessor.

e. Either find a lease rate that will give the financial lease a positive net advantage for both lessor and lessee, or show that no such lease rate exists.

f. Explain what your answer to part e implies about the tax costs and tax benefits of the financial lease when lease payments are made in advance.

MINICASE WILL LEASING FLY AT CONTINENTAL?

Several years ago, Continental Airlines (Continental) was looking to add two Boeing 757s to its fleet of more than 300 aircraft. Each plane would cost $125 million, but the two aircraft could be leased. The lease would have a term of 15 years and would require quarterly payments of $4 million in arrears for each aircraft. Leasing was attractive to Continental at that time because it had a total of $2.5 billion of net operating loss carryforwards. A loss can be carried forward for a maximum of 20 years. Continental's loss carryforwards were set to expire, some each year, over the next 14 years. At the time, Continental's capitalization was:

BOOK CAPITALIZATION (Dollar amounts in millions)	
Long-term bonds	$ 1,352
Capitalized leases	306
Total long-term debt	1,658
Preferred stock	283
Stockholders' equity	305
Total long-term capitalization	2,246
Short-term debt	221
Total capitalization	$ 2,467

Continental's cost of fully secured (80% of the value of the collateral) 15-year debt was 10%. Its cost of unsecured 15-year debt was 12%, and its WACC was 15%. Continental was uncertain about the residual value of a Boeing 757 at the end of the 15-year lease term, but it estimated the following possible values and probabilities:

Residual value ($ millions):	10	15	20	25	30	35	40	45	50
Probability (%):	5	10	10	15	20	15	10	10	5

QUESTIONS

1. Calculate the net advantage to leasing, using the expected residual value and assuming Continental can use all the tax benefits of ownership with a tax rate is 40% and straight-line depreciation to the expected residual value.
2. Calculate the net advantage to leasing, assuming Continental cannot use any of the tax benefits of ownership and the residual value is (i) the expected residual value, (ii) $50 million, and (iii) $10 million.
3. Determine the residual value that would make the net advantage to leasing equal zero, assuming Continental cannot use any of the tax benefits of ownership.
4. Suppose Continental believes it will not be in a taxpaying position for a decade or longer. Should it lease, or borrow and buy? Explain.
5. Suppose Continental believes it will not be in a taxpaying position for a decade or longer, and this lease includes the option to terminate the lease at any time without penalty. Should it lease, or borrow and buy? Explain.

21

DERIVATIVES AND HEDGING

Modern financial engineering emerged in the 1970s in response to a very real problem: Financial markets had become more volatile compared to the previous 20 years. Because this volatility could affect firm value, managers sought to avoid it. Initially many firms tried to build better forecasting models. If they could predict price changes, they could avoid the risk. Not surprisingly, these forecasting efforts were generally unsuccessful because of the Principle of Capital Market Efficiency. Putting into practice the Principle of Valuable Ideas, financial engineers developed a variety of derivative instruments that firms can use to manage financial risk.

Recall that a *derivative* is a financial instrument whose value depends on the price of some other asset. There are four basic types of derivatives: options, swaps, forwards, and futures. We call them the *basic building blocks* because they are used to build more complex derivatives and other securities. The basic building blocks can be used to analyze or "build" more complex securities. For example, recall that a convertible bond is a *hybrid security*, which can be viewed as being a "straight" bond and a call option on the issuer's common stock *or* as being common stock and a put option on the stock.

Organized options markets and financial futures markets were two of the most significant financial developments of the 1970s. The development of the swaps markets was one of the most significant developments of the 1980s. These new financial instruments increased the ability of investors to change their return distributions. Insurance protects against a potential but unlikely loss. You pay the insurance company to bear the risk. Similarly, these new financial markets made it possible to pay others to bear financial risk.

Here, we describe the basic types of derivatives and show how firms use them to manage their financial risks. We build on our discussion of futures, options, and hedging risk in this chapter to show you in Chapter 27 how firms use derivatives to hedge foreign exchange risk.

FOCUS ON PRINCIPLES

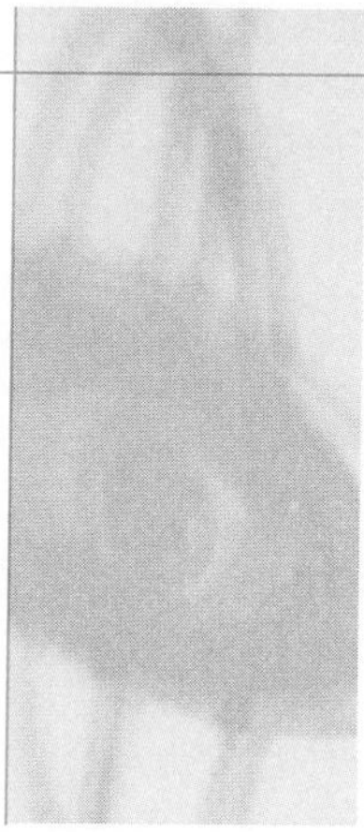

- *Valuable Ideas:* Look for opportunities to develop derivatives that enable firms to cope better with the financial risks they face.
- *Options:* Recognize the value of stock and other options.
- *Two-Sided Transactions:* Use derivatives to pay others to take risks. Derivatives do not eliminate financial risk; they only transfer it.
- *Risk-Return Trade-Off:* To transfer risk to another party, you must offer a return that fully compensates for the amount of risk transferred.
- *Capital Market Efficiency:* You cannot forecast movements in interest rates, commodity prices, and foreign exchange rates precisely because these financial prices have a significant random component in an efficient market. Use the financial markets' consensus forecasts.
- *Comparative Advantage:* Paying others to bear financial risk may be valuable if they can bear the risk more cheaply.

21.1 OPTIONS

The first basic building block we examine is the option. An option is an example of a derivative. A **derivative** is a financial instrument whose value depends on the price of some other asset. As you know, the value of a stock option depends on the price of the underlying shares.

Recall that an *option* gives the holder a right without an obligation. According to the Options Principle, that is why options are valuable. With a *call option* on a stock, you have the right to buy a specified amount of stock (usually 100 shares in the case of a standardized market-traded stock option) at a specified price within some stated time period. A *put option* provides the right to sell. The specified price is the *strike price.* These instruments are traded in the options markets.

Options Markets

Options are traded on organized exchanges and in the over-the-counter (OTC) market. The Chicago Board Options Exchange (CBOE) began operations in 1973. It initially traded only call options on about two dozen stocks. Trading volume grew rapidly, and so did the number of option contracts available. By January 1997, the CBOE listed puts and calls on 881 common stocks. Today it is the largest options exchange in the world in aggregate dollar value of contracts traded. Among U.S. securities exchanges, only the New York Stock Exchange (NYSE) is bigger. Stock options are also traded on four other exchanges: the American Stock Exchange, Philadelphia Stock Exchange, International Securities Exchange, and Pacific Stock Exchange. There is also an OTC market. It deals primarily in nonstandardized options.

Figure 21.1 shows a typical price quotation for options listed on an exchange. It comes from the *Wall Street Journal* and shows the previous day's trading in put and call options on Intel common stock. Newspapers usually provide quotations only for actively traded options. Intel's stock closed at \$22. The options have a strike price of \$15, \$20, \$25, \$30, or \$35. They expire the following October, January, or July. The Vol. (volume) column gives the number of contracts to buy or sell 100 shares traded that day. The column headed Last gives the last trading price. For example, the July 25 call last traded at \$0.65 per underlying share, or \$65 per contract. A total of 5,720 contracts to buy 572,000 shares traded that day.

On each options exchange, the members meet during trading hours on the floor of the exchange to buy and sell options. Floor brokers execute buy orders and sell orders for their customers. Each exchange employs clerks who observe the trading and transmit the latest trading information to other options exchanges and news services around the world.

FIGURE 21.1
A typical price quotation for listed options.

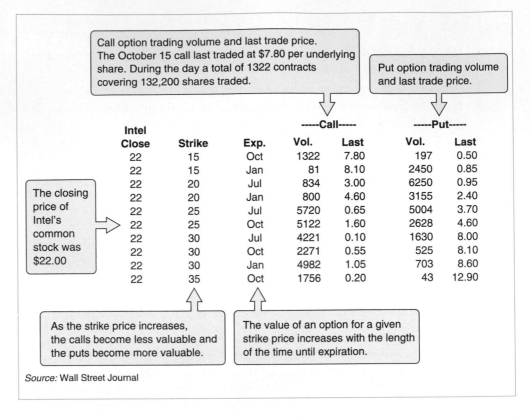

Call option trading volume and last trade price. The October 15 call last traded at $7.80 per underlying share. During the day a total of 1322 contracts covering 132,200 shares traded.

Put option trading volume and last trade price.

The closing price of Intel's common stock was $22.00

Intel Close	Strike	Exp.	-----Call----- Vol.	Last	-----Put----- Vol.	Last
22	15	Oct	1322	7.80	197	0.50
22	15	Jan	81	8.10	2450	0.85
22	20	Jul	834	3.00	6250	0.95
22	20	Jan	800	4.60	3155	2.40
22	25	Jul	5720	0.65	5004	3.70
22	25	Oct	5122	1.60	2628	4.60
22	30	Jul	4221	0.10	1630	8.00
22	30	Oct	2271	0.55	525	8.10
22	30	Jan	4982	1.05	703	8.60
22	35	Oct	1756	0.20	43	12.90

As the strike price increases, the calls become less valuable and the puts become more valuable.

The value of an option for a given strike price increases with the length of the time until expiration.

Source: Wall Street Journal

The five options exchanges jointly own the Options Clearing Corporation (OCC) and clear all their option trades through the OCC. Figure 21.2 shows how the OCC interposes itself between every option buyer and seller. The option buyer and seller agree on the price and strike a deal. At this point, the OCC steps in. It places itself between the two traders, effectively becoming both the buyer of the option from the writer and the writer of the option to the buyer. The OCC substitutes its promise to deliver for the option seller's promise to deliver. When an option holder exercises, the OCC arranges with a member firm whose clients have written that particular option to make good on the option obligation. The OCC stands behind this obligation. The OCC effectively makes all call option contracts written on a particular security that have the same strike price and the same expiration date perfect substitutes for one another. The same is true for put option contracts. This lowers transaction costs because it saves the cost of having to conduct a separate credit investigation for each seller.

FIGURE 21.2
The role of the OCC.

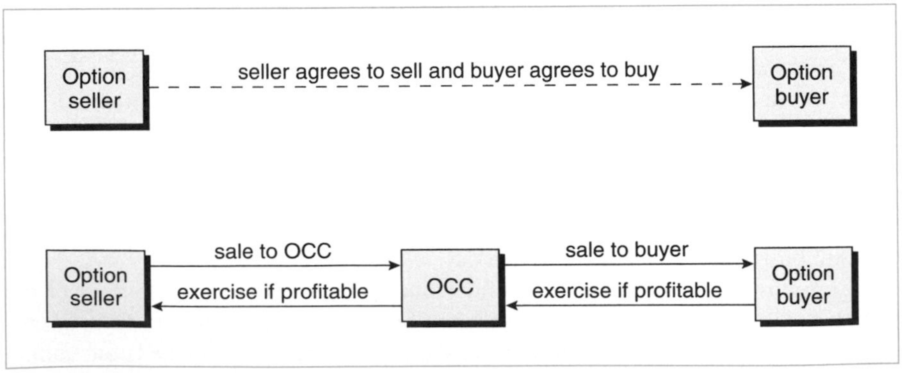

In recent years, the number of traded options has greatly increased. There are options on common stocks, of course. There are also traded options on foreign currencies, on debt instruments such as U.S. Treasury securities, on stock market indexes such as the Standard & Poor's 500 Index (S&P 500), and on futures contracts.

Over-the-Counter Options

The options that are traded on exchanges are standardized with respect to such features as strike price, expiration date, exercise style (for example, American or European), and settlement arrangements. This enhances their liquidity. But there is a drawback. If an investor or a firm wants a nonstandard option, it cannot obtain such an option on an exchange. The investor can try to obtain the option in the OTC market. Like the OTC market for stocks, the OTC market for options consists of securities dealers who craft customized options to meet investor demand. A potential option buyer calls an OTC dealer to negotiate an option contract's exercise price, expiration date, underlying stock, and so on and a mutually acceptable price for the option.

To compete with the OTC market, the CBOE introduced FLEX options. These allow some flexibility in designing options on the S&P 500, S&P 100, and Russell 2000 indexes. The OTC market still offers greater flexibility in option design.

Options and Financial Management

Options have a wide range of uses in financial management. We first introduced you to options in our discussion of the Options Principle in Chapter 2. In Chapter 12, we explored options in broad generalities. There, we explained the basis for valuing an option, and pointed out many places where options exist.

As we have said, firms often include an option in a new bond issue to redeem the bonds before maturity. The option to redeem is a call option. In Chapter 18, we described how some firms, especially in other countries, sell new common stock to their shareholders through rights offerings. Rights are call options.

Finally, recall that options exist in many situations, even though they are sometimes hard to spot. But keep in mind how important it is to look for options, because they affect value—in some cases dramatically.

An Option Pricing Model

Now let us take a look at how to value options. To keep matters simple, we will value only stock options. We will value calls first and then puts.

Fischer Black and Myron Scholes derived a very useful model for valuing options. The value of a call option, CALL, using the Black-Scholes option pricing model (OPM) is

$$\text{CALL} = P_0 N(d_1) - SN(d_2)e^{-\Delta tk} \tag{21.1}$$

where

$$d_1 = \frac{\ln(P_0 / S) + \Delta tk}{\sigma \Delta t^{1/2}} + \frac{\sigma \Delta t^{1/2}}{2} \tag{21.2}$$

$$d_2 = d_1 - \sigma \Delta t^{1/2} \tag{21.3}$$

and

$N(d)$ = the cumulative distribution function (cdf) for a standardized (mean = 0, σ = 1) normal random variable. This is the probability that an outcome is less than or equal to d. $N(d)$ is given in the table in Appendix B to this book for values of d from $d = -3.09$ to $d = 3.09$, in increments of 0.01.

σ = the standard deviation of the (continuously compounded) return on the underlying asset

Δt = the time (in years) until the option expires

k = the riskless APR with continuous compounding

S = the strike price of the option

P_0 = the current value of the underlying asset

ln = the natural (base e) logarithm function

Let's take a closer look at Equation (21.1). P_0 is the current share price; $Se^{-\Delta tk}$ is the present value of the strike price, which you would pay in the future if you exercise the call option; and $N(d_1)$ and $N(d_2)$ are probabilities. We know that for any given strike price, a call option is more valuable the higher the market price of the underlying asset. We also know that for any given asset price, a call option is less valuable the higher the strike price. Thus, it seems reasonable that CALL, the value of a call option, should increase with P_0 and decrease with S. The probabilities $N(d_1)$ and $N(d_2)$ take into account the uncertainty concerning the future share price and consequently, whether the option will ever be exercised, and if it is, what value will be realized. So although we cannot show you the complex mathematics that led Black and Scholes to their remarkable discovery, at least we hope you can see that the formula appears reasonable.

Using the Black-Scholes OPM is very practical for two reasons. First, except for σ, the parameter inputs needed are specified in the option contract or are readily observable in currently operating markets. Second, the model usually provides a very good approximation of the true value of an option, even though some of its assumptions may not be perfectly satisfied.

VALUING CALL OPTIONS As you might expect by now, violations of the perfect market assumption do not harm the model's usefulness. However, it may surprise you to find out that the distinction between an American and a European type of option is not important unless there are cash flows associated with the underlying asset before the option expires. Recall that you can exercise an American option any time during its life. Also, you are generally better off selling, rather than exercising, one prior to its expiration. Thus, with a few adjustments, you can usually use the Black-Scholes OPM to value American as well as European call options.

EXAMPLE Applying the Black-Scholes OPM to Value a Call Option

Suppose a non-dividend-paying stock is selling for \$28 per share. The standard deviation of the return from owning a share of this stock is estimated from the returns on the stock during a recent representative historical period and is found to be 0.30. The APR for the riskless return with continuous compounding is 6%. The option has a strike price of \$30, and there are nine months until expiration. What is a call option on this stock worth?

First, list the parameter values: $P_0 = 28$, $\sigma = 0.30$, $k = 0.06$, $S = 30$, and $\Delta t = 0.75$. Then $\sigma\Delta t^{1/2} = 0.259808$. From Equation (21.2), d_1 is

$$d_1 = \frac{\ln(P_0/S) + \Delta tk}{\sigma\Delta t^{1/2}} + \frac{\sigma\Delta t^{1/2}}{2} = \frac{\ln(28/30) + 0.75(0.06)}{0.259808} + \frac{0.259808}{2}$$

$$= -0.092349 + 0.129904 = 0.037555 \approx 0.04$$

From Equation (21.3):

$$d_2 = d_1 - \sigma\Delta t^{1/2} = 0.037555 - 0.259808 = -0.222253 \approx -0.22$$

From Appendix B, we have

$$N(d_1) = N(0.04) = 0.5160$$
$$N(d_2) = N(-0.22) = 0.4129$$

Finally, from Equation (21.1):

$$\text{CALL} = P_0 N(d_1) - SN(d_2)e^{-\Delta tk} = 28(0.5160) - 30(0.4129)e^{-0.045} = \$2.61$$

An option like this one should sell in the market for a price of about \$2.61.

EXAMPLE What Happens When the Share Price Falls?

Suppose the non-dividend-paying stock in the previous example was instead selling for \$26 per share. With everything else the same, we would have $P_0 = 26$, $\sigma = 0.30$, $k = 0.06$, $S = 30$, and $\Delta t = 0.75$. As before, $\sigma\Delta t^{1/2} = 0.259808$. From Equation (21.2), d_1 is

$$d_1 = \frac{\ln(P_0 / S) + \Delta tk}{\sigma\Delta t^{1/2}} + \frac{\sigma\Delta t^{1/2}}{2} = \frac{\ln(28/30) + 0.75(0.06)}{0.259808} + \frac{0.259808}{2}$$

$$= -0.377590 + 0.129904 = -0.247686 \approx -0.25$$

Equation (21.3) yields

$$d_2 = d_1 - \sigma\Delta t^{1/2} = -0.247686 - 0.259808 = -0.507494 \approx -0.51$$

From Appendix B, we have

$$N(d_1) = N(-0.25) = 0.4013$$
$$N(d_2) = N(-0.51) = 0.3050$$

Finally, from Equation (21.1),

$$\text{CALL} = P_0\, N(d_1) - SN(d_2)e^{-\Delta tk} = 26(0.4013) - 30(0.3050)e^{-0.045} = \$1.69$$

Although the option is \$2 farther out-of-the-money, its value decreases by less than \$2.

EXERCISE VALUE AND TIME PREMIUM OF A CALL OPTION Option value can be broken into two parts; the exercise (also called intrinsic) value and the time premium. If a call option is in-the-money ($P_0 > S$), the exercise value is $P_0 - S$. If the call option is out-of-the-money ($P_0 < S$), you will not exercise it and the exercise value is 0. Thus, the exercise value is the greater of $P_0 - S$ and 0.

$$\text{Exercise value of a call option} = \text{Maximum of } (P_0 - S, 0)$$

Prior to expiration, the market value of a call option generally exceeds its exercise value. We say that an option "is worth more alive than dead." The excess of the market value above the exercise value is called the time premium.

$$\text{Time premium of an option} = \text{Market value} - \text{Exercise value}$$

In these two call option examples, the option was out-of-the-money because the stock price ($28 for the first example and $26 for the second) was below the strike price ($30). The exercise value of these options is zero. The time premium of these options is the excess of the market value of these call options over the exercise value, which is $2.61 for the first example and $1.69 for the second.

VALUING PUT OPTIONS With put-call parity, the value of a put option can be expressed in terms of the value of a similar call option:[1]

$$\text{PUT} = \text{CALL} + Se^{-\Delta tk} - P_0 \tag{21.4}$$

You can value a put option by substituting Equation (21.1) into Equation (21.4).

EXAMPLE Valuing a Put Option

What is the value of a nine-month put option, with $S = \$30$, on a non-dividend-paying stock that is selling for $28 per share if $\sigma = 0.30$ and $k = 6\%$? We computed the value of a call option under the same conditions in our first example. It was $2.61. Therefore, from Equation (21.4):

$$\text{PUT} = \text{CALL} + Se^{-\Delta tk} - P_0 = 2.61 + (30)e^{-0.045} - 28 = \$3.29$$

Note that the option's time premium equals $1.29, which is its market value minus its exercise value.

Next let's redo the second example, finding the value of the put option if the stock price declines to $26:

$$\text{PUT} = \text{CALL} + Se^{-\Delta tk} - P_0 = 1.69 + (30)e^{-0.045} - 26 = \$4.37$$

The put option is $2 farther in-the-money. But the put option's value does not increase by $2.

EXERCISE VALUE AND TIME PREMIUM OF A PUT OPTION A put option has a positive exercise value only when it is in-the-money, that is, the stock price is below the strike price ($P_0 < S$). If a put option is out-of-the-money, the exercise value of the put option is zero. Thus, the exercise value of a put option is:

$$\text{Exercise value of a put option} = \text{Maximum of } (S - P_0, 0)$$

A put option's time premium is the market value minus the exercise value. For the put examples, when the stock price is $28, the strike price is $30, and the put value is $3.29, the exercise value is $2.00 and time premium is $1.29. When the stock price drops to $26 and the strike price and put value are $30 and $4.37, the exercise value is $4.00 and the time premium is $0.37.

Review

1. How does an increase in the strike price affect the value of a call option? A put option?
2. What is put-call parity?
3. What are the five variables that you use in the Black-Scholes option pricing model to value an option?
4. What are the exercise value and the time premium of a call option? Of a put option?

---

[1] *Put-call parity* was introduced in Chapter 12, and shows that the value of either option can be expressed in terms of the value of the other (and the present value of the strike price and the current value of the asset).

21.2 WARRANTS

A **warrant** is a long-term call option that is issued by a firm. It entitles the holder to buy shares of the firm's common stock at a stated price for cash. Firms, particularly smaller ones, often find it more attractive to issue convertible bonds, or bonds with warrants, than to issue straight debt. In addition, smaller firms often include warrants as a "sweetener" to a new issue of common stock or a privately placed debt issue.

A convertible bond (or convertible preferred share) entitles the holder to exchange the bond (or preferred share) for a stated number of shares of the issuing firm's common stock. Convertible securities thus incorporate a call option that lets the owner profit if the firm's share price goes up.

Recall that standardized call options traded in the options market are written by investors against outstanding shares of a firm's stock. By contrast, warrants are issued by the firm, often as part of a package that includes the issuer's common stock, preferred stock, or bonds. The firm issues new shares to investors who exercise their warrants. Warrants are like rights because the underlying security is newly issued equity. Warrants usually do not expire for several years, and some firms, such as Allegheny Corporation, have even issued perpetual warrants.

Main Features of Warrants

The provisions of a warrant are essentially the same as those of a conventional call option, except that new shares are created. A warrant specifies the underlying common stock, the number of shares, a strike price, an expiration date, and the option type (American or European). Sometimes a warrant contains an early redemption feature, which enables the issuer to trigger its exercise prior to the expiration date.

EXAMPLE An Issue of Warrants

A large and actively traded issue of warrants was sold by American Express Company in two *tranches* (parts). American Express distributed 932,000 common share purchase warrants to its common stockholders and then sold an additional 900,000 such warrants to the public at a price of $12.625 per warrant. Each American Express warrant entitled the holder to purchase, at any time within five years of the issue date, one share of American Express common stock at a strike price of $55 per share. The strike price was 17.0% over the previous closing price of American Express common stock. The terms of the warrant permitted American Express to accelerate the expiration date if the price of American Express's common stock traded at or above a price of $95 per share for a period of 10 consecutive trading days.

The American Express warrants were also redeemable at the firm's option beginning two years from the issue date at a price of $40 per warrant. This redemption feature, like the redemption feature on a convertible bond, permits the issuer to force exercise of the call option. Some warrants provide for a "step-up" or increase in the strike price. Warrants like those issued by American Express provide for adjustment of the strike price if the issuer pays a common stock dividend, splits its common stock, distributes some of its assets (other than cash dividends), or issues stockholders rights to purchase shares at a discount from the prevailing market price, and in some other circumstances.[2] However, as is generally the case, American Express warrant holders are not entitled to vote or to receive dividends, and the strike price is not adjusted for cash dividend payments to common stockholders.

[2]The strike price is usually adjusted only if the dilutive factors would require an adjustment of at least 5%. In addition, the $40 redemption price and the $95 acceleration price of the American Express warrants would be adjusted along with the strike price.

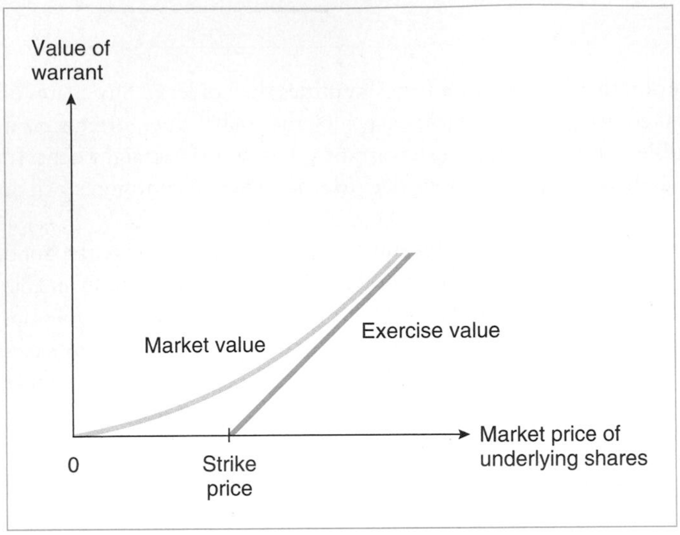

FIGURE 21.3
Relationship between the value of a warrant and the price of the underlying shares.

Financing with Warrants

Firms can sell warrants separately, as American Express did, or in combination with other securities. Because of the efficiency of the capital markets, when a firm issues warrants at their fair market price, the cash it receives is fair compensation for the potential equity interest it gives up. Nevertheless, issuing warrants may add value by reducing agency costs.[3] Including warrants along with an issue of debt allows lenders to share in the upside if the project financed with the debt issue is very profitable. As a result, lenders will accept a lower interest rate on the debt issue.

Valuing Warrants

Figure 21.3 illustrates the relationship between the value of a warrant and the price of the underlying shares.[4] Warrants are long-term call options. We can value them like any other call option. But there is one important adjustment. Issuing warrants is dilutive because new shares are created. We must take this dilution into account. To do so, divide the call option value by a dilution factor:

$$W = \frac{C}{1 + P} \tag{21.5}$$

where W is the value of the warrant, C is the value of a call option to purchase one common share, and P is the proportionate increase in the number of common shares that would result from exercising the warrants.

We use Equation (21.5) to value warrants *before* they are issued. How about after the issue? In an efficient market, their dilutive impact will be fully reflected in the issuer's common stock price, so $W = C$ *after* issuance.

Review

1. What are the major differences between a warrant and a conventional call option?
2. Why are warrants considered to be dilutive?

[3]See Chapter 13 for a discussion of optimal financial contracts.

[4]This is the same relationship described for other call options in Chapter 12.

21.3 CONVERTIBLE SECURITIES

The conversion features of convertible bonds and convertible preferred stock are very similar. In our discussion we will concentrate on convertible bonds, but our comments will also apply to most convertible preferred stock.

Main Features of Convertible Debt

A **convertible bond** is a bond that is convertible, at the option of the bondholder, into shares of the issuer's common stock. You can think of it simply as a straight bond with call options attached. Convertible debt has the same coupon rate, maturity, and optional redemption features that are typical in a straight bond. It also has the following conversion features:

- Each bond is convertible at any time prior to maturity into common stock at a stated *conversion price.* This (strike) price usually exceeds the issuer's share price at the time of issue. In other words, the conversion option is normally issued out-of-the-money. The conversion premium is generally between 10% and 20%. Dividing the face amount of the convertible bond by the conversion price gives the *conversion ratio.* It is the number of shares of common stock into which each bond can be converted. The conversion terms are normally fixed for the life of the issue, although some convertible securities provide for one or more step-ups in the conversion price over time.
- The conversion price is usually adjusted for stock splits, stock dividends, or rights offerings with a discounted offering price. It is also adjusted when the firm distributes assets (other than cash dividends) or indebtedness to its shareholders.
- Bondholders who convert do not receive accrued interest. Therefore, bondholders rarely convert voluntarily just before an interest payment date.
- If the bonds are called, the conversion option will expire just before (usually between three and ten days) the redemption date.

Valuing Convertible Bonds

A convertible bond can be modeled as a straight bond plus a nondetachable warrant. From the Options Principle, you know that the value of a warrant can never be negative. Therefore, in a perfect capital market environment, the value of a convertible bond can never fall below its value as a straight bond. Similarly, the value of a convertible bond can also never fall below its conversion value. Figure 21.4 illustrates the relationship among the bond value, conversion value, and actual market value of a convertible bond.

The market value of a convertible bond equals the sum of the bond value and the actual value of the conversion option. For low stock prices, the value of the straight bond increases as the stock price increases because the probability of default is declining. Once the probability of default is low (and stock prices are high), the straight bond price no longer increases with the stock price. Note in Figure 21.4 that the market value of the convertible bond always exceeds both the bond value and the conversion value. When the underlying share price rises above the conversion price, the conversion value exceeds the bond value. In that share price range, the actual market value of the convertible bond equals the bond value plus the exercise value of the conversion option plus the conversion option's time premium. When the underlying share price is very low, the convertible bond's market value approximates the bond value. When the share price is very high, the convertible bond's market value approximates the conversion value.

We can value a convertible bond by valuing the bond and warrant components separately. The value of a convertible bond exactly equals the sum of the two component values in a perfect capital market.

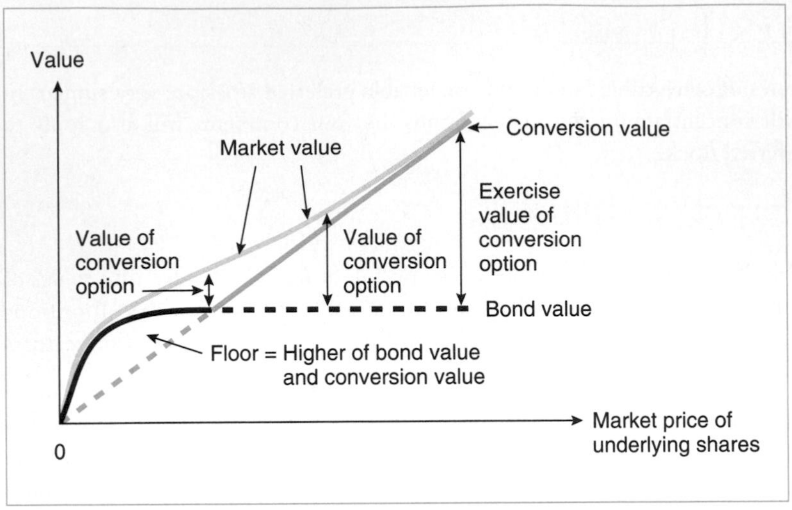

FIGURE 21.4
Bond value, conversion value, and actual market value of a convertible bond.

Convertible Preferred Stock

The main buyers of convertible securities are either entirely tax-exempt investors or those who cannot benefit directly from the corporate 70% dividends-received deduction. Consequently, under most market conditions, issuers of convertible securities have been able to obtain essentially the same terms (chiefly nominal annual interest or dividend rate and conversion premium) whether they issued the convertible security as debt or as preferred stock.

Convertible preferred stock is similar to convertible debt; it is preferred stock that is convertible at the holder's option into shares of the issuer's common stock. Issuers who are in a taxpaying position and expect to remain so for a number of years find it cheaper to issue convertible debt than convertible preferred stock. Interest payments are tax deductible, whereas dividend payments are not. The tax deductions reduce the cost of capital. Interest deductions are much less valuable to issuers who do not expect to be in a taxpaying position for a number of years. Of course, they are worthless if the issuer will *never* be able to claim them for tax purposes. Thus, in either case, nontaxpaying firms that wish to issue convertible securities issue convertible preferred stock.

Convertible preferred stock is usually perpetual, whereas convertible debt has a stated maturity and usually has a sinking fund. The rating agencies view perpetual convertible preferred stock as "true" equity for credit rating purposes.

Convertible Exchangeable Preferred Stock

A firm that is only temporarily not in an income-tax-paying position can issue *convertible exchangeable preferred stock.* Such securities are convertible preferred stock that is exchangeable at the option of the firm into convertible *debt* of the firm. The firm would exercise this option as soon as it becomes taxpaying. The nominal annual interest rate on the convertible debt equals the nominal annual dividend yield on the convertible preferred stock issue, and the issues have equivalent conversion terms. A nontaxpaying firm can reap the advantages of issuing convertible preferred stock while preserving the flexibility to reissue it in the form of debt should it become a taxpayer before the issue is converted.

Exchangeable Debentures

Firms have also issued bonds that are exchangeable for the common stock of another firm. The debentures are in effect "convertible" into the common stock of the other firm. But in all other respects, exchangeable debentures are like conventional convertible bonds. Exchangeable debentures may be attractive to a firm that owns a block of another firm's common stock when it would like to raise cash and intends to sell the block eventually. The firm may want to defer the sale, because it believes the shares will increase in value or because it wants to defer the capital gains tax liability.

Forced Conversions

Convertible bonds are normally callable subject to a schedule of fixed redemption (strike) prices that decline over the life of the issue. This call provision allows the issuer to force holders to convert the debt into common stock whenever the conversion value exceeds the call price. Most convertible bond indentures require the issuer to notify bondholders of the call prior to the redemption date, generally 30 days in advance. Securityholders can convert at any time during this notice period.

HOW FORCED CONVERSION WORKS As we have noted, the market value of a convertible bond always exceeds its conversion value unless the conversion option is about to expire. The difference between the market and conversion values reflects the conversion option's time premium. If the underlying common stock is non-dividend-paying, convertible bondholders never voluntarily convert, no matter how high the conversion value becomes. They can always realize greater value by selling the bond. Even when the underlying common stock is paying cash dividends, convertible bondholders do not voluntarily convert if the dividends they would receive after conversion are less than the interest they receive now.

Suppose the market value of the underlying common stock exceeds the call price. Calling the convertible issue motivates holders to convert, because converting is more profitable than tendering the bonds for cash redemption. A firm should follow the forced conversion strategy that maximizes shareholder wealth. If the firm calls convertible bonds when their conversion value is less than the effective call price, the bonds will not be converted, and wealth will be transferred from shareholders to bondholders. If the firm calls convertible bonds when the conversion value exceeds the call price, bondholders will simply convert. The forced conversion strategy that maximizes shareholder wealth is the one that minimizes bondholder value: In a perfect capital market, a firm should call convertible bonds when their conversion value reaches the *effective call price* (optional redemption price plus accrued interest).

Judged by the standards of the perfect capital market, most firms appear to wait "too long" to call their convertible bonds. They usually wait until the conversion value exceeds the call price by a seemingly wide margin—at least 20% is the practitioner's rule. Why do they behave this way? As we well know by now, actual markets are not perfect. In addition, if the market price of the issuer's common stock falls—and remains below the conversion price during the 30-day notice period—the redemption value will exceed the conversion value, and bondholders will surrender their bonds for cash rather than convert. In that case, the firm may have to raise enough cash to cover the cash redemption value on short notice. That could involve significant transaction costs. This explains why firms normally wait to call their convertible bonds until the conversion value exceeds the effective call price by a comfortable margin.

There is also an agency cost involved with trying to force conversion. A failed attempt is very embarrassing for the firm's executives and could even lead to someone being fired. This, of course, tends to bias the executives toward waiting for an even larger margin.

EXAMPLE Time Incorporated's Forced Conversion

Time Incorporated (now part of AOL Time Warner) called its Series C $4.50 cumulative convertible preferred stock for redemption at a price of $54.9375, including accrued dividends. The issue was convertible into 1.5152 shares of Time common stock at a conversion price of $33 per share. The market price of the common stock was $46.375, representing a 40.5% premium over the conversion price. Time was paying dividends on its common stock at the rate of $1.00 per share per year. A holder who converted at that time would suffer a decrease in annual dividend income amounting to \$2.98 (= 4.50 − [1.5152]1.00) per preferred share. Consequently, few holders had converted voluntarily.

The market value of the common stock provided a *redemption cushion* over the redemption price amounting to:

$$\text{Redemption cushion} = \frac{\begin{pmatrix}\text{Conversion}\\ \text{ratio}\end{pmatrix}\begin{pmatrix}\text{Market price of}\\ \text{common stock}\end{pmatrix} - \begin{matrix}\text{Redemption}\\ \text{price}\end{matrix}}{\text{Redemption price}} \tag{21.6}$$

$$= \frac{(1.5152)(46.375) - 54.9375}{54.9375} = 27.9\%$$

This cushion gave holders a strong incentive to convert when Time called the issue. With the assistance of investment bankers, the entire issue was converted.

Review

1. What is a convertible bond? What is convertible preferred stock? What are the main differences between them?
2. What are the main features of convertible debt?
3. What is convertible exchangeable preferred stock? Why do firms issue it?
4. What is forced conversion? Why do firms want to force conversions? What is the optimal time to force a conversion?

21.4 INTEREST RATE SWAPS

Often, a firm wishes to replace fixed-rate debt with floating-rate debt, or vice versa. Such a substitution involves transaction costs. The firm can avoid these by entering into an interest rate swap. The swap enables the firm to recharacterize an existing debt obligation rather than having to pay the cost of replacing it in its entirety.

A **swap** contract obligates two parties to exchange specified cash flows at specified intervals. In an **interest rate swap,** the cash flows are determined by two different interest rates.

Swaps were introduced in 1981, and their use has grown rapidly. Table 21.1 shows the growth in the interest rate swap market since 1987. The total notional principal amount involved in these transactions grew 86-fold. The market is still growing.

How an Interest Rate Swap Works

The two parties to an interest rate swap exchange interest payment obligations. One might be at a specified fixed rate, say 8%, and the other at a floating rate, say six-month LIBOR (London

TABLE 21.1
Interest rate swaps outstanding, 1987 to 2001.

	1987	1988	1989	1990	1991	1992	1993	1994	1995	1996	1997	1998	1999	2000	2001
Notional principal amount in billions of U.S. dollars	\$682	\$1,010	\$1,539	\$2,311	\$3,065	\$3,850	\$6,177	\$8,815	\$12,810	\$19,170	\$22,291	\$36,262	\$43,936	\$48,768	\$58,897

Source: International Swaps and Derivatives Association and Bank for International Settlements.

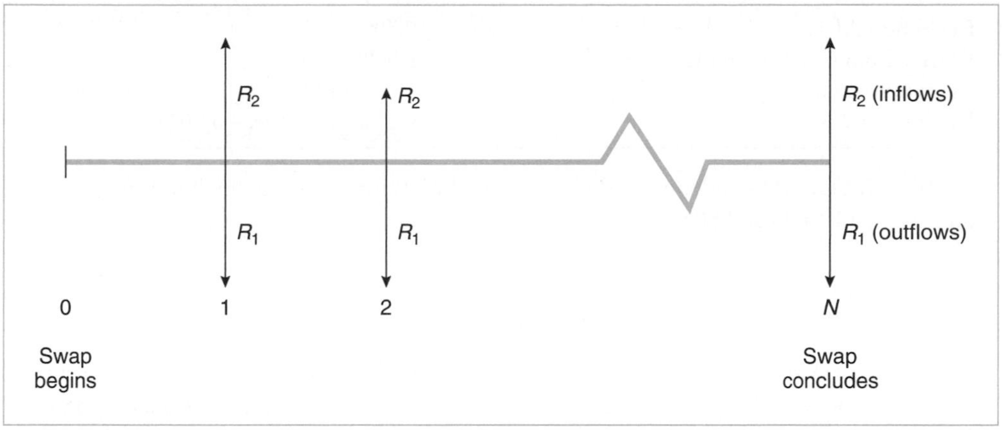

FIGURE 21.5
An interest rate swap.

Interbank Offer Rate, at which banks in the London money market lend each other funds). Or they might be different floating rates. In interest rate swaps, coupon payments, *but not the principal,* are swapped. The payments are based on a *notional principal amount;* it is only *notional* because the two parties do not exchange principal, they simply use the principal amounts to calculate the amounts of interest they owe each other. The interest payment obligations are conditional. If one party defaults, the other is released from its obligation.

Figure 21.5 illustrates an interest rate swap. In its simplest form, called a *fixed-rate–floating-rate swap,* one interest rate is fixed and the other is floating. One party pays out a series of cash flows determined by the fixed interest rate R_1. It receives a series of cash flows determined by the floating interest rate R_2. The cash flows for the other party are the mirror image of those shown in Figure 21.5.

A swap has lower default risk than a loan. Two features account for this. No principal changes hands, and the payments are netted. Each party calculates what it owes the other. The party owing the greater amount writes a check to the other for the difference.

EXAMPLE McDonald's Interest Rate Swap

Let's say that McDonald's Corporation enters into the following fixed-rate–floating-rate swap. It agrees to pay six-month LIBOR and to receive 8%, based on \$100 million notional. Net payments will be made semiannually. The amount of the first payment is determined on the swap date. LIBOR is 6%. Six months later, McDonald's receives a check for \$1,000,000 (= 100,000,000[0.08 − 0.06]/2). By then LIBOR has risen to 7%. Six months later, McDonald's receives a check for \$500,000 (= 100,000,000[0.08 − 0.07]/2). Assume LIBOR has risen further to 9%. At the end of the third period, McDonald's writes a check for \$500,000 (= 100,000,000[0.09 − 0.08]/2).

Interest rate swaps are used to change fixed-rate loans into floating-rate loans, and vice versa, or to change the index on a floating-rate loan.

EXAMPLE How Interest Rate Swaps Are Used

Suppose McDonald's issued \$100 million of 10-year fixed-rate bonds three years ago. The interest rate is 7.50%. The issue has seven years remaining. McDonald's now enters into a seven-year fixed-rate–floating-rate swap like the one in the previous example. Every six months McDonald's pays interest at a 7.50% rate on the bonds. It receives interest at an 8% rate and pays six-month LIBOR in the swap. Its net interest cost is

Pay bondholders	7.50%
Receive from swap counterparty	8.00%
Pay swap counterparty	6-month LIBOR
Net interest cost	6-month LIBOR – 0.50%

In effect, McDonald's has converted its fixed-rate bonds into floating-rate bonds paying six-month LIBOR minus 0.50%.

The Changing Market for Swaps

Swaps are not traded on exchanges. In the early days of the swap market, financial institutions arranged swaps by finding two counterparties who wanted to swap. The intermediary took no risk; it simply acted as agent. Swaps have evolved into a standardized product, and the intermediary's role has changed. It became important for intermediaries to put the transactions on their books. This exposed the intermediaries to default risk. The Principle of Comparative Advantage came into play. Commercial banks, with their greater capitalizations and comparative advantages in handling high-volume, standardized transactions and in extending credit, replaced investment banks as the main intermediaries.

Banks are the largest users of swaps. Table 21.2 shows the 10 largest swap users among U.S. banks in 2002.

Value Added by Interest Rate Swaps

In the 1980s, many market participants and academic researchers argued that comparative advantage was responsible for the rapid growth of the interest rate swap market.

THE COMPARATIVE ADVANTAGE ARGUMENT The argument went like this. Suppose a BBB-rated firm can borrow on a floating-rate basis at LIBOR plus 0.50% and on a fixed-rate basis at 12%. An AAA-rated bank can borrow at LIBOR or at 10.50%. The BBB-rated firm must pay a rate premium of 1.50% in the fixed-rate market but only 0.50% in the floating-rate market. The BBB-rated firm has a comparative advantage in the floating-rate market. The AAA-rated bank has

TABLE 21.2
Ten largest users of swaps, 2002.[a]

RANK	FIRM	NOTIONAL PRINCIPAL AMOUNT OUTSTANDING ($ MILLIONS)
1	J.P. Morgan Chase Bank	14,806,564
2	Bank of America	5,594,772
3	Citibank National Association	3,524,593
4	First Union National Bank	616,886
5	Bank One National Association	540,570
6	HSBC Bank USA	145,757
7	Bank of New York	141,886
8	Fleet National Bank	122,320
9	Wells Fargo Bank	83,137
10	LaSalle Bank National Association	57,477

[a]Notional amount of interest rate swaps and currency swaps outstanding at the end of the first quarter 2002.
Source: OCC Bank Derivatives Report: First Quarter 2002, Comptroller of the Currency, Washington, DC.

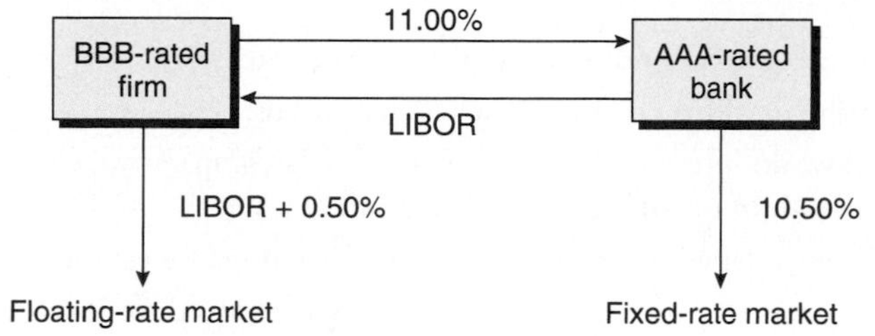

Firm's Net Interest Cost		Bank's Net Interest Cost	
Pay floating rate	LIBOR + 0.50%	Pay fixed rate	10.50%
Swap:		Swap:	
Pay	11	Receive	11
Receive	LIBOR	Pay	LIBOR
Net interest cost	11.50%	Net interest cost	LIBOR – 0.50%
Without swap	12.00%	Without swap	LIBOR
Savings	0.50%	Savings	0.50%

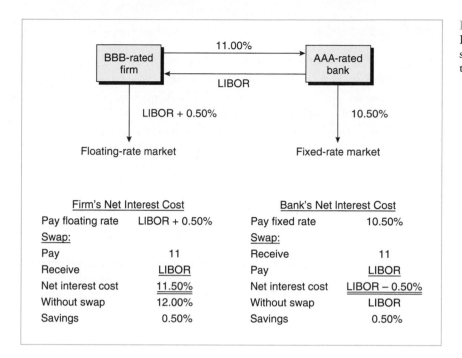

FIGURE 21.6
Fixed-rate–floating-rate swap and the comparative advantage argument.

a comparative advantage in the fixed-rate market. Suppose the bank borrows fixed rate, the firm borrows floating rate, and they swap. The firm agrees to pay the bank 11%, and the bank agrees to pay LIBOR. Figure 21.6 illustrates the swap and the net interest cost to each party.

The firm pays a net interest cost of 11.50%. It saves 0.50%. The bank pays LIBOR – 0.50% and also saves 0.50%. Sound too good to be true? It is! The argument is appealing. Unfortunately, it ignores arbitrage. With no barriers to capital flows, arbitrage would eventually eliminate any comparative advantage. Over time, the swap market would shrink, not grow!

A simple comparison of interest rates can be misleading. A swap is mutually beneficial only if it is superior *for each party* to a straight borrowing that is *identical in design and risk*. In a competitive market, there is no reason why the difference in floating rates for two firms should be the same as the difference in fixed rates. Consequently, there is also no reason why the fixed-rate–floating-rate differential should be the same for every firm. This differential depends on the firm's cash flow characteristics. If two firms differ, so will their fixed-rate–floating-rate differentials.

A BETTER EXPLANATION We think there is a better explanation for the growth of the interest rate swap market. Market imperfections, such as transaction costs, can explain much of the growth. Suppose a firm has information, which is not available to the market, that leads it to believe that its credit quality will improve. It is generally cheaper and easier to refund short-term debt than long-term debt. Issuing short-term floating-rate debt and swapping into fixed-rate debt will enable the firm to exploit its information advantage. In our example, suppose the BBB-rated firm's credit improves so that it can borrow at LIBOR + 0.25%. It replaces its bank loan facility with a new one, leaving the swap in place. Its cost of funds drops to 11.25% (= LIBOR + 0.25% + 11.00% − LIBOR).

We explain later how firms can use interest rate swaps to manage their interest rate risk exposure. Firms can enter into a swap with any number of large financial institutions. The success of swaps should therefore come as no surprise. Recall that the creation of a market for a security increases its liquidity, thus increasing its value by lowering transaction costs. The markets for swaps and other interest rate derivatives have grown with the increase in hedging by firms.

Review

1. What is an interest rate swap? How does one work?
2. Why do firms enter into interest rate swaps?
3. How do interest rate swaps add value? Is comparative advantage responsible for the growth in the interest rate swap market?
4. How are interest rate swaps useful in hedging interest rate risk?
5. Explain why an interest rate swap involves less default risk than simply exchanging two debt obligations?

21.5 FORWARDS AND FUTURES

You may think derivatives are new. Some are, but others are not. Futures contracts on commodities have been traded on organized exchanges since the 1860s. Forward contracts are even older. The Chicago Board of Trade (CBOT) opened in 1842. It initially traded forwards. It introduced commodity futures in 1865. Financial futures are newer. The International Monetary Market of the Chicago Mercantile Exchange (CME) introduced foreign currency futures in 1972 and interest rate futures in 1975.

Forward Contracts

As we said in Chapter 2, a **forward contract** obligates the holder to buy a specified amount of a particular asset at a stated price on a particular date in the future. All these terms are fixed at the time the forward contract is entered into. The specified future price is the *exercise price.* Most forward contracts are for commodities or currencies. (We discuss foreign exchange forwards in Chapter 27.)

At contract origination, the net present value of a forward contract is zero because the exercise price is set equal to the expected future price. Neither buyer nor seller will realize a profit unless the actual market price of the asset differs from the exercise price at maturity. If the actual price exceeds the exercise price, the contract holder profits. If the actual price is lower than the exercise price, the holder suffers a loss. Under the Principle of Two-Sided Transactions, the holder's gain (loss) is the contract seller's loss (gain).

EXAMPLE National Refining's Forward Contract

National Refining Corporation enters into a forward contract to purchase 10,000 barrels of oil at \$17 per barrel in 90 days from Lone Star Oil & Gas. The purchase obligation is \$170,000 (= [17]10,000). Suppose the price of oil is \$20 when the contract matures. National Refining realizes a profit of \$3 per barrel, or \$30,000.

A forward contract has two-sided default risk. Lone Star might fail to deliver the oil, and National Refining might fail to pay for it.[5] This credit risk is important in determining who is able to transact in the forward market. Access is usually limited to large corporations, governments, and other creditworthy parties.

[5]The CBOT developed futures contracts after many forward contracts defaulted.

Two other features of forward contracts are noteworthy. First, there are no intermediate cash flows. Value is conveyed only at maturity. Second, most forward contracts require *physical delivery* of the asset in exchange for the cash purchase price. However, some can be *cash settled,* which requires the party with the loss to pay that sum to the other party.

Futures Contracts

You may recall from Chapter 2 that the basic form of a futures contract is identical to that of a forward contract. A **futures contract** obligates the holder to buy a specified quantity of a particular asset at a specified exercise price at a specified date in the future. A futures contract differs from a forward contract with respect to realizing gains or losses. With a forward contract, gains or losses are realized only on the settlement date. With a futures contract, they are realized daily. Also, futures contracts are traded on organized exchanges, whereas forwards are traded over the counter. Futures contracts are actively traded on more than 60 exchanges in more than two dozen countries. There are futures contracts for agricultural commodities, precious metals, industrial commodities, currencies, stock market indexes, common stocks, and interest-bearing securities. These securities include Treasury bills, Treasury notes, Treasury bonds, and Eurodollar deposits. Stock futures began trading on the London International Financial Futures and Options Exchange in 2001 and started trading in the United States in 2002. Until that time, U.S. regulations forbade single stock futures out of concern that trading in them might disrupt the market for the underlying stocks.

Some futures contracts (notably agricultural futures) require physical delivery. Others (notably stock index futures and Eurodollar futures) are cash settled. In practice, few futures contracts are held to maturity and exercised. Most are closed out by doing a reverse trade on the futures exchange. For example, a person who bought a futures contract can close out the position by selling an identical contract.

MARKET FOR FUTURES Futures are traded on exchanges through open outcry. Trading takes place in a trading ring on the exchange floor. Exchange members who want to trade enter the ring and announce their intention to trade. When a buyer and seller agree on terms, the updated price is posted on a board near the trading ring.

Unlike the stock exchanges and the options markets, there are no central market makers on the futures exchanges. As a result, futures prices can exhibit considerable volatility. To limit this volatility, the futures exchanges have established price limits. Futures prices cannot change by more than the indicated limit on any particular day.

LOW DEFAULT RISK A futures contract has less default risk than a forward contract. Three features of futures markets are responsible. (1) Futures contracts are *marked to market* and *settled* at the end of every business day. When a futures contract loses value during the day, the holder pays the seller at the end of the day a sum equal to the day's loss. (2) There are *margin requirements.* Each buyer and seller must post a performance bond, which is adjusted daily. (3) There is a *clearinghouse.* Each party to a futures transaction really enters into a transaction with the clearinghouse. If either party defaults on a payment, the clearinghouse will make the payment. It first applies any funds in the defaulting party's margin account. If that is not enough, the clearinghouse covers the difference.

GREATER LIQUIDITY Futures contracts are more liquid than forward contracts for two reasons. Futures are standardized contracts, and they are traded on organized exchanges.

How an Interest Rate Futures Contract Works

We will use the Treasury bond futures contract to illustrate how an interest rate futures contract works. The underlying instrument is a hypothetical bond with a $100,000 par value, a 20-year maturity, and an 8% coupon. The contract price is quoted with respect to this bond. However, the contract seller can choose from among several actual Treasury bonds that are acceptable to deliver. Settlement is made by physical delivery.

EXAMPLE A Treasury Bond Futures Contract

Suppose you buy one contract, which specifies delivery in six months at a price of 96 (that is, 96% of the face amount, or $96,000 in total). You are said to be *long* the contract, and the seller is said to be *short* the contract. Each day, your position and the seller's position will be "marked to market" as the value of the futures contract changes. As interest rates go up, the value of the futures contract (the value of the 8% bond) goes down. As interest rates go down, the value of the futures contract goes up. Under the Principle of Two-Sided Transactions, as the value of your long position goes down, the value of the seller's short position goes up by the same amount. As the value of your long position goes up, the value of the seller's short position goes down by the same amount.

At the end of six months, you will take delivery of Treasury bonds in exchange for the $96,000 agreed-on price. Your gain (or loss) will depend on whether you can sell the bonds for more (or less) than the $96,000 you paid for them. If you do not want to take delivery, you can "close out your position" by selling one Treasury bond contract. The clearinghouse will net your long and short positions. If the 8% bond increased in value while you owned the futures contract, you will have a profit; in the opposite case, you will have a loss.

Growth of the Futures Market

Figure 21.7 illustrates the growth of the Treasury bond and Eurodollar CD futures markets between 1981 and 2001. The number of Treasury bond contracts traded grew eightfold between 1981 and 1998 to 112 million per year, but has since fallen by about half. The number of Eurodollar CD contracts traded grew many times faster to 184 million per year by 2001. Each Eurodollar CD contract is for $1 million, whereas each Treasury bond contract is for $100,000. Thus, the underlying principal amount is actually much greater in the Eurodollar futures market than in the Treasury bond futures market.

FIGURE 21.7
Yearly volume of financial futures contracts, 1981 to 2001.

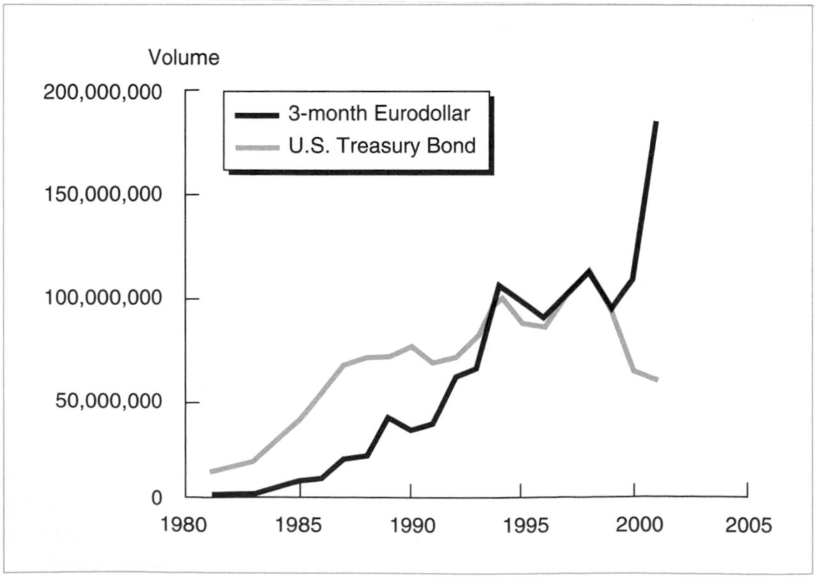

As we observed in the swap market, the interest rate futures markets have expanded because of the increase in hedging activity.

Review

1. Describe the main differences between a forward contract and a futures contract. What do they have in common?
2. Explain why a futures contract involves less default risk than a forward contract.
3. How does an interest rate futures contract work?
4. What factors account for the growth of the futures markets?

21.6 HEDGING

We have mentioned several times that derivatives are used in hedging and that an increase in hedging helps to explain the growth in the options, swaps, and futures markets. In Chapter 27, we show how a firm can use currency futures and options to hedge foreign exchange risk. Here, we show how firms use the instruments we have described to hedge other types of risk.

How a Hedge Works

A firm engages in hedging to reduce its sensitivity to changes in the price of a commodity, a foreign exchange rate, or an interest rate. Figure 21.8 illustrates the rationale for hedging. **Hedging** involves taking an offsetting position by buying or selling a financial instrument whose value changes in the opposite direction from the value of the asset being hedged. Suppose an increase in interest rates would decrease the value of the firm. In panel (a), the firm's value decreases as interest rates increase. This may be a result of interest rates increasing on floating-rate debt that the firm has outstanding. It might reflect a rise in long-term interest rates just as the firm is about to issue new bonds. You could also think of r as the price of jet fuel to an airline, or the cost of British pounds to a U.S. importer of British goods.

If the firm can take a position in a derivative whose value will increase as interest rates increase, it can neutralize the impact of the interest rate increase. In panel (b), the value of the hedge position follows the dashed line. The hedge position is carefully selected so that changes in its value offset changes in the value of the asset being hedged. Panel (b) illustrates a *perfect hedge.* The value changes offset each other precisely, so the value of the firm is unaffected. Perfect hedges are difficult to construct. Nevertheless, proper hedging should substantially reduce the firm's exposure to price risks.

EXAMPLE Hedging Gas Prices

It was reported a few years ago that because the spikes in the price of natural gas the preceding winter had sent home heating bills skyrocketing, utility regulators in several states had done an about-face on natural gas hedging. They had previously rejected any use of energy derivatives as too costly, but were now encouraging gas utilities to hedge to obtain more predictable prices for the next winter heating season.

Hedging with Options

Options provide an opportunity to hedge against a bad outcome while preserving the opportunity to benefit from a good outcome. Imagine that General Holding Company has purchased 1 million shares of Family Entertainment's common stock. General Holding would like to sell the

FIGURE 21.8
The rationale for hedging.

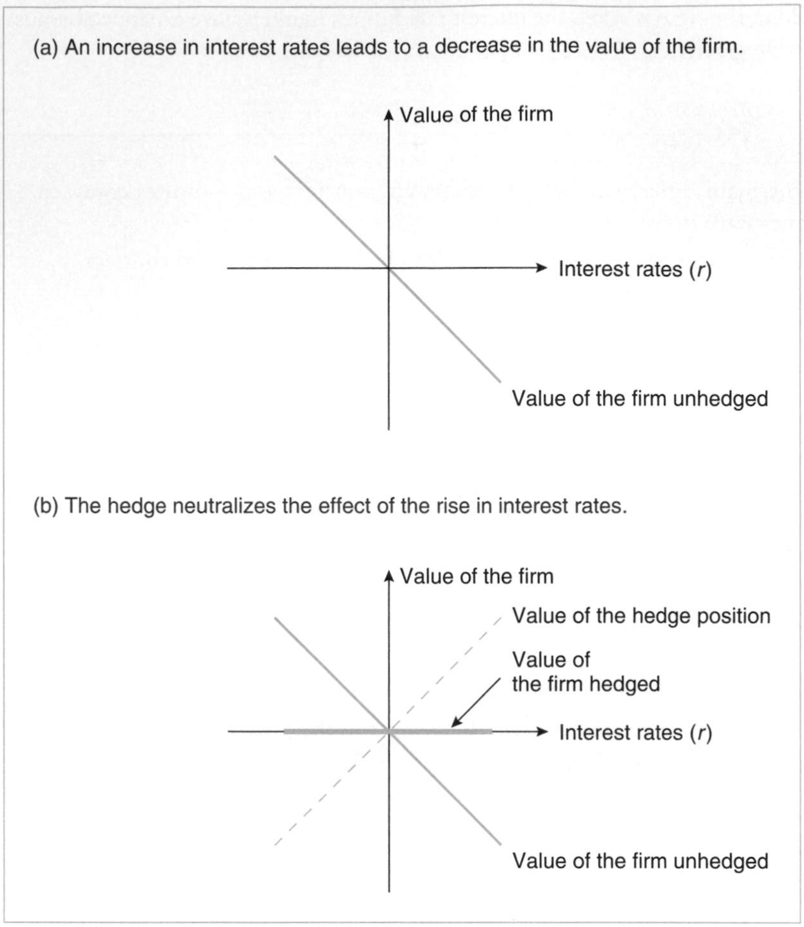

stock. However, it is near year-end. Deferring the sale would defer tax on the gain General Holding has realized. But General Holding is concerned that the shares might decline in value before year-end. Let us see how General Holding can hedge this risk.

EXAMPLE Using Options to Hedge at General Holding

General Holding can purchase put options. Family Entertainment's current share price is $28. If General Holding buys put options on 1 million shares at $28 per share, it will be fully hedged against risk of loss. Table 21.3 illustrates the possible outcomes. Suppose Family Entertainment's share price falls to $20. General Holding's 1 million shares lose $8 each. But the put is worth $8 per share. The gain just offsets the loss. On the other hand, if Family Entertainment's share price rises, General Holding has a gain. It has hedged against the risk of a loss without affecting its opportunity to benefit from a rise in Family Entertainment's share price.

Hedging is not costless, however. General Holding must pay the option seller. Why? The Principle of Two-Sided Transactions provides the answer. General Holding transfers the risk of loss to the option seller, who must be compensated in order to be willing to accept this risk. General Holding will purchase the put only if it believes that the price of the option is at least as great as the value it realizes by transferring the risk.

TABLE 21.3
Possible outcomes for General Holding's option hedge.

SHARE PRICE AT TIME OF SALE	GAIN OR (LOSS) ON SHARES		GAIN OR (LOSS) ON HEDGE		NET GAIN OR (LOSS)
	Per Share	Total	Per Share	Total	
$20	$(8)	$(8,000,000)	$8	$8,000,000	—
25	(3)	(3,000,000)	3	3,000,000	—
30	2	2,000,000	—	—	$2,000,000
35	7	7,000,000	—	—	7,000,000

There are many types of derivative instruments that are really options (even though "option" does not appear in the name). Three we should mention are interest rate caps, interest rate floors, and interest rate collars.

CAPS AND FLOORS An *interest rate cap* pays the holder if the specified interest rate (for example, three-month LIBOR) rises above a specified rate. A floating-rate borrower who buys a 7% cap will never have to pay more than 7%. Any period in which three-month LIBOR exceeds 7%, the seller of the cap contract pays the difference between the actual rate and 7% multiplied by the notional amount and the fraction of the year (in this case 0.25). The cap contract is like a call option on three-month LIBOR with a strike price of 7%. It hedges the contract holder against a rise in rates.

An *interest rate floor* places a lower limit on the interest rate. For example, an investor in floating-rate notes that pay three-month LIBOR + 1% who purchases a 4% floor contract can never receive less than 5% interest any period. The floor contract is like a put option on three-month LIBOR with a strike price of 4%. It hedges against a drop in rates.

COLLARS Finally, an *interest rate collar* is just a package consisting of a cap and a floor. For example, a 4%/7% collar consists of a 4% floor and a 7% cap. It hedges against rates falling outside a particular range.

Hedging with Interest Rate Swaps

A floating-rate borrower can hedge against a change in interest rates by entering into a swap to pay fixed and receive floating. The BBB-rated firm in the comparative advantage example entered into such a swap. The swap converted its interest cost from LIBOR + 0.50% floating to 11.50% fixed.

Hedging with Forwards and Futures

Because forwards and futures are basically identical in structure, we will present only a futures example. The critical factor in futures hedging is determining the hedge ratio. The *hedge ratio* is defined by

$$\text{Hedge ratio} = \frac{\text{Volatility of bond to be hedged}}{\text{Volatility of hedging instrument}} \tag{21.7}$$

EXAMPLE Hedging with Futures at PepsiCo

PepsiCo Inc. plans to issue $50 million of bonds. It needs one month to prepare the documentation, and it is concerned that interest rates might rise by a full percentage point before it can sell the issue. It could sell Treasury bond futures to hedge this risk.

CALCULATOR SOLUTION

Data Input	Function Key
60	N
5.5	I
5	PMT
100	FV
91.2751	**PV**

If it were prepared to issue debt immediately, it could sell 10% notes that mature in a lump sum at the end of 30 years. If its new-issue rate increases to 11%, the 10% issue will fall in value to \$91.2751 per \$100 par value:

$$PV = \sum_{t=1}^{60} \frac{5}{(1.055)^t} + \frac{100}{(1.055)^{60}} = 91.2751$$

The change in value is 8.7249 (= 100 − 91.2751).

CALCULATOR SOLUTION

Data Input	Function Key
40	N
4.5	I
4	PMT
100	FV
90.7992	**PV**

PepsiCo estimates that the yield on an 8% 20-year Treasury bond would also increase by 1%, from 9% currently to 10%. At a 9% yield, the 8% Treasury bond is worth \$90.7992 per \$100 par value:

$$PV = \sum_{t=1}^{40} \frac{4}{(1.045)^t} + \frac{100}{(1.045)^{40}} = 90.7992$$

CALCULATOR SOLUTION

Data Input	Function Key
40	N
5.0	I
4	PMT
100	FV
82.8409	**PV**

At a 10% yield, it is worth \$82.8409 per \$100 par value:

$$PV = \sum_{t=1}^{40} \frac{4}{(1.05)^t} + \frac{100}{(1.05)^{40}} = 82.8409$$

The change in value is 7.9583 (= 90.7992 − 82.8409).

From Equation (21.7), the hedge ratio is:

$$\text{Hedge ratio} = \frac{8.7249}{7.9583} = 1.0963$$

PepsiCo needs to sell short 1.0963 8% Treasury bonds for each bond to be hedged. PepsiCo needs to sell short

$$\text{Number of contracts} = (\text{Hedge ratio})\left(\frac{\text{Principal amount to be hedged}}{\text{Par value of hedging instrument}}\right) \tag{21.8}$$

Each futures contract covers \$100,000 principal amount of bonds, so

$$\text{Number of contracts} = (1.0963)\left(\frac{50{,}000{,}000}{100{,}000}\right) = 548 \text{ Treasury bond contracts}$$

To verify, suppose interest rates rise by 1%. The missed issuance opportunity will cost PepsiCo

$$0.087249(50{,}000{,}000) = \$4{,}362{,}450$$

But it will earn a profit on the futures contracts equal to

$$548(0.079583)100{,}000 = \$4{,}361{,}148$$

This profit offsets 99.97% of the opportunity cost.

Consider two other hedging situations. Suppose Delta Airlines is concerned about a possible rise in the cost of jet fuel. It could hedge by buying oil futures. Suppose Nike is about to receive payment in Euros for a large shipment of running shoes just like the ones you wear. It could sell Euro futures to hedge against the risk of a decline in the value of the Euro.

Corporate Use of Hedging

Surveys show that larger firms are more likely to use derivatives than smaller firms, and that mining firms and other primary producers are more likely to hedge than manufacturing or service firms. More than 80% of large firms hedge, but only about 10% of small firms do. Firms are more likely to hedge if they have higher leverage, greater interest rate or foreign exchange exposure, lower liquidity, or more research and development spending. These findings suggest that hedging reduces the likelihood of financial distress and lessens the asset substitution and underinvestment problems by reducing cash flow volatility. Empirical studies also suggest that the managers of large firms hedge to protect their wealth when they have a large part of it tied up in the firm's stock.

Review

1. Explain a firm's rationale for hedging? How does a hedge work?
2. A firm might win a contract to sell goods to a British firm in exchange for pounds sterling. How could it go about hedging its sterling/dollar foreign exchange risk?
3. A firm is considering borrowing on a floating-rate basis. How could it hedge its interest-rate risk?
4. What are interest rate caps and floors? How are they like options?
5. How could a firm use interest rate futures to hedge an upcoming issue of long-term debt?

SUMMARY

Financial markets have become more volatile in recent years, and firms actively seek ways to hedge their risk exposure. Financial engineers have responded by developing new hedging instruments. These do not eliminate risk. Rather, they transfer it to other parties who are willing to bear it at lower cost.

- There are four basic derivatives: options, swaps, forwards, and futures. They can be used to build more complex securities. Once you understand these basic building blocks, you will be able to analyze complex securities more easily.
- An option gives the holder a right without an obligation. A call option gives the right to buy, a put option the right to sell. Firms can issue call options, known as warrants, to raise equity. They can package them with debt to create convertible bonds or exchangeable bonds. Valuing options can be difficult. Various option valuation models have been developed. The Black-Scholes OPM is one that is widely used.
- The Black-Scholes OPM can be used to value options on stocks. It is also useful for valuing warrants and the option component of convertible bonds. Remember to adjust for the dilution factor when valuing warrants that have not yet been issued.
- Financing with convertible debt represents a form of what practitioners call deferred equity financing. The issue is debt until it is converted. A convertible bond derives its value from two sources: its value as a straight bond and the value of the underlying common stock into which it can be converted.
- Firms, particularly smaller ones, often find it advantageous to issue convertible bonds or bonds with warrants. These securities generally have lower agency costs than straight debt. If the firm pursues riskier projects, the option feature lets securityholders share in the payoff from really good outcomes.
- A firm that is not taxpaying, and does not expect to be in the foreseeable future, should issue convertible preferred stock rather than convertible debt. If it expects to become

taxpaying soon, it should consider issuing convertible exchangeable preferred stock. It can exchange convertible debt for the convertible preferred when it begins paying income taxes.

- In a perfect capital market, a convertible debt issue should be called for redemption, to force its conversion into common stock, when its conversion value reaches its effective call price (the optional redemption price plus accrued interest). With costly transactions, including the chance of a "failed conversion," firms usually call only when the conversion value exceeds the effective call price by at least 20%.
- Interest rate swaps entered the marketplace in 1981. Their use has grown rapidly. The two parties to a swap exchange interest but not principal. Payments are based on a notional principal amount. Swaps can be used to transform fixed-rate debt into floating-rate debt, and vice versa. Interest rate swaps are useful in hedging interest rate risk. The swaps market has grown in response to the increase in hedging by firms.
- A firm that wants to transform some fixed-rate debt into floating-rate debt should compare the cost of refunding the fixed-rate debt and the cost of entering into a fixed-rate–floating-rate swap. It should select the lower-cost alternative.
- Forwards and futures are contracts that obligate the holder to buy a specified amount of a particular asset at a stated price on a particular date in the future. Futures are standardized, forwards are not. Futures are exchange traded. Forwards are traded over-the-counter. Forwards allow greater flexibility in design, whereas futures are more liquid and have less default risk. Both are useful for hedging commodity price risk, foreign exchange risk, and interest rate risk.
- A firm can use derivatives to reduce its exposure to commodity price, foreign exchange, or interest rate risk. It should decide how much risk it wants to transfer. It should make sure that any transaction it considers will work properly. If it considers more than one alternative, it should select the one with the lowest cost.

EQUATION SUMMARY

$$\text{CALL} = P_0 N(d_1) - SN(d_2)e^{-\Delta tk} \tag{21.1}$$

$$d_1 = \frac{\ln(P_0/S) + \Delta tk}{\sigma \Delta t^{1/2}} + \frac{\sigma \Delta t^{1/2}}{2} \tag{21.2}$$

$$d_2 = d_1 - \sigma \Delta t^{1/2} \tag{21.3}$$

$$\text{PUT} = \text{CALL} + Se^{-\Delta tk} - P_0 \tag{21.4}$$

$$W = \frac{C}{1+P} \tag{21.5}$$

$$\text{Redemption cushion} = \frac{\begin{pmatrix}\text{Conversion}\\ \text{ratio}\end{pmatrix}\begin{pmatrix}\text{Market price of}\\ \text{common stock}\end{pmatrix} - \begin{matrix}\text{Redemption}\\ \text{price}\end{matrix}}{\text{Redemption price}} \tag{21.6}$$

$$\text{Hedge ratio} = \frac{\text{Volatility of bond to be hedged}}{\text{Volatility of hedging instrument}} \tag{21.7}$$

$$\text{Number of contracts} = (\text{Hedge ratio})\left(\frac{\text{Principal amount to be hedged}}{\text{Par value of hedging instrument}}\right) \tag{21.8}$$

QUESTIONS

1. What is a derivative?
2. What are the variables that affect the value of a call option?
3. What is the relationship between the value of a call option and a put option?
4. What is a warrant?
5. What is a convertible security?
6. Explain why a convertible bond can be viewed as a package consisting of a straight bond and warrants.
7. What is an interest rate swap?
8. Warrants are often referred to as "sweeteners" to a bond issue, as though the firm can "throw them into the deal" at no cost. Explain why it is, or is not, costless for the firm to include warrants with a bond issue.
9. Explain why futures contracts are similar to forward contracts. How are they different?
10. What is the basic rationale for hedging?
11. Explain how each of the following instruments is used to hedge interest rate risk: (a) Interest rate swap (b) Option to buy a bond (c) Interest rate future.

CHALLENGING QUESTIONS

12. Consider the following statement: A call option is a great way to make money. If the asset goes up in value, you get the increase, but if the asset goes down in value, you do not exercise the option and do not lose any money. Therefore, everyone should invest in call options. Is this statement true, false, or partly true and partly false? Explain why.
13. What type of option is a cap? What type of option is a floor? Explain how you could construct a collar using options.
14. We pointed out that common stock in a firm that has some debt can be viewed as a call option. Explain why.
15. Explain why a convertible bond can be viewed as a combination of (1) the underlying common stock that it is convertible into and (2) a put option exercisable at the conversion price.
16. Why does the time premium of an option increase (decrease) as the value of the underlying asset moves toward (away from) the strike price?
17. How could you use the put-call parity concept to arbitrage an overpriced put? An underpriced put?
18. Explain why it is possible to view an interest rate swap as a portfolio of forward contracts.
19. Explain why a futures contract can be viewed as a sequence of forward contracts.
20. A convertible bond can be modeled as a call option plus a straight bond. A warrant is a call option. In a perfect capital market environment, the combined market value of a warrant and a straight bond is identical to the market value of a comparable convertible bond. Explain why you might expect the market value of the warrant-bond combination to be somewhat greater than that of the comparable convertible bond. (*Hint:* This can be done using the Options Principle.)

PROBLEMS

LEVEL A (BASIC)

A1. (Exercise value and time premium of a call option) Microsoft stock is currently selling for $45.67 per share. What is the exercise value and the time premium of these two Microsoft options?

a. A call option with a strike price of $45 and a market value of $2.15.

b. A call option with a strike price of $50 and a market value of $0.40.

A2. (Exercise value and time premium of call or put options) What are the exercise values and the time premiums of the following options?

a. An Exxon Mobil call with a strike price of $35 and a market value of $1.80. Exxon Mobil stock is selling for $33.40.

b. An Exxon Mobil put with a strike price of $35 and a market value of $2.90. Exxon Mobil stock is selling for $33.40.

c. An IBM call with a strike price of $65 and a market value of $6.00. IBM stock is selling for $67.90.

d. An IBM put with a strike price of $65 and a market value of $3.30. IBM stock is selling for $67.90.

A3. (Exercise value and time premium of call or put options) What are the exercise values and the time premiums of the following options?

a. A Disney call with a strike price of $50 and a market value of $10. Disney stock is selling for $55.

b. A Disney put with a strike price of $50 and a market value of $1.50. Disney stock is selling for $55.

c. A Cisco call with a strike price of $15 and a market value of $0.40. Cisco stock is selling for $12.07.

d. A Cisco put with a strike price of $15 and a market value of $3.20. Cisco stock is selling for $12.07.

A4. (Put-call parity)

a. General Electric stock is selling for $29.65. A call option with a strike price of $30 is selling for $0.95, and the present value of the strike price is $29.80. What should a put with the same strike price and maturity be worth?

b. An IBM put has a strike price of $100, the stock price is $67.90, and the put price is $32.40. The present value of the strike price is $99.20. What should a $100 call with the same expiration be worth?

A5. (Put-call parity) A BankAmerica call option with a $60 strike price has a value of $6.30. The market price of the stock is $63.73, and the present value of the strike price is $59.70. What should be the value of a put option on BankAmerica with the same expiration and strike price?

A6. (Put-call parity)

a. Pfizer stock is selling for $30.45. A call option with a strike price of $30 is selling for $3.80, and the present value of the strike price is $29.20. What should a put with the same strike price and expiration be worth?

b. A Starbucks put option has a market price of $2.05 and a strike price of $20. The stock price is $19.09. The present value of the strike price is $19.60. What should a $20 call with the same expiration be worth?

A7. (Value of a convertible bond) OEM Corporation has a convertible bond outstanding that is convertible into 25 common shares. OEM common shares are selling for $40 per share. A similar nonconvertible bond would be expected to sell for about $950.

a. The convertible bond is selling for a premium of $50 above the greater of its conversion value and its straight-bond value. What is the market price of the convertible bond?

b. What is the value of the conversion option of the convertible bond?

c. OEM can call the bond and force conversion at a redemption price of $1,080. Should OEM call the bond today?

A8. (Value of a convertible bond) Xygot Co. has a convertible bond outstanding that is convertible into 20 common shares. Xygot common shares are selling for $35 per share. A similar nonconvertible bond would be expected to sell for about $900.

a. The convertible bond is selling for a premium of $75 above the greater of its conversion value and its straight-bond value. What is the market price of the convertible bond?

b. What is the value of the conversion option of the convertible bond?

c. Xygot can call the bond and force conversion at a redemption price of $1,050. Should Xygot call the bond today?

A9. (Value of a convertible bond) LMP Corporation has a convertible bond outstanding that is convertible into 50 common shares. LMP common shares are selling for $20 per share. A similar nonconvertible bond would be expected to sell for about $975.

a. The convertible bond is selling for a premium of $65 above the greater of its conversion value and its straight-bond value. What is the market price of the convertible bond?

b. What is the value of the conversion option of the convertible bond?

c. LMP can call the bond and force conversion at a redemption price of $1,080. Should LMP call the bond today?

A10. (Interest rate swap payments) Coke enters into a swap agreement where it agrees to pay a fixed 8.5% and receive LIBOR plus 0.5%. The notational amount is $300 million and the net payments are made semiannually.

a. What is Coke's cash payment or receipt if LIBOR is 6.00%?

b. What is Coke's cash payment or receipt if LIBOR is 10.00%?

A11. (Interest rate swap payments) Suppose that Intel enters into a swap agreement where it agrees to pay LIBOR plus 0.5% and it receives a fixed 8.0%. The notational amount is $100 million and the net payments are made semiannually.

a. What is Intel's cash flow if LIBOR is 6.00%?

b. What is Intel's cash flow if LIBOR is 8.50%?

A12. (Interest rate swap payments) PepsiCo enters into a swap agreement with TI where it agrees to pay a fixed 8% and receive LIBOR plus 0.5%. The notational amount is $100 million and the net payments are made semiannually.

a. What is PepsiCo's cash payment or receipt if LIBOR is 6.00%?

b. What is TI's cash payment or receipt if LIBOR is 10.00%?

A13. (Caps, floors, and collars) What will the holder of the following contracts pay or receive?

a. You buy a 9% interest rate cap to hedge against interest rate increases on a large bond. What do you pay or receive if the interest rate is 7%? 9.5%?

b. You buy a 5% floor. What do you pay or receive if the interest rate is 6%? 4.5%?

c. You buy a 5%/9% collar. What do you pay or receive if the interest rate is 4.5%, 6%, or 9.5%.

A14. (Caps, floors, and collars) What will the holder of the following contracts pay or receive?

a. You buy a 10% interest rate cap to hedge against interest rate increases on a large bond. What do you pay or receive if the interest rate is 8%? 10.5%?

b. You buy a 6% floor. What do you pay or receive if the interest rate is 7%? 5.5%?

c. You buy a 6%/9% collar. What do you pay or receive if the interest rate is 4.5%, 6%, or 9.5%.

A15. (Valuing a call option) Redo the Black-Scholes OPM example assuming $P_0 = 28$, $S = 30$, $\Delta t = 0.75$, $k = 0.06$, and $\sigma = 0.40$. (This is identical to the example in the text except that the standard deviation is larger.) Why has the value of the call option increased?

A16. (Valuing a call option) Redo problem A15 assuming $\Delta t = 2.00$. Why has the value of the call option increased?

A17. (Valuing a call option) Redo the Black-Scholes OPM example assuming $P_0 = 28$, $S = 30$, $\Delta t = 0.75$, $k = 0.06$, and $\sigma = 0.45$. (This is identical to the example in the text except that the standard deviation is larger.) Why has the value of the call option increased?

A18. (Valuing a call option) Redo problem A17 assuming $\Delta t = 2.5$. Why has the value of the call option increased?

LEVEL B

B1. (Call and put valuation) Suppose a stock is selling for $48.50 per share, the standard deviation of the return from owning a share of this stock is 24% per year, and the riskless return with continuous compounding is 5% APR. According to the Black-Scholes OPM:

a. What is a call option on this stock worth if the option has a strike price of $50 and eight months until expiration?

b. What is a put option on this stock worth if the option has a strike price of $50 and eight months until expiration?

c. What is a call option on this stock worth if the option has a strike price of $50 and four months until expiration?

d. What is a put option on this stock worth if the option has a strike price of $50 and four months until expiration?

B2. (Call and put valuation) Suppose a stock is selling for $45 per share, the standard deviation of the return from owning a share of this stock is 20% per year, and the riskless return with continuous compounding is 6% APR. According to the Black-Scholes OPM:

a. What is a call option on this stock worth if the option has a strike price of $50 and eight months until expiration?

b. What is a put option on this stock worth if the option has a strike price of $50 and eight months until expiration?

c. What is a call option on this stock worth if the option has a strike price of $50 and four months until expiration?

d. What is a put option on this stock worth if the option has a strike price of $50 and four months until expiration?

B3. (Put valuation) According to the Black-Scholes OPM, what is the value of a six-month put option with a strike price of $40 on stock selling for $37.75 if the standard deviation of the return to the stock is 28% per year and the riskless return with continuous compounding is 7% APR?

B4. (Put valuation) According to the Black-Scholes OPM, what is the value of a six-month put option with a strike price of $42 on stock selling for $35 if the standard deviation of the return to the stock is 30% per year and the riskless return with continuous compounding is 8% APR?

B5. (Call valuation, and time and exercise values) Suppose the standard deviation of a stock's return is 25% per year and the riskless return with continuous compounding is 6% APR. According to the Black-Scholes OPM:

a. What is a six-month call option on this stock worth if the strike price is $30 and the stock is currently selling for $28? What are the time and exercise values of this option?

b. What is a six-month call option on this stock worth if the strike price is $30 and the stock is currently selling for $32? What are the time and exercise values of this option?

c. What is a six-month call option on this stock worth if the strike price is $30 and the stock is currently selling for $34? What are the time and exercise values of this option?

B6. (Call valuation, and time and exercise values) Suppose the standard deviation of a stock's return is 25% per year and the riskless return with continuous compounding is 7% APR. According to the Black-Scholes OPM:

a. What is a six-month call option on this stock worth if the strike price is $40 and the stock is currently selling for $35? What are the time and exercise values of this option?

b. What is a six-month call option on this stock worth if the strike price is $40 and the stock is currently selling for $42? What are the time and exercise values of this option?

c. What is a six-month call option on this stock worth if the strike price is $40 and the stock is currently selling for $45? What are the time and exercise values of this option?

B7. (Call valuation for differing volatilities) Consider a nine-month call option with a strike price of $25 on a stock that currently sells for $25. According to the Black-Scholes OPM, if the riskless return with continuous compounding is 6% APR:

a. What is the value of this option if σ is 35%?

b. What is the value of this option if σ is 30%?

c. What is the value of this option if σ is 25%?

B8. (Call valuation for differing volatilities) Consider a nine-month call option with a strike price of $50 on a stock that currently sells for $50. According to the Black-Scholes OPM, if the riskless return with continuous compounding is 8% APR:

a. What is the value of this option if σ is 35%?

b. What is the value of this option if σ is 30%?

c. What is the value of this option if σ is 25%?

B9. (Call value for a deep out-of-the-money option) According to the Black-Scholes OPM, what is the value of a call option with a strike price of $110 and three months until expiration on an asset that has a current market value of $90 and a σ of 30% per year if k is 10%?

B10. (Call value for a deep out-of-the-money option) According to the Black-Scholes OPM, what is the value of a call option with a strike price of $100 and three months until expiration on an asset that has a current market value of $80 and a σ of 30% per year if k is 10%?

B11. (Call valuation for differing interest rates) Consider a six-month call option with a strike price of $20 on a stock that currently sells for $21. According to the Black-Scholes OPM, if σ is 30%:

a. What is the value of this option if k is 4%?

b. What is the value of this option if k is 7%?

c. What is the value of this option if k is 10%?

B12. (Call valuation for differing interest rates) Consider a six-month call option with a strike price of $30 on a stock that currently sells for $31. According to the Black-Scholes OPM, if σ is 30%:

a. What is the value of this option if k is 4%?

b. What is the value of this option if k is 7%?

c. What is the value of this option if k is 10%?

B13. (Call value, exercise value, and time premium) What is the current value of a European call option with an exercise price of $20 and an expiration date nine months from now if the stock is non-dividend-paying and is now selling for $24.38, the variance of the return on the stock is 0.48, and the riskless return is 6% APR? What is the current exercise value of this call option? What is the current time premium?

B14. (Call value, exercise value, and time premium) What is the current value of a European call option with an exercise price of $50 and an expiration date nine months from now if the stock is non-dividend-paying and is now selling for $57.25, the variance of the return on the stock is 0.5, and the riskless return is 6% APR? What is the current exercise value of this call option? What is the current time premium?

B15. (Interest rate swaps and comparative advantage) Tokai Bank can borrow at a fixed rate of 9% or at LIBOR. A manufacturing firm can borrow at a fixed rate of 12% or at LIBOR + 1%.

a. Is there a mutually advantageous opportunity to engage in an interest rate swap? Explain.

b. Suppose the bank offers to pay the manufacturing firm LIBOR in return for payments at 11-1/2%. How should the manufacturing firm respond?

c. The manufacturing firm proposes to pay 10-1/2% in return for LIBOR. Is such a swap advantageous for the bank?

d. What fraction of the net cost benefit does each party realize under the swap terms in part c?

B16. (Interest rate swaps and comparative advantage) Triple-A-rated Exxon Mobil Corporation can borrow at a fixed rate of 8.5% or at LIBOR + 0.10%. Single-B-rated Cajun Drilling Company can borrow fixed rate at 12% or floating rate at LIBOR + 2%.

a. Is there a mutually advantageous opportunity to engage in an interest rate swap? Explain.

b. Suppose Exxon Mobil proposes that Cajun pay 11% in return for LIBOR. Should Cajun accept the offer?

c. Suppose Exxon Mobil proposes that Cajun pay 9.5% in return for LIBOR. Should Cajun accept the offer?

B17. (Interest rate swaps and comparative advantage) Triple-A-rated General Motors Corporation can borrow at a fixed rate of 8.5% or at LIBOR + 0.10%. Single-B-rated KLG Inc. can borrow fixed rate at 12% or floating rate at LIBOR + 2%.

a. Is there a mutually advantageous opportunity to engage in an interest rate swap? Explain.

b. Suppose GM proposes that KLG pay 11% in return for LIBOR. Should KLG accept the offer?

c. Suppose GM proposes that KLG pay 9.5% in return for LIBOR. Should KLG accept the offer?

B18. (Hedging with a put option) Petrie Stores holds 200,000 shares of Toys 'R' Us common stock. It plans to sell the shares but would like to delay the sale for three months for tax reasons. Toys 'R' Us is trading at $40. The standard deviation of the return on the stock is 28% per year. The riskless return with continuous compounding is 6% APR. The stock is not expected to pay dividends for the next three months.

a. How could Petrie Stores hedge the risk of a decline in the Toys 'R' Us share price?

b. How much would an at-the-money put option on 200,000 shares cost?

c. How much would the put option cost with a strike price of $35?

d. Compare the advantages and disadvantages of the two option alternatives.

B19. (Interest rate cap) Dayton, Duvalier, and Dice (Three D) plans to acquire Neptune Candy Company through a leveraged buyout. It will borrow $1 billion of the purchase price from its banks. The interest rate is three-month LIBOR + 1%. Three D would like to protect against its interest cost rising above 10%.

a. How can Three D hedge this risk?

b. Suppose Three D buys a 9% interest rate cap contract. LIBOR varies over the next eight quarters as shown in the table below. How much interest does Three D pay each quarter?

Quarter	1	2	3	4	5	6	7	8
Three-month LIBOR (%)	7.50	6.75	8.50	10.25	11.50	12.25	9.75	7.50

c. How much does the party who sold the cap contract have to pay Three D each quarter?

B20. (Interest rate collar) An interest rate collar provides for an 8% floor and 10% cap. The notional amount is $100 million. The quarterly interest rates are shown in Problem B19. Calculate the amount of the payment the seller of the collar contract will make or receive each quarter.

B21. (Hedging a new bond issue) Duke plans to issue $100 million of bonds. It needs one month to prepare the documentation. It is concerned that interest rates might rise before it can sell the issue. Its current new-issue rate is 9% for 30-year bonds.

a. How could Duke use futures contracts to hedge this risk?

b. The yield on 8% 20-year Treasury bonds is 7.50%. Duke's treasurer estimates that the yield on these bonds will rise to 8.50% if Duke's borrowing cost rises to 10%. Calculate the hedge ratio.

c. Calculate the number of Treasury bond futures contracts Duke should sell to hedge its risk.

d. Calculate Duke's missed issuance opportunity cost and its profit on the futures contracts if interest rates rise by 1%.

e. Recalculate the hedge ratio, number of contracts, missed issuance opportunity cost, and profit on the futures contracts if the yield on 20-year Treasury bonds rises by 0.5% when Duke's borrowing cost rises by 1%.

B22. (Excel: Black-Scholes option pricing model) Your boss wants you to prepare and print out some tables for the value of Microsoft call options.

a. For the first table, assume that the maturity is three months, the risk-free interest rate is 5%, and the volatility (annual standard deviation) is 0.30. Use five rows with strike prices of 45, 50, 55, 60, and 65 and eight columns with stock prices of 48, 50, 52, 54, 56, 58, 60, and 62.

b. For the second table, assume the risk-free rate is 5%, the volatility (annual standard deviation) is 0.30, and the stock price is 52. Use five rows with strike prices of 45, 50, 55, 60, and 65 and four columns with maturities of 3, 6, 9, and 12 months.

B23. (Excel: Swaps) Holmes Heating has entered a three-year swap agreement starting today, March 1, with the Bank of New York. Holmes will pay the Bank of New York a rate of 7.0% APR in semiannual payments. The Bank of New York will pay Holmes the six-month LIBOR rate each six months, based on the rate at the first day of each six-month period. The notional principal is $120 million. Three possible interest rate paths for six-month LIBOR that could occur over the next three years are:

	PATH A	PATH B	PATH C
Today, Mar. 1	6.80%	6.80%	6.80%
6 months, Sept. 1	6.60	7.10	6.90
12 months, Mar. 1	7.20	7.40	6.60
18 months, Sept. 1	7.50	8.00	5.90
24 months, Mar. 1	7.10	8.60	5.80
30 months, Sept. 1	6.60	8.90	5.20

a. What are the net payments for Holmes and their dates assuming that LIBOR rates follow path A?

b. What are the net payments for Holmes and their dates assuming that LIBOR rates follow path B.

c. What are the net payments for Holmes and their dates assuming that LIBOR rates follow path C?

B24. (Excel: Swaps)

a. Johnson Controls has a $200 million debt on which it pays LIBOR plus 0.80% to its outside lenders. Johnson enters into a swap where it pays 6% and receives LIBOR under the terms of the swap. The net interest is paid/received semiannually. If LIBOR takes on the values in the table shown here, what is the total interest cost each six months (in dollars) and the APR for years 1, 2, and 3?

b. Trczinka Systems has a $50 debt on which it pays a fixed rate of 8.00% (APR, with semiannual interest payments). Trczinka enters into a swap where it pays LIBOR minus 0.50% and receives a fixed rate of 7.00%. The net interest is paid/received semiannually. If LIBOR assumes the values in the table, what is the total interest cost each six months (in dollars) and the APR for years 1, 2, and 3?

TIME (YEARS)	SIX-MONTH LIBOR (%)
0	5.8
0.5	6.2
1.0	7.0
1.5	7.3
2.0	7.8
2.5	8.4

LEVEL C (ADVANCED)

C1. (Implied standard deviation) What standard deviation of the return to a stock is implied by the Black-Scholes OPM for the following situation? A five-month call option with a strike price of $35 sells for $2.03, *k* is 6%, and the stock is currently selling for $32.75. (Do not solve this problem. Explain *how* you might solve it.)

C2. (Put-call parity) Use put-call parity to show that the combination of buying an asset, buying a put with a strike price of *S*, and selling a call with a strike price of *S* is equivalent to simply buying a riskless bond that has a maturity value of *S*.

C3. (Puzzle: Using options as alternative securities) Suppose you live in a state that has a usury law prohibiting interest charges above 9% APR, but current market rates are 18% APR for a project for which you have the opportunity to provide six-year debt financing. Show how you can use option contracts on an asset that is connected with the project to provide the project with a six-year "loan" of $250,000, from which you will earn the market rate of 18% per year with interest payments of $45,000 per year and a principal repayment of $250,000 at the end of six years.

C4. (Corporate use of options) The *Wall Street Journal* reported a few years ago that Dell Computer Corp. was having to pay $47 a share to repurchase shares of its stock that were trading in the market at around $24. It seems that over the years, Dell had sold put options on its own stock and told investors it would use the option premiums it received to offset the cost of issuing shares in its employee stock ownership plan. As long as its share price was rising, the puts expired worthless and Dell seemed to come out ahead. But Dell's share price had recently fallen, bringing millions of options into the money. In fact, Dell had written put options on 96 million shares at an average share price of $44, giving rise to a potential liability of $4.22 billion. Do you think Dell is hedging, or is it speculating, when it sells put options on its own stock to "offset" employee stock ownership plan expense?

MINICASE DERIVING PRIDE FROM ISSUING INNOVATIVE SECURITIES

Bally Entertainment Corporation (Bally) is one of the leading operators of casinos and casino hotels. It has casinos in Atlantic City, New Jersey; Las Vegas, Nevada; New Orleans, Louisiana; and Robinsville, Mississippi. Several years ago, Bally was considering issuing a new derivative instrument called PRIDES, which Merrill Lynch & Co. had developed. (To help protect its invention, Merrill Lynch also registered the PRIDES service mark.) A summary of terms for the proposed issue is provided below.

Bally's treasury department analyzed this unusual form of convertible preferred stock. In particular, they wanted to understand how the conversion feature worked. At the time, Bally's common stock was trading at $11.125 and was not paying cash dividends. The treasury staff gathered the following additional information and began their analysis of PRIDES:

Riskless return	5.50%
Volatility of the return on Bally's common stock (standard deviation)	0.40
Bally's new-issue rate for four-year preferred stock	10.75%

Securities:	Preferred Redeemable Increased Dividend Equity Securities (PRIDES), a form of convertible preferred stock.
Number of Shares:	13,500,000
Price per Share:	$11.125
Dividends:	Dividends are payable quarterly in arrears at the rate of $0.2225 per share. Dividends are cumulative.
Conversion:	
Mandatory:	After four years, each share of PRIDES not previously redeemed or converted will be mandatorily converted into one share of Bally's common stock plus the right to receive in cash all accrued but unpaid dividends.
Optional:	Unless previously redeemed (or mandatorily converted), each share of PRIDES is convertible at any time at the option of the holder into 0.82 share of Bally's common stock.
Optional Redemption:	Bally may not redeem shares of PRIDES prior to three years from the issue date. At any time after three years and prior to the mandatory conversion date, each share of PRIDES is redeemable at Bally's option. Upon any such redemption, each holder will receive for each share of PRIDES the *number* of Bally common shares equal to (1) the call price plus all accrued and unpaid dividends divided by (2) the current market price of Bally's common stock. However, this *number* can never be less than 0.82. The call price varies according to the following schedule:

Period	Call Price	Period	Call Price
Months 1–3	$11.348	Months 10–11	$11.181
Months 4–6	11.292	Month 12	11.125
Months 6–9	11.237		

PRIDES holders may convert PRIDES that are called for redemption on or before the redemption date.

Source: Bally Entertainment Corporation, *Prospectus for 13,500,000 Shares of 8% PRIDES Convertible Preferred Stock.*

QUESTIONS

1. Explain how the mandatory conversion feature in the PRIDES works. If Bally's common stock price is $20 in four years, explain why you think Bally would or would not use the mandatory conversion. If Bally's common stock price is $8 in four years, explain why you think Bally would or would not use the mandatory conversion.
2. Graph the value the holder of a share of PRIDES will realize at the end of four years as a function of the price of Bally's common stock on that date. Within which common stock price range on your graph will the PRIDES holder get: (i) The value of a share of Bally's common stock; (ii) $11.125 per PRIDES share regardless of Bally's share price; (iii) $11.125 plus 82% of the appreciation in Bally's share price above $13.567. Within which price range for the underlying common stock will a PRIDES holder voluntarily convert it into Bally common stock?
3. Explain how a share of PRIDES can be interpreted as a combination of a share of Bally's common stock plus a stream of cash dividends paying $0.2225 per quarter for four years minus the difference between two four-year call options, one with a strike price of $11.125 and the other with a strike price of $13.567, and minus also 0.18 of a four-year call option with a strike price of $13.567. Value each of these components and estimate the value of the PRIDES as of the date they were issued.
4. Do you think the PRIDES were overpriced or underpriced? What factor(s) might account for any overpricing or underpricing you found?

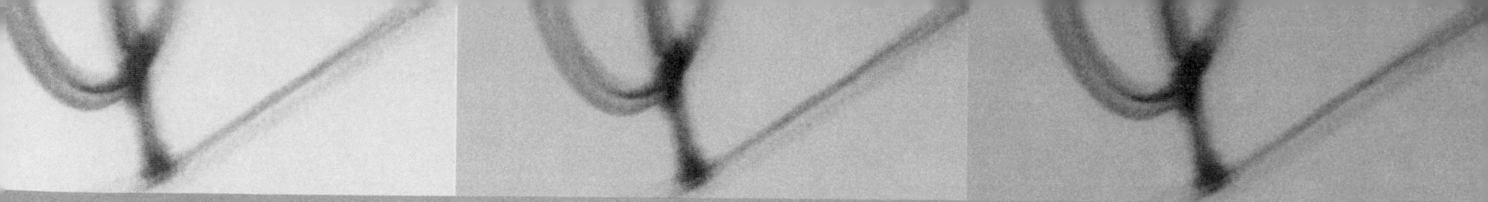

PART VI

WORKING CAPITAL MANAGEMENT

Many of a firm's day-to-day operating decisions involve its working capital, its *current* assets and liabilities. In Part VI, we apply the Principles of Finance to the problems of working capital management. Making good day-to-day management decisions is critical to maximizing stockholder wealth.

Chapter 22 deals with cash and working capital management. These are assets and liabilities the firm expects to receive and pay, respectively, in cash within a year. Managing them properly is important because it affects the firm's ability to meet its obligations as they come due.

Chapter 23 examines economic decisions about accounts receivable and inventories. A firm invests in both, along with its investments in fixed assets. We show how a firm can make sure that its investments in receivables and inventories are profitable.

Finally, Chapter 24 deals with financial planning, the problems of coordinating the firm's various financial activities. Careful planning can be critical; a firm must be prepared to deal with problems as they occur. A firm that does not plan for its future might find that it does not have one!

CASH AND WORKING CAPITAL MANAGEMENT

22

A checking account is a place to "collect" money between inflows and outflows. The account acts like a reservoir. It is useful because you can add money in any amount, say $87.35, and conveniently take it out in completely different amounts, say $11.52 and $34.27. The catch is that you cannot take out more than what is in the reservoir, so you have to manage the reservoir to make sure there is enough for the outflows. But you can arrange to have money added automatically, whenever you run short, by using "check-bouncing protection." Whenever money is added to your account to cover a check, you effectively take out a loan.

Many people also use a credit card. They can charge things and then get one bill for all their recent charges. They can pay the bill off entirely, or they may be able to pay only part of it, thereby extending their loan—at some cost.

Checking accounts, check-bouncing protection, and credit cards are just a few of the many tools available for managing your money. Firms use similar tools to manage their money. For example, firms create check-bouncing protection by establishing a credit line.

Suppose you have a choice. Which loan is cheaper, check-bouncing protection or credit card debt? The answer is to take the one with the lowest after-tax APY. In this chapter, we will tell you how a firm can answer such questions.

Firms make short-term financial decisions just about every day. Where should we borrow? Where should we invest our cash? How much liquidity should we have? The options come rapidly. Investment bankers want you to sell commercial paper, a bank wants to lend you money, and a supplier is willing to offer you trade credit. Which one is offering the best deal? Another bank wants you to purchase its lockbox services. Should you do it? After much complaining, your largest customer is threatening to stop doing business with you unless you immediately convert your ordering and invoicing systems over to EDI (electronic data interchange). How would that affect your costs and cash flow?

Working capital decisions are fast paced because they reflect a firm's day-to-day operations. The Principles of Finance, along with hard work and imagination, provide guidance for sound, value-maximizing decisions.

FOCUS ON PRINCIPLES

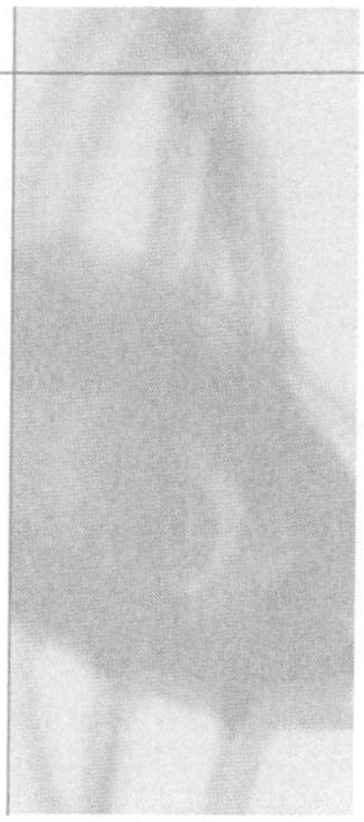

- *Time Value of Money:* Compare the benefits and costs of alternative uses and sources of money using after-tax APYs.
- *Incremental Benefits:* Calculate the incremental after-tax cash flows connected with working capital decisions.
- *Risk-Return Trade-Off:* Recognize that risk-return trade-off decisions are part of a firm's choice of financing working capital.
- *Options:* Look for hidden options and recognize their value, such as the option to refinance long-term debt.
- *Capital Market Efficiency:* Periodically evaluate routine capital market alternatives to make sure they continue to be competitive. Also, be careful to distinguish between routine transactions made in an efficient capital market and unique transactions that are not subjected to such intense competition. For example, decisions to grant credit or to use a particular supplier are essentially private, and so the prices and risks should be checked against those in a competitive marketplace.
- *Behavioral:* Use common industry practices as a starting place for operating efficiently.
- *Comparative Advantage:* Consider subcontracting business activities to outside vendors if the vendors can provide the services more cheaply and competently.
- *Two-Sided Transactions:* Do not act unethically to gain short-term profit at the expense of a supplier or a customer. Such behavior can damage or even destroy a profitable long-term relationship.

22.1 OVERVIEW OF WORKING CAPITAL MANAGEMENT

Much of a financial manager's time is devoted to **working capital management.** Recall that a firm's net working capital consists of its current assets minus its current liabilities. *Current assets,* principally cash and short-term securities, accounts receivable, and inventories, are assets that can normally be converted into cash within one year. *Current liabilities,* principally short-term borrowings, accounts payable, and taxes payable, are obligations that are expected to come due within one year. Working capital management involves all aspects of the administration of current assets and current liabilities.

The goal of working capital management is shareholder wealth maximization, avoiding negative-NPV decisions and seeking positive-NPV decisions. Some methods that managers use in practice to make working capital decisions do not rely on the principles of finance. Rather, they use imprecise rules of thumb or poorly constructed models. You should avoid such methods. Working capital decisions can and should be made to maximize shareholder wealth.

Working capital management involves making the appropriate investments in cash, marketable securities, receivables, and inventories, as well as the level and mix of short-term financing. Working capital management includes several basic business relationships.

- *Sales impacts.* The firm must determine appropriate levels of receivables and inventories. Granting easy credit to customers and keeping high inventories may help boost sales and fulfill orders quickly, but they raise costs.
- *Liquidity.* The firm must choose levels of cash and marketable securities, taking into account liquidity needs and any required compensating balances.
- *Relations with stakeholders.* Suppliers and customers are intimately affected by the management of working capital. Customers are concerned with quality, cost, availability, and the service

TABLE 22.1
Current assets and liabilities of all manufacturing corporations.

	PERCENTAGE OF TOTAL ASSETS					DOLLARS INVESTED IN 2001
	1960	1970	1980	1990	2001	
Current Assets						
Cash	6.0%	4.3%	2.8%	2.4%	4.0%	$ 187.9 billion
Marketable securities	4.8	0.7	2.5	2.0	2.2	106.2
Accounts receivable	15.6	17.3	17.0	13.9	9.8	463.3
Inventory	23.6	23.0	19.8	14.3	9.9	470.9
Other current assets	2.3	3.5	2.8	3.4	5.5	260.8
Total current assets	52.3%	48.8%	44.9%	36.0%	31.4%	$,1489.1 billion
Current Liabilities						
Notes payable	3.9%	6.3%	5.0%	6.2%	4.1%	$195.5 billion
Accounts payable	7.9	8.5	9.9	7.9	7.0	333.9
Accruals and other current liabilities	9.0	9.9	12.0	11.6	14.6	690.4
Total current liabilities	20.8%	24.7%	26.9%	25.7%	25.7%	$1,219.8 billion

Source: Quarterly Financial Report for Manufacturing, Mining, and Trade Corporations, U.S. Department of Commerce, various dates.

reputation of the firm. Likewise, the firm has similar concerns about its suppliers. The firm's reputation depends in large measure on how it manages its short-term assets and obligations.

- *Short-term financing mix.* The firm must choose the mix of short-term financing, as well as the proportions of short- and long-term financing, taking into account its profitability and risk objectives.

Table 22.1 shows the composition of the current assets and current liabilities for all U.S. manufacturing corporations in recent years. Notice the sheer size of the investment in short-term assets. The investment shown in the table is only for manufacturing firms; additional working capital is owned by wholesaling and retailing firms, service firms, and others. Also, notice that the percentage of total assets invested in short-term assets has declined substantially in recent years. Most of this decline in short-term assets has been accomplished by the reduction in the relative amount of inventories from "just-in-time" inventory management systems. Finally, notice that short-term debt of various types accounts for roughly 25% of the total financing of the firm.

Philosophies About Financing Working Capital

In its day-to-day operations, the firm must maintain adequate *liquidity.*[1] At the same time, it wants to operate as efficiently and profitably as possible. There is a tension between risk and return that manifests itself in managerial philosophies about how working capital should be financed. We can characterize a firm's philosophy about how it finances working capital as the maturity-matching approach, the conservative approach, and the aggressive approach.

MATURITY-MATCHING APPROACH TO FINANCING WORKING CAPITAL With maturity matching, the firm hedges its risk by matching the maturities of its assets and liabilities (panel A of Figure 22.1). The firm finances seasonal variations in current assets with current liabilities of the same maturity. It finances long-term assets by issuing long-term debt and equity securities. In addition, in most cases there is a permanent component of current assets. Inventories and receiv-

[1]Recall that liquidity refers to how quickly and easily assets can be bought or sold without loss of value. Cash is the most liquid asset.

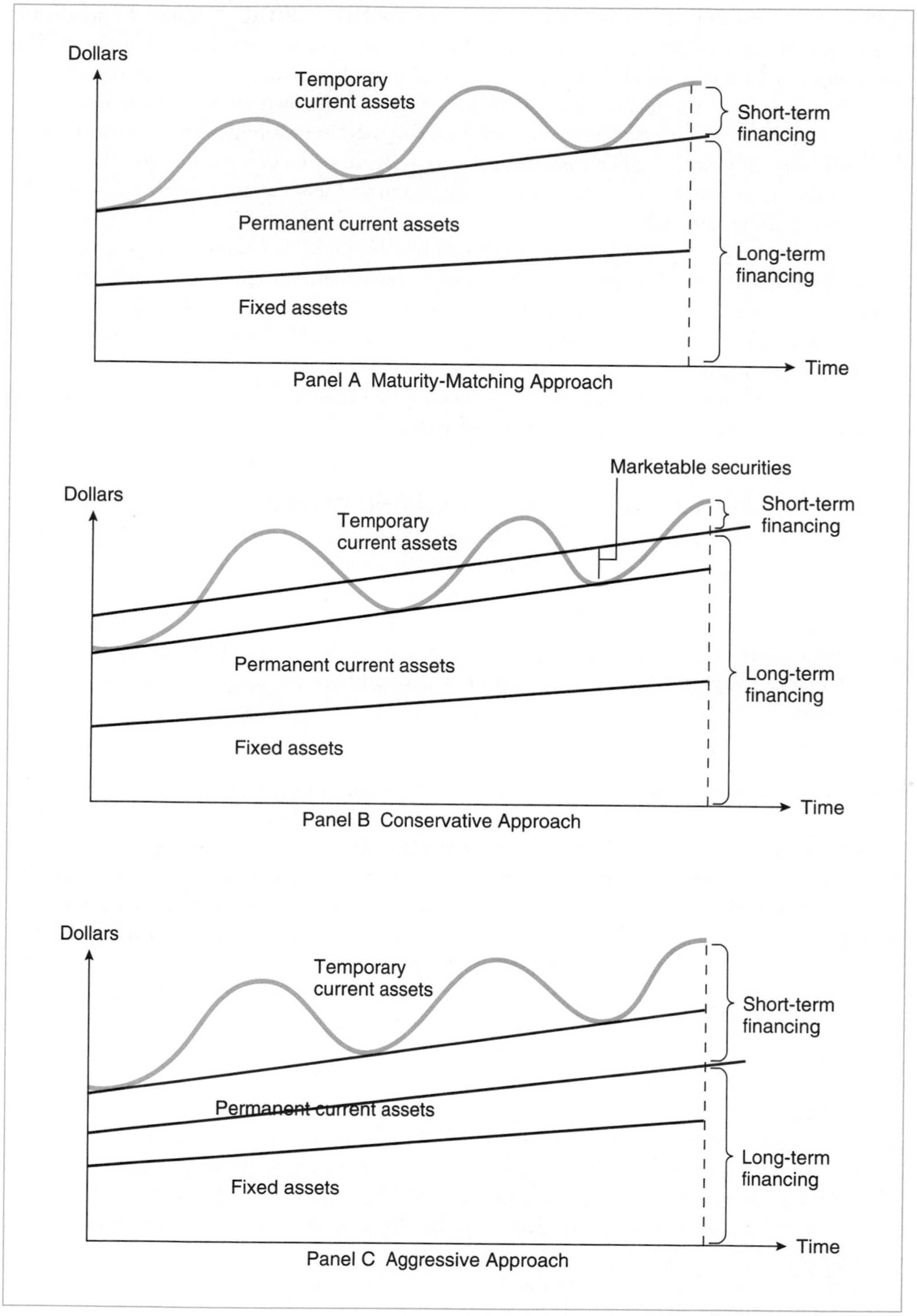

FIGURE 22.1
Three philosophies of financing working capital.

ables will remain above some minimum level. This permanent component of current assets is also financed with long-term capital. As panel A of Figure 22.1 illustrates, short-term borrowing (including temporary increases in payables as well as bank borrowing, commercial paper, etc.) mirrors the seasonal swings in current assets. Short-term borrowing under this sort of policy would fall to zero at seasonal low spots.

CONSERVATIVE APPROACH TO FINANCING WORKING CAPITAL Under the maturity-matching approach, a firm depends on short-term financing for its temporary current assets. The firm assumes that funds will always be available. It also gambles that their cost will not rise dramatically. If general economic conditions worsen or if the firm's own circumstances deteriorate, the firm might have trouble getting the money it needs. Another possibility is that funds are available, but only at a much higher cost. To guard against the risks of a credit shutoff or a cost increase, the conservative approach uses more long-term and less short-term financing than the maturity-matching approach.

The conservative approach is shown in panel B of Figure 22.1. Long-term financing is used to finance all of the firm's long-term assets, all of its permanent current assets, and some of its temporary current assets. As you can see in panel B, only when asset needs are high will the firm use short-term financing. At other times, when asset needs are low, the firm actually has more long-term financing than it has assets needed to operate the firm. At these times, the firm invests the excess funds in marketable securities. By financing a portion of its seasonal needs for funds on a long-term basis, the firm builds in a margin of safety.

AGGRESSIVE APPROACH TO FINANCING WORKING CAPITAL One problem with the maturity-matching and conservative approaches is that long-term funds generally cost more than short-term funds. The term structure is usually upward sloping. Because of this, many managers prefer an aggressive approach to financing working capital (Figure 22.1, panel C). The aggressive approach uses less long-term and more short-term financing. The goal is to raise profitability. We know from the Principle of Risk-Return Trade-Off that without some sort of market imperfection, higher expected profitability comes only at the expense of greater risk.

COSTS OF THE THREE APPROACHES TO FINANCING WORKING CAPITAL We can think of the maturity-matching approach as the base-case scenario. If interest rates rise unexpectedly, a firm using the aggressive approach loses relative to less aggressive (maturity-matching and conservative) firms. This is because firms with more long-term financing locked in at the lower rate will have lower financing costs. But if interest rates fall, the situation is reversed and the aggressive firm is a winner. This is because firms with more long-term financing may be stuck with either higher interest costs or the cost of refinancing.

Therefore, because of the possibility that funds might become more expensive or even unavailable, a firm without ready access to capital markets should be more conservative. The availability of financing at a fixed cost can be ensured by locking in long-term financing. In contrast, a firm with ready capital market access can be more aggressive.

Some managers gamble on the direction of interest rates. A manager who expects a decline in interest rates will use the aggressive approach. The aggressive manager shortens the average maturity of the firm's debt by financing more with short-term and less with long-term debt. A manager who expects interest rate increases will use the conservative approach. This manager lengthens the average maturity of the firm's debt by financing more with long-term and less with short-term debt.

If interest rates in fact move in the direction that the manager forecasts, the firm will realize additional profits. However, if interest rates move in the "wrong" direction, the interest rate gamble will backfire and the firm will be less profitable. On the basis of the Principle of Capital Market Efficiency, we caution against such gambling. Our recommendation is that the firm apply the Principle of Comparative Advantage instead. For example, a shoe firm might work on manufacturing higher-quality shoes at lower cost instead of guessing the direction of interest rate movement.

Review

1. What is working capital management? What are examples of major financial decisions that are made in working capital management?
2. Compare and contrast the maturity-matching, conservative, and aggressive approaches to financing working capital.
3. If a firm is afraid that its access to borrowing in the future might be restricted by its banks and other lenders, which of the three approaches should it follow?
4. Which approach benefits the firm if interest rates rise? Which one benefits the firm if interest rates fall?

22.2 CASH CONVERSION CYCLE

The **cash conversion cycle** is the length of time between the payment of accounts payable and the receipt of cash from accounts receivable.

Without credit, a firm's cash is tied up from the moment it purchases inventory until it collects its accounts receivable. Suppose a firm holds its inventory 50 days and collects its accounts receivable in 30 days. Then it would take 80 days for the original investment to be converted back into cash.

However, with supplier credit, the firm's money is not invested for the entire 80 days. Figure 22.2 illustrates this cycle with 20-day supplier credit. On day 0, goods are delivered from the supplier, go into inventory, and result in an account payable. In 50 days, the goods are sold for credit, and the accounts receivable are collected 30 days later, on day 80. However, the firm does not have to put up its own money until it pays its accounts payable on day 20. With 20-day supplier credit, the firm's cash is invested for 60 days, day 20 to day 80. Thus, in this instance, the cash conversion cycle is 60 days.

The cash conversion cycle is equal to the inventory conversion period, plus the receivables collection period, minus the payables deferral period:

$$\begin{matrix}\text{Cash}\\ \text{conversion}\\ \text{cycle}\end{matrix} = \begin{matrix}\text{Inventory}\\ \text{conversion}\\ \text{period}\end{matrix} + \begin{matrix}\text{Receivables}\\ \text{collection}\\ \text{period}\end{matrix} - \begin{matrix}\text{Payables}\\ \text{deferral}\\ \text{period}\end{matrix} \qquad (22.1)$$

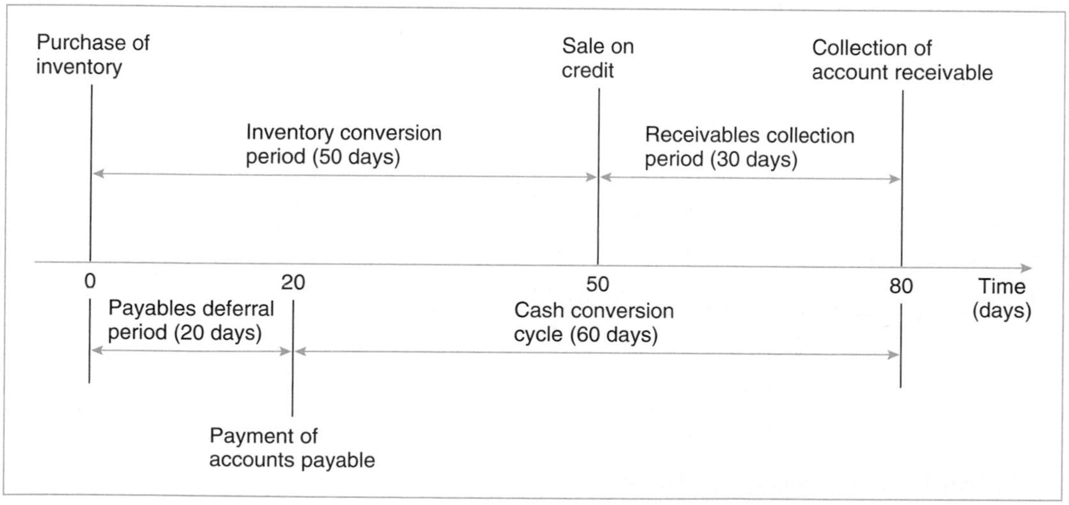

FIGURE 22.2
Cash conversion cycle.

The inventory conversion period is the average time between buying inventory and selling the goods:

$$\text{Inventory conversion period} = \frac{\text{Inventory}}{\text{Cost of sales / 365}} = \frac{365}{\text{Inventory turnover}} \tag{22.2}$$

The receivables collection period, or days' sales outstanding (DSO), is the average number of days it takes to collect on accounts receivable:

$$\text{Receivables collection period} = \frac{\text{Receivables}}{\text{Sales / 365}} = \frac{365}{\text{Receivables turnover}} \tag{22.3}$$

The payables deferral period is the average length of time between the purchase of the materials and labor that go into inventory and the payment of cash for these materials and labor:

$$\text{Payables deferral period} = \frac{\text{Accounts payable + Wages, benefits, and payroll taxes payable}}{\text{(Cost of sales + Selling, general, and administrative expenses) / 365}} \tag{22.4}$$

EXAMPLE Cash Conversion Cycle for Clark Pharmaceuticals

Suppose Clark Pharmaceuticals has the financial information given here. What is Clark's cash conversion cycle?

Inventory	Accounts receivable	Accounts payable	Wages, benefits, and payroll taxes payable	Sales	Cost of sales	Selling, general, and administrative expenses
\$1,400,000	\$1,700,000	\$400,000	\$100,000	\$20,000,000	\$10,000,000	\$1,000,000

Using Equation (22.2), the inventory conversion period is 51.1 days:

$$\text{Inventory conversion period} = \frac{1{,}400{,}000}{10{,}000{,}000 / 365} = 51.1 \text{ days}$$

Using Equation (22.3), the receivables collection period is 31.0 days:

$$\text{Receivables collection period} = \frac{1{,}700{,}000}{20{,}000{,}000 / 365} = 31.0 \text{ days}$$

Using Equation (22.4), the payables deferral period is

$$\text{Payables deferral period} = \frac{400{,}000 + 100{,}000}{(10{,}000{,}000 + 1{,}000{,}000) / 365} = 16.6 \text{ days}$$

Finally, using Equation (22.1), the cash conversion cycle is 65.5 days:

$$\text{Cash conversion cycle} = 51.1 + 31.0 - 16.6 = 65.5 \text{ days}$$

Review

1. What is the cash conversion cycle?
2. What happens to the cash conversion cycle when: (a) The inventory turnover increases? (b) The receivables turnover decreases? (c) A firm pays its accounts payable more quickly because credit terms have become less attractive?

22.3 CASH MANAGEMENT

Firms use increasingly sophisticated cash management systems to monitor their cash and marketable securities and maintain their needed liquidity at minimum cost. Cash and marketable securities are managed together, because marketable securities are so liquid and funds can be moved from one to the other quickly and cheaply. In fact, firms usually report only the total of the two on the balance sheet.

A firm's cash management decision can be broken into two parts. First, how much liquidity (cash plus marketable securities) should the firm have? Second, what should be the relative proportions of cash and marketable securities in maintaining that liquidity?

Demands for Money

There are three basic motives for holding cash: (1) the transactions demand, (2) the precautionary demand, and (3) the speculative demand.

The **transactions demand** is simply the need for cash to make everyday payments for such things as wages, raw materials, taxes, and interest. The transactions demand for cash exists because of imbalances between cash inflows and outflows. The need for transactions balances depends on the size of the firm. The larger the firm, the more transactions it makes. The transactions demand also depends on the timing of cash inflows and outflows. The more closely they match, the less cash is needed to maintain liquidity.

The **precautionary demand** is essentially the margin of safety required to meet unexpected needs. The more uncertain the cash inflows and outflows, the larger the precautionary balance should be.

Finally, the **speculative demand** is based on the desire to take advantage of unexpected profitable opportunities that require cash. This motive accounts for a smaller percentage of firm cash holdings than of individual cash holdings. For the most part, firms hold cash for transactions and precautionary reasons. Readily available bank borrowing can generally be used to meet the speculative demand for cash.

In addition to the three basic demands for cash, many firms hold cash in compensating balances. A **compensating balance** is an account balance that the firm agrees to maintain. It provides indirect payment to the bank for its loans or other services. Commercial banks may accept or require compensating balances in lieu of direct fees.

If a bank wants $1,000 of compensation for its services, the bank can simply charge a fee of $1,000. Alternatively, if the interest rate is 5%, a compensating balance of $20,000 left at the bank for one year would provide the same amount of indirect compensation to the bank (.05 [$20,000] = $1,000). Although direct fees are much more popular than they were in the past, a substantial amount of firm cash balances are still made up of compensating balances.

Short-Term Investment Alternatives

The following is a list of several types of marketable securities. They are shown in order of increasing level of risk and return.

- *U.S. Treasury securities. Treasury bills* (T-bills) have an original maturity of one year or less when they are issued. *Treasury notes* and *bonds* have an original maturity of one year or more. These securities have the lowest risk and greatest liquidity, but because of the risk-return trade-off, they also offer the lowest yield. Firms can buy and sell these securities directly. Firms can also invest in these securities for very short periods by using repurchase agreements, or *repos,* with securities dealers.
- *U.S. federal agency securities.* These securities are backed to varying degrees by the U.S. government. Many are nearly as liquid as U.S. Treasury securities but have a slightly higher risk and return.
- *Negotiable certificates of deposit.* Negotiable CDs are time deposits issued by domestic or foreign commercial banks that can be sold to a third party.[2] *Eurodollar certificates of deposit* generally have higher risk and return than domestic CDs.
- *Short-term tax-exempt municipals. Munis* are securities issued by state and local governments that are exempt from federal taxation. Several of these are short-term securities issued in anticipation of cash receipts. They are Tax Anticipation Notes (TANs), Revenue Anticipation Notes (RANs), and Bond Anticipation Notes (BANs).
- *Bankers' acceptances.* Bankers' acceptances are drafts that a commercial bank has "accepted." Their value is based on the accepting bank's credit standing.
- *Commercial paper.* These securities are unsecured promissory notes that corporations issue. Commercial paper seldom has an original maturity of more than 270 days.[3] Most commercial paper has an original maturity between 30 and 180 days and is issued only by very creditworthy corporations.
- *Preferred stock and money market preferred stock.* Preferred stock pays dividends that qualify for the 70% dividends-received deduction. Most preferred stocks are long-term securities subject to market value fluctuations. Money market preferred stock differs from other preferred stock. It is a short-term security that has a floating dividend rate that is reset frequently to reflect current interest rates. Therefore, like other short-term securities, it has lower risk and lower return and is less subject to market value fluctuations.

Transactions Demand Models

How much cash does a firm need to conduct its transactions? A simple and useful approach to answering this question treats cash management as an inventory management problem. In this approach, the firm manages its inventory of cash on the basis of the cost of holding cash (rather than marketable securities) and the cost of converting marketable securities to cash. The best policy minimizes the sum of these costs.

BAUMOL MODEL The Baumol cash management model assumes the firm can predict its future cash requirements with certainty, cash disbursements are spread uniformly over the period, the interest rate (the opportunity cost of holding cash) is fixed, and the firm pays a fixed transaction cost each time it converts securities to cash.

The Baumol model has a sawtooth pattern of cash balances, which is shown in Figure 22.3. The firm sells C dollars worth of marketable securities and deposits the funds in its checking account. The cash balance decreases steadily to zero as the cash is spent. Then the firm sells C dollars of marketable securities and deposits the funds in the checking account, and the pattern repeats itself. Over time, the average (mean) cash balance will be $C/2$. The opportunity cost of funds is the interest rate i times the average balance, or $iC/2$. Likewise, if each deposit is for C dol-

[2] Consumer CDs are usually nonnegotiable. They can only be sold back to the issuing bank.

[3] So long as its maturity does not exceed 270 days, commercial paper does not have to be registered with the Securities and Exchange Commission (SEC).

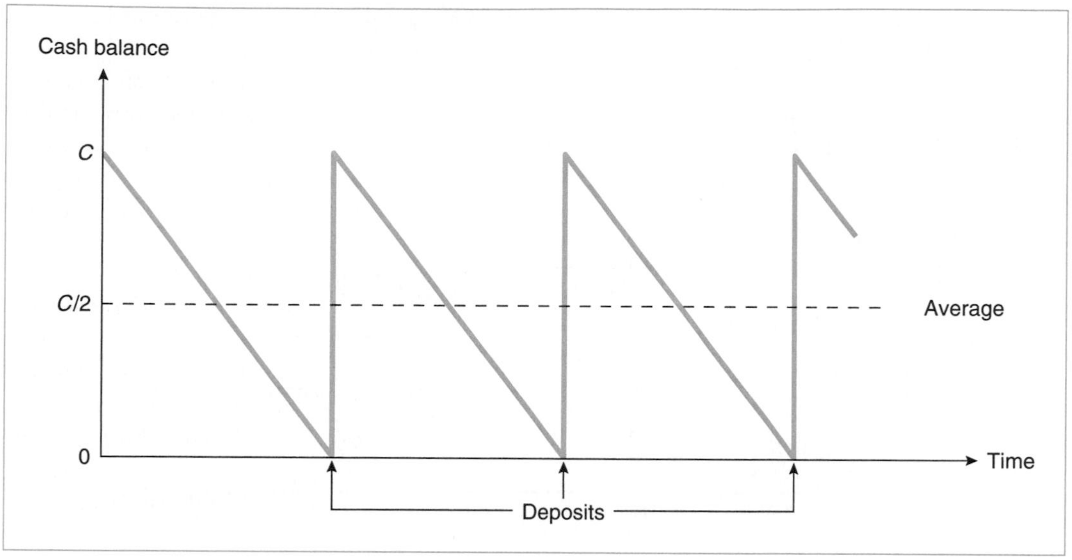

FIGURE 22.3
Cash balances with the Baumol model.

lars and the firm needs to deposit a total of T dollars in its account during the year, the total number of deposits (and the number of sawteeth per year in Figure 22.3) is equal to T/C. The annual transactions cost will be the cost per deposit times the number of deposits, which is bT/C.

The annual cost of meeting the transactions demand is the transactions cost plus the opportunity (time value) cost:

$$\text{Cost} = b\left[\frac{T}{C}\right] + i\left[\frac{C}{2}\right] \tag{22.5}$$

where

T = annual transactions volume in dollars (uniform through time)
b = fixed cost per transaction
i = annual interest rate
C = size of each deposit

The decision variable is C, the deposit size. Increasing C increases the average cash balance and the opportunity cost as well. However, increasing C reduces the number of deposits, thereby lowering the annual transactions cost. Figure 22.4 shows this tradeoff between the two costs. The best or optimal deposit size, C^*, provides the minimum total cost, Cost*.

The optimal deposit size is

$$C^* = \sqrt{\frac{2bT}{i}} \tag{22.6}$$

The optimal deposit size is a function of the transaction cost b, the annual transactions volume T, and the annual interest rate i. C^* is positively related to b and T and negatively related to i. Note that the optimal deposit size is not linearly related to these variables. For example, if T doubles, then the optimal deposit size will also increase—but it will not double.

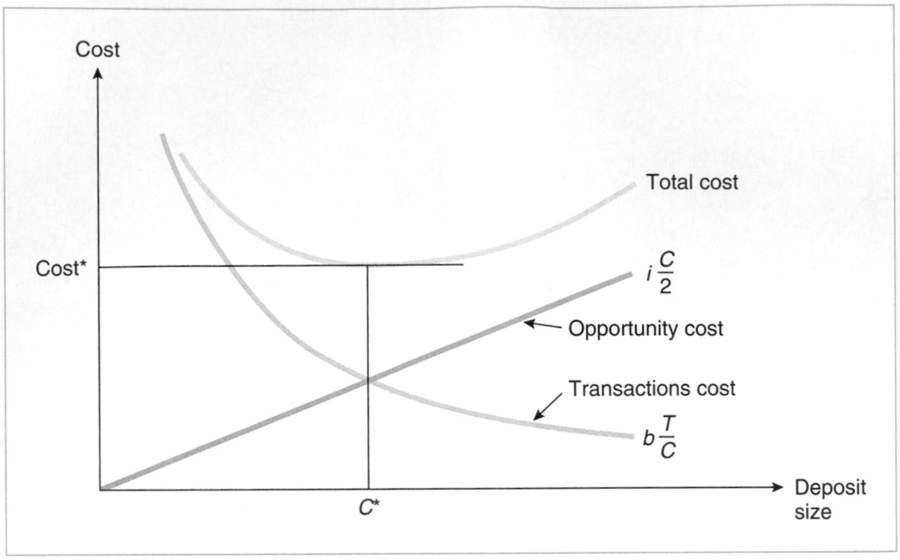

FIGURE 22.4
Annual costs for the Baumol model.

EXAMPLE Using the Baumol Model at Fox

Fox, Inc. needs $12 million in cash next year. It believes it can earn 12% per year on funds invested in marketable securities, and converting marketable securities to cash costs $312.50 per transaction. What does this imply for Fox?

Using Equation (22.6), Fox's optimal deposit size is

$$C^* = \sqrt{\frac{2bT}{i}} = \sqrt{\frac{2(312.50)(12{,}000{,}000)}{0.12}} = \$250{,}000$$

Using Equation (22.5), the annual cost is $30,000.

$$\text{Cost} = 312.50\left[\frac{12{,}000{,}000}{250{,}000}\right] + 0.12\left[\frac{250{,}000}{2}\right] = 15{,}000 + 15{,}000 = \$30{,}000$$

The subparts of the solution are: $T/C = 48$ = deposits per year; $b[T/C] = 312.50(48) =$ $15,000 = transactions costs per year; $C/2 =$ $125,000 = average cash balance; $i[C/2] = 0.12(125{,}000) =$ $15,000 = annual opportunity cost of funds. Fox would make about one deposit per week of $250,000. The average cash balance is $125,000, transactions costs are $15,000, opportunity costs are $15,000, and the total annual cost is $30,000.

MILLER-ORR CASH MANAGEMENT MODEL The Miller-Orr cash management model is more realistic than the Baumol model. It allows the daily cash flows to vary according to a probability function. For example, suppose we can assume that the net cash flow (combined inflows and outflows) follows a normal distribution with a mean of zero and a standard deviation of $50,000 per day. This incorporates the realistic uncertainty about future cash flows. Figure 22.5 illustrates the Miller-Orr model.

The Miller-Orr model uses two control limits and a return point. The lower control limit, LCL in the figure, is determined outside the model. The upper control limit, UCL, is $3Z$ above the lower control limit. The model uses a return point, RP, that is Z above LCL. The return point is the target level the firm returns to whenever the cash balance hits a control limit.

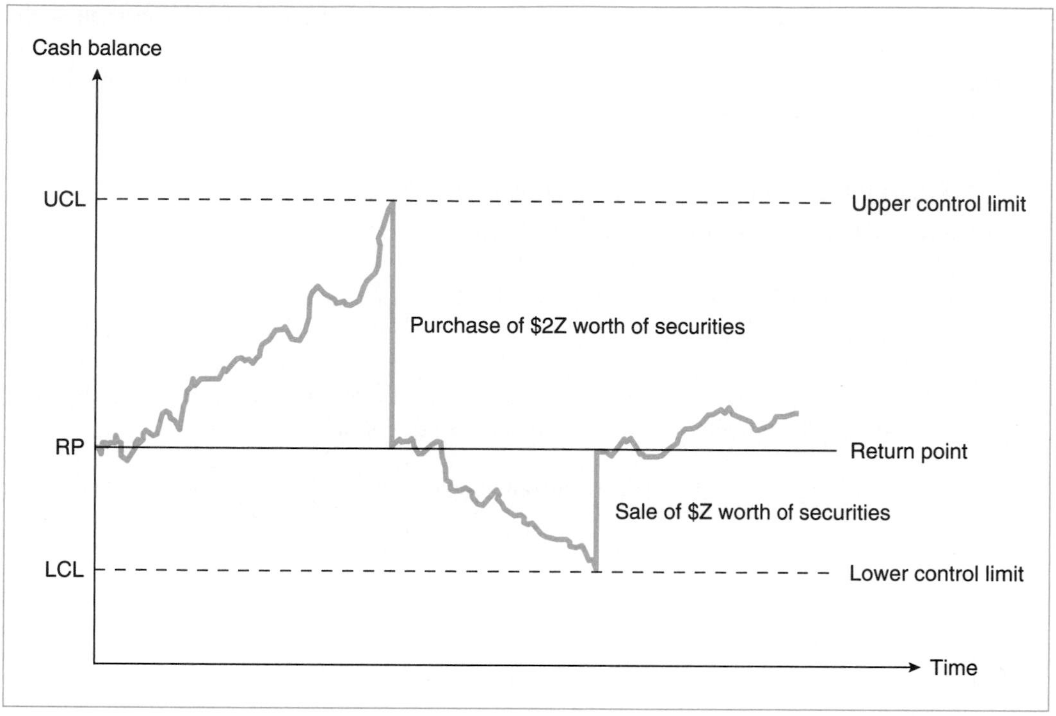

FIGURE 22.5
Cash balances with the Miller-Orr model.

When the cash balance hits LCL, the firm sells $\$Z$ of marketable securities and puts the money in the checking account. This brings the cash balance back up to the RP. Whenever the balance hits the upper limit, $\$2Z$ of marketable securities are purchased with money from the checking account, putting the balance back to RP. This procedure produces an average cash balance of LCL + (4/3)Z.

Although LCL is set outside the model, UCL and RP depend on LCL and on Z. RP is simply LCL + Z, and UCL equals LCL + 3Z. The variable Z depends on the cost per transaction, b, the interest rate per period, i, and the standard deviation of the net cash flows, σ. The interest rate and the standard deviation of cash flows must be defined for the same unit of time, which is most often per day. Z is then

$$Z = \left[\frac{3b\sigma^2}{4i}\right]^{1/3} \tag{22.7}$$

As we noted above, the return point, RP, upper control limit, UCL, and average cash balance are:

$$\text{RP} = \text{LCL} + Z$$

$$\text{UCL} = \text{LCL} + 3Z$$

$$\text{Average cash balance} = \text{LCL} + (4/3)Z$$

A higher cost per transaction or greater variation in the cash flow results in a larger Z and a larger difference between LCL and UCL. Likewise, a higher interest rate results in a smaller Z and a smaller range.

The Miller-Orr model is a good example of *management by exception.* Managers allow the cash balance to fluctuate within specified limits. Only when these limits are violated do managers take action, and that action is planned ahead of time. The model is useful for managing day-to-day cash balances needed to make routine transactions.

EXAMPLE Using the Miller-Orr Model at KFC

Suppose KFC has estimated the standard deviation of its daily cash flows (outflows minus inflows for the day) to be $\sigma = \$50{,}000$ per day. In addition, the cost of buying or selling marketable securities is \$100. The APR interest rate is 10%. Because of its liquidity requirements and compensating balance agreements, KFC has a lower control limit of \$100,000 on its cash balances. What would be KFC's upper control limit and return point, using the Miller-Orr model?

First, we find Z. We divide the APR interest rate by 365 to convert it to a daily rate because the variability of cash flows is expressed on a daily basis.

$$Z = \left[\frac{3b\sigma^2}{4i}\right]^{1/3} = \left[\frac{3(100)(50{,}000)^2}{4(.10\,/\,365)}\right]^{1/3} = \$88{,}125$$

Then we calculate the upper control limit and return point:

$$\text{UCL} = \text{LCL} + 3Z = 100{,}000 + 3(88{,}125) = \$364{,}375$$

$$\text{RP} = \text{LCL} + Z = 100{,}000 + 88{,}125 = \$188{,}125$$

If the cash balance falls to \$100,000, KFC sells $Z = \$88{,}125$ of securities and puts the cash in the cash account, thereby bringing the balance up to the RP of \$188,125. If the cash balance climbs to \$364,375, KFC buys $2Z = \$176{,}250$ of securities from cash, thereby reducing the cash balance to the RP of \$188,125 (= 364,375 − 176,250). KFC's average cash balance will be:

$$\text{Average cash balance} = \text{LCL} + (4/3)Z = 100{,}000 + (4/3)(88{,}125) = \$217{,}500$$

OTHER PRACTICAL CONSIDERATIONS IN CASH MANAGEMENT The Baumol and Miller-Orr models deal with optimizing a firm's cash transactions balances. Other factors not included in these models also affect cash balances. For example, a firm may have a compensating balance requirement. In such a case, the firm's average cash balance is the greater of the balance needed for transactions and the compensating balance requirement. The compensating balance is costly only when it is greater than the balance the firm would maintain anyway. Frequently, it is costly.

The optimal amount of marketable securities is the total liquidity desired minus cash balances. The firm invests in a variety of marketable securities, taking into account its possible future cash needs as well as the transaction costs, maturities, riskiness, and investment yields.

Some firms maintain unusually large portfolios of marketable securities. Although some of the portfolios may be maintained for liquidity purposes, responding to special tax situations may also be the motive. Sometimes firms have foreign operations in countries with different tax laws, and they can benefit by investing the cash abroad rather than returning it to the United States and paying U.S. income taxes on it.

Float

When you write a check, there is a delay before the funds are taken out of your checking account. This delay occurs because of the time your check is in the mail, the time needed to process the check, and the time it takes the banking system to remove the funds from your account. During this delay, you are benefiting from float. **Float** is the difference between the available or collected balance at the bank and the firm's book or ledger balance:

$$\text{Float} = \text{Available balance} - \text{Book balance} \qquad (22.8)$$

Float arises from timing differences that occur when you are paying your bills or collecting from customers. There are two kinds of float, disbursement float and collection float.

DISBURSEMENT FLOAT When you write a check, your book or ledger balance is reduced by the amount of the check, but your available or collected balance at the bank is not reduced until the check finally clears. This difference is **disbursement float.**

EXAMPLE Disbursement Float at Huskie Oil

Huskie Oil Corporation has $50,000 for both its book balance and its bank balance. If Huskie writes a $1,000 check that takes four days to clear, during this period, $1,000 of disbursement float has been created. Huskie's book balance declines by the amount of the check, from $50,000 to $49,000, but the bank balance is unchanged until the check clears. What is Huskie's float on this check?

Using Equation (22.8), the float is

$$\text{Float} = 50{,}000 - 49{,}000 = \$1{,}000$$

After the check clears, the book and bank balances are both $49,000, and there is no more disbursement float.

COLLECTION FLOAT Of course, float can be either positive or negative. Suppose you receive a check and deposit it in your bank. Until the funds are credited to your account, your book balance will be higher than your actual balance. In this case, you are experiencing **collection float.**

EXAMPLE Collection Float at Huskie Oil

Huskie has a $50,000 cash balance on both its ledger balance and its available bank balance. If Huskie receives a $5,000 check and deposits it in its checking account, funds are not made available on this particular check for two days. Its book balance increases by $5,000, but its bank balance is unchanged until the funds are finally available. What is the float?

Using Equation (22.8), the float is

$$\text{Float} = 50{,}000 - 55{,}000 = -\$5{,}000$$

This negative float of $5,000 is Huskie's collection float.

FLOAT MANAGEMENT TECHNIQUES Firms use several devices and procedures to manage float.

- *Wire transfers.* Large payments can be made with wire transfers instead of with paper checks. Sending a wire transfer is more expensive than writing and mailing a paper check, but a wire transfer reduces the cost of float because the transfer is immediate.
- *Zero balance accounts (ZBAs).* These are special disbursement accounts that maintain a zero balance. Funds are automatically transferred in when a check is presented on a ZBA.
- *Controlled disbursing.* This technique may use disbursing accounts at several banks in addition to the master account at the firm's lead bank. As with ZBAs, funds are put into the accounts on an as-needed basis. The banks notify the firm about what funds are needed. The firm then wires the needed funds to the banks. Conversely, the bank notifies the firm about excess funds and wires them out.
- *Centralized processing of payables.* By centralizing payables, a cash manager knows when all bills must be paid and can make sure that funds are available and bills are paid on time. Prompt bill paying leads to better relations with vendors. In addition, the firm avoids late penalties while reducing its cash balances.

- *Lockboxes.* Lockboxes are post office boxes to which a firm directs its incoming checks. A bank is engaged to open the lockbox several times per day, process the checks, and collect them. Cash managers face two problems: the choice of lockbox locations, and the assignment of customers to particular lockboxes. By strategically locating the lockboxes around the country and by using efficient banks, firms can reduce their float substantially. Float is reduced by shortening mail times (from customers to the lockbox), processing times (by using efficient banks), and availability times (the amount of time it takes for funds to be made available on checks after they are presented to banks).

EXAMPLE Cost of a Wire Transfer

You need to transfer \$100,000 from Houston to Chicago. If you mail a check, it will cost \$1.00 for postage and clearing the check, and it will take a total of five days for the funds to be transferred. During the money's five-day travel, you are suffering an opportunity cost, because the \$100,000 is not earning 3% APR interest. Alternatively, you could avoid the opportunity cost by wiring the money at a cost of \$12.00, which would instantaneously transfer the funds with no float. Which is cheaper?

$$\text{Cost} = \text{Fixed costs} + \text{Float costs}$$

$$\text{Cost of check} = \$1.00 + \$100{,}000(.03)(5/365) = \$1.00 + \$41.10 = \$42.10$$

$$\text{Cost of wire transfer} = \$12.00 + 0 = \$12.00$$

The wire transfer is substantially cheaper.

EXAMPLE Profitability of a Lockbox System at The Gap

Let us say The Gap currently collects all of its customer payments in Nashville. By going to a new lockbox system with boxes in Atlanta and St. Louis, The Gap expects to reduce the time from when customers mail their checks to when the funds are collected. It expects the time to fall from an average of eight days to an average of five days, a three-day savings. The Gap collects \$100,000 per day. The extra costs associated with the lockbox are \$12,000 per year. The Gap's opportunity cost of funds is 10% per year. What is the expected annual profit of using the new system?

$$\begin{aligned}
&\text{Reduction in float} = (100{,}000/\text{day})(3\text{ days}) &&= \$300{,}000\\
&\text{Value of float reduction} = 300{,}000(0.10) &&= 30{,}000\\
&\text{Less: Annual operating cost} &&= \underline{12{,}000}\\
&\text{Net before-tax profit of lockbox system} &&= \$18{,}000
\end{aligned}$$

The reduction in float of \$300,000 permanently frees up this amount of cash. Invested at 10%, this is worth \$30,000 per year. Subtracting the \$12,000 yearly cost of operating the system gives an expected before-tax profit of \$18,000 per year.

Review

1. What are the three basic motives for holding cash?
2. Describe three short-term investment alternatives.
3. Explain graphically and with equations (1) the Baumol cash management model and (2) the Miller-Orr cash management model.
4. What is float? What causes float? What are the two kinds of float? Explain how each of the following can help a firm manage its float: (a) wire transfers; (b) zero balance accounts; (c) controlled disbursing; (d) centralized processing of payables; (e) lockboxes.

22.4 SHORT-TERM FINANCING

The phrases *short-term funds* and *intermediate-term funds* refer to the original maturity of the debt obligation. Short-term funds are debt obligations that were originally scheduled for repayment within one year. Intermediate-term funds are debt obligations that were originally scheduled to mature between one and perhaps as many as 10 years from the date of issue. These time periods vary in practice.

Another useful distinction concerns the source of funds from which the loan is to be repaid. Firms typically arrange short-term loans to finance seasonal or temporary needs. Intermediate-term loans are to be repaid over a period of years. If the loan is short term (due in a year or less), lenders are mainly concerned with the firm's working capital position and its ability to liquidate current assets—collecting on receivables and reducing inventories according to seasonal patterns—to generate cash to meet the firm's current debt service obligations. For an intermediate-term loan, lenders are more concerned with the longer-term profitability of the firm's operations.

There are three main sources of short-term funds: *trade credit* (borrowing from suppliers), *bank loans* (borrowing from banks), and *commercial paper* (selling short-term debt securities in the open market). This section discusses each of these sources of short-term funds, describes how to estimate the cost of funds from each source, and provides a framework for comparing these costs on a consistent basis.

Trade Credit

Trade credit is credit extended by one firm to another. Businesses routinely grant trade credit on the sales of their goods and services. Purchasers of raw materials, manufactured products, and services are generally permitted to wait until after the goods or services are delivered to pay for them. Trade credit is the largest single source of short-term funds for businesses, representing approximately one-third of the current liabilities of nonfinancial firms. Because suppliers are often more liberal in extending credit than financial institutions, trade credit is a particularly important source of funds for small firms.

When extending trade credit, the seller specifies the period of time allowed for payment and often offers a **cash discount** if payment is made more quickly. For example, the terms "2/10, net 30" are frequently encountered; they mean the buyer can take a 2% cash discount if payment is made within 10 days (the *discount period*). Otherwise, the full amount is due within 30 days (the *net period*).

Trade credit can be a significant source of funds. For example, suppose a firm purchases \$50,000 worth of supplies each day on terms of 2/10, net 30. The firm always pays in exactly 10 days. In this case, the firm will owe its suppliers 10 times \$50,000, or \$500,000, less the 2% discount. Its suppliers are providing almost \$500,000 of funds the firm can use in its business. If the firm pays at the end of 30 days, the total amount of trade credit would be 30 days of purchases, which is approximately \$50,000 times 30, or \$1,500,000. More accurately, it is 0.98(1,500,000) = \$1,470,000.

COST OF TRADE CREDIT If no discount is offered, or if payment is made soon enough that the discount can be taken, there is no cost to the firm for the use of the supplier's credit. When cash discounts are offered but not taken, however, trade credit involves a cost. It should be obvious that when a firm offers a discount for early payment, the discounted price is the "real" price of the goods. That is, if the invoice is for \$100 and a 2% discount is offered for early payment, the "real" price is \$98. If the firm does not pay its bill within 10 days, it is effectively borrowing \$98 and paying \$2 interest for the loan by forgoing the discount. Figure 22.6 illustrates this.

Equation (4.10) is the formula for computing the APR. Similarly, the APR for trade credit is

$$\text{APR} = \left[\frac{\text{Discount\%}}{100\% - \text{Discount\%}}\right]\left[\frac{365}{\text{Total period} - \text{Discount period}}\right] \tag{22.9}$$

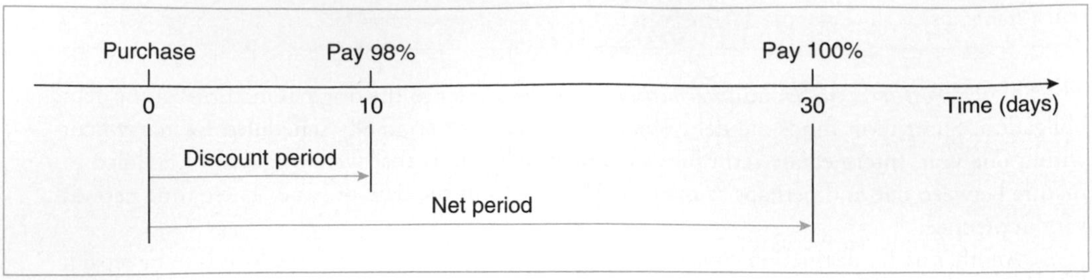

FIGURE 22.6
Cost of trade credit.

The APR formula is widely used, but of course it understates the true annual interest rate because it ignores the effect of interest compounding. The true interest cost is the APY, Equation (4.11), which for trade credit is

$$\text{APY} = \left[1 + \frac{\text{Discount\%}}{100\% - \text{Discount\%}}\right]^{\left[\frac{365}{\text{Total period} - \text{Discount period}}\right]} - 1 \qquad (22.10)$$

EXAMPLE Cost of Trade Credit for Radio Shack

What is the cost to Radio Shack if it skips the discount and pays at the end of the net period if credit terms are 2/10, net 30? Using Equation (22.9), the APR is

$$\text{APR} = \left[\frac{2\%}{100\% - 2\%}\right]\left[\frac{365}{30 - 10}\right] = 37.24\%$$

This example can be visualized with the help of Figure 22.6. Radio Shack would pay \$2 of interest on a \$98 loan. The loan is for only 20 days, so the loan is rolled over 365/(30− 10) = 365/20 = 18.25 times per year.

For such a high interest rate, the difference between the APR and the APY can be substantial. Using Equation (22.10), the APY is 44.59%:

$$\text{APY} = \left[1 + \frac{2\%}{100\% - 2\%}\right]^{\left[\frac{365}{30-10}\right]} - 1 = 44.59\%$$

CALCULATOR SOLUTION

Data Input	Function Key
0.05479 (=20/365)	N
98	PV
0	PMT
100	FV
44.59	I

As the Radio Shack example illustrates, trade credit can be very expensive when a cash discount is offered but not taken. So it is important to evaluate the implicit cost of not taking the discount. Other sources of credit may be quite a bit cheaper.

EFFECTIVE USE OF TRADE CREDIT Trade credit offers certain advantages as a source of short-term funds. It is readily available, at least to firms that regularly pay their suppliers on schedule. Also, it is informal. If the firm is now paying its bills within the discount period, it can get additional credit simply by delaying the payment until the end of the net period or perhaps later (but at the cost of forgoing the discount).

Trade credit is also more flexible than other means of short-term financing. The firm does not have to negotiate a loan agreement, pledge collateral, or adhere to a rigid repayment schedule. In particular, the consequences of delaying a payment beyond the net period are much less onerous than those resulting from failure to repay a bank loan on schedule. For these and other reasons, trade credit is particularly valuable to smaller firms, which often have difficulty obtaining credit elsewhere.

STRETCHING ACCOUNTS PAYABLE Firms may also "stretch" accounts payable by postponing payment beyond the end of the net period. Such stretching lowers the financing cost computed in Equations (22.9) and (22.10) because the loan period is extended without any increase in cost.

For example, with credit terms of 2/10, net 30, paying in 40 rather than 30 days lowers the APR from 37.24% to 24.83%. It lowers the APY from 44.59% to 27.86%. Suppliers sometimes tolerate such delinquencies during periods when the buyer has large seasonal funds requirements. To minimize any adverse consequences, however, the buyer should keep the supplier fully informed of its situation. It should also try to keep current on its repayment obligations with the supplier over the rest of the year.

Stretching the payments on accounts payable is a good example of the Principle of Two-Sided Transactions. Paying late may be a zero-sum game, and what you save for yourself is a cost imposed on your supplier. The buyer must be careful to avoid excessive stretching of accounts payable. Stretching may cause the firm to incur other implicit costs, such as a deterioration in its credit ratings, strained relations with suppliers, or both. These can lead to less attractive credit terms in the future and perhaps to higher prices as suppliers attempt to pass through to the buyer the cost of the buyer's delinquent payments. These implicit costs of trade credit, although difficult to estimate, should be carefully weighed. In particular, smaller firms that may at times rely heavily on trade credit for short-term financing should assess the implicit as well as explicit costs of the trade credit.

STATEMENT BILLING VERSUS INVOICE BILLING In many business relationships, particularly where the number of purchases is small, the supplier sends a separate bill for each purchase. This is called *invoice billing.* Obviously, this can result in a lot of paperwork.

In *statement billing,* several invoices are collected together into a single statement and the customer is asked to pay after the statement is presented. A common arrangement is monthly statements. The supplier's "month" might run from the 25th of one month until the 25th of the next month. On the 25th day of the month, the supplier collects all of the invoices over the last month and sends the statement with credit terms such as "2/10, net EOM." If the statement was prepared on April 25, this allows the customer to take a 2% discount if the bill is paid by the 10th of the next month, which is May 10th. If the discount is not taken, the net amount is due on EOM, the end of the month, which is May 31.

Review

1. What are the three main sources of short-term funds? What are the main differences among them? Which is the largest source?
2. What is trade credit? What are its advantages compared to other sources of short-term funds?
3. What does "3/10, net 20" mean?
4. What is the cost of trade credit when the borrower pays within the discount period?
5. Why does trade credit create an implicit cost when a firm does not pay within the discount period?

Secured and Unsecured Bank Loans

Commercial bank lending is second in importance to trade credit as a source of short-term financing. Commercial banks also provide intermediate-term financing (maturity between 1 and 10 years).

Banks provide loans in a wide variety of forms that are tailored to the specific needs of the borrower. Banks generally lend to their most creditworthy customers on an unsecured basis. But when a borrower represents a significant credit risk, the bank may ask it to provide some form of security, such as a lien on receivables or inventory. Finance companies also lend on a secured basis.

SHORT-TERM UNSECURED LOANS Short-term unsecured bank loans take one of three basic forms: a specific *transaction loan,* a *line of credit,* or a *revolving credit.* Such loans are generally regarded as "self-liquidating": The lender expects that the assets the firm purchases with the loan proceeds will generate sufficient cash to repay the loan within a year. Short-term unsecured loans are evidenced by a promissory note that specifies the amount of the loan, interest rate, and repayment terms. Short-term unsecured loans typically bear interest at a floating rate.

Banks make a **transaction loan** for a specific purpose. For example, a bank may lend a home builder funds to pay for building houses. The loan agreement requires the firm to repay the bank when the houses are sold.

A **line of credit** is an arrangement between a bank and a customer concerning the maximum loan balance the bank will permit the borrower at any one time. Banks normally extend credit lines for a one-year period, with one-year renewals granted as long as the bank continues to find the borrower's credit acceptable.

Banks generally do not like borrowers to use credit lines to cover their long-term funds requirements, so banks require borrowers to be out of bank debt periodically for some specified amount of time (for example, 30 consecutive days each year). Inability to meet such a requirement gives the bank an early warning of potential trouble. If the firm is unable to meet this requirement, the bank will insist that the firm get additional long-term financing to be able to meet it. Most credit lines are informal arrangements. If the prospective borrower's credit deteriorates, the bank is not legally obligated to advance funds.

A **revolving credit agreement** represents a legal commitment to lend up to a specified maximum amount any time during a specified period. In return for this legal commitment, the borrower must pay a *commitment fee,* typically between 0.25% and 0.5%, on the difference between the permitted maximum and the amount actually borrowed. This fee increases the firm's cost of borrowing and compensates the bank for committing itself to making extra funds available to the firm. Revolving credits are evidenced by short-term notes that usually mature in 90 days. The borrower can roll these over automatically as long as the notes mature no later than the date the revolving credit agreement expires. Revolving credits often extend beyond one year, and the borrower often has the option to convert the revolving credit to a term loan when the revolving credit expires.

TERM LOAN Bank term loans represent intermediate-term debt, but the similarity between their pricing and that of short-term bank loans makes it appropriate to discuss them in this chapter. A bank **term loan** is a loan for a specified amount that requires the borrower to repay it according to a specified schedule. A term loan generally matures in 1 to 10 years, but banks permit longer maturities under special circumstances. Repayment is normally at regular intervals in equal installments.

In some cases the loan may provide for a larger final payment, called a *balloon payment,* or simply repayment at maturity in one lump sum, called a *bullet maturity.* A loan with a bullet maturity is like a typical corporate bond. The interest is paid periodically over the life of the loan, but the principal is repaid in one lump sum at the end. Banks often extend revolving credits that the borrower can convert into a term loan. A three-year revolving credit convertible into a five-year term loan at the end of the third year is not uncommon. Term loans often carry a floating interest rate.

COST OF BANK FINANCING Except for a rather small percentage of loans that bear interest at a fixed rate, commercial banks charge interest at a rate that floats. Generally, the interest rate floats with the bank's **prime rate,** which is a benchmark rate that banks may use to price loans.[4]

[4]The prime rate used to be the interest rate banks charged their largest, most creditworthy customers. Currently, however, banks often lend to their best customers at below prime rate.

Banks often use other benchmark rates besides prime. These are usually based on the bank's cost of funding the loan. For example, commercial banks often offer their larger, more creditworthy customers the option of selecting interest rates based on (1) one of the London Interbank Offer Rates (LIBOR), the rates at which prime banks offer one another deposits in the London money market, or (2) the interest rate the bank pays on large certificates of deposit. The prime rate serves as the base lending rate in most cases.

A bank adjusts its prime rate to reflect changes in its cost of funds. In addition, commercial banks frequently offer loans at "money market rates" that are below prime to compete with the commercial paper market. Banks charge less creditworthy customers a higher rate, usually expressed as a percentage over prime, depending on the customer's credit standing. For example, if a bank's prime rate is 7%, then it might lend to a local manufacturing firm at prime plus 0.5%, or 7.5%, and to a local merchant at prime plus 2%, or 9%. The interest rates on these loans would vary with changes in the bank's prime rate. If the bank raises its prime rate to 7.5%, the interest rate on the manufacturing firm's loan would automatically become 8%, and the interest rate on the merchant's loan would automatically become 9.5%.

A compensating balance requirement, generally between 10% and 20% of the size of the loan, is required in addition to interest charges. This requirement may be a minimum, but more commonly it is a required *average* deposit balance during a particular interest period. Such an average gives the borrower greater flexibility, because a high balance one day can offset a low balance on another day. Compensating balance requirements are more common when credit is tight in the entire economy. In any case, a compensating balance adds to the cost of a loan in those instances where a firm has to maintain a higher cash balance than it otherwise would.

Despite the many differences in bank loan contracts, calculating the cost of a loan is not difficult. As with trade credit, we can calculate the APR. It is

$$\text{APR} = \left[\frac{\text{Net cost of loan}}{\text{Cash advance}}\right]\left[\frac{1}{f}\right] \tag{22.11}$$

where f is the fraction of a year that the loan is outstanding. For example, for a three-month loan, $f = 0.25$.

The APY is:

$$\text{APY} = \left[1 + \frac{\text{Net cost of loan}}{\text{Cash advance}}\right]^{1/f} - 1 = \left[\frac{\text{Net repayment}}{\text{Cash advance}}\right]^{1/f} - 1 \tag{22.12}$$

In the analysis that follows, we will give only the APR formulas based on Equation (22.11). In each case, the comparable APY formula would be based on Equation (22.12).

TRUE INTEREST COST WITH COMPENSATING BALANCES When interest is paid in arrears (that is, at the end of an interest period) and compensating balances are required, the true interest cost of the loan is higher than the rate quoted on the principal amount of the loan. The compensating balance reduces the effective loan proceeds, raising the cost of the usable funds. The higher interest cost with a compensating balance is

$$\text{APR} = \left[\frac{\text{Net cost of loan}}{\text{Cash advance}}\right]\left[\frac{1}{f}\right] = \left[\frac{\text{Interest charges}}{\text{Loan amount} - \text{Compensating balance}}\right]\left[\frac{1}{f}\right] = \left[\frac{rP}{P - B}\right]\left[\frac{1}{f}\right] \tag{22.13}$$

where

P = amount of the loan
f = loan term
r = interest rate on loan amount
B = increase in the firm's average cash balances due to the compensating balance requirement
rP = interest charges

The financing costs for this loan consist of interest charges, and the net loan proceeds are the loan amount reduced by the amount of the compensating balance requirement.

Equation (22.13) assumes the compensating balances do not earn interest, which is generally the case. But if the compensating balances earn some yield, *y*, the interest earned, *yB*, reduces the cost of the loan. In that case, the cost of the loan is

$$\text{APR} = \left[\frac{\text{Interest charges} - \text{Interest received}}{\text{Loan amount} - \text{Compensating balance}}\right]\left[\frac{1}{f}\right] = \left[\frac{rP - yB}{P - B}\right]\left[\frac{1}{f}\right] \tag{22.14}$$

EXAMPLE Loans with Compensating Balance Requirements

A Wendy's franchisee borrows $100,000 for one year. The bank charges interest at prime rate plus 0.50%. It also requires a 10% compensating balance, which the franchisee would not otherwise have kept. If the prime rate averages 11.50%, what is the APR?

Using Equation (22.13), the APR is

CALCULATOR SOLUTION

Data Input	Function Key
1	N
90,000	PV
0	PMT
102,000	FV
13.33	I

$$\text{APR} = \left[\frac{rP}{P - B}\right]\left[\frac{1}{f}\right] = \left[\frac{0.12(100{,}000)}{100{,}000 - 10{,}000}\right]\left[\frac{1}{1}\right] = \frac{12{,}000}{90{,}000} = 13.33\%$$

In the absence of any compensating balance requirements, the true interest cost would have been simply 12%. We can look at this problem another way.

The franchisee borrows $100,000 at the first of the year and repays the $112,000 at the end of the year. However, because $10,000 stays in the bank the whole year, the franchisee takes out only $90,000 at the first of the year and must pay $102,000 at the end. This produces a one-year interest rate of 13.33%.

Suppose the franchisee could deposit the compensating balance in a time deposit account earning 5% interest. Then the financing costs would be reduced by the amount of interest earned, which would be 5% of $10,000, or $500. The APR is now 12.78%:

CALCULATOR SOLUTION

Data Input	Function Key
1	N
90,000	PV
0	PMT
101,500 (=102,000 − 500)	FV
12.78	I

$$\text{APR} = \left(\frac{rP - yB}{P - B}\right)\left(\frac{1}{f}\right) = \left(\frac{0.12(100{,}000) - 0.05(10{,}000)}{100{,}000 - 10{,}000}\right)\left(\frac{1}{1}\right) = \frac{11{,}500}{90{,}000} = 12.78\%$$

TRUE INTEREST COST OF DISCOUNT NOTES Many loans are **discount loans,** which require the borrower to pay the interest in advance. The loan proceeds are reduced by the interest cost. The stated loan amount is *P*, but the borrower gets only $P - rPf$, where *f* is the borrowing period expressed as a fraction of a year and the interest rate *r* is referred to as the *discount rate.* Often, *f* is computed using a 360-day year. With an interest expense of *rPf*, the "true" loan amount is $P - rPf$. Adjusting for a loan period of *f*, the APR is

$$\text{APR} = \left(\frac{rPf}{P - rPf}\right)\left(\frac{1}{f}\right) = \frac{r}{1 - fr} \tag{22.15}$$

As you would expect, because of the time value of money, the true interest cost is higher when interest is paid in advance than when it is paid in arrears. If a compensating balance were also required, other adjustments would be needed as well.

EXAMPLE Famous Amos's Cost for a Discounted Loan

Famous Amos is paying interest on a discount basis at the rate of 12% per year for a $100,000, three-month loan. There is no compensating balance requirement. What is Famous Amos's true cost of this loan?

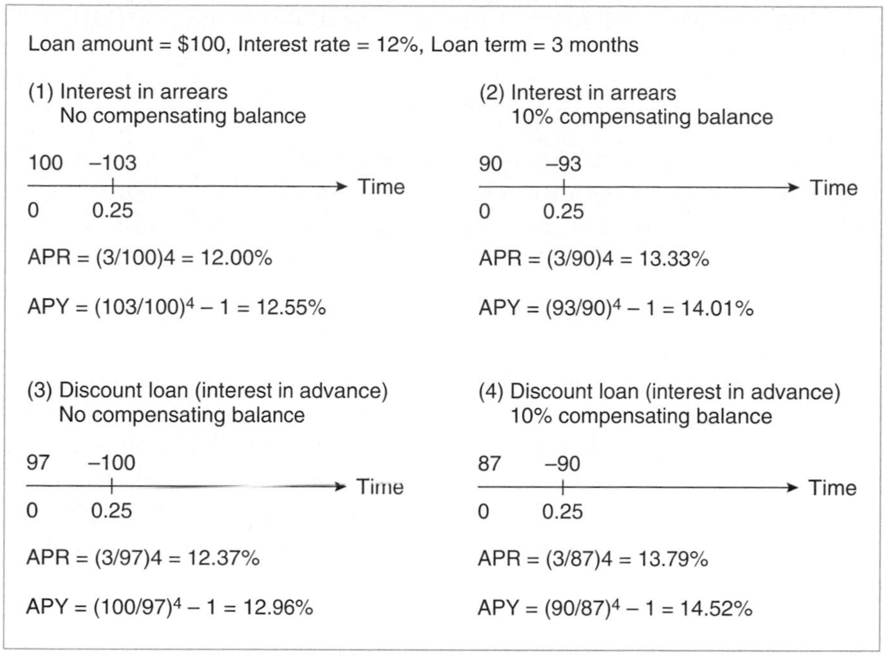

Loan amount = $100, Interest rate = 12%, Loan term = 3 months
(1) Interest in arrears
No compensating balance
100 −103
Time
0 0.25
APR = (3/100)4 = 12.00%
APY = (103/100)4 − 1 = 12.55%
(2) Interest in arrears
10% compensating balance
90 −93
Time
0 0.25
APR = (3/90)4 = 13.33%
APY = (93/90)4 − 1 = 14.01%
(3) Discount loan (interest in advance)
No compensating balance
97 −100
Time
0 0.25
APR = (3/97)4 = 12.37%
APY = (100/97)4 − 1 = 12.96%
(4) Discount loan (interest in advance)
10% compensating balance
87 −90
Time
0 0.25
APR = (3/87)4 = 13.79%
APY = (90/87)4 − 1 = 14.52%

FIGURE 22.7
Costs of four types of single-payment loans.

Using Equation (22.15), the APR is

$$\text{APR} = \frac{r}{1 - fr} = \frac{0.12}{1 - 0.12(0.25)} = \frac{0.12}{0.97} = 12.37\%$$

The APY is 12.96%.

CALCULATOR SOLUTION

Data Input	Function Key
0.25	N
97,000	PV
0	PMT
100,000	FV
12.96	I

SUMMARY OF COST OF SINGLE-PAYMENT LOANS Figure 22.7 summarizes the costs of four types of single-payment $100, three-month loans at 12% APR. The types are based on whether interest is paid in arrears (at the end of the year, cases 1 and 2) or in advance (a discount loan, cases 3 and 4) and on whether a compensating balance is required (cases 2 and 4) or not (cases 1 and 3). Figure 22.7 shows how the loan's APY is increased by compensating balances, or by paying interest on a discount basis.

THE APY FOR A DISCOUNTED INSTALLMENT LOAN Instead of a single-payment loan, the bank may require the borrower to repay the loan on an installment basis. The APY of an installment loan can be found by solving for the periodic interest rate and then annualizing it.

EXAMPLE Famous Amos's Cost for a Discounted Installment Loan

Suppose Famous Amos is borrowing another $100,000 at what the bank calls a 12% interest rate. In this case, the interest is discounted at 12% for three months (total discount of 3%). Amos will repay the loan in three installments of $25,000 each at the end of the first two months and $50,000 at the end of three months. So Amos gets $97,000 (= $100,000 − [0.12][0.25]100,000), and its true interest cost is the r that solves

$$97{,}000 = \frac{25{,}000}{(1 + r)} + \frac{25{,}000}{(1 + r)^2} + \frac{50{,}000}{(1 + r)^3}$$

CALCULATOR SOLUTION

Data Input	Function Key
12	N
1.3658	I
100	PV
0	PMT
117.68	FV

Solving for r gives $r = 1.3658\%$ per month. The APR is 16.39% (= [12]1.3658), and the APY is 17.68%.

Famous Amos's "12%" discounted installment loan illustrates vividly, once again, why it is so critical to understand and account for the exact terms of a loan agreement. Two loans with the same quoted interest rate may have substantially different APYs because of differences in how interest is calculated or differences in the timing of repayments.

SECURITY Commercial banks often ask lenders to provide security for their loans. When the bank is lending on a short-term basis, it may ask the borrower to pledge liquid assets, such as receivables, inventories, or marketable securities. The pledge of collateral may take the form of a "floating lien" against one or more classes of short-term assets without specifying them in detail. More commonly, banks will ask the borrower to specify in detail the collateral for the loan (such as a list of the receivables it is pledging). Depending on the quality of the receivables, a firm can usually borrow between 70% and 90% of the face value of the receivables it pledges. With inventories that are easily sold, a firm can usually borrow between 50% and 75% of the inventory's retail value.

For loans secured by receivables, commercial banks normally charge the prime rate plus a premium of up to 5 percentage points. The bank's cost of processing the receivables affects the rate it charges. The higher the processing cost, the higher the interest rate. However, there are normally no compensating balances on such loans. Interest rates on loans secured by inventory have a similar range. The premium is generally lower the higher the quality of the receivables or inventory pledged. Finance companies also make secured loans, but they usually do so at higher rates than commercial banks charge.

The main benefit from pledging is that a firm can borrow more than it could on an unsecured basis. In return, the firm incurs extra administrative and bookkeeping costs and sacrifices some degree of control over its receivables and inventories. In some cases, the borrower's customers repay their receivables directly to the bank. Pledged inventories are sometimes physically separated out and given special handling.

Commercial Paper

The largest, most creditworthy firms are able to borrow on a short-term basis by selling **commercial paper.** More than 4,000 firms issue this form of security. Commercial paper consists of unsecured promissory notes that have a maturity of up to 270 days. It is possible for commercial paper to have a maturity longer than 270 days, but such an issue would have to be placed privately or else registered with the Securities and Exchange Commission.

MARKET FOR COMMERCIAL PAPER Commercial paper is sold either directly or through dealers. Large industrial firms, utilities, and medium-size finance companies generally sell their paper through dealers, who typically charge a commission of 1/8 of 1% on an annualized basis. Such dealer-placed paper typically has a maturity of between 30 and 180 days. Principal buyers include other business firms, insurance companies, pension funds, and banks.

Roughly 40% of all commercial paper is sold directly to investors. Large finance companies, such as General Motors Acceptance Corporation or General Electric Capital, typically sell their paper directly. They tailor the maturities and the amounts of the notes to fit the needs of investors, who consist principally of corporations investing excess cash on a short-term basis. Maturities range from 1 to 270 days. In contrast to most industrial firms, the large finance companies use the commercial paper market as a permanent source of funds because of the finance companies' assets and the lower cost of commercial paper relative to bank financing.

EXAMPLE GE's Interest Plus Commercial Paper Substitute

General Electric Capital Corporation sells floating-rate demand notes in small denominations directly to investors. The interest rate floats weekly, and GE promises that the rate will always exceed the average rate on taxable U.S. money market funds. Investors can redeem them at any time. They are a cost-effective substitute for commercial paper because GE does not have to pay dealers to market them.

COMPUTING THE TRUE COST OF COMMERCIAL PAPER Interest on commercial paper is paid on a discount basis. For example, if 120-day prime commercial paper has a 12% discount rate, then the APR (based on a 360-day year), using Equation (22.15) is

$$\text{APR} = \frac{r}{1 - fr} = \frac{0.12}{1 - 0.12(120 / 360)} = 12.5\%$$

CALCULATOR SOLUTION

Data Input	Function Key
3	N
4.167 (12.5/3)	I
100	PV
0	PMT
113.03	FV

Because of the many different ways to state interest rates, we remind you yet again to compute carefully the APY of each alternative. The one with the lowest APY is the lowest-cost alternative. In this case, with an APR of 12.5%, the APY is 13.03%.

Issuers of commercial paper generally maintain a backup line of credit to provide insurance against any problems selling commercial paper. If a firm cannot pay off its commercial paper at maturity, the backup line of credit is used. For example, when Tyco International Ltd. was unable to roll over its commercial paper in spring 2002, the parent and its finance unit drew down $14.4 billion of bank credit lines to pay off the commercial paper. Banks generally charge an annualized fee of 1/4 to 1/2 of 1% for such backup lines, which increases the cost.

EXAMPLE GMAC's Cost of Commercial Paper

General Motors Acceptance Corporation (GMAC) issues $50 million of 90-day commercial paper at 10%. The paper is discounted, so GMAC receives $48.75 million (= 50 − [0.10][0.25]50). Using Equation (22.11), the APR is

$$\text{APR} = \left(\frac{1{,}250{,}000}{48{,}750{,}000}\right)\left(\frac{1}{0.25}\right) = \left(\frac{1{,}250{,}000}{48{,}750{,}000}\right)(4) = 10.26\%$$

GMAC "rolls over" its paper four times per year, selling new commercial paper to replace each issue as it matures.

Assuming that a backup line of credit costs 0.25% of the funds received and that legal and other out-of-pocket costs amount to another 0.50% per year, GMAC's total APR cost is

$$\text{Cost} = 10.26\% + 0.25\% + 0.50\% = 11.01\%$$

RATING CONSIDERATIONS The credit quality of commercial paper is rated by agencies such as Moody's Investors Service and Standard & Poor's. The agencies apply similar rating criteria. Moody's has two basic commercial paper rating categories: "Prime" and "Not Prime." The Prime category is subdivided into P-1 (highest quality), P-2, and P-3. Standard & Poor's has four basic commercial paper rating categories: A, B, C, and D. The A category corresponds to Moody's Prime category and is subdivided into A-1+ (highest), A-1, A-2, and A-3.

Paper with the highest rating, P-1/A-1+, carries the lowest cost of borrowing and the smallest chance of interrupted market access. At times the yield differential between P-1/A-1+ and P-3/A-3 rated paper has been more than two full percentage points. Furthermore, in market crises, the market for paper rated lower than P-1/A-1 can dry up. Even in the best of times, there is normally no market for commercial paper rated lower than P-3/A-3, and the market for commercial paper rated P-3/A-3 is very limited.

Firms with P-3/A-3 rated paper, and some firms with P-2/A-2 rated paper, may be able to lower their borrowing cost with an irrevocable letter of credit. The letter of credit is a form of insurance that raises the rating and lowers the interest rate. And, of course, if the present value of the interest savings exceeds the cost, this is a positive-NPV decision.

Contracting Costs, Agency Costs, and Short-term Debt

A variety of factors affect a firm's choice of amount and mix of short-term debt as well as the overall maturity structure of the firm's debt. These factors include (1) the cost of each source of funds, (2) the desired level of current assets, (3) the seasonal component of current assets, and (4) the extent to which a firm uses the maturity-matching approach to hedge its debt structure.

Beyond the basic factors just cited, several contracting costs and agency costs also affect the firm's use of short-term debt.

- *Flotation costs.* The costs of issuing long-term securities like bonds and common stock are generally much higher than the costs of arranging short-term borrowings. Consequently, the firm issues these long-term securities only infrequently. In the interim, firms borrow short term from banks or issue commercial paper. As these short-term borrowings build up, they are eventually replaced with long-term securities.
- *Restricted access to sources of long-term capital.* Legal restrictions limit the types of loans that institutional investors can make. It may not be attractive for smaller firms, or larger firms whose debt would be rated below investment grade, to sell long-term debt securities. They may have to rely on trade credit, bank financing, or borrowing from finance firms.
- *Less restrictive terms.* Public and private debt normally carry penalties for early repayment. Such a penalty is simply the cost of the "hidden" option to refinance. Because of this cost, the more likely a firm is to want to repay early, the more attractive bank financing becomes. Bank financing generally does not have such a penalty.
- *Bankruptcy costs.* Bankruptcy costs create a bias in favor of longer maturities, because every time short-term financing comes due, there is the "hidden" option to default. Shareholders must decide whether it is worthwhile to "repurchase" the assets from the debtholders or to "walk away."[5]
- *The firm's choice of risk level.* The firm's attitude toward risk will help determine its philosophy about financing its working capital and, more generally, its choice of short- versus long-term financing. Because of possible increases in interest rates, firms whose shareholders are not well diversified, as is often the case with owner-managed businesses, frequently choose the conservative approach.

Review

1. Why do banks often require a borrower to pledge receivables or inventory as security for a loan?
2. Does a compensating balance requirement always increase the cost of a bank loan? If not, when does it and when does it not?
3. Why is the true interest cost of a discounted loan always greater than the stated discount rate?
4. Describe the following four basic forms of bank loans: (a) Line of credit; (b) Revolving credit; (c) Transaction loan; (d) Term loan.
5. What is commercial paper? Who are the main issuers and who are the main investors?

[5]For more on this, see Chapters 12 and 13.

22.5 ELECTRONIC DATA INTERCHANGE (EDI)

More and more, an increasing volume of business transactions is being made using **electronic data interchange (EDI).** EDI is the exchange of information electronically, directly from one computer to another, in a structured format. By moving the information in this way, firms save time, personnel costs, materials costs, and costs due to errors.

Let us follow a simple business transaction to see the potential value of EDI. First, assume you want to buy something using traditional paper documents and mail delivery. You contact a supplier about availability and price. You then place an order. The supplier acknowledges the purchase order. When the goods are shipped, the supplier also sends shipping documents and an invoice. When it is time to pay, you send a check along with remittance information through the mail. After getting the check, the supplier credits your account and deposits the check in its bank. Finally, the money is transferred from your bank account to the supplier's.

Now consider the same transaction using EDI. In North America, the American National Standards Institute (ANSI) sets EDI standards for such things as invoices, shipping information, purchase orders, customer account information, requests for quotations, and many others.

Each step in the traditional paper-based process causes time delays and labor costs. In addition, the paper-based system is prone to errors. There are also uncertainties in paper-based systems because participants do not know the status of the transaction. By simplifying the process and sending information almost instantaneously, EDI reduces labor costs, substantially reduces errors, and makes possible a much higher degree of control over the firm's resources.

Using EDI, some firms have been able to operate with much lower investments in inventories, to provide their customers with better service, and to be more price competitive. In fact, the economic advantages of EDI are so compelling that some firms either require that all transactions be done with EDI or charge a fee, such as $50, for paper documents.

By increasing the availability and lowering the cost of high-quality information, EDI is changing the way firms manage their working capital assets. There are also some special kinds of EDI that can be considered a subset of the overall EDI architecture. Electronic funds transfer (EFT) is the transfer of money electronically from one bank to another. Financial EDI (FEDI) is the exchange of information between a bank and its customers (such as information about checks paid, account balances, lockbox information, and other things).

Review

1. What does EDI stand for? What is it and what are its advantages?
2. Which of the following will increase or decrease in an EDI system compared to a paper-based system? (a) The time between the sending and receipt of a purchase order; (b) The number of times that information must be keyed into the computer; (c) The number of errors that employees make in handling a customer's orders; (d) The amount of managerial control over resources such as inventory levels.

SUMMARY

- Working capital management is the management of the firm's short-term assets and liabilities.
- The cash conversion cycle is the length of time between when a firm pays its accounts payable and collects on its accounts receivable. The cash conversion cycle is equal to the inventory conversion period plus the receivables collection period minus the payables deferral period.

- Businesses need stores of cash for three reasons: to conduct ordinary transactions when cash flows are uneven (the transactions demand), to avert default on obligations (the precautionary demand), and to take advantage of investment opportunities (the speculative demand). Bank requirements for compensating balances also contribute to the demand for cash balances.
- The Baumol model and the Miller-Orr model are two well-known models that minimize the cost of accommodating the transactions demand for cash.
- Float is the difference between the checking account balance at the bank and the balance on the firm's ledgers; the available balance minus the book balance. Firms use zero balance accounts, wire transfers, controlled disbursing, centralized processing of payables, and lockboxes to manage float.
- Trade credit, bank loans, and commercial paper are the main sources of short-term financing. The APY of each source depends on the specific terms in its contract.
- Electronic data interchange is the direct exchange of information between the computers of two businesses. A wide variety of documents can be electronically exchanged with the structured formats in EDI.

EQUATION SUMMARY

$$\begin{matrix}\text{Cash}\\ \text{conversion}\\ \text{cycle}\end{matrix} = \begin{matrix}\text{Inventory}\\ \text{conversion}\\ \text{period}\end{matrix} + \begin{matrix}\text{Receivables}\\ \text{collection}\\ \text{period}\end{matrix} - \begin{matrix}\text{Payables}\\ \text{deferral}\\ \text{period}\end{matrix} \tag{22.1}$$

$$\begin{matrix}\text{Inventory}\\ \text{conversion}\\ \text{period}\end{matrix} = \frac{\text{Inventory}}{\text{Cost of sales / 365}} = \frac{365}{\text{Inventory turnover}} \tag{22.2}$$

$$\begin{matrix}\text{Receivables}\\ \text{collection}\\ \text{period}\end{matrix} = \frac{\text{Receivables}}{\text{Sales / 365}} = \frac{365}{\text{Receivables turnover}} \tag{22.3}$$

$$\begin{matrix}\text{Payables}\\ \text{deferral}\\ \text{period}\end{matrix} = \frac{\text{Accounts payable + Wages, benefits, and payroll taxes payable}}{\text{(Cost of sales + Selling, general, and administrative expenses) / 365}} \tag{22.4}$$

$$\text{Cost} = b\left[\frac{T}{C}\right] + i\left[\frac{C}{2}\right] \tag{22.5}$$

$$C^* = \sqrt{\frac{2bT}{i}} \tag{22.6}$$

$$Z = \left[\frac{3b\sigma^2}{4i}\right]^{1/3} \tag{22.7}$$

$$\text{Float} = \text{Available balance} - \text{Book balance} \tag{22.8}$$

$$\text{APR} = \left[\frac{\text{Discount\%}}{100\% - \text{Discount\%}}\right]\left[\frac{365}{\text{Total period} - \text{Discount period}}\right] \tag{22.9}$$

$$\text{APY} = \left[1 + \frac{\text{Discount\%}}{100\% - \text{Discount\%}}\right]^{\left[\frac{365}{\text{Total period} - \text{Discount period}}\right]} - 1 \quad (22.10)$$

$$\text{APR} = \left[\frac{\text{Net cost of loan}}{\text{Cash advance}}\right]\left[\frac{1}{f}\right] \quad (22.11)$$

$$\text{APY} = \left[1 + \frac{\text{Net cost of loan}}{\text{Cash advance}}\right]^{1/f} - 1 = \left[\frac{\text{Net repayment}}{\text{Cash advance}}\right]^{1/f} - 1 \quad (22.12)$$

$$\text{APR} = \left[\frac{\text{Net cost of loan}}{\text{Cash advance}}\right]\left[\frac{1}{f}\right] = \left[\frac{\text{Interest charges}}{\text{Loan amount} - \text{Compensating balance}}\right]\left[\frac{1}{f}\right] = \left[\frac{rP}{P - B}\right]\left[\frac{1}{f}\right] \quad (22.13)$$

$$\text{APR} = \left[\frac{\text{Interest charges} - \text{Interest received}}{\text{Loan amount} - \text{Compensating balance}}\right]\left[\frac{1}{f}\right] = \left[\frac{rP - yB}{P - B}\right]\left[\frac{1}{f}\right] \quad (22.14)$$

$$\text{APR} = \left(\frac{rPf}{P - rPf}\right)\left(\frac{1}{f}\right) = \frac{r}{1 - fr} \quad (22.15)$$

QUESTIONS

1. Cite and describe three alternative philosophies about how a firm finances its working capital.
2. Describe the cash conversion cycle and discuss its importance to working capital management.
3. Cite and describe three basic motives for holding cash.
4. Briefly describe the two types of transaction demand models.
5. Explain the concept of float.
6. List and describe five marketable securities that are available to a corporation that has funds to invest short term. Order them from the lowest risk (and return) to the highest.
7. Cite and describe three alternative types of short-term bank loans.
8. What does "2/10, net 30" mean?
9. What is electronic data interchange (EDI)? What are the principal economic advantages of EDI over the traditional paper-based system?

CHALLENGING QUESTIONS

10. What are the assumptions of the Baumol cash management model? What are the Miller-Orr model's assumptions?
11. Briefly explain how each of the following can be used to reduce a firm's float costs: (a) Wire transfers; (b) Zero balance accounts (ZBAs); (c) Controlled disbursing; (d) Centralized processing of payables; (e) Lockboxes.

12. What causes the differences between available balances and book balances?
13. Why do investors require firms issuing commercial paper to be of high creditworthiness?
14. Why are interest rates on short-term loans not necessarily comparable to each other? Give three possible reasons.

PROBLEMS

LEVEL A (BASIC)

A1. (Cash conversion cycle) Auburn Hair Products has an inventory turnover of six times per year, a receivables turnover of 10 times, and a payables turnover of 12 times. What is Auburn Hair's inventory conversion period, the receivables collection period, and the payables deferral period? What is the cash conversion cycle?

A2. (Cash conversion cycle) Baklava Baking Corporation is interested in its cash conversion cycle. A Baklava manager has assembled the data given here for your use. Estimate each of the following:

a. Inventory conversion period
b. Receivables collection period
c. Payables deferral period
d. Cash conversion cycle

INVENTORY	ACCOUNTS RECEIVABLE	ACCOUNTS PAYABLE	WAGES, BENEFITS, AND PAYROLL TAXES PAYABLE	SALES	COST OF SALES	SELLING, GENERAL, AND ADMIN-ISTRATIVE EXPENSES
$1,000,000	$800,000	$400,000	$150,000	$25,000,000	$10,000,000	$1,500,000

A3. (Cash conversion cycle) Dennis Lasser has collected some information about a food wholesaler in order to estimate its cash conversion cycle. The accumulated information is given. What will Dennis find the cash conversion cycle to be?

Inventory turnover = 10x	Inventory conversion period = 365/10 = 36.5 days
Receivables turnover = 20x	Receivables collection period = 365/20 = 18.25 days
Payables turnover = 25x	Payables deferral period = 365/25 = 14.6 days

A4. (Cash conversion cycle) Brooks Toy Company has an inventory turnover of 12 times per year, a receivables turnover of 20 times, and a payables turnover of 25 times. What is Brooks' inventory conversion period, the receivables collection period, and the payables deferral period? What is the cash conversion cycle?

A5. (Cash conversion cycle) Iomega Corporation is interested in its cash conversion cycle. An Iomega manager has assembled the data given here for your use. Estimate each of the following:

a. Inventory conversion period
b. Receivables collection period
c. Payables deferral period
d. Cash conversion cycle

INVENTORY	ACCOUNTS RECEIVABLE	ACCOUNTS PAYABLE	WAGES, BENEFITS, AND PAYROLL TAXES PAYABLE	SALES	COST OF SALES	SELLING, GENERAL, AND ADMIN-ISTRATIVE EXPENSES
$3,000,000	$1,200,000	$900,000	$2,300,000	$65,000,000	$40,000,000	$12,000,000

A6. (Cash conversion cycle) The Mennen Corporation is interested in examining its cash conversion cycle. Suppose a Mennen manager has assembled the following data for your use:

$1.00 million	Inventory
$0.80 million	Accounts receivable
$0.40 million	Accounts payable
$0.15 million	Wages, benefits, and payroll taxes payable
$25.0 million	Sales
$10.0 million	Cost of sales
$1.50 million	Selling, general, and administrative expenses

Estimate each of the following:

a. Inventory conversion period

b. Receivables collection period

c. Payables deferral period

d. Cash conversion cycle

A7. (Baumol cash management model) A firm projects a need for $2 million cash per month. Its projected 30-day investment yield is 9% per year. The cost of converting securities into cash is $300 per transaction.

a. How much cash would it raise each time it sells securities?

b. How often should the firm plan to sell securities?

c. What will be the average cash balance?

d. What is the annual opportunity cost of funds, transactions costs, and total costs?

A8. (Baumol cash management model) A firm projects a need for $1 million cash per month. Its projected 30-day investment yield is 12% APR. The cost of converting securities into cash is $500 per transaction.

a. How much cash would it raise each time it sells securities?

b. How often should the firm plan to sell securities?

c. What will be the average cash balance?

d. What is the annual opportunity cost of funds, transactions costs, and total costs?

A9. (Miller-Orr cash management model) Suppose that the cash flows of a firm are uncertain and have an estimated standard deviation of $100,000 per day. The interest rate is 9% per year and the cost of converting securities into cash or vice versa is $300 per transaction. The lower control limit is zero. (Hint: Convert the annual interest rate into a daily rate.)

a. Calculate the return point and upper control limit.

b. When and in what amounts should the firm buy and sell securities?

c. What is the average cash balance?

A10. (Miller-Orr cash management model) Suppose that the cash flows of a firm are uncertain and have an estimated standard deviation of $40,000 per day. The interest rate is 12% per year and the cost of converting securities into cash or vice versa is $1,000 per transaction. The lower control limit is zero.

a. Calculate the return point and upper control limit.

b. When and in what amounts should the firm buy and sell securities?

c. What is the average cash balance?

A11. (Float) Suppose a Footlocker franchisee has $20,000 in both its book balance and its bank balance. If the franchisee writes a $2,000 check that takes four days to clear, what is its disbursement float?

A12. (Float) Gerry Johnson writes a $100 check on Monday, a $200 check on Tuesday, and a $300 check on Wednesday. It takes exactly two days for the checks to be presented and funds taken from Gerry's account. What is Gerry's disbursement float on Monday, Tuesday, Wednesday, Thursday, and Friday?

A13. (Float) Suppose a firm has $100,000 in both its book balance and its bank balance. If the firm writes a $30,000 check that takes four days to clear, what is its disbursement float?

A14. (Cost of trade credit) Calculate the cost of skipping the discount and paying at the end of the net period for each of the following credit terms. Calculate the APR and the APY.

a. 1/10, net 30

b. 6/10, net 70

c. 2/15, net 45

A15. (Cost of trade credit) Trade credit terms are 2/10, net 40.

a. What is the true interest cost of skipping the discount and paying on day 40? Estimate both the APR and the APY.

b. If payment is stretched to day 55 (fifteen days late), calculate the true interest cost of skipping the discount if the supplier accepts the payment without penalty at that time. Again, estimate both the APR and the APY.

A16. (Cost of trade credit) Suppose you are offered trade credit terms of 1.5/15, net 50. What is the APR cost of this trade credit if you skip the discount and pay at the end of the net period? What would be the APR cost if you "stretched" the payable and paid after 75 days?

A17. (Float) Sandy Ritter writes a $500 check on Monday, a $700 check on Tuesday, and a $100 check on Wednesday. It takes exactly two days for the checks to be presented and funds taken from Sandy's account. What is Sandy's disbursement float on Monday, Tuesday, Wednesday, Thursday, and Friday?

A18. (Cost of bank loan) A bank loan agreement calls for an interest rate equal to prime rate plus 1%. If prime rate averages 9% and non-interest-earning compensating balances equal to 10% of the loan must be maintained, what are the APR and the APY of the loan assuming annual payments?

A19. (Cost of bank loan) A bank loan agreement calls for an interest rate equal to prime rate plus 2%. If prime rate averages 7% and non-interest-earning compensating balances equal to 15% of the loan must be maintained, what are the APR and the APY of the loan assuming annual payments?

A20. (Cost of short-term funds) D. M. Ferguson and Associates is considering three alternative sources of short-term funds shown below. What is the cost of each source?

1. Skipping the discount on accounts payable, the terms of which are 1/10, net 30.
2. Borrowing from the bank at 10%, interest in arrears, with a 20% compensating balance requirement.
3. Selling 90-day commercial paper, with a discount rate of 13%.

A21. (Cost of trade credit) Calculate the cost of skipping the discount and paying at the end of the net period for each of the following credit terms. Calculate the APR and the APY.

a. 5/10, net 50

b. 3/15, net 30

c. 2/10, net 20

A22. (Cost of trade credit) Trade credit terms are 1/15, net 30.

a. What is the true interest cost of skipping the discount and paying on day 30? Estimate both the APR and the APY.

b. If payment is stretched to day 60 (thirty days late), calculate the true interest cost of skipping the discount if the supplier accepts the payment without penalty at that time. Again, estimate both the APR and the APY.

A23. (Cost of trade credit) Suppose you are offered trade credit terms of 2/10, net 30. What is the APR cost of this trade credit if you skip the discount and pay at the end of the net period? What would be the APR cost if you "stretched" the payable and paid after 90 days?

A24. (Cost of commercial paper) The discount rate for a 54-day issue of commercial paper is 8.50%. What are the APR and the APY? Assume a 360-day year.

A25. (Cost of commercial paper) Specific Motors Acceptance Corporation sells medium-term commercial paper with a 180-day maturity. If SMAC sells the commercial paper at a discount rate of 11%, calculate the APR and APY. Assume a 360-day year.

A26. (Cost of commercial paper) The discount rate for a 100-day issue of commercial paper is 9%. What are the APR and the APY? Assume a 360-day year.

A27. (Cost of commercial paper) Intuit Technology Corporation (ITC) sells commercial paper with a 90-day maturity. If ITC sells the commercial paper at a discount rate of 10%, calculate the APR and APY. Assume a 360-day year.

A28. (Cost of wire transfer versus paper check) You need to transfer $250,000 from Houston to Chicago. If you mail a check, it will cost $1.00 for postage and clearing the check, and it will take a total of five days for the funds to be transferred. During the money's five-day travel, you will suffer an opportunity cost because the $250,000 is not earning 3% APY interest. Alternatively, you can avoid the opportunity cost by sending a wire transfer costing $12.00, which instantaneously transfers the funds with no float. Calculate the cost of each alternative. Which is cheaper?

A29. (Cost of wire transfer versus paper check) You need to transfer $500,000 from New York to Los Angeles. If you mail a check, it will cost $1.00 for postage and clearing the check, and it will take a total of six days for the funds to be transferred. During the money's six-day travel, you will suffer an opportunity cost because the $500,000 is not earning 2% APY interest. Alternatively, you can avoid the opportunity cost by sending a wire transfer costing $20.00, which instantaneously transfers the funds with no float. Calculate the cost of each alternative. Which is cheaper?

LEVEL B

B1. (Baumol cash management model) A firm uses the Baumol model and projects a need for $2 million cash per month. Its projected 30-day investment yield is 9% APR. The cost of converting securities into cash is $300 per transaction.

a. How much cash would the firm raise each time it sells securities?

b. How often should the firm plan to sell securities?

c. What will be the average cash balance?

d. What are the annual opportunity cost of funds, the annual transactions costs, and the annual total cost?

B2. (Baumol cash management model) Sturbens Electrical Systems pays its $4,000,000 annual payroll expenses out of a Wyoming bank. The disbursements are roughly uniform throughout the year. Sturbens makes deposits into the account from its master account in a Chicago bank. Each deposit involves a fixed cost of $200. The opportunity cost of funds is 4%, because the funds are earning 4% in Chicago and the corporate account in Wyoming receives no interest.

a. What is the optimal deposit size? What are the annual opportunity cost of funds, annual transactions cost, and annual total cost?

b. Assume that interest rates have risen substantially, and that Sturbens now has an opportunity cost of funds of 8%. If Sturbens continues to use the same deposit size that you determined in part a, what would be its annual opportunity cost of funds, annual transactions cost, and annual total cost?

c. Recompute the optimal deposit size assuming the new 8% opportunity cost. What are the opportunity cost, transactions cost, and total cost using the recomputed deposit size?

B3. (Baumol cash management model) A corporation projects a need for $10,000 of cash next year. It believes it can earn 12.5% per year on funds which are invested in marketable securities and that converting marketable securities to cash involves a cost of $1.00 per transaction.

a. What is the optimal deposit size using the Baumol model?

b. What is the average cash balance and the number of deposits per year?

c. What is the annual total cost, opportunity cost of funds, and transactions cost?

B4. (Baumol cash management model) A firm uses the Baumol model and projects a need for $5 million cash per month. Its projected 30-day investment yield is 12% APY. The cost of converting securities into cash is $200 per transaction.

a. How much cash would the firm raise each time it sells securities?

b. How often should the firm plan to sell securities?

c. What will be the average cash balance?

d. What are the annual opportunity cost of funds, the annual transactions costs, and the annual total cost?

B5. (Baumol cash management model) The Kryer Corporation pays its $20,000,000 annual payroll expenses out of a Los Angeles bank. The disbursements are roughly uniform throughout the year. Kryer makes deposits into the account from its master account in a Colorado bank. Each deposit involves a fixed cost of $150. The opportunity cost of funds is 5%, because the funds are earning 5% in Colorado and the corporate account in Los Angeles receives no interest.

a. What is the optimal deposit size? What are the annual opportunity cost of funds, annual transactions cost, and annual total cost?

b. Assume interest rates have risen substantially, and that Kryer now has an opportunity cost of funds of 7%. If Kryer continues to use the same deposit size that you determined in part a, what would be its annual opportunity cost of funds, annual transactions cost, and annual total cost?

c. Recompute the optimal deposit size assuming the new 7% opportunity cost. What are the opportunity cost, transactions cost, and total cost using the recomputed deposit size?

B6. (Float) The book and available balance for a firm's checking account for the last seven days is given here. What is the daily float? For the seven days, what is the average book balance, average available balance, and average float?

DAY	MONDAY	TUESDAY	WEDNESDAY	THURSDAY	FRIDAY	SATURDAY	SUNDAY
Book balance	$100,000	50,000	70,000	100,000	110,000	110,000	110,000
Available balance	$120,000	100,000	60,000	80,000	130,000	130,000	130,000

B7. (Float) The book and available balance for a firm's checking account for the last seven days is given here. What is the daily float? For the seven days, what is the average book balance, average available balance, and average float?

DAY	MONDAY	TUESDAY	WEDNESDAY	THURSDAY	FRIDAY	SATURDAY	SUNDAY
Book balance	$20,000	25,000	30,000	40,000	15,000	25,000	30,000
Available balance	$30,000	40,000	45,000	30,000	10,000	30,000	35,000

B8. (Float) Patin Risk Management Company writes the checks and makes the deposits indicated in the table below. Assume that when Patin writes a check, it takes three days for the check to clear and funds to be removed from Patin's available balance at the bank. When Patin makes a deposit, it takes one day for the funds to be made available at the bank. Indicate each day the amount of Patin's available balance at the bank, disbursement float, collection float, and total float.

DAY	CHECKS WRITTEN	DEPOSITS	BOOK BALANCE	AVAILABLE BALANCE	DISBURSE-MENT FLOAT	COLLEC-TION FLOAT	TOTAL FLOAT
1	0	0	10,000	10,000	0	0	0
2	500	1,000	10,500				
3	800	0	9,700				
4	800	0	8,900				
5	0	0	8,900				
6	0	2,000	10,900				
7	900	0	10,000				
8	0	0	10,000				
9	0	0	10,000				
10	0	0	10,000				

B9. (Float) Salem Packaging Company writes the checks and makes the deposits indicated in the table below. Assume that when Salem Packaging writes a check, it takes three days for the check to clear and funds to be removed from Salem Packaging's available balance at the bank. When Salem Packaging makes a deposit, it takes one day for the funds to be made available at the bank. Indicate each day the amount of Salem Packaging's available balance at the bank, disbursement float, collection float, and total float.

DAY	CHECKS WRITTEN	DEPOSITS	BOOK BALANCE	AVAILABLE BALANCE	DISBURSE-MENT FLOAT	COLLEC-TION FLOAT	TOTAL FLOAT
1	0	0	50,000	50,000	0	0	0
2	1,000	2,000	51,000				
3	1,500	0	49,500				
4	2,500	0	47,000				
5	0	0	47,000				
6	0	3,000	50,000				
7	1,300	0	48,700				
8	0	0	48,700				
9	0	0	48,700				
10	0	0	48,700				

B10. (Cost of wire transfer versus paper check) If you send money to firm headquarters with a wire transfer, it costs a fixed $10 and there is no float. On the other hand, if you write a check and mail it, the fixed cost is only $1.50 and the transfer of funds will occur in five days (due to mail times, processing times, and clearing times). The opportunity cost of funds is 8% per year. Assume a 365-day year.

a. What is the cost of a wire transfer and the cost of a paper check if the amount being forwarded to headquarters is $5,000?

b. What is the cost of a wire transfer and the cost of a paper check if the amount being forwarded to headquarters is $25,000?

c. What is the breakeven point between a wire transfer and paper check?

B11. (Cost of wire transfer versus paper check) If you send money to firm headquarters with a wire transfer, it costs a fixed $12.50 and there is no float. On the other hand, if you write a check and mail it, the fixed cost is only $1.00 and the transfer of funds will occur in three days (due to mail times, processing times, and clearing times). The opportunity cost of funds is 5.5% per year. Assume a 365-day year.

a. What is the cost of a wire transfer and the cost of a paper check if the amount being forwarded to headquarters is $5,000?

b. What is the cost of a wire transfer and the cost of a paper check if the amount being forwarded to headquarters is $50,000?

c. What is the breakeven point between a wire transfer and paper check?

B12. (Lockbox) The Denver Bakery Products Company currently collects all of its customer payments in Denver. By going to a new lockbox system with boxes in Denver, Boston, and Atlanta, Denver Bakery Products can reduce the total time it takes to convert customer payments into available funds by an average of 2.50 days. The firm collects an average of $120,000 per day. The extra costs associated with the lockbox system are $7,500 per year. The opportunity cost of funds is 6% per year. What is the expected annual profit of using the new system?

B13. (Lockbox) A Columbus bank has made a proposal to operate a lockbox for you. Checks cleared through the lockbox amount to $20,000 per day, and the lockbox will make these funds available to you 2.5 days faster.

a. If the Columbus bank will provide the lockbox services in exchange for a $30,000 compensating balance, is its proposal attractive?

b. Instead of a compensating balance, the bank proposes to provide lockbox services on a fee basis, charging an annual fee of $1,000 plus $.10 per check. You expect 40,000 checks per year to be processed through the lockbox. If the opportunity cost of funds is 6% per year, what is the annual profit associated with accepting the fee-based proposal?

c. Which is more profitable to you, the compensating balance proposal in part a or the fee-based proposal in part b?

B14. (Lockbox) National Distributing, Inc. currently collects all of its customer payments in its home state. By going to a new lockbox system with numerous boxes around the country, National Distributing can reduce the total time it takes to convert customer payments into available funds by an average of four days. The firm collects an average of $65,000 per day. The extra costs associated with the lockbox system are $2,000 per year. The opportunity cost of funds is 3.5% per year. What is the expected annual profit of using the new system?

B15. (Fees versus compensating balance) The bank services you receive cost $500 per month. You have a $100,000 average balance at the bank, on which the bank gives you earnings credits of 0.4% per month.

a. Is your compensating balance sufficient to cover your service charges? If not, how much additional money do you owe the bank?

b. What minimum compensating balance would cover your $500 service charge?

B16. (Fees versus compensating balance) The bank services you receive cost $1,500 per month. You have a $150,000 average balance at the bank, on which the bank gives you earnings credits of 0.6% per month.

a. Is your compensating balance sufficient to cover your service charges? If not, how much additional money do you owe the bank?

b. What minimum compensating balance would cover your $1,500 service charge?

B17. (Cost of bank loan) For a *one-year* loan of $100 with an APR interest rate of 15%, determine the cash flows and the APY for each of the following loans:

a. interest in arrears

b. discount loan

c. interest in arrears with a 10% compensating balance

d. discount loan with a 10% compensating balance

B18. (Cost of bank loan) For a *three-month* loan of $100 with an APR interest rate of 15%, determine the cash flows and the APY for each of the following loans:

a. interest in arrears

b. discount loan

c. interest in arrears with a 10% compensating balance

d. discount loan with a 10% compensating balance

B19. (Cost of bank loan) Jim Booth has discussed a $250,000 one-year loan with several different banks. What are the APR and the APY of each alternative? Which loan is the cheapest?

a. A 15% annual rate on a simple interest loan (interest in arrears), with no compensating balance and interest due at the end of the year.

b. An 11% annual rate on a simple interest loan (interest in arrears), with a 20% compensating balance requirement and interest due at the end of the year.

c. A 14% annual rate on a discount loan with no compensating balance. Interest is due at the beginning of the year.

B20. (Cost of bank loan) For a *one-year* loan of $100 with an interest rate of 10% APR, determine the cash flows and the APY for each of the following loans:

a. interest in arrears

b. discount loan

c. interest in arrears with a 10% compensating balance

d. discount loan with a 10% compensating balance

B21. (Cost of bank loan) For a *three-month* loan of $100 with an interest rate of 8% APR, determine the cash flows and the APY for each of the following loans:

a. interest in arrears

b. discount loan

c. interest in arrears with a 10% compensating balance

d. discount loan with a 10% compensating balance

B22. (Cost of installment loan) The Bank of Corpus Christi will give you an installment loan for $50,000 that will be repaid in twelve equal monthly installments. The loan is a 12% add-on loan, which means you must pay 12% on the original loan advance (not just the remaining balance). Your total payments will be $56,000 (the principal of $50,000 plus $6,000 of interest), so your monthly payment is $4,666.67. What APY are you paying on the loan?

B23. (Cost of bank loan) Barbara O'Connor has discussed a $15,000 one-year loan with several different banks. What are the APR and the APY of each alternative? Which loan is the cheapest?

a. A 14% annual rate on a simple interest loan (interest in arrears), with no compensating balance and interest due at the end of the year.

b. A 10% annual rate on a simple interest loan (interest in arrears), with a 15% compensating balance requirement and interest due at the end of the year.

c. A 16% annual rate on a discount loan with no compensating balance. Interest is due at the beginning of the year.

B24. (Cost of installment loan) A bank will give you an installment loan for $25,000 that will be repaid in twelve equal monthly installments. The loan is an 11% add-on loan, which means you must pay 11% on the original loan advance (not just the remaining balance). Your total payments will be $27,750 (the principal of $25,000 plus $2,750 of interest), so your monthly payment is $2,312.50. What APY are you paying on the loan?

B25. (Excel: Loan interest rate) Schoene Lighting Company is borrowing $2 million. The loan will be repaid in equal quarterly installments for the next three years. The interest rate is 9% APR. Schoene incurs $10,000 of loan setup costs at time zero, and must also make an insurance payment of 1.5% of the remaining loan balance at the first of each of the three years.

a. What are Schoene's net cash flows over the life of the loan?

b. What is the APR and the APY on the loan?

B26. (Excel: Float) Reeder Printing has a balance of $100,000 in its checkbook and a $100,000 available balance at its bank. When Reeder makes a deposit, funds are available in one day. When Reeder writes a check, it takes three days for the check to clear and for funds to be removed from the available bank balance. Assume that Reeder makes daily deposits of $20,000 and writes daily checks of $10,000 for the next 10 days. Then, for the following 10 days, Reeder makes daily deposits of $10,000 and writes daily checks of $20,000. Prepare a table showing the daily amounts for: checks written, checks deposited, the book balance, the available balance, disbursement float, collection float, and total float.

B27. (Excel: Cash management) DeFusco Partners uses a Miller-Orr model to manage its cash position. It has established a minimum cash balance of $200,000, a maximum cash balance of $800,000, and a return point of $400,000. The cash balance is currently $400,000. Whenever the daily cash balance reaches or falls outside of the control limits, DeFusco will purchase or sell marketable securities to bring the cash balance to the return point. Given the daily cash flows below (in $1,000s), calculate any needed security purchases or sales and the ending daily balance.

Day	1	2	3	4	5	6	7	8	9	10
Cash flow	−50	−75	−225	300	100	0	−50	−50	−175	50
Day	11	12	13	14	15	16	17	18	19	20
Cash flow	50	450	200	50	−50	−100	−25	−25	−100	−100

LEVEL C (ADVANCED)

C1. (Float) Gravel Shirt Company has daily deposits of $40,000 that take one day to clear, $80,000 that take two days to clear, and $30,000 that take three days to clear.

a. What is the average daily collection float?

b. What is the weighted average collection delay? (Weight the delays by the dollar volume of the deposits.)

c. If Gravel added a part-time evening clerk costing $15,000 per year, it could reduce the average collection delay by 0.30 days. If the opportunity cost of funds is 10% per year, what is the annual profitability of adding this clerk?

C2. (Float) Tarred Shirt Company has daily deposits of $100,000 that take one day to clear, $200,000 that take two days to clear, and $75,000 that take three days to clear.

a. What is the average daily collection float?

b. What is the weighted average collection delay? (Weight the delays by the dollar volume of the deposits.)

c. If Tarred added a part-time evening clerk costing $7,000 per year, it could reduce the average collection delay by 0.75 days. If the opportunity cost of funds is 10% per year, what is the annual profitability of adding this clerk?

C3. (Fees versus compensating balances) First Bank of New Orleans has the schedule of service charges given here. Your monthly usage of the services is also given.

a. What is your total service charge for the month?

b. The bank gives you earnings credits equal to the earnings credit rate times your available balance. If the earnings credit rate is 3.6% (0.3% per month) and your available balance is $300,000, how much in earnings credits did you accumulate during the month?

c. The bank will invoice you for the difference between service charges and earnings credits if the earnings credits are insufficient to cover the service charges. Excess earnings credits are lost. How much do you owe the bank?

d. What available balance is necessary to exactly cover your service charges for the month?

SERVICE	DEPOSITS	CHECKS CLEARED	WIRE TRANSFERS	ACCOUNT MAIN-TENANCE	ACH TRANS-ACTIONS	CON-SULTING
Per item	$0.50	0.15	15.00	25.00	0.05	200.00
Number	400	3000	10	6	1,000	0.5

C4. (Compensating balances and effective loan rates) Tom Sanders is a loan officer with Miami National Bank. The bank typically charges 8% APR on loans with a compensating balance requirement of 10%. In order to be competitive with other banks, Sanders will adjust the loan rate based on a customer's compensating balance level. A customer maintaining a balance greater than 10% will get a lower interest rate, and a customer with a balance lower than 10% will get a higher rate.

a. What is the effective interest rate on the typical loan with a nominal 8% interest rate and a 10% compensating balance?

b. Collins Construction would supply compensating balances of $150,000 and would like to borrow $2,000,000. What nominal interest rate should Sanders charge on the Collins loan in order to realize the same effective interest rate as the "typical" loan in part a?

c. Dussold Distributors would provide compensating balances of $200,00 and would like to borrow $1,000,000. What nominal interest rate should Sanders charge on the Dussold loan in order to realize the same effective interest rate as the "typical" loan in part a?

MINICASE SHORT-TERM FINANCING FOR BREAKFAST

Kellogg Company, the breakfast food people, manufactures its products in 20 countries and distributes them in more than 150 countries. Not too long ago, Kellogg was considering three short-term borrowing alternatives:

1. 90-day commercial paper at a 6.50% discount rate
2. Commercial bank loan with three interest rate alternatives:
   a. prime rate with interest payable quarterly
   b. three-month London Interbank Offer Rate (LIBOR) plus 0.25%
   c. three-month certificate of deposit (CD) rate plus 0.50%
3. Fixed-rate note maturing after two years and paying interest at the rate of 8% APR with interest payable semiannually

At the time, the prime rate was 10% APR, three-month LIBOR was 6% APR, and the three-month CD rate was 6% APR.

QUESTIONS

1. Consider the commercial paper alternative.
   a. What is the true interest cost (APY)?
   b. Kellogg has a policy of maintaining a backup line of credit for its commercial paper. The cost is 0.25% per year. What is the true interest cost of the commercial paper (APY), including the cost of the backup line?
   c. Assume the 90-day commercial paper rate is expected to increase to 6.75% after 90 days, to 7.00% 90 days thereafter, and to 7.50% 90 days thereafter. Borrowing for one year, calculate the APY of the commercial paper alternative, including the cost of the backup line.
2. Consider the commercial bank loan alternatives.
   a. Calculate the APY for each bank loan interest rate alternative. Which one is the cheapest?
   b. Suppose that the bank requires a 10% compensating balance. Calculate the APY for the bank loan, including the cost of the compensating balance.
   c. Suppose the prime rate is not expected to change over the next year, but three-month LIBOR is expected to increase by 0.30% every three months, and the three-month CD rate is expected to increase by 0.20% every three months. Borrowing for one year, calculate the APY for each bank loan alternative.
   d. Which is cheaper, issuing commercial paper or borrowing from the bank? Are there any options that might affect the value of one alternative or the other?
3. Compare the APYs for the fixed-rate note and the floating-rate alternatives. Which alternative is cheapest on this basis? How might interest-rate risk affect Kellogg's choice? Find the average interest cost (APR) for year 2 for the cheapest floating-rate alternative in question 2 that would make Kellogg indifferent to choosing between that alternative and issuing the two-year note. (This is called the *break-even rate.*)

23

Accounts Receivable and Inventory Management

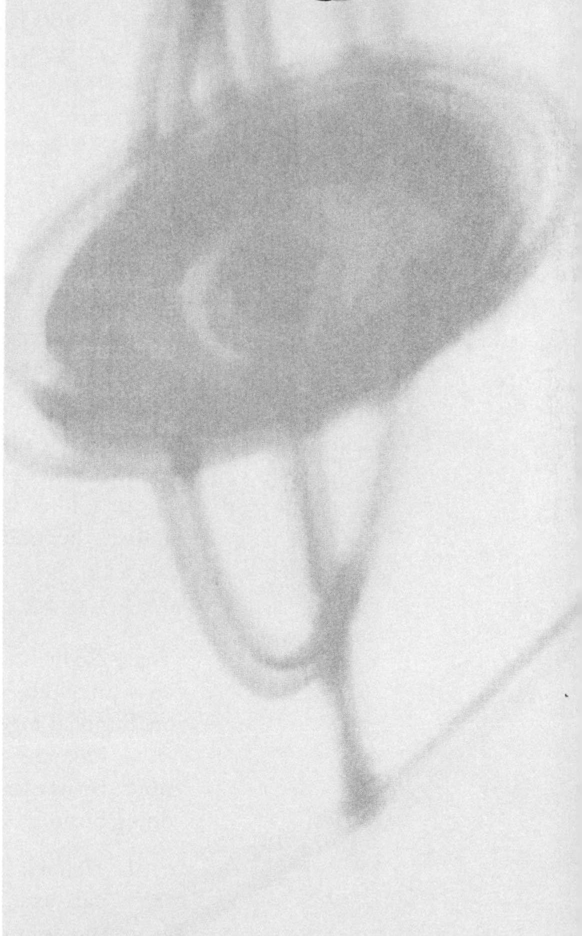

In this chapter, we discuss receivables and inventories, which are integral parts of working capital management. Receivables and inventories are important for several reasons. First, they make up a large investment in assets. Second, they represent a tremendous volume of transactions and decisions. Third, they involve a large proportion of jobs. Finally, receivables and inventories are important because if they are managed poorly, an otherwise healthy firm can be pushed into financial distress.

In practice, managing receivables and inventories often falls to new employees, including those who have just received their business degrees. From this vantage point, new managers apply the principles of finance to day-to-day decisions at the core of the business. Competent use of these resources is essential to the firm's short-term operation and long-term health. Therefore, inventory and receivables managers often work under close supervision. Employees who do well can earn promotion, and those who do poorly can find themselves out of work.

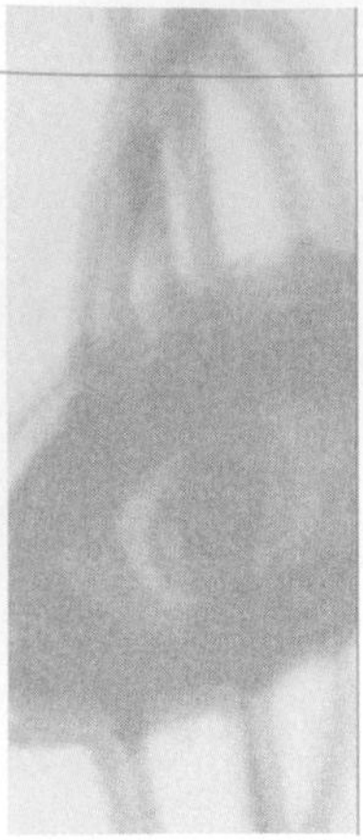

FOCUS ON PRINCIPLES

- *Incremental Benefits:* Calculate the incremental cash flows for receivables and inventory decisions.
- *Time Value of Money:* Compare the NPV of alternative receivables and inventory decisions.
- *Two-Sided Transactions:* Look for situations that are non-zero-sum games; these may be profitable for you *and* your supplier or customer. Receivables and inventory decisions can be used to reduce agency costs and transaction costs.
- *Self-Interested Behavior:* Carefully evaluate and monitor the creditworthiness of your credit customers as well as the quality of goods and services from your suppliers.
- *Comparative Advantage:* Consider subcontracting business activities to outside vendors if they can provide the services more cheaply and competently.
- *Behavioral:* Common industry practices provide a starting place for operating efficiently.

23.1 ACCOUNTS RECEIVABLE MANAGEMENT

Credit sales create accounts receivable. There are two types of credit: trade credit and consumer credit. Between firms, **trade credit** occurs when one firm buys goods or services from another without simultaneous payment. Such sales create an account receivable for the supplier (seller) and an account payable for the buying firm. **Consumer credit,** or retail credit, is created when a firm sells goods or services to a consumer without simultaneous payment.

Most business transactions use trade credit. At the retail level, payment mechanisms include cash, checks, credit extended by the retailer, and credit extended by a third party (such as MasterCard, Visa, or American Express). The use of trade credit and consumer credit is so commonplace that we tend to take it for granted. If you ask why firms grant credit, managers often say they must because competitors do. Although true, this response is simplistic and does not address the fundamental reasons for the extensive use of credit.

Why Is Credit So Pervasive?

Trade credit is effectively a loan from one firm to another. But it is a loan that is tied to a purchase, like the "special-financing" offers we explored in Chapter 4. The product and loan (credit) are bundled together. Why does this bundling occur?

One answer is that bundling controls agency costs that are created by market imperfections. By using trade credit, both sides of the transaction must be able to lower the cost or risk of doing business. Some specific market considerations follow.

1. *Financial intermediation.* Generally, the interest rate of a trade credit loan benefits both partners. It is lower than the customer's alternative borrowing rates but higher than short-term investment rates available to the supplier. A successful transaction makes the supplier a convenient and economical "bank" for the customer and makes the customer a reliable short-term investment for the supplier.
2. *Collateral.* Suppliers know how to handle the goods as collateral better than other lenders such as banks. When collateral is repossessed after a default on payment, the collateral is more valuable in the hands of a supplier, who has expertise in producing, maintaining, and marketing this collateral.
3. *Information costs.* A supplier may already possess the information needed to evaluate customer creditworthiness. A firm accumulates important information about its customers in its normal business relations. This same information may be a sufficient basis on which to

make credit-granting decisions. If a bank wants to lend to this same customer, making the credit-granting decision entails costs. Such costs give a supplier a cost advantage over a bank.

4. *Product quality information.* A supplier generally has better information than the customer about the quality of its products. If a supplier is willing to grant credit to customers who buy its products, this is a positive signal about product quality. Credit can provide a cheaply enforced product quality guarantee. If the product is of acceptable quality, the customer pays the trade credit on time. If the product is of low quality, the customer ships it back and refuses to pay. Of course, a supplier can offer a product quality guarantee, but this can be expensive and time consuming for a customer to enforce if payment has already been made. (For a highly reputable supplier who readily honors all guarantees, the extension of credit adds little as a product quality signal.)
5. *Employee opportunism.* Firms try to protect themselves from employee theft in a variety of ways. One is to separate the employees who authorize transactions, who physically handle products, and who handle the payments. This segregation of duties makes it much more difficult for dishonest employees to steal merchandise or money without being caught. Trade credit helps separate the various functions.
6. *Steps in the distribution process.* If a supplier sells to a customer, but the goods must pass through the hands of shippers (such as rail, truck, sea, or air transporters), then it is simply impractical to have payments exchanged at each step in the distribution process. By granting credit to the ultimate buyer, the payments mechanism bypasses all of the agents in the distribution process, requiring only one payment from the ultimate buyer to the original seller.
7. *Convenience, safety, and buyer psychology.* Sometimes it is inconvenient to pay at the time of purchase. Carrying a lot of cash increases the likelihood of being robbed as well as the possibility of losing or misplacing cash. Convenience and safety are important for both business and retail customers, but psychology is also important, especially at the retail level. Most retailers know that their customers would probably buy less if they had to pay with cash or check instead of with credit. "Plastic money" just does not seem like real money. Credit can be an important part of marketing.

The Basic Credit-Granting Decision

The basic analysis for credit-granting decisions is the same as for other financial decisions. Credit should be granted whenever granting credit is a positive-NPV decision.

$$\text{NPV} = \text{PV of future net cash inflows} - \text{Outlay}$$

For a simple credit-granting decision, the NPV is

$$\text{NPV} = \frac{pR}{(1+r)^t} - C \tag{23.1}$$

At time zero, we invest C in a credit sale. The investment might be the cost of goods sold and sales commissions. The sale amount is R, the probability of payment is p, and the expected payment is pR. The customer's probability of payment is estimated subjectively or with the help of statistical models. The payment is expected at time t. The required return is r. If the NPV is negative, then credit should not be granted. Of course, we would like a positive NPV.

We can also calculate an indifference (zero-NPV) payment probability, p^*. If a credit customer has a payment probability exceeding p^*, then granting credit has a positive NPV. This indifference payment probability is found by setting the NPV in Equation (23.1) equal to zero and solving for p^*:

$$p^* = \frac{C(1+r)^t}{R} \tag{23.2}$$

EXAMPLE Simple Credit-Granting Decision

Boy Scouts of America (BSA) has a customer who wants to purchase $1,000 of goods on credit. BSA estimates that the customer has a 95% probability of paying the $1,000 in three months and a 5% probability of a complete default (paying no cash at all). Assume an investment of 80% of the amount, made at the time of the sale, and a required return of 20% APY. What is the NPV of granting credit, and what is the indifference payment probability?

Using Equation (23.1), the NPV is $107.67:

$$\text{NPV} = \frac{pR}{(1+r)^t} - C = \frac{0.95(1{,}000)}{(1+0.20)^{0.25}} - 800 = 907.67 - 800 = \$107.67$$

Therefore, granting credit is profitable.

Using Equation (23.2), the indifference payment probability is 83.7%:

$$p^* = \frac{C(1+r)^t}{R} = \frac{800(1+0.20)^{0.25}}{1{,}000} = \frac{837.31}{1{,}000} = 83.7\%$$

This result is, of course, consistent with the NPV calculation. BSA's estimate of a 95% payment probability exceeds the indifference value of 83.7% and indicates that BSA should grant credit.

The NPV rule is the best method for evaluating credit-granting decisions. However, calculations can be quite complicated. The investment in the sale may not be made at time zero. In addition, the expected payments may occur at various times rather than at a single point in time. For example, with payment due in 30 days, the customer might have a 60% probability of paying in 30 days, a 30% probability of paying in 60 days, a 5% probability of paying in 90 days, and a 5% probability of never paying. No matter how complicated the situation, however, the NPV rule should be used.

Credit Policy Decisions

Credit policy affects a firm's revenues and costs. For example, consider a policy of granting credit more easily. A more liberal credit policy should increase the cost of goods sold, gross profit, bad debt expenses, the cost of carrying additional receivables, and administrative costs. However, the more liberal policy might or might not increase net profit. A policy's profitability depends on the incremental benefits and incremental costs. The benefits are the additional gross profits generated by the liberal policy. The increased costs are bad debt costs, carrying costs on increased receivables, and administrative costs.

Depending on the industry, credit policy can vary from being crucial to being irrelevant. A retail store may need a competitive policy to survive, whereas an electric utility must simply grant credit according to government regulation. Credit policy decisions involve all aspects of receivables management. They include (1) the choice of credit terms, (2) setting evaluation methods and credit standards, (3) monitoring receivables and taking actions for slow payment, and (4) controlling and administering the firm's credit functions.

Credit Terms

Credit terms are the contract between the supplier and credit customer specifying how the credit will be repaid. In our discussion of accounts payable in Chapter 22, we used the term "2/10, net 30." As the seller, you are now *offering* such credit terms instead of *receiving* them. For the 2/10, net 30 credit terms, you are offering a total **credit period** of 30 days from the date of the invoice, a **discount**

period of 10 days, and a 2% **discount** if paid on or before the discount period expires. The **invoice date** is usually the date the goods are shipped.

Although many alternative sets of credit terms are possible, a few sets of terms tend to be used in a particular industry. These credit terms reflect the industry's specific circumstances, as well as general economic conditions. The following box describes several basic types of commonly used credit terms.

Credit terms also specify the evidence of indebtedness. Most credit sales are made on an **open account** basis, which means that customers simply purchase what they want. The invoice they sign when receiving the shipment provides evidence that they received the goods and have accepted an obligation to pay. Suppliers usually establish a credit limit for each customer. It is the maximum total amount of outstanding invoices that the customer is permitted. If the cumulative bills reach the credit limit, further credit is denied until the customer makes a payment or obtains a higher credit limit. Credit limits are an effective way to limit the amount that can be lost to default.

For large purchases or nonregular customers, a customer may be required to sign a promissory note. Because of time and expense and the low risk of default, promissory notes are not used for routine sales.

Trade Credit Terms

CIA (cash in advance) and CBD (cash before delivery): Payment must be received before the order is shipped.

COD (cash on delivery): The shipper collects the payment (on behalf of the seller) upon delivery.

Cash: Payment is due when the goods are delivered. Unlike COD, cash terms allow the customer to mail a check for payment. Effectively, cash terms allow the customer up to about ten days to pay.

Standard Terms: "net 30" or "net 60" Payment is due in full 30 or 60 days from the date of the invoice.

Discount Terms: "2/10, net 30" Discount terms include a discount percent, discount payment date, and net date. The buyer can take a 2% discount if the payment is made by the 10th day following the invoice date. Otherwise, the full amount is due 30 days following the invoice date.

Prox Terms: "10th prox," "25th prox," "2/10, prox net 30" Prox or proximate refers to the next month. All invoices dated prior to a defined cutoff are to be paid by a date in the next month. Invoices with "10th prox" must be paid by the 10th of the next month and invoices with "25th prox" by the 25th of the next month. "2/10, prox net 30" means that invoices paid by the 10th of the next month receive a 2% discount. If payment is not made by the 10th, then the full amount is due by the 30th.

Seasonal Dating: "2/10, net 30, dating 120," or "2/10, net 30, 60 extra" For seasonal items such as sporting goods, some clothing, or Christmas items, payment is sometimes scheduled to be due near the buyer's selling season. The "dating 120" or the "60 extra" mean that the clock does not start until 120 or 60 days after the invoice date. Although seasonal dating does give buyers a longer time to pay, sellers benefit by encouraging buyers to make earlier purchase decisions. This lowers the seller's inventory costs by reducing the amount of time the goods spend in inventory.

Consignment: The seller ships the goods to the buyer, but the buyer is not required to pay until the goods have been sold or used.

(continued)

Letter of Credit: A letter of credit is an agreement where a financial institution (a bank or other financially strong party) substitutes its creditworthiness for that of the customer. The supplier can require a letter of credit when the payment risk is high. When the terms specified in the letter of credit are met, such as delivery of the goods, the bank will make payment on behalf of the customer. Letters of credit are frequently used in international trade.

Electronic Credit Terms: The seller is paid directly from the buyer's bank account by an automated clearing house (ACH) transaction. Transfer usually occurs right after delivery. Electronic credit terms reduce administrative costs and uncertainties about payment dates. They also reduce supplier accounts receivable and buyer accounts payable.

Review

1. What is trade credit? How is it different from consumer credit? Explain how both arise in the normal course of business transactions.
2. Why is credit so pervasive?
3. What should be the basis for credit-granting decisions?
4. What are the four main aspects of credit policy decisions?

23.2 CREDIT STANDARDS AND CREDIT EVALUATION

Credit standards are the criteria used to grant credit. They depend on the variables that determine the NPV of the sale: investment in the sale, probability of payment, required return, and payment period. A higher probability of default, delayed payments, and the necessity of expensive collection efforts all reduce the NPV.

Table 23.1 gives three pairs of numerical examples showing how each of these variables can cause a sale to be profitable or unprofitable. The first pair shows the effect of a lower probability of payment. The lower probability results in a negative NPV. The second pair shows the effect of delayed payment. The time value of money on a two-month payment delay more than eliminates

TABLE 23.1
Effects of default risk, delayed payments, and collection costs.

SALE	INVESTMENT	PROBABILITY OF PAYMENT	COLLECTION PERIOD	PV OF COLLECTION COSTS	COST OF FUNDS	NPV[a]
Effect of Default Risk						
\$1,000	\$ 850	.99	1 month	0	20%	\$125.07
\$1,000	\$ 850	.85	1 month	0	20%	−\$12.82
Effect of Delayed Payment						
\$2,000	\$1,925	.99	1 month	0	20%	\$25.14
\$2,000	\$1,925	.99	3 months	0	20%	−\$33.22
Effect of Collection Costs						
\$ 100	\$ 80	.95	1 month	\$ 5	20%	\$8.57
\$ 100	\$ 80	.95	1 month	\$20	20%	−\$6.43

[a]For example, $0.99(1{,}000)/(1.20)^{(1/12)} - 850 = \$125.07$.

the profit. The final pair emphasizes the role of collection costs. The present value of the collection costs is an added cost of the sale. Higher collection costs reduce the NPV and can even cause it to be negative. Collection costs have a fixed component, costs that are independent of the amount of the credit sale. These fixed administrative or collection costs often make small credit sales unprofitable.

Unfortunately, these individual factors that reduce the profitability of a credit sale often reinforce one another. For example, a customer who is likely to make late payments is also more likely to default and to require extra collection efforts. The management of credit policy includes establishing credit standards and then evaluating individual customers against these standards. To do this, managers must know how to analyze creditworthiness.

Sources of Credit Information

There are several valuable internal and external sources of information. The primary *internal sources* are:

1. A credit application, including references
2. The applicant's previous payment history, if credit has previously been extended
3. Information from sales representatives and other employees

Several important *external sources* of credit information include:

1. Financial statements for recent years. These financial statements can be analyzed to get insights into the customer's profitability, debt obligations, and liquidity.
2. Reports from credit rating agencies, such as Dun & Bradstreet Business Credit Services (D&B). These agencies supply credit appraisals of thousands of firms and estimates of their overall strength. D&B appraises the credit of a firm relative to that of other firms and assigns composite credit appraisal ratings between 1 ("high") and 4 ("limited").
3. Credit bureau reports. These reports provide factual information about whether a firm's financial obligations are overdue. Credit bureau reports also give information about any legal judgments against the firm.
4. Industry association credit files. Industry associations sometimes maintain credit files. Industry associations and your direct competitors are frequently willing to share credit information about customers.

Two basic approaches to evaluating a credit application are the *judgmental* approach and the *objective* approach. The judgmental approach uses a variety of credit information, as well as specific knowledge and experience, to reach a decision. The objective approach uses numerical cutoffs or scores that must be reached for credit to be granted. The "five C's of credit" are used with the judgmental approach. Credit scoring is an example of an objective approach.

Five C's of Credit

The **five C's of credit** are five general factors that credit analysts often consider when making a credit-granting decision.

1. *Character.* The commitment to meet credit obligations. Character is best measured by a credit applicant's prior payment history.
2. *Capacity.* The ability to meet credit obligations with current income. Capacity is evaluated by looking at the income or cash flows on the applicant's income statement or statement of cash flows.
3. *Capital.* The ability to meet credit obligations from existing assets if necessary. Capital is evaluated by looking at the applicant's net worth.

4. *Collateral.* The collateral that can be repossessed in the case of nonpayment. Collateral value depends on the cost of repossessing and on the possible resale value.
5. *Conditions.* General or industry economic conditions. Conditions external to the customer's business affect the credit-granting decision. For example, improving or deteriorating general economic conditions can change interest rates or the risk of granting credit. Likewise, conditions in a particular industry can affect the profitability of granting credit to a firm in that industry.

Credit-Scoring Models

Assessing a firm's ability to pay its debts is a complex judgment, because many factors affect creditworthiness. One tool many firms use is credit scoring. **Credit scoring** combines several financial variables into a single score, or index, that measures creditworthiness. The score is often a linear combination of several specific variables. An example of a score based on four financial variables could be

$$S = w_1X_1 + w_2X_2 + w_3X_3 + w_4X_4 = 2X_1 - 0.3X_2 + 0.1X_3 + 0.6X_4$$

where

X_1 = net working capital/sales (expressed as a percent) X_2 = debt/assets (%)
X_3 = assets/sales (%) X_4 = net profit margin (%)

The w's are the coefficients (or weights) that are multiplied by the X's (financial characteristics) to create the overall credit score. The positive coefficients for X_1, X_3, and X_4 mean that a higher value results in a higher credit score. The negative coefficient for X_2 means that a higher debt/assets ratio reduces the credit score.

EXAMPLE Calculating Credit Scores for a Business Customer

Using the credit-scoring equation just given, what are the credit scores for two customers with the following characteristics?

	CUSTOMER 1	CUSTOMER 2
X_1 = net working capital/sales (%)	15%	8%
X_2 = debt/assets (%)	40	55
X_3 = assets/sales (%)	105	110
X_4 = net profit margin (%)	12	9

Customer 1's credit score is 35.7.

$$S = 2.0(15) - 0.3(40) + 0.1(105) + 0.6(12) = 30 - 12 + 10.5 + 7.2 = 35.7$$

Customer 2's credit score is 15.9.

$$S = 2.0(8) - 0.3(55) + 0.1(110) + 0.6(9) = 16 - 16.5 + 11 + 5.4 = 15.9$$

If the firm expects a zero NPV for customers with a score of 25, customer 1 should get credit, but customer 2 should be denied credit.

Credit-scoring models are constructed by using sophisticated statistical methods to analyze the payment records of many past customers. Such models offer several advantages.

1. They enable the creditor to accept the clearly good customers and reject the clearly bad customers very quickly. The creditor can devote costly evaluation talent to analyzing the "close calls."
2. They allow different loan processors to apply consistent standards across all credit applicants. They also make changing the standard easy. For example, the firm could change the cutoff from 25 to 28, and this change would then apply equally to all loan applicants.
3. They are "objective" and can help the firm avoid bias or discrimination.

There are important disadvantages of credit-scoring models, too.

1. The models are only as good as the payment records used to construct the models. Many samples do not have a rich enough set of bad loans to build an effective scoring model. In addition, the models have to be updated occasionally. When the model is updated with a new sample, there is some "inbreeding" whereby the new model is built on data that eliminated many bad customers.
2. Credit-scoring models work best when applied to large populations of loan applicants. Consumer loan databases often include many thousands of loans, and credit-scoring models can be built readily. Unfortunately, the number of business loans in a database is often too small to be statistically reliable. Consequently, credit-scoring models are more often used for evaluating consumer loans than for evaluating business loans, which usually rely on judgmental methods.

Credit scoring is frequently used on consumer credit card applications and for personal loans and car loans. For a credit card application, the following scoring sheet (sometimes called a weighted application blank) is often used.

Telephone	Yes = 4 points, No = 0 points
Income	Above $40,000 = 3 points
	$20,000 to $40,000 = 2 points
	Below $20,000 = 0 points
Employment	More than three years with current employer = 3 points
	One to three years with current employer = 2 points
	Less than one year with current employer = 1 point
	Self-employed = 1 point
	Unemployed = 0 points
Residence	Own = 3 points
	Rent = 1 point
	More than three years at current address = 2 points
	One to three years at current address = 1 point
	Zero to one year at current address = 0 points
Credit report	Good = 10 points
	Fair = 4 points
	Bad = −5 points
	None = 0 points

EXAMPLE Consumer Credit-Scoring Model

Suppose Marcelle Welch is applying for a credit card. After graduating with her business degree, Marcelle has a new job earning $45,000 per year. She has just moved to her new job and has rented an apartment. Her telephone is connected, and she has a good credit report. What is her credit score using the credit-scoring system?

Telephone	4 points
Income	3
Employment	1
Residence	1
Credit report	10
Total score	19 points

If the cutoff is 15, Marcelle qualifies for the credit card.

Review

1. What are the main sources of credit information? Which are internal and which are external sources?
2. What are the five C's of credit? Explain how credit analysts use them to decide whether to grant credit.
3. Explain how a firm can use a credit-scoring model to decide whether to grant credit. How is such a model constructed?
4. What are the main advantages and disadvantages of using credit-scoring models to evaluate customer creditworthiness?

23.3 MONITORING ACCOUNTS RECEIVABLE

Monitoring accounts receivable is critical because of the size of the investment. If the quality is surprisingly high or low, several relevant questions arise: Are the firm's credit standards too low or too high? Has a change in general economic conditions affected customer creditworthiness? Is something fundamentally wrong with the evaluation system?

In any case, a reliable, early warning about deterioration of receivables can make it possible to take action. Conversely, a reliable, early indication of improvement in the quality of receivables might inspire the firm to be more liberal in its receivables policies.

Widely used techniques to monitor the quality of receivables include aging schedules, the average age of receivables, collection fractions, and receivables balance fractions. Let us take a look at each in turn.

Aging Schedules

An **aging schedule** is a table showing the total dollar amounts and the percentages of total accounts receivable that fall into several age classifications. It provides a picture of the quality of outstanding accounts receivable. Such schedules usually show those receivables that are 0 to 30 days old, 30 to 60 days old, 60 to 90 days old, and over 90 days old.

The following example shows how an aging schedule is prepared. All of the firm's outstanding invoices are collected and sorted according to their ages. These are then summarized on the aging schedule.

EXAMPLE Building an Aging Schedule for the Provo Palace

On September 30, the Provo Palace prepares a list of all of its outstanding invoices from its database system and sorts them by their original dates. The invoices for each month up to the current date are collected together and totaled, as shown in Table 23.2. As you can see, the September invoices, which are 0 to 30 days old, are substantially more than the previous months because most of the older invoices have already been collected.

TABLE 23.2
Aging schedule for Provo Palace.

OUTSTANDING INVOICES, SEPTEMBER 30

Invoice Number	Invoice Date	Invoice Amount		
1041	7/7	$ 1,200		
1049	7/13	1,000	$ 3,400	Total for July
1060	7/27	800		
1061	7/27	400		
1063	8/5	1,500		
1066	8/12	1,000		
1067	8/12	500		
1072	8/15	800	$ 8,300	Total for August
1073	8/16	1,200		
1080	8/23	1,200		
1083	8/25	1,500		
1084	8/26	600		
1087	9/2	1,000		
1089	9/5	1,400		
1090	9/5	500		
1092	9/7	1,000		
1093	9/10	1,200		
1094	9/14	700		
1095	9/15	400	$11,800	Total for September
1096	9/18	900		
1097	9/20	1,000		
1098	9/22	800		
1099	9/25	1,000		
1100	9/25	500		
1101	9/28	1,400		
Total		$23,500	$23,500	

AGING SCHEDULE, SEPTEMBER 30

AGE	AMOUNT	PERCENT
0–30 days	$11,800	50.2%
30–60 days	8,300	35.3
60–90 days	3,400	14.5
over 90 days	0	0
Total	$23,500	100.0%

Amounts are usually shown in both dollars and percentages. The percentage breakdown can be readily compared to previous aging schedule breakdowns to see if the current situation is different from past experience.

The aging schedule depends on the credit terms offered, customer payment habits, and trends in recent sales. For example, if a firm changes its credit terms, such as giving customers a longer credit period, the aging schedule will reflect this change. If customers are paying more quickly, the percentages in the youngest categories will increase and the percentages in the older categories will decrease. Likewise, a change in the firm's sales can affect the aging schedule. If sales increase during the current month, the percentage of 0 to 30 days receivables will increase. Conversely, a sales decrease tends to reduce the percentage of 0 to 30 days receivables.

Average Age of Accounts Receivable

In addition to an aging schedule, managers commonly compute an **average age of accounts receivable,** the average age of all of the firm's outstanding invoices. There are two common ways to make the computation. The first is to calculate the weighted average age of all individual outstanding invoices. The weights used are the percentages that the individual invoices represent out of the total amount of accounts receivable.

A simplified way to calculate the average age of accounts receivable is to use the aging schedule. Here, all receivables that are 0 to 30 days old are assumed to be 15 days old (the midpoint of 0 and 30), all receivables that are 30 to 60 days old are assumed to be 45 days old, and all receivables that are 60 to 90 days old are assumed to be 75 days old. Then the average age is computed by taking a weighted average of 15, 45, and 75. The weights are the percentages of receivables that are 0 to 30, 30 to 60, and 60 to 90 days old.

EXAMPLE Average Age of Accounts Receivable for Provo Palace

What is the average age of accounts receivable for Provo Palace?

Using the aging schedule in Table 23.2, and the midpoint for each category (for example, 15 for the 0 to 30 day category), we estimate that the weighted average is 34.29 days:

$$\text{Average age} = 0.502(15) + 0.353(45) + 0.145(75) = 7.53 + 15.885 + 10.875 = 34.29 \text{ days}$$

The same factors that affect an aging schedule will affect an average age. Changes in credit terms, payment habits, or sales levels can increase or decrease the average age.

Collection Fractions and Receivables Balance Fractions

Two other measures used to monitor the quality of receivables are collection fractions and receivables balance fractions. **Collection fractions** are the percentages of sales collected during various months. For example, the collection fractions show the percentage of June's sales that are collected in June, as well as the percentage collected in each month thereafter (July, August, and September). After a month's billings have all been collected, the collection fractions sum to 100%. The pattern of the collection fractions is compared to an expected or budgeted collection pattern to see whether collections are faster or slower than expected.

Receivables balance fractions are the percentages of a month's sales that remain uncollected (and part of accounts receivable) at the end of the month of sale and at the end of succeeding months. For example, receivables balance fractions would include the percentage of June's sales that remain outstanding at the end of June and in the months of July, August, and September. The key point to notice about collection fractions and receivables balance fractions (compared to aging schedules) is that collections and receivables outstanding are always expressed as a *percent of original sales.*

If sales go up or down after the given month, collections and receivables are always compared to their original month of sale instead of to later sales figures. Data from each month's sales are always treated separately. June's collection fractions and balance fractions are never mixed in with those of another month. Hence, collection fractions and receivables balance fractions are more reliable measures of quality than aging schedules, particularly when sales are increasing or decreasing. The following example illustrates how to use collection fractions and balance fractions to monitor the quality of receivables.

EXAMPLE Micro Systems's Collection Fractions and Receivables Balance Fractions

Micro Systems, Inc., expects its collection fractions and receivables balance fractions to be:

	COLLECTION FRACTION	BALANCE FRACTION
Original month	0.10	0.90
month t + 1	0.50	0.40
month t + 2	0.35	0.05
month t + 3	0.05	0.00

These expected fractions are based on the firm's credit terms and on its best estimate of what the payment habits of its customers should be. Note that the expected collection fractions sum to 1.00, but the balance fractions do not. The balance fraction declines from its previous value by the amount collected during the month.

Table 23.3 is a schedule showing monthly sales and the pattern of collections over several months tied back to the original month's sales. What are the collection fractions, receivables balance fractions, and dollar amounts of receivables outstanding that go with these data? How would you assess the behavior of collections and receivables compared to the expected fractions?

Panel A of Table 23.3 shows how each month's sales are subsequently collected. For example, December's $1,200 of sales were collected as follows: $110 in December, $550 in January, $420 in February, and $120 in March. Panel B shows the collection fractions that correspond to panel A. For example, December's sales collection fraction for December is 110/1,200 = 0.092. For January it is 550/1,200 = 0.458, for February 420/1,200 = 0.350, and for March 120/1,200 = 0.100.

Panel C shows this information in terms of receivables yet to be paid, the total and by age. For example, December's total accounts receivable of $1,570 is made up of remaining receivables of $1,090 from December sales, $420 from November sales, and $60 from October sales. The progression through panel C follows the diagonal, by subtracting the collections (panel A) according to the formula

Receivables from one month previous
−Collections from two months previous
Receivables from two months previous

For example, receivables in December from the previous month (420, in panel C) minus collections in January from two months previous (350, in panel A) equals receivables in January from two months previous (420 − 350 = 70, in panel C).

Panel D presents this information in terms of receivables balance fractions. The receivables balance fraction is the value in panel C divided by the original month's sales. For example, the receivables balance fractions in January are for the current month, one month previous, and two months previous: 0.910 (= 1,365/1,500), 0.450 (= 540/1,200), and 0.070 (= 70/1,000).

The collection fractions and receivables balance fractions are evaluated by comparing them to their expected sizes. In November, the collection fractions in panel B are exactly equal to the expected levels. Likewise, in November, the receivables balance fractions in panel D are equal to their expected levels. However, the quality of receivables then deteriorates. You can see that by the end of March, the collection fractions for the current month and the previous month are below expectations, and the collection fractions for late collections (from sales three months previous) are higher. It is taking longer to collect.

This collection slowdown also shows up in the receivables balance fractions for March in panel D. Because of delayed collections, the receivables balance fractions are higher than expected. Micro Systems may have a receivables problem. If its credit terms were not changed, it could be that the firm is granting credit to less creditworthy customers or is managing collections poorly.

TABLE 23.3
Collection fractions and receivables balance fractions.

MONTH SALES	**AUG 1,000**	**SEPT 1,000**	**OCT 1,000**	**NOV 1,000**	**DEC 1,200**	**JAN 1,500**	**FEB 1,800**	**MAR 2,000**
Panel A								
Collections from:								
Current month	100	100	100	100	110	135	160	175
Previous month		500	500	500	480	550	680	800
Two months previous			350	350	340	350	420	525
Three months previous				50	50	60	70	120
Total collections				1,000	980	1,095	1,330	1,620
								Collections of December sales
Panel B								
Collection fractions from:								
Current month	0.100	0.100	0.100	0.100	0.092	0.090	0.089	0.088
Previous month		0.500	0.500	0.500	0.480	+ 0.458	0.453	0.444
Two months previous			0.350	0.350	0.340	0.350	+ 0.350	0.350
Three months previous				0.050	0.050	0.060	0.070	+ 0.100 = 1.00
				Collections fractions for the month				Fractions of December sales collected
Panel C								
Accounts receivable from:								
Current month	900	900	900	900	1,090	1,365	1,640	1,825
Previous month		400	400	400	420	540	685	840
Two months previous			50	50	60	70	120	160
Three months previous				0	0	0	0	0
Total accounts receivable				1,350	1,570	1,975	2,445	2,825
Panel D								
Receivables balance fractions from:								
Current month	0.900	0.900	0.900	0.900	0.908	0.910	0.911	0.9125
Previous month		0.400	0.400	0.400	0.420	0.450	0.457	0.467
Two months previous			0.050	0.050	0.060	0.070	0.100	0.107
Three months previous				0.000	0.000	0.000	0.000	0.000
				Receivables balance fractions for the month				

Pursuing Delinquent Credit Customers

Your best credit customers pay their bills promptly and are very easy to deal with. A few credit customers will prove to be complete deadbeats, and it will be difficult to recover anything from them no matter how hard you try. Other customers fall in between these two extremes, and dealing successfully with these marginal credit customers can be a key to profitability.

Businesses follow a number of specific steps in the collection process, depending on how long overdue the account is, the size of the debt, and other factors. A typical collection process can include these steps.

1. *Letters.* When an account is overdue by a few days, a "friendly reminder" may be sent. If payment is not received, one or two more letters might be sent, with the tone of the letters becoming more severe and demanding.
2. *Telephone calls.* After the first couple of letters, the customer is phoned. If the customer is having financial troubles, a compromise might be worked out. A partial payment is better than no payment.
3. *Personal visits.* The salesperson who made the sale can visit the customer to request payment. Other special collectors besides the salesperson can be used.
4. *Collection agencies.* The account is turned over to a collection agency that specializes in collecting past due accounts. Collection agencies usually collect a fee, such as one half of whatever is recovered, and they recover only a fraction of the accounts they go after. So a firm's loss can be a very large portion of the accounts turned over.
5. *Legal proceedings.* If the bill is large enough, legal action may be used to obtain a judgment against the debtor.

The collection process can be viewed as a capital budgeting process wherein the firm wants to use the collection procedures that generate the highest NPV. When collection is viewed this way, there are a few important principles to follow. The sequence of collection efforts begins with the least expensive and proceeds to increasingly more expensive techniques only after earlier methods have failed. Letters may cost the firm only $0.50, whereas telephone calls may average $5.00, and personal visits may cost $20 to $100. Controlling the size of the investment in the collection effort can improve the NPV.

The early collection contacts are more upbeat and friendly, and the later contacts are not the least bit friendly. This is because many marginal customers will pay if asked and because future sales to these customers might be profitable. Once it becomes clear that there is limited potential for future profitable sales, collection efforts become much more aggressive.

Collection decisions follow capital budgeting principles. Sunk costs, which can be the uncollected investments made in goods sold, are eventually ignored. The collection sequence should be the one that results in the maximum NPV. Once the expected cash flow from continuing the collection effort is less than the additional cost of continuing, the correct decision is to stop pursuing the customer.

Changing Credit Policy

Credit policy can be changed by altering terms, standards, or collection practices. A change in credit policy can affect sales. It can also affect the cost of goods sold, bad debt expenses, carrying costs on accounts receivable, and other administrative costs. We can calculate the NPV of a credit policy change.

EXAMPLE The NPV of Changing Credit Policy

A firm currently uses credit terms of net 30. It is considering a switch to 2/10, net 30. The expected effects of this more liberal policy are:

	CURRENT POLICY	PROPOSED POLICY
Credit terms	net 30	2/10, net 30
Annual sales	$1,000,000	$1,050,000
Cost of sales (at time 0)	$600,000	$630,000
Bad debt losses	1.5% of sales	1.0% of sales
	0.015(1,000,000) = $15,000	0.01(1,050,000) = $10,500

(continued)

	CURRENT POLICY	PROPOSED POLICY
Collection pattern	1.5 months (98.5% pay here on average) (1.5% never pay)	0.5 months (70%) 1.5 months (29%) (1% never pay)
Required return	1% per month	1% per month
Sales less bad debt	\$985,000	\$1,039,500
Discounts taken	\$0	0.02(0.70)(1,050,000) = \$14,700
Sales less bad debt and discounts	\$985,000	\$1,024,800

The expected cash flows for the current policy are:

–600,000	985,000	
0	1.5 months	time

The current policy requires \$600,000 at time zero and has an expected inflow of \$985,000 (the sales of \$1,000,000 less 1.5% bad debt) in 1.5 months. At a required return of 1% per month, the NPV of one year's sales under the current policy is

$$\text{NPV(current policy)} = \frac{0.985(1{,}000{,}000)}{(1+0.01)^{1.5}} - 600{,}000 = 970{,}408 - 600{,}000 = \$370{,}408$$

The expected cash flows for the proposed policy are:

–630,000	720,300	304,5000	
0	0.5 months	1.5 months	time

The proposed policy results in a 5% increase in sales and cost of goods sold, an outlay of \$630,000 at time 0. Seventy percent of the customers pay early and take the 2% discount, resulting in a cash flow of .70(.98)(1,050,000) = \$720,300 at time 0.5 months. The balance of the paying customers, 29% of sales, pay in 1.5 months. These customers pay .29(1,050,000) = \$304,500. So the NPV of one year's sales for the proposed policy is:

$$\text{NPV(proposed policy)} = \frac{0.70(.98)(1,050,000)}{(1.01)^{0.5}} + \frac{0.29(1,050,000)}{(1.01)^{1.5}} - 630,000$$
$$= 716,725 + 299,989 - 630,000 = \$386,714$$

Because the proposed policy has the greater NPV (\$386,714 versus \$370,408), the firm would be better off with the proposed change in credit policy.

Most firms in an industry use similar credit policies. Competitive pressures, as well as similar contracting cost structures, tend to cause credit policies to be strikingly similar. Therefore, the Behavioral Principle can be useful. When you are considering your own credit policy, a good starting point is the credit policies of other firms in the industry. Then, on the basis of your own strategic directions or changing economic conditions, you should consider credit policies that might be better for your firm.

Review

1. How do firms monitor the quality of their receivables?
2. What does an aging schedule show? How is one prepared?
3. Explain how a firm can use collection fractions and receivables balance fractions to monitor its accounts receivable. Are they more useful as measures of quality than aging schedules?
4. Describe the five steps that are usually part of the collection process.
5. How can information about your main competitors' current credit policies be useful to your firm in setting its credit policy?

23.4 INVENTORY MANAGEMENT

Inventories play a crucial role in a firm's purchasing-production-marketing process. Some inventories are a physical necessity for the firm. For example, partly built cars must be on the assembly line. Oil in transit must fill up oil pipelines. Other inventories are buffer stocks that are necessary at several points in the purchasing-production-marketing process. If the food is not in the grocery store when customers want it, the store cannot sell it. Likewise, if needed parts are delayed or out of stock, an assembly line can be shut down. Some goods, such as grain or coal, are shipped in such large quantities that it can take a year or more to use up one shipment.

Manufacturing firms generally carry three types of inventories: raw materials, work in process, and finished goods. The size of a firm's raw materials inventories depends on factors such as the anticipated level of production, production seasonality, and supply reliability. The size of the firm's work-in-process inventories depends mainly on the overall length of each production cycle and the number of distinct stages in the cycle. Finally, the size of the firm's finished goods inventories depends primarily on the rate of sales (units of product per unit of time), cost of carrying the inventory, cost of ordering replacement stocks, and cost of running out of an item (lost sales cost). In general, larger inventories give the firm greater sales and operating flexibility, but they also cost more.

The Economic Order Quantity (EOQ) Model

A simple and useful inventory management model is the economic order quantity (EOQ) model. This model is derived in the following manner. Suppose that units are removed from inventory at a constant rate S (the rate at which goods are sold, in the case of finished goods inventories). Assume that there is a fixed reordering cost, F, per order regardless of the number of units reordered, and that it costs C to carry a unit in inventory for an entire period. Note that the EOQ model assumes *constant* inventory usage or sales, and *instantaneous* inventory replenishment.

Under these assumptions, the inventory level behaves as shown in Figure 23.1.[1] The inventory begins at Q units and is reduced at a constant rate until it reaches zero. At that point, the inventory is instantaneously replenished with another Q units, and the process starts over. Over the year, the inventory fluctuates between Q and zero, and the number of sawteeth in the figure is the number of orders per year.

[1] If Figure 23.1 looks familiar, that is probably because it is essentially identical to Figure 22.3, the Baumol cash management model. The two models have equivalent structures.

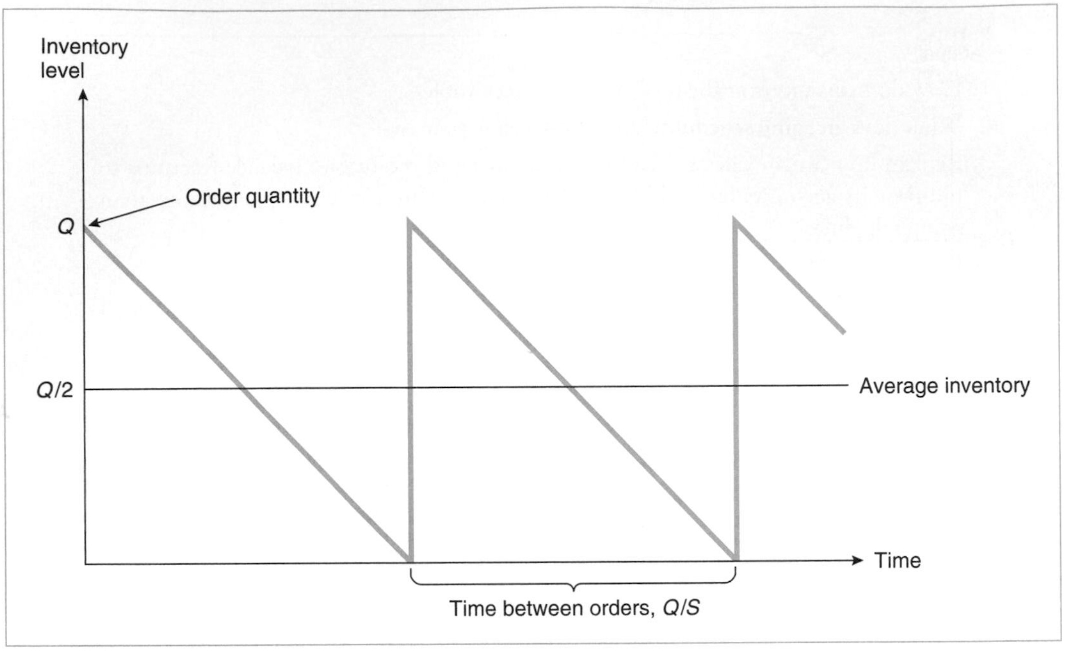

FIGURE 23.1
Inventory levels for the EOQ model.

The total annual cost is made up of two components, ordering cost and carrying cost. The ordering cost is the cost per order, F, times the number of orders per year. The number of orders per year is the annual usage (in units) divided by the order size, S/Q, so the annual ordering cost is $F(S/Q)$.

The annual carrying cost is the carrying cost per unit, C, times the average inventory, which is $Q/2$. Thus, the annual carrying cost is $C(Q/2)$.

The annual total cost is the sum of these two components:

$$\text{Total cost} = \text{Ordering cost} + \text{Carrying cost} = F\frac{S}{Q} + C\frac{Q}{2} \tag{23.3}$$

Figure 23.2 shows ordering cost and carrying cost as a function of Q, the order size, which is the decision variable. Note that an increase in Q increases the carrying cost but decreases the ordering cost. Total cost can be minimized by finding the order quantity that balances the two component costs. That order quantity is the **economic order quantity (EOQ),** as shown in Figure 23.2. The formula for EOQ is[2]

$$\text{EOQ} = \sqrt{\frac{2FS}{C}} \tag{23.4}$$

EXAMPLE Officemax's EOQ

Suppose Officemax sells personal copying machines at the rate of 1,800 units per year. The cost of placing one order is \$400, and it costs \$100 per year to carry a copier in inventory. What is Officemax's EOQ? Using the EOQ, find the average inventory, number of orders

[2]The form of the EOQ model is identical to the one for C^*, the optimal deposit size in the Baumol cash management model. So we will make your day and skip the mathematical derivation.

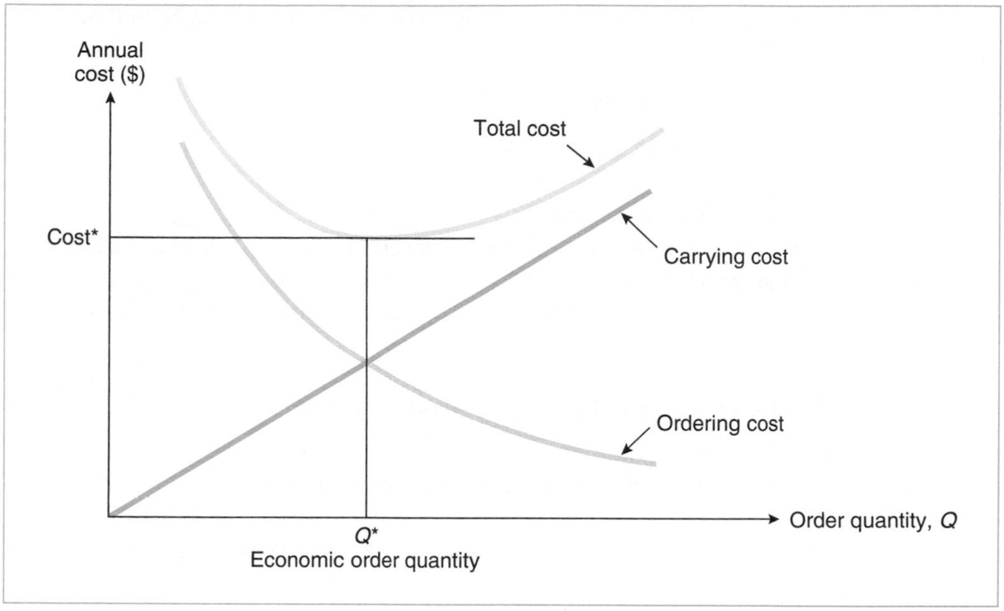

FIGURE 23.2
Annual costs for the EOQ model.

per year, time interval between orders, annual ordering cost, annual carrying cost, and annual total cost.

Using Equation (23.4), the EOQ is 120 copiers:

$$\text{EOQ} = \sqrt{\frac{2FS}{C}} = \sqrt{\frac{2(400)(1,800)}{100}} = \sqrt{14,400} = 120 \text{ copiers}$$

Average inventory = EOQ/2 = 120/2 = 60 copiers

Number of orders per year = S/EOQ = 1,800/120 = 15 times per year

Time interval between orders = EOQ/S = 120/1,800
= 0.0667 years ([0.0667]365 = 24.3 days)

Annual ordering cost = F(S/EOQ)= 400(1,800/120) = 400(15) = \$6,000

Annual carrying cost = C(EOQ/2) = 100(120/2) = 100(60) = \$6,000

Using Equation (23.3), Officemax's total annual cost is \$12,000.

$$\text{Total cost} = 400\frac{1,800}{120} + 100\frac{120}{2} = 6,000 + 6,000 = \$12,000$$

Note that the carrying cost and ordering cost are equal (\$6,000); this always holds for the EOQ.

Quantity Discounts

Many suppliers offer a quantity discount to encourage larger orders. For example, a supplier might offer a price discount for ordering 10,000 or more units. If your EOQ is currently more than the discount quantity, you get the discount without doing anything.

If your EOQ is less than the discount quantity, you have to increase your order size to get the discount. The trade-off is between higher inventory costs and a lower price for purchases. If the discounts exceed the cost of the extra inventory, then you should increase the order size to get the discounts. To analyze this decision, we can adjust the total cost function by adding in the price discounts:

$$\text{Total cost} = \text{Ordering cost} + \text{Carrying cost} - \text{Price discounts}$$

$$= F\frac{S}{Q} + C\frac{Q}{2} - dS \quad (23.5)$$

where *d* is the dollar price discount per unit.

The best order size is the one that provides the lowest total cost: either the result of using Equation (23.4) to find the EOQ without price discounts or the result of using Equation (23.5), which calculates the total cost outcome of ordering the larger quantity and getting the price discounts.

EXAMPLE The EOQ and Quantity Discounts at Officemax

Continuing our Officemax example, where the EOQ was 120, let us say the dealer offered a quantity discount of $3 per unit for orders of 200 or more. Should Officemax order 200 each time to get the discount?

Officemax must compare the total cost of ordering the larger quantity to get the discount with the total costs of ordering the EOQ. We calculated the total cost using the EOQ to be $12,000. Using Equation (23.5), the total cost of ordering 200 units each time is $8,200:

$$\text{Total cost} = 400\frac{1{,}800}{200} + 100\frac{200}{2} - 3.00(1{,}800) = 3{,}600 + 10{,}000 - 5{,}400 = \$8{,}200$$

The order size of 200 increases the inventory costs from $12,000 per year (with the EOQ) to $13,600 (= 3,600 + 10,000). The firm receives discounts of $3.00 per unit on *the entire year's purchases* (1,800 units). The total discounts received ($5,400) are more than the $1,600 increase in ordering and carrying costs. The total costs decline by $3,800 when the quantity discount is taken. Thus raising the order size to 200 is worth it.

Inventory Management with Uncertainty

The EOQ model makes simplifying assumptions: Future demand is known with certainty, inventory is used at a constant rate, and delivery is instantaneous (or equivalently, the lead time is known with certainty). Each factor, of course, actually has some uncertainty. A firm can protect itself from this uncertainty by maintaining **safety stocks**—that is, a buffer inventory.

Figure 23.3 shows the firm's inventory level over time, with a safety stock and other more realistic assumptions. In the figure, the firm uses inventory down to the reorder point. At the reorder point, the firm orders its EOQ, but there is a lead time until the order arrives. During this lead time, the firm might have a *stockout* if demand is large. A stockout occurs when the firm cannot immediately make a sale because of lack of inventory. Stockouts can create customer ill will and can cause lost sales. To guard against a stockout, the reorder point includes the expected lead-time demand plus a safety stock:

$$\text{Reorder point} = \text{Expected lead-time demand} + \text{Safety stock} \quad (23.6)$$

With uncertainties, annual inventory cost has three components:

$$\text{Annual cost} = \text{Ordering cost} + \text{Carrying cost} + \text{Stockout costs} \quad (23.7)$$

The expected stockout cost is the probability of a stockout times the cost of a stockout. A larger safety stock reduces the expected stockout cost but raises the reorder point. Thus a larger safety stock increases the inventory carrying cost, because the average inventory level is equal to

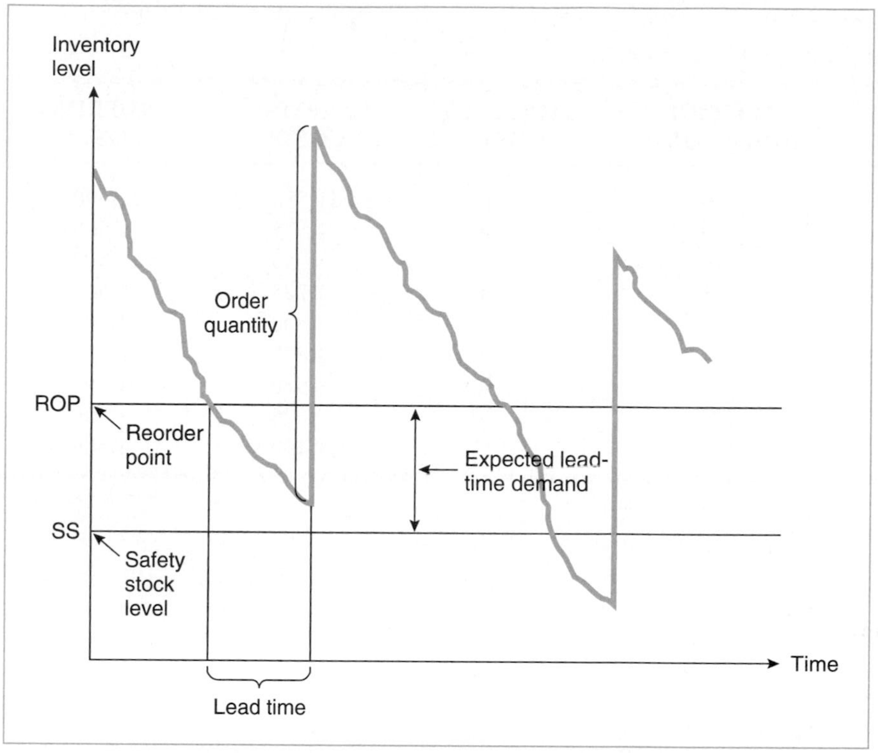

FIGURE 23.3
Inventory levels with uncertain demand and a safety stock.

EOQ/2 *plus* the safety stock. Again, there is a trade-off between costs. But again, the optimal inventory policy provides the lowest total cost.

EXAMPLE Order Quantity and Reorder Point at Oxford Arms

Oxford Arms sells bullet-proof vests through mail orders. Oxford sells 5,000 vests per year, with a fixed cost of \$60 per order, and a carrying cost of \$15 per unit average inventory. Oxford's EOQ is therefore 200 vests:

$$\text{EOQ} = \sqrt{\frac{2FS}{C}} = \sqrt{\frac{2(60)(5{,}000)}{15}} = \sqrt{40{,}000} = 200 \text{ vests}$$

This order quantity implies 25 orders per year (= 5,000/200) and an ordering cost of \$1,500 per year (= [25]60). What are Oxford's optimal safety stock and reorder point?

Oxford's average lead-time demand is 20 vests, so the reorder point will be the safety stock plus 20. The average inventory will be the safety stock plus EOQ/2 = 100. Oxford is considering several safety stock levels ranging from none to 30. Estimates of the expected stockout cost for various sizes of safety stock are given in Table 23.4.

Note in Table 23.4 that the expected stockout cost starts high and declines at a rapid but diminishing rate. Adding the first five units to the safety stock reduces the expected stockout cost by \$500, from \$1,200 to \$700. The annual carrying cost of the five units of safety stock is only \$75 (= [5]15), so the total cost declines by \$425 (= 500 − 75). As long as the expected stockout cost declines faster than the carrying cost increases, increasing the safety stock is beneficial. A safety stock of 20 and a reorder point of 40 provide the lowest total cost. This is the optimal safety stock and reorder point. Above this point, the incremental benefit of lower stockout cost is less than the incremental carrying cost of more inventory.

TABLE 23.4
Finding the reorder point and safety stock.

REORDER POINT[a]	SAFETY STOCK	AVERAGE INVENTORY[b]	STOCKOUT COST[c]	CARRYING COST[d]	ORDERING COST[e]	TOTAL COST[f]
20	0	100	$1,200	$1,500	$1,500	$4,200
25	5	105	700	1,575	1,500	3,775
30	10	110	450	1,650	1,500	3,600
35	15	115	250	1,725	1,500	3,475
40[g]	20[g]	120	150	1,800	1,500	3,450[g]
45	25	125	90	1,875	1,500	3,465
50	30	130	50	1,950	1,500	3,500
55	35	135	30	2,025	1,500	3,555
60	40	140	25	2,100	1,500	3,625

[a]Reorder point = Lead-time demand + Safety stock = 20 + Safety stock.
[b]Average inventory = $Q/2$ + Safety stock = 100 + Safety stock.
[c]Stockout cost is management's estimate for each safety stock level.
[d]Carrying cost = Average inventory times $15.
[e]Ordering cost = $F(S/Q)$ = $60(25) = $1,500.
[f]Total cost = Stockout cost + Carrying cost + Ordering cost.
[g]Indicates the cost-minimizing reorder point and safety stock.

ABC System of Inventory Control

The **ABC system of inventory control** categorizes inventory into one of three groups—A, B, or C—on the basis of critical need. The most important items are A items, and the least important are C items. For example, suppose 10% of inventory items make up 80% of the total inventory value. These might be the A items. The B items might compose 30% of the total *number* of items but only 15% of the total inventory value. The C items would be 60% of the number of items but would make up only 5% of total inventory value. Figure 23.4 shows the relationship between the number of items and their cumulative investment for the ABC inventory system.

Because they are the most critical, the A items are managed very carefully. The B items are managed with less care, and the C items are managed the least carefully. For example, for a car firm, engines, transmissions, and in fact all of the components of the cars under production are A items and are managed very carefully. On the other hand, office supplies, such as paper clips, pencils, and paper, are ordered when needed without much supervision.

Materials Requirement Planning (MRP) Systems

Firms often produce or supply more than one product, and each product may have a large number of components. Typically, this means the firm has multiple suppliers. Coordinating and scheduling can become complex, so firms rely on **materials requirement planning (MRP) systems.** MRP systems are computer-based systems that plan backward from the production schedule to make purchases and manage inventory. These large software systems combine information about the production process and the supply process to determine when the firm should place purchase orders. Done properly, MRP assures that production proceeds smoothly without interruptions due to inventory stockouts.

Just-in-Time (JIT) Inventory Systems

Just-in-time (JIT) inventory systems greatly reduce inventories. The philosophy of a JIT system is that materials should arrive exactly as they are needed in the production process. The system

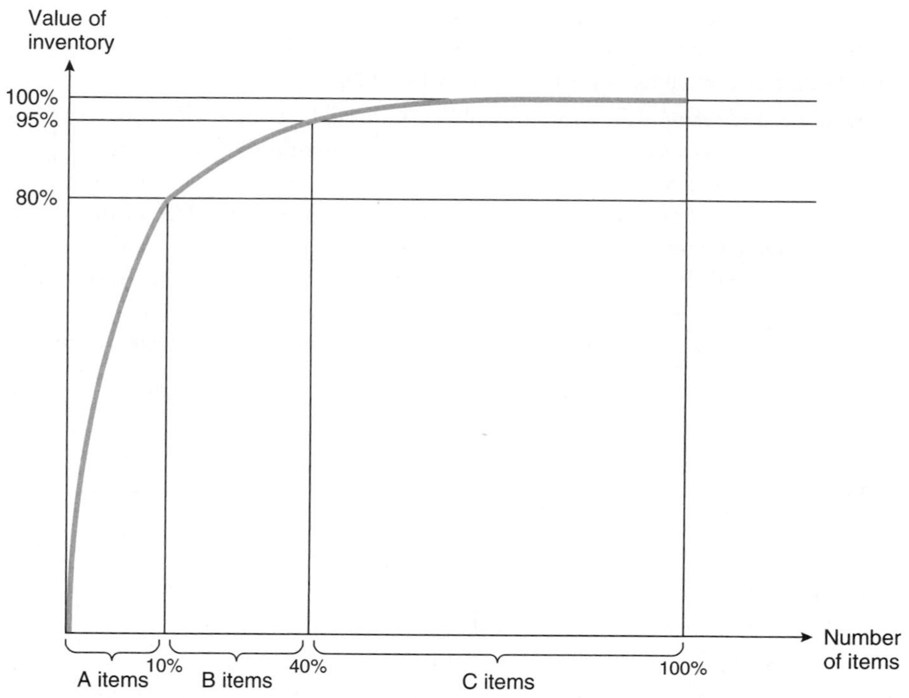

FIGURE 23.4
The ABC system of inventory control.

requires careful planning and scheduling, and extensive cooperation between suppliers and manufacturers is needed throughout the production process. All of this is facilitated by electronic data interchange (EDI), which we discussed in Chapter 22. A JIT system can reduce raw materials inventories, work-in-process inventories, and finished product inventories.

The success of a JIT system depends on several factors:

1. *Planning requirements.* JIT requires a coordinated, integrated plan for the entire firm. Recall that one of the basic functions of inventories is to serve as a buffer stock at various stages of the production process. By careful planning and scheduling, JIT systems practically eliminate these buffer stocks. The integrated operating environment of JIT can produce substantial savings. Of course, if a high degree of coordination and planning is impractical for a business, JIT does not work.
2. *Supplier relations.* The firm must work closely with its suppliers for JIT to be successful. Delivery schedules, quantities, quality, and instantaneous communication are all part of the system. The system requires frequent deliveries of the exact amounts needed and in the order required. Careful marking—often bar coding—is necessary. Therefore, there must be good relations.
3. *Setup costs.* The manufacturing process is redesigned to allow as much flexibility as possible by reducing the length of production runs. In manufacturing, there is often a fixed setup cost each time a production run begins. The optimal size of the production run is affected by the setup cost (much as inventory order costs are affected by the fixed order cost). By reducing these setup costs, the firm can use much smaller production runs and thus achieve more flexibility.
4. *Other cost factors.* Because JIT systems require careful monitoring and control, firms that employ JIT usually limit the number of their suppliers in order to reduce these costs. Many firms can reduce their inventory carrying costs and inventory setup costs by using

a JIT system. However, nothing is free. Suppliers are asked to improve quality, provide more frequent deliveries, sequence and barcode items in the shipments, and other such things. Suppliers' additional handling costs increase the prices they charge. The trade-off has been very profitable, however, for many firms that have adopted JIT.

5. *Impact on credit terms.* JIT systems would be impossible without electronic data interchange (EDI). Because many aspects of the purchasing-production-marketing process are now handled electronically, trade credit is also becoming automated. When electronic credit terms are used, payment is not made, say, 30 days after an invoice date. Rather, payment is made shortly—such as only one day—after delivery and use of materials. This essentially eliminates accounts payable for a firm, which was a major source of short-term financing. On the other hand, collecting electronically eliminates the supplier's accounts receivable. EDI also eliminates the costs and risks associated with paper-based payables and receivables systems.

Review

1. What is the EOQ (economic order quantity)? What cost does it minimize?
2. Explain how the EOQ is related to the rate at which items are removed from inventory, the fixed reordering cost, and the carrying cost.
3. What is safety stock, and what is its purpose?
4. Explain how a just-in-time (JIT) inventory system works. What factors determine how well it works? What is the purpose of such a system?

SUMMARY

- Accounts receivable and inventories are large investments in assets that support the firm's process of buying materials, transforming them into final products, and selling them. These investments, like capital budgeting projects, are measured in terms of their NPV. A firm should avoid negative-NPV decisions and seek out positive-NPV decisions.
- Trade credit is used as a device to reduce agency costs created by market imperfections.
- The NPV of granting credit is the present value of all of the expected cash flows that occur if credit is extended.
- An indifference payment probability can be derived where customers with a payment probability above this critical value are designated profitable (positive-NPV) customers.
- Credit policy includes the choice of (1) credit terms, (2) evaluation methods and credit standards, (3) the process of monitoring the quality of outstanding receivables and pursuing delinquent customers, and (4) administering the credit functions.
- A variety of credit terms have been designed to allow suppliers and customers to carry on mutually profitable associations. See the "Trade Credit Terms" box for several examples.
- The five C's of credit are character, capacity, capital, collateral, and conditions. Subjective credit evaluation methods use the five C's.
- Credit-scoring models create a single credit score for a customer. This score is supposed to be an objective measure of creditworthiness.
- Aging schedules, collection fractions, and receivables balance fractions are used to monitor the quality of outstanding accounts receivable.

- Pursuing delinquent credit customers is a balancing act between the cost of pursuit, the likelihood of maintaining a profitable relationship with a marginal customer, and the amount of cash that can be collected.
- Changing credit policies can be evaluated with the same NPV framework that is used for making basic credit-granting decisions. The optimal policy generates the largest NPV.
- The EOQ (economic order quantity) is the order size that minimizes the total inventory cost.
- When uncertainties in deliveries or demand exist, firms maintain safety stocks. The reorder point is the safety stock level plus the expected lead-time demand that provides the minimum total cost.
- The ABC system of inventory control categorizes inventory into three groups—A, B, and C—on the basis of critical need. The most important items (A items) are managed the most carefully. The relatively less important items (C items) are the least closely managed.
- Computer-based materials requirement planning (MRP) systems plan backward from production schedules to make purchases and plan inventories.
- Just-in-time (JIT) inventory systems schedule arrivals of materials exactly when they are needed. JIT systems can greatly reduce inventories. When electronic data interchange (EDI) is used with JIT, firms often reduce both their payables and receivables.

EQUATION SUMMARY

$$\text{NPV} = \frac{pR}{(1+r)^t} - C \tag{23.1}$$

$$p^* = \frac{C(1+r)^t}{R} \tag{23.2}$$

$$\text{Total cost} = \text{Ordering cost} + \text{Carrying cost} = F\frac{S}{Q} + C\frac{Q}{2} \tag{23.3}$$

$$\text{EOQ} = \sqrt{\frac{2FS}{C}} \tag{23.4}$$

$$\begin{aligned}\text{Total cost} &= \text{Ordering cost} + \text{Carrying cost} - \text{Price discounts}\\ &= F\frac{S}{Q} + C\frac{Q}{2} - dS\end{aligned} \tag{23.5}$$

$$\text{Reorder point} = \text{Expected lead-time demand} + \text{Safety stock} \tag{23.6}$$

$$\text{Annual cost} = \text{Ordering cost} + \text{Carrying cost} + \text{Stockout costs} \tag{23.7}$$

QUESTIONS

1. What is meant by the phrase 1/10, net 40?
2. Trade credit presumably exists because it allows two trading partners to reduce the costs and risks of doing business. Explain how each of the following examples can make trade credit mutually beneficial for a supplier and customer. (a) Suppliers know how to handle collateral

better than other lenders such as banks. (b) Suppliers already possess the information needed to evaluate creditworthiness. (c) The extension of credit is a positive signal about product quality. (d) Trade credit reduces employee opportunism.

3. Cite and discuss five reasons for the extensive use of trade credit.
4. Optical Supply Company offers credit terms of 2/10, net 60. If Optical Supply is considering a change in its credit terms to one of those indicated, explain whether the change should increase or decrease sales. (a) 2/10, net 30, (b) net 60, (c) 3/15, net 60, (d) 2/10, net 30, 30 extra
5. What are the five Cs of credit? Explain why each is relevant.
6. What is a credit-scoring model? What are possible advantages and disadvantages of using credit-scoring models?
7. Describe the steps involved in a typical collection process.
8. The basic economic order quantity (EOQ) model deals with which two of the following three costs? (1) ordering costs, (2) carrying costs, and (3) stockout costs
9. Explain the logic of an ABC system of inventory control.
10. What is meant by the term safety stocks? Why would a firm normally find it beneficial to maintain safety stocks in its inventory?
11. What is a materials requirement planning (MRP) system?
12. What are the factors on which the success of a JIT system depends?

CHALLENGING QUESTIONS

13. Explain how agency costs, created by market imperfections, can lead to the use of trade credit.
14. Why are credit-scoring models used more for consumer loans than for business loans?
15. Explain how a firm's inventory and accounts receivable management problems are like a capital budgeting problem.
16. Explain why trade credit is costless for the borrower when the funds are repaid before the end of the discount period.
17. How can granting credit to a person or firm with a poor credit record still be a positive-NPV investment?
18. Explain the difference between collection fractions and receivables balance fractions.
19. What benefits and costs should be analyzed when deciding the proper safety stock level?
20. Explain the similarities between the economic order quantity model and the Baumol model.
21. How does a just-in-time inventory system benefit a firm? What conditions are needed for its successful use?

PROBLEMS

LEVEL A (BASIC)

A1. (NPV of granting credit) A credit sale of $15,000 has a 95% probability of being repaid in two months and a 5% probability of a complete default. If the investment in the sale is $12,000 and the opportunity cost of funds is 15% per year, what is the NPV of granting credit?

A2. (NPV of granting credit) For each of the following items sold on credit, estimate the net present value of granting credit.

ITEM	SALE PRICE	INVESTMENT IN SALE	COLLECTION PERIOD	REQUIRED RETURN	PROBABILITY OF PAYMENT
Refrigerator	$1,200	$1,000	3 months	12%	0.80
Jewelry	300	150	12 months	14%	0.95
Stereo	800	550	6 months	13%	0.90

A3. (NPV of granting credit) A credit sale of $25,000 has a 97% probability of being repaid in three months and a 3% probability of a complete default. If the investment in the sale is $18,000 and the required return is 12% per year, what is the NPV of granting credit?

A4. (NPV of granting credit) For each of the following items sold on credit, estimate the net present value of granting credit.

ITEM	SALE PRICE	INVESTMENT IN SALE	COLLECTION PERIOD	REQUIRED RETURN	PROBABILITY OF PAYMENT
Clock	$ 350	$ 260	3 months	11%	0.85
Clothing	450	400	12 months	15%	0.93
Table	1,200	850	6 months	10%	0.90

A5. (Credit-granting decision) Benny Baggins is applying for a credit card. After graduating with his business degree, Benny started at a job two years ago and now earns $41,000 a year. He has been renting an apartment near work since he started at the job. His telephone is connected, but he only has a fair credit report. Using the credit card application scoring sheet given in the chapter, and a cutoff of 15 points, determine whether Benny would qualify for the credit card.

A6. (Credit-granting decision) Murfreesboro Air Handling Systems wants to buy 10 compressors from you at a price of $800 each. Your cost of supplying each compressor is $650, and you estimate that Murfreesboro has a 95% probability of paying you in two months. There is also a 5% probability that it will pay you nothing. Your opportunity cost of funds is 1.2% per month. Find (a) the expected payment from Murfreesboro, (b) the present value of the expected payment, and (c) the net present value of extending credit.

A7. (Breakeven payment probability) For each of the following items sold on credit, estimate the probability of payment that is required for the seller to break even (have a zero net present value from granting credit).

ITEM	SALE PRICE	INVESTMENT IN SALE	COLLECTION PERIOD	REQUIRED RETURN
Refrigerator	$1,200	$1,000	3 months	12%
Jewelry	300	150	12 months	14%
Stereo	800	550	6 months	13%

A8. (Breakeven payment probability) For each of the following items sold on credit, estimate the probability of payment that is required for the seller to break even (have a zero net present value from granting credit).

ITEM	SALE PRICE	INVESTMENT IN SALE	COLLECTION PERIOD	REQUIRED RETURN
Clock	$ 350	$ 260	3 months	11%
Clothing	450	400	12 months	15%
Table	1,200	850	6 months	10%

A9. (Economic order quantity model) Assume that annual usage is 12,000 units, that the fixed order cost is $60 per order, and that the carrying cost is $4 per unit average inventory. Find the average inventory, number of orders per year, carrying cost, ordering cost, and total cost for the order sizes indicated below.

ORDER SIZE (UNITS)	200	400	600	800	1,000
Average inventory	____	____	____	____	____
Orders per year	____	____	____	____	____
Annual carrying cost	____	____	____	____	____
Annual ordering cost	____	____	____	____	____
Total annual cost	____	____	____	____	____

A10. (Economic order quantity) Knoxville Accountants LLP consumes 100,000 packets of plain copier paper annually. The usage is roughly constant throughout the year. The carrying cost of this inventory is $2.00 per unit average inventory per year. The ordering and delivery cost is a fixed $100 per order.

a. What is the economic order quantity?

b. How many orders will be placed per year using the EOQ?

c. What is the average inventory level?

d. What is the total annual inventory cost?

A11. (Economic order quantity) Lake Charles Office Supply sells 10,000 boxes of photocopy paper per year. The ordering cost is $24 per order and the carrying cost is $3 per unit average inventory per year. Demand for the boxes is uniform through time and replenishment of inventory is instantaneous.

a. What is the economic order quantity?

b. What is the average inventory, number of orders per year, and the time interval between orders?

c. What is the annual carrying cost, ordering cost, and total cost?

A12. (Economic order quantity model) Assume that annual usage is 20,000 units, that the fixed order cost is $100 per order, and that the carrying cost is $15 per unit average inventory. Find the average inventory, number of orders per year, carrying cost, ordering cost, and total cost for the order sizes indicated below.

ORDER SIZE (UNITS)	1,000	1,200	1,400	1,600	1,800
Average inventory	____	____	____	____	____
Orders per year	____	____	____	____	____
Annual carrying cost	____	____	____	____	____
Annual ordering cost	____	____	____	____	____
Total annual cost	____	____	____	____	____

A13. (Economic order quantity) GMC consumes 10,000 barrels of lubricant annually. The usage is roughly constant throughout the year. The carrying cost of this inventory is $7.00 per unit average inventory per year. The ordering and delivery cost is a fixed $45 per order.

a. What is the economic order quantity?

b. How many orders will be placed per year using the EOQ?

c. What is the average inventory level?

d. What is the total annual inventory cost?

A14. (Value of JIT) Meridian Ceramics is studying the economics of converting its manufacturing over to a just-in-time system. There are several benefits and costs that must be weighed.

Total inventories are expected to decline by $4 million, saving an estimated $600,000 per year. Labor savings in tracking inventories are expected to save another $100,000 per year. The additional demands placed on Meridian's suppliers are expected to increase the cost of purchases by about 2% of annual purchases, about $250,000 per year. Equipment needed to operate the JIT system should cost about $150,000 per year. The system will facilitate a savings of $20,000 per year in administering the firm's billing and payables systems. Finally, the JIT system will allow Meridian to gain new customers that should add $300,000 annually to gross profits. If these estimates are correct, what would be the impact of a JIT system on Meridian's annual before-tax profits?

A15. (Value of JIT) Digital Manufacturing is considering converting its manufacturing over to a just-in-time system. There are several benefits and costs that must be weighed. Total inventories are expected to decline by $2 million, saving an estimated $250,000 per year. Labor savings in tracking inventories are expected to save another $36,000 per year. The additional demands placed on Digital's suppliers are expected to increase the cost of purchases by about 5% of annual purchases, about $150,000 per year. Equipment needed to operate the JIT system should cost about $90,000 per year. The system will facilitate a savings of $15,000 per year in administering the firm's billing and payables systems. Finally, the JIT system will allow Digital to gain new customers that should add $120,000 annually to gross profits. If these estimates are correct, what would be the impact of a JIT system on Digital's annual before-tax profits?

LEVEL B

B1. (NPV of extending credit) The Salt Lake Ski Company wants to make a $200,000 credit purchase from your firm. Your investment in the credit sale is 70% of the amount of the sale. You estimate that Salt Lake has a 95% probability of paying you on time, which is in three months, and a 5% probability of paying nothing. If the opportunity cost of funds is 18% per year, what is the net present value of granting credit?

B2. (NPV of extending credit) Squires Sports Equipment Company is selling $4,000 of rubber mats to the Springfield Fitness Center. Squires will invest $3,400 in the sale. Squires has credit terms of 2/10, net 30, and estimates that Springfield has a 50% probability of taking the discount and paying on day 10, a 40% probability of paying the net amount on day 30, and a 10% chance of defaulting. If Springfield Fitness defaults, Squires estimates that it will recover nothing. If the opportunity cost of funds is 12% compounded annually, what is the net present value of granting credit? Assume a 365-day year.

B3. (NPV of extending credit) Schenectady Printers, Inc. wants to make a $100,000 credit purchase from your firm. Your investment in the credit sale is 80% of the amount of the sale. You estimate that Schenectady Printers has a 95% probability of paying you on time, which is in four months, and a 5% probability of paying nothing. If the opportunity cost of funds is 14% per year, what is the net present value of granting credit?

B4. (NPV of extending credit) Kensen Audio Company is selling $10,000 of audio equipment to a local radio station. Kensen will invest $8,300 in the sale. Kensen has credit terms of 2/10, net 30, and estimates that the radio station has a 60% probability of taking the discount and paying on day 10, a 30% probability of paying the net amount on day 30, and a 10% chance of defaulting. If the radio station defaults, Kensen estimates that it will recover nothing. If the opportunity cost of funds is 12% compounded annually, what is the net present value of granting credit? Assume a 365-day year.

B5. (Changing credit policies) Vulcan Games is considering a new credit policy that has much more stringent credit standards. Vulcan's analysts estimate that the new policy will affect several key variables as shown below. Assume that the cost of goods sold is a cash outlay at time zero, and that the expected sales (net of bad debt) are collected at the end of the collection period. Which policy is better?

	CURRENT POLICY	PROPOSED POLICY
Annual sales	$15 million	$14 million
Cost of goods sold/Sales	72%	72%
Bad debt/Sales	4%	2%
Collection period	2 months (0.1667 years)	1 month (0.08333 years)
Required return	15%	15%

B6. (Changing credit policies) Jordon Ross is considering a new credit policy that has much more stringent credit standards. Ross's analysts estimate that the new policy will affect several key variables as shown below. Assume the cost of goods sold is a cash outlay at time zero, and the expected sales (net of bad debt) are collected at the end of the collection period. Which policy is better?

	CURRENT POLICY	PROPOSED POLICY
Annual sales	$1,500,000	$1,400,000
Cost of goods sold/Sales	72%	72%
Bad debt/Sales	4%	2%
Collection period	2 months (0.1667 years)	1 month (0.08333 years)
Required return	15%	15%

B7. (Changing credit policies) Conn Music Company is considering a new credit policy that has much more lenient credit standards. Sharon Conn estimates that the new policy will affect the several key variables as shown below. Assume that the cost of goods sold is a cash outlay at time zero, and that the expected sales (net of bad debt) are collected at the end of the collection period. Which policy is better?

	CURRENT POLICY	PROPOSED POLICY
Annual sales	$4.8 million	$6.0 million
Cost of goods sold/Sales	60%	60%
Bad debt/Sales	1%	3%
Collection period	3 months (.25 years)	4 months (1/3 year)
Required return	10%	10%

B8. (Aging schedule) The accounts receivable for the Boulder Skimobile Company include the following twelve invoices:

INVOICE	INVOICE DATE	AMOUNT
522	March 3	$1,200
530	March 12	1,800
533	April 2	600
540	April 4	2,400
544	April 12	1,800
548	April 25	1,200
550	May 5	1,200
551	May 8	2,400
552	May 12	1,200
553	May 15	1,800
554	May 16	2,400
555	May 27	1,200

Prepare an aging schedule as of May 31 for Boulder Skimobile in the following format:

AGE	ACCOUNTS RECEIVABLE	PERCENT
0–30 days	$xx,xxx	xx.x%
30–60 days	xx,xxx	xx.x
60–90 days	xx,xxx	xx.x
Total	$xx,xxx	100.0%

B9. (Aging schedule) The accounts receivable for the Miscellaneous Office Supply Company include the following twelve invoices:

INVOICE	INVOICE DATE	AMOUNT
48	January 3	$1,000
51	January 12	800
56	January 22	600
67	February 4	1,200
68	February 12	100
71	February 25	400
73	March 5	1,300
78	March 8	200
83	March 12	100
91	March 15	600
93	March 16	900
95	March 27	1,100

Prepare an aging schedule as of March 31 for Miscellaneous Office Supply Company. Use the format shown in problem B8.

B10. (Average age of accounts receivable) Wilson Licensing has the aging schedule shown below. Assume that the receivables in each age category have an age equivalent to the midpoint of the range. Calculate an average age of accounts receivable for Wilson Licensing.

AGE	ACCOUNTS RECEIVABLE	PERCENT
0–30 days	$400,000	53.33%
30–60 days	250,000	33.33
60–90 days	100,000	13.33
Total	$750,000	100.0%

B11. (Average age of accounts receivable) Baker & Sons Advertising Consultants has the aging schedule shown below. Assume that the receivables in each age category have an age equivalent to the midpoint of the range. Calculate an average age of accounts receivable for Baker & Sons.

AGE	ACCOUNTS RECEIVABLE	PERCENT
0–30 days	$ 25,000	25%
30–60 days	30,000	30
60–90 days	45,000	45
Total	$100,000	100%

B12. (Changing credit policies) The Deep River Company is considering the liberalization of its credit terms and credit standards in order to increase sales and, hopefully, profits. The ad hoc management team charged with evaluating this credit liberalization has gathered the information shown below. Assume that the cost of goods sold is equivalent to an investment at time zero and that the expected sales (net of bad debt) are received at the end of the predicted collection period. Which policy is more profitable for the Deep River Company?

	CURRENT POLICY	PROPOSED POLICY
Annual sales	$10 million	$11 million
Collection period	0.10 years	0.20 years
Bad debt/Sales	1%	2%
Cost of goods sold/Sales	85%	85%
Annual required return	15%	15%

B13. (Changing credit policies) Randy Jordan, Inc. is considering loosening its credit terms and credit standards in order to increase sales and, hopefully, profits. The management team evaluating this possibility has gathered the information shown below. Assume the cost of goods sold is equivalent to an investment at time zero and that the expected sales (net of bad debt) are received at the end of the predicted collection period. Which policy is more profitable?

	CURRENT POLICY	PROPOSED POLICY
Annual sales	$1,000,000	$1,100,000
Collection period	0.10 years	0.20 years
Bad debt/Sales	1%	2%
Cost of goods sold/Sales	85%	85%
Annual required return	15%	15%

B14. (Economic order quantity) Sartoris Steel Products uses 200,000 tons of coal per year. The carrying cost per unit average inventory is $10, and the fixed cost per order is $1,000.

a. What is the economic order quantity? What is the annual cost of using the EOQ?

b. The coal supplier will not ship partial carloads of coal, so Sartoris can only order coal in multiples of 1,000 tons. What should Sartoris use as the order quantity? What is the annual cost?

B15. (Economic order quantity) Waters Printing Company orders six rolls of paper every week. The ordering and setup cost is $500, and the annual carrying cost is $1,000 per unit average inventory. Assume a 52-week year.

a. What is the annual cost of ordering six rolls at a time?

b. What is the economic order quantity and the annual cost of using the EOQ?

c. Assume that Waters cannot order fractional rolls. If your EOQ in part b above was not an integer value, what is the annual cost of using the next integer-valued order size above the EOQ? What is the annual cost of using the closest integer-valued order size below the EOQ? What order size do you recommend?

B16. (Economic order quantity) Your annual usage is 50,000 units, the carrying cost per unit is $1, and the ordering cost is $250 per order.

a. What is the EOQ and the total annual cost?

b. Your warehouse will allow a maximum inventory level of 3,000 units. If the order size is constrained by this, what is the total annual cost?

c. What is the maximum annual rent you would pay for additional warehouse space that would relieve your warehouse space constraint?

B17. (Economic order quantity) Washington Furniture Manufacturers uses 500,000 tons of lumber per year. The carrying cost per unit average inventory is $50, and the fixed cost per order is $1,300.

a. What is the economic order quantity? What is the annual cost of using the EOQ?

b. The lumber supplier will not ship partial truckloads of lumber, so Washington can order lumber only in multiples of 1,000 tons. What should Washington use as the order quantity? What is the annual cost?

B18. (Economic order quantity) Fields Janitorial Services orders 100 bottles of cleaning solution every week. The ordering and setup cost is $55, and the annual carrying cost is $2 per unit average inventory. Assume a 52-week year.

a. What is the annual cost of ordering 100 bottles at a time?

b. What is the economic order quantity and the annual cost of using the EOQ?

c. Assume that Fields cannot order fractional bottles. If your EOQ in part b above was not an integer value, what is the annual cost of using the next integer-valued order size above the EOQ? What is the annual cost of using the closest integer-valued order size below the EOQ? What order size do you recommend?

B19. (Economic order quantity) Your annual usage is 25,000 units, the carrying cost per unit is $3, and the ordering cost is $75 per order.

a. What is the EOQ and the total annual cost?

b. Your warehouse will allow a maximum inventory level of 750 units. If the order size is constrained by this, what is the total annual cost?

c. What is the maximum annual rent you would pay for additional warehouse space that would relieve your warehouse space constraint?

B20. (Economic order quantity with quantity discounts) The annual usage of toggle switches is 10,000 units per year, at a uniform rate through the year. The ordering cost is $50 per order, and carrying cost is $4 per unit average inventory per year.

a. What is the economic order quantity? What is the annual cost using the EOQ?

b. If the supplier offers a quantity discount of $0.10 per unit if you order in quantities of 250 or more, what should you do? What is the annual cost of following your recommendation?

c. If the supplier offers a quantity discount of $0.10 per unit if you order in quantities of 1,000 or more, what should you do? What is the annual cost of following your recommendation?

B21. (Economic order quantity with quantity discounts) The annual usage of copy paper is 30,000 units per year, at a uniform rate through the year. The ordering cost is $100 per order, and carrying cost is $10 per unit average inventory per year.

a. What is the economic order quantity? What is the annual cost using the EOQ?

b. If the supplier offers a quantity discount of $0.10 per unit if you order in quantities of 500 or more, what should you do? What is the annual cost of following your recommendation?

c. If the supplier offers a quantity discount of $0.10 per unit if you order in quantities of 1,000 or more, what should you do? What is the annual cost of following your recommendation?

B22. (Reorder point) Alabama Central Hospital has established an economic order quantity for its obstetrics kits of 60 units. The lead time before orders arrive and are ready for use is four days. The average usage is four kits per day, and Alabama Central has determined that it would like to have a safety stock of 10 kits.

a. What is the expected lead-time demand?

b. What should Alabama Central use as its reorder point?

B23. (Reorder point) Auburn Manufacturing has established an economic order quantity for its part #5467 of 100 units. The lead time before orders arrive and are ready for use is two days. The average usage is 10 units per day, and Auburn Manufacturing has determined that it would like to have a safety stock of five units.

a. What is the expected lead-time demand?

b. What should Auburn Manufacturing use as its reorder point?

B24. (Safety stock) General Enzyme Company uses an average of five tons of beta medium per day. Because the lead time between a reorder and delivery is four days, expected lead-time demand is 20 tons. The economic order quantity is 80 tons. Because its usage is somewhat random, GE carries a safety stock to reduce the probability of a stockout. Based on the annual costs estimated here, which reorder point and safety stock would minimize total annual cost?

SAFETY STOCK	REORDER POINT	ORDERING COST	CARRYING COST	STOCKOUT COST
0	20	$10,000	$10,000	$12,000
5	25	10,000	12,500	7,000
10	30	10,000	15,000	4,000
15	35	10,000	17,500	2,000
20	40	10,000	20,000	1,000

B25. (Safety stock) New York Marketing uses an average of 2,000 advertising leaflets per day. Because the lead time between a reorder and delivery is six days, expected lead-time demand is 12,000 units. The economic order quantity is 20,000 units. Because its usage is somewhat random, New York Marketing carries a safety stock to reduce the probability of a stockout. Based on the annual costs estimated here, which reorder point and safety stock would minimize total annual cost?

SAFETY STOCK	REORDER POINT	ORDERING COST	CARRYING COST	STOCKOUT COST
0	12,000	$200	$200	$800
3,000	15,000	200	300	550
6,000	18,000	200	400	350
9,000	21,000	200	500	225
12,000	24,000	200	600	150

B26. (Excel: Order quantity with quantity discounts) UT STROBE Company uses 100,000 pounds of silica per year. The ordering cost is $500 per order, and the carrying cost is $20 per pound per year.

a. What is the economic order quantity and the total annual inventory cost using the EOQ?

b. UT STROBE can purchase silica in multiples of 1,000 pounds only. Furthermore, its supplier has offered a $0.15 per pound discount if UT STROBE will place an order size of at least 5,000 pounds. Prepare a table showing the ordering cost, carrying cost, discounts received, and total cost if the order size is 1,000, 2,000, 3,000, 4,000, 5,000, 6,000, 7,000, and 8,000 pounds.

B27. (Excel: Collection fractions and receivables balance fractions) Texas Chili Products collects 20% of its sales in the month of the sale, 50% in the month following the sale, 25% in the second month following sale, and 5% in the third month following sale.

a. For a given month's sales, what percent of that month's sales should be outstanding at the end of the sale month, in the first month after the sale, the second month after sale, and the third month after sale?

b. Assume that collections proceed as predicted. Calculate the level of accounts receivable for January, February, and March from the sales information given.

c. Provide an aging schedule for accounts receivable outstanding at the end of March.

MONTH	OCTOBER	NOVEMBER	DECEMBER	JANUARY	FEBRUARY	MARCH
Sales	$500	$500	$500	$500	$700	$900

LEVEL C (ADVANCED)

C1. (Credit scoring) The Flint Area Credit Union (FACU) uses a credit-scoring system to screen its car loan applications. It uses the following scoring system:

Telephone	yes +5	no 0		
Home	own (no mortgage) +6	own (mortgage) +3	rent +2	
Years at present address	<6 months 0	6 months −2 years +1	>2 years +2	
Monthly income	<1,000 +1	1,000–2,000 +2	2,000–3,500 +3	>3,500 +4
Years at present job	<6 months 0	6 months −2 years +1	>2 years +2	
Family size	1 +2	2 +5	3–5 +3	>5 +1
Previous loan experience	none 0	loan pmts on time +5	loan pmts late −5	
Account with FACU	yes +2	no 0		
Number of bank accounts	zero 0	1 +2	2 +3	>2 +4
Loan/Value ratio	<50% +4	50–75% +2	75–90% +1	>90% −3
Credit report	good +5	limited +2	poor −5	

FACU's disposition of a credit application is as follows:

0–20 points	deny credit
21–24 points	investigate further and base decision on the added information
25 or more points	grant credit

Apply the credit-scoring system to the following two loan applicants and decide the disposition of each loan request.

a. Jorge is buying a $20,000 car, putting $6,000 down and borrowing the remaining $14,000. Jorge has a telephone, is renting an apartment (where he has lived for three months), and is making $3,000 per month. He has been with his present employer for three years. He is single. He has a savings account with FACU and has two additional bank accounts. He has not previously borrowed from FACU. His credit report is good.

b. Flavia is buying a $24,000 car and is asking for a $23,000 loan to help her make the purchase. Flavia has a telephone, is renting an apartment (where she has lived for three years), and is making $2,400 per month. She has been with her present employer for 10 months. She is single. She has no accounts with FACU and has two bank accounts. Flavia has not previously borrowed from FACU. Her credit report is bad.

C2. (Credit scoring) The First National Bank (FNB) uses a credit-scoring system to screen its loan applications. It uses the following scoring system:

Telephone	yes +3	no 0		
Home	own (no mortgage) +4	own (mortgage) +2	rent +1	
Years at present address	<6 months 0	6 months − 2 years +1	>2 years +2	
Monthly income	<1,000 0	1,000–2,000 +1	2,000–3,500 +2	>3,500 +3
Years at present job	<6 months 0	6 months − 2 years +1	>2 years +2	
Family size	1 +0	2 +3	3–5 +2	>5 +1
Previous loan experience	none 0	loan pmts on time +3	loan pmts late −3	
Account with FNB	yes +1	no 0		
Number of bank accounts	zero 0	1 +1	2 +2	>2 +3
Loan/Value ratio	<50% +3	50–75% +2	75–90% +1	>90% 0
Credit report	good +3	limited 0	poor −3	

FNB's disposition of a credit application is as follows:

0–10 points	deny credit
11–15 points	investigate further and base decision on the added information
16 or more points	grant credit

Apply the credit-scoring system to the following two loan applicants and decide the disposition of each loan request.

a. Sarah is interested in taking out a loan. She needs $30,000 of which she is putting up $10,000 herself. She has a telephone and has lived at her present address for three years. Sarah owns the house she lives in and finished the mortgage payments two years ago. Her monthly income is $2,500, and she has been with her employer for one year. Sarah is married and has one child. She does not have an account with FNB but has one account in another bank. She has no previous loan experience, giving her a credit report with little information.

b. Jake is also interested in taking out a loan. Jake has a telephone and rents a small apartment where he has lived for twelve years. Jake makes $1,500 per month and has worked for the same employer for twenty years. Jake lives alone. Jake has an account with FNB and has previous loan experience with FNB. Jake was frequently late with payments on a previous loan with FNB. Jake has one bank account and plans to borrow $5,000 of the $6,000 he needs. Jake's overall credit report shows frequent missed payments and a bankruptcy filing.

C3. (EOQ and safety stocks) Brown Pontiac maintains an inventory of tires. The dealer uses tires at a constant rate of 1,000 per month. The dealer's cost of placing a new order is $500 per order. The cost of carrying a tire in inventory for a year is $12.

a. Calculate the economic order quantity.

b. Brown Pontiac has found that if it is out of stock when a customer arrives, it will make the eventual sale only 20% of the time. For each lost sale, Brown Pontiac loses the net margin of $30 per tire. Lost sales as well as back orders involve record-keeping costs of $10 per stockout. Brown Pontiac has estimated the benefit of maintaining safety stocks given below. What level of safety stock should Brown Pontiac maintain?

Safety stock	100	125	150	175	200
Stockouts per year	75	50	35	30	30

MINICASE MUSICAL CHAIRS AT HOME DEPOT

Just about everyone knows that the Home Depot has stores almost everywhere and sells a wide array of things. In fact, the firm operates more than 1,400 full-service stores in the U.S., Canada, Puerto Rico, and Mexico. Each store stocks between 40,000 and 50,000 different kinds of building materials, home improvement supplies, and lawn and garden products.

Not long ago, Home Depot was considering stocking a new deluxe toilet unit in its bathroom fixtures department. It was trying to broaden its product line to appeal to home-improvement contractors, and this item had recently been featured in *Architectural Digest.* The toilet seat contains a special feature. Sitting on the seat activates a system that sprays up a fine mist of air freshener and plays music. You can choose the scent and whatever musical selection moves you. (We are not making this up!)

The new toilet units had been test marketed successfully, and Home Depot estimated that sales would average 1,000 units per year. It would cost $100 to keep a unit in inventory for a year, and the fixed reordering cost would be $80. Home Depot's cost would be $500 per unit.

SAFETY STOCKS AND EXPECTED STOCKOUT COSTS

Reorder Point	Safety Stock	Expected Stockout Cost	Reorder Point	Safety Stock	Expected Stockout Costs
10	0	$350	20	10	$200
12	2	290	22	12	192
14	4	255	24	14	186
16	6	225	26	16	182
18	8	210	28	18	180

QUESTIONS

1. What is Home Depot's EOQ for the deluxe toilet units? Using the EOQ, what is the average inventory, number of orders per year, and the total annual cost of maintaining the inventory of deluxe toilet units? What would the EOQ be if expected sales were 2,000 units per year, ordering cost was $160, and the carrying cost was $200?
2. The average lead-time demand is 10 units. The table above shows how the expected annual stockout cost depends on the amount of safety stock. What is the optimal safety stock and reorder point?
3. The supplier of the deluxe toilet units has offered Home Depot a 2% discount if it orders 50 or more units each time. Should Home Depot order 50 units each time it buys?
4. Home Depot can sell 1,000 units per year at a price of $750 per unit. It estimates that it could sell 1,100 units per year if it dropped the price to $700, and that it would sell only 900 units if it raised the price to $800 per unit.
   a. What is Home Depot's EOQ assuming that the quantity discounts are available and that sales are 900 units/year or 1,100 units/year?
   b. What is the total annual inventory cost (including carrying cost, ordering cost, stockout cost, and discounts taken) for each of the three unit prices?
   c. Which price, $700, $750, or $800 per unit, maximizes the annual profit Home Depot can expect to earn from selling these deluxe toilet units?

24

FINANCIAL PLANNING

Financial planning creates a "blueprint" for the firm's future. Planning is necessary to (1) establish the firm's goals, (2) choose operating and financial strategies, (3) forecast operating results against which to monitor and evaluate performance, and (4) create contingent plans for dealing with possible future circumstances. Good financial planning involves all parts of the firm and its policies and decisions about such things as liquidity, working capital, inventories, capital budgeting projects, capital structure, and dividends.

A firm should not simply react to events as they unfold. It should be prepared to deal swiftly and effectively with both favorable and unfavorable developments. Competitive forces in the capital markets—and in other markets—make it difficult to find positive-NPV opportunities. However, mistakes and poor planning make negative-NPV outcomes an ever-present possibility!

In this chapter, we develop a framework for financial planning. We look at both short- and long-term planning models, because the typical short-term plan is simply a more detailed part of a firm's long-term plan.

FOCUS ON PRINCIPLES

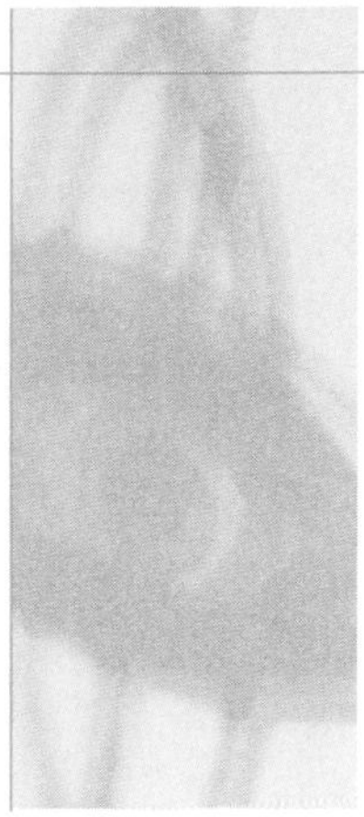

- *Valuable Ideas:* Use both bottom-up and top-down processes to increase the chance of finding valuable ideas.
- *Behavioral:* Use common industry practices as a good starting place for the planning process.
- *Self-Interested Behavior:* Carefully evaluate and monitor the financial plan's impact on the firm and its stakeholders.
- *Incremental Benefits:* Forecast the firm's cash flows, and analyze the incremental cash flows of alternative decisions.
- *Time Value of Money:* Compare the NPVs of alternative financial plans.
- *Two-Sided Transactions:* Look for situations that are not zero-sum games and thus may be profitable to you *and* your supplier or customer, perhaps by reducing agency costs and transaction costs.
- *Comparative Advantage:* Design the plan to take advantage of any opportunities you can find to use the firm's comparative advantages to create value.

24.1 THE FINANCIAL PLANNING PROCESS

A firm is a dynamic system. Decisions and policies about liquidity, working capital, inventories, capital budgeting projects, capital structure, and dividends (among other things) interact continually. Figure 24.1 illustrates this interaction in a flow-of-funds framework.

The main net source of funds is the firm's operations. The firm uses its fixed assets, together with labor, raw materials, and other inputs, to produce products and services to sell. Sales revenue minus cost of goods sold and operating expenses (such as selling, general, and administrative expenses) equals the firm's operating income. An important question in connection with financial planning is how operating income responds to increases in output. The answer depends on the firm's operating leverage. Recall from Chapter 11 that the higher the fixed-cost component of total costs, the greater is operating leverage.

Net income is left after interest expense and taxes are paid. Net income can be paid out as dividends, or it can be retained and reinvested. The firm's dividend policy determines the split between dividends and retained earnings. Dividend policy interacts with the firm's capital budget. A higher payout ratio increases the amount of external financing needed to meet the capital budget. Both of these policies in turn interact with the firm's capital structure policy. The combination of the firm's financing needs, its dividend policy, and its capital structure policy determines the mix of debt and equity in any required new external financing.

The firm's financing needs are determined mainly by its capital budget and internal cash generation. The capital budget is in turn affected by projected sales. Increased sales can require expenditures for expansions and new equipment. In addition, higher production rates cause machines to wear out faster, so the need for replacement investment also increases. Higher sales levels will also require additional investment in working capital.

The firm's planned investment in current assets (net of increases in payables), along with its liquidity policy, determines the net increase or decrease in short-term borrowing. The rest of the firm's borrowing needs, the residual, should be on a long-term basis. The firm might issue some preferred stock in addition to (or in place of) long-term debt, depending on its tax position and capital structure objectives. The firm's tax position is essentially the amount of tax deductions and credits from depreciation, depletion allowance, and interest expense.

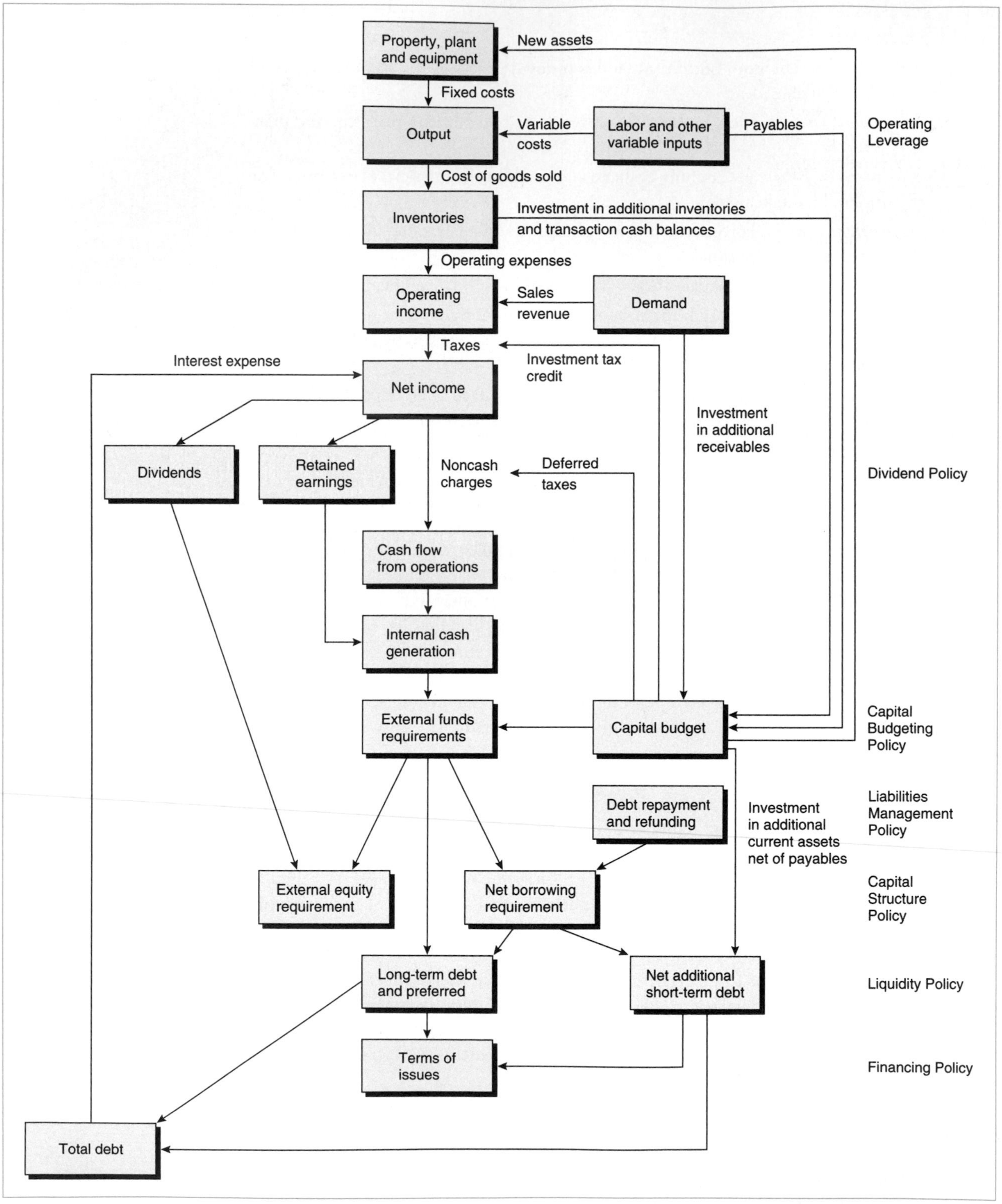

FIGURE 24.1
Interaction of financial decisions in a flow-of-funds framework.

The total long-term borrowing requirement includes the residual just noted plus any required debt repayments and planned early refunding. Finally, the terms of the debt (and/or preferred stock) issues must be determined in light of the firm's financing policy. Any resulting debt issuance changes the firm's interest expense. This will affect net income—and the planning "circle" is complete.

The process illustrated in Figure 24.1 is a continuing one. Remember, the firm's total sources of funds must equal its total uses of funds in any finite planning period. For relatively short periods of time, this equality might require either unintended changes in cash balances or unplanned short-term borrowing. But the firm should strive to avoid these inefficiencies through good financial planning. All six of the basic financial policies must be determined simultaneously. This requires certain trade-offs. These trade-offs can be analyzed within a financial planning model.

The Financial Plan

Figure 24.1 provides a starting point for financial planning. **Financial planning** is a process of evaluating the impact of alternative investing and financing decisions. Decisions, such as the firm's capital budget or a debt restructuring, are projected as part of a financial plan. Subsequent outcomes are measured against the plan.

A financial plan has inputs, a model, and outputs. Examples of inputs include projections of sales, collections, costs, interest rates, and exchange rates. The firm's current positions (cash balance, debt obligations, and so on) are also inputs. The model is a set of mathematical relationships among the inputs and outputs.

The outputs of a financial plan are pro forma financial statements and a set of budgets. **Pro forma financial statements** are projected (forecasted) financial statements. A **budget** is a detailed schedule of a financial activity, such as an advertising budget, a sales budget, or a capital budget.

Firms use both short- and long-term financial planning models. Models are classified by their planning horizon. A model's **planning horizon** is the length of time it projects into the future. "Short term" usually means a year or less. A five-year horizon is common for a long-term planning model, but some industries use a ten-year or longer horizon. For example, a forestry products firm might have a planning horizon of several decades.

Short-term models are detailed and very specific. Long-term models tend to be much less detailed.

A complete financial plan includes, at a minimum,

1. Clearly stated strategic, operating, and financial *objectives*
2. The *assumptions* on which the plan is based
3. Descriptions of the underlying *strategies*
4. *Contingency plans* for emergencies
5. *Budgets,* categorized and summarized in various ways, such as by time period, division, and type (for example, cash, advertising, and capital)
6. The *financing program,* categorized and summarized in various ways, such as by time period, sources of funds (for example, bonds, bank loans, and stock), and types of funds (for example, short-term versus long-term, and internal versus external)
7. A set of period-by-period *pro forma financial statements* for the entire planning horizon

Planning Cycles: Bottom-Up Versus Top-Down Planning Styles

Financial plans are updated on a regular basis, according to a planning cycle. Each update adds the latest information and renews the planning horizon—that is, it projects into the future by the length of the cycle. Short-term models might be updated monthly, weekly, or even daily. Long-term plans might be updated once, twice, or perhaps four times a year. Updates also vary in how thorough they are.

For example, a firm might update its short-term model by adding the latest data each week, although it might extend the planning horizon only once a month. In addition, the firm might review and make any changes in the model itself only once a year. Similar procedures are typical for long-term models.

Bottom-Up and Top-Down Planning

Plans and ideas can be generated through either a bottom-up or a top-down process. A bottom-up planning process starts at the product or production level and proceeds upward through the plant and division levels to top management. At each level, ideas are added, modified, and/or deleted. Managers at successively higher levels, who are in a position to take a broader view, should be able to see things that are not visible to the lower levels. Higher management levels can also propose efficient combinations or eliminations that are unlikely to be suggested by the affected employees.

The top-down planning process starts with the firm's top management and its strategic plans and goals and proceeds downward through the organization's levels. Top management makes strategic decisions. These decisions often create, increase, shrink, or eliminate such things as the firm's products, divisions, and international marketing efforts. Managers describe how strategic decisions will be implemented. At each successively lower managerial level, the required actions become more specific.

Critics of the bottom-up process say it often fails to produce a coherent strategy for the firm as a whole and can cause the firm to appear chaotic and poorly managed. Critics of the top-down process say it tends to exaggerate the role of top managers and often results in bad investments and missed opportunities because top management may not be in touch with what is going on "in the field." But the bottom-up and top-down processes actually complement one another. Good planning requires both. Ideally, valuable new ideas are supported no matter where or how they originate.

Phases of the Financial Planning Process

Financial planning has three phases: *formulating* the plan, *implementing* the plan, and *evaluating* performance. Involvement in the three phases depends on the manager's specific role. For example, salespersons may have special insights into marketing forecasts, and engineers may have special expertise in developing cost estimates. A financial plan should be formulated by using the kinds of bottom-up and top-down processes we just described.

In the implementation phase, budgets with specific objectives, resource allocations, and operating policies are used to clarify each manager's responsibilities for contributing to the firm's goals. During implementation, circumstances change and opportunities evolve. A firm should alter its plans to adapt to, and take advantage of, changing circumstances. Consequently, a good budgeting system should be *flexible.* A budget is simply part of a financial plan, and plans need to be adapted to new opportunities and circumstances.

In the evaluation phase, the firm compares its overall performance to the financial plan. Managers and their units are evaluated in terms of how well their performance compares to the objectives. In this process the conditions that actually prevailed, which can be very different from those expected and forecasted, are taken into account.

Benefits of Financial Planning

Of course, the goal of the planning process is to help maximize the value of the firm. Toward this end, there are several benefits a firm hopes to realize from the planning process:

1. *Standardizing assumptions.* The planning process can expose inconsistencies in decision-making methods. For example, when managers differ in their forecasts of future conditions, the more optimistic manager's plan will look better—even if there is no other difference between the plans. A similar problem occurs when managers use different required returns

to evaluate the same project. Such differences bias the planning process in favor of one manager's proposals. Planning requires explicit assumptions that can themselves be evaluated. Standardized assumptions then make it possible to compare alternative plans.

2. *Future orientation.* The planning process forces you to think about the future. Doing so generates new ideas and can help eliminate bad ones.
3. *Objectivity.* Because assumptions and models are made explicit, planning can expose decisions that are based on politics or emotions. Planning therefore increases the objective pursuit of organizational goals.
4. *Employee development.* The planning process includes input from many people. The ability to provide such input increases an employee's perceived stake in the firm. People who are empowered through the budgeting process may be better motivated to carry out the firm's plans. The planning process also educates participants about the firm. This fosters coordination and cooperation. It also helps prepare an employee for career advancement in the firm.
5. *Lender requirements.* Financial plans, sometimes very detailed, are necessary for borrowing—especially for the first time. Such plans indicate the use of the borrowed money and show the firm's expected future cash inflows and outflows, including the loan's interest and principal repayments.
6. *Better performance evaluation.* It is possible for a manager to make good decisions but to have bad performance because of an unexpected downturn in the economy. Similarly, bad decisions can have favorable outcomes as a result of just plain good luck. For example, when net income is higher than expected because interest rates and borrowing costs were lower than expected, the high performance is not due to superior managerial decision making. A financial plan provides a benchmark against which to identify reasons for the differences between outcomes and forecasts. Then the firm can avoid punishing good decisions because of bad outcomes or rewarding bad decisions because of good outcomes.
7. *Preparing for contingencies.* A good financial plan includes contingency plans for unlikely outcomes. The planning process can identify potential, if unlikely, conditions that would cause significant problems. This enables the firm to plan appropriate reactions should such an unlikely contingency occur. For example, the planning process might reveal a possible shortage of funds. The firm that has prearranged contingency financing will be able to continue to operate efficiently—regardless of its cash flow.

In the next section, we will discuss cash budgeting, which usually has a short-term planning horizon and focuses on the cash flows of the firm.

Review

1. What is financial planning? What benefits can a firm derive from it? Why is sound financial planning critical to a firm's success?
2. What are pro forma financial statements? How are they created?
3. What is a budget? How is it related to the firm's financial plan? What does each include?
4. Contrast top-down and bottom-up planning.

24.2 CASH BUDGETING

Cash budgeting is the process of projecting (forecasting) and summarizing the firm's cash inflows and outflows expected during the planning horizon. The cash budget also shows the monthly cash balances and any short-term borrowing used to cover cash shortfalls. Monthly cash budgets typically have a 6- to 12-month planning horizon. A positive net cash flow for a month can increase cash, reduce outstanding loans, or be used elsewhere in the business. Similarly, negative net cash flows can reduce cash or be offset with additional borrowing.

For the most part, cash budgets are used in short-term plans, so they include substantial detail. However, the amount of detail also depends on the size of the firm and on the present stage of projects in the planning horizon. Small firms are less complex, and their cash budgets are less detailed. Because of the complexity of larger firms, more detail is required to take into account all of the factors that affect their cash flows. Projections farther out in the planning horizon are less detailed.

Most cash budgets are based on sales forecasts because so many cash flows are tied to sales. Inflows from sales depend on the amount of sales and also on the proportion that are cash versus credit sales. The time delays involved in collecting on credit sales depend on credit terms and payment patterns.

Several variable cash outflows also depend on sales. The cost of goods sold reflects raw materials purchases, wages, and production costs for inventories based on anticipated sales. Selling costs, including commissions, are often directly linked to sales.

Other fixed cash expenditures do not fluctuate with current sales. These include capital expenditures; rent, lease, and debt payments; and some types of salaries and tax payments. Such fixed cash outflows are also included in the cash budget. Our next example shows how to create a cash budget.

EXAMPLE Cash Budgeting at the Monet Paint Company

The cash managers of Monet Paint are preparing a cash budget for the six months from April through September. Their cash management model is based on the following assumptions:

1. The recent and forecasted (April on) sales (in $1,000s) are:

FEB.	MAR.	APR.	MAY	JUN.	JUL.	AUG.	SEP.	OCT.
400	500	600	700	800	800	700	600	500

2. Twenty percent of sales is collected in the month of sale, 50% is collected in the month following the sale, and 30% is collected in the second month following the sale.
3. Purchases are 60% of sales, and purchases are paid for one month prior to sale.
4. Wages and salaries are 12% of sales and are paid in the same month as the sale.
5. Rent of $10,000 is paid each month. Additional cash operating expenses of $30,000 per month will be incurred for April through July, decreasing to $25,000 for August and September.
6. Tax payments of $20,000 and $30,000 are expected in April and July, respectively. A capital expenditure of $150,000 will occur in June, and the firm has a mortgage payment of $60,000 due in May.
7. The cash balance at the end of March is $150,000, and managers want to maintain a minimum balance of $100,000 at all times. The firm will borrow the amounts necessary to assure that the minimum balance is achieved. Any cash above the minimum will be used to pay off any loan balance until it is eliminated.

The cash budget in Table 24.1 is based on these assumptions. The top part of the table presents the cash receipts, which reflect the sales predicted in assumption 1 and the collection pattern in assumption 2. The cash disbursements for each month reflect the checks that must be written to satisfy assumptions 3 through 6. April's beginning cash balance is the end-of-March cash balance in assumption 7. Monthly net cash flows are total receipts minus total disbursements for the month.

The lower portion of Table 24.1 projects the beginning and ending cash balances for each month, amounts borrowed or repaid on short-term loans, and the cumulative short-term loan balance. It is important to follow the logic in this section of the cash budget.

TABLE 24.1
Cash budget for the Monet Paint Company.

	CASH BUDGET, APRIL–SEPTEMBER					
SALES	**April $600,000**	**May $700,000**	**June $800,000**	**July $800,000**	**August $700,000**	**September $600,000**
Cash Receipts						
Collections (current) 20%	$120,000	$140,000	$160,000	$160,000	$140,000	$120,000
(previous month) 50%	250,000	300,000	350,000	400,000	400,000	350,000
(2nd month previous) 30%	120,000	150,000	180,000	210,000	240,000	240,000
Total cash receipts	490,000	590,000	690,000	770,000	780,000	710,000
Cash Disbursements						
Purchases	420,000	480,000	480,000	420,000	360,000	300,000
Wages and salaries	72,000	84,000	96,000	96,000	84,000	72,000
Rent	10,000	10,000	10,000	10,000	10,000	10,000
Cash operating expenses	30,000	30,000	30,000	30,000	25,000	25,000
Tax installments	20,000			30,000		
Capital expenditure			150,000			
Mortgage payment		60,000				
Total cash disbursements	552,000	664,000	766,000	586,000	479,000	407,000
Ending Cash Balance						
Net cash flow	−62,000	−74,000	−76,000	184,000	301,000	303,000
Beginning cash balance	150,000	100,000	100,000	100,000	122,000	423,000
Available balance	88,000	26,000	24,000	284,000	423,000	726,000
Monthly borrowing	12,000	74,000	76,000			
Monthly repayment				162,000		
Ending cash balance	$100,000	$100,000	$100,000	$122,000	$423,000	$726,000
Cumulative loan balance	$ 12,000	$ 86,000	$162,000	$ 0	$ 0	$ 0

The monthly net cash flow plus the beginning balance for the month gives an available balance. The available balance is compared to the desired minimum $100,000 balance. If the available balance is too low, the firm borrows enough to bring the balance up to $100,000. Any amount above the minimum can be used to repay any outstanding short-term loans. The ending cash balance is the available balance plus the month's borrowing and minus the month's loan repayments. Finally, the cumulative loan balance is the previous month's loan balance plus any additional borrowing and minus any loan repayments this month. Note that Monet projects negative net cash flows for April, May, and June, which will require the firm to borrow each month and build up its loan balance. Beginning in July, the projected positive net cash flows will enable Monet to pay off its outstanding loan balance and to accumulate a substantial ending cash balance by the end of September.

The purpose of a cash budget is to ensure a firm's smooth financial operation over the planning horizon. The cash budget identifies the amounts and timing of any surplus or needed funds and is the basis for planning the firm's uses and sources of funds. For example, there is often a benefit to maturity matching short-term investments to particular cash needs that are identified in the cash budgeting process. Once these needs have been quantified, the firm can select from among the short-term investment alternatives discussed in Chapter 22.

Monet's cash budget is a monthly budget. It could be further divided into weekly or daily flows. There are cash flow patterns within the month, which can be incorporated into the daily or weekly budgets. For example, wage and salary cash flows will occur on predictable days. Similarly, payments for rent, loans, and even trade credit are often known in advance. These more detailed daily and weekly cash budgets enable a firm to monitor its short-term finances very closely.

Review

1. What is a cash budget? How is it created?
2. What is the typical planning horizon for a cash budget?
3. Why do firms prepare cash budgets?

24.3 PRO FORMA FINANCIAL STATEMENTS

Firms continually make decisions. For example, they choose the schedules, amounts, processes, innovations, and pricing connected with such things as their products, marketing, production, labor, and inventories. Before making such decisions—and to help them make the best ones—they want to know the effects of alternative choices. Although it is not possible to predict the future perfectly, the effects of many decisions can be predicted with reasonable accuracy.

Pro forma financial statements show the effects of the firm's decisions on its future financial statements. Firms use pro forma financial statements throughout the planning process to assess the effects of alternative decisions on various items of interest, such as sales and net income. In addition to helping in the decision-making process, pro forma statements also help the firm create contingent plans for responding to unexpected situations.

A complete financial plan includes a set of pro forma financial statements, which show the firm's planned financial position at regular points over the planning horizon. These statements are based on the actual decisions made as a result of the planning process, and on the agreed-upon sales and other forecasts. Our next example illustrates the use of pro forma financial statements.

EXAMPLE Pro Forma Financial Statements for Bluestem Crafts Stores

Bluestem Crafts operates several stores in medium-size towns in the Southwest. It has decided to expand into the Southeast. Pro forma financial statements for next year are shown in Table 24.2, along with the latest income statement and current balance sheet.

Bluestem forecasts increased sales and profits next year for existing stores. However, new stores are not expected to break even in their first year because of startup and extra promotional costs.

Cost of goods sold and the selling, general, and administrative expenses are expected to rise somewhat faster than sales. The result will be a small increase in earnings before interest and taxes and a correspondingly modest increase in net income. Because of a recent decline in interest rates, Bluestem expects interest expense to remain unchanged, even though total debt will increase. Bluestem is not planning any cash dividends during the next year.

Bluestem's balance sheet shows a \$5.8 million increase in assets as receivables, inventories, and fixed assets all increase. This increase in assets is financed with \$3.7 million of retained earnings, a \$600,000 increase in accounts payable, and a \$1.5 million increase in bank loans.

Income statements beyond next year are expected to show increased profitability as the new stores get over their "shakedown period" and become profitable. Of course, Bluestem may continue to expand, and future growth decisions will depend on the success of this year's new stores.

TABLE 24.2
Pro forma financial statements for Bluestem Crafts Stores.

INCOME STATEMENT	CURRENT	PROJECTED	CHANGE
Sales	$74,000,000	$95,000,000	$21,000,000
Less cost of goods sold	45,500,000	59,000,000	13,500,000
Less depreciation	500,000	600,000	100,000
Gross profit	28,000,000	35,400,000	7,400,000
Less selling & administrative expenses	21,000,000	28,000,000	7,000,000
Earnings before interest and taxes	7,000,000	7,400,000	400,000
Less interest	500,000	500,000	—
Earnings before taxes	6,500,000	6,900,000	400,000
Less taxes	3,000,000	3,200,000	200,000
Net income	3,500,000	3,700,000	200,000
Less cash dividends	—	—	—
Addition to retained earnings	$ 3,500,000	$ 3,700,000	$ 200,000

BALANCE SHEET	CURRENT	PROJECTED	CHANGE
Assets			
Cash and marketable securities	$ 3,000,000	$ 3,000,000	—
Accounts receivable	4,600,000	6,000,000	$ 1,400,000
Inventory	9,500,000	12,400,000	2,900,000
Total current assets	17,100,000	21,400,000	4,300,000
Net plant and equipment	6,500,000	8,000,000	1,500,000
Total assets	$23,600,000	$29,400,000	$ 5,800,000
Liabilities and Equity			
Accounts payable	$ 3,400,000	$ 4,000,000	$ 600,000
Bank loans	1,700,000	3,200,000	1,500,000
Other short-term debt	3,000,000	3,000,000	—
Total current liabilities	8,100,000	10,200,000	2,100,000
Long-term debt	3,500,000	3,500,000	—
Stockholders' equity	12,000,000	15,700,000	3,700,000
Total liabilities and equity	$23,600,000	$29,400,000	$ 5,800,000

In addition to pro forma financial statements, firms create many specialized budgets that show in greater detail each unit's resources and responsibilities. Table 24.3 lists statements and budgets that are often created in the planning process. For example, a sales budget provides sales forecasts in units and total revenues, shown in various ways such as by product, division, geographical region, and store. The production budget shows the planned quantities of various items to be produced. Planned production equals forecasted sales plus the desired ending inventory minus the beginning inventory. The purchasing budget specifies the quantities and costs of the necessary production input items. Of course, these and other budgets must be carefully coordinated.

Which budgets and statements managers are concerned with depends on their role in the firm. For example, top management and the board of directors often focus on the combined pro forma financial statements for the entire firm. These officials coordinate the firm's investing, financing, production, and liquidity; they must understand the entire firm's operations.

TABLE 24.3
Statements and budgets produced in the financial planning process.

Pro Forma Financial Statements	
Income statement	Projected revenues, expenses, net income, and additions to retained earnings
Balance sheet	Projected assets, liabilities, and equity
Statement of cash flows	Projected cash flows for operations, investing, and financing
Specialized Budgets	
Cash budget	Cash inflows, cash outflows, and cash balances
Sales budget	Planned sales in units and in dollar volume. Various sales budgets may be produced for different divisions, product lines, regions, and even individual stores and individuals
Production budget	Scheduled production (quantities and costs)
Purchasing budget	Planned purchases of the raw materials the firm uses in production, goods for resale, and supplies used in operating the firm
Advertising budget	Planned advertising campaigns and their cost
Capital budget	Purchase of long-term assets
R&D budget	Research-and-development plans for the period
Personnel training and recruiting budget	Planned expenses for training employees and recruiting new employees
Administrative budgets	Administrative expenses for each plant, store, department, or managerial unit in the organization

Middle managers need other kinds of information to do their specific jobs. Specialized budgets are provided for each managerial responsibility. For example, personnel managers are given training budgets for training current personnel and recruiting budgets for recruiting new employees. The recruiting budget has funds for advertising job opportunities, visiting college campuses, and hosting job candidates on visits to the firm.

Pro forma financial statements omit many details in order to provide a "big picture" of the firm. This big picture is important and is especially useful to the board of directors, CEO, CFO, and other top managers. But the many specialized budgets provide important detailed guidance to other employees. For example, a salesperson probably does not need to know the firm's leverage policy, liquidity objective, dividend policy, and the like. The salesperson, however, does need to know about the availability and prices of new and existing products and must be familiar with the resources available to help in selling them. Each of the firm's units and managers should have the budgets and parts of the financial plan that are relevant to their responsibilities.

Percent of Sales Forecasting Method

Although pro forma statements and budgets are very useful, they can be complex and time consuming to produce. Consequently, managers often use a shortcut method to create them: the percent of sales forecasting method. This method is a crude but easy way to estimate the funds required to finance growth.

Sales growth requires additional investments in receivables, inventories, and fixed assets, so the firm must have financing to grow. Some short-term financing comes spontaneously from the additional sales because accounts payable and accruals, such as wages and taxes payable, naturally increase with an increase in sales. Other financing can come from retained earnings. Any remaining necessary financing must come from other sources, such as additional borrowing.

THE PERCENT OF SALES FORECASTING FORMULA The percent of sales forecasting formula is based on the following equation:

$$\text{Additional financing needed} = \text{Required increase in assets} - \text{Increase in liabilities} - \text{Increase in retained earnings}$$

$$AFN = (A/S)gS_0 - (L/S)gS_0 - [M(1+g)S_0 - D] \tag{24.1}$$

where

AFN = additional financing needed
A/S = the increase in assets required per dollar increase in sales
L/S = the increase in liabilities provided per dollar increase in sales
S_0 = sales for the current year
g = growth in sales
M = net profit margin on sales
D = cash dividends planned for common stock

EXAMPLE Forecasting Financing Needs at Cohen Energy Management Systems

Cohen Energy Management Systems is a small firm with excellent growth opportunities. Cohen's sales last year were \$2 million. They are expected to grow 25% in the coming year to \$2.5 million. Cohen believes that it has access to \$250,000 of external capital and wants to know whether this is sufficient to finance its planned growth.

Cohen requires additional assets (receivables, inventories, and fixed assets) equal to 60% of the increase in sales. Short-term liabilities (accounts payable and other accruals) will increase by 10% of the sales increase. The net profit margin is 8%, and Cohen plans to pay a \$50,000 cash dividend next year.

Using Equation (24.1), the additional financing required is \$100,000:

$$\begin{aligned} \text{AFN} &= (0.60)500{,}000 - (0.10)500{,}000 - [(0.08)2{,}500{,}000 - 50{,}000] \\ &= 300{,}000 - 50{,}000 - 150{,}000 = \$100{,}000 \end{aligned}$$

From this, we can see that Cohen requires an additional \$300,000 of assets to support its sales growth. Spontaneous financing from short-term liabilities that increase with sales provides \$50,000 of the needed funds. After payment of the \$50,000 dividend from the expected net income of \$200,000, this year's retained earnings will provide \$150,000 of funds. This leaves a need for only \$100,000 more to finance the expected sales growth. Cohen will be fine, then, because it has access to up to \$250,000 of additional financing.

Cash Flow Break-Even Point

Over the planning horizon, the **cash flow break-even point** is the point below which the firm will need either to obtain additional financing or to liquidate some of its assets to meet its fixed costs (for example, salaries and administrative costs, interest and principal payments, and planned cash dividends). The existence of the cash flow break-even point is pivotal in that it "forces" the firm to address contingency plans for possible, but perhaps unlikely, bad outcomes.

The probability of falling below cash flow breakeven during a planning horizon provides a measure of the firm's total risk. This probability depends both on the variability of sales and on how close the firm is to its cash flow break-even point when adversity begins to set in.

It is important to keep the possible effects of financial leverage and operating leverage in mind when preparing the financial plan for a firm. Both are sources of risk. Therefore, to control the risk that it will be unable to meet, for example, its contractual debt payment obligations, a firm can, to whatever extent possible, (1) change its financial leverage, (2) change its operating leverage and, consequently, its break-even point, or (3) change some combination of the two. To the extent that a firm cannot control its operating leverage, the firm should use the planning process to control risk by creating contingency plans for dealing with bad outcomes.

Alternatives When Funds Are Inadequate

Many rapidly growing firms find themselves short of cash—even though they are profitable. In such cases, the firm has several options to consider:

1. *Reduce the growth rate.* The firm can choose to reduce its funds requirement to a manageable level by not fully meeting the demand for its product. One thing that might reduce demand is to raise the selling price. If implemented successfully, this approach has the added benefit of increasing the firm's income, which provides additional funds that can be reinvested to finance growth. (See our discussion of the price-setting option in Chapter 8.)
2. *Sell assets.* If there are any assets that are not required to run the firm, it can sell those assets and reinvest the proceeds. Such an alternative would need to be analyzed as a capital budgeting project under capital rationing. (See Chapter 8.)
3. *Obtain new external financing.* Among other things, a firm can issue new securities, arrange loans, lease or rent assets, or use venture capital financing. Because these choices can affect capital structure, they must be made in conjunction with the firm's capital structure policy. (See Chapter 15.)
4. *Reduce or stop paying dividends.* Cash dividends use funds that could otherwise be reinvested. However, there are many factors to consider before making this decision. (See our discussion of dividend policy in Chapter 17.)

Managers must weigh the benefits and costs of each alternative carefully before deciding on a course of action. An inappropriate course of action can be very costly to the firm. Consider this simple rule: An unprofitable firm that does not have substantial unused production capacity cannot grow itself into profitability.[1]

Growth does not usually increase the firm's return on its existing assets. Growth in the form of a simple expansion of existing operations would normally have a lower *rate* of return than the rate of return on existing assets. Growth is attractive—in spite of this lower return—only when the growth has a positive NPV, that is, when the expected return exceeds the required return. Growth can lead to disaster when it has a negative NPV. An unprofitable firm should consider the abandonment option if it is unable to move itself into profitability without growth.

It is also important to remember that rapid expansion is risky. Expansion often means sales in new markets or even sales of new products—both of which are likely to be riskier than the firm's current operations. Consequently, firms often limit their growth through capital rationing to control the firm's risk. (See our discussion of the potential benefits of capital rationing in Chapter 8.)

[1]A firm with substantial unused capacity might become profitable if it can grow. If it can expand sales, for example through better marketing, and earn a positive contribution margin on the increased sales, its *rate of return ratios* will improve. (See Chapter 3.)

Long-Term Planning Models

Thus far we have focused on short-term planning models. Firms also use long-term planning models, where the planning horizon depends on the nature of the industry. Most firms use a five- or ten-year planning horizon. Some industries, such as electric utilities, have even longer horizons. Long-term planning models incorporate the firm's strategic commitments of resources. They are built around periodic pro forma financial statements over the planning horizon.

EXAMPLE Whittaker Industries' Long-Term Planning Model

Whittaker Industries has a seven-year planning model that includes detailed financial statements for the next seven years. Some of the data from Whittaker's pro forma income statements, statements of cash flows, and balance sheets are summarized and presented in Table 24.4. This table provides a good overview of several of the firm's strategic decisions.

TABLE 24.4
Whittaker Industries' seven-year plan.

YEAR	1	2	3	4	5	6	7
Selected Income Statement Items							
Sales	60.00	62.00	65.00	80.00	95.00	105.00	110.00
Net income	3.00	3.10	3.25	4.00	4.75	5.25	5.50
Dividends	0.60	0.60	0.60	0.60	0.90	1.20	1.25
Statement of Cash Flow Summary							
Operating cash flow	6.50	6.25	6.50	7.50	6.50	7.50	8.00
Investing cash flow	−8.00	−9.00	−8.00	−2.00	−2.00	−4.00	−3.00
Financing cash flow	1.00	2.50	1.50	−4.00	−2.00	−2.00	−2.00
Total cash flow	−0.50	−0.25	−0.00	−1.50	−2.50	−1.50	−3.00
Balance Sheet Summary							
Cash	4.00	3.75	3.75	5.25	7.75	9.25	12.25
Receivables	9.00	9.30	9.75	12.00	14.25	15.75	16.50
Inventory	7.20	7.45	7.70	9.60	11.40	12.60	13.20
Total current assets	20.20	20.50	21.20	26.85	33.40	37.60	41.95
Net fixed assets	35.00	42.00	48.00	50.00	52.00	54.00	56.00
Total assets	55.20	62.50	69.20	76.85	85.40	91.60	97.95
Payables and accruals	3.60	3.72	3.90	4.80	5.70	6.30	6.60
Other short-term debt	10.00	12.00	13.00	6.00	6.85	7.50	7.75
Total current liabilities	13.60	15.72	16.90	10.80	12.55	13.80	14.35
Mortgages	12.00	12.00	12.00	19.00	19.00	19.00	19.00
Other long-term debt	14.40	17.08	19.95	23.30	26.25	27.15	28.70
Stockholders' equity	15.20	17.70	20.35	23.75	27.60	31.65	35.90
Total liabilities and equity	55.20	62.50	69.20	76.85	85.40	91.60	97.95
Selected Financial Ratios							
Sales/total assets	1.09	0.99	0.94	1.04	1.11	1.15	1.12
Current assets/current liabilities	1.49	1.30	1.25	2.49	2.66	2.72	2.92
Dividends/net income	20.0%	19.4%	18.5%	15.0%	18.9%	22.9%	22.7%
Net income/stockholders' equity	19.7	17.5	16.0	16.8	17.2	16.6	15.3
Total debt/total assets	72.5	71.7	70.6	69.1	67.7	65.4	63.3

The firm intends to expand over the next four years. You can see this in the large investing cash flow (the negative cash flow is an investment) for the first three years. Net fixed assets also increase substantially on the balance sheet in the early years of the plan. In the fourth year, some of the short-term debt expected to be accumulated to finance construction will be refinanced with long-term mortgages. Sales growth is expected to be slow for the first three years but much faster in years 4 through 6 of the plan. In year 7, sales growth is expected to taper off. The sales growth in years 4 through 6 is accompanied by planned increases in working capital. The firm plans to hold dividends constant for four years, until after the construction is completed and net income has begun increasing in response to the sales expansion. In years 5 and 6, if all goes well, the firm will be able to increase substantially the dividend on its common shares.

In the first three years of the plan, Whittaker's total asset turnover and current ratio fall slightly. Thereafter, these ratios improve. Late in the seven-year plan, the firm's overall financial health is expected to have improved to the point where other strategic decisions might be considered, such as additional growth, paying off debt, or repurchasing some common shares.

Review

1. How do firms use pro forma financial statements?
2. What role do business unit budgets play in the operation of the firm?
3. What is the relationship among the additional financing needed, the required increases in assets, the increase in liabilities, and the increase in retained earnings?
4. If a profitable but rapidly growing firm finds itself short of cash, what steps can it take to deal with the problem?

24.4 AUTOMATING FINANCIAL FORECASTING

Computer technology has greatly benefited cash budgeting and the entire planning process. Spreadsheet software lends itself to cash budgeting and pro forma financial statement analysis. You probably already know how to use a computer spreadsheet package. The main benefit of a spreadsheet is its flexibility. It can be updated very easily, which reduces the clerical burden. A spreadsheet is ideally suited to answer "what-if" questions. For example, changing the February sales projection would cause other changes that ripple through the entire annual cash budget. You can make such changes in seconds when you are using a spreadsheet.

An Example of an Automated Forecast

When Justin Case started his new job as treasurer of the You 'N' Me Toy Company (YNMTC), he found the firm did not have a formal cash budgeting system. The owner said "Don't worry, we have plenty of money in the bank." However, Mr. Case wanted to create a cash management model for the firm's activities just the same. (Somewhat surprisingly, the owner agreed, saying, "We need this model, Justin Case.")

YNMTC is a small manufacturer with a stable customer base and stable supplier relationships. Accurate cash inflow and cash outflow data are available. Table 24.5 shows the information Justin Case gathered. Justin then had to decide on the form of the model, what period(s) it would cover, and how frequently it would be updated.

In his accounting classes, Justin learned that accountants go to great lengths to avoid having an account with a negative balance. For example, they create what are called contra accounts for dealing with negative amounts. We in financial management do not feel so constrained. We recognize that an account with a negative balance can be equivalently viewed as being a positive amount on the other side of the balance sheet. The two sides are mirror images: A negative asset is a liability, and a negative

TABLE 24.5
Information about the You 'N' Me Toy Company, compiled by Justin Case.

1. The payment pattern for revenues is estimated to be as follows: 40% of sales are for cash, 10% are paid for 1 month after the sale, 50% are paid for 2 months after the sale, and bad debt is negligible.
2. The treasury department believes that the cash account should be set to start each month in the amount of $10,000 plus 60% of next month's salaries and wages plus 70% of this month's accounts payable. It also believes YNMTC can earn 0.6% per month on its short-term investments. The model will adjust the cash account with the short-term investment (borrowing) account.
3. YNMTC appears to purchase raw materials each month in the amount of 30% of the predicted sales for the month after next plus 20% of next month's predicted sales plus 10% of this month's sales. Purchases are paid for in the month following their purchase, and there are no discounts available to YNMTC from its suppliers. The cost of raw materials averages 60% of sales.
4. YNMTC pays salaries and wages of $7,000 plus 18% of this month's sales.
5. YNMTC is depreciating its net fixed assets at the rate of 1% of *net* fixed assets per month.
6. YNMTC pays a cash dividend of $2,000 every month.
7. The long-term debt on the YNMTC balance sheet carries a 12% APR, and payments are made quarterly in December, March, June, and September.
8. Taxes for YNMTC are at the rate of 35% of taxable income (including rebates for negative taxes). Taxes are paid monthly.
9. Sales in October and November of this year were $40,000 and $60,000, respectively. Sales forecasts for the next 11 months ($ thousands) are

DEC.	JAN.	FEB.	MAR.	APR.	MAY	JUN.	JUL.	AUG.	SEP.	OCT.
100.00	170.00	150.00	125.00	100.00	70.00	65.00	90.00	175.00	50.00	70.00

BALANCE SHEET AS OF NOVEMBER 30

Cash	$ 76.00	Accounts payable	$ 77.00
Short-term investments (borrowing)	70.00	Accrued interest	6.00
Accounts receivable	56.00	Long-term debt	300.00
Inventory	122.00	Common stock	70.00
Net fixed assets	391.00	Retained earnings	262.00
Total assets	$715.00	Liabilities + stockholders' equity	$715.00

liability is an asset. We can recognize the Principle of Two-Sided Transactions in this relationship. For example, "negative debt" is money someone else owes you—so it is an asset. Similarly, a "negative marketable security" is simply money you owe someone else—so it is a liability.

Justin used this fact to simplify his short-term financial planning model of YNMTC. He created a short-term investment (borrowing) account to use as a "plug" for balancing the balance sheet. The account consists of marketable securities when it is positive, but it becomes a short-term bank loan whenever it must be negative to make the balance sheet balance. A negative balance in this account indicates that the firm needs to arrange for more short-term financing.

Justin's short-term investment (borrowing) account simplifies the model-building process. Letting the account be positive *or* negative avoids the problem of automating "conditional" accounts. Conditional accounts require a more complex set of equations. For example, with the short-term investment (borrowing) account, if YNMTC is investing money (the account is positive), then the amount invested is shown as a current asset. But if YNMTC is borrowing money (that is, if the account is negative), then the amount is normally shown in an entirely different account as a current liability with a positive balance.

Table 24.6 presents output from Justin Case's automated financial planning model, based on the information in Table 24.5. The short-term investment (borrowing) account is projected to be negative in January and February. Thus, it seems that during January and February, YNMTC will have to either (1) obtain additional financing in the amounts indicated (the absolute value of

TABLE 24.6

Cash budget and pro forma income statements and balance sheets for the You 'N' Me Toy Company, based on the information in Table 24.5.

CASH BUDGET FOR DECEMBER THROUGH AUGUST

	Oct	Nov	Dec	Jan	Feb	Mar	Apr	May	Jun	Jul	Aug	Sep	Oct
SALES	40.00	60.00	100.00	170.00	150.00	125.00	100.00	70.00	65.00	90.00	175.00	50.00[a]	70.00[a]
A/R COLLECTIONS			66.00	108.00	127.00	150.00	127.50	100.50	83.00	77.50	111.50		
INTEREST INCOME			0.42	0.01	−0.13	−0.06	0.24	0.56	0.76	0.66	0.52		
CASH INFLOW			66.42	108.01	126.87	149.94	127.74	101.06	83.76	78.16	112.02		
PAYABLES PAID			77.00	89.00	84.50	70.00	53.50	43.50	47.00	77.00	59.00		
SALARIES & WAGES PAID			25.00	37.60	34.00	29.50	25.00	19.60	18.70	23.20	38.50	16.00[a]	
TAXES PAID			2.98	8.24	6.66	4.78	2.97	0.79	0.48	2.39	8.90		
INTEREST PAID			9.00	0.00	0.00	9.00	0.00	0.00	9.00	0.00	0.00		
DIVIDENDS PAID			2.00	2.00	2.00	2.00	2.00	2.00	2.00	2.00	2.00		
STARTING CASH			76.00	94.86	89.55	76.70	62.45	52.21	54.12	77.82	74.40		
ENDING CASH			94.86	89.55	76.70	62.45	52.21	54.12	77.82	74.40	53.55		
S-T INVESTMENT CHANGE (cash budget)			−68.42	−23.52	12.56	48.92	54.51	33.27	−17.12	−23.00	24.48		
S-T INVESTMENT CHANGE (balance sheet)			−68.42	−23.52	12.56	48.92	54.51	33.27	−17.12	−23.00	24.48		

MONTHLY PRO FORMA INCOME STATEMENTS

	Oct	Nov	Dec	Jan	Feb	Mar	Apr	May	Jun	Jul	Aug
SALES	40.00	60.00	100.00	170.00	150.00	125.00	100.00	70.00	65.00	90.00	175.00
COST OF RAW MATERIALS			60.00	102.00	90.00	75.00	60.00	42.00	39.00	54.00	105.00
SALARIES & WAGES			25.00	37.60	34.00	29.50	25.00	19.60	18.70	23.20	38.50
DEPRECIATION			3.91	3.87	3.83	3.79	3.76	3.72	3.68	3.64	3.61
INTEREST EXPENSE			3.00	3.00	3.00	3.00	3.00	3.00	3.00	3.00	3.00
INTEREST INCOME			0.42	0.01	−0.13	−0.06	0.24	0.56	0.76	0.66	0.52
TAXABLE INCOME			8.51	23.54	19.04	13.65	8.48	2.25	1.38	6.82	25.42
TAXES			2.98	8.24	6.66	4.78	2.97	0.79	0.48	2.39	8.90
NET INCOME			5.53	15.30	12.37	8.87	5.51	1.46	0.90	4.43	16.52
DIVIDENDS			2.00	2.00	2.00	2.00	2.00	2.00	2.00	2.00	2.00
CHANGE IN RETAINED EARNINGS			3.53	13.30	10.37	6.87	3.51	−0.54	−1.10	2.43	14.52

CURRENT BALANCE SHEET AND MONTHLY PRO FORMA BALANCE SHEETS

	Oct	Nov	Dec	Jan	Feb	Mar	Apr	May	Jun	Jul	Aug
CASH		76.00	94.86	89.55	76.70	62.45	52.21	54.12	77.82	74.40	53.55
S-T INVESTMENT (BORROWING)		70.00	1.58	−21.94	−9.38	39.53	94.04	127.31	110.19	87.19	111.66
ACCOUNTS RECEIVABLE		56.00	90.00	152.00	175.00	150.00	122.50	92.00	74.00	86.50	150.00
INVENTORY		122.00	151.00	133.50	113.50	92.00	75.50	80.50	118.50	123.50	67.00
NET FIXED ASSETS		391.00	387.09	383.22	379.39	375.59	371.84	368.12	364.44	360.79	357.19
TOTAL ASSETS		715.00	724.53	736.33	735.21	719.58	716.09	722.05	744.95	732.38	739.40
ACCOUNTS PAYABLE		77.00	89.00	84.50	70.00	53.50	43.50	47.00	77.00	59.00	48.50
ACCRUED INTEREST		6.00	0.00	3.00	6.00	0.00	3.00	6.00	0.00	3.00	6.00
LONG-TERM DEBT		300.00	300.00	300.00	300.00	300.00	300.00	300.00	300.00	300.00	300.00
COMMON STOCK		70.00	70.00	70.00	70.00	70.00	70.00	70.00	70.00	70.00	70.00
RETAINED EARNINGS		262.00	265.53	278.83	289.21	296.08	299.59	299.05	297.95	300.38	314.90
LIABILITIES + OWNERS' EQUITY		715.00	724.53	736.33	735.21	719.58	716.09	722.05	744.95	732.38	739.40

[a]Required for other computations.

TABLE 24.7

Spreadsheet equations for the output shown in Table 24.6. (The months of October through October are in columns D through P.)

LINE	COLUMN A	COLUMN F
3	CASH BUDGET FOR DECEMBER THROUGH AUGUST	
4		DEC
5	SALES	100.00
6	A/R COLLECTIONS	= 0.4*F5 + 0.1*E5 + 0.5*D5
7	INTEREST INCOME	= 0.006*E42
8	CASH INFLOW	= F6 + F7
9		
10	PAYABLES PAID	= E48
11	SALARIES & WAGES PAID	= 7.0 + 0.18*F5
12	TAXES PAID	= F32
13	INTEREST PAID	= E49 + F28[a]
14	DIVIDENDS PAID	2.00
15	STARTING CASH	= E41
16	ENDING CASH	= F41
17	S-T INVESTMENT CHANGE (cash budget)	= F15 − F16 + F8 − F10 − F11 − F12 − F13 − F14
18	S-T INVESTMENT CHANGE (balance sheet)	= F42 − E42
19		
20		
21		
22	MONTHLY PRO FORMA INCOME STATEMENTS	
23		DEC
24	SALES	= F5
25	COST OF RAW MATERIALS	= 0.6*F24
26	SALARIES & WAGES	= F11
27	DEPRECIATION	= 0.01*E45
28	INTEREST EXPENSE	= 0.01*E50
29	INTEREST INCOME	= F7
30	TAXABLE INCOME	= F24 − F25 − F26 − F27 − F28 + F29
31		
32	TAXES	= 0.35*F30
33	NET INCOME	= F30 − F32
34		
35	DIVIDENDS	= F14
36	CHANGE IN RETAINED EARNINGS	= F33 − F35
37		
38		
39	CURRENT BALANCE SHEET AND MONTHLY PRO FORMA BALANCE SHEETS	
40		DEC
41	CASH	= 10.0 + 0.6*G11 + 0.7*F48
42	S-T INVESTMENT (BORROWING)	= F53 − F41 − F43 − F44 − F45
43	ACCOUNTS RECEIVABLE	= 0.6*F5 + 0.5*E5
44	INVENTORY	= E44 + F48 − F25
45	NET FIXED ASSETS	= E45 − F27
46	TOTAL ASSETS	= F41 + F42 + F43 + F44 + F45
47		
48	ACCOUNTS PAYABLE	= 0.1*F5 + 0.2*G5 + 0.3*H5
49	ACCRUED INTEREST	= E49 + F28 − F13
50	LONG-TERM DEBT	= E50
51	COMMON STOCK	= E51
52	RETAINED EARNINGS	= E52 + F36
53	LIABILITIES + OWNERS' EQUITY	= F48 + F49 + F50 + F51 + F52

[a]This equation repeats every 3 months, with zero for the intervening months.

the negative balance), to maintain its target level for the cash account, or (2) allow the cash account to fall below the target.

Table 24.7 presents the spreadsheet equations (or data) in Justin's model for the first month of the planning period, December, which is shown in column F. In principle, the general form of such equations is simple:

$$\text{Ending balance} = \text{Starting balance} + \text{Increases} - \text{Decreases} \tag{24.2}$$

Of course, the "trick" to building the model is to identify correctly all the potential increases and decreases for a given account. For example, the inventory account increases with the purchase of raw materials and decreases with the sale of finished goods. A purchase of raw materials also increases accounts payable or decreases cash. And a sale of finished goods increases accounts receivable or increases cash.

Account changes in double-entry accounting always maintain the "balance" of the balance sheet. When the offsetting accounts are on the same side of the balance sheet, an increase in one account causes a decrease in the other, and vice versa. For example, a cash purchase of raw materials causes an increase in inventory and a decrease in cash. When the offsetting accounts are on opposite sides of the balance sheet, the changes are in the same direction. An increase in one account causes an increase in the other, and a decrease in one causes a decrease in the other. For example, a credit purchase of raw materials causes an increase in inventory and an increase in accounts payable.

Once he had entered the equations into the December column, Justin *block-copied* them into subsequent columns for January through August. Then he put in "corrections" for two of the model's rows: (1) Each sales forecast was entered separately, and (2) he put in zeros in line 13 for the months in which YNMTC does not make a cash interest payment.[2]

In the cash budget, Justin put in two different equations for the short-term investment change as a check on the model. The first equation (cash budget) tracks the actual cash flows. This change is the sum of the increases and decreases in short-term investment (borrowing). The second equation (balance sheet) is the change in short-term investment (borrowing) that results from forcing the balance sheet to balance. This second change is the short-term investment (borrowing) ending balance minus its starting balance. If these two equations do not produce the same answer, then there is an error—the model is not internally consistent.

"What-If" Questions: The Power of a Spreadsheet Package

After he had built the financial planning model shown in Tables 24.6 and 24.7, it occurred to Mr. Case that actual sales virtually never turn out to be what was expected. Therefore, he decided to consider the possibilities of higher- or lower-than-expected sales. Tables 24.8 and 24.9 present output from his model, assuming that sales are 80% and 120% of forecast levels, respectively.

Looking at Table 24.8, we see a case of "good news and bad news." The good news is that with lower-than-expected sales, YNMTC will not need to obtain additional financing to maintain its target level of cash; in none of the months is the short-term investment (borrowing) balance negative. The bad news is that total projected net income over the planning horizon declines from \$70,890 to \$41,130.

Similarly, Table 24.9 reveals that higher-than-expected sales will require an even greater amount of additional financing but that total projected net income increases from \$70,890 to \$100,660. Although growth can have its problems, You 'N' Me would be happy to have higher-than-expected sales but, true to his name, Justin Case also considered lower-than-expected sales to help create contingency plans.

---

[2]Note that unless you specify differently, the copy command maintains the relationship among the cells rather than maintaining specific cell identities. For example, if cell G6 has the equation [E5 + F4] in it, and you copy G6 to L12, the equation becomes [J11 + K10].

TABLE 24.8

Cash budget and pro forma income statements and balance sheets for the You 'N' Me Toy Company, with 80% of forecast sales.

CASH BUDGET FOR DECEMBER THROUGH AUGUST

	Oct	Nov	Dec	Jan	Feb	Mar	Apr	May	Jun	Jul	Aug	Sep	Oct
SALES	40.00	60.00	80.00	136.00	120.00	100.00	80.00	56.00	52.00	72.00	140.00	40.00[a]	56.00[a]
A/R COLLECTIONS			58.00	92.40	101.60	120.00	102.00	80.40	66.40	62.00	89.20		
INTEREST INCOME			0.42	0.09	0.01	0.06	0.28	0.54	0.69	0.60	0.48		
CASH INFLOW			58.42	92.49	101.61	120.06	102.28	80.94	67.09	62.60	89.68		
PAYABLES PAID			77.00	71.20	67.60	56.00	42.80	34.80	37.60	61.60	47.20		
SALARIES & WAGES PAID			21.40	31.48	28.60	25.00	21.40	17.08	16.36	19.96	32.20	14.20[a]	
TAXES PAID			1.44	5.65	4.40	2.89	1.44	−0.30	−0.54	0.98	6.19		
INTEREST PAID			9.00	0.00	0.00	9.00	0.00	0.00	9.00	0.00	0.00		
DIVIDENDS PAID			2.00	2.00	2.00	2.00	2.00	2.00	2.00	2.00	2.00		
STARTING CASH			76.00	78.73	74.48	64.20	52.80	44.61	46.14	65.10	62.36		
ENDING CASH			78.73	74.48	64.20	52.80	44.61	46.14	65.10	62.36	45.68		
S-T INVESTMENT CHANGE (cash budget)			−55.15	−13.59	9.29	36.57	42.83	25.83	−16.28	−19.20	18.78		
S-T INVESTMENT CHANGE (balance sheet)			−55.15	−13.59	9.29	36.57	42.83	25.83	−16.28	−19.20	18.78		

MONTHLY PRO FORMA INCOME STATEMENTS

	Oct	Nov	Dec	Jan	Feb	Mar	Apr	May	Jun	Jul	Aug
SALES	40.00	60.00	80.00	136.00	120.00	100.00	80.00	56.00	52.00	72.00	140.00
COST OF RAW MATERIALS			48.00	81.60	72.00	60.00	48.00	33.60	31.20	43.20	84.00
SALARIES & WAGES			21.40	31.48	28.60	25.00	21.40	17.08	16.36	19.96	32.20
DEPRECIATION			3.91	3.87	3.83	3.79	3.76	3.72	3.68	3.64	3.61
INTEREST EXPENSE			3.00	3.00	3.00	3.00	3.00	3.00	3.00	3.00	3.00
INTEREST INCOME			0.42	0.09	0.01	0.06	0.28	0.54	0.69	0.60	0.48
TAXABLE INCOME			4.11	16.14	12.58	8.27	4.13	−0.86	−1.55	2.79	17.67
TAXES			1.44	5.65	4.40	2.89	1.44	−0.30	−0.54	0.98	6.19
NET INCOME			2.67	10.49	8.17	5.38	2.68	−0.56	−1.01	1.82	11.49
DIVIDENDS			2.00	2.00	2.00	2.00	2.00	2.00	2.00	2.00	2.00
CHANGE IN RETAINED EARNINGS			0.67	8.49	6.17	3.38	0.68	−2.56	−3.01	−0.18	9.49

CURRENT BALANCE SHEET AND MONTHLY PRO FORMA BALANCE SHEETS

	Oct	Nov	Dec	Jan	Feb	Mar	Apr	May	Jun	Jul	Aug
CASH		76.00	78.73	74.48	64.20	52.80	44.61	46.14	65.10	62.36	45.68
S-T INVESTMENT (BORROWING)		70.00	14.85	1.26	10.55	47.12	89.95	115.78	99.50	80.29	99.07
ACCOUNTS RECEIVABLE		56.00	78.00	121.60	140.00	120.00	98.00	73.60	59.20	69.20	120.00
INVENTORY		122.00	145.20	131.20	115.20	98.00	84.80	88.80	119.20	123.20	78.00
NET FIXED ASSETS		391.00	387.09	383.22	379.39	375.59	371.84	368.12	364.44	360.79	357.19
TOTAL ASSETS		715.00	703.87	711.76	709.34	693.51	689.19	692.43	707.43	695.84	699.93
ACCOUNTS PAYABLE		77.00	71.20	67.60	56.00	42.80	34.80	37.60	61.60	47.20	38.80
ACCRUED INTEREST		6.00	0.00	3.00	6.00	0.00	3.00	6.00	0.00	3.00	6.00
LONG-TERM DEBT		300.00	300.00	300.00	300.00	300.00	300.00	300.00	300.00	300.00	300.00
COMMON STOCK		70.00	70.00	70.00	70.00	70.00	70.00	70.00	70.00	70.00	70.00
RETAINED EARNINGS		262.00	262.67	271.16	277.34	280.71	281.39	278.83	275.83	275.64	285.13
LIABILITIES + OWNERS' EQUITY		715.00	703.87	711.76	709.34	693.51	689.19	692.43	707.43	695.84	699.93

[a]Required for other computations.

TABLE 24.9

Cash budget and pro forma income statements and balance sheets for the You 'N' Me Toy Company, with 120% of forecast sales.

CASH BUDGET FOR DECEMBER THROUGH AUGUST

	Oct	Nov	Dec	Jan	Feb	Mar	Apr	May	Jun	Jul	Aug	Sep	Oct
SALES	40.00	60.00	120.00	204.00	180.00	150.00	120.00	84.00	78.00	108.00	210.00	60.00[a]	84.00[a]
A/R COLLECTIONS			74.00	123.60	152.40	180.00	153.00	120.60	99.60	93.00	133.80		
INTEREST INCOME			0.42	−0.07	−0.27	−0.18	0.19	0.59	0.83	0.73	0.56		
CASH INFLOW			74.42	123.53	152.13	179.82	153.19	121.19	100.43	93.73	134.36		
PAYABLES PAID			77.00	106.80	101.40	84.00	64.20	52.20	56.40	92.40	70.80		
SALARIES & WAGES PAID			28.60	43.72	39.40	34.00	28.60	22.12	21.04	26.44	44.80	17.80[a]	
TAXES PAID			4.52	10.83	8.92	6.66	4.49	1.87	1.51	3.79	11.60		
INTEREST PAID			9.00	0.00	0.00	9.00	0.00	0.00	9.00	0.00	0.00		
DIVIDENDS PAID			2.00	2.00	2.00	2.00	2.00	2.00	2.00	2.00	2.00		
STARTING CASH			76.00	110.99	104.62	89.20	72.10	59.81	62.10	90.54	86.44		
ENDING CASH			110.99	104.62	89.20	72.10	59.81	62.10	90.54	86.44	61.42		
S-T INVESTMENT CHANGE (cash budget)			−81.69	−33.45	15.83	61.26	66.19	40.70	−17.96	−26.81	30.18		
S-T INVESTMENT CHANGE (balance sheet)			−81.69	−33.45	15.83	61.26	66.19	40.70	−17.96	−26.81	30.18		

MONTHLY PRO FORMA INCOME STATEMENTS

	Oct	Nov	Dec	Jan	Feb	Mar	Apr	May	Jun	Jul	Aug
SALES	40.00	60.00	120.00	204.00	180.00	150.00	120.00	84.00	78.00	108.00	210.00
COST OF RAW MATERIALS			72.00	122.40	108.00	90.00	72.00	50.40	46.80	64.80	126.00
SALARIES & WAGES			28.60	43.72	39.40	34.00	28.60	22.12	21.04	26.44	44.80
DEPRECIATION			3.91	3.87	3.83	3.79	3.76	3.72	3.68	3.64	3.61
INTEREST EXPENSE			3.00	3.00	3.00	3.00	3.00	3.00	3.00	3.00	3.00
INTEREST INCOME			0.42	−0.07	−0.27	−0.18	0.19	0.59	0.83	0.73	0.56
TAXABLE INCOME			12.91	30.94	25.50	19.03	12.84	5.35	4.31	10.84	33.16
TAXES			4.52	10.83	8.92	6.66	4.49	1.87	1.51	3.79	11.60
NET INCOME			8.39	20.11	16.57	12.37	8.34	3.48	2.80	7.05	21.55
DIVIDENDS			2.00	2.00	2.00	2.00	2.00	2.00	2.00	2.00	2.00
CHANGE IN RETAINED EARNINGS			6.39	18.11	14.57	10.37	6.34	1.48	0.80	5.05	19.55

CURRENT BALANCE SHEET AND MONTHLY PRO FORMA BALANCE SHEETS

	Oct	Nov	Dec	Jan	Feb	Mar	Apr	May	Jun	Jul	Aug
CASH		76.00	110.99	104.62	89.20	72.10	59.81	62.10	90.54	86.44	61.42
S-T INVESTMENT (BORROWING)		70.00	−11.69	−45.14	−29.31	31.95	98.14	138.84	120.89	94.08	124.26
ACCOUNTS RECEIVABLE		56.00	102.00	182.40	210.00	180.00	147.00	110.40	88.80	103.80	180.00
INVENTORY		122.00	156.80	135.80	111.80	86.00	66.20	72.20	117.80	123.80	56.00
NET FIXED ASSETS		391.00	387.09	383.22	379.39	375.59	371.84	368.12	364.44	360.79	357.19
TOTAL ASSETS		715.00	745.19	760.90	761.07	745.64	742.99	751.67	782.47	768.91	778.87
ACCOUNTS PAYABLE		77.00	106.80	101.40	84.00	64.20	52.20	56.40	92.40	70.80	58.20
ACCRUED INTEREST		6.00	0.00	3.00	6.00	0.00	3.00	6.00	0.00	3.00	6.00
LONG-TERM DEBT		300.00	300.00	300.00	300.00	300.00	300.00	300.00	300.00	300.00	300.00
COMMON STOCK		70.00	70.00	70.00	70.00	70.00	70.00	70.00	70.00	70.00	70.00
RETAINED EARNINGS		262.00	268.39	286.50	301.07	311.44	317.79	319.27	320.07	325.11	344.67
LIABILITIES + OWNERS' EQUITY		715.00	745.19	760.90	761.07	745.64	742.99	751.67	782.47	768.91	778.87

[a]Required for other computations.

Review

1. Why is spreadsheet software so useful in preparing financial plans?
2. In building a financial planning spreadsheet model, why is it convenient to use a single item to represent both short-term investments (when the amount is positive) and short-term borrowing (when the amount is negative)?

SUMMARY

- Financial planning is an organized process of gathering information, analyzing alternative decisions, developing goals and plans, implementing the plans, and evaluating performance against those plans. The purpose of planning and budgeting is to draw out the best of the firm's units and individuals to achieve the firm's overall goals.
- The financial plan is a "blueprint" for the future.
- A firm should prepare a financial plan on a regular basis, preferably at least annually. Any firm that does not plan for its future may not have one.
- Financial planning has three phases: (1) the formulation phase where the plan is designed, (2) the implementation phase where the plan is put into action, and (3) the evaluation phase where future performance is measured against the plan.
- Top-down financial planning relies on top managers to dominate the strategic decisions, whereas a bottom-up planning style tends to make decisions based on ideas that percolate up from lower levels in the firm.
- Good financial planning uses both bottom-up and top-down processes to get the most out of the firm's units and individuals.
- Pro forma financial statements are used to summarize the overall impact on the firm of the production, marketing, and financing decisions that have been made.
- A firm's financial plan should consist of (1) a *long-term financial plan* that covers a period of at least three to five years, (2) a *short-term financial plan* that covers the coming year and agrees with the first year of the long-term plan, and (3) a detailed *cash budget* for the coming year.
- A complete financial plan includes, at a minimum,
  1. Clearly stated strategic, operating, and financial *objectives*
  2. The *assumptions* on which the plan is based
  3. Descriptions of the underlying *strategies*
  4. *Contingency plans* for emergencies
  5. *Budgets,* categorized and summarized in various ways, such as by time period, division, and type (for example, cash, advertising, purchasing, and capital)
  6. The *financing program,* categorized and summarized in various ways, such as by time period, sources of funds (for example, bonds, bank loans, stock), and types of funds (for example, short- versus long-term, internal versus external)
  7. A set of period-by-period *pro forma financial statements* for the entire planning horizon
- A firm's business units should be intimately involved in the planning process, with each unit preparing its own financial plan. The corporate staff must provide overall guidance by ensuring that all business units base their plans on a consistent set of assumptions (supplied by the corporate staff), checking the business unit plans for reasonableness, and consolidating the business unit plans into the overall financial plan for the firm.
- A cash budget summarizes the firm's expected cash inflows and outflows as well as its expected cash and loan balances.

- A firm should regularly (at least monthly) monitor its performance against the short-term plan and the cash budget.
- The *cash flow break-even point* over a planning horizon is a pivotal point for addressing contingency plans for possible, even if unlikely, bad outcomes.
- The probability of falling below cash flow break-even during a planning horizon provides a measure of the firm's total risk.
- Computer technology has greatly benefited cash budgeting and the entire planning process. Because of its flexibility, spreadsheet software lends itself to cash budgeting and the analysis of pro forma financial statements. Changes can be made easily and "what-if" questions can be readily investigated.

EQUATION SUMMARY

$$\begin{array}{c}\text{Additional} \\ \text{financing} \\ \text{needed}\end{array} = \begin{array}{c}\text{Required} \\ \text{increase} \\ \text{in assets}\end{array} - \begin{array}{c}\text{Increase} \\ \text{in liabilities}\end{array} - \begin{array}{c}\text{Increase in} \\ \text{retained} \\ \text{earnings}\end{array}$$

$$AFN = (A/S)gS_0 - (L/S)gS_0 - [M(1 + g)S_0 - D] \tag{24.1}$$

$$\text{Ending balance} = \text{Starting balance} + \text{Increases} - \text{Decreases} \tag{24.2}$$

QUESTIONS

1. What would a complete financial plan include, at a minimum?
2. What is the difference between bottom-up and top-down planning?
3. Assume that you are working for a business and one of your colleagues is whining that the business is wasting too much resources on its financial planning. Because this person is your friend, outline for him some of the major benefits of the financial planning process that, hopefully, justify its cost.
4. Indicate whether each of the following would typically increase or decrease a firm's need for additional external financing. (a) An increase in cash dividends, (b) An increase in the net profit margin, (c) A decrease in the credit period offered by the firm's suppliers, (d) A decrease in the credit period offered to the firm's customers, (e) An increase in corporate income tax rates.
5. A rapidly growing firm does not have access to sufficient external financing to accommodate its planned growth. What alternatives does it have to avoid running out of cash?
6. True or false?
   a. The three phases of the financial planning process are formulating the plan, implementing the plan, and evaluating performance.
   b. Top-down financial planning relies on top managers to dominate the strategic decisions whereas a bottom-up planning style tends to make decisions based on ideas that percolate up from lower levels in the firm.
   c. A major advantage of financial planning is that various managers are given an increase in flexibility and a reduction in accountability.
   d. Most U.S. firms have a very short-term planning horizon, seldom exceeding one year.
   e. In the implementation phase, every manager receives a copy of all of the pro forma financial statements and budgets.
   f. The use of computer technology and spreadsheet software in financial planning has greatly diminished in recent years.

7. What alternatives do profitable growth firms have when internal funds are insufficient to finance expansion?
8. What are the advantages in using a computer spreadsheet package for your financial planning (instead of doing it by hand, using a pencil and calculator)?

CHALLENGING QUESTIONS

9. Explain the ideas behind the percent of sales forecasting method.
10. Explain why spreadsheets are so powerful for conducting a "what-if" analysis.

PROBLEMS

LEVEL A (BASIC)

A1. (Cash budgeting) Steve Ferris has $6,000 in the bank and has a part-time job earning $500 per month. Estimates for his monthly college expenses for his senior year are given below. Steve has a loan agreement where his bank will lend him money when he runs out, such that he will eventually have a zero cash balance and will be accumulating a debt obligation. What is Steve's forecasted cash balance and loan balance for the nine months? How much will he owe when he graduates in May?

SEP.	OCT.	NOV.	DEC.	JAN.	FEB.	MAR.	APR.	MAY
$4,000	1,000	1,000	1,500	4,000	1,000	1,500	1,000	1,500

A2. (Cash budgeting) Tulsa Well Supply Company has a cash balance at the end of June of $1,200,000 and predicts the net cash flows (in $1,000s) given here for the next six months. If Tulsa must keep a cash balance of at least $1,000,000 at all times, when and how much will it need to borrow to maintain this minimum cash balance?

JUL.	AUG.	SEP.	OCT.	NOV.	DEC.
220	205	−325	−625	100	360

A3. (Cash budgeting) At the beginning of January, the South Carolina Sportsplex has $150,000 of cash on hand. The firm's forecasts of the cash flows for the first six months of the year are given below. The S.C. Sportsplex wants to maintain a cash balance of at least $100,000 at all times. If the balance falls below that level, the firm will borrow to bring its balance up to $100,000. If more than $100,000 of cash is available, it will use the excess to reduce its short-term borrowing.

Show the monthly net cash flow, borrowing (if any), loan repayments, cash balance, and cumulative borrowing balance.

Cash flows ($1,000s)

	JAN.	FEB.	MAR.	APR.	MAY	JUN.
Cash inflows	100	120	150	320	350	240
Cash outflows	150	180	200	290	240	180

A4. (Cash budgeting) Kathleen Barry has $5,000 in the bank and has a job earning $2,000 per month. Estimates for her monthly expenses are given below. Kathleen has a loan agreement where her bank will lend her money when she runs out, such that she will eventually have a zero cash balance and will be accumulating a debt obligation. What is Kathleen's forecasted cash balance and loan balance for the next nine months? How much will she owe in December?

APR.	MAY	JUN.	JUL.	AUG.	SEP.	OCT.	NOV.	DEC.
$3,000	5,000	2,000	6,000	3,000	2,000	3,000	4,000	3,000

A5. (Cash budgeting) Illinois Industrial Rental Co. has a cash balance at the end of January of $500,000 and predicts the net cash flows (in $1,000s) given here for the next six months. If Illinois must keep a cash balance of at least $300,000 at all times, when and how much will it need to borrow to maintain this minimum cash balance?

FEB.	MAR.	APR.	MAY	JUN.	JUL.
100	250	−300	−400	50	300

A6. (Additional financing needed) Rodeo Supply Company is planning to increase its sales by 20% next year. The sales increase will require a total additional investment in receivables, inventory, and fixed assets of $750,000. Increases in liabilities such as accounts payable and other accruals will supply $175,000 of financing. Rodeo also expects total profits of $225,000 next year and will not pay any cash dividends. How much external financing is required to finance the sales increase?

A7. (Additional financing needed) Chris Hughen is studying his firm's financing requirements for next year. Chris estimates that the firm must invest an additional $100 in assets and that short-term liabilities will increase spontaneously by $10. He also estimates that the firm will earn profits of $70 and that it has access to additional external financing of $50. What is the largest dividend that the firm can pay and still have adequate funds to finance its additional assets?

A8. (Additional financing needed) Johnson Supply Company is planning to increase its sales by 20% next year. The sales increase will require a total additional investment in receivables, inventory, and fixed assets of $450,000. Increases in liabilities such as accounts payable and other accruals will supply $75,000 of financing. Johnson also expects total profits of $300,000 next year and will not pay any cash dividends. How much external financing is required to finance the sales increase?

A9. (Additional financing needed) Michael Stevens is studying his firm's financing requirements for next year. Michael estimates that the firm must invest an additional $200 in assets and that short-term liabilities will increase by $30. He also estimates that the firm will earn profits of $95 and that it has access to additional external financing of $100. What is the largest dividend that the firm can pay and still have adequate funds to finance its additional assets?

LEVEL B

B1. (Percent of sales forecasting) Last year sales for Amalgamated Meat Loaf Company were $12,000,000. Several balance sheet items varied directly with sales as follows:

CASH	ACCOUNTS RECEIVABLE	INVENTORY	NET FIXED ASSETS	ACCOUNTS PAYABLE	OTHER ACCRUALS
3%	20%	15%	25%	10%	5%

The net profit margin for Amalgamated Meat Loaf is 6%, and the firm pays out an annual dividend equal to 25% of net income. The latest balance sheet is:

ASSETS		LIABILITIES AND OWNERS' EQUITY	
Cash	$ 360,000	Accounts payable	$1,200,000
Accounts receivable	2,400,000	Accruals	600,000
Inventory	1,800,000	Short-term loan	800,000
Total current assets	$4,560,000	Total current liabilities	$2,600,000
Net fixed assets	3,000,000	Long-term debt	1,000,000
Total assets	$7,560,000	Stockholders' equity	3,960,000
		Total liabilities and equity	$7,560,000

a. If sales increase by 25% to $15,000,000 next year, what additional financing is needed?

b. Assume that the additional financing needed is acquired by increasing the short-term loan. Create a projected balance sheet for next year for Amalgamated Meat Loaf.

B2. (Percent of sales forecasting) Last year sales for the Sally Forth Company were $12,000,000. Several balance sheet items varied directly with sales as follows:

CASH	ACCOUNTS RECEIVABLE	INVENTORY	NET FIXED ASSETS	ACCOUNTS PAYABLE	OTHER ACCRUALS
3%	20%	15%	25%	10%	5%

The net profit margin for Sally Forth is 6%, and the firm pays out an annual dividend equal to 25% of net income. The latest balance sheet is:

ASSETS		LIABILITIES AND OWNERS' EQUITY	
Cash	$ 360,000	Accounts payable	$1,200,000
Accounts receivable	2,400,000	Accruals	600,000
Inventory	1,800,000	Short-term loan	800,000
Total current assets	$4,560,000	Total current liabilities	$2,600,000
Net fixed assets	3,000,000	Long-term debt	1,000,000
Total assets	$7,560,000	Stockholders' equity	3,960,000
		Total liabilities and equity	$7,560,000

a. If sales increase by 50% to $18,000,000 next year, what additional financing is needed?

b. Assume the additional financing needed is acquired by increasing the short-term loan. Create a projected balance sheet next year for Sally Forth.

B3. (Pro forma financial statements) Columbus Distributors has the following balance sheet:

ASSETS		LIABILITIES AND OWNERS' EQUITY	
Cash	$ 500,000	Accounts payable	$ 1,000,000
Accounts receivable	3,500,000	Bank loan	1,500,000
Inventory	3,000,000	Long-term bond	2,000,000
Fixed assets	3,000,000	Stockholders' equity	5,500,000
Total assets	$10,000,000	Total liabilities and equity	$10,000,000

Next year Columbus Distributors is planning for a major sales increase of 40%. Sales are currently $15,000,000, and they should increase to $21,000,000 next year. Cash, receivables, and inventory will increase proportionally to sales. Fixed assets will increase by $500,000. Payables will also increase proportionally to sales. The bank loan will increase to $2,000,000. Sinking fund payments will decrease the bond balance by $200,000.

Columbus has a 6.0% profit margin and is expecting to pay a nominal dividend of $100,000 to its common stockholders.

Prepare a pro forma balance sheet for next year. Does the balance sheet show that extra external funds are needed, or that excess funds are available for investment?

B4. (Excel: Cash budgeting) Merrimack Resorts has projected the cash flows for the six months of April through September as given below. Prepare a schedule showing the monthly cash flow, borrowing, loan repayments, cash balance, and cumulative loan balance. Merrimack has a beginning cash balance of $150 and wishes to maintain a minimum cash balance of at least $100. If the firm has cash balances in excess of the minimum, the excess will be used to reduce any outstanding loan balances.

	APR.	MAY	JUN.	JUL.	AUG.	SEP.
Cash inflows	100	100	175	250	300	250
Cash outflows	200	200	250	250	175	125

B5. (Excel: Cash budgeting) LTS Inc. has projected the cash flows for the six months of April through September as given below. Prepare a schedule showing the monthly cash flow, borrowing, loan repayments, cash balance, and cumulative loan balance. LTS has a beginning cash balance of $200 and wishes to maintain a minimum cash balance of at least $100. If the firm has cash balances in excess of the minimum, the excess will be used to reduce any outstanding loan balances.

	APR.	MAY	JUN.	JUL.	AUG.	SEP.
Cash inflows	150	200	150	250	300	350
Cash outflows	100	100	300	450	350	250

B6. (Excel: Cash budgeting) The management team of Dark Adventures has tasked you with preparing a monthly cash budget for the six months from October through March. Because the sales of Dark Adventures are seasonal, peaking around the turn of the year, cash budgeting is critical to the firm. To facilitate your preparation of the cash budget, they have supplied you with the following information:

1. The recent and forecasted (starting in Oct.) sales (in $1,000s) are:

AUG.	SEP.	OCT.	NOV.	DEC.	JAN.	FEB.	MAR.	APR.
400	500	600	700	800	800	700	600	500

2. Twenty-five percent of sales is collected during the month of sale, 50% is collected in the month following the sale, and 25% is collected in the second month following the sale.
3. Purchases are 50% of sales and are paid for one month prior to sale.
4. Wages and salaries are 24% of sales and are paid in the same month as the sale.
5. Rent of $4,000 is paid each month. Additional cash operating expenses of $8,000 per month will be incurred for October and November, $20,000 for December and January, and $8000 for February and March.
6. Tax installments of $10,000 are planned for October and January. A capital expenditure of $100,000 will occur in October, and the firm has a mortgage payment of $5,000 due every month.
7. The cash balance at the end of September is $125,000, and managers want to maintain a minimum balance of $60,000 at all times. The firm will borrow the amounts neces-

sary to assure that the minimum balance is achieved. If the cash balance is above the minimum and there is still a loan balance from previous months, excess funds will be applied to the loan balance until it is eliminated.

B7. (Excel: Pro forma financial statements) Kennesaw Leisure Products has the following balance sheet (in $1,000s):

ASSETS		LIABILITIES AND OWNERS' EQUITY	
Cash	$ 50	Accounts payable	$ 70
Accounts receivable	220	Bank loan	180
Inventory	300	Long-term mortgage	200
Fixed assets	210	Stockholders' equity	330
Total assets	$780	Total liabilities and equity	$780

In the year just completed, Kennesaw had sales of $600,000, with net income of $60,000 and a net profit margin of 10%. The firm expects the same profit margin on next year's sales. Kennesaw paid no dividend this year and does not plan to pay one next year. Next year Kennesaw is planning on a substantial sales increase. Assume that cash, accounts receivable, inventory, and accounts payable will increase proportionally to the sales increase. Furthermore, the existing level of fixed assets is sufficient to accommodate the planned sales increase, the mortgage loan will be amortized by $10,000, and the bank loan cannot be increased.

a. Assume that sales increase by 10%. Prepare a pro forma balance sheet showing the firm's financial position at the end of next year. If the balance sheet does not otherwise balance, indicate on the balance sheet the amount of additional external funds that are needed or the excess funds that are available for investment.

b. Assume that sales increase by 20%. Prepare a pro forma balance sheet showing the firm's financial position at the end of next year. If the balance sheet does not otherwise balance, indicate on the balance sheet the amount of extra external funds that are needed or the excess funds that are available for investment.

B8. (Excel: Pro forma financial statements) Jim Balance Beam, Inc. has the following balance sheet (in $1,000s):

ASSETS		LIABILITIES AND OWNERS' EQUITY	
Cash	$100	Accounts payable	$120
Accounts receivable	240	Bank loan	200
Inventory	290	Long-term mortgage	220
Fixed assets	220	Stockholders' equity	310
Total assets	$850	Total liabilities and equity	$850

In the year just completed, Beam had sales of $750,000, with net income of $75,000 and a net profit margin of 10%. The firm expects the same profit margin on next year's sales. Beam paid no dividend this year and does not plan to pay one next year. Next year Beam is planning on a substantial sales increase. Assume that cash, accounts receivable, inventory, and accounts payable will increase proportionally to the sales increase. Furthermore, the existing level of fixed assets is sufficient to accommodate the planned sales increase, the mortgage loan will be amortized by $15,000, and the bank loan cannot be increased.

a. Assume that sales increase by 10%. Prepare a pro forma balance sheet showing the firm's financial position at the end of next year. If the balance sheet does not otherwise balance, indicate on the balance sheet the amount of additional external funds that are needed or the excess funds that are available for investment.

b. Assume that sales increase by 20%. Prepare a pro forma balance sheet showing the firm's financial position at the end of next year. If the balance sheet does not otherwise balance, indicate on the balance sheet the amount of extra external funds that are needed or the excess funds that are available for investment.

B9. (Percent of sales forecasting) Current sales of $1,000,000 are expected to increase by 20% next year. The investment in additional assets to finance this growth should be 150% of the sales increase. Short-term liabilities (such as accounts payable and other accruals) will provide financing equivalent to 15% of the sales increase. The firm's net income is predicted to be 20% of total sales, and the firm plans to pay a cash dividend equal to one-third of net income. How much additional financing is needed to finance the firm's growth?

B10. (Percent of sales forecasting) Lafayette Oil Company has current sales of $50 million. Lafayette estimates that an additional dollar of sales requires an investment of $1.25 and generates short-term financing of $0.15. Lafayette has an 8% net profit margin and expects to pay out dividends equal to 25% of its net profit. How much additional financing is needed if Lafayette plans to expand sales by 10% next year?

B11. (Excel: Percent of sales forecasting) Current sales of $500,000 are expected to increase by 10% next year. The investment in additional assets to finance this growth should be 90% of the sales increase. Short-term liabilities (such as accounts payable and other accruals) will provide financing equivalent to 10% of the sales increase. The firm's net income is predicted to be 20% of total sales, and the firm plans to pay a cash dividend equal to one-sixth of net income. How much additional financing is needed to finance the firm's growth?

LEVEL C (ADVANCED)

C1. (Excel: Pro forma financial statements) The table shows the income statement and balance sheet for the current year for Dellva Machine Products Company. The table also gives assumptions about what Dellva expects during the next year. Based on this information, complete the projected income statement and balance sheet for Dellva Machine Products.

INCOME STATEMENT	CURRENT	PROJECTED	ASSUMPTIONS FOR NEXT YEAR
Sales	$54,000,000	$	20% increase
Less cost of goods sold	25,000,000		20% increase
Less depreciation	1,500,000		$500,000 increase
Gross profit	$27,500,000	$	
Less selling and administrative expenses	16,000,000		$1,500,000 increase
Earnings before interest and taxes	$11,500,000	$	
Less interest	1,500,000		$1,000,000 increase
Earnings before taxes	$10,000,000	$	
Less taxes	4,500,000		45% of earnings before taxes
Net income	$ 5,500,000	$	
Less cash dividends	1,000,000		Unchanged
Addition to retained earnings	$ 4,500,000	$	

BALANCE SHEET	CURRENT	PROJECTED	ASSUMPTIONS FOR NEXT YEAR
Assets			
Cash and marketable securities	$ 2,000,000	$	See note below
Accounts receivable	4,500,000		$1,000,000 increase
Inventory	5,500,000	______	$1,000,000 increase
Total current assets	$12,000,000	$	
Net plant and equipment	8,000,000	______	$1,000,000 increase
Total assets	$20,000,000	$	
Liabilities and Equity			
Accounts payable	$ 2,500,000	$	$500,000 increase
Bank loans	2,000,000		See note below
Other short-term debt	1,500,000	______	Unchanged
Total current liabilities	$ 6,000,000	$	
Long-term debt	5,000,000		Unchanged
Stockholders' equity	9,000,000	______	Add new retained earnings
Total liabilities and equity	$20,000,000	$	

NOTE: Dellva wants cash and marketable securities to be at least $2,000,000. If the firm has more funds (from total liabilities and equity) than it needs for its planned assets, the excess funds will be added to cash and marketable securities. On the other hand, if the firm's asset requirements (total assets) exceed its total financing (total liabilities and equity not including bank loans), Dellva will use short-term bank loans to raise the needed funds. (In other words, the cash and marketable securities or bank loans accounts are the plug accounts that will cause the balance sheet to balance. Extra funds are invested in cash and marketable securities, or a funds shortage is covered by bank borrowing.)

C2. (Excel: Automated forecasts) Mathew T. Box, III, grandson of the founder and currently CEO of the M. T. Box Company, has been concerned about the firm's short-term financial management. The treasurer of M. T. Box, Mary Hoover, has gathered the following information and is asking you to create a cash budget, monthly pro forma income statements, and monthly pro forma balance sheets for the next six months for M. T. Box.

1. The payment pattern for revenues is estimated to be as follows: 20% of sales are for cash, 15% are paid for one month after the sale, 55% are paid for two months after the sale, 9% are paid for in three months, and 1% are uncollectible.
2. The cash account should be set to start each month in the amount of $15,000, plus 65% of next month's salaries and wages, plus 75% of this month's accounts payable. The cash account will be adjusted with the short-term investment (borrowing) account, and Mary Hoover believes M. T. Box can earn 9% APR on its short-term investments.
3. Purchases of raw materials each month are in the amount of 35% of the predicted sales for the month after next, plus 25% of next month's predicted sales, plus 8% of this month's sales. Purchases are paid for in the following month, and there are no discounts available from suppliers. The cost of raw materials averages 68% of sales.
4. The firm pays salaries and wages of $15,000 plus 14% of this month's sales.
5. Fixed assets are being depreciated at the rate of 1% of net fixed assets per month.
6. The firm pays a cash dividend of $2,000 every month.
7. The long-term debt on the balance sheet carries a 15% APR, and payments are made quarterly in December, March, June, and September.
8. Taxes are at the rate of 35% of taxable income (including rebates for negative taxes). Taxes are paid monthly.

9. Mary Hoover expects the firm to purchase $150,000 of fixed assets at the end of April.
10. Sales for October, November, and December of this year were $60,000, $90,000, and $150,000, respectively. Sales forecasted for the next eight months are (in $1,000s)

JAN.	FEB.	MAR.	APR.	MAY	JUN.	JUL.	AUG.
250	235	190	160	110	90	135	260

BALANCE SHEET AS OF DECEMBER 31 (IN $1,000s)

ASSETS		LIABILITIES AND OWNERS' EQUITY	
Cash	$ 170	Accounts payable	$ 160
Short-term investments (borrowing)	90	Accrued interest	0
Accounts receivable	195	Long-term debt	600
Inventory	157	Common stock	120
Net fixed assets	615	Retained earnings	347
Total assets	$1,227	Liabilities and stockholders' equity	$1,227

C3. (Excel: Automated forecasts) The following information has been gathered for Dunn Manufacturing, Inc. Ulysses R. Dunn, the founder, manager, and majority shareholder, is trying to get a "handle" on financial planning. Use the following information to create a cash budget, monthly pro forma income statements, and monthly pro forma balance sheets for the next nine months for Dunn Manufacturing and U. R. Dunn.

1. The payment pattern for revenues is estimated to be as follows: 20% of sales are for cash, 10% are paid for one month after the sale, 50% are paid for two months after the sale, 18% are paid for three months after the sale, and 2% are uncollectible.
2. The cash account is targeted to start each month in the amount of $20,000, plus 70% of next month's salaries and wages, plus 75% of this month's accounts payable. The cash account will be adjusted with the notes payable account, which currently costs 1.1% per month on the balance.
3. Dunn purchases raw materials each month in the amount of 40% of the predicted sales for the month after next, plus 10% of next month's predicted sales, plus 15% of this month's sales. Purchases are paid for in the following month, and there are no discounts available to Dunn from its suppliers. The cost of raw materials averages 65% of sales.
4. Dunn pays salaries and wages of $27,000 plus 10% of this month's sales.
5. Dunn is depreciating its net fixed assets at the rate of 0.9% of *net* fixed assets per month.
6. Dunn pays a cash dividend of $5,000 every month.
7. The long-term debt on the Dunn balance sheet carries a 12% APR, and payments are made quarterly in December, March, June, and September.
8. Taxes for Dunn Manufacturing are at the rate of 34% of taxable income (including rebates for negative taxes). Taxes are paid quarterly (end of December, March, June, and September) on the basis of what the tax liability is *expected to be over the next quarter.* The model you build must be used in conjunction with trial and error to determine the correct tax payments to avoid encountering the problem of circular reasoning (CIRC). (*Hint:* Initially, just let the taxes "use up" what is currently in the prepaid tax account and go negative.)
9. Dunn expects to purchase $275,000 worth of fixed assets at the end of July.

10. Sales for January, February, and March of this year were $320,000, $345,000, and $365,000, respectively. Sales forecasted for the next 11 months are (in $1,000s):

APR.	MAY	JUN.	JUL.	AUG.	SEP.	OCT.	NOV.	DEC.	JAN.	FEB.
410	430	350	325	300	220	265	290	375	350	370

BALANCE SHEET AS OF MARCH 31 (IN $1,000s)

ASSETS		LIABILITIES AND OWNERS' EQUITY	
Cash	$210	Accounts payable	$ 177
Accounts receivable	256	Notes payable	219
Inventory	437	Accrued interest	0
Prepaid taxes	43	Long-term debt	650
Other assets	15	Common stock	150
Net fixed assets	674	Retained earnings	439
Total assets	$1,635	Liabilities and owners' equity	$1,635

MINICASE PLANNING NEW MAGIC AT DISNEY

After its success domestically, the Walt Disney Company (Disney) decided to share its magic with the rest of the world. After successfully opening Tokyo Disneyland, Disney was moving around the world to create Euro Disneyland. The financing plan for Euro Disneyland included an initial public offering by the main project firm. The financing plan would change Euro Disneyland from an internally financed, privately owned project into a highly leveraged, publicly owned entity in which Disney would hold only a minority interest. The table below provides financial projections for the first five years of operations.

FINANCIAL PROJECTIONS FOR EURO DISNEYLAND (MILLIONS OF FRENCH FRANCS)

Year	1	2	3	4	5
Revenues					
Magic Kingdom[a]	FF4,246	FF4,657	FF5,384	FF5,853	FF6,415
Second theme park	0	0	0	0	3,128
Resort and property development	1,236	2,144	3,520	5,077	6,386
Total revenues	5,482	6,801	8,904	10,930	15,929
Operating expenses					
Magic Kingdom	2,643	2,836	3,161	3,370	3,641
Second theme park	0	0	0	0	1,794
Resort and property development	796	1,501	2,431	2,970	3,694
Total operating expenses	3,439	4,337	5,592	6,340	9,129
Operating income	2,043	2,464	3,312	4,490	6,800
Other expenses (income)					
Royalties	302	333	387	422	717
Preopening amortization	341	341	341	341	341
Depreciation	255	263	290	296	625
Interest expense	567	575	757	708	1,166
Interest and other income	(786)	(788)	(768)	(778)	(790)
Lease expense	958	950	958	962	975
Management incentive fees	55	171	477	963	1,820
Total other expenses (income)	1,692	1,845	2,442	2,914	4,854
Profit before taxation	351	619	870	1,676	1,946
Taxation	147	260	366	704	818
Net profit	FF204	FF359	FF504	FF972	FF1,128

[a]Includes the Magic Kingdom Hotel.
Source: Euro Disneyland S.C.A., Offer for Sale of 10,691,000 Shares, p. 36.

QUESTIONS

1. Using the format of the table as a guide, project the net profit for the following 20 years (years 6 to 25) based on the following assumptions:
   - Each class of revenue after year 5 grows at a 5% annual rate.
   - Each class of operating expenses after year 5 grows at a 5% annual rate.
   - In other expenses (income), royalties equal 5% of total revenues.
   - In other expenses (income), preopening amortization is zero after year 5.

- Annual depreciation, annual interest expense, annual interest and other income, and annual lease expense are constant after year 5.
- Management incentive fees grow at a 7.5% annual rate.
- Euro Disneyland's income tax rate is 42%.

2. Calculate the present value of Euro Disneyland's equity at time 0 (when the park opens) and at time −3 (the time of the initial public offering, three years before the opening). Use the following assumptions:
   - Dividends are 75% of net profit for years 1 to 25.
   - At the end of year 25, the terminal value of equity is worth 10 times the year's net profit.
   - Euro Disneyland's cost of equity capital is 15%.
3. Recalculate the value for Euro Disneyland estimated at time −3 for two cases where the assumptions are changed to the following:
   a. Revenues after year 5 grow at 6% and operating expenses grow at 5%.
   b. Revenues after year 5 grow at 5% and operating expenses grow at 6%.

PART VII

SPECIAL TOPICS

Part VII draws together concepts and techniques developed throughout the book. Growth through a merger or acquisition, which is a "mega" capital budgeting decision, is an important part of virtually every major firm's development. One firm should acquire another only if doing so creates value—that is, only if it is a positive-NPV investment. But an acquisition is a more complex capital budgeting decision because it involves special legal, tax, and accounting issues. In Chapter 25, we show how to apply DCF analysis and other useful techniques that incorporate these complexities to measure a proposed acquisition's NPV. We also draw on techniques developed in Part IV to deal with investment-financing interactions.

Bankruptcy is a natural part of a firm's life. In the face of intense competition, some firms succeed and others fail. Before actually failing, poor performers exhibit signs of *financial distress.* Financial distress occurs when the firm is in danger of not being able to pay its debts as they come due. Often a *financial restructuring,* either privately or in a formal bankruptcy, is required to resolve this condition. If the distress cannot be resolved, then the firm must be *liquidated.*

Our final chapter concerns international corporate finance. Firms with significant foreign operations must consider the special opportunities and risks—particularly the foreign exchange risk—that go along with multinational operations. We show how to apply the techniques developed in Parts II and V to evaluate international investment and financing opportunities. We also explain how firms use foreign exchange derivatives, which are similar to other derivatives we discussed in Part V, to hedge their foreign exchange risk.

Mergers and Acquisitions

25

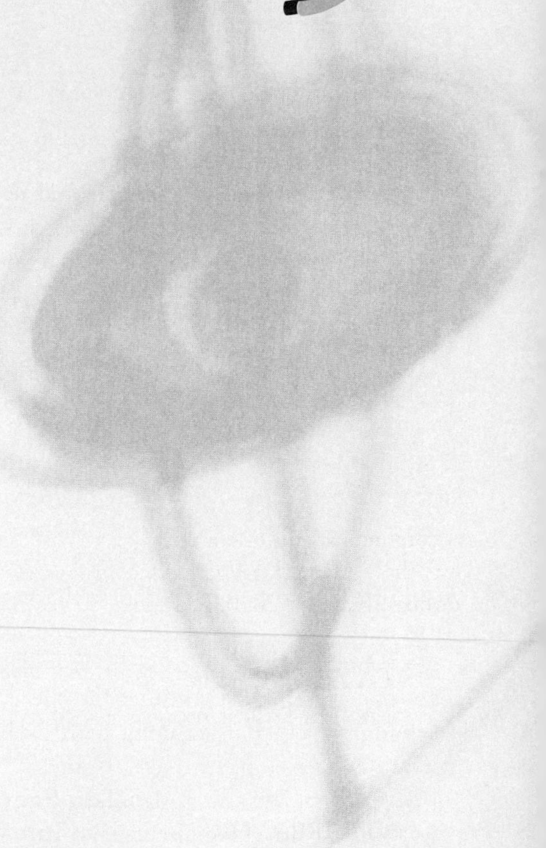

Acquisitions attract headlines, especially when there is a dramatic battle for control. Several years ago, the front page of the *Wall Street Journal* carried an article headlined "Bidding War: Offers for RJR Pit KKR and Shearson in a Battle for Turf," which announced the bid of Kohlberg Kravis Roberts & Company (KKR) for control of RJR Nabisco. Five days earlier, a management-led group had announced its intention to develop a proposal, in conjunction with Shearson Lehman Hutton, to acquire RJR Nabisco in a leveraged buyout (LBO) valued at $75 per common share. A leveraged buyout is an acquisition that is financed mainly (sometimes more than 90%) by debt. The KKR bid amounted to $90 per share. The battle for control unfolded over the ensuing six weeks. It involved three bidding groups, no fewer than 10 of the leading investment banks, and a veritable army of lawyers, information agents, accountants, and commercial banks. KKR finally prevailed when it offered to pay $109 per common share, 45% more than the management-led group's original proposal and an aggregate bid of $25 billion.

In this chapter, we show you how to analyze corporate acquisitions. An acquisition is like a "mega" capital budgeting project. As such, a firm should acquire another firm only if it will increase shareholder wealth. However, a corporate acquisition involves special legal, tax, and accounting issues. We explain how to tailor capital budgeting techniques to evaluate a corporate acquisition. We also describe other valuation techniques—especially comparative analysis—that are widely used in practice.

Agency problems are important in corporate acquisitions. How will the target respond? Based on the Principle of Self-Interested Behavior, we would expect that managers would not sit by passively when facing a possible acquisition of "their" firm. And in fact, corporate managers go to great lengths to erect barriers to forestall unwanted suitors from acquiring their firms (and perhaps eliminating their jobs in the process). We describe these measures and their potential impact on shareholder wealth.

FOCUS ON PRINCIPLES

- *Self-Interested Behavior:* Look for opportunities to make profitable acquisitions. Acquire another firm only if doing so increases shareholder wealth.
- *Two-Sided Transactions:* Acquiring another firm usually requires paying a premium over the prevailing market price large enough to get the acquiree's shareholders to sell their shares.
- *Comparative Advantage:* Recognize that a merger of firms that have different comparative advantages might have a positive NPV.
- *Behavioral Principle:* Look to comparable acquisitions for guidance regarding a reasonable price to pay for an acquisition.
- *Valuable Ideas:* Look for opportunities to redesign securities or the structure of an acquisition transaction to enhance value.
- *Incremental Benefits:* Calculate the net advantage of an acquisition on the basis of the incremental after-tax cash flows the acquisition will provide.
- *Risk-Return Trade-Off:* Merging two firms through an exchange of shares can benefit the bondholders of both firms, because their expected return increases and their risk decreases.
- *Diversification:* Diversifying through a conglomerate merger will benefit shareholders only if they could not achieve such diversification on their own.
- *Capital Market Efficiency:* The method of accounting for an acquisition does not affect the benefits shareholders derive from it.
- *Time Value of Money:* Use discounted-cash-flow analysis to measure the net advantage of an acquisition.

25.1 WHAT IS SPECIAL ABOUT A MERGER?

A corporate acquisition is usually a substantial capital investment for the acquiring firm. Table 25.1 lists the 10 largest merger and acquisition transactions that have taken place in the United States through year-end 2000. Because of its size, an acquisition can have a greater impact on shareholder

TABLE 25.1
The ten largest merger and acquisition transactions in the United States through year-end 2000.

ACQUIRING FIRM	ACQUIRED FIRM	APPROXIMATE PRICE PAID ($ BILLIONS)[a]	YEAR ANNOUNCED
Pfizer Inc.	Warner-Lambert Co.	116.7	1999
America Online Inc.	Time Warner Inc.[b]	101.0	2000
Exxon Corp.	Mobil Corp.	81.4	1998
SBC Communications Inc.	Ameritech Corp.	75.2	1998
Vodafone Group PLC-UK	AirTouch Communications Inc.	62.8	1999
Bell Atlantic Corp.	GTE Corp.	60.5	1998
British Petroleum Co. PLC-UK	Amoco Corp.	56.5	1998
AT&T Corp.	Tele-Communications Inc.	52.5	1998
Viacom Inc.	CBS Corp.	48.8	1999
AT&T Corp.	MediaOne Group Inc.	44.2	2000

[a]Based on the number of shares of common stock acquired.
[b]Statutory merger.
Source: Mergerstat Review.

wealth than other forms of capital investment. The analytical tools and basic decision rules of capital budgeting still apply. However, particular care must be taken in applying these tools because of the enormous size and complexity of the investment.

A corporate acquisition can take the form of either a merger or a consolidation. A **merger** involves a combination of two firms, the acquiror and the acquiree. The *acquiror* absorbs all the assets and liabilities of the acquiree and assumes the acquiree's business. The *acquiree* loses its independent existence, and becomes a subsidiary of the acquiror.

In a **consolidation,** two or more firms combine to form an entirely new entity. The distinction between acquiror and acquiree becomes blurred, because shares of each of the consolidated firms are exchanged for shares of the new firm. Both of the consolidating firms lose their independent existence, often becoming subsidiaries of the new firm or combining to become the new firm.

EXAMPLE Lockheed's and Martin Marietta's "Merger of Equals"

Several years ago, the federal defense budget for research and development, test and evaluation, and procurement had shrunk by almost two-thirds in real terms (dollars of constant purchasing power). This reduction placed pressure on aerospace/defense firms to consolidate to achieve production economies and remain competitive.

After about 10 years of shrinking federal defense budgets, Lockheed Corporation and Martin Marietta Corporation, two of the nation's leading aerospace firms, announced a consolidation, which they proclaimed a "merger of equals." They would form a new corporation, Lockheed Martin Corporation, which would have two special-purpose subsidiaries. One would be merged with and into Lockheed, and the other would be merged with and into Martin Marietta. As a result, Lockheed and Martin Marietta became wholly owned subsidiaries of Lockheed Martin.

When two firms of roughly equal size combine, they often choose to consolidate. When they are of unequal size, one firm acquires the other through merger. Usually the larger firm acquires the smaller, although this is not always the case. The distinction between a merger and a consolidation is important in a legal sense, but the same analytical techniques apply to both. Accordingly, we assume that one party to a corporate combination can be identified, or at least treated for analytical purposes, as the acquiror, and we use the terms *corporate acquisition* and *merger* interchangeably to refer to corporate combinations in general.

A merger involves the acquisition of an entire firm. Buying a firm, with its own portfolio of assets and its own liabilities, is more complicated than buying a new machine or building a new plant. In addition, complex tax issues must often be resolved. For these reasons, estimating the incremental cash flows is inherently more difficult than the measurement problems encountered in capital budgeting projects of the types discussed in Chapters 6, 7, and 8.

Also, how a firm finances an acquisition takes on added importance. The economics of the investment and how the firm finances it tend to interact because the acquisition can alter the acquiror's financial structure. Thus, estimating the required return is inherently more difficult in the case of corporate acquisitions than in other forms of capital investment. Yet accuracy is often crucial because of the large amount of money the acquiror must commit to the transaction.

There is an additional reason mergers represent a special form of capital investment. Firms usually have to make very quick decisions on the basis of incomplete information. In unfriendly situations, the acquiror may have only publicly available information on which to base a decision. In such cases, discounted-cash-flow analysis is difficult to apply. Consequently, the other valuation techniques that are used in practice to gauge the reasonableness of an acquisition price take on increased importance in such situations.

Review

1. What is a merger? What is a consolidation? How do they differ?
2. A corporate acquisition can be viewed as a special type of capital investment project. In what respects is it more complicated than a typical capital investment project?

25.2 WHY FIRMS MERGE

A firm may have a number of possible motives for seeking to merge with a particular firm. Each should be judged against the objective of maximizing shareholder wealth.

When Do Mergers Create Value?

The shareholders of an acquiring firm can benefit from a merger only if the two firms are worth more combined than separate. To provide a framework for discussion, suppose that acquiror and acquiree are worth V_A and V_B in total market value (that is, the total market value of their assets), respectively. They would be worth V_{AB} in total market value in combination. The acquiror must normally offer the acquiree's shareholders some premium, P_B, above V_B to induce them to sell their shares. The acquiror also incurs various costs and expenses. The **net advantage to merging (NAM)** to the acquiror's shareholders equals the difference between (1) the total market value of the firm postmerger net of the cost of completing the transaction and (2) the total market value of the firms before the merger:

$$\text{NAM} = [V_{AB} - (V_A + V_B)] - P_B - \text{Expenses} \tag{25.1}$$

If the net advantage to merging is positive, the merger would increase the wealth of the acquiror's shareholders. The term in brackets in Equation (25.1) represents what is commonly referred to as the merger's *synergistic effect.* The whole is worth more than the sum of the parts when it is positive. Under the Principle of Two-Sided Transactions, the premium P_B is both a gain to the acquiree's shareholders and a cost to the acquiror's shareholders. Even if the synergistic effect is positive, the acquiror's shareholders will benefit only if the premium P_B and the expenses are less than the synergistic benefits. One of the more interesting issues with mergers and acquisitions is the size of P_B in relation to $V_{AB} - (V_A + V_B)$. If P_B is large enough, NAM is negative. In that case, the acquiror will have "overpaid" for the acquisition.

EXAMPLE Calculating the Net Advantage to Merging

Firm A, with a total market value of $50 million, is planning to acquire firm B, which has a total market value of $15 million. Firm A estimates that the merged firm will be worth $75 million as a result of operating and other efficiencies. Firm A's investment bankers have advised that firm A will have to pay a $6 million premium in price to acquire firm B. Merger-related costs and expenses will amount to $1 million. Applying Equation (25.1), we find that the net advantage to merging is

$$\text{NAM} = [75 - (50 + 15)] - 6 - 1 = \$3 \text{ million}$$

Synergy creates $10 million of value (= 75 − [15 + 50]). Of this amount, $6 million is paid to firm B's shareholders, and $1 million covers expenses. Firm A's shareholders wind up with a net increase in wealth of $3 million. Thus, the merger would benefit both firms' shareholders.

Evidence suggests that mergers do tend to produce synergy, at least when the two firms are in the same industry, and that the stockholders of acquired firms tend to benefit handsomely. Target stockholders generally receive takeover premiums averaging between 30% and 50% for their shares. In contrast, the shareholders of acquiring firms tend to realize only very modest gains. This sharing of benefits is probably due to capital market efficiency, reflecting the impact (actual or potential) of competing acquirors.

Valid Motives for Merging

A merger can be economically beneficial only if the sum of the parts exceeds the whole. There are at least four situations in which this can happen.

ACHIEVE OPERATING EFFICIENCIES AND ECONOMIES OF SCALE Two firms may decide to merge in order to achieve *operating efficiencies* or to take advantage of *economies of scale.* The merged firms can eliminate duplicate facilities, operations, or departments.[1] Consider two airlines with overlapping routes. By merging their operations, they can better coordinate scheduling and eliminate excess capacity.

Achieving operating efficiencies is more likely to result from a horizontal or vertical merger than from a conglomerate merger. A **horizontal merger** combines two firms in the same line of business. A **vertical merger** involves integrating forward toward the consumer, or backward toward the source of supply, in a particular line of business. A **conglomerate merger** joins firms in unrelated businesses. The merger of two airlines is a horizontal merger. When a firm purchases one of its parts suppliers, that is a vertical merger. Most mergers in the United States since World War II have been of the conglomerate type.

One means of achieving operating efficiencies involves combining two firms that have complementary resources. For example, a small computer firm might have a skilled product engineering staff and one or more unique products but might lack management expertise and a strong sales staff. A second computer firm, perhaps older and larger, might have strong management and an established sales network but lack state-of-the-art products. A merger could be mutually beneficial because each firm has something the other firm needs. Such a case is an application of the Principle of Comparative Advantage. But a merger will be beneficial to both only if it enables each firm to obtain what it needs more cheaply than it could have if it had remained on its own.

Two firms in the same line of business might also merge in order to achieve economies of scale in production, distribution, or some other phase of their operation. Economies of scale occur when the average unit cost of goods sold decreases as output expands. For example, a higher volume of production might permit a firm to build larger, more efficient plants than the smaller ones it must build now. Achieving economies of scale in production is a key motive underlying most horizontal mergers.

EXAMPLE The Lockheed/Martin Marietta Horizontal Merger

The Lockheed-Martin Marietta combination described earlier was going to create a leading U.S. aerospace firm, which would have the economies of scale necessary to compete effectively in the global business environment. The boards of directors of the two firms expected the merger to enhance the combined firm's position in commercial markets, give rise to an estimated $200 million per year of pretax operating cost savings, and create a broader product platform on which to grow the combined business.

[1]Something to consider if you are thinking of pursuing a career in financial management: The financial staff of the acquiree is usually one of the first redundancies to be eliminated!

Operating efficiencies and economies of scale are the main sources of any synergy. A conglomerate merger has the least potential for generating them. In any case, one must be careful in assessing potential operating efficiencies and potential economies of scale. They may never be realized. For example, merging an insurance broker and a securities broker to achieve economies of distribution may fail to yield the anticipated benefits if the brokers cannot (or simply will not) sell each other's products.

EXAMPLE Potential Economies Are Not Always Realized

After Sears, Roebuck & Co. acquired Dean Witter Reynolds Inc., it placed Dean Witter stockbrokers in more than 300 of its approximately 850 retail stores nationwide. Dean Witter brokers complained about the "socks and stocks" marketing strategy, saying it was difficult to drum up business from people shopping for clothing, vacuum cleaners, and lawn mowers. Within a few years, Sears had reduced the number of Dean Witter outlets by more than two-thirds.

REALIZE TAX BENEFITS Suppose a firm has tax loss carryforwards it cannot fully use. Merging with a profitable firm that pays income taxes might prove mutually beneficial. Under some circumstances, the firm with a loss can use its tax loss carryforwards to shelter some—or perhaps all—of the profitable firm's income from taxation. For example, when the Penn Central Corporation emerged from bankruptcy, it was able to use its substantial tax loss carryforwards by acquiring tax-paying firms.[2]

There is another possible tax benefit. Consider a firm in a mature industry that is generating a large amount of free cash flow. If the firm distributes the cash to its shareholders, they will have to pay tax (unless shares are repurchased at a price that is less than the shareholders' tax basis in the shares). But they would not have to pay tax if the firm instead invests the cash in the shares of other firms. Whether the acquiror's shareholders truly gain depends on whether the acquisition has a positive net present value when compared to the other possible alternative uses of the cash.

CAPTURE SURPLUS CASH Mergers may be motivated by the acquiror's desire to use the acquiree's cash. Firms with substantial cash and a shortage of capital investment opportunities may therefore look like sitting ducks for acquisition unless they can invest the cash or distribute it to their shareholders.

GROW MORE QUICKLY OR MORE CHEAPLY A firm may find that it can grow more quickly or more cheaply by acquiring other firms than through internal development. It is generally quicker to obtain new products, new facilities, or a national distribution network by acquiring a firm that has already developed them. A firm may be able to acquire assets, such as oil and gas reserves, more cheaply by purchasing another firm than by developing—or in this case exploring for—its own. Acquiring a local firm may be the most cost-effective means of establishing a secure market position in a foreign market. The desire to secure a position in the U.S. market probably is largely responsible for the sharp increase in the number of foreign acquisitions of U.S. firms in recent years.

---

[2]Under current tax law, the merger must have a valid business purpose, apart from taxes, in order for the Internal Revenue Service to permit the profitable firm to use the other firm's tax net operating loss carryforwards (NOLs). The Tax Reform Act of 1986 tightened restrictions on one firm's ability to use another firm's NOLs to shelter part of its operating income from taxation following an acquisition. It is no longer possible for an acquiring firm to use its NOLs to shelter gain on the sale of the acquiree's assets (for example, assets in a subsidiary with a very low tax basis) following the corporate acquisition, which was one of the strategies Penn Central adopted.

EXAMPLE Sandoz A.G.'s Acquisition of Genetic Therapy Inc.

Sandoz A.G., one of the world's largest pharmaceutical firms, acquired Genetic Therapy Inc., which develops human gene therapy delivery systems. Sandoz paid $295 million for Genetic Therapy, whose annual sales revenues were just $17.2 million. Why would Sandoz pay such a high price for a relatively small firm? Genetic Therapy's research and development efforts were yielding promising opportunities—new product options—and options have value!

Questionable Motives for Merging

Firms also cite other motives for mergers. Three of the more questionable motives involve diversification, reducing the cost of debt, and increasing earnings per share.

DIVERSIFICATION Diversification is generally one of the main motives behind a conglomerate merger. At first glance, this motive seems reasonable because of the Principle of Diversification. But diversification will benefit the acquiror's shareholders *only if they could not achieve such diversification more cheaply on their own.*

EXAMPLE A Conglomerate Merger Might Not Increase Shareholder Wealth

Two firms plan to merge through an exchange of shares. The firms are in unrelated businesses, so there is no synergistic effect. Firm B has 1 million shares worth $40 each, and firm A has 3 million shares worth $20 each. Each firm is debt free. Firm A will issue two new shares of its stock (worth $20 each, for a total of $40) for each share of firm B (worth $40). (There is no merger premium in this case.) Table 25.2 shows the impact of the merger. The total market value of each firm is the weighted average of its value in the three possible states of the economy. For example, the value of firm B is

$$\text{Value of firm B} = 0.4(50) + 0.5(36) + 0.1(20) = \$40 \text{ million}$$

The value of firm A is calculated the same way. Merging firms A and B combines their respective values. The value of the combined firm is $100 million (= 60 + 40). Because there are 5 million shares, each share is worth $20 (= 100/5).

TABLE 25.2
Diversification through merging may not increase shareholder wealth (dollar amounts in millions except per-share amounts).

	NUMBER OF SHARES	TOTAL VALUE IN STATE: Boom	Stable Growth	Recession	TOTAL MARKET VALUE	SHARE PRICE
Probability		0.4	0.5	0.1		
Firm B	1 million[b]	$ 50	$36	$20	$ 40	$40
Firm A	3 million	75	54	30	60	20
Combined[a]	5 million[b]	125	90	50	100	20

[a]Firm A and Firm B combine through an exchange of shares. Firm A issues 2 million new shares in exchange for Firm B's 1 million outstanding shares.
[b]Firm B's 1 million shares are eliminated in exchange for 2 million shares of Firm A.

Suppose a shareholder owned 1,000 shares of firm B and 500 shares of firm A prior to the merger. Her shares were worth

$$\$50,000 = (40)(1000) + (20)(500)$$

Following the merger, she owns 2,500 shares of firm A (the original 500 shares plus 2,000 more received in exchange for her 1,000 shares of firm B), which are worth the same \$50,000 (= [20]2,500).

Shareholder wealth has not changed.[3]

The homemade diversification argument is like the homemade dividends argument given in Chapter 17 and the homemade borrowing (leverage) argument given in Chapter 15. They rest on the assumption that there are no market imperfections. Because there are, corporate diversification may create value. As already noted, diversifying at the firm level may be more tax efficient than paying out the excess cash to shareholders.

REDUCING THE COST OF DEBT A larger (merged) firm may achieve economies of scale in issuing securities. If the merged firm makes larger issues than the two firms would separately, the merger may result in lower transaction costs. However, lower issuance expenses are not likely to contribute much to the value of a merger.

Suppose two firms combine by exchanging shares. Such a merger can lower the combined firm's cost of borrowing but it can also benefit bondholders at the expense of shareholders. The problem here is the reverse of the problem of *claim dilution* with respect to capital structure. Stockholders can expropriate wealth from bondholders by diluting the bondholders' claim on the assets.[4]

This same phenomenon can work in reverse, against the stockholders. Diversification via merger can reduce the probability of bankruptcy and, consequently, the bondholders' required returns. The expected return to each class of the firms' debtholders increases, and their risk decreases because each firm effectively guarantees the debt of the other. It follows from the Principle of Risk-Return Trade-Off that the debtholders of each firm are unambiguously better off. But if the merger does not alter the two firms' combined returns, the stockholders must be worse off. The bondholders gain at the expense of stockholders, who are worse off despite the lower borrowing cost.

EXAMPLE A Conglomerate Merger Can Benefit Bondholders at the Expense of Stockholders

Table 25.3 illustrates how a conglomerate merger can benefit bondholders at the expense of shareholders. The conditions are the same as in Table 25.2 except that firm B now has \$30 million principal amount of debt. Firm B's bondholders will be paid in full in the boom and stable growth states. But there is only \$20 million available in the recession state. The bondholders get it all, but still come up short by \$10 million, and the shareholders get nothing. Therefore, the debt is worth only \$29 million.

If firm A and firm B merge, the combined cash flows of the two firms are available to service the debt. In the recession state, the bondholders will get paid in full as a result of the merger. In effect, firm A guarantees firm B's obligation to repay its bonds. This guarantee is

[3]Note that the merger might actually make her *worse off* if there are no close substitutes for each firm, because the merger in that case would reduce her investment opportunities. Before the merger, she owned the shares of the two firms in the ratio 4:1 by market value (\$40,000 of firm B and \$10,000 of firm A). They combine in the ratio 2:3 (\$40 million of firm B and \$60 million of firm A). After the merger, she effectively owns them in this new ratio.

[4]Claim dilution is explained more fully in Chapter 13.

TABLE 25.3
Financial synergy can benefit bondholders at the expense of stockholders (dollar amounts in millions).

	BOOM	STABLE GROWTH	RECESSION	TOTAL MARKET VALUE
Probability	0.4	0.5	0.1	
Firm B				
Debt	$ 30	$30	$20	$ 29
Equity	20	6	—	11
Total	$ 50	$36	$20	$ 40
Firm A				
Debt	$ —	$—	$—	$ —
Equity	75	54	30	60
Total	$ 75	$54	$30	$ 60
Combined				
Debt	$ 30	$30	$30	$ 30[a]
Equity	95	60	20	70[b]
Total	$125	$90	$50	$100

[a]Bondholder wealth increases by $1 (= 30 − 29) because bondholders are paid in full in each state as a result of the merger.
[b]Shareholder wealth decreases by $1 (= 60 + 11 − 70) because of the coinsurance effect.

referred to as the coinsurance effect of a merger. If both firms had debt, each would effectively guarantee the debt of the other.

The stock of the combined firm is worth $70 million. The sum of the values of the stock in each firm is $71 million (= $60 + 11). The shareholders of the two firms have collectively lost $1 million. What happened to this value? The $1 million of value was transferred to the bondholders. Their debt became more valuable because they will get paid in full regardless of the state of the economy. The merger transferred value from the bondholders to the stockholders through the coinsurance effect.

INCREASING EARNINGS PER SHARE A firm may be able to increase its earnings per share by choosing the right mix of cash and securities to pay the selling firm's shareholders. Some managers believe this is beneficial because they think it will increase the firm's share price. However, shareholders will benefit only if the net advantage to merging is positive.

Review

1. What is the net advantage to merging (NAM)? How is it calculated?
2. List four valid motives that firms may have for merging. Explain each one.
3. What is the difference between a horizontal merger and a vertical merger? How are they different from a conglomerate merger?
4. Two unrelated firms plan to merge. Their joint announcement says that the shareholders of both will benefit from diversification. Do you agree? Why or why not?
5. Firm A with high leverage acquires firm B with a debt-free capital structure. The firms exchange shares on the basis of their respective fair market values. Why might the shareholders of firm B object to this merger?

25.3 TECHNICAL ISSUES

When one firm acquires another, two sets of technical issues arise: the legal form of the transaction and its tax status.[5] These two sets of issues are interrelated.

Form of Transaction

There are three basic ways of accomplishing a corporate acquisition: (1) Merger or consolidation, (2) Purchase of stock, and (3) Purchase of assets.

MERGER OR CONSOLIDATION In a merger, the acquiror absorbs the acquiree. The acquiror automatically obtains all the assets and assumes all the liabilities of the acquiree, which loses its corporate existence. But suppose the acquiror wants the acquiree to survive as a separate entity. Then the acquiror can merge the acquiree with a special-purpose subsidiary. The acquiree becomes a wholly owned subsidiary of the acquiror.

A merger or consolidation must comply with each corporation's charter. Many corporate charters require a simple majority of the firm's shareholders to approve a merger or consolidation. Some require a two-thirds majority.

A merger or consolidation offers the most flexible means of structuring a tax-free acquisition. The tax bases of the acquiree's assets and liabilities remains the same. It is also generally easier and less costly to complete than either of the other two forms of acquisition.

PURCHASE OF STOCK An acquiror can purchase the acquiree's stock. It still obtains the acquiree's assets and liabilities, but no shareholders' meetings are involved. A prospective acquiror can also bypass management and make a **tender offer** directly to the firm's shareholders. It is only an *offer* to purchase; any shareholders who do not like the price offered can refuse to sell their shares. But if the price is high enough, the shareholders will sell. This can create problems for the acquiror, however. If the acquiror purchases fewer than 80% of the acquiree's voting securities, then it will not be able to consolidate the acquiree for tax purposes. Also, if any of the acquiree's shares remain outstanding, there is a minority interest in the subsidiary, which creates potential agency problems.[6]

PURCHASE OF ASSETS An acquiror can purchase only the selling firm's assets. The liabilities of the seller, other than those specifically assumed by the buyer, remain the responsibility of the seller. There is thus substantially less likelihood that hidden liabilities will be discovered after the transaction to the detriment of the buyer. There is also no problem with minority shareholders. In addition, the buyer's shareholders usually do not have to approve the transaction, and most corporate charters require only 50% approval by the seller's shareholders. The three main drawbacks to this structure are that (1) it is more difficult to achieve a tax-free transaction, (2) transferring the title of ownership to individual assets is costly and time consuming, and (3) distributing the cash proceeds to shareholders usually triggers an income tax liability to the shareholders in addition to any tax the firm may owe.

---

[5]There used to be a third issue, the accounting treatment. Statement of Financial Accounting Standards No. 141 ("Business Combinations") removed this issue by requiring purchase accounting for all mergers, so that firms can no longer use the pooling-of-interests method.

[6]Consequently, an acquiror that purchases shares from less than all of the acquiree's shareholders—for instance, through a tender offer—generally follows this purchase with a formal merger in order to eliminate the minority interest.

Antitrust Considerations

A merger transaction must comply with federal antitrust law, state antitakeover statutes, the corporate charter of each firm, and federal and state securities laws. There are three main federal antitrust statutes. The Clayton Act has become the chief weapon the government uses to contest mergers that it feels may lessen competition. It forbids a firm to purchase the assets or the stock of another firm if the purchase might substantially lessen competition, or tend to create a monopoly, in any line of commerce or in any section of the country.

EXAMPLE Texaco's Acquisition of Getty Oil

The federal government challenged the merger of Texaco and Getty Oil Company, the third and twelfth largest oil firms in the United States at the time, because of the two firms' overlapping gasoline marketing operations in the northeastern United States.

The actual percentage of potential mergers contested on antitrust grounds is small. Those involving very large firms, and horizontal acquisitions, appear to be the most likely to be challenged. Many of those that are questioned can survive the challenge by having the acquiror agree to sell assets in the affected market(s) to restore competition, as Texaco agreed to do.

Other Legal Considerations

Several other legal issues must be addressed in merger situations. For example, there are special rules relating to tender offers. Also, the acquiror should examine the indenture covenants for the acquiree's outstanding debt to determine whether any of its debt issues will have to be repaid at par upon a change in control.

Tax Considerations

The tax issues that arise in connection with mergers are very complex. All we can do is summarize some of the key aspects. The Internal Revenue Service assumes that an acquisition is taxable unless stringent conditions are met. In a **tax-free acquisition,** the selling shareholders are treated as having *exchanged* their old shares for substantially similar new shares. The acquiror's tax basis in each asset whose ownership is transferred in the transaction is the same as the acquiree's. Each selling shareholder who receives only stock does not have to pay any tax on the gain realized as a result of the acquisition until the shares are sold.

In a **taxable acquisition,** the selling shareholders are treated as having *sold* their shares. The acquiror can, if it wants, increase the tax basis in the assets it acquires to the fair market value of the consideration it pays to acquire them (including the fair market value of the acquiree's liabilities assumed by the acquiror).

From the seller's perspective, the main benefit of a tax-free transaction is deferral of tax on any gain realized on the sale of the business. The seller who receives stock in the acquiror also has a continuing equity interest in the enterprise and can share in any postmerger benefits. From the buyer's perspective, the main benefit of a tax-free transaction derives from the acquiror's ability to take advantage of the existing tax attributes of the acquiree, such as net operating loss carryforwards.

REQUIREMENTS FOR TAX-FREE TREATMENT The Internal Revenue Code imposes a variety of conditions that must be met for a transaction to be tax free. If these conditions are not met, the transaction is taxable. Figure 25.1 summarizes the requirements for tax-free treatment.

BUSINESS-PURPOSE TEST

The transaction must have a sound business purpose. It cannot be solely for tax reasons.

CONTINUITY-OF-BUSINESS TEST

The acquiror must continue to operate the acquiree's business.

MODE-OF-ACQUISITION AND MEDIUM-OF-PAYMENT TESTS
Merger or Consolidation

- Must qualify as a merger or consolidation under applicable state law.
- Acquiree's shareholders must receive at least 50% of the aggregate purchase price in stock of the acquiror (either common or preferred, either voting or nonvoting).

Stock-for-Stock Acquisition

- Acquiror can exchange only its voting stock or the voting stock of its parent.
- Acquiror must gain control of at least 80% of the aggregate voting interest in the acquiree and 80% of the total number of outstanding shares of each class of nonvoting stock.

Stock-for-Assets Acquisition

- Acquiror must obtain *substantially all* of the acquiree's assets in exchange for voting stock of the acquiror or voting stock of its parent.[a]
- Immediately after the stock-for-assets exchange, this voting stock must be distributed to the acquiree's shareholders in liquidation of the acquiree.

[a]If the acquiree is merged into a subsidiary of the acquiror (a so-called *subsidiary merger*), then the Code requires that (1) the medium-of-payment test be met using only stock of the parent firm and (2) the subsidiary acquire substantially all the assets of the acquiree. Under present IRS guidelines, *substantially all* means at least 90% of the fair market value of net assets and at least 70% of the fair market value of gross assets. If a subsidiary of the acquiror is merged into the acquiree (a *reverse subsidiary merger*), the Code requires that (1) at least 80% of the purchase price be paid in voting stock and (2) after the transaction the acquiror hold substantially all of its (pre-merger) assets and substantially all of the acquiree's (pre-merger) assets.

FIGURE 25.1
Requirements for tax-free treatment.

EXAMPLE Lockheed/Martin Marietta Tax-Free Combination

The Lockheed/Martin Marietta combination was structured so as to qualify as a tax-free exchange of shares. Each of Lockheed's 66,179,422 outstanding common shares was exchanged for 1.63 Lockheed Martin shares. Each of Martin Marietta's 100,680,090 outstanding common shares was exchanged for one Lockheed Martin share.

TO BE OR NOT TO BE TAX FREE A tax-free transaction benefits a shareholder who has a gain because it permits deferral of tax on the gain. A taxable transaction benefits a shareholder who has a loss and has sufficient taxable income to offset the loss because it creates a tax deduction. A taxable transaction also gives the acquiror greater flexibility in financing the acquisition. Under the

Principle of Two-Sided Transactions, the interests of the acquiror and those of the selling shareholders often conflict. The "high" market value of the assets that can make writing up their tax basis advantageous is likely to be reflected in a "high" share price for the acquiree, which creates the capital gain.

As a general rule, structuring an acquisition of a corporation as a taxable transaction in order to be able to write up the tax basis of the acquiree's assets is not a tax-effective strategy under current U.S. tax law.[7] The seller must pay tax on the difference between the purchase price received and its tax basis in the assets. In an efficient market, this tax liability will be reflected in the purchase price the buyer pays. Because this difference is then depreciated over several years, the net present value of the asset write-up must be negative.

Accounting Considerations

Acquisitions often involve difficult accounting issues. In an efficient capital market, the choice of accounting technique should not affect market value, because it does not affect cash flows. Nevertheless, professional managers often take great pains to structure transactions so as to achieve a particular accounting treatment.

Under the **purchase method** of accounting, one of the firms is identified as the acquiror. It is treated as having purchased the assets of the other firm. The purchase price, after adding the fair market value of the liabilities the acquiror assumes, is allocated to the acquired assets. Any excess of the purchase price over the fair market value of the net assets acquired is recorded as *goodwill.*[8]

EXAMPLE Purchase Accounting

Firm A acquires firm B, using cash from issuing \$60 million of new common stock. Table 25.4 shows the accounting impact. Firm B's fixed assets have a book value of \$30 million, but a fair market value of \$42 million. Its debt has a book value of \$10 million but is worth only \$7 million. Firm B's assets are written up by \$12 million. Its debt is written down by \$3 million. The acquisition eliminates firm B's book equity of \$40 million because firm B's shares are purchased and retired. The purchase price for firm B increases the merged firm's equity by \$60 million.

Table 25.4 also shows the calculation of goodwill. The fair market value of firm B's assets exceeds that of its liabilities by \$55 million. But firm A paid \$60 million. The \$5 million excess represents goodwill. You might think of goodwill as a firm's "franchise" value: the reputational capital it has built up for itself and its products through years of successful operation.

Review

1. What are the three basic ways of structuring a corporate acquisition? What are the distinguishing features of each approach?
2. What are the main differences between a tax-free acquisition and a taxable acquisition? Why would a seller with a low tax basis in stock prefer a tax-free acquisition, other things being equal?
3. Why do antitrust concerns sometimes arise in connection with mergers? Which type of merger is most likely to raise them?

---

[7]There are special tax rules that apply to S corporations and limited liability firms, which are taxed as partnerships. These special rules *can* make it mutually beneficial to both firms to write up the tax basis of the acquiree's assets.

[8]If there is a deficiency, it reduces the carrying value of long-term assets.

TABLE 25.4
Accounting for an acquisition: purchase method (dollar amounts in millions).

	FIRM B	FIRM A	ADJUSTMENTS	COMBINED
Assets				
Working capital	$20	$ 35		$ 55
Fixed assets	30	65	$+12$[a]	107
Goodwill	—	—	$+ 5$[b]	5
Total	$50	$100		$167
Liabilities and Equity				
Debt	$10	$ 25	$- 3$[c]	$ 32
Equity	40	75	-40[d]	
			$+60$[e]	135
Total	$50	$100		$167

[a]To record the write-up of Firm B's assets to fair market value.
[b]Calculation of goodwill:

Purchase price paid for Firm B's equity		$60
Fair market value of Firm B's assets	$62	
Fair market value of Firm B's liabilities	7	
Fair market value of Firm B's net assets		55
Goodwill		$ 5

[c]To revalue Firm B's debt to fair market value.
[d]The acquisition eliminates Firm B's equity.
[e]To record the equity Firm A issues to raise the cash to pay for Firm B.

25.4 COMPARATIVE ANALYSIS OF MERGERS

There are two main ways to value corporate acquisitions: by comparative analysis and by discounted-cash-flow analysis. The two approaches differ in one fundamental respect. Comparative analysis is an application of the Behavioral Principle. It is used to determine a "reasonable" price to pay: We infer the value from the prices that were paid for firms in comparable transactions. The discounted-cash-flow approach is used to calculate the impact of an acquisition on shareholder wealth, given a particular acquisition cost. It can also be used to estimate the maximum price an acquiror could pay without reducing the wealth of its shareholders. These two approaches are therefore complementary. When used properly together, they yield more useful information than either approach could separately.

The Merger Premium

The acquiror usually must pay a premium over the price at which the acquiree's shares are trading in the market (or would trade if the target firm were publicly held). The premium reflects the value of obtaining control of the acquiree. Comparative analysis can be used to determine a "reasonable" premium.

Investment bankers look at comparable acquisitions to gauge a reasonable premium to offer for the target firm's shares. This reflects the Behavioral Principle: Look to comparable acquisitions for guidance regarding a reasonable price to pay. The *premium paid* is defined as

$$\text{Premium paid} = \frac{\begin{array}{c}\text{Purchase price}\\\text{per share}\end{array} - \begin{array}{c}\text{Target's premerger}\\\text{share price}\end{array}}{\text{Target's premerger share price}} \tag{25.2}$$

The target's premerger share price is usually measured 30 days before the initial announcement date of the acquisition in order to prevent preannouncement effects from biasing the analysis. The required premium tends to vary from one industry to another, depending on the industry's prospects. It also varies from one firm to another within an industry, depending on that firm's financial and business characteristics and relative prospects. And the required premium may depend on the state of the stock market.

Premiums Paid in Past Deals

Table 25.5 shows the distribution of premiums paid in acquisitions for the period 1975 to 2000. The annual average premium has varied between a low of 35% in 1991 and a high of 50% in 1979 and again in 1980. The annual median premium has varied between a low of 27% in 1996 and a high of 48% in 1979. A recent study found that acquisition premiums during the 1974 to 1985 period were approximately double those of the 1963 to 1973 period, which was a period of

TABLE 25.5
Premiums paid in acquisitions of publicly traded firms, 1975–2000.

		PERCENT PREMIUM PAID OVER MARKET PRICE								DOW JONES INDUSTRIAL AVERAGE DURING YEAR	
		0.1–40.0		40.0–80.0		Over 80.0					
YEAR	NUMBER OF ACQUISITIONS	Number	%	Number	%	Number	%	AVERAGE PREMIUM	MEDIAN PREMIUM	High	Low
1975	129	74	57	38	30	17	13	41%	30%	881.81	632.04
1976	168	101	60	45	27	22	13	40	31	1014.79	858.71
1977	218	120	55	70	32	28	13	41	36	999.75	800.85
1978	240	116	48	90	38	34	14	46	42	907.74	742.12
1979	229	95	41	91	40	43	19	50	48	897.61	796.67
1980	169	75	44	61	36	33	20	50	45	1000.17	795.13
1981	166	80	48	54	33	32	19	48	42	1024.05	824.01
1982	176	80	45	66	37	30	18	47	44	1070.55	776.92
1983	168	101	60	53	32	14	8	38	34	1287.20	1027.04
1984	199	118	59	68	34	13	7	38	34	1286.64	1086.57
1985	331	231	70	71	21	29	9	37	28	1553.10	1184.96
1986	333	222	67	82	24	29	9	38	30	1955.60	1502.30
1987	237	155	65	66	28	16	7	38	31	2722.42	1738.74
1988	410	255	62	113	28	42	10	42	31	2183.50	1879.14
1989	303	187	62	88	29	28	9	41	29	2791.41	2144.64
1990	175	105	60	48	27	22	13	42	32	2999.75	2365.10
1991	137	92	67	35	26	10	7	35	29	3168.83	2470.30
1992	142	84	59	40	28	18	13	41	35	3413.21	3136.58
1993	173	110	64	48	28	15	9	39	33	3794.33	3241.95
1994	260	155	60	80	31	25	10	42	35	3978.36	3593.35
1995	324	214	66	77	24	33	10	45	29	5216.50	3838.10
1996	381	253	66	104	27	24	6	37	27	6560.90	5032.90
1997	487	340	69	119	24	28	6	36	28	8259.30	6442.50
1998	512	331	64	129	25	52	10	41	30	9338.00	7580.40
1999	723	430	59	221	31	72	10	43	35	11497.10	9120.90
2000	574	279	53	212	37	83	14	49	41	11252.80	9796.03
Total	7,364	3,823	52	2,169	30	792	11				

Source: Reprinted by permission of Mergerstat LP. www.mergerstat.com.

generally rising share prices. That study also found that the acquisition premium behaves countercyclically, varying inversely with the Standard & Poor's 500 Index.[9]

EXAMPLE Analysis of Premiums Paid

An acquisition target currently has 10,000,000 shares outstanding. They are trading at \$27. This gives the target a current market value of \$270 million. The acquiror's financial staff analyzes 10 recent acquisitions of firms in the same industry. It finds that the merger premiums fall between 50% and 66%. It also considers whether there has been any merger speculation or other factors that might have inflated the target's share price. It concludes there were none.

The premiums paid suggest that a reasonable acquisition value is between \$405 million (= [270]1.5) and \$448 million (= [270]1.66). A reasonable offering price would fall between \$40.50 (= 405/10) and \$44.80 (= 448/10) per share. Discounted-cash-flow analysis and tactical considerations will determine what price the acquiror should initially offer.[10]

Comparative Analysis

Investment bankers look at comparable acquisitions to determine a reasonable price for the acquiror to offer for the target firm's shares. They use a table like Table 25.6. Using such a table reflects the Behavioral Principle: Look to comparable acquisitions for guidance regarding a reasonable price to pay for an acquisition. The table provides the following pricing benchmarks for a carefully selected group of acquisitions of publicly traded firms:

$$\begin{matrix}\text{Multiple of}\\ \text{earnings paid}\end{matrix} = \frac{\text{Purchase price per share}}{\begin{matrix}\text{Target's fully diluted earnings per share}\\ \text{before extraordinary items}\end{matrix}} \tag{25.3}$$

$$\begin{matrix}\text{Multiple of}\\ \text{cash flow paid}\end{matrix} = \frac{\text{Purchase price per share}}{\begin{matrix}\text{Target's fully diluted cash flow per share}\\ \text{before extraordinary items}\end{matrix}} \tag{25.4}$$

$$\begin{matrix}\text{Multiple of}\\ \text{EBIT paid}\end{matrix} = \frac{\begin{matrix}\text{Aggregate purchase}\\ \text{price of equity}\end{matrix} + \begin{matrix}\text{Market value of}\\ \text{debt assumed}\end{matrix}}{\begin{matrix}\text{Target's earnings before interest and taxes (EBIT)}\\ \text{before extraordinary items}\end{matrix}} \tag{25.5}$$

$$\begin{matrix}\text{Multiple of}\\ \text{EBITDA paid}\end{matrix} = \frac{\begin{matrix}\text{Aggregate purchase}\\ \text{price of equity}\end{matrix} + \begin{matrix}\text{Market value of}\\ \text{debt assumed}\end{matrix}}{\begin{matrix}\text{Target's earnings before interest, taxes, depreciation}\\ \text{and amortization (EBITDA) before extraordinary items}\end{matrix}} \tag{25.6}$$

$$\begin{matrix}\text{Multiple of}\\ \text{book value paid}\end{matrix} = \frac{\text{Purchase price per share}}{\text{Target's book value per common share}} \tag{25.7}$$

[9]The reasons for this behavior are not entirely clear. One possibility is that takeovers occur when the target firm is undervalued. Undervaluation may be more severe during recessions (when share prices are depressed).

[10]Discounted-cash-flow analysis will indicate the maximum price the acquiror can afford to pay. The acquiror must then determine an appropriate bidding strategy. But do not offer the maximum initially—give yourself room to raise the bid later.

TABLE 25.6
Illustration of comparative analysis (dollar amounts in millions except per-share amounts).

ACQUIROR/ ACQUIREE[a]	INFORMATION ON ACQUIREE FOR LATEST 12 MONTHS PRIOR TO ACQUISITION: Net Revenue (5-year growth)	Net Income (5-year growth)	Cash Flow (5-year growth)	EBIT (5-year growth)	EBITDA (5-year growth)	Book Value	MARKET VALUE OF DEBT	PURCHASE PRICE PAID FOR EQUITY: Aggregate	Per Share	PURCHASE PRICE AS MULTIPLE OF: Earnings[b]	Cash Flow[b]	EBIT[c]	EBITDA[c]	Book Value[b]	PREMIUM PAID OVER MARKET PRICE ONE MONTH BEFORE ANNOUNCEMENT
Empire/	$600	$30	$42	$53	$58	$196	$ 93	—	—	—	—	—	—	—	—
Garden State (P)	(12.3%)	(11.2%)	(12.0%)	(11.9%)	(12.1%)										
Atlantic/	630	27	40	45	51	177	105	$410	$33.75	15.2*x*	10.3*x*	11.4*x*	10.1*x*	2.3*x*	60%
Crescent (P)	(10.9)	(11.0)	(10.3)	(10.4)	(10.2)										
Essex/	435	20	30	35	39	142	90	270	39.50	13.5	9.0	10.3	9.2	1.9	45
Trenton	(9.8)	(10.0)	(10.1)	(10.2)	(9.9)										
Sussex/	465	23	35	39	43	130	87	220	24.50	9.6	6.3	7.9	7.1	1.7	37
Brooklyn	(7.5)	(8.0)	(8.7)	(9.1)	(8.9)										
Madison/	833	42	60	80	86	281	175	730	55.25	17.4	12.2	11.3	10.5	2.6	66
Washington (P)	(12.9)	(12.6)	(13.2)	(12.9)	(13.3)										
Jersey/	610	29	45	52	60	197	100	450	27.63	15.5	10.0	10.6	9.2	2.3	55
Philadelphia (P)	(11.7)	(12.4)	(12.7)	(12.5)	(12.6)										
Morris/	720	32	42	58	64	210	90	441	38.25	13.8	10.5	9.2	8.3	2.1	53
Neptune (P)	(10.1)	(9.9)	(10.2)	(10.4)	(10.0)										
Salem/	415	17	22	30	34	121	75	302	43.50	17.8	13.7	12.6	11.1	2.5	62
Seaside (P)	(13.6)	(12.6)	(11.1)	(11.3)	(10.7)										
Worthington/	440	22	35	40	48	161	125	320	31.25	14.5	9.1	11.1	9.3	2.0	50
Homestead (P)	(11.4)	(11.7)	(11.0)	(11.1)	(10.5)										
Ludlow/	515	24	37	41	45	160	85	300	29.88	12.5	8.1	9.4	8.6	1.9	47
Quackenbush	(11.1)	(8.3)	(8.3)	(8.7)	(8.4)										
Warren/	550	25	37	42	45	130	110	285	44.00	11.4	7.7	9.4	8.8	2.2	43
Bergen	(10.8)	(8.7)	(9.0)	(9.1)	(8.8)										
For all the Comparables															
High	13.6%	12.6%	13.2%	12.9%	13.3%					17.8*x*	13.7*x*	12.6*x*	11.1*x*	2.6*x*	60%
Low	7.5	8.0	8.3	8.7	8.4					9.6	6.3	7.9	7.1	1.7	37
Average	11.0	10.5	10.5	10.6	10.3					14.1	9.7	10.3	9.2	2.2	51
For the Proprietary Pharmaceutical Manufacturers															
High	13.6%	12.6%	13.2%	12.9%	13.3%					17.8*x*	13.7*x*	12.6*x*	11.1*x*	2.6*x*	66%
Low	10.1	9.9	10.2	10.4	10.0					13.8	9.1	9.2	8.3	2.0	50
Average	11.8	11.7	11.4	11.4	11.2					15.7	11.0	11.0	9.8	2.3	58

[a](P) denotes proprietary pharmaceutical manufacturers.
[b]Based on the purchase price paid for equity.
[c]Based on the combined market value of debt and purchase price paid for equity.

The following ratio is often useful for firms that have substantial manufacturing facilities:

$$\text{Multiple of replacement cost paid} = \frac{\text{Aggregate purchase price of equity} + \text{Market value of debt assumed}}{\text{Replacement cost of target's assets}} \quad (25.8)$$

The following ratio is useful for natural resource firms whose assets often enjoy relatively liquid secondary markets (such as oil and gas reserves, timber and timberland, and so forth):

$$\text{Price paid per unit of resource} = \frac{\text{Aggregate purchase price of equity} + \text{Market value of debt assumed}}{\text{Number of units of resource target owns}} \quad (25.9)$$

In Equations (25.3) and (25.4), if the firm is in a highly cyclical industry, earnings per share and cash flow per share for each firm should be averaged over a period that corresponds to the length of one cycle. Also, if projected earnings are available for each firm as of its acquisition date, it is useful to calculate the multiple of earnings paid on both a historical basis and a projected basis. The multiple of EBIT (Equation (25.5)) and the multiple of EBITDA (Equation (25.6)) are usually more meaningful than the multiple of earnings (Equation (25.3)) or cash flow (Equation (25.4)) when the acquirees in the group of comparable transactions have significantly different capital structures. Differences in interest expense will affect earnings and cash flow but not EBIT and EBITDA.

In Equation (25.8), the replacement cost of the acquiree's assets can often be estimated from industry benchmarks (for example, proved developed crude oil reserves located in Texas have an average "finding cost" of so many dollars per barrel). In Equation (25.9), the number of units of resource the target owns is measured in physical units. Different resources can be combined by adopting some standard of equivalence. For example, an oil and gas firm's hydrocarbon reserves can be expressed on a "net equivalent barrel" basis by calculating the number of barrels of oil that would have the same market value as the firm's gas reserves. Then the price paid per unit of resource would be expressed in terms of dollars per net equivalent barrel.

EXAMPLE Comparative Analysis

Table 25.7 illustrates comparative analysis of Empire State's possible acquisition of Garden State. Empire State Pharmaceutical is a proprietary drug manufacturer with annual sales of \$1.2 billion. Empire State is considering acquiring another publicly traded proprietary drug manufacturer, Garden State Drugs. Garden State has annual sales of \$600 million. The acquisition would increase Empire State's sales by 50%. It would also lead to significant economies in marketing, and it could expand Empire State's product line more quickly than Empire State would be able to do by developing similar drugs on its own. The net benefit of the potential acquisition depends, of course, on how much Empire State would have to pay to acquire Garden State.

Garden State currently has 10,000,000 shares outstanding, which are trading at a price of \$27. This gives Garden State a current market value of \$270 million. Empire State's financial staff believes that there has been no merger speculation or other factors that might have inflated Garden State's share price. (If there had been, Empire State's financial staff would have to reduce the premium to be offered Garden State's shareholders.)

The comparative analysis table contains data for 10 carefully selected recent acquisitions of pharmaceutical firms that are similar to Garden State in terms of size and business and financial characteristics. Six are also proprietary drug manufacturers like Garden State.

TABLE 25.7
Estimated ranges of value for Garden State Drugs.

MULTIPLE	RANGE OF MULTIPLES	VALUE FOR GARDEN STATE ($ MILLIONS)	IMPLIED AGGREGATE PURCHASE PRICE ($ MILLIONS)
Earnings	13.8–17.8x	30	414–534
Cash flow	9.1–13.7	42	382–575
EBIT	9.2–12.6	53	395–575[a]
EBITDA	8.3–11.1	58	388–551[a]
Book value	2.0–2.6	196	392–510
Premium paid	50%–66%	270	405–448

[a]After subtracting the market value of Garden State's debt ($93 million).

Comparing the multiples and premiums paid for all 10 firms to those paid for proprietary drug manufacturers reveals that the proprietary manufacturers have commanded higher multiples and premiums. Empire State's financial staff therefore decides to base its calculations on the data concerning the proprietary drug firm acquisitions.

In terms of its growth (and other characteristics), Garden State compares very favorably with the six proprietary drug manufacturers. "Reasonable" acquisition multiples and a "reasonable" acquisition price would fall within the ranges shown in Table 25.7. The intersection of the six value ranges is $414 to $448 million. This analysis suggests a price per share in the range of $41.40 to $44.80 per Garden State share. Any price per share within this range would represent a reasonable price, in the sense that it would not be out of line with the prices acquirors have paid in comparable situations, an application of the Behavioral Principle.

Comparative analysis does not always work this smoothly. In many cases, it is difficult to identify a well-defined group of comparables. For example, the candidates may all be in different businesses. In such cases, careful judgment must be applied to determine an appropriate value range, for example, by eliminating less closely comparable firms from the table (as we did in the illustration).

Liquidation Approach

The potential liquidation value (or breakup value) of a firm should also be considered in a merger evaluation. A holding company that operates a number of essentially autonomous firms, or a firm that owns a number of dissimilar assets, investments, and other firms, can be valued by estimating the market value of each class of assets and subtracting the cost of repaying all liabilities:

$$LV = A - L - T - E \tag{25.10}$$

where LV is the liquidation value of the target, A is the liquidation value of all its assets, L is the cost of repaying all its debt and preferred stock obligations, T is the tax obligation incurred in connection with the liquidation, and E is the costs and expenses associated with the acquisition and liquidation.

The liquidation values estimated when applying Equation (25.10) should be based on the values that can be realized within a "reasonable" time frame, say one year, rather than in a "fire sale." Equations (25.3) through (25.7)—and in the case of subsidiaries that hold substantial natural resources, Equation (25.9)—can be used to value subsidiaries that are saleable within this reasonable time frame. Equation (25.2) can be used to value any subsidiaries that are publicly traded. The cost of repaying debt and redeeming preferred (and preference) stock will be specified in the documents governing those fixed-income obligations. Finally, the sale of assets usually triggers a corporate tax liability, and disposing of assets generally involves significant expenses.

Review

1. Explain how to use comparative analysis to estimate a reasonable price to pay for an acquisition. What is the rationale underlying this approach?
2. What is a merger premium, and how is it calculated? Why is it wise to calculate the merger premium using the share price 30 days before the initial announcement of the acquisition?
3. What is the multiple of earnings paid? multiple of cash flow paid? multiple of EBITDA paid? Why is the multiple of EBITDA paid more useful than the other two when the comparables have widely different capital structures?
4. Suppose a holding company has three operating subsidiaries. There is no other firm just like the holding company, but each of its subsidiaries has a number of competitors, each involved in only a single business. How would you use the liquidation approach to value this firm?

25.5 DISCOUNTED-CASH-FLOW ANALYSIS

We have pointed out that an acquisition is a special type of capital budgeting problem. A firm acquires another firm, instead of just one project. Even though acquisitions are more complex, discounted-cash-flow (DCF) analysis is still useful. We must be careful not to overlook any of the complexities that might affect shareholder value. When applied correctly, DCF analysis is helpful to an acquiror in deciding whether an acquisition would benefit its shareholders if it can buy the target for the price it is considering paying. DCF analysis is also useful in determining the maximum price the acquiror can afford to pay. We illustrate both uses of the technique in this section.

Table 25.8 illustrates how to use DCF analysis to evaluate Empire State's possible acquisition of Garden State, which we discussed earlier. We assume that Empire State has already decided that it would not be advantageous to step up the tax basis of Garden State's assets. Empire State elected to use a 10-year time horizon for its analysis. Projected amounts are rounded to the nearest million.

Determining the Net Acquisition Cost

The first step is to determine what it would cost Empire State to acquire Garden State. The **net acquisition cost (NAC)** is the investment the acquiror makes when it purchases the acquiree:

$$\begin{array}{l} \text{Cost of purchasing target's equity} \\ +\text{Transaction costs} \\ \underline{-\text{Target's excess assets}} \\ \text{Net investment in target's equity} \\ \underline{+\text{Cost of assuming target's debt}} \\ \text{Net acquisition cost (NAC)} \end{array} \qquad (25.11)$$

Let's take a closer look at each item in Equation (25.11).

COST OF PURCHASING TARGET'S EQUITY Garden State has 10,000,000 shares outstanding, at \$27 per share. Empire State plans to purchase all of Garden State's outstanding stock for cash through a tender offer at a price of \$48 per share (16 times earnings), which represents a 78% premium. Purchasing Garden State's shares will cost \$480 million.

TABLE 25.8
Discounted-cash-flow (DCF) analysis of the acquisition of Garden State Drugs (dollar amounts in millions).

YEAR	0	1	2	3	4	5	6	7	8	9	10
Purchase of equity[a]	$ 480.0	—	—	—	—	—	—	—	—	—	—
Cost of debt assumed	92.6	—	—	—	—	—	—	—	—	—	—
Transaction costs	5.0	—	—	—	—	—	—	—	—	—	—
Acquiree's excess cash	(35.0)	—	—	—	—	—	—	—	—	—	—
Net acquisition cost	$ 542.6										
Incremental Free Cash Flow:											
Revenue	—	$672	$753	$843	$944	$1,057	$1,184	$1,326	$1,486	$1,664	$1,864
Cost of goods sold[b]	—	336	376	421	472	529	592	663	743	832	932
SG&A	—	251	276	304	334	367	404	444	489	538	591
Depreciation (tax)	—	13	15	15	18	19	22	25	28	30	35
Pretax operating profit	—	72	86	103	120	142	166	194	226	264	306
Income taxes[c]	—	36	43	52	60	71	83	97	113	132	153
Net operating profit	—	36	43	51	60	71	83	97	113	132	153
Depreciation (tax)	—	13	15	15	18	19	22	25	28	30	35
Net operating cash flow	—	49	58	66	78	90	105	122	141	162	188
Net investment in working capital[d]	—	(15)	(18)	(20)	(25)	(28)	(32)	(36)	(40)	(43)	(50)
Investment in fixed assets	—	(22)	(25)	(30)	(35)	(40)	(45)	(50)	(50)	(50)	(50)
Operating economies net of taxes[e]	—	10	11	12	13	15	15	15	15	15	15
Incremental free cash flow	—	$ 22	$ 26	$ 28	$ 31	$ 37	$ 43	$ 51	$ 66	$ 84	$ 103
Terminal Value of Net Assets:											
Nondisposition basis[f]	—	—	—	—	—	—	—	—	—	—	$2,472
Disposition basis[g]	—	—	—	—	—	—	—	—	—	—	1,842
Incremental Net Cash Flow:											
Nondisposition basis	$(542.6)	$ 22	$ 26	$ 28	$ 31	$ 37	$ 43	$ 51	$ 66	$ 84	$2,575
Disposition basis	$(542.6)	$ 22	$ 26	$ 28	$ 31	$ 37	$ 43	$ 51	$ 66	$ 84	$1,945

$$\text{Required return} = \text{WACC} = r - T*Lr_d\left[\frac{1+r}{1+r_d}\right] = 0.1659 - 0.25(1/3)(0.12)\left[\frac{1.1659}{1.12}\right] = 15.55\%$$

IRR (Nondisposition basis) = 20.40%
IRR (Disposition basis) = 17.59%
NPV (Nondisposition basis) = $236.5 million
NPV (Disposition basis) = $88.0 million

[a]Estimated as 16 times prior year's earnings (a purchase price of $48.00 per share).
[b]Excluding depreciation.
[c]Assumes a 50% marginal income tax rate.
[d]Increase in inventories and receivables net of increase in payables.
[e]Estimated after-tax savings resulting from eliminating redundant overhead and redundant production facilities and marketing some of Garden State's products through Empire State's distribution network.
[f]Calculated as 16 times terminal year's earnings ($142.7 million) plus the amount of debt outstanding at the investment horizon ($188.3 million). This calculation assumes that Empire State does not sell the shares of Garden State; it continues to hold them (nondisposition case).
[g]Calculated as 16 times terminal year's earnings ($142.7 million) plus the amount of debt outstanding at the investment horizon ($188.3 million) and net of capital gains tax at a 34% rate (with a tax basis of $450 million) and net also of transaction costs ($10 million). This calculation assumes that Empire State sells the shares of Garden State at the end of the 10th year and pays any resulting tax liability if there is a gain (or receives a tax benefit if there is a loss on disposition).

COST OF ASSUMING TARGET'S DEBT Garden State currently has $100 million of debt outstanding, which bears interest at a 10% rate, payable annually in arrears. The debt matures in one lump sum at the end of 10 years and is callable at par. Empire State will be able to assume this debt.

Assuming the obligation for servicing Garden State's debt reduces the amount of new debt that Empire State can issue to finance (part of) the cost of the acquisition. Cash that Empire State uses to service the debt it assumes is not available to service new debt. In other words, assuming the 10% debt involves an opportunity cost. This opportunity cost equals the maximum amount of new debt that Empire State could issue, subject to the constraint that the after-tax period-by-period debt service payments of the hypothetical new issue are the same as those of Garden State's debt that Empire State would assume.[11]

If Empire State is permitted to assume the debt, *and* if the opportunity cost of assuming the debt is less than the cost of retiring it immediately, Empire State should assume the debt rather than retire it. Empire State should include the opportunity cost as part of the net acquisition cost. It must also be subtracted from the amount of new debt Empire State could otherwise issue to finance the acquisition. If instead the opportunity cost of assuming Garden State's debt is greater than the cost of retiring it immediately, the debt should be retired. The cost of retiring it must then be included in the net acquisition cost.

Empire State's pretax cost of a new debt issue (before issuance expenses) is 12%. Its marginal ordinary income tax rate is 50%. Assume the 10% debt would require after-tax interest payments of $5 million per year. Newly issued debt would have an after-tax interest cost of 6% per year. *The opportunity cost of assuming Garden State's outstanding debt equals the present value of the after-tax debt service with Empire's after-tax cost of debt serving as the discount rate:*

$$\text{PV(debt assumed)} = \sum_{t=1}^{10} \frac{5}{(1.06)^t} + \frac{100}{(1.06)^{10}} = \$92.6 \text{ million}$$

CALCULATOR SOLUTION	
Data Input	**Function Key**
10	N
6	I
5	PMT
100	FV
−92.6	**PV**

Because the cost of assuming the 10% debt is less than the $100 million cost of retiring it, Empire State is better off assuming the debt. The net advantage is $7.4 million (= 100.0 − 92.6).

HOW MUCH NEW DEBT CAN EMPIRE STATE ISSUE? Empire State's financial staff has studied the capital structure policies of large pharmaceutical firms in the manner described in Chapter 15. On the basis of that analysis, Empire State believes that it could finance the acquisition on a long-term basis with a debt-to-total-value ratio of 1/3 without any adverse impact on its senior debt rating or on how it might choose to finance other projects. The amount of new long-term debt that Empire State can issue is the amount it can have outstanding after the acquisition less the amount of debt displaced by the debt it assumes in the acquisition:

$$\begin{aligned}\text{Added debt} &= (L)\text{NAC} - \text{PV(debt assumed)} \qquad (25.12)\\ &= (1/3)542.6 - 92.6 = \$88.3 \text{ million}\end{aligned}$$

where L is the acquiror's target debt-to-total-value ratio. This calculation uses NAC = $542.6 million, which is calculated in Table 25.8.

TARGET'S EXCESS ASSETS AND TRANSACTION COSTS The gross cost of Empire State's acquisition before transaction costs is $572.6 million (= 480.0 + 92.6). However, after analyzing Garden State's financial statements, Empire State believes that Garden State has approximately $35 million of excess cash and marketable securities that it will be able to apply toward the purchase price. Empire State has estimated that investment bankers' fees and other expenses net of taxes will total $5 million.

Note that excess assets represent a potential pitfall. Firms like to pay as much of the acquisition cost as they can with the acquiree's cash. But what appears as excess cash may in fact be tied up as compensating balances, or it may be overseas and repatriating it could trigger a significant tax liability.

NET ACQUISITION COST Empire State's net acquisition cost of acquiring Garden State's net assets is $542.6 million. The calculation is shown in Table 25.8. It will be convenient for our

[11]This method of analysis, the debt service parity (DSP) approach, is described more fully in Chapter 19.

later discussion to reorder the items as in Equation (25.11) to identify separately Empire State's $450 million net investment in Garden State's equity:

Cost of purchasing target's equity	$480.0
+Transaction costs	5.0
−Target's excess assets	(35.0)
Net investment in target's equity	450.0
+Cost of assuming target's debt	92.6
Net acquisition cost (NAC)	$542.6

If the target's debt became payable immediately as a result of the acquisition, the cost of retiring target's debt would be the face amount, $100 million. In that case, the net acquisition cost would be $550 million (= 450 + 100). Whenever you evaluate the possible acquisition of a firm that has debt outstanding, check whether the acquisition will trigger immediate repayment. If it will, and assuming the debt would be cheaper than retiring it, you will probably want to find an alternative legal structure that will avoid triggering the repayment.

Incremental Free Cash Flow

Empire State believes that Garden State's revenue will grow at the rate of 12% per year, the historical growth rate. Empire State also believes that the cost of goods sold will grow at the same rate, whereas selling, general, and administrative expense (SG&A) will grow at 10% per year. Annual depreciation expense for tax purposes is estimated from Garden State's published financial reports and from Empire State's estimate of Garden State's required capital expenditure program. The forecasted operating economies represent Empire State's estimate of the benefits it will realize by eliminating redundant production facilities and from marketing some of Empire State's products through Garden State's distribution network.

There are some important potential pitfalls. It is easy to be too optimistic about the acquiree's growth prospects. It is also easy to be overly optimistic about the synergistic benefits from the merger. The more dissimilar the acquiree's and the acquiror's businesses, the more difficult it will be to find true synergies. It is also easy to underestimate the amount of investment that will be required. The older the acquiree's plant and equipment, the higher the required post-merger capital expenditures.

The projected incremental free cash flow stream is shown in Table 25.8. In year 1, net operating cash flow is expected to be $49 million. Empire State estimates that $15 million of this amount will have to be invested in additional inventories and receivables, and $22 million will have to be invested in fixed assets. It also believes that operating economies will provide $10 million of after-tax savings, leaving $22 million of incremental free cash flow. Empire State estimates that annual incremental free cash flow from Garden State's operations should grow to $103 million in year 10.

Terminal Value of Net Assets

An acquiree's terminal value is the estimated value of its net assets (total assets net of current liabilities, which equals the sum of shareholders' equity and long-term debt) at the end of the time period used in the acquisition analysis. We estimate terminal value by comparing the results of owning the acquiree with the results of selling it. For our example, the first case (nondisposition) assumes that Empire State continues to own Garden State for an indefinite period beyond the investment horizon. The second case (disposition) assumes that Empire State sells all the common stock of Garden State at the investment horizon. If Empire State were to sell Garden State after the investment horizon, the present value of any resulting tax liabilities would have to be taken into account. The value of Garden State in that case would lie between the two values estimated in the following paragraphs.

In the first case, Garden State's terminal value is estimated by applying an appropriate multiple to Garden State's pro forma earnings in year 10 estimated as though Garden State were on a stand-alone basis. Empire State would pay \$480 million to purchase Garden State's equity. Garden State's net income is \$30 million per year according to its latest income statement, an EPS of \$3. Using Equation (25.3), the purchase price represents a multiple of 16 times earnings:

$$\text{Multiple of earnings paid} = \frac{\text{Purchase price per share}}{\text{Target's fully diluted earnings per share before extraordinary items}} = \frac{48}{3} = 16$$

In year 10, Garden State would have \$100 million principal amount of 10% debt plus \$88.3 million of 12% debt, giving rise to \$10.3 million of after-tax interest expense (= [100(0.10) + 88.3(0.12)][0.50]). Subtracting this from Garden State's estimated year-10 net operating profit of \$153 million leaves \$142.7 million of earnings. Multiplying by 16.0 gives a terminal value of \$2,283.2 million for Garden State's equity. Adding the terminal value of Garden State's debt, \$188.3 million, gives the terminal value of Garden State's net assets:

$$\begin{aligned} \text{TV(NA)} &= \text{TV(equity)} + \text{TV(debt)} - \text{Taxes} - \text{Expenses} \qquad (25.13) \\ &= 2{,}283.2 + 188.3 - 0 - 0 = \$2{,}471.5 \text{ million} \end{aligned}$$

where TV(NA) is the terminal value of net assets, TV(equity) is the terminal value of shareholders' equity, TV(debt) is the terminal value of long-term debt (and capitalized leases and preferred stock) obligations, Taxes represents any taxes incurred in realizing the terminal value, and Expenses represents any other expenses incurred in realizing the terminal value. TV(NA) rounded to the nearest million is \$2,472 million, which appears in Table 25.8 as the terminal value of net assets on a nondisposition basis.

In the second case, tax liabilities and transaction costs must be taken into account. Empire State estimates that if it sold Garden State, it would incur \$10 million of transaction costs. Its net proceeds are \$2,273.2 million (= 2,283.2 − 10). Its tax basis equals what it pays to purchase Garden State's shares (that is, the net investment in target's shares after taking into account excess assets and transaction costs), \$450 million. Empire State would realize a long-term capital gain equal to the difference between the net proceeds from the sale of the equity and the net investment in the target's shares, \$1,823.2 million (= 2,273.2 − 450).[12] Empire State's financial staff estimates a future capital gains tax rate of 34%. Empire State would incur capital gains tax of \$620.0 million (= [0.34]1,823.2). Substituting into Equation (25.13), this leaves

$$\text{TV(NA)} = \$2{,}283.2 + 188.3 - 620.0 - 10 = \$1{,}841.5 \text{ million}$$

TV(NA) rounded to the nearest million is \$1,842 million, which appears in Table 25.8 as the terminal value of net assets on a disposition basis.

The calculation of terminal value is often critical. By assuming a high enough future multiple, an acquiror can justify any purchase price. But it seems more prudent to assume that the future acquisition multiple will be no greater than the current acquisition multiple, as we did in the illustration.

DCF Analysis

We have calculated the incremental net cash flow stream in Table 25.8. Next we must estimate the required return. As we have noted, an acquisition is a form of capital investment. Therefore we must estimate the weighted average cost of capital (WACC) for the acquisition. We will use the procedure outlined in Chapter 16 that assumes leverage rebalancing.

---

[12]Its original tax basis in the shares of Garden State equals the cost of purchasing the shares (\$480 million) plus transaction costs (\$5 million) minus the portion of the purchase price paid for with the target's excess cash (\$35 million). The net amount is \$450 million. The net sales proceeds realized upon the sale of the shares equal the sale price (\$2,283 million) net of transaction costs (\$10 million).

The debt ratio is $L = 1/3$. Empire State's financial staff has analyzed pharmaceutical firms comparable to Garden State. It estimated a required return to *unleveraged* equity of $r = 0.1659$, and a net-benefit-to-leverage factor $T^* = 0.25$. Finally, the cost of debt is $r_d = 0.12$. Substituting these values into Equation (16.9), the weighted average cost of capital formula, gives

$$\text{WACC} = 0.1659 - 0.25(1/3)(0.12)\left[\frac{1.1659}{1.12}\right] = 0.1555 = 15.55\%$$

Note that as in capital budgeting, the debt ratio is the acquiror's long-run target proportion of debt financing.

The incremental net cash flow stream is discounted at the required return WACC = 0.1555 to obtain the net present value of the acquisition, NPV(acquisition):

$$\text{NPV(acquisition)} = -\text{NAC} + \sum_{t=1}^{N} \frac{\text{CFAT}_t}{(1 + \text{WACC})^t} \tag{25.14}$$

where CFAT_t is the (unleveraged) incremental net cash flow during period t, and N is the investment horizon. CFAT_N includes the terminal value of the acquisition (at the investment horizon) estimated from Equation (25.13).

EXAMPLE Calculating the NPV of a Potential Acquisition

Applying Equation (25.14) to Empire State's proposed acquisition of Garden State indicates NPV(acquisition) = \$236.5 million on a nondisposition basis and NPV(acquisition) = \$88.0 million on a disposition basis. Both values are given at the bottom of Table 25.8. The WACC approach indicates that the acquisition of Garden State at a price representing 16 times Garden State's earnings would be profitable.

Calculating terminal value on both bases reveals the sensitivity of the acquisition decision to this value and, in this case, to the multiple applied to the terminal year's earnings. Note that the present value of the incremental net cash flow stream, exclusive of terminal value, is −\$346.1 million. The terminal value must be at least \$1,468.6 million ($= [346.1]1.1555^{10}$) for the NPV to be positive. The NPV of a proposed acquisition is usually very sensitive to the estimated terminal value. Therefore, it is important to consider carefully the assumptions made in arriving at the estimate. It is also wise to calculate the break-even terminal value, which makes NPV(acquisition) equal to zero.

Maximum Acquisition Price

There is one additional use for DCF analysis. We can calculate the maximum price the acquiror could afford to pay for the target. Given the incremental net cash flow stream and discount rate, the maximum price is the one that makes NPV(acquisition) equal to zero. Valuing Garden State on a disposition basis, Empire State could afford to pay approximately \$568.0 million (the original \$480 million price plus the \$88.0 million net present value), or \$56.80 (= 568/10) per share. At that price, Garden State's shareholders would experience a 110% gain (56.80 versus 27), whereas Empire State's shareholders would expect only to break even at best.[13]

[13]Empire State could actually afford to pay an even higher price before NPV becomes zero. A higher price increases Empire State's tax basis in Garden State's shares and reduces the future capital gains tax liability. For a purchase price of \$568.0 million, the tax liability would be \$590.0 million (= 0.34[2,273.2 − 538.0]); it would be \$620.0 million if the price paid for the stock were \$480 million.

Review

1. Explain why the cost of assuming the acquiree's debt should be included in the cost of purchasing the acquiree's net assets.
2. What is excess cash? Should you assume that all of the cash and marketable securities shown on the acquiree's balance sheet are available to pay part of the acquisition cost?
3. What are some of the pitfalls to avoid when you are projecting the acquiree's incremental after-tax cash flow?
4. What is the terminal value used in an acquisition analysis? How is it calculated?

25.6 THE MEDIUM OF PAYMENT

Acquirors usually pay for acquisitions in cash, stock, or some combination of the two. Achieving tax-free treatment requires that the acquiror pay at least 50% of the purchase price in its stock, although in many cases the acquiror has the flexibility to issue preferred stock instead of common stock.

Choice of Medium of Payment

Figure 25.2 breaks down merger transactions during the period 1981 to 2000 according to the medium of payment. Overall, 40% of the acquisitions were cash only, 32% were stock only, 1% were debt only, and the other 27% were paid for in a combination of stock, cash, and debt. The proportion of cash-only transactions fell sharply between 1988 and 1992 but also rose sharply between 1992 and 2000. The proportion involving a combination of stock, cash, and debt generally moved in the opposite direction. Combinations of stock and debt arise in two-tiered tender offers, wherein shareholders of the target usually get debentures in the second tier of the transaction. Combinations of cash and debt are common in acquisitions of privately held firms wherein the sellers often take a note from the buyers as part of the purchase price.

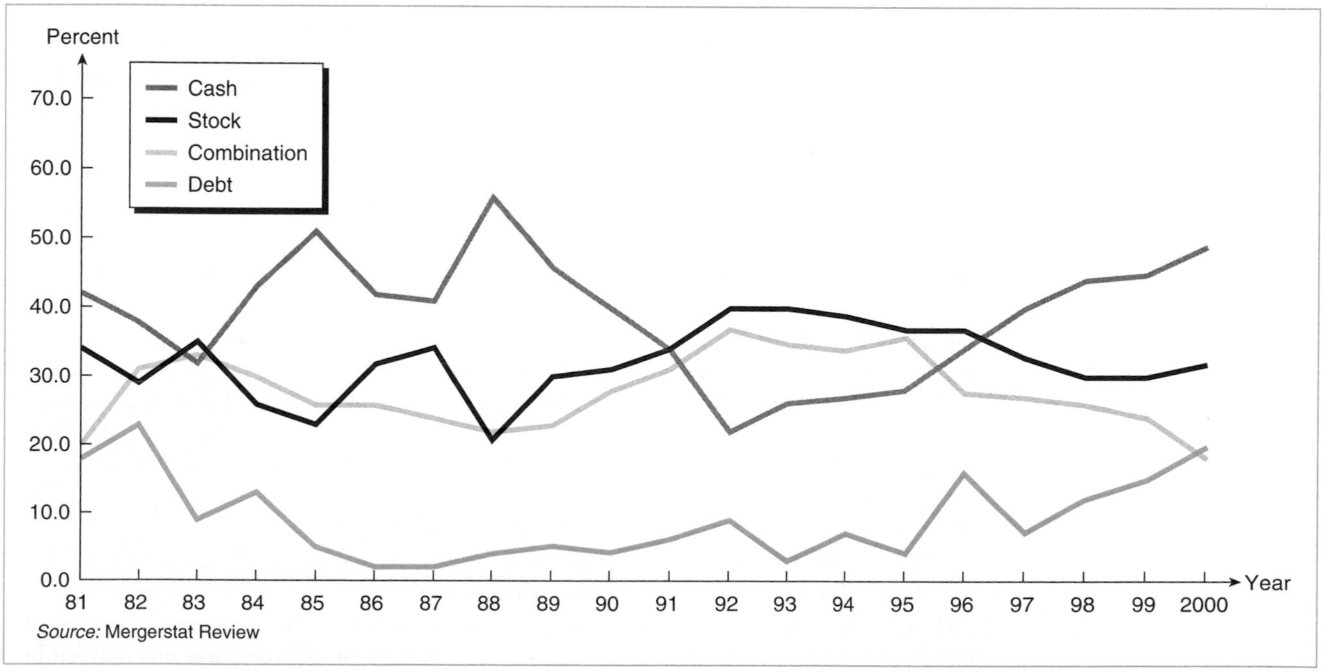

FIGURE 25.2
Trend in medium of payment, 1981–2000.

We expect the fraction of stock-only acquisitions to decrease because of the elimination of pooling-of-interest accounting for mergers, which we noted earlier. Many firms had favored that method of accounting, which could be used only for stock-only mergers (that also met the other requirements to use pooling). With the pooling alternative no longer available, it is likely there will be fewer stock-only mergers.

Common Stock and Net Acquisition Cost

Common stock tends to become a more popular medium of payment among acquirors during periods of rising stock prices. Acquirors are reluctant to pay in stock when they feel their shares are depressed in price. However, the shareholders of publicly traded acquirees, particularly the *risk arbitrageurs* who generally replace a significant portion of the public shareholders by buying their shares as soon as an acquisition is announced, prefer cash as the medium of payment. When an acquisition occurs, they want to take their profits and move on. Receiving cash saves them the trouble and cost of having to sell securities in the open market.

Acquirors often decide to pay in common stock, unless they think their share price is undervalued. That is, they think it is "cheaper" to pay in common stock than in cash. But whether it really is cheaper depends on (1) how the transaction is structured and (2) what happens to the share price after the transaction is announced.

Suppose Empire State wished to buy Garden State in an exchange of common stock. If managers of the two firms agreed on a fixed price of $480 million payable in Empire State common stock, the net acquisition cost would remain $542.6 million regardless of what happened to Empire State's share price. But in stock-for-stock acquisitions it is customary to negotiate an *exchange ratio*—that is, a given number of shares of Empire State for each share of Garden State. If the acquiror's share price subsequently increases, so does the net acquisition cost. Of course, if the acquiror's share price falls, the net acquisition cost falls also.

EXAMPLE Impact on the Net Acquisition Cost in a Stock-for-Stock Acquisition

Assume that Empire State has 50 million shares outstanding that are trading at a price of $32 each. Garden State has 10 million shares outstanding. Suppose Empire State offers to pay $48 for each Garden State share. It would have to exchange 1.5 (= 48/32) of its shares for each Garden State share. Empire State would have to issue 15 million (= [1.5]10) new shares. As a result, Garden State's former shareholders would own 23% (= 15/[15 + 50]) of Empire State after the acquisition. Suppose the exchange ratio is fixed. Suppose also that stock market investors believe the market value of Empire State's equity should be $2,168 million after the acquisition. This value is the sum of Empire State's current market value ($1,600 million) plus the value of the shares issued in exchange for Garden State's shares ($480 million) plus the NPV in the disposition case ($88.0 million). In that case, Empire State's share price would rise to $33.35 per share (= 2,168/65) and its cost of purchasing Garden State's shares would increase to $500.2 million (= 33.35[1.5]10) from $480 million. The fixed exchange ratio effectively appropriates 23% of the NPV (= [500.2 − 480]/88) for Garden State's former shareholders.

Let's assume instead that investors believe the market value of Empire State's equity after the merger should be only $1,950 million. Then Empire State's share price would fall to $30 (= 1,950/65), and its cost of purchasing Garden State's shares would fall to $450 million (= 30[1.5]10). Its net acquisition cost would fall from the $542.6 million in Table 25.8 to $512.6 million. In this way, Garden State's former shareholders would share the burden of the decline in value of Empire State's shares. Thus, an acquiror's shareholders are better off in a stock-for-stock transaction than in a cash-for-stock transaction if the acquiror overpays.

Acquirees realize they will share the burden of a decline in the acquiror's share price if the exchange ratio is fixed. As a result, acquirees often try to negotiate a *flexible exchange ratio* designed to assure them a fixed dollar price for their shares. For example, suppose Empire State's share price falls to $30 upon announcement of the acquisition, but the exchange ratio adjusts to 1.60 Empire State shares per Garden State share. Garden State's shareholders would still realize $48 (= [1.60]30) per share.

Dilution in Earnings per Share

There is one other factor to consider when common stock is the medium of payment. A publicly traded acquiror is usually concerned about an acquisition's impact on its future EPS. Paying for an acquisition with stock will usually decrease EPS when the target's price-earnings multiple exceeds the acquiror's. Issuing preferred stock or debt can reduce the impact, and possibly even raise EPS.

Table 25.9 illustrates the effect of different methods of payment. In the absence of any operating economies or other synergistic benefits, the market value of the combined entity is just the sum of the market values of the acquiror and the acquiree. The acquiror has the lower price-earnings multiple. When the acquiror pays entirely in common stock, it must issue 3,000,000 new shares. Its EPS falls to $4.62 (= [50,000,000 + 10,000,000]/[10,000,000 + 3,000,000]). However, its price-earnings multiple increases from 10.0*x* to 10.8*x*. If instead it borrows the $150,000,000 purchase price at 8% APR interest and its tax rate is 40%, after-tax interest is $7,200,000 (= 150,000,000[0.08][1 − 0.4]), and its EPS rises to $5.28 (= [50,000,000 + 10,000,000 − 7,200,000]/10,000,000). However, its price-earnings multiple decreases from 10.0*x* to 9.5*x*.

You should appreciate that as long as transactions take place in an efficient capital market, dilution in earnings per share will have only an accounting impact. Dilution is *not* an indicator of a proposed acquisition's impact on shareholder wealth. It should not affect which medium of payment the acquiror chooses.

Bond Rating

The method of payment can also have important capital structure effects. In Table 25.9, borrowing the entire amount increases the acquiror's leverage. Excessive leverage can reduce shareholder

TABLE 25.9
Illustration of the impact of an acquisition on reported earnings per share.

			COMBINED	
	ACQUIROR	ACQUIREE	Issues Stock[b]	Borrows and Pays Cash[c]
Market value				
Debt	—	—	—	$150,000,000
Stock	$500,000,000	$150,000,000[a]	$650,000,000	500,000,000
Total	$500,000,000	$150,000,000	$650,000,000	$650,000,000
Total earnings	$50,000,000	$10,000,000	$60,000,000	$52,800,000
Number of shares	10,000,000	5,000,000	13,000,000	10,000,000
Earnings per share	$ 5.00	$ 2.00	$ 4.62	$ 5.28
Share price	$50.00	$30.00[a]	$50.00	$50.00
Price-earnings ratio	10.0*x*	15.0*x*	10.8*x*	9.5*x*

[a]The premium paid is 25%.
[b]Acquiror issues 3,000,000 shares worth $50.00 each.
[c]Acquiror borrows $150,000,000 at 8% APR interest and pays cash for the acquiree's stock. After-tax interest expense is $7,200,000 (= 150,000,000[0.08][1 − 0.4]) assuming a 40% tax rate, which reduces combined earnings to $52,800,000 (= 60,000,000 − 7,200,000).

wealth, so a firm would be unwise to choose the debt-only alternative without first considering its impact on the firm's capital structure.

A firm that wishes to avoid having its bond rating downgraded will have to include enough common stock in the financing mix to achieve that goal. Bond covenants may also require including at least some common stock, either because they set an upper limit on the firm's debt ratio or because a rating downgrade would trigger an expensive increase in the interest rate on some of the firm's debt or a large redemption of debt.

Review

1. Over the last 20 years, what has been the most frequent medium of payment in corporate acquisitions? Are there any noticeable trends in use of the various methods of payment?
2. Why does paying for an acquisition with stock raise the cost of a positive-NPV acquisition and reduce the cost of a negative-NPV acquisition?

25.7 MERGER TACTICS

Many merger and acquisition transactions take place on a "friendly" basis. The two parties first agree to merge. Then they negotiate the legal form of the transaction, price, method of payment, and other terms. But many transactions are unfriendly. Management of the target may resist the potential acquiror's overtures. If they refuse to negotiate, the potential acquiror can take its offer directly to the target's shareholders along either of two avenues: a tender offer or a proxy contest. Managers and boards of directors have shown remarkable creativity in designing takeover defenses to thwart such threats to their security. You have probably heard the term *shark repellents,* which is used to describe them in the media.

Tender Offers

Few events in business pack as much drama—or engender as much bitterness—as a hostile tender offer by one firm for the shares of another. Recall that a tender offer is an offer to purchase shares of stock at a stated price from shareholders who are willing to sell shares at that price. The buyer decides on a tender price and on the other terms of the offer, files the tender offer documents with the Securities and Exchange Commission, and when the SEC clears these documents for distribution to security holders, the buyer publicly announces its offer to purchase their shares.

Tender offers may be either friendly or hostile to the target's management. In a hostile tender offer, the management of the target firm takes steps, often including litigation, to contest the offer. *Hostile raids* became an established acquisition strategy more than 25 years ago when one of the leading securities firms assisted International Nickel of Canada in a successful hostile tender offer for ESB.

Tender offers are frequently employed when incumbent management refuses to negotiate with the prospective acquiror. An example is the battle for control over RJR Nabisco, which is discussed in the next section. In other cases, management may be indifferent to a proposed acquisition. A tender offer lets the shareholders decide for themselves whether they like the acquiror's offer. Of course, a tender offer can seem very expensive because the tender price is usually substantially higher than the target's preoffer share price, and because tender offers are almost always made exclusively in cash.

ADVANTAGES OF TENDER OFFERS Cash tender offers present an acquiror with several potential advantages. First, a cash tender offer represents the quickest means of obtaining control of another firm. There are no terms to be negotiated and no securities to be registered. Tender offers also have a shorter minimum waiting period for government antitrust review. However, tender offers are regulated, and SEC rules do not permit an all-out blitzkrieg. The securities laws require disclosure (within 10 days) when an acquiror buys 5% or more of any class of a firm's equity securities, as well as disclosure of tender offers or exchange offers to acquire a class of equity securities of a publicly traded firm.

A second advantage is that a tender offer provides greater flexibility than other acquisition strategies. A firm can tender for just enough shares to give it effective control. In the case of a publicly traded firm whose shares are widely held, this may require tendering for only 20% to 40% of the outstanding shares. The acquiror can set conditions of the offer so that, for example, it does not have to buy any shares unless the required minimum number is tendered. Once the acquiror has purchased these shares, resistance on the part of the acquiree's management normally lessens. The acquiror can then structure a merger as a tax-free reorganization to achieve 100% ownership.

Third, a cash tender offer represents the simplest way for a foreign firm to buy a U.S. firm. U.S. investors would generally be reluctant to swap shares of a U.S. firm for securities of a foreign firm for legal and other reasons. A cash tender offer gets around this problem.

Fourth, open-market purchases of the target firm's stock followed by a cash tender offer give the potential acquiror an opportunity for profit. The cash tender price effectively puts a floor under the target's share price and alerts the financial community that the target firm is "in play." If a higher bidder emerges, the original bidder can take some consolation from the profits it realizes on the shares it owns.

CONTESTED TENDER OFFERS Tender offers are often contested by the target's management, which may mount an aggressive public relations campaign, file lawsuits, bid for the other firm's shares, and take other steps.

Unexpected tender offers are a source of concern to management. There is a 20-day minimum period that the tender offer must remain open, which seems painfully short to a firm that gets caught by surprise. In addition, current tender offer regulations require the target firm to disclose its response within 10 business days of the commencement of the offer.

Proxy Contests

Tender offers are expensive because the bidder must purchase enough shares to secure control. Alternatively, one or more individuals who oppose incumbent management can initiate a **proxy contest.** A *proxy* conveys the right to vote the shares of the person who grants the proxy. The dissidents solicit shareholders' proxies to vote their shares in favor of their own slate of directors at the next annual meeting of stockholders. However, a proxy fight is expensive and time consuming, and few succeed.

EXAMPLE Brooke Group's Proxy Battle with RJR Nabisco Management

Brooke Group, controlled by investor Bennett LeBow, and investor Carl Icahn tried unsuccessfully to convince the board of directors of RJR Nabisco to spin off the Nabisco food division to separate it from the firm's tobacco business. Nabisco's board expressed a willingness to consider the spinoff but said that it would need time to figure out how best to separate the two businesses.

Brooke Group responded by taking the first step in a proxy battle with RJR Nabisco's management by soliciting RJR Nabisco's shareholders on the issue. More than 50% of the firm's shareholders voted in favor of a resolution supporting an immediate spinoff and another resolution giving shareholders the right to call a special shareholders' meeting. However, these resolutions were not binding on the board, which still refused to agree to an immediate spinoff.

Brooke Group's next move was to announce that it would propose its own slate of dissident directors with a stated goal of spinning off the food business. Brooke Group made good on its announcement and launched a proxy contest but lost. The result left RJR Nabisco management in place to pursue its own strategy.

Shareholders seem to prefer cash in hand—especially when it represents a large premium over the prevailing share price—to the mere promise that the firm's financial prospects will improve in the future under new management. This observation is consistent with the Principle of Risk-Return Trade-Off. It is not surprising, then, that the vast majority of contests for control take the form of cash tender offers rather than proxy fights.

Defensive Tactics

Corporate managers often react negatively to unsolicited takeover bids. One would hope that their motive in doing so is to achieve the highest possible value for the firm's shares rather than merely exhibiting the Principle of Self-Interested Behavior to protect their jobs. The courts have generally held that the directors of a firm have a responsibility to obtain maximum value for shareholders. Corporate managers have devised a host of defensive tactics. Table 25.10 lists some of the more popular ones. These tactics include anticipatory steps that management and the board take to reduce the risk of getting blindsided. But such tactics can also entrench management. The poison pill has become controversial. In at least two cases, the Delaware Chancery Court ordered the board of directors to redeem poison pills in order to let shareholders choose between a restructuring plan supported by the board and an outside bidder's cash tender offer. The responsive tactics are more extreme, and many involve the sale of assets or securities.

IMPLICATIONS FOR SHAREHOLDER WEALTH The use of defensive tactics raises serious questions about how they affect shareholder wealth. If they entrench inefficient management, shareholder wealth must suffer. Studies have concluded that corporate charter amendments that authorize a staggered election of directors or supermajority voting do not adversely affect stock prices but that targeted share repurchases (greenmail) cause shareholders who do not receive favored treatment to suffer a loss of wealth.

THE AGENCY PROBLEM IN THE BID RESPONSE The managers' role in determining the firm's response to an unsolicited takeover bid reflects a potentially serious agency problem. Many firms have established golden parachutes in order to reduce this agency problem. A *golden parachute* provides generous payments to managers who lose their jobs as a result of a takeover. In some cases these payments have been substantial. For example, the RJR Nabisco leveraged buyout discussed in the next section resulted in payments to employees totaling $166 million. Golden parachutes are designed to align the objectives of shareholders and managers. However, because of the Principle of Self-Interested Behavior, if they are too generous, they could give management an incentive to sell the firm on terms that may not be the best ones for shareholders.

Review

1. What is a tender offer? How are tender offers used in battles for corporate control?
2. What are the main advantages of a tender offer as compared to alternative acquisition methods?
3. What is a proxy contest, and how does one work?
4. What are some of the defensive tactics that firms use in their efforts to ward off unwanted suitors?
5. What is a golden parachute? What agency problem is it designed to avoid? How might it create an agency problem of its own?

TABLE 25.10
Frequently used takeover defensive tactics.

DEFENSIVE TACTIC	DESCRIPTION
Anticipatory Tactics	
Dual class recapitalization	Firm distributes a second class of common stock that possesses superior voting rights (for example, 10 votes per share). New shares cannot be sold. Shareholders who wish to sell must exchange new shares for regular shares with only 1 vote per share. Over time, management's voting power increases as other shareholders sell their shares.
Employee stock ownership plan (ESOP)	Firm sells a large block of common stock (or voting preferred stock) to a company-sponsored ESOP and repurchases an equivalent number of common shares in the open market. Firm votes the ESOP's shares until they are distributed to employees, which typically takes place over several years.
Poison pill	Firm issues rights to its shareholders (typically, one nondetachable right per common share) that entitle the shareholders to purchase at one-half the market price (1) shares of the firm's common stock if a potential acquiror buys more than a specified percentage of the firm's shares (flip-in poison pill) or (2) shares of the acquiror's common stock following an acquisition of the firm (flip-over poison pill). The acquiree's board of directors can redeem the rights for a nominal sum (typically, $0.05 per right) if it approves of the acquisition.
Staggered election of directors	Firm's board of directors is divided into three equal classes. Only one class stands for reelection each year. A hostile raider cannot obtain control through a single proxy context.
Supermajority voting/ fair-price provision	Firm's charter is amended to require a supermajority (for example, 80%) of the firm's common shares to be voted in favor of a merger that has not been approved by the firm's board of directors. (If it is board-approved, a simple majority usually applies.) A fair-price provision allows the board of directors to waive the supermajority voting provision if the acquiror agrees to pay all shareholders the same price. The fair-price provision is designed to prevent a two-tier bid, in which shareholders who sell their shares in the initial tender often receive one price and the remaining shareholders who are "merged out" in the second stage receive a lower price.
Responsive Tactics	
Asset purchases or sales	Firm purchases assets that the bidder does not want or that would block the bidder by creating an antitrust problem. Firm sells the "crown jewel" assets that the bidder wants.
Leveraged recapitalization	Firm borrows a large sum of money and distributes the loan proceeds along with any other excess cash to its shareholders as a dividend. A recapitalization is designed to make it more difficult for a takeover raider to make the acquisition with borrowed funds.
Litigation	Firm files suit against the bidder alleging violation of state takeover statute(s), antitrust laws, securities laws, or other laws or regulations.
Pac-Man defense (or counter tender offer)	Firm makes a counterbid for the common stock of the potential acquiror.
Share repurchases or sales	Firm uses excess cash or borrows cash with which to finance a large share repurchase program. Alternatively, the firm might instead repurchase shares only from the takeover raider, any premium over fair market value representing "greenmail." As a third alternative, the firm can sell shares to a "friendly" third party.
Standstill agreement	Prospective acquiror agrees during the term of the agreement (1) not to increase its shareholdings above a specified percentage and, in many cases, (2) to vote its shares with management.

25.8 LEVERAGED BUYOUTS

A **leveraged buyout (LBO)** is an acquisition that is financed principally, sometimes more than 90%, by borrowing on a secured basis. Lenders look to the collateral value of the firm's assets as security for their loans. They look to the operating cash flow from these assets to service this debt. LBOs are often used to take a firm private.[14]

The RJR Nabisco Leveraged Buyout

When Kohlberg Kravis Roberts & Co. (KKR) acquired RJR Nabisco, it was a landmark transaction because it was the largest merger transaction ever accomplished.

When RJR Nabisco announced that a management group was contemplating paying about $75 per share in cash to acquire the firm, it meant an aggregate value of $17.6 billion. Four days later, KKR announced that it was offering to acquire the firm for $90 per share in cash and securities (plus $108 for each outstanding share of preferred stock). Several rounds of bidding ensued. KKR finally prevailed when it raised its bid to $109 per share ($81 of it in cash). The leveraged buyout cost $26 billion (including over $1 billion of transaction costs). KKR's common equity investment was a mere $1.5 billion, just 5.8% of the cost of the acquisition.

The transaction was so large that it caused a small blip in the U.S. money supply. Senior bank debt provided 49% of the funds. Subordinated lenders provided 19% of the funds. The new common stockholders provided 8% of the funds, $500 million in pay-in-kind extendible debt securities and $1.5 billion in common stock. The pay-in-kind securities permitted RJR Nabisco to pay interest on them in the form of additional notes rather than cash. The securities issued in a second merger step provided the remaining 24% of the funds.

Agency Problems and the RJR Nabisco LBO

The RJR Nabisco LBO illustrates two significant agency problems. First, the management-led group announced that it was contemplating bidding $75 per share—far below the $109 acquisition price. The relatively low initial bid undoubtedly reflects the Principle of Two-Sided Transactions: The better the deal for the managers, the worse the deal would be for the shareholders. If shareholders had sold their shares to the management-led group, that group would have reaped a windfall of $34 per share, or more than $7.5 billion in the aggregate. Fortunately, the board of directors immediately formed a special outside committee and took steps to enable the firm's shareholders to realize "full value" for their shares.

Second, the LBO caused RJR Nabisco's bonds to fall in price by approximately 20% to 30%. The fall in bond value reflected a transfer of wealth to the shareholders from the bondholders. This illustrates the problem of claim dilution with respect to capital structure, which we noted earlier. The huge amount of additional borrowing reduced the credit standing of the bonds because RJR Nabisco's assets and operating cash flow did not change. Soon after the LBO announcement, Moody's Investors Service downgraded the bonds from A-1 to Ba-2. Worse, the transaction sent shock waves through the corporate bond market as bond investors became concerned that other corporate bonds might be subject to similar *event risk.* Investors began to demand new protective bond covenants, called *super poison puts,* that would force issuers to redeem bonds at par in the event that a change in control occurred. Event risk is, of course, another form of agency cost. The demand for super poison puts represents the bondholders' attempt to reduce this cost.

---

[14]The advantages of being public or private are discussed in Chapter 18.

What Makes an Attractive LBO Candidate?

The ideal LBO candidate has relatively low operating risk. This permits the firm to take on an unusually high degree of financial risk. In addition, an issue of subordinated debt provides comfort to senior lenders, much like true equity. The actual financing structure for a leveraged buyout will depend crucially on the perceived riskiness of the firm's business, its cash flow characteristics, and the quality of its assets. These factors determine how much debt the firm's operations can support. Investment bankers (or leveraged buyout firms) try to determine the maximum amount of debt the firm's operations can support. The comparative approach, together with the DCF approach, will suggest a reasonable purchase price. This price, together with the firm's borrowing capacity, will indicate the maximum degree of leverage for the buyout.

Review

1. What is a leveraged buyout? What distinguishes it from other acquisitions?
2. Describe two agency problems that can arise in a leveraged buyout.
3. What is event risk? How do bond investors deal with it?

SUMMARY

- A merger represents a special form of capital budgeting decision. One firm acquires the entire portfolio of assets, and usually the liabilities as well, of another firm.
- A merger has special legal and tax consequences. It is larger, more complex, and thus more difficult to analyze than a single project.
- Firms have a variety of motives for merging, but a merger can benefit both the acquiror's shareholders and the acquiree's shareholders only if (1) the two firms are worth more together than they are apart and (2) the increase in value is large enough to offset the transaction costs involved. Merging benefits the acquiror's shareholders only if they can realize some of the net gain.
- Valid motives for merging include operating efficiencies and economies of scale, tax benefits, surplus cash, and more rapid growth or cheap assets.
- Questionable motives for merging include diversification, reducing the cost of debt financing, and increasing earnings per share.
- A proposed merger must comply with federal antitrust and securities laws and with each firm's charter. An acquiror can merge or consolidate with the acquiree, purchase the acquiree's stock, or purchase only (some portion of) the acquiree's assets.
- The acquiror must evaluate its tax position, the target's tax position, and the tax position of the target's shareholders and decide whether it prefers a tax-free transaction or a taxable transaction.
- Generally, the acquiror is also concerned about the accounting impact of an acquisition, even though the available evidence indicates that the choice of accounting method does not affect valuation. Acquirors often place a constraint on how much dilution in earnings per share they are willing to accept.
- The acquiror can use comparative analysis to determine a range of merger premiums—and a reasonable price range.

- The acquiror can use discounted-cash-flow (DCF) analysis to evaluate the net present value of the acquisition. DCF analysis can (and should!) also be used to determine the maximum price the acquiror can afford to pay (which is likely to depend on the legal form and tax status of the acquisition).
- The acquiror must decide how it wishes to pay for the acquisition: cash, common stock, other securities, or some combination. Its choice is restricted by the legal form of the transaction and the tax status it chooses. Common stock has a potential advantage in that the target's shareholders bear part of the risk that the acquiror has overpaid.
- Considering all its prior decisions and the probable response(s) of the target, the acquiror must decide how to proceed with the transaction, such as with a cash tender offer or a friendly proposal to merge. The defensive barriers the target has already erected affect this decision. Prior to proceeding with the transaction, the acquiror must comply with all applicable legal and regulatory requirements.
- A leveraged buyout (LBO) is an acquisition that is financed principally by borrowing on a secured basis.
- As the transaction proceeds—or as the battle for control unfolds—the acquiror may have to alter some of its earlier decisions if it finds that its objectives conflict with those of the target. But throughout this process, the acquiror must not lose sight of the fact that its ultimate objective is to maximize the wealth of its stockholders.

EQUATION SUMMARY

$$\text{NAM} = [V_{AB} - (V_A + V_B)] - P_B - \text{Expenses} \tag{25.1}$$

$$\text{Premium paid} = \frac{\text{Purchase price per share} - \text{Target's premerger share price}}{\text{Target's premerger share price}} \tag{25.2}$$

$$\text{Multiple of earnings paid} = \frac{\text{Purchase price per share}}{\text{Target's fully diluted earnings per share before extraordinary items}} \tag{25.3}$$

$$\text{Multiple of cash flow paid} = \frac{\text{Purchase price per share}}{\text{Target's fully diluted cash flow per share before extraordinary items}} \tag{25.4}$$

$$\text{Multiple of EBIT paid} = \frac{\text{Aggregate purchase price of equity} + \text{Market value of debt assumed}}{\text{Target's earnings before interest and taxes (EBIT) before extraordinary items}} \tag{25.5}$$

$$\text{Multiple of EBITDA paid} = \frac{\text{Aggregate purchase price of equity} + \text{Market value of debt assumed}}{\text{Target's earnings before interest, taxes, depreciation and amortization (EBITDA) before extraordinary items}} \tag{25.6}$$

$$\text{Multiple of book value paid} = \frac{\text{Purchase price per share}}{\text{Target's book value per common share}} \tag{25.7}$$

$$\text{Multiple of replacement cost paid} = \frac{\text{Aggregate purchase price of equity} + \text{Market value of debt assumed}}{\text{Replacement cost of target's assets}} \tag{25.8}$$

$$\text{Price paid per unit of resource} = \frac{\text{Aggregate purchase price of equity} + \text{Market value of debt assumed}}{\text{Number of units of resource target owns}} \tag{25.9}$$

$$\text{LV} = \text{A} - \text{L} - \text{T} - \text{E} \tag{25.10}$$

Cost of purchasing target's equity
+Transaction costs
−Target's excess assets
Net investment in target's equity (25.11)
+Cost of assuming target's debt
Net acquisition cost (NAC)

$$\text{Added debt} = (L)\text{NAC} - \text{PV(debt assumed)} \tag{25.12}$$

$$\text{TV(NA)} = \text{TV(equity)} + \text{TV(debt)} - \text{Taxes} - \text{Expenses} \tag{25.13}$$

$$\text{NPV(acquisition)} = -\text{NAC} + \sum_{t=1}^{N} \frac{\text{CFAT}_t}{(1 + \text{WACC})^t} \tag{25.14}$$

QUESTIONS

1. Define the following terms: (a) merger, (b) consolidation, (c) horizontal merger, (d) vertical merger, and (e) conglomerate merger.
2. Explain the valid motives that two firms may have for merging.
3. The Diversification Principle states that diversification is beneficial. Diversification is one of the main justifications managers give when undertaking conglomerate mergers. Explain why the justification is usually invalid notwithstanding the Diversification Principle.
4. How can a merger create financial synergy? How can it create business synergy? What is the difference between these two types of synergy?
5. How is the net advantage to merging usually divided between shareholders of acquirors and shareholders of acquirees?
6. Describe the three basic ways of structuring a corporate acquisition and explain the distinguishing features of each.
7. Describe the main differences between a tax-free acquisition and a taxable acquisition. Which of these does a seller generally prefer and which does a buyer generally prefer?
8. Define the term *tender offer,* and explain how a firm can acquire another firm through a tender offer. What are the main advantages of a tender offer relative to other acquisition methods?
9. Define the term *proxy contest,* and explain how an investor group can gain control of a firm through a proxy contest. What are the main disadvantages of a proxy contest relative to a cash tender offer?
10. Describe the main defensive tactics that firms have used in an effort to fight off unwanted suitors. How would you expect the use of such tactics to affect shareholder wealth? Describe the agency problem that arises in connection with defensive tactics to thwart unwanted bids.
11. What distinguishes a leveraged buyout from other types of acquisitions?

CHALLENGING QUESTIONS

12. Why is a flexible exchange ratio less risky for the shareholder of the selling firm (acquiree)?
13. Explain how acquiring a firm with past losses can be beneficial.
14. Explain how a merger can expropriate wealth from the shareholders to the bondholders.
15. Would it ever be in the selling shareholders' best interest to structure a taxable acquisition? Explain.
16. What are the advantages and disadvantages of the comparative approach over the liquidation approach when computing a premium for an acquisition?
17. Why is an accurate estimate of terminal value so important when using DCF analysis? What could potentially happen if the terminal value was overestimated? Underestimated?
18. An increase in EPS is a questionable motive for merging. What do you think about a merger that dilutes EPS?
19. Explain how the agency cost associated with managers blocking takeovers is resolved. Can this resolution lead to other agency costs?
20. In an LBO, a large amount of debt is used to finance the transaction. The debt usually has a fixed repayment schedule. Explain why the APV approach from Chapter 16 is a good technique to use when valuing an LBO.
21. At the time the Delaware Chancery Court ruled in favor of Time Inc. and let it proceed with its purchase of Warner Communications, Time's shares were trading at around $144 per share. Paramount Communications had bid $200 per share for Time's common stock. Time's board of directors refused to let the shareholders vote on the proposed Paramount Communications transaction and argued that their long-term strategy had greater value for the Time shareholders. After the court decision, Paramount withdrew its bid.
    a. What do Time's actions reveal about the existence of agency costs?
    b. How could you reconcile the board's argument that its long-term strategy has a present value in excess of $200 per share with the fact that the stock was trading at just $144 per share?

PROBLEMS

LEVEL A (BASIC)

A1. (Merger premium) Carbondale Scientific was worth $40 per share. What is the merger premium offered in the following two cases.
   a. Edwardsville Biotechnics offers $55 cash per share.
   b. Edwardsville Biotechnics offers 1.40 Edwardsville shares per Carbondale share. Edwardsville shares are worth $48 each following the takeover announcement.

A2. (Merger premium) Yukon Inc. was worth $80 per share. What is the merger premium offered in the following two cases.
   a. Alaska Inc. offers $87 cash per share.
   b. Alaska Inc. offers 1.50 Alaska Inc. shares per Yukon Inc. share. Alaska Inc. shares are worth $85 each following the takeover announcement.

A3. (Merger premium) Firm A has 4 million outstanding shares and a market price of $30 per share. Firm B has 1 million shares outstanding and a market price of $45 per share.
   a. Firm A offers 2.0 shares of its stock per share of firm B. If the price of firm A stays at $30 per share, what is the merger premium offered?
   b. Firm A offers 2.0 shares of its stock per share of firm B. If the price of firm A drops by $2 per share, what is the merger premium offered?

A4. (Merger premium) Firm A has 10 million outstanding shares and a market price of $52 per share. Firm B has 2.5 million shares outstanding and a market price of $68 per share.

a. Firm A offers 2.0 shares of its stock per share of firm B. If the price of firm A stays at $52 per share, what is the merger premium offered?

b. Firm A offers 2.0 shares of its stock per share of firm B. If the price of firm A drops by $5 per share, what is the merger premium offered?

A5. (Net advantage to merging) LSU Co. is acquiring TT Co. Prior to the merger, LSU's equity had a total value of $340 million and that of TT was worth $120 million. After the merger, LSU is expected to have a market value of $500 million. LSU is giving TT shareholders a $40 million premium for their shares. In addition, LSU incurred $6 million of acquisition costs.

a. What is the net advantage to merging for LSU?

b. What is the total synergistic effect in this merger? By how much did the synergy exceed the premium and other acquisition costs?

A6. (Net advantage to merging) Lucite Co. is acquiring Mt. Gear Co. Prior to the merger, Lucite's equity had a total value of $600 million and that of Mt. Gear was worth $220 million. After the merger, Lucite is expected to have a market value of $900 million. Lucite is giving Mt. Gear shareholders a $100 million premium for their shares. In addition, Lucite incurred $3 million of acquisition costs.

a. What is the net advantage to merging for Lucite?

b. What is the total synergistic effect in this merger? By how much did the synergy exceed the premium and other acquisition costs?

A7. (Net advantage to merging) Ace Homebuilding and Brace Homebuilding will merge. Ace has a total market value of $50 million, and Brace has a total market value of $75 million. Their merger will lead to operating efficiencies and will produce present value savings of $10 million.

a. What is the total market value of the merged firms?

b. If the merger would entail expenses amounting to $5 million, is there a net advantage to merging?

c. If Ace buys Brace's outstanding shares, paying Brace's common stockholders a $3 million premium, will the acquisition be advantageous to Ace's shareholders? How is the net advantage to merging divided between the two firms' shareholders?

A8. (Net advantage to merging) Case Janitorial Services and Byman Janitorial Services will merge. Case has a total market value of $100 million, and Byman has a total market value of $145 million. Their merger will lead to operating efficiencies and will produce present value savings of $25 million.

a. What is the total market value of the merged firms?

b. If the merger would entail expenses amounting to $12 million, is there a net advantage to merging?

c. If Case buys Byman's outstanding shares, paying Byman's common stockholders a $7 million premium, will the acquisition be advantageous to Case's shareholders? How is the net advantage to merging divided between the two firms' shareholders?

A9. (Net advantage to merging) Agrawal Services is acquiring Mandelker Manufacturing. Prior to the merger, Agrawal's equity had a total value of $170 million and that of Mandelker was worth $60 million. After the merger, Agrawal is expected to have a market value of $260 million. Agrawal gave Mandelker shareholders a $20 million premium for their shares. In addition, Agrawal incurred $3 million of acquisition costs.

a. What is the net advantage to merging for Agrawal?

b. What is the total synergistic effect in this merger? By how much did the synergy exceed the premium and other acquisition costs?

A10. (Earnings per share) Youhaul has 4,000,000 shares outstanding that are trading at $25 each. Z-Rocks has 2,000,000 shares outstanding that are trading at $20 each. Youhaul earns $2.00 per share, and Z-Rocks earns $2.50 per share. If the firms merge, their total combined earnings will be the same as before the merger.

a. Calculate each firm's price-earnings ratio.

b. Suppose Youhaul acquires Z-Rocks in a stock-for-stock swap based on current market values. What is the exchange ratio? What happens to Youhaul's earnings per share?

c. Suppose that Youhaul's managers (stupidly) believe that Youhaul is profiting as long as its earnings per share do not decline as a result of the merger. What is the maximum number of shares offered to Z-Rocks stockholders that they can issue and achieve this? What is the exchange ratio?

A11. (Earnings per share) Two firms plan to merge. Prior to the merger, the acquiror has earnings per share of $10 and a price-earnings ratio of 20. The acquiree has earnings per share of $4 and a price-earnings ratio of 10. The acquiror has 10 million shares of stock, and the acquiree has 5 million shares.

a. How many shares must the acquiror exchange for each of the acquiree's shares if the shares are exchanged at their respective market values (i.e., no premium).

b. Calculate the acquiror's earnings per share after the merger.

c. Calculate the acquiror's price-earnings ratio after the merger.

d. What conclusion can be drawn from parts b and c?

A12. (Earnings per share) Loop Company has 2,500 shares outstanding that are trading at $65 each. PRT has 500 shares outstanding that are trading at $55 each. Loop earns $5.00 per share, and PRT earns $3.00 per share. If the firms merge, their total combined earnings will be the same as before the merger.

a. Calculate each firm's price-earnings ratio.

b. Suppose Loop acquires PRT in a stock-for-stock swap based on current market values. What is the exchange ratio? What happens to PRT's earnings per share?

c. What is the maximum number of shares that can be offered to PRT stockholders that would not cause Loop's earnings per share to drop?

A13. (Comparative analysis) Fleming Corporation is planning to acquire Southwest Purveyors, a wholesale food distributor. Fleming's financial staff has gathered the data shown below regarding acquisitions involving firms in the food service industry. Price is the price paid in the acquisition. Southwest's latest 12 months' earnings are $35 million, its latest 12 months' cash flow is $48 million, and its current aggregate book value is $175 million. Calculate a reasonable range of acquisition values for Southwest.

ACQUIREE	BUSINESS	PRICE/ EARNINGS	PRICE/ CASH FLOW	PRICE/ BOOK VALUE
Ferri Foods	wholesale	8x	5.0x	1.5x
Chowderhead	fast food	12	6.2	2.2
Conrad's	wholesale	8	4.5	1.6
Puri Curry	fast food	11	7.0	2.1
Burtin's Bar	fast food	10	7.5	2.4
Foodmasters	wholesale	7	4.8	1.3

A14. (Earnings per share) Two firms plan to merge. Prior to the merger, the acquiror has earnings per share of $5 and a price-earnings ratio of 20. The acquiree has earnings per share of

$2 and a price-earnings ratio of 10. The acquiror has 10 million shares of stock, and the acquiree has 5 million shares.

a. How many shares must the acquiror exchange for each of the acquiree's shares if the shares are exchanged at their respective market values (i.e., no premium).

b. Calculate the acquiror's earnings per share after the merger.

c. Calculate the acquiror's price-earnings ratio after the merger.

d. What conclusion can be drawn from parts b and c?

A15. (Earnings per share) Lux Company has 1,000 shares outstanding that are trading at $50 each. MCD has 200 shares outstanding that are trading at $40 each. Lux earns $4 per share, and MCD earns $2 per share. If the firms merge, their total combined earnings will be the same as before the merger.

a. Calculate each firm's price-earnings ratio.

b. Suppose Lux acquires MCD in a stock-for-stock swap based on current market values. What is the exchange ratio? What happens to MCD's earnings per share?

c. What is the maximum number of shares that can be offered to MCD stockholders that would not cause Lux's earnings per share to drop?

LEVEL B

B1. (NPV of an acquisition) Firm A intends to acquire firm B. The acquisition will cost firm A $100 million. Firm A plans to install new management, "fix" the firm, and sell it at the end of five years. The projected incremental free cash flow stream firm A expects to realize from the acquisition, which reflects the anticipated operating improvements, is given below. In addition, the projected after-tax sales proceeds amount to $200 million.

a. Calculate the NPV of the acquisition assuming a 20% cost of capital.

b. Calculate the internal rate of return for the acquisition.

c. Calculate the payback period for the acquisition.

d. Should firm A proceed with the acquisition?

YEAR	1	2	3	4	5
Cash flow ($ millions)	10	20	30	40	50

B2. (NPV of an acquisition) Firm A intends to acquire firm B. The acquisition will cost firm A $200 million. Firm A plans to install new management, "fix" the firm, and sell it at the end of six years. The projected incremental free cash flow stream firm A expects to realize from the acquisition, which reflects the anticipated operating improvements, is given below. In addition, the projected after-tax sales proceeds amount to $410 million.

a. Calculate the NPV of the acquisition assuming a 15% cost of capital.

b. Calculate the internal rate of return for the acquisition.

c. Calculate the payback period for the acquisition.

d. Should firm A proceed with the acquisition?

YEAR	1	2	3	4	5	6
Cash flow ($ millions)	40	40	40	40	40	40

B3. (Effect of a merger on bondholders) Two firms in unrelated businesses plan to merge. There are three possible states of the economy. The table below shows the returns to the shareholders of each firm and the debtholders of firm B in each state of the economy. Firm B has $50 million principal amount of debt, and firm A has no debt.

a. What is each firm worth?

b. A merger would not produce any operating efficiencies or economies of scale. What is the merged firm worth? What is the debt of the merged firm worth? What is the equity of the merged firm worth?

c. Should the firms merge?

	BOOM	STABLE GROWTH	RECESSION
Probability	0.3	0.5	0.2
Firm A Equity	$200 million	$100 million	$25 million
Firm B			
Debt	$50 million	$50 million	$25 million
Equity	$100 million	$50 million	—

B4. (Effect of a merger on bondholders) Suppose the two firms in Problem B3 are in the same industry and a merger will produce $30 million of synergistic benefits (in all three states of the economy) but requires $2 million of expenses.

a. How will a merger affect the bondholders?

b. How will a merger affect the shareholders of each firm?

c. Should the firms merge?

B5. (Purchase accounting) The purchase price in an acquisition is $275 million. Consultants estimate that the fair market value of the assets acquired is $180 million. Investment bankers estimate that the fair market value of the liabilities assumed in the acquisition is $30 million. Calculate the amount of goodwill.

B6. (Purchase accounting) The purchase price in an acquisition is $100 million. Consultants estimate that the fair market value of the assets acquired is $90 million. Investment bankers estimate that the fair market value of the liabilities assumed in the acquisition is $20 million. Calculate the amount of goodwill.

B7. (Comparative analysis) Louisiana Fried Chicken (LFC) is hoping to acquire Arkansas Fried Chicken (AFC). LFC has gathered the following information regarding recent acquisitions of comparable restaurant chains (dollar amounts in millions):

ACQUISITION	MARKET VALUE OF DEBT	PRICE PAID FOR EQUITY	EARNINGS	EBIT	EBITDA
1	$225	$450	$30	$ 80	$110
2	150	600	50	100	125
3	175	350	25	85	85
4	25	375	35	50	65
5	110	330	30	55	70
6	50	450	45	60	85

a. Calculate the multiples of earnings, EBIT, and EBITDA paid for each firm.

b. AFC has no debt. Which of the three multiples in part a is most useful for gauging a reasonable price to pay for AFC?

c. AFC's earnings are $50 million, its EBIT is $75 million, and its EBITDA is $100 million. What is a reasonable range of acquisition values? Why do the three ratios appear to give inconsistent value ranges?

B8. (Takeover premium paid) National Permanent Credit Corporation just acquired Specific Capital Corporation. National paid $50 per Specific share. Specific's closing share price 30 days prior to the merger announcement was $35. Calculate the premium paid.

B9. (Takeover premium paid) Unity Corporation just acquired Boxer Corporation. Unity paid $85 per Boxer share. Boxer's closing share price 30 days prior to the merger announcement was $78. Calculate the premium paid.

B10. (Valuing a takeover target) International Oil Company has oil and gas reserves consisting of 25 million barrels of oil and 60 billion cubic feet of natural gas. Judging by the prices at which oil and gas reserves have recently sold, one barrel of oil is equivalent to 6,000 cubic feet of natural gas.

a. Calculate the number of barrels of oil equivalent in International's reserves.

b. Regal Oil Corporation is contemplating a bid for International based on the value of International's assets. Petroleum reserves have recently sold for $8.50 per barrel of oil equivalent, and Regal estimates that International's other assets are worth $52.5 million. Calculate the estimated value of International's assets.

B11. (Valuing a takeover target) Shipper Oil Company has oil and gas reserves consisting of 15 million barrels of oil and 45 billion cubic feet of natural gas. Judging by the prices at which oil and gas reserves have recently sold, one barrel of oil is equivalent to 4,500 cubic feet of natural gas.

a. Calculate the number of barrels of oil equivalent in Shipper's reserves.

b. Standard Oil Corporation is contemplating a bid for Shipper based on the value of Shipper's assets. Petroleum reserves have recently sold for $9.50 per barrel of oil equivalent, and Standard estimates that Shipper's other assets are worth $62.5 million. Calculate the estimated value of Shipper's assets.

B12. (NPV of an acquisition) Razorback Computer Corporation is preparing to make a bid for the common shares of Windy City Software. Razorback would acquire the shares for cash but not write up Windy City's assets. Windy City has 5 million shares outstanding, which are trading at a price of $30 per share and a price-earnings multiple of 10. Windy City has $50 million principal amount of 8% debt, which pays interest annually in arrears and matures in a lump sum at the end of six years. Razorback's marginal income tax rate is 40%. Razorback estimates that it will have to pay a 50% premium to acquire Windy City and also pay $3 million of after-tax transaction costs. Windy City has no excess cash. Razorback's target debt-to-value ratio is 25%, its pretax cost of new debt is 12%, its cost of capital for the acquisition is 16.5%, and the incremental free cash flow stream for the next six years is given below.

a. Calculate the NPV of the acquisition on a nondisposition basis, assuming the estimated year-6 earnings before interest and taxes (EBIT) is $125 million and using the acquisition multiple based on a purchase price of $45 per share to calculate the terminal value.

b. Calculate the NPV of the acquisition on a disposition basis, using the same assumptions as in part a and assuming no transaction costs for the sale.

c. Should Razorback make the acquisition if it has to pay $45 per share?

d. What is the maximum price Razorback can afford to pay on a disposition basis with a six-year investment horizon?

YEAR	1	2	3	4	5	6
Cash flow ($ millions)	25	30	35	40	45	50

B13. (NPV of an acquisition) Razorback Computer Corporation in Problem B12 has determined that the net-benefit-to-leverage factor $T^* = 0.25$, and the *unleveraged* beta for

Windy City Software's equity is 1.5. The riskless return is 6%, and the risk premium on the market portfolio is 8%.

a. Calculate the cost of capital for Razorback's acquisition using Equation (16.9).

b. Calculate the NPV of the acquisition on a nondisposition basis, assuming the debt issued to finance the acquisition matures in a lump sum at the end of six years.

c. Calculate the NPV of the acquisition on a disposition basis, assuming the debt issued to finance the acquisition matures in a lump sum at the end of six years.

B14. (Earnings per share) Firm A has 1,000,000 shares outstanding that are trading at $25 each. Firm B has 2,000,000 shares outstanding that are trading at $50 each. Firm A earns $2.50 per share, and firm B earns $4.00 per share.

a. Calculate each firm's price-earnings ratio.

b. Suppose firm B acquires firm A in a stock-for-stock swap based on current market values. What happens to firm B's earnings per share? Does that mean that firm B's shareholders are better off as a result of the merger? Explain.

B15. (Earnings per share) Firm A has 1,500,000 shares outstanding that are trading at $35 each. Firm B has 2,500,000 shares outstanding that are trading at $70 each. Firm A earns $3.50 per share, and firm B earns $5.00 per share.

a. Calculate each firm's price-earnings ratio.

b. Suppose firm B acquires firm A in a stock-for-stock swap based on current market values. What happens to firm B's earnings per share? Does that mean that firm B's shareholders are better off as a result of the merger? Explain.

B16. (Effect of a merger on bondholders) With regard to Empire State's acquisition of Garden State in Section 25.5, suppose Garden State's new issue rate is 13%.

a. What is the market value of the $100 million of outstanding bonds?

b. Would the acquisition help or hurt Garden State's bondholders?

c. What is the cause of this transfer of wealth?

B17. (Effect of a merger on bondholders) With regard to Empire State's acquisition of Garden State in Section 25.5, suppose Garden State's new issue rate is 14%.

a. What is the market value of the $100 million of outstanding bonds?

b. Would the acquisition help or hurt Garden State's bondholders?

c. What is the cause of this transfer of wealth?

B18. (Acquisition value) American Car Rental has agreed to acquire Big Apple Car Rental. American's financial staff has gathered the following data regarding acquisitions involving firms in the automobile industry:

ACQUIREE	BUSINESS	PRICE/ EARNINGS	PRICE/ CASH FLOW	(DEBT & EQUITY)/ EBITDA	PRICE/ BOOK VALUE
Central	rental	10x	5.8x	8.2x	1.5x
Eastern	manufacturing	7	4.3	6.5	1.2
Western	manufacturing	6	4.0	6.3	1.1
South Central	rental	11	6.7	8.9	1.6
Southwestern	rental	12	7.8	7.9	1.4
Panhandle	manufacturing	8	4.9	6.9	1.3

Price is the price paid in the acquisition. Big Apple's latest 12 months' earnings are $25 million, latest 12 months' cash flow is $40 million, latest 12 months' EBITDA is $30 million, and current aggregate book value is $175 million. Calculate a reasonable range of acquisition values for Big Apple.

B19. (NPV of an acquisition) Big Sky Airlines would like to acquire Far West Commuter Air and integrate Far West's route structure into its system. Big Sky would acquire Far West's shares for cash but not write up Far West's assets. Far West has 2 million shares outstanding. Its share price was $24 prior to rumors of the merger. Its EPS is $4, and it has no debt and no excess cash. Big Sky's debt-to-value ratio is 42%. Its pretax cost of debt is 14% (annual interest), its cost of equity is 21%, and its marginal income tax rate is 40%. The net-benefit-to-leverage factor $T^* = 0.25$, and the *unleveraged* cost of equity capital in the airlines industry is 14.07%. If Big Sky acquires Far West, it expects a year-8 earnings before interest and taxes (EBIT) of $75 million and the incremental free cash flows as given below.

a. Calculate the NPV of the acquisition on a nondisposition basis, assuming Big Sky pays a 1/3 premium for Far West's shares, $500,000 of after-tax acquisition expenses, and using the acquisition multiple to calculate the terminal value.

b. Calculate the NPV of the acquisition on a disposition basis under the same assumptions as in part a and assuming an eight-year investment horizon.

c. Should Big Sky make the acquisition if it has to pay a 1/3 premium for Far West's shares?

YEAR	1	2	3	4	5	6	7	8
Cash flow ($ millions)	6	10	12	14	18	22	25	30

B20. (Calculating exchange ratios) Ajax Air Products and Central Combustion have agreed to an exchange of common stock under which Ajax would acquire Central. Ajax's common stock is trading at $40 per share, and Central's common stock is trading at $20 per share. Each firm has 10 million shares outstanding.

a. Calculate the exchange ratio assuming Ajax does not pay a premium.

b. Calculate the exchange ratio assuming Ajax pays a 25% premium to acquire Central.

c. If the exchange ratio determined in part b is fixed and the announcement of the merger causes Ajax's share price to fall 10%, by how much would you expect Central's share price to change?

B21. (Calculating exchange ratios) Bell Corporation and National Corporation have agreed to an exchange of common stock under which Bell would acquire National. Bell's common stock is trading at $80 per share, and National's common stock is trading at $40 per share. Each firm has 10 million shares outstanding.

a. Calculate the exchange ratio assuming Bell does not pay a premium.

b. Calculate the exchange ratio assuming Bell pays a 25% premium to acquire National.

c. If the exchange ratio determined in part b is fixed and the announcement of the merger causes Bell's share price to fall 10%, by how much would you expect National's share price to change?

B22. (Excel: APV of an acquisition) Excelsior Paper Products Company is considering acquiring the Spring Lake Greeting Card Company. Excelsior would have to pay $100 million (including after-tax transaction costs) for Spring Lake, 90% of which it would borrow at a 10% annual interest rate. The $100 million purchase price represents a multiple of 8 times this year's CFAT (EBIT$[1 - T]$). Excelsior's marginal income tax rate is 40%. Its debt-to-value ratio is 50%. Spring Lake's CFAT is expected to grow at the rate of 10% per year into the foreseeable future. All CFAT will be used first to pay interest, next to repay principal (until the acquisition loan is fully repaid), and then to pay dividends. The *unleveraged* cost of equity capital for similar acquisitions is 15%, and the net-benefit-to-leverage factor $T^* = 0.32$. Calculate the APV (adjusted present value, see Chapter 16) of the acquisition, assuming a six-year investment horizon and using the acquisition multiple to calculate the terminal value.

LEVEL C (ADVANCED)

C1. (Valuing combinations) Arnold Electronics and Beard Oil and Gas plan to combine through merger. Neither firm has any debt. The merger will involve a share-for-share exchange, and there will be no transaction costs. Arnold has total market value $V_A =$ \$100 million, and Beard has total market value $V_B =$ \$200 million. There are no synergistic effects that will result from the merger.

a. What is the maximum value the combined firms could have following the merger?

b. Suppose that if there were no merger, Arnold's shares and Beard's shares would be expected to provide annual returns of 20% and 25%, respectively. Further suppose that there exist two other firms, one of whose shares are a perfect substitute for Arnold's and the other of whose shares are a perfect substitute for Beard's. What must be the expected return on the shares of the merged firm in a perfect market environment?

c. Show that if the shares of the merged firm were trading at a price that would provide an expected annual return of 23%, market agents could earn a pure arbitrage profit. Explain how this could be accomplished, and quantify the profit.

d. Suppose instead that neither the Arnold shares nor the Beard shares has a close substitute. Show that the value of the combined firms following the merger must be less than \$300 million.

C2. (Effect of a merger on bondholders) Two firms are identical, including their capital structures. Each faces two possible states of nature, which are equally likely: F (favorable) or U (unfavorable). The returns to the stockholders of each firm and the returns to debtholders are identical in each state but the likelihood that state F will occur for firm A and the likelihood that it will occur for firm B are uncorrelated. For each firm, debtholders have a prior claim to the first \$140 of income. The returns in each state are:

RETURN TO	RETURN IN STATE F	RETURN IN STATE U	EXPECTED RETURN	STANDARD DEVIATION
Firm	200	100	150	50
Debtholders	140	100	120	20
Stockholders	60	0	30	30

a. Specify the set of possible outcomes for the merged firm, for the former debtholders of each firm, and for the former stockholders of each firm following a merger through an exchange of shares.

b. Show that each class of debtholders is better off as a result of the merger.

c. Show that each class of stockholders is worse off as a result of the merger.

d. What conclusions can be drawn from parts b and c?

C3. (Excel: APV of an acquisition) Reconsider Razorback's acquisition of Windy City in Problem B12. Assume Razorback borrowed \$200 million of the purchase price at 14% under terms that called for \$20 million principal payment at the end of each year.

a. Calculate the APV (adjusted present value, see Chapter 16) of the acquisition, assuming all of the other conditions given in the problem are the same.

b. Calculate the APV of the acquisition, assuming the terminal value is based on the preacquisition multiple with all the other assumptions the same.

C4. (Excel: NPV of an acquisition) Radnor Publishing would like to acquire Excelsior Publishing from The Miami Media Group. Radnor estimates that the net acquisition cost, before any depreciation recapture, would be $125 million. Radnor estimates that Excelsior's incremental free cash flow is currently $15 million and is growing at 15% per annum into the foreseeable future before allowing for any asset write-up. Radnor believes it could sell Excelsior at the end of 10 years at a multiple of 125/15 = 8.33 times incremental free cash flow. The Miami Media Group acquired Excelsior one year ago for $100 million, which represents its current tax basis in Excelsior's stock. Excelsior's tax basis in its assets is $25 million because Excelsior's assets consist primarily of goodwill. Radnor's marginal income tax rate is 40%, and its cost of capital for the acquisition is 16%.

a. Calculate Radnor's NPV of acquiring Excelsior's common stock for $125 million cash assuming that Radnor can write up Excelsior's assets to $50 million and pay only $10 million in depreciation recapture taxes.

b. Calculate Radnor's NPV of acquiring Excelsior's common stock for $125 million common stock. [*Hint:* the transaction is tax free.]

c. Would Miami Media prefer a taxable transaction or a tax-free transaction? Calculate the difference in taxes payable.

d. How would you recommend that Miami Media and Radnor structure the acquisition: taxable or tax free?

MINICASE IS THE LOCKHEED/MARTIN MARIETTA MERGER DEFENSIBLE?

Three of the examples in the chapter involve aspects of the Lockheed/Martin Marietta merger of several years ago, and provide background for this case. Recall that the merger of Lockheed and Martin Marietta was to involve the formation of a new corporation, Lockheed Martin Corporation (Lockheed Martin). Each of Lockheed's 66,179,422 outstanding common shares would be exchanged for 1.63 Lockheed Martin shares. Martin Marietta's 100,680,090 outstanding common shares would be exchanged for Lockheed Martin shares on a share-for-share basis. In addition, General Electric Company held 20 million shares of Martin Marietta convertible preferred stock, which could be converted into 28,941,466 shares of common stock. Under the merger terms, GE would exchange its preferred stock for 20 million shares of Lockheed Martin convertible preferred stock, which would be convertible into 28,941,466 shares of Lockheed Martin.

Lockheed Martin intended to pay cash dividends of $0.35 per share per quarter. Lockheed had paid $0.57 per share per quarter, and Martin Marietta had paid $0.24 per share per quarter. Lockheed's financial advisor noted that the ratios of Lockheed's average closing stock price to Martin Marietta's average closing stock price for various historical periods ending just prior to the announcement of the merger were

LAST 5 YEARS	LAST 3 YEARS	LAST 2 YEARS	LAST 12 MONTHS	LAST 6 MONTHS	LAST 3 MONTHS	LAST 30 DAYS	LATEST CLOSING PRICE
1.609	1.597	1.567	1.484	1.438	1.444	1.380	1.309

The table below provides summary income statements and balance sheets for Lockheed and Martin Marietta for the latest 12 months preceding the merger.

	LOCKHEED	MARTIN MARIETTA	ADJUSTMENTS
Net sales	$13,025	$10,276	$(116)[a]
Cost of sales	(12,144)	(9,329)	116[a]
Earnings from operations	881	947	
Other income and expenses, net	(6)	203	
Interest expense	(160)	(120)	
Pretax income	715	1,030	
Income taxes	(272)	(415)	
Net income	$ 443	$ 615	
Weighted average shares (millions)	63.5	125.9[b]	
Assets			
Current assets	$ 4,116	$ 3,325	
Long-term assets	4,909	5,668	
Total assets	$ 9,025	$ 8,993	
Liabilities and Stockholders' Equity			
Current liabilities	$ 2,723	$ 2,156	
Long-term debt	1,906	1,347	
Other long-term liabilities	1,707	2,220	
Preferred stock	—	1,000	
Common stockholders' equity	2,689	2,270	
Total liabilities and stockholders' equity	$ 9,025	$ 8,993	

[a]Intercompany sales.
[b]Fully diluted.
Source: Lockheed Corporation and Martin Marietta Corporation, *Joint Proxy Statement.*

QUESTIONS

1. Prepare a pro forma income statement and pro forma balance sheet for Lockheed Martin.
2. Calculate the impact on earnings per share for Lockheed shareholders and for Martin Marietta shareholders.
3. Calculate the percentages of Lockheed Martin that the former stockholders of Lockheed and Martin Marietta will each own assuming the Martin Marietta convertible preferred stock (i) is, and (ii) is not, converted.
4. Immediately prior to the announcement of the proposed terms of the merger (but several months after the two firms' intention to merge had been announced), Lockheed's closing share price was \$74.125, and Martin Marietta's closing share price was \$45.25
   a. What is the total equity value of Lockheed Martin before allowing for the effect of the operating cost savings? (*Hint:* Treat the convertible preferred stock as though it had been converted.)
   b. How would the operating cost savings affect the value of the firm? (Assume a 40% income tax rate.)
5. How would the merger affect Lockheed's and Martin Marietta's bondholders?
6. How would the merger affect the dividend income of Lockheed's and Martin Marietta's shareholders?
7. Are the proposed exchange ratios fair to (i) Lockheed's shareholders and (ii) Martin Marietta's shareholders?
8. Lockheed and Martin Marietta described their combining as a merger of equals. Do you think this is an accurate description of the transaction? Explain.

26

FINANCIAL DISTRESS

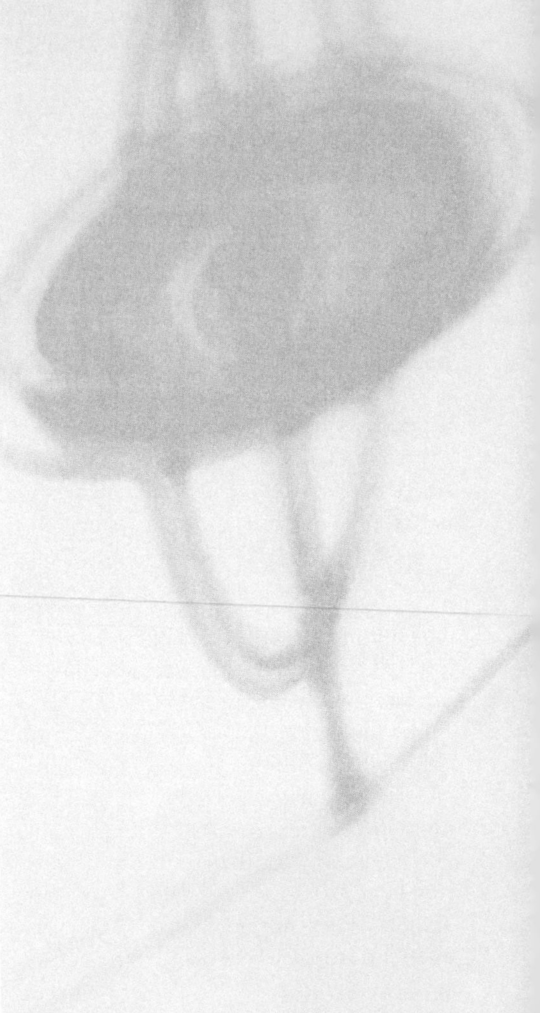

When a firm borrows money, it enters into a contract to pay interest and repay principal in a timely manner. When the firm does not generate enough cash to pay its debt, lenders take steps to make the borrower meet its obligations. If the firm finds it cannot correct the situation, it will try to renegotiate the terms of the loan. And if that proves impossible, the firm may have no choice but to file for bankruptcy. **Bankruptcy** is a legal process for liquidating, reorganizing the claims on, or transferring to its creditors, a firm's assets to settle its debt obligations under bankruptcy court supervision.

The term *bankruptcy* has its origin in medieval Italy. When a merchant did not pay his debts, lenders would destroy his trading bench. The word "bankruptcy" comes from the Italian term for broken bench, *banca rotta.*

Today, bankruptcy law offers two ways to resolve financial distress: (1) reorganization and (2) liquidation. **Reorganization** (under Chapter 11 of the bankruptcy code) creates a plan to restructure the debtor's business and restore its financial health. **Liquidation** (under Chapter 7 of the bankruptcy code) is a more extreme solution. Under liquidation, the debtor stops operating the business, its assets are sold, usually piecemeal, and the cash proceeds are paid to the firm's creditors according to strict rules of priority. We discuss both forms of bankruptcy, but emphasize reorganization because U.S. bankruptcy law favors it. However, the bankruptcy laws of most other countries favor liquidation.

FOCUS ON PRINCIPLES

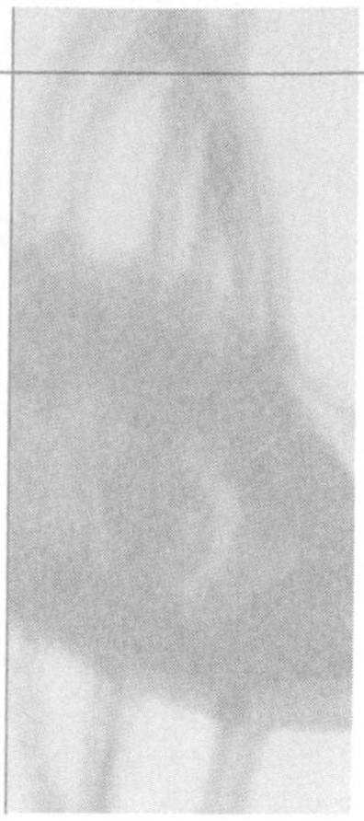

- *Self-Interested Behavior:* When involved in a reorganization, look for opportunities to increase the value of what you recover. The other parties will do the same!
- *Two-Sided Transactions:* Increasing your recovery comes at the expense of what some other party to the reorganization will recover.
- *Valuable Ideas:* Look for opportunities to redesign securities or other features of a plan of reorganization to enhance value.
- *Options:* Use the option to default only when it is beneficial to do so.
- *Risk-Return Trade-Off:* Obtaining debtholder consents to modify the terms of a bond indenture requires compensation for the added risk they face.
- *Capital Market Efficiency:* Value a security based on the price at which it would trade in an active market.
- *Time Value of Money:* Use discounted-cash-flow analysis to determine whether reorganization is preferable to liquidation, and to compare alternative plans of reorganization.

26.1 CORPORATE FINANCIAL DISTRESS AND ITS CONSEQUENCES

Recent experience has taught us an important lesson: Even very large firms can fail. Recent experience has also highlighted the risk in leveraged buyouts. In a leveraged buyout, investors acquire a firm largely using borrowed money. Leveraged buyouts, which became popular in the 1980s, offered equity investors the opportunity to earn exceptionally high returns. But under the Principle of Risk-Return Trade-Off, leveraged buyouts also had an exceptionally high risk of financial distress. This became evident in the 1990s, when many of these firms began to fail because of their crushing debt loads.

Corporate Financial Distress Since 1990

The number of business failures accelerated in 1990 to 1992 (Figure 26.1). Business failures rose by 21% in 1990, by 45% in 1991, and by 10% in 1992. The aggregate liabilities of firms entering bankruptcy increased by 33% in 1990 to \$56 billion and by 73% in 1991 to \$96.8 billion. Both the number and the aggregate liabilities of firms entering bankruptcy have fallen since 1992, although the number of firms entering remains high. As the number and size of bankruptcies grew, bankruptcy came to be regarded as a more acceptable strategy for dealing with financial distress. In 2001, a record 143 publicly traded firms filed for bankruptcy.

Not only has the number of bankruptcies increased sharply, but unprecedented numbers of very large firms have failed. Table 26.1 lists the 20 largest U.S. bankruptcies through the middle of 2002. The bankruptcies come in waves, with several large ones in 2001–2002. They also cluster in industries, where banks, telecommunications firms, and retailers share economic difficulties at the same times.

Four Aspects of Financial Distress

A firm is in **financial distress** when it is having significant trouble paying its debts as they come due. A variety of terms are used to describe a financially distressed firm. Four of the more widely used terms are *bankrupt, in default, failed,* and *insolvent.* They have different shades of meaning.

A firm is *bankrupt* when it has filed a petition for relief from its creditors under the bankruptcy code, or when it has consented to a filing by its creditors. A firm is *in default* when it violates

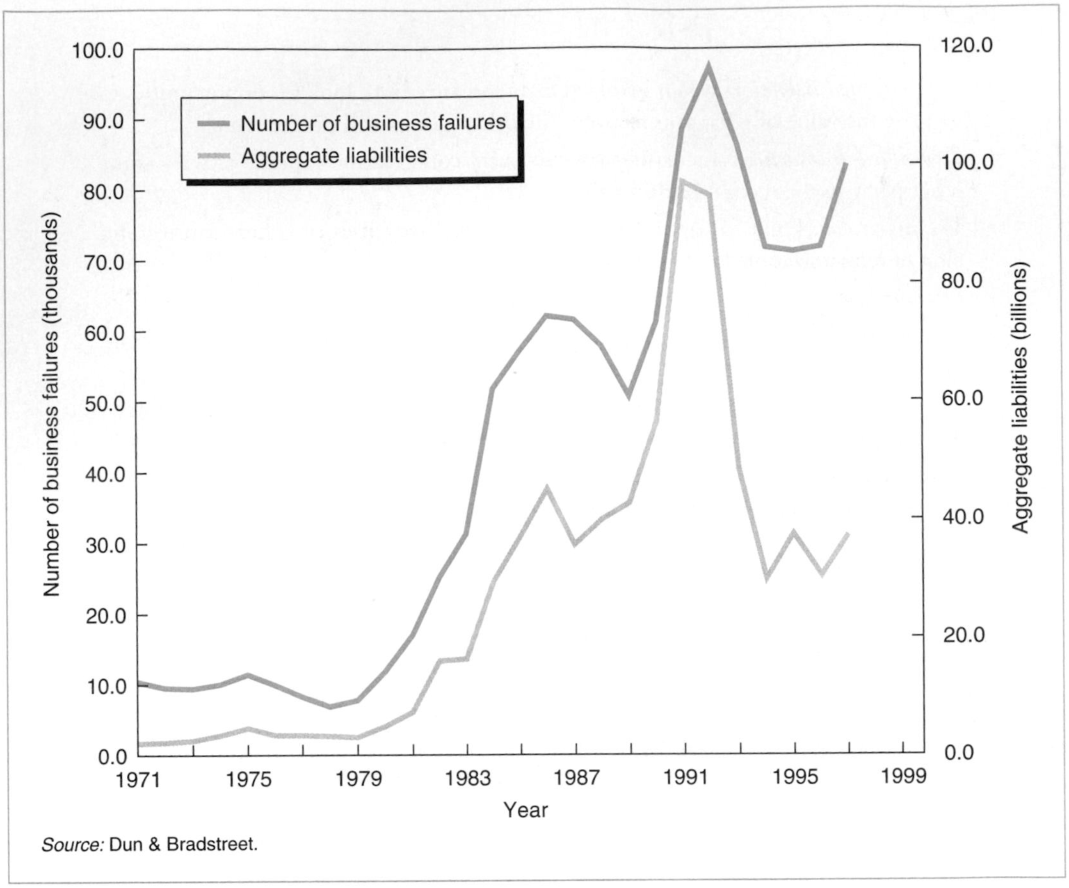

FIGURE 26.1
Number of business failures and aggregate liabilities of firms entering bankruptcy, 1971–1997.

one of the terms of a loan agreement or bond indenture. A firm is said to have *failed* if it meets one of several criteria created by Dun & Bradstreet, a leading provider of information about distressed firms. A firm is *insolvent* when it is unable to pay its debts. It is useful to distinguish between technical insolvency and bankruptcy insolvency. Technical insolvency occurs because of a lack of cash. Bankruptcy insolvency occurs when the firm's total liabilities exceed the fair market value of its total assets. Technical insolvency may be just a temporary condition. Bankruptcy insolvency usually indicates a more serious distressed condition.

Causes of Business Failure

Financial distress results from a deterioration in a firm's business. There can be many causes. Poor management, unwise expansion, intense competition, too much debt, massive litigation, and unfavorable contracts are just a few of the possible causes.

Managerial inexperience and incompetence are the leading causes of corporate business failure. Table 26.2 reports the results of two Dun & Bradstreet surveys. In the earlier survey, lack of management experience, unbalanced experience, or outright management incompetence caused 94% of business failures. The later survey used a different set of categories. Nevertheless, managerial incompetence is probably responsible for most of the failures charged to "industry weakness," "insufficient profits," or "financial factors."

TABLE 26.1
The largest U.S. bankruptcies.

RANK	COMPANY	BANKRUPTCY DATE	ASSETS ($ MILLIONS)
1	Worldcom, Inc.*	07/21/2002	103,914
2	Enron Corp.**	12/02/2001	63,392
3	Conseco, Inc.	12/18/2002	61,392
4	Texaco, Inc.	04/12/1987	35,892
5	Financial Corp. of America	09/09/1988	33,864
6	Global Crossing Ltd.	01/28/2002	25,511
7	UAL Corp.	12/09/2002	25,197
8	Adelphia Communications	06/25/2002	24,409
9	Pacific Gas and Electric Co.	04/06/2001	21,470
10	MCorp	03/31/1989	20,228
11	Kmart Corp.	01/22/2002	17,007
12	NTL, Inc.	05/08/2002	16,834
13	First Executive Corp.	05/13/1991	15,193
14	Gibraltar Financial Corp.	02/08/1990	15,011
15	FINOVA Group, Inc., (The)	03/07/2001	14,050
16	HomeFed Corp.	10/22/1992	13,885
17	Southeast Banking Corporation	09/20/1991	13,390
18	Reliance Group Holdings, Inc.	06/12/2001	12,598
19	Imperial Corp. of America	02/28/1990	12,163
20	Federal-Mogul Corp.	10/01/2001	10,150
21	First City Bancorp. of Texas	10/31/1992	9,943
22	First Capital Holdings	05/30/1991	9,675
23	Baldwin-United	09/26/1983	9,383

Source: The Bankruptcy Yearbook & Almanac (Boston, Mass.: New Generation Research) or BankruptcyData.com.

TABLE 26.2
Causes of business failure.

Poor Management	Financial Factors
Lack of experience	Burdensome debt
Incompetence	Heavy operating costs
Economic Factors	Insufficient capital
Industry weakness	Neglect
Insufficient profits	Disaster
Inadequate sales	Strategy
Not competitive	Fraud

Source: Business Failure Record, Dun & Bradstreet.

EXTERNAL FACTORS Factors external to the firm can also play a role. For example, intense competition within the U.S. airline industry has made it difficult for any airline, regardless of management quality, to make money. This undoubtedly contributed to the bankruptcy of UAL, parent of United Airlines, in 2002. Nevertheless, how quickly and effectively management responds to changing conditions in the product and financial markets determines to a great extent which firms survive and which do not.

TABLE 26.3
Age of failed businesses.

	PROPORTION OF TOTAL FAILURES							
	1980		1990		1993		1997	
Age (years)	**Percent**	**Cumulative**	**Percent**	**Cumulative**	**Percent**	**Cumulative**	**Percent**	**Cumulative**
1 or less	0.9%	0.9%	9.0%	9.0%	7.1%	7.1%	10.7%	10.7%
2	9.6	10.5	11.2	20.2	8.5	15.6	10.1	20.8
3	15.3	25.8	11.2	31.4	8.8	24.4	8.7	29.5
4	15.4	41.2	10.0	41.4	7.9	32.3	7.8	37.3
5	12.4	53.6	8.4	49.8	7.4	39.7	7.0	44.3
6	8.9	62.5	7.2	57.0	6.5	46.2	5.9	50.2
7	6.3	68.8	5.3	62.3	5.9	52.1	5.3	55.5
8	5.2	74.0	4.5	66.8	5.5	57.6	5.0	60.5
9	4.3	78.3	3.8	70.6	5.0	62.6	4.0	64.5
10	3.4	81.7	3.5	74.1	4.3	66.9	3.7	68.2
over 10	18.3	100.0	25.9	100.0	33.1	100.0	31.8	100.0
Number of failures	11,742		60,747		86,133		83,384	

Source: Business Failure Record, Dun & Bradstreet.

AGE OF THE FIRM Younger firms are more likely to fail than older firms. Younger firms have less experience. They also tend to be smaller and less well capitalized than older firms in the same industry. Table 26.3 shows the breakdown of business failures according to the age of the firm at the time of the bankruptcy filing. Approximately half of the business failures in 1980 and 1990 were of firms no more than five years old. The percentage was 44% in 1997. The likelihood of failure increases in years 2 and 3, and falls after that.

Review

1. What is the main difference between reorganization and liquidation under the bankruptcy code?
2. What happened to the number and aggregate size of business failures in the period 1990 to 1997?
3. What is financial distress? What aspects of financial distress are involved when a firm is bankrupt? in default? failed? insolvent?
4. What are the main causes of financial distress? To what extent are factors internal to the firm and external to it responsible?
5. How does the likelihood of financial distress vary with the age of the firm? For which years is the likelihood of failure greatest?

26.2 A LITTLE HISTORY

Until modern times, the legal system generally favored creditors and treated a financially distressed debtor quite harshly. The first official laws covering bankruptcy were adopted in England in 1542 under King Henry VIII. The law treated a bankrupt individual as a criminal. Punishments ranged from imprisonment in debtors' prison to the death penalty in more serious cases!

Origins of U.S. Bankruptcy Law

In the United States, three federal bankruptcy laws were adopted during the 19th century. Each was enacted in response to some sort of financial panic and was repealed after the panic ended. These laws were designed to help creditors recover as much of their loans as possible.

Current U.S. bankruptcy law favors reorganizing the financially distressed debtor. The Bankruptcy Act of 1898 was the first U.S. bankruptcy law to give firms in distress the option of being protected from their creditors. The firm could be placed in what is called an equity receivership and reorganized under court supervision. Otherwise it had to be liquidated. The equity receivership structure proved to be costly and ineffective. There was no provision for an independent, objective review of the plan of reorganization, as there is today. In keeping with the Principle of Self-Interested Behavior, often a debtor and a friendly creditor would initiate an equity receivership and push through a plan that favored that creditor over the others. Debtors could even offer cash payoffs to powerful dissenters to secure their consent to the proposed plan!

Evolution

The Great Depression produced a large number of bankruptcies and led to the Chandler Act of 1938. This law substantially improved the procedures for reorganizing distressed firms. It required the court to hold hearings on a proposed plan and provided greater protection for creditors.

The bankruptcy rules were overhauled again with passage of the Bankruptcy Reform Act of 1978. The new law replaced the old Chapters X and XI with a new Chapter 11. It established a bankruptcy court system and substantially improved bankruptcy procedures. It made it easier, quicker, and less costly for public firms to seek relief from their creditors while they try to reorganize. Under Chapter 11, the debtor usually continues to operate its business with existing management. The exception is when the bankruptcy court determines that a disinterested trustee should be appointed. This may be for cause[1] or because it would be in the best interests of the creditors or shareholders.

Recent Developments

In 1991, Congress enacted a new provision of the Bankruptcy Code, entitled Chapter 10. This new section allows small and medium-sized businesses to reorganize under a "fast-track Chapter 11" procedure. It is intended to reduce the delay and expense of a Chapter 11 reorganization.

Three years later, Congress enacted the Bankruptcy Reform Act of 1994. This act contains provisions designed to expedite the bankruptcy process. However, U.S. bankruptcy law continues to draw criticism. Bankruptcy is a slow and expensive process. Expect further changes to the bankruptcy law in the future!

Review

1. Does the current U.S. bankruptcy law favor reorganizing the debtor or liquidating it?
2. What were some of the changes brought about by the Bankruptcy Reform Act of 1978?
3. What is the main purpose of the new Chapter 11 of the bankruptcy code?

26.3 EARLY DETECTION OF FINANCIAL DISTRESS

As a firm's financial condition worsens, it begins to show signs of financial distress. Losses begin to occur. Interest coverage worsens. The firm's operations start to absorb more cash than they generate. Net working capital may turn negative. The debt level tends to rise relative to cash flow.

[1]Cause includes fraud, dishonesty, incompetence, or gross mismanagement.

The debt-to-equity ratio also tends to increase. This deterioration will reveal itself in a worsening of the firm's key financial ratios. Thus, changes in a firm's financial ratios can be used to predict the onset of financial distress.

Multiple Discriminant Analysis

Almost without exception, early studies that used financial ratios to predict corporate bankruptcy tried to pick a single financial ratio that worked best. But it seems unlikely that any single financial ratio will work best for all industries and in all situations.

Multiple discriminant analysis (MDA) is a more appropriate technique for predicting corporate bankruptcy, because it uses more than one variable. MDA places a firm into one of two or more groups based upon the firm's individual characteristics. In bankruptcy prediction, MDA tries to distinguish between two groups, bankrupt and nonbankrupt firms.

MDA is applied in the following manner. A set of financial ratios are calculated for groups of bankrupt and nonbankrupt firms. MDA then determines the discriminant function that best distinguishes between the groups. The discriminant function is of the form $Z = V_1X_1 + V_2X_2 + \cdots + V_nX_n$. The discriminant function transforms the individual financial ratios into a single discriminant score, or Z-score. The Z-score is then used to classify the firm as "bankrupt" or "nonbankrupt." In this equation, V_1, V_2, and so forth are discriminant coefficients or weights, and X_1, X_2, and so forth are the financial ratios. The MDA technique determines the set of discriminant coefficients, V_i, that maximizes the percentage of firms that are correctly classified.

Figure 26.2 shows a two-variable analysis. Measures of profitability and liquidity are plotted for a sample of nonbankrupt (•) and bankrupt (○) firms. MDA selects the weights so as to

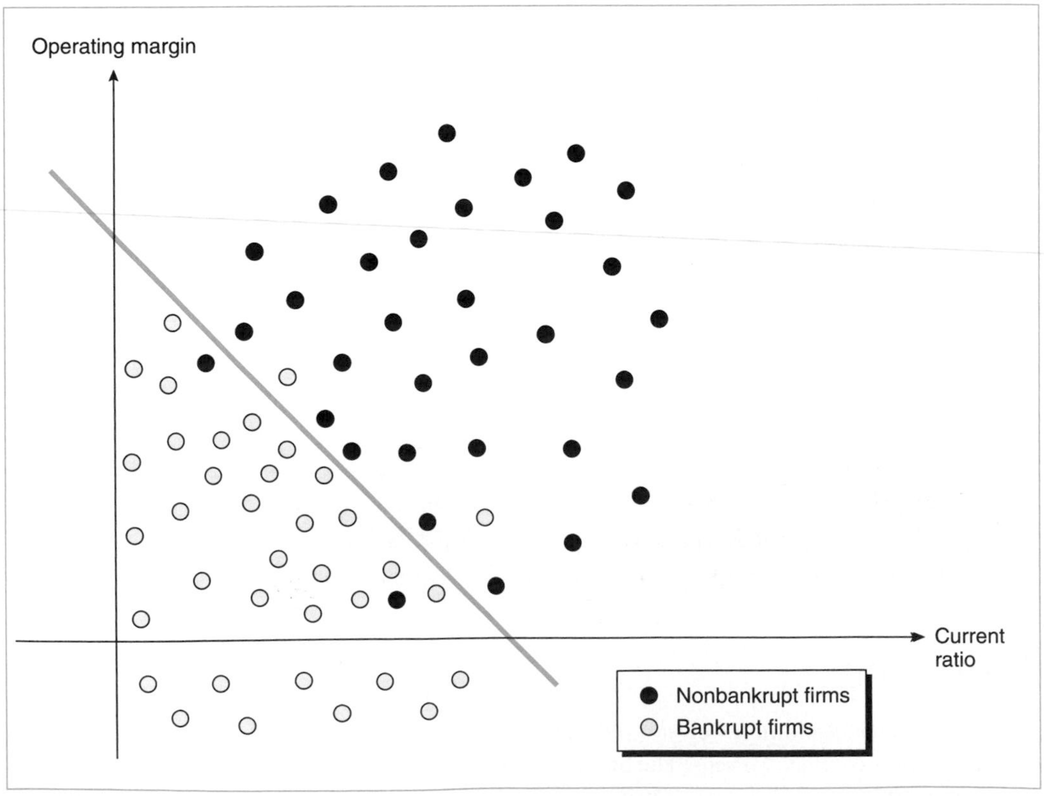

FIGURE 26.2
Applying discriminant analysis.

position the line where it distinguishes best between bankrupt and nonbankrupt firms. The discriminant function is used to calculate a *Z*-score for a firm in order to assign it to one of the two groups. This procedure effectively compares the financial profile of an individual firm to the financial profiles of the groups of bankrupt and nonbankrupt firms.[2]

Altman's Z-Score Model

Edward Altman developed a *Z*-score model based on five financial ratios. Altman's *Z*-score model is:[3]

$$Z = 0.012X_1 + 0.014X_2 + 0.033X_3 + 0.006X_4 + 0.999X_5 \qquad (26.1)$$

where

X_1 = net working capital/total assets
X_2 = retained earnings/total assets
X_3 = earnings before interest and taxes/total assets
X_4 = market value of equity/book value of total liabilities
X_5 = sales/total assets
Z = *Z*-score

The greater a firm's *Z*-score, the lower its risk of going bankrupt.

EXAMPLE Applying the *Z*-score Model

Suppose that Plexus, a manufacturer of luxury cars, has the following financial ratios:

$$X_1 = 15\% \quad X_2 = 30\% \quad X_3 = 17\% \quad X_4 = 225\% \quad X_5 = 1.5$$

Substituting into the *Z*-score model (26.1) gives

$$Z = 0.012(15) + 0.014(30) + 0.033(17) + 0.006(225) + 0.999(1.5) = 4.01$$

In order to interpret this *Z*-score, we need to examine the Z scores of Altman's samples of bankrupt and nonbankrupt firms. He found that $Z = 2.675$ discriminated best between bankrupt and nonbankrupt firms (in the sense that it minimized the number of misclassifications). However, he also found that there was a zone of uncertainty between $Z = 1.81$ and $Z = 2.99$ within which errors in classification would occur for firms within one year prior to bankruptcy. Thus, the range of Z values can be divided into three intervals:

Z-SCORE	PREDICTION
$Z > 2.99$	Firm will not fail within one year
$1.81 \le Z \le 2.99$	Gray area within which it is difficult to discriminate effectively
$Z < 1.81$	Firm will fail within one year

The *Z*-score model predicts that Plexus will not fail within the next year.

---

[2]The *Z*-score model can also be used to predict the likelihood that a reorganized debtor might fail if it is capitalized in a particular manner. It is thus a potentially useful tool in assessing the feasibility of a proposed plan of reorganization.

[3]Values for the variables X_1 through X_4 should be entered as absolute percentage values. For example, if a firm has a ratio of net working capital to total assets (X_1) of 10%, X_1 should be entered as 10.0% and not 0.10. Variable X_5 (sales to total assets) should be entered as a ratio. For example, a sales-to-total-assets ratio of 200% should be entered as 2.0.

Classification Accuracy

Studies have found that Equation (26.1) is not as accurate when it is used to predict bankruptcy in more recent time periods. The mix of variables and the coefficient values tend to change over time. We offer two practical suggestions. Anyone using a *Z*-score model should reestimate the discriminant function regularly to ensure that it is up to date. Second, a *Z*-score model is likely to be most reliable when it is applied to firms within a particular industry. For example, a bankruptcy prediction model could be estimated for the oil and gas industry.

Other Indicators of Distress

In addition to financial ratios, there are four other useful indicators of distress. (1) There are derivatives, called credit-default swaps, that investors purchase to insure against default risk. When credit-default swaps written on a firm's debt rise sharply in price, investors are signaling greater concern about that firm's risk of defaulting. (The derivatives market predicted Enron's distress far ahead of the rating agencies.) (2) A firm's debt falls sharply in price. (3) A firm suddenly has to draw down all of its standby credit lines to pay off commercial paper, which it is unable to roll over. (4) A firm announces that it has engaged one of the leading bankruptcy-advisory investment banks. It would only do that if it were considering bankruptcy.

Review

1. What is MDA?
2. What does a firm's *Z*-score measure? How reliable is it?
3. Based on Altman's original model, what would a *Z*-score of 1.50 indicate? a *Z*-score of 4.50? a *Z*-score of 2.50?
4. Why is it important to reestimate the discriminant function regularly?
5. What are four indicators of financial distress (in addition to worsening credit ratios)?

26.4 REORGANIZATION OUTSIDE BANKRUPTCY

Bankruptcy is time-consuming and expensive. For these reasons, financially distressed firms usually try to reorganize outside bankruptcy before filing for bankruptcy.

Reorganization Techniques

A firm can restructure its liabilities outside bankruptcy in one of three ways: (1) exchange new securities for existing securities, (2) solicit securityholders' consent to modify the terms of existing securities, and (3) repurchase existing securities for cash. Each technique requires the firm to persuade its securityholders to alter the terms of their investment in the firm.

Exchange Offers

If a firm finds itself unable to service its debt, it can offer to exchange new securities for some of the outstanding debt. These new securities might consist of common stock, preferred stock, or new debt securities with a lower interest rate or a longer repayment schedule. These transactions reduce the firm's leverage ratio and its debt obligations.

Many firms conducted exchange offers in more recent years to deal with a ticking time bomb in their capital structures. Two examples of such time bombs are interest-rate-reset notes[4] and pay-in-kind debentures.[5] If the interest-rate-reset feature or requirement to pay debt service in cash will substantially increase the firm's debt service requirements, eliminating a substantial part of the debt may be necessary to avert a financial crisis.

EXAMPLE RJR Nabisco's Exchange Offer

RJR Nabisco's LBO (leveraged buyout) created an issue of convertible debentures and an issue of exchangeable debentures. Each issue had both a pay-in-kind feature and an interest-rate-reset feature. RJR Nabisco had $20 billion of debt outstanding, including nearly $6.0 billion of pay-in-kind interest-rate-reset securities. About a year after the LBO, the interest rate on the convertible debentures reset to 17.375% and the interest rate on the exchangeable debentures reset to 17%.

RJR Nabisco immediately took steps to reduce its debt. It offered to exchange $333 of cash and $667 stated value of convertible preferred stock for each convertible debenture and for each exchangeable debenture. It also repurchased other debt for cash. The deleveraging program retired $6.9 billion of debt. These steps eventually helped RJR Nabisco regain an investment-grade rating.

Amending the Terms of Outstanding Securities

A firm may try to amend its indenture if it can no longer satisfy some of the terms. For example, a firm might no longer satisfy a covenant to maintain a specified minimum net worth. The firm can solicit the written consent of the debtholders to relax or, perhaps, eliminate the restrictive covenant. Of course, to obtain their consent, the firm might have to pay cash or increase the interest rate on the debt.

Repurchasing Securities for Cash

Repurchases for cash by a financially troubled firm are unusual. Such a firm usually does not have enough cash on hand and would probably have trouble arranging credit. Yet, some voluntary debt reductions have taken the form of cash repurchases of outstanding debt. This can get rid of a particularly troublesome debt issue.

Creating Incentives to Participate

A financially distressed firm can create incentives—either positive or negative—to encourage bondholders to agree to an out-of-court restructuring. As a positive incentive, the firm can offer to exchange new securities with a higher interest rate, shorter maturity, senior ranking (with the new securities possibly being secured), or stronger covenants than the outstanding securities. It can also offer a cash incentive.

As a negative incentive, a firm might structure the exchange offer such that nonexchanging holders would find their securities contractually or structurally subordinated to the new securities

[4]Interest-rate-reset notes provide for a resetting of the interest rate on a specified date, usually two or three years after issuance. The interest rate must be reset to an interest rate that will make the securities worth 101% of their principal amount. If the reset issue is large relative to the firm's capitalization, the interest rate reset could itself cause the firm's financial condition to deteriorate. It could even be enough to push the firm "over the edge."

[5]Pay-in-kind debentures pay interest in the form of additional notes for some specified period. Interest payment obligations are thus deferred (to a period when the issuer expects to be better able to service its debt). But if the improvement in operating cash flow does not occur, the initial cash-pay date can threaten serious financial distress.

if the exchange offer succeeds. Or the firm might combine a consent solicitation with an exchange offer: Bondholders would receive the new securities only if enough of them agreed to modify the covenants of the old bonds. The modification reduces the covenant protection for bondholders who refuse to exchange. A firm might also threaten to file for bankruptcy if the exchange offer fails.

The Holdout Problem

Holdouts are holders of outstanding securities who refuse to exchange their securities for new ones. In keeping with the Principle of Self-Interested Behavior, they hope to get a better deal. Holdouts can usually benefit because the firm's ability to pay the holdouts in full will improve if the exchange offer succeeds. Holdouts benefit at the expense of exchanging bondholders.

Firms employ a variety of techniques to discourage holdouts. They use the incentives and disincentives just discussed. Many have also used a prepackaged bankruptcy. This strategy is discussed later in the chapter. It is often effective in dealing with the holdout problem, because all holders of the outstanding securities are bound by the terms of the plan once the bankruptcy court confirms it.

Review

1. Cite three ways that a firm can restructure its liabilities outside bankruptcy.
2. How can a firm use an exchange offer to restructure its liabilities? Why did RJR Nabisco feel it was necessary to do this not too long after its LBO?
3. Why does amending restrictive covenants involve making a payment to the debtholders?
4. What are holdouts, and why are they a problem when a firm is trying to restructure its liabilities? How can a firm discourage holdouts?

26.5 CHAPTER 11 OF THE BANKRUPTCY CODE—REORGANIZATION

The guiding principle of Chapter 11 reorganizations is that a debtor should be given the opportunity to negotiate with its creditors and achieve a consensual plan of reorganization *provided that the going-concern value of the reorganized debtor exceeds its liquidation value.* Even though a firm may not be able to meet its current financial obligations, it may still be able to operate profitably after its debts are restructured. Chapter 11 gives the debtor the opportunity to determine whether restructuring is feasible and in the best interest of its creditors.

EXAMPLE Reorganization Value Versus Liquidation Value

Consider a steel manufacturer with just a single steel mill. The scrap value of the mill is well below its book value. The firm owes \$100 million, the economy is in a recession, and the firm cannot cover its interest payment obligations. The scrap value of the mill plus the value of the land it occupies would provide a total liquidation value of \$30 million. The firm expects that once the economy recovers from the recession, it will be able to earn a competitive return on its steelmaking assets. The present value of the expected cash flows is \$60 million. The steel manufacturer cannot service \$100 million of debt, and the amount of its liabilities exceeds the value of its assets. But liquidation would be wasteful. The going-concern value is more than the liquidation value, so a higher value can be realized through reorganization.

Reorganization in Bankruptcy

Chapter 11 offers a debtor the opportunity to freeze its debts while it attempts to negotiate a reorganization plan with creditors. Reorganization is an administrative procedure. It allows a distressed, but otherwise economically viable, firm to survive as a going concern. The objective of this process is to preserve the going-concern value of the debtor.

DEBTOR IN POSSESSION Table 26.4 describes the Chapter 11 process. The firm commences this process by filing a *petition for relief.* The firm then becomes a **debtor in possession.** It is in possession of the same assets and business it had before the bankruptcy filing. It can continue to operate its business with the same officers and the same board of directors it had before.

TABLE 26.4
How Chapter 11 works in a successful reorganization.

HOW CHAPTER 11 WORKS

Firm Files for Chapter 11 Protection

A firm files for Chapter 11 protection from its creditors either when it is no longer able to pay its debts as they come due or when it anticipates future liabilities that it will not be able to meet. It has usually attempted an out-of-court restructuring but failed to achieve one.

The Chapter 11 Bankruptcy Process

The bankruptcy judge issues an automatic stay.

The firm becomes a *debtor in possession.* The firm operates its business as before the bankruptcy filing except that the bankruptcy court must approve all significant decisions. All debts are frozen. Creditors are precluded from seizing the debtor's property or trying to enforce collection. Lawsuits are suspended.

Different creditor classes form committees.

Generally, the largest seven creditors within each class of creditors are appointed to the committee. Equityholders may also form a single committee or one committee for preferred stockholders and one for common stockholders, if the firm has preferred stock outstanding. The creditors committee(s) can ask the bankruptcy court to appoint an examiner to investigate possible fraud or mismanagement. They can also petition the bankruptcy court to appoint a trustee to run the firm.

The committees and the debtor negotiate a plan of reorganization.

For the first 120 days after filing for bankruptcy, the firm has the exclusive right to propose a plan of reorganization. Thereafter, unless the bankruptcy court extends the period of exclusivity, any interested party can submit a plan.

Creditors approve the proposed plan of reorganization.

Generally, each class of creditors must approve the plan.[a] A majority of the creditors holding at least two-thirds of the bonds in the class who vote must approve the plan in order for the class to accept it.

The bankruptcy court confirms the plan of reorganization.

The reorganization plan must satisfy the requirements of the bankruptcy code before the bankruptcy court can confirm it.

Reorganized Firm Emerges from Bankruptcy

The reorganized debtor must execute the plan of reorganization. The debtor emerges from Chapter 11 when it has satisfied the conditions in the plan.

[a]The *cramdown* exception is described in the text.

AUTOMATIC STAY The bankruptcy code imposes an *automatic stay* of any further efforts by creditors to collect their debts, or by secured creditors to seize the collateral securing their loans. This is one of the fundamental protections provided to debtors by the bankruptcy code. The automatic stay stops all collection efforts, all foreclosure actions, and all harassment against the debtor. It enables the debtor to hold on to its assets while it strives to put together a plan of reorganization.

Review

1. What is the guiding principle of Chapter 11 in the bankruptcy code?
2. What is a debtor in possession? What is it required to do in bankruptcy?
3. What does an automatic stay accomplish?

Plan of Reorganization

The main objective of the Chapter 11 process is to come up with a *plan of reorganization.* It is crucial to the firm's survival as a going concern. The plan of reorganization contains a business plan for the firm, establishes a new capital structure, shows how the old debts will be paid off, and provides for the distribution of cash, new securities, and other consideration among the firm's creditors and shareholders. The plan must satisfy requirements specified in the bankruptcy code in order for a bankruptcy court to confirm it.

PRIORITY The liabilities, called *claims,* and equity interests are classified in order of decreasing priority, as follows.

1. *Administrative expenses,* such as legal, accounting, and trustee fees
2. *Priority claims,* which are unsecured claims created in the ordinary course of business and certain "small" claims (for example, wages up to $2,000 per person earned within 90 days of the filing)
3. Secured debt
4. Unsecured senior debt
5. Subordinated debt
6. Preferred stock
7. Common stock

ABSOLUTE PRIORITY The **absolute priority doctrine** holds that the assets of the debtor should be distributed among creditors and shareholders according to the hierarchy just listed. A more senior claim must be paid in full before a junior claim is permitted to receive *any* distribution. Liquidations must follow absolute priority. However, senior creditors in a reorganization often find it expedient, in practice, to allow the plan to deviate from absolute priority. Making a small distribution to a dissenting class can benefit senior creditors when that achieves their support and speeds up the reorganization process.

REQUIREMENTS FOR CONFIRMATION A plan of reorganization must be *feasible* and it must satisfy four basic standards of *fairness.* Table 26.5 summarizes these requirements.

PLAN ACCEPTANCE A class of claims accepts a proposed plan of reorganization if (1) more than one-half of the number of creditors who vote and (2) creditors holding at least two-thirds of the

TABLE 26.5
Summary of the requirements for confirming a plan of reorganization.

SUMMARY OF THE REQUIREMENTS FOR CONFIRMING A PLAN OF REORGANIZATION

1. The plan must be feasible.
   - The reorganized debtor must have positive net worth.
   - It is unlikely that the reorganized debtor will wind up back in bankruptcy in the foreseeable future.
2. The plan cannot discriminate unfairly among creditors of equal classes.
3. At least one class of creditors must accept the plan.
   - Need at least two-thirds approval in amount of allowed claims that vote *and*
   - Need more than one-half approval in number of allowed claims that vote.
4. The plan must satisfy the fair-and-equitable test.
   - If an *impaired* class votes against the plan and would receive less than the full amount of its claims under the plan, all junior classes must get nothing under the plan.[a]
   - If an *unimpaired* class votes against the plan, it is treated as having approved the plan.
5. The plan must satisfy the best-interests-of-creditors test.
   - If the holder of a claim or interest votes against the plan, the claim holder must receive at least as much under the plan as the holder would receive if the debtor were liquidated.

[a]A class is impaired when it will receive cash and securities that are worth less than the amount of its claims.

amount of claims belonging to that class that vote, approve the plan. A class of equityholders accepts a plan if at least two-thirds of the number of outstanding shares that are voted are cast in favor of the plan. Creditors and shareholders who do not vote are ignored when applying these tests.

CRAMDOWN The **cramdown** procedure permits the bankruptcy court to confirm a proposed plan over the objections of one or more classes of creditors. The plan must pass the following test. If a class rejects the plan, (1) it must provide the holders with property whose value is at least equal to the allowed amount of their claims or else (2) no junior class receives anything.[6]

EXAMPLE Cramdown

Olympic Computer Company is preparing a plan of reorganization. Table 26.6 provides Olympic Computer's latest balance sheet. The firm has 1,000 shares of preferred stock with a par value of $100 per share and a liquidation value of $110 per share. It has 1,000 shares of common stock with no par value. It also has $3 million of bank debt (secured by accounts receivable), $2 million of mortgage debt (secured by machinery, equipment, and real estate), and $3 million of subordinated debt (expressly subordinated to the bank debt).

Suppose that an appraisal of Olympic Computer's assets reveals a liquidation value of $1 million for the machinery, equipment, and real estate, $2 million for the receivables, and $1 million for the inventory. The mortgage holder would be paid $1 million, leaving a $1 million deficiency. The banks would be paid $2 million, also leaving a $1 million deficiency. Suppose that administrative claims and tax claims total $1 million. Table 26.7 shows how the available assets would compare to the unsecured claims in a Chapter 7 liquidation.

There is $1 million of cash but $9 million of unsecured claims. Unsecured claimants would be entitled to a cash distribution equal to 1/9 of their claims. Because of the subordination

[6]A cramdown plan satisfies the absolute priority doctrine.

TABLE 26.6
Balance sheet of Olympic Computer Company.

OLYMPIC COMPUTER COMPANY
Balance Sheet before Reorganization
($ millions)

Assets		Liabilities and Stockholders' Equity	
Cash	$1.0	Accounts payable	$4.0
Accounts receivable[a]	3.0	Bank debt	3.0
Inventory	2.0	Subordinated debt[c]	3.0
Fixed assets[b]	1.0	Mortgage bonds	2.0
Real estate[b]	1.0	Preferred stock	0.1
		Common stock	(4.1)
Total assets	$8.0	Total liabilities and stockholders' equity	$8.0

[a]Pledged to secure the bank debt.
[b]Pledged to secure the mortgage bonds.
[c]Subordinated to the bank debt.

provision, the bank debt is entitled to the share that would otherwise be paid to subordinated debt. Therefore, the banks would be entitled to 4/9 of the cash distribution, and the subordinated debtholders would get nothing.

A careful analysis of Olympic Computer reveals that it has a value of $6 million on a going-concern basis. Suppose also that the $1 million of cash is not needed to run the business. Then Olympic Computer's *reorganization value*—its value as a going concern plus the value of any excess assets—is $7 million.

TABLE 26.7
Distributions to Olympic Computer creditors in liquidation.

DISTRIBUTIONS TO OLYMPIC COMPUTER CREDITORS IN LIQUIDATION
($ millions)

Available Cash		Unsecured Claims	
Cash on balance sheet	$1.0	Accounts payable	$4.0
Liquidation of assets	4.0	Banks' deficiency	1.0
Administrative & tax claims	(1.0)	Subordinated debt	3.0
Secured interests	(3.0)	Mortgagee's deficiency	1.0
Total cash available	$1.0	Total unsecured claims	$9.0

CASH DISTRIBUTIONS

	Secured Claim	Unsecured Claim	Total Distribution
Trade creditors	—	$0.444	$0.444
Banks	$2.0	0.444	2.444
Subordinated debtholders	—	—	—
Mortgage bondholders	1.0	0.112	1.112
Total	$3.0	$1.0	$4.0

TABLE 26.8
Distributions to Olympic Computer creditors in a cramdown.

DISTRIBUTIONS TO OLYMPIC COMPUTER CREDITORS IN A CRAMDOWN
($ millions)

Available Consideration		**Unsecured Claims**	
Going-concern value	$6.0	Accounts payable	$4.0
Cash on balance sheet	1.0	Banks' deficiency	1.0
Administrative & tax claims	(1.0)	Subordinated debt	3.0
Secured interests	(3.0)	Mortgagee's deficiency	1.0
Total available consideration	$3.0	Total unsecured claims	$9.0

DISTRIBUTIONS

	Secured Claim	**Unsecured Claim**	**Total Distribution**
Trade creditors	—	$1.333	$1.333
Banks	$2.0	1.0	3.0
Subordinated debtholders	—	0.333	0.333
Mortgage bondholders	1.0	0.334	1.334
Preferred stockholders	—	—	—
Common stockholders	—	—	—
Total	$3.0	$3.0	$6.0

Table 26.8 illustrates the distributions that would occur in a cramdown. Subtracting $1 million of administrative and tax claims and $3 million for the secured claims from the $7 million of reorganization value leaves $3 million available for distribution to the unsecured claims. These claims total $9 million. Unsecured claims can thus realize 33 cents on the dollar. Note that because Olympic Computer is insolvent, the preferred stockholders and common stockholders will not receive anything in a cramdown.

Trade creditors receive $1.333 million. Because of the subordination provision, subordinated debtholders must pay over to the banks the lesser of (1) their entire share or (2) enough to repay the banks in full. That is, a class of creditors cannot receive an amount that exceeds their claims. The subordination provision makes an additional $1.333 million available for the banks. However, $1 million brings their total distributions to $3 million, the amount of their original claims. The $0.333 million excess remains with the subordinated debtholders. The mortgage bondholders receive 3/9 of their $1 million deficiency, or $0.334 million. Adding this to the $1 million they receive from the sale of machinery, equipment, and real estate results in a total distribution of $1.334 million.

Advantages and Disadvantages of Reorganizing Under Chapter 11

A reorganization under Chapter 11 has several advantages and disadvantages compared to an out-of-court restructuring. They are summarized in Table 26.9.

On balance, a private out-of-court restructuring can save significant direct and indirect costs. It does so mainly by avoiding the delays inherent in a bankruptcy restructuring. The private alternative is more likely to work when the debtor's liabilities are concentrated in the hands of a fairly small number of banks or other large, sophisticated financial institutions.

TABLE 26.9
Advantages and disadvantages of reorganizing under Chapter 11.

ADVANTAGES	DISADVANTAGES
1. Filing the bankruptcy petition automatically stays all creditor collection efforts.	**1.** The debtor's business is disrupted for some period of time, in part because the debtor cannot pay pre-petition creditors. Some of its former vendors, suppliers, and customers may decline to do business with a bankrupt firm.
2. The bankruptcy process provides the debtor with a single forum—bankruptcy court—for conducting negotiations and resolving disputes.	**2.** A debtor in possession must meet stringent reporting requirements.
3. The bankruptcy court can authorize debtor-in-possession financing for working capital purposes.	**3.** The bankruptcy court must approve all transactions outside the ordinary course of business.
4. The bankruptcy court can authorize the debtor in possession to reject unfavorable leases and other contracts.	**4.** A bankruptcy filing may trigger the filing of claims that would not have been asserted in an out-of-court restructuring (for example, a claim concerning a potential environmental cleanup liability).
5. All claims (including contingent claims) can be dealt with at one time and a plan developed for discharging them.	**5.** The need for official committees to represent creditors and stockholders, as well as legal and financial advisors for these committees (paid for by the debtor), can make bankruptcy much more expensive than an out-of-court restructuring.
6. Interest stops accruing on unsecured claims.	**6.** The debtor's management might lose control of the firm through either the appointment of a trustee or the adoption of a creditors' reorganization plan.
7. Claims resulting from the rejection of leases or contracts are capped.	
8. If a proposed plan has been accepted by at least two-thirds in dollar amount of claims, and by more than one-half in number of claims, actually voting in each class of creditors, the bankruptcy court can confirm it over the objection of dissenting creditors.	
9. Even if a class of creditors rejects the plan, the court can still confirm it under the cramdown rules.	
10. Once the plan is confirmed, all of the debtor's creditors and stockholders are bound by its terms.	
11. Restructuring through bankruptcy may enable the debtor to avoid having to pay taxes on the income that results when debt is retired at less than its face amount.	

Review

1. What is the main purpose of the plan of reorganization? For how long does the debtor have the exclusive right to file one with a bankruptcy court?
2. What is the absolute priority doctrine? Is it ever violated in a reorganization? In a liquidation?
3. List the five main requirements a plan of reorganization must satisfy before a bankruptcy court can confirm it.
4. What does it mean to say that a plan of reorganization is feasible?
5. Explain the fair-and-equitable test, and the best-interests-of-creditors test.
6. What are the main advantages and disadvantages of reorganizing under Chapter 11?

26.6 PREPACKAGED PLANS OF REORGANIZATION

In a **prepackaged bankruptcy,** the debtor and creditors negotiate a plan of reorganization and then file it along with the bankruptcy petition. A prepackaged bankruptcy attempts to combine the advantages—and avoid the disadvantages—of the bankruptcy process and out-of-court restructurings. The requirements for confirming a prepackaged plan are the same as in a traditional reorganization.

The prepackaged bankruptcy process has some advantages relative to alternative methods of reorganization. (1) Approval is easier to obtain. Exchange offers usually require 90% or 95% of the debtholders to accept the exchange offer. The bankruptcy code sets lower acceptance levels. (2) The confirmed plan is binding on all debtholders, whether they vote to accept the plan or not. (3) Filing for bankruptcy often permits the debtor to realize tax advantages that are not available in an out-of-court restructuring. (4) Filing for bankruptcy allows the debtor to reject burdensome leases and other contracts.

EXAMPLE Crystal Oil Company's Prepackaged Bankruptcy

The first significant prepackaged bankruptcy was that of Crystal Oil Company, an independent oil and gas producer headquartered in Louisiana, in 1986. It emerged from bankruptcy less than three months later with its capital structure completely reorganized. Total indebtedness was reduced from $277 million to $129 million. Debtholders received common stock, convertible notes, convertible preferred stock, and warrants to purchase common stock in exchange for the old debt.

Crystal Oil's reorganization plan had been presented to creditors three months prior to the bankruptcy filing. All seven classes of public debtholders accepted the plan. However, Crystal Oil's two most senior creditors, Bankers Trust and Halliburton Company, did not initially accept the plan. Both had liens on Crystal Oil's oil and gas properties. Bankers Trust eventually accepted a revised plan. Halliburton never did. The Bankruptcy Court approved the plan over Halliburton's objection.

The prepackaged process works best when there is only one class of creditors that will be disadvantaged by the plan, and when the debtor can obtain the approval of that class before the bankruptcy filing. If a debtor has a large number of separate classes of creditors, the negotiations might be very time-consuming. The debtor might have to file for bankruptcy before it is able to get all the acceptances it needs. Also, trade creditors (because of their general lack of sophistication) often resist prepackaging attempts. If the debtor can pay them in full, the prepackaged strategy stands a greater chance of succeeding. Generally, prepackaged bankruptcies work best for holding companies with at most a few classes of debt and few trade creditors.

Review

1. What is a prepackaged bankruptcy? How does it work?
2. What are the four main advantages of a prepackaged bankruptcy?
3. When does the prepackaged process work best?

26.7 CHAPTER 7 OF THE BANKRUPTCY CODE—LIQUIDATION

When the prospects for reorganizing a debtor are so poor that it would be unreasonable to invest further time, effort, and financial resources in the effort, the only alternative is liquidation. The firm or its creditors file a petition under Chapter 7 (bankruptcy with intent to liquidate the firm). In some cases, the parties to a Chapter 11 cannot agree upon a plan of reorganization and decide to convert to a Chapter 7. Pan Am Corporation and Eastern Airlines are examples.

Liquidation is preferable to reorganization when selling the debtor's assets in liquidation would produce value that exceeds the debtor's reorganization value. Usually, the key variables are time and risk. For instance, the financial advisors of the debtor may believe that the realizable economic value of the debtor will eventually exceed the liquidation value. But suppose the value to be realized and the time it would take are highly uncertain. In that case, the expected present value of the debtor's assets as a going concern might be less than their currently realizable liquidation value. Then liquidation is in the best interest of creditors.

Liquidation Value

Liquidation value does not necessarily mean the amount of cash the debtor's estate would realize through a forced sale of the debtor's assets. Rather, it refers to the amount that could be realized through an orderly sale. Liquidation value is usually lower than reorganization value. For example, inventories of items that are protected by manufacturer warranties, such as electronic goods, will be heavily discounted in the event of liquidation.

Liquidation value must generally be estimated for each asset class. The aggregate liquidation value of all of the debtor's assets, less the costs of the liquidation process, is then compared to the reorganization value. Reorganization value can be estimated by applying the valuation techniques covered in Chapter 25.

Table 26.7 illustrates the distributions to creditors in a Chapter 7 bankruptcy. The absolute priority doctrine must be followed in a liquidation. Recall that under this doctrine, claims with a higher priority must be paid in full before junior claims can receive anything. If the going-concern value of Olympic Computer was $4 million, then liquidation would be in the best interest of creditors.

Liquidation Process

Liquidation can take the form of either an assignment or a formal court-supervised liquidation. Assignment is a private method of disposition. Assets are assigned to a trustee, usually selected by the creditors, who liquidates them, usually by auction. Proceeds from the sale are then distributed to the creditors. The firm ceases to exist.[7] Rarely are the funds realized sufficient to pay off all creditors' claims in full. Equity investors generally have their investments in the debtor wiped out. Assignment is usually faster and less costly than the more rigid court-supervised liquidation procedure.

Review

1. When will it be better to liquidate a debtor than to attempt a reorganization?
2. What do we mean by the term *liquidation value* of a debtor's assets?
3. Must the absolute priority doctrine be followed in a liquidation?

---

[7]Thus, the creditors never assume ownership of the firm, as they usually do following a reorganization.

26.8 AN INTERNATIONAL PERSPECTIVE

Bankruptcy laws vary greatly from country to country.[8] As we have seen, U.S. bankruptcy law emphasizes reorganizing a distressed firm. In contrast, most other nations place more emphasis on recovering creditors' funds and favor liquidation over reorganization, although this is changing. Recent reforms have favored reorganization, simplified payment priorities, brought secured creditors into the process, and increased cross-border cooperation. For example, recent bankruptcy legislation in Canada has struck a better balance between the rights of creditors and debtors by providing a new, more effective mechanism for reorganization. In Germany, a new reorganization process is similar to that of the United States. It provides for a decision period at the start of every bankruptcy case to determine whether to liquidate or attempt to reorganize the debtor.

The failures of large multinational firms that can file for bankruptcy protection in more than one country, as Maxwell Communication and Olympia & York Development did, will increase the pressure for international bankruptcy reform. In response, the United Nations Commission on International Trade Law recently adopted a Model Law on Cross-Border Insolvency, which is gradually being incorporated into bankruptcy laws. We think the U.S. will conform its law to this model.

Bankruptcy Around the World

Figure 26.3 compares the actual number of business bankruptcies in a recent year and the number of business bankruptcies per capita in 12 industrial nations. France had more business

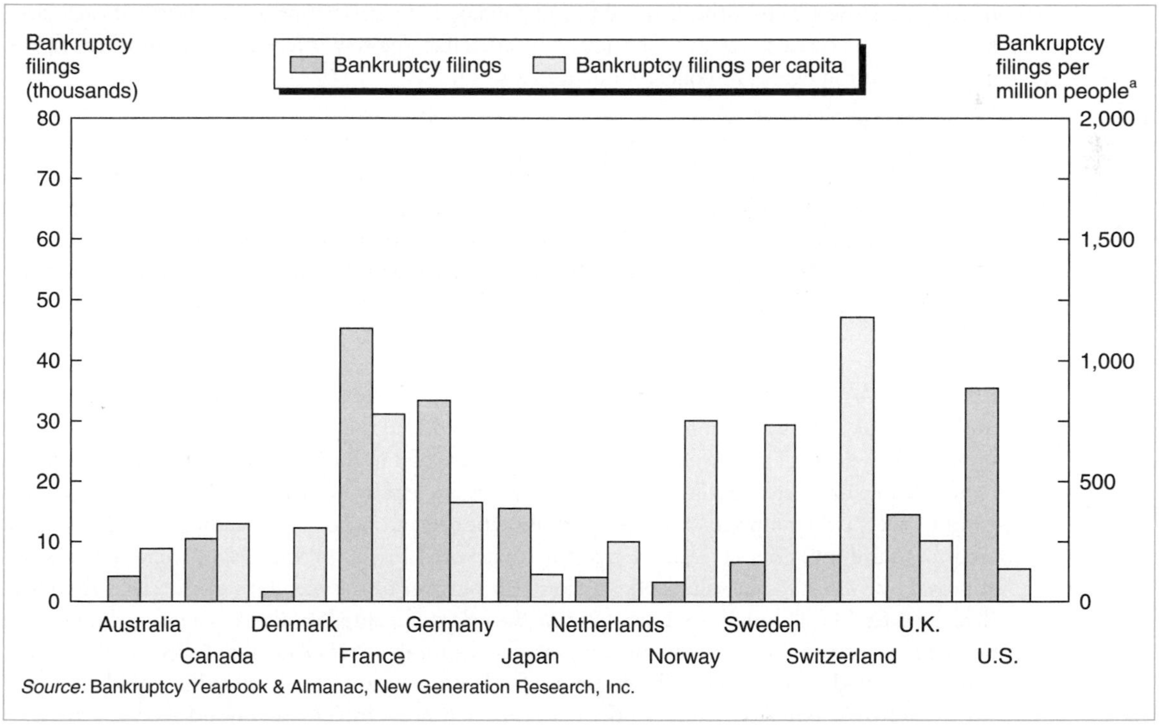

[a]Number of business bankruptcy filings per million people.

FIGURE 26.3
Business bankruptcies in 12 countries.

[8]A good source of information concerning the bankruptcy laws of different countries is *Multinational Commercial Insolvency* published by the American Bar Association.

bankruptcies than the United States. Relative to the size of the countries, Switzerland, France, and Norway had the greatest number of business bankruptcies.

In the balance of this section, we discuss the bankruptcy laws of Canada and Mexico, to illustrate different national approaches to resolving financial distress.

Bankruptcy in Canada

In Canada there are three possible strategies for reorganizing a distressed firm: (1) informal restructuring, (2) restructuring under the Companies' Creditors Arrangement Act (CCAA), and (3) reorganization under the Bankruptcy and Insolvency Act (BIA, enacted in 1992). Informal out-of-court restructurings in Canada are similar to those in the United States.

REORGANIZATION UNDER THE CCAA The CCAA has been described as one of the most unusual reorganization laws in the world.[9] Adopted during the Great Depression, it was designed for reorganizing large, insolvent public firms with complicated debt structures. But bankruptcy professionals in Canada were dissatisfied with the old, pre-BIA bankruptcy law. They decided to apply the CCAA to small and medium-sized bankruptcies as well as large ones.

The CCAA has evolved into a rough equivalent of U.S. Chapter 11. For example, the CCAA allows for a stay against both secured and unsecured creditors although it is not automatic; the debtor must apply to the court. There are other important differences. The CCAA lacks rules for classifying creditors. It also lacks the detailed procedures of Chapter 11. There is no cram-down or other means of dealing with dissenting creditors. A proposed plan of reorganization must be approved by two-thirds in value and a majority in number of the members of each class, including unaffected classes. If it is rejected by any class, the stay is lifted and creditors are free to move against the debtor to collect on their loans.

EXAMPLE Olympia & York's Bankruptcy

Several years ago, Olympia & York (O&Y) filed for protection under the CCAA for 29 affiliated firms (mostly subsidiaries), five of which also filed for protection under Chapter 11 in the United States. After months of difficult negotiations, O&Y presented a restructuring plan. A significantly amended plan was approved by creditors and the courts about five months later.

REORGANIZATION UNDER THE BIA An insolvent firm can file for protection from creditors under the BIA. Creditor actions are automatically stayed, and the debtor must offer a proposal to its unsecured creditors. The firm may also submit the proposal to the secured creditors, but this is not required. The unsecured creditors can be treated as a single class. If each class of unsecured creditors votes to accept the proposal, and the court also approves it, it becomes binding on all unsecured creditors (and any class of secured creditors that voted to accept it). Class acceptance requires approval by two-thirds in value and a majority in number of the members of the class who voted (like Chapter 11). The proposal is not binding on a class of secured creditors that either did not vote or voted to reject. They are free to move against the debtor to seize collateral or collect on their loans. If the unsecured creditors reject the proposal, the debtor is automatically placed in liquidation.

The BIA shifted the focus of the bankruptcy process in Canada toward reorganization. It was intended to replace the CCAA. But the CCAA affords considerable flexibility in handling reorganizations, which many bankruptcy professionals in Canada find advantageous. Due to the CCAA's popularity, the Canadian government has not repealed it.

---

[9]E. Bruce Leonard, "Commercial Organizations Under the Bankruptcy and Insolvency Act—Canada," in *Multinational Commercial Insolvency,* Chicago: American Bar Association, 1993, p. F-2.

Bankruptcy in Mexico

Mexico recently enacted a new bankruptcy law that provides for both reorganization and liquidation and is very similar to the U.S. bankruptcy code. Under the first alternative, the debtor requests the bankruptcy court to order a suspension of payments. That order halts debt payments and gives the debtor time to try to negotiate a preventive agreement and a payment plan with its creditors under the supervision of a "conciliator." At least two-thirds in amount and a majority in number of the holders of secured and unsecured claims who vote must approve the agreement. If the creditors reject the agreement, the firm must be liquidated.

A suspension of payments is similar to a U.S. Chapter 11 bankruptcy in that creditors are stayed from enforcing their claims, and the debtor continues to operate its business under court supervision while it negotiates with creditors. The new law includes a cramdown provision just like U.S. law: the plan is binding on all creditors of every class, including those who do not agree to the plan. It also provides that sales of assets for less than market value or repayment of debt before it comes due that occur within 270 days of the bankruptcy filing are presumed fraudulent and may be reclaimed by the debtor.

Review

1. In what critical respect does U.S. bankruptcy law differ from the bankruptcy laws of most other countries?
2. How is reorganization under the Companies' Creditors Arrangement Act of Canada similar to a U.S. Chapter 11 reorganization? How is it different?
3. How is a suspension of payments under Mexican bankruptcy law similar to the automatic stay under U.S. Chapter 11? How is it different?

SUMMARY

- A firm seeks protection from its creditors under Chapter 11 when it is no longer able to pay its debts as they come due, or when it anticipates future liabilities that it will not be able to meet. Chapter 11 has a guiding principle. A debtor should be given the opportunity to negotiate with its creditors and achieve a plan of reorganization, provided that the value of the reorganized debtor exceeds its liquidation value.
- An out-of-court restructuring is normally less expensive and less time-consuming than a Chapter 11 reorganization.
- When a distressed firm's liquidation value exceeds its reorganization value, it should file for liquidation under Chapter 7.
- A debtor undergoing reorganization under Chapter 11 has the exclusive right to propose a plan of reorganization for 120 days from the date it filed the bankruptcy petition. It must ensure that the plan it proposes complies with the requirements for plan confirmation contained in the bankruptcy code.
- Financial distress does not occur without warning. Creditors can use multiple discriminant analysis (MDA) to predict a firm's financial distress.
- A prepackaged bankruptcy has several advantages over an out-of-court restructuring. It is an effective way to deal with the holdout problem.
- Absolute priority is not always observed in bankruptcy. In many cases, making a small distribution to a dissenting class will be advantageous to senior creditors. Buying their support is likely to speed up the reorganization process and reduce expenses.

- It is not necessary to secure the approval of every class of creditors in Chapter 11. The bankruptcy code contains a cramdown provision to deal with dissenting class(es). Cramdown should be used when it is cheaper than increasing the distributions to the dissenting class(es).

EQUATION SUMMARY

$$Z = 0.012X_1 + 0.014X_2 + 0.033X_3 + 0.006X_4 + 0.999X_5 \tag{26.1}$$

QUESTIONS

1. Define "corporate financial distress."
2. What are some useful indicators of impending corporate financial distress?
3. What is the purpose of the bankruptcy code? When should a firm file for bankruptcy?
4. How do a Chapter 7 liquidation and a Chapter 11 reorganization differ?
5. What is the main cause of corporate financial distress? What role do factors outside the firm play?
6. How does the age of the firm affect the probability of bankruptcy?
7. What is the basic premise of Chapter 11?
8. Explain the meaning of the following terms: (a) debtor in possession, (b) automatic stay, (c) plan of reorganization, (d) consensual plan of reorganization, (e) cramdown, and (f) prepackaged bankruptcy.
9. What is the purpose of the cramdown provision?
10. Under what circumstances will: (a) Reorganization be preferred over liquidation? (b) Liquidation be preferred over reorganization?
11. Under what circumstances is a prepackaged bankruptcy attempt most likely to succeed?
12. Explain what is meant by the absolute priority doctrine. What are the arguments for and against enforcing absolute priority in reorganization?
13. Why can we not rely on just one variable to predict bankruptcy?
14. Describe the positive and negative incentives a financially distressed firm can use to encourage securityholders to participate in an exchange offer.
15. What is a holdout? How can holdouts frustrate the financial reorganization process?
16. What are the main advantages and disadvantages of an out-of-court restructuring compared to bankruptcy?
17. What are the five basic conditions a plan of reorganization must staisfy to be confirmed by the bankruptcy court?

CHALLENGING QUESTIONS

18. What is multiple discriminant analysis (MDA)? Why is it used to predict financial distress?
19. What role does valuation play in the bankruptcy process? Explain how the DCF approach could be used to determine reorganization value.
20. How has the addition of Chapter 11 to the bankruptcy code potentially reduced the costs of bankruptcy?
21. Should the increase in the number of bankruptcy filings since the Bankruptcy Reform Act of 1978 was enacted be a cause for concern?

22. How would the following classes of claims and interests be ordered for bankruptcy purposes:
    (a) Accounts payable
    (b) Legal fees due to the bankruptcy process
    (c) First mortgage bonds
    (d) Common stock
    (e) Unsecured bank debt
    (f) Second mortgage bonds
    (g) Bank debt secured by current assets
    (h) Preferred stock
    (i) Debentures subordinated to all bank debt
    (j) Tax claims
23. How is the growing importance of financial intermediaries likely to affect the reorganization process?

PROBLEMS

LEVEL A (BASIC)

A1. (Altman *Z*-score) Suppose a firm's financial statements indicate the following financial ratio values:

$$X_1 = 5\% \quad X_2 = 10\% \quad X_3 = -5\% \quad X_4 = 50\% \quad X_5 = 1.05$$

a. Calculate the *Z*-score using the Altman model, Equation (26.1).

b. Is the firm likely to go bankrupt within one year?

A2. (Altman *Z*-score) Suppose a firm's financial statements indicate the following financial ratio values:

$$X_1 = 5\% \quad X_2 = 20\% \quad X_3 = 2\% \quad X_4 = 110\% \quad X_5 = 1.25$$

a. Calculate the *Z*-score using the Altman model, Equation (26.1).

b. Is the firm likely to go bankrupt within one year?

A3. (Liquidation versus reorganization) A firm's liquidation value is $80 million. Under reorganization, its annual after-tax operating cash flows will be $10 million indefinitely. If the appropriate discount rate is 10%, should the firm liquidate or reorganize?

A4. (Liquidation versus reorganization) A firm is deciding whether to file a Chapter 7 or Chapter 11 bankruptcy. Its liquidation value is $125 million. Under reorganization, the firm will generate $13 million per year indefinitely. If the required return is 12%, should the firm file for bankruptcy under Chapter 7 or Chapter 11?

A5. (Liquidation versus reorganization) Pinto Brothers, Inc. is in financial distress. If Pinto reorganizes, the following cash flows ($1,000,000s) are expected:

YEAR	1	2	3	4	5
CF	100	120	140	160	180

If the liquidation value is $600 million and the opportunity cost of funds is 10%, should Pinto liquidate or reorganize?

A6. (Liquidation versus reorganization) The firm you work for is trying to decide whether to file a Chapter 7 or a Chapter 11 bankruptcy. If it chooses to reorganize, the following future cash flows ($1,000,000s) are expected:

YEAR	1	2	3	4	5
CF	20	25	30	35	40

The appropriate discount rate is 13%. The liquidation value of the firm is $100 million. Should the firm file a Chapter 7 or a Chapter 11 bankruptcy?

LEVEL B

B1. (Value of debt received in a reorganization) A reorganization plan provides that creditors will receive new debt. It will pay a 10% coupon annually and mature in a lump sum at the end of 10 years. The debtor's financial advisors estimate that the required return for the new debt is 16%. What is the new debt worth as a percentage of its face amount?

B2. (Value of debt received in a reorganization) A reorganization plan provides that creditors will receive new debt. It will pay a 12% coupon annually and mature in a lump sum at the end of 15 years. The debtor's financial advisors estimate that the required return for the new debt is 15%. What is the new debt worth as a percentage of its face amount?

B3. (Distributions in bankruptcy) In the cramdown example presented in the chapter, suppose that Olympic Computer's subordinated debt is subordinated not only to the bank debt but also to the accounts payable and the mortgage bonds. How would the distributions in a cramdown change?

B4. (Distributions in bankruptcy) A firm had assets worth $700 million. It borrowed $100 million, which was secured by a mortgage on it newest factory. The firm also borrowed $200 million on an unsecured basis. The firm subsequently goes bankrupt, and its assets are worth just $150 million. Its newest factory can only be sold for $50 million. Who gets what?

B5. (Distributions in bankruptcy) A firm had assets worth $100 million. It borrowed $20 million, which was secured by a mortgage on its newest land acquisition. The firm also borrowed $15 million on an unsecured basis. The firm subsequently goes bankrupt, and its assets are worth just $20 million. Its newest land acquisition can only be sold for $10 million. Who gets what?

B6. (Liquidation) Boris Baking is in bankruptcy. Because it is worth less as a going concern than in liquidation, the firm will be liquidated. The firm's balance sheet prior to bankruptcy is:

ASSETS		LIABILITIES AND STOCKHOLDERS' EQUITY	
Cash	$ 500	Accounts payable	$1,500
Accounts receivable	2,000	Bank loan	1,500
Inventory	2,000	Mortgage bond	4,000
Fixed assets	5,000	Subordinated debenture	2,500
		Preferred stock	500
		Common stock	(500)
Total assets	$9,500	Total liabilities and equity	$9,500

The bank loan is secured by accounts receivable and the mortgage bond is secured by fixed assets. The subordinated debenture is subordinated to the mortgage bond. The liquidation values for the assets are $500 for cash, $1,600 for accounts receivable, $1,000 for inventory, and $2,500 for fixed assets. How will the $5,600 total liquidation value be allocated among the firm's claimants? Assume that there are $500 of administrative expenses (for legal and accounting fees) and that absolute priority is followed.

B7. (Liquidation) Downtown Crafts is in bankruptcy. Because it is worth less as a going concern than in liquidation, the firm will be liquidated. The firm's balance sheet prior to bankruptcy is:

ASSETS		LIABILITIES AND STOCKHOLDERS' EQUITY	
Cash	$ 250	Accounts payable	$ 750
Accounts receivable	1,000	Bank loan	750
Inventory	1,000	Mortgage bond	2,000
Fixed assets	2,500	Subordinated debenture	1,250
		Preferred stock	250
		Common stock	(250)
Total assets	$4,750	Total liabilities and equity	$4,750

The bank loan is secured by accounts receivable and the mortgage bond is secured by fixed assets. The subordinated debenture is subordinated to the mortgage bond. The liquidation values for the assets are $250 for cash, $800 for accounts receivable, $500 for inventory, and $1,250 for fixed asscts. IIow will the $2,800 total liquidation value be allocated among the firm's claimants? Assume that there are $250 of administrative expenses (for legal and accounting fees) and that absolute priority is followed.

B8. (Standards of fairness) Divided Airlines Corporation has $100 million of subordinated debentures outstanding, which are expressly subordinated to the firm's bank debt. Outstanding bank debt totals $500 million. It also has $200 million of accounts payable. Divided Airlines goes bankrupt. The fair market value of its assets is estimated to be $600 million. The firm proposes in its plan of reorganization to pay the banks $400 million, the trade creditors $150 million, and the subordinated debenture holders $50 million.

a. Against whom does the proposed plan discriminate unfairly?

b. Suppose the bank creditors vote to reject the proposed plan. Can it meet the fair-and-equitable test?

B9. (Standards of fairness) Assume the same facts as in problem B8. A revised plan of reorganization proposes to pay the banks $500 million, the trade creditors $100 million, and the subordinated debenture holders nothing.

a. Against whom does the revised plan discriminate unfairly?

b. Suppose the trade creditors vote to reject the plan. Could it be crammed down?

B10. (Standards of fairness) Assume the same facts as in problem B8 except that Divided Airlines is worth $700 million. The banks propose a plan of reorganization in which they would be paid $500 million, the trade creditors would be paid $175 million, and the subordinated debenture holders would be paid $25 million. Against whom does the plan discriminate unfairly?

B11. (Excel: Altman *Z*-score) Create a spreadsheet model that uses the Altman model to evaluate the likelihood of failure for a firm with the five inputs (X_1= net working capital/total assets, X_2= retained earnings/total assets, X_3= EBIT/total assets, X_4= market value of equity/book value of total liabilities, and X_5= sales/total assets). Use the equation $Z = 0.012X_1 + 0.014X_2 + 0.033X_3 + 0.006X_4 + 0.999X_5$. If the computed Z is greater than 2.99, print "unlikely to fail." If it is between 1.81 and 2.99, print "gray area." If Z is less than 1.81, print "likely to fail."

Evaluate the following six firms based on the five input variables:

FIRM	X_1	X_2	X_3	X_4	X_5
1	10%	35%	13%	150%	0.90
2	4%	−10%	−7%	3%	1.20
3	5%	20%	10%	70%	0.80
4	2%	26%	12%	55%	1.10
5	4%	50%	8%	60%	0.90
6	8%	1%	4%	25%	0.80

B12. (Excel: Liquidation) Dude Realty is in bankruptcy. Because Dude is worth less as a going concern than in liquidation, the firm will be liquidated. The firm's balance sheet prior to bankruptcy is:

ASSETS		LIABILITIES AND STOCKHOLDERS' EQUITY	
Cash	$ 400	Accounts payable	$1,000
Accounts receivable	2,000	Bank loan	1,800
Inventory	1,000	Mortgage bond	2,000
Fixed assets	3,000	Subordinated debenture	2,200
		Preferred stock	300
		Common stock	(900)
Total assets	$6,400	Total liabilities and equity	$6,400

The bank loan is secured by accounts receivable and the mortgage bond is secured by fixed assets. The subordinated debenture is subordinated to the mortgage bond. The liquidation values for the assets are $400 for cash, $1,600 for accounts receivable, and $500 for inventory. The liquidation value of the fixed assets is expected to be somewhere between $1,000 and $2,500. Prepare a spreadsheet showing how the total liquidation value will be allocated among the firm's claimants. Assume that the liquidation value of the fixed assets assumes one of four values: $1,000, $1,500, $2,000, and $2,500. Assume that there are $300 of administrative expenses (for legal and accounting fees) and that absolute priority is followed. In your model, put the types of claimants in the rows and use four columns for the differing liquidation values for fixed assets.

LEVEL C (ADVANCED)

C1. (Cramdown and negotiation) Local Business Machines Corporation is a distressed manufacturer of personal computers. Its balance sheet is shown in Table 26.10, and its income statement for the latest 12-month period is shown in Table 26.11. Income statements for the prior five years show a steady stream of significant losses. Lately, Local Business Machines has been selling assets to meet interest payments.

a. Is the fair market value of Local Business Machine's assets likely to differ from their book value? Explain.

b. Assume that the fair market value of the accounts receivable and inventory is $16 million each, plant and equipment is $25 million, and other assets is $2 million. How would value be distributed in a cramdown situation?

c. What issues would each of the classes of claims holders be likely to raise as they negotiate a plan of reorganization?

C2. (Financial distress and bankruptcy) Dissipated Technologies Corporation has a capital structure consisting of (1) $5 million principal amount of secured debt due in 10 years, (2) $2.5 million of unsecured debentures due in one year, and (3) common stock. Dissipated Technologies defaults on an interest payment to the unsecured debenture holders. They elect, through their trustee, to accelerate the debt. (How can they do this?) The debenture holders bring suit and obtain a judgment. Dissipated Technologies, not having any cash, cannot pay. Under a cross-default provision in the secured debt's indenture, its maturity is accelerated. The secured creditor demands payment. Dissipated Technologies, still without cash, refuses. The debenture holders begin attachment proceedings on Dissipated Technologies' unpledged property. The secured creditor begins a proceeding to arrange for a sheriff's sale of the property (about one-half of the property of Dissipated Technologies) on which it has a lien. The proceeds of such a sale would be used to satisfy its claim.

TABLE 26.10
Balance sheet of Local Business Machines Corporation.

LOCAL BUSINESS MACHINES CORPORATION
Balance Sheet Before Reorganization
($ millions)

Assets		**Liabilities and Shareholders' Equity**	
Current Assets:		Current Liabilities:	
Cash	$ 10	Bank debt due within one year[a]	$ 50
Accounts receivable	20	Account payable	30
Inventory	20	Total current liabilities	80
Total current assets	50		
		Long-term debt:	
Plant and equipment	100	10% senior debentures	20
Less accumulated depreciation	(60)	9% mortgage bonds due 2006[b]	20
	40	14% subordinated debentures due 1997[c]	30
Other assets	10	Total long-term debt	70
		Accumulated shareholders' deficit	(50)
Total assets	$100	Total liabilities and shareholders' equity	$100

[a]Secured by accounts receivable and inventory.
[b]Secured by all plant and equipment.
[c]Subordinated to senior debentures and bank debt.

TABLE 26.11
Income statement for Local Business Machines Corporation.

LOCAL BUSINESS MACHINES CORPORATION

Income Statement for the Latest 12 Months
($ millions)

Gross sales	$100
Cost of goods sold	(90)
Gross profit	10
Depreciation	(5)
Income before interest expense	5
Interest expense	(12)
Loss	$ (7)

a. Dissipated Technologies files a bankruptcy petition. The debenture holders' and secured creditor's proceedings stop. Why? Does any section of the bankruptcy code require this?

Dissipated Technologies proposes the following reorganization plan: (1) The secured creditor will have her maturity reinstated and interest payments will be paid when due under the old indenture. Her lien on Dissipated Technologies' property will continue. One interest payment was missed during the reorganization proceedings. She will be paid the missed interest payment with an added premium for the delay. (2) The unsecured creditors will receive six annual installments of $600,000 each. (3) The common stockholders will remain as such. Dissipated Technologies is valued at $6 million.

b. The secured creditor objects to the plan. The unsecured creditors and shareholders accept the plan. Can the bankruptcy court confirm the plan over the secured creditor's objection?

c. Suppose instead that one debenture holder (out of the 100 debenture holders in all) holding 25% of the principal amount of the outstanding debentures objects but the secured creditor accepts the plan. Can the bankruptcy court confirm the plan over the debenture holder's objection?

d. Suppose instead that all the debenture holders object whereas the secured creditor again accepts the plan. Can the plan be confirmed?

e. What did the balance sheet of Dissipated Technologies look like? What would it look like if the plan is confirmed?

MINICASE CRYSTAL OIL'S PREPACKAGED BANKRUPTCY

Crystal Oil Company (Crystal Oil) was engaged mainly in crude oil and natural gas exploration and production. A worldwide decline in the demand for crude oil and natural gas led to a decline in oil and gas prices, which threatened Crystal Oil's ability to meet its debt service obligations. The firm sold many properties as well as its refinery assets, greatly reduced its exploration activities, and cut back its investments in producing properties in an effort to cope with its financial problems. It then restructured some of its debt by (1) extending the maturity of a large trade payable to Halliburton Company by two years; (2) exchanging approximately $125 million face amount of new 15% notes and 7,418,000 shares of its common stock for approximately $234 million face amount of old debentures, which reduced its annual interest cost by $12.7 million; and (3) exercising its option to pay interest on the new 15% notes in common stock rather than cash.

Crystal Oil had negative income for several years. As its troubles mounted, it lost $213.7 million in the first half of that year, having also lost $67.8 million in the previous year. As a result of these losses, its balance sheet had a large negative stockholders' equity:

BALANCE SHEET
(Dollar amounts in thousands)

Current assets	$ 21,721	Total liabilities	$370,961
Long-term assets	104,332	Stockholders' equity	(244,908)
Total assets	$126,053	Total capitalization	$126,053

At that point, Crystal Oil was no longer in compliance with some of its debt covenants, had defaulted on a scheduled interest payment, and suspended all payments on its secured trade debt to Halliburton. This was followed by defaulting on scheduled interest payments for four other debt issues.

Crystal Oil finally concluded that it could not continue as a going concern unless it substantially reduced its outstanding debt and put together a plan of reorganization. The plan would reduce the outstanding face amount of debt from $277.4 million to $129.0 million (with a fair market value of $75.8 million). The holders of the old debt that would be eliminated would receive a combination of new notes, new preferred stock, new common stock, and new warrants. Crystal Oil presented its plan to Bankers Trust, Halliburton, and all its unsecured creditors. It asked these creditors to vote on the plan. If it could get enough favorable votes, it would file the prepackaged plan along with a voluntary petition for reorganization under Chapter 11, and simultaneously seek the plan's immediate confirmation. Under the plan, the capitalization of the reorganized Crystal Oil would be as shown in the following table (dollar amounts in thousands):

New bank note (issued to Bankers Trust)	$ 43,651
New Halliburton note (issued to Halliburton)	10,278
New convertible secured notes	21,114
Other liabilities	747
Total liabilities	75,790
Preferred stockholders' equity	1,170
Common stockholders' equity	53,268
Total capitalization	$130,228

The upper part of the table below shows the distributions to creditors and stockholders under the proposed plan and, alternatively, what they could expect to get if Crystal Oil were liquidated. The lower part provides a statement of projected cash flows for Crystal Oil. Year 1 is the current year, which is about half over.

DISTRIBUTIONS TO CRYSTAL OIL'S CREDITORS AND SHAREHOLDERS UNDER THE PROPOSED PLAN OF REORGANIZATION (DOLLAR AMOUNTS IN THOUSANDS)

CLASS OF CLAIMS OR INTERESTS	LIQUIDATION (000s)	New Blank Note	New Halliburton Note	New Convertible Notes	Other Liabilities	New Preferred Stock	New Common Stock and Warrants	Total
Bankers Trust	$43,864	$43,651	—	—	—	—	$ 213	$ 43,864
Halliburton	10,515	—	$10,278	—	—	—	237	10,515
15% Notes[1]	14,919	—	—	$21,114	—	$20,784	1,730	43,628
Other liabilities[2]	22	—	—	—	$747	—	—	747
Debentures[3]	—	—	—	—	—	27,761	1,252	29,013
Common stock	—	—	—	—	—	—	2,461	2,461
								$130,228

PROJECTED CASH FLOWS (DOLLAR AMOUNTS IN THOUSANDS)

	Year 1	Year 2	Year 3	Year 4	Year 5	Year 6	Year 7	Year 8	Year 9	Year 10	Year 11
Cash at beginning of year	$ 9,231	$ 3,153	$ 4,000	$ 3,362	$ 4,000	$10,795	$24,708	$34,720	$52,470	$57,939	$60,167
Cash flow from operations before debt expense	24,683	18,696	25,752	24,903	26,464	23,469	20,928	19,307	17,396	13,276	6,007
Planned capital expenditures	(6,957)	(1,736)	(13,733)	(6,287)	(10,412)	(9,451)	(10,827)	(1,483)	(1,868)	(1,003)	(675)
Cash available for debt service	26,957	20,113	16,019	21,978	20,052	24,813	34,809	52,544	67,998	70,212	65,499
Debt service	(23,804)	(16,113)	(12,657)	(17,978)	(9,257)	(105)	(89)	(74)	(10,059)	(10,045)	(55,122)
Cash at end of year	$ 3,153	$ 4,000	$ 3,362	$ 4,000	$10,795	$24,708	$34,720	$52,470	$57,939	$60,167	$10,377

[1] Ranks junior to the Bankers Trust and Halliburton debt.
[2] Ranks junior to the secured portion of the 15% Notes and to the Bankers Trust and Halliburton debt.
[3] Ranks junior to all other liabilities.
Source: Crystal Oil Company, *Disclosure Statement.*

QUESTIONS

1. Describe Crystal Oil's situation in terms of being (a) bankrupt, (b) in default, (c) failed, (d) insolvent.
2. Based on the information given in the lower part of the table, explain whether you think the proposed plan satisfies the feasibility and best-interests-of-creditors tests.
3. The 15% notes had 234 claimants with an aggregate claim of $134,542,000. What must happen for the class of claims to vote in favor of Crystal Oil's plan? If the plan went through, the holders of the 15% notes would receive only $43,628,000. How do you explain the distribution of $2,461,000 to common stockholders?
4. If the classes of debenture holders (there are actually two such classes) vote to reject the plan, could it still pass the fair-and-equitable test? Could it pass this test if just one of the debenture holder classes votes to reject?
5. The discussion in the Crystal Oil Company's prepackaged bankruptcy example in the chapter noted that Halliburton never accepted Crystal Oil's plan, but that the bankruptcy court approved it anyway. How could that happen?

27

INTERNATIONAL CORPORATE FINANCE

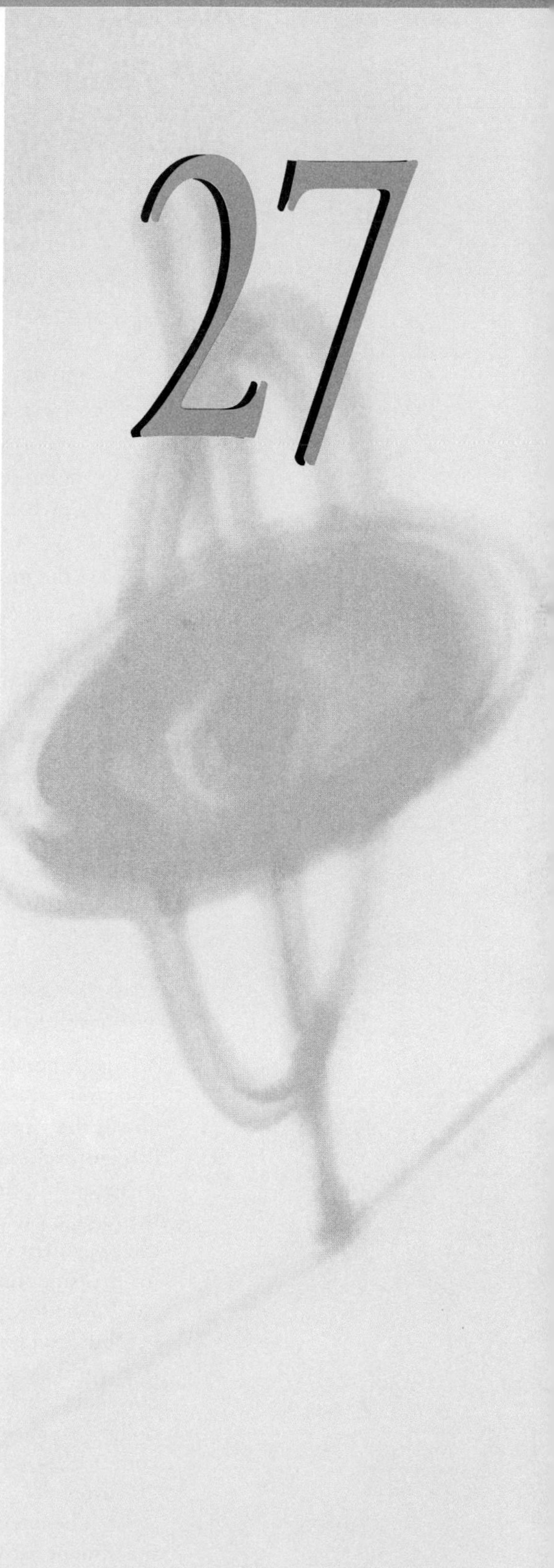

Successful firms today have a global perspective and operate in many countries. As a result, the distinction between U.S. firms and foreign firms has become blurred as the leading firms have evolved into truly **multinational firms.** When Germany's Daimler-Benz AG combined with Chrysler Corp. of the U.S. in 1998, Chrysler Corp. Chairman Robert Eaton said, "This is not going to be a German company; it is not going to be an American company; it's going to be a multinational company." Daimler-Chrysler was the first major non-North American firm to trade the same 'ordinary' common shares on the NYSE as it did in its home market (Frankfurt, Germany).

The Coca-Cola Company sells its familiar soft drink virtually everywhere and derives two-thirds of its sales and three-quarters of its operating profits outside the United States. Exxon Mobil Corporation produces oil and gas in the North Sea, off Norway and the United Kingdom, and in Australia, Indonesia, and Malaysia. The Walt Disney Company has huge theme parks located near Paris and Tokyo. Australia's News Corporation owns the Fox Broadcasting Network, Twentieth Century Fox film studio, HarperCollins Publishers, and TV Guide. Japan's Toyota Motor Corporation manufactures automobiles in California, Indiana, and Kentucky.

The Principles of Finance do not stop at the border. They apply no matter where the firm has its base and where it operates. The fundamental goal of a multinational firm also remains unchanged: Maximize shareholder wealth. The main complication concerns foreign currencies, but multinational firms must also contend with changing interest rates and inflation rates among countries. Multinational firms must manage the complex risks they face.

In this chapter, we explain how the foreign exchange markets operate and describe the methods they offer to help manage foreign exchange risk. We also show how to take foreign exchange risk into account when evaluating proposed capital budgeting projects and analyzing foreign-currency-denominated financing alternatives.

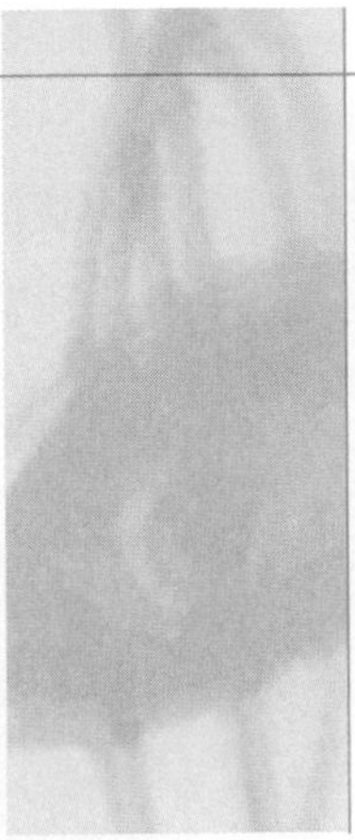

FOCUS ON PRINCIPLES

- *Self-Interested Behavior:* Seek out investments that offer the greatest expected risk-adjusted real return.
- *Two-Sided Transactions:* You can use derivatives to transfer foreign exchange risk to others. Derivatives do not eliminate risk; they only transfer it.
- *Valuable Ideas:* Look for opportunities to invest in positive-NPV projects in foreign markets or to develop derivatives or design arrangements that enable firms to cope better with the risks they face in their foreign operations. Also, look for opportunities to develop new positive-NPV financing mechanisms.
- *Comparative Advantage:* Transfer foreign exchange risk to other parties if they are willing to bear these risks more cheaply.
- *Options:* Recognize the value of hidden options in a situation, such as the foreign exchange options in some derivative instruments.
- *Incremental Benefits:* Calculate the net advantage of a foreign project on the basis of the incremental after-tax cash flows the project will provide.
- *Risk-Return Trade-Off:* To transfer risk to another party, you must offer a return that fully compensates for the amount of risk transferred.
- *Diversification:* Diversifying internationally is valuable when the returns from a foreign investment are not perfectly correlated with the returns on any subset of the U.S. market portfolio.
- *Capital Market Efficiency:* You cannot forecast foreign exchange rate movements precisely. You should use forward rates as quoted in the foreign exchange market rather than internal exchange rate forecasts.
- *Time Value of Money:* Use discounted-cash-flow analysis to measure the net present value of a foreign investment project.

27.1 THE FOREIGN EXCHANGE MARKET

A large American department store chain has signed an agreement to import fine English china. The contract calls for the American firm to pay the British exporting firm in British pounds. To do so, the American firm must purchase British pounds in the foreign exchange market. The **foreign exchange market** is the market that trades one country's currency for another country's currency. In our example, the American firm would exchange U.S. dollars for British pounds in the foreign exchange market and pay the exporter's invoice. Alternatively, if the contract had specified payment in U.S. dollars, the exporter would have received dollars and then sold the dollars for British pounds in the foreign exchange market.

The foreign exchange market is the world's largest financial market. It is a worldwide market, but London, New York, and Tokyo are the major centers of activity. The larger commercial banks and the central banks are the principal market participants, and firms generally buy and sell currencies through a commercial bank. Most of the trading takes place in five currencies: U.S. dollar ($), euro (€), Swiss franc (SF), Japanese yen (¥), and British pound (£). The euro is the common currency of the countries that make up the European Monetary Union. Table 27.1 lists 20 currencies and their symbols.

The foreign exchange market is an over-the-counter market. The large commercial banks and investment banks are the major participants. Some other participants include: importers, who need foreign currency to pay for the goods they import; money managers, who buy and sell foreign stocks and bonds; and multinational firms, who invest in facilities and sell goods in foreign markets.

TABLE 27.1
Twenty currencies and their symbols.

COUNTRY	CURRENCY	SYMBOL	COUNTRY	CURRENCY	SYMBOL
Argentina	Peso	Arg$	Japan	Yen	¥
Australia	Dollar	$A	Mexico	Peso	Mex$
Botswana	Pula	P	Poland	Zloty	PLN
Canada	Dollar	Can$	Russia	Ruble	Rb
Chile	Peso	Ch$	Saudi Arabia	Riyal	SRIs
Denmark	Krone	DKr	South Africa	Rand	R
European Monetary Union	Euro	€	South Korea	Won	W
Hong Kong	Dollar	HK$	Switzerland	Franc	SFr
India	Rupee	Rs	United Kingdom	Pound	£
Israel	New Shekel	NIS	United States	Dollar	$

Exchange Rates

An **exchange rate** is the price of one country's currency expressed in terms of another country's currency. For example, a rate of $1.70 per £1 means that 1 pound costs $1.70 (£1 = $1.70). Put somewhat differently, 1 U.S. dollar costs 0.5882 pounds, because 1/1.70 = 0.5882 ($1 = £0.5882). The exchange rate can be expressed equivalently in terms of either dollars per pound or pounds per dollar.

An exchange rate is used to convert an amount expressed in one currency into another.

EXAMPLE Using an Exchange Rate to Convert from One Currency to Another

Your sorority can buy a used two-decker London bus for £15,000. (You will use it to drive everyone to home football games and other important events.) The exchange rate is $1.70 per £1. How many dollars will you need to buy it?

Purchasing the bus will cost $25,500 (= [15,000]1.70).

The U.S. dollar-pound exchange rate can be expressed equivalently in terms of either dollars per pound or pounds per dollar. The exchange rates could also be expressed indirectly in terms of a third currency—say, the Swiss franc: SF1.50/$ and SF2.55/£. Figure 27.1 illustrates these currency relationships. Given any two, it is easy to find the third.

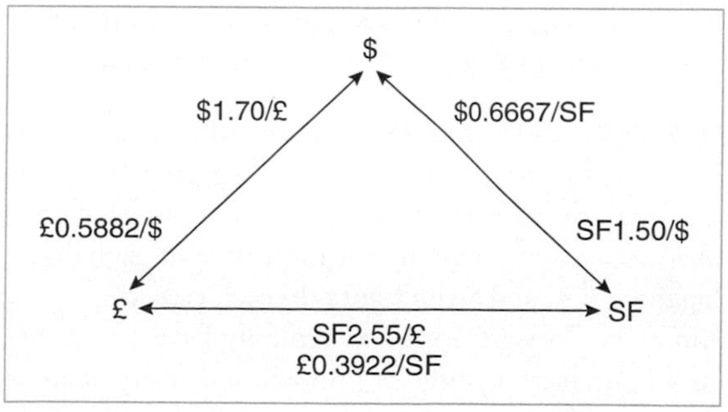

FIGURE 27.1
The relationship among the values of three currencies.

The direct and indirect methods of expressing an exchange rate are equivalent. In our example, the dollar-pound exchange rate implicit in the exchange rates SF1.50/$ and SF2.55/£ is £0.5882/$ (or equivalently, $1.70/£) because

$$\frac{\frac{\text{SF}1.50}{\$}}{\frac{\text{SF}2.55}{£}} = \frac{£0.5882}{\$}$$

If the equivalence did not hold, there would be a riskless arbitrage opportunity.

EXAMPLE A Riskless Currency Arbitrage Opportunity

Suppose British pounds are trading at a price of SF2.60/£ in Switzerland and $1.70/£ in New York while Swiss francs are trading for SF1.50/$ in New York. In that case, the pound would be overvalued in Switzerland relative to the other two currencies. A foreign exchange trader who purchases $100 worth of pounds in New York would obtain £58.82 (= [100]0.5882). Selling the pounds in Switzerland would yield SF152.93 (= [58.82]2.60). The Swiss francs could be sold in New York for $101.96 (= [152.93]0.6667), yielding a riskless arbitrage profit of $1.96 per $100 invested.

In practice in foreign exchange trading, all exchange rates are expressed in terms of the U.S. dollar. For example, SF1 = $0.66, €1 = $0.90, £1 = $1.70, and so on. Traders find it convenient to quote exchange rates indirectly in terms of a single currency, the U.S. dollar.

Types of Foreign Exchange Transactions

There are five types of foreign exchange transactions: spot transactions, forward transactions, currency futures, currency swaps, and currency options. Let's take a look at each.

IMMEDIATE TRANSACTIONS **Spot trades** involve the purchase and sale of a currency for "immediate" delivery, which actually occurs two business days after the trade takes place. Figure 27.2 illustrates what a typical table of foreign exchange rates published in a financial newspaper looks like. The table furnishes the *spot foreign exchange rates* quoted by Reuters for trading amounts of $1 million or greater as of 4 P.M. the preceding two trading days. For example, the British pound is quoted in the table at £1 = $1.4599 for Friday and £1 = $1.4601 for Thursday, indicating a slight decrease in the value of the pound (relative to the dollar) between Thursday and Friday.

The table also reports currency *cross rates* for actively traded currencies. They show the value of any currency in terms of any other currency. For example, considering the Canadian dollar (CdnDlr)-U.S. dollar ($) exchange rate, CdnDlr1.5330 = $1 (in the upper left-hand corner) is equivalent to $0.65232 = CdnDlr1 (in the lower right-hand corner).

FORWARD CONTRACTS A **forward contract** covers the purchase and sale of an item, such as a currency, for *future* delivery based on a price (the exchange rate) that is agreed to *today.* When the forward contract involves a currency, it is referred to as a *currency forward.* Figure 27.2 shows *forward exchange rates* in addition to spot exchange rates for British pounds, Canadian dollars, Japanese yen, and Swiss francs. In each case, the rates are shown for 30-, 90-, and 180-day forward contracts. Forward contracts typically have a term between 1 and 52 weeks. For example, a firm could purchase pounds for immediate delivery at an exchange rate of £1 = $1.4599 on Friday. On that same day, a firm could also contract for 30-day delivery at an exchange rate of £1 = $1.4574,

KEY CURRENCY CROSS RATES

	Dollar	Euro	Pound	SFranc	Peso	Yen	CdnDlr
Canada	1.5330	1.4470	2.2380	0.9840	.15739	.01233	—
Japan	124.36	117.38	181.55	79.820	12.768	—	81.122
Mexico	9.7400	9.1936	14.219	6.2516	—	.07832	6.3536
Switzerland	1.558	1.4706	2.2745	—	.15996	.01253	1.0163
U. K.	.68500	.6466	—	.4397	.07033	.00551	.44682
Euro	1.05940	—	1.5467	.68000	.10877	.00852	.69109
U. S.	—	.9439	1.4599	.64185	.10267	.00804	.65232

EXCHANGE RATES

The New York foreign exchange mid-range rates below apply to trading among banks in amounts of $1 million and more, as quoted at 4 p.m. Eastern time by Reuters and other sources.

	U.S. $ equiv.		Currency per U.S. $	
Country	*Fri.*	*Thurs.*	*Fri.*	*Thurs.*
Argentina (Peso)-y	.2732	.2725	3.6600	3.6700
Australia (Dollar)	.5719	.5756	1.7487	1.7372
Bahrain (Dinar)	2.6525	2.6525	.3770	.3770
Brazil (Real)	.3791	.3758	2.6380	2.6610
Britain (Pound)	1.4599	1.4601	.6850	.6849
1-month Forward	1.4574	1.4576	.6862	.6861
3-months Forward	1.4516	1.4519	.6889	.6888
6-months Forward	1.4433	1.4435	.6929	.6928
Canada (Dollar)	.6523	.6522	1.5330	1.5333
1-month Forward	.6519	.6518	1.5339	1.5343
3-months Forward	.6508	.6507	1.5365	1.5368
6-months Forward	.6491	.6491	1.5405	1.5407
Chile (Peso)	.001513	.001509	660.95	662.75
China (Renminbi)	.1208	.1208	8.2770	8.2770
Colombia (Peso)	.0004271	.0004282	2341.50	2335.20
Czech. Rep. (Koruna) commercial rate	.03082	.03089	32.445	32.371
Denmark (Krone)	.1270	.1272	7.8720	7.8630
Ecuador (U. S. dollar)	1.0000	1.0000	1.0000	1.0000
Hong Kong (Dollar)	.1282	.1282	7.7998	7.7997
Hungary (Forint)	.003908	.003920	255.88	255.10
India (Rupee)	.02041	.02042	49.000	49.980
Indonesia (Rupiah)	.0001127	.0001106	8875	9045
Israel (Shekel)	.1996	.2009	5.0100	4.9780
Japan (Yen)	.008041	.008049	124.36	124.24
1-month Forward	.008053	.008061	124.17	124.05
3-months Forward	.008079	.008087	123.77	123.66
6-months Forward	.008123	.008131	123.11	122.99
Jordon (Dinar)	1.4124	1.4124	.7080	.7080
Kuwait (Dinar)	3.2884	3.2884	.3041	.3041
Lebanon (Pound)	.0006607	.0006607	1513.50	1513.50
Malaysia (Ringgit)-b	.2632	.2632	3.8001	3.8001
Malta (Lira)	2.2962	2.2983	.4355	.4351
Mexico (Peso) Floating rate	.1027	.1026	9.7400	9.7425

Continued on next page

FIGURE 27.2
Foreign exchange rate tables.

	U.S. $ equiv.		Currency per U.S. $	
Country	*Fri.*	*Thurs.*	*Fri.*	*Thurs.*
New Zealand (Dollar)	.4889	.4912	2.0454	2.0358
Norway (Krone)	.1270	.1273	7.8711	7.8542
Pakistan (Rupee)	.01663	.01663	60.125	60.125
Peru (new Sol)	.2882	.2883	3.4698	3.4685
Philippines (Peso)	.01975	.01964	50.640	50.925
Poland (Zloty)	.2488	.2499	4.0200	4.0010
Russia (Ruble)-a	.03182	.03182	31.425	31.425
Saudi Arabia (Riyal)	.2666	.2666	3.7504	3.7509
Singapore (Dollar)	.5581	.5568	1.7917	1.7960
Slovak Rep. (Koruna)	.02116	.02129	47.257	46.979
South Africa (Rand)	.1016	.1021	9.8450	9.7935
South Korea (Won)	.0008143	.0008163	1228.00	1225.00
Sweden (Krona)	.1023	.1031	9.7705	9.6998

	U.S. $ equiv.		Currency per U.S. $	
Country	*Fri.*	*Thurs.*	*Fri.*	*Thurs.*
Switzerland (Franc)	.6418	.6417	1.5580	1.5583
1-month Forward	.6422	.6421	1.5572	1.5575
3-months Forward	.6428	.6427	1.5556	1.5560
6-months Forward	.6437	.6436	1.5534	1.5537
Taiwan (Dollar)	.02940	.02939	34.010	34.020
Thailand (Baht)	.02360	.02354	42.380	42.475
Turkey (Lira)	.00000068	.00000069	1463000	1450000
United Arab (Dirham)	.2723	.2723	3.6730	3.6730
Uruguay (Peso) Financial	.05763	.05814	17.351	17.200
Venezuela (Bolivar)	.000873	.000854	1145.50	1170.50
SDR	1.2917	1.2885	.7742	.7761
Euro	.9439	.9456	1.0594	1.0575

Special Drawing Rights (SDR) are based on exchange rates for the U.S., British, and Japanese currencies. Source: International Monetary Fund.
a–Russian Central Bank rate. b–Government rate. y–Floating rate.

FIGURE 27.2
(concluded)

called the forward exchange rate, and for 180-day delivery at a forward rate of £1 = $1.4433. A firm entering into a 30-day forward contract on Friday to purchase British pounds would agree to exchange $1.4574 per pound when the contract settles one month later.

Note that the forward rates for pounds ($1.4574 or $1.4433) are lower than the spot rate ($1.4599). In the next section we explain why. If a firm purchased pounds for 30-day delivery, it would get more pounds for its dollar than it would in a spot purchase (£0.6862/$ versus £0.6850/$). The pound is said to trade at a *forward discount* relative to the dollar, because forward pounds are "cheaper" than spot pounds. In Figure 27.2, note that the Japanese yen is trading at a *forward premium* relative to the dollar, because forward yen are more expensive than spot yen. This forward premium or discount can be expressed on a nominal annualized basis as

$$\text{Forward premium} = 12\left(\frac{\text{30-Day forward rate} - \text{Spot rate}}{\text{Spot rate}}\right) = n\left(\frac{f_t - s_0}{s_0}\right) \qquad (27.1)$$

The premium is $f_t - s_0$, which is converted to a fractional premium by dividing by s_0, and then annualized by multiplying by the number of such periods in a year. Using the 30-day forward exchange rate for UK pounds, the annualized forward premium is:

$$\text{Forward premium} = 12\left(\frac{1.4574 - 1.4599}{1.4599}\right) = -2.05\%$$

The forward premium of −2.05% can also be expressed as a forward discount of 2.05%.

EXAMPLE A Forward Contract

Instead of buying a bus today, your sorority is going to take delivery and pay for the bus in 180 days. If you must pay £15,000 in 180 days, and the 180-day forward exchange rate for pounds is $1.6800 per pound, how many dollars will it cost you to buy the bus?

Purchasing the pounds forward will cost $25,200 (= [15,000]1.6800). You will pay this amount in 180 days to take delivery of the £15,000, which you will then use to buy the bus.

Forward contracts can be customized to suit a corporation's particular requirements as to amount, currency, settlement date, and other matters. Voiding a forward contract, however, is difficult and is subject to negotiation with the other party to the contract.

CURRENCY FUTURES Currency futures markets also exist. Currency futures are like currency forwards except that a **futures contract** is standardized and exchange traded. A **currency future** is a futures contract that is denominated in a particular foreign currency. Because of this standardization, currency futures generally are less costly to trade and enjoy more liquid markets than (non-exchange-traded) forward contracts. With a futures contract, a firm can close out its position at any time simply by selling the contract (or repurchasing the contract if the firm had previously sold it). The choice between a forward contract and a futures contract thus involves a trade-off. Forward contracts can be customized, but futures contracts have greater liquidity and lower transaction costs.

Currency futures, like currency forwards, have premiums or discounts that reflect market expectations of exchange rates at future dates.

CURRENCY SWAPS In the fourth type of foreign exchange transaction, the **currency swap,** two parties swap equivalent amounts of two currencies and agree to exchange a series of specified payment obligations denominated in one currency for payment obligations denominated in the other. When payments are due, one party generally pays the other the difference in value caused by changes in the exchange rate. Currency swaps can be arranged directly between two firms seeking to borrow in each other's home currency. More commonly, firms swap currency with commercial banks, which are in a better position to effect such transactions.

EXAMPLE A Currency Swap

Imperial Chemicals Industries PLC (ICI), a British firm, would like to make an investment in the United States. Exxon Mobil is an American firm that would like to make an investment in the United Kingdom. The firms can borrow in their respective national currencies and enter into a currency swap. Suppose a 10-year British pound loan to ICI requires a 12% APR, whereas a 10-year U.S. dollar loan to Exxon Mobil requires a 9% APR. Exxon Mobil and ICI agree to exchange interest and principal payment obligations.

TABLE 27.2
Exxon Mobil's debt service stream (currency amounts in millions).

	YEAR 0		YEARS 1–10		YEAR 10	
	$	£	$	£	$	£
Borrow $	+100					
Swap $ for £	−100	+62.5				
Interest on $ loan			−9			
Swap payments			+9	−7.5	+100	−62.5
Repay $ loan					−100	
Net cash flow	0	+62.5	0	−7.5	0	−62.5

Suppose each firm needs the equivalent of $100 million. Each firm borrows this sum in its home currency, and the two firms enter into a currency swap. Exxon Mobil's debt service stream (assuming the debt matures in a lump sum and pays annual interest) under a currency swap arrangement with ICI is given in Table 27.2.

In this example, Exxon Mobil borrows $100 million and exchanges the $100 million with ICI for £62.5 million. In each of the subsequent 10 years, Exxon Mobil agrees to pay ICI £7.5 million (= [0.12]62.5), and ICI agrees to pay Exxon Mobil $9 million (= [0.09]100). Exxon Mobil then makes an interest payment of $9 million on its loan. At the time of the last interest payment, Exxon Mobil agrees to pay ICI £62.5 million, and ICI agrees to pay Exxon Mobil $100 million. Exxon Mobil then pays $100 million to its creditors to repay its loan. The payment obligations of ICI and Exxon Mobil are netted: On the basis of prevailing exchange rates, one party will have to write the other party a check for the net amount owed when each payment is due.

The currency swap effectively converts Exxon Mobil's $100 million 9% U.S. dollar loan into a £62.5 million 12% British pound loan.

Why does a currency swap offer a cost advantage over simply borrowing the needed foreign currency directly in the foreign capital market? Briefly, the answer is market imperfections. Tax asymmetries and national regulations can restrict international capital flows and restrict the free flow of capital across national boundaries. These frictions lead to differences in relative borrowing costs that give a comparative advantage to the two firms, or (as is more often the case recently) to a firm and one of its commercial banks, to engage in a currency swap.

CURRENCY OPTIONS A forward contract or a futures contract obligates the parties to make the foreign currency exchange specified in the contract. In contrast, a **currency option** conveys the *right* to buy (in the case of a call option) or sell (for a put option) a specified amount of a particular foreign currency at a stated price within a specified time period. Commercial banks sell customized currency options; standardized currency options are traded on option exchanges.

The optionholder's gain will depend on the change in the exchange rate. The maximum loss, however, is limited to the cost of the option, because the optionholder does not have to actually make the exchange.[1]

[1]For more on options, see Chapters 12 and 21.

Review

1. What is the foreign exchange market?
2. What is an exchange rate? If the dollar-pound rate is \$1.75/£, what is it when expressed in pounds per dollar?
3. What is a spot exchange rate? What is a forward exchange rate?
4. What is a currency future? How is it different from a currency forward?
5. What is a currency swap? How can a firm use a currency swap to convert a dollar loan into, say, a euro loan?

27.2 HEDGING AGAINST FOREIGN EXCHANGE RISKS

When some of the cash flows a firm expects to receive, or anticipates having to pay, are denominated in a foreign currency, the firm faces foreign exchange risk. **Foreign exchange risk** (or foreign currency risk) is the risk that the value of a cash flow will change as a result of a change in the exchange rate. For example, suppose that Boeing has a contract to sell two aircraft to British Airways. The contract calls for delivery of both in one year against payment in British pounds. The value of the contract is £200 million. Suppose the spot dollar-pound exchange rate expected one year hence is £1 = \$1.60. Then the aircraft contract has an expected value of \$320 million. But suppose the dollar-pound exchange rate is £1 = \$1.50 when British Airways makes payment. In that case, British Airways will still pay £200 million, but Boeing will receive only \$300 million when it converts the pounds into dollars.

Exchange Rate Volatility

The exchange rates between the major currencies are not fixed by government policy. Rather, they can float up or down in response to supply and demand. The central bank of each major country does intervene in the foreign exchange market from time to time. It buys or sells its currency in order to smooth exchange rate fluctuations. It tries to keep its exchange rate at a level it deems appropriate. For example, it may wish to reduce its exchange rate in order to boost exports. However, intervention can affect the situation only temporarily when exchange rates are floating. Attempts to force a different exchange rate are soon swamped by market forces.

Figure 27.3 shows how the values of the Australian dollar, British pound, euro, and Japanese yen moved in relation to the U.S. dollar between 1990 and 2001. All four currencies exhibit considerable volatility.

Hedging Techniques

Boeing can eliminate its foreign currency risk exposure by hedging. **Hedging** means establishing a financial position whose change in value will offset a recognized risk. To create a foreign exchange hedge, Boeing should enter into a foreign currency transaction that would generate an offsetting gain in case the pound's value depreciated relative to the expected future spot rate before receipt of payment (a \$20 million gain if the pound were to depreciate to \$1.50/£).[2] We will explain two basic foreign currency hedging techniques: (1) forward market transactions and (2) currency option transactions.

[2]You can read more about hedging in Chapter 21.

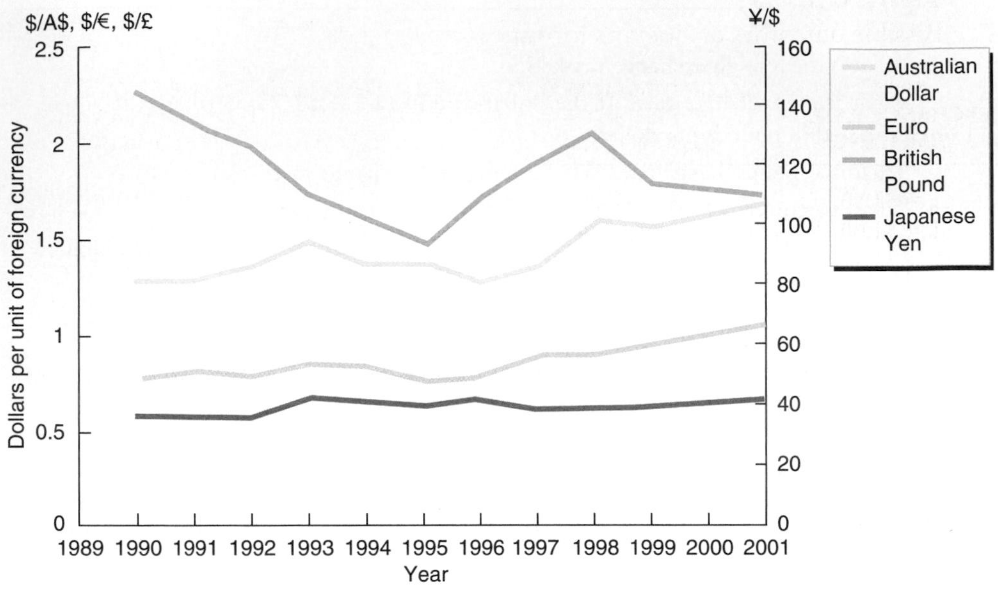

Source: Federal Reserve Bulletin.

FIGURE 27.3
Exchange rate fluctuations for four currencies relative to the U.S. dollar, 1990–2001 (currency amounts in millions).

Before describing them, we should mention one other strategy for Boeing that you may have thought of. Boeing could negotiate payment in U.S. dollars. But the Principle of Two-Sided Transactions should indicate why invoicing in dollars does not eliminate foreign currency risk. It eliminates *Boeing's* foreign currency risk exposure—but transfers it to British Airways, which must now pay in dollars. The Principle of Risk-Return Trade-Off implies that the risk transfer will require compensation to British Airways in the form of a reduced transaction price.

Let us see how forward market transactions can be used to hedge foreign currency risk.

EXAMPLE Hedging Foreign Currency Risk in the Forward Market

Boeing could hedge its foreign currency risk exposure by selling a £200 million forward contract for delivery in one year. That strategy converts the £200 million receivable into a known dollar amount. Suppose the one-year forward rate is £1 = $1.60. Then the forward sale will net Boeing $320 million one year hence. Table 27.3 shows the consequences to Boeing of hedging in this manner in three different future exchange rate scenarios.

Suppose the British pound depreciates to £1 = $1.50. Boeing receives £200 million from British Airways, which is worth $300 million. But Boeing delivers the £200 million under the forward contract for $320 million. There is a $20 million profit ($320 − 300) on the forward contract that restores the value of the contract to the originally expected $320 million value. Suppose instead the British pound appreciates to £1 = $1.70. The £200 million Boeing receives is worth $340 million. But it must deliver pounds at an exchange rate of £1 = $1.60 to settle the forward contract. The $20 million loss on the forward contract leads to a net (of gain or loss on hedging) realized value of $320 million on the aircraft contract. Indeed, regardless of what happens to the spot rate one year hence, Boeing will realize $320 million because of the forward contract. Losses are avoided—but so are gains—under a forward contract hedge.

TABLE 27.3
Possible outcomes of Boeing's forward market hedge.

SPOT EXCHANGE RATE, 1 YEAR HENCE	VALUE OF ORIGINAL CONTRACT (MILLIONS)	GAIN (LOSS) ON FORWARD CONTRACT (MILLIONS)	NET REALIZED DOLLAR VALUE (MILLIONS)
£1 = $1.50	£200 = $300	$20	$320
£1 = $1.60	£200 = $320	—	320
£1 = $1.70	£200 = $340	(20)	320

Forward market transactions are useful for hedging foreign currency risk exposures that are certain as to amount and timing. But life is not always quite so simple.

Suppose that Boeing and Airbus are competing for the order and that British Airways will not make a decision for several weeks (while it studies the bids). If Boeing sells pounds forward but does not win the contract, it will lose money if the British pound appreciates. Boeing can avoid this outcome and still hedge its foreign currency risk by purchasing an option to sell £200 million at a stated exchange rate in one year. The most Boeing can lose in that case is the cost of the option.

Currency options are a useful hedging tool when the quantity of foreign currency to be received or paid is uncertain. The following rules indicate how to choose between forward contracts and currency options.

- When the quantity of foreign currency to be received (paid) is known, sell (buy) the currency forward.
- When the quantity is unknown, buy an option to sell (buy) enough of the foreign currency to cover the maximum amount of foreign currency that might be received (paid).

Review

1. What is foreign exchange risk? What is hedging?
2. Explain how a firm can use a forward market transaction to hedge foreign currency risk.
3. Explain how a firm can use currency options to hedge foreign currency risk.

27.3 INTERNATIONAL INTEREST RATES AND EXCHANGE RATES

As we have seen in our discussion of currency swaps, interest rates are not the same in every market. One factor affecting interest rates is the exchange rate between currencies. Even in a perfect capital market, interest rates and exchange rates would be closely linked. This relationship is referred to as interest rate parity. **Interest rate parity** is the relationship between the spot and forward exchange rates and the interest rates for two countries. The following example illustrates this interaction.

EXAMPLE Relationship Between International Interest Rates and Exchange Rates

Suppose you have the following two investment alternatives. You can buy a one-year U.S. dollar-denominated note that pays 10% interest at maturity, or a one-year British pound-denominated note that pays 12% interest at maturity. Which would you select?

You cannot answer the question until you take into account how many pounds you get for your dollars today, and how many dollars you would get for your pounds one year from today. The forward exchange market provides the needed information.

Suppose the dollar-pound spot rate is \$1.70/£ and the one-year forward rate is \$1.60/£. The pound is trading at a forward discount. This example will demonstrate why. If you invest \$1,000 in the U.S. dollar-denominated note, you will receive \$1,100 at maturity. If you instead convert the \$1,000 into British pounds at the spot rate, you will receive £588.24 (= 1,000/1.70). If you purchase the British pound-denominated note, then you will receive £658.83 (= [588.24]1.12) at maturity. By selling the pounds forward, you would ensure that the £658.83 would purchase \$1,054.13. The dollar-denominated note is the more profitable investment.

Moreover, you can earn a riskless arbitrage profit by borrowing British pounds, selling them in the spot market for U.S. dollars, investing the dollars at 10%, and selling the dollars you will receive at maturity forward against the pound.

If you borrowed £588.24 and bought \$1,000 (= [588.24]1.70), the investment of those dollars would yield \$1,100, which would produce £687.50 (= 1,100/1.60) under the forward contract. After paying £70.59 (= [588.24]0.12) of interest and repaying the British pound borrowing, you have a £28.67 (= 687.50 − 588.24 − 70.59) arbitrage profit. Arbitrage will continue until the interest rate differential is equivalent to the differential between the spot and forward rates. The interest rate differential between U.S. dollars and British pounds for investments of identical risk can be expressed in ratio form as[3]

$$\frac{1 + r_{£}}{1 + r_{\$}}$$

where $r_{£}$ and $r_{\$}$ are the pound and dollar interest rates, respectively. The differential between the spot exchange rate (s_0) and the forward exchange rate (f_t) can be expressed as

$$\frac{s_0}{f_t}$$

Interest rate parity holds that

$$\frac{1 + r_{£}}{1 + r_{\$}} = \frac{s_0}{f_t} \tag{27.2}$$

Please note that for Equation (27.2), the exchange rates are "direct" quotes, which are the \$/£, or U.S. dollars per pound. The direct quote is the price of foreign currency in dollars. In this example, interest rate parity would hold if arbitrage activity raises the one-year forward rate to \$1.67/£, for then

$$\frac{1 + r_{£}}{1 + r_{\$}} = \frac{1.12}{1.10} = 1.02 = \frac{\$1.70/£}{\$1.67/£} = \frac{s_0}{f_1}$$

Interest rate parity requires the difference between the forward and spot exchange rates to offset the difference between the interest rates in the two countries. *It ensures that a forward currency discount exactly offsets the higher interest rate on comparable investments in that currency.* If U.S. dollar-denominated investments provide a higher interest rate, then the British pound would trade

---

[3]The interest rates $r_{£}$ and $r_{\$}$ both apply to the same period of time as the time between the spot and forward quotes, for example, one year in this case. If the forward rate is three months or six months forward, the interest rates should be for three or six months, respectively.

at a forward premium. In that case, the larger number of dollars to be received upon future sale of pounds would fully compensate for the lower British interest rate. Evidence indicates that interest rate parity normally holds, at least to a close approximation, in the major currency markets.

Review

1. What is interest rate parity?
2. The spot exchange rate is \$0.7432 = 1 Canadian dollar, and the 180-day forward rate is \$0.7518 = 1 Canadian dollar. Which country should have the higher interest rate, the U.S. or Canada?
3. The spot exchange rate is \$0.6085 = 1 Swiss franc and the 180-day forward rate is \$0.6159 = 1 Swiss franc. Should the interest rate be higher in Switzerland or the U.S.?

27.4 INTERNATIONAL INFLATION RATES AND EXCHANGE RATES

Inflation rates also affect exchange rates and interest rates. Suppose a loaf of bread costs \$1 in the United States. What should it cost in Britain? According to the law of one price, \$1 should also buy a loaf of bread in Britain and in every other market. This will happen only if the foreign exchange rate between two currencies adjusts by the difference in the rates of inflation in the countries that issued the two currencies. If the inflation rate is 3% in the United States and 5% in Britain, then the British pound would have to fall by (1.05/1.03) − 1, or about 2% per year, for the (equivalent) dollar price of bread to remain the same in both countries.

The condition just described is referred to as purchasing power parity.[4] It is formally stated in terms of expected inflation rates. **Purchasing power parity** requires that the expected difference in inflation rates equals the difference between the spot exchange rate now and the spot exchange rate expected in the future. The difference in expected inflation rates is expressed in ratio form as

$$\frac{1 + E[i_{£}]}{1 + E[i_{\$}]}$$

where E is the expected value of the quantity in brackets, and $i_{£}$ and $i_{\$}$ are the British and U.S. inflation rates, respectively. This ratio must equal the difference between the spot exchange rate (s_0), expressed in dollars per pound, and the expected future spot exchange rate ($E[s_t]$) which is[5]

$$\frac{s_0}{E[s_t]}$$

Purchasing power parity holds that

$$\frac{1 + E[i_{£}]}{1 + E[i_{\$}]} = \frac{s_0}{E[s_t]} \qquad (27.3)$$

For Equation (27.3), the exchange rates are "direct" quotes, which are the \$/£, or U.S. dollars per pound.

[4]Purchasing power parity differs from the law of one price in that the law of one price refers to individual goods, whereas purchasing power parity refers to the general price level for all goods, for example, as measured by the consumer price index.

[5]The inflation rates $i_{£}$ and $i_{\$}$ both apply to the same period of time, for example, both might be one-year inflation rates. The exchange rate $E[s_t]$ is the one expected to hold at the end of this period.

EXAMPLE Relationship Between International Inflation Rates and Exchange Rates

Let us continue the previous example. Suppose the expected inflation rate is 8% in the United States and 10% in Britain. If the current spot rate is \$1.70 = £1, purchasing power parity will hold if the expected spot rate one year forward is \$1.67 = £1. Equation (27.3) can be used to solve for the expected spot rate:

$$\frac{1 + E[i_{£}]}{1 + E[i_{\$}]} = \frac{s_0}{E[s_1]}$$

$$\frac{1.10}{1.08} = \frac{\$1.70/£}{E[s_1]}$$

$$E[s_1] = \$1.67/£$$

Purchasing power parity ensures that the expected change in the spot exchange rate offsets the difference between the expected inflation rates in the two countries. *The higher inflation rate is fully offset by the expected rate of depreciation of that country's currency.*

Review

1. Explain what purchasing power parity means.
2. The spot exchange rate is \$0.9553 = 1 Brazilian real. If the expected inflation rate is lower in the United States than in Brazil, should the expected future spot rate be higher or lower than the current spot rate? (Assume the rates are quoted in dollars per real.)
3. The spot rate is \$0.7026 = 1 Swiss franc. If the Swiss inflation rate is expected to be lower than that in the U.S., what is expected to happen to the future spot rate?

27.5 UNBIASED FORWARD RATES AND THE INTERNATIONAL FISHER EFFECT

There are two other conditions that will hold in a well-behaved market. One links forward and spot exchange rates. The other explains how real interest rates relate.

Unbiased Forward Exchange Rates

Suppose foreign exchange market participants do not care about risk, that is, they are risk neutral. Then the forward rate would depend solely on what market participants expect the future spot rate to be. For example, suppose the expected spot rate for British pounds is £1 = \$1.50. What would be the forward rate? It would have to be £1 = \$1.50. If it were higher than this rate, everyone would want to sell pounds, but no one would be willing to sell dollars forward. If it were lower than this rate, everyone would want to sell dollars, but no one would be willing to sell pounds forward. Therefore, the *unbiased forward exchange rate* condition states that the expected spot exchange rate equals the forward rate:

$$E[s_t] = f_t \tag{27.4}$$

This condition does not require the actual future spot rate to equal the historical forward rate. Foreign exchange market participants are not assumed to be perfect forecasters. All that is required is that, on average, the forward rate equals the future spot rate. Evidence shows that it does. However, the evidence also indicates that when the forward rate predicts a sharp change (either up or down) in the spot rate, the forecast change tends to overstate the actual change. Thus, the forward rate is not *always* an unbiased predictor of the future spot rate.

International Fisher Effect

In Chapter 7, we saw that the required return in nominal terms (r_n) results from simply compounding the required real return (r_r) and the *expected* inflation rate (i):

$$(1 + r_n) = (1 + r_r)(1 + i)$$

so that

$$1 + r_r = \frac{1 + r_n}{1 + i}$$

Many years ago, Irving Fisher argued that the nominal interest rate observed in the financial markets fully reflects investors' collective expectation regarding the inflation rate. It does so in order to compensate them for inflation's effects on the real value of their investments. This phenomenon is now called the *Fisher effect.* It follows from the Principle of Self-Interested Behavior: Investors seek out investments that offer the greatest expected risk-adjusted real return. Arbitrage ensures that in a perfect capital market, two debt instruments denominated in different currencies but of equivalent risk will offer the same expected real return.

If the Fisher effect holds, then the difference in nominal interest rates must equal the difference in expected inflation rates:

$$\frac{1 + r_£}{1 + r_\$} = \frac{1 + E[i_£]}{1 + E[i_\$]} \qquad (27.5)$$

We refer to Equation (27.5) as the **international Fisher effect** because it follows from the (domestic) Fisher effect.

Equation (27.5) follows from Equations (27.2), (27.3), and (27.4). The four relationships are mutually consistent. If any three of them hold, then they must all hold.

EXAMPLE International Fisher Effect

Let's continue the investments example. We know that $r_£ = 0.12$, $r_\$ = 0.10$, $i_£ = 0.10$, and $i_\$ = 0.08$. We can verify that Equation (27.5) holds:

$$\frac{1.12}{1.10} \approx 1.02 \approx \frac{1.10}{1.08}$$

Interpretation of the International Fisher Effect

Rewrite Equation (27.5) as

$$\frac{1 + r_£}{1 + E[i_£]} = \frac{1 + r_\$}{1 + E[i_\$]} = 1 + r_r$$

The international Fisher effect says that the real interest rate is the same in every country.

There is little empirical evidence concerning the international Fisher effect. As a general rule, the countries with the highest inflation rates also tend to have the highest interest rates. Thus, real interest rates vary less than nominal interest rates. As we have noted, there are various impediments to the free international flow of capital. As a result, arbitrage activity cannot achieve a single real interest rate that applies in all market segments.

Review

1. What is the unbiased forward exchange rate condition?
2. The one-year forward rate is 121 Japanese yen per U.S. dollar. According to the unbiased forward exchange rate condition, what is an unbiased estimate of the spot rate in one year?
3. What is the international Fisher effect?
4. The interest rate is higher in Mexico than in the United States. How does the international Fisher effect account for this?

27.6 INTERNATIONAL CAPITAL BUDGETING DECISIONS

Firms should evaluate foreign investment opportunities using the same principles they apply to domestic projects. A foreign project, however, involves several complications. The incremental after-tax cash flows are denominated in foreign currencies. These foreign currencies may not be freely convertible into U.S. dollars. Foreign investment projects may also entail a risk of expropriation by the host country's government. In addition, foreign taxes must be considered, the cost of capital for a foreign project may differ from that for a domestic project, and there may be a cost advantage to raising funds in the foreign country or in the international capital market.

After cash flows are adjusted for these factors, a firm has two alternative methods of applying the NPV criterion to foreign projects. The first is to calculate the incremental cash flows in the local currency, convert them into dollars at appropriate projected foreign exchange rates, and discount at the dollar-denominated required return. The second method is to do the entire NPV calculation in the local currency and then convert the foreign-currency-denominated NPV into dollars at the current exchange rate. The two procedures, applied correctly, will produce the same NPV.

Estimating the Incremental Cash Flows

So long as a firm can hedge its foreign currency risk exposure, it should not use internal foreign exchange forecasts to make investment decisions. It should use the forward rates quoted in the foreign exchange market. If forward rates are not available far enough into the future, then the firm should use the key relationships between interest rates, exchange rates, and inflation rates to estimate expected future spot exchange rates.

EXAMPLE The Incremental After-Tax Cash Flows for AlliedSignal's Swiss Project

AlliedSignal Inc. is considering building a plant in Switzerland to manufacture automotive parts for the Central European market. The plant is expected to cost SF50 million. AlliedSignal's project staff has projected the following incremental after-tax cash flows in Swiss francs:

YEAR	1	2	3	4	5
Cash flow (SF millions)	15	17	20	20	17

The current dollar-franc exchange rate is SF1 = \$0.60. This implies a \$30 million (= [0.60]50) project cost. AlliedSignal can project future exchange rates by applying the key relationships between interest rates, exchange rates, inflation rates, and expected future spot exchange rates.

Suppose the one-year riskless return is 8% in the United States (the equivalent annual one-year Treasury note rate) and 6% in Switzerland, and that the expected inflation rate in the United States is 5% per year for each of the next five years. Under interest rate parity, Equation (27.2), and unbiased forward exchange rates, Equation (27.4), the expected spot rate one year hence satisfies

$$\frac{1.06}{1.08} = \frac{\$0.60}{E[s_1]}$$
$$E[s_1] = \$0.6113$$

Under purchasing power parity, Equation (27.3),

$$\frac{1 + E[i_{SF}]}{1.05} = \frac{0.60}{0.6113}$$
$$1 + E[i_{SF}] = 1.03059$$

The expected inflation rate in Switzerland for the next year is 3.059%. Suppose the real interest rate is expected to remain constant over the next five years in each country. Then the projected Swiss inflation rate is 3.059% per annum for each of the next five years. AlliedSignal should check to make sure that its cash flow forecast is consistent with a 3.059% Swiss inflation rate.

Under purchasing power parity, Equation (27.3), the expected spot exchange rate t years hence ($1 \le t \le 5$) satisfies

$$E[s_t] = \$0.60\left[\frac{1.05}{1.03059}\right]^t$$

The projected Swiss franc cash flows can be converted into U.S. dollars:

YEAR	1	2	3	4	5
Cash flow (SF millions)	15	17	20	20	17
Exchange rate (\$/SF)	0.6113	0.6228	0.6345	0.6465	0.6586
Cash flow (\$ millions)	9.17	10.59	12.69	12.93	11.20

LACK OF CONVERTIBILITY Unlike Switzerland, many foreign countries place restrictions on a firm's ability to convert local currency into dollars or other "hard" currencies. This is often the case in Third World countries that have very limited hard currency reserves. If the free cash flow is not freely convertible into U.S. dollars—that is, if the U.S. parent is not free to convert the foreign currency into U.S. dollars and transfer the dollars outside the foreign country—then the annual cash flows may overstate the true benefits that the project sponsor can expect to realize. Recall from Chapter 6 that the NPV calculation implicitly assumes that interim cash flows can be reinvested at the project's cost of capital. When the local currency is not freely convertible into U.S. dollars, the incremental cash flow stream should reflect the actual expected U.S. dollar cash remittances (including interest on reinvested balances that can be remitted in U.S. dollars) at the time the project sponsor expects to realize these U.S. dollar flows.

EXPROPRIATION AND OTHER POLITICAL RISKS Investing in a foreign country entails political risk. An incoming foreign government might not honor a previous government's agreement to permit convertibility. Or the foreign government might impose discriminatory taxes. Worst of all, it might expropriate the firm's property for its own use (euphemistically called "nationalization").

Political risks should be incorporated into discounted-cash-flow analysis by adjusting the incremental cash flows, rather than by adjusting the discount rate.

EXAMPLE Adjusting for Political Risk

Suppose that the expected cash flows for a project are

YEAR	1	2	3	4
Cash flow ($ millions)	20	30	30	40

The project sponsor fears there is a 50% probability that the project will be expropriated at the end of two years when a new government may come to power. The expected cash flow stream to be discounted becomes

YEAR	1	2	3	4
Cash flow ($ millions)	20	30	15	20

Calculating the probability of expropriation is highly subjective. But that does not mean the risk should be ignored. If expropriation risk is significant, it is important to gauge the sensitivity of NPV to the probability of expropriation. Break-even analysis—determining the probability of expropriation during any particular year that would reduce the NPV to zero—is often used.

Domestic Currency Approach

Returning to the AlliedSignal example, we would like to demonstrate calculating the project's NPV with both the domestic currency approach and the foreign currency approach. To use the domestic currency approach, the cash flows are converted into U.S. dollars, and an appropriate risk-adjusted discount rate is estimated. Then the NPV can be calculated.

EXAMPLE Calculating the NPV for AlliedSignal's Swiss Investment

AlliedSignal's marginal income tax rate for the project is 23.8%. The pretax cost of debt for the project is 10% based on a project debt ratio (L) of 25%, or $r_d = 0.10$. The debt ratio is consistent with AlliedSignal's capital structure objective. Next we use the CAPM to calculate AlliedSignal's required return on equity.

AlliedSignal calculates a (leveraged) project beta of 1.10. The riskless return is 8%, and the expected return on the market portfolio is 16.6%. The (leveraged) required return on equity for the project is

$$r_e = 8 + 1.10(16.6 - 8) = 17.46\%$$

The required return for the dollar-denominated incremental cash flow stream is the weighted average cost of capital:

$$\text{WACC} = 0.25(1 - 0.238)(0.1) + 0.75(0.1746) = 15.00\%$$

The project NPV is

$$\begin{aligned} \text{NPV} &= -30.0 + \frac{9.17}{1.15} + \frac{10.59}{(1.15)^2} + \frac{12.69}{(1.15)^3} + \frac{12.93}{(1.15)^4} + \frac{11.20}{(1.15)^5} \\ &= \$7.29 \text{ million} \end{aligned}$$

Foreign Currency Approach

We can verify that calculating the project NPV in Swiss francs does not alter the dollar NPV. First, we calculate the approximate Swiss franc required return. Then we discount the cash flows in Swiss francs, and finally, convert the present value to dollars.

Based on the international Fisher effect, the required return in Swiss francs must satisfy the relationship

$$\frac{1 + r_{SF}}{1 + r_{\$}} = \frac{1 + r^*_{SF}}{1 + r^*_{\$}}$$

where r_{SF} and $r_{\$}$ are the one-year riskless returns, and r^*_{SF} and $r^*_{\$}$ are the required returns in SF and \$, respectively. Then

$$\frac{1.06}{1.08} = \frac{1 + r^*_{SF}}{1.15} \quad or\ r^*_{SF} = 12.87\%$$

The NPV of the project in Swiss francs is

$$\begin{aligned} NPV &= -50.0 + \frac{15.00}{1.1287} + \frac{17.00}{(1.1287)^2} + \frac{20.00}{(1.1287)^3} + \frac{20.00}{(1.1287)^4} + \frac{17.00}{(1.1287)^5} \\ &= SF12.15 \text{ million} \end{aligned}$$

Converting this amount to U.S. dollars gives

$$SF12.15 \text{ million}(\$0.60/SF) = \$7.29 \text{ million}$$

Properly used, the domestic and foreign currency approaches produce the same result.

Review

1. Describe the two alternative methods of applying the NPV criterion to foreign capital budgeting projects. Should they both lead to the same NPV? Why?
2. How can you allow for expropriation risk in the NPV analysis of a foreign capital budgeting project?

27.7 FINANCING FOREIGN INVESTMENTS

Today, bond issues are regularly launched in New York, London, or Japan and traded almost immediately in every time zone. Increasingly, domestic debt and equity issues are sold overseas as well as in the United States, and foreign debt and equity issues are also sold in the United States. The capital markets have become global, and for this reason, it is important for financial managers to maintain a global perspective when raising funds.

A firm that wants to borrow funds to finance a foreign capital budgeting project can (1) borrow U.S. dollars in the United States and export the funds to the foreign country, (2) borrow U.S. dollars in the Eurobond market, (3) borrow in the foreign country, or (4) borrow in whichever currency and in whichever market affords the lowest interest cost. The fourth strategy is particularly tempting, but is also very risky, as many *former* corporate treasurers will attest!

Financing in the Eurobond Market

In addition to the separate domestic capital markets, there is a large supranational Eurobond market. A *Eurobond* is a bond that a firm or some other type of issuer sells outside the country in whose currency it is denominated. In financial circles, the prefix "Euro" means "outside of." For example, Eurodollar bonds are denominated in U.S. dollars and issued, held, and traded outside the United States. Eurobonds exist in U.S. dollars, Canadian dollars, the euro, Swiss francs, Japanese yen, British pounds, and many other currencies.

EXAMPLE GE Capital's Eurobond Financing

Recently, General Electric Capital raised 1.6 billion British pounds, 1.275 billion Swiss francs, 235 million Swedish krona, 2.75 billion euros, 450 million Danish krone, 1.5 billion Czech krona, 130 billion Japanese yen, 2.1 billion Australian dollars, 100 million New Zealand dollars, and 100 million Canadian dollars in the Eurobond market.

LONG-TERM LOANS Eurobonds have become a major source of capital. The Eurobond market is a large unregulated market; it is basically free of the restrictions that apply to domestic offerings. The Eurobond market is a viable alternative to the domestic capital market for a firm that wants to raise short-term or long-term funds. From time to time, U.S. firms have found it advantageous to sell entire bond issues in the Eurobond market, rather than domestically, and to borrow in different currencies. A few years ago, the World Bank introduced *global bonds,* which are designed to qualify for immediate trading in any domestic capital market and in the Eurobond market, and hence to reach the broadest group of investors. In all these cases, the issuer enters the Eurobond market hoping to exploit an opportunity to raise funds at a lower cost than domestically.

SHORT-TERM LOANS In addition to issuing Eurobonds to raise long-term funds, firms can also borrow short-term funds in the Euroloan market. The interest rate on such loans is usually tied to one of the LIBOR interest rates. The *London Interbank Offered Rate,* or *LIBOR,* is the interest rate at which large international banks lend each other funds in the London money market. Most loans consist of Eurodollars, which are U.S. dollar deposits in banks outside the United States. But loans are also granted in other currencies. Most Eurodollar loans are overnight. The overnight rate is referred to as *overnight LIBOR.* But banks also lend each other Eurodollars for longer periods, such as for one week at *7-day LIBOR,* for one month at *1-month LIBOR,* and so on. There are similar interest rates for other Eurocurrencies, such as Euribor (euro interbank offered rate), sterling (British pound) LIBOR, Swiss franc LIBOR, and so on.

Dollar LIBOR is important in the commercial loan market. Many short-term loans, including in the United States, bear interest at a rate tied to LIBOR. For example, the interest rate on a loan might be stated as 3-month LIBOR plus 1%. The interest rate adjusts quarterly. If 3-month LIBOR increases to 6% from 5%, the interest rate increases to 7% from 6%. Similarly, floating-rate Eurobonds usually have an interest rate that is tied to LIBOR.

FOREIGN BONDS A *foreign bond* is issued by a foreign firm or government in the country in whose currency it is denominated. For example, *Yankee bonds* are denominated in U.S. dollars and issued in the United States by foreign firms or governments. They are different from Eurobonds. A U.S. firm sells Eurobonds outside the United States; a foreign firm sells Yankee bonds in the United States. Other examples of foreign bonds are Bulldog bonds (issued in Britain), Matador bonds (Spain), Rembrandt bonds (Netherlands), and Samurai bonds (Japan). Foreign bonds often face tougher restrictions and disclosure standards than bonds sold by domestic issuers. As a result, the Eurobond market has grown more rapidly than the markets for foreign bonds.

Choice of Currency

AlliedSignal could borrow \$30 million and purchase SF50 million, or it could borrow SF50 million. Borrowing dollars to fund a Swiss franc investment entails foreign exchange risk. If

AlliedSignal borrows dollars and the Swiss franc depreciates relative to the dollar, the firm's Swiss automotive plant will be worth fewer dollars. Also, in that case, AlliedSignal will have to dedicate a larger proportion of its franc-denominated project cash flow to service its U.S. dollar-denominated debt. The opposite would occur if the franc appreciated relative to the dollar. AlliedSignal can hedge against this foreign exchange risk by borrowing in francs.

Interest rate parity implies that when credit risk is held constant, any difference in nominal *pretax* yields between two different currencies is exactly offset by the expected change in the spot exchange rate during the term of the loan. The currency of borrowing does not matter. Income taxes or international capital market frictions can cause the choice of currency to make a difference, however. For example, government-imposed capital controls can create opportunities to reduce a borrower's after-tax cost of debt by choosing one currency over another.

EXAMPLE Calculating AlliedSignal's Cost of Borrowing in a Foreign Currency

Suppose that AlliedSignal can borrow five-year funds in U.S. dollars for its new plant at an interest rate of 10% APR or five-year funds in Swiss francs at an interest rate of 8% APR. The franc-denominated loan calls for sinking fund payments of SF10 at the end of years 2 and 3 and SF15 at the end of years 4 and 5. First we verify that the pretax dollar cost of debt (before transaction costs) is 10%. Table 27.4 presents AlliedSignal's debt service in U.S. dollars. The cost of debt is the return c that solves the equation

$$0 = -30.0 + \frac{2.4452}{1+c} + \frac{8.7192}{(1+c)^2} + \frac{8.3754}{(1+c)^3} + \frac{11.2491}{(1+c)^4} + \frac{10.6693}{(1+c)^5}$$

so that $c = 10.0\%$. (c is like an internal rate of return, IRR.)

AlliedSignal's marginal ordinary income tax rate is 50% on both its U.S. income and its Swiss income. Its after-tax cost of debt on the U.S. dollar loan (before transaction costs) is $0.10(1 - 0.5) = 5.00\%$.

Suppose instead that AlliedSignal borrows and repays the Swiss francs through its Swiss subsidiary. Its after-tax cost of debt, expressed in terms of dollars, is given in Table 27.5. In this case, the cost of debt is the return c that solves the equation

$$0 = -30.0 + \frac{1.2226}{1+c} + \frac{7.4736}{(1+c)^2} + \frac{7.3602}{(1+c)^3} + \frac{10.4733}{(1+c)^4} + \frac{10.2742}{(1+c)^5}$$

so that $c = 5.96\%$.

TABLE 27.4
AlliedSignal's debt service in U.S. dollars.

YEAR	1	2	3	4	5
Principal amount (SF millions)	50.00	50.00	40.00	30.00	15.00
Interest at 8% (SF millions)	4.00	4.00	3.20	2.40	1.20
Principal payment (SF millions)	—	10.00	10.00	15.00	15.00
Total debt service (SF millions)	4.00	14.00	13.20	17.40	16.20
Exchange rate ($/SF)	0.6113	0.6228	0.6345	0.6465	0.6586
Debt service ($ millions)	2.4452	8.7192	8.3754	11.2491	10.6693

TABLE 27.5
After-tax debt service for AlliedSignal's Swiss franc loan.

YEAR	1	2	3	4	5
Debt service (SF millions):					
Principal payment	—	10.00	10.00	15.00	15.00
Interest payment	4.00	4.00	3.20	2.40	1.20
Tax saving (at 50%)	(2.00)	(2.00)	(1.60)	(1.20)	(0.60)
Total	2	12	11.6	16.2	15.6
Exchange rate	0.6113	0.6228	0.6345	0.6465	0.6586
Debt service ($ millions)	1.2226	7.4736	7.3602	10.4733	10.2742

The after-tax cost of the loan in Swiss francs exceeds the after-tax cost of the U.S. dollar loan. Note that the franc is appreciating relative to the dollar, but only the actual interest expense, not the cost to AlliedSignal of repaying the more expensive francs, is tax deductible.

As a rule, borrowing in the weaker currency usually minimizes the expected after-tax cost of debt. That is, interest rate parity applies to pretax yields, not after-tax yields. Also, it is normally cheaper to borrow in high-tax-rate countries. However, neither statement is *always* true. We recommend that when evaluating alternative currency borrowing options, you calculate the after-tax cost of each before deciding which to select.

American Depository Receipts

As with debt, a firm can raise equity in its domestic capital market, in one of the foreign national capital markets, or in the Euromarket. Likewise, foreign firms can raise equity in the United States.

A foreign firm can raise funds in the United States by issuing *American depository receipts,* or ADRs. An ADR is a security that represents ownership of shares of a foreign common stock. The foreign shares are held in trust, which issues the ADRs in the United States. ADRs are publicly traded, and their price is expressed in U.S. dollars. An agent bank converts each dividend into U.S. dollars before paying it to U.S. shareholders. Foreign firms like ADRs because the securities laws are less demanding for ADRs than for shares issued directly to U.S. investors. There are more than 2,100 separate issues of ADRs.

Review

1. What is the Eurobond market? Are there Eurobond markets for bonds denominated in other currencies besides U.S. dollars? Name a few.
2. Why might it be advantageous to borrow in one currency rather than another?
3. Taking tax factors into account, is it usually better to borrow in a weaker currency or in a stronger currency? In a high-tax-rate country or a low-tax-rate country?
4. What are ADRs? Where are they issued and traded? If you look up the price of an ADR, in what currency will it be quoted?

SUMMARY

- A multinational firm's objective is the same as that of a purely domestic firm: to maximize shareholder wealth.
- International dimensions are increasingly relevant to financial decisions. An international financial manager needs additional analytical tools to cope with complications in the form of cash flows denominated in foreign currencies, foreign political risk, foreign government regulations and capital constraints, and foreign tax systems. Managers need these tools to take advantage of opportunities that are available in the foreign exchange market and in foreign capital markets to reduce foreign exchange risk. Information can be obtained from those markets that enables a financial manager to ensure that financial decisions are not biased, perhaps unknowingly, by foreign exchange rate factors.
- A critical first step toward developing these tools involves understanding the four key international financial market relationships: interest rate parity, purchasing power parity, unbiased forward exchange rates, and the international Fisher effect.
  1. Interest rate parity requires the difference between the forward and spot exchange rates to offset the difference between the interest rates in the two countries.
  2. Purchasing power parity states that the difference between the expected inflation rates in two countries equals the expected change in the spot exchange rate.
  3. The unbiased forward exchange rate condition states that the forward exchange rate equals the expected future spot exchange rate.
  4. The international Fisher effect holds that real rates of interest must be the same in all the world's capital markets.

  These four relationships do not hold exactly because of government regulations and other market imperfections. But they are a useful approximation to reality and represent a good starting point for analysis.
- The foreign exchange market offers a low-cost means of hedging foreign exchange risk. International financial managers would be wise to utilize this relatively cheap insurance and not to speculate on exchange rate movements. We explained how to use forward and futures contracts and currency options to reduce or eliminate exposure to foreign exchange risk.
- International capital budgeting projects involve foreign exchange considerations. Because of the four key international financial market relationships, it makes no difference which currency is used in the calculations.
  1. The foreign currency approach involves estimating cash flows in the foreign currency, calculating an NPV in the foreign currency at the foreign currency required return, and then converting the foreign currency NPV to the domestic currency.
  2. The domestic currency approach involves converting the foreign cash flows into the domestic currency, and then calculating a domestic currency NPV at the domestic currency required return.
- The incremental cash flow stream and the discount rate should be calculated with respect to the same currency; which currency does not matter so long as the key international financial market relationships all hold. In particular, ensure that the inflation rate implicit in the forecast cash flow stream is consistent with purchasing power parity.
- A foreign project can be financed in the sponsoring firm's domestic capital market, in the Eurobond market, in the host country's capital market, or in some other country's capital market. The cost of funds for each alternative should be calculated after tax on a consistent basis. It should be expressed in terms of the same currency, the same frequency of compounding, and so forth. The firm should select the lowest-cost alternative, taking into consideration any particular benefit from hedging foreign exchange, political, or other risks.

- A firm should not always borrow in the currency that has the lowest stated interest rate. That currency is likely to appreciate, which can offset the apparent saving.
- Trading on U.S. exchanges in American Depository Receipts (ADRs), representing shares of foreign firms, has become very significant.

EQUATION SUMMARY

$$\text{Forward premium} = 12\left(\frac{\text{30-day forward rate} - \text{Spot rate}}{\text{Spot rate}}\right) = n\left(\frac{f_t - s_0}{s_0}\right) \tag{27.1}$$

$$\frac{1 + r_{£}}{1 + r_{\$}} = \frac{s_0}{f_t} \tag{27.2}$$

$$\frac{1 + E[i_{£}]}{1 + E[i_{\$}]} = \frac{s_0}{E[s_t]} \tag{27.3}$$

$$E[s_t] = f_t \tag{27.4}$$

$$\frac{1 + r_{£}}{1 + r_{\$}} = \frac{1 + E[i_{£}]}{1 + E[i_{\$}]} \tag{27.5}$$

QUESTIONS

1. Explain the important differences between a forward contract for a particular foreign currency and a futures contract for the same currency. What are the relative advantages of each?
2. Explain each of the following relationships: (a) interest rate parity, (b) purchasing power parity, (c) unbiased forward exchange rates, and (d) equality of expected real returns.
3. What happens if the conditions required for unbiased forward exchange rates to hold are satisfied in the market for U.S. dollars and British pounds but: (a) The forward rate (expressed as \$ per £) is greater than the expected future spot rate (expressed as \$ per £). (b) The forward rate (expressed as \$ per £) is less than the expected future spot rate (expressed as \$ per £).
4. Explain which of the following represents the stronger requirement: (a) the forward rate always equals the expected future spot rate, or (b) the forward rate always equals the future spot rate.
5. Explain why a corporate treasurer would be unwise to follow a policy of always borrowing in whichever currency affords the lowest stated interest rate.
6. Suppose the Japanese yen-Canadian dollar spot exchange rate is ¥1 = CD0.012 and the expected spot rate one year hence is ¥ = CD0.015. What is the relationship between the expected inflation rates in Japan and Canada for the coming year?
7. You are going to receive 120 million yen in three months. How would you hedge this amount with forwards?

CHALLENGING QUESTIONS

8. Equation (27.1) shows how to calculate the annualized forward premium with a 30-day forward rate and the spot rate. How would the formula be modified for a 60-day forward or a 180-day forward?

9. Show that if interest rate parity, purchasing power parity, and unbiased forward exchange rates all hold, then so does the international Fisher effect. What happens when any one of the first three parity relationships fails to hold?
10. Suppose the expected average annual inflation rates in Canada and Great Britain over the next five years are 7% and 10%, respectively. Interest rate parity and purchasing power parity hold, and forward exchange rates are unbiased. What is the relationship between the five-year interest rates in Canada and Great Britain?
11. Show that if any one of the four parity relationships fails to hold, at least one other must also fail to hold.
12. Explain how to make an arbitrage profit when interest rate parity does not hold.

PROBLEMS

LEVEL A (BASIC)

A1. (Currency cross rates) Consider the following exchange rates: \$0.005872 = 1 Hungarian forint; \$0.03797 = 1 Philippines peso; \$0.9511 = 1 euro.

a. How many forints, pesos, and euros are equivalent to \$1.00?

b. How many forints equal one peso? How many pesos equal one euro? How many euros equal one forint?

A2. (Currency cross rates) Consider the following exchange rates: \$0.3245 = 1 Brazilian real; \$0.02787 = 1 Indian rupee; \$0.7432 = 1 Canadian dollar.

a. How many reals, rupees, and Canadian dollars are equivalent to \$1.00?

b. How many reals equal one rupee?

c. How many rupees equal one Canadian dollar?

d. How many Canadian dollars equal one real?

A3. (Currency cross rates) Consider the following exchange rates: \$0.1208 = 1 Chinese renminbi; \$0.01931 = 1 Philippines peso; \$0.0008322 = 1 South Korean won.

a. How many renminbis, pesos, and won are equivalent to \$1.00?

b. How many renminbis equal one peso? How many pesos equal one won? How many won equal one renminbi?

A4. (Interest rate parity) The spot rate is \$0.7432 = 1 Canadian dollar and the 180-day forward rate is \$0.7518 = 1 Canadian dollar. If the interest rate in the U.S. is 5.00% APR, what should be the interest rate in Canada?

A5. (Interest rate parity) The spot rate is \$1.6403 = 1£ and the 180-day forward rate is \$1.6344 = 1£ . If the interest rate in the U.S. is 5.00% APR, what should be the interest rate in the U.K.?

A6. (Interest rate parity) The spot rate is \$0.6341 = 1 Canadian dollar and the 180-day forward rate is \$0.6304 = 1 Canadian dollar. If the interest rate in the U.S. is 2.50% APR, what should be the interest rate in Canada?

A7. (Purchasing power parity) The spot rate is \$.7500 per Swiss franc. If the inflation rates are 3.5% in the U.S. and 1.5% in Switzerland, what is the expected spot rate in one year?

A8. (Purchasing power parity) The spot rate is \$0.70 per Swiss franc. If the inflation rates are 5.5% in the U.S. and 2.5% in Switzerland, what is the expected spot rate in one year?

A9. (Currency cross rates) Using the foreign currency cross rates in Figure 27.2:

a. Find the price of a Canadian dollar in Swiss francs.

b. Find the price of a Swiss franc in Canadian dollars.

c. Show that the currency cross rates in a and b are equivalent.

A10. (Forward premiums or discounts) Using the foreign exchange rates for Friday in Figure 27.2:

a. Is the Canadian dollar trading at a forward discount or at a forward premium to the U.S. dollar? Calculate the annualized forward premium or discount based on the 30-day, 90-day, and 180-day forwards.

b. Is the Japanese yen trading at a forward discount or at a forward premium to the U.S. dollar? Calculate the annualized forward premium or discount based on the 30-day, 90-day, and 180-day forwards.

A11. (Currency cross rates) The Swiss franc-Japanese yen exchange rate is SF1 = ¥96.18. The Swiss franc-euro exchange rate is SF1 = €0.680. What is the Japanese yen-euro exchange rate?

A12. (Currency cross rates) The Swiss franc-Japanese yen exchange rate is SF1 = ¥103.61. The Swiss franc-euro exchange rate is SF1 = €0.645. What is the Japanese yen-euro exchange rate?

A13. (Purchasing power parity) The dollar-pound exchange rate is £1 = $2.00. The expected rates of inflation in the United States and Great Britain are 4% and 8% APR, respectively. Calculate the one-year forward exchange rate required under purchasing power parity.

A14. (Purchasing power parity) The dollar-pound exchange rate is £1 = $1.87. The expected rates of inflation in the United States and Great Britain are 5% and 7% APR, respectively. Calculate the one-year forward exchange rate required under purchasing power parity.

A15. (International Fisher effect) Suppose the interest rates in the United States and Switzerland are 8% and 4% APR, respectively, and the projected inflation rates are 5% and 1% APR, respectively. Verify that Equation (27.5) holds. What is the real interest rate?

A16. (Purchasing power parity) The spot rate is $0.03183 per Russian ruble. If the inflation rates are 3% in the U.S. and 7% in Russia, what is the expected spot rate in one year?

A17. (International Fisher effect) Suppose the interest rates in the United States and New Zealand are 8% and 6% APR, respectively, and the projected inflation rates are 4% and 2% APR, respectively. Verify that Equation (27.5) holds. What is the real interest rate?

A18. (Hedging) Using the Boeing example, show that if the future spot rate is £1 = $1.25, the forward contract hedge will produce a net realized dollar value of $320 million. Show that the same result occurs if the future spot rate is £1 = $2.00.

A19. (Hedging) Using the Boeing example, show that if the future spot rate is £1 = $1.00, the forward contract hedge will produce a net realized dollar value of $320 million. Show that the same result occurs if the future spot rate is £1 = $3.00.

A20. (NPV versus IRR criterion) Calculate the U.S. dollar and Swiss franc internal rates of return for AlliedSignal's automotive plant and apply the IRR criterion. Which criterion is superior, IRR or NPV?

LEVEL B

B1. (Currency cross rates) The table of currency cross rates is partially filled in. Fill in the missing exchange rates. The values in the table are the units of the foreign currency of the country in a particular row equivalent to the currency in the column. For example, in the Japan row and Dollar column, 120.98 yen = $1.00. In the U.S. row and the Yen column, $0.00827 = 1 yen, which is the reciprocal of 120.98.

KEY CURRENCY CROSS RATES

	DOLLAR	EURO	POUND	PESO	YEN	CAND
Canada	1.5798	_	_	_	_	......
Japan	120.98	_	_	_	......	_
Mexico	9.7495	_	_	......	_	_
U.K.	.65330	_	......	_	_	_
Euro	1.0346	......	_	_	_	_
U.S.	......	.9666	1.5306	.10257	.00827	.63299

B2. (Currency cross rates) The table of currency cross rates is partially filled in. Fill in the missing exchange rates. The values in the table are the units of the foreign currency of the country in a particular row equivalent to the currency in the column.

KEY CURRENCY CROSS RATES

	DOLLAR	POUND	PESO	YEN	EURO	CAND
Canada	1.4125	–	–	–	–	......
Euro	1.1044	–	–	–	......	–
Japan	106.52	–	–	......	–	–
Mexico	8.5621	–	......	–	–	–
U.K.	.71544	......	–	–	–	–
U.S.	......	1.3977	.11679	.00939	.90547	.70796

B3. (International borrowing cost) A firm faces two borrowing alternatives. It can issue six-year debt domestically that bears a 10% APR coupon and that matures in a lump sum at the end of six years. Issuance expenses are 1% of the principal amount. Alternatively, it can issue a 10-1/4% Eurobond that matures in a lump sum at the end of six years. Issuance expenses are 1.25% of the principal amount. The issuer's tax rate is 50%. The domestic debt pays a semiannual coupon and the Eurobond pays an annual coupon.

a. Calculate the after-tax cost of the domestic issue.

b. Calculate the after-tax cost of the Eurobond issue, and express this cost on an equivalent semiannually compounded basis.

c. Which issue is cheaper? Explain.

B4. (International borrowing cost) A firm faces two borrowing alternatives. It can issue 10-year debt domestically that bears a 12% APR coupon and that matures in a lump sum at the end of 10 years. Issuance expenses are 3% of the principal amount. Alternatively, it can issue a 14% Eurobond that matures in a lump sum at the end of 10 years. The domestic bond pays a semiannual coupon and the Eurobond pays an annual coupon. Issuance expenses are 1% of the principal amount. The issuer's tax rate is 50%.

a. Calculate the after-tax cost of the domestic issue.

b. Calculate the after-tax cost of the Eurobond issue, and express this cost on an equivalent semiannually compounded basis.

c. Which issue is cheaper?

B5. (International borrowing cost) Look back at AlliedSignal's cost of borrowing in Swiss francs. Suppose AlliedSignal's marginal ordinary income tax rate is 34%. Ignore issuance expenses.

a. Calculate the after-tax cost of the U.S. dollar-denominated issue.

b. Calculate the after-tax cost of the Swiss-franc-denominated issue expressed in U.S. dollars.

B6. (Interest rate parity) The three-month riskless interest rate in U.S. dollars is 8% APR. The three-month riskless interest rate in Swiss francs is 3% APR. The dollar-franc exchange rate is SF1 = \$0.66.

a. Calculate the three-month forward rate required under interest rate parity.

b. Suppose the three-month forward rate is SF1 = \$0.68. Describe how a riskless arbitrage profit could be earned.

c. Quantify the profit in both dollars and Swiss francs.

B7. (Interest rate parity) The three-month riskless interest rate in U.S. dollars is 10% APR. The three-month riskless interest rate in Swiss francs is 5% APR. The dollar-franc exchange rate is SF1 = \$0.75.

a. Calculate the three-month forward rate required under interest rate parity.
b. Suppose the three-month forward rate is SF1 = \$0.77. Describe how a riskless arbitrage profit could be earned.
c. Quantify the profit in both dollars and Swiss francs.

B8. (Interest rate parity) The spot rate for U.S. dollars and Canadian dollars is \$1 = CD1.50. The one-year forward rate is \$1 = CD1.40.
a. Under interest rate parity, what is the one-year U.S. dollar interest rate if the one-year Canadian dollar interest rate is 5%?
b. Under interest rate parity, what is the one-year Canadian dollar interest rate if the one-year U.S. dollar interest rate is 10%?
c. What mathematical relationship must hold between the U.S. dollar and Canadian dollar one-year interest rates if interest rate parity prevails?

B9. (Interest rate parity) The spot rate for U.S. dollars and Canadian dollars is \$1 = CD1.70. The one-year forward rate is \$1 = CD1.60.
a. Under interest rate parity, what is the one-year U.S. dollar interest rate if the one-year Canadian dollar interest rate is 6%?
b. Under interest rate parity, what is the one-year Canadian dollar interest rate if the one-year U.S. dollar interest rate is 12%?
c. What mathematical relationship must hold between the U.S. dollar and Canadian dollar one-year interest rates if interest rate parity prevails?

B10. (Arbitrage opportunity) Gold is selling for \$310.00/oz. in New York and £207.0/oz. in London.
a. Suppose it were costless to transport gold between New York and London. What would the dollar-pound exchange rate have to be if the law of one price is to hold?
b. Suppose the dollar-pound exchange rate is £1 = \$1.70. Describe how arbitrageurs could realize a riskless arbitrage profit.
c. Quantify the profit in both dollars and British pounds.

B11. (Arbitrage opportunity) Silver is selling for \$6.00/oz. in New York and £3.60/oz. in London.
a. Suppose it were costless to transport silver between New York and London. What would the dollar-pound exchange rate have to be if the law of one price is to hold?
b. Suppose the dollar-pound exchange rate is £1 = \$2.00. Describe how arbitrageurs could realize a riskless arbitrage profit.
c. Quantify the profit in both dollars and British pounds.

B12. (Unbiased forward exchange rates) The Swiss franc-Canadian dollar spot exchange rate is SF1 = CD1.20. The one-year forward rate is SF1 = CD1.30.
a. What is your best estimate of the spot rate expected one year from now?
b. If the expected spot rate were SF1 = CD1.40, would anyone want to sell Swiss francs forward? to sell Canadian dollars forward?
c. If the expected spot rate were SF1 = CD1.10, would anyone want to sell Swiss francs forward? to sell Canadian dollars forward?

B13. (Unbiased forward exchange rates) The Swiss franc-Canadian dollar spot exchange rate is SF1 = CD1.40. The one-year forward rate is SF1 = CD1.55.
a. What is your best estimate of the spot rate expected one year from now?
b. If the expected spot rate were SF1 = CD1.45, would anyone want to sell Swiss francs forward? to sell Canadian dollars forward?
c. If the expected spot rate were SF1 = CD1.30, would anyone want to sell Swiss francs forward? to sell Canadian dollars forward?

B14. (Hedging transactions) TransAtlantic Airlines (TAA) expects to receive €5 million from a German tour operator in 30 days. Because TAA's expenses are in U.S. dollars, the firm wishes to hedge its foreign currency risk. The current spot exchange rate is €1 = $0.90, and the 30-day forward exchange rate is €1 = $0.87.

a. How many U.S. dollars should TAA expect to receive if it does not hedge?

b. Suppose the spot exchange rate at the time the tour operator pays is €1 = $0.84. How much would hedging have saved TAA?

c. If 30-day interest rates are 10% APR in the United States and Germany, would TAA be better off (1) borrowing euros for 30 days, investing them, and using the €5 million it receives to repay the loan or (2) selling €5 million forward to hedge its risk?

d. If the 30-day interest rates in the United States and Germany are 10% and 14% APR, respectively, would TAA be better off borrowing euros for 30 days and using the €5 million to repay the loan, or selling €5 million forward?

B15. (Interest rate parity) In problem B14, suppose the 30-day interest rate in the United States is 12% APR. What would the 30-day interest rate have to be in Germany in order for TAA to be indifferent between (1) entering into a 30-day forward contract and (2) borrowing euros for 30 days and using the €5 million to repay the loan?

B16. (Purchasing power parity) Consider again AlliedSignal's proposed automotive plant. What are the expected real rates of interest in Switzerland and in the United States? Why must these rates of interest be equal when interest rate parity and purchasing power parity hold and forward exchange rates are unbiased?

B17. (International capital budgeting) With AlliedSignal's proposed automotive plant, suppose that the projected riskless interest rates (APR) in the United States and Switzerland are as given here.

a. Calculate the spot exchange rates expected one, two, three, four, and five years hence.

b. Calculate the projected incremental cash flow stream in dollars on the basis of the projected spot exchange rates in part a.

c. Calculate the NPV of the project based on the cash flow stream in part b.

MATURITY (YEARS)	1	2	3	4	5
United States	8%	9%	9%	10%	10%
Switzerland	6%	7%	8%	9%	10%

B18. (International borrowing cost) Verify that if AlliedSignal can deduct for tax purposes the appreciation in the cost of francs that must be repaid, its after-tax cost of the franc-denominated loan, expressed in U.S. dollars, closely approximates the after-tax cost of the U.S. dollar-denominated loan, 5.00%.

B19. (International capital budgeting) Northern Chemical Company is considering building a petrochemical plant in Scotland. The plant would cost $100 million. The projected incremental cash flow stream is given below. The current spot exchange rate is £1 = $1.50. The one-year riskless return is 8% in the United States and 12% in the United Kingdom. The expected inflation rate in the United States is 5% per annum for the next seven years. The expected inflation rate in the United Kingdom is constant over this time period, too.

a. What is the expected inflation rate in the United Kingdom for the next seven years?

b. Calculate the expected spot exchange rates for each of the next seven years.

c. Calculate the projected incremental cash flow stream in dollars.

d. If the dollar required return is 14%, what is the NPV in dollars?

e. Calculate the British pound required return.

f. Calculate the NPV in British pounds.

g. Are the project NPVs in parts d and f equal? Explain.

YEAR	1	2	3	4	5	6	7
Cash flow (£ millions)	30	40	40	50	50	50	50

B20. (Excel: International capital budgeting) Work Problem B19 using a spreadsheet for all parts.

B21. (Excel: International borrowing cost) General Instrument can borrow in U.S. dollars at an APY of 8.0%. General Instrument can also borrow in euros at 10%. Assume the loan amount is $100 million.

a. For a four-year bullet loan with annual installments, what are the annual payments and the APY in dollars?

b. For a four-year bullet loan, what are the annual payments and APY in euros? The spot rate is $0.95/€.

c. Assume the forward rates are $0.935/€ for one year, $0.930/€ for two years, $0.915/€ for three years, and $0.900/€ for four years. What are the dollar-equivalent cash flows of the euro loan and the dollar-equivalent APY?

LEVEL C (ADVANCED)

C1. (Forward interest rates) The two-year interest rate is 10% APR semiannually compounded. The one-year interest rate is 8% APR semiannually compounded. If there is no opportunity for riskless arbitrage, what is the one-year forward interest rate?

C2. (Forward interest rates) The two-year interest rate is 9% APR semiannually compounded. The one-year interest rate is 8% APR semiannually compounded. If there is no opportunity for riskless arbitrage, what is the one-year forward interest rate?

C3. (Hedging transactions) Generalize the Boeing example to demonstrate that:

a. The net realized dollar value will be $320 million regardless of the future spot exchange rate when the British pounds are sold forward.

b. The net realized dollar value will be $320 million regardless of the future spot exchange rate when the British pounds are sold spot and the dollar proceeds invested at an interest rate that satisfies interest rate parity.

C4. (Law of one price) *The Economist* recently reported the following prices for a Big Mac hamburger in different countries, along with the exchange rates.

a. Calculate the exchange rates implied by the law of one price.

b. Are the prices consistent with the law of one price?

c. How would you interpret your answers to parts a and b? Are exchange rates out of equilibrium? Is the law of one price invalid? Or is there some other explanation?

COUNTRY	PRICE OF BIG MAC	EXCHANGE RATE
Australia	A$3.00	A$1.86/US$
Britain	£1.99	£0.69/US$
Canada	C$3.33	C$1.57/US$
Euro Area	€18.5	€1.12/US$
Japan	¥262	¥130/US$
United States	$2.46	—

MINICASE INTERNATIONAL FINANCING AT EMERSON ELECTRIC

Emerson Electric Company (Emerson) manufactures a broad range of electrical and electronic equipment. It has about 200 subsidiaries that operate in more than two dozen countries. Emerson is placing increased emphasis on its international operations, and international sales have increased to more than 20% of its total. As part of its international strategy, Emerson has shifted from exporting domestically produced items to manufacturing goods offshore, and nearly doubled its number of foreign plants.

Emerson wants to raise $65 million (or the equivalent in a foreign currency) to finance its overseas expansion. Its debt is rated triple-A, and thus it should be able to borrow funds in virtually any market it chooses. Emerson's investment banker has presented several financing alternatives. These alternatives include three possible two-year debt issues, each with a bullet maturity:

1. A domestic U.S. dollar issue bearing a coupon rate of 8.65% APR (with interest payable semiannually in arrears)
2. A Swiss franc-denominated Eurobond issue bearing a coupon rate of 4.60% APR (with interest payable annually in arrears)
3. A domestic issue denominated in New Zealand dollars bearing a coupon rate of 18.55% APR (with interest payable semiannually in arrears)

Emerson has subsidiaries operating in both Switzerland and New Zealand, and it realizes free cash flow in Swiss francs and New Zealand dollars. Nevertheless, it intends to hedge fully its currency risk exposure if it issues non-U.S. dollar debt. Its investment banker has said Emerson would be able to purchase Swiss francs and New Zealand dollars in the futures market at the following prices:

Months forward	6	12	18	24
Swiss francs/ U.S. dollar	1.510	1.470	1.440	1.410
New Zealand dollars/ U.S. dollar	1.905	1.992	2.079	2.166

The spot foreign exchange rates are 1.530 Swiss francs per U.S. dollar and 1.762 New Zealand dollars per U.S. dollar.

QUESTIONS

1. How would you explain the pattern of decreasing forward exchange rates for Swiss francs and the pattern of increasing forward exchange rates for New Zealand dollars? Explain why the Swiss franc issue may not be the least expensive, and why the New Zealand dollar issue may not be the most expensive, in spite of their interest rates.
2. What principal amount of foreign-currency-denominated bonds would Emerson have to issue to raise $65 million, assuming it issues bonds denominated in Swiss francs or New Zealand dollars? Specify the debt-service stream (principal and interest) for each alternative and express it in equivalent amounts of U.S. dollars.
3. Calculate the cost of borrowing for each alternative. Which of the three borrowing alternatives has the lowest cost?
4. Suppose the three debt issues require the following flotation costs, which are tax-deductible in the United States on a straight-line basis over the life of each issue: 1% for the Swiss franc issue, 0.75% for the New Zealand dollar issue, and 0.50% for the U.S. dollar issue. Assume a 40% income tax rate for Emerson. Which of the three alternatives has the lowest after-tax cost?

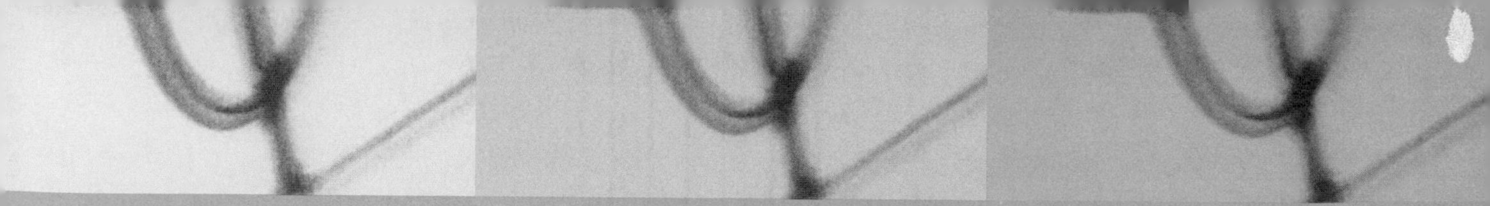

APPENDIX A

USING A BUSINESS CALCULATOR

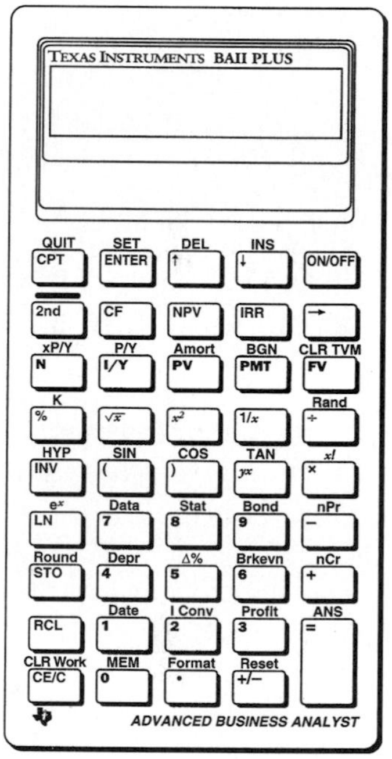

A business calculator is an absolute must in today's corporate environment whether you are doing finance, accounting, marketing, production, strategy, or human resource management. You can easily learn to make the time-value-of-money calculations we illustrate here. However, with just a little more effort, you can also learn to do so much more with your calculator, such as calculating averages, standard deviations, depreciation, linear regression coefficients, and breakeven amounts. The list is almost endless.

There are many different business calculators on the market today. The one you choose depends on your own personal preferences. We have chosen the Texas Instruments BAII PLUS to illustrate the use of a business calculator.

Key strokes are illustrated by boxes. An unshaded box indicates the function shown on the face of the key. For example, the four-key stroke sequence [3] [+] [2] [=] adds the numbers 3 and 2 using the blue keys with + and = on them. A shaded box preceded by a [2nd] indicates the function shown in cream above the key. For example, [4] [2nd] [*x!*] computes 4 factorial (4 times 3 times 2 times 1) using the secondary function shown above the times key, which is the blue key with × on it.

ASSUMED PAYMENTS PER PERIOD *(VERY IMPORTANT)*

Your calculator can assume any number of payments per period. For simplicity, our calculations here, and throughout the book, *always* assume the mode is set to 1.00. For example, if there are 12 monthly payments per year over 5 years, we make the conversion and use N = 60.

To set your calculator for use with our calculations:

[2nd] [P/Y] [1] [ENTER] [CE/C] [CE/C]

This setting continues indefinitely (even though the calculator is turned off and on) until it is changed.

DECIMAL PLACE DISPLAY

Your calculator always *calculates* with 9-digit accuracy. However, the numbers it displays depend on the number of decimal places to which you have it set. Our calculations generally display 2, 3, or 4 decimal places.

To set the number of decimal places displayed to three:

[2nd] [Format] [3] [ENTER] [the display will show: DEC = □ 3.000] [CE/C] [CE/C]

This setting also continues indefinitely (even though the calculator is turned off and on) until it is changed.

END-OF-PERIOD ANNUITY CASH FLOWS

Your calculator can assume that annuity cash flows occur either at the end of the period or at the beginning of the period. For simplicity, our calculations *always* assume the mode is set to end-of-period annuity cash flows. If a small BGN appears above the number display, the mode is set to beginning-of-period annuity cash flows. Otherwise, the mode is already set to end-of-period annuity cash flows.

To set the mode to end-of-period annuity cash flows:

[2nd] [BGN] [the display should show BGN; if it shows END, hit [CE/C]]
[2nd] [SET] [CE/C] [CE/C]

This setting also continues indefinitely (even though the calculator is turned off and on) until it is changed.

EXAMPLES

Present Value of a Single Future Cash Flow

The present value of $5,000 to be received in 4 years at 12% APY is $3,177.59:

[4] [N] [1] [2] [I/Y] [0] [PMT] [5] [0] [0] [0] [FV] [CPT] [PV] = −3,177.59

Future Value of a Current Amount

The future value of $2,000 to be received in 7 years at 9% APY is $3,656.08:

[7] [N] [9] [I/Y] [2] [0] [0] [0] [PV] [0] [PMT] [CPT] [FV] = −3,656.08

Present Value of an Annuity

The present value of $200 per month for 5 years (60 months) at 9% APR (0.75% per month) is $9,634.67:

[6] [0] [N] [.] [7] [5] [I/Y] [2] [0] [0] [PMT] [0] [FV] [CPT] [PV] = −9,634.67

Future Value of an Annuity

The future value of $50 per week for 3 years (156 weeks) at 6% APR (0.5% per week) is $11,772.37:

[1] [5] [6] [N] [.] [5] [I/Y] [0] [PV] [5] [0] [PMT] [CPT] [FV] = −11,772.37

Annuity Cash Flows for a Present Value

The monthly payments for a $100,000 20-year (240 months) mortgage at 8.16% APR (0.68% per month) are $846.43:

[2] [4] [0] [N] [.] [6] [8] [I/Y] [1] [0] [0] [0] [0] [0] [PV] [0] [FV] [CPT] [PMT] = −846.43

Annuity Cash Flows for a Future Value

Suppose you are going to save some money from the paycheck you get every 2 weeks, and you will earn 4.42% APR (0.17% per 2-week period) on your savings. To save up $10,000 over 2.5 years (65 pay periods), you will need to put aside $145.63 from each paycheck:

[6] [5] [N] [.] [1] [7] [I/Y] [0] [PV] [1] [0] [0] [0] [0] [FV] [CPT] [PMT] = −145.63

Interest Rate for a Present Value

A $15,000 10-year (120-month) loan requiring monthly payments of $206.96 has an APR of 11.04%:

[1] [2] [0] [N] [1] [5] [0] [0] [0] [PV] [2] [0] [6] [.] [9] [6] [+/−] [PMT] [0] [FV] [CPT] [I/Y] =
0.92 [×] [1] [2] [=] 11.04

Interest Rate for a Future Value

To save $1,000,000 by investing $155.50 per month for 35 years (420 months), your investments must earn an APR of 12.00%:

[4] [2] [0] [N] [0] [PV] [1] [5] [5] [6] [5] [0] [+/−] [PMT] [1] [0] [0] [0] [0] [0] [0] [FV] [CPT] [I/Y]
= 1.00 [×] [1] [2] [=] 12.00

Present Value of Annuity Cash Flows and a Future Value

The present value of a 10%-coupon ($50 semiannually) corporate bond that pays $1,000 at maturity in 8 years (16 semiannual periods) and has a yield to maturity of 12% (6% semiannually) is $898.94:

[1] [6] [N] [6] [I/Y] [5] [0] [PMT] [1] [0] [0] [0] [FV] [CPT] [PV] = −898.94

Interest Rate for Annuity Cash Flows and a Future Value

The yield to maturity of a 6%-coupon ($30 semiannually) corporate bond that pays $1,000 at maturity in 5.5 years (11 semiannual periods) and currently sells for $833.87 is 10%:

[1] [1] [N] [8] [3] [3] [.] [8] [7] [+/−] [PV] [3] [0] [PMT] [1] [0] [0] [0] [FV] [CPT] [I/Y] =
5.00 [×] [2] [=] 10.00

NPV and IRR for Uneven Cash Flows

CF0	CF1	CF2	CF3	CF4	CF5
−110,000	45,000	45,000	45,000	10,000	60,000

The NPV at a cost of capital of 12% and the IRR for the above cash flows from a capital budgeting project are $38,483.20 and 25.73%, respectively:

[CE/C] [CE/C] [CF] [2nd] [CLR Work] [1] [1] [0] [0] [0] [0] [+/−] [ENTER] [↓] [4] [5] [0] [0]

[0] [ENTER] [↓] [3] [3 is the number of times the cash flow repeats] [ENTER] [↓] [1] [0] [0]

[0] [0] [ENTER] [↓] [ENTER] [↓] [6] [0] [0] [0] [0] [ENTER] [↓] [ENTER] [2nd] [QUIT]
[all the cash flows have been entered]

[NPV] [1] [2] [12 is the cost of capital (required return)] [ENTER] [↓] [CPT] = 38,483.20

[IRR] [CPT] = 25.73

at a 20% cost of capital, the NPV is $13,726.85:

[NPV] [2] [0] [ENTER] [↓] [CPT] = 13,726.85

APPENDIX B

CUMULATIVE DISTRIBUTION FUNCTION FOR THE STANDARD NORMAL RANDOM VARIABLE

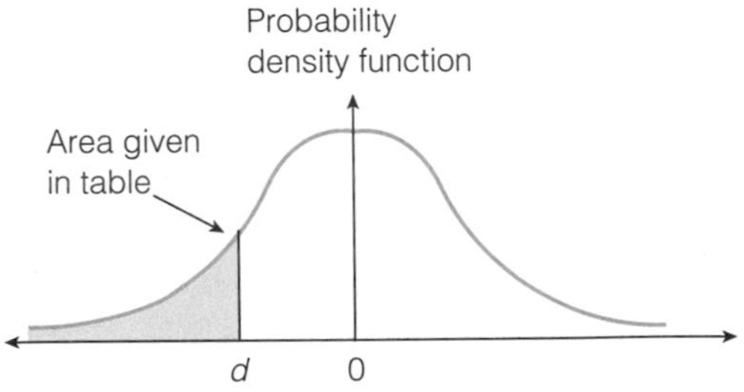

For example, N[−1.15] = .1251 and N[1.57] = .9418

d	0.00	0.01	0.02	0.03	0.04	0.05	0.06	0.07	0.08	0.09
−3.0	.0013	.0013	.0013	.0012	.0012	.0011	.0011	.0011	.0010	.0010
−2.9	.0019	.0018	.0018	.0017	.0016	.0016	.0015	.0015	.0014	.0014
−2.8	.0026	.0025	.0024	.0023	.0023	.0022	.0021	.0021	.0020	.0019
−2.7	.0035	.0034	.0033	.0032	.0031	.0030	.0029	.0028	.0027	.0026
−2.6	.0047	.0045	.0044	.0043	.0041	.0040	.0039	.0038	.0037	.0036
−2.5	.0062	.0060	.0059	.0057	.0055	.0054	.0052	.0051	.0049	.0048
−2.4	.0082	.0080	.0078	.0075	.0073	.0071	.0069	.0068	.0066	.0064
−2.3	.0107	.0104	.0102	.0099	.0096	.0094	.0091	.0089	.0087	.0084
−2.2	.0139	.0136	.0132	.0129	.0125	.0122	.0119	.0116	.0113	.0110
−2.1	.0179	.0174	.0170	.0166	.0162	.0158	.0154	.0150	.0146	.0143
−2.0	.0227	.0222	.0217	.0212	.0207	.0202	.0197	.0192	.0188	.0183
−1.9	.0287	.0281	.0274	.0268	.0262	.0256	.0250	.0244	.0239	.0233
−1.8	.0359	.0351	.0344	.0336	.0329	.0322	.0314	.0307	.0301	.0294
−1.7	.0446	.0436	.0427	.0418	.0409	.0401	.0392	.0384	.0375	.0367
−1.6	.0548	.0537	.0526	.0516	.0505	.0495	.0485	.0475	.0465	.0455
−1.5	.0668	.0655	.0643	.0630	.0618	.0606	.0594	.0582	.0571	.0559
−1.4	.0808	.0793	.0778	.0764	.0749	.0735	.0721	.0708	.0694	.0681
−1.3	.0968	.0951	.0934	.0918	.0901	.0885	.0869	.0853	.0838	.0823
−1.2	.1151	.1131	.1112	.1093	.1075	.1056	.1038	.1020	.1003	.0985
−1.1	.1357	.1335	.1314	.1292	.1271	.1251	.1230	.1210	.1190	.1170
−1.0	.1587	.1563	.1539	.1515	.1492	.1469	.1446	.1423	.1401	.1379
−0.9	.1841	.1814	.1788	.1762	.1736	.1711	.1685	.1660	.1635	.1611
−0.8	.2119	.2090	.2061	.2033	.2005	.1977	.1949	.1922	.1894	.1867
−0.7	.2420	.2389	.2358	.2327	.2296	.2266	.2236	.2206	.2177	.2148
−0.6	.2743	.2709	.2676	.2643	.2611	.2578	.2546	.2514	.2483	.2451
−0.5	.3085	.3050	.3015	.2981	.2946	.2912	.2877	.2843	.2810	.2776
−0.4	.3446	.3409	.3372	.3336	.3300	.3264	.3228	.3192	.3156	.3121
−0.3	.3821	.3783	.3745	.3707	.3669	.3632	.3594	.3557	.3520	.3483
−0.2	.4207	.4168	.4129	.4090	.4052	.4013	.3974	.3936	.3897	.3859
−0.1	.4602	.4562	.4522	.4483	.4443	.4404	.4364	.4325	.4286	.4247
−0.0	.5000	.4960	.4920	.4880	.4840	.4801	.4761	.4721	.4681	.4641

d	0.00	0.01	0.02	0.03	0.04	0.05	0.06	0.07	0.08	0.09
0.0	.5000	.5040	.5080	.5120	.5160	.5199	.5239	.5279	.5319	.5359
0.1	.5398	.5438	.5478	.5517	.5557	.5596	.5636	.5675	.5714	.5753
0.2	.5793	.5832	.5871	.5910	.5948	.5987	.6026	.6064	.6103	.6141
0.3	.6179	.6217	.6255	.6293	.6331	.6368	.6406	.6443	.6480	.6517
0.4	.6554	.6591	.6628	.6664	.6700	.6736	.6772	.6808	.6844	.6879
0.5	.6915	.6950	.6985	.7019	.7054	.7088	.7123	.7157	.7190	.7224
0.6	.7257	.7291	.7324	.7357	.7389	.7422	.7454	.7486	.7517	.7549
0.7	.7580	.7611	.7642	.7673	.7704	.7734	.7764	.7794	.7823	.7852
0.8	.7881	.7910	.7939	.7967	.7995	.8023	.8051	.8078	.8106	.8133
0.9	.8159	.8186	.8212	.8238	.8264	.8289	.8315	.8340	.8365	.8389
1.0	.8413	.8439	.8461	.8485	.8508	.8531	.8554	.8577	.8599	.8621
1.1	.8643	.8665	.8686	.8708	.8729	.8749	.8770	.8790	.8810	.8830
1.2	.8849	.8869	.8888	.8907	.8925	.8944	.8962	.8980	.8997	.9015
1.3	.9032	.9049	.9066	.9082	.9099	.9115	.9131	.9147	.9162	.9177
1.4	.9192	.9207	.9222	.9236	.9251	.9265	.9279	.9292	.9306	.9319
1.5	.9332	.9345	.9357	.9370	.9382	.9394	.9406	.9418	.9429	.9441
1.6	.9452	.9463	.9474	.9484	.9495	.9505	.9515	.9525	.9535	.9545
1.7	.9554	.9564	.9573	.9582	.9591	.9599	.9608	.9616	.9625	.9633
1.8	.9641	.9649	.9656	.9664	.9671	.9678	.9686	.9693	.9699	.9706
1.9	.9713	.9719	.9726	.9732	.9738	.9744	.9750	.9756	.9761	.9767
2.0	.9773	.9778	.9783	.9788	.9793	.9798	.9803	.9808	.9812	.9817
2.1	.9821	.9826	.9830	.9834	.9838	.9842	.9846	.9850	.9854	.9857
2.2	.9861	.9864	.9868	.9871	.9875	.9878	.9881	.9884	.9887	.9890
2.3	.9893	.9896	.9898	.9901	.9904	.9906	.9909	.9911	.9913	.9916
2.4	.9918	.9920	.9922	.9925	.9927	.9929	.9931	.9932	.9934	.9936
2.5	.9938	.9940	.9941	.9943	.9945	.9946	.9948	.9949	.9951	.9952
2.6	.9953	.9955	.9956	.9957	.9959	.9960	.9961	.9962	.9963	.9964
2.7	.9965	.9966	.9967	.9968	.9969	.9970	.9971	.9972	.9973	.9974
2.8	.9974	.9975	.9976	.9977	.9977	.9978	.9979	.9979	.9980	.9981
2.9	.9981	.9982	.9982	.9983	.9984	.9984	.9985	.9985	.9986	.9986
3.0	.9987	.9987	.9987	.9988	.9988	.9989	.9989	.9989	.9990	.9990

APPENDIX C

ANSWERS TO SELECTED PROBLEMS

CHAPTER 2

B1. $4,523.49

B3. $22,106.81

B5. a. $11,000; $10,000
b. $12,000; $10,909.09
c. $11,000; $9,166.67

B7. $3,259.84

B9. a. $50,000; Yes; $48,500; 3133%
b. −$15,000; No

B11. Sell as is; $2,100,000

C1. a. 20%; 100%; −100%
b. −15%; −100%; 200%

CHAPTER 3

B1. a. $170 million; $300 million
b. $200 million; $300 million
c. $170 million d. $160 million
e. $70 million; $100 million
f. $330 million; $(160) million; $(170) million

B3. a. $10,200 thousand
b. $1,700 thousand c. $8,500 thousand

B5. a. $400 million; $475 million
b. $975 million; $1,175 million
c. $275 million

B7. a. $2,123,300 b. 34%; 34%

B9. a. $2,250; 15%; 15%
b. $14,493.75; 27.5%; 22.3%
c. $31,862.25; 30.5%; 26.1%

C1. $750,000; Economic income includes changes in market values of assets.

C3. a. $127,000; 27% b. $119,092; 19.1%

CHAPTER 4

B1. 8.0%

B3. a. $7,360.09 b. $11,469.92
c. $15,761.86 d. $16,617.55
e. $16,666.67

B5. a. $5,667,797.62 b. 28.3%

B7. $9,244,236.98

B9. a. 0.11% b. 5.72% c. 5.88%

B11. a. $3,178.27 b. $3,338.38

B13. $1,900.79

B15. a. 18.39% b. $3,551.70
c. $5,893.61

B17. a. 0.80% b. 9.60% c. 10.03%

B19. a. 8.16% b. 23.87% c. 6.18%

B21. a. 16.18% b. 9.42%

B23. a. 0.62% b. 7.44% c. 7.70%

B25. $9,314.76

B27. $1,151.26

B29. $33,668.65

B31. $21,568.14

B33. $9,883.46

B35. $7,644.63

B37. 12.0%

B39. In 8 years

B41. a. 17.67 years b. 8.04 years
c. 4.96 years

B43. 17.0%

B45. $16,257.54

B47. $5,425.23

B49. a. 1.0% b. 12.0% c. 12.68%

B51. a. $572.49 b. No

B53. Borrow and pay the cash price.

B55. $320.65

B57. $16,790.88
B59. The financing deal
B61. a. $635.99 c. 9.38%
C1. $169.79
C3. a. $61,857.64 b. $32.64
C5. $47,908.26
C7. $290.18
C9. $362.73
C11. $33,052.88
C13. $10,182.49
C15. 3.53%
C17. $2,119.82
C19. $77.88
C21. $2,268,400.09

CHAPTER 5

B1. 8.10%; 8.26%
B3. 5.18%; 10.63%
B5. October 10, 2020
B7. January 18, 2020
B9. a. $1,208.29 b. 9.34% c. 9.44%
B11. 4.77%
B13. 12.14%
B15. 9.20%
B17. 3.33%
B19. 3.33%
B21. a. $1,010.61; $1,059.42; $1,097.27
b. $1,020.18; $1,116.03; $1,195.42
c. $1,001.17; $1,006.39; $1,010.18
d. Interest rate risk is higher for longer maturity bonds.
B23. a. $1,009.57; $1,062.81; $1,115.57
b. $990.57; $941.74; $901.04
c. $954.17; $747.35; $623.84
d. Interest rate risk is higher for longer maturity bonds.
B25. a. −5.48% b. 23.32%
B27. a. $12.65 b. $7.70
B29. a. $24.84 b. $13.15
B31. $26.19
B33. $176.21
B35. 10.58%
B37. a. $866.78 b. 9.72%
C1. a. 13.5%; 13.95%
b. 13.32%; 13.64%
c. 13.4%; 13.85%
C3. −$0.16
C5. 18.24%; 12.00%; Risk; Diversification
C7. a. 16.20% b. 16.20%

CHAPTER 6

B1. a. 0% b. $9.09 c. Yes
B3. No. It has a negative NPV.
B5. $2.57 million
B7. a. −$10.11 million
b. −$3.37 per share
B9. a. N, M, L, K
b. $26.79; $29.79; $32.97; $39.80 c. Yes
B11. a. $2,679.46; $1,339.73
b. 21.86%; 21.86% c. 1.2679; 1.2679
d. 16.73%; 16.73%
e. 2.5 years; 2.5 years
f. A; It has a higher NPV.
B13. a. R2 b. Size difference c. 12.12%
B15. a. 3 years b. 3.51 years
c. $32,110.17 d. 1.1835
e. 17.09% f. 14.73%
B17. a. $39,456.29 b. −$518.50
B19. a. $24.90; Yes b. 20.28%; Yes
c. 2.5 years; Nothing
B21. a. $87.75; Yes
b. −31.12%; Yes c. 0
d. Select the project with the highest NPV.
B23. B because it has a higher NPV.
B25. a. $85,369.03; $82,095.97
b. 44.83%; 48.40% c. 18.15% d. A
B27. a. A: $300.00; $209.19; $133.97; $71.00; $17.75; −$27.68 B: $500.00; $322.70; $183.01; $71.75; −$17.75; −$90.40
b. $133.97; $183.01
c. 21.86%; 18.92%
d. 15.09%; $69.94 e. B
B29. Yes.
B31. a. $72.73; 50.00%; $100.53; 25.99%
b. 1: $85.71; $72.73; $60.87; $50; $40; $30.77; $22.22; $14.29; $6.90; $0
c. 2: $145.54; $100.53; $63.01; $31.48; $4.80; −$17.93; −$37.42; −$54.23; −$68.79; −$81.48
C1. a. $0.31; 15.31%; $2.51; 16.97% b. Both
c. Both d. B
C3. The existence of a discounted payback period guarantees a positive (or zero) NPV.

CHAPTER 7

B1. a. \$6,065.26 b. \$8,000.00 c. Expense
B3. \$24,996.05
B5. a. −\$101,750
b. \$33,498.57; \$38,252.37; \$25,581.27; \$22,417.77; \$19,250.00
c. \$26,000 d. \$22,944.69
B7. \$94,183.52
B9. −\$271,547.85
B11. a. \$57,006.23 b. \$57,006.23
B13. \$681.91
B15. \$2,529,798.59
B17. a. \$240,000; \$1,474,696.11
b. \$300,000; \$843,370.13 c. 68.63%
B19. a. \$500,000; \$70,000; \$500,000
b. \$122,891.34 c. \$4,622,891.34
B21. B; It has a lower EAC.
B23. \$1,030,800
B25. b. \$990,537; 26.24%
C1. Japanese
C3. \$13,793.94
C5. −\$38,388.43; −\$22,119.05; −\$51,912.10; −\$20,874.62; −\$66,801.79; −\$21,074.01; −\$83,256.20; −\$21,962.78

CHAPTER 8

B1. B
B3. \$0
B5. a. \$200,000 b. \$350,000
B7. Sell
B9. \$33,333.33
B11. a. No b. \$10,000,000
c. \$5,703,281.15
B13. a. A b. B
B15. b. 12.33% c. \$3,016.95
C1. $TR = (2{,}538{,}000 \times Q_D^{2})^{1/3}$; MR = MC = \$0.387
C3. a. \$106.81
b. Rational for 2nd outcome; \$123.82

CHAPTER 9

B1. \$49.50
B3. 8%; 16%
B5. a. 1: 15.2%; 12.16; 3.49% 2:14.4%; 31.84; 5.64% 3: 10%; 1.6; 1.26%
b. Return: 1, 2, 3 Risk: 3, 1, 2
B7. a. 4.8%; 3.3% b. 57.76; 37.41
c. −311.53 d. −0.14
B9. \$79.40
C1. a. 1, 2, 3, 7 b. 7
c. Invest 60.24% in risk-free asset and 39.76% in portfolio 7; 11.63%
d. Borrow 19.02% at risk-free rate and invest 119.02% in portfolio 7; 14.88%
C5. 216.32%

CHAPTER 10

B1. 3.92
B3. 14.14%
B5. 25.90%
B7. 1.25; 10%
B9. 12%
B11. 14.48%
B13. a. 1.44 b. 17.52%
C1. a. 9.75%; 15.00% b. 1.49
c. 11.59%
C3. a. 0.697 c. Yes

CHAPTER 11

B1. 15.0%
B3. 28.20%
B5. 20%; 80%
B7. 47.62%; 52.38%
B9. B, C
B11. 13.72%
B15. 14.5%
B17. a. 5.46% b. 11.88% c. 8.58%
B19. a. 4.52% b. 15.60% c. 12.22%
B21. 13.60%
B23. Select project B.
C1. a. 0.91 b. 19.06% c. 14.53%
C3. a. 0.97 b. 1.29
c. 13.76%; 16.32%
C5. 1.45

CHAPTER 12

B1. a. \$1,080 b. \$240 c. \$0; No
B3. −2.87%; −100.00% 4.17%; −100.00% 11.11%; −100.00% 11.11%; 66.67% 11.11%; 233.33%

B5. $742,924.53
B7. $9,142.62
B9. a. $20; $15 b. $5; $0 c. $25; $25
C1. a. $1.90 b. $1.90 c. $1.95
d. The simple option model calculated a slightly lower put price than put-call parity.
C3. a. $100 b. $100 c. 25%

CHAPTER 13

B1. a. $10 million; $100 million
b. $0; $70 million
c. −$10 million; $80 million
d. $5 million; $75 million
e. Asset substitution
B3. $437,000
B5. a. $22,500; $300,000
b. $75,000; $450,000
c. $26,250; $150,000; $87,500; $225,000
d. The plan with the higher bonus
B7. a. $200,000 b. $175,000
B9. a. $500 b. $400
B11. $0
B13. a. $0; $0; $0; $500,000 b. −$500,000; −$200,000; −$300,000; $300,000
C1. a. $20 million b. $17.14 million
C3. a. $22 million; $100 million
b. $0; $82 million
c. −$10 million; $92 million
d. $5.5 million; $86.5 million e. Yes
C5. a. $6,000; $4,000; $0; $0; $5,880; $3,920
b. $6,000; $3,000; $6,000; $4,000
c. $120; −$900; Debtholders
C7. a. 13.33% b. 15.20%

CHAPTER 14

B1. a. $24,000 b. 10.67% c. 11.94%
B3. a. $270,000 b. −$330,000 c. $2.70
B5. a. $80,000 b. −$70,000 c. $1.60

CHAPTER 15

B1. 18.17%
B5. a. $5,000 b. $3,500
c. $3,920; 35.71% d. $3,149.89
e. $3,317.89 f. $5,000
B7. Either; Symmetric
B9. a. 14.82% b. 12.76%
c. 13.43% d. 1.57
C3. If the risk-free rate (APR) is greater than 14.76%

CHAPTER 16

B1. a. 3.25 − 4.30; 50 − 65; 25 − 32
B5. $243,486.99
B7. 12.89%
B9. a. 14.16% b. 14.38%
B11. 16.73%
B13. a. $613,702.06 b. 0.2785
c. 22.54% d. 22.76%

CHAPTER 17

B1. a. 80% b. 1,600
B5. a. Yes; It is now $0.50 per presplit share
b. Stock price increase
B7. No effect
B9. a. 39.375% b. Firms in cyclical businesses
B11. 4
B13. a. $22.50 b. Wealth has been expropriated from other shareholders.
B15. a. $1,000,000 increase b. $0.56 decrease
c. $1,000,000 decrease
d. Greenmail expropriates shareholder wealth.
B17. $0.41
C1. a. $8,000,000 decrease; $4,000,000 decrease
b. If shareholders do not have any other investment opportunities such that $r \times (1 - T) > r_f$

CHAPTER 18

B1. a. 8.33% b. 8.41% c. 8.71%
B3. $29.67
B5. a. $21.75; 15.23 b. $0.82
c. The firm does not have broad market appeal or has highly concentrated ownership.
d. Time to complete and lack of new investors
B7. 7.26%
B9. a. $1 increase b. 50,000
c. $10,000 increase d. No
B11. a. 5% b. Buy 60,000 shares
B13. a. $19,600,000; $1.96 b. $25,360,000; $1.95 c. $23,920,000; $1.71

CHAPTER 19

B1. a. $50; $50; $50; $50; $50; $50; $50; $550; $50; $550
b. 12.70%

B3. a. $100; $102.50; $105; $107.50; $1,110
b. 10.45% c. 6.90%

B5. a. 9.37%; 9.45%; 9.32%
b. Eurobond offering
c. Eurobonds are harder to redeem before maturity

B7. $55 million

B9. $800 million

B11. 8.8 years

B13. a. 9.84% b. 9 years c. 6.27 years

B15. −$1,194,770.49

B17. a. 2.72; 6.95; 7.35; 10
b. 0.52%; 1.32%; 1.40%; 1.90%
c. The percentage change is approximately (9% − 8.8%) × duration

C1. a. 7.92% b. 8.12%

C3. a. $11,996,650.11
b. NA decreases by $300,000

CHAPTER 20

B3. $17,279.03

B5. Yes; Leasing

B7. $0.46

B9. a. $25,000; −$4,000; −$4,000; −$4,000; −$4,000; −$4,000; −$4,000; −$4,000; −$9,000
b. −$226.30; Borrow and buy
c. −$1,363.33; Borrow and buy
d. −$186.88; Borrow and buy; $45.52; Lease

B11. a. $500,958.64 b. $2,108,462.65
c. $1,137,442.28 d. Yes

B13. 22.31%

B15. a. $19,441.59
b. $9,818.77; Present value of depreciation tax credit is different
c. $19,056.80

CHAPTER 21

B1. a. $3.74 b. $3.60 c. $2.40 d. $3.08

B3. $3.35

B5. a. $1.54; $1.54; $0 b. $3.82; $1.82; $2.00 c. $5.49; $1.49; $4.00

B7. a. $3.50 b. $3.12 c. $2.74

B9. $0.88

B11. a. $2.49 b. $2.66 c. $2.84

B13. $8.16; $4.38; $3.78

B15. a. Yes. b. Reject offer c. Yes
d. Bank 75%; Manufacturer 25%

B17. a. Yes b. No c. Yes

B19. a. Buy an interest rate cap
b. 8.5%; 7.75%; 9.5%; 10%; 10%; 10%; 10%; 8.5%
c. $0; $0; $0; $3,125,000; $6,250,000; $8,125,000; $1,875,000; $0

B21. a. Sell interest futures b. 0.95459
c. 955 d. $9,460,000; $9,464,050
e. 1.8405; 1,840; $9,460,000; $9,457,600

B23. a. −$120,000; −$240,000; $120,000; $300,000; $60,000; −$240,000
b. −$120,000; $60,000; $240,000; $600,000; $960,000; $1,140,000
c. −$120,000; −$60,000; −$240,000; −$660,000; −$720,000; −$1,080,000

C1. Trial and error

CHAPTER 22

B1. a. $400,000 b. About every 6 days
c. $200,000
d. $18,000; $18,000; $36,000

B3. a. $400 b. $200; 25 c. $50; $25; $25

B5. a. $346,410.16; $8,660.25; $8,660.25; $17,320.50
b. $12,124.36; $8,660.25; $20,784.61
c. $10,246.95; $10,246.95; $20,493.90

B7. $10,000; $15,000; $15,000; −$10,000; −$5,000; $5,000; $5,000; $26,428.57; $31,428.57; $5,000

B11. a. $12.50; $3.26 b. $12.50; $23.60
c. $25,439.40

B13. a. Yes b. −$2,000
c. Compensating balance proposal

B15. a. No; $100 b. $125,000

B17. a. $100; −$115; 15%
b. $85; −$100; 17.65%
c. $90; −$105; 16.67% d. $75; −$90; 20%

B19. a. 15% b. 13.75%
c. 16.28%; The second loan is cheapest

B21. a. $100; −$102; 8.24%
b. $98; −$100; 8.42%
c. $90; −$92; 9.19% d. $88; $90; 9.41%

B23. a. 14% b. 11.76% c. 19.05%

B25. b. 21.20%; 22.94%

C1. a. $290,000 b. 1.93 days c. −$10,500
C3. a. $1,100 b. $900 c. $200
d. $366,666.67

CHAPTER 23

B1. $42,298.50
B3. $10,940.08
B5. Proposed policy
B7. Proposed policy
B9. $4,200; $1,700; $2,400; $8,300; 50.60%; 20.48%; 28.92%
B11. 51 days
B13. Current policy
B15. a. $29,000 b. 17.66 rolls; $17,663.52
c. $17,666.67; $17,676.47; 18 rolls
B17. a. 5,099 tons; $254,950.98
b. 5,000 tons; $255,000
B19. a. 1,118; $3,354.10 b. $3,625
c. $270.90
B21. a. 774.6; $7,745.97 b. 774.6; $4,745.97
c. 1,000; $5,000
B23. a. 20 units b. 25 units
B25. 21,000; 9,000
B27. a. 80%; 30%; 5%; 0%
b. $575; $735; $955
c. $720; $210; $25; 75.39%; 21.99%; 2.62%
C1. a. 27; Grant credit b. 10; Deny credit
C3. a. 1,000 units b. 175 units

CHAPTER 24

B1. a. $765,000
B3. External funds are needed.
B7. a. $6,000 available for investment
b. $38,000 additional external financing needed
B9. $110,000
B11. $0

CHAPTER 25

B1. a. $59.34 b. 34.45%
c. 4 years d. Yes
B3. a. $115 million; $100 million
b. $215 million; $50 million; $165 million
c. No
B5. $125 million
B7. a. 15; 12; 14; 10.7; 11; 10; 8.4; 7.5; 6.2; 8.0; 8.0; 8.3; 6.1; 6.0; 6.2; 6.2; 6.3; 5.9
b. Multiple of EBITDA
c. $580 − $630 million; Differences in interest and depreciation expenses
B9. 8.97%
B11. a. 25 million barrels b. $300 million
B13. a. 17.21% b. $292.69 million
c. $71.94 million
B15. a. 10; 14 b. 12.82; no
B17. a. $79.14 million b. Help c. Risk
B19. a. $145.91 million b. $76.15 million
c. Yes
B21. a. 1: 1/2 b. 1: 5/8 c. −10%
C1. a. $300 million b. 23.33%
c. $0.10 / share
C3. a. $299.1 million b. $164.65 million

CHAPTER 26

B1. 71%
B3. Trade creditors receive $2,000,000; Banks receive $500,000; Mortgage holders receive $500,000
B5. Secured debt holders receive $14 million; Unsecured debt holders receive $6 million
B7. Trade creditors receive $150; Banks receive $750; Mortgage holders receive $1,650
B9. a. Trade creditors b. Yes
B11. Gray; Likely; Gray; Gray; Gray; Likely
C1. a. Yes b. Trade creditors receive $8.68; Banks receive $31.31; Mortgage holders receive $20; Senior debenture holders receive $9.01

CHAPTER 27

B3. a. 5.25% b. 5.27%
c. Domestic; Lower issuance costs, lower coupon
B5. a. 6.6% b. 7.26%
B7. a. $0.76 b. Covered interest arbitrage
c. $1.45 / $100 (3 mos.); SF 1.88 / SF 133.33 (3 mos.)
B9. a. 12.63% b. 5.41%
c. $r_{us} = 1/16 + 17/16 \times r_{cd}$
B11. a. $1.67 / £
b. Buy NY silver; Sell London silver
c. $1.20 / oz; £0.60 / oz
B13. a. SF 1 = CD 1.55 b. Yes; No c. Yes; No
B15. 53.8% APR

B17. a. \$0.6113 / SF; \$0.6227 / SF; \$0.6285 / SF; \$0.6343 / SF; \$0.6343 / SF
b. −\$30; \$9.17; \$10.59; \$12.57; \$12.69; \$10.78
c. \$6.86 million

B19. a. 8.89%
b. \$1.45 / £; \$1.39 / £; \$1.34 / £; \$1.30 / £; \$1.25 / £; \$1.21 / £; \$1.16 / £
c. −\$100; \$43.39; \$55.79; \$53.80; \$64.85; \$62.53; \$60.30; \$58.14
d. \$138.88 million
e. 18.22%
f. £92.59 million
g. Yes; \$1.50 / £ × £92.59 = \$138.88

B21. a. \$8; \$8; \$8; \$108; 8.0%
b. 10.53; 10.53; 10.53; 115.83; 10.0%
c. \$9.84; \$9.80; \$9.63; \$104.21; 8.54%

C1. 12.04%

GLOSSARY

Abandonment option The option of terminating an investment earlier than originally planned.

ABC system of inventory control An inventory management system that categorizes inventory into one of three groups—A, B, or C—on the basis of critical need.

Absolute priority doctrine The requirement that any distribution of a debtor's assets should be strictly according to claim priority.

Acid test ratio The difference between current assets and inventories divided by current liabilities.

Adjusted present value (APV) A method that determines total value by adding the "basic" present value of unleveraged cash flows to the present value of net benefits to leverage.

Agency cost view (of capital structure) The argument that the various agency costs create a complex environment in which total agency costs are at a minimum with some, but less than 100%, debt financing.

Agency costs The incremental costs of having an agent make decisions for a principal.

Agency problem A potential conflict of interest in a principal-agent relationship.

Agency theory The analysis of principal-agent relationships, wherein one person, an *agent*, acts on behalf of another person, a *principal*.

Agent The decision maker in a principal-agent relationship.

Aging schedule A table of accounts receivable broken down into age categories (such as 0–30 days, 30–60 days, and 60–90 days), which is used to see whether customer payments are keeping close to schedule.

American option An option that can be exercised at any time during its life.

Annual percentage rate (APR) The periodic rate times the number of periods in a year. For example, 2% per quarter is an 8% APR.

Annual percentage yield (APY) The effective (true) annual rate of return. The APY is the rate you actually earn or pay in one year, taking into account the effect of compounding. For example, as shown in Table 4-3, 1% per month is a 12.68% APY.

Annual report A report issued annually by a firm. It includes, at a minimum, an income statement, a balance sheet, a statement of cash flows, and accompanying notes.

Annuity A series of identical cash flows each period for n periods.

Annuity due An *annuity* with n payments, wherein the first payment is made at time $t = 0$ and the last payment is made at time $t = n - 1$.

APR See *Annual percentage rate.*

APT See *Arbitrage pricing theory.*

APV See *Adjusted present value.*

APY See *Annual percentage yield.*

Arbitrage The act of buying and selling an asset simultaneously, where the sale price is larger than the purchase price, so that the difference provides a riskless profit.

Arbitrage pricing theory (APT) A theory of asset pricing in which the risk premium is based on a specified set of risk factors in addition to (or other than) the correlation with the expected excess return on the market portfolio.

Arbitragers Persons who search for and exploit arbitrage opportunities. Also spelled *arbitrageurs.*

Asset activity ratios Ratios that measure how effectively the firm is managing its assets.

Asset-based financing Methods of financing in which lenders and equity investors look principally to the cash flow from a particular asset or set of assets for a return on, and the return of, their investment.

Asset substitution A firm's investing in assets that are riskier than those that the debtholders expected.

Asymmetric Lacking equivalence, such as the unequal tax treatment of interest expense and dividend payments.

Asymmetric information Information that is known to some people but not to others.

Average age of accounts receivable The weighted average age of all the firm's outstanding invoices.

Average collection period The approximate number of days required to collect a firm's accounts receivable. Also called *days' sales outstanding.*

Average life The effective maturity of a debt issue, taking into account the effect of sinking fund payments.

Average tax rate Taxes as a fraction of income; total taxes divided by total taxable income.

Balance sheet A statement of a firm's financial position at one point in time, including its assets and the claims on those assets by creditors (liabilities) and owners (stockholders' equity).

Balance sheet identity Total Assets = Liabilities + Stockholders' Equity.

Balloon payment A debt payment that is larger than the loan's other payments. It is typically the final payment that repays the outstanding balance of the loan.

Bankruptcy A formal legal process under which a firm experiencing financial difficulty is protected from its creditors while it works out a plan to settle its debt obligations under the supervision of the bankruptcy court.

Bankruptcy cost view (of capital structure) The argument that expected indirect and direct bankruptcy costs offset the other benefits from leverage so that the optimal amount of leverage is less than 100% debt financing.

Benefit-cost ratio The present value of the future cash flows divided by the initial investment. Also called the *profitability index.*

Beta A linear measure of how much an individual asset contributes to the standard deviation of the market portfolio; calculated as the covariance between the return on the asset and the return on the market portfolio, divided by the variance of the return on the market portfolio.

Bond A long-term obligation for borrowed money; that is, a long-term *debt security.*

Bond covenant A contractual provision in a bond indenture. A positive covenant requires certain actions. A negative covenant limits certain actions.

Bond indenture The explicit legal contract for a bond.

Bond refunding Replacing an outstanding bond before its maturity with a new bond.

Book value The net amount (net book value) for something shown in accounting statements.

Break-even point An accounting term defined as the point at which the total contribution margin equals the total fixed costs of producing a product or service.

Budget A detailed schedule of a financial activity, such as an advertising budget, a sales budget, or a capital budget.

Bullet maturity Refers to debt that requires repayment of the entire principal at maturity.

Business risk The inherent or fundamental risk of a business, without regard to financial risk. Also called *operating risk.*

Call option The right to *buy* something at a given price during the life of the option.

Call provision A provision that gives the firm the right to repay the bonds before the maturity date.

Capital-asset-pricing model (CAPM) A model for determining the *required return* on an asset, taking into account the risk of the asset. A model for specifying the risk-return trade-off in the capital markets.

Capital budget A firm's set of planned capital expenditures.

Capital budgeting The process of choosing the firm's long-term capital investments.

Capital gain The difference between what an asset is sold for and its book value, typically referring to an asset that has been owned for a sufficiently long time, such as a year or more.

Capital gains yield The price change portion of a stock's return.

Capital lease A lease obligation that has to be capitalized on the face of the balance sheet.

Capital market A market in which securities are bought and sold.

Capital market efficiency Reflects the relative amount of wealth wasted in making transactions. An efficient capital market allows the transfer of assets with little wealth loss.

Capital market imperfections view (of capital structure) The view that issuing debt is generally valuable but that the firm's optimal choice of capital structure is a dynamic process that involves the other views of capital structure (net corporate/personal tax, agency cost, bankruptcy cost, and pecking order), which result from considerations of asymmetric taxes, asymmetric information, and transaction costs.

Capital market line (CML) The line of investment possibilities extending outward from the *riskless rate*, r_f, and passing through the expected return on the *market portfolio.*

Capital rationing Placing one or more limits on (rationing) the amount of new investment undertaken by a firm, either by using a higher cost of capital or by setting a maximum on parts of, and/or the entirety of, the capital budget.

Capital structure The makeup of the liabilities and stockholders' equity side of the balance sheet, especially the ratio of debt to equity and the mixture of short and long maturities.

Capitalization rate A stock's *required return.*

CAPM See *Capital-asset-pricing model.*

Cash budget A forecasted summary of a firm's expected cash inflows and cash outflows as well as its expected cash and loan balances.

Cash budgeting The process of preparing the *cash budget.*

Cash conversion cycle The length of time between a firm's purchase inventory and the receipt of cash from its accounts receivable.

Cash discount An incentive offered to purchasers of a firm's product for payment within a specified time period, such as 10 days.

Cash flow after tax The *net operating cash flow.*

Cash-flow break-even point The point below which the firm will need either to obtain additional financing or to liquidate some of its assets to meet its fixed costs (for example, salaries and administrative costs, interest and principal payments, and planned cash dividends).

Cash flow coverage ratio The number of times that financial obligations (for interest, principal payments, preferred stock dividends, and rental payments) are covered by earnings before interest, taxes, rental payments, and depreciation.

Cash ratio The proportion of a firm's assets held as cash.

Characteristic line The plot of the periodic excess return on a stock (the difference between the return on the stock and the riskless return) and the excess return on the market portfolio.

Clientele effect The grouping of investors who have a preference that the firm follow a particular financing policy, such as the amount of leverage it uses.

Closing price The price of a financial security in the last trade before the market closed.

Collateral Assets that can be repossessed if the borrower defaults.

Collection float The negative float that is created between the time when you deposit a check in your account and the time when funds are made available.

Collection fractions The percentage of a given month's sales collected during the month of sale and each month following the sale.

Collective wisdom The combination (net result) of all of the individual opinions about a stock's value.

Commercial paper A promissory note sold by a large, creditworthy corporation in large denominations with maturities of 1 day to 270 days.

Common-base-year analysis The representing of accounting information over multiple years as percentages of amounts in an initial year.

Common-size analysis The representing of balance sheet items as percentages of assets and of income statement items as percentages of sales.

Common stock A proportional equity ownership interest — that is, a proportionate residual ownership interest—in a corporation. Common stock is the most junior security a corporation can issue.

Compensating balance An excess balance that is left at a bank to provide indirect compensation for loans extended or other bank services.

Competitive bidding A securities offering process in which securities firms submit competing bids to the issuer for the securities the issuer wishes to sell.

Compound interest Interest paid on previously earned interest as well as on the principal.

Compounding frequency The number of compounding periods in a year. For example, quarterly compounding has a compounding frequency of 4.

Conglomerate merger A merger involving two or more firms that are in unrelated businesses.

Consolidation The combining of two or more firms to form an entirely new entity.

Consumer credit Credit granted by a firm to consumers for the purchase of goods or services. Also called *retail credit*.

Contingent claim A claim that can be made only if one or more specified outcomes occur—that is, a claim that is contingent on the value of some other asset or on a particular occurrence.

Conventional project A project with a negative initial cash flow (an outflow), which is expected to be followed by one or more future positive cash flows (cash inflows).

Convertible bond A bond that, at the option of its owner, can be exchanged for a contractually specified number of shares of the firm's common stock.

Corporate financial management The application of financial principles within a corporation to create and maintain value through decision making and proper resource management.

Corporate tax view (of capital structure) The argument that double (corporate and individual) taxation of equity returns makes debt a cheaper financing method.

Corporation A legal "person" that is separate and distinct from its owners. A corporation is allowed to own assets, incur liabilities, and sell securities, among other things.

Correlation coefficient The covariance between two random variables divided by the product of the standard deviations of those random variables.

Cost of capital The required return for a capital budgeting project.

Cost of limited partner capital The discount rate that equates the after-tax inflows with outflows for capital raised from limited partners.

Coupon payments A bond's interest payments.

Coupon rate A bond's annual percentage rate.

Covariance The mathematical expectation of the product of two random variables' deviations from their means.

Covenants Provisions in a *bond indenture* (or *preferred stock agreement*) that require the bond (or preferred stock) issuer to take certain specified actions (*affirmative covenants*) or to refrain from taking certain specified actions (*negative covenants*).

Coverage ratios Ratios that show the amount of funds available to "cover" a particular financial obligation compared to the size of that obligation.

Cramdown The ability of the bankruptcy court to confirm a *plan of reorganization* over the objections of some classes of creditors.

Credit period The length of time for which the customer is granted credit.

Credit scoring A statistical technique wherein several financial characteristics are combined to form a single score to represent a customer's creditworthiness.

Crossover point A cost of capital at which two projects have equal NPV.

Currency future A *financial future* contract for the delivery of a stated amount of a specified foreign currency.

Currency option An *option* to buy or sell foreign currency.

Currency swap An agreement to swap a series of specified payment obligations denominated in one currency for a series of specified payment obligations denominated in a different currency.

Current assets Assets that are expected to become cash within one year.

Current liabilities Liabilities that mature, or are expected to be paid off, within one year.

Current ratio A liquidity ratio that measures the number of times a firm's current assets cover its current liabilities.

Current yield The annual coupon payment divided by the closing price.

Days' sales in inventory ratio The average number of days' worth of sales that is held in inventory.

Days' sales outstanding (DSO) The approximate number of days required to collect a firm's accounts receivable. Also called *average collection period*.

Debenture Long-term bonds (typically of longer than 10-year maturity) not secured by specific assets.

Debt/equity ratio Total debt divided by total common stockholders' equity; the amount of debt per dollar of equity.

Debt ratio Total debt divided by total assets; the fraction of the assets of the firm that are financed by debt.

Debt service coverage ratio Earnings before interest and income taxes plus one-third of rental charges, divided by interest expense plus one-third of rental charges plus the quantity principal repayments divided by one minus the tax rate. See Equation (16.3).

Debtor in possession A firm that is continuing to operate its business under Chapter 11 bankruptcy protection.

Deductive reasoning The use of a general fact to provide accurate information about a specific situation.

Deferred annuity An annuity where the first payment is more than one period in the future.

Derivatives Securities that derive their value from another asset.

Dilution Reduction in earnings per common share resulting from a financial transaction.

Disbursement float The positive float that is created between the time when a check is written and the time when it is finally cleared out of the checking account.

Discount The percent a customer can deduct from the net amount of the bill if payment is made before the end of the *discount period*.

Discount bond A bond that is selling for less than its par value.

Discount loans Loans which require the borrower to pay the interest in advance.

Discount period The period during which a customer can deduct the *discount* from the net amount of the bill when making payment.

Discount rate A generic term for a rate of return that measures the time value of money.
Discounted basis Selling something on a discounted basis is selling it below what its value will be at maturity, so that the difference makes up all or part of the interest.
Discounted-cash-flow (DCF) analysis The process of valuing capital budgeting projects by discounting their future expected cash flows.
Discounted-cash-flow (DCF) framework The valuing of an asset by discounting its expected future cash flows at some discount rate.
Discounted payback The length of time it takes for an investment's *discounted* future cash flows to equal the investment's initial cost.
Dividend policy An established guide for the firm to determine the amount of money it will pay out as dividends.
Dividend reinvestment plan A firm-sponsored program that enables common stockholders to pool their dividends (and, in many cases, supplementary cash) for reinvestment in shares of the firm's common stock.
Dividend yield The dividend income portion of a stock's return; more specifically, the dividend per share divided by the share price.
Duration The time until the "average" dollar of present value is received from an asset.
Dutch auction tender offer A "reverse" tender process, wherein shareholders can offer to sell shares at prices within a specified range.
EAA See *Equivalent annual annuity.*
EAC See *Equivalent annual cost.*
Earning power Earnings before interest and taxes (EBIT) divided by total assets.
Earnings before interest and taxes (EBIT) Operating profit plus nonoperating profit, such as investment income, calculated before the deduction of interest and income taxes.
Earnings yield The earnings per share divided by the market price per share; equals the reciprocal of the price/earnings ratio.
Economic order quantity (EOQ) The order quantity that minimizes total inventory costs.
Efficiency Reflects the amount of wasted energy.
Efficient frontier The combinations of securities portfolios that maximize expected return for any given level of risk or, equivalently, minimize risk for any given level of expected return.
Efficient portfolio A portfolio that provides the highest expected return for a given amount of risk and the lowest risk for a given expected return.
Electronic data interchange (EDI) The exchange of information electronically, directly from one firm's computer to another's, in a structured format.
Enhancement An innovation that has a positive impact on one or more of a firm's existing products.
EOQ See *Economic order quantity.*
Equity An ownership interest in a firm.
Equityholders Those holding some shares of the firm's equity. Also called *stockholders* and *shareholders.*
Equity multiplier Total assets divided by total common stockholders' equity; the amount of total assets per dollar of equity.
Equivalent annual annuity (EAA) The equivalent amount per year for some number of years that has a present value equal to a given amount.
Equivalent annual cost (EAC) The equivalent cost per year of owning an asset over its entire life.
Eurobond A bond that is sold outside the country in whose currency the bond is denominated.
Eurodollar bond market The market for U.S. dollar-denominated bonds outside the United States.
European option An option that can be exercised only at its expiration.
Events of default Contractually specified events that allow lenders to demand immediate repayment of a debt.
Exchange offer An offer by the firm to give one security, such as a bond or preferred stock, in exchange for another security, such as shares of common stock.
Exchange rate The price of one country's currency expressed in terms of another country's currency.
Ex-dividend date The date beginning on which a dividend is not paid to a new owner of a share of the stock.
Exercise To make the exchange specified in the option contract.
Exercise value The amount of advantage over a current market transaction provided by an in-the-money option.
Expected return The return one would expect to earn on an asset if it were purchased.
Expiration The time when the option contract ceases to exist (expires).
Extra or special dividends A dividend that is paid in addition to a firm's "regular" quarterly dividend, either at the same time as one of the quarterly dividends or at some other time.
Face value The amount of money to be repaid at the end of the bond's life. Also called *par value.*
Fair price A price that does not favor either the buyers' or the sellers' side of the transaction—that is, a zero-NPV investment.
Financial distress When a firm is having significant trouble paying its debts as they come due.
Financial intermediary A firm that purchases financial securities and pays for them by issuing claims against itself (its own financial securities).
Financial lease See *Capital lease.*
Financial leverage The degree to which a firm's assets are financed by debt as opposed to equity.
Financial planning The process of evaluating the investing and financing options available to the firm. It includes attempting to make optimal decisions, projecting the consequences of these decisions for the firm in the form of a financial plan, and then comparing future performance against that plan.
Financial ratio The result of dividing one financial statement item by another. Ratios help analysts interpret financial statements by focusing on specific relationships.
Financial risk Risk that is created by financial leverage, which is the financial makeup, or *capital structure*, of the firm.
Financial security A standardized financial asset, such as common stock, preferred stock, bond, convertible bond, or financial future; a contract that provides for the exchange of money at various times.
Financing decisions Decisions concerning the liabilities and stockholders' equity (right) side of the firm's balance sheet, such as the decision to issue bonds.
Fixed asset turnover ratio The ratio of sales to fixed assets.
Fixed charge coverage ratio Generally, the number of times that interest charges

and rental payments are covered by earnings before interest, taxes, and rental payments. More specifically, earnings before interest and income taxes plus one-third of rental charges, divided by interest expense plus one-third of rental charges. See Equation (16.2).

Fixed-price tender offer A one-time offer to purchase a stated number of shares at a stated fixed price above the current market price.

Float The difference between the firm's available or collected balance at its bank and the firm's book or ledger balance.

Foreign currency risk The risk that the value of one currency expressed in terms of another currency—the foreign exchange rate—may fluctuate over time.

Foreign exchange market The market within which one country's currency is traded for another country's currency.

Foreign exchange risk See *Foreign currency risk.*

Forward contract A contract to exchange a stated amount of a specified asset for cash at a specific future date.

Free rider A follower who avoids the cost and expense of finding the best course of action by simply mimicking the behavior of a leader who, for example, makes investments.

Frictions The "stickiness" in making transactions; the total "hassle," including the time, effort, money, and associated tax effects of gathering information and making a transaction such as buying stock or borrowing money.

Future investment opportunities The options to identify additional, more valuable investment opportunities in the future that result from a current opportunity or operation.

Futures contract A standardized forward contract that is traded in a futures market.

Future-value annuity factor Equation (4.5) without PMT.

Future-value factor Equation (4.3) without PV.

Future-value formula Equation (4.3).

General cash offer A *public offering* made to investors at large.

Generally accepted accounting principles (GAAP) A technical accounting term that encompasses the conventions, rules, and procedures necessary to define accepted accounting practice at a particular time.

Greenmail A firm's paying a takeover raider a premium to repurchase shares from the raider.

Gross profit margin Gross profit divided by sales, which is the amount of each sales dollar left over after paying the cost of goods sold.

Gross spread The fraction of the (gross) proceeds of an underwritten securities offering that is paid as compensation to the underwriters of the offering.

Gross underwriting spread See *Gross spread.*

"Hard" capital rationing Capital rationing that under no circumstances can be violated.

Hedging Reducing the risk of an investment through the use of financial security transactions.

Holding period The amount of time money is invested in a particular asset.

Homemade dividend Sale of some shares of stock to get cash that would be similar to getting a cash dividend.

Horizontal merger A merger involving two or more firms in the same industry that are both at the same stage in the production cycle—that is, two or more competitors.

Human capital The unique capabilities and expertise of individuals.

In-the-money Said of an option that currently would provide an advantage, if exercised.

Income statement A financial statement that reports the income, expenses, and profit (or loss) for a specific interval of time, usually a year or a quarter of a year.

Independent project A project that can be chosen without requiring or precluding any other investment.

Inductive reasoning The attempt to use information about a specific situation to draw a general conclusion.

Informational efficiency The speed and accuracy with which prices reflect new information.

Initial public offering (IPO) A first-time public issuing of stock in a corporation.

Interest coverage ratio Earnings before interest and income taxes divided by interest expense. See Equation (16.1).

Interest rate parity A theory of relative exchange rates that states that the difference in interest rates in two currencies for a stated period should just offset the difference between the spot foreign exchange rate and the forward exchange rate corresponding to that period.

Interest-rate risk The risk of a change in the value of a bond because of a change in the interest rate.

Interest rate swap An agreement to swap interest payment obligations.

Internal rate of return (IRR) The expected return of a capital budgeting project.

International Fisher effect A theory that holds that the difference between the interest rates in two currencies should just offset the difference between the expected inflation rates in the two countries that issued the currencies.

Inventory turnover ratio An asset turnover ratio that shows how many times inventory turns over in a year.

Investment banker A *financial intermediary* that specializes in marketing new securities issues and assisting with *mergers.*

Investment decisions Decisions concerning the asset (left) side of the firm's balance sheet, such as the decision to offer a new product.

Investment-grade ratings A long-term debt rating in one of the four highest rating categories.

Investment tax credit A provision of the tax code that permits a firm that makes qualifying capital expenditures to credit a specified percentage of those expenditures against its income tax liability for the period in which the qualifying expenditures are made. The Tax Reform Act of 1986 eliminated the investment tax credit, but the credit has been eliminated and restored several times during the postwar period.

Investments As a discipline, the study of financial securities, such as stocks and bonds, from the investor's viewpoint. This area deals with the firm's financing decision, but from the other side of the transaction.

Invoice date Usually the date when goods are shipped. Payment dates are set relative to the invoice date.

Just-in-time (JIT) inventory systems Systems that schedule materials to arrive exactly as they are needed in the production process.

Lease A long-term rental agreement; a form of secured long-term debt.

Lessee An entity that leases an asset from another entity.

Lessor An entity that leases an asset to another entity.

Letter of credit A form of guarantee of payment issued by a bank; used to guarantee the payment of interest and repayment of principal on bond issues.

Leverage The use of debt financing.

Leverage ratios Generally, measures of the relative contribution of stockholders and creditors, and of the firm's ability to pay financing charges. More specifically, the ratio of the value of the firm's debt to the total value of the firm.

Leverage rebalancing Making transactions to adjust (rebalance) a firm's leverage ratio back to its target.

Leveraged buyout The purchase of a firm that is financed with a very high proportion of debt.

Leveraged lease A lease arrangement under which the lessor borrows a large proportion of the funds needed to purchase the asset and grants the lenders a lien on the asset and a pledge of the lease payments to secure the borrowing.

Liability A debt claim against the firm's assets.

Limited liability Limitation of possible loss to what has already been invested.

Limited liability company A company which offers limited liability, like a corporation, but is normally taxed like a partnership.

Limited partnership A partnership that includes one or more partners who have *limited liability*.

Line of credit An *informal* arrangement between a bank and a customer establishing a maximum loan balance that the bank will permit the borrower to maintain.

Liquidation When a firm's business is terminated, all its assets are sold and the proceeds are used to pay its creditors, and any leftover proceeds are distributed to its shareholders.

Liquidity The extent to which something can be sold quickly and easily without loss of value.

Liquidity ratios Ratios that measure a firm's ability to meet its short-term financial obligations on time.

Long-term In accounting information, one year or more.

Management's discussion A report from management to the stockholders that accompanies the firm's financial statements in the annual report. This report explains the period's financial results and enables management to discuss other ideas that may not be apparent in the financial statements in the annual report.

Managerial decisions Decisions concerning the operation of the firm, such as the choice of firm size, firm growth, and employee compensation.

Marginal tax rate The tax rate applied to the last, or marginal, dollar of income.

Market portfolio A value-weighted portfolio of every asset in a market.

Market risk premium The difference between the expected return on the market portfolio and the riskless return.

Market-to-book ratio The ratio of the market price per share to the book value per share.

Market value The price for which something could be bought or sold in a reasonable length of time, where "reasonable length of time" is defined in terms of the item's liquidity.

Market value ratios Ratios that relate the market price of the firm's common stock to selected financial statement items.

Materials requirement planning (MRP) systems Computer-based systems that plan backward from the production schedule to make purchases and manage inventory levels.

Maturity The end of a bond's life.

Maturity date The date a bond's life ends; the date by which it must be fully repaid.

Max function A mathematical function that selects the item of greatest value from a list.

Mean The *expected value* of a *random variable*.

Merger A combination of two firms in which the *acquiror* absorbs all the assets and liabilities of the *acquiree* and assumes the acquiree's business.

Monitor To seek information about an agent's behavior; a device that provides such information.

Moral hazard A situation wherein an agent can take unseen actions for personal benefit when such actions are costly to the principal.

Mortgage bond A bond that is secured by a lien on one or more specific assets.

Multinational firms Firms that operate in more than one country.

Mutually exclusive Two projects that cannot both be undertaken; that is, choosing one precludes choosing the other.

Negative covenant (of a bond) A *bond covenant* that limits or prohibits altogether certain actions unless the bondholders agree.

Negotiated offering An offering of securities for which the terms, including underwriters' compensation, have been negotiated between the issuer and the underwriters.

Net acquisition cost (NAC) The cost of purchasing the target's equity plus transaction costs plus the cost of assuming the target's debt minus the target's excess assets. See Equation (25.11).

Net advantage to leasing The net present value of entering into a lease financing arrangement rather than borrowing the necessary funds and buying the asset.

Net advantage to merging The difference in total post- and pre-merger market value minus the cost of the merger.

Net book value The current book value of an asset or liability; that is, its original book value net of any accounting adjustments such as depreciation.

Net operating cash flow The change in periodic revenue minus the change in periodic cash operating expense connected with undertaking the project minus also the tax liability on revenue net of cash operating expenses.

Net present value (NPV) The present value of the expected future cash flows minus the cost.

Net profit margin Net income divided by sales; the amount of each sales dollar left over after all expenses have been paid.

Net salvage value The after-tax net cash flow for terminating the project.

Nonconventional project A project in which the cash flow pattern is different in some way from conventional projects.

Nondiversifiability of human capital The difficulty of diversifying one's *human capital* (the unique capabilities and expertise of individuals) and employment effort.

Nonoperating cash flows Cash flows not associated with operations.

Note A debt obligation with an initial maturity between one and ten years.

Notes to the financial statements A detailed set of notes immediately following the financial statements that explain and expand on the information in the financial statements.

NPV See *Net present value.*

NPV profile A graph of NPV as a function of the discount rate.

Open account A credit account where the customer makes purchases and the signed invoices are evidence of indebtedness.

Operating lease A lease obligation that does not have to be capitalized on the face of the balance sheet.

Operating risk The inherent or fundamental risk of a firm, without regard to *financial risk*. The risk that is created by *operating leverage*. Also called *business risk*.
Opportunity cost The difference between the value of a course of action and the value of the next best alternative.
Optimal contract The contract that balances the three types of agency costs (contracting, monitoring, and misbehavior) against one another to minimize the total cost.
Option A right to do something without an obligation to do it.
Ordinary annuity A kind of annuity where the payments occur at the end of each period.
Original maturity The length of a bond's life when it is issued.
Out-of-the-money Said of an option that currently would provide a disadvantage, if exercised.
Par value The amount of money to be repaid for a bond at the end of its life. The par value is also called the *face value*.
Partnership Shared ownership among two or more individuals, some of whom may, but do not necessarily, have limited liability. See *Limited partnership*.
Payback The length of time it takes to recover the initial cost of a project, without regard to the time value of money.
Payment date The date on which each *shareholder of record* will be sent a check for the declared dividend.
Payout ratio Generally, the proportion of earnings paid out to common stockholders as cash dividends. More specifically, the firm's cash dividend divided by the firm's earnings in the same period.
Pecking-order view (of capital structure) The argument that external financing transaction costs, especially those associated with the problem of adverse selection, create a dynamic environment in which firms have a preference, or pecking, order of preferred sources of financing, when all else is equal. Internally generated funds are the most preferred, new debt is next, debt-equity combinations are next, and new external equity is the least preferred source.
Perfect market view (of capital structure) Analysis of a decision (capital structure), in a perfect capital market environment, that shows the irrelevance of capital structure in a perfect capital market.
Perpetuity An infinite annuity. A series of identical cash flows each period forever.
Perquisites Personal benefits, including direct benefits, such as the use of a firm car or expense account for personal business, and indirect benefits, such as an up-to-date office decor.
Personal tax view (of capital structure) The argument that the difference in personal tax rates between income from debt and income from equity eliminates the disadvantage from the double taxation (corporate and personal) of income from equity.
Planning horizon The length of time a model projects into the future.
Portfolio (1) The collection of securities that an investor owns. (2) The collection of real and financial assets that a firm owns.
Positive covenant (of a bond) A *bond covenant* that specifies certain actions the firm must take. Also called an *affirmative covenant*.
Postaudit A set of procedures for evaluating a capital budgeting decision after the fact.
Postponement option The option of postponing a project without eliminating the possibility of undertaking it.
Precautionary demand (for money) The need to meet unexpected or extraordinary contingencies with a buffer stock of cash.
Premium bond A bond that is selling for more than its par value.
Prepackaged bankruptcy A *bankruptcy* in which a debtor and its creditors prenegotiate a *plan of reorganization* and then file it along with the bankruptcy petition.
Present-value annuity factor Equation (4.6) without PMT.
Present-value factor Equation (4.4) without FV.
Present-value formula Equation (4.4).
Price-earnings ratio, or P/E A stock's market price per share divided by the firm's annual earnings per share.
Primary market A market consisting of newly created securities.
Primary offering A firm selling some of its own newly issued shares to investors.
Prime rate The benchmark interest rate that banks charge large, creditworthy firms.
Principal (1) The total amount of money being borrowed. (2) The party affected by agent decisions in a principal-agent relationship.
Principal-agent relationship A situation that can be modeled as one person, an *agent*, who acts on behalf of another person, a *principal*.
Private placement The sale of securities directly to investors (often institutions) without a *public offering*.
Pro forma statement A financial statement showing the forecast (or projected) operating results or impact of a particular transaction, as in pro forma income statements in the *long-term financial plan* or the pro forma *balance sheet* for a share repurchase.
Profitability index (PI) The present value of the future cash flows divided by the initial investment. Also called the *benefit-cost ratio*.
Profitability ratios Ratios that focus on the profitability of the firm. *Profit margins* measure performance in relation to sales, and *rate of return ratios* measure performance relative to some measure of the size of the investment.
Progressive tax system A tax system wherein the average tax rate increases for some increases in income but never decreases with an increase in income.
Project financing A form of asset-based financing in which a firm finances a discrete set of assets (project) on a stand-alone basis.
Prospectus A legal disclosure document that must be distributed both to purchasers and to persons whose purchase interest is solicited in connection with a public offering of securities.
Proxy contest A battle for the control of a firm in which the dissident group seeks, from the firm's other shareholders, the right to vote those shareholders' shares in favor of the dissident group's slate of directors.
Purchase method A method of accounting for a *merger* or *consolidation* in which one of the firms is identified as the acquiror.
Purchasing power parity A theory of relative exchange rates that states that the expected difference in inflation rates for two countries over some period must equal the differential between the spot exchange rate currently prevailing and the spot exchange rate expected at the end of the period.
Pure-discount bond A bond that will make only one payment of principal and interest. Also called a *zero-coupon bond*.
Put an option To *exercise* a put option.

Put-call parity The relationship between the value of a put option and the value of a call option.
Put option The right to *sell* something at a given price during the life of the option.
Pyramid scheme An illegal, fraudulent scheme in which a con artist convinces victims to invest by promising an extraordinary return but simply uses newly invested funds to pay off any investors who insist on terminating their investment.
Quick (acid test) ratio A liquidity ratio that measures the number of times a firm can cover its current liabilities using its current assets (but not including its inventories, which are less liquid).
Realized return The return that is actually gotten over a given time period.
Receivables balance fractions The percentage of a month's sales that remain uncollected (and part of accounts receivable) at the end of the month of sale and at the end of succeeding months.
Receivables turnover ratio The number of times receivables turn over in a year, measured as the total annual credit sales divided by the current accounts receivable balance.
Record date A date established to determine who will actually get the dividend check for a share of stock, in case the share is sold between when the dividend is declared and when it is paid.
Registration statement A legal document that is filed with the Securities and Exchange Commission to register securities for public offering.
Reinvestment rate assumption The return that the cash flows from a capital budgeting project are expected (assumed) to earn from being reinvested.
Remaining maturity The length of time remaining until a bond's maturity.
Reorganization Creating a plan to restructure a debtor's business and restore its financial health.
Replacement cycle The frequency with which an asset is replaced by an equivalent asset.
Required return The minimum *expected return* you would require to be willing to purchase the asset (that is, to make the investment).
Return on assets (ROA) Net income divided by total assets.
Return on equity (ROE) Net income available to common stockholders divided by common stockholders' equity.
Revolving credit agreement A *legal* commitment wherein a bank promises to lend a customer up to a specified maximum amount during a specified period.
Rights issue The process of offering common stock to existing shareholders by issuing *rights*.
Risk-averse Choosing lower risk when alternative returns are equal, or choosing higher returns when alternative risks are equal.
Risk class A group of capital budgeting projects that all have approximately the same amount of risk.
Risky debt Debt that has some possibility of not being fully repaid on time.
Rule 144A private placement The sale of unregistered securities to one or more investment banks, which then resell them to qualified institutional buyers (QIBs), or the direct sale to QIBs.
Safety stock Inventory buffer stock that a firm holds to hedge uncertainties in delivery times, usage, or sales.
Sale-and-lease-back An agreement to sell an asset and lease it back from the purchaser.
Salvage value The before-tax difference between the sale price of the assets and the clean-up and removal expenses.
Seasoned offering A public issuing of shares by a corporation that already has shares that are trading in the capital markets.
Secondary market A market where securities that are already outstanding are traded.
Secondary offering Shareholders (usually insiders or large institutions) selling previously issued shares they own to investors at large in an offering that has been registered with the *SEC*.
Security market line (SML) The linear relationship between required return and beta.
Semi-strong form of capital market efficiency Prices reflect all *publicly available* information about an asset's value.
Sensitivity analysis Varying key parameters of a process to determine the sensitivity of outcomes to that variation.
Set-of-contracts model A model that describes the firm as a collection of implicit and explicit contracts among the *stakeholders*.
Share repurchase A firm's purchase of its own shares of stock.
Shareholder wealth maximization Maximizing the value of the firm to its owners. For a publicly traded firm, the value of the firm to its owners is the market value of the shares owned.
Shareholders Those holding some shares of the firm's equity. Also called *stockholders* and *equityholders*.
Shelf registration The process of registering a two-year inventory of securities by filing a single registration statement.
Shirking An agent's putting forth less than "full effort."
Short-term Typically, less than a year.
Simple interest Interest that is received on the initial principal amount only, rather than compounded.
Simulation The use of a mathematical model to imitate a situation many times in order to estimate the likelihood of various possible outcomes.
Sinking fund A bond provision specifying principal repayments prior to the maturity date.
"Soft" capital rationing Capital rationing that under certain circumstances can be violated or even viewed as made up of targets rather than absolute constraints.
Sole proprietorship A firm wherein a single individual owns all the firm's assets directly and is responsible for all its liabilities.
Specific risk The standard deviation of an investment's return.
Speculative demand (for money) The need for cash to take advantage of investment opportunities that may arise.
Speculative-grade rating A long-term debt rating other than an *investment-grade rating*.
Spot market A market to trade today an asset that is also traded on a futures market.
Spot trade The purchase or sale of a foreign currency, commodity, or other item for "immediate" delivery.
Stakeholder Anyone with a legitimate claim of any sort on the firm, such as stockholders, bondholders, creditors, employees, customers, the community, and the government.
Standard deviation The square root of the *variance*.
Stock and bond guide A document that contains detailed information about stocks and bonds.
Stock dividends A bookkeeping reapportioning of the claim size of a share of stock so that there are more shares and each share has a proportionately smaller ownership interest. For example, if a

firm declares a 5% stock dividend, a shareholder will receive 5 new shares for every 100 shares owned. Money from the retained earnings account is transferred to the "Paid-in Capital" and "Capital Contributed in Excess of Par Value" accounts.

Stock split A bookkeeping reapportioning of the claim size of a share of stock so that there are more shares and each share has a proportionately smaller ownership interest. For example, if a firm declares a 2-for-1 stock split, then each shareholder owns twice as many shares, but each new share has half the claim size of each old share. The stock's par value per share is adjusted to reflect the change, but no money is transferred among balance sheet accounts.

Stockholders Those holding some shares of the firm's equity. Also called *shareholders* and *equityholders.*

Stockholders' equity Residual ownership claims against the firm's assets.

Strike price The price specified in the option contract for buying or selling the underlying asset. That is, the asset is exchanged for the strike price.

Strong form of capital market efficiency Prices reflect *all* information that exists about an asset's value.

Sunk cost A cost that has already been incurred and cannot be altered by subsequent decisions. Previously incurred sunk costs can be ignored when making most decisions.

Swap An agreement to exchange specified payment obligations, such as an *interest rate swap.*

Syndicate A group of securities firms formed to share the underwriting risk in connection with an *underwritten offering* of securities.

Target payout ratio A *payout ratio* objective that a firm sets to guide its dividend policy.

Tax asymmetry A situation in which two parties to a transaction are taxed at different rates and can structure the transaction (or their relationship) to reduce their collective tax bill.

Tax-free acquisition A *merger* or *consolidation* in which (1) the acquiror's tax basis in each asset whose ownership is transferred in the transaction is generally the same as the acquiree's and (2) each seller who receives only stock does not have to pay any tax on the gain he realizes until the shares are sold.

Tax-timing option The option to sell an asset and claim a loss for tax purposes or not to sell the asset and defer a capital gain tax.

Taxable acquisition A *merger* or *consolidation* that is not a *tax-free acquisition.* The selling shareholders are treated as having sold their shares.

Tender offer A general offer to purchase securities that is made publicly and directly to all holders of the desired securities.

Tender offer premium The premium offered above the current market price in a tender offer.

Term loan A bank loan, typically with a floating interest rate, for a specified amount that matures in between one and ten years and requires a specified repayment schedule.

Term structure (1) The yield curve for zero-coupon U.S. Treasury securities. (2) The general relationship between debt maturity and interest rates.

Time premium of an option The value of an option beyond its current exercise value representing the optionholder's control until expiration, the risk of the underlying asset, and the riskless return.

Times-interest-earned ratio The ratio of EBIT to interest expense, also called the *interest coverage ratio.*

Total asset turnover ratio The ratio of sales to total assets.

Trade credit Credit granted by a firm to another firm for the purchase of goods or services.

Traders Persons engaged in short-term speculation.

Trading Buying and selling securities.

Transaction costs The time, effort, and money necessary to make a transaction, including such things as commission fees and the cost of physically moving the asset from seller to buyer.

Transaction loan A loan extended by a bank for a specific purpose. In contrast, lines of credit and revolving credit agreements involve loans that can be used for various purposes.

Transactions demand (for money) The need to accommodate a firm's expected cash transactions.

Transferable put right An option issued by the firm to its shareholders to sell the firm one share of its common stock at a fixed price (the strike price) within a stated period (the time to maturity). The put right is "transferable" because it can be traded in the capital markets.

Underinvestment The mirror image of the *asset substitution problem,* wherein stockholders refuse to invest in low-risk assets to avoid shifting wealth from themselves to the debtholders.

Underlying asset The asset that an option gives the optionholder the right to buy or to sell.

Underwrite To guarantee, as to guarantee the issuer of securities a specified price by entering into a purchase and sale agreement.

Underwriter A party that guarantees the proceeds to the firm from a security sale, thereby in effect taking ownership of the securities.

Urgency A dangerous but widely used method of allocating resources in which a firm puts off making a capital budgeting decision until it is left with no choice but to make the investment.

Value additivity Prevails when the value of the whole (a group of assets) exactly equals the sum of the values of the parts (the individual assets).

Variance The mathematical expectation of the squared deviations from the mean. See Equation (9.3).

Vertical merger A merger in which one firm acquires another that is in the same industry but at another stage in the production cycle—for example, the acquiree serves as a supplier to the acquiror or purchases the acquiror's goods or services.

WACC See *Weighted average cost of capital.*

Warrant A long-term call option issued by a firm on its own stock.

Weak form of capital market efficiency Prices reflect information about an asset's value that is *contained in past asset market prices.*

Weighted average cost of capital (WACC) The weighted average of financing costs for a financing package that would allow a project to be undertaken.

Working capital Current assets minus current liabilities.

Working capital management The management of current assets and current liabilities.

Working capital ratio Net working capital expressed as a proportion of sales.

World market portfolio A portfolio that includes all the capital assets in the world.

Yield to call (YTC) The annual percentage rate of a bond, assuming it will be paid off at a particular call date.

Yield to maturity (YTM) The annual percentage rate that equates a bond's market price to the present value of its promised future cash flows.

Zero-coupon bond A bond that will make only one payment of principal and interest. Also called a *pure-discount bond.*

Zero-sum game A type of game wherein one player can gain only at the expense of another player.

INDEX

D

G

H

I

J

K

L

M